X

Oxford
esol
Dictionary

OXFORD
UNIVERSITY PRESS

OXFORD
UNIVERSITY PRESS

Great Clarendon Street, Oxford OX2 6DP

Oxford University Press is a department of the University of Oxford. It furthers the University's objective of excellence in research, scholarship,and education by publishing worldwide in

Oxford New York

Auckland Cape Town Dar es Salaam Hong Kong Karachi Kuala Lumpur Madrid Melbourne Mexico City Nairobi New Delhi Shanghai Taipei Toronto

With offices in

Argentina Austria Brazil Chile Czech Republic France Greece Guatemala Hungary Italy Japan Poland Portugal Singapore South Korea Switzerland Thailand Turkey Ukraine Vietnam

OXFORD and OXFORD ENGLISH are registered trademarks of Oxford University Press in the UK and in certain other countries

© Oxford University Press 2006

Database right Oxford University Press (maker)

First published 2006

Also published as *Oxford Essential Dictionary*

2009 2008 2007 2006

6 5 4 3 2 1

The British National Corpus is a collaborative project involving Oxford University Press, Longman, Chambers, the Universities of Oxford and Lancaster and the British Library

ISBN-13: 978 0 19 431734 4
ISBN-10: 0 19 431734 X

ACKNOWLEDGEMENTS

Edited by: Alison Waters, assisted by Victoria Bull

Advisory Board: Dr Keith Brown; Prof Guy Cook; Dr Alan Cruse; Ruth Gairns; Moira Runcie; Prof Gabriele Stein; Dr Norman Whitney; Prof Henry Widdowson

We would like to thank the following for their permission to reproduce photographs: Bananastock P4 (girl's face); *Corel* A–Z illustrations, P1 (ferry, helicopter, lorry, plane, ship, train), P2 (cow, budgie, cat, dog, donkey, goose, horse, parrot, peacock, sheep, turkey), P3 (elephant, jaguar, koala, lion, polar bear, rhinoceros, tiger), P6 (milk, milkshake, orange juice, water), P7 (chicken, pizza, beef, soup, stew), P8 (apple, bananas, grapes, orange), P9 (celery, lettuce, peppers), P14 (baseball, canoe, cricket, football, rugby, skating, surfing, swimming, windsurfing), P15 (cycling, judo, horse riding, snooker, snowboarding, working out); *Corbis* A–Z illustrations, P3 (bear), P15 (sunset); *Getty Images* A–Z illustrations, P1 (underground), P2 (chicken, hamster, guinea pigs, pig), P5 (leotard, shorts), P6 (biscuits, herbs, olives, salt and pepper), P7 (fast food, pasta), P8 (coconut, half-lemon, melon, pineapple, strawberry), P9 (beans, sprouts), P11 (classroom), P12 (doctor, farmer, judge, plumber, policeman, vet, waiter), P13 (all images), P14 (basketball, waterskiing), P15 (bowling, hiking, skateboarding, yoga), P16 (flood, fog, icicles); *Hemera Technologies Inc.* A–Z illustrations, P5 (pyjamas, skirt, suit), P6 (coffee, tea), P7 (cereal, ice cream, kebab, pancakes, quiche, salad, spaghetti), P8 (pear), P11 (bin, computer), P12 (dentist); *Ingram Publishing* A–Z illustrations, P3 (crocodile, giraffe, hippopotamus, leopard, wolf), P6 (cake), P7 (hotdog), P8 (plum), P9 (beetroot, cucumber), P11 (calculator); *iStockphoto.com* P6 (butter), P7 (fish, rice), P9 (garlic); *John Foxx* P6 (jam); *Peter Burgess* P11 (exercise book); *Punchstock* P12 (carpenter, chef, nurse, painter, teacher), P16 (wind); *Rubberball* P4 (boy, girl standing), P5 (dress); *Stockbyte* A–Z illustrations, P6 (cracker, doughnut, eggs, noodles, vinegar), P7 (curry, fish and chips), P8 (blackcurrants, dates, gooseberries), P9 (tomato)

Illustrations: Lorna Barnard, Jeremy Bays, David Burroughs, Martin Cox, Mark Dunn, David Eaton, Gay Galsworthy, Karen Hiscock, Margaret Jones, Richard Lewington, Martin Lonsdale/Hardlines, Vanessa Luff, Kevin Maddison, Martin Shovel, Technical Graphics Department OUP, Harry Venning, Graham White, Michael Woods

Maps © Oxford University Press

Text capture, processing and typesetting by Oxford University Press

Printed in China

423 0

Contents

Guide to the dictionary

Finding words and phrases

The **2000 keywords** (= the most important words to learn) are clearly marked and there is a list of them at the back of the dictionary.

easy 0̶ /'iːzi/ *adjective* (easier, easiest)
1 not difficult to do or understand: *The homework was very easy.* ◇ *English isn't an easy language to learn.*
2 without problems or pain: *He has had an easy life.* ⊃ OPPOSITE **difficult, hard**
take it easy, take things easy to relax and not worry or work too much: *After my exams I'm going to take it easy for a few days.*

Idioms and **phrasal verbs** (which have a special meaning) are shown below the main words.

Words with the **same spelling**, but different parts of speech, have different numbers.

smoke[1] 0̶ /sməʊk/ *noun* (no plural)
the grey, white or black gas that you see in the air when something is burning: *The room was full of smoke.* ◇ *cigarette smoke*

smoke[2] 0̶ /sməʊk/ *verb* (smokes, smoking, smoked /sməʊkt/)
to breathe in smoke through a cigarette, etc. and let it out again; to use cigarettes, etc. in this way, as a habit: *He was smoking a cigar.* ◇ *Do you smoke?*
▶ **smoker** /'sməʊkə(r)/ *noun*: *Her parents are both **heavy smokers** (= they smoke a lot).*

Related words are given below the main word.

Grammar

speak 0̶ /spiːk/ *verb* (speaks, speaking, spoke /spəʊk/, has spoken /'spəʊkən/)
1 to say things; to talk to somebody: *Please speak more slowly.* ◇ *Can I **speak to** John Smith, please?*

the **forms of a verb.** We show the *he/she* form, the *–ing* form, the *past tense* (and the *past participle* of irregular verbs).

To make the plural of most nouns, you add –s (for example girl, girl**s**). For all other nouns, we give you full information. Some nouns have a completely different **plural form**, or there is a change to the spelling.

knife 0̶ /naɪf/ *noun* (plural knives /naɪvz/)
a sharp metal thing with a handle that you use to cut things or to fight: *a knife and fork*

clothes 0̶ /kləʊðz/ *noun* (plural)
things like trousers, shirts and coats that you wear to cover your body: *She was **wearing** new **clothes**.* ◇ *Take off those wet clothes.*

Some nouns are always **plural.** We give you extra help with these.

Sometimes a noun has **no plural** form and it cannot be used with *a* or *an*.

information 0̶ /ˌɪnfə'meɪʃn/ *noun* (no plural)
facts about people or things: *Can you give me some **information about** trains to London?*

the **part of speech** (for example *noun*, *verb* or *adjective*)

🔎 GRAMMAR
Be careful! You cannot say 'an information'. You say **some information** or a **piece of information**: *She gave me an interesting piece of information.*

Nouns with no plural form often have notes giving extra information about grammar.

busy 0— /ˈbɪzi/ *adjective* (busier, busiest)
1 with a lot of things that you must do; working or not free: *Mr Jones can't see you now – he's busy.*

Comparative and **superlative** forms are given, unless they are formed with *more* or *most* (for example beautiful, more beautiful).

Understanding and using words

anticlockwise /ˌænti'klɒkwaɪz/
(*British*) (*American* counterclockwise)
adjective, adverb
in the opposite direction to the hands of a clock: *Turn the handle anticlockwise.*

Both **British English** and **American English** are given.

Example sentences help you to understand a word and show you how it is used.

pronunciation and **stress**

best man /ˌbest'mæn/ *noun* (*no plural*)
a man at a wedding who helps the man who is getting married (the **bridegroom**)

Related words help you to build your vocabulary.

clever 0— /ˈklevə(r)/ *adjective*
(cleverer, cleverest)
quick at learning and understanding things
⊃ SAME MEANING **intelligent**: *a clever student* ⊃ OPPOSITE **stupid**

meaning (or definition)

Many **opposites** and **synonyms** (= words with the same meaning) are given.

🔎 **WORD BUILDING** notes show you related words and help build your vocabulary.

🔎 **SPEAKING** Some words are used only in **formal** situations and there may be a word that is used more often, especially in **speech**.

🔎 **SPELLING** and **PRONUNCIATION** notes help you remember how to spell a word and tell you how to pronounce difficult words.

🔎 **WHICH WORD?** notes show you the difference between words that you might confuse.

🔎 **CULTURE** notes tell you about life in Britain and the US.

cat 0— /kæt/ *noun*
1 a small animal with soft fur that people keep as a pet

🔎 **WORD BUILDING**
A young cat is called a **kitten**. A cat **purrs** when it is happy. When it makes a loud noise, it **miaows**: *My cat miaows when she's hungry.*

assist /əˈsɪst/ *verb* (assists, assisting, assisted) (*formal*)
to help somebody: *The driver assisted her with her suitcases.*

🔎 **SPEAKING**
Help is the word that we usually use.

piece 0— /piːs/ *noun*

🔎 **SPELLING**
Remember! **I** comes before **E** in **piece**. Use the phrase **a piece of pie** to help you remember.

daughter 0— /ˈdɔːtə(r)/ *noun*

🔎 **PRONUNCIATION**
The word **daughter** sounds like **water**, because we don't say the letters **gh** in this word.

pile¹ 0— /paɪl/ *noun*

🔎 **WHICH WORD?**
Pile or **heap**?
A **pile** may be tidy or untidy. A **heap** is untidy.

English /ˈɪŋglɪʃ/ *noun*

🔎 **CULTURE**
Be careful! The people of **Scotland** (the **Scots**) and the people of **Wales** (the **Welsh**) are **British**, not **English**.

Dictionary Quiz

This quiz shows how your **Oxford dictionary** can help you.
You will find the answers to all these questions in the dictionary.

Meanings

1 On which part of your body do you wear **wellingtons**?

2 When is **Boxing Day**?

The dictionary explains the meanings of words in simple language. The example sentences also help you to understand words and use them correctly. Words marked with a key are important words for you to learn. There is a list of the 2000 keywords at the back of the dictionary.

Vocabulary

3 What is a young **goat** called?

There are hundreds of notes that give useful extra vocabulary or show the differences between words.

4 What is the opposite of **wide**?

The dictionary has a lot of photos and pictures that help you understand words and build your vocabulary. As well as the pictures in the main part of the dictionary, there is a 16-page Picture Dictionary section in the middle with colour pictures of things like clothes, food and drink, and the weather.

5 *I bought this book in the library.* In this sentence, the word **library** is wrong. What is the right word?

6 What is the name of the central part of a **tree**, that grows up from the ground?

7 What is the name of this fruit?

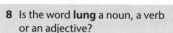

Grammar

8 Is the word **lung** a noun, a verb or an adjective?

You can check if a new word is a noun, a verb, an adjective, etc. by looking in the dictionary.

9 Is it correct to say: *Can you give me some **advices**?*

The dictionary gives you extra help with some nouns. For example, it gives irregular and difficult noun plurals and tells you if a word cannot be used in the plural.

10 What is the past tense of the verb **break**?

The important verb forms are listed for each verb, and there is a list of irregular verbs with their past tenses and past participles on pages 484–485.

11 What is the *-ing* form of the verb **hit**?

12 How do you spell the plural of **party**?

13 Do the words **son** and **sun** have the same sound?

14 Does **enough** sound like **though** or **tough**?

15 How do you *say* this **date**: 4 July, 2010?

16 What is the name of the exam that all British pupils must take in secondary school?

17 Is **Yours faithfully** the correct ending to a formal or an informal letter?

18 Name three young farm animals.

19 On which part of your body is your **nostril**?

20 What is the word for a person who comes from **Spain**?

Spelling

You can use the dictionary to check how to spell a word, and it also shows changes in the spelling of other forms of the word, for example the plurals of nouns and the -*ing* forms of verbs.

Pronunciation

The dictionary gives the pronunciation of words, and on page viii you will find help with reading the phonetic symbols. There are also notes to help you with words that have the same sound or words that are difficult to pronounce.

Extra information

The blue Study Pages in the middle give useful information on topics like dates, education and writing letters and emails. The colourful Picture Dictionary section shows you groups of related words in topic areas such as animals and the body. At the end of the dictionary you will find helpful lists of words such as geographical names and irregular verbs.

Answers

1 your feet
2 26 December
3 a kid
4 narrow
5 bookshop/bookstore
6 the trunk
7 a pineapple
8 a noun
9 No. (The word 'advice' does not have a plural form.)
10 broke
11 hitting
12 parties
13 yes
14 tough
15 the fourth of July (or July the fourth), two thousand and ten
16 General Certificate of Secondary Education (GCSE)
17 formal
18 lamb, foal, calf
19 nose, face
20 a Spaniard

Phonetic symbols

Vowels

iː	see	/siː/		ʌ	cup	/kʌp/
i	happy	/ˈhæpi/		ɜː	bird	/bɜːd/
ɪ	sit	/sɪt/		ə	about	/əˈbaʊt/
e	ten	/ten/		eɪ	say	/seɪ/
æ	cat	/kæt/		əʊ	go	/ɡəʊ/
ɑ	father	/ˈfɑːðə(r)/		aɪ	five	/faɪv/
ɒ	got	/ɡɒt/		aʊ	now	/naʊ/
ɔː	saw	/sɔː/		ɔɪ	boy	/bɔɪ/
ʊ	put	/pʊt/		ɪə	near	/nɪə(r)/
u	situation	/ˌsɪtʃuˈeɪʃn/		eə	hair	/heə(r)/
uː	too	/tuː/		ʊə	pure	/pjʊə(r)/

Consonants

p	pen	/pen/		s	so	/səʊ/
b	bad	/bæd/		z	zoo	/zuː/
t	tea	/tiː/		ʃ	shoe	/ʃuː/
d	did	/dɪd/		ʒ	vision	/ˈvɪʒn/
k	cat	/kæt/		h	hat	/hæt/
ɡ	got	/ɡɒt/		m	man	/mæn/
tʃ	chain	/tʃeɪn/		n	no	/nəʊ/
dʒ	jam	/dʒæm/		ŋ	sing	/sɪŋ/
f	fall	/fɔːl/		l	leg	/leg/
v	van	/væn/		r	red	/red/
θ	thin	/θɪn/		j	yes	/jes/
ð	this	/ðɪs/		w	wet	/wet/

(ˈ) shows the strong stress: it is in front of the part of the word that you say most strongly, for example **because** /bɪˈkɒz/.

(ˌ) shows a weaker stress. Some words have a part that is said with a weaker stress as well as a strong stress, for example **OK** /ˌəʊ ˈkeɪ/.

(r) at the end of a word means that in British English you say this sound only when the next word begins with a vowel sound. In American English, you always pronounce this 'r'.

Some words, for example **at** and **must**, have two pronunciations. We give the usual pronunciation first. The second pronunciation must be used when the word is stressed, and is also often used when the word is at the end of a sentence. For example:
This book is for /fə(r)/ *Lisa.*
Who is this book for? /fɔː(r)/

A a

A, a /eɪ/ *noun* (*plural* A's, a's /eɪz/)
the first letter of the English alphabet: '*Apple*' *begins with an 'A'.*

a 0—π /ə; eɪ/ (*also* an /ən; æn/) *article*
1 one or any: *Would you like a drink?* ◇ *A dog has four legs.* ◇ *He's a teacher.*
2 each, or for each: *She phones her mother three times a week.* ◇ *Calls cost 16p a minute.*

🔎 **WHICH WORD?**

A or **an**?
You use **an** in front of words that start with a vowel sound. Be careful! It is the sound that is important, not the spelling. For example, words like *euro* and *university* and words that begin with a silent 'h', like *hour*, take **a** instead of **an**. Look at these examples: *a box* ◇ *an apple* ◇ *a singer* ◇ *an hour* ◇ *a university* ◇ *an MP* ◇ *a euro* ◇ *an umbrella*.

abandon /ə'bændən/ *verb* (abandons, abandoning, abandoned /ə'bændənd/)
1 to leave somebody or something completely: *He abandoned his car in the snow.*
2 to stop doing something before it is finished: *When the rain started, we abandoned our game.*

abbey /'æbi/ *noun* (*plural* abbeys)
a building where religious men or women (called **monks** and **nuns**) live or lived

abbreviate /ə'briːvieɪt/ *verb* (abbreviates, abbreviating, abbreviated)
to make a word shorter by not saying or writing some of the letters: *The word 'telephone' is often abbreviated to 'phone'.*

abbreviation /ə,briːvi'eɪʃn/ *noun*
a short form of a word: *TV is an abbreviation for 'television'.*

abdomen /'æbdəmən/ *noun* (formal)
the front middle part of your body, which contains your stomach

ability 0—π /ə'bɪləti/ *noun* (*plural* abilities)
the power and knowledge to do something: *She has the ability to pass the exam, but she must work harder.*

able 0—π /'eɪbl/ *adjective*
be able to do something to have the power and knowledge to do something: *Will*

you be able to come to the party? ◇ *Is Simon able to swim?* ⊃ OPPOSITE **unable** ⊃ Look at **can**.

abnormal /æb'nɔːml/ *adjective*
different from what is normal or usual, in a way that worries you or that is unpleasant: *They thought the boy's behaviour was abnormal.*

aboard /ə'bɔːd/ *adverb, preposition*
on or onto a ship, train, bus or plane: *Are all the passengers aboard the ship?* ◇ *Welcome aboard flight 603 to Nairobi.*

abolish /ə'bɒlɪʃ/ *verb* (abolishes, abolishing, abolished /ə'bɒlɪʃt/)
to stop or end something by law: *The Americans abolished slavery in 1863.*
▸ **abolition** /,æbə'lɪʃn/ *noun* (no plural): *the abolition of hunting*

about 0—π /ə'baʊt/ *preposition, adverb*
1 a little more or less than; a little before or after: *She's about 30 years old.* ◇ *There were about 2,000 people at the concert.* ◇ *I got there at about two o'clock.*
2 of; on the subject of: *a book about cats* ◇ *We talked about the problem.* ◇ *What are you thinking about?*
3 (*also* around) in a lot of different directions or places: *The children were running about in the garden.* ◇ *There were books lying about on the floor.*
4 almost; nearly: *Dinner is just about ready.*
5 (*also* around) in a place; here: *It was late and there weren't many people about.*
be about to do something to be going to do something very soon: *The film is about to start.*

above 0—π /ə'bʌv/ *preposition, adverb*
1 in or to a higher place; higher than somebody or something: *I looked up at the sky above.* ◇ *My bedroom is above the kitchen.* ◇ *There is a picture on the wall above the fireplace.* ⊃ OPPOSITE **below**
2 more than a number or price: *children aged ten and above* ⊃ OPPOSITE **below, under**
above all more than any other thing; what is most important: *He's handsome and intelligent and, above all, he's kind!*

abroad 0—π /ə'brɔːd/ *adverb*
in or to another country: *She lives abroad.* ◇ *Are you going abroad this summer?*

abrupt /ə'brʌpt/ *adjective*
1 sudden and unexpected: *an abrupt change of plan*

2 seeming rude and unfriendly: *I'm sorry for being so abrupt with you.*
▸ **abruptly** /ə'brʌptli/ ***adverb***: *The conversation ended abruptly.*

absence /'æbsəns/ ***noun*** (*no plural*)
a time when a person or thing is not there: *I am doing Julie's job in her absence.*

absent /'æbsənt/ ***adjective***
not there ➲ SAME MEANING **away**: *He was absent from work yesterday because he was ill.*

absent-minded /ˌæbsənt 'maɪndɪd/ ***adjective***
often forgetting or not noticing things, perhaps because you are thinking about something else ➲ SAME MEANING **forgetful**: *Grandma is getting more absent-minded as she gets older.*

absolute /'æbsəlu:t/ ***adjective***
complete: *I've never played chess before. I'm an absolute beginner.* ◇ *The whole trip was an absolute disaster.*

absolutely 🔑 /'æbsəlu:tli/ ***adverb***
1 completely: *It's absolutely freezing outside!*
2 /ˌæbsə'lu:tli/ (used when you are strongly agreeing with somebody) yes; certainly: *'It is a good idea, isn't it?' 'Oh, absolutely!'*

absorb /əb'sɔ:b; əb'zɔ:b/ ***verb*** (**absorbs, absorbing, absorbed** /əb'sɔ:bd; əb'zɔ:bd/)
to take in something like liquid or heat, and hold it: *The dry ground absorbed all the rain.*

absorbent /əb'sɔ:bənt; əb'zɔ:bənt/ ***adjective***
able to take in and hold something, especially liquid: *an absorbent cloth*

absorbing /əb'sɔ:bɪŋ; əb'zɔ:bɪŋ/ ***adjective***
very interesting: *an absorbing book*

abstract /'æbstrækt/ ***adjective***
1 about an idea, not a real thing: *abstract thought*
2 not like a real thing: *an abstract painting*

absurd /əb'sɜ:d/ ***adjective***
so silly that it makes you laugh: *The guards look absurd in that new uniform.* ◇ *Don't be absurd! I can't possibly do all this work in one day.* ➲ SAME MEANING **ridiculous**

abuse¹ /ə'bju:z/ ***verb*** (**abuses, abusing, abused** /ə'bju:zd/)
1 to use something in a wrong or bad way: *The manager often abuses her power.*
2 to say rude things to somebody: *The player got a red card for abusing the referee.*
3 to be cruel or unkind to somebody: *The children were abused by their father.*

abuse² /ə'bju:s/ ***noun*** (*no plural*)
1 using something in a wrong or bad way: *the dangers of drug abuse*
2 rude words: *The lorry driver shouted abuse at the cyclist.* ◇ *racial abuse*
3 being cruel or unkind to somebody: *The child had suffered verbal and physical abuse.*

academic /ˌækə'demɪk/ ***adjective***
connected with education, especially in schools and universities: *Our academic year begins in September.*

accelerator /ək'seləreɪtə(r)/ ***noun***
the part of a vehicle that you press with your foot when you want it to go faster: *She put her foot down on the accelerator and overtook the bus.*

accent /'æksent/ ***noun***
1 the way a person from a certain place or country speaks a language: *She speaks English with an American accent.*
2 saying one word or part of a word more strongly than another: *In the word 'because', the accent is on the second part of the word.*
3 (in writing) a mark, usually above a letter, that changes the sound of the letter: *Fiancé has an accent on the 'e'.*

accept 🔑 /ək'sept/ ***verb*** (**accepts, accepting, accepted**)

> **SPELLING**
> Remember! Don't confuse **accept** with **except**, which sounds nearly the same.

1 to say 'yes' when somebody asks you to have or do something: *Please accept this present.* ◇ *I accepted the invitation to his party.*
2 to believe that something is true: *She can't accept that her son is dead.*

acceptable 🔑 /ək'septəbl/ ***adjective***
allowed by most people; good enough: *It's not acceptable to make so many mistakes.*

acceptance /ək'septəns/ ***noun*** (*no plural*)
taking something that somebody offers you or asks you to have: *Her quick acceptance of the offer surprised me.*

access¹ /'ækses/ ***noun*** (*no plural*)
a way to go into a place or to use something: *We don't **have access to** the garden from our flat.* ◇ *Do you **have access to** a computer at home?*

access² /'ækses/ ***verb*** (**accesses, accessing, accessed** /'æksest/)
(*computing*) to find information on a computer: *Click on the icon to access a file.*

accident 🔑 /'æksɪdənt/ ***noun***
something bad that happens by chance: *I **had an accident** when I was driving to work – my car hit a tree.* ◇ *I'm sorry I broke your watch – it was an accident.*

by accident by chance; not because you planned it: *I took Jane's book by accident. I thought it was mine.*
▶ **accidentally** /ˌæksɪ'dentəli/ *adverb*: *He accidentally broke the window.*

accidental /ˌæksɪ'dentl/ *adjective*
If something is **accidental**, it happens by chance and is not planned: *Police do not know if the plane crash was accidental or caused by a bomb.*

accommodation /əˌkɒmə'deɪʃn/ *noun*
(*no plural*)

> 🔍 SPELLING
> Remember! You spell **accommodation** with **CC** and **MM**.

a place to stay or live: *It's difficult to find cheap accommodation in London.*

> 🔍 GRAMMAR
> **Accommodation** has no plural. We cannot say 'I will help you find an accommodation.'
> Sometimes it is better to use a different phrase instead. In this case we could say, 'I will help you to find somewhere to live.'

accompany /ə'kʌmpəni/ *verb*
(accompanies, accompanying, accompanied /ə'kʌmpənid/)
1 (*formal*) to go with somebody to a place: *Four teachers accompanied the class on their school trip.*
2 to happen at the same time as something else: *Thunder is usually accompanied by lightning.*
3 to play music while somebody sings or plays another instrument: *You sing and I'll accompany you on the guitar.*

accomplish /ə'kʌmplɪʃ/ *verb*
(accomplishes, accomplishing, accomplished /ə'kʌmplɪʃt/)
to succeed in doing something difficult that you planned to do ⊃ SAME MEANING **achieve**: *The first part of the plan has been safely accomplished.*

accord /ə'kɔːd/ *noun* (*no plural*)
of your own accord because you want to, not because somebody has asked you: *She left the job of her own accord.*

according to 0ᴛ /ə'kɔːdɪŋ tə; before a, e, i, o or u ə'kɔːdɪŋ tu: or tu/ *preposition*
as somebody or something says: *According to Mike, this film is really good.* ◇ *The church was built in 1395, according to this book.*

account¹ 0ᴛ /ə'kaʊnt/ *noun*
1 words that somebody says or writes about

something that happened: *She gave the police a full account of the robbery*
2 an arrangement with a bank which lets you keep your money there: *I paid the money into my account.* ◇ *to open an account*
3 accounts (*plural*) lists of all the money that a person or business receives and pays: *Who keeps (= writes) the accounts for your business?*
on account of something because of something: *Our school was closed on account of bad weather.*
on no account, not on any account not for any reason: *On no account should you walk home on your own.*
take account of something, take something into account to remember something when you are thinking about other things: *John is always last, but you must take his age into account – he is much younger than the other children.*

account² /ə'kaʊnt/ *verb*
account for something
1 to explain or give a reason for something: *How can you account for the missing pieces?*
2 to make the amount that is mentioned: *Sales to Africa accounted for 60% of our total sales last year.*

accountant /ə'kaʊntənt/ *noun*
a person whose job is to make lists of all the money that people or businesses receive and pay: *Nicky is an accountant.*

accuracy /'ækjərəsi/ *noun* (*no plural*)
the quality of being exactly right, with no mistakes

accurate /'ækjərət/ *adjective*
exactly right; with no mistakes: *He gave an accurate description of the thief.*
⊃ OPPOSITE **inaccurate**
▶ **accurately** /'ækjərətli/ *adverb*: *The map was accurately drawn.*

accuse 0ᴛ /ə'kjuːz/ *verb* (accuses, accusing, accused /ə'kjuːzd/)
to say that somebody has done something wrong or broken the law: *His classmates accused him of cheating in the exam.* ◇ *She was accused of murder.*
▶ **accusation** /ˌækju'zeɪʃn/ *noun*: *The accusations were not true.*

accustomed /ə'kʌstəmd/ *adjective*
familiar with something and accepting it as normal or usual ⊃ SAME MEANING **used to**: *My eyes slowly grew accustomed to the dark.*

ace /eɪs/ *noun*
a PLAYING CARD (= one of 52 cards used for playing games) which has only one shape on it. An **ace** has either the lowest or the

A

highest value in a game of cards: *the ace of hearts*

ache¹ /eɪk/ *verb* (aches, aching, ached /eɪkt/)

to hurt; to give you pain: *She was aching all over.* ◇ *My legs ached after the long walk.*

ache² /eɪk/ *noun* (no plural)

a pain that lasts for a long time: *If you eat all those sweets, you'll get stomach ache.* ◇ *She's got earache.*

> 🔎 **GRAMMAR**
>
> We often use **ache** with a part of the body.
> In British English, we usually use **ache** without 'a' or 'an': *I've got backache.* But we always say 'a headache': *I've got a terrible headache.*
> In American English, we usually use **ache** with 'a' or 'an', especially when talking about a particular attack of pain: *I have an awful toothache.*

achieve 0‑ŋ /əˈtʃiːv/ *verb* (achieves, achieving, achieved /əˈtʃiːvd/)

to do or finish something well after trying hard: *He worked hard and achieved his aim of becoming a doctor.*

achievement /əˈtʃiːvmənt/ *noun*

something that somebody has done after trying hard: *Climbing Mount Everest was his greatest achievement.*

acid 0‑ŋ /ˈæsɪd/ *noun*

(in chemistry) a liquid substance that burns things or makes holes in metal

acid rain /ˌæsɪd ˈreɪn/ *noun* (no plural)

rain that has chemicals in it from factories, for example. It causes damage to trees, rivers and buildings.

acknowledge /əkˈnɒlɪdʒ/ *verb* (acknowledges, acknowledging, acknowledged /əkˈnɒlɪdʒd/)

1 to agree or accept that something is true: *He acknowledged that he had made a mistake.*

2 to write to somebody who has sent you a letter, etc. to say that you have received it: *She never acknowledged my letter.*

▶ **acknowledgement** /əkˈnɒlɪdʒmənt/ *noun*: *I didn't receive an acknowledgement of my application.*

acne /ˈækni/ *noun* (no plural)

a skin problem, common among young people, that causes red spots, especially on the face

acorns

acorn /ˈeɪkɔːn/ *noun*

a small nut with a base like a cup. **Acorns** grow on large trees (called **oak trees**).

acquaintance /əˈkweɪntəns/ *noun*

a person that you know a little but who is not a close friend

acquire /əˈkwaɪə(r)/ *verb* (acquires, acquiring, acquired /əˈkwaɪəd/) (formal)

to get or buy something: *He acquired some English from listening to pop songs.*

acre /ˈeɪkə(r)/ *noun*

a unit for measuring an area of land; about 4050 square metres: *a farm of 40 acres*

acrobat /ˈækrəbæt/ *noun*

a person who performs difficult acts such as walking on high ropes, especially in a CIRCUS (= a show that travels to different towns)

across 0‑ŋ /əˈkrɒs/ *adverb, preposition*

1 from one side to the other side of something: *We walked across the field.* ◇ *A smile spread across her face.* ◇ *The river was about twenty metres across.*

2 on the other side of something: *There is a bank just across the road.*

> 🔎 **WHICH WORD?**
>
> **Across** or **over**?
> We can use **across** or **over** to mean 'on or to the other side': *I ran across the road.* ◇ *I ran over the road.*
> We usually use **over** to talk about crossing something high: *Adam climbed over the wall.*
> With 'room' we usually use **across**: *I walked across the room.*

act¹ 0‑ŋ /ækt/ *verb* (acts, acting, acted)

1 to do something, or to behave in a certain way: *Doctors acted quickly to save the boy's life after the accident.* ◇ *Stop acting like a child!*

2 to pretend to be somebody else in a play, film or television programme

➔ SAME MEANING **perform**

act as something to do the job of another person, usually for a short time: *He acted as manager while his boss was ill.*

act² 0‑ŋ /ækt/ *noun*

1 a thing that you do: *an act of kindness*

> 🔎 **WHICH WORD?**
>
> **Act**, **action** or **activity**?
> **Act** and **action** can have the same meaning: *It was a brave act.* ◇ *It was a*

brave action.
Act, but not **action**, can be followed by
of: *It was an act of bravery.*
We say **activity** for something that is
done regularly: *I like outdoor activities such
as walking and cycling.*

2 one of the main parts of a play or an
OPERA (= a musical play): *This play has five
acts.*
3 a law that a government makes: *an act of
Parliament*
4 behaviour that hides your true feelings:
*She seems very happy, but she's just putting
on an act.*
in the act (of doing something) while
doing something wrong: *I caught him in the
act of stealing the money.*

acting /'æktɪŋ/ *noun* (no plural)
being in plays or films: *Have you ever done
any acting?*

action 0̄ /'ækʃn/ *noun*
1 (no plural) doing things, especially for a
particular purpose: *Now is the time for action!
◇ If we don't **take action** quickly, it'll be too
late!*
2 (plural **actions**) something that you do:
The little girl copied her mother's actions.
3 (no plural) exciting things that happen:
*I like films with a lot of action in them. ◇ an
action-packed film*
in action doing something; working: *We
watched the machine in action.*

active 0̄ /'æktɪv/ *adjective*
1 If you are **active**, you are always busy and
able to do a lot of things: *My grandmother is
75 but she's still very active.*
2 (grammar) when the person or thing
doing the action is the subject of a sentence
or verb: *In the sentence 'The dog bit him', the
verb is active.* ⊃ You can also say 'The verb is
in the active'. ⊃ OPPOSITE **passive**

activity 0̄ /æk'tɪvəti/ *noun*
1 (no plural) a lot of things happening and
people doing things: *On the day of the
festival there was a lot of activity in the streets.*
2 (plural **activities**) something that you do,
usually regularly and because you enjoy it:
The hotel offers a range of leisure activities.

actor 0̄ /'æktə(r)/ *noun*
a man or woman who acts in plays, films or
television programmes

actress 0̄ /'æktrəs/ *noun* (plural
actresses)
a woman who acts in plays, films or
television programmes

actual 0̄ /'æktʃuəl/ *adjective*
that really happened; real: *The actual
damage to the car was not as bad as we'd
feared. ◇ They seemed to be good friends but
in actual fact they hated each other.*

actually 0̄ /'æktʃuəli/ *adverb*
1 really; in fact: *You don't actually believe her,
do you? ◇ I can't believe I'm actually going to
Australia!*
2 a word that you use to disagree politely or
when you say something new: *I don't agree. I
thought the film was very good, actually. ◇
'Let's go out tonight.' 'Actually, I'd like to stay
in and watch a film.'*

> 🔎 WHICH WORD?
> Be careful! **Actually** does **not** mean
> 'now'.
> We can say **currently**, **at present** or **at
> the moment** instead: *He's currently
> working in China. ◇ I'm studying for my
> exams at the moment.*

acute /ə'kju:t/ *adjective*
very serious; very great: *an acute shortage of
food*

acute angle /ə,kju:t 'æŋgl/ *noun*
(maths) an angle of less than 90° ⊃ Look also
at **obtuse angle** and **right angle**.

AD /,eɪ 'di:/ *abbreviation*
AD in a date shows that it was after Christ
was born: *1066 AD* ⊃ Look at **BC**.

ad 0̄ /æd/ *noun* (informal) short for
ADVERTISEMENT

adapt /ə'dæpt/ *verb* (adapts, adapting,
adapted)
1 to change the way that you do things
because you are in a new situation: *He has
adapted very well to being at a new school.*
2 to change something so that you can use
it in a different way: *The car was adapted for
use as a taxi.*

adaptable /ə'dæptəbl/ *adjective*
able to change in a new situation: *He'll soon
get used to his new school. Children are very
adaptable.*

add 0̄ /æd/ *verb* (adds, adding, added)
1 to put something with something else:
*Mix the flour with the milk and then add the
eggs. ◇ Add your name to the list.*
2 to put numbers together so that you get a
total: *If you add 2 and 5 together, you get 7.
◇ Add $10 to the total, to cover postage and
packing.* ⊃ OPPOSITE **subtract**
3 to say something more: *'Go away – and
don't come back again,' she added.*
add up to find the total of several numbers:
The waiter hadn't added up the bill correctly.

A B C D E F G H I J K L M N O P Q R S T U V W X Y Z

A
B
C
D
E
F
G
H
I
J
K
L
M
N
O
P
Q
R
S
T
U
V
W
X
Y
Z

add up to something to have as a total: *How much does all the shopping add up to?*

addict /'ædɪkt/ *noun*
a person who cannot stop wanting something that is bad for them: *a drug addict*

addicted /ə'dɪktɪd/ *adjective*
not able to stop wanting something that is bad for you: *He is **addicted to** heroin.*

addition /ə'dɪʃn/ *noun*
1 (*no plural*) putting numbers together: *We learnt addition and subtraction at primary school.*
2 (*plural* additions) a thing or person that is added to something: *They have a new **addition to** their family* (= a new baby).
in addition, in addition to something as well as: *He speaks five languages in addition to English.*

address¹ 0-ᴡ /ə'dres/ *noun* (*plural* addresses)

🔍 SPELLING
Remember! You spell **address** with **DD** and **SS**.

1 the number of the building and the name of the street and town where somebody lives or works: *Her address is 18 Wilton Street, London NW10.* ◇ *Are you still living at that address?*
2 (*computing*) a group of words and symbols that tells you where you can find somebody or something using a computer: *What's your email address?*

address² /ə'dres/ *verb* (addresses, addressing, addressed /ə'drest/)
1 to write on a letter or package the name and address of the person you are sending it to: *The letter was **addressed to** Alison Waters.*
2 to make a formal speech to a group of people: *The President will address the assembly.*

adequate /'ædɪkwət/ *adjective*
enough for what you need: *They are very poor and do not have adequate food or clothing.* ⊃ OPPOSITE **inadequate**

adjective /'ædʒɪktɪv/ *noun*
(*grammar*) a word that you use with a noun, that tells you more about it: *In the sentence 'This soup is hot', 'hot' is an adjective.*

adjust /ə'dʒʌst/ *verb* (adjusts, adjusting, adjusted)
to make a small change to something, to make it better: *You can adjust the height of this chair.*

administration /əd,mɪnɪ'streɪʃn/ *noun* (*no plural*)
controlling or managing something, for example a business, an office or a school

admiral /'ædmərəl/ *noun*
a very important officer in the navy

admire 0-ᴡ /əd'maɪə(r)/ *verb* (admires, admiring, admired /əd'maɪəd/)
to think or say that somebody or something is very good: *I really **admire** you **for** doing such a difficult job.* ◇ *They were admiring the view from the top of the tower.*
▶ **admiration** /,ædmə'reɪʃn/ *noun* (*no plural*): *I have great admiration for her work.*

admission /əd'mɪʃn/ *noun*
1 (*no plural*) allowing somebody to go into a school, club, public place, etc.: *There is no **admission to** the park after 8 p.m.* ◇ *All those who were not wearing a tie were **refused** admission to the club.*
2 (*no plural*) the amount of money that you have to pay to go into a place: *Admission to the zoo is €10.*
3 when you agree that you did something wrong or bad: *an **admission of** guilt*

admit 0-ᴡ /əd'mɪt/ *verb* (admits, admitting, admitted)
1 to say that you have done something wrong or that something bad is true: *He admitted stealing the money.* ◇ *I admit that I made a mistake.* ⊃ OPPOSITE **deny**
2 to allow somebody or something to go into a place: *This ticket admits one person to the museum.*

adolescence /,ædə'lesns/ *noun* (*no plural*)
the period of a person's life between being a child and becoming an adult

adolescent /,ædə'lesnt/ *noun*
a young person who is developing from a child into an adult ⊃ SAME MEANING **teenager**

adopt /ə'dɒpt/ *verb* (adopts, adopting, adopted)
to take the child of another person into your family and treat them as your own child by law: *They adopted Micky after his parents died.*

adore /ə'dɔː(r)/ *verb* (adores, adoring, adored /ə'dɔːd/)
to love somebody or something very much: *She adores her grandchildren.*

adult 0-ᴡ /'ædʌlt; ə'dʌlt/ *noun*
a person or an animal that has grown to the full size; not a child: *Adults as well as children will enjoy this film.*
▶ **adult** *adjective*: *an adult ticket* ◇ *adult education*

advance[1] /əd'vɑːns/ *noun*
progress or a new development in
something: *major **advances in** computer
technology*
in advance before something happens:
*You should book tickets for the concert well in
advance.*

advanced /əd'vɑːnst/ *adjective*
of or for somebody who is already good at
something; difficult: *an advanced English
class*

advantage 0ᴛ /əd'vɑːntɪdʒ/ *noun*
something that helps you or that is useful:
*One **advantage of** camping is that it's cheap.*
⊃ OPPOSITE **disadvantage**
take advantage of something to make
good use of something to help yourself: *Buy
now and take advantage of these special
prices!*

adventure /əd'ventʃə(r)/ *noun*
something exciting that you do or that
happens to you: *She wrote a book about her
adventures in Africa.*

adventurous /əd'ventʃərəs/ *adjective*
An **adventurous** person likes to do exciting,
dangerous things.

adverb /'ædvɜːb/ *noun*
(*grammar*) a word that tells you how, when
or where something happens: *In the sentence
'Please speak slowly','slowly' is an adverb.*

advert /'ædvɜːt/ *noun short for*
ADVERTISEMENT

advertise /'ædvətaɪz/ *verb* (advertises,
advertising, advertised /'ædvətaɪzd/)
to put information in a newspaper, on
television, on a wall, etc., to make people
want to buy something or do something:
I saw those trainers advertised in a magazine.
◇ *It's very expensive to advertise on television.*

advertisement 0ᴛ /əd'vɜːtɪsmənt/
(*also informal* ad, advert) *noun*
information in a newspaper, on television,
on the Internet, on a wall, etc. that makes
people want to buy something or do
something: *an **advertisement for** a new kind
of chocolate bar*

advertising /'ædvətaɪzɪŋ/ *noun* (*no
plural*)
telling people about things to buy: *He works
in advertising.* ◇ *The magazine gets a lot of
money from advertising.*

advice 0ᴛ /əd'vaɪs/ *noun* (*no plural*)
words that you say to help somebody decide
what to do: *The book **gives** some good **advice
on** travelling abroad.* ◇ *I **took** the doctor's
advice (= I did what the doctor told me to
do) and stayed in bed.*

advise 0ᴛ /əd'vaɪz/ *verb* (advises,
advising, advised /əd'vaɪzd/)

to tell somebody what you think they should
do: *The doctor **advised** him **to** lose weight.*
▶ **adviser** (*British*) (*American* advisor)
/əd'vaɪzə(r)/ *noun* a person who gives
advice to a company, government, etc.

aerials

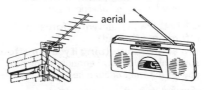

aerial

aerial /'eəriəl/ *noun* (*British*) (*American*
antenna)
a long metal stick on a building, car, etc. that
receives radio or television signals

aerobics /eə'rəʊbɪks/ *noun* (*no plural*)
physical exercises that people often do in
classes, with music

aeroplane /'eərəpleɪn/ *noun* (*American*
airplane) (*British and American also* **plane**)
a vehicle with wings that can fly through the
air ⊃ Look at the note at **plane**.

aerosol /'eərəsɒl/ *noun*
a container with liquid in it. You press a
button to make the liquid come out in a lot
of very small drops.

affair /ə'feə(r)/ *noun*
1 (*plural* **affairs**) something that happens;
an event: *The wedding was a very quiet affair.*
2 **affairs** (*plural*) important events and
situations: *the minister for foreign affairs* ◇ *We
talked about **current affairs** (= the political
and social events that are happening at the
present time)*
3 (*no plural*) something private that you do
not want other people to know about: *What
happened between us is my affair. I don't want
to talk about it.*
4 (*plural* **affairs**) a sexual relationship

A

between two people, usually one that is secret: *Her husband was **having an affair**.*

affect 0→ /əˈfekt/ *verb* (affects, affecting, affected)

🔍 SPELLING

Be careful! Don't confuse **affect**, which is a verb, with **effect**, which is a noun. If you **affect** something then you have an **effect** on it.

to make something or somebody change in a particular way, especially a bad way: *Smoking can affect your health.* ◇ *His parents' divorce affected the child deeply.*

affection /əˈfekʃn/ *noun* (no plural)
the feeling of loving or liking somebody: *She has great **affection for** her aunt.*

affectionate /əˈfekʃənət/ *adjective*
showing that you love or like somebody very much: *a very affectionate child*
▶ **affectionately** /əˈfekʃənətli/ *adverb*:
He smiled at his son affectionately.

afford 0→ /əˈfɔːd/ *verb* (affords, affording, afforded)
can afford something If you **can afford something**, you have enough money to pay for it: *I can't afford a holiday this year.*

afraid 0→ /əˈfreɪd/ *adjective*
If you are **afraid** of something, it makes you feel fear: *Some people are **afraid of** snakes.* ◇ *I was afraid to open the door.*
I'm afraid … a polite way of saying that you are sorry: *I'm afraid I've broken your calculator.* ◇ *I'm afraid that I can't come to your party.*

after¹ 0→ /ˈɑːftə(r)/ *preposition*
1 later than somebody or something: *Jane arrived after dinner.* ◇ *After doing my homework, I went out.*
2 behind or following somebody or something: *Ten comes after nine.* ◇ *Close the door after you.*
3 trying to get or catch somebody or something: *The police officer ran after her.*
after all
1 used when you thought something different would happen: *I was worried about the exam, but it wasn't difficult after all.*
2 used to mean 'do not forget': *She doesn't understand. After all, she's only two.*
be after something to be trying to get or find something: *What kind of work are you after?*

after² /ˈɑːftə(r)/ *conjunction, adverb*
at a time later than somebody or something: *We arrived after the film had started.* ◇ *Jane left at ten o'clock and I left soon after.*

afternoon 0→ /ˌɑːftəˈnuːn/ *noun*
the part of a day between midday (= 12 o'clock) and the evening: *We had lunch and in the afternoon we went for a walk.* ◇ *I saw Jane this afternoon.* ◇ *Yesterday afternoon I went shopping.* ◇ *I'll see you on Monday afternoon.*

🔍 GRAMMAR

We usually say **in the afternoon**: *We went to Windsor Castle in the afternoon.* If we include a day or date then we use **on**: *We went shopping on Monday afternoon.*

aftershave /ˈɑːftəʃeɪv/ *noun* (no plural)
a liquid with a nice smell that men sometimes put on their faces after they SHAVE (= cut the hair off their face)

afterwards 0→ /ˈɑːftəwədz/ *adverb*
later; after another thing has happened: *We had dinner and went to see a film afterwards.*

again 0→ /əˈgen/ *adverb*
1 one more time; once more: *Could you say that again, please?* ◇ *I will never see him again.*
2 in the way that somebody or something was before: *You'll soon feel well again.*
again and again many times: *I've told you again and again not to do that!*

against 0→ /əˈgenst/ *preposition*
1 on the other side in a game, fight, etc.: *They played against a football team from another village.*
2 If you are against something, you do not agree with it: *Many people are against the plan.*
3 touching somebody or something for support: *I put the ladder against the wall.*
4 to stop something: *Have you had an injection against the disease?*

age 0→ /eɪdʒ/ *noun*
1 (*plural* ages) the amount of time that somebody or something has been in the world: *She is seven **years of age**.* ◇ *I started work **at the age of** 16.*

🔍 SPEAKING

When we want to ask someone's **age**, we say **How old are you?**
To say your age, you say **I am 10.** or **I'm 10 years old.** (but NOT 'I am 10 years.')

2 (no plural) being old: *Her hair was grey with age.*
3 (*plural* ages) a certain time in history: *the computer age* ◇ *the history of art through the ages* ◇ *the **Stone Age** (= when people used stone tools)*

4 ages (*plural*) (*informal*) a very long time: *We waited ages for a bus.* ◇ *She's lived here for ages.*

aged 0‑ /eɪdʒd/ *adjective*
of the age mentioned: *They have two children, aged three and five.*

agency /'eɪdʒənsi/ *noun* (*plural* **agencies**)
the work or office of somebody who does business for others: *A travel agency plans holidays for people.*

agenda /ə'dʒendə/ *noun*
a list of all the things to be talked about in a meeting: *The next item **on the agenda** is the school sports day.*

agent /'eɪdʒənt/ *noun*
a person who does business for another person or for a company: *An actor's agent tries to find work for actors and actresses.* ◇ *a travel agent*

aggressive /ə'gresɪv/ *adjective*
If you are **aggressive**, you are ready to argue or fight: *He often gets aggressive after drinking alcohol.*

ago 0‑ /ə'gəʊ/ *adverb*
before now; in the past: *His wife died five years ago.* ◇ *I learned to drive a long time ago.*
long ago a very long time in the past: *Long ago there were no cars or aeroplanes.*

agony /'ægəni/ *noun* (*plural* **agonies**)
very great pain: *He screamed **in agony**.*

agree 0‑ /ə'griː/ *verb* (**agrees, agreeing, agreed** /ə'griːd/)
1 to have the same opinion as another person about something: *Martin thinks we should go by train but I don't agree.* ◇ *I **agree with** you.* ➜ OPPOSITE **disagree**
2 to say 'yes' when somebody asks you to do something: *Amy **agreed to** give me the money.* ➜ OPPOSITE **refuse**
3 to decide something with another person: *We **agreed to** meet on March 3rd.* ◇ *Liz and I **agreed on** a price.*

agreement 0‑ /ə'griːmənt/ *noun*
1 (*no plural*) having the same opinion as somebody or something: *She nodded her head **in agreement**.*
➜ OPPOSITE **disagreement**
2 (*plural* **agreements**) a plan or decision that two or more people have made together: *The leaders **reached an agreement** after five days of talks.*

agriculture /'ægrɪkʌltʃə(r)/ *noun* (*no plural*)
keeping animals and growing plants for food ➜ SAME MEANING **farming**

▶ **agricultural** /ˌægrɪ'kʌltʃərəl/ *adjective*: *agricultural workers*

ahead 0‑ /ə'hed/ *adverb*
1 in front of somebody or something: *We could see a light **ahead** of us.*
2 before or more advanced than somebody or something: *Inga and Nils arrived a few minutes **ahead** of us.* ◇ *London is about five hours ahead of New York.*
3 into the future: *He's got a difficult time **ahead** of him.* ◇ *We must **think ahead** and make a plan.*
4 winning in a game, competition, etc.: *Italy were one goal ahead at half time.*
go ahead used to give somebody permission to do something: *'Can I borrow your bike?' 'Sure, go ahead.'*

aid /eɪd/ *noun* (*no plural*)
1 help, or something that gives help: *He walks **with the aid of** a stick.* ◇ *She wears a **hearing aid** (= a small thing that you put in your ear so you can hear better).*
2 money, food, etc. that is sent to a country or to people in order to help them: *We sent aid to the earthquake victims.*
in aid of somebody or something for somebody or something, especially for a charity: *a concert in aid of Children in Need*

AIDS (*British also* **Aids**) /eɪdz/ *noun* (*no plural*)
a very serious illness which destroys the body's ability to fight other illnesses: *the AIDS virus*

aim[1] 0‑ /eɪm/ *noun*
something that you want and plan to do; a purpose: *Kate's aim is to find a good job.*

aim[2] 0‑ /eɪm/ *verb* (**aims, aiming, aimed** /eɪmd/)
1 to try or plan to do something: *He's aiming to leave at nine o'clock.*
2 to plan something for a certain person or group: *This book is **aimed at** teenagers.*
3 to point something, for example a gun, at somebody or something that you want to hit: *The farmer **aimed** his gun **at** the rabbit and fired.*

air[1] 0‑ /eə(r)/ *noun* (*no plural*)
1 the mixture of gases that surrounds the earth and that you take in through your nose and mouth when you breathe: *Please open a window — I need some **fresh air**.*
2 the space around and above things: *He threw the ball up **into the air**.*
3 travel or transport in an aircraft: *It's more expensive to travel **by air** than by train.* ◇ *an air ticket*

A
B
C
D
E
F
G
H
I
J
K
L
M
N
O
P
Q
R
S
T
U
V
W
X
Y
Z

on air, **on the air** on the radio or on television: *This radio station is on the air 24 hours a day.*

air conditioning /'eə kəndɪʃnɪŋ/ *noun* (*no plural*)
a system that keeps the air in a room, building, car, etc. cool and dry
▶ **air-conditioned** /'eə kəndɪʃnd/ *adjective*: air-conditioned offices

aircraft 0-ₘ /'eəkrɑːft/ *noun* (*plural* aircraft)
any vehicle that can fly, for example a plane

air force /'eə fɔːs/ *noun*
the aircraft that a country uses for fighting, and the people who fly them

air hostess /'eə həʊstəs/ *noun* (*plural* air hostesses)
a woman whose job is to look after people on a plane: *Alison is an air hostess.*
◔ SAME MEANING **stewardess**

airline /'eəlaɪn/ *noun*
a company that takes people or things to different places by plane: *Which airline are you flying with?*

airmail /'eəmeɪl/ *noun* (*no plural*)
the system of sending letters, packages, etc. by plane: *I sent the parcel by airmail.* ◇ *I sent it airmail.*

airplane /'eəpleɪn/ *American English for* AEROPLANE

airport 0-ₘ /'eəpɔːt/ *noun*
a place where people get on and off planes, with buildings where passengers can wait: *I'll meet you at the airport.*

aisle /aɪl/ *noun*
a way between lines of seats in a church, plane, etc.

alarm¹ /ə'lɑːm/ *noun*
1 (*no plural*) a sudden feeling of fear: *He heard a noise, and jumped out of bed in alarm.*
2 (*plural* alarms) something that tells you about danger, for example by making a loud noise: *Does your car have an alarm?* ◇ *a burglar alarm* ◇ *a fire alarm*
3 = ALARM CLOCK ◔ Look also at **false alarm**.

alarm² /ə'lɑːm/ *verb* (alarms, alarming, alarmed /ə'lɑːmd/)
to make somebody or something feel suddenly frightened or worried: *The noise alarmed the bird and it flew away.* ◇ *She was alarmed to hear that Peter was ill.*

alarm clock /ə'lɑːm klɒk/ (*also* alarm) *noun*
a clock that makes a noise to wake you up: *She set the alarm clock for half past six.*

alarm clock

hand

album /'ælbəm/ *noun*
1 a collection of songs on one CD, tape, etc.: *The band are about to release their third album.* ◔ Look at **single**.
2 a book in which you can keep stamps, photographs, etc. that you have collected: *a photograph album*

alcohol 0-ₘ /'ælkəhɒl/ *noun* (*no plural*)
1 the clear liquid in drinks such as beer and wine that can make people drunk
2 drinks like wine, beer, etc. that contain alcohol

alcoholic 0-ₘ /ˌælkə'hɒlɪk/ *adjective*
containing alcohol: *an alcoholic drink*

> 🔎 **WORD BUILDING**
> Drinks without alcohol are called **soft drinks**.

alert¹ /ə'lɜːt/ *adjective*
watching, listening, etc. for something with all your attention: *A good driver is always alert.*

A level /'eɪ levl/ *noun*
an exam that students in Britain take when they are about eighteen. You usually take **A levels** in two, three or four subjects and you need good results (called **grades**) if you want to go to university. **A level** is short for **Advanced level**. ◔ Look at **GCSE**.

algebra /'æld ʒɪbrə/ *noun* (*no plural*)
a type of mathematics in which letters and symbols are used to represent numbers

alien /'eɪliən/ *noun*
1 (*formal*) a person who comes from another country: *an illegal alien*
2 a person or an animal that comes from another planet: *aliens from outer space*

alight /ə'laɪt/ *adjective*
on fire; burning: *A cigarette set the petrol alight.*

alike /ə'laɪk/ *adjective, adverb*
1 very similar: *The two sisters are very alike.*
2 in the same way: *The book is popular with adults and children alike.*

alive 0ᴎ /əˈlaɪv/ *adjective*
living; not dead: *Are your grandparents alive?*

all¹ 0ᴎ /ɔːl/ *adjective, pronoun*
1 every part of something; the whole of something: *She's eaten all the bread.* ◇ *It rained all day.*
2 every one of a group: *All cats are animals but not all animals are cats.* ◇ *I invited thirty people to the party, but not **all of** them came.* ◇ *Are you all listening?*
3 everything that; the only thing that: *All I've eaten today is one banana.*
(not) at all in any way: *I didn't enjoy it at all.*

all² 0ᴎ /ɔːl/ *adverb*
completely: *She lives all alone.* ◇ *He was dressed all in black.*
all along from the beginning: *I knew all along that she was lying.*
all over everywhere: *We've looked all over for that ring.*

allergic /əˈlɜːdʒɪk/ *adjective*
having an ALLERGY: *He's **allergic to** cow's milk.*

allergy /ˈælədʒi/ *noun (plural allergies)*
a medical condition that makes you ill when you eat, touch or breathe something that does not normally make other people ill: *She has an **allergy to** cats.*

alley /ˈæli/ *noun (plural alleys)*
a narrow path between buildings

alliance /əˈlaɪəns/ *noun*
an agreement between countries or groups of people to work together and help each other

alligator /ˈælɪɡeɪtə(r)/ *noun*
a big long animal with sharp teeth. *Alligators* live in the lakes and rivers of the US and China.

allow 0ᴎ /əˈlaʊ/ *verb* (allows, allowing, allowed /əˈlaʊd/)
to say that somebody can have or do something: *My parents allow me to stay out late at weekends.* ◇ *Smoking is not allowed in most cinemas.* ◇ *You're not allowed to park your car here.*

> 🔎 **WHICH WORD?**
> **Allow** or **let**?
> **Allow** is used in both formal and informal English.
> **Let** is very common in spoken English. You **allow somebody to do something**, but you **let somebody do something** (without 'to'): *Jenny was*

allowed to stay up late last night. ◇ *Her parents **let her stay up late** last night.*
In written English you can use **permit**: *Smoking is not permitted in this building.*

all right 0ᴎ /ˌɔːl ˈraɪt/ (*also informal* alright) *adjective, adverb, exclamation*
1 good, or good enough: *Is everything all right?*
2 well; not hurt: *I was ill, but I'm all right now.*
3 used to say 'yes, I agree' when somebody asks you to do something: *'Can you get me some stamps?' 'All right.'*

ally /ˈælaɪ/ *noun (plural allies)*
a person or country that agrees to help another person or country, for example in a war

almond /ˈɑːmənd/ *noun*
a flat pale nut that you can eat ➔ Look at the picture at **nut**.

almost 0ᴎ /ˈɔːlməʊst/ *adverb*
nearly; not quite: *It's almost three o'clock.* ◇ *I almost fell into the river!*

alone 0ᴎ /əˈləʊn/ *adjective, adverb*
1 without any other person
➔ SAME MEANING **on your own**, **by yourself**: *I don't like being alone in the house.* ◇ *My grandmother lives alone.*
2 only: *You alone can help me.*

> 🔎 **WHICH WORD?**
> **Alone** or **lonely**?
> **Alone** means that you are not with other people: *She lived alone in a flat near the city centre.*
> **Lonely** means that you are unhappy because you are not with other people: *He felt lonely at the new school without his old friends.*

along¹ 0ᴎ /əˈlɒŋ/ *preposition*
1 from one end of something towards the other end: *We walked along the road.*
2 in a line next to something long: *There are trees along the river bank.*

along² 0ᴎ /əˈlɒŋ/ *adverb*
1 forward: *He drove along very slowly.*
2 (*informal*) with somebody: *We're going for a walk. Why don't you **come along** too?*

alongside /əˌlɒŋˈsaɪd/ *preposition, adverb*
next to something: *Put your bike alongside mine.* ◇ *Nick caught up with me and rode alongside.*

aloud /əˈlaʊd/ *adverb*
in a normal speaking voice that other people can hear: *I read the story aloud to my sister.*

A B C D E F G H I J K L M N O P Q R S T U V W X Y Z

A
B
C
D
E
F
G
H
I
J
K
L
M
N
O
P
Q
R
S
T
U
V
W
X
Y
Z

alphabet 0–🔊 /ˈælfəbet/ **noun**
all the letters of a language: *The English
alphabet starts with A and ends with Z.*

alphabetical /ˌælfəˈbetɪkl/ **adjective**
in the order of the alphabet: *Put these words
in alphabetical order* (= with words
beginning with A first, then B, then C, etc.).
▶ **alphabetically** /ˌælfəˈbetɪkli/ **adverb**:
The books are listed alphabetically.

already 0–🔊 /ɔːlˈredi/ **adverb**
before now or before then: *'Would you like
some lunch?' 'No, thank you – I've already
eaten.'* ◇ *We ran to the station but the train
had already left.*

> 🔎 **WHICH WORD?**
>
> **Already** or **yet**?
> **Yet** means the same as **already**, but you
> only use **yet** in negative sentences and
> questions: *I have finished this book already.*
> ◇ *I haven't finished this book yet.* ◇ *Have
> you finished the book yet?*

alright /ɔːlˈraɪt/ (*informal*) = ALL RIGHT

also 0–🔊 /ˈɔːlsəʊ/ **adverb**
as well; too: *He plays several instruments and
also writes music.* ◇ *The food is wonderful, and
also very cheap.*

> 🔎 **WHICH WORD?**
>
> **Also**, **too** or **as well**?
> You use **also** in writing, but you usually
> use **too** or **as well** in spoken English.
> **Also** usually goes before a main verb or
> after 'is', 'are', 'were', etc.: *He also enjoys
> reading.* ◇ *He has also been to Australia.*
> **Too** and **as well** usually go at the end of a
> phrase or sentence: *We're going to the
> cinema tomorrow. Would you like to come
> too?* ◇ *I really love this song, and I liked the
> first one as well.*

alter /ˈɔːltə(r)/ **verb** (**alters, altering,
altered** /ˈɔːltəd/)
to make something different in some way; to
change: *We've altered our plans and will now
stay for a week instead of ten days.* ◇ *He had
altered so much I hardly recognized him.*

alteration /ˌɔːltəˈreɪʃn/ **noun**
a small change: *We want to **make** a few
alterations to the house before we move in.*

alternate¹ /ɔːlˈtɜːnət/ **adjective**
1 with first one thing, then the other, then
the first thing again, etc.: *The cake had
alternate layers of fruit and cream.*
2 one out of every two: *He works alternate
weeks* (= he works the first week, he doesn't
work the second week, he works again the
third week, etc.).

3 (*American*) (*British* **alternative**) that you
can use, do, etc. instead of something else:
an alternate plan

alternate² /ˈɔːltəneɪt/ **verb**
If two things **alternate**, first one thing
happens and then the other and then the
first thing happens again, etc.: *She seemed to
alternate between loving him and hating him.*

alternative¹ /ɔːlˈtɜːnətɪv/ **adjective**
that you can use, do, etc. instead of
something else: *The road was closed so we
had to find an alternative route.*

alternative² /ɔːlˈtɜːnətɪv/ **noun**
a thing that you can choose instead of
another thing: *We could go by train – the
alternative is to take the car.*

alternatively /ɔːlˈtɜːnətɪvli/ **adverb**
used to talk about a second possible thing
you can do: *We can go by bus. Alternatively, I
could take the car.*

although 0–🔊 /ɔːlˈðəʊ/ **conjunction**

> 🔎 **PRONUNCIATION**
>
> The word **although** ends with the same
> sound as **go**.

1 in spite of something: *Although she was ill,
she went to work.*
2 but: *I love dogs, although I wouldn't have
one as a pet.* ➲ SAME MEANING **though**

altogether /ˌɔːltəˈɡeðə(r)/ **adverb**
1 completely: *I don't altogether agree with
you.*
2 counting everything or everybody: *There
were ten of us altogether.*

aluminium /ˌæljəˈmɪniəm/ (*British*)
(*American* **aluminum** /əˈluːmɪnəm/) **noun**
(*no plural*)
a light, silver-coloured metal

always 0–🔊 /ˈɔːlweɪz/ **adverb**
1 at all times; every time: *I have always lived
in London.* ◇ *The train is always late.*
2 for ever: *I will always remember that day.*
3 again and again: *My sister is always
borrowing my clothes!*

> 🔎 **GRAMMAR**
>
> **Always** usually goes before the main
> verb or after 'is', 'are', 'were', etc.: *He
> always wears those shoes.* ◇ *Fiona is always
> late.*
> **Always** can go at the beginning of a
> sentence when you are telling somebody
> to do something: *Always stop and look
> before you cross the road.*

am *form of* BE

a.m. (*American also* A.M.) /ˌeɪ 'em/ *abbreviation*
You use **a.m.** after a time to show that it is between midnight and midday: *I start work at 9 a.m.* ⊃ You use **p.m.** for times between midday and midnight.

amateur /'æmətə(r)/ *noun*
a person who does a sport or an activity because they enjoy it, but not for money as a job: *Only amateurs can take part in the tournament.* ⊃ OPPOSITE **professional**
▶ **amateur** *adjective*: *an amateur photographer*

amaze /ə'meɪz/ *verb* (amazes, amazing, amazed /ə'meɪzd/)
to surprise somebody very much; to be difficult for somebody to believe: *It amazes me that anyone could be so stupid!*

amazed /ə'meɪzd/ *adjective*
very surprised: *She was **amazed to** discover the truth about her father.* ◇ *I was **amazed at** her knowledge of French literature.*

amazement /ə'meɪzmənt/ *noun* (*no plural*)
great surprise: *She looked at me in amazement.*

amazing /ə'meɪzɪŋ/ *adjective*
If something is **amazing**, it surprises you very much and is difficult to believe.
⊃ SAME MEANING **incredible**: *He has shown amazing courage.* ◇ *I've got an amazing story to tell you.*
▶ **amazingly** /ə'meɪzɪŋli/ *adverb*: *Jo plays the violin amazingly well.*

ambassador /æm'bæsədə(r)/ *noun*
an important person who represents his or her country in a foreign country: *the British Ambassador to Italy*

> 🔎 WORD BUILDING
> An ambassador works in an **embassy**.

ambition /æm'bɪʃn/ *noun*
1 something that you really want to do: *My ambition is to become a doctor.*
2 (*no plural*) a very strong wish to be successful, to have power, etc.: *Louise is intelligent, but she has no ambition.*

ambitious /æm'bɪʃəs/ *adjective*
A person who is **ambitious** wants to be successful, to have power, etc.

ambulance /'æmbjələns/ *noun*
a vehicle that takes people who are ill or hurt to hospital

American football /ə,merɪkən 'fʊtbɔːl/ (*British*) (*American* **football**) *noun* (*no plural*)
a game that is played by two teams of eleven

players who kick, throw or carry the ball to the end of the field. The players wear special clothing to protect their heads and bodies.

ammunition /ˌæmju'nɪʃn/ *noun* (*no plural*)
things that you throw or fire from a gun to hurt people or damage things: *They had no more ammunition.*

among

A house among some trees   **A small house between two large ones.**

among 0̄ /ə'mʌŋ/ (*also* amongst /ə'mʌŋst/) *preposition*
1 in the middle of a group of people or things: *I often feel nervous when I'm among strangers.*
2 in a particular group of people or things: *There is a lot of anger among students about the new law.*
3 for or by more than two things or people: *He divided the money among his six children.*

> 🔎 WHICH WORD?
> **Among** or **between**?
> We use **among** when we are talking about more than two people or things: *You're among friends here.*
> If there are only two people or things, we use **between**: *Sarah and I divided the cake between us.* ◇ *I was standing between Alice and Cathy.*

amount¹ 0̄ /ə'maʊnt/ *noun*
how much there is of something: *He spent a large amount of money.*

amount² /ə'maʊnt/ *verb* (amounts, amounting, amounted)
amount to something to make a certain amount when you add everything together: *The cost of the repairs amounted to £500.*

amp /æmp/ *noun*
a measure of electricity

amplifier /'æmplɪfaɪə(r)/ *noun*
an electrical machine that makes sounds louder

amuse 0̄ /ə'mjuːz/ *verb* (amuses, amusing, amused /ə'mjuːzd/)
1 to make somebody smile or laugh: *Rick's joke did not amuse his mother.*

A
B
C
D
E
F
G
H
I
J
K
L
M
N
O
P
Q
R
S
T
U
V
W
X
Y
Z

2 to keep somebody happy and busy: *We played games to amuse ourselves on the long journey.*

amused /ə'mjuːzd/ *adjective*
thinking that something is funny and wanting to laugh or smile: *He was amused to see how seriously she took the game.*

amusement /ə'mjuːzmənt/ *noun* (*no plural*)
the feeling that you have when something makes you laugh or smile: *We watched* **in amusement** *as the dog chased its tail.*

amusement park /ə'mjuːzmənt pɑːk/ *noun*
a large park which has a lot of things that you can ride and play on and many different activities to enjoy

amusing 0→ /ə'mjuːzɪŋ/ *adjective*
Something or somebody that is **amusing** makes you smile or laugh: *an amusing story* ⊃ SAME MEANING **funny**

an 0→ /ən; æn/ *article*
1 one or any: *I ate an apple.*
2 each, or for each: *It costs £2 an hour to park your car here.* ⊃ Look at the note at **a**.

anaesthetic (*British*) (*American* **anesthetic**) /ˌænəs'θetɪk/ *noun*
a drug that a doctor gives you so that you will not feel any pain during an operation: *The patient will be* **under anaesthetic** *for about an hour.*

analyse (*British*) (*American* **analyze**) /'ænəlaɪz/ *verb* (**analyses, analysing, analysed** /'ænəlaɪzd/)
to look at or think about the different parts of something carefully so that you can understand it: *They will analyse the statistics.*

analysis /ə'næləsɪs/ *noun* (*plural* **analyses** /ə'næləsiːz/)
the process of carefully examining the different parts of something: *Some samples of the water were sent to a laboratory* **for analysis**.

ancestor /'ænsestə(r)/ *noun*
Your **ancestors** are the people in your family who lived a long time before you: *My ancestors came from Norway.*

anchor /'æŋkə(r)/ *noun*
a heavy metal thing that you drop into the water from a boat to moving away

anchor

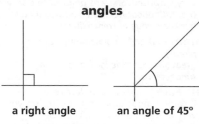

ancient 0→ /'eɪnʃənt/ *adjective*
very old; from a time long ago: *ancient buildings*

and 0→ /ənd; ænd/ *conjunction*
a word that joins words or parts of sentences together: *fish and chips* ◊ *The cat was black and white.* ◊ *They sang and danced all evening.*

anesthetic *American English for* ANAESTHETIC

angel /'eɪndʒl/ *noun*
a spirit who carries messages from God. In pictures, **angels** are usually dressed in white and they have wings.

anger 0→ /'æŋgə(r)/ *noun* (*no plural*)
the strong feeling that you have when something has happened or somebody has done something that you do not like: *She was shaking with anger.*

angles

a right angle   an angle of 45°

angle 0→ /'æŋgl/ *noun*

> 🔎 SPELLING
>
> Remember! You spell **angle** with **L** before **E**. You spell **angel** with **E** before **L**.

the space between two lines that meet. **Angles** are measured in degrees: *an angle of 40°*

> 🔎 WORD BUILDING
>
> A **right angle** measures exactly 90°. An **acute angle** measures less than 90° and an **obtuse angle** measures more than 90°.

angry 0→ /'æŋgri/ *adjective* (**angrier, angriest**)
If you are **angry**, you feel or show anger: *My father was* **angry with** *me when I got home late.*
▶ **angrily** /'æŋgrəli/ *adverb*: '*Somebody has taken my book!*' *she shouted angrily.*

animal 0→ /'ænɪml/ *noun*
1 any living thing that can move and feel but is not a person, a bird, a fish or an insect: *Cats, horses and rats are animals.* ⊃ Look at Picture Dictionary pages **P2-P3**.
2 any living thing that can move and feel,

including people, birds, etc.: *Humans are social animals.*

animated /ˈænɪmeɪtɪd/ *adjective*
1 full of interest and energy: *an animated discussion* ➪ SAME MEANING **lively**
2 If a film is **animated**, drawings or models of people and animals are made to look as if they can really move and talk: *animated cartoons*

animation /ˌænɪˈmeɪʃn/ *noun* (*no plural*)
the process of making films, videos and computer games in which drawings or models of people and animals seem to move: *computer animation*

ankle /ˈæŋkl/ *noun*
the part of your leg where it joins your foot ➪ Look at Picture Dictionary page **P4**.

anniversary /ˌænɪˈvɜːsəri/ *noun* (*plural* anniversaries)
a day that is exactly a year or a number of years after a special or important event: *Today is their 25th wedding anniversary.* ◇ *It happened on the anniversary of her husband's death.* ➪ Look at the note at **birthday**.

announce 0̶ᴡ /əˈnaʊns/ *verb*
(announces, announcing, announced /əˈnaʊnst/)
to tell a lot of people something important: *The teacher announced the winner of the competition.* ◇ *She announced that she was going to have a baby.*

announcement /əˈnaʊnsmənt/ *noun*
important information that somebody tells a lot of people: *Ladies and gentlemen, I'd like to make an announcement.*

announcer /əˈnaʊnsə(r)/ *noun*
a person whose job is to tell us about programmes on radio or television

annoy 0̶ᴡ /əˈnɔɪ/ *verb* (annoys, annoying, annoyed /əˈnɔɪd/)
to make somebody a little angry: *It really annoys me when my brother leaves his clothes all over the floor.* ◇ *Close the door if the noise is annoying you.*

annoyance /əˈnɔɪəns/ *noun* (*no plural*)
the feeling of being a little angry: *She could not hide her annoyance when I arrived late.*

annoyed 0̶ᴡ /əˈnɔɪd/ *adjective*
a little angry: *I was annoyed when he forgot to phone me.* ◇ *My dad is annoyed with me.*

annoying 0̶ᴡ /əˈnɔɪɪŋ/ *adjective*
If a person or thing is **annoying**, they make you a little angry: *It's annoying when people don't listen to you.*

annual /ˈænjuəl/ *adjective*
1 that happens or comes once every year: *There is an annual meeting in June.*
2 for a period of one year: *Their annual income* (= the money they earn in a year) *is less than $20000.*
▶ **annually** /ˈænjuəli/ *adverb*: *Payment will be made annually.*

anonymous /əˈnɒnɪməs/ *adjective*
1 If a person is **anonymous**, other people do not know their name: *An anonymous caller told the police about the bomb.*
2 If something is **anonymous**, you do not know who did, gave or made it: *She received an anonymous letter.*

anorak /ˈænəræk/ *noun*
a short coat with a covering for your head (called a **hood**) that protects you from rain, wind and cold

anorak

another 0̶ᴡ
/əˈnʌðə(r)/ *adjective, pronoun*
1 one more thing or person of the same kind: *Would you like another drink?* ◇ *I like these cakes – can I have another one?*
2 a different thing or person: *I can't see you tomorrow – can we meet another day?* ◇ *If you've already seen that film, we can go and see another.*

answer[1] 0̶ᴡ /ˈɑːnsə(r)/ *noun*

🔎 **PRONUNCIATION**
The word **answer** sounds like **dancer** because we don't say the letter **w** in this word.

1 something that you say or write when you answer somebody or something: *Thanks for the offer but the answer is still no.* ◇ *Have you had an answer to your letter?*
2 when somebody opens the door or picks up the telephone because somebody has knocked or rung: *I knocked on the door and waited but there was no answer.*
3 a way of stopping a problem: *I didn't have any money so the only answer was to borrow some.*
4 the correct reply to a question in a test or an exam: *What was the answer to question 4?* ◇ *All the answers are at the back of the book.*

answer[2] 0̶ᴡ /ˈɑːnsə(r)/ *verb* (answers, answering, answered /ˈɑːnsəd/)
1 to say or write something back when somebody has asked you something or written to you: *I asked him if he was hungry*

A B C D E F G H I J K L M N O P Q R S T U V W X Y Z

A

but he didn't answer. ◊ I couldn't answer all the exam questions.
2 to write a letter to somebody who has written to you ➲ SAME MEANING **reply**: She didn't answer my letter.
answer the door to open the door when somebody knocks or rings: Can you answer the door, please?
answer the telephone to pick up the telephone when it rings, and speak
answering machine /'ɑːnsərɪŋ mə,ʃiːn/ (British also **answerphone** /'ɑːnsəfəʊn/) **noun**
a machine that answers the telephone for you and keeps messages so that you can listen to them later: He wasn't at home, so I left a message **on** his **answerphone**.

ant /ænt/ **noun**
a very small insect that lives in big groups in the ground and works very hard

antelope

antelope /'æntɪləʊp/ **noun**
a wild animal with long horns and long thin legs, that can run fast

antennae

antenna | wing

shell | antenna

bee   snail

antenna /æn'tenə/ **noun** (plural **antennae** /æn'teniː/)
1 one of the two long thin parts on the heads of some insects, and of some animals that live in shells, which they use to feel and touch things
2 American English for AERIAL

anti- /'ænti/ **prefix**
against; not: an anti-smoking campaign

antibiotic /,æntibaɪ'ɒtɪk/ **noun**
a medicine which fights illness in a person's body: The doctor gave me some antibiotics for a chest infection.

anticipate /æn'tɪsɪpeɪt/ **verb**
(**anticipates, anticipating, anticipated**)
to think that something will happen and be

ready for it: We didn't anticipate so many problems.

anticipation /æn,tɪsɪ'peɪʃn/ **noun** (no plural)
excited feelings about something that is going to happen: They queued outside the stadium **in** excited **anticipation**.

anticlockwise /,ænti'klɒkwaɪz/ (British) (American **counterclockwise**) **adjective, adverb**
in the opposite direction to the hands of a clock: Turn the handle anticlockwise.
➲ OPPOSITE **clockwise**

antique /æn'tiːk/ **noun**
an old thing that is worth a lot of money: These chairs are antiques.
▶ **antique adjective**: an antique vase

anxiety /æŋ'zaɪəti/ **noun** (plural **anxieties**)
a feeling of worry and fear

anxious /'æŋkʃəs/ **adjective**
1 worried and afraid: She's anxious because her daughter hasn't arrived yet.
2 If you are **anxious** to do something, you want to do it very much: My family are anxious to meet you.
▶ **anxiously** /'æŋkʃəsli/ **adverb**: We waited anxiously.

any¹ 0🔦 /'eni/ **adjective, pronoun**
1 a word that you use instead of 'some' in questions and after 'not' and 'if': Have you got any money? ◊ I don't speak any Spanish. ◊ She asked if I had any milk. ◊ I want some chocolate but there isn't any. ➲ Look at the note at **some**.
2 used for saying that it does not matter which thing or person you choose: Come any day next week. ◊ Take any book you want.

any² 0🔦 /'eni/ **adverb**
used in negative sentences or questions to make an adjective or an adverb stronger: I can't walk any faster. ◊ Is your dad feeling any better? ◊ I don't want any more.

anybody 0🔦 /'enibɒdi/ another word for ANYONE

anyhow /'enihaʊ/ another word for ANYWAY

any more /,eni 'mɔː(r)/ (British) (British and American also **anymore**) **adverb**
used at the end of negative sentences and questions to mean 'now': She doesn't live here any more. ◊ Why doesn't he speak to me any more?

anyone 0🔦 /'eniwʌn/ (also **anybody**) **pronoun**
1 used in questions and negative sentences to mean 'any person': There wasn't anyone

there. ◇ *Did you see anyone you know?* ◇
Would anyone like more to eat?
2 any person; it does not matter who:
Anyone can learn to swim.

anyplace /'enipleɪs/ *American English for*
ANYWHERE

anything 0̶ʀ /'eniθɪŋ/ *pronoun*
1 used in questions and negative sentences
to mean 'a thing of any kind': *Is there
anything in that box?* ◇ *I can't see anything.* ◇
*'Would you like **anything else**?' asked the
waitress.*
2 any thing or things; it does not matter
what: *I'm so hungry, I could eat anything!* ◇ *I'll
do anything you say.*
not anything like somebody or
something not the same as somebody or
something in any way: *She isn't anything like
her sister.*

anyway 0̶ʀ /'eniweɪ/ (*also* anyhow)
adverb
1 a word that you use when you give a
second, more important reason for
something: *I don't want to go out tonight and
anyway I haven't got any money.*
2 in spite of something else: *It was very
expensive but she bought it anyway.* ◇ *I'm
afraid I'm busy tonight, but thanks for the
invitation anyway.*
3 a word that you use when you start to talk
about something different or when you go
back to something you talked about earlier:
*That's what John told me. Anyway, how are
you?*

anywhere 0̶ʀ /'eniweə(r)/ (*British*)
(*American* anyplace) *adverb*
1 used in negative sentences and in
questions instead of 'somewhere': *I can't find
my pen anywhere.* ◇ *Are you going anywhere
this summer?*
2 in, at or to any place, when it does not
matter where: *Just put the box down
anywhere.*

apart 0̶ʀ /ə'pɑːt/ *adverb*
1 away from the others; away from each
other: *The two houses are 500 metres apart.* ◇
My mother and father live apart now.
2 into parts: *He took my radio apart to
repair it.*
apart from somebody or **something**
except for: *There's nobody here, apart from
me.* ◇ *I like all vegetables apart from carrots.*

apartment 0̶ʀ /ə'pɑːtmənt/ *American
English for* FLAT²

ape /eɪp/ *noun*
an animal like a big MONKEY (= an animal
that lives in hot countries and can climb

trees), with no tail and with long arms. There
are different types of **ape**: *Gorillas and
chimpanzees are apes.* ⊅ Look at the pictures
at **chimpanzee** and **gorilla**.

apologize /ə'pɒlədʒaɪz/ *verb*
(apologizes, apologizing, apologized
/ə'pɒlədʒaɪzd/)
to say that you are sorry about something
that you have done: *I **apologized to** John **for**
losing his book.*

apology /ə'pɒlədʒi/ *noun* (*plural*
apologies)
words that you say or write to show that you
are sorry about something you have done:
Please accept my apologies.

apostrophe /ə'pɒstrəfi/ *noun*
the sign (') that you use in writing

> **🔎 GRAMMAR**
>
> You use an **apostrophe** to show that you
> have left a letter out of a word or that a
> number is missing, for example in *I'm* (= I
> am) and *'05* (= 2005).
> You also use it to show that something
> belongs to somebody or something: *the
> boy's room.*
> If the **apostrophe** comes after the letter
> *s*, it shows that there is more than one
> person: *the boys' room* (= a room which is
> shared by two or more boys).

appalling /ə'pɔːlɪŋ/ *adjective*
very bad; terrible: *appalling cruelty*

apparent /ə'pærənt/ *adjective*
easy to see or understand; clear: *It was
apparent that she didn't like him.*
⊅ SAME MEANING **obvious**

apparently /ə'pærəntli/ *adverb*
You use **apparently** to talk about what
people say, or how something appears,
when you do not know if it is true or not:
Apparently, he's already been married twice. ◇
He was apparently undisturbed by the news.

appeal¹ /ə'piːl/ *noun*
1 (*no plural*) a quality that makes somebody
or something attractive or interesting: *I can't
understand the appeal of stamp collecting.*
2 asking a lot of people for money, help or
information: *The police **made an appeal for**
witnesses to come forward.*

appeal² /ə'piːl/ *verb* (appeals, appealing,
appealed /ə'piːld/)
1 to ask in a serious way for something that
you want very much: *Aid workers in the
disaster area **appealed for** food and clothing.*
2 to be attractive or interesting to
somebody: *Living in a big city doesn't **appeal
to** me.*

A B C D E F G H I J K L M N O P Q R S T U V W X Y Z

A
B
C
D
E
F
G
H
I
J
K
L
M
N
O
P
Q
R
S
T
U
V
W
X
Y
Z

appear 0☞ /ə'pɪə(r)/ *verb* (appears, appearing, appeared /ə'pɪəd/)
1 to seem: *She appears to be very happy at her new school.* ◊ *It appears that I was wrong.*
2 to suddenly be seen; to come into sight: *The sun suddenly appeared from behind a cloud.* ◊ *We waited for an hour but he didn't appear.* ➔ OPPOSITE **disappear**

appearance 0☞ /ə'pɪərəns/ *noun*
1 the way that somebody or something looks or seems: *A new hairstyle can completely change your appearance.*
2 the coming of somebody or something; when somebody or something is seen: *Jane's appearance at the party surprised everybody.* ◊ *Is this your first appearance on television?*

appetite /'æpɪtaɪt/ *noun*
the feeling that you want to eat: *Swimming always gives me an appetite* (= makes me hungry).

appetizer /'æpɪtaɪzə(r)/ *noun* American English for STARTER

applaud /ə'plɔːd/ *verb* (applauds, applauding, applauded)
to make a noise by hitting your hands together to show that you like something: *We all applauded loudly at the end of the song.*

applause /ə'plɔːz/ *noun* (*no plural*)
when a lot of people hit their hands together to show that they like something: *There was loud applause from the audience.*

apple 0☞ /'æpl/ *noun*
a hard round fruit with green or red skin ➔ Look at Picture Dictionary page **P8**.

appliance /ə'plaɪəns/ *noun*
a useful machine for doing something in the house: *Washing machines and irons are electrical appliances.*

applicant /'æplɪkənt/ *noun*
a person who APPLIES (= asks) for a job or a place at university, for example: *There were six applicants for the job.*

application /ˌæplɪ'keɪʃn/ *noun*
1 writing to ask for something, for example a job: *Applications for the job should be made to the Personnel Manager.*
2 (*computing*) a computer program that is designed to do a particular job

application form /ˌæplɪ'keɪʃn fɔːm/ *noun*
a special piece of paper that you write on when you are trying to get something, for example a job: *Please fill in the application form.*

apply 0☞ /ə'plaɪ/ *verb* (applies, applying, applied /ə'plaɪd/)
1 to write to ask for something: *Simon has applied for a place at university.*
2 to be about somebody or something; to be important to somebody or something: *This law applies to all children over the age of sixteen.*

appoint /ə'pɔɪnt/ *verb* (appoints, appointing, appointed)
to choose somebody for a job or position: *The bank has appointed a new manager.*

appointment /ə'pɔɪntmənt/ *noun*
1 an arrangement to see somebody at a particular time: *I've got an appointment with the doctor at ten o'clock.* ◊ *You can telephone to make an appointment.*
2 (*formal*) a job ➔ **Job** is the word that we usually use.

appreciate /ə'priːʃieɪt/ *verb* (appreciates, appreciating, appreciated)
1 to enjoy something or understand how good somebody or something is: *Van Gogh's paintings were only appreciated after his death.* ◊ *My boss doesn't appreciate me.*
2 to understand that a situation is difficult: *I appreciate your problem, but I can't help you.*
3 to be grateful for something that somebody has done for you: *Thank you for your help. I appreciate it.*

appreciation /əˌpriːʃi'eɪʃn/ *noun* (*no plural*)
1 understanding and enjoyment of how good somebody or something is: *She shows little appreciation of good music.*
2 the feeling of being grateful for something that somebody has done for you: *We gave her some flowers to show our appreciation for her hard work.*

apprentice /ə'prentɪs/ *noun*
a young person who is learning to do a job: *an apprentice electrician*

approach¹ /ə'prəʊtʃ/ *verb* (approaches, approaching, approached /ə'prəʊtʃt/)
to come near to somebody or something in distance or time: *As you approach the village, you'll see a church on your right.* ◊ *The exams were approaching.*

approach² /ə'prəʊtʃ/ *noun*
1 (*plural* **approaches**) a way of doing something: *This is a new approach to learning languages.*
2 (*no plural*) coming near or nearer to somebody or something: *the approach of winter*

appropriate 0☞ /ə'prəʊpriət/ *adjective*
suitable or right for a particular situation,

person, etc.: *Jeans and T-shirts are not* **appropriate for** *a job interview.*
⊃ OPPOSITE **inappropriate**
▶ **appropriately** /ə'prəupriətli/ *adverb*: *Please come appropriately dressed.*

approval 0‑ʀ /ə'pruːvl/ *noun* (*no plural*)
feeling, showing or saying that something or somebody is good or right: *Tania's parents* **gave** *the marriage their* **approval.**
⊃ OPPOSITE **disapproval**

approve 0‑ʀ /ə'pruːv/ *verb* (**approves,** **approving, approved** /ə'pruːvd/)
to think or say that something or somebody is good or right: *My parents don't* **approve of** *my friends.* ◇ *She doesn't approve of smoking.*
⊃ OPPOSITE **disapprove**

approximate /ə'prɒksimət/ *adjective*
almost correct but not exact: *The approximate time of arrival is three o'clock.*

approximately /ə'prɒksimətli/ *adverb*
about; more or less: *I live approximately two miles from the station.* ⊃ SAME MEANING **roughly**

apricot /'eɪprɪkɒt/ *noun*
a small soft yellow or orange fruit with a large stone inside

April 0‑ʀ /'eɪprəl/ *noun*
the fourth month of the year

apron /'eɪprən/
noun
a thing that you wear over the front of your clothes to keep them clean, especially when you are cooking

apron

aquarium
/ə'kweəriəm/ *noun*
1 a large glass container filled with water, in which fish are kept
2 a building where people can go to see fish and other water animals

arch /ɑːtʃ/ *noun* (*plural* **arches**)
a part of a bridge, building or wall that is in the shape of a half circle

archaeologist (*British*) (*American* **archeologist**) /ˌɑːki'ɒlədʒɪst/ *noun*
a person who studies or knows a lot about ARCHAEOLOGY

archaeology (*British*) (*American* **archeology**) /ˌɑːki'ɒlədʒi/ *noun* (*no plural*)
the study of the past by looking at objects or

arches

parts of old buildings that are found in the ground

architect /'ɑːkɪtekt/ *noun*
a person whose job is to design and plan buildings

architecture /'ɑːkɪtektʃə(r)/ *noun* (*no plural*)
1 the study of designing and making buildings: *He has a degree in architecture.*
2 the design or style of a building or buildings: *Do you like modern architecture?*

are *form of* BE

area 0‑ʀ /'eəriə/ *noun*
1 a part of a town, country or the world: *Do you live in this area?* ◇ *the desert areas of North Africa*
2 the size of a flat place. If a room is three metres wide and four metres long, it has an **area** of twelve square metres.
3 a space that you use for a particular activity: *The restaurant has a non-smoking area* (= a part where you must not smoke).

arena /ə'riːnə/ *noun* (*plural* **arenas**)
a place with seats around it where you can watch sports or concerts

aren't /ɑːnt/ *short for* ARE NOT

argue 0‑ʀ /'ɑːɡjuː/ *verb* (**argues,** **arguing, argued** /'ɑːɡjuːd/)
1 to talk angrily with somebody because you do not agree: *My parents* **argue** *a lot* **about** *money.* ◇ *I often* **argue with** *my brother.*
2 to say why you think something is right or wrong: *Billy* **argued that** *war is not the answer.*

argument 0‑ʀ /'ɑːɡjumənt/ *noun*
an angry discussion between people who do not agree with each other: *They* **had** *an* **argument about** *where to go on holiday.* ◇ *I had an* **argument with** *my father.*

arise /ə'raɪz/ *verb* (**arises, arising, arose** /ə'rəʊz/, **arisen** /ə'rɪzn/) (*formal*)
If a problem or difficult situation **arises**, it happens or starts to exist.

A

arithmetic /əˈrɪθmətɪk/ *noun* (*no plural*) (*maths*) working with numbers, for example by adding or multiplying, to find the answer to a sum: *I'm not very good at **mental arithmetic**.*

arm 0⊸ /ɑːm/ *noun*
the part of your body from your shoulder to your hand: *Put your arms in the air.* ◇ *He was carrying a book under his arm.* ⤳ Look at Picture Dictionary **P4**.
arm in arm with your arm holding another person's arm: *The two friends walked arm in arm.*

armchair
/ˈɑːmtʃeə(r)/ *noun*
a soft comfortable chair with side parts where you can put your arms: *She was asleep in an armchair.*

armed /ɑːmd/ *adjective*
carrying a gun or other weapon: *an armed robber* ◇ *Are the police armed in your country?*

the armed forces /ðɪ ˌɑːmd ˈfɔːsɪz/ *noun* (*plural*)
a country's soldiers who fight on land, at sea or in the air

armour (*British*) (*American* **armor**)
/ˈɑːmə(r)/ *noun* (*no plural*)
metal clothes that men wore long ago to cover their bodies when they were fighting: *a suit of armour*

armpit /ˈɑːmpɪt/ *noun*
the part of your body under your arm, where your arm joins your body ⤳ Look at Picture Dictionary page **P4**.

arms /ɑːmz/ *noun* (*plural*)
guns, bombs and other weapons for fighting

army 0⊸ /ˈɑːmi/ *noun* (*plural* **armies**)
a large group of soldiers who fight on land in a war: *He **joined the army** when he was 17.* ◇ *the British Army*

> 🔎 **WORD BUILDING**
>
> A soldier who fights on land is **in the army**, one who fights at sea is **in the navy** and a soldier who fights in the air is **in the air force**.
> The **army**, the **navy** and the **air force** together are called **the armed forces**.

arose *form of* ARISE

around 0⊸ /əˈraʊnd/ *preposition, adverb*
1 (*also* **round**) in or to different places or in different directions: *Her clothes were lying around the room.* ◇ *We walked around for an hour looking for a restaurant.* ◇ *The children were running around the house.*
2 (*also* **round**) in the opposite direction or in another direction: *Turn around and go back the way you came.*
3 (*also* **round**) on or to all sides of something, often in a circle: *We sat around the table.* ◇ *He ran around the track.* ◇ *There is a wall around the garden.*
4 in a place; near here: *Is there a bank around here?* ◇ *Is Helen around? I want to speak to her.*
5 (*also* **about**) a little more or less than; a little before or after: *I'll see you around seven* (= at about 7 o'clock).

arrange 0⊸ /əˈreɪndʒ/ *verb* (**arranges**, **arranging**, **arranged** /əˈreɪndʒd/)
1 to make a plan for the future: *I have arranged to meet Tim at six o'clock.* ◇ *We arranged a big party for Debbie's birthday.*
2 to put things in a certain order or place: *Arrange the chairs in a circle.*

arrangement 0⊸ /əˈreɪndʒmənt/ *noun*
1 a plan or preparation that you make so that something can happen in the future: *They are **making** the **arrangements** for their wedding.*
2 a group of things put together so that they look nice: *a flower arrangement*

arrest¹ 0⊸ /əˈrest/ *verb* (**arrests**, **arresting**, **arrested**)
When the police **arrest** somebody, they take that person away to ask them questions about a crime: *The man was **arrested for** carrying a weapon.*

arrest² /əˈrest/ *noun*
the act of arresting somebody: *The police **made** five **arrests**.* ◇ *The wanted man is now **under arrest*** (= has been arrested).

arrival /əˈraɪvl/ *noun*
coming to a place: *My brother met me at the airport **on** my **arrival**.*
⤳ OPPOSITE **departure**

arrive 0⊸ /əˈraɪv/ *verb* (**arrives**, **arriving**, **arrived** /əˈraɪvd/)
1 to come to a place: *What time did you arrive home?* ◇ *What time does the train **arrive in** Paris?* ◇ *They **arrived at** the station ten minutes late.* ⤳ OPPOSITE **leave**, **depart**

> 🔎 **GRAMMAR**
>
> Be careful! We use **arrive in** with the name of a town or country and **arrive at** with a building such as a station, an airport or a school.

2 to come or happen: *Summer has arrived!*

B C D E F G H I J K L M N O P Q R S T U V W X Y Z

arrogant /ˈærəgənt/ *adjective*
A person who is **arrogant** thinks that they are better and more important than other people.

arrows

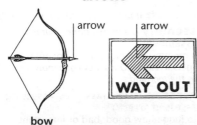

arrow   arrow

WAY OUT

bow

arrow Oₘ /ˈærəʊ/ *noun*
1 a long thin piece of wood or metal with a point at one end.

> 🔎 **WORD BUILDING**
> You shoot an **arrow** by pulling back the string on a curved piece of wood called a **bow** and then letting go. You try to hit a **target**.

2 the sign (←) that shows where something is or where you should go: *The arrow is pointing left.*

art Oₘ /ɑːt/ *noun*
1 (*no plural*) making beautiful things, like paintings and drawings: *He's studying art at college.*
2 (*no plural*) beautiful things like paintings and drawings that somebody has made: *modern art ◊ an art gallery*
3 the arts (*plural*) things like films, plays and literature: *How much money does the government spend on the arts?*
4 (*no plural*) a skill, or something that needs skill: *the art of letter writing*
5 arts (*plural*) the subjects you can study at school or university which are not science subjects, for example history or languages: *She has an arts degree.*

artery /ˈɑːtəri/ *noun* (*plural* arteries)
one of the tubes in your body that carry blood away from your heart to other parts of your body ⊃ Look at **vein**.

arthritis /ɑːˈθraɪtɪs/ *noun* (*no plural*)
a disease which causes pain when you bend your arms, fingers, etc.

artichoke /ˈɑːtɪtʃəʊk/ *noun*
a green vegetable with a lot of thick pointed leaves that looks like a flower. You eat the bottom part of the leaves and its centre when it is cooked. ⊃ Look at Picture Dictionary **P9**.

article Oₘ /ˈɑːtɪkl/ *noun*
1 a piece of writing in a newspaper or magazine: *Did you read the article about young fashion designers?*
2 a thing: *Many of the articles in the shop are half-price. ◊ articles of clothing* (= things like skirts, coats and trousers)
3 (*grammar*) the words *a* and *an* (called the **indefinite article**) or *the* (called the **definite article**)

artificial Oₘ /ˌɑːtɪˈfɪʃl/ *adjective*
not natural or real, but made by people: *artificial flowers*

artificial intelligence /ˌɑːtɪfɪʃl ɪnˈtelɪdʒəns/ *noun* (*no plural*) (*abbr.* **AI**)
(*computing*) the study of the way in which computers can copy the way humans think

artist Oₘ /ˈɑːtɪst/ *noun*
a person who paints or draws pictures: *Monet was a famous French artist.*

artistic Oₘ /ɑːˈtɪstɪk/ *adjective*
good at painting, drawing or making beautiful things: *He's very artistic — his drawings are excellent.*

as Oₘ /əz; æz/ *conjunction, preposition*
1 while something else is happening: *Just as I was leaving the house, the phone rang.*
2 as ... as words that you use to compare people or things; the same amount: *Paul is as tall as his father. ◊ I haven't got as many clothes as you have. ◊ I'd like it done as soon as possible.*
3 used to say that somebody or something has a particular job or purpose: *She works as a secretary for a big company. ◊ I used my shoe as a hammer.*
4 in the same way: *Please do as I tell you!*
5 because: *As she was ill, she didn't go to school.*

asap /ˌeɪ es eɪ ˈpiː/ *abbreviation* (*informal*)
as soon as possible: *I'd like the report on my desk asap.*

ash /æʃ/ *noun* (*no plural*)
the grey powder that is left after something has burned: *cigarette ash*

ashamed Oₘ /əˈʃeɪmd/ *adjective*
feeling sorry and unhappy because you have done something wrong, or because you are not as good as other people: *I was ashamed about lying to my parents. ◊ She was ashamed of her old clothes.*

ashore /əˈʃɔː(r)/ *adverb*
onto the land from the sea or a river: *We left the boat and went ashore.*

A B C D E F G H I J K L M N O P Q R S T U V W X Y Z

A

ashtray /ˈæʃtreɪ/ *noun*
a small dish for cigarette ASH and the ends of cigarettes

aside /əˈsaɪd/ *adverb*
on or to one side; away: *He put the letter aside while he did his homework.*

ask 0̄ᵣ /ɑːsk/ *verb* (asks, asking, asked /ɑːskt/)
1 to try to get an answer by using a question: *I asked him what the time was.* ◊ *'What's your name?' she asked.* ◊ *Liz asked the teacher a question.*
2 to say that you would like somebody to do something for you: *I asked Sara to drive me to the station.*
3 to try to get permission to do something: *I asked my teacher if I could go home.* ◊ *I asked if I could go home early.*
4 to invite somebody to go somewhere with you: *Mark has asked me to a party on Saturday.*
ask for somebody to say that you want to speak to somebody: *Phone this number and ask for Mrs Green.*
ask for something to say that you want somebody to give you something: *He asked for a new bike for his birthday.*

asleep 0̄ᵣ /əˈsliːp/ *adjective*
sleeping: *The baby is asleep in the bedroom.* ◊ *He fell asleep* (= started sleeping) *in front of the fire.* ◊ OPPOSITE **awake**

> 🔎 **WHICH WORD?**
>
> **Asleep** or **sleeping**?
> We usually say someone is **asleep**, not **sleeping**.
> We use **go to sleep** or **fall asleep** to talk about starting to sleep: *Laura fell asleep as soon as she got into bed.* ◊ *Tom read for half an hour before he went to sleep.*
> You use **sleeping**, not **asleep**, before a noun: *She put the sleeping child in his cot.*

asparagus /əˈspærəgəs/ *noun* (no plural)
thin green plants with pointed ends that are eaten as a vegetable ◊ Look at Picture Dictionary **P9**.

aspect /ˈæspekt/ *noun*
one of the qualities or parts of a situation, idea, problem, etc.: *Spelling is one of the most difficult aspects of learning English.*

aspirin /ˈæsprɪn/ *noun*
a medicine that stops pain: *I took an aspirin for my headache.*

assassinate /əˈsæsɪneɪt/ *verb* (assassinates, assassinating, assassinated)
to kill an important or famous person: *John F. Kennedy was assassinated in 1963.*

▶ **assassination** /əˌsæsɪˈneɪʃn/ *noun*: *an assassination attempt*

assault /əˈsɔːlt/ *verb* (assaults, assaulting, assaulted)
to attack or hurt somebody: *He assaulted a policeman.*
▶ **assault** *noun*: *an assault on an old lady*

assembly /əˈsembli/ *noun* (plural assemblies)
a meeting of a big group of people for a special reason: *Our school assembly is at 9.30 in the morning.*

assess /əˈses/ *verb* (assesses, assessing, assessed /əˈsest/)
to judge how good, bad or important something is: *It's difficult to assess the effects of the price rises.*
▶ **assessment** /əˈsesmənt/ *noun*: *I made a careful assessment of the risks involved.*

assignment /əˈsaɪnmənt/ *noun*
a job or piece of work that somebody is given to do: *You have to complete three written assignments each term.*

assist /əˈsɪst/ *verb* (assists, assisting, assisted) (formal)
to help somebody: *The driver assisted her with her suitcases.*

> 🔎 **SPEAKING**
> **Help** is the word that we usually use.

assistance /əˈsɪstəns/ *noun* (no plural) (formal)
help: *I can't move this piano without your assistance.*

assistant /əˈsɪstənt/ *noun*
a person who helps somebody in a more important position: *Ms Dixon is not here today. Would you like to speak to her assistant?* ◊ Look also at **shop assistant**.

associate /əˈsəʊʃieɪt/ *verb* (associates, associating, associated)
to make a connection between things or people in your mind: *Most people associate Austria with snow and skiing.* ◊ *These illnesses are associated with smoking.*

association /əˌsəʊʃiˈeɪʃn/ *noun*
a group of people who join or work together for a special reason: *the Football Association*

assume /əˈsjuːm/ *verb* (assumes, assuming, assumed /əˈsjuːmd/)
to think that something is true although you are not really sure: *Jo is not here today, so I assume that she is ill.*

assure /əˈʃʊə(r)/ *verb* (assures, assuring, assured /əˈʃʊəd/)
to tell somebody what is true or certain so

that they feel less worried: *I assure you that the dog isn't dangerous.*

asterisk /'æstərɪsk/ *noun*
the symbol (*) that you use to make people notice something in a piece of writing

asthma /'æsmə/ *noun* (*no plural*)
an illness which makes breathing difficult: *He had an asthma attack.*

astonish /ə'stɒnɪʃ/ *verb* (astonishes, astonishing, astonished /ə'stɒnɪʃt/)
to surprise somebody very much: *The news astonished everyone.*

astonished /ə'stɒnɪʃt/ *adjective*
very surprised: *I was astonished to hear that he was getting married.*

astonishing /ə'stɒnɪʃɪŋ/ *adjective*
If something is **astonishing**, it surprises you very much: *an astonishing story*

astonishment /ə'stɒnɪʃmənt/ *noun* (*no plural*)
a feeling of great surprise: *He looked at me in astonishment when I told him the news.*

astronaut /'æstrənɔːt/ *noun*
a person who works and travels in space

astronomer /ə'strɒnəmə(r)/ *noun*
a person who studies or knows a lot about ASTRONOMY

astronomy /ə'strɒnəmi/ *noun* (*no plural*)
the study of the sun, moon, planets and stars

at 0️⃣ /ət; æt/ *preposition*
1 a word that shows where: *They are at school. ◇ Jane is at home. ◇ The answer is at the back of the book.*
2 a word that shows when: *I go to bed at eleven o'clock. ◇ At night you can see the stars.*
3 towards somebody or something: *Look at the picture. ◇ I smiled at her. ◇ Somebody threw an egg at the President.*
4 a word that shows what somebody is doing or what is happening: *The two countries are at war. ◇ We were hard at work.*
5 a word that shows how much, how fast, how old, etc.: *We were travelling at about 50 miles per hour. ◇ He left school at sixteen (= when he was sixteen years old).*
6 a word that shows how well somebody or something does something: *I'm not very good at maths.*
7 because of something: *We laughed at his jokes.*
8 (*computing*) the symbol **@** which is used in email addresses after a person's name ⊃ Look at the note at **dot**.

ate *form of* EAT

athlete /'æθliːt/ *noun*
a person who is good at sports like running or jumping, especially one who takes part in

sports competitions: *Athletes from all over the world go to the Olympic Games.*

athletic /æθ'letɪk/ *adjective*
having a fit, strong and healthy body

athletics /æθ'letɪks/ *noun* (*plural*)
sports like running, jumping and throwing

atlas /'ætləs/ *noun* (*plural* atlases)
a book of maps: *an atlas of the world*

ATM /ˌeɪ tiː 'em/ *American English for* CASH MACHINE

atmosphere 0️⃣ /'ætməsfɪə(r)/ *noun* (*no plural*)
1 the atmosphere the mixture of gases around the earth: *pollution of the atmosphere*
2 the air in a place: *a smoky atmosphere*
3 the feeling that places or people give you: *The atmosphere in the office was very friendly.*

atom /'ætəm/ *noun*
one of the very small things that everything is made of: *Water is made of atoms of hydrogen and oxygen.* ⊃ Look also at **molecule.**

atomic /ə'tɒmɪk/ *adjective*
1 of or about ATOMS: *atomic physics*
2 using the great power that is made by breaking ATOMS: *an atomic bomb ◇ atomic energy*

attach /ə'tætʃ/ *verb* (attaches, attaching, attached /ə'tætʃt/)
to join or fix one thing to another thing: *I attached the photo to the letter.*

attached /ə'tætʃt/ *adjective*
liking somebody or something very much: *We've grown very attached to this house.*

attachment /ə'tætʃmənt/ *noun*
1 a strong feeling of love or liking for somebody or something: *a child's strong attachment to its parents*
2 (*computing*) a document that you send to somebody using email

attack¹ 0️⃣ /ə'tæk/ *noun*
1 a violent act which is done in order to hurt somebody or damage something: *There was a terrorist attack on the city.*
2 a time when you are ill: *an attack of flu*

attack² 0️⃣ /ə'tæk/ *verb* (attacks, attacking, attacked /ə'tækt/)
to start fighting or hurting somebody or something: *The army attacked the town. ◇ The old man was attacked and his money was stolen.*

attempt /ə'tempt/ *verb* (attempts, attempting, attempted)
to try to do something that is difficult ⊃ SAME MEANING **try**: *He attempted to sail round the world.*

A

▶ **attempt** *noun*: She **made no attempt** to help me. ◇ a brave **attempt at** breaking the world record

attend /ə'tend/ *verb* (attends, attending, attended)
to go to or be present at a place where something is happening: Did you attend the meeting?

attendance /ə'tendəns/ *noun*
1 (no plural) being present at a place, for example at school: **Attendance at** these lectures is compulsory.
2 (plural attendances) the number of people who go to an organized event: Cinema attendances have risen again recently.

attendant /ə'tendənt/ *noun*
a person whose job is to serve or help people in a public place: a car park attendant

attention 0— /ə'tenʃn/ *noun* (no plural)
looking or listening carefully and with interest: I shouted in order to **attract** her **attention** (= make her notice me). ◇ Can I have your **attention**, please? (= please listen to me)
pay attention look or listen carefully: Please pay attention to what I'm saying.

attic /'ætɪk/ *noun*
the room or space under the roof of a house ⊃ SAME MEANING **loft**: My old clothes are in a box in the attic. ⊃ Look at Picture Dictionary page **P10**.

attitude /'ætɪtjuːd/ *noun*
the way you think or feel about something: What's your **attitude to** marriage?

attorney /ə'tɜːni/ American English for LAWYER

attract 0— /ə'trækt/ *verb* (attracts, attracting, attracted)
1 to make somebody like somebody or something: He was **attracted to** her. ◇ I had always been **attracted by** the idea of working abroad.
2 to make somebody or something come somewhere: Moths are attracted to light. ◇ The new film has attracted a lot of publicity.

attraction /ə'trækʃn/ *noun*
1 (no plural) a feeling of liking somebody or something very much: I can't understand his attraction to her.
2 (plural attractions) something that makes people come to a place: Buckingham Palace is a major **tourist attraction**.

attractive 0— /ə'træktɪv/ *adjective*
1 A person who is **attractive** is nice to look at: He's very attractive. ⊃ Look at the note at **beautiful**.
2 Something that is **attractive** pleases you

or interests you: That's an attractive offer. ⊃ OPPOSITE **unattractive**

aubergine /'əʊbəʒiːn/ *noun* (British) (American **eggplant**)
a large purple vegetable that is white inside ⊃ Look at Picture Dictionary **P9**.

auction /'ɔːkʃn/ *noun*
a sale where each thing is sold to the person who will give the most money for it
▶ **auction** *verb* (auctions, auctioning, auctioned /'ɔːkʃnd/) to sell something at an AUCTION

audience /'ɔːdiəns/ *noun*
the people who are watching or listening to a film, play, concert, programme, etc.

audio /'ɔːdiəʊ/ *adjective*
connected with the recording of sound: audio tapes

audio-visual /ˌɔːdiəʊ 'vɪʒuəl/ *adjective*
using both sound and pictures: audio-visual aids for the classroom

August 0— /'ɔːgəst/ *noun*
the eighth month of the year

aunt 0— /ɑːnt/ *noun* (also informal auntie, aunty /'ɑːnti/)

> 🔊 **PRONUNCIATION**
> The word **aunt** sounds like **plant**.

the sister of your mother or father, or the wife of your uncle: Aunt Mary

au pair /ˌəʊ 'peə(r)/ *noun* (British)
a young person who lives with a family in a foreign country in order to learn the language. An **au pair** looks after the children and helps in the house.

authentic /ɔː'θentɪk/ *adjective*
real and true: That's not an authentic Van Gogh painting – it's just a copy.

author /'ɔːθə(r)/ *noun*
a person who writes books or stories: Who is your favourite author?

authority /ɔː'θɒrəti/ *noun*
1 (no plural) the power to tell people what they must do: The police have the **authority to** stop cars.
2 (plural authorities) a group of people that tell other people what they must do: the city authorities

autobiography /ˌɔːtəbaɪ'ɒgrəfi/ *noun* (plural autobiographies)
a book that a person has written about their life

autograph /'ɔːtəgrɑːf/ *noun*
a famous person's name, which they themselves have written: He asked Madonna for her autograph.

automatic /ˌɔːtəˈmætɪk/ *adjective*
1 If a machine is **automatic**, it can work by itself, without people controlling it: *automatic doors*
2 that you do without thinking: *Breathing is automatic.*
▶ **automatically** /ˌɔːtəˈmætɪkli/ *adverb*: *This light comes on automatically at five o'clock.*

automobile /ˈɔːtəməbiːl/ *American English* for CAR

autumn 0➡ /ˈɔːtəm/ *noun* (British) (*American* **fall**)
the part of the year between summer and winter: *In autumn, the leaves begin to fall from the trees.* ➲ Look at Picture Dictionary page **P16**.

available 0➡ /əˈveɪləbl/ *adjective*
ready for you to use, have or see: *I phoned the hotel to ask if there were any rooms available.* ◇ *I'm sorry – the manager is not available this afternoon.*

avalanche /ˈævəlɑːnʃ/ *noun*
a very large amount of snow that falls quickly down the side of a mountain

avenue /ˈævənjuː/ (*abbr.* **Ave.**) *noun*
a wide road or street: *I live in Connaught Avenue.* ◇ *Burnham Ave.*

average¹ /ˈævərɪdʒ/ *noun*
1 (*plural* **averages**) the result you get when you add two or more amounts together and then divide the total by the number of amounts you added: *The average of 2, 3 and 7 is 4 (2 + 3 + 7 = 12, and 12 ÷ 3 = 4).*
2 (*no plural*) the normal amount, quality, etc.: *On average, I buy a newspaper about twice a week.*

average² /ˈævərɪdʒ/ *adjective*
1 (used about a number) found by calculating the AVERAGE¹(1): *The average age of the students is 19.*
2 normal or usual: *The average student gets around 5 hours of homework a week.*

avoid 0➡ /əˈvɔɪd/ *verb* (**avoids, avoiding, avoided**)
1 to stop something happening; to try not to do something: *He always tried to avoid an argument if possible.* ◇ *She has to avoid eating too much chocolate.*
2 to stay away from somebody or something: *We crossed the road to avoid our teacher.*

awake 0➡ /əˈweɪk/ *adjective*
not sleeping: *The children are still awake.*
➲ OPPOSITE **asleep**

award¹ /əˈwɔːd/ *noun*
a prize or money that you give to somebody who has done something very well: *She won the award for best actress.*

award² /əˈwɔːd/ *verb* (**awards, awarding, awarded**)
to officially give a prize to somebody: *He was awarded first prize in the writing competition.*

aware 0➡ /əˈweə(r)/ *adjective*
If you are **aware** of something, you know about it: *He's not aware of the problem.* ◇ *I was aware that somebody was watching me.*
➲ OPPOSITE **unaware**

away 0➡ /əˈweɪ/ *adverb*
1 to or in another place: *She ran away from him.* ◇ *He put his books away.*
2 from a place: *The sea is two miles away.*
3 not here ➲ SAME MEANING **absent**: *Tim is away from school today because he is ill.*
4 in the future: *Our holiday is only three weeks away.*

awesome /ˈɔːsəm/ *adjective*
1 very impressive and perhaps rather frightening: *an awesome sight*
2 (*American, informal*) very good, enjoyable, etc. ➲ SAME MEANING **great**: *I just bought this awesome new CD!* ◇ *Wow! That's totally awesome!*

awful /ˈɔːfl/ *adjective*
very bad: *The pain was awful.* ◇ *What awful weather!* ➲ Look at the note at **bad**.

awfully /ˈɔːfli/ *adverb*
very ➲ SAME MEANING **terribly**: *It was awfully hot.* ◇ *I'm awfully sorry!*

awkward /ˈɔːkwəd/ *adjective*
1 difficult or causing problems: *This big box will be awkward to carry.* ◇ *an awkward question*
2 not comfortable; embarrassing: *I felt awkward at the party because I didn't know anybody.*
4 not able to move your body in an easy way: *He's very awkward when he dances.*

axe (*British*) (*American* **ax**) /æks/ *noun*
a tool for cutting wood: *He chopped down the tree with an axe.*

B b

B, b /biː/ *noun* (*plural* B's, b's /biːz/)
the second letter of the English alphabet: '*Ball*' begins with a '*B*'.

BA /ˌbiː ˈeɪ/ *noun*
the certificate that you receive when you complete a university or college course in an ARTS subject (= a subject that is not a science subject). **BA** is short for 'Bachelor of Arts'.
➜ Look also at **BSc**.

baby 0➥ /ˈbeɪbi/
baby
noun (*plural* babies)

a very young child:
*She's going to **have
a baby**.* ◇ *a baby boy*
◇ *a baby girl*

baby carriage
/ˌbeɪbi ˈkærɪdʒ/
American English for
PRAM

babysit /ˈbeɪbisɪt/
verb (**babysits,
babysitting, babysat** /ˈbeɪbisæt/)
to look after a child while the parents are not at home

babysitter /ˈbeɪbisɪtə(r)/ *noun*
a person who looks after a child while the parents are not at home

bachelor /ˈbætʃələ(r)/ *noun*
1 a man who has never married
2 Bachelor a person who has a university degree (= they have finished the course and passed all their exams): *a Bachelor of Science*

back¹ 0➥ /bæk/
back
noun

1 the part of a person or an animal that is between the neck and the bottom: *He lay **on his back** and looked up at the sky.* ◇ *She was standing **with her back** to me so I couldn't see her face.*

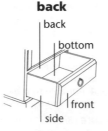

back
bottom
front
side

➜ Look at Picture Dictionary page **P4**.
2 the part of something that is behind or furthest from the front: *The answers are **at the back** of the book.* ◇ *Write your address **on the back** of the cheque.* ◇ *We sat **in the back** of the car.*

back to front
back to front
with the back part where the front should be: *You've got your sweater on back to front.*

behind somebody's back when somebody is not there, so that they do not know about it: *Don't talk about Kate behind her back.*

back² 0➥ /bæk/ *adjective*
furthest from the front: *the back door* ◇ *back teeth*

back³ 0➥ /bæk/ *adverb*
1 in or to the place where somebody or something was before: *I'll **be back** (= I will return)* *at six o'clock.* ◇ ***Go back** to sleep.* ◇ *We walked to the shops and back.*
2 away from the front: *I looked **back** to see if she was coming.* ◇ *Could everyone **move back** a bit, please?* ➜ OPPOSITE **forward**
3 as a way of returning or answering something: *He **paid** me the money **back**.* ◇ *I wrote her a letter, but she didn't **write back**.* ◇ *I was out when she rang, so I **phoned** her **back**.*
back and forth from one place to another and back again, many times: *She travels back and forth between London and Glasgow.*

back⁴ /bæk/ *verb* (**backs, backing, backed** /bækt/)
1 to move backwards or to make something move backwards: *She backed the car out of the garage.*
2 to give help or support to somebody or something: *They're backing their school team.*
back away to move away backwards: *Sally backed away **from** the big dog.*
back out to not do something that you promised or agreed to do: *You promised you would come with me. You can't back out **of** it now!*
back something up
1 to say or show that something is true: *All the evidence backed up what the woman had said.*
2 (*computing*) to make a copy of information in your computer that you do not want to lose

backbone /ˈbækbəʊn/ *noun*
the line of bones down the back of your body ➜ SAME MEANING **spine**

background /ˈbækɡraʊnd/ *noun*
1 the things at the back in a picture: *This is a photo of my house with the mountains **in the background**.* ➔ OPPOSITE **foreground**
2 the type of family that a person comes from and the education and experience that they have: *She's **from** a poor **background**.*

backpack

backpack (*British also* **rucksack**)

backpack¹ /ˈbækpæk/ *noun*
a large bag that you carry on your back when you are travelling ➔ SAME MEANING **rucksack**

backpack² /ˈbækpæk/ *verb*
to go walking or travelling with your clothes, etc. in a BACKPACK

> 🔎 **SPEAKING**
> You say **go backpacking** when you talk about spending time backpacking: *We went backpacking round Europe last summer.*

backside /ˈbæksaɪd/ *noun* (*informal*)
the part of your body that you sit on ➔ SAME MEANING **bottom**

backstroke /ˈbækstrəʊk/ *noun* (*no plural*)
a way of swimming on your back

backup /ˈbækʌp/ *noun*
1 extra help or support that you can get if necessary: *The police had backup from the army.*
2 (*computing*) a copy of information that you have put in your computer and which you do not want to lose

backward /ˈbækwəd/ *adjective*
1 in the direction behind you: *a backward step*
2 slow to learn or change: *Our teaching methods are backward compared to some countries.*

backwards 0🔑 /ˈbækwədz/ (*also* **backward** /ˈbækwəd/) *adverb*
1 towards a place or a position that is behind: *Could everybody take a step backwards?* ➔ OPPOSITE **forwards**
2 with the back or the end first: *If you say the alphabet backwards, you start with 'Z'.*

backwards and forwards first in one direction and then in the other, many times: *The dog ran backwards and forwards, fetching sticks.*

backyard /ˌbækˈjɑːd/ *noun* (*American*)
the area behind and around a house, including the garden

bacon /ˈbeɪkən/ *noun* (*no plural*)
long thin pieces of meat from a pig: *We had bacon and eggs for breakfast.*

bacteria /bækˈtɪəriə/ *noun* (*plural*)
very small things that live in air, water, earth, plants and animals. Some **bacteria** can make us ill.

bad 0🔑 /bæd/ *adjective* (**worse**, **worst**)
1 not good or nice: *The weather was very bad.* ◇ *He's had some bad news – his uncle has died.* ◇ *a bad smell*
2 serious: *She had a bad accident.*
3 not done or made well: *bad driving*
4 not able to work or do something well: *My eyesight is bad.* ◇ *He's a bad teacher.*
5 too old to eat; not fresh: *bad eggs*

> 🔎 **WORD BUILDING**
> If something is very bad, you can say **awful**, **dreadful** or **terrible**: *I've had a dreadful day.*
> Something that is unpleasant or somebody who is unkind is **horrible**: *He's always saying horrible things to me.*

bad at something If you are **bad at something**, you cannot do it well: *I'm very bad at sports.*
bad for you If something is **bad for you**, it can make you ill: *Smoking is bad for you.*
go bad to become too old to eat: *This fish has gone bad.*
not bad (*informal*) quite good: *'What was the film like?' 'Not bad.'*
too bad (*informal*) words that you use to say that you cannot change something: *'I want to go out.' 'Too bad – you can't!'*

badges

Dr. N. Norton

badge

A
B
C
D
E
F
G
H
I
J
K
L
M
N
O
P
Q
R
S
T
U
V
W
X
Y
Z

badge /bædʒ/ *noun*
a small piece of metal, cloth or plastic with a design or words on it that you wear on your clothes: *All employees must wear a name badge.* ➔ Look at the picture on page **27**.

badger
/'bædʒə(r)/ *noun*
an animal with
black and white
lines on its head
that lives in holes in
the ground and comes out at night

badger

badly 0ᴿ /'bædli/ *adverb* (**worse, worst**)
1 in a way that is not good enough; not well: *She played badly.* ◊ *These clothes are badly made.*
2 very much: *I badly need a holiday.* ◊ *He was badly hurt in the accident.*

badminton

shuttlecock

racket

badminton /'bædmɪntən/ *noun* (*no plural*)
a game for two or four players who try to hit a kind of light ball with feathers on it (called a **shuttlecock**) over a high net, using a RACKET (= a piece of equipment which you hold in your hand): *Do you want to play badminton?*

bad-tempered 0ᴿ /ˌbæd 'tempəd/ *adjective*
often angry or impatient: *Her neighbour was a bad-tempered old man.*

bag 0ᴿ /bæg/ *noun*
a thing made of cloth, paper, leather, etc., for holding and carrying things: *He put the apples in a **paper bag**.* ◊ *a plastic **shopping bag*** ➔ Look also at **carrier bag** and **handbag**.

bagel /'beɪgl/ *noun*
a type of bread roll
in the shape of a
ring

bagel

baggage
/'bægɪdʒ/ *noun* (*no plural*)
bags and suitcases that you take with you when you travel: *We put all our baggage in*

the car. ➔ SAME MEANING **luggage** ➔ Look at the note at **luggage**.

baggy /'bægi/ *adjective*
If clothes are **baggy**, they are big and loose: *He was wearing baggy trousers.*

bagpipes /'bægpaɪps/ *noun* (*plural*)
a musical instrument that is often played in Scotland

bait /beɪt/ *noun* (*no plural*)
food that is used to catch animals or fish with

bake /beɪk/ *verb* (**bakes, baking, baked** /beɪkt/)
to cook food, for example bread or cakes, in an oven: *My brother baked a cake for my birthday.*

baked beans /ˌbeɪkt 'biːnz/ *noun* (*plural*)
white BEANS cooked in tomato sauce, that you buy in a tin ➔ Look at Picture Dictionary page **P7**.

baked potato /ˌbeɪkt pə'teɪtəʊ/ (*plural* **baked potatoes**) (*also* **jacket potato**) *noun*
a whole potato cooked in its skin in an oven: *a baked potato and beans* ➔ Look at Picture Dictionary page **P7**.

baker /'beɪkə(r)/ *noun*
1 a person who makes and sells bread and cakes
2 **baker's** a shop that sells bread and cakes: *I went to the baker's to buy some bread.* ➔ Look at Picture Dictionary page **P13**.

bakery /'beɪkəri/ *noun* (*plural* **bakeries**)
a place where bread and cakes are baked to be sold in shops

balance¹ 0ᴿ /'bæləns/ *noun*
1 (*no plural*) when two things are the same, so that one is not bigger or more important, for example: *You need a **balance between** work and play.* ➔ OPPOSITE **imbalance**
2 (*no plural*) the ability to keep steady with an equal amount of weight on each side of the body: *I struggled to **keep my balance** on my new skates.* ◊ *She cycled round the corner, **lost her balance** and fell off.*
3 (*plural* **balances**) the amount of money that is left after you have used some money: *I must check my **bank balance** (= find out how much I have in my account).*

balance² /'bæləns/ *verb* (**balances, balancing, balanced** /'bælənst/)
to put your body or something else into a position where it is steady and does not fall: *He balanced the bag on his head.* ◊ *She balanced on one leg.*

balcony

/'bælkəni/ *noun*
(*plural* **balconies**)
a small platform on
the outside wall of a
building, above the
ground, where you
can stand or sit

balcony

bald /bɔːld/

adjective
with no hair or not
much hair: *My dad is
going bald* (= losing
his hair). ⊃ Look at the picture at **hair**.

ball 0━ /bɔːl/ *noun*

1 a round thing that you use in games and
sports: *Throw the ball to me.* ◇ *a football* ◇ *a
tennis ball*
2 any round thing: *a ball of string* ◇ *a
snowball*
3 a big formal party where people dance

ballerina /ˌbæləˈriːnə/ *noun*

a woman who dances in BALLETS

ballet /'bæleɪ/ *noun*

a kind of dancing that tells a story with music
but no words: *I went to see a ballet.* ◇ *Do you
like ballet?*

ballet dancer /'bæleɪ dɑːnsə(r)/ *noun*

a person who dances in BALLETS

balloon /bəˈluːn/ *noun*

1 a small coloured rubber thing that you
blow air into and use as a toy or for
decoration: *We are going to hang balloons
around the room for the party.*
2 (*also* **hot-air balloon**) a big thing like a
balloon that flies in the sky, carrying people
in a container (called a **basket**) underneath:
I would like to go up in a balloon. ⊃ Look at
Picture Dictionary **P1**.

ballot /'bælət/ *noun*

when people choose somebody or
something by writing secretly on a piece of
paper: *We held a ballot to choose a new
president.*

ballpoint /'bɔːlpɔɪnt/ (*also* **ballpoint pen**

/ˌbɔːlpɔɪnt 'pen/) *noun*
a pen that has a very small ball at the end
that rolls the ink onto the paper
⊃ SAME MEANING **Biro** ⊃ Look at Picture
Dictionary page **P11**.

bamboo /ˌbæmˈbuː/ *noun* (*plural*

bamboos)
a tall plant that grows in hot countries and is
often used for making furniture: *a bamboo
chair* ◇ *bamboo shoots* (= young bamboo
plants that can be eaten)

ban /bæn/ *verb* (bans, banning, banned

/bænd/)
to say that something must not happen; to
not allow something: *The film was banned.*
▶ **ban** *noun*: *There is a ban on smoking in
restaurants.*

banana /bəˈnɑːnə/ *noun*

a long curved yellow fruit ⊃ Look at Picture
Dictionary page **P8**.

band 0━ /bænd/ *noun*

1 a group of people who play music
together: *a rock band* ◇ *a jazz band*
2 a thin flat piece of material that you put
around something: *I put an elastic band
round the letters to keep them together.* ◇ *The
hat had a red band round it.*
3 a line of colour or material on something
that is different from the rest of it: *She wore a
red jumper with a green band across the
middle.*

bandage¹

/'bændɪdʒ/ *noun*
a long piece of
white cloth that you
tie around a part of
the body that is hurt

bandage

bandage

bandage²

/'bændɪdʒ/ *verb*
(bandages,
bandaging,
bandaged
/'bændɪdʒd/)
to put a BANDAGE
around a part of the
body: *The nurse
bandaged my foot.*

Band-Aid™ /'bænd eɪd/ *American English

for* PLASTER(3)

bandit /'bændɪt/ *noun*

a person who attacks and robs people who
are travelling: *They were killed by bandits in
the mountains.*

bang¹ /bæŋ/ *verb* (bangs, banging,

banged /bæŋd/)
to make a loud noise by hitting something
hard or by closing something: *He banged his
head on the ceiling.* ◇ *Don't bang the door!*

bang² /bæŋ/ *noun*

1 a sudden very loud noise: *He shut the door
with a bang.*
2 a short, strong knock or hit, especially one
that causes pain and injury: *He fell and got a
bang on the head.*
3 bangs (*plural*) *American English for*
FRINGE(1)

A
B
C
D
E
F
G
H
I
J
K
L
M
N
O
P
Q
R
S
T
U
V
W
X
Y
Z

A

B

C

D

E

F

G

H

I

J

K

L

M

N

O

P

Q

R

S

T

U

V

W

X

Y

Z

banister /ˈbænɪstə(r)/ *noun*
a long piece of wood or metal that you hold on to when you go up or down stairs ➜ Look at the picture at **staircase**.

bank¹ 0─➤ /bæŋk/ *noun*
1 a place that keeps money safe for people: *I've got £500 in the bank.*
2 the land along the side of a river: *People were fishing along the banks of the river.*

bank² /bæŋk/ *verb* (banks, banking, banked /bæŋkt/)
to keep your money in a particular bank: *Who do you bank with?*
bank on someone or **something** to expect and trust someone to do something, or something to happen: *The boss might give you the day off but I wouldn't bank on it.*

bank account /ˈbæŋk əkaʊnt/ *noun*
an arrangement that you have with a bank that lets you keep your money there: *I'd like to open a bank account.*

> 🔍 **WORD BUILDING**
>
> If you have a **bank account** you can **deposit** money (**pay** it **in**) or **withdraw** it (**take** it **out**): *I'd like to withdraw £50, please.*
> If you don't want to **spend** your money, you can **save** it (keep it in the bank).

banker /ˈbæŋkə(r)/ *noun*
a person who owns a bank or who has an important job in a bank

bank holiday /ˌbæŋk ˈhɒlədeɪ/ *noun*
(*British*)
a public holiday, for example Christmas Day, New Year's Day, etc.

banking /ˈbæŋkɪŋ/ *noun* (*no plural*)
the type of business done by banks: *She chose a career in banking.*

banknote /ˈbæŋknəʊt/ *noun*
a piece of paper money: *These are German banknotes.*

bankrupt /ˈbæŋkrʌpt/ *adjective*
not able to continue in business because you cannot pay the money that you owe: *His business went bankrupt after a year.*

banner /ˈbænə(r)/ *noun*
a long piece of cloth with words on it. People carry **banners** to show what they think: *The banner said 'Stop the war'.*

baptism /ˈbæptɪzəm/ *noun*
a religious ceremony when somebody is BAPTIZED

baptize /bæpˈtaɪz/ *verb* (baptizes, baptizing, baptized /bæpˈtaɪzd/)
to put water on somebody and give them a

name, to show that they belong to the Christian Church

bars

bar code

bar of soap

bar of chocolate

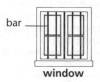
bar
bar
bar stool
bar
window

bar¹ 0─➤ /bɑː(r)/ *noun*
1 a place where people can go and buy drinks, especially alcoholic drinks: *There's a bar in the hotel.*
2 a long, high table where you buy drinks in a bar or pub: *We stood at the bar.*
3 a place where you can get a particular kind of food or drink: *a coffee bar ◇ a sandwich bar* ➜ Look at the note at **restaurant**.
4 a small block of something hard: *a bar of soap ◇ a bar of chocolate*
5 a long thin piece of metal: *There were iron bars on the windows.*

bar² /bɑː(r)/ *verb* (bars, barring, barred /bɑːd/)
1 to put something across a place so that people cannot pass: *A line of police barred the road.*
2 to say officially that somebody must not do something or go somewhere: *He was barred from the club for fighting.*

barbecue /ˈbɑːbɪkjuː/ *noun* (*abbr.* **BBQ**)
a party where you cook food on a fire outside: *We had a barbecue on the beach.*

barbed wire

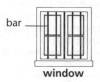

barbed wire /ˌbɑːbd ˈwaɪə(r)/ *noun* (*no plural*)
wire with a lot of sharp points on it. Some fences are made of **barbed wire**.

barber /ˈbɑːbə(r)/ ***noun***
1 a person whose job is to cut men's hair
2 **barber's** a shop where men go to get their hair cut

bar code /bɑː kəʊd/ ***noun***
a pattern of black lines that is printed on things you buy. It contains information that a computer reads to find the price.

bare /beə(r)/ ***adjective***
1 (used about a part of the body) with no clothes covering it: *He had **bare feet*** (= he wasn't wearing shoes or socks).
2 without anything covering it or in it: *They had taken the paintings down, so the walls were all bare.*

barefoot // ***adjective***, ***adverb***
with no shoes or socks on your feet: *The children ran barefoot along the beach.*

barely /ˈbeəli/ ***adverb***
almost not; only just ➲ SAME MEANING **hardly**: *She barely ate anything.*

bargain¹ /ˈbɑːgən/ ***noun***
something that is cheaper than usual: *At just £10, the dress was a real bargain!*

bargain² /ˈbɑːgən/ ***verb*** (**bargains**, **bargaining**, **bargained** /ˈbɑːgənd/)
to try to agree on the right price for something: *I think she'll sell the car for less if you **bargain with** her.*

barge /bɑːdʒ/ ***noun***
a long boat with a flat bottom for carrying things or people on rivers or CANALS (= artificial rivers)

bark

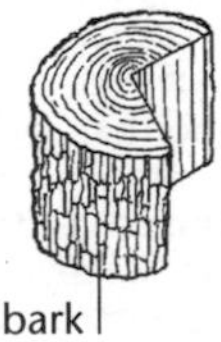

bark¹ /bɑːk/ ***noun***
1 (*no plural*) the hard surface of a tree
2 (*plural* **barks**) the short loud sound that a dog makes

bark² /bɑːk/ ***verb*** (**barks**, **barking**, **barked** /bɑːkt/)
If a dog **barks**, it makes short loud sounds: *The dog always **barks at** people it doesn't know.*

barley /ˈbɑːli/ ***noun*** (*no plural*)
a plant that we use for food and for making beer and some other drinks

barmaid /ˈbɑːmeɪd/ ***noun*** (*British*) (*American* **bartender**)
a woman who serves drinks in a bar or pub

barman /ˈbɑːmən/ ***noun*** (*plural* **barmen** /ˈbɑːmən/) (*American also* **bartender**)
a man who serves drinks in a bar or pub

barn /bɑːn/ ***noun***
a large building on a farm for keeping crops or animals in

barracks /ˈbærəks/ ***noun*** (*plural*)
a building or group of buildings where soldiers live: *an army barracks*

barrel /ˈbærəl/ ***noun***
1 a big container for liquids, with round sides and flat ends: *a beer barrel* ◇ *a barrel of oil*
2 the long metal part of a gun that a bullet goes through

barricade /ˌbærɪˈkeɪd/ ***noun***
a line of things arranged across a road, etc. to stop people from getting past
▶ **barricade** ***verb*** (**barricades**, **barricading**, **barricaded**): *He barricaded the door to keep the police out.*

barrier /ˈbæriə(r)/ ***noun***
a wall or fence that stops you going somewhere: *You must show your ticket at the barrier before you get on the train.*

bartender /ˈbɑːtendə(r)/ *American English for* BARMAID *or* BARMAN

base¹ 0━ /beɪs/ ***noun***
1 the bottom part of something; the part that something stands on: *The lamp has a heavy base.* ◇ *the **base of** a column*
2 a person's or a company's main home or office: *She travels all over the world but London is her base.*
3 a place where soldiers in the army, navy, etc. live and work: *an army base*

base² 0━ /beɪs/ ***verb*** (**bases**, **basing**, **based** /beɪst/)
be based somewhere If a person or a company **is based in** a place, that is where they have their main home or office
base something on something to make or develop something, using another thing as a starting point: *The film is based on a true story.*

baseball /ˈbeɪsbɔːl/ ***noun***
1 (*no plural*) a game in which two teams hit a ball with a wooden stick (called a **bat**) and then score points by running round four fixed points (called **bases**) on a large field: *We played baseball in the park.* ➲ Look at Picture Dictionary page **P14**.
2 (*plural* **baseballs**) a ball for playing this game

basement /ˈbeɪsmənt/ ***noun***
part of a building that is under the level of the ground: *a basement flat*

bases¹ /ˈbeɪsɪz/ *plural of* BASE

bases² /ˈbeɪsiːz/ *plural of* BASIS

bash /bæʃ/ ***verb*** (**bashes**, **bashing**, **bashed** /bæʃt/) (*informal*)
to hit somebody or something very hard: *I fell and bashed my knee.*

basic 0⃛ /'beisik/ *adjective*
1 most important and necessary: *A person's basic needs are food, clothes and a place to live.*
2 simple; including only what is necessary: *This course teaches basic computer skills.*

basically /'beisikli/ *adverb*
in the most important ways: *She's a little strange but basically a very nice person.*

basin /'beisn/ *noun*
1 = WASHBASIN
2 a round bowl for cooking or mixing food

basis 0⃛ /'beisis/ *noun* (*plural* bases /'beisi:z/)
1 the most important part or idea, from which something grows: *Her notes formed the **basis of** a book.*
2 the way something is done or organized: *We meet **on a regular basis** (= often).*

basket /'bɑːskɪt/ **basket**
noun
a container made of thin sticks or thin pieces of plastic or metal, that you use for holding or carrying things: *a shopping basket ◇ a bread basket* ⊃ Look also at **waste-paper basket**.

basketball /'bɑːskɪtbɔːl/ *noun*
1 (*no plural*) a game for two teams of five players who try to throw a ball into a high net ⊃ Look at Picture Dictionary page **P14**.
2 (*plural* basketballs) a ball for playing this game

bass /beis/ *adjective*
with a deep sound: *She plays the bass guitar. ◇ a bass drum*

bat¹ /bæt/ *noun*
1 a piece of wood for hitting the ball in a game like BASEBALL or TABLE TENNIS

> 🔎 **WHICH WORD?**
> The thing that you use to hit the ball has different names in different sports.
> You use a **bat** in baseball, cricket and table tennis.
> You use a **racket** to play badminton, squash and tennis.
> To play golf, you use a **club** and to play hockey, you use a **stick**.

2 an animal like a mouse with wings. **Bats** come out and fly at night.

bat² /bæt/ (bats, batting, batted) *verb*
to try to hit a ball in games like BASEBALL or CRICKET: *He bats very well.*

batch /bætʃ/ *noun* (*plural* batches)
a group of things: *She made a batch of cakes.*

bath 0⃛ /bɑːθ/ *noun* (*plural* baths /bɑːðz/)
1 (*British*) (*American* bathtub) a large container that you fill with water and sit in to wash your body ⊃ Look at Picture Dictionary page **P10**.
2 washing your body in a bath: *I **had a bath** this morning.*

bathe /beɪð/ *verb* (bathes, bathing, bathed /beɪðd/)
1 to wash a part of your body carefully: *He bathed the cut on his finger.*
2 to swim in the sea or in a lake or river: *On hot days we often bathe in the lake.*

> 🔎 **SPEAKING**
> It is more usual nowadays to say **go swimming**.

bathrobe /'bɑːθrəʊb/ *noun*
a piece of clothing, like a loose soft coat, that you put on after having a bath or shower

bathroom 0⃛ /'bɑːθruːm/ *noun*
1 (*British*) a room where you can wash and have a bath or shower ⊃ Look at Picture Dictionary page **P10**.
2 (*American*) a room with a toilet in it: *Can I **go to the bathroom** (= use the toilet)?* ⊃ Look at the note at **toilet**.

bathtub /'bɑːθtʌb/ *American English for* BATH(1)

battery /'bætri/ **batteries**
noun (*plural* batteries)
a thing that gives electricity. You put **batteries** inside things like toys, radios and cars to make them work.

battle¹ /'bætl/ *noun*
1 a fight between armies in a war: *the battle of Waterloo*
2 trying very hard to do something difficult: *After three years, she lost her **battle against** cancer.*

battle² /'bætl/ *verb* (battles, battling, battled /'bætld/)
to try very hard to do something difficult: *The doctors battled to save her life.*

bay /beɪ/ *noun* (*plural* bays)
a part of the coast where the land goes in to form a curve: *There was a ship in the bay. ◇ the Bay of Bengal*

be

present tense		short forms	negative short forms
I	**am**/æm/	**I'm**	**I'm not**
you	**are**/ɑː(r)/	you**'re**	you **aren't**
he/she/it	**is**/ɪz/	he**'s**/she**'s**/it**'s**	he/she/it **isn't**
we	**are**	we**'re**	we **aren't**
you	**are**	you**'re**	you **aren't**
they	**are**	they**'re**	they **aren't**

past tense		present participle	past participle
I	**was** /wɒz/	**being**	**been**
you	**were** /wɜː(r)/		
he/she/it	**was**		
we	**were**		
you	**were**		
they	**were**		

BC /ˌbiː ˈsiː/ *abbreviation*
'BC' in a date shows it was before Christ was born: *Julius Caesar died in 44 BC.* ➷ Look at **AD**.

be 0–ᴡ /bi; biː/ *verb*
1 there is/there are to exist or be present in a place: *There are a lot of trees in our garden.* ◇ *I tried phoning them but there was no answer.* ◇ *Is there a post office near here?*
2 a word that you use to give the position of somebody or something or the place where they are: *Jen's* (= Jen is) *in her office.* ◇ *Where are the scissors?*
3 a word that you use when you are giving the name of people or things, describing them or giving more information about them: *I'm* (= I am) *Ben.* ◇ *The film was excellent.* ◇ *John is a doctor.* ◇ *Roberta's Italian.* ◇ *'What colour is your car?' 'It's red.'* ◇ *Today is Friday.*
4 a word that you use to talk about the age of somebody or something or to talk about time: *'How old is she?' 'She's twelve.'* ◇ *Her birthday was in May.* ◇ *It's six o'clock.*
5 a word that you use with another verb: *'What are you doing?' 'I'm* (= I am) *reading.'*
6 a word that you use with part of another verb to show that something happens to somebody or something: *This cheese is made in France.* ◇ *The house was built in 1910.*
7 a word that shows that something must or will happen: *You are to go to bed immediately!*

beach 0–ᴡ /biːtʃ/ *noun* (*plural* **beaches**)
a piece of land next to the sea that is covered with sand or stones: *a sandy beach* ◇ *We lay on the beach in the sun.*

bead /biːd/ *noun*
a small ball of wood, glass or plastic with a hole in the middle. **Beads** are put on a string to make jewellery.

beak /biːk/ *noun*
the hard pointed part of a bird's mouth ➷ Look at the picture at **bird**.

beam¹ /biːm/ *noun*
1 a line of light: *a laser beam*
2 a long heavy piece of wood that holds up a roof or ceiling

beam² /biːm/ *verb* (**beams, beaming, beamed** /biːmd/)
to have a big happy smile on your face

bean /biːn/ *noun*
a seed, or a seed container, that we use as food: *green beans* ◇ *coffee beans* ➷ Look at Picture Dictionary page **P9**.

bear¹ 0–ᴡ /beə(r)/ *verb* (**bears, bearing, bore** /bɔː(r)/, **has borne** /bɔːn/)
1 to be able to accept something unpleasant without complaining: *The pain was difficult to bear.*
2 to hold somebody or something up so that they do not fall: *The ice is too thin to bear your weight.*
can't bear somebody or something
to hate somebody or something: *I can't bear this music.* ◇ *He can't bear having nothing to do.*

bear² /beə(r)/ *noun*
a big wild animal with thick fur ➷ Look at Picture Dictionary page **P3**.

beard 0–ᴡ /bɪəd/ *noun*
the hair on a man's chin: *He has got a beard.* ➷ Look at the picture on the next page.

beast /biːst/ *noun*
1 (*formal*) a wild animal

> 🔊 **SPEAKING**
> **Animal** is the word that we usually use.

2 an unkind or cruel person

A
B
C
D
E
F
G
H
I
J
K
L
M
N
O
P
Q
R
S
T
U
V
W
X
Y
Z

beard

| beard

beat¹ 0—ा /biːt/ *verb* (beats, beating, beat, has beaten /'biːtn/)
1 to win a fight or game against a person or group of people: *Daniel always beats me at tennis.* ◇ *Our team was beaten 2–1.*
2 to hit somebody or something very hard many times: *She beats her dog with a stick.* ◇ *The rain was beating on the roof.*
3 to make the same sound or movement many times: *His heart was beating fast.*
4 to mix food quickly with a fork, for example: *Beat the eggs and sugar together.*
beat somebody up to hit or kick somebody hard, many times: *He was badly beaten up by a gang of youths.*

beat² /biːt/ *noun*
a sound that comes again and again: *We heard the beat of the drums.* ⊃ Look at **heartbeat**.

beautician /bjuː'tɪʃn/ *noun*
a person whose job is to give special treatments to your face and body to make you look good

beautiful 0—ा /'bjuːtɪfl/ *adjective*
1 very pretty or attractive: *a beautiful woman*

> 🔎 **WORD BUILDING**
> When we talk about people, we usually say **beautiful** and **pretty** for women and girls, and **handsome** and **good-looking** for men and boys.
> **Attractive** can be used for both.

2 very nice to see, hear or smell
⊃ SAME MEANING **lovely**: *Those flowers are beautiful.* ◇ *What a beautiful song!*
▶ **beautifully** /'bjuːtɪfli/ *adverb*: *Louis sang beautifully.*

beauty 0—ा /'bjuːti/ *noun* (no plural)
the quality of being beautiful: *She was a woman of great beauty.* ◇ *the beauty of the mountains*

because 0—ा /bɪ'kɒz/ *conjunction*
for the reason that: *He was angry because I was late.*

because of something as a result of something or someone: *We stayed at home because of the rain.*

beckon /'bekən/ *verb* (beckons, beckoning, beckoned /'bekənd/)
to move your finger to show that you want somebody to come nearer

become 0—ा /bɪ'kʌm/ *verb* (becomes, becoming, became /bɪ'keɪm/, has become)
to begin to be something: *She became a doctor in 1982.* ◇ *The weather is becoming colder.*

> 🔎 SPEAKING
> In conversation, we usually say **get** instead of **become** with adjectives. It is less formal: *The weather is getting colder.* ◇ *She got nervous as the exam date came closer.*

what became of…? used to ask what has happened to somebody or something: *What became of that student who used to live with you?*

bed 0—ा /bed/ *noun*
1 a thing that you sleep on: *It was time to go to bed.* ◇ *The children are in bed.* ◇ *to make the bed* (= to make it ready for somebody to sleep in)

> 🔎 **WORD BUILDING**
> A bed for one person is called a **single bed** and a bed for two people is called a **double bed**.
> Children often sleep in **bunk beds**, which are two single beds built with one above the other.

2 the bottom of a river or the sea

bed and breakfast /,bed ən 'brekfəst/ (*abbr.* B and B *or* B & B) /,biː ən 'biː/ *noun* (British)
a private house or small hotel where you pay for a room to sleep in and a meal the next morning: *I stayed in a bed and breakfast.*

bedclothes /'bedkləʊðz/ *noun* (plural)
the sheets and covers that you use on a bed

bedroom 0—ा /'bedruːm/ *noun*
a room where you sleep ⊃ Look at Picture Dictionary page **P10**.

bedside /'bedsaɪd/ *noun* (no plural)
the area that is next to a bed: *She sat at his bedside all night long.* ◇ *A book lay open on the bedside table.*

bedsit /'bedsɪt/ (*also* **bedsitter** /,bed'sɪtə(r)/) *noun*
one room that you live and sleep in

beds

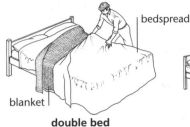
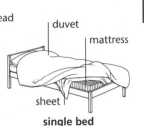

bedspread   duvet   mattress

pillow   blanket   sheet

bunk beds   **double bed**   **single bed**

bedspread /'bedspred/ *noun*
an attractive cover for a bed that you put on top of the sheets and other covers ⊃ Look at the picture at **bed**.

bedtime /'bedtaɪm/ *noun*
the time when somebody usually goes to bed

bee /biː/ *noun*
a black and yellow insect that flies and makes a sweet food that we eat (called **honey**)

bee

beef /biːf/ *noun* (*no plural*)
meat from a cow: *roast beef* ⊃ Look at the note at **cow** ⊃ Look at Picture Dictionary page **P7**.

beefburger /'biːfbɜːgə(r)/ *noun* (British)
another word for HAMBURGER

beehive /'biːhaɪv/ *noun*
a thing that BEES live in

been 0ᴡ /biːn; bɪn/
1 *form of* BE
2 *form of* GO¹
have been to to have gone to a place and come back again: *Have you ever been to Scotland?*

> 🔎 **WHICH WORD?**
>
> **Been** or **gone**?
> If somebody has **been** to a place, they have travelled there and returned: *I've been to Scotland three times.* ◇ *You were a long time. Where have you been?*
> If somebody has **gone** to a place, they have travelled there and they are still there now: *Judy isn't here. She's gone to Scotland.* ◇ *Mum's gone out, but she'll be back soon.*

beer 0ᴡ /bɪə(r)/ *noun*
1 (*no plural*) an alcoholic drink made from grain: *a pint of beer*

2 (*plural* **beers**) a glass, bottle or can of beer: *Three beers, please.*

beetle /'biːtl/ *noun*
an insect with hard wings and a shiny body

beetroot /'biːtruːt/ *noun* (British) (*American* **beet** /biːt/)
a round dark red vegetable that you cook before you eat it ⊃ Look at Picture Dictionary page **P9**.

before¹ 0ᴡ /bɪ'fɔː(r)/ *preposition, conjunction*
1 earlier than somebody or something; earlier than the time that: *He arrived before me.* ◇ *I said goodbye before I left.* ◇ *Ellen worked in a hospital before getting this job.* ◇ *They should be here **before long** (= soon).*
2 in front of somebody or something: *B comes before C in the alphabet.*
⊃ OPPOSITE **after**

before² /bɪ'fɔː(r)/ *adverb*
at an earlier time; in the past: *I've never met them before.* ◇ *I've seen this film before.*

beforehand /bɪ'fɔːhænd/ *adverb*
at an earlier time than something: *Tell me beforehand if you are going to be late.*

beg /beg/ *verb* (**begs, begging, begged** /begd/)
1 to ask somebody for something especially in an anxious way because you want or need it very much: *She **begged** me **to** stay with her.* ◇ *He **begged for** help.*
2 to ask for money or food because you are very poor: *There are a lot of people begging in the streets.*
I beg your pardon (formal) I am sorry: *I beg your pardon, could you say that again?*

beggar /'begə(r)/ *noun*
a person who asks other people for money or food

begin 0ᴡ /bɪ'gɪn/ *verb* (**begins, beginning, began** /bɪ'gæn/, **has begun** /bɪ'gʌn/)
1 to start to do something or start to happen ⊃ SAME MEANING **start**: *I'm*

A
B
C
D
E
F
G
H
I
J
K
L
M
N
O
P
Q
R
S
T
U
V
W
X
Y
Z

beginning to feel cold. ◇ *The film begins at 7.30.*

2 to start in a particular way: *The name John begins with a 'J'.* ⊃ OPPOSITE **end**

to begin with at first; at the beginning: *To begin with they were very happy.*

🔎 **WHICH WORD?**

Begin or **start**?
Begin and **start** both mean the same thing, but **start** is more often used in speaking: *Shall we eat now? I'm starting to feel hungry.*

---

beginner /bɪˈgɪnə(r)/ *noun*
a person who is starting to do or learn something

beginning 0─┅ /bɪˈgɪnɪŋ/ *noun*
the time or place where something starts; the first part of something: *I didn't see the beginning of the film.* ⊃ OPPOSITE **end**

begun form of BEGIN

behalf /bɪˈhɑːf/ *noun*
on behalf of somebody, **on somebody's behalf** for somebody; in the place of somebody: *Mr Smith is away, so I am writing to you on his behalf.*

behave 0─┅ /bɪˈheɪv/ *verb* (behaves, behaving, behaved /bɪˈheɪvd/)
to do and say things in a certain way: *They behaved very kindly towards me.* ◇ *The children behaved badly all day.*
behave yourself to be good; to do and say the right things: *Did the children behave themselves?*

behaviour 0─┅ (British) (American behavior) /bɪˈheɪvjə(r)/ *noun* (no plural)
the way you are; the way that you do and say things: *He was sent out of the class for bad behaviour.*

behind 0─┅ /bɪˈhaɪnd/ *preposition, adverb*
1 at or to the back of somebody or something: *I hid behind the wall.* ◇ *I drove off and Jim followed behind.*
2 slower or less good than somebody or something; slower or less good than you should be: *She is behind with her work because she is often ill.*
3 in the place where somebody or something was before: *I got off the train and left my bag behind* (= on the train).

beige /beɪʒ/ *adjective*
with a light brown colour

being¹ form of BE

being² /ˈbiːɪŋ/ *noun*
a person or living thing: *a being from another planet*

belief 0─┅ /bɪˈliːf/ *noun*
a sure feeling that something is true or real: *his belief in God* ◇ *Divorce is contrary to their religious beliefs.*

believable /bɪˈliːvəbl/ *adjective*
that you can believe
⊃ OPPOSITE **unbelievable**

believe 0─┅ /bɪˈliːv/ *verb* (believes, believing, believed /bɪˈliːvd/)
1 to feel sure that something is true; to feel sure that what somebody says is true: *Long ago, people believed that the earth was flat.* ◇ *She says she didn't take the money. Do you believe her?*
2 to think that something is true or possible, although you are not certain: *'Does Mick still work here?' 'I believe so.'*
believe in somebody or **something** to feel sure that somebody or something exists: *Do you believe in ghosts?*

bell 0─┅ /bel/ *noun*
a metal thing that makes a sound when something hits or touches it: *The church bells were ringing.* ◇ *I rang the bell and he answered the door.*

bell

belly /ˈbeli/ *noun* (plural **bellies**)
the part of your body between your chest and your legs ⊃ SAME MEANING **stomach**

belong 0─┅ /bɪˈlɒŋ/ *verb* (belongs, belonging, belonged /bɪˈlɒŋd/)
1 to be somebody's: *'Who does this pen belong to?' 'It belongs to me.'*
2 to be a member of a group or an organization: *Do you belong to any political party?*
3 to have its right or usual place: *That chair belongs in my room.*

belongings /bɪˈlɒŋɪŋz/ *noun* (plural)
the things that you own: *They lost all their belongings in the fire.*

below 0─┅ /bɪˈləʊ/ *preposition, adverb*
1 in or to a lower place than somebody or something: *From the plane we could see the mountains below.* ◇ *He dived below the surface of the water.* ◇ *Do not write below this line.*
⊃ OPPOSITE **above**
2 less than a number or price: *The temperature was below zero.*

belt 0️⃣ /belt/ *noun*
a long piece of cloth or leather that you wear around the middle of your body ➔ Look also at **safety belt** and **seat belt**.

bench /bentʃ/
noun (*plural*
benches)
a long seat for two
or more people,
usually made of
wood: *They sat on a
park bench.*

bench

bend

He is **bending** down.
(*also* **bending** over)

She is **bending**
a spoon.

bend¹ 0️⃣ /bend/ *verb* (**bends, bending, bent** /bent/, **has bent**)
1 to make something that was straight into a curved shape: *Bend your legs!*
2 to be or become curved: *The road bends to the left.*
bend down, bend over to move your body forward and down: *She bent down to put on her shoes.*

bend² /bend/ *noun*
a part of a road or river that is not straight: *Drive slowly – there's a bend in the road.*

beneath 0️⃣ /bɪˈniːθ/ *preposition, adverb*
in or to a lower place than somebody or something ➔ SAME MEANING **below, underneath**: *From the tower, they looked down on the city beneath.* ◇ *The boat sank beneath the waves.* ➔ OPPOSITE **above**

benefit¹ 0️⃣ /ˈbenɪfɪt/ *noun*
1 (*plural* **benefits**) something that is good or helpful: *What are the **benefits** of having a computer?* ◇ *I did it **for your benefit** (= to help you).*
2 (*no plural*) (*British*) money that the government gives to people who are ill or poor or who do not have a job: *housing benefit*

benefit² /ˈbenɪfɪt/ *verb* (**benefits, benefiting, benefited** *or* **benefitting, benefitted**)
to be good or helpful for somebody: *The new law will benefit families with children.*
benefit from something to get something good or useful from something: *She will benefit from a holiday.*

bent¹ *form of* BEND¹

bent² /bent/ *adjective*
not straight; curved: *Do this exercise with your knees bent.* ◇ *This knife is bent.*
➔ OPPOSITE **straight**

beret /ˈbereɪ/ *noun*
a soft flat round hat

berry /ˈberi/ *noun* (*plural* **berries**)
a small soft fruit with seeds in it: *Those berries are poisonous.* ◇ *raspberries*

beside 0️⃣ /bɪˈsaɪd/ *preposition*
at the side of somebody or something ➔ SAME MEANING **next to**: *Come and sit beside me.*

besides¹ /bɪˈsaɪdz/ *preposition*
as well as somebody or something; if you do not count somebody or something: *We have lots of things in common besides music.*

besides² /bɪˈsaɪdz/ *adverb*
also: *I don't really want to go. Besides, it's too late now.*

best¹ 0️⃣ /best/ *adjective* (**good, better, best**)
better than all others: *This is the best ice cream I have ever eaten!* ◇ *Tom is my **best** friend.* ◇ *Jo's the best player on the team.*
➔ OPPOSITE **worst**

best² 0️⃣ /best/ *adverb*
1 most well: *I work best in the morning.*
2 more than all others ➔ SAME MEANING **most**: *Which picture do you like best?*
➔ OPPOSITE **least**

best³ 0️⃣ /best/ *noun* (*no plural*)
the person or thing that is better than all others: *Mike and Ian are good at tennis but Paul is the best.*
all the best words that you use when you say goodbye to somebody, to wish them success
do your best to do all that you can: *I don't know if I can finish the work today, but I'll do my best.*

best man /ˌbest ˈmæn/ *noun* (*no plural*)
a man at a wedding who helps the man who is getting married (the **bridegroom**)

best-seller /ˌbest ˈselə(r)/ *noun*
a book or other product that is bought by large numbers of people

bet /bet/ *verb* (bets, betting, bet, has bet)
to risk money on a race or a game by saying
what the result will be. If you are right, you
win money: *I bet you £5 that our team will win.*
I bet (*informal*) I am sure: *I bet it will rain
tomorrow.* ◇ *I bet you can't climb that tree.*
▶ **bet** *noun*: *I lost the bet.*

betray /bɪ'treɪ/ *verb* (betrays, betraying,
betrayed /bɪ'treɪd/)
to harm your friends or your country by
giving information to an enemy: *She
betrayed the whole group to the secret police.*

better¹ 0ᴡ /'betə(r)/ *adjective* (good,
better, best)
1 of a higher standard or quality; not as bad
as something else: *This book is better than
that one.*
2 less ill: *I was ill yesterday, but I feel better
now.* ⊃ OPPOSITE **worse**

better² 0ᴡ /'betə(r)/ *adverb*
in a more excellent or pleasant way; not as
badly: *You speak French better than I do.*
be better off to be happier, richer, etc.:
I'm better off now that I've got a new job. ◇
You look ill – you'd be better off in bed.
had better ought to; should: *You'd better
go now if you want to catch the train.*

between 0ᴡ /bɪ'twiːn/ *preposition,
adverb*
1 in the space in the middle of two things or
people: *The letter B comes between A and C.* ◇
I sat between Sylvie and Bruno. ◇ *I see her most
weekends but not very often in between.*
⊃ Look at the note at **among**.
2 to and from two places: *The boat sails
between Dover and Calais.*
3 more than one thing but less than another
thing: *The meal will cost between £20 and
£25.*
4 after one time and before the next time: *I'll
meet you between 4 and 4.30.*
5 for or by two or more people or things: *We
shared the cake between us* (= each of us had
some cake).
6 a word that you use when you compare
two people or things: *What is the difference
between 'some' and 'any'?*

beware /bɪ'weə(r)/ *verb*
beware of somebody or **something**
to be careful because somebody or
something is dangerous: *Beware of the dog!*
(= words written on a sign)

bewildered /bɪ'wɪldəd/ *adjective*
If you are **bewildered**, you do not
understand something or you do not know
what to do. ⊃ SAME MEANING **confused**:
*I was completely bewildered by his sudden
change of mood.*

beyond 0ᴡ /bɪ'jɒnd/ *preposition, adverb*
on the other side of something; further than
something: *The road continues beyond the
village up into the hills.* ◇ *We could see the lake
and the mountains beyond.*

bib /bɪb/ *noun*
a piece of cloth or plastic that a baby wears
under its chin when it is eating

the Bible /ðə 'baɪbl/ *noun*
the book of great religious importance to
Christian and Jewish people

bicycle

handlebars
saddle
spoke
wheel
tyre (British)
tire (American)
pedal
chain

bicycle 0ᴡ /'baɪsɪkl/ (*also informal* **bike**)
noun
a vehicle with two wheels. You sit on a
bicycle and move your legs to make the
wheels turn: *Can you ride a bicycle?*

bid¹ /bɪd/ *verb* (bids, bidding, bid, has bid)
to offer some money because you want to
buy something: *He bid $10 000 for the
painting.*

bid² /bɪd/ *noun*
an offer of money for something that you
want to buy: *She made a bid of £250 for
the vase.*

big 0ᴡ /bɪg/ *adjective* (bigger, biggest)
1 not small; large: *Milan is a big city.* ◇ *This
shirt is too big for me.* ◇ *How big is your flat?*
⊃ OPPOSITE **small**
2 great or important: *a big problem*
3 older: *Amy is my big sister.*
⊃ OPPOSITE **little**

bike /baɪk/ *noun* (*informal*)
a bicycle or a motorbike: *I go to school by
bike.*

bikini /bɪ'kiːni/ *noun*
a piece of clothing in two pieces that women
wear for swimming

bilingual /ˌbaɪ'lɪŋgwəl/ *adjective*
1 able to speak two languages equally well:
Their children are bilingual.
2 having or using two languages: *a bilingual
dictionary*

bill ⊙ /bɪl/ *noun*
1 (*British*) (*American* **check**) a piece of paper that shows how much money you must pay for something: *Can I have the bill, please?* (= in a restaurant)
2 *American English for* NOTE¹(3): *a ten-dollar bill*

billfold /'bɪlfəʊld/ *American English for* WALLET

billion ⊙ /'bɪljən/ *number*
1 000 000 000; one thousand million: *five billion pounds* ◇ *The company is worth **billions** of dollars.*

> 🔎 **GRAMMAR**
> We say **five billion dollars** (without 's'), but **billions of** dollars.

bin /bɪn/ *noun*
a thing that you put rubbish in: *Put your rubbish in the bin.* ➩ Look also at **dustbin**.

bind /baɪnd/ *verb* (**binds, binding, bound** /baʊnd/, **has bound**)
to tie string or rope round something to hold it firmly: *They bound the prisoner's arms and legs together.*

bingo /'bɪŋgəʊ/ *noun* (*no plural*)
a game where each player has a card with numbers on it. When the person who controls the game says all the numbers on your card, you win the game.

binoculars   **binoculars**
/bɪ'nɒkjələz/ *noun*
(*plural*)
special glasses that
you use to see
things that are far
away ➩ Look at
telescope.

biodegradable /ˌbaɪəʊdɪ'greɪdəbl/ *adjective*
Biodegradable substances can go back into the earth and so do not damage the environment.

biography /baɪ'ɒgrəfi/ *noun* (*plural* **biographies**)
the story of a person's life, that another person writes: *a biography of Nelson Mandela* ➩ Look at **autobiography**.

biology ⊙ /baɪ'ɒlədʒi/ *noun* (*no plural*)
the study of the life of animals and plants: *Biology is my favourite subject.*
▶ **biologist** /baɪ'ɒlədʒɪst/ *noun* a person who studies **biology**

bird ⊙ /bɜːd/ *noun*
an animal with feathers and wings: *Gulls and sparrows are birds.*

> 🔎 **WORD BUILDING**
> Most birds can **fly** and **sing**. They build **nests** and **lay eggs**.
> There are many different types of **bird**. Here are some of them: chicken, eagle, ostrich, parrot, pigeon, seagull.

bird

bird flu /'bɜːd fluː/ *noun* (*no plural*)
a serious illness that birds, especially chickens, can catch and which can be spread from birds to humans and can cause death

bird of prey /ˌbɜːd əv 'preɪ/ *noun*
a bird that catches and eats other birds and small animals: *Eagles are birds of prey.*

Biro™ /'baɪrəʊ/ *noun* (*plural* **Biros**)
a pen with a very small ball at the end that rolls ink onto the paper ➩ SAME MEANING **ballpoint**

birth ⊙ /bɜːθ/ *noun*

> 🔎 **PRONUNCIATION**
> The word **birth** sounds like **earth**.

the time when a baby comes out of its mother; being born: *the birth of a baby* ◇ *What's your **date of birth*** (= the date when you were born)?
give birth to have a baby: *My sister gave birth to her second child last week.*

birthday ⊙ /'bɜːθdeɪ/ *noun* (*plural* **birthdays**)
the day each year that is the same as the date when you were born: *My birthday is on May 2nd.* ◇ *a birthday present* ◇ *Happy Birthday!*

> 🔎 **CULTURE**
> On your birthday people say **Happy Birthday!**
> Family and friends give you cards and presents. You can have a **birthday party**, and a **birthday cake** with candles.
> Your **18th birthday** is important because that is when you legally become an adult.
> An **anniversary** is not the same as a

A
B
C
D
E
F
G
H
I
J
K
L
M
N
O
P
Q
R
S
T
U
V
W
X
Y
Z

A
B
C
D
E
F
G
H
I
J
K
L
M
N
O
P
Q
R
S
T
U
V
W
X
Y
Z

birthday. It is the day in each year which is the same date as an important event that happened in the past: *We celebrated our tenth wedding anniversary.*

biscuit 0̶ᴡ /'bɪskɪt/ (*British*) (*American* **cookie**) *noun*
a kind of small thin hard cake that is usually sweet: *a packet of biscuits* ◇ *a chocolate biscuit* ⊃ Look at Picture Dictionary page **P6**.

bishop /'bɪʃəp/ *noun*
an important priest in the Christian church, who looks after all the churches in a large area

bit 0̶ᴡ /bɪt/ *noun*
1 a small piece or amount of something: *Would you like a bit of cake?* ◇ *Some bits of the film were very funny.*
2 a bit a little: *You look a bit tired.*
3 a bit a short time: *Let's wait a bit.*
4 (*computing*) a unit of information that is stored in a computer's memory
a bit of a... (*informal*) used when talking about unpleasant things to mean 'rather a': *It's a bit of a long way to the station.*
bit by bit slowly or a little at a time: *Bit by bit, I started to feel better.*
quite a bit (*informal*) a lot: *It must have rained quite a bit in the night.*

bite¹ 0̶ᴡ /baɪt/ *verb* (**bites**, **biting**, **bit** /bɪt/, **has bitten** /'bɪtn/)
1 to cut something with your teeth: *That dog bit my leg!*
2 If an insect or snake **bites** you, it hurts you by pushing a small sharp part into your skin: *I've been bitten by mosquitoes.*

bite² /baɪt/ *noun*
1 a piece of food that you can put in your mouth: *He took a bite of his sandwich.*
2 a painful place on your skin made by an insect or an animal: *a snake bite*

bitter 0̶ᴡ /'bɪtə(r)/ *adjective*
1 angry and sad about something that has happened: *He felt very bitter about losing his job.*
2 **Bitter** food has a sharp unpleasant taste: *The coffee was bitter.*
3 very cold: *a bitter wind*
▶ **bitterness** /'bɪtənəs/ *noun* (*no plural*): *The strike caused great bitterness.*

bizarre /bɪ'zɑ:(r)/ *adjective*
very strange ⊃ SAME MEANING **weird**: *He has a bizarre sense of humour.*
▶ **bizarrely** /bɪ'zɑ:li/ *adverb*: *bizarrely dressed teenagers*

black¹ 0̶ᴡ /blæk/ *adjective* (**blacker**, **blackest**)
1 with the colour of the sky at night: *a black dog*
2 belonging to a race of people with dark skins: *Martin Luther King was a famous black leader.*
3 without milk: *black coffee*

black² /blæk/ *noun*
1 the colour of the sky at night: *She was dressed in black.*
2 a person who belongs to a race of people with dark skins
black and white with the colours black, white and grey only: *We watched a black and white film on TV.*

blackberry /'blækbəri/ *noun* (*plural* **blackberries**)
a small soft black fruit that grows on a bush

blackbird /'blækbɜ:d/ *noun*
a bird with black feathers

blackboard /'blækbɔ:d/ *noun*
a dark board that a teacher writes on with a white substance (called **chalk**): *Look at the blackboard.* ⊃ Look at Picture Dictionary page **P12**.

blackcurrant /ˌblæk'kʌrənt/ *noun*
a small round black fruit that grows on a bush ⊃ Look at Picture Dictionary page **P8**.

black eye /ˌblæk 'aɪ/ *noun*
a dark area of skin around a person's eye where somebody or something has hit them: *He got a black eye in a fight.*

blackmail /'blækmeɪl/ *noun* (*no plural*)
saying that you will tell something bad about somebody if they do not give you money or do something for you
▶ **blackmail** *verb* (**blackmails**, **blackmailing**, **blackmailed** /'blækmeɪld/): *She blackmailed him into giving her thousands of pounds.*

blacksmith /'blæksmɪθ/ *noun*
a person whose job is to make and repair things made of iron

blade /bleɪd/ *noun*
1 the flat sharp part of something such as a knife or a tool ⊃ Look at the picture at **knife**.
2 a long thin leaf of a plant such as grass: *a blade of grass*

blame 0̶ᴡ /bleɪm/ *verb* (**blames**, **blaming**, **blamed** /bleɪmd/)
to say that a certain person or thing made something bad happen: *The other driver blamed me for the accident.*
▶ **blame** *noun* (*no plural*): *Eve took the blame for the mistake.*

bland /blænd/ *adjective*
1 ordinary and not very interesting: *I find her songs rather bland.*
2 Bland food does not have a strong taste: *a bland diet of rice and fish*

blank /blæŋk/ *adjective*
1 with no writing, pictures or anything else on it: *a blank piece of paper*
2 If your face is **blank**, it shows no feelings or understanding: *I asked her a question, but she just gave me a blank look.*

blanket /ˈblæŋkɪt/ *noun*
a thick cover that you put on a bed ⊃ Look at the picture at **bed**.

blast[1] /blɑːst/ *noun*
1 when a bomb explodes: *Two people were killed in the blast.*
2 a sudden movement of air: *a blast of cold air*
3 a sudden loud noise: *The driver gave a few blasts on his horn.*

blast[2] /blɑːst/ *verb* (blasts, blasting, blasted)
to make a hole in something with an explosion: *They blasted through the mountain to make a tunnel.*

blast-off /ˈblɑːst ɒf/ *noun* (no plural)
the time when a SPACECRAFT (= a vehicle that travels into space) leaves the ground

blaze[1] /bleɪz/ *verb* (blazes, blazing, blazed /bleɪzd/)
to burn strongly and brightly: *a blazing fire*

blaze[2] /bleɪz/ *noun*
a large and often dangerous fire: *It took firefighters four hours to put out the blaze.*

blazer /ˈbleɪzə(r)/ *noun*
a jacket. **Blazers** sometimes show which school or club you belong to.

bleak /bliːk/ *adjective* (bleaker, bleakest)
1 A **bleak** situation is not hopeful or encouraging: *The country's future looks bleak.*
2 cold and grey: *It was a bleak winter's day.*

bleed /bliːd/ *verb* (bleeds, bleeding, bled /bled/, has bled)
to lose blood: *I've cut my hand and it's bleeding.*

blend /blend/ *verb* (blends, blending, blended)
1 to mix: *Blend the sugar and the butter together.*
2 to look or sound good together: *These colours blend very well.*
▶ **blend** *noun*: *This is a blend of two different kinds of coffee.*

bless /bles/ *verb* (blesses, blessing, blessed /blest/)
to ask for God's help for somebody or

something: *The priest blessed the young couple.*
Bless you! words that you say to somebody when they SNEEZE (= make a loud noise through their nose)

blew *form of* BLOW[1]

blind[1] /blaɪnd/ *adjective*
not able to see: *My grandad is going blind.* ◇ *He trains guide dogs for the blind* (= people who are not able to see).
▶ **blindness** /ˈblaɪndnəs/ *noun* (no plural): *The disease can cause blindness.*

blinds

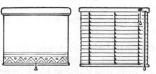

blind[2] /blaɪnd/ *noun*
a piece of cloth or other material that you pull down to cover a window

blindfold /ˈblaɪndfəʊld/ *noun*
a piece of cloth that you put over somebody's eyes so that they cannot see
▶ **blindfold** /ˈblaɪndfəʊld/ *verb* (blindfolds, blindfolding, blindfolded): *The prisoners were blindfolded and pushed into vans.*

blink /blɪŋk/ *verb* (blinks, blinking, blinked /blɪŋkt/)
to shut and open your eyes very quickly
▶ **blink** *noun* ⊃ Look at **wink**.

blister /ˈblɪstə(r)/ *noun*
a small painful place on your skin, that is full of liquid. Rubbing or burning can cause **blisters**: *My new shoes gave me blisters.*

blizzard /ˈblɪzəd/ *noun*
a very bad storm with snow and strong winds

blob

soap
blob

blob /blɒb/ *noun*
a small amount of a thick liquid: *There are blobs of paint on the floor.*

A
B
C
D
E
F
G
H
I
J
K
L
M
N
O
P
Q
R
S
T
U
V
W
X
Y
Z

block¹ 0🔗 /blɒk/ *noun*
1 a big heavy piece of something, with flat sides: *a **block of** wood* ◇ *The bridge is made of concrete blocks.*
2 a big building with a lot of offices or flats inside: *an office block* ◇ *a block of flats*
3 a group of buildings with streets all round it: *We drove round the block looking for the hotel.*
4 a thing that stops somebody or something from moving forward: *The police have put road blocks around the town.*

block² /blɒk/ *verb* (blocks, blocking, blocked /blɒkt/)
to stop somebody or something from moving forward: *A fallen tree blocked the road.*

block capitals /ˌblɒk ˈkæpɪtlz/ *noun*
big letters such as 'ABC' rather than 'abc': *Please write your name **in block capitals**.*

blog /blɒg/ *noun*
a personal record that somebody puts on their website saying what they do every day and what they think about things
▶ **blogger** /ˈblɒgə(r)/ *noun* a person who writes a BLOG

bloke /bləʊk/ *noun* (*British, informal*)
a man: *He's a really nice bloke.*

blonde /blɒnd/ (*also* blond) *adjective*
with light-coloured hair: *She is tall and blonde.* ◇ *He's got blond hair.*
▶ **blonde** *noun* a woman who has **blonde** hair: *She's a natural blonde.*

blood 0🔗 /blʌd/ *noun* (*no plural*)
the red liquid inside your body

blood vessel /ˈblʌd vesl/ *noun*
one of the tubes in your body that blood flows through

bloody /ˈblʌdi/ *adjective* (bloodier, bloodiest)
1 covered with blood: *a bloody nose*
2 with a lot of killing: *It was a bloody war.*

bloom /bluːm/ *verb* (blooms, blooming, bloomed /bluːmd/)
to produce flowers: *Roses bloom in the summer.*

blossom /ˈblɒsəm/ *noun* (*no plural*)
the flowers on a tree, especially a fruit tree: *The apple tree is covered in blossom.*
▶ **blossom** *verb* (blossoms, blossoming, blossomed /ˈblɒsəmd/): *The cherry trees are blossoming.*

blouse /blaʊz/ *noun*
a piece of clothing like a shirt that a woman or girl wears on the top part of her body: *She was wearing a blue skirt and a white blouse.*

blow¹ 0🔗 /bləʊ/ *verb* (blows, blowing, blew /bluː/, has blown /bləʊn/)

🔊 **PRONUNCIATION**
The word **blow** sounds like **go**.

1 When air or wind **blows**, it moves: *The wind was blowing from the sea.*
2 to move something through the air: *The wind **blew** my hat **off**.*
3 to send air out from your mouth: *Please blow into this tube.*
4 to send air out from your mouth into a musical instrument, for example, to make a noise: *The referee blew his whistle.*
blow up, blow something up
1 to explode or make something explode, for example with a bomb: *The plane blew up.* ◇ *They blew up the station.*
2 to fill something with air: *We blew up some balloons for the party.*
blow your nose to clear your nose by **blowing** strongly through it onto a piece of cloth or paper (called a **handkerchief**).

blow² /bləʊ/ *noun*
1 a hard hit from somebody's hand or a weapon: *He felt a blow on the back of his head.*
2 something that happens suddenly and that makes you very unhappy: *Her father's death was a terrible blow.*

blue 0🔗 /bluː/ *adjective* (bluer, bluest)
having the colour of a clear sky when the sun shines: *He wore a blue shirt.* ◇ *dark blue curtains* ◇ *Her eyes are bright blue.*
▶ **blue** *noun*: *She was dressed **in blue**.*

blunt /blʌnt/ *adjective*
1 with an edge or point that is not sharp: *This pencil is blunt.* ⊃ OPPOSITE **sharp**
2 If you are **blunt**, you say what you think in a way that is not polite.

blur /blɜː(r)/ *verb* (blurs, blurring, blurred /blɜːd/)
to make something less clear: *If you move while you are taking the photo, it will be blurred.*

blush /blʌʃ/ *verb* (blushes, blushing, blushed /blʌʃt/)
If you **blush**, your face suddenly becomes red, for example because you are shy: *She blushed when he looked at her.*

boar /bɔː(r)/ (*also* wild boar) *noun*
a wild pig

board¹ 0🔗 /bɔːd/ *noun*
1 a long thin flat piece of wood: *I nailed a board across the broken window.* ◇ *floorboards*
2 a flat piece of wood, for example, that you use for a special purpose: *There is a list of*

names on the noticeboard. ◇ *a chessboard*
◇ *an ironing board* ➔ Look at **blackboard**.
3 a group of people who have a special job,
for example controlling a company: *the
board of directors*
on board on a ship or a plane: *How many
passengers are on board?*

board² /bɔːd/ *verb* (**boards, boarding,
boarded**)
to get on a ship, bus, train or plane: *We
boarded the plane at Gatwick.* ◇ *Flight BA 193
to Lisbon is now boarding* (= is ready for
passengers to get on).

boarding card /'bɔːdɪŋ kɑːd/ *noun*
a card that you must show when you get on
a plane or a ship

boarding school /'bɔːdɪŋ skuːl/ *noun*
a school where the pupils live

boast /bəʊst/ *verb* (**boasts, boasting,
boasted**)
to talk in a way that shows you are too proud
of something that you have or something
that you can do: *He's always boasting about
what a good footballer he is.*

boats

mast

sail

motorboat

yacht　　　　　**dinghy**

boat 0-ๆ /bəʊt/ *noun*
a small vehicle for travelling on water: *a fishing
boat* ◇ *We travelled by boat.* ➔ Look at **ship**.

bob /bɒb/ *verb* (**bobs, bobbing, bobbed**
/bɒbd/)
to move quickly up and down: *The boats in
the harbour were bobbing up and down in
the water.*

body 0-ๆ /'bɒdi/ *noun* (*plural* **bodies**)
1 the whole physical form of a person or an
animal: *the human body* ➔ Look at Picture
Dictionary page **P4**.
2 all of a person or animal except the legs,
arms and head: *The baby mice have thin
bodies and big heads.*
3 a dead person: *The police found a body in
the river.*

bodybuilding /'bɒdibɪldɪŋ/ *noun* (no
plural)
making the muscles of your body bigger and
stronger by exercise

bodyguard /'bɒdigɑːd/ *noun*
a person or group of people whose job is to
keep an important person safe: *The
President's bodyguards all carry guns.*

boil 0-ๆ /bɔɪl/ *verb* (**boils, boiling, boiled**
/bɔɪld/)
1 When a liquid **boils**, it becomes very hot
and makes steam and bubbles: *Water boils at
100°C.*
2 to heat a liquid until it **boils**: *I boiled some
water for the pasta.*
3 to cook something in **boiling** water: *Boil
the rice in a pan.* ◇ *a boiled egg*
boil over to boil and flow over the sides of
a pan: *Don't let the milk boil over.*

boiler /'bɔɪlə(r)/ *noun*
a big metal container that heats water for a
building

boiling /'bɔɪlɪŋ/ (*also* **boiling hot**)
adjective
very hot: *I'm boiling.* ◇ *It's boiling hot in here.*

bold /bəʊld/ *adjective* (**bolder, boldest**)
brave and not afraid: *It was very bold of you to
ask for more money.*
► **boldly** /'bəʊldli/ *adverb*: *He boldly said
that he disagreed.*

bolt /bəʊlt/ *noun*
1 a piece of metal that you move across a
door to lock it
2 a thick metal pin
that you use with
another piece of
metal (called a **nut**)
to fix things
together
► **bolt** *verb* (**bolts,
bolting, bolted**) to lock a door by putting a
bolt across it

bolt

bolt

nut

bomb¹ 0-ๆ /bɒm/ *noun*
a thing that explodes and hurts or damages
people or things: *Aircraft dropped bombs on
the city.* ◇ *A bomb went off* (= exploded) *at
the station.*

bomb² /bɒm/ *verb* (**bombs, bombing,
bombed** /bɒmd/)
to attack people or a place with **bombs**: *The
city was bombed in the war.*

bone 0-ๆ /bəʊn/ *noun*
one of the hard white parts inside the body
of a person or an animal: *She broke a bone in
her foot.* ◇ *This fish has a lot of bones in it.*

bonfire /'bɒnfaɪə(r)/ *noun*
a big fire that you make outside

A
B
C
D
E
F
G
H
I
J
K
L
M
N
O
P
Q
R
S
T
U
V
W
X
Y
Z

Bonfire Night /'bɒnfaɪə naɪt/ *noun* (*no plural*)
In Britain, **Bonfire Night** is the evening of 5 November, when people have a party outside with a BONFIRE and FIREWORKS (= things that explode in the sky with coloured lights and loud noises).

bonnet /'bɒnɪt/ *noun*
1 (*British*) (*American* **hood**) the front part of a car that covers the engine ⊃ Look at Picture Dictionary page **P1**.
2 a soft hat that you tie under your chin

book¹ 0‑ /bʊk/ *noun*
a thing that you read or write in, that has a lot of pieces of paper joined together inside a cover: *I'm reading a book by George Orwell.* ◇ *an exercise book* (= a book that you write in at school)

book² /bʊk/ *verb* (**books, booking, booked** /bʊkt/)
to arrange to have or do something later: *We booked a table for six at the restaurant.* ◇ *The hotel is fully booked* (= all the rooms are full).

bookcase

bookcase /'bʊkkeɪs/ *noun*
a piece of furniture that you put books in

booking /'bʊkɪŋ/ *noun* (*British*)
an arrangement that you make to travel somewhere, go to the theatre, etc. in the future: *When did you make your booking?*

booking office /'bʊkɪŋ ɒfɪs/ *noun*
a place where you buy tickets

booklet /'bʊklət/ *noun*
a small thin book that gives information about something

bookshop /'bʊkʃɒp/ *noun* (*British*) (*American* **bookstore** /'bʊkstɔ:(r)/)
a shop that sells books ⊃ Look at Picture Dictionary page **P13**.

boom¹ /bu:m/ *noun*
(*business*) a period in which something increases or develops very quickly: *a boom in car sales*

boom² /bu:m/ *verb* (**booms, booming, boomed** /bu:md/)
to make a loud deep sound: *We heard the guns booming in the distance.*

boost /bu:st/ *verb* (**boosts, boosting, boosted**)
to make something increase in number, value, or strength: *Lower prices have boosted sales.* ◇ *What can we do to boost her confidence* (= make her feel more confident)?

boot 0‑ /bu:t/ *noun*
1 a shoe that covers your foot and ankle and sometimes part of your leg ⊃ Look at the pictures at **shoe** and **ski**.
2 (*British*) (*American* **trunk**) the part of a car where you can put bags and boxes, usually at the back ⊃ Look at Picture Dictionary page **P1**.

border 0‑ /'bɔ:də(r)/ *noun*
1 a line between two countries: *You need a passport to cross the border.* ⊃ Look at **boundary**.
2 a line along the edge of something: *a white tablecloth with a blue border*

bore¹ form of BEAR¹

bore² /bɔ:(r)/ *verb* (**bores, boring, bored** /bɔ:d/)
1 to make somebody feel bored, especially by talking too much: *He bores everyone with his long stories.*
2 to make a thin round hole in something: *These insects bore holes in wood.*

bore³ /bɔ:(r)/ *noun*
a person who talks a lot in a way that is not interesting

bored 0‑ /bɔ:d/ *adjective*
not interested; unhappy because you have nothing interesting to do: *I'm bored with this book.* ◇ *The children were bored stiff* (= extremely bored).

> 🔎 **WHICH WORD?**
> **Bored** or **boring**?
> If you have nothing to do, or if what you are doing does not interest you, then you are **bored**: *Grace was so bored that she went home.*
> The person or thing that makes you feel like this is **boring**: *The film was very boring.*

▶ **boredom** /'bɔ:dəm/ *noun* (*no plural*):
I started to eat too much out of boredom.

boring 0‑ /'bɔ:rɪŋ/ *adjective*
not interesting: *That lesson was so boring!*

born ⦿ /bɔːn/ *adjective*
be born to start your life: *He was born in 1990.* ◇ *Where were you born?*

borne *form of* BEAR¹

borrow/lend

He's **borrowing** some money from his mother.   She's **lending** her son some money.

borrow ⦿ /ˈbɒrəʊ/ *verb* (**borrows, borrowing, borrowed** /ˈbɒrəʊd/)
to take and use something that you will give back after a short time: *I borrowed some books **from** the library.* ◇ *Can I borrow your pen?*

> 🔎 **WHICH WORD?**
>
> **Borrow** or **lend**?
> If you **borrow** something, you have it for a short time and you must give it back: *I borrowed a CD from Alexi for the weekend.* If you **lend** something, you give it to someone for a short time: *Alexi lent me a CD for the weekend.*

boss¹ /bɒs/ *noun* (*plural* **bosses**) (*informal*)
a person who controls a place where people work and tells people what they must do: *I asked my boss for a holiday.*

boss² /bɒs/ *verb* (**bosses, bossing, bossed** /bɒst/)
boss somebody about, boss somebody around to tell somebody what to do, in a way that annoys them: *I wish you'd stop bossing me about.*

bossy /ˈbɒsi/ *adjective* (**bossier, bossiest**)
A **bossy** person likes to tell other people what to do: *My sister is very bossy.*

both ⦿ /bəʊθ/ *adjective, pronoun*
the two; not only one but also the other: *Hold it in both hands.* ◇ *Both her brothers are doctors.* ◇ *Both of us like dancing.* ◇ *We both like dancing.*
both ... and not only ... but also: *She is both rich and intelligent.*

bother¹ /ˈbɒðə(r)/ *verb* (**bothers, bothering, bothered** /ˈbɒðəd/)
1 to spend extra time or energy doing

something: *Don't **bother about** the washing-up – I'll do it later.* ◇ *He didn't even **bother to** say goodbye.*
2 to annoy or worry somebody, especially when they are doing something else: *Don't bother me now – I'm busy!* ◇ *Is this music bothering you?* ◇ ***I'm sorry to bother you**, but there's someone on the phone for you.*
can't be bothered If you **can't be bothered** to do something, you do not want to do it because it is too much work: *I can't be bothered to do my homework now.*

bother² /ˈbɒðə(r)/ *noun* (*no plural*)
something that causes you difficulty
⮕ SAME MEANING **trouble**: *'Thanks for your help!' 'It was no bother.'*

bottle ⦿ /ˈbɒtl/ *noun*
a glass or plastic container for liquids, with a thin part at the top: *a beer bottle* ◇ *They drank two **bottles of** water.*

glass   bottle

bottle bank /ˈbɒtl bæŋk/ *noun*
a large container in a public place where people can leave old empty bottles so that the glass can be used again (**recycled**)

bottom¹ ⦿ /ˈbɒtəm/ *noun*
1 the lowest part of something: *They live at **the bottom of** the hill.* ◇ *The book was at the bottom of my bag.* ◇ *Look at the picture at the bottom of the page.* ⮕ OPPOSITE **top** ⮕ Look at the picture at **back**.
2 the last part of something; the end: *The bank is at the bottom of the road.*
⮕ OPPOSITE **top**
3 the lowest position compared to other people or groups: *I was always at the bottom of the class in maths.* ⮕ OPPOSITE **top**
4 the part of your body that you sit on ⮕ Look at Picture Dictionary page **P4**.

bottom² /ˈbɒtəm/ *adjective*
lowest: *Put the book on the bottom shelf.*
⮕ OPPOSITE **top**

bought *form of* BUY

boulder /ˈbəʊldə(r)/ *noun*
a very big rock

bounce /baʊns/ *verb* (**bounces, bouncing, bounced** /baʊnst/)
1 (used about a ball) to move away quickly after hitting something hard; to make a ball

A
B
C
D
E
F
G
H
I
J
K
L
M
N
O
P
Q
R
S
T
U
V
W
X
Y
Z

do this: *The ball **bounced off** the wall.* ◇ *The boy was bouncing a basketball.*
2 to jump up and down many times: *The children were bouncing on their beds.*

bounce

bound¹ *form of* BIND

bound² /baʊnd/ *adjective*
bound to certain to do something: *She works very hard, so she is bound to pass the exam.*
bound for going to a place: *This ship is bound for Hong Kong.*

bound³ /baʊnd/ *verb* (**bounds, bounding, bounded**)
to run with long steps: *The dog bounded up the steps.*

boundary /ˈbaʊndri/ *noun* (*plural* **boundaries**)
a line between two places: *This fence is the **boundary between** the two gardens.* ➔ Look at **border**.

bouquet /buˈkeɪ/ *noun*
a group of flowers that is arranged in an attractive way: *He gave her a bouquet of roses.*

bow¹ /baʊ/ *verb* (**bows, bowing, bowed** /baʊd/)

> ♪ **PRONUNCIATION**
> With this meaning, the word **bow** sounds like **now**.

to bend your head or body forward to show respect: *The actors bowed at the end of the play.*
▸ **bow** *noun*: *He gave a bow and left the room.*

bows

violin | bow

bow

arrow

bow

bow² /bəʊ/ *noun*

> ♪ **PRONUNCIATION**
> With these meanings, the word **bow** sounds like **go**.

1 a curved piece of wood with a string between the two ends. You use a **bow** to send arrows through the air.
2 a knot with two loose round parts and two loose ends that you use when you are tying shoes, etc.
3 a long thin piece of wood with hair stretched across it that you use for playing some musical instruments: *a violin bow*

bowl¹ 0— /bəʊl/ *noun*
a deep round dish that is used for holding food or liquids: *a sugar bowl* ◇ *a bowl of soup*

bowl

bowl² /bəʊl/ *verb* (**bowls, bowling, bowled** /bəʊld/)
(in games such as CRICKET) to throw a ball so that somebody can hit it

bowling /ˈbəʊlɪŋ/ *noun* (*no plural*)
a game in which you roll a heavy ball down a special track towards a group of wooden objects shaped like bottles and try to knock them all down: *We go bowling every Friday night.* ➔ Look at Picture Dictionary page **P14**.

bow tie /ˌbəʊ ˈtaɪ/ *noun*
a tie in the shape of a BOW²(2) that some men wear on formal occasions

box¹ 0— /bɒks/ *noun* (*plural* **boxes**)
a container with straight sides. A box often has a lid: *Put the books in a cardboard box.* ◇ *a box of chocolates* ◇ *a box of matches* ➔ Look at the picture at **container**.

box² /bɒks/ *verb* (**boxes, boxing, boxed** /bɒkst/)
to fight with your hands, wearing thick gloves, as a sport

boxer /ˈbɒksə(r)/ *noun*
a person who BOXES as a sport: *Muhammad Ali was a famous boxer.*

boxer shorts /ˈbɒksə ʃɔːts/ (*also* **boxers** /ˈbɒksəz/) *noun* (*plural*)
men's underwear that looks like a pair of short trousers

boxing /ˈbɒksɪŋ/ *noun* (*no plural*)
the sport of fighting with your hands, wearing thick gloves

Boxing Day /ˈbɒksɪŋ deɪ/ *noun*
the day after Christmas Day; 26 December

A **B** C D E F G H I J K L M N O P Q R S T U V W X Y Z

box office /'bɒks ɒfɪs/ *noun*
a place where you buy tickets in a theatre or cinema

boy 0➝ /bɔɪ/ *noun (plural boys)*
a male child; a young man: *They have three children, two boys and a girl.* ◇ *The older boys at school used to tease him.*

boyfriend 0➝ /'bɔɪfrend/ *noun*
a boy or man who somebody has a romantic relationship with: *She has had a lot of boyfriends.*

Boy Scout /,bɔɪ 'skaʊt/ *American English for* SCOUT(2)

bra /brɑː/ *noun (plural bras)*
a thing that a woman wears under her other clothes to cover and support her breasts

bracelet

bracelet /'breɪslət/ *noun*
a pretty piece of metal, wood or plastic that you wear around your arm

brackets /'brækɪts/ *noun (plural)*
two marks, ( ) or [ ], that you put round extra information in a piece of writing: *(This sentence is written in brackets.)*

brag /bræg/ *verb (brags, bragging, bragged* /brægd/*)*
to talk in a way that shows you are too proud of something that you have or something that you can do ⇒ SAME MEANING **boast**: *She's always bragging about how clever she is.*

braid /breɪd/ *American English for* PLAIT

Braille *(also* braille*)* /breɪl/ *noun (no plural)*
a system of printing using little round marks that blind people can read by touching the page

brain 0➝ /breɪn/ *noun*
the part inside the head of a person or an animal that thinks and feels: *The brain controls the rest of the body.*

brainy /'breɪni/ *adjective (brainier, brainiest) (informal)*
clever: *Laura's even brainier than her sister.*

brake¹ /breɪk/ *noun*
the part of a vehicle that you use to make it go slower or stop: *I put my foot on the brake.*

brake² /breɪk/ *verb (brakes, braking, braked* /breɪkt/*)*
to use a **brake**: *A child ran into the road and the driver braked suddenly.*

branch 0➝ /brɑːntʃ/ *noun (plural branches)*
1 one of the parts of a tree that grow out from the thick main part (called the **trunk**)
2 an office or a shop that is part of a big company: *This bank has branches all over the country.*

brand /brænd/ *noun*
the name of a product that a certain company makes: *Which brand of coffee do you buy?*

brand new /,brænd 'njuː/ *adjective*
completely new: *a brand new car*

brandy /'brændi/ *noun*
1 *(no plural)* a strong alcoholic drink made from wine
2 *(plural brandies)* a glass of **brandy**

brass /brɑːs/ *noun (no plural)*
a yellow metal: *brass buttons*

brave 0➝ /breɪv/ *adjective (braver, bravest)*
ready to do dangerous or difficult things without fear: *brave soldiers* ◇ *Try to be brave.*
▶ **bravely** *adverb*: *He fought bravely in the war.*
▶ **bravery** /'breɪvəri/ *noun (no plural)*: *He won a medal for bravery.*

bread

a loaf of bread

bread 0➝ /bred/ *noun (no plural)*

food made from flour and baked in an oven: *I bought a loaf of bread.* ◇ *a slice of bread and butter*

breadth /bredθ/ *noun*
how far it is from one side of something to the other ⇒ SAME MEANING **width** ⇒ The adjective is **broad**.

A

break¹ 0━┳ /breɪk/ *verb* (breaks, breaking, broke /brəʊk/, has broken /ˈbrəʊkən/)

1 to make something go into smaller pieces, for example by dropping it or hitting it: *He broke the window.* ◇ *She has broken her arm.*

2 to go into smaller pieces, for example by falling or hitting: *I dropped the cup and it broke.*

3 to stop working; to damage a machine so that it stops working: *You've broken my watch.*

4 to do something that is against the law or against what has been agreed or promised: *People who break the law must be punished.* ◇ *I never break my promises.*

break down

1 If a machine or car **breaks down**, it stops working: *We were late because our car broke down.*

2 If a person **breaks down**, they start to cry: *He broke down when he heard the news.*

break in, break into something to go into a place by breaking a door or window so that you can steal something: *Thieves broke into the house. They broke in through a window.*

break off to take away a piece of something by breaking it: *He broke off a piece of chocolate for me.*

break out

1 to start suddenly: *A fire broke out last night.*

2 to get free from a place like a prison: *Four prisoners broke out of the jail last night.*

break up (*British*) to start the school holidays: *We break up at the end of July.*

break up with somebody to end a relationship with somebody: *Susy broke up with her boyfriend last week.*

break² /breɪk/ *noun*

1 a short time when you stop doing something: *We worked all day without a break.*

2 a place where something opens or has broken: *The sun shone through a break in the clouds.*

breakdown /ˈbreɪkdaʊn/ *noun*
a time when a machine, car, etc. stops working: *We had a breakdown on the motorway.*

breakfast 0━┳ /ˈbrekfəst/ *noun*
the first meal of the day: *I had breakfast at seven o'clock.*

breast /brest/ *noun*

> 🔎 **PRONUNCIATION**
> The word **breast** sounds like **test**.

1 one of the two soft round parts of a woman's body that can give milk

2 the front part of a bird's body

breaststroke
/ˈbreststrəʊk/ *noun*
(*no plural*)
a way of swimming
on your front: *Can
you do breaststroke?* ➔ Look also at **crawl**.

breaststroke

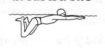

breath 0━┳ /breθ/ *noun*
taking in or letting out air through your nose and mouth: *Take a deep breath.*

hold your breath to stop breathing for a short time: *We all held our breath as the winner was announced.*

out of breath breathing very quickly: *She was out of breath after climbing the stairs.*

breathe 0━┳ /briːð/ *verb* (breathes, breathing, breathed /briːðd/)
to take in and let out air through your nose and mouth: *The doctor told me to breathe in and then breathe out again slowly.*

breathless /ˈbreθləs/ *adjective*
breathing quickly or with difficulty: *Running made them hot and breathless.*

breed¹ /briːd/ *verb* (breeds, breeding, bred /bred/, has bred)

1 When animals **breed**, they produce young animals: *Birds breed in the spring.*

2 to keep animals so that they will produce baby animals: *They breed horses on their farm.*

breed² /briːd/ *noun*
a kind of animal: *There are many different breeds of dog.*

breeze /briːz/ *noun*
a light wind

brewery /ˈbruːəri/ *noun* (*plural breweries*)
a place where beer is made

bribe /braɪb/ *noun*
money or a present that you give to somebody to make them do something for you, especially something dishonest
▶ **bribe** *verb* (bribes, bribing, bribed /braɪbd/): *The prisoner bribed the guard to let him go free.*

brick 0━┳ /brɪk/ *noun*
a small block of CLAY (= a type of earth) that has been baked until it is hard. **Bricks** are used for building: *a brick wall*

bricklayer /ˈbrɪkleɪə(r)/ *noun*
a person whose job is to build things with bricks

bride /braɪd/ *noun*
a woman on the day of her wedding

bridegroom /'braɪdgruːm/ (*also* **groom**) *noun*
a man on the day of his wedding

bridesmaid /'braɪdzmeɪd/ *noun*
a girl or woman who helps a BRIDE at her wedding

bridge

bridge 0̄ /brɪdʒ/ *noun*
a thing that is built over a road, railway or river so that people, trains or cars can cross it: *We walked over the bridge.*

brief 0̄ /briːf/ *adjective* (**briefer**, **briefest**)
short or quick: *a brief telephone call* ◇ *Please be brief.*
in brief in a few words: *Here is the news in brief* (= words said on a radio or television programme).
▶ **briefly** /'briːfli/ *adverb*: *He had spoken to Emma only briefly.*

briefcase /'briːfkeɪs/ *noun*
a flat case that you use for carrying papers, especially when you go to work

briefcase

bright 0̄ /braɪt/ *adjective* (**brighter**, **brightest**)
1 with a lot of light: *It was a bright sunny day.* ◇ *That lamp is very bright.*
2 with a strong colour: *a bright yellow shirt*
3 clever: *She is the brightest child in the class.*
▶ **brightly** /'braɪtli/ *adverb*: *brightly coloured clothes*
▶ **brightness** /'braɪtnəs/ *noun* (*no plural*): *the brightness of the sun*

brighten /'braɪtn/ *verb* (**brightens**, **brightening**, **brightened** /'braɪtnd/) (*also* **brighten up**)
to become brighter or happier; to make something brighter: *Her face brightened when she saw him.* ◇ *These flowers will brighten the room up.*

brilliant /'brɪliənt/ *adjective*
1 with a lot of light; very bright: *brilliant sunshine*
2 very intelligent: *a brilliant student*
3 (*British, informal*) very good: *The film was brilliant!*
▶ **brilliance** /'brɪliəns/ *noun* (*no plural*): *the brilliance of the light*
▶ **brilliantly** /'brɪliəntli/ *adverb*: *She played brilliantly.*

brim /brɪm/ *noun*
1 the edge around the top of something like a cup, bowl or glass: *The glass was **full to the brim**.*
2 the wide part around the bottom of a hat

bring

Bring the newspaper.

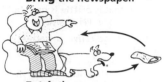

Fetch the newspaper.

Take the newspaper.

bring 0̄ /brɪŋ/ *verb* (**brings**, **bringing**, **brought** /brɔːt/, **has brought**)
1 to take something or somebody with you to a place: *Could you bring me a glass of water?* ◇ *Can I bring a friend to the party?*
2 to make something happen: *Money doesn't always bring happiness.*
bring something back
1 to return something: *I've brought back the book you lent me.*
2 to make you remember something: *These old photographs bring back a lot of happy memories.*
bring somebody up to look after a child until they are grown up: *He was brought up by his aunt after his parents died.*
bring something up
1 to be sick, so that food comes up from your stomach and out of your mouth
2 to start to talk about something: *Can you bring up this problem at the next meeting?*

A
B
C
D
E
F
G
H
I
J
K
L
M
N
O
P
Q
R
S
T
U
V
W
X
Y
Z

A
B
C
D
E
F
G
H
I
J
K
L
M
N
O
P
Q
R
S
T
U
V
W
X
Y
Z

🔍 **WHICH WORD?**

Bring, take or **fetch**?
You **bring** something with you to the place where you are going: *Bring your holiday photos to show me.* ◇ *He always brings me flowers.* ◇ *Can I bring a friend to the party?*
You **take** something to a different place: *Don't forget to take your passport.* ◇ *Take an umbrella when you go out today.*
You go somewhere to **fetch** someone or something and **bring** them back: *I'm going to fetch Sally from the airport.* ◇ *I'll fetch you a drink from the kitchen.*

brisk /brɪsk/ *adjective* (brisker, briskest)
quick and using a lot of energy: *We went for a brisk walk.*

bristle /ˈbrɪsl/ *noun*
a short thick hair like the hair on a brush

brittle /ˈbrɪtl/ *adjective*
Something that is **brittle** is hard but breaks easily: *This glass is very brittle.*

broad /brɔːd/ *adjective* (broader, broadest)
large from one side to the other
➔ SAME MEANING **wide**: *a broad river* ➔ The noun is **breadth**. ➔ OPPOSITE **narrow**

broadband /ˈbrɔːdbænd/ *noun* (no plural)
(computing) (used about an Internet connection) able to send and receive a lot of information quickly: *Have you got broadband?*

broadcast /ˈbrɔːdkɑːst/ *verb* (broadcasts, broadcasting, broadcast, has broadcast)
to send out sound or pictures by radio or television: *The Olympics are broadcast live around the world.*
▶ **broadcast** *noun*: *a news broadcast*
▶ **broadcaster** /ˈbrɔːdkɑːstə(r)/ *noun* a person whose job is to talk on radio or television

broad-minded /ˌbrɔːd ˈmaɪndɪd/ *adjective*
happy to accept ways of life and beliefs that are different from your own
➔ OPPOSITE **narrow-minded**

broccoli /ˈbrɒkəli/ *noun* (no plural)
a vegetable with green or purple flowers that you eat ➔ Look at Picture Dictionary page **P9**.

brochure /ˈbrəʊʃə(r)/ *noun*
a thin book with pictures of things you can buy or places you can go on holiday: *a travel brochure*

broke (also **broken**) *forms of* BREAK¹

broken 0̄ /ˈbrəʊkən/ *adjective*
in pieces or not working: *a broken window* ◇ *'What's the time?' 'I don't know – my watch is broken.'* ◇ *The TV is broken.* ➔ The verb is **break**.

bronze /brɒnz/ *noun* (no plural)
a dark red-brown metal: *a bronze medal*

brooch /brəʊtʃ/ *noun* (plural **brooches**)
a piece of jewellery with a pin at the back that you wear on your clothes

broom /bruːm/ *noun*
a brush with a long handle that you use for cleaning the floor ➔ Look at the picture at **brush**.

brother 0̄ /ˈbrʌðə(r)/ *noun*
a man or boy who has the same parents as you: *My younger brother is called Mark.* ◇ *Gavin and Nick are brothers.* ◇ *Have you got any brothers and sisters?*

brother-in-law /ˈbrʌðər ɪn lɔː/ *noun* (plural **brothers-in-law**)
1 the brother of your wife or husband
2 the husband of your sister ➔ Look at **sister-in-law**.

brought *form of* BRING

brow /braʊ/ *noun* (formal)
the part of your face above your eyes
➔ SAME MEANING **forehead**

brown 0̄ /braʊn/ *adjective, noun* (browner, brownest)
having the colour of earth or wood: *brown eyes* ◇ *I go brown* (= my skin becomes brown) *as soon as I sit in the sun.*
▶ **brown** *noun*: *Brown suits you* (= makes you look good).

browser /ˈbraʊzə(r)/ *noun*
(computing) a program that lets you look at pages on the Internet: *a Web browser*

bruise /bruːz/ *noun*
a dark mark on your skin that comes after something hits it
▶ **bruise** *verb* (bruises, bruising, bruised /bruːzd/): *He fell and bruised his leg.*

brush¹ 0̄ /brʌʃ/ *noun* (plural **brushes**)
a thing that you use for cleaning, painting or making your hair tidy: *a clothes brush.*

brush² 0̄ /brʌʃ/ *verb* (brushes, brushing, brushed /brʌʃt/)
to clean or tidy something with a **brush**: *I brush my teeth twice a day.* ◇ *Brush your hair!*

brushes

dustpan and brush

hairbrush   paintbrushes

broom   toothbrush

Brussels sprout /ˌbrʌslz ˈspraʊt/ (*also* sprout) *noun*
a very small round green vegetable consisting of a tight ball of leaves ➔ Look at Picture Dictionary page **P9**.

brutal /ˈbruːtl/ *adjective*
very cruel: *a brutal murder*
▶ **brutally** /ˈbruːtəli/ *adverb*: *She was brutally attacked.*

BSc /ˌbiː es ˈsiː/ *noun*
the certificate that you receive when you complete a university or college course in a science subject. **BSc** is short for 'Bachelor of Science' ➔ Look also at **BA**.

bubble[1] ⟵ /ˈbʌbl/ *noun*
a small ball of air or gas inside a liquid: *The children **blew bubbles** under the water.*

bubble[2] /ˈbʌbl/ *verb* (**bubbles, bubbling, bubbled** /ˈbʌbld/)
to make a lot of **bubbles**: *When water boils, it bubbles.*

bucket /ˈbʌkɪt/ *noun*
a round metal or plastic container with a handle. You use a **bucket** for carrying water, for example.

bucket

buckle /ˈbʌkl/ *noun*
a metal or plastic thing on the end of a belt or on a shoe that you use for fastening it ➔ Look at the picture at **shoe**.

bud /bʌd/ *noun*
a leaf or flower before it opens: *The trees are covered in buds.* ➔ Look at the picture at **plant**.

Buddhism /ˈbʊdɪzəm/ *noun* (*no plural*)
the religion that is based on the teaching of Buddha

Buddhist /ˈbʊdɪst/ *noun*
a person who follows the religion of BUDDHISM
▶ **Buddhist** *adjective*: *a Buddhist temple*

budge /bʌdʒ/ *verb* (**budges, budging, budged** /bʌdʒd/)
to move a little or to make something move a little: *I tried to move the rock but it wouldn't budge.*

budgerigar /ˈbʌdʒərigɑː(r)/ (*also informal* **budgie** /ˈbʌdʒi/) *noun*
a small blue or green bird that people often keep as a pet ➔ Look at Picture Dictionary page **P2**.

budget /ˈbʌdʒɪt/ *noun*
a plan of how much money you will have and how you will spend it: *We have a weekly budget for food.*
▶ **budget** *verb* (**budgets, budgeting, budgeted**): *I am budgeting very carefully because I want to buy a new car.*

buffalo /ˈbʌfələʊ/ *noun* (*plural* **buffalo**)
a large wild animal that looks like a cow with long curved horns ➔ Look at Picture Dictionary page **P3**.

buffet /ˈbʊfeɪ/ *noun*
a meal when all the food is on a big table and you take what you want: *a buffet lunch*

bug /bʌg/ *noun*
1 a small insect
2 an illness that is not serious: *I've caught a bug.*
3 a fault in a machine, especially a computer system or program

buggy /ˈbʌgi/ *noun* (*plural* **buggies**)
(*British*) (*American* **stroller**)
a chair on wheels in which a young child is pushed along ➔ SAME MEANING **pushchair** ➔ Look at the picture at **pushchair**.

build ⟵ /bɪld/ *verb* (**builds, building, built** /bɪlt/, **has built**)
to make something by putting parts together: *He built a wall in front of the house.*
◇ *The bridge is built of stone.*

builder /ˈbɪldə(r)/ *noun*
a person whose job is to make buildings

building ⟵ /ˈbɪldɪŋ/ *noun*
a structure with a roof and walls. Houses, schools, churches and shops are all **buildings**.

A

B

C

D

E

F

G

H

I

J

K

L

M

N

O

P

Q

R

S

T

U

V

W

X

Y

Z

building society /ˈbɪldɪŋ səsaɪəti/ *noun*
(*British*) (*plural* **building societies**)
a kind of bank that lends you money when
you want to buy a house or flat

built *form of* BUILD

bulb /bʌlb/ *noun*
1 (*also* **light bulb**) the glass part of an
electric lamp that gives light
2 a round thing that some plants grow
from: *a tulip bulb* ➲ Look at the picture at
plant.

bulge /bʌldʒ/ *verb* (**bulges, bulging,
bulged** /bʌldʒd/)
to go out in a round shape from something
that is usually flat: *My stomach is bulging – I
have to get some exercise.*
▶ **bulge** *noun*: *a bulge in the wall*

bulky /ˈbʌlki/ *adjective* (**bulkier, bulkiest**)
big, heavy and difficult to carry: *a bulky
parcel*

bull /bʊl/ *noun*
the male of the cow and of some other
animals ➲ Look at the picture at **cow**.

bulldog /ˈbʊldɒg/ *noun*
a strong dog with short legs and a large
head

bulldozer
/ˈbʊldəʊzə(r)/ *noun*
a big heavy
machine that moves
earth and makes
land flat

bulldozer

bullet ⓞⲧ /ˈbʊlɪt/ *noun*
a small piece of metal that comes out of a
gun: *The bullet hit him in the leg.*

bulletin board /ˈbʊlətɪn bɔːd/ *American
English for* NOTICEBOARD

bully /ˈbʊli/ *noun* (*plural* **bullies**)
a person who hurts or frightens a weaker
person
▶ **bully** *verb* (**bullies, bullying, bullied**
/ˈbʊlid/): *She was bullied by the older girls at
school.*

bum /bʌm/ *noun* (*informal*)
1 (*British*) the part of your body that you
sit on

> 🔊 **SPEAKING**
> Some people think this word is quite
> rude. **Bottom** is the more usual word.

2 (*American*) a person who has no home or
job and who asks other people for money or
food

bump¹ /bʌmp/ *verb* (**bumps, bumping,
bumped** /bʌmpt/)
1 to hit somebody or something when you
are moving: *She bumped into a chair.*
2 to hit a part of your body against
something hard: *I bumped my knee on the
table.*
bump into somebody to meet
somebody by chance: *I bumped into David
today.*

bump² /bʌmp/ *noun*
1 the action or sound of something hitting a
hard surface: *He fell and hit the ground with a
bump.*
2 a round raised area on your body where
you have hit it: *I've got a bump on my head.*
3 a small part on something flat that is
higher than the rest: *The car hit a bump in the
road.*

bumper /ˈbʌmpə(r)/ *noun*
a bar on the front and back of a car which
helps to protect the car if it hits something.
➲ Look at Picture Dictionary page **P1**.

bumpy /ˈbʌmpi/ *adjective* (**bumpier,
bumpiest**)
not flat or smooth: *We had a bumpy flight.* ◇
The road was very bumpy.
➲ OPPOSITE **smooth**

bun /bʌn/ *noun*
a small round cake or piece of bread

bunch /bʌntʃ/ *noun* (*plural* **bunches**)
a group of things that grow together or that
you tie or hold together: *a bunch of grapes* ◇
two bunches of flowers

bundle /ˈbʌndl/ *noun*
a group of things that you tie or wrap
together: *a bundle of old newspapers*

bungalow /ˈbʌŋgələʊ/ *noun* (*British*)
a house that has only one floor, with no
upstairs rooms

bunk /bʌŋk/ *noun*
1 a narrow bed that is fixed to a wall, for
example on a ship or train
2 (*also* **bunk bed**) one of a pair of single
beds built one on top of the other ➲ Look at
the picture at **bed**.

bunny /ˈbʌni/ *noun* (*plural* **bunnies**)
a child's word for RABBIT(= a small animal
with long ears)

buoy /bɔɪ/ *noun* (*plural* **buoys**)
a thing that floats in the sea to show ships
where there are dangerous places

burden /ˈbɜːdn/ *noun*
something that you have to do that causes
worry, difficulty or hard work: *I don't want to
be a burden to my children when I'm old.*

burger

burger /'bɜːgə(r)/ *noun*
meat cut into very small pieces and made into a flat round shape, that you eat between two pieces of bread
➲ SAME MEANING **hamburger**: *a burger and chips*

burglar /'bɜːglə(r)/ *noun*
a person who goes into a building to steal things

burglarize /'bɜːgləraɪz/ *American English for* BURGLE

burglary /'bɜːgləri/ *noun* (*plural* burglaries)
the crime of going into a house to steal things: *He was arrested for burglary.*

burgle /'bɜːgl/ *verb* (burgles, burgling, burgled /'bɜːgld/) (*American* burglarize)
to go into a building illegally, usually using force, and steal from it: *Our house was burgled.*

burial /'beriəl/ *noun*
the time when a dead body is put in the ground ➲ The verb is **bury**.

buried (*also* buries) forms of BURY

burn¹ 0➡ /bɜːn/ *verb* (burns, burning, burnt /bɜːnt/ *or* burned /bɜːnd/, has burnt *or* has burned)
1 to make flames and heat; to be on fire: *Paper burns easily.* ◊ *She escaped from the burning building.*
2 to harm or destroy somebody or something with fire or heat: *I burnt my fingers on a match.* ◊ *We burned the wood on the fire.*
burn down, **burn something down** to burn, or to make a building burn, until there is nothing left: *Their house burnt down.*

burn² /bɜːn/ *noun*
a place on your body where fire or heat has hurt it: *I've got a burn on my arm.*

burnt /bɜːnt/ *adjective*
damaged by burning: *burnt food* ◊ *Her hand was badly burnt.*

burp /bɜːp/ *verb* (burps, burping, burped /bɜːpt/)
to make a noise from your mouth when air suddenly comes up from your stomach: *He burped loudly.*
▶ **burp** *noun*: *I heard a loud burp.*

burrow /'bʌrəʊ/ *noun*
a hole in the ground where some animals, for example RABBITS (=small animals with long ears), live

burst¹ 0➡ /bɜːst/ *verb* (bursts, bursting, burst, has burst)
1 to break open suddenly or to make something do this: *The bag was so full that it burst.* ◊ *He burst the balloon.*
2 to go or come suddenly: *Steve burst into the room.*
burst into something to start doing something suddenly: *She read the letter and burst into tears* (= started to cry). ◊ *The car burst into flames* (= started to burn).
burst out laughing to suddenly start to laugh: *When she saw my hat, she burst out laughing.*

burst² /bɜːst/ *noun*
something that happens suddenly and quickly: *a burst of laughter*

bury 0➡ /'beri/ *verb* (buries, burying, buried /'berid/, has buried)

🔊 **PRONUNCIATION**
The word **bury** sounds like **very**.

1 to put a dead body in the ground ➲ The noun is **burial**.
2 to put something in the ground or under something: *The dog buried the bone in the garden.*

buses

bus

double-decker bus

bus 0➡ /bʌs/ *noun* (*plural* buses)
a large vehicle that carries a lot of people along the road and stops often so they can get on and off: *We went to town by bus.* ◊ *Where do you get off the bus?*

🔊 **WORD BUILDING**
You can get on or off a **bus** at a **bus stop** and the place where most bus routes start

A B C D E F G H I J K L M N O P Q R S T U V W X Y Z

A
B
C
D
E
F
G
H
I
J
K
L
M
N
O
P
Q
R
S
T
U
V
W
X
Y
Z

is the **bus station**.
The **bus driver** will take the money (your **fare**) and give you your **ticket**.
You can buy a **single ticket** for a one-way journey or a **return ticket** if you want to come back again: *Return to Woodstock, please.*
Note that we travel **on the bus** or by **bus**: *'How do you get to school?' 'By bus.'*

bush 0━ /bʊʃ/ *noun*
1 (*plural* **bushes**) a plant like a small tree with a lot of branches: *a rose bush*
2 the bush (*no plural*) wild country with a lot of small trees in Africa or Australia

business 0━ /ˈbɪznəs/ *noun*
1 (*no plural*) buying and selling things: *I want to go into business when I leave school.*
◇ *Business is not very good this year.*
2 (*plural* **businesses**) a place where people sell or make things, for example a shop or factory
3 the work that you do as your job: *The manager will be away on business next week.*
◇ *a business trip*
it's none of your business, mind your own business words that you use to tell somebody rudely that you do not want to tell them about something private: *'Where are you going?' 'Mind your own business!'*

businessman /ˈbɪznəsmæn; ˈbɪznəsmən/ *noun* (*plural* **businessmen** /ˈbɪznəsmen/)
a man who works in business, especially in a top position

businesswoman /ˈbɪznəswʊmən/ *noun* (*plural* **businesswomen** /ˈbɪznəswɪmɪn/)
a woman who works in business, especially in a top position ➪ Look at Picture Dictionary page **P12**.

bus stop /ˈbʌs stɒp/ *noun*
a place where buses stop and people get on and off

busy 0━ /ˈbɪzi/ *adjective* (**busier, busiest**)
1 with a lot of things that you must do; working or not free: *Mr Jones can't see you now – he's busy.*
2 with a lot of things happening: *I had a busy morning.* ◇ *The shops are always busy at Christmas.*
3 (used about a telephone) being used ➪ SAME MEANING **engaged**: *The line is busy – I'll try again later.*
▶ **busily** /ˈbɪzɪli/ *adverb*: *He was busily writing a letter.*

but¹ 0━ /bət; bʌt/ *conjunction*
a word that you use to show something different: *My sister speaks French but I don't.*

◇ *He worked hard but he didn't pass the exam.*
◇ *The weather was sunny but cold.*

but² /bət; bʌt/ *preposition*
except: *She eats nothing but chocolate.*

butcher /ˈbʊtʃə(r)/ *noun*
1 a person who sells meat
2 **butcher's** a shop that sells meat: *She went to the butcher's for some lamb chops.* ➪ Look at Picture Dictionary page **P13**.

butter 0━ /ˈbʌtə(r)/ *noun* (*no plural*)
a soft yellow food that is made from milk. You put it on bread or use it in cooking: *She spread butter on the bread.* ➪ Look at Picture Dictionary page **P6**.
▶ **butter** *verb* (**butters, buttering, buttered** /ˈbʌtəd/) to put butter on bread: *I buttered the toast.*

butterfly

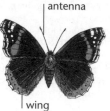

antenna

wing

butterfly /ˈbʌtəflaɪ/ *noun* (*plural* **butterflies**)
an insect with big coloured wings

buttock /ˈbʌtək/ *noun*
one of the two parts of your body that you sit on

buttons

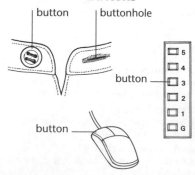

button   buttonhole

button

button

5
4
3
2
1
G

button 0━ /ˈbʌtn/ *noun*
1 a small round thing on clothes that holds them together. You push it through a small hole (called a **buttonhole**).
2 a small thing on a machine, that you push: *Press this button to ring the bell.*

buy 0⃞ /baɪ/ *verb* (buys, buying, bought /bɔːt/, has bought)

> 🔍 **PRONUNCIATION**
> The word **buy** sounds like **my**.

to give money to get something: *I bought a new watch.* ◇ *He* **bought** *the car* **from** *a friend.* ⊃ Look at **sell**.

buzz /bʌz/ *verb* (buzzes, buzzing, buzzed /bʌzd/)
to make the sound that a flying insect such as a BEE (= a black and yellow insect) makes: *A fly was buzzing against the window.*
▶ **buzz** *noun* (*plural* **buzzes**): *the buzz of insects.*

by¹ 0⃞ /baɪ/ *preposition*
1 very near ⊃ SAME MEANING **beside**: *The telephone is by the door.* ◇ *They live by the sea.*
2 a word that shows who or what did something: *a painting by Matisse* ◇ *She was caught by the police.*

3 using or doing something: *I go to work by train.* ◇ *He paid* **by cheque.** ◇ *You turn the computer on by pressing this button.*
4 as a result of something: *I got on the wrong bus* **by mistake.** ◇ *We met* **by chance.**
5 not later than ⊃ SAME MEANING **before**: *I must finish this work by six o'clock.*
6 from one side of somebody or something to the other ⊃ SAME MEANING **past**: *He walked* **by** *me without speaking.*
7 used for showing the measurements of an area: *The table is six feet by three feet* (= six feet long and three feet wide).

by² /baɪ/ *adverb*
past: *She drove by without stopping.*

bye 0⃞ /baɪ/ (*also* **bye-bye** /ˌbaɪ ˈbaɪ/) *exclamation*
goodbye: *Bye! See you tomorrow.*

byte /baɪt/ *noun*
(*computing*) a unit of information in a computer

A
B
C
D
E
F
G
H
I
J
K
L
M
N
O
P
Q
R
S
T
U
V
W
X
Y
Z

Cc

C, c /si:/ *noun*
1 (*plural* C's, c's /si:z/) the third letter of the English alphabet: *'Car' begins with a 'C'.*
2 C *short way of writing* CELSIUS, CENTIGRADE

cab /kæb/ *noun*
1 *another word for* TAXI
2 the part of a lorry, train or bus where the driver sits

cabbage /'kæbɪdʒ/ *noun*
a large round vegetable with thick green or white leaves ➲ Look at Picture Dictionary page **P9**.

cabin /'kæbɪn/ *noun*
1 a small bedroom on a ship
2 the part of a plane where people sit: *the passengers in the first-class cabin*
3 a small simple house made of wood: *a log cabin at the edge of the lake*

cabinet /'kæbɪnət/ *noun*
1 (*plural* cabinets) a piece of furniture that you can keep things in: ◇ *a filing cabinet* (= one that you use in an office to keep documents in) *a bathroom cabinet* ➲ Look at Picture Dictionary page **P10**.
2 the Cabinet (*no plural*) a group of the most important people in the government

cable /'keɪbl/ *noun*
1 a strong thick metal rope
2 a wire that carries electricity or messages
3 (*also* cable television /ˌkeɪbl 'telɪvɪʒn/) (*also* cable TV /ˌkeɪbl ti:'vi:/) (*no plural*) a way of sending television programmes along wires in the ground

cactus /'kæktəs/ *noun* (*plural* cactuses *or* cacti /'kæktaɪ/)
a plant with a lot of sharp points that grows in hot dry places

cactus

cafe (*also* café) /'kæfeɪ/ *noun*
a place where you can buy a drink and something to eat

cafeteria /ˌkæfə'tɪəriə/ *noun*
a restaurant where you choose and pay for your meal and then carry it to a table. Places like factories, colleges and hospitals often have **cafeterias**.

caffeine /'kæfi:n/ *noun* (*no plural*)
the substance in coffee and tea that makes you feel more active and awake ➲ Look at **decaffeinated**.

cage /keɪdʒ/ *noun*
a place with bars round it where animals or birds are kept so that they cannot escape

cake 0— /keɪk/ *noun*
a sweet food that you make from flour, eggs, sugar and butter and bake in the oven: *a chocolate cake* ◇ *Would you like a piece of cake?* ➲ Look at Picture Dictionary page **P6**.

calculate 0— /'kælkjuleɪt/ *verb*
(calculates, calculating, calculated)
to find an amount or a number by using mathematics: *Can you calculate how much the holiday will cost?*

calculation /ˌkælkju'leɪʃn/ *noun*
finding an answer by using mathematics

calculator /'kælkjuleɪtə(r)/ *noun*
a small electronic instrument that you use for CALCULATING numbers ➲ Look at Picture Dictionary page **P11**.

calendar /'kælɪndə(r)/ *noun*
a list of the days, weeks and months of one year

calf /kɑ:f/ *noun* (*plural* calves /kɑ:vz/)
1 the back of your leg, below your knee
2 a young cow ➲ Look at the note and the picture at **cow**.

call¹ 0— /kɔ:l/ *verb* (calls, calling, called /kɔ:ld/)
1 to give a name to somebody or something: *They called the baby Sophie.*
2 to speak loudly and clearly so that somebody who is far away can hear you: *'Breakfast is ready,' she called.* ◇ *She called out the names of the winners.*
3 to telephone somebody: *I'll call you later.* ◇ *Who's calling, please?*
4 to ask somebody to come: *He was so ill that we had to call the doctor.*
5 to make a short visit: *I'll call in to see you this evening.* ◇ *Can you call round later? I've got something for you.*
be called to have as a name: *'What is your teacher called?' 'She's called Mrs Gray.'*
call somebody back to telephone somebody again: *I can't talk now – I'll call you back later.*
call collect *American English for* REVERSE THE CHARGES
call for somebody (*British*) to go to somebody's house on your way to a place so that they can come with you: *Rosie usually calls for me in the morning and we walk to school together.*

call something off to say that a planned activity or event will not happen: *The football match was called off because of the bad weather.* ⊃ SAME MEANING **cancel**

call² 0→ /kɔːl/ *noun*
1 an act of using the telephone or a conversation on the telephone: *I got a call from James.* ◊ *I haven't got time to talk now – I'll give you a call later.*
2 a loud cry or shout: *a call for help*
3 a short visit to somebody: *The doctor has several calls to make this morning.*

call box /'kɔːl bɒks/ *noun* (plural call boxes) *another word for* PHONE BOX

calm¹ 0→ /kɑːm/ *adjective* (calmer, calmest)

> ℗ **PRONUNCIATION**
> The word **calm** sounds like **arm**, because we don't say the letter **l** in this word.

1 quiet, and not excited or afraid: *Try to keep calm – there's no danger.*
2 without big waves: *a calm sea*
3 without much wind: *calm weather*
▶ **calmly** /'kɑːmli/ *adverb*: *He spoke calmly about the accident.*

calm² /kɑːm/ *verb* (calms, calming, calmed /kɑːmd/)
calm down to become less afraid or excited; to make somebody less afraid or excited: *Calm down and tell me what happened.*

calorie /'kæləri/ *noun*
a unit for measuring the energy value of food. Food that has a lot of **calories** in it can make you fat: *a low-calorie drink*

calves *plural of* CALF

camcorder /'kæmkɔːdə(r)/ *noun*
a camera that you can carry around and use for recording moving pictures and sound

came *form of* COME

camel

hump

camel /'kæml/ *noun*
a large animal with one or two round parts (called **humps**) on its back. **Camels** carry people and things in hot dry places.

camera 0→ /'kæmərə/ *noun*
a thing that you use for taking photographs or moving pictures: *I need a new film for my camera.*

camp¹ 0→ /kæmp/ *noun*
a place where people live in tents for a short time

camp² 0→ /kæmp/ *verb* (camps, camping, camped /kæmpt/)
to live in a tent for a short time: *The children camped in the garden overnight.*

> ℗ **SPEAKING**
> It is more usual to say **go camping** when you mean that you are living in a tent on holiday: *We went camping last summer.*

campaign¹ /kæm'peɪn/ *noun*
a plan to do a number of things in order to get a special result: *a campaign to stop people smoking*

campaign² /kæm'peɪn/ *verb* (campaigns, campaigning, campaigned)
to take part in planned activities in order to get a special result: *The school is campaigning for new computer equipment.*

camping 0→ /'kæmpɪŋ/ *noun* (no plural)
sleeping or spending a holiday in a tent: *Camping is no fun when it rains.*

campsite /'kæmpsaɪt/ *noun*
a place where you can stay in a tent

campus /'kæmpəs/ *noun* (plural campuses)
the area where the buildings of a college or university are: *the college campus*

can¹ 0→ /kən; kæn/ *modal verb*

> ℗ **GRAMMAR**
> The negative form of **can** is **cannot** or **can't**: *She can't swim.*
> The past tense of **can** is **could**: *We could see the sea from our hotel room.*
> The future tense of **can** is **will be able to**: *You will be able to see it if you stand on this chair.*

1 to be able to do something; to be strong enough, clever enough, etc. to do something: *She can speak three languages.* ◊ *Can you ski?*
2 to be possible or likely to happen: *It can be very cold in the mountains in winter.*
3 a word that you use with verbs like 'see', 'hear', 'smell' and 'taste': *I can smell something burning.* ◊ *'What's that noise?' 'I can't hear anything.'*
4 to be allowed to do something: *You can go now.* ◊ *Can I have some more soup, please?*

A B C D E F G H I J K L M N O P Q R S T U V W X Y Z

A B **C** D E F G H I J K L M N O P Q R S T U V W X Y Z

◇ *The doctor says she can't go back to school yet.*
5 a word that you use when you ask somebody to do something: *Can you tell me the time, please?* ⊃ Look at the note at **modal verb**.

can² 0–ᵣ /kæn/ *noun*
a metal container for food or drink that keeps it fresh: *a can of lemonade*

> 🔎 **WHICH WORD?**
>
> **Can** or **tin**?
> In British English we usually use the word **tin** when it contains food: *a tin of soup.*
> **Can** is used for drinks: *Two cans of lemonade, please.*
> In American English **can** is used for both food and drink: *a can of beans.*

⊃ Look at the picture at **container**.

canal /kə'næl/ *noun*
a path that is made through the land and filled with water so that boats can travel on it: *the Suez Canal*

canary /kə'neəri/ *noun* (*plural* **canaries**)
a small yellow bird that people often keep as a pet

cancel /'kænsl/ *verb* (*British* **cancels, cancelling, cancelled** /'kænsld/) (*American* **canceling, canceled**)
to say that a planned activity or event will not happen: *The singer was ill, so the concert was cancelled.*

cancellation /ˌkænsə'leɪʃn/ *noun*
a decision that a planned activity or event will not happen: *the cancellation of the President's visit*

cancer /'kænsə(r)/ *noun*
a very dangerous illness that makes some very small parts in the body (called **cells**) grow too fast: *Smoking can cause cancer.*

candidate
/'kændɪdət/ *noun*
1 a person who wants to be chosen for something: *There were a lot of candidates for the job.*
2 (*British*) a person who is taking an exam

candle /'kændl/ *noun*
a round stick of WAX (= solid oil or fat) with a piece of string in the middle (called a **wick**) that burns to give light

candle

candle —
candlestick |

candlestick /'kændlstɪk/ *noun*
a thing that holds a CANDLE

candy 0–ᵣ /'kændi/ *American English for* SWEET²(1)

cane /keɪn/ *noun*
the long central part of some plants, for example BAMBOO (= a tall tropical plant), that can be used for making furniture: *sugar cane* ◇ *a cane chair*

canned /kænd/ *adjective*
in a can: *canned drinks*

cannibal /'kænɪbl/ *noun*
a person who eats other people

cannon /'kænən/ *noun*
an old type of big gun that fires big stone or metal balls

cannot 0–ᵣ /'kænɒt/ *form of* CAN¹

canoe

canoe /kə'nu:/ *noun*
a light narrow boat for one or two people that you move through the water using a flat piece of wood (called a **paddle**)

> 🔎 **SPEAKING**
>
> When you talk about using a canoe, you often say **go canoeing**: *We went canoeing on the river.* ⊃ Look at Picture Dictionary **P14**.

can't /kɑːnt/ *short for* CANNOT

canteen /kæn'tiːn/ *noun*
the place like a restaurant where people eat when they are at school or work

canvas /'kænvəs/ *noun* (*no plural*)
a strong heavy cloth, used for making tents, bags and sails, and for painting pictures on

canyon /'kænjən/ *noun*
a deep valley with steep sides of rock

cap /kæp/ *noun*
1 a soft hat with a hard curved part at the front: *a baseball cap* ⊃ Look at Picture Dictionary page **P5**.
2 a thing that covers the top of a bottle or tube: *Put the cap back on the bottle.*

capable 0–ᵣ /'keɪpəbl/ *adjective*
1 able to do something: *You are capable of passing the exam if you work harder.*
2 able to do things well: *a capable student* ⊃ OPPOSITE **incapable**

capacity /kə'pæsəti/ *noun* (*plural* **capacities**)
how much a container or space can hold: *a tank with a capacity of 1 000 litres*

cape /keɪp/ *noun*
1 a piece of clothing that covers your body and your arms, but does not have separate sleeves
2 a high part of the land that goes out into the sea: *the Cape of Good Hope*

capital ⊶ /'kæpɪtl/ *noun*
1 the most important city in a country, where the government is: *Tokyo is the capital of Japan.*
2 (*no plural*) (*business*) a large amount of money that you use to start a business, etc.: *When she had enough capital, she bought a shop.*
3 (*also* **capital letter**) a big letter of the alphabet, used at the beginning of sentences: *Please fill in the form* **in capitals.** ◇ *Names of people and places begin with a capital letter.*

capital punishment /ˌkæpɪtl 'pʌnɪʃmənt/ *noun* (*no plural*)
punishment by death for serious crimes

capsize /kæp'saɪz/ *verb* (**capsizes, capsizing, capsized** /kæp'saɪzd/)
If a boat **capsizes**, it turns over in the water: *During the storm, the boat capsized.*

captain /'kæptɪn/ *noun*
1 the person who is in charge of a ship or an aircraft: *The captain sent a message by radio for help.*
2 the leader of a group of people: *He's the captain of the school basketball team.*

caption /'kæpʃn/ *noun*
the words above or below a picture in a book or newspaper, that tell you about it

captive /'kæptɪv/ *noun*
a person who is not free ⊃ SAME MEANING **prisoner**

captivity /kæp'tɪvəti/ *noun* (*no plural*)
being kept in a place that you cannot leave: *Wild animals are often unhappy* **in captivity.**

capture /'kæptʃə(r)/ *verb* (**captures, capturing, captured** /'kæptʃəd/)
to catch somebody and keep them somewhere so that they cannot leave: *The police captured the criminals.*
▶ **capture** *noun* (*no plural*): *the capture of the escaped prisoners*

car ⊶ /kɑː(r)/ *noun*
1 (*British*) (*American also* **automobile**) a vehicle with four wheels, usually with enough space for four or five people: *She*

travels to work **by car.** ⊃ Look at Picture Dictionary page **P1**.
2 *American English for* CARRIAGE(1)

caravan
/'kærəvæn/ (*British*)
(*American* **trailer**)
noun
a large vehicle that is pulled by a car.
You can sleep, cook, etc. in a **caravan** when you are travelling or on holiday

caravan

carbohydrate /ˌkɑːbəʊ'haɪdreɪt/ *noun*
one of the substances in food, for example sugar, that gives your body energy: *Bread and rice contain carbohydrates.*

carbon /'kɑːbən/ *noun* (*no plural*)
the chemical that coal and diamonds are made of and that is in all living things

carbon dioxide /ˌkɑːbən daɪ'ɒksaɪd/ *noun* (*no plural*)
a gas that has no colour or smell that people and animals breathe out

card ⊶ /kɑːd/ *noun*
1 a piece of thick paper with writing or pictures on it: *We send birthday cards and postcards to our friends.* ⊃ Look also at **credit card** and **phonecard**.
2 (*also* **playing card**) one of a set of 52 cards (called a **pack of cards**) that you use to play games: *Let's have* **a game of cards.** ◇ *They often* **play cards** *in the evening.*

> 🔎 **WORD BUILDING**
>
> A **pack of cards** has four groups of thirteen cards, called **suits**.
> Two suits are red (**hearts** and **diamonds**) and two are black (**clubs** and **spades**).

⊃ Look at the picture at **playing card**.

cardboard ⊶ /'kɑːdbɔːd/ *noun* (*no plural*)
very thick paper that is used for making boxes, etc.

cardigan /'kɑːdɪgən/ *noun*
a piece of clothing which fastens at the front like a jacket and is usually made of wool
⊃ Look at the note at **sweater**.

care[1] ⊶ /keə(r)/ *noun* (*no plural*)
thinking about what you are doing so that you do not make a mistake or break something: *Wash these glasses* **with care!**
care of somebody = C/O
take care
1 to be careful: *Take care when you cross the road.*

A B C D E F G H I J K L M N O P Q R S T U V W X Y Z

2 (*informal*) used when you are saying 'goodbye' to somebody: *Bye now! Take care!*

take care of somebody or **something** to look after somebody or something; to do what is necessary: *She is taking care of her sister's baby today.* ◇ *Don't worry about cooking the dinner – I'll take care of it.*

care² 0ᴍ /keə(r)/ *verb* (cares, caring, cared /keəd/)

to think that somebody or something is important: *The only thing he **cares about** is money.* ◇ *I don't care who wins – I'm not interested in football.*

> 🗩 **SPEAKING**
>
> It is not polite to say **I don't care**, **Who cares?** or **I couldn't care less**.
> You can say **I don't mind** instead: *Would you like tea or coffee? – I don't mind.*

care for somebody to do the things for somebody that they need: *After the accident, her parents cared for her until she was better.*

career 0ᴍ /kə'rɪə(r)/ *noun*
a job that you learn to do and then do for many years: *He is considering a **career in** teaching.* ◇ *His career was always more important to him than his family.*

careful 0ᴍ /'keəfl/ *adjective*
thinking about what you are doing so that you do not make a mistake or have an accident: *Careful! The plate is very hot.* ◇ ***Be careful!** There's a car coming.* ◇ *He's a careful driver.*
▶ **carefully** /'keəfəli/ *adverb*: *Please listen carefully.*

careless 0ᴍ /'keələs/ *adjective*
not thinking enough about what you are doing so that you make mistakes: *Careless drivers can cause accidents.*
▶ **carelessly** /'keələsli/ *adverb*: *She threw her coat carelessly on the floor.*
▶ **carelessness** /'keələsnəs/ *noun* (no plural)

caretaker /'keəteɪkə(r)/ (*British*) (*American* janitor) *noun*
a person whose job is to look after a large building like a school or a block of flats

cargo /'kɑːgəʊ/ *noun* (*plural* cargoes)
the things that a ship or plane carries: *a cargo of wheat*

carnation /kɑː'neɪʃn/ *noun*
a pink, white or red flower with a nice smell

carnival /'kɑːnɪvl/ *noun*
a public festival that takes place in the streets with music and dancing: *the Rio carnival*

carol /'kærəl/ *noun*
a Christian song that people sing at Christmas

carousel /'kærə'sel/ *American English for* MERRY-GO-ROUND ➲ Look at the picture at **merry-go-round**.

car park /'kɑː pɑːk/ (*British*) (*American* parking lot) *noun*
an area or a building where you can leave your car for a time

carpenter /'kɑːpəntə(r)/ *noun*
a person whose job is to make things from wood ➲ Look at Picture Dictionary page **P12**.
▶ **carpentry** /'kɑːpəntri/ *noun* (no plural) making things from wood

carpet 0ᴍ /'kɑːpɪt/ *noun*
a soft covering for a floor that is often made of wool and is usually the same size as the floor ➲ Look at Picture Dictionary page **P10**.

carriage /'kærɪdʒ/ *noun*
1 (*British*) (*American* car) one of the parts of a train where people sit: *The carriages at the back of the train were empty.* ➲ Look at the picture at **train¹**.
2 a road vehicle, usually with four wheels, that is pulled by horses and was used in the past to carry people: *The Queen rode in a carriage through the streets of the city.*

carried *form of* CARRY

carrier bag /'kæriə bæg/ (*also* carrier) *noun*
a bag made from plastic or paper that you use for carrying shopping

carrot /'kærət/ *noun*
a long thin orange vegetable ➲ Look at Picture Dictionary page **P9**.

carry 0ᴍ /'kæri/ *verb* (carries, carrying, carried /'kærid/, has carried)
1 to hold something and take it to another place or keep it with you: *He carried the suitcase to my room.* ◇ *I can't carry this box – it's too heavy.* ◇ *Do the police carry guns in your country?*

> 🗩 **WHICH WORD?**
>
> **Carry** or **wear**?
> You use **wear**, not **carry**, to talk about having clothes on your body: *She is wearing a red dress and carrying a black bag.*

2 to move people or things: *Special fast trains carry people to the city centre.*
carry on to continue: *Carry on with your work.* ◇ *If you carry on to the end of this road, you'll see the post office on the right.*

carry out something to do or finish what you have planned: *The bridge was closed while they carried out the repairs.*

cart /kɑːt/ *noun*
1 (*American*) = TROLLEY
2 a wooden vehicle with wheels that a horse usually pulls

carton /ˈkɑːtn/ *noun*
a container made of very thick paper (called **cardboard**) or plastic: *a carton of milk*
➲ Look at the picture at **container**.

cartoon /kɑːˈtuːn/ *noun*
1 a funny drawing, for example in a newspaper
2 a film that tells a story by using moving drawings instead of real people and places: *a Mickey Mouse cartoon*

carve /kɑːv/ *verb* (carves, carving, carved /kɑːvd/)
1 to cut wood or stone to make a picture or shape: *Her father carved a little horse for her out of wood.*
2 to cut meat into thin pieces after you have cooked it

case ⊶ /keɪs/ *noun*
1 a situation or an example of something: *In some cases, students had to wait six months for their exam results.* ◊ *There were four cases of this disease in the school last month.*
2 a crime that the police must find an answer to: *a murder case*
3 a question that people in a court of law must decide about: *a divorce case*
4 a container or cover for keeping something in: *Put the camera back in its case.* ◊ *a pencil case* ➲ Look at Picture Dictionary page **P11**. ➲ Look also at **briefcase** and **suitcase**.
in any case words that you use when you give a second reason for something
➲ SAME MEANING **anyway**: *I don't want to see the film, and in any case I'm too busy.*
in case because something might happen: *Take an umbrella in case it rains.*
in that case if that is the situation: *'There's no coffee.' 'Well, in that case we'll have tea.'*

cash¹ ⊶ /kæʃ/ *noun* (no plural)
money in coins and notes: *Are you paying in cash or by cheque?* ➲ Look at the note at **money**.

cash² /kæʃ/ *verb* (cashes, cashing, cashed /kæʃt/)
to give somebody a cheque and get money for it: *I'd like to cash some traveller's cheques, please.*

cash desk /ˈkæʃ desk/ *noun* (*British*)
the place in a shop where you pay for things

cashier /kæˈʃɪə(r)/ *noun*
the person whose job is to take or give out money in a bank, shop or hotel

cash machine /ˈkæʃ məʃiːn/ (*British*) (*British also* Cashpoint™ /ˈkæʃpɔɪnt/) (*American* ATM) *noun*
a machine that you can get money from by using a special plastic card

cassette /kəˈset/ *noun*

> 🔎 SPELLING
> Remember! You spell **cassette** with **SS** and **TT**.

a plastic box with special tape inside for recording and playing sound or pictures: *a video cassette*

cassette player /kəˈset pleɪə(r)/ (*also* cassette recorder /kəˈset rɪˌkɔːdə(r)/) *noun*
a machine that can record sound or music on tape and play it again later

cast¹ /kɑːst/ *verb* (casts, casting, cast, has cast)
to choose an actor for a particular part in a film or a play: *She always seems to be cast in the same sort of role.*
cast a spell to use magic words that have the power to change somebody or something: *The witch cast a spell on the handsome prince.*

cast² /kɑːst/ *noun*
all the actors in a film, play, etc.: *The whole cast was excellent.*

castle ⊶ /ˈkɑːsl/ *noun*
a large old building that was built in the past to keep people safe from attack: *Windsor Castle*

casual /ˈkæʒuəl/ *adjective*
1 showing that you are not worried about something; relaxed: *She gave us a casual wave as she passed.*
2 (used about clothes) not formal: *I wear casual clothes like jeans and T-shirts when I'm not at work.*
▶ **casually** /ˈkæʒuəli/ *adverb*: *They chatted casually on the phone.*

casualty /ˈkæʒuəlti/ *noun*
1 (*plural* casualties) a person who is hurt or killed in an accident or a war
2 (*no plural*) (*British also* casualty department /ˈkæʒuəlti dɪpɑːtmənt/) (*American* ER, emergency room) the place in a hospital where you go if you have been hurt in an accident or if you have suddenly become ill: *The victims were rushed to casualty.*

A
B
C
D
E
F
G
H
I
J
K
L
M
N
O
P
Q
R
S
T
U
V
W
X
Y
Z

A
B
C
D
E
F
G
H
I
J
K
L
M
N
O
P
Q
R
S
T
U
V
W
X
Y
Z

cat

tail
whiskers
claw
paw
cat
kitten

cat ⌐ /kæt/ *noun*

1 a small animal with soft fur that people keep as a pet

🔍 **WORD BUILDING**

A young cat is called a **kitten**.
A cat **purrs** when it is happy. When it makes a loud noise, it **miaows**: *My cat miaows when she's hungry.*

2 a wild animal of the cat family: *the big cats, such as tigers and lions*

catalogue (*British*) (*American* **catalog**) /'kætəlɒg/ *noun*

a complete list of all the things that you can buy or see somewhere: *an online catalogue*

catastrophe /kə'tæstrəfi/ *noun*

a sudden disaster that causes great suffering or damage: *major catastrophes such as floods and earthquakes*

catch ⌐ /kætʃ/ *verb* (**catches, catching, caught** /kɔːt/, **has caught**)

1 to take and hold something that is moving: *He threw the ball to me and I caught it.*
2 to find and hold somebody or something: *They caught a fish in the river.* ◇ *The man ran so fast that the police couldn't catch him.*
3 to see somebody when they are doing something wrong: *They caught the thief stealing the painting.*
4 to be early enough for a bus, train, etc. that is going to leave: *You should run if you want to catch the bus.* ⊃ OPPOSITE **miss**
5 to get an illness: *She caught a cold.*
6 to let something be held tightly: *I caught my fingers in the door.*
catch fire to start to burn: *The house caught fire.*
catch up, **catch somebody up** to do something quickly so that you are not behind others: *If you miss a lesson, you can do some work at home to catch up.* ◇ *Quick! Run after the others and catch them up.*

category /'kætəgəri/ *noun* (*plural* **categories**)

a group of people or things that are similar to each other: *The results can be divided into three main categories.*

caterpillar /'kætəpɪlə(r)/ *noun*

a small animal with a long body and a lot of legs. A **caterpillar** later becomes an insect with large coloured wings (called a **butterfly**).

cathedral /kə'θiːdrəl/ *noun*

a big important church

Catholic /'kæθlɪk/ = ROMAN CATHOLIC

cattle /'kætl/ *noun* (*plural*)

cows that are kept for their milk or meat: *a herd* (= a group) *of cattle*

caught form of CATCH

cauliflower /'kɒliflaʊə(r)/ *noun*

a large vegetable with green leaves outside and a round white part in the middle ⊃ Look at Picture Dictionary page **P9**.

cause[1] ⌐ /kɔːz/ *noun*

🔍 **PRONUNCIATION**

The word **cause** sounds like **doors**.

1 a thing or person that makes something happen: *Bad driving is the cause of most road accidents.*
2 something that people care about and want to help: *They gave the money to a good cause – it was used to build a new hospital.*

cause[2] ⌐ /kɔːz/ *verb* (**causes, causing, caused** /kɔːzd/)

to be the reason why something happens: *What caused the accident?* ◇ *The fire was caused by a cigarette.*

caution /'kɔːʃn/ *noun* (*no plural*)

great care, because of possible danger: *Caution! Wet floor.*

cautious /'kɔːʃəs/ *adjective*

careful because there may be danger: *He has always been cautious about driving at night.*
▶ **cautiously** /'kɔːʃəsli/ *adverb*: *He cautiously pushed open the door and looked into the room.*

cave /keɪv/ *noun*

a large hole in the side of a mountain or under the ground: *Thousands of years ago, people lived in caves.*

CD ⌐ /,siː 'diː/ *noun* (*also* **disc**)

a small, round piece of hard plastic on which you can record sound or store information

CD player /,siː 'diː pleɪə(r)/ *noun*

a machine that you use to play CDs

CD-ROM /ˌsiː diː ˈrɒm/ *noun*
a CD on which you can store large amounts of information, sound and pictures, to use on a computer ➔ **CD-ROM** is short for 'compact disc read-only memory'.

cease /siːs/ *verb* (ceases, ceasing, ceased /siːst/) (*formal*)
to stop: *Fighting in the area has now ceased.*

ceiling 0️⃣ /ˈsiːlɪŋ/ *noun*

> 🔍 **PRONUNCIATION**
> The word **ceiling** sounds like **feeling**.

the top part of the inside of a room

> 🔍 **SPELLING**
> **IE** or **EI**?
> When the sound is /iː/ (which rhymes with 'be'), the rule is **I before E, except after C**, so **ceiling** is spelled with **EI**.

celebrate 0️⃣ /ˈselɪbreɪt/ *verb* (celebrates, celebrating, celebrated)
to do something to show that you are happy for a special reason or because it is a special day: *If you pass your exams, we'll have a party to celebrate.* ◇ *Grandma celebrated her 90th birthday last week.*

celebration 0️⃣ /ˌselɪˈbreɪʃn/ *noun*
a time when you enjoy yourself because you have a special reason to be happy: *birthday celebrations*

celery /ˈseləri/ *noun* (*no plural*)
a vegetable with long green and white sticks that can be eaten without being cooked: *a stick of celery* ➔ Look at Picture Dictionary page **P9**.

cell 0️⃣ /sel/ *noun*
1 a small room for one or more prisoners in a prison or police station
2 the smallest part of any living thing. All plants and animals are made up of **cells**: *red blood cells*

cellar /ˈselə(r)/ *noun*
a room in the part of a building that is under the ground ➔ Look at Picture Dictionary page **P10**.

cello

cello /ˈtʃeləʊ/ *noun* (*plural* cellos)
a large wooden musical instrument with strings. You sit down to play it and hold it between your knees.

cellphone /ˈselfəʊn/ *American English for* MOBILE PHONE

Celsius /ˈselsiəs/ (*also* centigrade) *noun* (*no plural*) (*abbr.* C)
a way of measuring temperature. Water freezes at 0° **Celsius** and boils at 100° **Celsius**: *The temperature tonight will fall to 2°C* (= We say 'two degrees Celsius'). ➔ Look also at **Fahrenheit**.

cement /sɪˈment/ *noun* (*no plural*)
a grey powder that becomes hard like stone when you mix it with water and leave it to dry. **Cement** is used in building for sticking bricks or stones together or for making very hard surfaces.

cemetery /ˈsemətri/ *noun* (*plural* cemeteries)
an area of ground where dead people are put under the earth

cent 0️⃣ /sent/ *noun*
a small coin that people use in many countries around the world. There are 100 **cents** in a dollar or a euro.

center *American English for* CENTRE

centigrade /ˈsentɪɡreɪd/ *another word for* CELSIUS

centilitre (*British*) (*American* centiliter) /ˈsentɪliːtə(r)/ *noun* (*abbr.* cl)
a measure of liquid. There are 100 **centilitres** in a **litre**: *250cl*

centimetre 0️⃣ (*British*) (*American* centimeter) /ˈsentɪmiːtə(r)/ *noun* (*abbr.* cm)
a measure of length. There are 100 **centimetres** in a **metre**.

central 0️⃣ /ˈsentrəl/ *adjective*
in the middle part of something: *central London*

central heating /ˌsentrəl ˈhiːtɪŋ/ *noun* (*no plural*)
a system for heating a building from one main point. Air or water is heated and carried by pipes to all parts of the building.

centre 0️⃣ (*British*) (*American* center) /ˈsentə(r)/ *noun*
1 the part in the middle of something: *the city centre* ◇ *The flower has a yellow centre with white petals.*
2 a place where people come to do a particular activity: *a shopping centre* ◇ *Our town has a new sports centre.*

century 0️⃣ /ˈsentʃəri/ *noun* (*plural* centuries)
a period of 100 years: *People have been making wine in this area for centuries.* ◇ *We*

A
B
C
D
E
F
G
H
I
J
K
L
M
N
O
P
Q
R
S
T
U
V
W
X
Y
Z

A | B | **C** | D | E | F | G | H | I | J | K | L | M | N | O | P | Q | R | S | T | U | V | W | X | Y | Z

are living at the beginning of the twenty-first century.

cereal /ˈsɪəriəl/ *noun*
1 (*plural* cereals) a plant that farmers grow so that we can eat the grain (= the seed): *Wheat and oats are cereals.*
2 (*no plural*) a food made from grain, that you can eat for breakfast with milk: *a bowl of cereal with milk* ⊃ Look at Picture Dictionary page **P7**.

ceremony 0̶ₘ /ˈserəməni/ *noun* (*plural* ceremonies)
a formal public or religious event: *the opening ceremony of the Olympic Games* ◇ *a wedding ceremony*

certain 0̶ₘ /ˈsɜːtn/ *adjective*
1 sure about something; without any doubt: *I'm certain that I've seen her before.* ◇ *Are you certain about that?*
⊃ OPPOSITE **uncertain**
2 used for talking about a particular thing or person without saying what or who they are: *Do you want the work to be finished by a certain date?* ◇ *It's cheaper to telephone at certain times of the day.*
for certain without any doubt: *I don't know for certain where she is.*
make certain to check something so that you are sure about it: *Please make certain that the window is closed before you leave.*

certainly 0̶ₘ /ˈsɜːtnli/ *adverb*
1 without any doubt ⊃ SAME MEANING **definitely**: *She is certainly the best swimmer in the team.*
2 used when answering questions to mean 'of course': *'Will you open the door for me, please?' 'Certainly.'* ◇ *'Are you going to apologize?' 'Certainly not!'*

certificate 0̶ₘ /səˈtɪfɪkət/ *noun*
an important piece of paper that shows that something is true: *Your birth certificate shows when and where you were born.*

chains

clasp
link
chain
chain

chain¹ 0̶ₘ /tʃeɪn/ *noun*
a line of metal rings that are joined together: *Round her neck she wore a gold chain.* ◇ *My bicycle chain is broken.* ⊃ Look at the picture at **bicycle**.

chain² /tʃeɪn/ *verb* (chains, chaining, chained /tʃeɪnd/)
to attach somebody or something to a place with a **chain**: *The dog was chained to a tree.*

chair 0̶ₘ /tʃeə(r)/ *noun*
1 a piece of furniture for one person to sit on, with four legs, a seat and a back: *a table and four chairs* ⊃ Look at Picture Dictionary page **P10**.
2 = CHAIRPERSON

chairperson /ˈtʃeəpɜːsn/ *noun* (*also* chair, chairman /ˈtʃeəmən/ chairwoman /ˈtʃeəwʊmən/)
a person who controls a meeting

chalk /tʃɔːk/ *noun* (*no plural*)
1 a type of soft white rock
2 a white or coloured stick of **chalk** that you use for writing or drawing: *The teacher picked up a piece of chalk.*

challenge¹ 0̶ₘ /ˈtʃælɪndʒ/ *noun*
1 a new or difficult thing that makes you try hard: *Climbing the mountain will be a real challenge.*
2 an invitation to fight or play a game against somebody

challenge² /ˈtʃælɪndʒ/ *verb* (challenges, challenging, challenged /ˈtʃælɪndʒd/)
1 to refuse to accept a set of rules; to say that you think somebody or something is wrong: *She does not like anyone challenging her authority.*
2 to ask somebody to play a game with you or fight with you to see who wins: *The boxer challenged the world champion to a fight.*

champagne /ʃæmˈpeɪn/ *noun* (*no plural*)
a French white wine with a lot of bubbles

champion /ˈtʃæmpiən/ *noun*
a person who is the best at a sport or game: *a chess champion* ◇ *the world champion*

championship /ˈtʃæmpiənʃɪp/ *noun*
a competition to find the best player or team in a sport or game: *Our team won the championship this year.*

chance 0̶ₘ /tʃɑːns/ *noun*
1 (*no plural*) a possibility that something may happen: *There's no chance that she'll come now.* ◇ *She has a good chance of becoming team captain.* ◇ *He doesn't stand* (= have) *a chance of passing the exam.*
2 (*plural* chances) a time when you can do something ⊃ SAME MEANING **opportunity**:

*It was their last **chance to** escape.* ◇ *Be quiet and **give** her **a chance** to explain.*
3 (*no plural*) when something happens that you cannot control or that you have not planned ⊃ SAME MEANING **luck**: *We must plan this carefully. I don't want to **leave** anything **to chance**.* ◇ *We met **by chance** at the station.*
no chance (*informal*) used to say that there is no possibility of something happening: *'Perhaps your mum will give you the money.' 'No chance!'*
take a chance to do something when it is possible that something bad may happen because of it: *We may lose money but we'll just have to take that chance.*

change¹ 0̄ᴡ /tʃeɪndʒ/ *verb* (**changes, changing, changed** /tʃeɪndʒd/)
1 to become different: *She has changed a lot since the last time I saw her – she looks much older.* ◇ *Water **changes into** ice when it gets very cold.*
2 to make something different: *At this restaurant they change the menu every week.*
3 to put or take something in place of another thing: *My new watch didn't work, so I took it back to the shop and changed it.* ◇ *I went to the bank to change my euros into dollars.* ◇ *Can you change a £5 note please? I need some pound coins.*
4 (*also* **get changed**) to put on different clothes: *I need to change before I go out.* ◇ *You need to get changed for football.*
5 to get off a train or bus and get on another one: *I have to change trains at Kings Cross.*

change² 0̄ᴡ /tʃeɪndʒ/ *noun*
1 (*plural* **changes**) when something becomes different: *The new government has **made** a lot of **changes**.* ◇ *There has been a **change in** the weather.*
2 (*no plural*) the money that you get back if you pay more than the amount something costs: *If a newspaper costs 60p and you pay with a pound coin, you will get 40p change.*
3 (*no plural*) small pieces of money; coins: *I haven't got any change.*
for a change because you want something different: *Today we had lunch in a restaurant for a change.*

channel /'tʃænl/ *noun*
1 a TV station: *Which channel is the film on?*
2 a long narrow place where water can go: *the English Channel* (= the sea between England and France)

chaos /'keɪɒs/ *noun* (*no plural*)
when everything is confused and nothing is organized: *The house was **in chaos** after the party.*

chapel /'tʃæpl/ *noun*
a room or a small church where Christians go to speak to God (to pray)

chapter /'tʃæptə(r)/ *noun*
one of the parts of a book: *Turn to Chapter 4.*

character 0̄ᴡ /'kærəktə(r)/ *noun*
1 (*no plural*) the qualities that make somebody or something different from other people or things: *He has a strong character.* ◇ *The new factory will change the character of the village.*
2 (*plural* **characters**) a person in a book, play or film: *Homer Simpson is a famous cartoon character.*

characteristic 0̄ᴡ /ˌkærəktə'rɪstɪk/ *noun*
a quality that somebody or something has: *personal characteristics such as age, height and weight*

charge¹ 0̄ᴡ /tʃɑːdʒ/ *noun*
1 the money that you must pay for something: *There is a **charge of** £50 for the use of the hall.* ◇ *We deliver **free of charge**.* ⊃ Look at the note at **price**.
2 when the police say that somebody has done something wrong: *a murder charge*
be in charge of somebody or **something** to take care of or be responsible for somebody or something: *Tim is in charge of his baby brother while his mother is out.*

charge² 0̄ᴡ /tʃɑːdʒ/ *verb* (**charges, charging, charged** /tʃɑːdʒd/)
1 to ask somebody to pay a certain price for something: *The garage charged me £200 for the repairs.*
2 to say that somebody has done something wrong: *The police have **charged** him **with** murder.*
3 to run quickly and with a lot of force: *The bull charged.* ◇ *The children charged into the room.*

charity 0̄ᴡ /'tʃærəti/ *noun*
1 (*plural* **charities**) an organization that collects money to help people who need it: *The Red Cross is a charity.* ◇ *They give a lot of money to charity.*
2 (*no plural*) being kind and helping other people

charm¹ /tʃɑːm/ *noun*
1 (*no plural*) a quality that makes people like you: *He was a man of great charm.*
2 (*plural* **charms**) a small thing that you wear because you think it will bring good luck: *She wears a chain with a lucky charm on it.*

A

B

C

D

E

F

G

H

I

J

K

L

M

N

O

P

Q

R

S

T

U

V

W

X

Y

Z

charm² /tʃɑːm/ *verb* (charms, charming, charmed /tʃɑːmd/)
to make somebody like you: *The baby charmed everybody with her smile.*

charming /ˈtʃɑːmɪŋ/ *adjective*
very pleasant or attractive: *a charming little village*

chart /tʃɑːt/ *noun*
1 a drawing that gives information about something: *a temperature chart*
2 a map of the sea or the sky

chase 0-π /tʃeɪs/ *verb* (chases, chasing, chased /tʃeɪst/)
to run behind somebody or something and try to catch them: *The dog chased the cat around the garden.* ◇ *The police chased after the thief but he escaped.*
▶ **chase** *noun*: *The film includes an exciting car chase.*

chat¹ /tʃæt/ *verb* (chats, chatting, chatted)
to talk in a friendly, informal way to somebody: *We chatted on the phone for a few minutes.*

chat² /tʃæt/ *noun*
a friendly talk: *Let's have a chat about it later.*

chat room /ˈtʃæt ruːm/ *noun*
an area on the Internet where you can join in a discussion with other people

chatter /ˈtʃætə(r)/ *verb* (chatters, chattering, chattered /ˈtʃætəd/)
to talk quickly about things that are not very important: *Stop chattering and finish your work.*

cheap 0-π /tʃiːp/ *adjective* (cheaper, cheapest)
costing little money: *That restaurant is very good and quite cheap.* ◇ *Computers are getting cheaper all the time.*
⊃ OPPOSITE **expensive**

cheat 0-π /tʃiːt/ *verb* (cheats, cheating, cheated)
to do something that is not honest or fair: *She cheated in the exam – she copied her friend's work.*
▶ **cheat** *noun* a person who **cheats**: *That man's a liar and a cheat.*

check¹ 0-π /tʃek/ *verb* (checks, checking, checked /tʃekt/)
1 to look at something to see that it is right, good or safe: *Do the sums and then use a calculator to check your answers.* ◇ *Before driving off, I checked the oil and water.* ◇ *Check that all the windows are closed before you leave.*
2 *American English for* TICK¹(2)

check in to tell the person at the desk in a hotel or an airport that you have arrived: *I have to check in an hour before my flight.*
check out to pay your bill and leave a hotel

check² 0-π /tʃek/ *noun*
1 a look to see that everything is right, good or safe: *They do regular safety checks on all their products.* ◇ *a security check*
2 a pattern of squares; one of the squares in a pattern: *a shirt with blue and red checks*
3 *American English for* CHEQUE
4 *American English for* BILL(1)
5 (*also* **check mark** /ˈtʃek mɑːk/) *American English for* TICK²(1)

checkbook *American English for* CHEQUEBOOK

checked /tʃekt/ *adjective*
with a pattern of squares: *a checked shirt*

checked

checkers /ˈtʃekəz/ *American English for* DRAUGHTS

checkout /ˈtʃekaʊt/ *noun*
the place in a large shop where you pay for things: *a supermarket checkout*

check-up /ˈtʃek ʌp/ *noun*
a general examination by a doctor to make sure that you are healthy: *You should visit your dentist for a check-up twice a year.*

cheek 0-π /tʃiːk/ *noun*
1 (*plural* **cheeks**) one of the two soft parts of your face below your eyes ⊃ Look at Picture Dictionary page **P4**.
2 (*no plural*) (*British*) talk or behaviour that people think is annoying, rude or not showing respect: *What a cheek! Somebody has eaten my sandwiches.*

cheeky /ˈtʃiːki/ *adjective* (cheekier, cheekiest) (*British*)
not polite and not showing respect
⊃ SAME MEANING **rude**: *Don't be so cheeky!* ◇ *She was punished for being cheeky to a teacher.*

cheer¹ /tʃɪə(r)/ *noun*
a loud shout that shows that you are pleased: *The crowd gave a loud cheer as the singer came onto the stage.*

cheer² /tʃɪə(r)/ *verb* (cheers, cheering, cheered /tʃɪəd/)
to shout to show that you like something or

to encourage somebody: *The crowd cheered loudly when the players ran onto the pitch.*
cheer up, **cheer somebody up** to become or to make somebody happier: *Cheer up! You'll feel better soon.* ◇ *We gave Julie some flowers to cheer her up.*

cheerful /'tʃɪəfl/ *adjective*
happy: *a cheerful smile* ◇ *You don't look very cheerful today. What's the matter?*

cheers /tʃɪəz/ *exclamation* (*informal*)
1 a word that people say to each other as they hold up their glasses to drink: '*Cheers,*' *she said, raising her glass.*
2 (*British*) goodbye
3 (*British*) thank you

cheese 0‑π /tʃiːz/ *noun*
a yellow or white food made from milk: *bread and cheese* ➋ Look at Picture Dictionary page **P6**.

chef /ʃef/ *noun*
a professional cook, especially the head cook in a hotel or restaurant ➋ Look at Picture Dictionary page **P12**.

chemical¹ 0‑π /'kemɪkl/ *adjective*
connected with chemistry or chemicals: *a chemical experiment*

chemical² 0‑π /'kemɪkl/ *noun*
a solid or liquid substance that is used or produced in a chemical process

chemist /'kemɪst/ *noun*
1 (*British*) (*American, British also* **pharmacist**) a person who prepares and sells medicines
2 **chemist's** (*British*) (*American* **drugstore**) a shop that sells medicines, soap and other personal goods: *I'm just going to the chemist's to get my tablets.* ➋ Look at Picture Dictionary page **P13**.
3 a person who studies chemistry

chemistry 0‑π /'kemɪstri/ *noun* (*no plural*)
the science that studies gases, liquids and solids to find out what they are and how they behave

cheque 0‑π (*British*) (*American* **check**) /tʃek/ *noun*

🔍 **PRONUNCIATION**
The word **cheque** sounds like **neck**.

a piece of paper from a bank that you can write on and use to pay for things: *I gave him a cheque for £50.* ◇ *Can I pay by cheque?* ➋ Look at the picture at **money**.

chequebook /'tʃekbʊk/ (*British*) (*American* **checkbook**) *noun*
a book of CHEQUES

cherry /'tʃeri/ *noun* (*plural* **cherries**)
a small round red or black fruit that has a large seed inside it (called a **stone**) ➋ Look at Picture Dictionary page **P8**.

chess /tʃes/ *noun* (*no plural*)
a game that two people play on a board with black and white squares on it (called a **chessboard**). Each player has sixteen pieces that can be moved around the board in different ways.

chest 0‑π /tʃest/ *noun*
1 the top part of the front of your body ➋ Look at Picture Dictionary page **P4**.
2 a large strong box with a lid that you use for storing or carrying things

chest of drawers /ˌtʃest əv 'drɔːz/ *noun* (*plural* **chests of drawers**)
a large piece of furniture with parts that you can pull out (called **drawers**). A **chest of drawers** is usually used for keeping clothes in. ➋ Look at Picture Dictionary page **P10**.

chew /tʃuː/ *verb* (**chews**, **chewing**, **chewed** /tʃuːd/)
to use your teeth to break up food in your mouth when you are eating: *You should chew your food thoroughly.*

chewing gum /'tʃuːɪŋ ɡʌm/ *noun* (*no plural*)
a sweet sticky substance that you can CHEW for a long time

chick /tʃɪk/ *noun*
a baby bird, especially a baby chicken: *a hen with her chicks* ➋ Look at the picture at **shell**.

chicken 0‑π /'tʃɪkɪn/ *noun*
1 (*plural* **chickens**) a bird that people often keep for its eggs and its meat ➋ Look at Picture Dictionary page **P2**.

🔍 **WORD BUILDING**
A female **chicken** is called a **hen** and a male chicken is called a **cock**. A young chicken is a **chick**.

2 (*no plural*) the meat from this bird: *roast chicken* ➋ Look at Picture Dictionary page **P7**.

chickenpox /'tʃɪkɪnpɒks/ *noun* (*no plural*)
a disease, especially of children. When you have **chickenpox** you feel very hot and get red spots on your skin that make you want to scratch.

A B C D E F G H I J K L M N O P Q R S T U V W X Y Z

A
B
C
D
E
F
G
H
I
J
K
L
M
N
O
P
Q
R
S
T
U
V
W
X
Y
Z

chief¹ 0📠 /tʃiːf/ *adjective*
most important: *Bad driving is one of the chief causes of road accidents.*

chief² 0📠 /tʃiːf/ *noun*
the leader or ruler of a group of people: *the chief of an African tribe* ◇ *police chiefs*

chiefly /'tʃiːfli/ *adverb*
not completely, but mostly
⊃ SAME MEANING **mainly**: *His success was due chiefly to hard work.*

child 0📠 /tʃaɪld/ *noun* (*plural* children /'tʃɪldrən/)
1 a young boy or girl: *There are 30 children in the class.*
2 a daughter or son: *Have you got any children?* ◇ *One of her children got married last year.*

childhood /'tʃaɪldhʊd/ *noun* (*no plural*)
the time when you are a child: *She had a happy childhood.*

childish /'tʃaɪldɪʃ/ *adjective*
like a child ⊃ SAME MEANING **immature**: *Don't be so childish! It's only a game.*

childminder /'tʃaɪldmaɪndə(r)/ *noun* (British)
a person whose job is to look after a child while his or her parents are at work

chilli (British) (American chili) /'tʃɪli/ *noun* (*plural* chillies *or* chilies)
a small green or red vegetable that has a very strong hot taste: *chilli powder*

chilly /'tʃɪli/ *adjective* (chillier, chilliest)
cold: *a chilly morning*

chime /tʃaɪm/ *verb* (chimes, chiming, chimed /tʃaɪmd/)
to make the sound that a bell makes: *The clock chimed midnight.*

chimney /'tʃɪmni/ *noun* (*plural* chimneys)
a large pipe over a fire that lets smoke go outside into the air ⊃ Look at Picture Dictionary page **P10**.

chimpanzee /ˌtʃɪmpænˈziː/ *noun*
an African animal like a large MONKEY with no tail

chimpanzee

chin 0📠 /tʃɪn/ *noun*
the part of your face below your mouth ⊃ Look at Picture Dictionary page **P4**.

china /'tʃaɪnə/ *noun* (*no plural*)
a hard white material made from earth, or things like plates and cups that are made from this: *a china cup*

chip¹ /tʃɪp/ *noun*
1 (*British*) (*British and American also* French fry, fry) a thin piece of potato cooked in hot oil: *We had fish and chips for lunch.* ⊃ Look at Picture Dictionary page **P7**.
2 *American English for* CRISP²
3 the place where a small piece of wood, stone or other material has broken off a larger piece: *This dish has a chip in it.*
4 a very small thing inside a computer that makes it work ⊃ SAME MEANING **microchip**

chip² /tʃɪp/ *verb* (chips, chipping, chipped /tʃɪpt/)
to break a small piece off something hard: *I chipped a cup.*

chirp /tʃɜːp/ *verb* (chirps, chirping, chirped /tʃɜːpt/)
to make the short high sound that small birds make

chocolate

chocolate 0📠 /'tʃɒklət/ *noun*
1 (*no plural*) a dark brown sweet food that is made seeds (called cocoa beans) that grow on trees in hot countries: *Do you like chocolate?* ◇ *a bar of chocolate* ◇ *a chocolate cake*
2 (*plural* chocolates) a sweet made of chocolate: *a box of chocolates*

choice 0📠 /tʃɔɪs/ *noun*
1 (*plural* choices) the act of between two or more people or things: *You made the right choice.*
3 (*no plural*) the right or chance to choose: *We have no choice. We have to leave.*
3 (*plural* choices) the things that you can choose from: *The cinema has a choice of six different films.*

choir /ˈkwaɪə(r)/ *noun*
a group of people who sing together: *a school choir*

choke /tʃəʊk/ *verb* (chokes, choking, choked /tʃəʊkt/)
to not be able to breathe because something is in your throat: *He was choking on a fish bone.*

choose 0⟶ /tʃuːz/ *verb* (chooses,
choosing, chose /tʃəʊz/, has chosen
/'tʃəʊzn/)
to decide which thing or person you want:
She chose the chocolate cake. ◇ *Mike had to
choose between getting a job or going to
college.* ⊅ The noun is **choice**.

chop

chop¹ /tʃɒp/ *verb* (chops, chopping,
chopped /tʃɒpt/)
to cut something into pieces with a knife,
etc.: *Chop the meat up into small pieces.* ◇ *We
chopped some wood for the fire.*

chop² /tʃɒp/ *noun*
a thick slice of meat with a piece of bone in
it: *a lamb chop*

chopsticks /'tʃɒpstɪks/ *noun* (*plural*)
a pair of thin sticks that are used for eating
with, especially in some Asian countries

chord /kɔːd/ *noun*
two or more musical notes that are played at
the same time

chorus /'kɔːrəs/ *noun* (*plural* choruses)
a part of a song that you repeat

chose *form of* CHOOSE

chosen *form of* CHOOSE

Christ /kraɪst/ = JESUS

christen /'krɪsn/ *verb* (christens,
christening, christened /'krɪsnd/)
to give a name to a baby and make him or
her a member of the Christian church in a
special ceremony ⊅ Look also at **baptize**.

christening /'krɪsnɪŋ/ *noun*
the ceremony when a baby is CHRISTENED

Christian /'krɪstʃən/ *noun*
a person who believes in Jesus Christ and
what He taught
▶ **Christian** *adjective*: *the Christian church*

Christianity /ˌkrɪstiˈænəti/ *noun* (*no
plural*)
the religion that follows what Jesus Christ
taught

Christmas /'krɪsməs/ *noun*
the period of time around and including 25
December, when Christians remember the
birth of Christ: *Merry Christmas!* ◇ *Where are
you spending Christmas this year?*

> *𝒫* **CULTURE**
>
> Christmas is a very important festival in
> Britain and the US.
> The day before **Christmas Day** is called
> **Christmas Eve**, and the day after is
> called **Boxing Day**.
> Many children believe that **Father
> Christmas** (also called **Santa Claus**)
> visits them at Christmas to bring
> presents.
> People send **Christmas cards** and give
> presents to their friends and family. Many
> people go to church at Christmas and
> sing **carols**.
> We put special trees (called **Christmas
> trees**) in our homes and decorate them
> with coloured lights and other pretty
> things.
> On **Christmas Day** we eat **Christmas
> dinner**, a special meal with roast turkey
> (= a large bird) and **Christmas pudding**
> (= a kind of cake made with dried fruit).
> **Christmas** is sometimes written
> informally as **Xmas**.

chubby /'tʃʌbi/ *adjective*
slightly fat in a pleasant way: *a baby with
chubby cheeks*

chunk /tʃʌŋk/ *noun*
a large piece of something: *a chunk of cheese*

church 0⟶ /tʃɜːtʃ/ *noun* (*plural*
churches)
a building where Christians go to speak to
God (to pray): *They go to church every
Sunday.*

> *𝒫* **GRAMMAR**
>
> When we talk about going to a ceremony
> (a **service**) in a church we say **in church**,
> **to church** or **at church** without 'a' or
> 'the': *Was Mr Poole at church today?*
> We use **a** or **the** to talk about the
> building: *the church where we got married*
> ◇ *a historic church.*

churchyard /'tʃɜːtʃjɑːd/ *noun*
a piece of land around a church, often used
for burying dead people in ⊅ Look also at
cemetery and **graveyard**.

cigar /sɪˈɡɑː(r)/ *noun*
a thick roll of dried leaves (called **tobacco**)
that some people smoke. **Cigars** are larger
than cigarettes.

A
B
C
D
E
F
G
H
I
J
K
L
M
N
O
P
Q
R
S
T
U
V
W
X
Y
Z

A

cigarette 0̲ₘ /ˌsɪgəˈret/ *noun*
a thin tube of white paper filled with dried
leaves (called **tobacco**), that some people
smoke: *He smokes two packets of cigarettes
a day.*

B

C

cinema 0̲ₘ /ˈsɪnəmə/ (*British*) (*American*
movie theater) *noun*
a place where you go to see a film: *Let's go to
the cinema tonight.*

D

E

> 🔎 **CULTURE**
>
> In American English, you use **movie
> theater** to talk about the building where
> you see a film but **the movies** when you
> are talking about going to see a film
> there: *There are five movie theaters in this
> town. ◇ Let's go to the movies this evening.*

F

G

H

I

J

circle

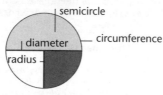

circle 0̲ₘ /ˈsɜːkl/ *noun*
a round shape; a ring: *There are 360 degrees
in a circle.*

K

L

M

N

circular /ˈsɜːkjələ(r)/ *adjective*
with the shape of a circle ➔ SAME MEANING
round: *a circular table*

O

P

circulate /ˈsɜːkjəleɪt/ *verb* (circulates,
circulating, circulated)
to move around: *Blood **circulates round** the
body.*

Q

circulation /ˌsɜːkjəˈleɪʃn/ *noun* (no plural)
the movement of blood around the body

R

circumference /səˈkʌmfərəns/ *noun*
the distance around a circle ➔ Look at the
picture at **circle**.

S

T

circumstances /ˈsɜːkəmstənsɪz/ *noun*
(plural)
the facts that are true in a particular situation
in or **under no circumstances** never;
not for any reason: *Under no circumstances
should you go out alone at night.*
in or **under the circumstances** as the
result of a particular situation: *It's not an ideal
solution, but it's the best we can do in the
circumstances.*

U

V

W

X

Y

circus /ˈsɜːkəs/ *noun* (plural circuses)
a show in a big tent, with a performance by a
group of people and trained animals

Z

citizen /ˈsɪtɪzn/ *noun*
a person who belongs to a country or a city:
She became an American citizen in 1995.

citrus fruit /ˈsɪtrəs fruːt/
a fruit such as an orange or a lemon ➔ Look
at Picture Dictionary page **P8**.

city 0̲ₘ /ˈsɪti/ *noun* (plural cities)
a big and important town: *the city of Rome ◇
the city centre*

civil /ˈsɪvl/ *adjective*
1 connected with the people who live in a
country: *civil disorder* (= involving groups of
people within the same country)
2 connected with the state, not with the
army or the Church: *a civil wedding* (= not a
religious one)

civilian /səˈvɪliən/ *noun*
a person who does not belong to a military
organization or the police

civilization /ˌsɪvəlaɪˈzeɪʃn/ *noun*
the way people live together in a society
with laws, education and a government: *the
ancient civilizations of Greece and Rome*

civilized /ˈsɪvəlaɪzd/ *adjective*
(used about a society) well-organized and
having a high level of social and cultural
development

civil rights /ˌsɪvl ˈraɪts/ *noun* (plural)
a person's legal rights to freedom and to
equal treatment in society

civil servant /ˌsɪvl ˈsɜːvənt/ *noun*
a person who works in THE CIVIL SERVICE

the civil service /ðə ˌsɪvl ˈsɜːvɪs/ *noun*
(no plural)
the government departments in a country,
and the people who work for them

civil war /ˌsɪvl ˈwɔː(r)/ *noun*
a war between groups of people who live in
the same country

cl *short way of writing* CENTILITRE

claim[1] /kleɪm/ *verb* (claims, claiming,
claimed /kleɪmd/)
1 to say that something is true: *He **claims**
that he did the work without help.*
2 to ask for something because it is yours: *If
nobody claims the camera you found, you can
have it.*

claim[2] /kleɪm/ *noun*
1 saying that something is true: *Nobody
believed his claim that he had found the money
on the street.*
2 something that you ask for because you
think you have a right to it: *The workers are
making a claim for better pay.*

clang /klæŋ/ *verb* (clangs, clanging, clanged /klæŋd/)
to make a loud sound, like metal when you hit it with something: *The iron gates **clanged** shut.*

clap /klæp/ *verb* (claps, clapping, clapped /klæpt/)
to hit your hands together to make a noise, usually to show that you like something: *At the end of the concert the audience clapped loudly.*

clarinet
/ˌklærə'net/ *noun*
a musical instrument made of wood with holes in it. You play it by blowing into it.

clarinet

clash¹ /klæʃ/ *noun*
(*plural* clashes)
1 a fight or a serious argument: *a clash between police and demonstrators*
2 a loud noise that you make by hitting two metal objects together

clash² /klæʃ/ *verb* (clashes, clashing, clashed /klæʃt/)
1 to fight or argue about something: *Police **clashed with** demonstrators outside the Town Hall.*
2 to happen at the same time: *The match **clashed with** my swimming lesson, so I couldn't watch it.*
3 If colours **clash**, they do not look nice together: *That red tie **clashes with** your shirt.*

clasp¹ /klɑːsp/ *verb* (clasps, clasping, clasped /klɑːspt/)
to hold somebody or something tightly
➲ SAME MEANING **grip**: *He clasped the child in his arms.*

clasp² /klɑːsp/ *noun*
a metal object that fastens or holds something together: *the clasp on a necklace*
➲ Look at the picture at **chain**.

class 0̶ₘ /klɑːs/ *noun* (*plural* classes)
1 a group of children or students who learn together: *There is a new girl in my class.* ◇ *The whole class passed the exam.*
2 the time when you learn something with a teacher ➲ SAME MEANING **lesson**: *Classes begin at nine o'clock.* ◇ *You mustn't eat **in class** (= during the lesson).*
3 a group of people or things that are the same in some way: *There are many different classes of animals.*
4 how good, comfortable, etc. something is: *It costs more to travel **first class**.*

classic /'klæsɪk/ *noun*
a book, film or piece of music that is so good that it is still popular many years after it was written or made: *'Alice in Wonderland' is a children's classic.*

classical /'klæsɪkl/ *adjective*
1 in a style that people have used for a long time because they think it is good
➲ SAME MEANING **traditional**: *classical dance* ➲ OPPOSITE **modern**
2 connected with ancient Greece or Rome: *classical Greek architecture*
3 **classical** music is serious and important: *I prefer pop music to classical music.*

classmate /'klɑːsmeɪt/ *noun*
a person who is in the same class as you at school or college

classroom /'klɑːsruːm/ *noun*
a room where you have lessons in a school or college ➲ Look at Picture Dictionary page **P11**.

clatter /'klætə(r)/ *verb* (clatters, clattering, clattered /'klætəd/)
to make the loud noise of hard things hitting each other: *The knives and forks clattered to the floor.*
▶ **clatter** *noun* (*no plural*): *the clatter of horses' hoofs*

clause /klɔːz/ *noun*
(*grammar*) a part of a sentence that has a verb in it: *The sentence 'After we had finished eating, we went out.' contains two clauses.*

claw /klɔː/ *noun*
one of the hard pointed parts on the feet of some animals and birds: *Cats have sharp claws.* ➲ Look at the pictures at **bird**, **cat** and **lion**.

clay /kleɪ/ *noun* (*no plural*)
a kind of heavy earth that becomes hard when it is dry: *clay pots*

clean¹ 0̶ₘ /kliːn/ *adjective* (cleaner, cleanest)
not dirty: *clean clothes* ◇ *Are your hands clean?* ➲ OPPOSITE **dirty**

clean² 0̶ₘ /kliːn/ *verb* (cleans, cleaning, cleaned /kliːnd/)
to remove the dirt or marks from something; to make something clean: *Sam helped his mother to clean the kitchen.* ◇ *Don't forget to **clean your teeth** before you go to bed.*
▶ **clean** *noun* (*no plural*): *The car needs a clean.*

🔎 **WORD BUILDING**
When you **clean** or tidy your home, you **do the housework** or **do the cleaning**. You **wash** something with water and

A
B
C
D
E
F
G
H
I
J
K
L
M
N
O
P
Q
R
S
T
U
V
W
X
Y
Z

often soap. You **dust** a surface with a **duster** (= a dry cloth). You **sweep** the floor with a **brush**.

cleaner /'kliːnə(r)/ *noun*
a person whose job is to clean people's houses or other buildings: *an office cleaner*

clear¹ 0—ㅠ /klɪə(r)/ *adjective* (clearer, clearest)
1 easy to see, hear or understand: *She spoke in a loud, clear voice.* ◇ *These instructions aren't very clear.* ◇ **It's clear that** *he's not happy.* ◇ *I* **made it clear** *to him that he was not welcome here any more.*
2 easy to see through: *clear glass*
3 free from marks: *a clear sky* (= without clouds) ◇ *clear skin* (= without spots)
4 with nothing blocking the way: *Most roads are now* **clear of** *snow.*

clear² 0—ㅠ /klɪə(r)/ *verb* (clears, clearing, cleared /klɪəd/)
1 to remove things from a place because you do not want or need them there: *They cleared the snow from the path.* ◇ *When you have finished your meal,* **clear the table** (= take away the dirty plates).
2 to become **clear**: *It rained in the morning, but in the afternoon the sky cleared.*
clear off (*informal*) to go away: *He got angry and told them to clear off.*
clear something out to make something empty and clean by removing things or throwing things away that you do not want
clear up, **clear something up** to make a place clean and tidy: *She helped me to clear up after the party.* ◇ *Clear up your own mess!*

clearly 0—ㅠ /'klɪəli/ *adverb*
1 in a way that is easy to see, hear or understand: *Please speak louder – I can't hear you very clearly.* ◇ *The notes explain very clearly what you have to do.*
2 without any doubt ◘ SAME MEANING **obviously**: *She is clearly very intelligent.*

clerk /klɑːk/ *noun*
1 a person whose job is to do written work or look after accounts in an office, a bank or shop
2 *American English for* SHOP ASSISTANT

clever 0—ㅠ /'klevə(r)/ *adjective* (cleverer, cleverest)
quick at learning and understanding things ◘ SAME MEANING **intelligent**: *a clever student* ◘ OPPOSITE **stupid**
▶ **cleverly** /'klevəli/ *adverb*: *The book is cleverly written.*

click¹ /klɪk/ *verb* (clicks, clicking, clicked /klɪkt/)
1 to make a short sharp sound: *The door clicked shut.*
2 (*computing*) to press one of the buttons on a computer mouse: *To open a file,* **click on the** *menu.* ◇ *Click the OK button to start.* ◘ Look at **double-click**.

click² /klɪk/ *noun*
1 a short sharp sound: *the click of a switch*
2 (*computing*) the act of pressing a button on a computer mouse: *You can do this with a click of the mouse.*

client /'klaɪənt/ *noun*
a person who pays another person, for example a lawyer, for help or advice

cliff

cliff /klɪf/ *noun*
the high steep side of a hill by the sea

climate 0—ㅠ /'klaɪmət/ *noun*
the normal weather conditions of a place: *Coffee will not grow in a cold climate.*

climax /'klaɪmæks/ *noun* (*plural* climaxes)
the most important part of something or of a period of time: *Winning an Oscar was the* **climax of** *his career.*

climb 0—ㅠ /klaɪm/ *verb* (climbs, climbing, climbed /klaɪmd/)

🔎 **PRONUNCIATION**
The word **climb** sounds like **time**.

1 to go up towards the top of something: *They climbed the mountain.* ◇ *The cat climbed to the top of the tree.*
2 to move to or from a place when it is not easy to do it: *The boys climbed through a hole in the fence.*
3 to move to a higher place: *The road climbs steeply.*
▶ **climb** *noun* (no plural): *It was a long climb to the top of the mountain.*

climber /'klaɪmə(r)/ *noun*
a person who climbs mountains or rocks as a sport: *a rock climber*

climbing /'klaɪmɪŋ/ *noun* (*no plural*)
the sport of climbing mountains or rocks: *They usually go climbing in their holidays.*

cling /klɪŋ/ *verb* (clings, clinging, clung /klʌŋ/, has clung)
to hold tightly or stick to somebody or something: *The girl was crying and clinging to her mother.* ◊ *His wet clothes clung to his body.*

clinic /'klɪnɪk/ *noun*
a place where you can go to get special help from a doctor

clip¹ /klɪp/ *noun*
a small piece of metal or plastic for holding things together or in place: *a hair clip* ◌ Look at **paper clip**.

clip² /klɪp/ *verb* (clips, clipping, clipped /klɪpt/)
to join something to another thing with a CLIP: *Clip the photo to the letter.* ◊ *Do your earrings clip on?*

cloak /kləʊk/ *noun*
a long loose coat that does not have separate sleeves

cloakroom /'kləʊkruːm/ *noun*
a room in a public building where you can leave your coat or bag

clock 0⃤ /klɒk/ *noun*
a thing that shows you what time it is: *an alarm clock*

> 🔎 **WORD BUILDING**
> A small clock that you wear on your wrist is called a **watch**.
> You say that a clock or watch is **fast** if it shows a time that is later than the real time. You say that it is **slow** if it shows a time that is earlier than the real time.

◌ Look at the picture at **watch**.

clockwise /'klɒkwaɪz/ *adjective, adverb*
in the direction that the hands of a clock move: *Turn the handle clockwise.* ◌ OPPOSITE **anticlockwise** (*British*), **counterclockwise** (*American*)

close¹ 0⃤ /kləʊz/ *verb* (closes, closing, closed /kləʊzd/)

> 🔎 **PRONUNCIATION**
> When the word **close** is a verb, it has a /z/ sound, as in **grows** or **nose**.
> When the word **close** is an adjective, it has an /s/ sound, as in **dose**.

1 to shut: *Please close the window.* ◊ *Close your eyes!* ◊ *The door closed quietly.*

2 to stop being open, so that people cannot go there: *What time does the bank close?*
◌ OPPOSITE **open**

close down, close something down
to stop all business at a shop, factory, etc.: *The shop closed down when the owner died.* ◊ *Health inspectors have closed the restaurant down.*

close² 0⃤ /kləʊs/ *adjective, adverb* (closer, closest)

1 near: *We live close to the station.* ◊ *The photographer asked us to stand closer together* (= with less space between us).

2 If people are **close**, they know each other well and like each other very much: *I'm very close to my sister.* ◊ *John and I are close friends.*

3 (used about a competition or race) only won by a small amount: *a close match*

4 careful: *Take a close look at this picture.*

▶ **closely** /'kləʊsli/ *adverb*: *Paul entered, closely followed by Mike.* ◊ *We watched her closely* (= carefully).

closed 0⃤ /kləʊzd/ *adjective*
not open ◌ SAME MEANING **shut**: *The shops are closed on Sundays.* ◊ *Keep your eyes closed.* ◌ OPPOSITE **open**

closet /'klɒzɪt/ *noun* (*American*)
a space in a wall with a door that reaches the ground, used for storing clothes, shoes, etc.: *a walk-in closet*

cloth 0⃤ /klɒθ/ *noun*

1 (*no plural*) material made of wool, cotton, etc. that you use for making clothes and other things

> 🔎 **SPEAKING**
> **Material** is the word we usually use: *Gloria bought some material to make a dress.*

2 a piece of **cloth** that you use for a special job: *Do you have a cloth I can use to wipe the floor with?* ◌ Look at **tablecloth**.

clothes 0⃤ /kləʊðz/ *noun* (*plural*)
things like trousers, shirts and coats that you wear to cover your body: *She was wearing new clothes.* ◊ *Take off those wet clothes.*

> 🔎 **SPEAKING**
> If you want to describe one thing that you wear, you call it **an item of clothing** or a **piece of clothing**: *A kilt is an item of clothing worn in Scotland.*

A B C D E F G H I J K L M N O P Q R S T U V W X Y Z

A

clothing 0→ /'kləʊðɪŋ/ *noun* (*no plural*)
clothes, especially a particular type of
clothes: *You will need waterproof clothing.*

B

C

> 🔍 **WHICH WORD?**
> **Clothing** is more formal than **clothes**.

D

cloud 0→ /klaʊd/ *noun*
1 a white or grey shape in the sky that is
made of small drops of water: *Look at those
dark clouds. It's going to rain.* ⊃ Look at
Picture Dictionary page **P16**.
2 a large collection of dust or smoke that
looks like a **cloud**: *clouds of smoke*

E

F

G

cloudy /'klaʊdi/ *adjective* (cloudier,
cloudiest)
If the weather is **cloudy**, the sky is full of
clouds: *a cloudy day*

H

I

clove /kləʊv/ *noun*
1 the small dried flower of a tree that grows
in hot countries, used as a spice in cooking.
Cloves look like small nails.
2 one of the small separate sections of
GARLIC (= a vegetable of the onion family
with a strong taste and smell, used in
cooking): *Crush two cloves of garlic.*

J

K

L

clown /klaʊn/ *noun*
a person who wears funny clothes and a big
red nose and does silly things to make
people laugh

M

N

club¹ 0→ /klʌb/ *noun*
1 a group of people who do something
together, or the place where they meet:
*I **belong to** the golf **club**.*
2 (*also* **nightclub**) a place where people,
especially young people, go and listen to
music, dance, etc.
3 a heavy stick with one thick end, used as a
weapon
4 a long thin stick that is used for hitting a
ball when playing GOLF (= a game played on
grass in which you hit a small ball into a
number of holes) ⊃ Look at the note at **bat**.
4 **clubs** (*plural*) the group of playing cards
(called a **suit**) that have the shape ♣ on
them: *the three of clubs* ⊃ Look at the picture
at **playing card**.

O

P

Q

R

S

T

U

V

club² /klʌb/ *verb* (clubs, clubbing,
clubbed /klʌbd/)
club together to give money so that a
group of people can buy something: *We all
clubbed together to buy him a leaving present.*
go clubbing (*British, informal*) to go out to
places where there is music and dancing
(called **nightclubs**): *They go clubbing every
Saturday night.*

W

X

Y

Z

clue /klu:/ *noun*
something that helps to find the answer to a

problem, or to know the truth: *The police are
looking for clues to help them find the missing
man.* ⊃ Look at the picture at **crossword
puzzle**.
not have a clue (*informal*) to know
nothing about something: *'What's his
name?' 'I haven't a clue.'*

clumsy /'klʌmzi/ *adjective* (clumsier,
clumsiest)
If you are **clumsy**, you often drop things or
do things badly because you do not move in
an easy or careful way: *I'm so clumsy! I've just
broken a glass.*
▶ **clumsily** /'klʌmzəli/ *adverb*: *He clumsily
knocked the cup off the table.*

clung *form of* CLING

clutch¹ /klʌtʃ/ *verb* (clutches, clutching,
clutched /klʌtʃt/)
to hold something tightly ⊃ SAME MEANING
grip: *The child clutched his mother's hand.*

clutch² /klʌtʃ/ *noun*
(in a vehicle) the part that your foot presses
while your hand moves the stick that
changes the engine speed

cm *short way of writing* CENTIMETRE

Co. /kəʊ/ *short for* COMPANY(1)

c/o /ˌsiː ˈəʊ/ *abbreviation*
You use **c/o** (short for **care of**) when you are
writing to somebody who is staying at
another person's house: *Ms S Garcia, c/o Mr
Michael Nolan*

coach¹ /kəʊtʃ/ *noun* (plural coaches)
1 a person who trains a person or team in a
sport: *a baseball coach*
2 (*British*) a comfortable bus for taking
people on long journeys: *It's cheaper to travel
by coach than by train.*
3 (*British*) one of the parts of a train where
people sit ⊃ SAME MEANING **carriage**
4 a vehicle with four wheels that is pulled by
horses ⊃ SAME MEANING **carriage**: *The
Queen travelled to the wedding in the royal
coach.*

coach² /kəʊtʃ/ *verb* (coaches, coaching,
coached /kəʊtʃt/)
to teach somebody to play a sport or do
something better: *She is coaching the team
for the Olympics.*

coal 0→ /kəʊl/ *noun* (*no plural*)
a hard black substance that comes from
under the ground and gives out heat when
you burn it: *Put some more coal on the fire.*
⊃ Look at the picture at **fireplace**.

coarse /kɔːs/ *adjective* (coarser, coarsest)
made of thick pieces so that it is not smooth:
coarse sand ◇ coarse material
⊃ OPPOSITE **fine**

coast 0̄ /kəʊst/ *noun*
the part of the land that is next to the sea:
Their house is near the coast. ◇ *The city is on the west coast of France.*

coastguard /ˈkəʊstɡɑːd/ *noun*
a person whose job is to watch the sea and ships and help people who are in danger

coastline /ˈkəʊstlaɪn/ *noun*
the edge of the land next to the sea: *a rocky coastline*

coat¹ 0̄ /kəʊt/ *noun*
1 a piece of clothing that you wear over your other clothes when you are outside: *Put your coat on – it's cold today.* ➔ Look at Picture Dictionary page **P5**.
2 the hair or fur that covers an animal: *a dog with a smooth coat* ➔ Look at the picture at **lion**.

coat² /kəʊt/ *verb* (coats, coating, coated)
to put a thin covering of something over another thing: *Their shoes were coated with mud.*

coat hanger

coat hanger /ˈkəʊt hæŋə(r)/ (*also* hanger) *noun*
a curved piece of wood, plastic or wire, with a hook at the top, that you hang clothes on

cobweb /ˈkɒbweb/ *noun*
a net that a spider makes to catch insects

cock /kɒk/ *noun* (*British*) (*American* rooster)
an adult male chicken ➔ Look at the note at **chicken**.

cockerel /ˈkɒkərəl/ *noun*
a young male chicken

cockpit /ˈkɒkpɪt/ *noun*
the part of a plane where the pilot sits

cockroach /ˈkɒkrəʊtʃ/ *noun* (*plural* cockroaches)
a large brown insect that you find in houses, especially dirty ones

cocktail /ˈkɒkteɪl/ *noun*
a drink usually made of alcohol and fruit juices mixed together. It can also be made without alcohol: *a cocktail bar*

cocoa /ˈkəʊkəʊ/ *noun* (*no plural*)
1 a dark brown powder made from the seeds (called cocoa beans) of a tree that

grows in hot countries. **Cocoa** is used in making chocolate.
2 a drink of hot milk mixed with this powder: *a cup of cocoa*

coconut /ˈkəʊkənʌt/ *noun*
a large fruit that grows on trees in hot countries. **Coconuts** are brown and hard on the outside, and they have sweet white food and liquid inside. ➔ Look at Picture Dictionary page **P8**.

cod /kɒd/ *noun* (*plural* cod)
a large fish that lives in the sea and that you can eat

code /kəʊd/ *noun*
1 a way of writing secret messages, using letters, numbers or special signs: *The list of names was written in code.*
2 a group of numbers or letters that helps you find something: *What's the code* (= the telephone number) *for Paris?*
3 a set of rules for a group of people: *the Highway Code* (= the rules for driving on the roads)

coffee 0̄ /ˈkɒfi/ *noun*
1 (*no plural*) a brown powder made from the seeds (called coffee beans) of a tree that grows in hot countries. You use it for making a drink.
2 (*no plural*) a drink made by adding hot water to this powder: *Would you like coffee or tea?* ◇ *a cup of coffee* ➔ Look at Picture Dictionary page **P6**.
3 (*plural* coffees) a cup of this drink: *Two coffees, please.*

🔎 **WORD BUILDING**
White coffee has milk in it and **black** coffee has no milk.

coffee table /ˈkɒfi teɪbl/ *noun*
a small low table that you put magazines, cups or other similar things on ➔ Look at Picture Dictionary page **P10**.

coffin /ˈkɒfɪn/ *noun*
a box that a dead person's body is put in

coil¹ /kɔɪl/ *verb* (coils, coiling, coiled /kɔɪld/)
to make something into a lot of circles that are joined together: *The snake coiled itself round a branch.*

coil² /kɔɪl/ *noun*
a long piece of rope or wire that goes round in circles: *a coil of rope* ➔ Look at the picture at **rope**.

coin 0̄ /kɔɪn/ *noun*
a piece of money made of metal: *a pound coin* ➔ Look at the picture and the note at **money**.

A B **C** D E F G H I J K L M N O P Q R S T U V W X Y Z

coincidence /kəʊˈɪnsɪdəns/ *noun*
two or more similar things happening at the same time or in the same place by chance, in a surprising way: *What a coincidence! I was thinking about you when you phoned!*

coincidental /kəʊˌɪnsɪˈdentl/ *adjective*
happening by chance; not planned

cold[1] 0🔊 /kəʊld/ *adjective* (colder, coldest)
1 not hot or warm; with a low temperature: *Put your coat on – it's cold outside.* ◇ *I'm cold. Will you put the heater on?* ◇ *hot and cold water* ➔ OPPOSITE **hot**

> 🔎 **WHICH WORD?**
>
> **Cool, cold** or **freezing**?
> **Cool** means quite cold, especially in a pleasant way: *It's hot outside but it's nice and cool in here.*
> **Freezing** means extremely cold, often in an unpleasant way: *It's absolutely freezing outside.*

2 not friendly or kind: *She gave him a cold, hard look.*
▶ **coldly** /ˈkəʊldli/ *adverb*: *She looked at me coldly.*

cold[2] 0🔊 /kəʊld/ *noun*
1 (*no plural*) cold weather: *Don't go out in the cold.*
2 (*plural* colds) a common illness of the nose and throat. When you have a **cold**, you often cannot breathe through your nose and your throat hurts: *I've got a cold.* ◇ *Come in out of the rain, or you'll catch a cold.*

collapse /kəˈlæps/ *verb* (collapses, collapsing, collapsed /kəˈlæpst/)
to fall down suddenly: *The building collapsed in the earthquake.* ◇ *She collapsed in the street and was rushed to hospital.*
▶ **collapse** *noun*: *the collapse of the bridge*

collar /ˈkɒlə(r)/ *noun*
1 the part of your clothes that goes round your neck ➔ Look at the pictures at **lace** and **shirt**.
2 a band that you put round the neck of a dog or cat

colleague /ˈkɒliːɡ/ *noun*
a person who works with you

collect 0🔊 /kəˈlekt/ *verb* (collect, collecting, collected)
1 to take things from different people or places and put them together: *The waiter collected the dirty glasses.*
2 to bring together things that are the same in some way, to study or enjoy them: *My son collects stamps.*
3 (*British*) to go and bring somebody or

something from a place: *She collects her children from school at 3.30.*

collection 0🔊 /kəˈlekʃn/ *noun*
1 a group of similar things that somebody has brought together: *The Tate Gallery has a large collection of modern paintings.* ◇ *a CD collection*
2 taking something from a place or from people: *rubbish collections*

collector /kəˈlektə(r)/ *noun*
a person who collects things as a hobby or as a job: *a stamp collector* ◇ *a ticket collector at a railway station*

college 0🔊 /ˈkɒlɪdʒ/ *noun*
1 a place where you can go to study after you have left school: *She's going to college next year.* ◇ *My brother is at college.*
2 a part of a university: *Kings College, London* ➔ Look at the note at **school**.

collide /kəˈlaɪd/ *verb* (collides, colliding, collided)
to move fast towards somebody or something and hit them hard
➔ SAME MEANING **crash**: *The two trucks collided.* ◇ *He ran along the corridor and collided with his teacher.*

collision /kəˈlɪʒn/ *noun*
when things or people **collide**
➔ SAME MEANING **crash**: *The driver of the car was killed in the collision.*

colon /ˈkəʊlən/ *noun*
the mark (:) that you use in writing, for example before a list

colonel /ˈkɜːnl/ *noun*
an officer of a high level in the army

colony /ˈkɒləni/ *noun* (*plural* colonies)
a country or an area that is ruled by another country: *Kenya was once a British colony.*

color, colored, colorful *American English for* COLOUR, COLOURED, COLOURFUL

colour[1] 0🔊 (*British*) (*American* color) /ˈkʌlə(r)/ *noun*
Red, blue, yellow and green are all **colours**: *'What colour are your new shoes?' 'Black.'* ◇ *The leaves change colour in autumn.*

> 🔎 **WORD BUILDING**
>
> Some words that we use to talk about colour are **light, pale, dark, deep** and **bright**.

colour[2] (*British*) (*American* color) /ˈkʌlə(r)/ *verb* (colours, colouring, coloured /ˈkʌləd/)
to put colour on something, for example by painting it: *The children coloured their pictures with crayons.*

coloured 0⃞ (*British*) (*American* colored) /'kʌləd/ *adjective*

having a particular colour or different colours: *She was wearing a brightly coloured jumper.* ◇ *coloured paper*

colourful (*British*) (*American* colorful) /'kʌləfl/ *adjective*

with a lot of bright colours: *The garden is very colourful in summer.*

column 0⃞ /'kɒləm/ *noun*

1 a tall solid piece of stone that supports part of a building

2 a long thin section of writing on one side or part of a page: *Each page of this dictionary has two columns.*

comb¹ /kəʊm/ *noun*

comb

a flat piece of metal or plastic with thin parts like teeth. You use it to make your hair tidy.

comb² /kəʊm/ *verb* (combs, combing, combed /kəʊmd/)

to make your hair tidy with a COMB: *Have you combed your hair?*

combination 0⃞ /ˌkɒmbɪ'neɪʃn/ *noun*

two or more things joined together
⊃ SAME MEANING **mixture**: *The building is a combination of new and old styles.*

combine 0⃞ /kəm'baɪn/ *verb* (combined, combining, combined /kəm'baɪnd/)

to join; to mix two or more things together: *The two schools combined and moved to a larger building.*

come 0⃞ /kʌm/ *verb* (comes, coming, came /keɪm/, has come)

1 to move towards the person who is speaking or the place that you are talking about: *Come here, please.* ◇ *The dog came when I called him.* ◇ *Here comes Colin* (= Colin is coming). ◇ *I'm sorry, but I can't come to your party.*

2 to arrive at or reach a place: *If you go along that road, you will come to the river.* ◇ *A letter came for you this morning.*

3 to go somewhere with the person who is speaking: *I'm going to a party tonight. Do you want to come with me?*

4 to be in a particular position: *June comes after May.*

come about to happen: *How did this situation come about?*

come across something to find something when you are not looking for it: *I came across these old photos yesterday.*

come apart to break into pieces: *This old coat is coming apart.*

come back to return: *What time will you be coming back?*

come down to fall or become lower: *The price of oil is coming down.*

come from somewhere or **something**
1 The place that you **come from** is where you were born or where you live: *I come from Japan.* ◇ *Where do you come from?*
2 to be made from something or produced somewhere: *Wool comes from sheep.*

come in to enter a place: *Come in and sit down.*

come off something to become removed from something: *The handle has come off this cup.*

come on!, come along! words that you use for telling somebody to hurry or to try harder: *Come on! We'll be late!*

come out to appear: *The rain stopped and the sun came out.* ◇ *His first novel came out in 2004.*

come round to visit a person at their house not very far away: *Come round for lunch on Saturday.*

how come ...? (*informal*) why or how...?: *How come you're here so early?*

to come in the future: *You'll regret it in years to come.*

comedian /kə'miːdiən/ *noun*
a person whose job is to make people laugh

comedy /'kɒmədi/ *noun* (*plural* comedies)
a funny play or film

comet /'kɒmɪt/ *noun*
a thing in the sky that moves around the sun. A **comet** looks like a bright star with a tail.

comfort¹ /'kʌmfət/ *noun*
1 (*no plural*) having everything your body needs; being without pain or problems: *They have enough money to live in comfort.*
2 (*plural* comforts) a person or thing that helps you or makes life better: *Her children were a comfort to her when she was ill.*

comfort² /'kʌmfət/ *verb* (comforts, comforting, comforted)
to make somebody feel less unhappy or worried: *A mother was comforting her crying child.*

comfortable 0⃞ /'kʌmftəbl/ *adjective*
1 nice to sit in, to be in, or to wear: *This is a very comfortable bed.* ◇ *comfortable shoes*
2 physically relaxed; with no pain or worry: *Sit down and make yourself comfortable.*
⊃ OPPOSITE **uncomfortable**

A B C D E F G H I J K L M N O P Q R S T U V W X Y Z

A

▶ **comfortably** /'kʌmftəbli/ *adverb*: *If you're all sitting comfortably, then I'll begin.*

B

comic[1] /'kɒmɪk/ (*also* comical /'kɒmɪkl/) *adjective*
funny: *a comic scene in a play*

comic[2] /'kɒmɪk/ *noun*
a magazine for children, with pictures that tell a story

D

comma /'kɒmə/ *noun* (*plural* commas)
a mark (,) that you use in writing to separate parts of a sentence or things in a list

E

F

command[1] 0—ᵣ /kə'mɑːnd/ *noun*
1 (*plural* commands) words that tell you that you must do something
ᕕ SAME MEANING **order**: *The soldiers must obey their general's commands.*
2 (*plural* commands) an instruction to a computer to do something: *Use the Find command to look for a word in the file.*
3 (*no plural*) the power to tell people what to do ᕕ SAME MEANING **control**: *Who is in command of this ship?*

G

H

I

J

K

command[2] /kə'mɑːnd/ *verb* (commands, commanding, commanded)
to tell somebody that they must do something ᕕ SAME MEANING **order**: *He commanded us to leave immediately.*

L

M

comment[1] 0—ᵣ /'kɒment/ *noun*
something that you say that shows what you think about something: *She made some interesting comments about the film.*

N

O

comment[2] 0—ᵣ /'kɒment/ *verb*
(comments, commenting, commented)
to say what you think about something: *A lot of people at school commented on my new watch.*

P

Q

commentary /'kɒməntri/ *noun* (*plural* commentaries)
when somebody describes an event while it is happening, especially on the radio or television: *a sports commentary*

R

S

commentator /'kɒmənteɪtə(r)/ *noun*
a person who gives a COMMENTARY on the radio or television

T

U

commerce /'kɒmɜːs/ *noun* (*no plural*)
the business of buying and selling things

V

commercial[1] /kə'mɜːʃl/ *adjective*
connected with buying and selling things: *commercial law*

W

X

commercial[2] /kə'mɜːʃl/ *noun*
an advertisement on the television or radio

Y

commit /kə'mɪt/ *verb* (commits, committing, committed)
to do something bad: *This man has committed a very serious crime.*

Z

commitment /kə'mɪtmənt/ *noun*
1 (*plural* commitments) a promise to do something: *When I make a commitment, I always stick to it.*
2 (*no plural*) being prepared to give a lot of your time and attention to something: *I admire his commitment to his work.*

committed /kə'mɪtɪd/ *adjective*
prepared to give a lot of your time and attention to something: *We are committed to raising standards in schools.*

committee /kə'mɪti/ *noun*

🔍 SPELLING
Remember! You spell **committee** with **MM**, **TT** and **EE**.

a group of people that other people choose to discuss or decide something: *She's on the planning committee.*

common[1] 0—ᵣ /'kɒmən/ *adjective*
(commoner, commonest)
1 happening often or found in many places: *Jackson is a common English name.*
ᕕ OPPOSITE **rare**
2 shared by two or more people or by everybody in a group: *They share a common interest in photography.*

common[2] /'kɒmən/ *noun*
a piece of land that everybody can use: *We went for a walk on the common.*
have something in common to be like somebody in a certain way, or to have the same interests as somebody: *Paul and I are good friends. We have a lot in common.*

common sense /ˌkɒmən 'sens/ *noun* (*no plural*)
the ability to think about things and do the right thing and not make stupid mistakes: *Jane's got no common sense. She lay in the sun all day and got sunburnt.*

communicate 0—ᵣ /kə'mjuːnɪkeɪt/ *verb* (communicates, communicating, communicated)
to share and exchange information, ideas or feelings with somebody: *Parents often find it difficult to communicate with their children.*

communication 0—ᵣ /kəˌmjuːnɪ'keɪʃn/ *noun*
1 (*no plural*) sharing or exchanging information, feelings or ideas with somebody: *Communication is difficult when two people don't speak the same language.*
2 communications (*plural*) ways of sending or receiving information, especially telephones, radio, computers, etc.: *a communications satellite*

community 0🔑 /kə'mjuːnəti/ *noun*
(*plural* communities)
1 all the people who live in a place; the place where they live: *Life in a small fishing community is very different from life in a big city.*
2 a group of people who join together, for example because they have the same interests or religion: *the Asian community in Britain*

commute /kə'mjuːt/ *verb* (commutes, commuting, commuted)
to travel a long way from home to work every day: *She lives in the country and commutes to London.*
▶ **commuter** /kə'mjuːtə(r)/ *noun* a person who **commutes**

compact disc /ˌkɒmpækt 'dɪsk/ *noun*
= CD

companion /kəm'pæniən/ *noun*
a person who travels with you or spends time with you

company 0🔑 /'kʌmpəni/ *noun*
1 (*plural* companies) a group of people who work together to make or sell things: *an advertising company*

> 🖊 **WRITING**
>
> In names, **company** is written with a capital letter. The abbreviation is **Co.**: *the Walt Disney Company* ◇ *Milton and Co.*

2 (*no plural*) being with a person or people: *I always enjoy Mark's company*
keep somebody company to be or go with somebody: *Please stay and keep me company for a while.*

comparable /'kɒmpərəbl/ *adjective*
similar in size or quality to something else: *Salaries here are comparable to salaries paid by other companies.*

comparative /kəm'pærətɪv/ *noun*
(*grammar*) the form of an adjective or adverb that shows more of something: *The comparative of 'bad' is 'worse'.*
▶ **comparative** *adjective*: *'Longer' is the comparative form of 'long'.* ➲ Look at **superlative**.

compare 0🔑 /kəm'peə(r)/ *verb*
(compares, comparing, compared /kəm'peəd/)
to think about or look at people or things together so that you can see how they are different: *Compared to the place where I grew up, this town is exciting.* ◇ *Steve is quite tall, compared with his friends.* ◇ *Compare your answers with your neighbour's.*

comparison 0🔑 /kəm'pærɪsn/ *noun*
looking at or understanding how things are different or the same: *It's hard to make comparisons between athletes from different sports.*
by or **in comparison with somebody** or **something** when you compare two or more people or things: *In comparison with many other people, they're quite rich.*

compartment /kəm'pɑːtmənt/ *noun*
1 one of the sections which a part of a train (called a **carriage**) is divided into: *He found an empty first-class compartment.*
2 a separate part inside a box, bag or other container: *The suitcase had a secret compartment at the back.*

compasses

north
north-west   north-east
west   east
south-west   south   south-east

compass   **compass or a pair of compasses**

compass /'kʌmpəs/ *noun* (*plural* compasses)
1 a thing for finding direction, with a needle that always points north: *You need a map and a compass.*
2 (*also* compasses) (*plural*) an instrument with two long thin parts joined together at the top that is used for drawing circles: *Use a pair of compasses.*

compete /kəm'piːt/ *verb* (competes, competing, competed)
to try to win a race or a competition: *The world's best athletes compete in the Olympic Games.*

competition 0🔑 /ˌkɒmpə'tɪʃn/ *noun*
1 (*plural* competitions) a game or test that people try to win: *I entered the painting competition and won first prize.*
2 (*no plural*) trying to win or be better than somebody else: *We were in competition with a team from another school.*

competitive /kəm'petətɪv/ *adjective*
1 in which people or organizations COMPETE against each other: *competitive sports*
2 wanting to win or be better than other people: *She's very competitive.*

competitor /kəm'petɪtə(r)/ *noun*
a person who is trying to win a competition

A
B
C
D
E
F
G
H
I
J
K
L
M
N
O
P
Q
R
S
T
U
V
W
X
Y
Z

complain 0̄─┓ /kəmˈpleɪn/ *verb*
(complains, complaining, complained /kəmˈpleɪnd/)
to say that you do not like something or that you are unhappy about something: *She is always complaining about the weather.* ◇ *He complained to the waiter that his soup was cold.*

complaint 0̄─┓ /kəmˈpleɪnt/ *noun*
when you say that you do not like something: *We made a complaint to the hotel manager about the dirty rooms.*

complete¹ 0̄─┓ /kəmˈpliːt/ *adjective*
1 in every way ⟹ SAME MEANING **total**: *Their visit was a complete surprise.*
2 with none of its parts missing ⟹ SAME MEANING **whole**: *I've got a complete set of Shakespeare's plays.*
⟹ OPPOSITE **incomplete**
3 finished: *The work is complete.*
⟹ OPPOSITE **incomplete**

complete² 0̄─┓ /kəmˈpliːt/ *verb*
(completes, completing, completed)
to finish doing or making something: *She was at university for two years but she did not complete her studies.* ◇ *When will the new building be completed?*

completely 0̄─┓ /kəmˈpliːtli/ *adverb*
in every way ⟹ SAME MEANING **totally**: *The money has completely disappeared.* ◇ *I completely forgot that it was your birthday!*

complex¹ /ˈkɒmpleks/ *adjective*
difficult to understand because it has a lot of different parts ⟹ SAME MEANING **complicated**: *a complex problem*
⟹ OPPOSITE **simple**

complex² /ˈkɒmpleks/ *noun* (*plural* complexes)
a group of buildings: *a sports complex*

complicated 0̄─┓ /ˈkɒmplɪkeɪtɪd/ *adjective*
difficult to understand because it has a lot of different parts: *I can't explain how to play the game. It's too complicated.*
⟹ OPPOSITE **simple**

complication /ˌkɒmplɪˈkeɪʃn/ *noun*
something that makes a situation more difficult

compliment /ˈkɒmplɪmənt/ *noun*
something nice that you say about somebody: *People often pay her compliments on her piano playing.*
▶ **compliment** /ˈkɒmplɪment/ *verb*
(compliments, complimenting, complimented): *They complimented Frank on his cooking.*

compose /kəmˈpəʊz/ *verb* (composes, composing, composed /kəmˈpəʊzd/)
to write something, especially music: *Verdi composed many operas.*
be composed of something to be made or formed from different parts or people: *Water is composed of oxygen and hydrogen.*

composer /kəmˈpəʊzə(r)/ *noun*
a person who writes music: *My favourite composer is Mozart.*

composition /ˌkɒmpəˈzɪʃn/ *noun*
a piece of writing or music

compound /ˈkɒmpaʊnd/ *noun*
1 something that is made of two or more parts: *Salt is a chemical compound.*
2 (*grammar*) a word that is made from two or more other words: *'Hairdryer' and 'car park' are compounds.*

comprehension /ˌkɒmprɪˈhenʃn/ *noun*
(*no plural*)
understanding something that you hear or read: *a test in listening comprehension*

comprehensive school
/ˌkɒmprɪˈhensɪv skuːl/ (*also* comprehensive) *noun*
(in Britain) a school for pupils of all levels of ability between the ages of 11 and 18

compromise /ˈkɒmprəmaɪz/ *noun*
an agreement between people when each person gets part, but not all, of what they wanted: *After long talks, the workers and management reached a compromise.*

compulsory /kəmˈpʌlsəri/ *adjective*
If something is **compulsory**, you must do it: *School is compulsory for all children between the ages of five and sixteen.*
⟹ OPPOSITE **optional**

computer 0̄─┓ /kəmˈpjuːtə(r)/ *noun*
a machine that can store and find information, calculate amounts and control other machines: *All the work is done by computer.* ◇ *He spends a lot of time on the computer, sending emails.* ◇ *a computer program* (= information that tells a computer what to do) ◇ *They play computer games every evening.* ⟹ Look at Picture Dictionary page **P11**.

conceal /kənˈsiːl/ *verb* (conceals, concealing, concealed /kənˈsiːld/) (*formal*)
to hide something: *They concealed the bomb in a suitcase.*

🔊 SPEAKING
Hide is the word that we usually use.

conceited /kənˈsiːtɪd/ *adjective*
too proud of yourself and what you can do

concentrate 0➡ /'kɒnsntreɪt/ *verb*
(concentrates, concentrating, concentrated)
to give all your attention to something: *Stop looking out of the window and **concentrate on** your work! ◇ Be quiet and let him concentrate.*

concentration /,kɒnsn'treɪʃn/ *noun* (*no plural*)
the ability to give all your attention to something: *You need total concentration for this type of work.*

concern¹ /kən'sɜːn/ *verb* (concerns, concerning, concerned /kən'sɜːnd/)
1 to be important or interesting to somebody ➲ SAME MEANING **affect**: *Please pay attention because this information concerns all of you.*
2 to be about something: *The story concerns the prince's efforts to rescue Pamina.*
3 to worry somebody: *It concerns me that she is always late.*

concern² /kən'sɜːn/ *noun*
1 (*no plural*) worry: *There is a lot of concern about this problem.*
2 (*plural* concerns) something that is important or interesting to somebody: *Her problems are not my concern.*

concerned /kən'sɜːnd/ *adjective*
worried about something: *They are very **concerned about** their son's health.*

concerning /kən'sɜːnɪŋ/ *preposition* (*formal*)
about something: *He asked several questions concerning the future of the company.*

concert 0➡ /'kɒnsət/ *noun*
a public performance of music: *a rock concert*

conclude /kən'kluːd/ *verb* (concludes, concluding, concluded)
1 to decide something, after you have studied or thought about it: *The report concluded that the working conditions were unsafe. ◇ May I conclude by thanking our guest speaker.*
2 (*formal*) to end or make something end: *The Prince concluded his tour with a visit to a local hospital.*

conclusion 0➡ /kən'kluːʒn/ *noun*
what you believe or decide after thinking carefully about something: *We came to the conclusion that you were right all along.*

concrete /'kɒŋkriːt/ *noun* (*no plural*)
a hard grey material used for building things: *a concrete wall*

condemn /kən'dem/ *verb* (condemns, condemning, condemned /kən'demd/)
1 to say strongly that somebody or

something is very bad or wrong: *Many people condemned the government's decision.*
2 to say that somebody must be punished in a certain way ➲ SAME MEANING **sentence**: *The murderer was condemned to death.*

condition 0➡ /kən'dɪʃn/ *noun*
1 (*no plural*) the state that somebody or something is in: *The car was cheap and in good condition, so I bought it.*
2 conditions (*plural*) the situation in which people live, work or do things: *The prisoners lived in terrible conditions.*
3 (*plural* conditions) something that must happen before another thing can happen: *One of the conditions of the job is that you agree to work on Saturdays.*
on condition that... only if: *You can go to the party on condition that you come home before midnight.*

conduct¹ /kən'dʌkt/ *verb* (conducts, conducting, conducted)
1 to organize or do an activity: *They are going to conduct an experiment.*
2 to stand in front of a group of musicians and control what they do: *The orchestra was conducted by Peter Jones.*
3 to show somebody where to go: *She conducted us on a tour of the museum.*

conduct² /'kɒndʌkt/ *noun* (*no plural*) (*formal*)
the way somebody behaves
➲ SAME MEANING **behaviour**

conductor /kən'dʌktə(r)/ *noun*
1 a person who stands in front of a group of musicians and controls what they do
2 (*British*) a person who sells or checks people's tickets on a bus or train

cones

| cone (*British* also **fir cone**) | ice cream cone | traffic cone |

cone /kəʊn/ *noun*
1 a shape with one flat round end and one pointed end
2 the hard fruit of some trees (called pine and fir): *a pine cone*

conference /'kɒnfərəns/ *noun*
a large meeting, where many people with the same job or interests come together to

A discuss their views: *an international conference on* climate change

confess /kən'fes/ *verb* (confesses, confessing, confessed /kən'fest/)
to say that you have done something wrong ⊃ SAME MEANING **admit**: *She confessed that she had stolen the money.* ◇ *He confessed to the crime.* ⊃ OPPOSITE **deny**

confession /kən'feʃn/ *noun*
when you say that you have done something wrong: *She made a full confession to the police.*

confidence 0ᴍ /'kɒnfɪdəns/ *noun* (no plural)
the feeling that you can do something well: *She answered the questions with confidence.* ◇ *I'm sure you'll pass the exam. I have great confidence in you.*
in confidence If somebody tells you something **in confidence**, it is a secret.

confident 0ᴍ /'kɒnfɪdənt/ *adjective*
sure that you can do something well, or that something will happen: *I'm confident that our team will win.*

confidential /ˌkɒnfɪ'denʃl/ *adjective*
If somebody tells you something that is **confidential**, you should keep it a secret and not tell other people: *confidential information*

confirm /kən'fɜːm/ *verb* (confirms, confirming, confirmed /kən'fɜːmd/)
to say that something is true or that something will happen: *Please write and confirm the date of your arrival.*

confirmation /ˌkɒnfə'meɪʃn/ *noun* (no plural)
saying that something is true or will definitely happen

conflict¹ /'kɒnflɪkt/ *noun*
a fight or an argument

conflict² /kən'flɪkt/ *verb*
to disagree or be different: *These results conflict with earlier research results.*

confuse 0ᴍ /kən'fjuːz/ *verb* (confuses, confusing, confused /kən'fjuːzd/)
1 to mix somebody's ideas, so that they cannot think clearly or understand: *They confused me by asking so many questions.*
2 to think that one thing or person is another thing or person: *I often confuse Lee with his brother. They look so similar.*
▶ **confusing** /kən'fjuːzɪŋ/ *adjective*
difficult to understand: *This map is very confusing.*

confused 0ᴍ /kən'fjuːzd/ *adjective*
not able to think clearly: *The waiter got*

confused and brought everybody the wrong drink!

confusion /kən'fjuːʒn/ *noun* (no plural)
not being able to think clearly or understand something: *He looked at me in confusion when I asked him a question.*

congratulate /kən'grætʃuleɪt/ *verb* (congratulates, congratulating, congratulated)
to tell somebody that you are pleased about something that they have done: *I congratulated Sue on passing her exam.*

congratulations /kənˌgrætʃu'leɪʃnz/ *noun* (plural)
something you say to somebody when you are pleased about something they have done: *Congratulations on your new job!*

congress /'kɒŋgres/ *noun*
1 (plural **congresses**) a large formal meeting of many people to talk about important things
2 Congress (no plural) a group of people who make the laws in some countries, for example in the US

> 🔎 CULTURE
> The US **Congress** is made up of two groups; the **Senate** and the **House of Representatives**.

conjunction /kən'dʒʌŋkʃn/ *noun*
(grammar) a word that joins other words or parts of a sentence: *'And', 'or' and 'but' are conjunctions.*

conjuror /'kʌndʒərə(r)/ *noun*
a person who does clever tricks that seem to be magic ⊃ SAME MEANING **magician**: *The conjuror pulled a rabbit out of a hat.*

connect 0ᴍ /kə'nekt/ *verb* (connects, connecting, connected)
to join one thing to another thing: *This wire connects the DVD player to the television.* ◇ *The two cities are connected by a motorway.*

connection 0ᴍ /kə'nekʃn/ *noun*
1 the way that one thing is joined or related to another: *We had a bad connection on the phone so I couldn't hear him very well.* ◇ *Is there a connection between violence on TV and crime?*
2 a train, plane or bus that leaves a place soon after another arrives, so that people can change from one to the other: *The train was late, so I missed my connection.*
in connection with something (formal) about something: *A man has been arrested in connection with the murder of the teenager.*

A B C D E F G H I J K L M N O P Q R S T U V W X Y Z

conscience /'kɒnʃəns/ *noun*
the feeling inside you about what is right
and wrong: *He has a **guilty conscience*** (= he
feels that he has done something wrong).

conscientious /ˌkɒnʃi'enʃəs/ *adjective*
careful to do things correctly and well: *She's
a very conscientious student.*

conscious 0🔑 /'kɒnʃəs/ *adjective*
1 If you are **conscious** of something, you
know about it. ➲ SAME MEANING **aware**:
*I was **conscious that** somebody was
watching me.*
2 awake and able to see, hear, feel and
think: *The patient was conscious during the
operation.* ➲ OPPOSITE **unconscious**

consciousness /'kɒnʃəsnəs/ *noun* (no
plural)
the state of being able to see, hear, feel and
think: *As she fell, she hit her head and **lost
consciousness**.*

consent¹ /kən'sent/ *noun* (no plural)
agreeing to let somebody do something
➲ SAME MEANING **permission**: *Her parents
gave their **consent to** the marriage.*

consent² /kən'sent/ *verb* (consent,
consenting, consented) (*formal*)
to agree to something: *He finally **consented
to** his daughter's marriage.*

consequence /'kɒnsɪkwəns/ *noun*
a result of something that has happened:
Their actions had terrible consequences. ◇ *I've
just bought a car and, **as a consequence**, I've
got no money.*

consequently /'kɒnsɪkwəntli/ *adverb*
because of that ➲ SAME MEANING
therefore: *He didn't do any work, and
consequently failed the exam.*

conservation /ˌkɒnsə'veɪʃn/ *noun* (no
plural)
taking good care of the world and its forests,
lakes, plants and animals: *the **conservation** of
the rainforests*

conservative /kən'sɜːvətɪv/ *adjective*
1 not liking change or new ideas
➲ SAME MEANING **traditional**: *the
conservative opinions of his parents*
2 **Conservative** (*politics*) belonging to or
connected with THE CONSERVATIVE PARTY

the Conservative Party /ðə
kən'sɜːvətɪv pɑːti/ *noun* (*also* **the Tory
Party**)
(*politics*) one of the important political
parties in Britain ➲ Look at **the Labour
Party** and **the Liberal Democrats**.

consider 0🔑 /kən'sɪdə(r)/ *verb*
(considers, considering, considered
/kən'sɪdəd/)
1 to think carefully about something: *I'm
considering applying for another job.* ◇ *We
must consider what to do next.*
2 to think that something is true: *I consider
her to be a good teacher.*
3 to think about the feelings of other people
when you do something: *I can't move to
Australia! I have to consider my family.*

considerable /kən'sɪdərəbl/ *adjective*
(*formal*)
great or large: *The car cost a considerable
amount of money.*
▶ **considerably** /kən'sɪdərəbli/ *adverb*:
My flat is considerably smaller than yours.

considerate /kən'sɪdərət/ *adjective*
A person who is **considerate** is kind, and
thinks and cares about other people: *Please
be more considerate and don't play loud music
late at night.* ➲ OPPOSITE **inconsiderate**

consideration /kənˌsɪdə'reɪʃn/ *noun* (no
plural)
1 (*formal*) thinking carefully about
something ➲ SAME MEANING **thought**: *After
a lot of consideration, I decided not to accept
the job.*
2 being kind, and caring about other
people's feelings: *He shows no **consideration
for** anybody else.*
take something into consideration
to think carefully about something when
you are deciding: *We must take the cost into
consideration when planning our holiday.*

consist 0🔑 /kən'sɪst/ *verb* (consists,
consisting, consisted)
consist of something to be made from
two or more things; to have things as parts:
Jam consists of fruit and sugar.

consistent /kən'sɪstənt/ *adjective*
always the same: *His work isn't very
consistent.* ➲ OPPOSITE **inconsistent**
▶ **consistently** /kən'sɪstəntli/ *adverb*: *We
must try to keep a consistently high standard.*

console¹ /kən'səʊl/ *verb* (consoles,
consoling, consoled /kən'səʊld/)
to make somebody happier when they are
sad or disappointed ➲ SAME MEANING
comfort

console² /'kɒnsəʊl/ *noun*
a piece of equipment with buttons and
switches on it which you connect to a
computer to play games

consonant /'kɒnsənənt/ *noun*
any letter of the alphabet except *a, e, i, o* and
u: *The letters 't', 'm', 's' and 'b' are all
consonants.* ➲ Look at **vowel**.

A
B
C
D
E
F
G
H
I
J
K
L
M
N
O
P
Q
R
S
T
U
V
W
X
Y
Z

constable /'kʌnstəbl/ *noun*
an ordinary police officer

constant /'kɒnstənt/ *adjective*
happening all the time: *the constant noise of traffic*
▸ **constantly** *adverb*: *The situation is constantly changing.*

constituency /kən'stɪtjuənsi/ *noun*
(*plural* **constituencies**) (*British*)
a town or an area and the people who live in it. Each **constituency** chooses one person in the government (called a **Member of Parliament**).

constitution /ˌkɒnstɪ'tjuːʃn/ *noun*
the laws of a country, a state or an organization

construct /kən'strʌkt/ *verb* (**constructs, constructing, constructed**)
to build something: *The bridge was constructed out of stone.*

🔎 SPEAKING
Build is the word that we usually use.

construction /kən'strʌkʃn/ *noun*
1 (*no plural*) building something: *the construction of a new airport*
2 (*plural* **constructions**) (*formal*) something that people have built

consul /'kɒnsl/ *noun*
a person who works in a foreign city and helps people from his or her country who are living or visiting there

consult /kən'sʌlt/ *verb* (**consults, consulting, consulted**)
to ask somebody or to look in a book when you want to know something: *If the pain doesn't go away, you should consult a doctor.*

consultant /kən'sʌltənt/ *noun*
a person who knows a lot about a subject and gives advice to other people about it: *a firm of management consultants*

consume /kən'sjuːm/ *verb* (**consumes, consuming, consumed** /kən'sjuːmd/)
(*formal*) to eat, drink or use something: *This car consumes a lot of fuel.*

consumer /kən'sjuːmə(r)/ *noun*
a person who buys or uses something: *Consumers want more information about the food they buy.*

consumption /kən'sʌmpʃn/ *noun* (*no plural*)
eating, drinking or using something: *This car has a high fuel consumption* (= it uses a lot of fuel).

contact¹ 0̰ /'kɒntækt/ *noun* (*no plural*)
meeting, talking to or writing to somebody:

Until Jane went to school, she had little contact with other children. ◇ *Are you still* **in contact** with the people you met on holiday? ◇ *Doctors* **come into contact with** (= meet) *a lot of people.*

contact² 0̰ /'kɒntækt/ *verb* (**contacts, contacting, contacted**)
to telephone or write to somebody, or go to see them: *If you see this man, please contact the police.*

contact lens /'kɒntækt lenz/ *noun* (*plural* **contact lenses**)
a small round piece of thin plastic that you wear in your eye so that you can see better
つ Look at **glasses**.

contagious /kən'teɪdʒəs/ *adjective*
A **contagious** disease passes from one person to another person if they touch each other. つ Look at **infectious**.

contain 0̰ /kən'teɪn/ *verb* (**contains, containing, contained** /kən'teɪnd/)
to have something inside: *This box contains pens and pencils.* ◇ *Chocolate contains a lot of sugar.*

container 0̰ /kən'teɪnə(r)/ *noun*
a thing that you can put other things in. Boxes, bottles and packets are all **containers**. つ Look at the picture on the next page.

contemporary¹ /kən'temprəri/ *adjective*
1 belonging to the same time as somebody or something else
2 belonging to the present time
つ SAME MEANING **modern**: *contemporary art*

contemporary² /kən'temprəri/ *noun*
(*plural* **contemporaries**)
a person who lives or does something at the same time as somebody else

content /kən'tent/ *adjective*
happy or satisfied with what you have: *She is not* **content with** *the money she has – she wants more.*

contented /kən'tentɪd/ *adjective*
happy or satisfied, especially because your life is good: *a contented smile*

contents /'kɒntents/ *noun* (*plural*)
what is inside something: *I poured the* **contents of** *the bottle into a bowl.* ◇ *The* **contents page** *of a book tells you what is in it.*

contest /'kɒntest/ *noun*
a game or competition that people try to win: *a boxing contest*

contestant /kən'testənt/ *noun*
a person who tries to win a CONTEST: *There are six contestants in the race.*

containers

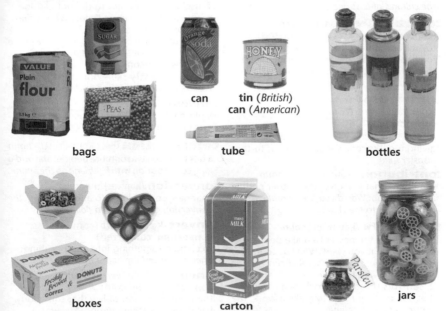

bags

can
tin (*British*)
can (*American*)

tube

bottles

boxes

carton

jars

context /'kɒntekst/ *noun*
the words that come before and after another word or sentence: *You can often understand the meaning of a word by looking at its context.*

continent /'kɒntɪnənt/ *noun*
one of the seven main areas of land in the world, for example Africa, Asia or Europe
▸ **continental** /,kɒntɪ'nentl/ *adjective*: *a continental climate*

continual /kən'tɪnjuəl/ *adjective*
happening often: *We have had continual problems with this machine.*
▸ **continually** /kən'tɪnjuəli/ *adverb*: *He is continually late for work.*

continue 0ᴍ /kən'tɪnju:/ *verb*
(continues, continuing, continued /kən'tɪnju:d/)
1 to not stop happening or doing something: *We continued working until five o'clock. ◇ The rain continued all afternoon.*
2 to go further in the same direction: *We continued along the path until we came to the river.*
3 to start again after stopping: *Let's have lunch now and continue the meeting this afternoon.*

continuous 0ᴍ /kən'tɪnjuəs/ *adjective*
not stopping: *a continuous line ◇ a continuous noise*

▸ **continuously** /kən'tɪnjuəsli/ *adverb*: *It rained continuously for five hours.*

contraceptive /,kɒntrə'septɪv/ *noun*
a drug or an object that stops a woman from becoming pregnant
▸ **contraception** /,kɒntrə'sepʃn/ *noun*
(*no plural*) the ways of stopping a woman from becoming pregnant

contract 0ᴍ /'kɒntrækt/ *noun*
an official piece of paper that says that somebody agrees to do something: *The company has signed a contract to build the new road.*

contradict /,kɒntrə'dɪkt/ *verb*
(contradicts, contradicting, contradicted)
to say that something is wrong or not true: *I didn't dare contradict him, but I think he was wrong.*

contrary¹ /'kɒntrəri/ *adjective*
contrary to something very different from something; opposite to something: *He didn't stay in bed, contrary to the doctor's orders.*

contrary² /'kɒntrəri/ *noun* (*no plural*)
on the contrary the opposite is true; certainly not: *'You look ill.' 'On the contrary, I feel fine!'*

contrast¹ 0ᴍ /'kɒntrɑ:st/ *noun*
a difference between things that you can see

A B **C** D E F G H I J K L M N O P Q R S T U V W X Y Z

clearly: *There is an obvious **contrast between** the cultures of East and West.*

contrast² 0— /kən'trɑːst/ *verb*
(contrasts, contrasting, contrasted)
to look at or think about two or more things together and see the differences between them: *The book **contrasts** life today **with** life 100 years ago.*

contribute 0— /kən'trɪbjuːt; 'kɒntrɪbjuːt/ *verb* (contributes, contributing, contributed)
to give something when other people are giving too: *We **contributed** £10 each **to** the disaster fund.*

contribution /ˌkɒntrɪ'bjuːʃn/ *noun*
something that you give when other people are giving too: *Would you like to **make** a **contribution** **to** the charity?*

control¹ 0— /kən'trəʊl/ *noun*
1 (*no plural*) the power to make people or things do what you want: *Who has **control of** the government? ◇ The driver **lost control** and the bus went into the river.*
2 controls (*plural*) the parts of a machine that you press or move to make it work: *the controls of an aeroplane*
be or **get out of control** to be or become impossible to deal with: *The situation got out of control and people started fighting.*
be in control to have the power or ability to deal with something: *The police are now in control of the area after last night's violence.*
be under control If things **are under control**, you are able to deal with them successfully: *Don't worry, everything's under control.*

control² 0— /kən'trəʊl/ *verb* (controls, controlling, controlled /kən'trəʊld/)
to make people or things do what you want: *He can't control his dog. ◇ This switch controls the heating.*
▶ **controller** /kən'trəʊlə(r)/ *noun* a person who controls something: *an air traffic controller*

controversial /ˌkɒntrə'vɜːʃl/ *adjective*
Something that is **controversial** makes people argue and disagree with each other: *a controversial new law*

controversy /'kɒntrəvɜːsi; kən'trɒvəsi/ *noun* (*plural* controversies)
public discussion and disagreement about something: *The government's plans caused a lot of controversy.*

convenience /kən'viːniəns/ *noun* (*no plural*)
being easy to use or making things easy for somebody: *For convenience, I usually do all my shopping in the same place.*

convenient /kən'viːniənt/ *adjective*
1 useful, easy or quick to do; not causing problems: *Let's meet on Friday. What's the most convenient time for you?*
2 near to a place or easy to get to: *The house is very convenient for the station.*
⊃ OPPOSITE **inconvenient**
▶ **conveniently** /kən'viːniəntli/ *adverb*: *We live conveniently close to the shops.*

convent /'kɒnvənt/ *noun*
a place where religious women (called nuns) live and work

conversation 0— /ˌkɒnvə'seɪʃn/ *noun*
a talk between two or more people: *She **had a** long **conversation with** her friend on the phone.*

conversion /kən'vɜːʃn/ *noun*
changing something into another thing: *the conversion of pounds into dollars*

convert /kən'vɜːt/ *verb* (converts, converting, converted)
to change something into another thing: *They **converted** the house **into** two flats.*

convict /kən'vɪkt/ *verb* (convicts, convicting, convicted)
to decide in a court of law that somebody has done something wrong: *She was **convicted of** murder and sent to prison.*

convince 0— /kən'vɪns/ *verb*
(convinces, convincing, convinced /kən'vɪnst/)
to make somebody believe something: *I couldn't **convince** him **that** I was right.*

convinced /kən'vɪnst/ *adjective*
completely sure about something: *I'm **convinced that** I have seen her somewhere before.*

cook¹ 0— /kʊk/ *verb* (cooks, cooking, cooked /kʊkt/)
to make food ready to eat by heating it: *My father cooked the dinner. ◇ I am learning to cook.*
▶ **cooked** /kʊkt/ *adjective*: *cooked chicken*

🔎 WORD BUILDING
There are many ways to cook food.
You can **bake** bread and cakes and you can **roast** meat in an **oven**.
You can **boil** vegetables in a **saucepan**.
You can **fry** fish, eggs, etc. in a **frying pan**.

cook² /kʊk/ *noun*
a person who cooks: *She works as a cook in a big hotel. ◇ He is a good cook.*

cooker 0— /'kʊkə(r)/ (*British*) (*American* stove) *noun*
a piece of kitchen equipment for cooking

using electricity or gas. It has places for heating pans on the top and an oven for cooking food inside it: *an electric cooker* ➲ Look at Picture Dictionary page **P10**.

cookery /'kʊkəri/ *noun* (*no plural*)
the skill or activity of preparing and cooking food: *cookery lessons*

cookie 0̶ᴋ /'kʊki/ *American English for* BISCUIT ➲ Look at Picture Dictionary page **P6**.

cooking 0̶ᴋ /'kʊkɪŋ/ *noun* (*no plural*)
1 making food ready to eat: *Who does the cooking in your family?*
2 the food that you cook: *He missed his mother's cooking when he left home.*

cool¹ 0̶ᴋ /kuːl/ *adjective* (**cooler**, **coolest**)
1 a little cold; not hot or warm: *cool weather* ◇ *I'd like a cool drink.* ➲ Look at the note at **cold**.
2 not excited or angry ➲ SAME MEANING **calm**
3 (*informal*) very good or fashionable: *Those are cool shoes you're wearing!*
4 (*informal*) People say **Cool!** to show that they think something is a good idea: '*We're planning to go out for lunch tomorrow.*' '*Cool!*'

cool² /kuːl/ *verb* (**cools**, **cooling**, **cooled** /kuːld/)
to make something less hot; to become less hot: *Take the cake out of the oven and leave it to cool.*
cool down
1 to become less hot: *We swam in the river to cool down after our long walk.*
2 to become less excited or angry

cooperate /kəʊˈɒpəreɪt/ *verb* (**cooperates**, **cooperating**, **cooperated**)
to work together with someone else in a helpful way: *The two companies agreed to cooperate with each other.* ◇ *If everyone cooperates, we'll be finished by lunchtime.*

cooperation /kəʊˌɒpəˈreɪʃn/ *noun* (*no plural*)
help that you give by doing what somebody asks you to do: *Thank you for your cooperation.*

cooperative /kəʊˈɒpərətɪv/ *adjective*
helpful by doing what you are asked to do

cope /kəʊp/ *verb* (**copes**, **coping**, **coped** /kəʊpt/)
to deal with something, although it is difficult: *He finds it difficult to cope with all the pressure at work.*

copied *form of* COPY²

copies *form of* COPY

copper /'kɒpə(r)/ *noun* (*no plural*)
a common metal with a colour between brown and red: *copper wire*

copy¹ 0̶ᴋ /'kɒpi/ *noun* (*plural* **copies**)
1 a thing that is made to look exactly like another thing: *This isn't a real painting by Van Gogh. It's only a copy.* ◇ *The secretary made two copies of the letter.*
2 one example of a book or newspaper: *Two million copies of this newspaper are sold every day.*

copy² 0̶ᴋ /'kɒpi/ *verb* (**copies**, **copying**, **copied** /'kɒpid/, **has copied**)
1 to write, draw or make something exactly the same as something else: *The teacher asked us to copy the list of words into our books.*
2 to do or try to do the same as somebody else ➲ SAME MEANING **imitate**: *He copies everything his brother does.*

cord /kɔːd/ *noun*
1 strong thick string
2 *American English for* FLEX

core

apples

core /kɔː(r)/ *noun*
the middle part of some kinds of fruit, where the seeds are: *an apple core*

cork /kɔːk/ *noun*
1 (*no plural*) a light soft material that comes from the outside of a particular tree

corkscrew

A
B
C
D
E
F
G
H
I
J
K
L
M
N
O
P
Q
R
S
T
U
V
W
X
Y
Z

2 (*plural* **corks**) a round piece of **cork** that you put in a bottle to close it

corkscrew /'kɔːkskruː/ *noun*
a thing that you use for pulling CORKS out of bottles

corn /kɔːn/ *noun* (*no plural*)
1 (*British*) the seeds of plants that are grown for their grain, for example WHEAT
2 *American English for* MAIZE

corner

The lamp is in the corner.

The bank is on the corner.

corner 0— /'kɔːnə(r)/ *noun*
a place where two lines, walls or roads meet: *Put the lamp **in the corner** of the room.* ◇ *The shop is **on the corner** of East Avenue and Union Street.* ◇ *He drove **round the corner** at top speed.*

cornflakes /'kɔːnfleɪks/ *noun* (*plural*)
small pieces of dried food that you eat with milk and sugar for breakfast

corporation /ˌkɔːpə'reɪʃn/ *noun*
a big company

corpse /kɔːps/ *noun*
the body of a dead person

correct¹ 0— /kə'rekt/ *adjective*
right or true; with no mistakes: *What is the correct time, please?* ◇ *All your answers were correct.* ⊃ OPPOSITE **incorrect**
▶ **correctly** /kə'rektli/ *adverb*: *Have I spelt your name correctly?*
⊃ OPPOSITE **incorrectly**

correct² 0— /kə'rekt/ *verb* (**corrects, correcting, corrected**)
to show where the mistakes are in something and make it right: *The class did the exercises and the teacher corrected them.* ◇ *Please correct me if I make a mistake.*

correction /kə'rekʃn/ *noun*
a change that makes something right or better: *The teacher **made** a few **corrections** to my essay.*

correspond /ˌkɒrə'spɒnd/ *verb* (**corresponds, corresponding, corresponded**)
to be the same, or almost the same, as something: *Does the name on the envelope **correspond with** the name inside the letter?*

correspondence /ˌkɒrə'spɒndəns/ *noun* (*no plural*)
the letters a person sends and receives: *Her secretary reads all her correspondence.*

corridor /'kɒrɪdɔː(r)/ *noun*
a long narrow part inside a building with rooms on each side of it

cosmetics /kɒz'metɪks/ *noun* (*plural*)
special powders or creams that you use on your face or hair to make yourself more beautiful

cost¹ 0— /kɒst/ *noun*
1 (*plural* **costs**) the money that you have to pay for something: *The cost of the repairs was very high.* ⊃ Look at the note at **price**.
2 (*no plural*) what you lose or give to have another thing: *He saved the child **at the cost** of his own life.*
at all costs no matter what you must do to make it happen: *We must win at all costs.*

cost² 0— /kɒst/ *verb* (**costs, costing, cost, has cost**)
1 to have the price of: *This plant cost $4.* ◇ *How much did the book cost?*
2 to make you lose something: *One mistake cost him his job.*

costly /'kɒstli/ *adjective* (**costlier, costliest**)
costing a lot of money ⊃ SAME MEANING **expensive**: *The repairs will be very costly.*

costume /'kɒstjuːm/ *noun*
the special clothes that people wear in a country or at a certain time: *The actors wore beautiful costumes.* ◇ *the national costume of Japan* ⊃ Look also at **swimming costume**.

cosy (*British*) (*American* **cozy**) /'kəʊzi/ *adjective* (**cosier, cosiest**)
warm and comfortable: *a cosy room*

cot /kɒt/ (*British*) (*American* **crib**) *noun*
a bed with high sides for a baby ⊃ Look at **cradle**.

cottage /'kɒtɪdʒ/ *noun*
a small house in the country ⊃ Look at the picture at **path**.

cotton 0— /'kɒtn/ *noun* (*no plural*)
1 a natural cloth or thread that is made from the soft white hairs around the seeds of a plant that grows in hot countries: *a cotton shirt* ◇ *a reel of cotton*
2 *American English for* COTTON WOOL

cotton wool /ˌkɒtn 'wʊl/ *noun* (*no plural*) (*British*) (*American* cotton)

soft light material made from cotton that you often use for cleaning your skin: *The nurse cleaned the cut with cotton wool.*

couch /kaʊtʃ/ *noun* (*plural* couches)

a long comfortable seat for two or more people to sit on ➔ SAME MEANING **sofa**

couch potato /'kaʊtʃ pəteɪtəʊ/ *noun* (*informal*)

a person who spends a lot of time sitting and watching television

cough[1] 0̄ᴍ /kɒf/ *verb* (coughs, coughing, coughed /kɒft/)

> 🔎 **PRONUNCIATION**
>
> The word **cough** sounds like **off**.

to send air out of your throat with a sudden loud noise: *The smoke made me cough.*

cough[2] 0̄ᴍ /kɒf/ *noun*

when you send air out of your throat with a sudden loud noise: *I've got a bad cough.* ◇ *He gave a little cough before he started to speak.*

could 0̄ᴍ /kʊd/ *modal verb*

> 🔎 **PRONUNCIATION**
>
> The word **could** sounds like **good**, because we don't say the letter **l** in this word.

1 the word for 'can' in the past: *He could run very fast when he was young.* ◇ *I could hear the birds singing.*

2 a word that you use to ask something in a polite way: *Could you open the door?* ◇ *Could I have another drink, please?*

3 a word that shows what is or may be possible: *I don't know where Mum is. She could be in the kitchen.* ◇ *It could rain tomorrow.* ➔ Look at the note at the entry for **modal verb**.

couldn't /'kʊdnt/ *short for* COULD NOT: *It was dark and I couldn't see anything.*

could've /'kʊdəv/ (*informal*) *short for* COULD HAVE: *He could've gone to university but he didn't want to.*

council /'kaʊnsl/ *noun*

a group of people who are chosen to work together and to make rules and decide things: *The city council is planning to widen the road.*

councillor (*British*) (*American* councilor) /'kaʊnsələ(r)/ *noun*

a member of a COUNCIL

count[1] 0̄ᴍ /kaʊnt/ *verb* (counts, counting, counted)

1 to say numbers one after the other in the correct order: *The children are learning to count from one to ten.*

2 to look at people or things to see how many there are: *I have counted the chairs – there are 32.*

3 to include somebody or something when you are finding a total: *There were twenty people on the bus, not counting the driver.*

4 to be important or accepted: *Every point in this game counts.* ◇ *Your throw won't count if you go over the line.*

count on somebody or **something** to feel sure that somebody or something will do what you want: *Can I count on you to help me?*

count[2] /kaʊnt/ *noun*

a time when you count things: *After an election there is a count of all the votes.*

keep count of something to know how many there are of something: *Try to keep count of the number of tickets you sell.*

lose count of something to not know how many there are of something

countable /'kaʊntəbl/ *adjective*

(*grammar*) **Countable** nouns are ones that you can use in the plural or with *a* or *an*, for example *chair* and *idea*. ➔ OPPOSITE **uncountable**

counter /'kaʊntə(r)/ *noun*

1 a long high table in a shop, bank or bar, that is between the people who work there and the customers: *The man **behind the counter** in the bank was very helpful.*

2 a small round thing that you use when you play some games

counterclockwise /ˌkaʊntə'klɒkwaɪz/ *American English for* ANTICLOCKWISE

countless /'kaʊntləs/ *adjective*

very many: *I have tried to phone him countless times.*

country 0̄ᴍ /'kʌntri/ *noun*

1 (*plural* countries) an area of land with its own people and government: *France, Spain and other European countries*

> 🔎 **WHICH WORD?**
>
> **Country** or **nation**?
> These words are very similar, but we use **nation** when we want to refer to the people as well as the land: *The whole nation seemed to be watching the match on TV.*

2 the country (*no plural*) land that is away from towns and cities: *Do you live in the town or **in the country**?*

A

countryside 0̶ₘ /'kʌntrisaɪd/ *noun*
(*no plural*)
land with fields, woods, farms, etc., that is
away from towns and cities: *There are
magnificent views over open countryside.*

B

county /'kaʊnti/ *noun* (*plural* **counties**)
one of the parts of Britain, Ireland or the US
which has its own local government: *the
county of Oxfordshire ◇ Orange County,
California*

C

D

couple 0̶ₘ /'kʌpl/ *noun*
1 a couple two or a small number of people
or things: *I invited a couple of friends to lunch.
◇ I'll be back in a couple of minutes.*
2 two people who are married or in a
romantic relationship: *A young couple live
next door.*

E

F

coupon /'kuːpɒn/ *noun*
a small piece of paper that you can use to
buy things at a lower price, or that you can
collect and use instead of money to buy
things

G

H

I

J

courage /'kʌrɪdʒ/ *noun* (*no plural*)
not being afraid, or not showing that you are
afraid when you do something dangerous or
difficult ⟳ SAME MEANING **bravery**: *She
showed great courage in the face of danger.*
▸ **courageous** /kə'reɪdʒəs/ *adjective*
⟳ SAME MEANING **brave**: *a courageous
young man*

K

L

M

N

courgette /kɔː'ʒet/ (*British*) (*American
zucchini*) *noun*
a long vegetable that is green on the outside
and white on the inside ⟳ Look at Picture
Dictionary page **P9**.

O

P

course 0̶ₘ /kɔːs/ *noun*
1 (*plural* **courses**) a set of lessons on a
certain subject: *He's taking a course in
computer programming.*
2 (*no plural*) the direction that something
moves in: *We followed the course of the river. ◇
The plane had to change course because of
the storm.*
3 (*no plural*) the time when something is
happening: *The telephone rang six times
during the course of the evening.*
4 (*plural* **courses**) one separate part of a
meal: *a three-course meal ◇ I had chicken for
my main course.*
5 (*plural* **courses**) a piece of ground for
some kinds of sport: *a golf course ◇ a
racecourse*
of course certainly: *Of course I'll help you. ◇
'Can I use your telephone?' 'Of course you
can.' ◇ 'Are you angry with me?' 'Of course
not!'*

Q

R

S

T

U

V

W

X

Y

coursebook /'kɔːsbʊk/ *noun* (*British*)
a book that teachers and students use in
class

Z

court 0̶ₘ /kɔːt/ *noun*
1 the place where a judge or a group of
people (called a **jury**) decide if a person has
done something wrong, and what the
punishment will be: *The man will appear in
court tomorrow.*
2 a piece of ground where you can play
certain sports: *a tennis court ◇ a basketball
court* ⟳ Look at the note at **pitch**.

courteous /'kɜːtiəs/ *adjective*
polite and showing respect for other people

courtesy /'kɜːtəsi/ *noun* (*no plural*)
polite behaviour that shows respect for
other people

court of law /ˌkɔːt əv 'lɔː/ *noun* (*plural
courts of law*) (*British also* **law court**)
a place where a judge or a group of people
(called a **jury**) decide if somebody has done
something wrong, and what the
punishment will be

courtyard /'kɔːtjɑːd/ *noun*
an open space without a roof, inside a
building or between buildings

cousin 0̶ₘ /'kʌzn/ *noun*
the child of your aunt or uncle ⟳ You use the
same word for both male and female cousins.

cover¹ 0̶ₘ /'kʌvə(r)/ *verb* (**covers**,
covering, covered /'kʌvəd/)
1 to put one thing over another thing to
hide it or to keep it safe or warm: *Cover the
floor with a newspaper before you start
painting. ◇ She covered her head with a scarf.*
2 to be all over something or somebody:
*Snow covered the ground. ◇ The children were
covered in mud.*

cover² 0̶ₘ /'kʌvə(r)/ *noun*
1 a thing that you put over another thing,
for example to keep it safe: *The computer has
a plastic cover.*
2 the outside part of a book or magazine:
*The book had a picture of a film star on the
cover* (= the front cover).

coveralls /'kʌvərɔːlz/ *American English for*
OVERALLS

covering 0̶ₘ /'kʌvərɪŋ/ *noun*
something that covers another thing: *There
was a thick covering of snow on the ground.*

cow 0̶ₘ /kaʊ/ *noun*
a big female farm animal that is kept for its
milk or meat ⟳ Look at Picture Dictionary
page **P2**.

> 🔎 **WORD BUILDING**
> The male is called a **bull** and a young cow
> is called a **calf**.
> Meat from a cow is called **beef** and meat
> from a calf is called **veal**.

cow

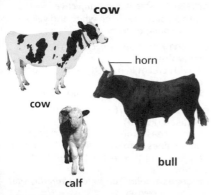

horn

cow

bull

calf

coward /'kaʊəd/ *noun*
a person who is afraid when there is danger or a problem

cowboy /'kaʊbɔɪ/ *noun*
a man who rides a horse and looks after cows in some parts of the US

cozy *American English for* COSY

crab

shell

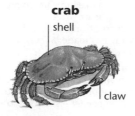

claw

crab /kræb/ *noun*
an animal that lives in and near the sea. It has a hard shell and ten legs.

crack¹ /kræk/ *verb* (cracks, cracking, cracked /krækt/)
1 to break, but not into separate pieces: *The glass will crack if you pour boiling water into it.* ◇ *This cup is cracked.*
2 to make a sudden loud noise
crack down on somebody or **something** to become stricter when dealing with bad or illegal behaviour: *The police are cracking down on drug dealers.*

crack² /kræk/ *noun*
1 a thin line on something where it has broken, but not into separate pieces: *There's a crack in this glass.*
2 a narrow space between two things or two parts of something: *a crack in the curtains*
3 a sudden loud noise: *a crack of thunder*

cracker /'krækə(r)/ *noun*
1 a thin dry biscuit that you can eat with cheese ⊃ Look at Picture Dictionary page **P6**.

2 a long round thing made of coloured paper with a small present inside. It makes a loud noise when two people pull the ends away from each other: *We often pull crackers at Christmas parties.*

crackle /'krækl/ *verb* (crackles, crackling, crackled /'krækld/)
to make a lot of short sharp sounds: *Dry wood crackles when you burn it.*

cradle /'kreɪdl/ *noun*
a small bed for a baby which can be moved from side to side ⊃ Look at **cot**.

craft /krɑːft/ *noun*
a job or activity for which you need skill with your hands: *Pottery is a traditional craft.*

craftsman /'krɑːftsmən/ *noun* (plural craftsmen /'krɑːftsmən/)
a person who is good at making things with their hands

crafty /'krɑːfti/ *adjective* (craftier, craftiest)
clever at getting what you want in a way that is not completely honest

cram /kræm/ *verb* (crams, cramming, crammed /kræmd/)
to push too many people or things into a small space: *She crammed her clothes into a bag.*

cramp /kræmp/ *noun* (no plural)
a sudden pain that you get in a muscle, for example in your leg, which makes it difficult to move

crane

crane /kreɪn/ *noun*
a big machine with a long metal arm for lifting heavy things

crash¹ 0͞ʒ /kræʃ/ *noun* (plural crashes)
1 an accident when something that is moving hits another thing: *He was killed in a car crash.* ◇ *a plane crash*
2 a loud noise when something falls or hits another thing: *I heard a crash as the tree fell.*

A
B
C
D
E
F
G
H
I
J
K
L
M
N
O
P
Q
R
S
T
U
V
W
X
Y
Z

A
B
C
D
E
F
G
H
I
J
K
L
M
N
O
P
Q
R
S
T
U
V
W
X
Y
Z

crash² 0🔊 /kræʃ/ *verb* (crashes, crashing, crashed /kræʃt/)

1 to have an accident in a car or other vehicle and hit something: *The bus* **crashed** *into a tree.* ◊ *I crashed my father's car.*
2 to fall or hit something with a loud noise: *The tree crashed to the ground.*
3 If a computer **crashes**, it suddenly stops working.

crash helmet /'kræʃ helmɪt/ *noun*
a hard hat that you wear when riding a motorbike to protect your head

crate /kreɪt/ *noun*
a big box for carrying bottles or other things

crawl

crawl¹ /krɔ:l/ *verb* (crawls, crawling, crawled /krɔ:ld/)
to move slowly on your hands and knees or with your body close to the ground: *Babies crawl before they can walk.* ◊ *A spider crawled across the floor.*

crawl² /krɔ:l/ *noun* (no plural)
a way of swimming on your front ⊃ Look also at **breaststroke**.

crayon /'kreɪən/ *noun*
a soft, thick, coloured pencil: *The children were drawing pictures with crayons.*

crazy 0🔊 /'kreɪzi/ *adjective* (crazier, craziest) (*informal*)
1 stupid; not sensible: *You must be crazy to ride a bike at night with no lights.*
2 very angry: *My mum will* **go crazy** *if I get home late.*
3 If you are **crazy about** something or somebody, you like them very much: *She's crazy about football.* ◊ *He's crazy about her.*
⊃ SAME MEANING **mad**

creak /kri:k/ *verb* (creaks, creaking, creaked /kri:kt/)
to make a noise like a door that needs oil, or like an old wooden floor when you walk on it
▶ **creak** *noun*: *The door opened with a creak.*

cream¹ 0🔊 /kri:m/ *noun*
1 (*no plural*) the thick liquid on the top of milk
2 (*plural* creams) a thick liquid that you put on your skin, for example to keep it soft: *hand cream*

cream² 0🔊 /kri:m/ *adjective*
with a colour between white and yellow: *She was wearing a cream dress.*

creamy /'kri:mi/ *adjective* (creamier, creamiest)
1 with cream in it, or thick and smooth like cream: *a creamy sauce*
2 having a colour like cream: *creamy skin*

crease /kri:s/ *verb* (creases, creasing, creased /kri:st/)
If you **crease** something, or it **creases**, untidy lines or folds appear in it: *Don't sit on my jacket – you'll crease it.* ◊ *This shirt creases easily.*
▶ **crease** *noun*: *You need to iron this shirt – it's full of creases.*

create 0🔊 /kri'eɪt/ *verb* (creates, creating, created)
to make something happen or exist: *Do you believe that God created the world?* ◊ *The government plans to create more jobs for young people.*

creation /kri'eɪʃn/ *noun*
1 (*no plural*) making something new: *the creation of the world*
2 (*plural* creations) a new thing that somebody has made: *Mickey Mouse was the creation of Walt Disney.*

creative /kri'eɪtɪv/ *adjective*
A person who is **creative** has a lot of new ideas or is good at making new things: *She's a very good painter – she's so creative.*

creator /kri'eɪtə(r)/ *noun*
a person who makes something new: *Walt Disney was the creator of Mickey Mouse.*

creature /'kri:tʃə(r)/ *noun*
any living thing that is not a plant: *birds, fish and other creatures* ◊ *This story is about creatures from another planet.*

credit¹ /'kredɪt/ *noun* (no plural)
1 a way of buying something where you pay for it later: *I bought the television* **on credit.**
2 having money in an account: *No bank charges are made if your account is* **in credit.**
3 saying that somebody has done something well: *I did all the work but John got all* **the credit for** *it!*

credit² /'kredɪt/ (credits, crediting, credited) *verb*
to add money to somebody's bank account: *$500 has been credited to your account.*

credit card 0🔊 /'kredɪt kɑːd/ *noun*
a plastic card from a bank that you can use to buy something and pay for it later: *Can I pay* **by credit card?** ⊃ Look at the picture at **money**.

creep /kriːp/ *verb* (creeps, creeping, crept /krept/, has crept)
to move quietly and carefully so that nobody hears or sees you: *I crept into the room where the children were sleeping.* ◇ *The cat crept towards the bird.*

creepy /ˈkriːpi/ *adjective* (creepier, creepiest) (*informal*)
making you feel nervous or afraid
➲ SAME MEANING **scary**: *a creepy ghost story*

crept *form of* CREEP

crescent /ˈkresnt; ˈkreznt/ *noun*
1 the shape of the moon when it is less than half a circle ➲ Look at the picture at **shape**.
2 a street or line of houses with a curved shape: *I live at 34 Elgin Crescent.*

crest /krest/ *noun*
the top part of a hill or a wave: *surfers riding the **crest** of the wave*

crew /kruː/ *noun*
all the people who work on a ship or a plane

crib /krɪb/ *American English for* COT

cricket /ˈkrɪkɪt/ *noun*
1 (*no plural*) a game for two teams of eleven players who try to hit a small hard ball with a piece of wood (called a **bat**) on a large field (called a **pitch**): *We watched a cricket match.* ➲ Look at Picture Dictionary page **P14**. ➲ Look at the note at **bat**.
2 (*plural* **crickets**) a small brown insect that jumps and makes a loud high noise by rubbing its wings together
▶ **cricketer** /ˈkrɪkɪtə(r)/ *noun* a person who plays CRICKET

cried *form of* CRY¹

cries *form of* CRY

crime 0— /kraɪm/ *noun*
something that somebody does that is against the law: *Murder and robbery are serious crimes.* ◇ *They had **committed** a crime.*

criminal¹ 0— /ˈkrɪmɪnl/ *adjective*
connected with crime: *Deliberate damage to public property is a **criminal offence**.* ◇ *She is studying criminal law.*

criminal² 0— /ˈkrɪmɪnl/ *noun*
a person who does something that is against the law

crimson /ˈkrɪmzn/ *adjective*
with a dark red colour, like blood

cripple /ˈkrɪpl/ *verb* (cripples, crippling, crippled /ˈkrɪpld/)
to damage somebody's body so that they cannot walk or move normally: *She was crippled in an accident.*

crisis 0— /ˈkraɪsɪs/ *noun* (*plural* crises /ˈkraɪsiːz/)
a time when something very dangerous or serious happens: *a political crisis*

crisp¹ /krɪsp/ *adjective* (crisper, crispest)
1 hard and dry: *If you keep the biscuits in a tin, they will stay crisp.*
2 fresh and not soft: *crisp apples*

crisps

crisp² /krɪsp/ (*British*) (*American* **chip, potato chip**) *noun*
a very thin piece of potato cooked in hot oil and eaten cold. **Crisps** are sold in bags and have many different flavours: *a packet of crisps*

critic /ˈkrɪtɪk/ *noun*
1 a person who says that somebody or something is wrong or bad: *critics of the government*
2 a person who writes about a book, film or play and says if they like it or not: *The critics loved his new film.*

critical /ˈkrɪtɪkl/ *adjective*
1 If you are **critical** of somebody or something, you say that they are wrong or bad: *They were very **critical of** my work.*
2 very important ➲ SAME MEANING **crucial**: *We have reached a critical stage in our negotiations.*
3 very serious or dangerous: *The patient is in a **critical** condition.*
▶ **critically** /ˈkrɪtɪkli/ *adverb*: *She's critically ill.*

criticism 0— /ˈkrɪtɪsɪzəm/ *noun*
what you think is bad about somebody or something: *I listened to all their criticisms of my plan.*

criticize /ˈkrɪtɪsaɪz/ *verb* (criticizes, criticizing, criticized /ˈkrɪtɪsaɪzd/)
to say that somebody or something is wrong or bad: *She was **criticized for** not following orders.*

croak /krəʊk/ *verb* (croaks, croaking, croaked /krəʊkt/)
1 If a FROG (= a small green animal that lives in or near water) **croaks**, it makes a low rough sound.
2 to speak in a low rough voice: *'My throat's really sore,'* *he croaked.*
▶ **croak** *noun*

crockery /ˈkrɒkəri/ *noun* (*no plural*)
plates, cups and dishes

A B C D E F G H I J K L M N O P Q R S T U V W X Y Z

A B **C** D E F G H I J K L M N O P Q R S T U V W X Y Z

crocodile /ˈkrɒkədaɪl/ *noun*
a big animal with a long tail and a big mouth with sharp teeth. **Crocodiles** live in rivers in hot countries: *A crocodile is a reptile.* ➔ Look at Picture Dictionary page **P3**.

crooked /ˈkrʊkɪd/ *adjective*
not straight: *She has crooked teeth.* ➔ Look at the picture at **straight**.

crop /krɒp/ *noun*
all the plants of one kind that a farmer grows at one time: *There was a good **crop of** potatoes last year.* ◇ *Rain is good for the crops.*

cross¹ 0‑ᴡ /krɒs/ *noun* (plural **crosses**)
1 a mark like X or †: *The cross on the map shows where I live.*
2 something with the shape X or †: *She wears a cross* (= a symbol of the Christian religion) *around her neck.*

cross² /krɒs/ *verb* (**crosses, crossing, crossed** /krɒst/)
1 to go from one side of something to the other: *Be careful when you cross the road.*
2 to put one thing over another thing: *She sat down and **crossed** her **legs**.*
cross something out to draw a line through a word or words, for example because you have made a mistake: *I crossed the word out and wrote it again.*

cross³ /krɒs/ *adjective*
angry ➔ SAME MEANING **annoyed**: *I was **cross with** her because she was late.*

crossing /ˈkrɒsɪŋ/ *noun*
a place where you can cross over something, for example a road or a river

crossroads /ˈkrɒsrəʊdz/ *noun* (plural **crossroads**)
a place where two roads meet and cross each other

crosswalk /ˈkrɒswɔːk/ *American English for* PEDESTRIAN CROSSING

crossword puzzle

clues

crossword /ˈkrɒswɜːd/ (*also* **crossword puzzle** /ˈkrɒswɜːd pʌzl/) *noun*
a game where you have to write words in square spaces across and down the page

crouch /kraʊtʃ/ *verb* (**crouches, crouching, crouched** /kraʊtʃt/)
to bend your legs and back so that your body is close to the ground: *I crouched under the table to hide.*

crow /krəʊ/ *noun*
a large black bird that makes a loud noise

crowd¹ 0‑ᴡ /kraʊd/ *noun*
a lot of people together: *There was a large crowd at the football match.*

crowd² /kraʊd/ *verb* (**crowds, crowding, crowded**)
to come together in a big group: *The journalists **crowded round** the film star.*

crowded 0‑ᴡ /ˈkraʊdɪd/ *adjective*
full of people: *The streets were very crowded.* ◇ *a crowded bus*

crown¹ /kraʊn/ *noun*
a circle made of valuable metal and stones (called **jewels**) that a king or queen wears on his or her head

crown² /kraʊn/ *verb* (**crowns, crowning, crowned** /kraʊnd/)
to put a **crown** on the head of a new king or queen, as a sign that he or she is the new ruler: *Elizabeth II **was crowned** in 1952.*

crucial /ˈkruːʃl/ *adjective*
very important ➔ SAME MEANING **critical**: *a crucial moment*

crude /kruːd/ *adjective* (**cruder, crudest**)
1 simple and not showing much skill or care: *The method was crude but effective.*
2 rude in a way that many people do not like: *crude jokes*

cruel 0‑ᴡ /ˈkruːəl/ *adjective* (**crueller, cruellest**)
A person who is **cruel** is unkind and likes to hurt other people or animals: *I think it's cruel to keep animals in cages.*
▸ **cruelly** /ˈkruːəli/ *adverb*: *He was cruelly treated when he was a child.*

cruelty /ˈkruːəlti/ *noun* (*no plural*)
behaviour that is unkind and hurts other people or animals

cruise¹ /kruːz/ *noun*
a holiday when you travel on a ship and visit a lot of different places: *They **went on a** world cruise.*

cruise² /kruːz/ *verb* (**cruises, cruising, cruised** /kruːzd/)
to travel on a ship as a holiday, visiting different places: *They cruised around the Caribbean.*

crumb /krʌm/ *noun*
a very small piece of bread, cake or biscuit

crumble /ˈkrʌmbl/ *verb* (**crumbles, crumbling, crumbled** /ˈkrʌmbld/)
to break into very small pieces: *The old castle walls are crumbling.*

crumple /ˈkrʌmpl/ *verb* (crumples, crumpling, crumpled /ˈkrʌmpld/)
to be pressed or to press something into an untidy shape: *She crumpled the paper into a ball and threw it away.*

crunch /krʌntʃ/ *verb* (crunches, crunching, crunched /krʌntʃt/)
1 to make a loud noise when you eat something that is hard: *She crunched her apple noisily.*
2 to make a noise like the sound of something being crushed: *The snow crunched under our feet as we walked.*

crush 0🔊 /krʌʃ/ *verb* (crushes, crushing, crushed /krʌʃt/)
to press something very hard so that you break or damage it: *She sat on my hat and crushed it.*

crust /krʌst/ *noun*
the hard part on the outside of bread ⊃ Look at the picture at **bread**.
▶ **crusty** /ˈkrʌsti/ *adjective* with a hard crust: *fresh crusty bread*

crutch /krʌtʃ/ *noun* (plural crutches)
a long stick that you put under your arm to help you walk when you have hurt your leg: *He broke his leg and now he's on crutches.* ⊃ Look at the picture at **plaster**.

cry¹ 0🔊 /kraɪ/ *verb* (cries, crying, cried /kraɪd/, has cried)
1 to have drops of water falling from your eyes because you are unhappy or hurt: *The baby cries a lot.*
2 to shout or make a loud noise: '*Help!*' he cried. ◇ *She cried out in pain.*

cry² 0🔊 /kraɪ/ *noun* (plural cries)
a loud noise that you make to show strong feelings such as pain, fear or excitement: *He gave a cry of pain.* ◇ *We heard her cries and ran to help.*

crystal /ˈkrɪstl/ *noun*
1 a shape that some substances make when they become solid: *salt crystals*
2 a kind of rock that looks like glass

cub /kʌb/ *noun*
a young animal such as a LION, a BEAR, a FOX, etc.

cube /kjuːb/ *noun*
1 a shape like a box with six square sides all the same size
2 the number that you get if you multiply a number by itself twice: *The cube of 5 (= 5³) is 125 (= 5 x 5 x 5).*
▶ **cubic** /ˈkjuːbɪk/ *adjective*: *a cubic metre (= a space like a cube that is one metre long on each side)*

cubicle /ˈkjuːbɪkl/ *noun*
a small room that is made by separating off part of a larger room: *a shower cubicle*

cuckoo /ˈkʊkuː/ *noun* (plural cuckoos)
a bird that makes a sound like its name

cucumber /ˈkjuːkʌmbə(r)/ *noun*
a long vegetable with a green skin, that we often eat in salads. ⊃ Look at Picture Dictionary page **P9**.

cuddle /ˈkʌdl/ *verb* (cuddles, cuddling, cuddled /ˈkʌdld/)
to hold somebody or something in your arms to show love ⊃ SAME MEANING **hug**: *He cuddled his baby.*
▶ **cuddle** *noun*: *I gave her a cuddle.*

cuff /kʌf/ *noun*
the end part of a sleeve, near your hand ⊃ Look at the picture at **shirt**.

cultivate /ˈkʌltɪveɪt/ *verb* (cultivates, cultivating, cultivated)
1 to use land for growing plants: *Only a small area of the island was cultivated.*
2 to keep and care for plants
▶ **cultivation** /ˌkʌltɪˈveɪʃn/ *noun* (no plural): *cultivation of the land*

cultural /ˈkʌltʃərəl/ *adjective*
1 connected with the ideas, customs and way of life of a group of people or a country: *There are many cultural differences between our two countries.* ⊃ Look at **multicultural**.
2 connected with art, music or literature

culture 0🔊 /ˈkʌltʃə(r)/ *noun*
1 (plural cultures) the customs, ideas and way of life of a group of people or a country: *the language and culture of the Aztecs*
2 (no plural) art, music, literature and the theatre: *The city is a centre of culture.*

cunning /ˈkʌnɪŋ/ *adjective*
clever; good at making people believe something that is not true: *Their plan was quite cunning.*

cup 0🔊 /kʌp/ *noun*
1 a small round container with a handle, that you can drink from: *a cup and saucer*
2 a large metal thing like a cup, that you get for winning a sport

cupboard 0🔊 /ˈkʌbəd/ *noun*
a piece of furniture with shelves and doors, where you keep things like clothes or food ⊃ Look at Picture Dictionary page **P10**.

curb¹ American English for KERB

curb² /kɜːb/ *verb* (curbs, curbing, curbed /kɜːbd/)
to control or limit something, especially something bad: *He needs to learn to curb his temper.*

cups

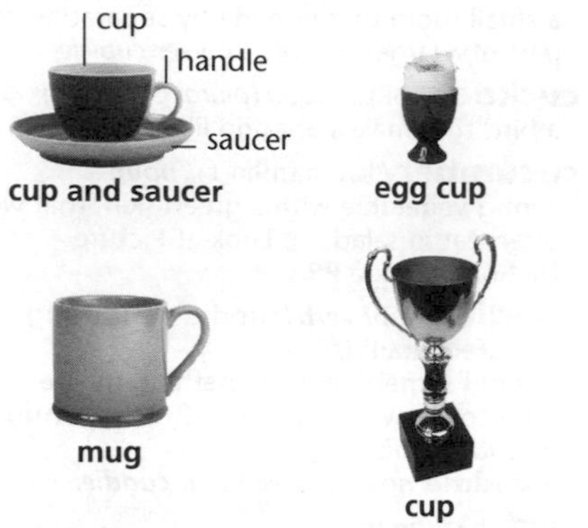
cup
handle
saucer
cup and saucer
egg cup
mug
cup

cure¹ /kjʊə(r)/ ***verb*** **(cures, curing, cured** /kjʊəd/)
1 to make a sick person well again: *The doctors can't cure her.*
2 to make an illness go away: *Can this disease be cured?*

cure² /kjʊə(r)/ ***noun***
something that makes an illness go away: *a* ***cure for*** *cancer*

curiosity /ˌkjʊəriˈɒsəti/ ***noun*** (*no plural*)
wanting to know about things: *I was full of curiosity about the letter.*

curious /ˈkjʊəriəs/ ***adjective***
1 If you are **curious**, you want to know about something: *They were very* ***curious about*** *the people who lived upstairs.*
2 strange or unusual: *There was a curious mixture of people in the audience.*
▸ **curiously** /ˈkjʊəriəsli/ ***adverb***: *'Where are you going?' she asked curiously.*

curl¹ /kɜːl/ ***verb*** **(curls, curling, curled** /kɜːld/)
to form or make something form into a round or curved shape: *Does your hair curl naturally?*
curl up to put your arms, legs and head close to your body: *The cat curled up by the fire.*

curl² /kɜːl/ ***noun***
a piece of hair in a round shape

curly 0┳ /ˈkɜːli/ ***adjective*** **(curlier, curliest)**
with a lot of CURLS ➲ OPPOSITE **straight**: *He's got curly hair.* ➲ Look at the picture at **hair**.

currant /ˈkʌrənt/ ***noun***
a very small black dried fruit that is used in cooking

currency /ˈkʌrənsi/ ***noun*** (*plural* **currencies**)
the money that a country uses: *The currency of the United States is the dollar.*

current¹ /ˈkʌrənt/ ***adjective***
happening or used now: *current fashions*
▸ **currently** /ˈkʌrəntli/ ***adverb*** now; at the moment: *He is currently working in Saudi Arabia.*

current² /ˈkʌrənt/ ***noun***
1 air or water that is moving: *It is dangerous to swim here because of the strong current.*
2 electricity that is going through a wire

curriculum /kəˈrɪkjələm/ ***noun*** (*plural* **curricula** /kəˈrɪkjələ/ *or* **curriculums**)
all the subjects that you study in a school or college: *Latin is not* ***on the curriculum*** *at our school.* ➲ Look at **syllabus**.

curriculum vitae /kəˌrɪkjələm ˈviːtaɪ/ = CV

curry /ˈkʌri/ ***noun*** (*plural* **curries**)
an Indian dish of meat or vegetables cooked with spices and often eaten with rice: *a chicken curry* ➲ Look at Picture Dictionary page **P7**.

curse /kɜːs/ ***noun***
1 a rude word that some people use when they are very angry ➲ SAME MEANING **swear word**
2 a word or phrase that has a magic power to make something bad happen: *The family seemed to be* ***under a curse*** (= lots of bad things happened to them).
▸ **curse** ***verb*** **(curse, cursing, cursed** /ˈkɜːst/) to use rude language because you are angry: *When he stood up, he hit his head and cursed loudly.*

cursor /ˈkɜːsə(r)/ ***noun***
(*computing*) a small sign on a computer screen that shows where on the screen you are working

curtain 0┳ /ˈkɜːtn/ ***noun***
a piece of cloth that you can move to cover a window: *Could you* ***draw the curtains*** (= open or close the curtains), *please?*

curtains

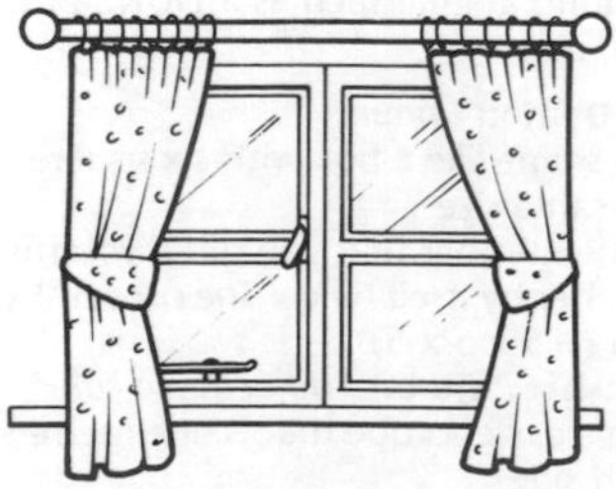

curve

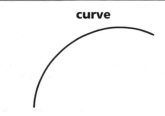

curve¹ 0ᴛ /kɜːv/ *noun*
a line that is not straight; a bend

curve² /kɜːv/ *verb* (curves, curving, curved /kɜːvd/)
to make a round shape; to bend: *The road curves to the right.*
▸ **curved** /kɜːvd/ *adjective*: *a table with curved legs* ◇ *a curved line*

cushion /'kʊʃn/ *noun*
a cloth bag filled with something soft, which you put on a chair ⊃ Look at Picture Dictionary page **10**.

custard /'kʌstəd/ *noun (no plural)*
a sweet yellow sauce made with milk. You eat it with fruit or other sweet dishes.

custom 0ᴛ /'kʌstəm/ *noun*
something that a group of people usually do: *the custom of giving presents at Christmas.*
◇ *It is the custom in that country for women to marry very young.*

customer 0ᴛ /'kʌstəmə(r)/ *noun*
a person who buys things from a shop

customs /'kʌstəmz/ *noun (plural)*
the place at an airport or a port where you must show what you have brought with you from another country: *a customs officer*

cut¹ 0ᴛ /kʌt/ *verb* (cuts, cutting, cut, has cut)
1 to break or damage something with something sharp, for example a knife or scissors: *I cut the string and opened the parcel.*
◇ *I cut the apple in half* (= into two parts). ◇ *She cut her finger on some broken glass.*
2 to take one piece from something bigger using a knife or scissors: *Can you cut me a piece of cake, please?*
3 to make something shorter with a knife or scissors: *Have you had your hair cut?*
be cut off to be kept alone, away from other people: *Our house was cut off from the village by the snow.*
cut down on something to use, do or buy less of something: *You should cut down on sweets and chocolate.*
cut something down to **cut** something so that it falls down: *We cut down the old tree.*

cut something off to stop the supply of something: *The workmen cut off the electricity.*
cut something out to take something from the place where it was by using scissors, etc.: *I cut the picture out of the newspaper.*
cut something up to **cut** something into pieces with a knife, etc.

cut² 0ᴛ /kʌt/ *noun*
1 an injury on the skin, made by something sharp like a knife: *He had a deep cut on his leg.*
2 a hole or opening in something, made with something sharp: *Make a small cut in the material.*
3 making something smaller or less: *a cut in government spending* ◇ *job cuts*

cute /kjuːt/ *adjective* (cuter, cutest)
pretty and attractive: *What a cute little puppy!*

cutlery /'kʌtləri/ *noun (no plural)* (*British*) (*American* **flatware**)
knives, forks and spoons that you use for eating

CV /ˌsiː 'viː/ (*British*) (*American* **résumé**) *noun*
a written list of your education and work experience that you send when you are trying to get a new job: *Send a full CV with your job application.* ⊃ **CV** is the short way of writing the Latin words **curriculum vitae**.

cyberspace /'saɪbəspeɪs/ *noun (no plural)*
a place that is not real where emails go when you send them from one computer to another

cycle¹ /'saɪkl/ *noun*
a bicycle ⊃ SAME MEANING **bike**: *We went for a cycle ride at the weekend.* ◇ *a cycle shop*

cycle² /'saɪkl/ *verb* (cycles, cycling, cycled /'saɪkld/)
to ride a bicycle: *I cycle to school every day.*

cycling /'saɪklɪŋ/ *noun (no plural)*
the sport or activity of riding a bicycle: *We go cycling most weekends.* ⊃ Look at Picture Dictionary page **P15**.

cyclist /'saɪklɪst/ *noun*
a person who rides a bicycle: *He's a keen cyclist* (= he likes cycling).

cyclone /'saɪkləʊn/ *noun*
a very strong wind that moves in a circle and causes a storm

cylinder /'sɪlɪndə(r)/ *noun*
a long round shape, like a tube or a tin of food
▸ **cylindrical** /sɪ'lɪndrɪkl/ *adjective*: *a cylindrical shape*

A B **C** D E F G H I J K L M N O P Q R S T U V W X Y Z

Dd

D, d /diː/ *noun* (*plural* D's, d's /diːz/)
the fourth letter of the English alphabet: *'Dog' begins with a 'D'.*

dab /dæb/ *verb* (dabs, dabbing, dabbed /dæbd/)
to touch something lightly and quickly: *She dabbed the cut with cotton wool.*

dad /dæd/ *noun* (*informal*)
father: *Hello, Dad.* ◇ *This is my dad.*

daddy /'dædi/ *noun* (*plural* daddies)
a word for 'father' that children use

daffodil /'dæfədɪl/ *noun*
a yellow flower that grows in spring

daft /dɑːft/ *adjective* (dafter, daftest)
(*British, informal*)
silly: *I think you're daft to work for nothing!* ◇ *Don't be daft!*

dagger /'dægə(r)/ *noun*
a short pointed knife that people use as a weapon ➔ Look also at **sword**.

daily /'deɪli/ *adjective, adverb*
happening or coming every day or once a day: *There are daily flights between London and Tokyo.* ◇ *a daily newspaper* ◇ *The museum is open daily from 9 a.m. to 5 p.m.*

dainty /'deɪnti/ *adjective* (daintier, daintiest)
small and pretty: *a dainty little girl*

dairy /'deəri/ *noun* (*plural* dairies)

> 🔎 SPELLING
>
> Be careful! Don't confuse **dairy** and **diary**. You spell **dairy** with **AI**.

a place where milk is kept or where milk products like butter and cheese are made

daisy

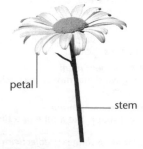

petal
stem

daisy /'deɪzi/ *noun* (*plural* daisies)
a small flower with a yellow centre, which usually grows wild in grass

dam /dæm/ *noun*
a wall that is built across a river to hold the water back

damage¹ 0️⃣ /'dæmɪdʒ/ *noun* (*no plural*)
harm or injury that is caused when something is broken or spoiled: *He had an accident, but he didn't do any damage to his car.*

damage² 0️⃣ /'dæmɪdʒ/ *verb* (damages, damaging, damaged /'dæmɪdʒd/)
to break or harm something: *The house was badly damaged by fire.*
▶ **damaging** /'dæmɪdʒɪŋ/ *adjective*: *Cars have a damaging effect on the environment.*

damn /dæm/ *exclamation*
a rude word that people sometimes use when they are angry: *Damn! I've lost my key!*

damp /dæmp/ *adjective* (damper, dampest)
a little wet: *a cold damp house*

dance¹ 0️⃣ /dɑːns/ *verb* (dances, dancing, danced /dɑːnst/)
to move your body to music: *Ian dances well.* ◇ *I danced with her all night.*
▶ **dancing** /'dɑːnsɪŋ/ *noun* (*no plural*): *Will there be dancing at the party?*

dance² 0️⃣ /dɑːns/ *noun*
1 movements that you do to music
2 a party where people dance: *My parents met at a dance.*

dancer 0️⃣ /'dɑːnsə(r)/ *noun*
a person who dances: *Nureyev was a famous ballet dancer.* ◇ *I'm not a very good dancer.*

dandelions

dandelion /'dændɪlaɪən/ *noun*
a small yellow wild flower

dandruff /'dændrʌf/ *noun* (*no plural*)
small pieces of dead skin in a person's hair

danger 0—¬ /'deɪndʒə(r)/ *noun*
1 (*no plural*) the possibility that something bad may happen: *You may be in danger if you travel alone late at night.*
2 (*plural* dangers) a person or thing that may bring harm or trouble: *Smoking is a danger to health.*

dangerous 0—¬ /'deɪndʒərəs/ *adjective*
A person or thing that is **dangerous** may hurt you: *It's dangerous to drive a car at night without any lights.* ◊ *a dangerous illness*
▶ **dangerously** *adverb*: *She drives dangerously.*

dare /deə(r)/ *verb* (dares, daring, dared /deəd/)

> 🔎 **GRAMMAR**
> The negative is **daren't** /deənt/ or **don't dare** or **doesn't dare**: *They daren't ask her for any more money.* ◊ *He doesn't dare tell anyone that he's broken a window.* In the past tense it is **didn't dare**.

dare do something to be brave enough to do something: *I daren't tell Mum that I've lost her key.* ◊ *I didn't dare ask for more money.*
dare somebody to do something to ask somebody to do something dangerous or silly to see if they are brave enough: *I dare you to jump off that wall!*
don't you dare words that you use for telling somebody very strongly not to do something: *Don't you dare read my letters!*
how dare you words that show you are very angry about something that somebody has done: *How dare you speak to me like that!*

daring /'deərɪŋ/ *adjective*
not afraid to do dangerous things: *a daring attack* ⊃ SAME MEANING **brave**

dark¹ 0—¬ /dɑːk/ *adjective* (darker, darkest)
1 with no light, or not much light: *It was so dark that I couldn't see anything.* ◊ *It gets dark very early in the winter.*
⊃ OPPOSITE **light**
2 A **dark** colour is nearer to black than to white: *a dark green skirt* ◊ *He's got dark brown eyes.* ⊃ OPPOSITE **light**, **pale**
3 A person who is **dark** has brown or black hair or skin: *a thin, dark woman*
⊃ OPPOSITE **fair**

dark² 0—¬ /dɑːk/ *noun* (*no plural*)
the **dark** where there is no light: *Cats can see in the dark.* ◊ *Are you afraid of the dark?*
after dark after the sun goes down in the evening

before dark before the sun goes down in the evening: *Make sure you get home before dark.*

darkness /'dɑːknəs/ *noun* (*no plural*)
when there is no light: *The whole house was in darkness.*

darling /'dɑːlɪŋ/ *noun*
a name that you call somebody that you love: *Are you all right, darling?*

dart /dɑːt/ *verb* (darts, darting, darted)
to move quickly and suddenly: *He darted across the road.*

darts

dart   dartboard

darts /dɑːts/ *noun* (*plural*)
a game in which you throw a small metal arrow (called a **dart**) at a round board with numbers on it (called a **dartboard**)

dash¹ /dæʃ/ *noun* (*plural* dashes)
1 a sudden short run somewhere: *The robber made a dash for the door.*
2 a mark (–) that you use in writing

dash² /dæʃ/ *verb* (dashes, dashing, dashed /dæʃt/)
to run quickly somewhere: *I dashed into a shop when it started to rain.* ◊ *I must dash – I'm late for work.*

dashboard /'dæʃbɔːd/ *noun*
the part of a car in front of the driver where most of the switches and controls are

data /'deɪtə/ *noun* (*plural*)
facts or information: *We are studying the data that we have collected.*

database /'deɪtəbeɪs/ *noun*
information that is stored in a computer in an organized system that lets you look at it and use it in different ways: *Information about every car is stored in the police database.*

date 0—¬ /deɪt/ *noun*
1 the number of the day, the month and sometimes the year: *'What's the date today?' 'The first of February.'* ◊ *Today's date is 11 December 2004.* ◊ *What is your date of birth?*
⊃ Look at Study Page **S8**.
2 a romantic meeting when two people go out somewhere: *He's asked her out on a date.*
3 a small sweet brown fruit that comes from

A B C D E F G H I J K L M N O P Q R S T U V W X Y Z

a tree which grows in hot countries ⟳ Look at Picture Dictionary page **P8**.

out of date

1 not modern: *The machinery they use is completely out of date.*

2 too old, so that you cannot use it: *This ticket is out of date.*

up to date

1 modern: *The new kitchen will be right up to date, with all the latest gadgets.*

2 with the newest information: *Is this list of names up to date?*

daughter 0🔑 /'dɔ:tə(r)/ *noun*

> 🔎 **PRONUNCIATION**
>
> The word **daughter** sounds like **water**, because we don't say the letters **gh** in this word.

a girl or woman who is somebody's child: *They have two daughters and a son.* ◇ *My oldest daughter is a doctor.*

daughter-in-law /'dɔ:tər ɪn lɔ:/ *noun* (plural **daughters-in-law**)
the wife of your son

dawn /dɔ:n/ *noun*
the time in the early morning when the sun comes up

day 0🔑 /deɪ/ *noun* (plural **days**)

1 a time of 24 hours from midnight to the next midnight: *There are seven days in a week.* ◇ *I went to Italy for a few days.* ◇ *'What day is it today?' 'Tuesday.'*

> 🔎 **WORD BUILDING**
>
> The days of the week are: **Monday**, **Tuesday**, **Wednesday**, **Thursday**, **Friday**, **Saturday**, **Sunday**.

2 the time when it is light outside: *Most people work during the day and sleep at night.*

3 a time in the past: *In my grandparents' day, not many people had cars.*

one day

1 on a certain day in the past: *One day, a letter arrived.*

> 🔎 **SPEAKING**
>
> We often use **one day** at the beginning of a story.

2 (*also* **some day**) at some time in the future: *I hope to become a doctor one day.* ◇ *Some day I'll be rich and famous.*

the day after tomorrow not tomorrow, but the next day

the day before yesterday not yesterday, but the day before

the other day a few days ago: *I went to London the other day.*

these days (*informal*) used to talk about the present, especially when you are comparing it with the past: *These days kids grow up so quickly.* ⟳ SAME MEANING **nowadays**

daybreak /'deɪbreɪk/ *noun* (no plural)
the time of day when light first appears

daydream /'deɪdri:m/ *noun*
happy thoughts that make you forget about what you should be doing now: *She stared out of the window, lost in a daydream.*
▶ **daydream** (daydreams, daydreaming, daydreamed /'deɪdri:md/) *verb*: *He daydreamed about being so rich that he could buy anything he wanted.*

daylight /'deɪlaɪt/ *noun* (no plural)
the light from the sun during the day: *These colours look different in daylight.*

day off /ˌdeɪ 'ɒf/ *noun* (plural **days off**)
a day when you do not go to work or school

daytime /'deɪtaɪm/ *noun* (no plural)
the time when it is day and not night: *I prefer to study in the daytime and go out in the evening.*

dazzle /'dæzl/ *verb* (dazzles, dazzling, dazzled /'dæzld/)
If a light **dazzles** you, it shines brightly in your eyes so that you cannot see for a short time: *I was dazzled by the car's lights.*

dead¹ 0🔑 /ded/ *adjective*

1 not alive now: *All my grandparents are dead.* ◇ *Throw away those dead flowers.* ◇ *Survivors helped to bury the dead* (= the dead people).

2 (*informal*) very quiet: *This town is dead: everywhere is closed after ten o'clock at night.*

a dead end a street that is only open at one end

dead² /ded/ *adverb* (*informal*)
completely or very: *I'm dead tired.*

deadline /'dedlaɪn/ *noun*
a day or time before which you must do something: *The deadline for finishing this essay is next Tuesday.*

deadly¹ /'dedli/ *adjective* (deadlier, deadliest)
Something that is **deadly** may kill people or other living things: *a deadly weapon*

deadly² /'dedli/ *adverb* (*informal*)
extremely: *I'm deadly serious.*

deaf /def/ *adjective*
not able to hear anything or not able to hear very well: *My grandma's starting to go deaf.* ◇ *television subtitles for the deaf* (= people who cannot hear)
▶ **deafness** /'defnəs/ *noun* (no plural): *In old age she was troubled by deafness.*

A
B
C
D
E
F
G
H
I
J
K
L
M
N
O
P
Q
R
S
T
U
V
W
X
Y
Z

deafen /'defn/ *verb* (deafens, deafening, deafened /'defnd/)
to make a very loud noise so that somebody cannot hear well: *We were deafened by the loud music.*

deal¹ ∘━ /di:l/ *verb* (deals, dealing, dealt /delt/, has dealt)
1 to give cards to players in a game of cards: *Start by dealing seven cards to each player.*
2 to buy and sell something in business: *Our firm **deals with** customers all over the world.* ◊ *We **deal in** insurance.*
deal out to give something to a number of people: *The profits will be dealt out among us.*
deal with something
1 to take action in a particular situation in order to solve a problem or do a particular job: *I am too busy to deal with this problem now.*
2 to be about a special subject: *The first chapter of the book deals with letter writing.*

deal² /di:l/ *noun*
an agreement, usually about buying, selling or working: *Let's **make a deal** – I'll help you today if you help me tomorrow.*
a good deal *or* **a great deal** a lot: *I've spent a great deal of time on this report.*

dealer /'di:lə(r)/ *noun*
a person who buys and sells things: *a car dealer*

dear¹ ∘━ /dɪə(r)/ *adjective* (dearer, dearest)

> 🔎 **PRONUNCIATION**
> The word **dear** sounds just like **deer**.

1 Dear a word that you use before a person's name at the beginning of a letter: *Dear Mr Carter, …* ◊ *Dear Sir or Madam, …*
2 that you love very much: *She was a dear friend.*
3 (*British*) costing a lot of money
⊃ SAME MEANING **expensive**: *Those strawberries are too dear.* ⊃ OPPOSITE **cheap**

dear² /dɪə(r)/ *exclamation*
something you say if you are surprised, upset or disappointed: *Oh dear! It's started raining again.* ◊ *Dear me! What a mess!*

dear³ /dɪə(r)/ *noun* (*informal*)
a word that you use when you are speaking to somebody that you love: *Hello, dear.*

death ∘━ /deθ/ *noun*
when a life finishes: *He became manager of the company after his father's death.* ◊ *There are thousands of deaths in car accidents every year.*

deathly /'deθli/ (deathlier, deathliest) *adjective*
like death: *There was a deathly silence.*

debate /dɪ'beɪt/ *noun*
a public meeting where people talk about something important
▶ **debate** *verb* (debates, debating, debated): *Politicians will be debating the new law later this week.*

debit card /'debɪt kɑːd/ *noun*
a plastic card that you can use to pay for things directly from your bank account: *Can I pay **by debit card**?*

debt ∘━ /det/ *noun*
money that you must pay back to somebody: *The company has borrowed a lot of money and it still has debts.*
in debt If you are **in debt**, you must pay money to somebody.

decade /'dekeɪd/ *noun*
a period of ten years: *The country has become richer in the past decade.*

decaffeinated /ˌdiː'kæfɪneɪtɪd/ *adjective*
(used about coffee or tea) with all or most of the CAFFEINE (= the substance that makes you feel awake) taken out: *I only drink decaffeinated coffee in the evenings.*

decay /dɪ'keɪ/ *verb* (decays, decaying, decayed /dɪ'keɪd/)
to become bad or be slowly destroyed: *If you don't clean your teeth, they will decay.*
▶ **decay** *noun* (*no plural*): *tooth decay*

deceive /dɪ'siːv/ *verb* (deceives, deceiving, deceived /dɪ'siːvd/)

> 🔎 **SPELLING**
> Remember! When the sound is /iː/ (which rhymes with 'be', there is a spelling rule: **I before E, except after C** so you spell **deceive** with **EI** (not **IE**).

to deliberately make somebody believe something that is not true: *She **deceived** me **into** thinking she was a police officer.* ◊ *You're deceiving yourself if you think he'll change his mind.*

December ∘━ /dɪ'sembə(r)/ *noun*
the twelfth month of the year

decent /'diːsnt/ *adjective*
1 good enough; right: *You can't wear jeans for a job interview — you should buy some decent clothes.*
2 honest and good: *decent people*

decide ∘━ /dɪ'saɪd/ *verb* (decides, deciding, decided)
to choose something after thinking about the possibilities: *I can't decide what colour to*

A

paint my room. ◇ *We've **decided to** go to France for our holidays.* ◇ *She **decided that** she didn't want to come.*

B

C

decimal /ˈdesɪml/ *noun*
part of a number, written after a small round mark (called a **decimal point**): *Three quarters written as a decimal is 0.75.*

D

E

𝒫 SPEAKING
We say '0.75' as 'nought point seven five'.

F

decision 0━ /dɪˈsɪʒn/ *noun*
choosing something after thinking; deciding: *I must **make a decision about** what I'm going to do when I leave school.*

G

H

deck /dek/ *noun*
1 one of the floors of a ship, plane or bus: *He stood on the lower deck of the ship and looked out to sea.*
2 (*American*) (*British* **pack**) a set of 52 cards for playing games

I

J

K

deckchair
/ˈdektʃeə(r)/ *noun*
a chair that you use outside, for example on the beach. You can fold it up and carry it.

deckchair

L

M

N

declare 0━ /dɪˈkleə(r)/ *verb* (declares, declaring, declared /dɪˈkleəd/)
1 to say very clearly what you think or what you will do, often to a lot of people: *He **declared that** he was not a thief.* ◇ *The country **declared war** on its enemy.*
2 In an airport or port you **declare** things that you have bought in another country so that you can pay tax on them: *Have you anything to declare?*
▶ **declaration** /ˌdekləˈreɪʃn/ *noun*: *a declaration of independence*

O

P

Q

R

S

decorate 0━ /ˈdekəreɪt/ *verb*
(decorates, decorating, decorated)
1 to make something look nicer by adding beautiful things to it: *We decorated the room with flowers.*
2 to put paint or paper on the walls of a room: *I am decorating the kitchen.*

T

U

V

decoration /ˌdekəˈreɪʃn/ *noun*
a beautiful thing that you add to something to make it look nicer: *Christmas decorations*

W

X

decrease /dɪˈkriːs/ *verb* (decreases, decreasing, decreased /dɪˈkriːst/)
to become or to make something smaller or less: *The number of people in the village has decreased from 200 to 100.*
↻ OPPOSITE **increase**
▶ **decrease** /ˈdiːkriːs/ *noun*: *There was a*

Y

Z

decrease in the number of people living in the village. ↻ OPPOSITE **increase**

deed /diːd/ *noun* (*formal*)
a thing that somebody does that is usually very good or very bad: *Doing the shopping for her grandmother was a good deed.*

deep 0━ /diːp/ *adjective* (deeper, deepest)
1 Something that is **deep** goes down a long way: *Be careful: the water is very deep.* ◇ *There were deep cuts in his face.* ↻ Look at the picture at **shallow**.
2 You use **deep** to say or ask how far something is from the top to the bottom: *The hole was about six metres deep and three metres wide.* ↻ The noun is **depth**.
3 A **deep** sound is low and strong: *He has a deep voice.* ↻ OPPOSITE **high**
4 A **deep** colour is strong and dark: *She has deep blue eyes.* ↻ OPPOSITE **pale** or **light**
5 If you are in a **deep** sleep, it is difficult for somebody to wake you up: *She was in such a deep sleep that she didn't hear me calling her.*
6 Deep feelings are very strong: *deep sadness*

deeply 0━ /ˈdiːpli/ *adverb*
strongly or completely: *They were deeply disturbed by the accident.* ◇ *He is sleeping very deeply.*

deer /dɪə(r)/ *noun* (*plural* deer)

𝒫 PRONUNCIATION
The word **deer** sounds just like **dear**.

a wild animal that eats grass and has horns that look like branches (called antlers).

deer

defeat 0━
/dɪˈfiːt/ *verb*
(defeats, defeating, defeated)
to win a fight or game against a person or group of people: *The army defeated the rebels.*
▶ **defeat** *noun*: *It was another defeat for the team.*

defence (*British*) (*American* **defense**)
/dɪˈfens/ *noun*
fighting against people who attack, or keeping away dangerous people or things: *They fought the war **in defence of** their country.*

defend /dɪˈfend/ *verb* (defends, defending, defended)
1 to fight to keep away people or things that attack: *They **defended** the city **against** the enemy.*
2 to say that somebody has not done something wrong: *My sister defended me when my father said I was lazy.* ◇ *He had a lawyer to defend him in court.*
3 to try to stop another person or team scoring goals or points in a game

defense *American English for* DEFENCE

defiant /dɪˈfaɪənt/ *adjective*
refusing to do what somebody tells you: *From the age of fifteen she became more defiant.*

defied (*also* defies) *forms of* DEFY

define /dɪˈfaɪn/ *verb* (defines, defining, defined /dɪˈfaɪnd/)
to say what a word means: *How do you define 'rich'?*

definite 0ᵣ /ˈdefɪnət/ *adjective*
Something that is **definite** is clear, fixed and unlikely to change. ⊃ SAME MEANING **certain**: *I want a definite answer, 'yes' or 'no'.* ◇ *There has been a definite change in her attitude.*

definite article /ˌdefɪnət ˈɑːtɪkl/ *noun*
(*grammar*) in English grammar, the word 'the' ⊃ Look at **indefinite article**.

definitely 0ᵣ /ˈdefɪnətli/ *adverb*
certainly: *I'll definitely consider your advice.* ◇ *It's definitely the best restaurant in the town.*

definition /ˌdefɪˈnɪʃn/ *noun*
a group of words that tell you what another word means

defy /dɪˈfaɪ/ *verb* (defies, defying, defied /dɪˈfaɪd/, has defied)
If you **defy** somebody or something, you do something that they say you should not do: *She defied her parents and stayed out all night.*

degree 0ᵣ /dɪˈɡriː/ *noun*
1 a measurement of temperature: *Water boils at 100 degrees Celsius (100° C).*
2 a measurement of angles (= the space between two lines that meet): *There are 90 degrees (90°) in a right angle.*
3 Universities and colleges give **degrees** to students who have completed special courses there: *She has a **degree in** Mathematics.*

delay¹ /dɪˈleɪ/ *noun* (*plural* delays)
a time when somebody or something is late: *There was a long delay at the airport.* ◇ *You must pay the money **without delay** (= immediately).*

delay² /dɪˈleɪ/ *verb* (delays, delaying, delayed /dɪˈleɪd/)
1 to make somebody or something late: *My train was delayed for two hours because of the bad weather.*
2 to not do something until a later time: *Can we delay our meeting until next week?*

delete /dɪˈliːt/ *verb* (deletes, deleting, deleted)
to remove something that is written or that is stored on a computer: *I deleted some important files on my computer by accident.*

deliberate /dɪˈlɪbərət/ *adjective*
If something is **deliberate** then it is planned and not done by mistake: *Was it an accident or was it deliberate?*

deliberately 0ᵣ /dɪˈlɪbərətli/ *adverb*
If you do something **deliberately**, you wanted or planned to do it: *The police think that somebody started the fire deliberately.*

delicate /ˈdelɪkət/ *adjective*
1 If something is **delicate**, you can break or damage it very easily: *I've got delicate skin, so I use special soap.*
2 light and pleasant; not strong: *delicate colours like pale pink and pale blue* ◇ *The food had a delicate flavour.*

delicatessen /ˌdelɪkəˈtesn/ *noun*
a shop that sells special, unusual or foreign food, especially cold cooked meat and cheeses

delicious /dɪˈlɪʃəs/ *adjective*
very good to eat: *This soup is delicious.*

delight¹ /dɪˈlaɪt/ *noun* (no plural)
great happiness ⊃ SAME MEANING **joy**: *The children shrieked **with delight** when they saw the puppy.*

delight² /dɪˈlaɪt/ *verb* (delights, delighting, delighted)
to make somebody very pleased or happy

delighted /dɪˈlaɪtɪd/ *adjective*
very pleased or happy: *I'm delighted to meet you.*

delightful /dɪˈlaɪtfl/ *adjective*
very pleasant or attractive ⊃ SAME MEANING **lovely**: *We stayed in a delightful little hotel.*

deliver 0ᵣ /dɪˈlɪvə(r)/ *verb* (delivers, delivering, delivered /dɪˈlɪvəd/)
to take something to the place where it must go: *The postman delivered two letters this morning.*
▸ **delivery** /dɪˈlɪvəri/ *noun* (*plural* deliveries): *We are waiting for a delivery of bread.*

A B C **D** E F G H I J K L M N O P Q R S T U V W X Y Z

A
B
C
D
E
F
G
H
I
J
K
L
M
N
O
P
Q
R
S
T
U
V
W
X
Y
Z

demand¹ 0‑ /dɪˈmɑːnd/ *noun*
saying strongly that you must have
something: *a **demand** for higher pay*
in demand wanted by a lot of people:
Good teachers are always in demand.

demand² 0‑ /dɪˈmɑːnd/ *verb*
(demands, demanding, demanded)
to say strongly that you must have
something: *The workers are demanding more
money.* ◇ *She demanded to see the manager.*

demo /ˈdeməʊ/ *noun* (*plural* demos)
(*informal*) short for DEMONSTRATION: *All the
students went on the demo.*

democracy /dɪˈmɒkrəsi/ *noun* (*plural*
democracies)
1 a system of government where the people
choose their leader by voting
2 a country with a government that the
people choose

democrat /ˈdeməkræt/ *noun*
1 a person who wants DEMOCRACY
2 Democrat (*politics*) a person in the
Democratic Party in the US ➔ Look at
Republican.

democratic /ˌdeməˈkrætɪk/ *adjective*
If a country, etc. is **democratic**, all the
people in it can choose its leaders or decide
about the way it is organized.

the Democratic Party /ðə
ˌdeməˈkrætɪk pɑːti/ *noun* (*no plural*)
(*politics*) one of the two main political parties
in the US ➔ Look at **the Republican Party**.

demolish /dɪˈmɒlɪʃ/ *verb* (demolishes,
demolishing, demolished /dɪˈmɒlɪʃt/)
to break a building so that it falls down: *The
warehouse is due to be demolished next year.*
▸ **demolition** /ˌdeməˈlɪʃn/ *noun* (*no
plural*): *The demolition of the factory will make
room for more houses.*

demonstrate /ˈdemənstreɪt/ *verb*
(demonstrates, demonstrating,
demonstrated)
1 to show something clearly: *He
demonstrated how to operate the machine.*
2 to walk or stand in public with a group of
people to show that you have strong
feelings about something ➔ SAME MEANING
protest: *Thousands of people demonstrated
against the war.*

demonstration /ˌdemənˈstreɪʃn/ (*also
informal* demo) *noun*
1 a group of people walking or standing
together in public to show that they have
strong feelings about something: *anti-
government demonstrations*
2 showing how to do something, or how
something works: *He gave us a cookery
demonstration.*

den /den/ *noun*
the place where a wild animal lives

denied (*also* denies) forms of DENY

denim /ˈdenɪm/ *noun* (*no plural*)
strong cotton material that is used for
making jeans and other clothes. **Denim** is
often blue: *a denim jacket* ➔ Look at Picture
Dictionary page **P5**.

dense /dens/ *adjective*
1 with a lot of things or people close
together: *dense forests*
2 thick and difficult to see through: *The
accident happened in dense fog.*

dent /dent/ *noun*
a place where a flat surface, especially metal,
has been hit and pushed in but not broken:
There's a big dent in the side of my car.
▸ **dent** *verb* (dents, denting, dented):
I dropped the tin and dented it.

dental /ˈdentl/ *adjective*
connected with teeth: *dental care*

dentist 0‑ /ˈdentɪst/ *noun*
1 a person whose job is to look after your
teeth ➔ Look at Picture Dictionary page **P12**.
➔ Look at the note at **tooth**.
2 the dentist's (*no plural*) the place where
a dentist works: *I have to go to the dentist's
today.*

deny /dɪˈnaɪ/ *verb* (denies, denying,
denied /dɪˈnaɪd/, has denied)
to say that something is not true: *He **denied**
that he had stolen the car.* ◇ *They denied
breaking the window.* ➔ OPPOSITE admit

deodorant /diˈəʊdərənt/ *noun*
a liquid that you put on your body to stop
bad smells

depart /dɪˈpɑːt/ *verb* (departs, departing,
departed)
to leave a place: *The next train to Birmingham
departs from platform 3.*

⌕ SPEAKING
It is more usual to say **leave**.

➔ OPPOSITE **arrive**

department 0‑ /dɪˈpɑːtmənt/ *noun*
one of the parts of a university, school,
government, shop, big company, etc.: *The
book department is on the second floor.* ◇ *the
sales department*

department store /dɪˈpɑːtmənt stɔː(r)/
noun
a big shop that sells a lot of different things:
*Harrods is a famous department store in
London.*

departure /dɪˈpɑːtʃə(r)/ *noun*
leaving a place: *Passengers should check in at*

least one hour before departure.
⊃ OPPOSITE **arrival**

depend 0–ᴡ /dɪˈpend/ *verb* (depends, depending, depended)
depend on somebody or **something**
1 to need somebody or something: *She still depends on her parents for money because she hasn't got a job.*
2 to trust somebody; to feel sure that somebody or something will do what you want: *I know I can depend on my friends to help me.*
it depends, **that depends** words that you use to show that something is not certain: *I don't know whether I'll see him. It depends what time he gets here.* ◊ *'Can you lend me some money?' 'That depends. How much do you want?'*

dependant /dɪˈpendənt/ *noun*
a person, especially a child, who depends on another person for a home, food, money, etc.: *Do you have any dependants?*

dependent /dɪˈpendənt/ *adjective*
If you are **dependent** on somebody or something, you need them: *A baby is completely dependent on its parents.*

deposit[1] /dɪˈpɒzɪt/ *noun*
1 money that you pay to show that you want something and that you will pay the rest later: *We paid a deposit on the flat.*
2 extra money that you pay when you rent something. You get it back if you do not damage or lose what you have rented: *If you damage the car they will keep your deposit.*
3 money that you pay into a bank: *I'd like to make a deposit, please.*

deposit[2] /dɪˈpɒzɪt/ *verb* (deposits, depositing, deposited)
to put something somewhere to keep it safe: *The money was deposited in the bank.*

depot /ˈdepəʊ/ *noun*
a place where a lot of goods or vehicles are stored

depress /dɪˈpres/ *verb* (depresses, depressing, depressed /dɪˈprest/)
to make somebody feel sad: *This wet weather really depresses me.*

depressed /dɪˈprest/ *adjective*
very unhappy for a long period of time: *He's been very depressed since he lost his job.*

depressing /dɪˈpresɪŋ/ *adjective*
Something that is **depressing** makes you feel very unhappy: *That film about the war was very depressing.*

depression /dɪˈpreʃn/ *noun* (no plural)
a feeling of unhappiness that lasts for a long time: *She often suffers from depression.*

depth /depθ/ *noun*
how deep something is; how far it is from the top of something to the bottom: *What is the depth of the swimming pool?* ◊ *The hole was 2m in depth.* ⊃ The adjective is **deep**.

deputy /ˈdepjəti/ *noun* (*plural* deputies)
the person in a company, school, etc., who does the work of the leader when they are not there: *a deputy headmaster*

derivative /dɪˈrɪvətɪv/ *noun*
a word that is made from another word: *'Sadness' is a derivative of 'sad'.*

descend /dɪˈsend/ *verb* (descends, descending, descended) (*formal*)
to go down: *The plane started to descend.*

> 🗩 SPEAKING
>
> It is more usual to say **go down**.

descendant /dɪˈsendənt/ *noun*
Your **descendants** are your children, your children's children (called **grandchildren**) and everybody in your family who lives after you: *Queen Elizabeth II is a descendant of Queen Victoria.*

descent /dɪˈsent/ *noun*
going down: *The plane began its descent to Munich airport.*

describe 0–ᴡ /dɪˈskraɪb/ *verb* (describes, describing, described /dɪˈskraɪbd/)
to say what somebody or something is like or what happened: *Can you describe the man you saw?* ◊ *She described the accident to the police.*

description 0–ᴡ /dɪˈskrɪpʃn/ *noun*
words that tell what somebody or something is like or what happened: *I gave the police a description of the thief.*

desert[1] 0–ᴡ /ˈdezət/ *noun*

> ✎ SPELLING
>
> Remember! You spell **desert** with one **S**.

a large, dry area of land with very few plants: *the Sahara Desert*

desert[2] /dɪˈzɜːt/ *verb* (deserts, deserting, deserted)
to leave a person or place when it is wrong to go: *He deserted his wife and children.*

deserted /dɪˈzɜːtɪd/ *adjective*
empty, because all the people have left: *At night the streets are deserted.*

desert island /ˌdezət ˈaɪlənd/ *noun*
an island where nobody lives, in a hot part of the world

A B C **D** E F G H I J K L M N O P Q R S T U V W X Y Z

A

deserve /dɪˈzɜːv/ *verb* (deserves, deserving, deserved /dɪˈzɜːvd/)
to be good or bad enough to have something: *You have worked very hard and you deserve a rest.* ◇ *They stole money from old people, so they deserve to go to prison.*

B

C

D

design¹ 0ᵐ /dɪˈzaɪn/ *noun*

> 🔊 PRONUNCIATION
> The word **design** sounds like **fine**, because we don't say the letter **g** in this word.

E

F

1 a drawing that shows how to make something: *Have you seen the designs for the new shopping centre?*
2 a pattern of lines, shapes and colours on something: *The wallpaper has a design of blue and green squares on it.*

G

H

I

design² 0ᵐ /dɪˈzaɪn/ *verb* (designs, designing, designed /dɪˈzaɪnd/)
to draw a plan that shows how to make something: *The building was designed by a German architect.*

J

K

designer /dɪˈzaɪnə(r)/ *noun*
a person whose job is to make drawings that show how something will be made: *a fashion designer*

L

M

desire 0ᵐ /dɪˈzaɪə(r)/ *noun*
a feeling of wanting something very much: *a desire for peace*

N

O

desk

P

Q

R

S

T

U

desk 0ᵐ /desk/ *noun*
1 a type of table, often with drawers, that you sit at to write or work: *The pupils took their books out of their desks.*
2 a table or place in a building where somebody gives information, etc.: *Ask at the information desk.*

V

W

X

despair /dɪˈspeə(r)/ *noun* (no plural)
a feeling of not having hope: *He was in despair because he had no money and nowhere to live.*
▶ **despair** *verb* (despairs, despairing,

Y

Z

despaired /dɪˈspeəd/): *We began to despair of ever finding somewhere to live.*

desperate /ˈdespərət/ *adjective*
1 If you are **desperate**, you have no hope and you are ready to do anything to get what you want: *She is so desperate for a job that she will work anywhere.*
2 very serious: *There is a desperate need for food in some parts of Africa.*
▶ **desperately** /ˈdespərətli/ *adverb*: *He is desperately unhappy.*

desperation /ˌdespəˈreɪʃn/ *noun* (no plural)
the feeling of having no hope, that makes you do anything to get what you want: *In desperation, she sold her ring to get money for food.*

despise /dɪˈspaɪz/ *verb* (despises, despising, despised /dɪˈspaɪzd/)
to hate somebody or something: *I despise people who tell lies.*

despite /dɪˈspaɪt/ *preposition*
although something happened or is true; not noticing or not caring about something ⊃ SAME MEANING **in spite of**: *We decided to go out despite the bad weather.*

dessert /dɪˈzɜːt/ *noun*

> 🔊 SPELLING
> Remember! You spell **dessert** with **SS**.

something sweet that you eat at the end of a meal ⊃ SAME MEANING **pudding**: *We had ice cream for dessert.*

dessertspoon /dɪˈzɜːtspuːn/ *noun*
a spoon that you use for eating DESSERTS ⊃ Look at the picture at **spoon**.

destination /ˌdestɪˈneɪʃn/ *noun*
the place where somebody or something is going: *They were very tired when they finally reached their destination.*

destroy 0ᵐ /dɪˈstrɔɪ/ *verb* (destroys, destroying, destroyed /dɪˈstrɔɪd/)
to break something completely so that you cannot use it again or so that it is gone: *The house was destroyed by fire.*

destruction /dɪˈstrʌkʃn/ *noun* (no plural)
breaking something completely so that you cannot use it again or so that it is gone: *the destruction of the city by bombs*

detach /dɪˈtætʃ/ *verb* (detaches, detaching, detached /dɪˈtætʃt/)
to separate something from another thing that it is joined to: *Please complete and detach the form below.* ⊃ OPPOSITE **attach**

detached /dɪˈtætʃt/ *adjective*
A **detached** house stands alone and is not joined to any other house.

detail 0̄ /'diːteɪl/ *noun*
1 one of the very small parts that make the whole of something: *Tell me quickly what happened – I don't need to know all the details.*
2 **details** (*plural*) information about something: *For more details, please telephone this number.*
in detail with all the small parts: *Tell me about your plan in detail.*

detailed /'diːteɪld/ *adjective*
giving a lot of information: *a detailed description*

detect /dɪ'tekt/ *verb* (detects, detecting, detected)
to discover or notice something that is difficult to see: *The tests detected a small amount of blood on his clothes.*

detective /dɪ'tektɪv/ *noun*
a person whose job is to find out who did a crime. **Detectives** are usually police officers: *Sherlock Holmes is a famous detective in stories.*

detention /dɪ'tenʃn/ *noun*
the punishment of being kept at school after the other children have gone home: *They can't give me a detention for this.*

detergent /dɪ'tɜːdʒənt/ *noun*
a powder or liquid that you use for washing things

deteriorate /dɪ'tɪəriəreɪt/ *verb* (deteriorates, deteriorating, deteriorated)
to get worse: *Her health deteriorated as she got older.*

determination 0̄ /dɪ,tɜːmɪ'neɪʃn/ *noun* (*no plural*)
being certain that you want to do something: *She has shown great determination to succeed.*

determined 0̄ /dɪ'tɜːmɪnd/ *adjective*
very certain that you want do something: *She is determined to win the match.*

detest /dɪ'test/ *verb* (detests, detesting, detested)
to hate somebody or something: *They have always detested each other.*

detour /'diːtʊə(r)/ *noun*
a longer way to a place when you cannot go by the usual way: *The bridge was closed so we had to make a detour.*

devastate /'devəsteɪt/ *verb* (devastates, devastating, devastated)
1 to destroy something or damage it very badly: *War devastated the country.*
2 to make somebody extremely upset and

shocked: *This tragedy has devastated the community.*
▸ **devastating** /'devəsteɪtɪŋ/ *adjective*: *The storm had a devastating effect on the island.*

develop 0̄ /dɪ'veləp/ *verb* (develops, developing, developed /dɪ'veləpt/)
1 to grow slowly, increase, or change into something else; to make somebody or something do this: *Children develop into adults.*
2 to begin to have something: *She developed the disease at the age of 27.*
3 When a photograph is **developed**, special chemicals are used on the film so that you can see the picture.

developing country /dɪ,veləpɪŋ 'kʌntri/ *noun*
a country that is poor and is just starting to have modern industries

development 0̄ /dɪ'veləpmənt/ *noun*
1 (*no plural*) becoming bigger or more complete; growing: *We studied the development of babies in their first year of life.*
2 (*plural* **developments**) something new that happens: *There are new developments in science almost every day.*

device /dɪ'vaɪs/ *noun*
a tool or piece of equipment that you use for doing a special job: *a device for opening tins*

devil /'devl/ *noun* **the Devil** (*no plural*)
the most powerful evil spirit, according to some religions

devote /dɪ'vəʊt/ *verb* (devotes, devoting, devoted)
to give a lot of time or energy to something: *She devoted her life to helping the poor.*

devoted /dɪ'vəʊtɪd/ *adjective*
If you are **devoted** to somebody or something, you love them very much: *John is devoted to his wife and children.*

dew /djuː/ *noun* (*no plural*)
small drops of water that form on plants and grass in the night: *In the morning, the grass was wet with dew.*

diabetes /,daɪə'biːtiːz/ *noun* (*no plural*)
a disease that makes it difficult for your body to control the level of sugar in your blood

diagonal /daɪ'ægənl/ *adjective*
If you draw a **diagonal** line from one corner of a square to another, you make two triangles. ⊃ Look at the picture at **line**.
▸ **diagonally** /daɪ'ægənəli/ *adverb*: *Walk diagonally across the field to the far corner and then turn left.*

A
B
C
D
E
F
G
H
I
J
K
L
M
N
O
P
Q
R
S
T
U
V
W
X
Y
Z

A
B
C
D
E
F
G
H
I
J
K
L
M
N
O
P
Q
R
S
T
U
V
W
X
Y
Z

diagram 0—┱ /'daɪəgræm/ *noun*
a picture that explains something: *This diagram shows all the parts of an engine.*

dial¹ /'daɪəl/ *noun*
a round part of a clock or other piece of equipment with numbers or letters on it which shows the time, speed, temperature, etc.: *Check the tyre pressure on the dial.*

dial² /'daɪəl/ *verb* (*British* **dials, dialling, dialled** /'daɪəld/) (*American* **dialing, dialed**)
to use a telephone by pushing buttons or turning the **dial** to call a number: *You have dialled the wrong number.*

dialect /'daɪəlekt/ *noun*
the form of a language that people speak in one part of a country: *a local dialect*

dialogue (*British*) (*American* **dialog**) /'daɪəlɒg/ *noun*
words that people say to each other in a book, play or film

diameter /daɪ'æmɪtə(r)/ *noun*
a straight line across a circle, through the centre ⊃ Look at the picture at **circle**.

diamond 0—┱ /'daɪəmənd/ *noun*
1 a hard stone that looks like clear glass and is very expensive: *The ring has a large diamond in it.* ◇ *a diamond necklace*
2 the shape ♦ ⊃ Look at the picture at **shape**.
3 diamonds (*plural*) the group of playing cards (called a **suit**) that have red ♦ shapes on them: *the eight of diamonds* ⊃ Look at the picture at **playing card**.

diaper /'daɪəpə(r)/ *American English for* **NAPPY**

diarrhoea (*American* **diarrhea**) /ˌdaɪə'rɪə/ *noun* (*no plural*)
an illness that makes you go to the toilet very often: *an attack of diarrhoea*

diary /'daɪəri/ *noun* (*plural* **diaries**)

> 🔎 SPELLING
>
> Be careful! Don't confuse **diary** and **dairy**. You spell **diary** with **IA**.

1 a book where you write what you are going to do: *I'll look in my diary to see if I'm free tomorrow.*
2 a book where you write what you have done each day: *Do you keep a diary* (= write in a diary every day)*?*

dice /daɪs/ *noun* (*plural* **dice**)
a small piece of wood or plastic with spots on the sides for playing games: *Throw the dice.*

dice

dictate /dɪk'teɪt/ *verb* (**dictates, dictating, dictated**)
to say words so that another person can write them: *She dictated a letter to her secretary.*

dictation /dɪk'teɪʃn/ *noun*
words that you say or read so that another person can write them down: *We had a dictation in English today* (= a test when we wrote down what the teacher said).

dictator /dɪk'teɪtə(r)/ *noun*
a person who has complete control of a country

dictionary 0—┱ /'dɪkʃənri/ *noun* (*plural* **dictionaries**)
a book that gives words from A to Z and explains what each word means: *Look up the words in your dictionary.*

did *form of* DO

didn't /'dɪdnt/ *short for* DID NOT

die 0—┱ /daɪ/ *verb* (**dies, dying, died** /daɪd/, *has* **died**)
to stop living: *People, animals and plants die if they don't have water.* ◇ *She died of cancer.*
be dying for something (*informal*) to want to have something very much: *It's so hot! I'm dying for a drink.*
be dying to do something to want to do something very much: *My brother is dying to meet you.*
die down to slowly become less strong: *The storm died down.*

diesel /'diːzl/ *noun*
1 (*no plural*) a type of heavy oil that is used in some engines instead of petrol: *a diesel engine* ◇ *a taxi that runs on diesel*
2 (*plural* **diesels**) a vehicle that uses **diesel**: *My new car's a diesel.*

diet /'daɪət/ *noun*
1 the food that you usually eat: *It is important to have a healthy diet.*
2 special foods that you eat when you are ill or when you want to get thinner: *You'll need to go on a diet if you want to lose some weight.*

difference 0—┱ /'dɪfrəns/ *noun*
the way that one thing is not the same as another thing: *What's the difference between*

this computer and that cheaper one? ◇ What's the **difference in** price between these two bikes? ◇ Sarah looks exactly like her sister – I can't **tell the difference** between them.

make a difference to change or have an effect on somebody or something: *Marriage made a big difference to her life.*

make no difference, **not make any difference** to not change anything; to not be important: *It makes no difference to us if the baby is a girl or a boy.*

different 0ᵐ /'dɪfrənt/ *adjective*
1 not the same: *These two shoes are different sizes!* ◇ *Cricket is different from baseball.*
2 many and not the same: *They sell 30 different sorts of ice cream.*
▶ **differently** /'dɪfrəntli/ *adverb*: *He's very quiet at home but he behaves differently at school.*

difficult 0ᵐ /'dɪfɪkəlt/ *adjective*
1 not easy to do or understand: *a difficult problem* ◇ *The exam was very difficult.* ◇ *It's difficult to learn a new language.*
⊃ OPPOSITE **easy**
2 A person who is **difficult** is not easy to please or will not do what you want: *She's a very difficult child.*

difficulty 0ᵐ /'dɪfɪkəlti/ *noun* (plural difficulties)
a problem; something that is not easy to do or understand: *I have difficulty understanding German.* ◇ *My grandfather walks with difficulty now.*

dig

spade

dig 0ᵐ /dɪg/ *verb* (digs, digging, dug /dʌg/, has dug)
to move earth and make a hole in the ground: *You need to dig the garden before you plant the seeds.* ◇ *They dug a tunnel through the mountain for the new railway.*

dig something up to take something from the ground by **digging**: *They dug up some Roman coins in their field.*

digest /daɪ'dʒest/ *verb* (digests, digesting, digested)
When your stomach **digests** food, it changes it so that your body can use it.
▶ **digestion** /daɪ'dʒestʃən/ *noun* (no plural): *Vegetables are usually cooked to help digestion.*

digital /'dɪdʒɪtl/ *adjective*
1 using an electronic system that changes sounds or pictures into numbers before it stores or sends them: *a digital camera*
2 A **digital** clock or watch shows the time in numbers.

dignified /'dɪgnɪfaɪd/ *adjective*
behaving in a calm, serious way that makes other people respect you

dignity /'dɪgnəti/ *noun* (no plural)
calm and serious behaviour that makes other people respect you: *to behave with dignity*

dilemma /dɪ'lemə; daɪ'lemə/ *noun*
a situation when you have to make a difficult choice between two things: *to be in a dilemma*

dilute /daɪ'luːt; daɪ'ljuːt/ *verb* (dilutes, diluting, diluted)
to add water to another liquid: *You need to dilute this paint before you use it.*

dim /dɪm/ *adjective* (dimmer, dimmest)
not bright or clear: *The light was so dim that we couldn't see anything.*
▶ **dimly** /'dɪmli/ *adverb*: *The room was dimly lit and full of smoke.*

din /dɪn/ *noun* (no plural)
a very loud, unpleasant noise: *Stop making that terrible din!*

dinghy /'dɪŋi/ *noun* (plural dinghies)
a small open boat ⊃ Look at the picture at **boat**.

dining room /'daɪnɪŋ ruːm/ *noun*
a room where people eat ⊃ Look at Picture Dictionary page **P10**.

dinner 0ᵐ /'dɪnə(r)/ *noun*
the largest meal of the day. You have **dinner** in the evening, or sometimes in the middle of the day: *What time do you usually have dinner?* ◇ *What's for dinner?* ⊃ Look at the note at **meal**.

dinosaur /'daɪnəsɔː(r)/ *noun*
a big wild animal that lived a very long time ago: *dinosaur fossils*

dip /dɪp/ *verb* (dips, dipping, dipped /dɪpt/)
to put something into a liquid for a short

time and then take it out again: *Dip your hand in the water to see how hot it is.*

diploma /dɪˈpləʊmə/ *noun*
a piece of paper that shows you have passed an exam or finished special studies: *a teaching diploma*

diplomat /ˈdɪpləmæt/ *noun*
a person whose job is to speak and do things for their country in another country

diplomatic /ˌdɪpləˈmætɪk/ *adjective*
1 connected with managing relations between countries: *diplomatic talks*
2 careful not to say or do things that may make people unhappy or angry ○ SAME MEANING **tactful**: *a diplomatic answer*

direct¹ 0ᴍ /dəˈrekt; daɪˈrekt/ *adjective, adverb*
1 as straight as possible, without turning or stopping: *Which is the most direct route to the town centre from here?* ◇ *We got a **direct flight** (= a flight that does not stop) to Bangkok.* ◇ *The 6.45 train goes direct to Oxford.*
2 from one person or thing to another person or thing with nobody or nothing between them: *You should keep this plant out of direct sunlight.* ◇ *They are in direct contact with the hijackers.* ⊃ Look at **indirect**.

direct² 0ᴍ /dəˈrekt; daɪˈrekt/ *verb*
(directs, directing, directed)
1 to manage or control somebody or something: *A policeman was in the middle of the road, directing the traffic.*
2 to be in charge of actors in a play or a film: *The movie was directed by Quentin Tarantino.*
3 to tell somebody how to get to a place: *Can you **direct** me **to** the station, please?*

direction 0ᴍ /dəˈrekʃn; daɪˈrekʃn/ *noun*
1 where a person or thing is going or looking: *They got lost because they went **in** the wrong **direction**.*
2 directions (*plural*) words that tell you how to get to a place or how to do something: *Let's stop and **ask for directions**.* ◇ *Simple directions for building the model are printed on the box.*

directly 0ᴍ /dəˈrektli; daɪˈrektli/ *adverb*
in a direct line or way: *He refused to answer my question directly.* ◇ *The supermarket is directly opposite the bank.* ◇ *Lung cancer is directly related to smoking.*

direct object /dəˌrekt ˈɒbdʒekt; daɪˌrekt ˈɒbdʒekt/ *noun*
(*grammar*) the person or thing that is directly affected by the action of a verb:

In 'I met him in town', the word 'him' is the direct object.

director /dəˈrektə(r); daɪˈrektə(r)/ *noun*
1 a person who controls a business or a group of people
2 a person in charge of a film or play who tells the actors what to do

directory /dəˈrektəri; daɪˈrektəri/ *noun*
(*plural* **directories**)
1 a book or list of people's addresses and telephone numbers: *a telephone directory*
2 (*computing*) a file containing a group of other files or programs in a computer

dirt 0ᴍ /dɜːt/ *noun* (*no plural*)
a substance that is not clean, for example mud or dust: *The children came in from the garden covered in dirt.*

dirty 0ᴍ /ˈdɜːti/ *adjective* (**dirtier, dirtiest**)
not clean: *Your hands are dirty – go and wash them!*

dis- /dɪs/ *prefix*
Dis- at the beginning of a word usually means 'not': *disagree* ◇ *dishonest*

disability /ˌdɪsəˈbɪləti/ *noun* (*plural* **disabilities**)
a physical or mental condition that means you cannot use a part of your body completely or easily, or that you cannot learn easily: *people with severe learning disabilities*

disabled /dɪsˈeɪbld/ *adjective*
not able to use a part of your body well: *Peter is disabled – he lost a leg in an accident.* ◇ *The hotel has improved facilities for **the disabled** (= people who are disabled).*

disadvantage 0ᴍ /ˌdɪsədˈvɑːntɪdʒ/ *noun*
a problem that makes something difficult or less good: *One **disadvantage of** living in the country is the lack of public transport.*

disagree 0ᴍ /ˌdɪsəˈɡriː/ *verb*
(disagrees, disagreeing, disagreed /ˌdɪsəˈɡriːd/)
to have a different opinion from somebody else: *I said it was a good film, but Jason **disagreed with** me.* ◇ *My sister and I **disagree about** everything!* ⊃ OPPOSITE **agree**

disagreement 0ᴍ /ˌdɪsəˈɡriːmənt/ *noun*
a situation where people have different opinions about something and often argue: *My parents sometimes **have disagreements about** money.*

disappear 0̶⃗ /ˌdɪsəˈpɪə(r)/ *verb*
(disappears, disappearing, disappeared /ˌdɪsəˈpɪəd/)

> 🔎 **SPELLING**
>
> Remember! You spell **disappear** with one **S** and **PP**.

If a person or thing **disappears**, they go away so people cannot see them: *The sun disappeared behind the clouds.* ◇ *The police are looking for a woman who disappeared on Sunday.* ➔ OPPOSITE **appear**
▸ **disappearance** /ˌdɪsəˈpɪərəns/ *noun*: *Everybody was worried about the child's disappearance.*

disappoint 0̶⃗ /ˌdɪsəˈpɔɪnt/ *verb*
(disappoints, disappointing, disappointed)
to make you sad because what you wanted did not happen: *I'm sorry to disappoint you, but I can't come to your party.*

disappointed 0̶⃗ /ˌdɪsəˈpɔɪntɪd/ *adjective*

> 🔎 **SPELLING**
>
> Remember! You spell **disappointed** with one **S** and **PP**.

If you are **disappointed**, you feel sad because what you wanted did not happen: *Sue was disappointed when she didn't win the prize.*

disappointing 0̶⃗ /ˌdɪsəˈpɔɪntɪŋ/ *adjective*
If something is **disappointing**, it makes you feel sad because it is not as good as you hoped: *disappointing exam results*

disappointment 0̶⃗ /ˌdɪsəˈpɔɪntmənt/ *noun*
1 (*no plural*) a feeling of sadness because what you wanted did not happen: *She couldn't hide her disappointment when she lost the match.*
2 (*plural* disappointments) something that makes you sad because it is not what you hoped: *Sarah's party was a disappointment – only four people came.*

disapproval /ˌdɪsəˈpruːvl/ *noun* (*no plural*)
a feeling that something is bad or that somebody is behaving badly: *She shook her head in disapproval.* ➔ OPPOSITE **approval**

disapprove /ˌdɪsəˈpruːv/ *verb*
(disapproves, disapproving, disapproved /ˌdɪsəˈpruːvd/)
to think that somebody or something is bad:

*Joe's parents **disapproved of** his new girlfriend.* ➔ OPPOSITE **approve**

disaster 0̶⃗ /dɪˈzɑːstə(r)/ *noun*
1 something very bad that happens and that may hurt a lot of people: *Floods and earthquakes are natural disasters.*
2 a very bad situation or event: *Our holiday was a disaster! It rained all week!*

disastrous /dɪˈzɑːstrəs/ *adjective*
very bad; that causes great trouble: *The heavy rain brought disastrous floods.*

disc (*American* disk) /dɪsk/ *noun*
1 a round flat object: *He wears an identity disc around his neck.*
2 = CD: *This recording is available on disc or cassette.*

discipline /ˈdɪsəplɪn/ *noun* (*no plural*)
teaching you to control yourself and follow rules: *Children learn discipline at school.*
▸ **discipline** *verb* (disciplines, disciplining, disciplined /ˈdɪsəplɪnd/): *You must discipline yourself to work harder.*

disc jockey /ˈdɪsk dʒɒki/ *noun* (*abbr.* DJ)
a person whose job is to play records and talk about music on the radio or in a club

disco /ˈdɪskəʊ/ *noun* (*plural* discos)
a place where people dance and listen to pop music

disconnect /ˌdɪskəˈnekt/ *verb*
(disconnects, disconnecting, disconnected)
to stop a supply of water, gas or electricity going to a piece of equipment or a building: *Your phone will be disconnected if you don't pay the bill.* ➔ OPPOSITE **connect**

discount /ˈdɪskaʊnt/ *noun*
money that somebody takes away from the price of something to make it cheaper: *Students often get a **discount** on rail travel.*

discourage /dɪsˈkʌrɪdʒ/ *verb*
(discourages, discouraging, discouraged /dɪsˈkʌrɪdʒd/)
to make somebody not want to do something: *Jane's parents tried to **discourage** her **from** leaving school.*
➔ OPPOSITE **encourage**
▸ **discouraging** /dɪsˈkʌrɪdʒɪŋ/ *adjective*
making you feel less confident about something: *The results were discouraging.*
➔ OPPOSITE **encouraging**

discover 0̶⃗ /dɪˈskʌvə(r)/ *verb*
(discovers, discovering, discovered /dɪˈskʌvəd/)
to find or learn something for the first time: *Who discovered Australia?* ◇ *I was in the shop when I discovered that I did not have any money.*

A B C D E F G H I J K L M N O P Q R S T U V W X Y Z

discovery /dɪˈskʌvəri/ *noun* (*plural* discoveries)
finding or learning something for the first time: *Scientists have **made** an important new discovery.*

discriminate /dɪˈskrɪmɪneɪt/ *verb* (discriminates, discriminating, discriminated)
to treat one person or a group in a worse way than others: *This company **discriminates against** women – it pays them less than men for doing the same work.*
▶ **discrimination** /dɪˌskrɪmɪˈneɪʃn/ *noun* (*no plural*): *religious discrimination* (= treating somebody in an unfair way because their religion is not the same as yours)

discuss 0🔒 /dɪˈskʌs/ *verb* (discusses, discussing, discussed /dɪˈskʌst/)
to talk about something: *I discussed the problem with my parents.*

discussion 0🔒 /dɪˈskʌʃn/ *noun*
talking about something seriously or deeply: *We **had** an interesting **discussion about** politics.*

disease 0🔒 /dɪˈziːz/ *noun*
an illness, especially one that you can catch from another person: *Malaria and measles are diseases.*

disgrace /dɪsˈɡreɪs/ *noun* (*no plural*)
when other people stop thinking well of you, because you have done something bad: *He's **in disgrace** because he stole money from his brother.*

disgraceful /dɪsˈɡreɪsfl/ *adjective*
Something that is **disgraceful** is very bad, making other people feel sorry and embarrassed: *The way the football fans behaved was disgraceful.*

disguise¹ /dɪsˈɡaɪz/ *verb* (disguises, disguising, disguised /dɪsˈɡaɪzd/)
to change the appearance of somebody or something so that people will not know who or what they are: *They **disguised** themselves **as** guards and escaped from the prison.*

disguise² /dɪsˈɡaɪz/ *noun*
things that you wear so that people do not know who you are: *She is so famous that she has to go shopping **in disguise**.*

disgust¹ 0🔒 /dɪsˈɡʌst/ *noun* (*no plural*)
a strong feeling of not liking something: *They left the restaurant **in disgust** because the food was so bad.*

disgust² 0🔒 /dɪsˈɡʌst/ *verb* (disgusts, disgusting, disgusted)
to make somebody have a strong feeling of not liking something: *The violence in the film really disgusted me.*

disgusted 0🔒 /dɪsˈɡʌstɪd/ *adjective*
If you are **disgusted**, you have a strong feeling of not liking something: *I was disgusted to find a fly in my soup.*

disgusting 0🔒 /dɪsˈɡʌstɪŋ/ *adjective*
very unpleasant: *What a disgusting smell!*

dish 0🔒 /dɪʃ/ *noun* (*plural* dishes)
1 a container for food. You can use a **dish** to cook food in an oven, or to put food on the table.
2 the dishes (*plural*) all the plates, bowls, cups, etc. that you must wash after a meal: *I'll wash the dishes.*
3 a part of a meal: *We had a fish dish and a vegetarian dish.*

dishcloth /ˈdɪʃklɒθ/ *noun*
a cloth used for washing dirty dishes

dishonest 0🔒 /dɪsˈɒnɪst/ *adjective*
A person who is **dishonest** says things that are not true, or steals or cheats.
⊃ OPPOSITE **honest**

dishwasher /ˈdɪʃwɒʃə(r)/ *noun*
a machine that washes things like plates, glasses, knives and forks ⊃ Look at Picture Dictionary page **P10**.

disinfectant /ˌdɪsɪnˈfektənt/ *noun*
a liquid that you use for cleaning something very well

disk 0🔒 /dɪsk/ *noun*
(*computing*) a flat piece of plastic that stores information for use by a computer ⊃ Look also at **floppy disk** and **hard disk**.

disk drive /ˈdɪsk draɪv/ *noun*
(*computing*) a piece of electrical equipment that passes information to or from a computer disk

diskette /dɪsˈket/ *noun*
(*computing*) a small flat plastic object that you can put in your computer's DISK DRIVE to record and keep information
⊃ SAME MEANING **floppy disk**

dislike /dɪsˈlaɪk/ *verb* (dislikes, disliking, disliked /dɪsˈlaɪkt/) (*formal*)
to not like somebody or something: *I dislike getting up early.*
▶ **dislike** *noun*: *I have a strong **dislike of** hospitals.*

disloyal /dɪsˈlɔɪəl/ *adjective*
not supporting your friends, family, country, etc.: *He was accused of being **disloyal to** the government.* ⊃ OPPOSITE **loyal**

dismal /'dɪzməl/ *adjective*
very bad and making you feel sad: *It was a wet, dismal day.*

dismay /dɪs'meɪ/ *noun* (no plural)
a strong feeling of surprise and worry: *John looked at me **in dismay** when I told him about the accident.*
▶ **dismayed** /dɪs'meɪd/ *adjective*: *I was dismayed to find that somebody had stolen my bike.*

dismiss /dɪs'mɪs/ *verb* (dismisses, dismissing, dismissed /dɪs'mɪst/)
1 (*formal*) to make somebody leave their job ⊃ SAME MEANING **sack** or **fire**: *He was dismissed for stealing money from the company.*
2 to allow somebody to leave a place: *The lesson finished and the teacher dismissed the class.*

disobedient /ˌdɪsə'biːdiənt/ *adjective*
not doing what somebody tells you to do: *a disobedient child* ⊃ OPPOSITE **obedient**
▶ **disobedience** /ˌdɪsə'biːdiəns/ *noun* (no plural) ⊃ OPPOSITE **obedience**

disobey /ˌdɪsə'beɪ/ *verb* (disobeys, disobeying, disobeyed /ˌdɪsə'beɪd/)
to not do what somebody tells you to do: *She disobeyed her parents and went to the party.* ⊃ OPPOSITE **obey**

disorganized /dɪs'ɔːgənaɪzd/ *adjective*
badly planned or not tidy: *The meeting was very disorganized.* ⊃ OPPOSITE **organized**

dispenser /dɪ'spensə(r)/ *noun*
a machine or container that you can get things like money or drinks from: *a cash dispenser at a bank* ◊ *a soap dispenser*

display¹ /dɪ'spleɪ/ *verb* (displays, displaying, displayed /dɪ'spleɪd/)
to show something so that people can see it: *All kinds of toys were displayed in the shop window.*

display² /dɪ'spleɪ/ *noun* (plural displays)
something that people look at: *a firework display*
on display in a place where people can see it and where it will attract attention: *The paintings are on display in the museum.*

dispose /dɪ'spəʊz/ *verb* (disposes, disposing, disposed /dɪ'spəʊzd/)
dispose of something to throw something away or give something away because you do not want it: *Where can I dispose of this rubbish?*
▶ **disposal** /dɪ'spəʊzl/ *noun* (no plural): *the disposal of nuclear waste*

dispute /dɪ'spjuːt; 'dɪspjuːt/ *noun*
an argument or disagreement between people with different ideas: *There was a dispute about which driver caused the accident.*

dissatisfied /ˌdɪs'sætɪsfaɪd/ *adjective*
not pleased with something: *I am very **dissatisfied with** your work*
⊃ OPPOSITE **satisfied**

dissolve /dɪ'zɒlv/ *verb* (dissolves, dissolving, dissolved /dɪ'zɒlvd/)
If a solid **dissolves**, it becomes part of a liquid: *Sugar dissolves in water.*

distance 0━ /'dɪstəns/ *noun*
1 how far it is from one place to another place: *It's a short **distance from** my house to the station.* ◊ *We usually measure distance in miles or kilometres.*
2 a place that is far from somebody or something: ***From a distance**, he looks quite young.* ◊ *I could see a light **in the distance**.*

distant /'dɪstənt/ *adjective*
far away in space or time: *distant countries*

distinct /dɪ'stɪŋkt/ *adjective*
1 easy to hear, see or smell; clear: *There is a distinct smell of burning in this room.*
2 clearly different: *English and Welsh are two distinct languages.*
▶ **distinctly** /dɪ'stɪŋktli/ *adverb* very clearly: *I distinctly heard him say his name was Robert.*

distinguish /dɪ'stɪŋgwɪʃ/ *verb* (distinguishes, distinguishing, distinguished /dɪ'stɪŋgwɪʃt/)
to see, hear, etc. the difference between two things or people: *Some people can't **distinguish between** me and my twin sister.*

distinguished /dɪ'stɪŋgwɪʃt/ *adjective*
famous or important: *a distinguished actor*

distract /dɪ'strækt/ *verb* (distracts, distracting, distracted)
If a person or thing **distracts** you, they stop you thinking about what you are doing: *The noise distracted me from my homework.*

distress /dɪ'stres/ *noun* (no plural)
1 a strong feeling of pain or sadness
2 being in danger and needing help: *a ship in distress*
▶ **distress** *verb* (distresses, distressing, distressed /dɪ'strest/) *It distressed her to see her mother crying.*

distressing /dɪ'stresɪŋ/ *adjective*
making you feel sad or upset: *The news of her death was extremely distressing.*

distribute /dɪ'strɪbjuːt/ *verb* (distributes, distributing, distributed)
to give or send things to each person: *New books are distributed on the first day of school.*
▶ **distribution** /ˌdɪstrɪ'bjuːʃn/ *noun* (no plural): *the distribution of newspapers*

A B C D E F G H I J K L M N O P Q R S T U V W X Y Z

A

district /'dɪstrɪkt/ *noun*
a part of a country or town: *the City of London's financial district*

B

C

disturb 0━ /dɪ'stɜ:b/ *verb* (disturbs, disturbing, disturbed /dɪ'stɜ:bd/)
1 to stop somebody doing something, for example thinking, working or sleeping: *I'm sorry to disturb you, but there's a phone call for you.* ◇ *Do not disturb* (= a notice that you put on a door to tell people not to come in).
2 to worry somebody: *We were disturbed by the news that John was ill.*

D

E

F

disturbance /dɪ'stɜ:bəns/ *noun*
1 a thing that stops you doing something, for example thinking, working or sleeping
2 when a group of people fight or make a lot of noise and trouble: *The football fans were causing a disturbance outside the stadium.*

G

H

I

disused /,dɪs'ju:zd/ *adjective*
not used any more: *a disused railway line*

J

ditch /dɪtʃ/ *noun* (*plural* **ditches**)
a long narrow hole at the side of a road or field that carries away water

K

L

dive /daɪv/ *verb*
(dives, diving, dived /daɪvd/)
1 to jump into water with your arms and head first: *Sam dived into the pool.*
2 to swim underwater wearing breathing equipment, collecting or looking at things: *The main purpose of his holiday to Greece was to go diving.*
3 to go to a deeper level underwater: *The birds were diving for fish.*
▶ **diving** *noun* (*no plural*): *The resort has facilities for sailing, waterskiing and diving.*

M

N

O

diving

diving board

swimming costume

P

Q

R

S

T

U

diver /'daɪvə(r)/ *noun*
a person who works underwater: *Police divers found a body in the lake.*

V

diversion /daɪ'vɜ:ʃn/ *noun*
a way that you must go when the usual way is closed: *There was a diversion around the town because of a road accident.*

W

X

divert /daɪ'vɜ:t/ *verb* (diverts, diverting, diverted)
to make something go a different way: *Our flight was diverted to another airport because of the bad weather.*

Y

Z

divide 0━ /dɪ'vaɪd/ *verb* (divides, dividing, divided)
1 to share or cut something into smaller parts: *The teacher divided the class into groups of three.* ◇ *The book is divided into ten chapters.*
2 to go into parts: *When the road divides, go left.*
3 to find out how many times one number goes into a bigger number: *36 divided by 4 is 9 (36 ÷ 4 = 9).*

divided highway /dɪ,vaɪdɪd 'haɪweɪ/
American English for DUAL CARRIAGEWAY

divine /dɪ'vaɪn/ *adjective*
of, like or from God or a god: *a divine message*

diving board /'daɪvɪŋ bɔ:d/ *noun*
a board at the side of a swimming pool that you use to jump into the water ⊃ Look at the picture at **dive**.

division 0━ /dɪ'vɪʒn/ *noun*
1 (*no plural*) sharing or cutting something into parts: *the division of Germany after the Second World War*
2 (*no plural*) (*maths*) finding out how many times one number goes into a bigger number ⊃ Look at **multiplication**.
3 (*plural* **divisions**) one of the parts of a big company: *He works in the sales division.*

divorce /dɪ'vɔ:s/ *noun*
the end of a marriage by law: *They are getting a divorce.*
▶ **divorce** *verb* (divorces, divorcing, divorced /dɪ'vɔ:st/): *He divorced his wife.* ⊃ We often say **get divorced**: *They got divorced last year.*
▶ **divorced** *adjective*: *I'm not married – I'm divorced.*

DIY /,di: aɪ 'waɪ/ *noun* (*no plural*) (*British*)
making, painting or repairing things in your house yourself: *a DIY store* (= where you can buy materials for DIY) ⊃ **DIY** is short for 'do-it-yourself'.

dizzy /'dɪzi/ *adjective* (dizzier, dizziest)
If you feel **dizzy**, you feel that everything is turning round and round and that you are going to fall: *The room was very hot and I started to feel dizzy.*

DJ /,di: 'dʒeɪ/ *short for* DISC JOCKEY

do¹ 0━ /du:/ *verb* (does /dʌz/, doing, did /dɪd/, has done /dʌn/)
1 to carry out an action: *What are you doing?* ◇ *He did the cooking.* ◇ *What did you do with my key?* (= where did you put it?)
2 to have a job or study something: *'What do you do?' 'I'm a doctor.'* ◇ *She's doing physics, biology and chemistry for A level.*

do

present tense		negative short forms		past tense
I	**do**	I	**don't**	**did** /dɪd/
you	**do**	you	**don't**	
he/she/it	**does** /dʌz/	he/she/it	**doesn't**	present participle
we	**do**	we	**don't**	**doing**
you	**do**	you	**don't**	
they	**do**	they	**don't**	past participle
				done /dʌn/

3 to finish something; to find the answer: *I have done my homework.* ◇ *I can't do this sum – it's too difficult.*
4 to be good enough; to be enough: *Will this soup do for dinner?*

> 🔎 **WHICH WORD?**
>
> **Do** or **make**?
> We use the verb **do** for many of the jobs we do at home.
> We **do the shopping**, **the cleaning**, **the washing** and **the ironing**.
> We always use **make** for beds: *Make your bed after breakfast.*

be or **have to do with somebody** or **something** to be connected with somebody or something: *I'm not sure what his job is – I think it's something to do with computers.* ◇ *Don't read that letter. It has nothing to do with you!*
could do with something to want or need something: *I could do with a drink.*
do something up (*British*)
1 to fasten something: *Do up the buttons on your shirt.* ⊃ OPPOSITE **undo**
2 to clean and repair something to make it look newer: *They bought an old house and now they are doing it up.*

do² 0̄ɰ /duː; də/ *verb* (does /dʌz/, doing, did /dɪd/, has done /dʌn/)
1 a word that you use with another verb to make a question: *Do you want an apple?*
2 a word that you use with another verb when you are saying 'not': *I like football but I don't* (= do not) *like tennis.*
3 a word that you use in place of saying something again: *She doesn't speak English, but I do* (= I speak English). ◇ *'I like football.'* *'So do I.'* ◇ *'I don't speak Chinese.'* *'Neither do I.'*
4 a word that you use before another verb to make it stronger: *You do look nice!*

dock /dɒk/ *noun*
a place by the sea or a river where ships go so that people can move things on and off them or repair them
▶ **dock** (docks, docking, docked /dɒkt/) *verb* (used about a ship) to sail into a port

and stop at the **dock**: *The ship had docked at Lisbon.*

doctor 0̄ɰ /'dɒktə(r)/ *noun*
1 a person whose job is to make sick people well again: *Doctor Waters sees patients every morning.* ⊃ Look at Picture Dictionary page **P12**.

> 🔎 **SPEAKING**
>
> When we talk about visiting the doctor, we say **go to the doctor's**: *If you're feeling ill, you should go to the doctor's.*

2 a person who has the highest degree from a university ⊃ When you write 'Doctor' as part of a person's name the short form is **Dr**.

document 0̄ɰ /'dɒkjumənt/ *noun*
1 an official paper with important information on it: *a legal document*
2 (*computing*) a computer file that contains writing

documentary /ˌdɒkju'mentri/ *noun* (*plural* **documentaries**)
a film about true things: *I watched an interesting documentary about Japan on TV last night.*

dodge /dɒdʒ/ *verb* (dodges, dodging, dodged /dɒdʒd/)
to move quickly to avoid something or somebody: *He ran across the busy road, dodging the cars.*

does *form of* DO

doesn't /'dʌznt/ *short for* DOES NOT

dogs

dog   puppies

A
B
C
D
E
F
G
H
I
J
K
L
M
N
O
P
Q
R
S
T
U
V
W
X
Y
Z

dog 0—¬ /dɒg/ *noun*
an animal that many people keep as a pet or to guard buildings

> 🔍 **WORD BUILDING**
> A young dog is called a **puppy**.

➔ Look at the picture on page **P15**.

doll /dɒl/ *noun*
a toy like a very small person

dollar 0—¬ /'dɒlə(r)/ *noun* (*symbol* $)

> 🔍 **SPELLING**
> Remember! You spell **dollar** with **AR**.

a unit of money that people use in the US, Canada, Australia and some other countries. There are 100 **cents** in a dollar: *You will be paid in American dollars.*

dolphin

dolphin /'dɒlfɪn/ *noun*
an intelligent animal that lives in the sea

dome /dəʊm/ *noun*
the round roof of a building: *the dome of St Paul's Cathedral in London*

domestic /də'mestɪk/ *adjective*
1 not international; only inside one country: *a domestic flight* (= to a place in the same country)
2 connected with the home or family: *Cooking and cleaning are domestic jobs.* ◇ *Many cats and dogs are domestic animals* (= animals that live in your home with you).

dominate /'dɒmɪneɪt/ *verb* (dominates, dominating, dominated)
to control somebody or something because you are stronger or more important: *The Italian team dominated throughout the second half of the game.*

domino /'dɒmɪnəʊ/ *noun* (*plural* dominoes)
one of a set of small flat pieces of wood or plastic, used to play a game (called dominoes)

donate /dəʊ'neɪt/ *verb* (donates, donating, donated)
to give something, especially money, to people who need it: *They donated $10 000 to the hospital.*
▸ **donation** /dəʊ'neɪʃn/ *noun*: *He made a donation to the charity.*

dominoes

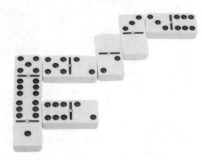

done *form of* DO

donkey /'dɒŋki/ *noun* (*plural* donkeys)
an animal like a small horse with long ears
➔ Look at Picture Dictionary page **P2**.

donor /'dəʊnə(r)/ *noun*
somebody who gives something to help a person or an organization

don't /dəʊnt/ *short for* DO NOT

doodle /'du:dl/ *verb* (doodles, doodling, doodled /'du:dld/)
to make small drawings, especially when you are bored or thinking about something else: *I often doodle when I'm on the phone.*

doom /du:m/ *noun* (*no plural*)
death or a terrible event in the future that you cannot avoid

door 0—¬ /dɔ:(r)/ *noun*
the way into a building or room; a piece of wood, glass or metal that you use to open and close the way in to a building, room, cupboard, car, etc.: *Can you close the door, please?* ◇ *Sophie knocked on the door. 'Come in,' Peter said.* ◇ *There is somebody at the door.* ◇ *Will you answer the door* (= go to open the door when somebody knocks or rings the bell)? ➔ A house often has a **front door** and a **back door**. ➔ Look at the picture at **house**.
next door in the next house, room or building: *Mary lives next door to us.*
out of doors outside; not in a building: *Farmers spend a lot of time out of doors.*

doorbell /'dɔ:bel/ *noun*
a bell outside a house that you ring to tell people inside that you want to go in

doorknob /'dɔ:nɒb/ *noun*
a round object on a door that you use to open and close it

doormat /'dɔ:mæt/ *noun*
a piece of material on the floor in front of a door for cleaning your shoes on

doorstep /'dɔ:step/ *noun*
a step in front of a door outside a building ⊃ Look at Picture Dictionary page **P10**.

doorway /'dɔ:weɪ/ *noun*
an opening for going into a building or room: *Mike was waiting in the doorway when they arrived.*

dormitory /'dɔ:mətri/ *noun* (*plural* **dormitories**)
a big bedroom for a lot of people, usually in a school

dose /dəʊs/ *noun*
an amount of medicine that you take at one time: *Take a large dose of medicine before you go to bed.*

dot /dɒt/ *noun*
a small round mark: *The letter 'i' has a dot over it.*

> *🔎* SPEAKING
> We use **dot** when we say a person's email address. For the address **ann@smith.co.uk** we say 'Ann **at** smith **dot** co **dot** uk'.

on the dot at exactly the right time: *Please be here at nine o'clock on the dot.*

dotted line /,dɒtɪd 'laɪm/ *noun*
a line of DOTS that sometimes shows where you have to write something: *Please sign* (= write your name) *on the dotted line.* ⊃ Look at the picture at **wavy**.

double¹ 0̄ₐ /'dʌbl/ *adjective*

> *🔎* PRONUNCIATION
> The word **double** sounds like **bubble**.

1 two times as much or as many: *a double portion of chips*
2 with two parts that are the same: *double doors ◇ Does 'necessary' have double 's'? ◇ My phone number is double four nine five one* (= 44951).
3 made for two people or things: *a double bed ◇ a double room* ⊃ Look at **single**.

double² /'dʌbl/ *verb* (**doubles, doubling, doubled** /'dʌbld/)
to become, or make something become, twice as much or as many: *The price of petrol has almost doubled in two years.*

double bass /,dʌbl 'beɪs/ *noun*
the largest musical instrument with strings, that you usually play standing up

double-click /,dʌbl 'klɪk/ *verb* (**double-clicks, double-clicking, double-clicked** /,dʌbl 'klɪkt/)
to quickly press a button twice on a computer control (called a **mouse**): *To start the program, just double-click on the icon.*

double-decker /,dʌbl 'dekə(r)/ *noun*
a bus with two levels ⊃ Look at the picture at **bus**.

doubt¹ 0̄ₐ /daʊt/ *noun*

> *🔎* PRONUNCIATION
> The word **doubt** sounds like **out**, because we don't say the letter **b** in this word.

a feeling that you are not sure about something: *She says the story is true but I have my doubts about it.*
in doubt not sure: *If you are in doubt, ask your teacher.*
no doubt I am sure: *Paul isn't here yet, but no doubt he will come later.*

doubt² /daʊt/ *verb* (**doubts, doubting, doubted**)
to not feel sure about something; to think that something is probably not true or probably will not happen: *I doubt if he will come.*

doubtful /'daʊtfl/ *adjective*
not certain or not likely: *It is doubtful whether he will walk again.*

doubtless /'daʊtləs/ *adverb*
almost certainly: *Doubtless she'll be late!*

dough /dəʊ/ *noun* (*no plural*)
flour, water and other things mixed together, for making bread

doughnut (*American also* donut) /'dəʊnʌt/ *noun*
a small round cake that is cooked in oil ⊃ Look at Picture Dictionary page **P6**.

dove

dove /dʌv/ *noun*
a bird that is often used as a sign of peace

down 0̄ₐ /daʊn/ *adverb, preposition*
1 in or to a lower place; not up: *The sun goes down in the evening. ◇ We ran down the hill. ◇ Put that box down on the floor.*
2 from standing to sitting or lying: *Sit down. ◇ Lie down on the bed.*
3 at or to a lower level: *Prices are going down. ◇ Turn that music down!* (= so that it is not so loud)
4 along: *He lives just down the street. ◇ Go down the road till you reach the traffic lights.*
5 on paper; on a list: *Write these words down. ◇ Have you got me down for the trip?*

A B C D E F G H I J K L M N O P Q R S T U V W X Y Z

A

downhill /ˌdaʊnˈhɪl/ *adverb*
down, towards the bottom of a hill: *My bicycle can go fast downhill.*

B

C

download /ˌdaʊnˈləʊd/ *verb*
(downloads, downloading, downloaded)
(*computing*) If you **download** a computer program or information from the Internet, you make a copy of it on your own computer: *I downloaded some music files from the Internet.*

D

E

F

downstairs 0ᴖ /ˌdaʊnˈsteəz/ *adverb*
to or on a lower floor of a building: *I went downstairs to make breakfast.*
▶ **downstairs** *adjective*: *She lives in the downstairs flat.* ⊃ OPPOSITE **upstairs**

G

H

downtown /ˌdaʊnˈtaʊn/ *adverb*
(*American*)
in or towards the centre of a city, especially its main business area: *She works downtown.*

I

J

downwards 0ᴖ /ˈdaʊnwədz/ (*also* **downward** /ˈdaʊnwəd/) *adverb*
towards the ground or towards a lower level: *She was lying face downwards on the grass.* ⊃ OPPOSITE **upwards**

K

L

doze /dəʊz/ *verb* (dozes, dozing, dozed /dəʊzd/)
to sleep lightly for a short time: *My grandfather was dozing in his armchair.*
doze off to go to sleep, especially during the day: *I dozed off in front of the television.*
▶ **doze** *noun*: *She had a doze after lunch.*

M

N

O

dozen /ˈdʌzn/ *noun* (*plural* dozen)
twelve: *a dozen red roses* ◇ *two dozen boxes* ◇ *half a dozen eggs*
dozens of a lot of: *They've invited dozens of people to the party.*

P

Q

R

Dr *short way of writing* DOCTOR

draft, drafty *American English for* DRAUGHT, DRAUGHTY

S

drag

T

U

V

W

drag /dræg/ *verb* (drags, dragging, dragged /drægd/)
1 to pull something along the ground slowly, often because it is heavy: *He couldn't lift the sack, so he dragged it out of the shop.*
2 If something **drags**, it seems to go slowly because it is not interesting: *Time drags when you're waiting for a bus.*

X

Y

Z

dragon /ˈdrægən/ *noun*
a big, dangerous animal with fire in its mouth, that you only find in stories

dragonfly /ˈdrægənflaɪ/ *noun* (*plural* dragonflies)
an insect that often flies near water and that has four wings and a long, thin body

drain¹ /dreɪn/ *verb* (drains, draining, drained /dreɪnd/)
1 to let liquid flow away from something, so that it becomes dry: *Drain and rinse the pasta.*
2 to become dry because liquid is flowing away: *Leave the dishes to drain.*
3 to flow away: *The water drained away slowly.*

drain² /dreɪn/ *noun*
a pipe that carries away dirty water from a building: *The drain is blocked.* ⊃ Look at the picture at **kerb.**

drainpipe /ˈdreɪnpaɪp/ *noun*
a pipe that takes water from the roof of a building to a DRAIN when it rains ⊃ Look at Picture Dictionary page **P10.**

drama /ˈdrɑːmə/ *noun*
1 (*plural* dramas) a story that you watch in the theatre or on television, or listen to on the radio: *a TV drama*
2 (*no plural*) the study of plays and acting: *She went to drama school.*
3 (*plural* dramas) an exciting thing that happens: *There was a big drama at school when one of the teachers fell in the swimming pool!*

dramatic /drəˈmætɪk/ *adjective*
1 sudden, great or exciting: *The finish of the race was very dramatic.*
2 of plays or the theatre: *a dramatic society*
▶ **dramatically** /drəˈmætɪkli/ *adverb*: *Prices went up dramatically.*

dramatist /ˈdræmətɪst/ *noun*
a person who writes plays

drank *form of* DRINK¹

draught (*British*) (*American* draft) /drɑːft/ *noun*
cold air that comes into a room: *Can you shut the window? I can feel a draught.*
▶ **draughty** (*British*) (*American* drafty) /ˈdrɑːfti/ *adjective* (draughtier, draughtiest): *a draughty old house*

draughts /drɑːfts/ *noun* (*plural*) (*British*) (*American* checkers)
a game that two people play with round flat pieces on a board that has black and white squares on it: *Do you want a game of draughts?*

draw¹ 0➖ /drɔː/ *verb* (draws, drawing, drew /druː/, has drawn /drɔːn/)

> 🔍 **PRONUNCIATION**
> The word **draw** sounds like **more**.

1 to make a picture with a pen or a pencil: *She drew a picture of a horse.* ◇ *He has drawn a car.* ◇ *My sister draws well.*
2 to pull or take something from a place: *I drew my chair up closer to the fire.* ◇ *He drew a knife from his pocket.*
3 to pull something to make it move: *The carriage was drawn by two horses.*
4 to open or close curtains: *I switched on the light and drew the curtains.*
5 to move or come: *The train drew into the station.*
6 to end a game with the same number of points for both players or teams: *Liverpool and Tottenham drew in last Saturday's match.*
draw back to move away from somebody or something: *He came close but she drew back.*
draw something out to take money out of a bank: *I drew out £50 before I went shopping.*
draw up to come to a place and stop: *A taxi drew up outside the house.*
draw something up to write something: *They drew up a list of people who they wanted to invite.*

draw² /drɔː/ *noun*
the result of a game when both players or teams have the same number of points: *The football match ended in a 1–1 draw.*

drawer

— drawer

chest of drawers

drawer 0➖ /drɔː(r)/ *noun*

> 🔍 **PRONUNCIATION**
> The word **drawer** sounds like **four**.

a thing like a box that you can pull out from a cupboard or desk, for example: *There's some paper in the top drawer of my desk.*

drawing 0➖ /ˈdrɔːɪŋ/ *noun*
1 (*plural* drawings) a picture made with a pen or a pencil, but not paint: *He did a drawing of the old farmhouse.*
2 (*no plural*) the art of drawing pictures with a pen or a pencil: *Katherine is very good at drawing.*

drawing pin /ˈdrɔːɪŋ pɪn/ *noun* (British) (American **thumbtack**)
a short pin with a flat round top, that you use for fastening paper to a wall or board: *I put the poster up with drawing pins.*

drawn form of DRAW¹

dread /dred/ *verb* (dreads, dreading, dreaded)
to be very afraid of something that is going to happen: *I'm dreading the exams.*

dreadful /ˈdredfl/ *adjective*
very bad: *I had a dreadful journey – my train was two hours late!*

dreadfully /ˈdredfəli/ *adverb*
very: *I'm dreadfully sorry, but I must go now.*

dream¹ 0➖ /driːm/ *noun*
1 pictures or events which happen in your mind when you are asleep: *I had a dream about school last night.*

> 🔍 **WORD BUILDING**
> A bad or frightening dream is called a **nightmare**.

2 something nice that you hope for: *His dream was to give up his job and live in the country.*

dream² 0➖ /driːm/ *verb* (dreams, dreaming, dreamt /dremt/ or dreamed /driːmd/, has dreamt or has dreamed)
1 to have a picture or idea in your mind when you are asleep: *I dreamt about you last night.* ◇ *I dreamt that I was flying.*
2 to hope for something nice in the future: *She dreams of becoming a famous actress.*

dreary /ˈdrɪəri/ *adjective*
not at all interesting or attractive: *His voice is so dreary that it sends me to sleep.*

dress¹ 0➖ /dres/ *noun*
1 (*plural* dresses) a piece of clothing with a top part and a skirt, that a woman or girl wears ➪ Look at Picture Dictionary page **P5**.
2 (*no plural*) clothes: *The group of dancers wore Bulgarian national dress.*

dress² 0➖ /dres/ *verb* (dresses, dressing, dressed /drest/)
1 to put clothes on yourself or another person: *I got dressed and went downstairs for breakfast.* ◇ *She dressed quickly and went out.*

◇ *He washed and dressed the baby.*
⊃ OPPOSITE **undress**
2 to wear a particular style, type or colour of clothes: *She dresses like a film star.* ◇ *He was **dressed in** black.*
dress up
1 to put on your best clothes: *They dressed up to go to the theatre.*
2 to put on special clothes for fun, so that you look like another person or a thing: *The children dressed up **as** ghosts.*

dressing /'dresɪŋ/ *noun*
1 a thing for covering a part of your body that is hurt: *You should put a dressing on that cut.*
2 a sauce for food, especially for salads

dressing gown /'dresɪŋ gaʊn/ *noun*
(*British*) (*American* **robe**)
a piece of clothing like a loose coat with a belt, which you wear before or after a bath, before you get dressed in the morning, etc.: *She got up and put on her dressing gown.*

dressing table /'dresɪŋ teɪbl/ *noun*
(*British*)
a piece of bedroom furniture like a table with drawers and a mirror

drew *form of* DRAW¹

dried *form of* DRY²

drier
1 *form of* DRY¹
2 = DRYER

dries *form of* DRY²

driest *form of* DRY¹

drift /drɪft/ *verb* (drifts, drifting, drifted)
to move slowly in the air or on water: *The empty boat drifted out to sea.* ◇ *The balloon drifted away.*

drill /drɪl/ *noun*
a tool that you use for making holes: *an electric drill* ◇ *a dentist's drill*
▶ **drill** *verb* (drills, drilling, drilled /drɪld/): *Drill two holes in the wall.*

drink¹ 0— /drɪŋk/ *verb* (drinks, drinking, drank /dræŋk/, has drunk /drʌŋk/)
1 to take in liquid, for example water, milk or coffee, through your mouth: *What do you want to drink?* ◇ *She was drinking a cup of tea.*
2 to drink alcohol: *'Would you like some wine?' 'No, thank you. I don't drink.'*

drink² 0— /drɪŋk/ *noun*
1 liquid, for example water, milk or coffee, that you take in through your mouth: *Would you like a drink?* ◇ *Can I **have a drink** of water?*
2 drink with alcohol in it, for example beer

or wine: *There was lots of food and drink at the party.*

drip /drɪp/ *verb* (drips, dripping, dripped /drɪpt/)
1 to fall slowly in small drops: *Water was dripping through the roof.*
2 If something **drips**, liquid falls from it in small drops: *The tap is dripping.*

drive¹ 0— /draɪv/ *verb* (drives, driving, drove /drəʊv/, has driven /'drɪvn/)
1 to control a car, bus, etc. and make it go where you want to go: *Can you drive?* ◇ *She usually drives to work.*
2 to take somebody to a place in a car: *My parents drove me to the airport.*

drive² 0— /draɪv/ *noun*
1 a journey in a car: *It's a long drive from London to Edinburgh.* ◇ *We went for a drive in my sister's car.*
2 a wide hard path or private road that goes from the street to one house: *You can park your car in the drive.*
3 (*computing*) the part of a computer that reads and stores information: *I saved my work on the C: drive*

drive-in /'draɪv ɪn/ *noun* (*American*)
a place where you can go to eat or to watch a film while you are sitting in your car

driven *form of* DRIVE¹

driver 0— /'draɪvə(r)/ *noun*
a person who controls a car, bus, train, etc.: *John is a good driver.* ◇ *a taxi driver*

driver's license /'draɪvəz laɪsns/
American English for DRIVING LICENCE

driving /'draɪvɪŋ/ *noun* (*no plural*)
controlling a car, bus, etc.: *Driving in the fog can be dangerous.*

driving licence /'draɪvɪŋ laɪsns/ (*British*)
(*American* **driver's license**) *noun*
an official document that shows that you are allowed to drive a car, etc.

driving test /'draɪvɪŋ test/ *noun*
a test that you have to pass before you get your DRIVING LICENCE

droop /druːp/ *verb* (droops, drooping, drooped /druːpt/)
to bend or hang down: *Flowers droop if you don't put them in water.*

drop¹ 0— /drɒp/ *verb* (drops, dropping, dropped /drɒpt/)
1 to let something fall: *I dropped my watch and it broke.*
2 to fall: *The glass dropped from her hands.*
3 to become lower or less: *The temperature has dropped.*
4 (*also* **drop off**) to stop your car and let

somebody get out: *Could you drop me at the station?* ◇ *He dropped me off at the bus stop.*
5 to stop doing something: *I'm going to drop geography* (= stop studying it) *at school next year.*

drop in to visit somebody who does not know that you are coming: *We were in the area so we thought we'd drop in and see you.*

drop off to fall asleep: *She dropped off in front of the TV.*

drop out to stop doing something with a group of people: *I dropped out of the football team after I hurt my leg.*

drop

drop² 0—ᵤ /drɒp/ *noun*
1 a very small amount of liquid: *drops of rain* ◇ *a drop of blood*
2 a fall in the amount or level of something: *a **drop** in temperature* ◇ *a drop in prices*

drought /draʊt/ *noun*
a long time when there is not enough rain: *Thousands of people died in the drought.*

drove form of DRIVE¹

drown /draʊn/ *verb* (drowns, drowning, drowned /draʊnd/)
to die under water because you cannot breathe; to make somebody die in this way: *The boy fell in the river and drowned.* ◇ *Twenty people were drowned in the floods.*

drowsy /ˈdraʊzi/ *adjective*
feeling tired and wanting to sleep: *The heat made him very drowsy.*

drug 0—ᵤ /drʌg/ *noun*
1 an illegal chemical substance that people take because it makes them feel happy or excited: *He doesn't smoke or **take drugs**.* ◇ *Her daughter is **on drugs** (= regularly using illegal drugs).* ◇ *Heroin is a dangerous drug.*
2 a chemical substance used as a medicine, that you take when you are ill to make you better: *drug companies* ◇ *Some drugs can only be obtained with a prescription from a doctor.*

drug addict /ˈdrʌg ædɪkt/ *noun*
a person who cannot stop using drugs

drugstore /ˈdrʌgstɔː(r)/ *noun*
a shop in the US where you can buy medicines and a lot of other things

drums

drumstick

drum /drʌm/ *noun*
1 a musical instrument that you hit with special sticks (called **drumsticks**) or with your hands: *He plays the drums in a band.*
2 a big round container for oil: *an oil drum*

drummer /ˈdrʌmə(r)/ *noun*
a person who plays a DRUM

drunk¹ form of DRINK¹

drunk² 0—ᵤ /drʌŋk/ *adjective*
If a person is **drunk**, they have drunk too much alcohol: *He **gets drunk** every Friday night.*

dry¹ 0—ᵤ /draɪ/ *adjective* (drier, driest)
1 with no water or liquid in it or on it: *The washing isn't dry yet.* ↻ OPPOSITE **wet**
2 with no rain: *dry weather* ↻ OPPOSITE **wet**
3 not sweet: *dry white wine*

dry 0—ᵤ² /draɪ/ *verb* (dries, drying, dried /draɪd/, has dried)
to become or make something dry: *Our clothes were drying in the sun.* ◇ *Dry your hands on this towel.*

dry out to become completely dry: *Leave your shoes by the fire to dry out.*

dry up
1 (used about rivers, lakes, etc.) to become completely dry: *There was no rain for several months and all the rivers dried up.*
2 to dry things like plates, knives and forks with a towel after you have washed them: *If I wash the dishes, could you dry up?*

dry-clean /ˌdraɪ ˈkliːn/ *verb* (dry-cleans, dry-cleaning, dry-cleaned /ˌdraɪ ˈkliːnd/)
to make clothes clean by using chemicals, not water: *I **had** my suit **dry-cleaned**.*

dry-cleaner's /ˌdraɪ ˈkliːnəz/ *noun*
a shop where you take clothes and other things to be DRY-CLEANED ↻ Look at Picture Dictionary page **P13**.

A B C **D** E F G H I J K L M N O P Q R S T U V W X Y Z

A

B

D

C

E

F

G

H

I

J

K

L

M

N

O

P

Q

R

S

T

U

V

W

X

Y

Z

dryer (*also* **drier**) /'draɪə(r)/ *noun*
a machine for drying something: *Take the clothes out of the washing machine and put them in the dryer.* ◇ *a hairdryer*

dual carriageway /ˌdjuːəl ˈkærɪdʒweɪ/ *noun* (*British*) (*American* **divided highway**)
a wide road with a narrow piece of land or a fence between the two lines of traffic

duchess /'dʌtʃəs/ *noun* (*plural* **duchesses**)
a woman who has a very high position in society or who is married to a DUKE (= a man of the highest social position): *the Duchess of York*

duck

duck¹ /dʌk/ *noun*
a bird that lives on and near water. You often see **ducks** on farms or in parks.

> 🔍 **WORD BUILDING**
> A young duck is called a **duckling**.

duck² /dʌk/ *verb* (**ducks, ducking, ducked** /dʌkt/)
to move your head down quickly, so that something does not hit you or so that somebody does not see you: *He saw the ball coming towards him and ducked.*

duckling /'dʌklɪŋ/ *noun*
a young DUCK

due /djuː/ *adjective*
1 because of something; caused by something: *The accident was **due to** bad driving.*
2 If something is **due** at a certain time, you expect it to happen or come then: *When's the baby due?* ◇ *The new road is **due to** open in April.*
3 If an amount of money is **due**, you must pay it: *My rent is **due** at the beginning of the month.*
4 ready for something: *My car is **due for** a service.*

duet /dju'et/ *noun*
music for two people to sing or play on musical instruments: *James and Olivia sang a duet.*

dug *form of* DIG

duke /djuːk/ *noun*
a man who has a very high position in

society in some parts of Europe ➲ Look at **duchess**.

dull /dʌl/ *adjective* (**duller, dullest**)
1 not interesting or exciting ➲ SAME MEANING **boring**: *Life is never dull in a big city.*
2 not bright: *It was a dull, cloudy day.*
3 not strong or loud: *a dull pain*

dumb /dʌm/ *adjective*
1 not able to speak: *She was born **deaf and dumb**.*
2 (*informal*) not intelligent; stupid: *That was a dumb thing to do!*

dummy /'dʌmi/
(*plural* **dummies**)
noun (*British*)
(*American* **pacifier**)
a small rubber object that you put in a baby's mouth to stop it crying

dummy

dump /dʌmp/ *verb* (**dumps, dumping, dumped** /dʌmpt/)
1 to take something to a place and leave it there because you do not want it: *They dumped their rubbish by the side of the road.*
2 to put something down without being careful: *Don't dump your clothes on the floor!*
▶ **dump** *noun* a place where people take things they do not want

dune /djuːn/ *noun*
a small hill of sand near the sea or in a desert

dungarees /ˌdʌŋɡəˈriːz/ *noun* (*plural*) (*British*)
trousers with a part that covers the top of your body: *a new pair of dungarees*

dungeon /'dʌndʒən/ *noun*
a prison under the ground, for example in a castle

during 0━ /'djʊərɪŋ/ *preposition*
1 all the time that something is happening: *The sun gives us light during the day.*
2 at some time while something else is happening: *She died during the night.* ◇ *I fell asleep during the film.*

dusk /dʌsk/ *noun* (*no plural*)
the time in the evening when it is nearly dark

dust¹ 0━ /dʌst/ *noun* (*no plural*)
dry dirt that is like powder: *The old table was covered in dust.*

dust² /dʌst/ *verb* (**dusts, dusting, dusted**)
to take dust off something with a cloth: *I dusted the furniture.*

dustbin

dustbin /'dʌstbɪn/ *noun* (*British*) (*American* garbage can, trash can)
a large container for rubbish that you keep outside your house

duster /'dʌstə(r)/ *noun*
a cloth that you use for taking the dust off furniture

dustman /'dʌstmən/ *noun* (*plural* dustmen /'dʌstmən/) (*British*)
a person whose job is to take away rubbish from outside people's houses

dustpan

brush

dustpan /'dʌstpæn/ *noun*
a flat container with a handle that you use for getting dust or rubbish off the floor: *Have you got a dustpan and brush?*

dusty /'dʌsti/ *adjective* (dustier, dustiest)
covered with dust: *The furniture was very dusty.*

duty 0̶ᴡ /'djuːti/ *noun* (*plural* duties)
1 something that you must do because it is part of your job or because you think it is right: *It's your **duty to** look after your parents when they get older.* ◊ *One of the duties of a secretary is to type letters.*
2 money (called **tax**) that you pay to the government when you bring things into a country from another country
off duty not working: *The police officer was off duty.*
on duty working: *Some nurses at the hospital are on duty all night.*

duty-free /ˌdjuːti 'friː/ *adjective*, *adverb*
Duty-free goods are things that you can bring into a country without paying money to the government. You can buy goods **duty-free** on planes or ships and at airports.

duvet /'duːveɪ/ *noun* (*British*)
a thick warm cover for a bed. **Duvets** are often filled with feathers. ⊃ Look at the picture at **bed**.

DVD 0̶ᴡ /ˌdiː viː 'diː/ *noun*
a small plastic disk that you record films and music on. You can play a **DVD** on a computer or a special machine (called a **DVD player**): *Is the film available on DVD?*

dwarf /dwɔːf/ *noun*
1 a person, animal or plant that is much smaller than the usual size
2 (in children's stories) a very small person: *Snow White and the Seven Dwarfs*

dye *verb* (dyes, dyeing, dyed /daɪd/)
to change the colour of something by using a special liquid or substance: *She dyed her hair blonde.*
▶ **dye** *noun* a substance that you use to change the colour of something, for example cloth or hair: *purple hair dye*

dying *form of* DIE

dynamite /'daɪnəmaɪt/ *noun* (*no plural*)
a powerful substance that can explode: *a stick of dynamite*

A B C D E F G H I J K L M N O P Q R S T U V W X Y Z

E e

E, e /iː/ *noun* (*plural* E's, e's /iːz/)
the fifth letter of the English alphabet: '*Egg*' *begins with an* '*E*'.

each 0⊸ /iːtʃ/ *adjective, pronoun*
every person or thing in a group: *Each student buys a book and a tape.* ◇ *He gave a present to* **each of** *the children.* ◇ *These T-shirts are £5 each.*

each other

They are looking at each other.

each other 0⊸ /ˌiːtʃ ˈʌðə(r)/ *pronoun*
used for saying that somebody does the same thing as another person: *Gary and Susy looked at each other* (= Gary looked at Susy and Susy looked at Gary).

eager /ˈiːgə(r)/ *adjective*
If you are **eager** to do something, you want to do it very much. ⊃ SAME MEANING **keen**: *She's eager to help with the party.*
▶ **eagerly** /ˈiːgəli/ *adverb*: *The children were waiting eagerly for the film to begin.*
▶ **eagerness** /ˈiːgənəs/ *noun* (*no plural*): *I couldn't hide my eagerness to get home.*

eagle /ˈiːgl/ *noun*
a very large bird that can see very well. It catches and eats small birds and animals.

eagle

beak

ear 0⊸ /ɪə(r)/ *noun*
one of the two parts of your body that you use to hear with: *Elephants have big ears.*
⊃ Look at Picture Dictionary page **P4**.

earache /ˈɪəreɪk/ *noun* (*no plural*)
pain inside your ear: *I've got earache.*

earl /ɜːl/ *noun*
a British man who has a high social position

early 0⊸ /ˈɜːli/ *adjective, adverb* (**earlier, earliest**)
1 near the beginning of a period of time: *Come in the early afternoon.* ◇ *She was in her early twenties* (= aged between 20 and about 23 or 24). ◇ *I have to get up early tomorrow.*
2 before the usual or right time: *The train arrived ten minutes early.* ◇ *You're early! It's only half past six.* ◇ *I was early for the lesson.*
⊃ OPPOSITE **late**
have an early night to go to bed earlier than usual: *I'm really tired, I think I'll have an early night.*

earn 0⊸ /ɜːn/ *verb* (**earns, earning, earned** /ɜːnd/)
1 to get money by working: *How much do teachers earn in your country?* ◇ *She earns about £1500 a month.*
2 to get something because you have worked well or done something good: *You've earned a holiday!*

earnings /ˈɜːnɪŋz/ *noun* (*plural*)
money that you earn by working

earphones /ˈɪəfəʊnz/ *noun* (*plural*) = HEADPHONES

earring /ˈɪərɪŋ/ *noun*
a piece of jewellery that you wear on your ear: *a pair of silver earrings*

earrings

earth 0⊸ /ɜːθ/ *noun* (*no plural*)
1 *usually* **the earth, the Earth** this world; the planet that we live on: *The moon travels round the earth.* ◇ *They live in one of the hottest places* **on earth**.
2 the substance that plants grow in ⊃ SAME MEANING **soil**: *Cover the seeds with earth.*
how, who, what, where, etc. on earth? (*informal*) used in questions when you are very surprised or want to say something very strongly: *What on earth are you doing?* ◇ *Where on earth is Paul? He's two hours late!*

earthquake /ˈɜːθkweɪk/ *noun*
a sudden strong shaking of the ground

ease[1] /iːz/ *noun* (*no plural*)
be or **feel at ease** to be or feel comfortable and relaxed: *Everyone was so friendly that I felt completely at ease.*
with ease with no difficulty
⊃ SAME MEANING **easily**: *She answered the questions with ease.*

the earth
northern hemisphere

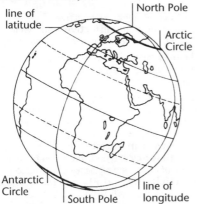

line of latitude — North Pole — Arctic Circle — Antarctic Circle — South Pole — line of longitude

southern hemisphere

ease² /iːz/ *verb*
to become or to make something less painful or serious: *They waited for the rain to ease.* ◇ *This should ease the pain.*

easel /'iːzl/ *noun*
a frame that an artist uses to hold a picture while it is being painted

easily 0━┓ /'iːzəli/ *adverb*
with no difficulty: *I can easily ring and check the time of the film.* ◇ *He passed the test easily.* ➔ The adjective is **easy**.

east 0━┓ /iːst/ *noun* (*no plural*) (*abbr.* E)
1 the direction you look in to see the sun come up in the morning: *Which way is east?* ◇ *There was a cold wind from the east.* ➔ Look at the picture at **compass**.
2 the East the countries of Asia, for example China and Japan
▶ **east** *adjective*, *adverb*: *They live on the east coast.* ◇ *an east wind* (= that comes from the east) ◇ *We travelled east.*

Easter /'iːstə(r)/ *noun* (*no plural*)
a Sunday in March or April, and the days around it, when Christians think about Christ coming back to life: *I'm going on holiday at Easter.*

> 🔎 **CULTURE**
> **Easter** is a popular festival, with many traditions in Britain and the US.
> People think about new life and the coming of spring. They celebrate this by eating chocolate eggs.
> The Monday after **Easter** is called '**Easter Monday**'. In Britain, this is a public holiday.

Easter egg /'iːstər eg/ *noun*
an egg made of chocolate that people give as a present at EASTER

eastern 0━┓ /'iːstən/ *adjective*
in, of or from the east of a place: *eastern Scotland*

easy 0━┓ /'iːzi/ *adjective* (easier, easiest)
1 not difficult to do or understand: *The homework was very easy.* ◇ *English isn't an easy language to learn.*
2 without problems or pain: *He has had an easy life.* ⊃ OPPOSITE **difficult**, **hard**
take it easy, **take things easy** to relax and not worry or work too much: *After my exams I'm going to take it easy for a few days.*

eat 0━┓ /iːt/ *verb* (eats, eating, ate /et/, has eaten /'iːtn/)
1 to put food in your mouth and swallow it: *Have you eaten all the chocolates?* ◇ *Do you want something to eat?*
2 to have a meal: *What time shall we eat?*
eat out to have a meal in a restaurant: *We don't eat out very often.*

echo /'ekəʊ/ *noun* (*plural* echoes)
a sound that a surface such as a wall sends back so that you hear it again
▶ **echo** *verb* (echoes, echoing, echoed /'ekəʊd/): *His footsteps echoed in the empty hall.*

eclipse /ɪ'klɪps/ *noun*
1 a time when the moon comes between the earth and the sun so that we cannot see the sun's light
2 a time when the earth comes between the sun and the moon so that we cannot see moon's light

ecology /i'kɒlədʒi/ *noun* (*no plural*)
the relationship between living things and everything around them; the study of this subject
▶ **ecological** /ˌiːkə'lɒdʒɪkl/ *adjective*: *an ecological disaster*
▶ **ecologist** /i'kɒlədʒɪst/ *noun* a person who studies or knows a lot about ECOLOGY

economic /ˌiːkə'nɒmɪk; ˌekə'nɒmɪk/ *adjective*
connected with the way that people and countries spend money and make, buy and sell things: *The country has serious economic problems.*

> 🔎 **WHICH WORD?**
> Be careful! **Economical** has a different meaning.

economical /ˌiːkə'nɒmɪkl; ˌekə'nɒmɪkl/ *adjective*
costing or using less time, money, etc. than usual: *This car is very economical to run* (= it

A B C D **E** F G H I J K L M N O P Q R S T U V W X Y Z

A

does not use a lot of petrol).

▶ **economically** /ˌiːkəˈnɒmɪkli; ˌekəˈnɒmɪkli/ *adverb*: *The service could be run more economically.*

economics /ˌiːkəˈnɒmɪks; ˌekəˈnɒmɪks/ *noun* (*no plural*)
the study of the way that people and countries spend money and make, buy and sell things

economist /ɪˈkɒnəmɪst/ *noun*
a person who studies or knows a lot about ECONOMICS

economy /ɪˈkɒnəmi/ *noun* (*plural* economies)
1 the way that a country spends its money and makes, buys and sells things: *the economies of Japan and Germany*
2 using money or things well and carefully: *We need to make some economies.*

edge 0→ /edʒ/ *noun*
1 the part along the end or side of something: *She stood at the water's edge.* ◇ *the edge of the table*
2 the sharp part of a knife or tool
be on edge to be nervous or worried

edible /ˈedəbl/ *adjective*
good or safe to eat: *The food was barely edible* (= almost too bad to eat).

edition /ɪˈdɪʃn/ *noun*
one of a number of books, magazines or newspapers that appear at the same time: *the evening edition of the newspaper*

editor /ˈedɪtə(r)/ *noun*
a person whose job is to prepare or control a book or a newspaper before it is printed

educate 0→ /ˈedʒukeɪt/ *verb* (educates, educating, educated)
1 to teach somebody at a school or college: *Where was she educated?*
2 to give people information about something: *We must educate young people about the dangers of smoking.*

education 0→ /ˌedʒuˈkeɪʃn/ *noun* (*no plural*)
teaching somebody at a school or college: *He had a good education.* ◇ *Education is extremely important.*
▶ **educational** /ˌedʒuˈkeɪʃənl/ *adjective*: *an educational video*

eel /iːl/ *noun*
a long fish that looks like a snake

effect 0→ /ɪˈfekt/ *noun*
a change that happens because of

something: *We are studying the effects of heat on different metals.* ◇ *Her shouting had little effect on him.*

effective /ɪˈfektɪv/ *adjective*
Something that is **effective** works well: *Cycling is an effective way of keeping fit.*

effectively /ɪˈfektɪvli/ *adverb*
in a way that gets the result you wanted: *She dealt with the situation effectively.*

efficient /ɪˈfɪʃnt/ *adjective*
working well without making mistakes or wasting energy: *Our secretary is very efficient.* ◇ *an efficient way of working*
◑ OPPOSITE **inefficient**
▶ **efficiency** /ɪˈfɪʃnsi/ *noun* (*no plural*): *ways of increasing efficiency at the factory*
▶ **efficiently** /ɪˈfɪʃntli/ *adverb*: *Try to use your time more efficiently.*

effort 0→ /ˈefət/ *noun*
the physical or mental energy that you need to do something: *Thank you for all your efforts.* ◇ *He made an effort to arrive on time.*

EFL /ˌiː ef ˈel/ *abbreviation* (*British*)
EFL is short for 'English as a foreign language' (= the teaching of English to people who speak other languages) ◑ Look at **ESL** and **ESOL**.

e.g. /ˌiː ˈdʒiː/ *abbreviation* short for FOR EXAMPLE: *popular sports, e.g. football, tennis and swimming*

egg

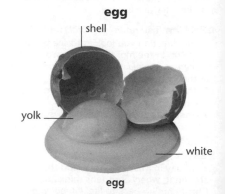

shell

yolk

white

egg

egg 0→ /eg/ *noun*
1 a round or OVAL (= almost round) object that has a baby bird, fish, insect or snake inside it: *The hen has laid an egg.*
2 an **egg** that we eat, especially from a chicken: *a boiled egg* ◑ Look at Picture Dictionary page **P6**.

egg cup /ˈeg kʌp/ *noun*
a small cup that holds a boiled egg while you are eating it ◑ Look at the picture at **cup**.

B
C
D
E
F
G
H
I
J
K
L
M
N
O
P
Q
R
S
T
U
V
W
X
Y
Z

eggplant /'eɡplɑːnt/ *American English for*
AUBERGINE

eight 0-π /eɪt/ *number* 8

eighteen 0-π /ˌeɪˈtiːn/ *number* 18
▶ **eighteenth** /ˌeɪˈtiːnθ/ *pronoun,
adjective, adverb* 18th: *He met Emma just
before his eighteenth birthday.*

eighth 0-π /eɪtθ/ *pronoun, adjective,
adverb, noun*
1 8th
2 one of eight equal parts of something; ⅛

eighty 0-π /'eɪti/ *number*
1 80
2 the eighties (*plural*) the numbers, years
or temperature between 80 and 89
in your eighties between the ages of 80
and 89
▶ **eightieth** /'eɪtiəθ/ *pronoun, adjective,
adverb* 80th: *My grandpa just celebrated his
eightieth birthday.*

either¹ 0-π /'aɪðə(r); 'iːðə(r)/ *adjective,
pronoun*
1 one of two things or people: *There is cake
and ice cream. You can have either.* ◇ *Either of
us will help you.*
2 each: *There are trees along either side of the
street.*

either² 0-π /'aɪðə(r); 'iːðə(r)/ *adverb*
(used in sentences with 'not') also: *Lydia
can't swim and I can't either.*
either ... or words that show two different
things or people that you can choose: *You
can have either tea or coffee.* ◇ *I will either
write or telephone.*

elaborate /ɪˈlæbərət/ *adjective*
not simple; with a lot of different parts
➲ SAME MEANING **complicated**: *The carpet
has a very elaborate pattern.*
▶ **elaborately** /ɪˈlæbərətli/ *adverb*: *The
rooms were elaborately decorated.*

elastic /ɪˈlæstɪk/ *noun* (*no plural*)
material that becomes longer when you pull
it and then goes back to its usual size: *This
skirt needs some new elastic in the waist.*
▶ **elastic** *adjective*: *elastic material*

elastic band /ɪˌlæstɪk ˈbænd/ *noun*
(*British*)
a thin circle of rubber that you use for
holding things together ➲ SAME MEANING
rubber band

elbow /'elbəʊ/ *noun*
the part in the middle of your arm where it
bends: *She fell and broke her elbow.* ➲ Look at
Picture Dictionary page **P4**.

elder /'eldə(r)/ *adjective*
older, especially of two members of the same
family: *My elder brother lives abroad.*

elderly /'eldəli/ *adjective*
(used about people) a polite way of saying
'old': *an elderly lady*

eldest /'eldɪst/ *adjective*
oldest of three or more people, especially
members of the same family: *Their eldest son
is at university.*

elect /ɪˈlekt/ *verb* (elects, electing,
elected)
to choose somebody to be a leader by
voting for him or her: *The new president was
elected last year.*

election 0-π /ɪˈlekʃn/ *noun*
a time when people choose somebody to be
a leader by voting for him or her: *The election
will be held on Wednesday.*

> 🔎 CULTURE
>
> In Britain, **general elections** are held
> about every five years.
> Voters in each area must choose one
> person from a list of **candidates** (= a
> person who wants to be elected) to be
> the **Member of Parliament** for that
> area. The head of the UK government is
> called the **Prime Minister**.
> In the US, **Presidential elections** are
> held every four years. The head of the US
> government is called the **President**.

electric 0-π /ɪˈlektrɪk/ *adjective*
using or providing electricity: *an electric
cooker* ◇ *an electric socket*

electrical 0-π /ɪˈlektrɪkl/ *adjective*
of or using electricity: *an electrical appliance*
(= a machine that uses electricity)

electrician /ɪˌlekˈtrɪʃn/ *noun*
a person whose job is to make and repair
electrical systems and equipment: *John's
an electrician. He'll be able to mend the light
for you.*

electricity 0-π /ɪˌlekˈtrɪsəti/ *noun* (*no
plural*)
power that comes through wires. **Electricity**
can make heat and light and makes
machines work.

electric shock /ɪˌlektrɪk ˈʃɒk/ *noun*
a sudden painful feeling that you get if
electricity goes through your body

electronic 0-π /ɪˌlekˈtrɒnɪk/ *adjective*
Electronic equipment includes things like
computers and televisions. They use
electricity and very small electrical parts

A B C D E F G H I J K L M N O P Q R S T U V W X Y Z

A B C D E F G H I J K L M N O P Q R S T U V W X Y Z

(called **microchips** and **transistors**) to make them work: *an electronic calculator*

electronics /ɪˌlek'trɒnɪks/ *noun* (*no plural*)
the technology that is used to make things like computers and televisions: *the electronics industry*

elegant /'elɪɡənt/ *adjective*
with a beautiful style or shape: *She looked very elegant in her new black dress.* ◇ *elegant furniture*

element /'elɪmənt/ *noun*
1 an important part of something: *Cost was an important element in our decision.*
2 a simple chemical, for example iron or gold: *Water is made of the elements hydrogen and oxygen.*

elementary /ˌelɪ'mentri/ *adjective*
connected with the early stages of learning; not difficult: *an elementary dictionary* ◇ *elementary physics*

elementary school /ˌelɪ'mentri skuːl/ *noun* (*American*) (*British* **primary school**)
a school for children aged six to eleven

elephant

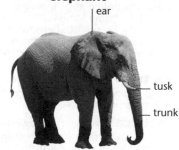

ear

tusk

trunk

elephant /'elɪfənt/ *noun*
a very big wild animal from Africa or Asia, with a long nose (called a **trunk**) that hangs down ⇨ Look at Picture Dictionary page **P3**.

elevator /'elɪveɪtə(r)/ *American English for* LIFT² (1)

eleven 0🔧 /ɪ'levn/ *number* 11
▶ **eleventh** /ɪ'levnθ/ *pronoun, adjective, adverb* 11th

elf /elf/ *noun* (*plural* **elves** /elvz/)
a very small person in stories who has pointed ears and magic powers

eliminate /ɪ'lɪmɪneɪt/ *verb* (**eliminates, eliminating, eliminated**)
to remove something that is not needed or wanted: *We must try to eliminate waste.*

else 0🔧 /els/ *adverb*
1 more; extra: *What else would you like?* ◇ *Is anyone else coming to the party?*
2 different: *This cafe's full, let's go somewhere else.* ◇ *It's not mine – it must be somebody else's.* ◇ *There was nothing else to eat so we had eggs again.*

> **GRAMMAR**
> You use **else** after words like **anybody**, **nothing** and **somewhere**, and after question words like **where** and **who**.

or else if not, then ⇨ SAME MEANING **otherwise**: *Go now, or else you'll be late.*

elsewhere /ˌels'weə(r)/ *adverb*
in or to another place: *He can't find a job near home so he's looking elsewhere.*

elves *plural of* ELF

email 0🔧 (*also* e-mail) /'iːmeɪl/ *noun*
1 (*no plural*) a system for sending messages from one computer to another: *to send a message by email* ◇ *What's your email address?*
2 (*plural* **emails**) a message that is written on one computer and sent to another: *I'll send you an email.*
▶ **email** (*also* e-mail) *verb* (**emails, emailing, emailed** /'iːmeɪld/): *Email me when you arrive.* ◇ *I'll email the documents to her.*

embarrass 0🔧 /ɪm'bærəs/ *verb*
(**embarrasses, embarrassing, embarrassed** /ɪm'bærəst/)
to make somebody feel shy or worried about what other people think of them: *Please don't embarrass me in front of my friends.*

embarrassed 0🔧 /ɪm'bærəst/ *adjective*

> **SPELLING**
> Remember! You spell **embarrassed** with **RR** and **SS**.

If you are **embarrassed**, you feel shy or worried about what other people think of you: *He felt embarrassed at being the centre of attention.*

embarrassing 0🔧 /ɪm'bærəsɪŋ/ *adjective*
Something that is **embarrassing** makes you feel EMBARRASSED: *I couldn't remember her name – it was so embarrassing!*

embarrassment 0🔧 /ɪm'bærəsmənt/ *noun* (*no plural*)
the feeling that you have when you are EMBARRASSED: *His face was red with embarrassment.*

embassy /'embəsi/ *noun* (*plural* **embassies**)
a group of people whose job is to speak and act for their government in another country, or the building where they work: *To get a visa, you should apply to the American embassy.*

embrace /ɪm'breɪs/ *verb* (**embraces, embracing, embraced** /ɪm'breɪst/) (*formal*)
to put your arms around somebody to show that you love them ⊃ SAME MEANING **hug**: *She embraced each member of her family in turn.*

embroider /ɪm'brɔɪdə(r)/ *verb* (**embroiders, embroidering, embroidered** /ɪm'brɔɪdəd/)
to decorate cloth by sewing patterns on it
▶ **embroidered** /ɪm'brɔɪdəd/ *adjective*: *an embroidered blouse*

embroidery

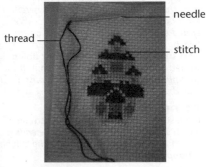

thread — needle — stitch

embroidery /ɪm'brɔɪdəri/ *noun* (*no plural*)
patterns that are sewn onto cloth to decorate it

embryo /'embriəʊ/ *noun* (*plural* **embryos**)
a human or animal when it is starting to grow before it is born

emerald /'emərəld/ *noun*
a green JEWEL (= very valuable stone): *an emerald ring*
▶ **emerald** (*also* **emerald green** /ˌemərəld 'griːn/) *adjective* bright green: *an emerald green dress*

emerge /i'mɜːdʒ/ *verb* (**emerges, emerging, emerged** /ɪ'mɜːdʒd/)
to come out from a place: *The moon emerged from behind the clouds.*

emergency 0̄͞ʊ /i'mɜːdʒənsi/ *noun* (*plural* **emergencies**)
a sudden dangerous situation, when people need help quickly: *Come quickly, doctor! It's an emergency!* ◊ *In an emergency phone 999*

for help. ◊ *an emergency exit* (= a way out of a building that can be used in an emergency)

emergency room /i'mɜːdʒənsi ruːm/ (*also* **ER** /ˌiː 'ɑː(r)/) *noun* (*American*) (*British* **casualty department**)
the place in a hospital where you go if you have been hurt in an accident or if you have suddenly become ill

emigrate /'emɪɡreɪt/ *verb* (**emigrates, emigrating, emigrated**)
to leave your country and go to live in another country: *They emigrated to Australia in the 1980s.*
▶ **emigration** /ˌemɪ'ɡreɪʃn/ *noun* (*no plural*): *emigration by poor people in search of work* ⊃ Look at **immigration**.

emotion 0̄͞ʊ /ɪ'məʊʃn/ *noun*
a strong feeling, for example love or anger: *They expressed mixed emotions at the news.*

emotional /ɪ'məʊʃənl/ *adjective*
1 connected with feelings: *emotional problems*
2 showing strong feelings, sometimes by crying: *He got very emotional when we said goodbye.*

empathy /'empəθi/ *noun* (*no plural*)
the ability to understand how other people feel

emperor /'empərə(r)/ *noun*
a man who rules a group of countries (called an empire): *the Emperor Napoleon* ⊃ Look at **empress**.

emphasis /'emfəsɪs/ *noun* (*plural* **emphases** /'emfəsiːz/)
special importance that is given to something ⊃ SAME MEANING **stress**: *Our school places a lot of emphasis on science.*

emphasize /'emfəsaɪz/ *verb* (**emphasizes, emphasizing, emphasized** /'emfəsaɪzd/)
to say something strongly to show that it is important ⊃ SAME MEANING **stress**: *She emphasized the importance of hard work.*

empire /'empaɪə(r)/ *noun*
a group of countries that is controlled by one country: *the Roman Empire*

employ 0̄͞ʊ /ɪm'plɔɪ/ *verb* (**employs, employing, employed** /ɪm'plɔɪd/)
to pay somebody to do work for you: *The factory employs 800 workers.* ⊃ Look at **unemployed**.

employee /ɪm'plɔɪiː/ *noun*
a person who works for somebody: *This company treats its employees very well.*

A
B
C
D
E
F
G
H
I
J
K
L
M
N
O
P
Q
R
S
T
U
V
W
X
Y
Z

employer /ɪm'plɔɪə(r)/ *verb*
a person or company that pays other people to do work

employment /ɪm'plɔɪmənt/ *noun* (*no plural*)
having a job that you are paid to do: *It can be hard for young people to find employment .*
➔ Look at **unemployment**.

empress /'emprəs/ *noun* (*plural* empresses)
a woman who rules a group of countries (called an **empire**), or the wife of an EMPEROR (= a man who rules a group of countries)

empty¹ 0̅ᴡ /'empti/ *adjective* (emptier, emptiest)
with nothing or nobody inside or on it: *The hall was almost empty.* ◇ *an empty box.*
➔ Look at the picture at **full**.

empty² 0̅ᴡ /'empti/ *verb* (empties, emptying, emptied /'emptid/, has emptied)
1 to take everything out of something: *The waiter emptied the ashtrays.* ◇ *We emptied our bags out onto the floor.*
2 to become **empty**: *The film finished and the cinema started to empty.*

enable /ɪ'neɪbl/ *verb* (enables, enabling, enabled /ɪ'neɪbld/) (*formal*)
to make it possible for somebody to do something: *Your help enabled me to finish the job.*

enclose /ɪn'kləʊz/ *verb* (encloses, enclosing, enclosed /ɪn'kləʊzd/)
1 to put something inside a letter or package: *I enclose a cheque for €100.*
2 to put something, for example a wall or fence, around a place on all sides: *The prison is enclosed by a high wall.*

encourage 0̅ᴡ /ɪn'kʌrɪdʒ/ *verb* (encourages, encouraging, encouraged /ɪn'kʌrɪdʒd/)
to give somebody hope or help so that they do something or continue doing something: *We encouraged him to write a book about his adventures.* ➔ OPPOSITE **discourage**
▶ **encouragement** /ɪn'kʌrɪdʒmənt/ *noun* (*no plural*): *Kim's parents have always given her a lot of encouragement.*
▶ **encouraging** /ɪn'kʌrɪdʒɪŋ/ *adjective*: *Ann's school report is very encouraging.*

encyclopedia /ɪnˌsaɪklə'piːdiə/ *noun* (*plural* encyclopedias)
a book or CD that gives information about a lot of different things: *an encyclopedia of world history*

end¹ 0̅ᴡ /end/ *noun*
the furthest or last part of something: *Turn right at the end of the street.* ◇ *They were sitting at the other end of the room.* ◇ *I'm going on holiday at the end of June.* ◇ *We were sad because the holiday was coming to an end.*
end to end in a line with the ends touching: *They put the tables end to end.*
for ... on end for a very long time: *He watches TV for hours on end.*
in the end finally; at last: *In the end it was midnight when we got home.*
make ends meet to have enough money for your needs: *After her husband died it was difficult to make ends meet.*
put an end to something to stop something happening: *We must put an end to this terrible war.*

end² 0̅ᴡ /end/ *verb* (ends, ending, ended)
to stop or to finish something: *What time does the film end?* ◇ *The road ends here.* ◇ *Most adverbs in English end in '-ly'.* ◇ *We ended our holiday with a few days on the beach.*
end up to finally be in a place or doing something when you did not plan it: *If she continues to steal, she'll end up in prison.* ◇ *I ended up doing all the work myself.*

ending /'endɪŋ/ *noun*
the last part of something, for example a word, story or film: *Nouns with the ending '—ch' form the plural with '—es'.* ◇ *The film has a happy ending.*

endless /'endləs/ *adjective*
never stopping or finishing; very long: *The journey seemed endless.*
▶ **endlessly** /'endləsli/ *adverb*: *He talks endlessly about nothing.*

endure /ɪn'djʊə(r)/ *verb* (endures, enduring, endured /ɪn'djʊəd/) (*formal*)
to suffer something that is painful or uncomfortable, usually without complaining
➔ SAME MEANING **bear**: *The pain was almost too great to endure.*

enemy 0̅ᴡ /'enəmi/ *noun* (*plural* enemies)
1 a person who hates you: *He has made a lot of enemies.*
2 the enemy (*no plural*) the army or country that your country is fighting against in a war: *The enemy is attacking from the north.*

energetic /ˌenə'dʒetɪk/ *adjective*
full of energy so that you can do a lot of things

energy 0→ /'enədʒi/ *noun* (no plural)
1 the ability to be active without getting tired: *Children are usually **full of energy**.*
2 the power from electricity, gas, coal, etc. that is used to make machines work and to make heat and light: *It is important to try to **save energy**.* ◇ *atomic energy*

engaged /ɪn'ɡeɪdʒd/ *adjective*
1 If two people are **engaged**, they have agreed to get married: *Louise is **engaged to** Michael.* ◇ *They **got engaged** last year.*
2 (*British*) (*American* **busy**) (used about a telephone) being used: *I tried to phone him but his number was engaged.*

engagement /ɪn'ɡeɪdʒmənt/ *noun*
an agreement to marry somebody

engine 0→ /'endʒɪn/ *noun*
1 a machine that makes things move: *a car engine*
2 the front part of a train which pulls the rest. ⊃ Look at the picture at **train¹**.

engineer /ˌendʒɪ'nɪə(r)/ *noun*
a person whose job is to plan, make or repair things like machines, roads or bridges: *My brother is an electrical engineer.*

engineering /ˌendʒɪ'nɪərɪŋ/ *noun* (no plural)
planning and making things like machines, roads or bridges: *She's studying chemical engineering at college.*

English /'ɪŋɡlɪʃ/ *noun*
1 (*no plural*) the language that is spoken in Britain, the US, Canada, Australia, etc.: *Do you speak English?*
2 the English (*plural*) the people of England

> **🔎 CULTURE**
> Be careful! The people of **Scotland** (the **Scots**) and the people of **Wales** (the **Welsh**) are **British**, not **English**.

enjoy 0→ /ɪn'dʒɔɪ/ *verb* (enjoys, enjoying, enjoyed /ɪn'dʒɔɪd/)
to like something very much: *I enjoy playing football.* ◇ *Did you enjoy your dinner?*
enjoy yourself to be happy; to have a good time: *I really enjoyed myself at the party.*

enjoyable 0→ /ɪn'dʒɔɪəbl/ *adjective*
Something that is **enjoyable** makes you happy: *Thank you for a very enjoyable evening.*

enjoyment 0→ /ɪn'dʒɔɪmənt/ *noun* (no plural)
a feeling of enjoying something
⊃ SAME MEANING **pleasure**: *I get a lot of enjoyment from travelling.*

enlarge /ɪn'lɑːdʒ/ *verb* (enlarges, enlarging, enlarged /ɪn'lɑːdʒd/)
to make something bigger: *Reading will enlarge your vocabulary.*
▶ **enlargement** /ɪn'lɑːdʒmənt/ *noun*: *an enlargement of a photograph*

enormous /ɪ'nɔːməs/ *adjective*
very big ⊃ SAME MEANING **huge**: *an enormous dog*

enormously /ɪ'nɔːməsli/ *adverb*
very or very much: *The film was enormously successful.*

enough 0→ /ɪ'nʌf/ *adjective, pronoun, adverb*

> **🔎 PRONUNCIATION**
> The word **enough** sounds like **stuff**, because sometimes the letters **-gh** sound like **f**, in words like **enough**, **rough** and **tough**.

as much or as many as you need: *There isn't enough food for ten people.* ◇ *You're too thin – you don't eat enough.* ◇ *Is she old enough to drive?*

> **🔎 GRAMMAR**
> If you have **enough** of something you have the right amount: *There's enough cake for everyone.*
> In negative sentences **enough** means 'less than': *The coffee isn't hot enough.* For 'more than' we use **too**: *The coffee is too hot.*

⊃ Look at the picture at **too**.

enquire (*British*) (*American* **inquire**) /ɪn'kwaɪə(r)/ *verb* (enquires, enquiring, enquired /ɪn'kwaɪəd/) (*formal*)
to ask for information about something ⊃ SAME MEANING **ask**: *Could you enquire about train times?*
enquire into something to find out information about something: *Journalists have been enquiring into his past.*

enquiry *noun* (*British*) (*American* **inquiry**) /ɪn'kwaɪəri/ (*plural* **enquiries**) (*formal*)
a question that you ask to get information about something: *I'll make some enquiries about dance classes.*

enrol (*British*) (*American* **enroll**) /ɪn'rəʊl/ *verb* (enrols, enrolling, enrolled /ɪn'rəʊld/)
to join a group, for example a school, college, course or club. You usually pay money (called a **fee**) when you **enrol**: *I've enrolled on an English course.* ⊃ In American English, you say: *I've enrolled in an English course.*

A
B
C
D
E
F
G
H
I
J
K
L
M
N
O
P
Q
R
S
T
U
V
W
X
Y
Z

ensure (British) (American **insure**) /ɪnˈʃʊə(r)/ *verb* (**ensures**, **ensuring**, **ensured** /ɪnˈʃʊəd/) (*formal*)
to make certain that something happens ⊃ SAME MEANING **make sure**: *Please ensure that all the lights are switched off before you leave.*

enter 0= /ˈentə(r)/ *verb* (**enters**, **entering**, **entered** /ˈentəd/)
1 (*formal*) to come or go into a place: *They stopped talking when she entered the room.* ◊ *Do not enter without knocking.*

> 🔊 SPEAKING
> In this sense, it is more usual to say **go in** or **come in**.

2 to give your name to somebody because you want to do something like take an exam or run in a race: *I entered a competition last month and won a prize.*
3 to put information on paper or in a computer: *Please enter your name and address at the top of the form.* ◊ *I've entered the data onto the computer.*

enterprise /ˈentəpraɪz/ *noun*
a new plan, project or business: *a business enterprise*

entertain 0= /ˌentəˈteɪn/ *verb* (**entertains**, **entertaining**, **entertained** /ˌentəˈteɪnd/)
1 to give food and drink to visitors in your house: *We're entertaining friends this evening.*
2 to say or do things that other people find interesting or funny: *She entertained us all with her funny stories.*

entertainer /ˌentəˈteɪnə(r)/ *noun*
a person whose job is to help people have a good time, for example by singing, dancing or telling jokes

entertaining /ˌentəˈteɪnɪŋ/ *adjective*
funny and interesting: *The talk was informative and entertaining.*

entertainment 0= /ˌentəˈteɪnmənt/ *noun* (*no plural*)
anything that ENTERTAINS people, for example films, concerts or television: *There isn't much entertainment for young people in this town.*

enthusiasm 0= /ɪnˈθjuːziæzəm/ *noun* (*no plural*)
a strong feeling of wanting to do something or liking something: *The pupils showed great enthusiasm for the new project.*

enthusiastic 0= /ɪnˌθjuːziˈæstɪk/ *adjective*
full of enthusiasm: *The kids are very enthusiastic about sport.*

entire /ɪnˈtaɪə(r)/ *adjective*
whole or complete: *We spent the entire day on the beach.*

entirely /ɪnˈtaɪəli/ *adverb*
completely: *That is an entirely different question.* ◊ *I entirely agree with you.*

entrance 0= /ˈentrəns/ *noun*
1 (*plural* **entrances**) the door, gate or opening where you go into a place: *I'll meet you at the entrance to the museum.*
2 (*plural* **entrances**) coming or going into a place: *He made his entrance onto the stage.*
3 (*no plural*) the right to go into a place: *They were refused entrance to the club because they were wearing jeans.*

entry /ˈentri/ *noun*
1 (*no plural*) the act of going into a place: *The thieves gained entry* (= got in) *through a window.*
2 (*no plural*) the right to go into a place: *There's a sign that says 'No Entry'.* ◊ *They were refused entry into the country.*
3 (*plural* **entries**) a person or thing that is entered in a competition: *The standard of the entries was very high.*

envelopes

envelope /ˈenvələʊp/ *noun*
a paper cover for a letter: *Have you written his address on the envelope?*

envied (*also* **envies**) forms of ENVY

envious /ˈenviəs/ *adjective*
wanting what somebody else has: *She's envious of her sister's success.* ⊃ The noun and verb are both **envy**.

environment 0= /ɪnˈvaɪrənmənt/ *noun*

> ✏️ SPELLING
> Be careful! Remember to put **N** before **M** in **environment**.

1 everything around you: *Children need a happy home environment.*
2 the environment (*no plural*) the air, water, land, animals and plants around us: *We must do more to protect the environment.*
▶ **environmental** /ɪnˌvaɪrən'mentl/ *adjective*: *We talked about pollution and other environmental problems.*

environmentalist
/ɪnˌvaɪrən'mentəlɪst/ *noun*
a person who tries to protect the ENVIRONMENT

environmentally friendly
/ɪnˌvaɪrənmentəli 'frendli/ (*also*
environment-friendly /ɪnˌvaɪrənmənt
'frendli/) *adjective*
(used about things you buy) not harming the ENVIRONMENT: *environmentally friendly packaging*

envy /'envi/ *noun* (*no plural*)
a sad or angry feeling of wanting what another person has ⊃ SAME MEANING **jealousy**: *I couldn't hide my envy of her success.* ◇ *They looked with envy at her new clothes.*
▶ **envy** *verb* (**envies, envying, envied** /'envid/, **has envied**): *I envy you! You always seem so happy!*

epic /'epɪk/ *noun*
a long film or book that contains a lot of action: *His latest film is a historical epic.*

epidemic /ˌepɪ'demɪk/ *noun*
a disease that many people in a place have at the same time: *a flu epidemic*

episode /'epɪsəʊd/ *noun*
a programme on radio or television that is part of a longer story: *You can see the final episode of the series on Monday.*

equal¹ 0📻 /'iːkwəl/ *adjective*
the same in size, amount, value or level as something or somebody else: *Women want equal pay for equal work.* ◇ *Divide the pie into six equal pieces.*

equal² 0📻 /'iːkwəl/ *verb* (*British* **equals, equalling, equalled** /'iːkwəld/) (*American* **equaling, equaled**)
1 to be exactly the same amount as something: *Two plus two equals four (2+2=4).*
2 to be as good as somebody or something: *This achievement is unlikely ever to be equalled.*

equal³ /'iːkwəl/ *noun*
a person who has the same ability or rights as somebody else: *She treats everyone as her equal.*

equality /i'kwɒləti/ *noun* (*no plural*)
being the same or having the same rights: *People are still fighting for racial equality.*

equally 0📻 /'iːkwəli/ *adverb*
1 in the same way: *Diet and exercise are equally important.*
2 in equal parts or amounts: *The money was divided equally among her four children.*

equator /i'kweɪtə(r)/ *noun* (*no plural*)
the line on maps around the middle of the world. Countries near the **equator** are very hot.

equip /i'kwɪp/ *verb* (**equips, equipping, equipped** /i'kwɪpt/)
to get or have all the things that are needed for doing something: *Before setting out, they equipped themselves with a map.* ◇ *The kitchen is well equipped.*

equipment 0📻 /i'kwɪpmənt/ *noun* (*no plural*)
special things that you need for doing something: *sports equipment*

🔎 **GRAMMAR**
Equipment does not have a plural. If you are talking about one item, you say 'a piece of equipment'.

ER /ˌiː 'ɑː(r)/ *abbreviation* (*American*) short for EMERGENCY ROOM

er /ɜː(r)/ *exclamation* (*British*)
used in writing to show the sound that a person makes when they cannot decide what to say next: *Er, do you want to come with us?*

eraser /i'reɪzə(r)/ *American English for* RUBBER(2)

erect¹ /i'rekt/ *adjective* (*formal*)
standing or pointing straight up: *He stood with his head erect.*

erect² /i'rekt/ *verb* (**erects, erecting, erected**) (*formal*)
to build something or to make something stand up straight: *Police erected barriers to keep the crowds back.*

erotic /i'rɒtɪk/ *adjective*
causing sexual excitement: *an erotic film*

errand /'erənd/ *noun*
a short journey to do something for somebody, for example to buy something from a shop: *I've got to run a few errands for my mum.*

error 0📻 /'erə(r)/ *noun* (*formal*)
something that is done wrong
⊃ SAME MEANING **mistake**: *The letter was sent to the wrong address because of a computer error.* ◇ *I think you have made an error in calculating the total.*

A
B
C
D
E
F
G
H
I
J
K
L
M
N
O
P
Q
R
S
T
U
V
W
X
Y
Z

erupt /ɪˈrʌpt/ *verb* (erupts, erupting, erupted)
When a VOLCANO (= a mountain with a hole in the top) **erupts**, smoke, hot rocks or liquid rock (called lava) suddenly come out: *When Mount Vesuvius erupted, it buried Pompeii.*
▶ **eruption** /ɪˈrʌpʃn/ *noun*: *a volcanic eruption*

escalator /ˈeskəleɪtə(r)/ *noun*
moving stairs that carry people up and down

escape¹ 0🔑 /ɪˈskeɪp/ *verb* (escapes, escaping, escaped /ɪˈskeɪpt/)
1 to get free from somebody or something: *The bird escaped from its cage.* ◇ *Two prisoners escaped, but were later caught.*
2 to manage to avoid something dangerous or unpleasant: *The pilot escaped death by seconds.*

escape² /ɪˈskeɪp/ *noun*
escaping from a place or a dangerous or unpleasant situation: *As soon as he turned his back, she would make her escape.* ◇ *She had a lucky escape* (= something bad almost happened to her) *when a lorry crashed into her car.*

escort¹ /ˈeskɔːt/ *noun*
one or more people or vehicles that go with somebody to protect them: *The President always travels with an armed escort.*

escort² /ɪˈskɔːt/ *verb* (escorts, escorting, escorted)
to go with somebody, for example to protect them or to make sure that they arrive somewhere: *The police escorted him out of the building.*

ESL /ˌiː es ˈel/ *abbreviation*
ESL is short for 'English as a second language' (= the teaching of English to speakers of other languages who are living in a country where people speak English).
➔ Look at **EFL**.

ESOL /ˈiːsɒl/ *abbreviation* (*British*)
ESOL is short for 'English for speakers of other languages' (= the teaching of English to speakers of other languages). ➔ Look also at **EFL**.

especially 0🔑 /ɪˈspeʃəli/ *adverb*
1 more than usual or more than others: *I hate getting up early, especially in winter.* ◇ *She loves animals, especially horses.*
2 for a particular person or thing: *I bought these flowers especially for you.*

essay /ˈeseɪ/ *noun*
a short piece of writing about a particular subject: *Our teacher asked us to write an essay on our favourite author.*

essential /ɪˈsenʃl/ *adjective*
If something is **essential**, it is completely necessary and you must have or do it: *It is essential that you work hard for this exam.*

establish /ɪˈstæblɪʃ/ *verb* (establishes, establishing, established /ɪˈstæblɪʃt/)
to start something new: *The school was established in 1852.*

estate /ɪˈsteɪt/ *noun*
1 a large piece of land in the country that one person or family owns
2 (*British*) land with a lot of houses or factories on it: *We live on a housing estate.* ◇ *an industrial estate* (= where there are a lot of factories)

estate agent /ɪˈsteɪt eɪdʒənt/ (*British*) (*American* real estate agent) *noun*
a person whose job is to sell buildings and land for other people

estate car /ɪˈsteɪt kɑː(r)/ *noun* (*British*) (*American* station wagon)
a long car with a door at the back and space behind the back seat for carrying things

estimate¹ /ˈestɪmət/ *noun*
a guess about the size or cost of something before you have all the facts and figures: *Can you give me a rough estimate of how many people will be there?*

estimate² /ˈestɪmeɪt/ *verb* (estimates, estimating, estimated)
to say how much you think something will cost, how big something is, or how long it will take to do something: *The builders estimated that it would take a week to repair the roof.*

estuary /ˈestʃuəri/ *noun* (*plural* estuaries)
the wide part of a river where it goes into the sea: *the Thames Estuary*

etc. 0🔑 *abbreviation* /ˌet ˈsetərə/
You use **etc.** at the end of a list to show that there are other things but you are not going to name them all: *Remember to take some paper, a pen, etc.*

eternal /ɪˈtɜːnl/ *adjective*
existing or continuing for ever: *They believe in eternal life* (= life after death).

ethnic /ˈeθnɪk/ *adjective*
connected with or belonging to a particular race of people: *London is home to many different ethnic minorities.*

euro 0🔑 /ˈjʊərəʊ/ (*plural* euros) *noun* (*symbol* €)
money that is used in many countries of the European Union: *All prices are in euros.*

European /ˌjʊərə'piːən/ *adjective*
from or connected with Europe: *European languages*
▶ **European** *noun*: *Many Europeans settled here in the nineteenth century.*

the European Union /ðə ˌjʊərəpiːən 'juːniən/ *noun* (*no plural*) (*abbr.* EU)
an organization of European countries that encourages TRADE (= the buying and selling of goods) between its members

evacuate /ɪ'vækjueɪt/ *verb* (evacuates, evacuating, evacuated)
to take people away from a dangerous place to a safer place: *The area near the factory was evacuated after the explosion.*
▶ **evacuation** /ɪˌvækju'eɪʃn/ *noun*: *the evacuation of cities during the war*

evaporate /ɪ'væpəreɪt/ *verb* (evaporates, evaporating, evaporated)
If a liquid **evaporates**, it changes into a gas: *Water evaporates if you heat it.*

eve /iːv/ *noun*
the day before a special day: *24 December is* **Christmas Eve**. ◇ *I went to a party on* **New Year's Eve** (= 31 December).

even¹ 0-₩ /'iːvn/ *adverb*
1 a word that you use to say that something is surprising: *The game is so easy that even a child can play it.* ◇ *He didn't laugh – he didn't even smile.*
2 a word that you use to make another word stronger: *Their house is even smaller than ours.*
even if it does not change anything if: *Even if you run, you won't catch the bus.*
even so although that is true: *I didn't have any lunch, but even so I'm not hungry.*
even though although: *I went to the party, even though I was tired.*

even² /'iːvn/ *adjective*
1 flat and smooth: *The game must be played on an even surface.* ⊃ OPPOSITE **uneven**
2 the same; equal: *Sara won the first game and I won the second, so we're even.*
3 Even numbers can be divided exactly by two: *4, 6 and 8 are even numbers.*
⊃ OPPOSITE **odd**
get even with somebody (*informal*) to hurt somebody who has hurt you

evening 0-₩ /'iːvnɪŋ/ *noun*
the part of the day between the afternoon and when you go to bed: *What are you doing* **this evening**? ◇ *Most people watch television* **in the evening**. ◇ *John came on Monday evening.*

event 0-₩ /ɪ'vent/ *noun*
1 something important that happens: *My sister's wedding was a big event for our family.*
2 a race or competition: *The next event will be the high jump.*

eventually 0-₩ /ɪ'ventʃuəli/ *adverb*
after a long time: *The bus eventually arrived two hours late.*

ever 0-₩ /'evə(r)/ *adverb*
at any time: '*Have you ever been to Africa?*' '*No, I haven't.*' ◇ *I* **hardly ever** (= almost never) *see Peter any more.*
ever since in all the time since: *I have known Lucy ever since we were children.*
ever so, **ever such a** (*informal*) very: *I'm ever so hot.* ◇ *It's ever such a good film.*
for ever for all time; always: *I will love you for ever.*

evergreen /'evəɡriːn/ *noun*
a tree or bush that has green leaves all the year

every 0-₩ /'evri/ *adjective*
1 all of the people or things in a group: *She knows every student in the school.*
2 used for saying how often something happens: *He phones* **every evening**. ◇ *I see Robert* **every now and then** (= sometimes, but not often). ◇ *She comes* **every other day** (= for example on Monday, Wednesday and Friday but not on Tuesday or Thursday).

everybody 0-₩ /'evribɒdi/ (*also* everyone) *pronoun*
each person; all people: *Everybody knows Tom.* ◇ *Everybody has a chance to win.*

> 🔎 WHICH WORD?
> **Everybody** or **somebody**?
> You use **somebody** for one person: *Somebody is singing outside my window.* You use **everybody** for all people: *Everybody was singing 'Happy Birthday'.*

everyday /'evrideɪ/ *adjective*
normal; not special: *Computers are now part of* **everyday life**.

everyone 0-₩ /'evriwʌn/ *pronoun* =
EVERYBODY: *If everyone is here then we can start.*

everything 0-₩ /'evriθɪŋ/ *pronoun*
each thing; all things: *Sam lost everything in the fire.* ◇ *Everything in that shop is very expensive.*

everywhere 0-₩ /'evriweə(r)/ *adverb*
in all places or to all places: *I've looked everywhere for my pen, but I can't find it.*

evidence 0-₩ /'evɪdəns/ *noun* (*no plural*)
the facts, signs or objects that make you

A
B
C
D

E

F
G
H
I
J
K
L
M
N
O
P
Q
R
S
T
U
V
W
X
Y
Z

believe that something is true: *The police searched the room, looking for evidence.* ◇ *There is **evidence of** a link between smoking and cancer.*

> 🔍 **GRAMMAR**
> **Evidence** does not have a plural so we cannot say 'an evidence'. Instead we say 'a piece of evidence'.

give evidence to say what you know about somebody or something in a court of law: *The man who saw the accident will give evidence in court.*

evident /'evɪdənt/ *adjective*
easy to see or understand ⊃ SAME MEANING **obvious**: *It was **evident that** the damage was very serious.*

evidently /'evɪdəntli/ *adverb*
clearly ⊃ SAME MEANING **obviously**: *She was evidently very upset.*

evil 0🔑 /'iːvl/ *adjective*
morally bad and cruel: *an evil person*

exact 0🔑 /ɪg'zækt/ *adjective*
completely correct: *We need to know the exact time the incident occurred.*

exactly 0🔑 /ɪg'zæktli/ *adverb*
1 You use **exactly** when you are asking for or giving information that is completely correct. ⊃ SAME MEANING **precisely**: *Can you tell me exactly what happened?* ◇ *It cost exactly £10.*
2 in every way or detail ⊃ SAME MEANING **just**: *This shirt is exactly what I wanted.*
3 You use **exactly** to agree with somebody: *'So you mean somebody in this room must be the murderer?' 'Exactly.'*

exaggerate 0🔑 /ɪg'zædʒəreɪt/ *verb*
(exaggerates, exaggerating, exaggerated)

> ✏️ **SPELLING**
> Remember! You spell **exaggerate** with **GG**.

to say that something is bigger, better, worse, etc. than it really is: *Don't exaggerate! I was only two minutes late, not twenty.*
▸ **exaggeration** /ɪg,zædʒə'reɪʃn/ *noun*: *It's a bit of an exaggeration to say she can't speak English!*

exam 0🔑 /ɪg'zæm/ *noun*
a test of what you know or can do: *We've got an English exam next week.*

> 🔍 **WORD BUILDING**
> You **sit** or **take** an exam. If you do well, you **pass**, and if you do badly, you **fail**: *I took my exams in June.* ◇ *'Did you pass all your exams?' 'No, I failed History. I've got to take it again in December.'*

examination 0🔑 /ɪg,zæmɪ'neɪʃn/ *noun*
1 an act of looking carefully at somebody or something: *a medical examination.*
2 (*formal*) = EXAM

examine 0🔑 /ɪg'zæmɪn/ *verb*
(examines, examining, examined /ɪg'zæmɪnd/)
1 to look carefully at something or somebody: *The doctor examined her but could find nothing wrong.* ◇ *Have the car examined by an expert before you buy it.*
2 (*formal*) to ask questions to find out what somebody knows or what they can do: *You will be **examined on** everything you have learnt this year.*

example 0🔑 /ɪg'zɑːmpl/ *noun*
something that shows what other things of the same kind are like: *This dictionary gives many **examples of** how words are used in sentences.*
for example used for giving an example: *Do you speak any other languages, for example French or German?* ⊃ The short way of writing 'for example' is **e.g.**

exasperated /ɪg'zæspəreɪtɪd/ *adjective*
very annoyed or angry: *They were exasperated by all the delays.*

exceed /ɪk'siːd/ *verb* (exceeds, exceeding, exceeded)
to be more than a particular number or amount: *The weight must not exceed 20 kilos.* ⊃ The noun is **excess**.

excellent 0🔑 /'eksələnt/ *adjective*

> ✏️ **SPELLING**
> Remember! You spell **excellent** with **LL**.

very good: *She speaks excellent Spanish.*

except 0🔑 /ɪk'sept/ *preposition*

> 🔍 **WHICH WORD?**
> Be careful! Don't confuse **except** with **accept**, which sounds very similar.

not including somebody or something: *The restaurant is open every day except Sunday.* ◇ *Everyone went to the party except for me.*
except that apart from the fact that: *I don't know what he looks like, except that he's very tall.*

exception /ɪkˈsepʃn/ *noun*
a person or thing that is not the same as the others: *Most of his films are good but this one is an exception.*
with the exception of somebody or **something** except ➔ SAME MEANING **apart from**: *I like all vegetables with the exception of cabbage.*

exceptional /ɪkˈsepʃənl/ *adjective*
very good: *She is an exceptional pianist.*
▸ **exceptionally** /ɪkˈsepʃənəli/ *adverb*: *He was an exceptionally bright student.*

excess /ɪkˈses/ *noun* (*no plural*)
more than is necessary or usual: *An excess of stress can make you ill.*
▸ **excess** /ˈekses/ *adjective*: *Cut any excess fat off the meat.* ➔ The verb is **exceed**.

exchange¹ 0̶ₘ /ɪksˈtʃeɪndʒ/ *noun*
giving or receiving something in return for something else: *a useful exchange of information* ◇ *We can offer free accommodation in exchange for some help in the house.* ➔ Look at **stock exchange**.

exchange² 0̶ₘ /ɪksˈtʃeɪndʒ/ *verb*
(exchanges, exchanging, exchanged /ɪksˈtʃeɪndʒd/)
to give one thing and get another thing for it: *I would like to exchange this skirt for a bigger size.* ◇ *We exchanged phone numbers.*

exchange rate /ɪksˈtʃeɪndʒ reɪt/ *noun*
how much money from one country you can buy with money from another country: *The exchange rate is 1.4 euros to the pound.*

excite /ɪkˈsaɪt/ *verb* (excites, exciting, excited)
to make a person feel very happy or enthusiastic so that they are not calm: *Please don't excite the children too much or they won't sleep tonight.*

excited 0̶ₘ /ɪkˈsaɪtɪd/ *adjective*
not calm, for example because you are happy about something that is going to happen: *He's getting very excited about his holiday.*

excitement 0̶ₘ /ɪkˈsaɪtmənt/ *noun* (*no plural*)
a feeling of being excited: *There was great excitement in the stadium before the match began.*

exciting 0̶ₘ /ɪkˈsaɪtɪŋ/ *adjective*
Something that is **exciting** makes you have strong feelings of happiness and enthusiasm: *an exciting film* ◇ *Her new job sounds very exciting.*

exclaim /ɪkˈskleɪm/ *verb* (exclaims, exclaiming, exclaimed /ɪkˈskleɪmd/)
to say something suddenly and loudly because you are surprised or angry: *'I don't believe it!' she exclaimed.*
▸ **exclamation** /ˌekskləˈmeɪʃn/ *noun*: *He gave an exclamation of surprise.*

exclamation mark /ˌekskləˈmeɪʃn mɑːk/ (*British*) (*American* **exclamation point** /ˌekskləˈmeɪʃn pɔɪnt/) *noun*
a mark (!) that you use in writing to show loud or strong words, or surprise

exclude /ɪkˈskluːd/ *verb* (excludes, excluding, excluded)
1 to deliberately not include something: *The price excludes air fares.* ➔ OPPOSITE **include**
2 to not allow a person to enter a place or do an activity: *Students were excluded from the meeting.*

excluding 0̶ₘ /ɪkˈskluːdɪŋ/ *preposition*
without: *The meal cost £35, excluding drinks.*
➔ OPPOSITE **including**

excursion /ɪkˈskɜːʃn/ *noun*
a short journey to see something interesting or to enjoy yourself ➔ SAME MEANING **trip**: *We're going on an excursion to the seaside on Sunday.*

excuse¹ 0̶ₘ /ɪkˈskjuːs/ *noun*

> 🔎 **PRONUNCIATION**
> When the word **excuse** is a noun, it ends with a sound like **juice** or **loose**.
> When the word **excuse** is a verb, it ends with a sound like **shoes** or **choose**.

words you say or write to explain why you have done something wrong: *You're late! What's your excuse this time?* ◇ *There's no excuse for rudeness.*

excuse² 0̶ₘ /ɪkˈskjuːz/ *verb* (excuses, excusing, excused /ɪkˈskjuːzd/)
used when you are saying sorry for something that is not very bad: *Please excuse us for being late – we missed the bus.*
excuse me You use **excuse me** when you want to stop somebody who is speaking, or when you want to speak to somebody you do not know. You can also use **excuse me** to say that you are sorry: *Excuse me, could you tell me the time?* ◇ *Did I stand on your foot? Excuse me.*

execute /ˈeksɪkjuːt/ *verb* (executes, executing, executed)
to kill a person as a legal punishment: *He was executed for murder.*
▸ **execution** /ˌeksɪˈkjuːʃn/ *noun*: *the execution of prisoners*

A
B
C
D
E
F
G
H
I
J
K
L
M
N
O
P
Q
R
S
T
U
V
W
X
Y
Z

executive /ɪgˈzekjətɪv/ *noun*
an person who has an important position in a business or organization

exercise¹ 0⇥ /ˈeksəsaɪz/ *noun*
1 (*no plural*) moving your body to keep it strong and well: *Swimming is very good exercise.*
2 (*plural* **exercises**) a special movement that you do to keep your body strong and well: *This exercise is good for your back.*
3 (*plural* **exercises**) a piece of work that you do to learn something: *Please do exercises 1 and 2 for homework.*

exercise² /ˈeksəsaɪz/ *verb* (**exercises**, **exercising**, **exercised** /ˈeksəsaɪzd/)
to move your body to keep it strong and well: *They exercise in the park every morning.*

exercise book /ˈeksəsaɪz bʊk/ *noun*
a book that you use at school for writing in ⊃ Look at Picture Dictionary page **P11**.

exhaust¹ /ɪgˈzɔːst/ *noun*
1 (*no plural*) the waste gas that comes out of a vehicle, an engine or a machine: *car exhaust fumes*
2 (*also* **exhaust pipe** /ɪgˈzɔːst paɪp/) (*British*) (*American* **tailpipe**) a pipe through which waste gases come out, for example on a car ⊃ Look at Picture Dictionary page **P1**.

exhaust² /ɪgˈzɔːst/ *verb* (**exhausts**, **exhausting**, **exhausted**)
to make you feel very tired: *The long journey exhausted us.*
▶ **exhausted** /ɪgˈzɔːstɪd/ *adjective*: *I'm exhausted – I think I'll go to bed.*

exhausting /ɪgˈzɔːstɪŋ/ *adjective*
making you feel very tired: *Teaching young children can be exhausting.*

exhibit /ɪgˈzɪbɪt/ *verb* (**exhibits**, **exhibiting**, **exhibited**)
to show something in a public place for people to look at: *Her photographs have been exhibited all over the world.*

exhibition 0⇥ /ˌeksɪˈbɪʃn/ *noun*
a group of things that are arranged in a place so that people can look at them: *an exhibition of paintings by Monet*

exile /ˈeksaɪl/ *noun*
1 (*no plural*) having to live away from your own country, especially for political reasons or as a punishment: *Napoleon spent the last years of his life in exile.*
2 (*plural* **exiles**) a person who has to live away from their own country

exist 0⇥ /ɪgˈzɪst/ *verb* (**exists**, **existing**, **existed**)
to be real; to live: *Does life exist on other planets?* ◊ *That word does not exist.*

existence /ɪgˈzɪstəns/ *noun* (*no plural*)
being real; existing: *This is the oldest Latin manuscript in existence.*

exit /ˈeksɪt/ *noun*
a way out of a building: *Where is the exit?* ◊ *an emergency exit*

exotic /ɪgˈzɒtɪk/ *adjective*
strange or interesting because it comes from another country: *exotic fruits*

expand /ɪkˈspænd/ *verb* (**expands**, **expanding**, **expanded**)
to become bigger or to make something bigger: *Metals expand when they are heated.* ◊ *We hope to expand the business this year.*
▶ **expansion** /ɪkˈspænʃn/ *noun* (*no plural*): *The city's rapid expansion has caused a lot of problems.*

expect 0⇥ /ɪkˈspekt/ *verb* (**expects**, **expecting**, **expected**)
1 to think that somebody or something will come or that something will happen: *I'm expecting a letter.* ◊ *We expected it to be hot in South Africa, but it was quite cold.* ◊ *She's expecting a baby* (= she is going to have a baby) *in June.*
2 If you are **expected** to do something, you must do it: *I am expected to work every Saturday.*
3 (*British, informal*) to think that something will happen or is probably true: *I expect she'll be late. She usually is.* ◊ *They haven't had lunch yet, so I expect they're hungry.* ◊ *'Is Ian coming?' 'Oh yes, I expect so.'*

expectation /ˌekspekˈteɪʃn/ *noun*
a belief that something will happen: *Against all expectations, we enjoyed ourselves.*

expedition /ˌekspəˈdɪʃn/ *noun*
a journey to find or do something special: *an expedition to the South Pole*

expel /ɪkˈspel/ *verb* (**expels**, **expelling**, **expelled** /ɪkˈspeld/)
to send somebody away from a school, a club or a country: *The boys were expelled from school for smoking.*

expense /ɪkˈspens/ *noun*
1 the cost of something: *Having a car is a big expense.*
2 **expenses** (*plural*) money that you spend on a certain thing: *The company pays our travelling expenses.*

expensive 0⇥ /ɪkˈspensɪv/ *adjective*
Something that is **expensive** costs a lot of money: *expensive clothes* ◊ *The meal was very expensive.* ⊃ OPPOSITE **cheap**

experience¹ 0⇥ /ɪkˈspɪəriəns/ *noun*
1 (*no plural*) knowing about something because you have seen it or done it: *She has*

four years' teaching experience. ◇ *Do you have much* **experience of** *working with children?*
2 (*plural* **experiences**) something that has happened to you: *He wrote a book about his experiences in Africa.*

experience² 0🛒 /ɪk'spɪəriəns/ *verb*
(**experiences, experiencing, experienced** /ɪk'spɪəriənst/)
If you **experience** something, it happens to you: *Everyone experiences failure at some time in their lives.*

experienced /ɪk'spɪəriənst/ *adjective*
If you are **experienced**, you know about something because you have done it many times before: *She's an experienced driver.*
⊃ OPPOSITE **inexperienced**

experiment 0🛒 /ɪk'sperɪmənt/ *noun*
a scientific test that you do to find out what will happen or to see if something is true: *They have to* **do experiments** *to find out if the drug is safe for humans.*
▸ **experiment** *verb* (**experiments, experimenting, experimented**): *I don't think it's right to* **experiment on** *animals.*

expert 0🛒 /'eksp3:t/ *noun*
a person who knows a lot about something: *He's an* **expert on** *Shakespeare.* ◇ *a computer expert*

explain 0🛒 /ɪk'spleɪn/ *verb* (**explains, explaining, explained** /ɪk'spleɪnd/)
1 to tell somebody about something so that they understand it: *The teacher usually* **explains** *the new words* **to** *us.* ◇ *He* **explained** **how** *to use the machine.*

> 🔎 GRAMMAR
> We say 'Explain **it to me**'. It is wrong to say 'Explain me it'.

2 to give a reason for something: *I* **explained** **why** *we needed the money.*

explanation 0🛒 /ˌeksplə'neɪʃn/ *noun*
something that helps somebody understand something, or a reason for something: *Did they* **give** *any* **explanation for** *their behaviour?*

explode 0🛒 /ɪk'spləʊd/ *verb* (**explodes, exploding, exploded**)
to burst suddenly with a very loud noise: *A bomb exploded in the city centre, killing two people.* ⊃ The noun is **explosion**.

exploit /ɪk'splɔɪt/ *verb* (**exploits, exploiting, exploited**)
to treat somebody badly to get what you want: *Some employers exploit foreign workers, making them work long hours for low pay.*

explore 0🛒 /ɪk'splɔː(r)/ *verb* (**explores, exploring, explored** /ɪk'splɔːd/)
to travel around a new place to learn about it: *They explored the area on foot.*
▸ **exploration** /ˌeksplə'reɪʃn/ *noun*: *the exploration of space*

explorer /ɪk'splɔːrə(r)/ *noun*
a person who travels around a new place to learn about it: *The first European explorers arrived in America in the 15th century.*

explosion 0🛒 /ɪk'spləʊʒn/ *noun*
the sudden bursting and loud noise of something such as a bomb exploding: *There was an explosion and pieces of glass flew everywhere.* ⊃ The verb is **explode**.

explosive /ɪk'spləʊsɪv/ *adjective*
Something that is **explosive** can cause an explosion: *an explosive gas*
▸ **explosive** *noun* a substance that can make things explode

export¹ /ɪk'spɔːt/ *verb* (**exports, exporting, exported**)
to sell things to another country: *Japan* **exports** *cars* **to** *Britain.* ⊃ OPPOSITE **import**
▸ **exporter** /ek'spɔːtə(r)/ *noun*: *the world's biggest exporter of oil* ⊃ OPPOSITE **importer**

export² /'ekspɔːt/ *noun*
1 (*no plural*) selling things to another country: *These cars are made* **for export.**
2 (*plural* **exports**) something that you sell to another country: *The country's main exports are tea and cotton.*
⊃ OPPOSITE **import**

expose /ɪk'spəʊz/ *verb* (**exposes, exposing, exposed** /ɪk'spəʊzd/)
to show something that is usually covered or hidden: *A baby's skin should not be* **exposed** **to** *the sun for too long.* ◇ *The newspaper exposed his terrible secret.*

express¹ /ɪk'spres/ *verb* (**expresses, expressing, expressed** /ɪk'sprest/)
to say or show how you think or feel: *She expressed her ideas well.*

express² /ɪk'spres/ *adjective*
that goes or is sent very quickly: *an express letter* ◇ *an express coach*
▸ **express** *adverb*: *I sent the parcel express.*

express³ /ɪk'spres/ (*plural* **expresses**)
(*also* **express train**) *noun*
a fast train that does not stop at all stations

expression 0🛒 /ɪk'spreʃn/ *noun*
1 the look on your face that shows how you feel: *an expression of surprise*
2 a word or group of words; a way of saying something: *The expression 'to drop off' means 'to fall asleep'.*

A B C D E F G H I J K L M N O P Q R S T U V W X Y Z

A B C D **E** F G H I J K L M N O P Q R S T U V W X Y Z

expressway /ɪkˈspreswei/ *American English for* MOTORWAY

exquisite /ɪkˈskwɪzɪt/ *adjective*
extremely beautiful: *She has an exquisite face.*

extend /ɪkˈstend/ *verb* (extends, extending, extended)
1 to make something longer or bigger: *I'm extending my holiday for another week.*
2 to reach or stretch over an area: *The park extends as far as the river.*

extension /ɪkˈstenʃn/ *noun*
1 (*British*) a part that you add to something to make it bigger: *They've built an extension on the back of the house.*
2 one of the telephones in a building that is connected to the main telephone: *Can I have extension 4110, please?*

extensive /ɪkˈstensɪv/ *adjective*
large in area or amount: *The house has extensive grounds.* ◇ *Many buildings suffered extensive damage.*

extent /ɪkˈstent/ *noun* (*no plural*)
how big something is: *I had no idea of the **full extent of** the problem* (= how big it was).
to a certain extent, to some extent used to show that you do not think something is completely true: *I agree with you to a certain extent.*

exterior /ɪkˈstɪəriə(r)/ *noun*
the outside part of something, especially a building: *We painted the exterior of the house white.* ➲ OPPOSITE **interior**
▶ **exterior** *adjective*: *an exterior door* ➲ OPPOSITE **interior**

external /ɪkˈstɜːnl/ *adjective*
on, of or from the outside: *external walls* ➲ OPPOSITE **internal**

extinct /ɪkˈstɪŋkt/ *adjective*
If a type of animal or plant is **extinct**, it does not exist now: *Dinosaurs **became extinct** millions of years ago.*

extinguish /ɪkˈstɪŋɡwɪʃ/ *verb* (extinguishes, extinguishing, extinguished /ɪkˈstɪŋɡwɪʃt/) (*formal*)
to make something stop burning
➲ SAME MEANING **put out**: *It took several hours to extinguish the fire.*

extra 0ーᵤ /ˈekstrə/ *adjective, adverb*
more than what is usual: *I've put an extra blanket on your bed because it's cold tonight.* ◇ *The room costs £30 and you have to pay extra for breakfast.*

extraordinarily /ɪkˈstrɔːdnrəli/ *adverb*
extremely: *She's extraordinarily clever.*

extraordinary /ɪkˈstrɔːdnri/ *adjective*
very unusual or strange: *What an extraordinary thing to say!*

extravagant /ɪkˈstrævəɡənt/ *adjective*
If you are **extravagant**, you spend too much money: *He's terribly extravagant – he goes everywhere by taxi.*
▶ **extravagance** /ɪkˈstrævəɡəns/ *noun* (*no plural*) the act or habit of spending too much money: *There are no limits to his extravagance.*

extreme 0ーᵤ /ɪkˈstriːm/ *adjective*
1 very great or strong: *the extreme cold of the Arctic*
2 If you say that a person is **extreme**, you mean that their ideas are too strong.
3 as far away as possible: *They came from the extreme north of Scotland.*

extremely 0ーᵤ /ɪkˈstriːmli/ *adverb*
very: *He's extremely good-looking.*

the eye

eyebrow | eyelid
eyelash | pupil

eye 0ーᵤ /aɪ/ *noun*
one of the two parts in your head that you see with: *She's got blue eyes.* ◇ *Open your eyes!*
catch somebody's eye
1 to make somebody look at you: *Try to catch the waiter's eye the next time he comes this way.*
2 If something **catches your eye**, you see it suddenly: *Her bright yellow hat caught my eye.*
in somebody's eyes in the opinion of somebody: *Richard is 42, but in his mother's eyes, he's still a little boy!*
keep an eye on somebody or **something** to look after or watch somebody or something: *Will you keep an eye on my bag while I go to the toilet?*
see eye to eye with somebody to agree with somebody: *Mr Harper doesn't always see eye to eye with his neighbours.*

eyebrow /ˈaɪbraʊ/ *noun*
one of the two lines of hair above your eyes
➲ Look at the picture at **eye**.

eyelash /'aɪlæʃ/ (*also* lash) *noun* (*plural* eyelashes)
one of the hairs that grow in a line on your EYELID: *She's got beautiful long eyelashes.* ⊃ Look at the picture at **eye**.

eyelid /'aɪlɪd/ *noun*
the piece of skin that can move to close your eye ⊃ Look at the picture at **eye**.

eyesight /'aɪsaɪt/ *noun* (*no plural*)
the ability to see: *Your eyesight is very good.*

A
B
C
D
E
F
G
H
I
J
K
L
M
N
O
P
Q
R
S
T
U
V
W
X
Y
Z

F f

F, f /ef/ *noun*
1 (*plural* F's, f's /efs/) the sixth letter of the English alphabet: '*Father*' *begins with an* '*F*'.
2 F *short way of writing* FAHRENHEIT

fable /'feɪbl/ *noun*
a short story, usually about animals, that teaches people a lesson (called a **moral**)

fabric /'fæbrɪk/ *noun*
cloth that is used for making things such as clothes and curtains: *cotton fabrics*

fabulous /'fæbjələs/ *adjective*
very good ⊃ SAME MEANING **wonderful**:
The food smells fabulous!

face¹ 0🔑 /feɪs/ *noun*
1 the front part of your head: *Have you washed your face?* ◇ *She had a smile on her face.* ⊃ Look at Picture Dictionary page **P4**.
2 the front or one side of something: *a clock face* ◇ *He put the cards face down on the table.*
face to face If two people are face to face, they are looking straight at each other: *They stood face to face.*
keep a straight face to not smile or laugh when something is funny: *I couldn't keep a straight face when he dropped his watch in the soup!*
make or **pull a face** to move your mouth and eyes to show that you do not like something: *She made a face when she saw what was for dinner.*
to somebody's face If you say something **to somebody's face**, you say it when that person is with you: *I wanted to say that I was sorry to her face, not on the phone.*

face² 0🔑 /feɪs/ *verb* (**faces, facing, faced** /feɪst/)
1 to have your face or front towards something: *Can you all face the front of the class, please?* ◇ *My bedroom faces the garden.*
2 to deal with an unfriendly person or a difficult situation: *I can't face going to work today – I feel too ill.*
let's face it (*informal*) we must agree that it is true: *Let's face it – you're not very good at maths.*

facilities /fə'sɪlətiz/ *noun* (*plural*)
a service, building, piece of equipment, etc. that makes it possible to do something: *Our school has very good sports facilities.*

fact 0🔑 /fækt/ *noun*
something that you know has happened or is true: *It's a fact that the earth travels around the sun.*
in fact, **in actual fact** used to show that something is true; really: *I thought she was Swedish, but in actual fact she's from Norway.* ◇ *I think I saw him – in fact, I'm sure I did.*

factory 0🔑 /'fæktri/ *noun* (*plural* **factories**)
a place where people make things, usually with machines: *He works at the car factory.*

fade /feɪd/ *verb* (**fades, fading, faded**)
to become lighter in colour or less strong: *Will this shirt fade when I wash it?* ◇ *The cheers of the crowd faded away.*

Fahrenheit /'færənhaɪt/ *noun* (*no plural*) (*abbr.* F)
a way of measuring temperature. Water freezes at 32° **Fahrenheit** and boils at 212° **Fahrenheit**: *110°F*

fail¹ 0🔑 /feɪl/ *verb* (**fails, failing, failed** /feɪld/)
1 to not pass an exam or test: *She failed her driving test again.* ◇ *How many students failed last term?* ⊃ OPPOSITE **pass**
2 to try to do something but not be able to do it: *He played quite well but failed to win the match.* ⊃ OPPOSITE **succeed**
3 to not do something that you should do: *The driver failed to stop at a red light.*

fail² /feɪl/ *noun*
without fail certainly: *Be there at twelve o'clock without fail!*

failure 0🔑 /'feɪljə(r)/ *noun*
1 (*no plural*) lack of success: *The search for the missing children ended in failure.*
2 (*plural* **failures**) a person or thing that does not do well: *I felt that I was a failure because I didn't have a job.*
⊃ OPPOSITE **success**

faint¹ /feɪnt/ *adjective* (**fainter, faintest**)
1 not clear or strong: *We could hear the faint sound of music in the distance.*
2 If you feel **faint**, you feel that you are going to fall, for example because you are ill or tired.

faint² /feɪnt/ *verb* (**faints, fainting, fainted**)
to suddenly become unconscious for a short time, for example because you are weak, ill or shocked: *She fainted as soon as she saw the blood.*

fair¹ 0‑⊓ /feə(r)/ *adjective* (fairer, fairest)
1 treating people equally or in the right way: *They didn't get a fair trial.* ◇ *It's not fair! I have to go to bed before my sister!*
➲ OPPOSITE **unfair**
2 quite good or quite large: *They have a fair chance of winning.* ◇ *They've invited a fair number of people to their party.*
3 (used about a person's skin or hair) light in colour: *He's got fair hair.* ➲ OPPOSITE **dark**
4 (used about the weather) bright and not raining

fair² /feə(r)/ *noun*
1 (*also* **funfair**) a place outdoors where you can ride on big machines and play games to win prizes. **Fairs** usually travel from town to town.
2 a large event where people and businesses show and sell the things they make: *a book fair* ◇ *a world trade fair*

fairly 0‑⊓ /'feəli/ *adverb*
1 quite; not very: *She speaks French fairly well.* ◇ *I'm fairly certain it was him.*
2 in a way that is right and honest: *This company treats its workers fairly.*
➲ OPPOSITE **unfairly**

fairy

wing

fairy /'feəri/ *noun* (*plural* **fairies**)
a very small person in stories. **Fairies** have wings and can do magic.

fairy tale /'feəri teɪl/ (*also* **fairy story** /'feəri stɔːri/ *plural* **fairy stories**) *noun*
a story for children that is about magic

faith /feɪθ/ *noun*
1 (*no plural*) feeling sure that somebody or something is good, right or honest: *I've got great faith in your ability to do the job* (= I'm sure that you can do it).
2 (*plural* **faiths**) a religion: *the Muslim faith*

faithful /'feɪθfl/ *adjective*
always ready to help your friends and to do what you have promised to do: *a faithful friend*

faithfully /'feɪθfəli/ *adverb*
Yours faithfully words that you write at the end of a formal letter, before your name ➲ Look at Study Page **S14**.

fake /feɪk/ *noun*
a copy of something that seems real but is not: *This painting is not really by Van Gogh – it's a fake.*
▸ **fake** *adjective*: *a fake passport*

fall¹ 0‑⊓ /fɔːl/ *verb* (falls, falling, fell /fel/, has fallen /'fɔːlən/)
1 to go down quickly towards the ground: *The book fell off the table.* ◇ *She fell down the stairs and broke her arm.*
2 (*also* **fall over**) to suddenly stop standing: *He slipped on the ice and fell.* ◇ *I fell over and hurt my leg.*
3 to become lower or less: *In the desert the temperature falls quickly at night.* ◇ *Prices have fallen again.* ➲ OPPOSITE **rise**
fall apart to break into pieces: *The chair fell apart when I sat on it.*
fall asleep to start sleeping: *She fell asleep in the armchair.*
fall behind to become slower than others, or not do something when you should do it: *She's falling behind with her school work.*
fall for somebody to begin to love somebody: *He has fallen for someone he met on holiday.*
fall in love with somebody to begin to love somebody: *He fell in love with Anna the first time they met.*
fall out with somebody to argue with somebody so that you stop being friends: *Jane has fallen out with her best friend.*
fall through If a plan **falls through**, it does not happen.

fall² 0‑⊓ /fɔːl/ *noun*
1 a sudden drop from a higher place to a lower place: *He had a fall from his horse.*
2 becoming lower or less: *a fall in the price of oil*
3 **falls** (*plural*) a place where water falls from a high place to a low place
➲ SAME MEANING **waterfall**: *the Victoria Falls*
4 *American English for* AUTUMN

fallen *form of* FALL¹

false /fɔːls/ *adjective*
1 not true; wrong: *She gave a false name to the police.* ◇ *A spider has eight legs – true or false?* ➲ OPPOSITE **true**
2 not real or not natural: *He has false teeth* (= teeth that are made of plastic).
false alarm a warning about something bad that does not happen: *Everyone thought there was a fire, but it was a false alarm.*

A
B
C
D
E
F
G
H
I
J
K
L
M
N
O
P
Q
R
S
T
U
V
W
X
Y
Z

A
B
C
D
E
F
G
H
I
J
K
L
M
N
O
P
Q
R
S
T
U
V
W
X
Y
Z

fame /feɪm/ *noun* (*no plural*)
being known by many people ⊃ The adjective is **famous**.

familiar ○ₜ /fə'mɪliə(r)/ *adjective*
that you know well: *I heard a familiar voice in the next room.* ◇ *I'm not familiar with this computer.* ⊃ OPPOSITE **unfamiliar**

family ○ₜ /'fæməli/ *noun* (*plural families*)
1 parents and children: *How many people are there in your family?* ◇ *My family have all got red hair.* ◇ *His family lives on a farm.*

> *ρ* CULTURE
> Sometimes **family** means not just parents and children but other people too, for example grandparents, aunts, uncles and cousins.

2 a group of plants or animals: *Lions belong to the cat family.*

family name /'fæməli neɪm/ *noun*
the name that is shared by members of a family ⊃ SAME MEANING **surname** ⊃ Look at the note at **name**.

family tree /ˌfæməli 'triː/ *noun*
a plan that shows all the people in a family

famine /'fæmɪn/ *noun*
A **famine** happens when there is not enough food in a country: *There is a famine in many parts of Africa.*

famous ○ₜ /'feɪməs/ *adjective*
known by many people: *Oxford is famous for its university.* ◇ *Marilyn Monroe was a famous actress.* ⊃ The noun is **fame**.

fans

fan¹ /fæn/ *noun*
1 a person who likes somebody or something, for example a singer or a sport, very much: *She was a big fan of the Beatles.* ◇ *football fans*
2 a thing that moves the air to make you cooler: *an electric fan*

fan² /fæn/ *verb* (**fans, fanning, fanned** /fænd/)
to make somebody or something cooler by

moving the air: *I fanned my face with the newspaper.*

fanatic /fə'nætɪk/ *noun*
a person who is very enthusiastic about something and may have extreme or dangerous opinions: *He's a football fanatic.* ◇ *a religious fanatic*

fancy¹ /'fænsi/ *verb* (**fancies, fancying, fancied** /'fænsid/, **has fancied**) (*British, informal*)
1 to feel that you would like something: *Do you fancy a drink?* ◇ *I don't fancy going.*
2 to like somebody in a sexual way: *She fancied her friend's brother.*
3 a word that shows you are surprised: *Fancy seeing you here!*

fancy² /'fænsi/ *adjective* (**fancier, fanciest**)
not simple or ordinary: *She wore a very fancy hat to the wedding.* ◇ *a fancy restaurant*

fancy dress /ˌfænsi 'dres/ *noun* (*no plural*) (*British*)
clothes that you wear at a party so that you look like a different person or a thing: *He wants to go in fancy dress.* ◇ *It was a fancy dress party so I went as Charlie Chaplin.*

fantastic /fæn'tæstɪk/ *adjective* (*informal*)
very good; wonderful ⊃ SAME MEANING **great** or **brilliant**: *We had a fantastic holiday.*

fantasy /'fæntəsi/ *noun* (*plural* **fantasies**)
something nice that you think about and that you hope will happen, although it is very unlikely ⊃ SAME MEANING **dream**: *It was just a fantasy.* ◇ *She was living in a fantasy world.*

FAQ /ˌef eɪ 'kjuː/ *abbreviation*
FAQ is used in writing to mean 'frequently asked questions'.

far¹ ○ₜ /fɑː(r)/ *adverb* (**farther** /'fɑːðə(r)/ or **further** /'fɜːðə(r)/, **farthest** /'fɑːðɪst/ or **furthest** /'fɜːðɪst/)
1 a long way from somewhere: *My house isn't far from the station.* ◇ *It's too far to drive in one day.* ◇ *I walked much further than you.*
2 You use **far** to ask about the distance from one place to another place: *How far is it to the coast from here?*

> *ρ* WHICH WORD?
> We usually use **far** only in questions and negative sentences, and after **too** and **so**. In other sentences we use **a long way**: *It's a long way to walk – let's take the bus.*

3 very much: *He's far taller than his brother.* ◇ *That's far too expensive.*
as far as... to a place: *We walked as far as*

the village and then came back. ◇ I read as far as the second chapter.

as far as I know used when you think something is true, but you are not certain: *As far as I know, she's coming, but I may be wrong.*

by far You use **by far** to show that a person or thing is much better, bigger, etc. than anybody or anything else: *She's by far the best player in the team.*

far from it (*informal*) certainly not; just the opposite: *'Are you upset?' 'Far from it – I'm delighted.'*

far from something almost the opposite of something; not at all: *I'm far from certain.*

so far until now: *So far the work has been easy.*

far² 0🔧 /fɑː(r)/ *adjective* (farther /ˈfɑːðə(r)/ or further /ˈfɜːðə(r)/, farthest /ˈfɑːðɪst/ or furthest /ˈfɜːðɪst/)

1 a long way away: *Let's walk – it's not far.* ⊃ OPPOSITE **near**

🔎 **WHICH WORD?**

We only use **far** in questions or negative forms: *Is it far to the beach?* In positive statements we say **a long way**: *He lives a long way from the station.*

2 a long way from the centre in the direction mentioned: *Who's that on the far left of the photo?*

fare /feə(r)/ *noun*
the money that you pay to travel by bus, train, plane, etc.: *My bus fare has gone up.*

farewell /ˌfeəˈwel/ *noun* (*formal*)
goodbye: *We're having a farewell party for Vanessa.*

farm 0🔧 /fɑːm/ *noun*
land and buildings where people keep animals and grow crops: *They work on a farm.* ◇ *farm animals*

farmer 0🔧 /ˈfɑːmə(r)/ *noun*
a person who owns or looks after a farm ⊃ Look at Picture Dictionary page **P12**.

farmhouse /ˈfɑːmhaʊs/ *noun*
the main house on a farm

farming 0🔧 /ˈfɑːmɪŋ/ *noun* (*no plural*)
managing a farm or working on it: *farming methods*

farmyard /ˈfɑːmjɑːd/ *noun*
the area beside the main house on a farm, with buildings or walls around it

farther 0🔧 (*also* **farthest**) forms of FAR

fascinate /ˈfæsɪneɪt/ *verb* (fascinates, fascinating, fascinated)
to attract or interest somebody very much: *China has always fascinated me.* ◇ *I've always been fascinated by his ideas.*

fascinating /ˈfæsɪneɪtɪŋ/ *adjective*
very interesting: *She told us fascinating stories about her life.*

fascination /ˌfæsɪˈneɪʃn/ *noun* (*no plural*)
when you find something or somebody very interesting: *The girls listened in fascination.*

fashion 0🔧 /ˈfæʃn/ *noun*
a way of dressing or doing something that people like and try to copy for a time: *Bright colours are back in fashion.* ◇ *Some styles never go out of fashion.* ◇ *a fashion show*

fashionable 0🔧 /ˈfæʃnəbl/ *adjective*
popular or in a popular style at the time: *She was wearing a fashionable black hat.* ⊃ OPPOSITE **old-fashioned** or **unfashionable**
▶ **fashionably** /ˈfæʃnəbli/ *adverb*: *He was always fashionably dressed.*

fashion designer /ˈfæʃn dɪzaɪnə(r)/ *noun*
a person whose job is to design clothes

fast¹ 0🔧 /fɑːst/ *adjective* (faster, fastest)
1 moving, happening or doing something very quickly: *the fastest rate of increase for many years* ◇ *a fast learner*

🔎 **WHICH WORD?**

Fast or **quick**?
We say **fast** for a person or thing that moves at great speed: *a fast car* ◇ *a fast train* ◇ *a fast worker.*
We say **quick** for something that is done in a short time: *a quick answer* ◇ *a quick visit* ◇ *a quick meal.*

2 If a clock or watch is **fast**, it shows a time that is later than the real time: *My watch is five minutes fast.* ⊃ OPPOSITE **slow**

fast² 0🔧 /fɑːst/ *adverb* (faster, fastest)
1 quickly: *Don't drive so fast!* ◇ *I can't go any faster.* ⊃ OPPOSITE **slowly**
2 firmly or deeply: *The baby was fast asleep.* ◇ *The car was stuck fast in the mud.*

fast³ /fɑːst/ *verb* (fasts, fasting, fasted)
to not eat food for a certain time: *Muslims fast during Ramadan.*

fasten 0🔧 /ˈfɑːsn/ *verb* (fastens, fastening, fastened /ˈfɑːsnd/)
1 to join or close something so that it will

not come open: *Please fasten your seat belts.* ◇ *Can you fasten this suitcase for me?*
2 to fix or tie one thing to another thing: *Fasten this badge to your jacket.*

fastener /'fɑːsnə(r)/ *noun*
a thing that joins together two parts of something: *The fastener on my skirt has just broken.*

fast food /ˌfɑːst 'fuːd/ *noun* (no plural)
hot food that is served very quickly in special restaurants, and often taken away to be eaten in the street ⊃ Look at Picture Dictionary page **P7**.

fat¹ 0ᵐ /fæt/ *adjective* (fatter, fattest)
with a large round body: *You'll get fat if you eat so much.* ⊃ OPPOSITE **slim** or **thin**

> 🔎 **WORD BUILDING**
> It is not polite to say somebody is **fat**. It is better to say **large** or **plump**: *She's a rather large lady.* ◇ *He's a bit plump.* You can say **chubby** to describe babies and children: *a chubby little girl.*

fat² 0ᵐ /fæt/ *noun*
1 (no plural) the soft white substance under the skins of animals and people: *Cut the fat off the meat.*
2 (plural **fats**) the substance containing oil that we get from animals, plants, or seeds and use for cooking: *foods which are low in fat* ◇ *Heat some fat in a frying pan.*

fatal /'feɪtl/ *adjective*
1 Something that is **fatal** causes death: *a fatal car accident*
2 Something that is **fatal** has very bad results: *I made the fatal mistake of signing a document without reading it properly.*
▸ **fatally** /'feɪtəli/ *adverb*: *She was fatally injured in the crash.*

fate /feɪt/ *noun*
1 (plural **fates**) the things, especially bad things, that will happen or have happened to somebody or something: *What will be the fate of the prisoners?*
2 (no plural) the power that some people believe controls everything that happens: *It was fate that brought them together again after twenty years.*

father 0ᵐ /'fɑːðə(r)/ *noun*
a man who has a child: *Where do your mother and father live?* ⊃ Look at **dad** and **daddy**.

Father Christmas /ˌfɑːðə 'krɪsməs/ *noun*
an old man with a red coat and a long white beard. Children believe that he brings presents at Christmas.

fatherhood /'fɑːðəhʊd/ *noun* (no plural)
being a father

father-in-law /'fɑːðər ɪn lɔː/ *noun* (plural **fathers-in-law**)
the father of your husband or wife

faucet /'fɔːsɪt/ *American English for* TAP²

fault 0ᵐ /fɔːlt/ *noun*
1 (no plural) If something bad is your **fault**, you made it happen: *It's her fault that we are late.* ◇ *It's my fault for being careless.*
2 (plural **faults**) something that is wrong or bad in a person or thing: *There is a serious fault in the machine.*

faultless /'fɔːltləs/ *adjective*
without any mistakes ⊃ SAME MEANING **perfect**: *a faultless performance*

faulty /'fɔːlti/ *adjective*
not working well: *This light doesn't work – the switch is faulty.*

favor *American English for* FAVOUR

favorite *American English for* FAVOURITE

favour 0ᵐ (British) (American **favor**) /'feɪvə(r)/ *noun*
something that you do to help somebody: *Would you do me a favour and open the door?* ◇ *Could I ask you a favour – will you take me to the station this evening?*
be in favour of something to like or agree with something: *Are you in favour of higher taxes on cigarettes?*

favourable (British) (American **favorable**) /'feɪvərəbl/ *adjective*
good, suitable, or acceptable: *She made a favourable impression on his parents.*

favourite¹ 0ᵐ (British) (American **favorite**) /'feɪvərɪt/ *adjective*
Your **favourite** person or thing is the one that you like more than any other: *What's your favourite food?*

favourite² 0ᵐ (British) (American **favorite**) /'feɪvərɪt/ *noun*
a person or thing that you like more than any other: *I like all chocolates but these are my favourites.*

fax /fæks/ *noun* (plural **faxes**)
a copy of a letter, etc. that you send by telephone lines using a special machine (called a **fax machine**): *They need an answer today so I'll send a fax.*
▸ **fax** *verb* (faxes, faxing, faxed /fækst/)
to send somebody a **fax**: *Can you fax the drawings to me?*

fear¹ 0ᵐ /fɪə(r)/ *noun*
the feeling that you have when you think that something bad might happen: *I have a*

terrible **fear of** dogs. ◇ He was shaking **with fear**. ◇ My fears for his safety were unnecessary.

fear² /fɪə(r)/ *verb* (fears, fearing, feared /fɪəd/)
1 to be afraid of somebody or something: *We all fear illness and death.*

> 🔎 **SPEAKING**
>
> It is more usual to say **be afraid of** or **be frightened of** somebody or something.

2 (*formal*) to feel that something bad might happen: *I fear we will be late.*

fearful /'fɪəfl/ *adjective* (*formal*)
afraid or worried about something: *They were fearful that they would miss the plane.*

fearless /'fɪələs/ *adjective*
not afraid of anything

feast /fiːst/ *noun*
a large special meal for a lot of people: *a wedding feast*

feat /fiːt/ *noun*
something you do that is clever, difficult or dangerous: *Climbing Mount Everest was an amazing feat.*

feather 0━
/'feðə(r)/ *noun*
one of the light, soft things that grow in a bird's skin and cover its body

feather

feature 0━
/'fiːtʃə(r)/ *noun*
1 an important part of something: *Pictures are a feature of this dictionary.*
2 one of the parts of your face, for example your eyes, nose or mouth: *Her eyes are her best feature.*
3 a newspaper or magazine article or TV programme about something: *The magazine has a special feature on education.*

February 0━ /'februəri/ *noun*
the second month of the year

fed form of FEED

federal /'fedərəl/ *adjective*
used for describing a political system in which a group of states or countries are joined together under a central government, but also have their own governments: *a federal system of rule* ◇ *the Federal Government of the United States*

fed up /ˌfed 'ʌp/ *adjective* (*informal*)
bored or unhappy, especially with a situation

that has continued for too long: *What's the matter? You look really fed up.* ◇ *I'm **fed up with** waiting – let's go.*

fee /fiː/ *noun*
1 the money you pay for professional advice or service from private doctors, lawyers, schools, universities, etc.: *We can't afford private school fees.* ◇ *Most ticket agencies will **charge** a small **fee**.*
2 the money that you pay to do something, for example to join a club or visit a museum: *There is no **entrance fee** to the gallery.*

feeble /'fiːbl/ *adjective* (feebler, feeblest)
not strong ⊃ SAME MEANING **weak**: *a feeble old man*

feed 0━ /fiːd/ *verb* (feeds, feeding, fed /fed/, has fed)
to give food to a person or an animal: *The baby's crying – I'll go and feed her.*

feedback /'fiːdbæk/ *noun* (no plural)
advice or information about how well or badly you have done something: *The teacher will **give** you **feedback on** the test.*

feel 0━ /fiːl/ *verb* (feels, feeling, felt /felt/, has felt)
1 to know something because your body tells you: *How do you feel?* ◇ *I don't feel well.* ◇ *I'm feeling tired.* ◇ *He felt somebody touch his arm.*
2 used for saying how something seems when you touch it or experience it: *The water felt cold.* ◇ *This towel feels wet – can I have a dry one?* ◇ *My coat **feels like** leather, but it's not.*
3 to touch something in order to find out what it is like: *Feel this wool – it's really soft.*
4 to have an opinion about something ⊃ SAME MEANING **believe**: *I **feel that** we should talk about this.*
5 to try to find something with your hands instead of your eyes: *She **felt** in her pocket **for** some matches.*
feel like something to want something: *Do you feel like going for a walk?* ◇ *I don't feel like going out tonight.*

feeling 0━ /'fiːlɪŋ/ *noun*
1 (*plural* **feelings**) something that you feel inside yourself, like happiness or anger: *a **feeling of** sadness*
2 (*no plural*) the ability to feel in your body: *I was so cold that I had no feeling in my feet.*
3 (*plural* **feelings**) an idea that you are not certain about: *I **have a feeling that** she isn't telling the truth.*
hurt somebody's feelings to do or say something that makes somebody sad: *Don't tell him you don't like his shirt – you'll hurt his feelings.*

A

feet *plural of* FOOT

fell *form of* FALL¹

B

fellow¹ /ˈfeləʊ/ *noun* (*informal*)
a man: *What is that fellow doing?*

C

fellow² /ˈfeləʊ/ *adjective*
used for saying that somebody is the same as
you in some way: *her fellow students*

D

E

felt¹ *form of* FEEL

felt² /felt/ *noun* (*no plural*)
a type of soft thick cloth

felt-tip pen /ˌfelt tɪp ˈpen/ *noun*
a pen with a soft point ⊃ Look at Picture
Dictionary page **P11**.

G

female 0ᴛ /ˈfiːmeɪl/ *adjective*
belonging to the sex that can have babies:
female students
▶ **female** *noun*: *My cat is a female.* ⊃ Look
at **male**.

H

I

feminine /ˈfemənɪn/ *adjective*
1 typical of a woman or right for a woman:
feminine clothes
2 (*grammar*) (in some languages) belonging
to a certain class of nouns, adjectives or
pronouns: *The German word for a flower is
feminine.* ⊃ Look at **masculine**.

J

K

L

M

N

fence

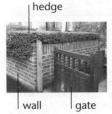

hedge

wall   gate   fence

O

P

Q

R

fence 0ᴛ /fens/ *noun*
a thing like a wall that is made of pieces of
wood or metal. **Fences** are put round
gardens and fields.

S

fern /fɜːn/ *noun*
a plant with long thin leaves and no flowers
that grows in wet areas

T

U

ferocious /fəˈrəʊʃəs/ *adjective*
violent and aggressive ⊃ SAME MEANING
fierce: *a ferocious wild animal*

V

W

ferry /ˈferi/ *noun* (*plural* **ferries**)
a boat that takes people or things on short
journeys across a river or sea: *We went by
ferry.* ⊃ Look at Picture Dictionary page **P1**.

X

Y

fertile /ˈfɜːtaɪl/ *adjective*
1 If soil is **fertile**, plants grow well in it.
2 Somebody who is **fertile** is able to have
babies.

Z

fertilizer /ˈfɜːtəlaɪzə(r)/ *noun*
food for plants

festival 0ᴛ /ˈfestɪvl/ *noun*
1 a series of public events, for example
concerts and shows, in one place: *the Cannes
Film Festival*
2 a time when people celebrate something,
especially a religious event: *Christmas is an
important Christian festival.*

fetch /fetʃ/ *verb* (**fetches**, **fetching**,
fetched /fetʃt/)
to go and bring back somebody or
something: *Can you fetch me my bag?* ◇ *I'll
fetch your coat for you.* ◇ *I went to fetch Andy
from the station.*

fête /feɪt/ (*British*) *noun*
an event where you can buy things and play
games, often organized to get money for a
particular purpose: *the school fête*

fetus *American English for* FOETUS

fever /ˈfiːvə(r)/ *noun*
If you have a **fever**, your body is too hot
because you are ill. ⊃ SAME MEANING
temperature
▶ **feverish** /ˈfiːvərɪʃ/ *adjective* If you are
feverish, your body is too hot because you
are ill.

few 0ᴛ /fjuː/ *adjective, pronoun* (**fewer**,
fewest)
not many: *Few people live to the age of 100.* ◇
There are fewer buses in the evenings. ◇ **Few of**
the players played well.
a few some, but not many: *Only a few
people came to the meeting.* ◇ *I have read a
few of her books.*
quite a few quite a lot: *It's been a good few
years since I saw him last.*

fiancé /fiˈɒnseɪ/ *noun*
A woman's **fiancé** is the man she has
promised to marry.

fiancée /fiˈɒnseɪ/ *noun*
A man's **fiancée** is the woman he has
promised to marry.

fib /fɪb/ *noun* (*informal*)
something you say that you know is not true;
a small lie: *Don't tell fibs!*
▶ **fib** (**fibs**, **fibbing**, **fibbed** /fɪbd/) *verb*
(*informal*) to tell a small lie: *I was fibbing
when I said I liked her hat.*

fibre (*British*) **fiber** (*American*) /ˈfaɪbə(r)/
noun
1 (*no plural*) the part of your food that helps
to move other food through your body and
keep you healthy: *Dried fruits are high in
fibre.*
2 (*plural* **fibres**) one of the many thin
threads that form a material: *cotton fibres*

fiction /'fɪkʃn/ *noun* (*no plural*)
stories that somebody writes and that are
not true: *I enjoy reading fiction.*

fiddle /'fɪdl/ *verb* (fiddles, fiddling,
fiddled /'fɪdld/)
to touch something a lot with your fingers,
because you are bored or nervous: *Stop
fiddling with your pen and do some work!*

fidget /'fɪdʒɪt/ *verb* (fidgets, fidgeting,
fidgeted)
to keep moving your body, hands, or feet
because you are nervous, excited, or bored:
Sit still and stop fidgeting!

field 0‑ᴡ /fiːld/ *noun*
1 a piece of land used for animals or for
growing crops, usually surrounded by a
fence, trees, etc.
2 an area of study or knowledge: *Dr Smith is
an expert in her field.*
3 a piece of land used for something special:
a sports field ◇ *an airfield* (= a place where
planes land and take off)

field hockey /'fiːld hɒki/ *American English
for* HOCKEY

fierce /fɪəs/ *adjective* (fiercer, fiercest)
1 angry and wild: *a fierce dog*
2 very strong: *the fierce heat of the sun*

fifteen 0‑ᴡ /,fɪf'tiːn/ *number* 15
▶ **fifteenth** /,fɪf'tiːnθ/ *pronoun, adjective,
adverb* 15th

fifth 0‑ᴡ /fɪfθ/ *pronoun, adjective, adverb*
1 5th
2 one of five equal parts of something; ⅕

fifty 0‑ᴡ /'fɪfti/ *number*
1 50
2 the fifties (*plural*) the numbers, years or
temperature between 50 and 59: *He was
born in the fifties* (= in the 1950s).
in your fifties between the ages of 50 and
59: *Her husband died when she was in her
fifties.*
▶ **fiftieth** /'fɪftiəθ/ *pronoun, adjective,
adverb* 50th

fig /fɪg/ *noun*
a soft sweet fruit
that is full of small
seeds

fig

fight¹ 0‑ᴡ /faɪt/
verb (fights,
fighting, fought
/fɔːt/, has fought)
1 When people
fight, they try to hurt or kill each other: *Our
grandfather fought in the war.* ◇ *My brothers
are always fighting.*

2 to try very hard to stop something: *He
fought against the illness for two years.*
3 to try very hard to do or get something:
*The workers are **fighting for** better pay.*
4 to argue: *It's not worth **fighting about**
money.*

fight² 0‑ᴡ /faɪt/ *noun*
when people try to hurt or kill each other:
*Don't **get into a fight**.* ◇ *A fight broke out
between the two gangs.*

fighter /'faɪtə(r)/ *noun*
1 (*also* **fighter plane** /'faɪtə pleɪn/) a fast
plane that shoots at other planes during
a war
2 a person who fights

figure 0‑ᴡ /'fɪgə(r)/ *noun*
1 one of the symbols (0–9) that we use to
show numbers: *Shall I write the numbers in
words or figures?*
2 an amount or price: *What are our sales
figures for Spain this year?*
3 the shape of a person's body: *She's got a
good figure.*
4 a shape of a person that you cannot see
clearly: *I saw a tall figure outside the window.*
5 figures (*plural*) (*informal*) working with
numbers to find an answer
➾ SAME MEANING **mathematics**: *I'm not
very good at figures.*

figure of speech /,fɪgər əv 'spiːtʃ/ *noun*
(*plural* **figures of speech**)
a word or phrase used in a different way
from its usual meaning to create a particular
effect: *I didn't really mean that she was mad –
it was just a figure of speech.*

files

file¹ 0‑ᴡ /faɪl/ *noun*
1 a box or cover for keeping papers in
2 a collection of information that is stored in
a computer and that has a particular name:
*Did you save your file? ◇ You can delete that
file now.*
3 a tool with rough sides that you use for
making things smooth: *a nail file*
in single file in a line with each person
following the one in front: *The children
walked into the hall in single file.*

file² /faɪl/ *verb* (files, filing, filed /faɪld/)
1 to put papers in their correct place, for
example in a cover or drawer: *Can you file
these letters, please?*

A
B
C
D
E
F
G
H
I
J
K
L
M
N
O
P
Q
R
S
T
U
V
W
X
Y
Z

2 to walk in a line, one behind the other: *The students filed into the classroom.*
3 to make something smooth using a tool with rough sides: *She filed her nails.*

filing cabinet

file

filing cabinet /'faɪlɪŋ kæbɪnət/ *noun*
(*British*)
a piece of office furniture with large drawers, in which you keep documents

fill 0🔑 /fɪl/ *verb* (fills, filling, filled /fɪld/)
1 to make something full: *Can you fill this glass with water, please?*
2 to become full: *His eyes filled with tears.*
fill something in, fill something out to write facts or answers in the spaces that have been left for them: *She gave me a form and told me to fill it in.*
fill up, fill something up to become full or to make something completely full: *The room soon filled up.* ◇ *He filled up the tank with petrol.*

filling /'fɪlɪŋ/ *noun*
1 the substance that a dentist uses to fill a hole in your tooth: *I've got three fillings in my teeth.*
2 the food that is put inside a sandwich, cake, etc.: *a choice of sandwich fillings* ◇ Look at the picture at **pie.**

film¹ 0🔑 /fɪlm/ *noun*
1 (*British*) (*American* **movie**) a story shown in moving pictures that you see on television or at the cinema: *Let's go and see a film.*
2 the thin plastic that you use in a camera for taking photographs: *I bought a roll of black and white film.*

film² 0🔑 /fɪlm/ *verb* (films, filming, filmed /fɪlmd/)
to use a camera to make moving pictures of a story, news, etc.: *A TV company are filming outside my house.*

film star /'fɪlm stɑː(r)/ (*British*) (*American* **movie star**) *noun*
an actor or actress who is famous for being in films

filter /'fɪltə(r)/ *noun*
a thing used for holding back the solid parts in a liquid or gas: *a coffee filter*
▶ **filter** *verb* (filters, filtering, filtered /'fɪltəd/): *Filter the water before you drink it.*

filthy /'fɪlθi/ *adjective* (filthier, filthiest)
very dirty: *Go and wash your hands. They're filthy!*

fin /fɪn/ *noun*
one of the thin flat parts on a fish that help it to swim ◇ Look at the pictures at **fish** and **shark.**

final¹ 0🔑 /'faɪnl/ *adjective*
not followed by any others
◇ SAME MEANING **last**: *This will be our final lesson.*

final² 0🔑 /'faɪnl/ *noun*
1 the last game or race in a competition, for the winners of the earlier games or races: *We've got through to the final.*
2 finals (*plural*) (*British*) the exams in your last year at university

finally 0🔑 /'faɪnəli/ *adverb*
1 after a long time ◇ SAME MEANING **in the end**: *After a long wait the bus finally arrived.*
2 used before saying the last thing in a list: *And finally, I would like to thank my parents for all their help.*

finance¹ /'faɪnæns/ *noun*
1 (*no plural*) money, or the activity of managing money: *an expert in finance* ◇ *the French Minister of Finance*
2 finances (*plural*) the money that you have and that you can spend: *You need to sort out your finances.*

finance² /'faɪnæns/ *verb* (finances, financing, financed /'faɪnænst/)
to give the money that is needed to pay for something: *The building was financed by the government.*

financial 0🔑 /faɪ'nænʃl/ *adjective*
connected with money: *financial problems*

find 0🔑 /faɪnd/ *verb* (finds, finding, found /faʊnd/, has found)
1 to see or get something after looking or trying: *I can't find my glasses.* ◇ *She hasn't found a job yet.* ◇ *Has anybody found the answer to this question?*
2 to see or get something that you did not expect: *I found some money in the street.* ◇ *I woke up and found myself in hospital.*

3 used for talking about your opinion or experience: *I didn't find that book very interesting.* ◇ *He finds it difficult to sleep at night.*

find something out to get information about something: *Can you find out what time the train leaves?* ◇ *Has she found out that you broke the window?*

fine¹ 0— /faɪn/ *adjective* (finer, finest)
1 beautiful or of good quality: *There's a fine view from the cathedral.* ◇ *This is one of Monet's finest paintings.*
2 well or happy: *'How are you?' 'Fine, thanks. And you?'*
3 used for saying that something is good or acceptable ⊃ SAME MEANING **OK**: *'Let's meet on Monday.' 'Fine.'* ◇ *'Do you want some more milk in your coffee?' 'No, that's fine.'*
4 not raining ⊃ SAME MEANING **sunny**: *I hope it stays fine for our picnic.*
5 very thin: *I've got very fine hair.*
⊃ OPPOSITE **thick**
6 made of very small pieces: *Salt is finer than sugar.* ⊃ OPPOSITE **coarse**

fine² /faɪn/ *noun*
money that you must pay because you have done something wrong: *You'll get a fine if you park your car there.*
▸ **fine** *verb* (fines, fining, fined /faɪnd/) to make somebody pay a fine: *I was fined £100 for speeding* (= driving too fast).

finger 0— /ˈfɪŋɡə(r)/ *noun*
one of the five parts at the end of your hand ⊃ Look at Picture Dictionary page **P4**.
keep your fingers crossed to hope that somebody or something will be successful: *I'll keep my fingers crossed for you in your exams.*

fingernail /ˈfɪŋɡəneɪl/ *noun*
the thin hard part at the end of your finger ⊃ Look at the picture at **fist**.

fingerprint /ˈfɪŋɡəprɪnt/ *noun*
the mark that a finger makes when it touches something: *The police found his fingerprints on the gun.*

fingertip /ˈfɪŋɡətɪp/ *noun*
the end of your finger ⊃ Look at the picture at **hand**.

finish¹ 0— /ˈfɪnɪʃ/ *verb* (finishes, finishing, finished /ˈfɪnɪʃt/)
1 to stop doing something: *I finish work at half past five.* ◇ *Hurry up and finish your dinner!* ◇ *Have you finished cleaning your room?*
2 to stop happening: *School finishes at four o'clock.* ⊃ OPPOSITE **begin** or **start**

finish something off to do or eat the last part of something: *He finished off the bread.*
finish with something to stop needing or using something: *Have you finished with that book?*

finish² /ˈfɪnɪʃ/ *noun* (plural finishes)
the last part or the end of something
⊃ OPPOSITE **start**: *There was a dramatic finish to the race.*

fir /fɜː(r)/ (*also* fir tree /ˈfɜː triː/) *noun*
a tall tree with thin sharp leaves (called **needles**) that do not fall off in winter

fire¹ 0— /ˈfaɪə(r)/ *noun*
1 the heat and bright light that comes from burning things: *Many animals are afraid of fire.* ◇ *There was a big fire at the factory last night.*
2 burning wood or coal that you use for keeping a place warm or for cooking: *They lit a fire to keep warm.*
3 a machine that uses electricity or gas to keep a room warm: *Switch on the fire.*
catch fire to start to burn: *She dropped her cigarette and the chair caught fire.*
on fire burning: *My house is on fire!*
put out a fire to stop something from burning: *We put out the fire with buckets of water.*
set fire to something, **set something on fire** to make something start to burn: *Somebody set the house on fire.*

fire² 0— /ˈfaɪə(r)/ *verb* (fires, firing, fired /ˈfaɪəd/)
1 to shoot with a gun: *The soldiers fired at the enemy.*
2 to tell somebody to leave their job ⊃ SAME MEANING **sack**: *He was fired because he was always late for work.*

fire alarm /ˈfaɪər əlɑːm/ *noun*
a bell that rings to tell people that there is a fire

fire brigade /ˈfaɪə brɪˌɡeɪd/ (*British*) (*American* fire department /ˈfaɪə dɪpɑːtmənt/) *noun*
a group of people whose job is to stop fires: *Call the fire brigade!*

fire engine /ˈfaɪər endʒɪn/ (*American also* fire truck /ˈfaɪə trʌk/) *noun*
a vehicle that takes people and equipment to stop fires

fire escape /ˈfaɪər ɪskeɪp/ *noun*
stairs on the outside of a building that people can go down if there is a fire

A B C D E F G H I J K L M N O P Q R S T U V W X Y Z

fire extinguisher /'faɪər ɪkˌstɪŋgwɪʃə(r)/ *noun*
a metal container with water or chemicals inside for stopping small fires

firefighter /'faɪəfaɪtə(r)/ *noun*
a person whose job is to stop fires

fireman /'faɪəmən/ (*plural* firemen /'faɪəmən/) *noun*
a man whose job is to stop fires

fireplace

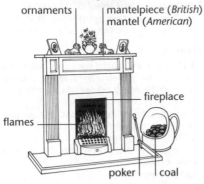

ornaments
mantelpiece (*British*)
mantel (*American*)
fireplace
flames
poker | coal

fireplace /'faɪəpleɪs/ *noun*
the place in a room where you light a fire

fire station /'faɪə steɪʃn/ *noun*
a building where fire engines are kept

fire truck *American English for* FIRE ENGINE

firework /'faɪəwɜːk/ *noun*
a thing that explodes with coloured lights and loud noises, used for entertainment: *We watched a firework display in the park.*

firm[1] 0🔔 /fɜːm/ *noun*
a group of people working together in a business ⊃ SAME MEANING **company**: *My father works for a building firm.*

firm[2] 0🔔 /fɜːm/ *adjective* (firmer, firmest)
1 Something that is **firm** is quite hard or does not move easily: *Wait until the glue is firm.* ◊ *The shelf isn't very firm, so don't put too many books on it.*
2 showing that you will not change your ideas: *She's very firm with her children* (= she makes them do what she wants). ◊ *a firm promise*
▶ **firmly** /'fɜːmli/ *adverb*: *Nail the pieces of wood together firmly.* ◊ *'No,' she said firmly.*

first[1] 0🔔 /fɜːst/ *adjective*
before all the others: *January is the first month of the year.* ◊ *You've won first prize!*

first[2] 0🔔 /fɜːst/ *adverb*
1 before all the others: *I arrived at the house first.* ◊ *Mike came first* (= he won) *in the competition.*
2 for the first time: *I first met Paul in 1996.*
3 before doing anything else: *First fry the onions, then add the potatoes.*
at first at the beginning: *At first she was afraid of the water, but she soon learned to swim.*
first of all before anything else: *I'm going to cook dinner, but first of all I need to buy some food.*

first[3] 0🔔 /fɜːst/ *noun* (*no plural*) *pronoun*
the first a person or thing that comes earliest or before all others: *I was the first to arrive at the party.*

first aid /ˌfɜːst 'eɪd/ *noun* (*no plural*)
medical help that you give to somebody who is hurt, before a doctor comes

first class /ˌfɜːst 'klɑːs/ *noun* (*no plural*)
1 the part of a train, plane, etc. that it is more expensive to travel in: *I got a seat in first class.*
2 (*British*) the fastest, most expensive way of sending letters
▶ **first class** *adverb*: *How much does it cost to send it first class?* ⊃ Look at **second class** and at the note at **stamp**.

first-class /ˌfɜːst 'klɑːs/ *adjective*
1 excellent: *a first-class player* ◊ *I know a place where the food is first-class.*
2 connected with the best and most expensive way of travelling on a train, plane or ship: *a first-class cabin*
3 (*British*) connected with the fastest, most expensive way of sending letters: *a first-class stamp*

first floor /ˌfɜːst 'flɔː(r)/ *noun* the first floor
1 (*British*) the floor of a building above the floor that is level with the street: *I live in a flat on the first floor.*
2 (*American*) (*British* **ground floor**) the floor of a building that is level with the street

firstly /'fɜːstli/ *adverb*
used when you are giving the first thing in a list: *We were angry firstly because he didn't come, and secondly because he didn't phone.*

first name /'fɜːst neɪm/ (*British*) (*American* given name) *noun*
the first of your names that come before your family name: *'What is Mr Carter's first name?' 'Paul.'* ⊃ Look at the note at **name**.

fish[1] 0🔔 /fɪʃ/ *noun* (*plural* fish or fishes)
an animal that lives and breathes in water, and has thin flat parts (called fins) that help it to swim: *I caught a big fish.* ◊ *We had fish and chips for dinner.* ⊃ Look at Picture Dictionary page **P7**.

A
B
C
D
E
F
G
H
I
J
K
L
M
N
O
P
Q
R
S
T
U
V
W
X
Y
Z

🔎 WORD BUILDING

There are many different types of **fish**. Here are some of them: cod, eel, goldfish, salmon, sardine, shark. Do you know any others?

fish

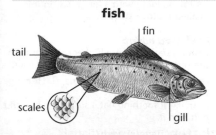

tail — fin — scales — gill

fish² 0ᵤ /fɪʃ/ *verb* (fishes, fishing, fished /fɪʃt/)
to try to catch fish

🔎 GRAMMAR

When you talk about spending time fishing as a sport, you often say **go fishing**: *I go fishing at weekends.*

▶ **fishing** /'fɪʃɪŋ/ *noun* (*no plural*): *Fishing is a major industry in Iceland.*

fisherman /'fɪʃəmən/ *noun* (*plural* **fishermen** /'fɪʃəmən/)
a person who catches fish as a job or sport

fishing rod /'fɪʃɪŋ rɒd/ *noun*
a long thin stick with a thin thread (called a **line**) and a hook, used for catching fish

fist

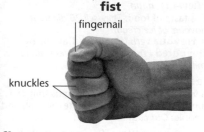

fingernail
knuckles

fist /fɪst/ *noun*
a hand with the fingers closed tightly: *She banged on the door with her fist.*

fit¹ 0ᵤ /fɪt/ *verb* (fits, fitting, fitted)
1 to be the right size or shape for somebody or something: *I tried the dress on, but it didn't fit.* ◇ *This key doesn't fit the lock.*
2 to put or fix something somewhere: *They fitted a smoke alarm to the ceiling.* ◇ *Can you fit these pieces of the puzzle together?*
fit somebody or **something in**
1 to find time to do something or see somebody: *The doctor can fit you in at 10.30.*

2 to find or have enough space for somebody or something: *We can't fit in any more chairs.*

fit² 0ᵤ /fɪt/ *adjective* (fitter, fittest)
1 healthy and strong: *I keep fit by jogging every day.*
2 good enough ⊃ SAME MEANING **suitable**: *This food isn't fit to eat.* ◇ *Do you think she's fit for the job?* ⊃ OPPOSITE **unfit**

fit³ /fɪt/ *noun*
1 a sudden illness in which somebody becomes unconscious and may make violent movements
2 when you cannot stop laughing, coughing, or feeling angry: *We were in fits of laughter.* ◇ *a fit of anger*

fitness /'fɪtnəs/ *noun* (*no plural*)
being healthy and strong

five 0ᵤ /faɪv/ *number* 5

fix 0ᵤ /fɪks/ *verb* (fixes, fixing, fixed /fɪkst/)
1 to put something in a place so that it will not move: *We fixed the shelf to the wall.*
2 to decide a date or an amount for something ⊃ SAME MEANING **set**: *They've fixed a date for the wedding.*
3 to repair something: *The light isn't working – can you fix it?*

fixed 0ᵤ /fɪkst/ *adjective*
1 already decided: *a fixed price*
2 not changing: *He has such fixed ideas that you can't discuss anything with him.*

fizzy /'fɪzi/ *adjective* (fizzier, fizziest)
(used about a drink) containing many small bubbles of gas: *Do you like fizzy drinks?*

flags

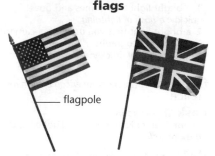

flagpole

flag 0ᵤ /flæg/ *noun*
a piece of cloth with a pattern on it which is joined to a stick (called a **flagpole**). Every country has its own **flag**: *The flag is flying for the Queen's birthday.*

A   **flake** /fleɪk/ *noun*
a small thin piece of something: *huge flakes*
B   *of snow*

C   **flame** 0‑ᴡ /fleɪm/ *noun*
a hot bright pointed piece of fire: *The house*
was in flames (= burning). ◇ *The paper burst*
D   *into flames* (= began to burn). ⊃ Look at the
picture at **fireplace**.

E   **flap**¹ /flæp/ *noun*
a piece of material, paper, etc. that is fixed to
something at one side only, often covering
F   an opening: *the flap of the envelope*

G   **flap**² /flæp/ *verb* (**flaps, flapping, flapped**
/flæpt/)
H   to move or to make something move up and
down or from side to side: *The sails of the*
I   *boat flapped in the wind.* ◇ *The bird flapped*
its wings.

J   **flare**¹ /fleə(r)/ *verb* (**flares, flaring, flared**
/fleəd/)
flare up
K   **1** to suddenly burn more strongly
2 to suddenly start or get worse: *The pain*
L   *flared up again.*

flare² /fleə(r)/ *noun*
M   a thing that produces a bright light or flame,
used especially as a signal

N   **flash**¹ 0‑ᴡ /flæʃ/ *verb* (**flashes, flashing,**
flashed /flæʃt/)
O   **1** to send out a bright light that comes and
goes quickly; to make something do this: *The*
P   *light kept flashing on and off.* ◇ *She flashed her*
headlights at the other driver.
2 to appear and disappear very quickly, or to
Q   make something do this: *I saw something*
flash past the window. ◇ *They flashed the*
R   *answer up on the TV screen.*

S   **flash**² 0‑ᴡ /flæʃ/ *noun* (*plural* **flashes**)
1 a bright light that comes and goes
quickly: *a flash of lightning*
T   **2** a bright light that you use with a camera
for taking photographs
U   **in a flash** very quickly: *The weekend was*
over in a flash.

V   **flashlight** /'flæʃlaɪt/ *American English for*
TORCH

W   **flask** /flɑːsk/ *noun*
a container for keeping a liquid hot or cold: *a*
X   **flask** *of coffee*

Y   **flat**¹ 0‑ᴡ /flæt/ *adjective* (**flatter, flattest**)
1 smooth, with no parts that are higher or
lower than the rest: *The countryside in*
Z   *Holland is very flat.* ◇ *a flat surface*
2 A tyre that is **flat** does not have enough air
inside it.

flat² 0‑ᴡ /flæt/ *noun* (*British*) (*American*
apartment)
a group of rooms for living in, usually on one
floor of a house or big building

> 🔎 **WORD BUILDING**
>
> A tall building with a lot of flats in it is
> called a **block of flats**.

flat³ /flæt/ *adverb*
with no parts that are higher or lower than
the rest: *He lay flat on his back on the floor.*

flatten /'flætn/ *verb* (**flattens, flattening,**
flattened /'flætnd/)
to make something flat: *I sat on the box and*
flattened it.

flatter /'flætə(r)/ *verb* (**flatters,**
flattering, flattered /'flætəd/)
1 to say nice things about somebody,
because you want them to do something
2 If you are **flattered** by something, you
like it because it makes you feel important:
I'm flattered that she wants my advice.

flattering /'flætərɪŋ/ *adjective*
making somebody look or sound more
attractive or important than they really are:
flattering remarks

flattery /'flætəri/ *noun* (*no plural*)
nice things that somebody says when they
want you to do something

flatware /'flætweə(r)/ *American English for*
CUTLERY

flavour 0‑ᴡ (*British*) (*American* **flavor**)
/'fleɪvə(r)/ *noun*
the taste of food: *They sell 20 different*
flavours of ice cream.
▶ **flavour** *verb* (**flavours, flavouring,**
flavoured /'fleɪvəd/): *chocolate-flavoured*
milk

flea /fliː/ *noun*
a very small insect without wings that can
jump and that lives on and bites animals and
people: *Our cat has got fleas.*

flee /fliː/ *verb* (**flees, fleeing, fled** /fled/,
has fled)
to run away from something bad or
dangerous: *During the war, thousands of*
people fled the country.

fleece /fliːs/ *noun*
1 the wool coat of a sheep
2 a jacket or sweater made from a type of
soft warm cloth (also called **fleece**)

fleet /fliːt/ *noun*
a big group of ships

flesh /fleʃ/ *noun* (*no plural*)
the soft part of your body under your skin

🔎 **WORD BUILDING**
The flesh of an animal that we eat is called **meat**.

flew form of FLY¹

flex /fleks/ *noun* (British) (*plural* **flexes**) (American **cord**)
a piece of wire covered with plastic, which carries electricity to electrical equipment

flexible /'fleksəbl/ *adjective*
1 able to change easily: *We can start earlier if you like – I can be flexible.* ◇ *flexible working hours*
2 able to bend easily without breaking

flies
1 form of FLY¹
2 plural of FLY²

flight ⊶ /flaɪt/ *noun*
1 (*plural* **flights**) a journey in a plane: *Our flight leaves at 10 a.m.* ◇ *a direct **flight from** London **to** Singapore*
2 (no plural) flying: *Have you ever seen an eagle **in flight**?*
3 a group of steps: *We carried the sofa up a **flight of stairs**.*

flight attendant /'flaɪt ətendənt/ *noun*
a person whose job is to serve and take care of passengers on a plane

fling /flɪŋ/ *verb* (**flings, flinging, flung** /flʌŋ/, has **flung**)
to throw something carelessly or with great force: *She flung her coat on the chair.*

flip-flop /'flɪp flɒp/ (American **thong**) *noun*
a simple open shoe with a narrow piece of material that goes between your big toe and the toe next to it

flippant /'flɪpənt/ *adjective*
not serious about important things: *a flippant answer*

flipper /'flɪpə(r)/ *noun*
1 a flat part of the body of some sea animals which they use for swimming: *Seals have flippers* ➔ Look at the picture at **seal**.
2 a flat rubber shoe that you wear to help you swim fast underwater ➔ Look at the picture at **scuba-diving**.

flirt /flɜːt/ *verb* (**flirts, flirting, flirted**)
to behave as if you like somebody in a sexual way: *Jo was **flirting with** him at the party.*
▶ **flirt** *noun* a person who **flirts** a lot with different people

float ⊶ /fləʊt/ *verb* (**floats, floating, floated**)
1 to stay on top of a liquid: *Wood floats on water.* ➔ OPPOSITE **sink**

2 to move slowly in the air: *Clouds were floating across the sky.*

flock /flɒk/ *noun*
a group of sheep or birds: *a flock of geese* ➔ Look at **herd**.

flood¹ ⊶ /flʌd/ *noun*
1 When there is a **flood**, a lot of water covers the land: *Many homes were destroyed in the flood.* ➔ Look at Picture Dictionary page **P16**.
2 a lot of something: *The child was in **floods of tears*** (= crying a lot).

flood² /flʌd/ *verb* (**floods, flooding, flooded**)
to fill a place with water; to be filled or covered with water: *A pipe burst and flooded the kitchen.*

floodlight /'flʌdlaɪt/ *noun*
a powerful light that is used outside, for example near a building or for sports

floor ⊶ /flɔː(r)/ *noun*
1 the part of a room that you walk on: *There weren't any chairs so we sat **on the floor**.*
2 all the rooms at the same height in a building: *I live **on the** top **floor**.* ◇ *Our hotel room was on the sixth floor.*

🔎 **WHICH WORD?**
The part of a building that is on the same level as the street is called the **ground floor** in British English and the **first floor** in American English.

floorboard /'flɔːbɔːd/ *noun*
a long flat piece of wood in a wooden floor ➔ Look at Picture Dictionary page **P10**.

floppy disk /ˌflɒpi 'dɪsk/ (*also* **floppy**) (*plural* **floppies**) *noun*
a small flat piece of plastic that stores information for a computer

florist /'florɪst/ *noun*
1 a person who owns or works in a shop that sells flowers
2 florist's a shop that sells flowers

flour ⊶ /'flaʊə(r)/ *noun* (no plural)

🔎 **PRONUNCIATION**
The word **flour** sounds just like **flower**.

soft white or brown powder that we use to make bread, cakes, etc.

flourish /'flʌrɪʃ/ *verb* (**flourishes, flourishing, flourished** /'flʌrɪʃt/)
to develop or grow successfully: *Their business is flourishing.* ◇ *These plants flourish in a sunny position.*

A

B

C

D

E

F

G

H

I

J

K

L

M

N

O

P

Q

R

S

T

U

V

W

X

Y

Z

flow¹ 0̶ /fləʊ/ *noun* (*no plural*)
a steady, continuous movement of something in one direction: *I used a handkerchief to stop the flow of blood.* ◇ *the steady flow of traffic through the city*

flow² 0̶ /fləʊ/ *verb* (flows, flowing, flowed /fləʊd/)
to move in a steady, continuous way in one direction: *This river flows into the North Sea.*

flower 0̶ /ˈflaʊə(r)/ *noun*
the brightly coloured part of a plant that comes before the seeds or fruit: *She gave me a bunch of flowers.* ⊃ Look at the picture at **plant**.

> 🔎 **WORD BUILDING**
> There are many different types of **flower**. Here are some of them: carnation, daffodil, daisy, rose, tulip, violet. Do you know any others?

flowerpot /ˈflaʊəpɒt/ *noun*
a container in which you grow plants

flowery /ˈflaʊəri/ (*also* **flowered** /ˈflaʊəd/) *adjective*
covered or decorated with flowers: *She was wearing a flowery dress.*

flown *form of* FLY¹

flu /fluː/ *noun* (*no plural*)
an illness like a very bad cold that makes your body sore and hot: *I think I've got flu.*

fluent /ˈfluːənt/ *adjective*
1 able to speak easily and correctly: *Ramon is fluent in English and French.*
2 spoken easily and correctly: *She speaks fluent Arabic.*
▶ **fluently** /ˈfluːəntli/ *adverb*: *She speaks five languages fluently.*

fluff /flʌf/ *noun* (*no plural*)
very light, soft pieces of wool, cotton, or fur, or very light and soft new feathers

fluffy /ˈflʌfi/ *adjective* (fluffier, fluffiest)
feeling or looking very light and soft: *a fluffy kitten* ◇ *fluffy clouds*

fluid /ˈfluːɪd/ *noun*
a liquid: *The doctor told her to drink plenty of fluids.*

flung *form of* FLING

flush /flʌʃ/ *verb* (flushes, flushing, flushed /flʌʃt/)
1 to clean a toilet by pressing or pulling a handle that sends water through it: *Remember to flush the toilet.*
2 If you **flush**, your face goes red because you are embarrassed or angry: *He flushed with anger.*

flute

flute /fluːt/ *noun*
a musical instrument that you hold out to the side and play by blowing

flutter /ˈflʌtə(r)/ *verb* (flutters, fluttering, fluttered /ˈflʌtəd/)
to make a quick, light movement through the air: *Flags fluttered in the breeze.*

fly¹ 0̶ /flaɪ/ *verb* (flies, flying, flew /fluː/, has flown /fləʊn/)
1 to move through the air: *In autumn some birds fly to warmer countries.*
2 to make an aircraft move through the air: *A pilot is a person who flies an aircraft.*
3 to travel in a plane: *I'm flying to Abu Dhabi tomorrow.*
4 to move quickly: *The door suddenly flew open and John came in.* ◇ *A stone came flying through the window.*

fly² 0̶ /flaɪ/ *noun*
(*plural* **flies**)
1 a small insect with two wings
2 (*British also* **flies**) the part where you fasten a pair of trousers at the front: *Your fly is undone!*

fly

flying 0̶ /ˈflaɪɪŋ/ *adjective*
able to fly: *flying insects*
with flying colours with great success; very well: *They all passed the exam with flying colours.*

flying saucer /ˌflaɪɪŋ ˈsɔːsə(r)/ *noun*
a flying object that some people think they have seen, and that they think has come from another planet

flyover /ˈflaɪəʊvə(r)/ (*British*) (*American* **overpass**) *noun*
a bridge that carries a road over other roads

foal /fəʊl/ *noun*
a young horse

foam /fəʊm/ *noun* (*no plural*)
a lot of very small white bubbles that you see when you move liquid quickly

focus¹ /ˈfəʊkəs/ *verb* (focuses, focusing, focused /ˈfəʊkəst/)

1 to give all your attention to something: *to focus on a problem*

2 to move part of a camera, etc. so that you can see things through it clearly

focus² /ˈfəʊkəs/ *noun* (no plural)

special attention that is given to somebody or something: *It was the main focus of attention at the meeting.*

in focus, **out of focus** If a photograph is **in focus**, it is clear. If it is **out of focus**, it is not.

foetus (British) (American **fetus**) /ˈfiːtəs/ (plural **foetuses**, **fetuses**) *noun*

a young human or animal that is still growing inside its mother's body

fog /fɒg/ *noun* (no plural)

thick cloud which forms close to the ground, and which is difficult to see through: *The fog will clear by late morning.* ⊃ Look at Picture Dictionary page **P16**.

▶ **foggy** /ˈfɒgi/ *adjective* (**foggier**, **foggiest**): *a foggy day* ◇ *It was very foggy this morning.*

foil /fɔɪl/ *noun* (no plural)

thin metal paper that is used for covering food: *Wrap the meat in foil and put it in the oven.*

fold¹ 0̄ᴡ /fəʊld/ *verb* (folds, folding, folded) (*also* **fold up**)

fold

She's **folding**   a **folding**
paper.   chair

1 to bend something so that one part is on top of another part: *I folded the letter and put it in the envelope.* ◇ *Fold up your clothes.* ⊃ OPPOSITE **unfold**

2 to be able to be made smaller in order to be carried or stored more easily: *a folding chair* ◇ *This table folds up flat.*

fold your arms If you **fold** your arms, you cross them in front of your chest: *She folded her arms and waited.*

fold your arms

He **folded**
his arms.

fold² 0̄ᴡ /fəʊld/ *noun*

a line that is made when you bend cloth or paper

folder /ˈfəʊldə(r)/ *noun*

1 a cover made of cardboard or plastic for keeping papers in

2 a collection of information or files on one subject that is stored in a computer or on a disk

folk /fəʊk/ *noun* (plural) (British) (American **folks**)

people: *There are a lot of old folk living in this village.*

folk dance /ˈfəʊk dɑːns/ *noun*

a traditional dance: *the folk dances of Turkey*

folk song /ˈfəʊk sɒŋ/ *noun*

a traditional song

follow 0̄ᴡ /ˈfɒləʊ/ *verb* (follows, following, followed /ˈfɒləʊd/)

1 to come or go after somebody or something: *Follow me and I'll show you the way.* ◇ *I think that car is following us!* ◇ *The film will be followed by the news.*

2 to go along a road, path, etc.: *Follow this road for about a mile and then turn right.*

3 to do what somebody says you should do: *I'd like you all to follow my instructions carefully.*

4 to understand something: *Has everyone followed the lesson so far?*

as follows as you will now hear or read: *The dates of the meetings will be as follows: 21 March, 3 April, 19 April.*

following 0̄ᴡ /ˈfɒləʊɪŋ/ *adjective*

next: *I saw him the following day.*

fond /fɒnd/ *adjective* (fonder, fondest)

be fond of somebody or **something** to like somebody or something a lot: *They are very fond of their uncle.*

food 0̄ᴡ /fuːd/ *noun* (no plural)

things that people or animals eat: *Let's go and get some food – I'm hungry.* ◇ *They gave the horses food and water.*

fool¹ /fuːl/ *noun*
a person who is silly or who does something silly: *You fool! You forgot to lock the door!*
make a fool of yourself to do something that makes you look silly in front of other people: *He always makes a fool of himself at parties.*

fool² /fuːl/ *verb* (fools, fooling, fooled /fuːld/)
to make somebody believe something that is not true ⊃ SAME MEANING **trick**: *You can't fool me! I know you're lying!*
fool about, fool around to do silly things: *Stop fooling about with that knife.*

foolish /ˈfuːlɪʃ/ *adjective*
stupid or silly: *a foolish mistake*
▸ **foolishly** /ˈfuːlɪʃli/ *adverb*: *I foolishly forgot to bring a coat.*

feet

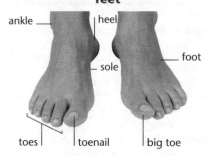

ankle • heel • foot • sole • toes • toenail • big toe

foot 0-π /fʊt/ *noun*
1 (*plural* **feet** /fiːt/) the part of your leg that you stand on: *I've been walking all day and my feet hurt.*
2 (*plural* **foot** or **feet**) (*abbr.* ft) a measure of length (= 30.48 centimetres). There are twelve INCHES in a **foot**: '*How tall are you?*' '*Five foot six* (= five feet and six inches).'

> 🔎 **CULTURE**
>
> In the past, people in Britain used **inches**, **feet**, **yards** and **miles** to measure distances. In the US, people still use these measurements.
> In Britain people now use both **centimetres** and **metres** as well as **feet** and **inches** but usually use **miles** instead of **kilometres**.

3 the lowest part of something ⊃ SAME MEANING **the bottom**: *She was standing at the foot of the stairs.*
on foot walking: *Shall we go by car or on foot?*
put your feet up to rest: *If you're tired, put your feet up and listen to some music.*

put your foot down (*informal*) to say strongly that something must or must not happen: *My mum put her foot down when I asked if I could stay out all night.*
put your foot in it (*informal*) to say or do something by accident that makes somebody embarrassed or upset

football 0-π /ˈfʊtbɔːl/ *noun*
1 (*no plural*) (*British*) (*American and British also* **soccer**) a game for two teams of eleven players who try to kick a round ball into the other team's goal on a field (called a **football pitch**): *Peter's playing in a football match tomorrow.* ⊃ Look at Picture Dictionary page **P14**.
2 *American English for* AMERICAN FOOTBALL
3 (*plural* **footballs**) a ball for playing this game

footballer /ˈfʊtbɔːlə(r)/ *noun*
a person who plays football: *a professional footballer*

footpath /ˈfʊtpɑːθ/ *noun*
a path in the country for people to walk on

footprint /ˈfʊtprɪnt/ *noun*
a mark that your foot or shoe makes on the ground

footstep /ˈfʊtstep/ *noun*
the sound of a person walking: *I heard footsteps and then a knock on the door.*

for¹ 0-π /fə(r); fɔː(r)/ *preposition*
1 a word that shows who will get or have something: *These flowers are for you.*
2 a word that shows how something is used or why something is done: *We had fish and chips for dinner.* ◇ *Take this medicine for your cold.* ◇ *He was sent to prison for murder.*
3 a word that shows how long something has been happening: *She has lived here for 20 years.* ⊃ Look at the note at **since**.
4 a word that shows how far somebody or something goes: *We walked for miles* (= a very long way).
5 a word that shows where a person or thing is going: *Is this the train for Glasgow?*
6 a word that shows the person or thing you are talking about: *It's time for us to go.*
7 a word that shows how much something is: *I bought this book for £9.*
8 a word that shows that you like an idea: *Some people were for the strike and others were against it.* ⊃ OPPOSITE **against**
9 on the side of somebody or something: *He plays football for Italy.*
10 with the meaning of: *What is the word for 'table' in German?*

for² /fə(r)/ *conjunction* (*formal*)
because: *She was crying, for she knew they could never meet again.*

🔎 SPEAKING
Because and as are the words that we usually use.

forbid /fəˈbɪd/ *verb* (forbids, forbidding, forbade /fəˈbæd/, has forbidden /fəˈbɪdn/)
to say that somebody must not do something: *My parents have forbidden me to see him again.* ◇ *Smoking is forbidden* (= not allowed) *inside the building.*
➔ OPPOSITE **allow**

force¹ 0🔊 /fɔːs/ *noun*
1 (*no plural*) power or strength: *He was killed by the force of the explosion.* ◇ *I lost the key so I had to open the door by force.*
2 (*plural* forces) a group of people, for example the police or soldiers, who do a special job: *the police force*

force² 0🔊 /fɔːs/ *verb* (forces, forcing, forced /fɔːst/)
1 to make somebody do something that they do not want to do: *They forced him to give them the money.*
2 to do something by using a lot of strength: *The thief forced the window open.*

forecast¹ /ˈfɔːkɑːst/ *noun*
what somebody thinks will happen, based on the information that is available: *The weather forecast said that it would rain today.*

forecast² /ˈfɔːkɑːst/ *verb* (forecasts, forecasting, forecast, has forecast)
to say what you think will happen, based on the information that is available
➔ SAME MEANING **predict**: *They've forecast rain tomorrow.*
▶ **forecaster** /ˈfɔːkɑːstə(r)/ *noun*: *She's a weather forecaster on TV.*

foreground /ˈfɔːɡraʊnd/ *noun*
the part of a picture that seems nearest to you: *The man in the foreground is my father.*
➔ OPPOSITE **background**

forehead /ˈfɔːhed/ *noun*
the part of your face above your eyes ➔ Look at Picture Dictionary page **P4**.

foreign 0🔊 /ˈfɒrən/ *adjective*
belonging to or connected with a country that is not your own: *We've got some foreign students staying at our house.* ◇ *a foreign language*

foreigner /ˈfɒrənə(r)/ *noun*
a person from another country ➔ Look at the note at **stranger**.

forename /ˈfɔːneɪm/ *noun* (*formal*)
your first name ➔ Look at the note at **name**.

foresee /fɔːˈsiː/ *verb* (foresees, foreseeing, foresaw /fɔːˈsɔː/, has foreseen /fɔːˈsiːn/)
to know or guess what will happen in the future ➔ SAME MEANING **predict**: *Nobody could have foreseen what would happen.*

forest 0🔊 /ˈfɒrɪst/ *noun*
a large area of land covered with trees: *We went for a walk in the forest.*

🔎 WORD BUILDING
A forest is larger than a **wood**. A **jungle** is a forest in a very hot country.

forever /fərˈevə(r)/ (*also* for ever) *adverb*
1 for all time ➔ SAME MEANING **always**: *I will love you forever.*
2 (*informal*) very often: *I can't read because he is forever asking me questions!*

forgave *form of* FORGIVE

forge /fɔːdʒ/ *verb* (forges, forging, forged /fɔːdʒd/)
to make an illegal copy of something in order to cheat people: *The passport had been forged.*
forge somebody's signature to sign another person's name, pretending to be that person

forgery /ˈfɔːdʒəri/ *noun*
1 (*no plural*) the crime of making an illegal copy of something in order to cheat people
2 (*plural* forgeries) something that has been copied in order to cheat people: *This painting is not really by Picasso – it's a forgery.*

forget 0🔊 /fəˈɡet/ *verb* (forgets, forgetting, forgot /fəˈɡɒt/, has forgotten /fəˈɡɒtn/)
1 to not remember something: *I've forgotten her name.* ◇ *Don't forget to do your homework!*
2 to not bring something with you: *I had forgotten my glasses.*
3 to stop thinking about something: *Forget about your exams and enjoy yourself!*

forgetful /fəˈɡetfl/ *adjective*
often forgetting things ➔ SAME MEANING **absent-minded**: *My grandmother had become rather forgetful.*

forgive 0🔊 /fəˈɡɪv/ *verb* (forgives, forgiving, forgave /fəˈɡeɪv/, has forgiven /fəˈɡɪvn/)
to stop being angry with somebody for a bad thing that they did: *I can't forgive him for behaving like that.*

forgiveness /fəˈɡɪvnəs/ *noun* (*no plural*)
the fact that you stop being angry with somebody for a bad thing that they did: *He begged for forgiveness.*

forgot, forgotten *forms of* FORGET

A B C D E F G H I J K L M N O P Q R S T U V W X Y Z

A
B
C
D
E
F
G
H
I
J
K
L
M
N
O
P
Q
R
S
T
U
V
W
X
Y
Z

forks

fork 0̄̄ /fɔːk/ *noun*

1 a thing with long points at one end, that you use for putting food in your mouth
2 a large tool with points at one end, that you use for digging the ground
3 a place where a road or river divides into two parts: *When you get to the fork in the road, go left.*

form¹ 0̄̄ /fɔːm/ *noun*

1 a type of something: *Cars, trains and buses are all forms of transport.*
2 a piece of paper with spaces for you to answer questions: *You need to fill in this form to get a new passport.* ➲ Look at Study Page **S16**.
3 the shape of a person or thing: *a cake in the form of a car*
4 one of the ways you write or say a word: *'Forgot' is a form of 'forget'.*
5 (*British*) a class in a school: *Which form are you in?*

form² 0̄̄ /fɔːm/ *verb* (**forms, forming, formed** /fɔːmd/)

1 to make something or to give a shape to something: *We formed a line outside the cinema.* ◇ *In English we usually form the past tense by adding 'ed'.*
2 to grow or take shape: *Ice forms when water freezes.*
3 to start a group or an organization: *The club was formed last year.*

formal 0̄̄ /'fɔːml/ *adjective*

You use **formal** language or behave in a **formal** way at important or serious times and with people you do not know very well: *'Yours faithfully' is a formal way of ending a letter.* ◇ *I wore a suit and tie because it was a formal dinner.* ➲ OPPOSITE **informal**
▸ **formally** /'fɔːməli/ *adverb*: '*How do you do?' she said formally.*

former /'fɔːmə(r)/ *adjective*

1 of a time before now: *the former Prime Minister*
2 the former the first of two things or people: *He had to choose between losing his job and losing his family. He chose the former.* ➲ OPPOSITE **the latter**

formerly /'fɔːməli/ *adverb*

before this time: *Sri Lanka was formerly called Ceylon.*

formula /'fɔːmjələ/ *noun* (*plural* **formulae** /'fɔːmjʊliː/ or **formulas**)

1 a group of letters, numbers or symbols that show a rule in mathematics or science: *The formula for finding the area of a circle is πr^2.*
2 a list of the substances that you need to make something: *The formula for the new drug has not yet been made public.*

fort /fɔːt/ *noun*

a strong building that was made to protect a place against its enemies

fortieth *number form of* FORTY

fortnight /'fɔːtnaɪt/ *noun* (*British*)

a period of two weeks: *I'm going on holiday for a fortnight.*
▸ **fortnightly** /'fɔːtnaɪtli/ *adjective*, *adverb*: *We have fortnightly meetings.*

fortress /'fɔːtrəs/ *noun* (*plural* **fortresses**)

a large strong building that was made to protect a place against its enemies

fortunate /'fɔːtʃənət/ *adjective*

lucky: *I was very fortunate to get the job.*
➲ OPPOSITE **unfortunate**
▸ **fortunately** /'fɔːtʃənətli/ *adverb*
➲ SAME MEANING **luckily**: *Fortunately, nobody was hurt in the accident.*

fortune /'fɔːtʃuːn/ *noun*

1 (*no plural*) things that happen that you cannot control ➲ SAME MEANING **luck**: *I had the good fortune to get the job.*
2 (*plural* **fortunes**) a lot of money: *He made a fortune selling old cars.*
tell somebody's fortune to say what will happen to somebody in the future: *The old lady said she could tell my fortune by looking at my hand.*

forty 0̄̄ /'fɔːti/ *number*

🔎 **SPELLING**

Remember! There is a **U** in **four**, but no **U** in **forty**.

1 40
2 the forties (*plural*) the numbers, years or temperature between 40 and 49
in your forties between the ages of 40 and 49: *I think my teacher must be in his forties.*
▸ **fortieth** /'fɔːtiəθ/ *pronoun*, *adjective*, *adverb* 40th

forward¹ 0̄̄ /'fɔːwəd/ (*also* **forwards**) /'fɔːwədz/ *adverb*

in the direction that is in front of you: *Move forwards to the front of the train.*
➲ OPPOSITE **backwards**
look forward to something to wait for something with pleasure: *We're looking forward to seeing you again.*

forward² /'fɔːwəd/ *verb* (forwards, forwarding, forwarded)
to send a letter that you receive at one address to another address: *Could you forward all my post to me while I'm abroad?*

fossil /'fɒsl/ *noun*
a part of a dead plant or an animal that has been in the ground for a very long time and has turned into rock

foster /'fɒstə(r)/ *verb* (fosters, fostering, fostered /'fɒstəd/)
1 (*formal*) to let a good feeling or situation develop: *The aim is to foster good relations between the two countries.*
2 to look after another person's child in your home for a time, without becoming their legal parent ⊃ Look at **adopt**.
▶ **foster** *adjective*: *her foster parents* ◇ *their foster child*

fought *form of* FIGHT

foul¹ /faʊl/ *adjective*
1 dirty, or with a bad smell or taste: *What a foul smell!*
2 very bad: *We had foul weather all week.*

foul² /faʊl/ (fouls, fouling, fouled /faʊld/) *verb*
(in sport) to do something to another player that is not allowed: *Johnson was fouled twice.*
▶ **foul** *noun*: *He was sent off for a foul on the goalkeeper.*

found¹ *form of* FIND

found² /faʊnd/ *verb* (founds, founding, founded)
to start a new organization: *This school was founded in 1865.*
▶ **founder** /'faʊndə(r)/ *noun* a person who starts a new organization: *the founder and president of the company*

foundation /faʊn'deɪʃn/ *noun*
1 **foundations** (*plural*) the bricks or stones that form the solid base of a building, under the ground
2 (*no plural*) the act of starting a new organization

fountain

fountain /'faʊntən/ *noun*
water that shoots up into the air and then falls down again. You often see **fountains** in gardens and parks.

fountain pen /'faʊntən pen/ *noun*
a pen that you fill with ink ⊃ Look at Picture Dictionary page **P11**.

four Oᴍ /fɔː(r)/ *number* 4
on all fours with your hands and knees on the ground: *We went through the tunnel on all fours.*
▶ **fourth** /fɔːθ/ *pronoun, adjective, adverb* 4th

fourteen Oᴍ /ˌfɔː'tiːn/ *number* 14
▶ **fourteenth** /ˌfɔː'tiːnθ/ *pronoun, adjective, adverb* 14th

fox

fox /fɒks/ *noun* (*plural* foxes)
a wild animal like a small dog with a long thick tail and red fur

fraction /'frækʃn/ *noun*
1 an exact part of a number: ¼ (= a quarter) and ⅓ (= a third) *are fractions.*
2 a very small part of something: *For a fraction of a second I thought the car would crash.*

fracture /'fræktʃə(r)/ *noun*
a break in one of your bones: *She had a fracture of the arm.*
▶ **fracture** *verb* (fractures, fracturing, fractured /'fræktʃəd/): *She fell and fractured her ankle.*

fragile /'frædʒaɪl/ *adjective*
A thing that is **fragile** breaks easily: *Be careful with those glasses. They're very fragile.*

fragment /'frægmənt/ *noun*
a very small piece that has broken off something: *There were **fragments of** glass everywhere.*

fragrance /'freɪɡrəns/ *noun*
a pleasant smell: *The flowers are chosen for their delicate fragrance.*

fragrant /'freɪɡrənt/ *adjective*
having a pleasant smell: *The air was fragrant.*

frail /freɪl/ *adjective* **(frailer, frailest)**
not strong or healthy ➾ SAME MEANING
weak: *a frail old woman*

frame[1] 0️⃣ /freɪm/ *noun*
1 a thin piece of wood or metal round the edge of a picture, window, mirror, etc.
2 strong pieces of wood or metal that give something its shape: *the frame of the bicycle*
3 the metal or plastic round the edge of a pair of glasses ➾ Look at the picture at **glasses**.
frame of mind that way that you feel at a particular time ➾ SAME MEANING **mood**: *I'm not in the right frame of mind for a party.*

frame[2] /freɪm/ *verb* **(frames, framing, framed** /freɪmd/**)**
to put a picture in a frame: *Let's have this photograph framed.*

framework /'freɪmwɜːk/ *noun*
the strong part of something that gives it shape: *The bridge has a steel framework.*

frank /fræŋk/ *adjective* **(franker, frankest)**
saying exactly what you think.
➾ SAME MEANING **honest** or **truthful**: *To be frank, I don't like your shirt.*
▶ **frankly** /'fræŋkli/ *adverb*: *Tell me frankly what you think of my work.*

fraud /frɔːd/ *noun*
1 (*no plural*) doing things that are not honest to get money: *His father was sent to prison for fraud.*
2 (*plural* **frauds**) a person or thing that is not what they seem to be: *He said he was a police officer but I knew he was a fraud.*

fray /freɪ/ *verb* **(frays, fraying, frayed** /freɪd/**)**
If cloth **frays**, the threads become loose at the edges: *frayed trousers*

freak /friːk/ *noun*
1 (*informal*) a person with a very strong interest in something: *a health freak* ◇ *a computer freak*
2 a person who looks strange or behaves in a very strange way

freckles /'freklz/ *noun* (*plural*)
small light brown spots on a person's skin: *A lot of people with red hair have freckles.*

free[1] 0️⃣ /friː/ *adjective, adverb* **(freer, freest)**
1 able to go where you want and do what you want: *After five years in prison she was finally free.* ◇ *We set the bird free* (= let it go) *and it flew away.*
2 If something is **free**, you do not have to pay for it: *We've got some free tickets for the concert.* ◇ *Children under five travel free on trains.*

3 not busy: *Are you free this afternoon?* ◇ *I don't have much free time.*
4 not being used: *Excuse me, is this seat free?*
free from something, free of something without something bad: *She was finally free from pain.*

free[2] 0️⃣ /friː/ *verb* **(frees, freeing, freed** /friːd/**)**
to make somebody or something free: *He was freed after ten years in prison.*

freedom 0️⃣ /'friːdəm/ *noun* (*no plural*)
being free: *They gave their children too much freedom.*

freeway /'friːweɪ/ *American English for* MOTORWAY

freeze 0️⃣ /friːz/ *verb* **(freezes, freezing, froze** /frəʊz/**, has frozen** /'frəʊzn/**)**
1 to become hard because it is so cold. When water **freezes**, it becomes ice.
2 to make food very cold so that it stays fresh for a long time: *frozen vegetables*
3 to stop suddenly and stay very still: *The cat froze when it saw the bird.*
freeze to death to be so cold that you die

freezer /'friːzə(r)/ *noun*
an electric container which keeps food very cold so that it stays fresh for a long time ➾ Look at **fridge**. ➾ Look at Picture Dictionary page **P10**.

freezing /'friːzɪŋ/ *adjective*
very cold: *Can you close the window? I'm freezing!*

freezing point /'friːzɪŋ pɔɪnt/ *noun* (*no plural*)
the temperature at which a liquid freezes: *Water has a freezing point of 0° Celsius.*

freight /freɪt/ *noun* (*no plural*)
things that lorries, ships, trains and planes carry from one place to another: *a freight train*

French fry /ˌfrentʃ 'fraɪ/ *American English for* CHIP[1](1)

frequent /'friːkwənt/ *adjective*
happening often: *His visits became less frequent.*
▶ **frequently** /'friːkwəntli/ *adverb*
(*formal*) ➾ SAME MEANING **often**: *Simon is frequently late for school.*

fresh 0️⃣ /freʃ/ *adjective* **(fresher, freshest)**
1 (used especially about food) made or picked not long ago; not frozen or in a tin: *I'll make some fresh coffee.* ◇ *Eat plenty of fresh fruit and vegetables.*
2 new or different: *fresh ideas*

3 clean and cool: *Open the window and let some **fresh air** in.*

4 (used about water) not containing salt; not from the sea

▶ **freshly** /ˈfreʃli/ *adverb*: *freshly baked bread*

Friday ⦿ /ˈfraɪdeɪ/ *noun*

the day of the week after Thursday and before Saturday ⮑ Look at the note at **day**.

fridge /frɪdʒ/ (*also formal* **refrigerator**) *noun*

a metal container, usually electric, which keeps food cold, but not frozen: *Can you put the milk in the fridge?* ⮑ Look at **freezer**. ⮑ Look at Picture Dictionary page **P10**.

fried *form of* FRY

friend ⦿ /frend/ *noun*

> 🔊 **PRONUNCIATION**
>
> The word **friend** sounds like **send**, because we don't say the letter **i** in this word.

a person that you like and know very well: *David is my **best friend**. ◇ We are very good friends.*

make friends with somebody to become a friend of somebody: *Have you made friends with any of the students in your class?*

friendly ⦿ /ˈfrendli/ *adjective*

(friendlier, friendliest)

kind and helpful: *My neighbours are very friendly.* ⮑ OPPOSITE **unfriendly**

be friendly with somebody to be somebody's friend: *Jane is friendly with their daughter.*

friendship ⦿ /ˈfrendʃɪp/ *noun*

the state of being friends with somebody: *a close friendship ◇ Your friendship is very important to me.*

fries *form of* FRY

fright /fraɪt/ *noun*

a sudden feeling of fear: *I hope I didn't **give** you a **fright** when I shouted.*

frighten ⦿ /ˈfraɪtn/ *verb* (frightens, frightening, frightened /ˈfraɪtnd/)

to make somebody feel afraid
⮑ SAME MEANING **scare**: *Sorry, did I frighten you?*

frightened ⦿ /ˈfraɪtnd/ *adjective*

afraid ⮑ SAME MEANING **scared**: *He's frightened of spiders.*

frightening ⦿ /ˈfraɪtnɪŋ/ *adjective*

making you feel afraid: *That was the most frightening film I have ever seen.*

frill /frɪl/ *noun*

a narrow piece of cloth with a lot of folds which decorates the edge of a shirt, dress, etc.: *a white blouse with frills at the cuffs*

▶ **frilly** /ˈfrɪli/ *adjective*: *a frilly skirt*

fringe /frɪndʒ/ *noun*

1 (*British*) (*American* **bangs**) the short hair that hangs down above your eyes ⮑ Look at the picture at **hair**.

2 a line of loose threads that decorate the edge of a piece of cloth or carpet

frizzy /ˈfrɪzi/ *adjective* (frizzier, frizziest) *adjective*

(used about hair) with a lot of small tight curls

fro /frəʊ/ *adverb*

to and fro first one way and then the other way, many times: *She rocked the baby to and fro.*

frog /frɒg/ *noun*

frog

a small green animal that lives in and near water. **Frogs** have long back legs and they can jump.

from ⦿ /frəm; frɒm/ *preposition*

1 a word that shows where somebody or something starts: *We travelled from New York to Boston. ◇ She began to walk away from him. ◇ The tickets cost from $15 to $35.*

2 a word that shows when something starts: *The shop is open from 9.30 until 5.30.*

3 a word that shows who gave or sent something: *I had a letter from Lyn. ◇ I borrowed a dress from my sister.*

4 a word that shows where somebody lives or was born: *I come from Spain.*

5 a word that shows what is used to make something: *Paper is made from wood.*

6 a word that shows how far away something is: *The house is two miles from the village.*

7 a word that shows how something changes: *The sky changed from blue to grey.*

8 a word that shows why: *Children are dying from this disease.*

9 a word that shows difference: *My book is different from yours.*

front ⦿ /frʌnt/ *noun*

the side or part of something that faces forwards and that you usually see first: *The book has a picture of a lion **on the front**. ◇ John and I sat **in the front of** the car and the children sat in the back.* ⮑ Look at the picture at **back**.

A B C D E **F** G H I J K L M N O P Q R S T U V W X Y Z

A B C D E F G H I J K L M N O P Q R S T U V W X Y Z

in front of somebody or **something**
1 further forward than another person or thing: *Alice was sitting in front of her mother on the bus.*
2 when other people are there: *Please don't talk about it in front of my parents.*
▶ **front** *adjective*: *the front door ◇ the front seat of a car*

frontier /'frʌntɪə(r)/ *noun*
the line where one country joins another country

frost /frɒst/ *noun*
ice like white powder that covers the ground when the weather is very cold: *There was a frost last night.*
▶ **frosty** /'frɒsti/ *adjective* (frostier, frostiest): *a frosty morning*

frosting /'frɒstɪŋ/ *American English for* ICING

frown /fraʊn/ *verb* (frowns, frowning, frowned /fraʊnd/)
to show feelings of anger or worry by making lines appear above your nose: *John frowned at me when I came in. 'You're late,' he said.*
▶ **frown** *noun*: *She looked at me with a frown.*

froze *form of* FREEZE
frozen¹ *form of* FREEZE

frozen² 0̄ /'frəʊzn/ *adjective* (*informal*)
1 (used about food) kept at a very cold temperature so that it stays fresh for a long time: *frozen peas*
2 (used about people) very cold: *I'm frozen stiff.*

fruit 0̄ /fruːt/ *noun*

> 🔍 **PRONUNCIATION**
> The word **fruit** sounds like **boot**.

the part of a plant or tree that holds the seeds. Oranges and apples are types of **fruit**.
➩ Look at Picture Dictionary page **P8**.

> 🔍 **GRAMMAR**
> Be careful! We do not usually say 'a fruit'. We say 'a piece of fruit' or 'some fruit ': *Would you like a piece of fruit? ◇ 'Would you like some fruit?' 'Yes please – I'll have a pear.'*

> 🔍 **WORD BUILDING**
> There are many different types of **fruit**. Here are some of them: apple, banana, date, lemon, mango, strawberry. Do you know any others?

frustrating /frʌ'streɪtɪŋ/ *adjective*
making you angry because you cannot do

what you want to do: *It's very frustrating when you can't say what you mean in a foreign language.*

fry 0̄ /fraɪ/ *verb* (fries, frying, fried /fraɪd/, has fried)
to cook something in hot oil: *Fry the onions in butter. ◇ fried eggs*

frying pan
/'fraɪɪŋ pæn/
(*British*) (*American* frypan /'fraɪpæn/)
noun
a flat metal container with a long handle that you use for frying food

frying pan

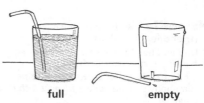

handle

ft *short way of writing* FOOT(2)

fuel 0̄ /'fjuːəl/
noun (*no plural*)
anything that you burn to make heat or power. Wood, coal and oil are kinds of **fuel**.

fulfil (*British*) (*American* fulfill) /fʊl'fɪl/ *verb* (fulfils, fulfilling, fulfilled /fʊl'fɪld/)
to do what you have planned or promised to do: *Jane fulfilled her dream of travelling around the world.*

full   **empty**

full 0̄ /fʊl/ *adjective* (fuller, fullest)
1 with a lot of people or things in it, so that there is no more space: *My glass is full. ◇ The bus was full so we waited for the next one. ◇ These socks are full of holes.*
2 (*British also* full up) having had enough to eat: *'Would you like anything else to eat?' 'No thank you, I'm full.'*
3 complete; with nothing missing: *Please tell me the full story.*
4 as much, big, etc. as possible: *The train was travelling at full speed.*
in full completely; with nothing missing: *Please write your name in full.*

full moon /ˌfʊl 'muːn/ *noun*
the time when you can see all of the moon

full stop /ˌfʊl 'stɒp/ *noun* (*British*) (*American* period)
a mark (.) that you use in writing to show the

end of a sentence, or after the short form of a word

full-time /ˌfʊl ˈtaɪm/ *adjective, adverb*
for all the normal working hours of the day or week: *My mother has a full-time job.* ◇ *Do you work full-time?* ⊃ Look at **part-time**.

fully 0̄ᴍ /ˈfʊli/ *adverb*
completely; totally: *The hotel was fully booked.*

fun 0̄ᴍ /fʌn/ *noun (no plural)*
pleasure and enjoyment; something that you enjoy: *Sailing is good fun.* ◇ *I'm just learning English for fun.* ◇ *Have fun* (= enjoy yourself)*!*
make fun of somebody to laugh about somebody in an unkind way: *The other children make fun of him because he wears glasses.*

function¹ /ˈfʌŋkʃn/ *noun*
the special work that a person or thing does: *The function of the heart is to send blood round the body.*

function² /ˈfʌŋkʃn/ *verb* (functions, functioning, functioned /ˈfʌŋkʃnd/)
to work: *The car engine will not function without oil.*

fund /fʌnd/ *noun*
money that will be used for something special: *a fund to help homeless people* ◇ *The school wants to raise funds for new computers.*

fundamental /ˌfʌndəˈmentl/ *adjective*
most important; from which everything else develops ⊃ SAME MEANING **basic**: *There is a fundamental difference between the two points of view.*

fund-raising /ˈfʌnd reɪzɪŋ/ *noun (no plural)*
the activity of collecting money for a particular use: *fund-raising activities at school*

funeral /ˈfjuːnərəl/ *noun*
the time when a dead person is buried or burned

funfair /ˈfʌnfeə(r)/ *noun* = FAIR² (1)

fungus /ˈfʌŋgəs/ *noun* (fungi /ˈfʌŋgiː; ˈfʌŋgaɪ/)
any plant without leaves, flowers or green colouring, that grows on other plants or on other surfaces. MUSHROOMS are **fungi**.

funnel /ˈfʌnl/ *noun*
1 a tube that is wide at the top to help you pour things into bottles
2 a large pipe on a ship or railway engine that smoke comes out of

funny 0̄ᴍ /ˈfʌni/ *adjective* (funnier, funniest)
1 making you laugh or smile ⊃ SAME MEANING **amusing**: *a funny story* ◇ *He's so funny!*
2 strange or surprising: *There's a funny smell in this room.*

fur 0̄ᴍ /fɜː(r)/ *noun (no plural)*
the soft thick hair that covers the bodies of some animals
▶ **furry** /ˈfɜːri/ *adjective* (furrier, furriest): *a furry animal*

furious /ˈfjʊəriəs/ *adjective*
very angry: *My parents were furious with me.*

furnace /ˈfɜːnɪs/ *noun*
a very hot fire in a closed place, used for heating metals, making glass, etc.

furnished /ˈfɜːnɪʃt/ *adjective*
with furniture already in it: *I rented a furnished flat in the town centre.*

furniture 0̄ᴍ /ˈfɜːnɪtʃə(r)/ *noun (no plural)*
tables, chairs, beds, etc.: *They've bought some furniture for their new house.* ◇ *All the furniture is very old.*

> 🔎 **GRAMMAR**
> **Furniture** does not have a plural, so we cannot say 'a furniture'. We say 'a piece of furniture' to talk about a single item: *The only piece of furniture in the room was a large bed.*

further 0̄ᴍ /ˈfɜːðə(r)/ *adjective, adverb*
1 at or to a greater distance ⊃ SAME MEANING **farther**: *The hospital is further down the road.* ◇ *We couldn't go any further because the road was closed.*
2 more; extra: *Do you have any further questions?*

further education /ˌfɜːðər edʒuˈkeɪʃn/ *noun* (abbr. FE) (British)
education for people who have left school but who are not at university ⊃ Look at **higher education**.

furthest 0̄ᴍ form of FAR

fury /ˈfjʊəri/ *noun (no plural)* (formal)
very strong anger: *She was filled with fury.*

fuse /fjuːz/ *noun*
a small wire inside a piece of electrical equipment that stops it from working if too much electricity goes through it

fuss¹ /fʌs/ *noun (no plural)*
a lot of excitement or worry about small things that are not important: *He makes a fuss when I'm five minutes late.*

A
B
C
D
E
F
G
H
I
J
K
L
M
N
O
P
Q
R
S
T
U
V
W
X
Y
Z

make a fuss of somebody to pay a lot of attention to somebody: *Grandad always makes a fuss of me.*

fuss² /fʌs/ *verb* (fusses, fussing, fussed /fʌst/)
to worry and get excited about small things that are not important: *Stop fussing!*

fussy /ˈfʌsi/ *adjective* (fussier, fussiest)
caring a lot about small things that are not important, and difficult to please: *Rod is fussy about his food* (= there are many things that he will not eat).

future¹ 0̶ₘ /ˈfjuːtʃə(r)/ *noun*
1 the time that will come: *Nobody knows what will happen in the future.* ◇ *The company's future is uncertain.*
2 the future (*no plural*) (*grammar*) the form of a verb that shows what will happen after now ➔ Look at **past** and **present**.
in future from now on: *You must work harder in future.*

future² 0̶ₘ /ˈfjuːtʃə(r)/ *adjective*
happening or existing in the time that will come: *Have you met John's future wife?*

G g

G, g /dʒiː/ *noun* (plural G's, g's /dʒiːz/)
the seventh letter of the English alphabet:
'*Girl*' begins with a '*G*'.

g² *abbreviation* short way of writing GRAM: *It
weighs 100g.*

gadget /ˈɡædʒɪt/ *noun*
a small machine or useful tool: *Their kitchen is
full of electrical gadgets.*

gain 0ₘ /ɡeɪn/ *verb* (gains, gaining,
gained /ɡeɪnd/)
1 to get something that you want or need: *I
gained useful experience from that job.*
2 to get more of something: *I have **gained**
weight* recently.

galaxy /ˈɡæləksi/ *noun* (plural galaxies)
a very large group of stars and planets

gale /ɡeɪl/ *noun*
a very strong wind: *The trees were blown
down in the gale.*

gallery /ˈɡæləri/ *noun* (plural galleries)
a place where people can look at or buy art:
an art gallery

gallon /ˈɡælən/ *noun*
a unit for measuring liquid. In the UK it is
equal to about 4.5 litres; in the US it is equal
to about 3.8 litres. ➲ Look at the note at
pint.

gallop /ˈɡæləp/ *verb* (gallops, galloping,
galloped /ˈɡæləpt/)
When a horse **gallops**, it runs very fast: *The
horses galloped round the field.*

gamble /ˈɡæmbl/ *verb* (gambles,
gambling, gambled /ˈɡæmbld/)
1 to try to win money by playing games that
need luck: *He gambled a lot of money on the
last race.*
2 to take a risk, hoping that something will
happen: *We **gambled on** the weather staying
fine.*
▶ **gamble** *noun* something that you do
without knowing if you will win or lose: *We
took a gamble, and it paid off* (= was
successful).
▶ **gambling** /ˈɡæmblɪŋ/ *noun* (no plural):
He had heavy gambling debts.

gambler /ˈɡæmblə(r)/ *noun*
a person who tries to win money by playing
games that need luck

game 0ₘ /ɡeɪm/ *noun*
1 (plural games) something you play that
has rules: *Shall we have a **game of** football?*
◇ *Let's **play a game**!* ◇ *computer games*

2 (no plural) wild animals or birds that
people kill for sport or food

game show /ˈɡeɪm ʃəʊ/ *noun*
a television programme in which people
play games or answer questions to win
prizes

gang¹ /ɡæŋ/ *noun*
1 an organized group of criminals: *a gang of
criminals*
2 a group of young people who spend a lot
of time together and often cause trouble or
fight against other groups: *street gangs*
3 (informal) a group of friends: *The whole
gang is coming tonight.*

gang² /ɡæŋ/ *verb* (gangs, ganging,
ganged /ɡæŋd/)
gang up on or **against somebody** to
join together in a group to hurt or frighten
somebody: *At school the older boys ganged up
on him and called him names.*

gangster /ˈɡæŋstə(r)/ *noun*
a member of a group of criminals

gangway /ˈɡæŋweɪ/ *noun*
1 (British) the long space between rows of
seats in a cinema, theatre, etc. ➲ Look at
aisle.
2 a bridge that you use for getting on or off
a ship

gaol /dʒeɪl/ *noun* (British) another word for
JAIL

gap /ɡæp/ *noun*
a space in something or between two
things; a space where something should be:
*The goats got out through a **gap in** the fence.*
◇ *Leave a **gap between** your car and the next.*
◇ *Fill in the gaps in the text.*

gape /ɡeɪp/ *verb* (gapes, gaping, gaped
/ɡeɪpt/)
to look at somebody or something with your
mouth open because you are surprised: *She
gaped at me in astonishment.*

gaping /ˈɡeɪpɪŋ/ *adjective*
wide open: *There was a gaping hole in the
fence.*

garage /ˈɡærɑːʒ/ *noun*
1 a building where you keep your car
2 a place where vehicles are repaired and
where you can buy a car or buy petrol and oil

garbage 0ₘ /ˈɡɑːbɪdʒ/ *American English
for* RUBBISH

garbage can /ˈɡɑːbɪdʒ kæn/ *American
English for* DUSTBIN

A
B
C
D
E
F
G
H
I
J
K
L
M
N
O
P
Q
R
S
T
U
V
W
X
Y
Z

garden 0🔑 /'gɑːdn/ *noun*
1 (*British*) (*American* **yard**) a piece of land by your house where you can grow flowers, fruit, and vegetables: *Let's have lunch in the garden.* ⊃ Look at Picture Dictionary page **P10**.
2 gardens (*plural*) a public park: *Kensington Gardens*
▸ **garden** *verb* (**gardens, gardening, gardened** /'gɑːdnd/) to work in a garden: *My mother was gardening all weekend.*
▸ **gardening** /'gɑːdnɪŋ/ *noun* (*no plural*) the work that you do in a garden to keep it looking attractive

gardener /'gɑːdnə(r)/ *noun*
a person who works in a garden

garlic /'gɑːlɪk/ *noun* (*no plural*)
a plant like a small onion with a strong taste and smell, that you use in cooking ⊃ Look at Picture Dictionary page **P9**.

garment /'gɑːmənt/ *noun* (*formal*)
a piece of clothing

gas 0🔑 /gæs/ *noun*
1 (*plural* **gases**) a substance like air that is not a solid or a liquid: *Hydrogen and oxygen are gases.*
2 (*no plural*) a **gas** with a strong smell, that you burn to make heat: *Do you use electricity or gas for cooking?* ◇ *a gas fire*
3 (*also* **gasoline** /'gæsəliːn/) *American English* for PETROL

gasp /gɑːsp/ *verb* (**gasps, gasping, gasped** /gɑːspt/)
to breathe in quickly and noisily through your mouth: *She gasped in surprise when she heard the news.* ◇ *He was gasping for air when they pulled him out of the water.*
▸ **gasp** *noun*: *a gasp of surprise*

gas station /'gæs steɪʃn/ *American English* for PETROL STATION

gate 0🔑 /geɪt/ *noun*
1 a thing like a door in a fence or wall, that opens so that you can go through: *Please close the gate.* ⊃ Look at the picture at **fence**.
2 a door in an airport that you go through to reach the plane: *Please go to gate 15.*

gateway /'geɪtweɪ/ *noun*
a way in or out of a place

gather /'gæðə(r)/ *verb* (**gathers, gathering, gathered** /'gæðəd/)
1 to come together in a group: *We all gathered round to listen to the teacher.*
2 to bring together things that are in different places: *Can you gather up all the books and papers?*

3 to believe or understand something: *I gather that you know my sister.*

gathering /'gæðərɪŋ/ *noun*
a time when people come together; a meeting: *a family gathering* ◇ *There was a large gathering outside the palace.*

gauge¹ /geɪdʒ/ *noun*
an instrument that measures how much of something there is: *Where is the petrol gauge in this car?*

gauge² /geɪdʒ/ *verb* (**gauges, gauging, gauged** /geɪdʒd/)
to judge, calculate, or guess something: *It was hard to gauge the mood of the audience.*

gave form of GIVE

gay /geɪ/ *adjective*
attracted to people of the same sex
⊃ SAME MEANING **homosexual**

gaze /geɪz/ *verb* (**gazes, gazing, gazed** /geɪzd/)
to look at somebody or something for a long time: *She sat and gazed out of the window.* ◇ *He was gazing at her.* ⊃ Look at the note at **stare**.

GCSE /ˌdʒiː siː es 'iː/ *noun*
an examination in one subject that children at schools in the UK take when they are 16: *I've got eight GCSEs.* ⊃ 'GCSE' is short for **General Certificate of Secondary Education**. ⊃ Look at **A level**.

gear /gɪə(r)/ *noun*
1 (*plural* **gears**) the parts in a car engine or a bicycle that control how fast the wheels turn round: *You need to change gear to get up the hill in this car.*
2 (*no plural*) special clothes or equipment that you need for a job or sport: *camping gear*

geek /giːk/ *noun* (*informal*)
a person who spends a lot of time on a particular interest and who is not popular or fashionable ⊃ SAME MEANING **nerd**: *a computer geek*

geese plural of GOOSE

gel /dʒel/ *noun* (*no plural*)
1 a thick liquid that you put on your hair to keep it in shape: *hair gel*
2 a thick liquid that you can use to wash your body instead of soap: *shower gel*

gem /dʒem/ *noun*
a stone that is very valuable and can be made into jewellery ⊃ SAME MEANING **jewel**

gender /'dʒendə(r)/ *noun*
the fact of being male or female

gene /dʒiːn/ *noun*
one of the parts inside a cell that control what a living thing will be like. **Genes** are

passed from parents to children: *The colour of your eyes is decided by your genes.* ➔ Look at **genetic**.

general¹ 0️⃣ /'dʒenrəl/ *adjective*
1 of, by or for most people or things: *Is this car park for general use?*
2 not in detail: *Can you give me a general idea of what the book is about?*
in general usually: *I don't eat much meat in general.*

general² /'dʒenrəl/ *noun*
a very important officer in the army

general election /ˌdʒenrəl ɪ'lekʃn/ *noun*
a time when people choose a new government: *Did you vote in the last general election?*

general knowledge /ˌdʒenrəl 'nɒlɪdʒ/ *noun* (*no plural*)
what you know about a lot of different things

generally 0️⃣ /'dʒenrəli/ *adverb*
usually; mostly: *I generally get up at about eight o'clock.*

generate /'dʒenəreɪt/ *verb* (generates, generating, generated)
to make something such as heat or electricity: *Power stations generate electricity.*

generation /ˌdʒenə'reɪʃn/ *noun*
all the people in a family, group or country who were born at about the same time: *This photo shows three generations of my family.* ◇ *The younger generation don't seem to be interested in politics.*

generator /'dʒenəreɪtə(r)/ *noun*
a machine that produces electricity

generosity /ˌdʒenə'rɒsəti/ *noun* (*no plural*)
liking to give things to other people

generous 0️⃣ /'dʒenərəs/ *adjective*
always ready to give people things or to spend money: *a generous gift* ◇ *It was generous of your parents to pay for the meal.* ➔ OPPOSITE **mean**
▶ **generously** /'dʒenərəsli/ *adverb*: *Please give generously.*

genetic /dʒə'netɪk/ *adjective*
connected with the parts in the cells of living things (called **genes**) that control what a person, animal or plant will be like: *The disease has a genetic origin.*

genetics /dʒə'netɪks/ *noun* (*no plural*)
the scientific study of the way that the development of living things is controlled by qualities that have been passed on from parents to children ➔ Look at **gene**.

genie /'dʒiːni/ *noun*
a spirit with magic powers, especially one that lives in a bottle or a lamp

genius /'dʒiːniəs/ *noun* (*plural* geniuses)
a very clever person: *Einstein was a genius.*

gentle 0️⃣ /'dʒentl/ *adjective* (gentler, gentlest)
1 quiet and kind: *Be gentle with the baby.* ◇ *a gentle voice*
2 not strong or unpleasant: *It was a hot day, but there was a gentle breeze* (= a soft wind).
▶ **gently** /'dʒentli/ *adverb*: *She stroked the kitten very gently.*

gentleman /'dʒentlmən/ *noun* (*plural* gentlemen /'dʒentlmən/)
1 a man who is polite and kind to other people: *He's a real gentleman.*
2 (*formal*) a polite way of saying 'man': *There is a gentleman here to see you.* ◇ **Ladies and gentlemen**... (= at the beginning of a speech) ➔ Look at **lady**.

gents /dʒents/ *noun* (*no plural*) (*British, informal*)
the gents a public toilet for men: *Do you know where the gents is, please?* ➔ Look at **ladies**.

genuine /'dʒenjuɪn/ *adjective*
real and true: *The painting was found to be genuine.* ➔ OPPOSITE **fake**
▶ **genuinely** /'dʒenjuɪnli/ *adverb* really: *Do you think he's genuinely sorry?*

geography /dʒi'ɒɡrəfi/ *noun* (*no plural*)
the study of the Earth and everything on it, such as mountains, rivers, land and people
▶ **geographical** /ˌdʒiːə'ɡræfɪkl/ *adjective*: *There is a list of geographical names* (= names of countries, seas, etc.) *at the back of this dictionary.*

geology /dʒi'ɒlədʒi/ *noun* (*no plural*)
the study of rocks and soil and how they were made
▶ **geologist** /dʒi'ɒlədʒɪst/ *noun* a person who studies or knows a lot about GEOLOGY

geometry /dʒi'ɒmətri/ *noun* (*no plural*)
the study in mathematics of things like lines, shapes and angles

geranium /dʒə'reɪniəm/ *noun*
a plant with red, white or pink flowers

germ /dʒɜːm/ *noun*
a very small living thing that can make you ill: *flu germs*

German measles /ˌdʒɜːmən 'miːzlz/ *noun* (*no plural*)
a disease that causes red spots all over the body: *Jane's got German measles.*

gesture¹ /'dʒestʃə(r)/ *noun*
a movement of your head or hand to show

how you feel or what you want: *The boy made a **rude gesture** before running off.*

gesture² /ˈdʒestʃə(r)/ *verb*
to point at something or make a sign to somebody: *She asked me to sit down and **gestured towards** a chair.*

get 0ᴜ /get/ *verb* (**gets, getting, got** /gɒt/, **has got**) (*British*) (*American* **has gotten** /ˈgɒtn/)
1 to buy or take something: *Will you get some bread when you go shopping?*
2 to receive something: *I got a lot of presents for my birthday.*
3 to go and bring back somebody or something ➲ SAME MEANING **fetch**: *Jenny will get the children from school.*
4 to become: *He is getting fat.* ◇ *Mum got angry.* ◇ *It's getting cold.*
5 to arrive somewhere: *We **got to** London at ten o'clock.*
6 a word that you use with part of another verb to show that something happens to somebody or something: *She got caught by the police.*
7 to make somebody do something: *I **got** Peter **to** help me.*
8 to start to have an illness: *I think I'm getting a cold.*
9 to travel on something such as a train or a bus: *I didn't walk – I got the bus.*
10 to understand or hear something: *I don't **get** the joke.*
get away with something to do something bad and not be punished for it: *He lied but he got away with it.*
get back to return: *When did you get back from your holiday?*
get in to reach a place ➲ SAME MEANING **arrive**: *My train got in at 7.15.*
get in, get into something to climb into a car: *Tom got into the car.*
get off, get off something to leave something such as a train, bus, or bicycle: *Where did you get off the bus?*
get on
1 words that you use to say or ask how well somebody does something: *Patrick is getting on well at school.* ◇ *How did you get on in the exam?*
2 to become old: *My grandfather is getting on – he's nearly 80.*
get on, get onto something to climb onto a bus, train, or bicycle: *I got on the train.*
get on with somebody to live or work in a friendly way with somebody: *We get on well with our neighbours.*
get out, get out of something to leave a car: *I opened the door and got out.*

get out of something to not do something that you do not like: *I'll come swimming with you if I can get out of cleaning my room.*
get something out to take something from the place where it was: *She opened her bag and got out a pen.*
get over something to become well or happy again after you have been ill or sad: *He still hasn't got over his wife's death.*
get through to be able to speak to somebody on the telephone: *I tried to ring Kate but I couldn't get through.*
get through something to use or finish a certain amount of something: *I got through a lot of work today.*
get together to meet; to come together in a group: *The whole family got together for Christmas.*
get up
1 to stand up: *He got up to let an elderly lady sit down.*
2 to get out of bed: *What time do you usually get up?*
get up to something
1 to do something, usually something bad: *I must go and see what the children are getting up to.*
2 to reach a particular place, for example in a book: *I've got up to page 180.*

ghetto /ˈgetəʊ/ *noun* (*plural* **ghettos** or **ghettoes**)
a part of a city where many poor people live

ghost /gəʊst/ *noun*
the form of a dead person that a living person thinks they see: *Do you believe in ghosts?*
▶ **ghostly** /ˈgəʊstli/ *adjective*: *ghostly noises*

giant¹ /ˈdʒaɪənt/ *noun*
(in stories) a very big tall person

giant² /ˈdʒaɪənt/ *adjective*
very big: *a giant insect*

gift 0ᴜ /gɪft/ *noun*
1 something that you give to or get from somebody ➲ SAME MEANING **present**: *This week's magazine comes with a special free gift.* ➲ Look at the picture at **present²**.
2 the natural ability to do something well: *She has a **gift** for languages.*

gigantic /dʒaɪˈgæntɪk/ *adjective*
very big: *gigantic trees*

🔎 **WORD BUILDING**
Other words that also mean 'very big' are: **enormous**, **huge** and **massive**.

giggle /ˈgɪgl/ *verb* (giggles, giggling, giggled /ˈgɪgld/)
to laugh in a silly way: *The children couldn't stop giggling.*
▶ **giggle** *noun*: *There was a giggle from the back of the class.*

gill /gɪl/ *noun*
the part on each side of a fish that it breathes through ⊃ Look at the picture at **fish**.

ginger¹ /ˈdʒɪndʒə(r)/ *noun* (no plural)
a plant with a hot strong taste, that is used in cooking: *a ginger biscuit*

ginger² /ˈdʒɪndʒə(r)/ *adjective*
with a colour between brown and orange: *My brother has got ginger hair.*

Gipsy /ˈdʒɪpsi/ = GYPSY

giraffe /dʒəˈrɑːf/ *noun*
a big animal from Africa with a very long neck and long legs ⊃ Look at Picture Dictionary page **P3**.

girl 0̶ₘ /gɜːl/ *noun*
a female child; a young woman: *They have three children, two girls and a boy.* ◇ *I lived in this house as a girl.*

girlfriend 0̶ₘ /ˈgɜːlfrend/ *noun*
a girl or woman who somebody has a romantic relationship with: *Have you got a girlfriend?*

Girl Guide /ˌgɜːl ˈgaɪd/ (*British*) = GUIDE¹(4)

Girl Scout /ˌgɜːl ˈskaʊt/ *American English* for GUIDE¹(4)

give 0̶ₘ /gɪv/ *verb* (gives, giving, gave /geɪv/, has given /ˈgɪvn/)
1 to let somebody have something: *She gave me a watch for my birthday.* ◇ *I gave my ticket to the man at the door.* ◇ *Give the letter to your mother when you've read it.*
2 to make a sound or movement: *Jo gave me an angry look.* ◇ *He gave a shout.* ◇ *She gave him a kiss.*
3 to make somebody have or feel something: *That noise is giving me a headache.* ◇ *Whatever gave you that idea?*
give something away to give something to somebody without getting money for it: *I've given all my old clothes away.*
give somebody back something, **give something back to somebody** to return something to somebody: *Can you give me back that book I lent you?*
give in to accept or agree to something that you did not want to accept or agree to: *My parents finally gave in and said I could go to the party.*

give something in (*British*) to give something to the person who is collecting it: *We have to give our essays in today.*
give something out to give something to a lot of people: *Could you give out these books to the class, please?*
give up to stop trying to do something: *I give up – what's the answer?*
give something up to stop doing or having something: *He's trying to give up smoking.*

given name /ˈgɪvn neɪm/ *another word for* FIRST NAME

glacier /ˈglæsiə(r)/ *noun*
a large river of ice that moves slowly down a mountain

glad /glæd/ *adjective*
happy about something ⊃ SAME MEANING **pleased**: *He was glad to see us.*

> 🔎 **WORD BUILDING**
> You are usually **glad** or **pleased** about a particular event or situation: *I'm glad that he's feeling better.* ◇ *I'm pleased to say that you've passed your exam.*
> You use **happy** to describe a state of mind: *I always feel happy when the sun is shining* or before a noun: *a happy child.*

▶ **gladly** /ˈglædli/ *adverb* If you do something **gladly**, you are happy to do it: *I'll gladly help you.*

glamorous /ˈglæmərəs/ *adjective*
attractive in an exciting way: *a glamorous model* ◇ *Making films is less glamorous than people think.*

glamour (*British*) (*American* **glamor**) /ˈglæmə(r)/ *noun* (no plural)
the quality of seeming to be more exciting and attractive than ordinary things and people: *Young people are attracted by the glamour of city life.*

glance¹ /glɑːns/ *verb* (glances, glancing, glanced /glɑːnst/)
to look quickly at somebody or something: *Sue glanced at her watch.* ⊃ Look at the note at **gaze**.

glance² /glɑːns/ *noun*
a quick look: *a glance at the newspaper*
at a glance immediately; with only a quick look: *I could see at a glance that he was ill.*

glare¹ /gleə(r)/ *verb* (glares, glaring, glared /gleəd/)
1 to look at somebody in an angry way: *He glared at the children.*
2 to shine with a bright light that hurts your eyes: *The sun glared down.*

A B C D E F **G** H I J K L M N O P Q R S T U V W X Y Z

glare² /gleə(r)/ *noun*
1 (*no plural*) strong light that hurts your eyes: *the glare of the car's headlights*
2 (*plural* **glares**) a long, angry look: *I tried to say something, but he gave me a glare.*

glaring /'gleərɪŋ/ *adjective*
1 very bad and easy to notice: *The article was full of glaring mistakes.*
2 A **glaring** light is very bright and hurts your eyes: *a glaring white light*

glass 0‒ /glɑːs/
noun

glass

1 (*no plural*) hard material that you can see through. Bottles and windows are made of **glass**: *I cut myself on some broken glass.* ◇ *a glass jar*
2 (*plural* **glasses**) a

a glass of milk

thing made of glass that you drink from: *Could I have **a glass of** milk, please?* ◇ *a wine glass*

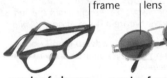

glasses

frame | lens

a pair of glasses   a pair of sunglasses

glasses 0‒ /'glɑːsɪz/ *noun* (*plural*)
two pieces of glass or plastic (called **lenses**) in a frame that people wear over their eyes to help them see better: *Does she **wear glasses**?*
➔ Look also at **sunglasses**.

🔎 **GRAMMAR**
Be careful! You cannot say 'a glasses'. You can say **a pair of glasses**: *I need a new pair of glasses* or *I need some new glasses.*

gleam /gliːm/ *verb* (**gleams**, **gleaming**, **gleamed** /gliːmd/)
to shine with a soft light: *The moonlight gleamed on the lake.*
▶ **gleam** *noun*: *I could see a gleam of light through the trees.*

glee /gliː/ *noun* (*no plural*)
a feeling of happiness, especially when something bad happens to somebody else: *She couldn't hide her glee when her rival came last.*

glide /glaɪd/ *verb* (**glides**, **gliding**, **glided**)
1 to move smoothly and quietly: *The dancers glided across the floor.*

2 to fly in a GLIDER: *I always wanted to go gliding.*

glider /'glaɪdə(r)/ *noun*
a plane without an engine

glimmer /'glɪmə(r)/ *noun*
1 a small, weak light
2 a small sign of something: *There's still a glimmer of hope.*
▶ **glimmer** *verb* (**glimmers**, **glimmering**, **glimmered** /'glɪməd/): *A light glimmered in the distance.*

glimpse /glɪmps/ *noun*
a view of somebody or something that is quick and not clear: *I **caught a glimpse of** myself in the mirror.*
▶ **glimpse** *verb* (**glimpses**, **glimpsing**, **glimpsed** /glɪmpst/): *I just glimpsed him in the crowd.*

glisten /'glɪsn/ *verb* (**glistens**, **glistening**, **glistened** /'glɪsnd/)
(used about wet surfaces) to shine: *His eyes glistened with tears.*

glitter /'glɪtə(r)/ *verb* (**glitters**, **glittering**, **glittered** /'glɪtəd/)
to shine brightly with a lot of small flashes of light: *The broken glass glittered in the sun.*
▶ **glitter** *noun* (*no plural*): *the glitter of jewels*

glittering /'glɪtərɪŋ/ *adjective*
1 very impressive or successful: *a glittering career*
2 shining with a lot of small flashes of light

global /'gləʊbl/ *adjective*
of or about the whole world: *Pollution is a global problem.*

global warming /ˌgləʊbl 'wɔːmɪŋ/ *noun* (*no plural*)
the fact that the earth's atmosphere is getting hotter because of increases in certain gases ➔ Look at **greenhouse effect**.

globe /gləʊb/ *noun*
1 (*plural* **globes**) a round object with a map of the world on it
2 **the globe** (*no plural*) the world: *He's travelled all over the globe.*

gloomy /'gluːmi/ *adjective* (**gloomier**, **gloomiest**)
1 dark and sad: *What a gloomy day!*
2 sad and without hope: *He's feeling very gloomy because he can't get a job.*
▶ **gloomily** /'gluːmɪli/ *adverb*: *She looked gloomily out of the window at the rain.*

glorious /'glɔːriəs/ *adjective*
1 (*formal*) famous and full of GLORY: *a glorious history*
2 wonderful or beautiful: *The weather was glorious.*

glory /'glɔːri/ *noun* (*no plural*)
1 FAME (= being known by many people) and respect that you get when you do great things: *The winning team came home covered in glory.*
2 great beauty: *Autumn is the best time to see the forest in all its glory.*

glossary /'glɒsəri/ *noun* (*plural* glossaries)
a list of difficult words and their meanings, especially at the end of a book

glossy /'glɒsi/ *adjective* (glossier, glossiest)
smooth and shiny: *glossy hair*

gloves

a pair of gloves

glove ⚬━ /glʌv/ *noun*
a thing that you wear to keep your hand warm or safe: *I need a new pair of gloves.* ◇ *rubber gloves*

glow /gləʊ/ *verb* (glows, glowing, glowed /gləʊd/)
to send out soft light or heat without flames or smoke: *His cigarette glowed in the dark.*
▸ **glow** *noun*: *the glow of the sky at sunset*

glowing /'gləʊɪŋ/ *adjective*
saying that somebody or something is very good: *His teacher wrote a glowing report about his work.*

glue¹ /gluː/ *noun* (*no plural*)
a thick liquid that you use for sticking things together

glue² /gluː/ *verb* (glues, gluing, glued /gluːd/)
to stick one thing to another thing with glue: *Glue the two pieces of wood together.*

glum /glʌm/ *adjective* (glummer, glummest)
sad and quiet: *Why are you looking so glum?*
▸ **glumly** /'glʌmli/ *adverb*

GM /ˌdʒiː ˈem/ *abbreviation*
(used about food and plants) grown from cells whose parts that contain information (called **genes**) have been changed: *GM crops* ➔ 'GM' is short for **genetically modified**.

GMT /ˌdʒiː em ˈtiː/ *abbreviation*
the time system that is used in Britain during the winter and for calculating the time in other parts of the world ➔ 'GMT' is short for **Greenwich Mean Time**.

gnaw /nɔː/ *verb* (gnaws, gnawing, gnawed /nɔːd/)
to bite something for a long time: *The dog was gnawing a bone.*

go¹ ⚬━ /gəʊ/ *verb* (goes, going, went /went/, **has gone** /gɒn/)
1 to move from one place to another: *I went to London by train.* ◇ *Her new car goes very fast.*
2 to travel to a place to do something: *Paul has gone shopping.* ◇ *Are you going to Dave's party?* ◇ *I'll go and make some coffee.*
3 to leave a place: *I must go now – it's four o'clock.* ◇ *What time does the train go?*
4 to become: *Her hair has gone grey.*
5 to have as its place: *'Where do these plates go?' 'In that cupboard.'*
6 to lead to a place: *Does this road go to the station?*
7 (used about a machine, etc.) to work: *Jane dropped the clock and now it doesn't go.*
8 to happen in a certain way: *How is your new job going?* ◇ *The week went very quickly.*
9 to disappear: *My headache has gone.*
10 to be or look good with something else ➔ SAME MEANING **match**: *Does this jumper go with my skirt?*
11 to make a certain sound: *Cows go 'moo'.*
be going to
1 words that show what you plan to do in the future: *Joe's going to cook the dinner tonight.*
2 words that you use when you are sure that something will happen in the future: *It's going to rain.*
go ahead to begin or continue to do something: *'Can I borrow your pen?' 'Sure, go ahead.'*
go away to leave a person or place; to leave the place where you live for at least one night: *Go away! I'm doing my homework.* ◇ *They have gone away for the weekend.*
go back to return to a place where you were before: *We're going back to school tomorrow.*
go by to pass: *The holidays went by very quickly.*

A

B

C

D

E

F

G

H

I

J

K

L

M

N

O

P

Q

R

S

T

U

V

W

X

Y

Z

go down well to be something that people like: *The film went down very well in the US.*

go off

1 to explode: *A bomb went off in the station today.*

2 When food or drink **goes off**, it becomes too old to eat or drink: *This milk has gone off – it smells horrible.*

go off somebody or **something** to stop liking somebody or something: *I've really gone off meat lately.*

go on

1 to happen: *What's going on?*

2 to continue: *I went on working.*

3 words that you use when you want somebody to do something: *Oh, go on! Come to the party with me!*

go out

1 to leave the place where you live or work for a short time, returning on the same day: *I went out for a walk.* ◇ *We're going out tonight.*

2 to stop shining or burning: *The fire has gone out.*

go out with somebody to have somebody as a boyfriend or girlfriend: *She's going out with a boy at school.*

go over something to look at or explain something carefully from the beginning to the end ⊃ SAME MEANING **go through something**: *Go over your work before you give it to the teacher.*

go round

1 to be enough for everybody: *Is there enough wine to go round?*

2 to go to somebody's home: *We're going round to Jo's this evening.*

go through something

1 to look at or explain something carefully from the beginning to the end ⊃ SAME MEANING **go over something**: *The teacher went through our homework.*

2 to have a bad experience: *She went through a difficult time when her mother was ill.*

go up to become higher or more ⊃ SAME MEANING **rise**: *The price of petrol has gone up again.* ⊃ Look at the note at **been**.

go² /gəʊ/ *noun* (*plural* **goes**) (*British*)
the time when a person should move or play in a game or an activity ⊃ SAME MEANING **turn**: *Get off the bike – it's my go!*

have a go (*British, informal*) to try to do something: *I'll have a go at mending your bike.*

in one go (*informal*) all together at one time: *They ate the packet of biscuits all in one go.*

goal

goalkeeper

goal 0̶ /gəʊl/ *noun*

1 the place where the ball must go to win a point in a game like football: *He kicked the ball into the goal.*

2 a point that a team wins in a game like football when the ball goes into the goal: *Liverpool won by three goals to two.*

3 something that you want to do very much: *She has finally **achieved** her **goal** of taking part in the Olympics.*

goalkeeper /ˈgəʊlkiːpə(r)/ *noun*
a player in a game like football who tries to stop the ball from going into the goal

goat

kid

goat /gəʊt/ *noun*
an animal with horns. People keep **goats** for their milk. ⊃ A young goat is called a **kid**.

god 0̶ /gɒd/ *noun*

1 God (*no plural*) the one great spirit that Christians, Jews and Muslims believe made the world: *Do you believe in God?*

2 (*plural* **gods**) a spirit or force that people believe has power over them and nature: *Mars was the Roman god of war.*

goddess /ˈgɒdes/ *noun* (*plural* **goddesses**)
a female god: *Venus was the Roman goddess of love.*

godparent /ˈgɒdpeərənt/ (*also* **godfather** /ˈgɒdfɑːðə(r)/ **godmother** /ˈgɒdmʌðə(r)/) *noun*
a person that parents choose to help their

child and teach them about the Christian religion

goes *form of* GO¹

goggles /ˈɡɒɡlz/ *noun* (*plural*)
big glasses that you wear so that water, dust, or wind cannot get in your eyes: *I always wear goggles when I swim.* ➔ Look at the picture at **ski**.

going *form of* GO¹

gold 0-ᴙ /ɡəʊld/ *noun* (*no plural*)
a yellow metal that is very valuable: *Is your ring made of gold?* ◇ *a gold watch*
▸ **gold** *adjective* with the colour of gold: *gold paint*

golden /ˈɡəʊldən/ *adjective*
1 made of gold: *a golden crown*
2 with the colour of gold: *golden hair*

goldfish /ˈɡəʊldfɪʃ/ *noun* (*plural* **goldfish**)
a small orange fish that people keep as a pet

golf /ɡɒlf/ *noun* (*no plural*)
a game that you play by hitting a small ball into holes with a long stick (called a **golf club**): *My mother plays golf on Sundays.*
▸ **golfer** /ˈɡɒlfə(r)/ *noun*: *He's a keen golfer.*
➔ Look at Picture Dictionary page **P15**.

golf course /ˈɡɒlf kɔːs/ *noun*
a large piece of land, covered in grass, where people play GOLF

gone *form of* GO¹

good¹ 0-ᴙ /ɡʊd/ *adjective* (**better**, **best**)
1 done or made very well: *It's a good knife – it cuts very well.* ◇ *The film was **really good**.*
2 pleasant or enjoyable ➔ SAME MEANING **nice**: *Did you have a good time?* ◇ *The weather was very good.*
3 able to do something well: *She's a good driver.* ◇ *James is very good at tennis.*
4 kind, or doing the right thing: *It's good of you to help.* ◇ *The children were very good while you were out.*
5 right or suitable: *This is a good place for a picnic.*
6 having a useful or helpful effect: *Fresh fruit and vegetables are good for you.*
7 a word that you use when you are pleased: *Is everyone here? Good. Now let's begin.*

> 🔎 SPEAKING
> We often say **brilliant**, **fantastic**, **great** or **terrific** instead of 'very good'.

➔ The adverb is **well**.

good² 0-ᴙ /ɡʊd/ *noun* (*no plural*)
something that is right or helpful: *They know the difference between good and bad.*
be no good, **not be any good** to not be useful: *This jumper isn't any good. It's too*

small. ◇ *It's no good asking Mum for money – she hasn't got any.*
do somebody good to make somebody well or happy: *It will do you good to go to bed early tonight.*
for good for ever: *She has left home for good.*

good afternoon /ˌɡʊd ɑːftəˈnuːn/ *exclamation* (*formal*)
words that you say when you see or speak to somebody in the afternoon

> 🔎 SPEAKING
> We sometimes just say **Afternoon**: '*Good afternoon, Alison.*' '*Afternoon, Colin.*'
> When we see friends we usually say **Hello** or **Hi** instead of **Good morning** or **Good afternoon**.
> When we meet somebody we don't know for the first time we say **How do you do?** or **Pleased to meet you**.

goodbye 0-ᴙ /ˌɡʊdˈbaɪ/ *exclamation*
a word that you say when somebody goes away, or when you go away: *Goodbye! See you tomorrow.*

> 🔎 SPEAKING
> We sometimes just say **Bye**: *Bye, Paddy. See you tomorrow.*

good evening /ˌɡʊd ˈiːvnɪŋ/ *exclamation* (*formal*)
words that you say when you see or speak to somebody in the evening

> 🔎 SPEAKING
> We sometimes just say **Evening**: '*Good evening, Mr James.*' '*Evening, Miss Evans.*'

good-looking /ˌɡʊd ˈlʊkɪŋ/ *adjective*
(used about people) nice to look at: *He's a good-looking boy.* ➔ SAME MEANING **attractive** ➔ Look at the note at **beautiful**.

good morning /ˌɡʊd ˈmɔːnɪŋ/ *exclamation* (*formal*)
words that you say when you see or speak to somebody in the morning ➔ Look at the note at **good afternoon**.

> 🔎 SPEAKING
> We sometimes just say **Morning**: '*Good morning, Jack.*' '*Morning.*'

goodness /ˈɡʊdnəs/ *noun* (*no plural*)
1 being good or kind
2 something in food that is good for your health: *Fresh vegetables have a lot of goodness in them.*
for goodness' sake words that show anger: *For goodness' sake, hurry up!*

A B C D E F **G** H I J K L M N O P Q R S T U V W X Y Z

A
B
C
D
E
F
G
H
I
J
K
L
M
N
O
P
Q
R
S
T
U
V
W
X
Y
Z

goodness, **goodness me** words that show surprise: *Goodness! What a big cake!*
thank goodness words that show you are happy because a problem or danger has gone away: *Thank goodness it's stopped raining.*

goodnight /ˌɡʊdˈnaɪt/ *exclamation*
words that you say when you leave somebody in the evening or when somebody is going to bed

> 🗩 SPEAKING
> We sometimes just say **Night** or **Night night**: *'Goodnight, Giles. Sleep well.'* *'Night.'*

goods 0🛒 /ɡʊdz/ *noun* (*plural*)
1 things that you buy or sell: *That shop sells electrical goods.*
2 things that a train or lorry carries: *a goods train*

goose /ɡuːs/ *noun* (*plural* **geese** /ɡiːs/)
a big bird with a long neck. People keep **geese** on farms for their eggs and meat. ⊃ Look at Picture Dictionary page **P2**.

gooseberry /ˈɡʊzbəri/ *noun* (*plural* **gooseberries**)
a small green fruit with a sharp taste ⊃ Look at Picture Dictionary page **P8**.

gorgeous /ˈɡɔːdʒəs/ *adjective* (*informal*)
very good or attractive ⊃ SAME MEANING **lovely**: *The weather was gorgeous!* ◇ *What a gorgeous dress!*

gorilla

gorilla /ɡəˈrɪlə/ *noun*
an African animal like a very big black MONKEY

gory /ˈɡɔːri/ *adjective* (**gorier**, **goriest**)
full of violence and blood: *It's the goriest film I've ever seen.*

gosh /ɡɒʃ/ *exclamation*
a word that shows surprise: *Gosh! What a big house!*

gossip /ˈɡɒsɪp/ *noun* (*no plural*)
talk about other people that is often unkind or not true: *Have you heard the latest gossip about her?*
▶ **gossip** *verb* (**gossips**, **gossiping**, **gossiped** /ˈɡɒsɪpt/): *They were gossiping about Jane's new boyfriend.*

got form of GET

gotten /ˈɡɒtn/ (*American*) form of GET

govern /ˈɡʌvn/ *verb* (**governs**, **governing**, **governed** /ˈɡʌvnd/)
to officially rule or control a country or part of a country: *Britain is governed by Parliament.*

government 0🛒 /ˈɡʌvənmənt/ *noun*
often **the Government** the group of people who officially rule or control a country: *The leaders of the European governments are meeting today in Brussels.*

> 🗩 GRAMMAR
> **Government** can be used with a singular or a plural verb: *The Government has failed to act.* ◇ *The Government are discussing the problem.*

governor /ˈɡʌvənə(r)/ *noun*
1 a person who rules or controls part of a country (especially in the US): *the Governor of California*
2 a person who controls a place like a prison or school

gown /ɡaʊn/ *noun*
1 a long dress that a woman wears at a special time: *a ball gown*
2 a long loose piece of clothing that people wear to do a special job. Judges, doctors and teachers sometimes wear **gowns**.

gown

GP /ˌdʒiː ˈpiː/ *noun*
a doctor who treats all types of illnesses and works in a town or village, not in a hospital ⊃ **GP** is short for 'General Practitioner'.

grab /græb/ *verb* (grabs, grabbing, grabbed /græbd/)
to take something in a rough and sudden way: *The thief grabbed her bag and ran away.*

grace /greɪs/ *noun* (*no plural*)
1 a beautiful way of moving: *She dances with grace.*
2 thanks to God that people say before or after they eat: *Let's say grace.*

graceful /'greɪsfl/ *adjective*
A person or thing that is **graceful** moves in a smooth and beautiful way: *a graceful dancer*
▶ **gracefully** /'greɪsfəli/ *adverb*: *He moves very gracefully.*

gracious /'greɪʃəs/ *adjective*
(used about people's behaviour) kind and polite: *a gracious smile*
▶ **graciously** /'greɪʃəsli/ *adverb*: *She accepted the invitation graciously.*

grade¹ 0⟿ /greɪd/ *noun*
1 the level or quality of something: *Which grade of petrol does your car use? ◇ We use only high-grade materials.*
2 a number or letter that a teacher gives for your work to show how good it is
➔ SAME MEANING **mark**: *She got very good grades in all her exams.*
3 (*American*) (*British* year) a class in a school in the US where all the children are the same age: *My sister is in the fifth grade.*

grade² /greɪd/ *verb* (grades, grading, graded)
to sort things or people into sizes or kinds: *The eggs are graded by size.*

gradual /'grædʒuəl/ *adjective*
happening slowly: *There has been a gradual increase in prices.* ➔ OPPOSITE **sudden**

gradually /'grædʒuəli/ *adverb*
slowly, over a long period of time: *Life gradually returned to normal.*

graduate¹ /'grædʒuət/ *noun*
1 a person who has finished studying at a university or college and who has passed their last exams: *an Oxford graduate*
2 (*American*) a person who has finished their school studies: *a high school graduate*

graduate² /'grædʒueɪt/ *verb* (graduates, graduating, graduated)
to finish your studies at a university or college and pass your last exams: *I graduated from Exeter University last year.*

graffiti /grə'fiːti/ *noun* (*plural*)
words or pictures that people write or draw on walls: *The walls were covered with graffiti.*

graffiti

grain 0⟿ /greɪn/ *noun*
1 (*no plural*) the seeds of a plant that we eat, for example rice or WHEAT: *The animals are fed on grain.*
2 (*plural* **grains**) a very small hard piece of something: *a grain of sand ◇ grains of rice*

gram 0⟿ (*also* gramme) /græm/ (*abbr.* g) *noun*
a measure of weight. There are 1 000 **grams** in a **kilogram**: *30 g of butter*

grammar 0⟿ /'græmə(r)/ *noun* (*no plural*)

> 🔍 SPELLING
> Remember! You spell **grammar** with **AR** at the end, not **ER**.

the rules that tell you how to put words together when you speak or write

grammar school /'græmə skuːl/ *noun*
(in Britain, especially in the past) a school for children between the ages of 11 and 18 who are good at studying

grammatical /grə'mætɪkl/ *adjective*
1 connected with grammar: *What is the grammatical rule for making plurals in English?*
2 correct because it follows the rules of grammar: *The sentence 'They is happy' is not grammatical.*
▶ **grammatically** /grə'mætɪkli/ *adverb*: *The sentence is grammatically correct.*

gran /græn/ *noun* (*British, informal*)
grandmother

grand /grænd/ *adjective* (grander, grandest)
very big, important or rich: *They live in a grand house in the centre of London.*

grandad /'grændæd/ *noun* (*British, informal*)
grandfather

grandchild /'græntʃaɪld/ *noun* (*plural* **grandchildren** /'græntʃɪldrən/)
the child of your son or daughter

A B C D E F G H I J K L M N O P Q R S T U V W X Y Z

A

granddaughter 0── /'grændɔːtə(r)/
noun
the daughter of your son or daughter

B

grandfather 0── /'grænfɑːðə(r)/ (*also
informal*) grandpa /'grænpɑː/) *noun*
the father of your mother or father

C

D

grandmother 0── /'grænmʌðə(r)/
(*also informal*) grandma /'grænmɑː/) *noun*
the mother of your mother or father

E

F

grandpa *another word for* GRANDFATHER

grandparent /'grænpeərənt/ *noun*
the mother or father of your mother or
father

G

H

grandson 0── /'grænsʌn/ *noun*
the son of your son or daughter

I

granny (*also* grannie /'græni/) *noun*
(*plural* grannies) (*informal*)
grandmother

J

K

grant¹ /grɑːnt/ *verb* (grants, granting,
granted) (*formal*)
to give somebody what they have asked for:
They granted him a visa to leave the country.
take somebody or **something for
granted** to be so used to somebody or
something that you forget you are lucky to
have them: *We tend to take our comfortable
lives for granted.*

L

M

N

O

grant² /grɑːnt/ *noun*
money that you are given for a special
reason: *a student grant* (= to help pay for
study at university)

P

Q

grapes

R

S

T

U

V

W

a bunch of grapes

X

grape /greɪp/ *noun*
a small green or purple fruit that we eat or
make into wine: *a bunch of grapes* ⊃ Look at
Picture Dictionary page **P8**.

Y

Z

grapefruit /'greɪpfruːt/ *noun* (*plural*
grapefruit *or* grapefruits)
a fruit that looks like a big orange, but is
yellow ⊃ Look at Picture Dictionary page **P8**.

graphs

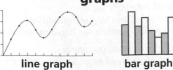

line graph   bar graph

graph /grɑːf/ *noun*
a picture that shows how numbers or
amounts are different from each other

graphics /'græfɪks/ *noun* (*plural*)
drawings, pictures and diagrams, especially
those which are produced by a computer

grasp /grɑːsp/ *verb* (grasps, grasping,
grasped /grɑːspt/)
1 to hold something tightly: *Claire grasped
my arm to stop herself from falling.*
2 to understand something: *He couldn't
grasp what I was saying.*
▸ **grasp** *noun* (*no plural*): *The ball fell from
my grasp.*

grass 0── /grɑːs/ *noun* (*no plural*)
a plant with thin green leaves that covers
fields and gardens. Cows and sheep eat
grass: *Don't walk on the grass.*
▸ **grassy** /'grɑːsi/ *adjective* covered with
grass

grasshopper /'grɑːshɒpə(r)/ *noun*
an insect that can jump high in the air and
makes a sound with its back legs

grate /greɪt/ *verb* (grates, grating,
grated)
If you **grate** food, you rub it over a metal
tool (called a **grater**) so that it is in very
small pieces: *Can you grate some cheese?* ◊
grated carrot

grateful 0── /'greɪtfl/ *adjective*
If you are **grateful**, you feel or show thanks
to somebody: *We are grateful to you for the
help you have given us.* ⊃ The noun is
gratitude. ⊃ OPPOSITE **ungrateful**

grater /'greɪtə(r)/ *noun*
a kitchen tool with holes in it that is used to
cut food into very small pieces by rubbing it
across its surface

gratitude /'grætɪtjuːd/ *noun* (*no plural*)
the feeling of wanting to thank somebody
for something: *We gave David a present to
show our gratitude for all his help.*

grave¹ /greɪv/ *noun*
a hole in the ground where a dead person's
body is buried: *We put flowers on the grave.*
⊃ Look at **tomb**.

grave² /greɪv/ *adjective* (graver, gravest) (*formal*)
very bad or serious: *The children were in **grave** danger.*

🔎 SPEAKING
Serious is the word that we usually use.

gravel /'grævl/ *noun* (*no plural*)
very small stones that are used for making paths and roads

gravestone /'greɪvstəʊn/ *noun*
a piece of stone on a GRAVE that shows the name of the dead person

graveyard /'greɪvjɑːd/ *noun*
a piece of land, usually near a church, where dead people are buried

gravity /'grævəti/ *noun* (*no plural*)
the force that pulls everything towards the earth

gravy /'greɪvi/ *noun* (*no plural*)
a hot brown sauce that you eat with meat

gray 0️⃣ *American English for* GREY

graze /greɪz/ *verb* (grazes, grazing, grazed /greɪzd/)
1 to eat grass: *The sheep were grazing in the fields.*
2 to hurt your skin by rubbing it against something rough: *He fell and grazed his arm.*
▶ **graze** *noun*: *She's got a **graze** on her knee.*

grease /griːs/ *noun* (*no plural*)
fat from animals, or any thick substance that is like oil: *You will need very hot water to get the grease off these plates.*

greasy /'griːsi/ *adjective* (greasier, greasiest)
covered with or containing a lot of GREASE: *Greasy food is not good for you.* ◇ *greasy hair*

great 0️⃣ /greɪt/ *adjective* (greater, greatest)

🔎 PRONUNCIATION
The word **great** sounds like **late**.

1 very large: *It's a great pleasure to meet you.*
2 important or special: *Einstein was a great scientist.*
3 (*informal*) very; very good: *He knows **a great many** people.* ◇ *There's a **great big** dog in the garden!* ◇ *They are great friends.*
4 (*informal*) very nice or enjoyable
⊃ SAME MEANING **wonderful**: *I had a great weekend.* ◇ *It's **great to** see you!*

great- /greɪt/ *prefix*
a word that you put before other words to show some members of a family. For example, your **great-grandmother** is the mother of your grandmother or

grandfather, and your **great-grandson** is the son of your grandson or granddaughter.

greatly /'greɪtli/ *adverb*
very much: *I wasn't greatly surprised to see her there.*

greed /griːd/ *noun* (*no plural*)
the feeling that you want more of something than you need

greedy /'griːdi/ *adjective* (greedier, greediest)
A **greedy** person wants or takes more of something than they need: *She's so greedy – she's eaten all the chocolates!*

green¹ 0️⃣ /griːn/ *adjective* (greener, greenest)
1 with the colour of leaves and grass: *My brother has green eyes.* ◇ *a dark green shirt*
2 covered with grass or other plants: *green fields*
3 connected with protecting the environment or the natural world: *green products* (= that do not damage the environment)

green² /griːn/ *noun*
the colour of leaves and grass: *She was dressed in green.*

greengrocer /'griːnɡrəʊsə(r)/ *noun*
1 a person who sells fruit and vegetables
2 greengrocer's a shop that sells fruit and vegetables

greenhouse /'griːnhaʊs/ *noun* (*plural* greenhouses /'griːnhaʊzɪz/)
a building made of glass, where plants grow

the greenhouse effect /ðə 'griːnhaʊs ɪfekt/ *noun* (*no plural*)
the problem of the earth's atmosphere getting warmer all the time because of the harmful gases that go into the air

greenhouse gas /ˌgriːnhaʊs 'gæs/ *noun* (*plural* greenhouse gases)
one of the harmful gases that are making the earth's atmosphere get warmer

green onion /ˌgriːn 'ʌnjən/ *noun*
American English for SPRING ONION

greet /griːt/ *verb* (greets, greeting, greeted)
to say hello when you meet somebody: *He greeted me with a smile.*

greeting /'griːtɪŋ/ *noun*
1 friendly words that you say when you meet somebody: *'Hello' and 'Good morning' are greetings.*
2 greetings (*plural*) friendly words that you write to somebody at a special time: *a greetings card* (= a card that you send at Christmas or on a birthday, for example)

grew form of GROW

grey 0— (American also **gray**) /greɪ/
adjective (**greyer**, **greyest**)
with a colour like black and white mixed
together: a grey skirt ◇ The sky was grey.
◇ He's starting to **go grey** (= to have grey
hair).
▸ **grey noun**: He was dressed in grey.

grid /grɪd/ **noun**
lines that cross each other to make squares,
for example on a map

grief /griːf/ **noun** (no plural)
great sadness, especially because somebody
has died

grieve /griːv/ **verb** (**grieves**, **grieving**,
grieved /griːvd/)
to feel great sadness, especially because
somebody has died: She is **grieving for** her
dead son.

grill¹ /grɪl/ **noun**
the part of a cooker, or a special metal
object, that you use to you GRILL food

grill² /grɪl/ **verb** (**grills**, **grilling**, **grilled**
/grɪld/)
to cook food such as meat and fish on metal
bars under or over heat: grilled steak

grim /grɪm/ **adjective** (**grimmer**,
grimmest)
1 (used about a person) very serious and not
smiling: a grim expression
2 (used about a situation) very bad and
making you feel worried: The news is grim.

grin /grɪn/ **verb** (**grins**, **grinning**, **grinned**
/grɪnd/)
to have a big smile on your face: She **grinned**
at me.
▸ **grin noun**: He had a big grin on his face.

grind /graɪnd/ **verb** (**grinds**, **grinding**,
ground /graʊnd/, **has ground**)
to make something into very small pieces or
powder by crushing it: They **ground** the
wheat **into** flour. ◇ ground coffee

grip /grɪp/ **verb** (**grips**, **gripping**, **gripped**
/grɪpt/)
to hold something tightly: Marie gripped my
hand as we crossed the road.
▸ **grip noun** (no plural): He kept a **tight grip**
on the rope.

gripping /ˈgrɪpɪŋ/ **adjective**
very exciting, in a way that holds your
attention: a gripping adventure film

grit /grɪt/ **noun** (no plural)
very small pieces of stone

groan /grəʊn/ **verb** (**groans**, **groaning**,
groaned /grəʊnd/)
to make a deep sad sound, for example

because you are unhappy or in pain: 'I've got
a headache,' he groaned.
▸ **groan noun**: She gave a groan, then lay
still.

grocer /ˈgrəʊsə(r)/ **noun**
1 a person who has a shop that sells food
and other things for the home
2 **grocer's** a shop that sells food and other
things for the home ➌ Look at Picture
Dictionary page **P13**.

groceries /ˈgrəʊsəriz/ **noun** (plural)
food and other things for the home that you
buy regularly: Can you help me unload the
groceries from the car, please?

groom /gruːm/ **noun**
1 a person whose job is to look after horses
2 a man on the day of his wedding
➌ SAME MEANING **bridegroom**

groove /gruːv/ **noun**
a long thin cut in the surface of something
hard

grope /grəʊp/ **verb** (**gropes**, **groping**,
groped /grəʊpt/)
to try to find something by using your
hands, when you cannot see: He **groped**
around for the light switch.

ground¹ form of GRIND

ground² 0— /graʊnd/ **noun**
1 (no plural) the surface of the earth: We sat
on the ground to eat our picnic. ◇ The ground
was too dry for the plants to grow.
2 (plural **grounds**) a piece of land that is
used for something special: a sports ground ◇
a playground (= a place where children play)
3 **grounds** (plural) the land around a large
building: the grounds of the hospital

ground floor /ˌgraʊnd ˈflɔː(r)/ **noun**
(British) (American **first floor**)
the part of a building that is at the same level
as the street: My office is **on the ground floor**.

group 0— /gruːp/ **noun**

> 🔎 **PRONUNCIATION**
> The word **group** sounds like **loop**.

1 a number of people or things together:
A **group of** people were standing outside
the shop.
2 a number of people who play music
together ➌ SAME MEANING **band**

grow 0— /grəʊ/ **verb** (**grows**, **growing**,
grew /gruː/, **has grown** /grəʊn/)
1 to become bigger: Children grow very
quickly.
2 When a plant **grows** somewhere, it lives
there: Oranges grow in warm countries.
3 to plant something in the ground and

look after it: *We grow vegetables in our garden.*
4 to allow your hair or nails to grow: *Mark has grown a beard.*
5 to become ⊃ SAME MEANING **get**: *It was growing dark.*
grow into something to get bigger and become something: *Kittens grow into cats.*
grow out of something to become too big to do or wear something: *She's grown out of her shoes.*
grow up to become an adult; to change from a child to a man or woman: *I want to be a doctor when I grow up.*

growl /graʊl/ *verb* (growls, growling, growled /graʊld/)
If a dog **growls**, it makes a low angry sound: *The dog growled at the stranger.*
▶ **growl** *noun*: *The dog gave a low growl.*

grown-up /'grəʊn ʌp/ *noun*
a man or woman, not a child
⊃ SAME MEANING **adult**: *Ask a grown-up to help you.*
▶ **grown-up** /ˌgrəʊn 'ʌp/ *adjective*: *She has a grown-up son.*

growth 0̄⊸ /grəʊθ/ *noun* (no plural)
the process of getting bigger: *A good diet is important for children's growth.* ◇ *population growth*

grub /grʌb/ *noun*
1 (*plural* grubs) a young insect when it comes out of the egg
2 (*no plural*) (*informal*) food

grubby /'grʌbi/ *adjective* (grubbier, grubbiest)
dirty: *grubby hands*

grudge /grʌdʒ/ *noun*
a feeling of anger towards somebody, because of something bad that they have done to you in the past: *I don't bear him a grudge about what happened.*

gruesome /'gruːsəm/ *adjective*
very unpleasant and shocking: *a gruesome murder*

grumble /'grʌmbl/ *verb* (grumbles, grumbling, grumbled /'grʌmbld/)
to say many times that you do not like something: *She's always grumbling about her boss.*

grumpy /'grʌmpi/ *adjective* (grumpier, grumpiest)
a little angry ⊃ SAME MEANING **bad-tempered**: *She gets grumpy when she's tired.*

grunt /grʌnt/ *verb* (grunts, grunting, grunted)
to make a short rough sound, like a pig makes
▶ **grunt** *noun*: *He gave a grunt of pain.*

guarantee¹ /ˌgærən'tiː/ *noun*
1 a promise that something will happen: *I want a guarantee that you will do the work today.*
2 a written promise by a company that it will repair a thing you have bought, or give you a new one, if it goes wrong: *a two-year guarantee* ◇ *The computer is still under guarantee.*

guarantee² /ˌgærən'tiː/ *verb* (guarantees, guaranteeing, guaranteed /ˌgærən'tiːd/)
1 to promise that something will be done or will happen: *I can't guarantee that I will be able to help you, but I'll try.*
2 to say that you will repair a thing that somebody buys, or give them a new one, if it goes wrong: *The television is guaranteed for three years.*

guard¹ 0̄⊸ /gɑːd/ *noun*

> 🔍 **PRONUNCIATION**
> The word **guard** just like the beginning of the word **garden**.

1 a person who keeps somebody or something safe from other people, or who stops somebody from escaping: *There are security guards outside the bank.* ◇ *The soldiers were on guard outside the palace* (= guarding the palace).
2 (*British*) (*American* **conductor**) a person whose job is to look after people and things on a train
be on your guard to be ready if something bad happens

guard² 0̄⊸ /gɑːd/ *verb* (guards, guarding, guarded)
to keep somebody or something safe from other people, or to stop somebody from escaping: *The house was guarded by two large dogs.*

guardian /'gɑːdiən/ *noun*
a person who looks after a child with no parents

guerrilla /gə'rɪlə/ *noun*
a person who is not in an army but who fights secretly against the government or an army

guess 0̄⊸ /ges/ *verb* (guesses, guessing, guessed /gest/)
to give an answer when you do not know if it is right: *Can you guess how old he is?*
▶ **guess** *noun* (*plural* guesses): *If you don't know the answer, have a guess!*

guest 0̄⊸ /gest/ *noun*
1 a person that you invite to your home or to a party or special event: *There were 200 guests at the wedding.*
2 a person who is staying in a hotel

A B C D E F **G** H I J K L M N O P Q R S T U V W X Y Z

guest house /'gest haʊs/ *noun* (*plural* guest houses /'gest haʊzɪz/)
a small hotel

guidance /'gaɪdns/ *noun* (*no plural*)
help and advice: *I want some guidance on how to find a job.*

guide¹ ⊶ /gaɪd/ *noun*
1 a book that tells you about something, or how to do something: *a guide to birdwatching*
2 (*also* guidebook /'gaɪdbʊk/) a book that tells you about a place you are visiting: *a guide to Bangkok*
3 a person who shows other people where to go and tells them about a place: *The guide took us round the castle.*
4 Guide (*also* Girl Guide) (*British*) (*American* Girl Scout) a member of a special club for girls (called the Girl Guides) which does a lot of activities with them, for example camping

guide² ⊶ /gaɪd/ *verb* (guides, guiding, guided)
to show somebody where to go or what to do: *He guided us through the busy streets to our hotel.*

guilt /gɪlt/ *noun* (*no plural*)
1 the feeling you have when you know that you have done something wrong: *She felt terrible guilt after stealing the money.*
2 the fact of having broken the law: *The police could not prove his guilt.*
⊃ OPPOSITE innocence

guilty ⊶ /'gɪlti/ *adjective* (guiltier, guiltiest)
1 If you feel guilty, you feel that you have done something wrong: *I feel guilty about lying to her.*
2 If you are guilty, you have broken the law: *He is guilty of murder.* ⊃ OPPOSITE innocent

guinea pig /'gɪni pɪg/ *noun*
1 a small animal with short ears and no tail, that people often keep as a pet ⊃ Look at Picture Dictionary page P2.
2 a person who is used in an experiment

guitar /gɪ'tɑː(r)/ *noun*
a musical instrument with strings: *I play the guitar in a band.*
▸ guitarist /gɪ'tɑːrɪst/ *noun* a person who plays the GUITAR

gulf /gʌlf/ *noun*
a large part of the sea that has land almost all the way around it: *the Gulf of Mexico*

gull /gʌl/ (*also* seagull) *noun*
a large grey or white bird that lives by the sea

guitars

bass guitar

guitar   electric guitar

gulp /gʌlp/ *verb* (gulps, gulping, gulped /gʌlpt/)
to eat or drink something quickly: *He gulped down a cup of tea and left.*
▸ gulp *noun*: *She took a gulp of coffee.*

gum /gʌm/ *noun*
1 (*plural* gums) Your gums are the hard pink parts of your mouth that hold the teeth.
2 (*no plural*) thick liquid that you use for sticking pieces of paper together
⊃ SAME MEANING glue ⊃ Look also at chewing gum.

gun ⊶ /gʌn/ *noun*
a weapon that shoots out pieces of metal (called bullets) to kill or hurt people or animals: *He aimed the gun at the bird and fired.*

gunman /'gʌnmən/ *noun* (*plural* gunmen /'gʌnmən/)
a man who uses a gun to rob or kill people

gush /gʌʃ/ *verb* (gushes, gushing, gushed /gʌʃt/)
to flow out suddenly and strongly: *Blood was gushing from the cut in her leg.*

gust /gʌst/ *noun*
a sudden strong wind: *A gust of wind blew his hat off.*

guts /gʌts/ *noun* (*plural*) (*informal*)
the courage to do something difficult or unpleasant: *It takes guts to admit you're wrong.*

gutter /'gʌtə(r)/ *noun*
1 a pipe under the edge of a roof to carry away water when it rains
2 the lower part at the edge of a road where water is carried away when it rains

guy /gaɪ/ *noun*
1 (*informal*) a man: *He's a nice guy!*
2 guys (*plural*) (*informal*) used when speaking to a group of men and women or boys and girls: *Come on guys, let's go.*

gym /dʒɪm/ *noun*
  1 (*plural* **gyms**) (*also formal* **gymnasium**
  /dʒɪm'neɪziəm/) a room or building with
  equipment for doing physical exercise
  2 (*no plural*) = GYMNASTICS: *a gym class*

gymnastics /dʒɪm'næstɪks/ *noun* (*also*
  gym) (*no plural*)
  exercises for your body: *a gymnastics
  competition*

⊃ Look at Picture Dictionary page **P15**.
▶ **gymnast** /'dʒɪmnæst/ *noun* a person
who does GYMNASTICS

Gypsy (*also* **Gipsy**) /'dʒɪpsi/ *noun* (*plural*
Gypsies)
Gypsies are people who travel around from
one place to another and live in homes with
wheels (called **caravans**).

A
B
C
D
E
F
G
H
I
J
K
L
M
N
O
P
Q
R
S
T
U
V
W
X
Y
Z

H h

H, h /eɪtʃ/ *noun* (*plural* H's, h's /'eɪtʃɪz/)
the eighth letter of the English alphabet:
'*Hat*' begins with an '*H*'.

habit 0̃ /'hæbɪt/ *noun*
something that you do very often: *Smoking is
a bad habit.* ◇ *She's got a **habit of** phoning me
when I'm in bed.*

habitat /'hæbɪtæt/ *noun*
the natural place where a plant or an animal
lives

hack /hæk/ *verb* (hacks, hacking, hacked
/hækt/)
1 to cut something or somebody in a rough
and violent way: *I hacked the dead branches
off the tree.*
2 to use a computer to get into somebody
else's computer in order to damage it or get
secret information: *He **hacked into** the bank's
computer system.*

had *form of* HAVE

hadn't /'hædnt/ *short for* HAD NOT

haggle /'hægl/ *verb* (haggles, haggling,
haggled /'hægld/)
to argue with somebody until you agree
about the price of something: *Tourists were
haggling over the price of a carpet.*

ha! ha! /ˌhɑː 'hɑː/ *exclamation*
words that you write to show that somebody
is laughing

hail /heɪl/ *noun* (*no plural*)
frozen rain that falls in small hard balls
(called **hailstones**)

▶ **hail** *verb* (hails, hailing, hailed /heɪld/):
It's hailing.

hair 0̃ /heə(r)/ *noun*
1 (*no plural*) all the hairs on a person's head:
She's got long black hair.
2 (*plural* **hairs**) one of the long thin things
that grow on the skin of people and animals:
There's a hair in my soup.

🔎 WORD BUILDING

You wash your hair with **shampoo** and
make it tidy with a **hairbrush** or a **comb**.
Some words that you can use to talk
about the colour of a person's hair are
black, **dark**, **brown**, **ginger**, **red**, **fair**,
blonde and **grey**.

---

hairbrush /'heəbrʌʃ/ *noun* (*plural*
hairbrushes)
a brush that you use to make your hair tidy
⊃ Look at the picture at **brush**.

haircut /'heəkʌt/ *noun*
1 when somebody cuts your hair: *I need a
haircut.*
2 the way that your hair is cut: *I like your new
haircut.*

hairdresser /'heədresə(r)/ *noun*
1 a person whose job is to wash, cut and
arrange people's hair ⊃ Look at **barber**.
2 **hairdresser's** the place where you go to
have your hair cut: *I'm going to the
hairdresser's tomorrow.*

hair

She has a ponytail.

She has long,
straight hair.

fringe (*British*)
bangs (*American*)

She has pigtails/plaits (*British*)
braids (*American*).

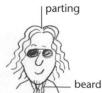

parting

beard

He has wavy hair.

He has short,
curly hair.

moustache (*British*)
mustache (*American*)

He is bald.

hairdryer (*also* hairdrier) /ˈheədraɪə(r)/ *noun*
a machine that dries your hair by blowing hot air on it

hairstyle /ˈheəstaɪl/ *noun*
the way that your hair is cut and arranged

hairy /ˈheəri/ *adjective* (hairier, hairiest)
covered with a lot of hair: *He has got very hairy legs.*

half¹ 0🔑 /hɑːf/ *noun, adjective, pronoun* (*plural* halves /hɑːvz/)

> 🔍 **PRONUNCIATION**
>
> The word **half** sounds like **staff**, because we don't say the letter **l** in this word.

one of two equal parts of something; ½: *Half of six is three.* ◊ *I lived in that flat for two and a half years.* ◊ *The journey takes an hour and a half.* ◊ *I've been waiting more than half an hour.* ◊ *She gave me half of her apple.* ◊ *Half this money is yours.*
in half so that there are two equal parts: *Cut the cake in half.* ⟳ The verb is **halve**.

half past

It's **half past** nine.

half² 0🔑 /hɑːf/ *adverb*
50%; not completely: *The bottle is half empty.* ◊ *He's half German* (= one of his parents is German).
half past 30 minutes after an hour on the clock: *It's half past nine.*

half-price /ˌhɑːf ˈpraɪs/ *adjective, adverb*
for half the usual price: *You can get half-price tickets one hour before the show.*

half-term /ˌhɑːf ˈtɜːm/ *noun* (British)
a short school holiday in the middle of a three-month period of school (called a **term**)

half-time /ˌhɑːf ˈtaɪm/ *noun* (no plural)
a short time in the middle of a game like football, when play stops

halfway /ˌhɑːfˈweɪ/ *adverb*
in the middle: *They live **halfway between** London and Oxford.* ◊ *She went out **halfway through** the lesson.*

hall 0🔑 /hɔːl/ *noun*
1 the room in a house that is near the front door and has doors to other rooms: *You can leave your coat in the hall.* ⟳ Look at Picture Dictionary page **P10**.
2 a big room or building where a lot of people meet: *a concert hall* ◊ *We did our exams in the school hall.*

hallo = HELLO

Halloween (*also* Hallowe'en) /ˌhæləʊˈiːn/ *noun* (no plural)
the night of 31 October

> 🔍 **CULTURE**
>
> People used to believe that dead people appeared from their graves at **Halloween**. Children now dress up as witches, ghosts, etc. and go to people's houses saying '**trick or treat**' and the people give them sweets.

halt /hɔːlt/ *noun* (no plural)
come to a halt to stop: *The car came to a halt in front of the school.*
▶ **halt** *verb* (halts, halting, halted)
(*formal*): *She halted just outside the gate.*

halve /hɑːv/ *verb* (halves, halving, halved /hɑːvd/)
to divide something into two parts that are the same: *There were two of us, so I halved the orange.* ⟳ The noun is **half**.

halves plural of HALF

ham /hæm/ *noun* (no plural)
meat from a pig's leg that you can keep for a long time because salt or smoke was used to prepare it ⟳ Look at the note at **pig**.

hamburger /ˈhæmbɜːɡə(r)/ *noun* (*also* **burger**)
meat cut into very small pieces and made into a flat round shape. You often eat it in a round piece of bread (called a **roll**): *A hamburger and chips, please.*

hammer

A
B
C
D
E
F
G
H
I
J
K
L
M
N
O
P
Q
R
S
T
U
V
W
X
Y
Z

hammer¹ 0🔑 /'hæmə(r)/ *noun*
a tool with a handle and a heavy metal part,
that you use for hitting nails into things
➲ Look at the picture on page **185**.

hammer² /'hæmə(r)/ *verb* (hammers,
hammering, hammered /'hæməd/)
1 to hit something with a hammer:
I hammered the nail into the wood.
2 to hit something hard: *He hammered on
the door until somebody opened it.*

hammock /'hæmək/ *noun*
a bed made of cloth or rope that you hang
up at the two ends

hamster /'hæmstə(r)/ *noun*
a small animal that people keep as a pet. A
hamster can keep food in the sides of its
mouth. ➲ Look at Picture Dictionary page
P2.

hand

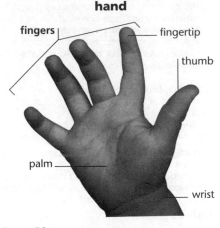

fingers | fingertip
thumb
palm
wrist

hand¹ 0🔑 /hænd/ *noun*
1 (*plural* hands) the part at the end of your
arm that has four **fingers** and a **thumb**: *She
held the letter in her hand.*
2 a hand (*no plural*) (*informal*) some help:
*Could you give me a hand with my
homework?* ◇ *Do you need a hand?*
3 (*plural* hands) one of the parts of a clock
or watch that move to show the time ➲ Look
at the picture at **alarm clock**.
by hand without using a machine: *The
curtains were made by hand.*
get out of hand to become difficult to
control: *The party got out of hand.*
hand in hand with your hand in another
person's hand: *They were walking hand in
hand.*
hands up
1 put one hand in the air if you can answer
the question
2 put your hands in the air because
somebody has a gun

hold hands

They're **holding hands.**

hold hands to have another person's hand
in your hand
in good hands well looked after: *Don't
worry – your son is in good hands.*
on hand near and ready to help: *There is a
doctor on hand 24 hours a day.*
**on the one hand ... on the other
hand** words that show the good and bad
things about something: *On the one hand
cars are very useful; on the other hand they
cause an awful lot of pollution.*

hand² /hænd/ *verb* (hands, handing,
handed)
to put something into somebody's hand:
Can you hand me the scissors, please? ◇
I handed the money to the shop assistant.
hand something down to pass
something from an older person to a
younger one: *He never had any new clothes –
they were all handed down from his older
brothers.*
hand something in to give something to
somebody: *The teacher asked us to hand in
our homework.*
hand something out to give something
to many people: *Please hand out these books.*
hand something over to give
something to somebody: *'Hand over your
weapons!'*

handbag /'hændbæg/ *noun* (*British*)
(*American* purse)
a small bag that a woman uses for carrying
things like money and keys

handcuffs /'hændkʌfs/ *noun* (*plural*)
two metal rings with a chain that the police
put on a prisoner's arms so that they cannot
use their hands

handful /'hændfʊl/ *noun*
1 as much as you can hold in one hand: *a
handful of stones*

2 a small number: *Only a handful of people came to the meeting.*

handicap /'hændikæp/ *noun*
1 something that makes it more difficult for you to do something: *Not being able to drive is a bit of a handicap.*
2 another word for DISABILITY
▶ **handicapped** /'hændikæpt/ *adjective*
another word for DISABLED

handkerchief /'hæŋkətʃɪf/ *noun* (*also informal* **hanky, hankie**)
a square piece of cloth or paper that you use for clearing (**blowing**) your nose

handles

handles   knobs

knob

VOLUME

door handle

knob

handle

knob

handle¹ 0⃞ /'hændl/ *noun*
the part of a thing that you hold in your hand: *I turned the handle and opened the door.* ◇ *Hold that knife by the handle.*

handle² 0⃞ /'hændl/ *verb* (**handles, handling, handled** /'hændld/)
1 to touch something with your hands: *Always wash your hands before you handle food.*
2 to control or deal with somebody or something: *He's not very good at handling pressure.*

handlebars /'hændlbɑːz/ *noun* (*plural*)
the part at the front of a bicycle or motorbike that you hold when you are riding it ➔ Look at the picture at **bicycle**.

handmade /ˌhænd'meɪd/ *adjective*
made by a person, not by a machine: *handmade chocolates*

handsome /'hænsəm/ *adjective*
attractive ➔ SAME MEANING **good-looking**: *a handsome man* ➔ Look at the note at **beautiful**.

hands-on /ˌhændz 'ɒn/ *adjective*
doing something yourself, rather than watching somebody else do it: *She needs some hands-on experience.*

handwriting /'hændraɪtɪŋ/ *noun* (*no plural*)
the way you write: *Her handwriting is difficult to read.*

handy /'hændi/ *adjective* (**handier, handiest**)
1 useful: *This bag will be handy for carrying my books.*
2 near and easy to find or reach: *Have you got a pen handy?*
come in handy to be useful: *Don't throw that box away – it might come in handy.*

hang 0⃞ /hæŋ/ *verb*
1 (**hangs, hanging, hung** /hʌŋ/, **has hung**) to fix something, or to be fixed, at the top so that the lower part is free: *Hang your coat up in the hall.* ◇ *I hung the washing on the line to dry.*
2 (**hangs, hanging, hanged** /hæŋd/, **has hanged**) to kill yourself or another person by putting a rope around the neck and allowing the body to drop downwards: *She was hanged for murder.*
hang about, hang around (*informal*) to stay somewhere with nothing special to do: *My plane was late so I had to hang about in the airport all morning.*
hang on (*informal*) to wait for a short time: *Hang on – I'm not ready.*
hang on to somebody or **something** to hold somebody or something firmly: *Hang on to your purse.*
hang up to end a telephone call by putting the telephone down

hanger /'hæŋə(r)/ *noun* (*also* **coat hanger**)
a piece of metal, wood or plastic with a hook. You use it for hanging clothes on. ➔ Look at the picture at **coat hanger**.

hang-glider /'hæŋ glaɪdə(r)/ *noun*
1 a very large piece of material on a frame, which you hang from and fly through the air
2 a person who does HANG-GLIDING
▶ **hang-gliding** /'hæŋ glaɪdɪŋ/ *noun* (*no plural*): *I'd love to try hang-gliding.* ➔ Look at Picture Dictionary page **P15**.

hanky (*also* **hankie** /'hæŋki/) *noun* (*plural* **hankies**) (*informal*)
another word for HANDKERCHIEF

happen 0⃞ /'hæpən/ *verb* (**happens, happening, happened** /'hæpənd/)
to take place, usually without being planned first: *How did the accident happen?* ◇ *Did you hear what happened to me yesterday?*

happen to do something to do something by chance: *I happened to meet Tim yesterday.*

happily /'hæpɪli/ *adverb*
1 in a happy way: *Everyone was smiling happily.*
2 it is lucky that ⊃ SAME MEANING **fortunately**: *Happily, the accident was not serious.* ⊃ OPPOSITE **unhappily**

happiness Oᴛ /'hæpɪnəs/ *noun* (*no plural*)
the feeling of being happy

happy Oᴛ /'hæpi/ *adjective* (happier, happiest)
1 feeling pleased or showing that you are pleased: *She looks very happy.* ◇ *That was one of the happiest days of my life.*
⊃ OPPOSITE **unhappy** or **sad** ⊃ Look at the note at **glad**.
2 a word that you use to say that you hope somebody will enjoy a special time: *Happy New Year!* ◇ *Happy Christmas!* ◇ *Happy Birthday!*

harbour (*British*) (*American* **harbor**) /'hɑːbə(r)/ *noun*
a place where ships can stay safely in the water

hard¹ Oᴛ /hɑːd/ *adjective* (harder, hardest)
1 not soft: *These apples are very hard.* ◇ *I couldn't sleep because the bed was too hard.*
⊃ OPPOSITE **soft**
2 difficult to do or understand: *The exam was very hard.* ◇ *hard work* ⊃ OPPOSITE **easy**
3 full of problems: *He's had a hard life.*
⊃ OPPOSITE **easy**
4 not kind or gentle: *She is very hard on her children.* ⊃ OPPOSITE **soft**

hard² Oᴛ /hɑːd/ *adverb*
1 a lot: *She works very hard.* ◇ *You must try harder!*
2 strongly: *It's raining hard.* ◇ *She hit him hard.*

hardback /'hɑːdbæk/ *noun*
a book with a hard cover ⊃ Look at **paperback**.

hard disk /,hɑːd 'dɪsk/ *noun*
(*computing*) a disk inside a computer that stores information (called **data**) and programs

harden /'hɑːdn/ *verb* (hardens, hardening, hardened /'hɑːdnd/)
to become hard: *Wait for the cement to harden.*

hard-hearted /,hɑːd 'hɑːtɪd/ *adjective*
not kind to other people and not thinking about their feelings

hardly Oᴛ /'hɑːdli/ *adverb*
almost not; only just: *She spoke so quietly that I could hardly hear her.* ◇ *There's hardly any* (= almost no) *coffee left.* ◇ *We hardly ever go out nowadays.*

hardware /'hɑːdweə(r)/ *noun* (*no plural*)
the electronic parts of a computer system, rather than the programs that work on it ⊃ Look at **software**.

hare /heə(r)/ *noun*
an animal like a RABBIT (= a small animal with long ears). **Hares** are bigger and have longer ears and can run very fast. ⊃ Look at the picture at **rabbit**.

harm¹ Oᴛ /hɑːm/ *noun* (*no plural*)
hurt or damage: *Make sure the children don't come to any harm.*
there is no harm in doing something nothing bad will happen if you do something: *I don't know if she'll help you, but there's no harm in asking.*

harm² Oᴛ /hɑːm/ *verb* (harms, harming, harmed /hɑːmd/)
to hurt or damage somebody or something: *These chemicals harm the environment.*

harmful Oᴛ /'hɑːmfl/ *adjective*
Something that is **harmful** can hurt or damage people or things: *Strong sunlight can be harmful to young babies.*

harmless /'hɑːmləs/ *adjective*
not dangerous: *Don't be frightened – these insects are harmless.*

harmony /'hɑːməni/ *noun*
1 (*no plural*) a state of agreement or of living together in peace: *The different races live together in harmony.*
2 (*plural* harmonies) musical notes that sound nice together: *They sang in harmony.*

harp

harp /hɑːp/ *noun*
a large musical instrument that has many strings stretching from the top to the bottom of a frame. You play the **harp** with your fingers.

A B C D E F G **H** I J K L M N O P Q R S T U V W X Y Z

harsh /hɑːʃ/ *adjective* (harsher, harshest)
1 not kind; cruel: *a harsh punishment*
2 rough and unpleasant to see or hear: *a harsh voice*
▶ **harshly** /'hɑːʃli/ *adverb*: *Alec laughed harshly.*

harvest /'hɑːvɪst/ *noun*
1 the time when grain, fruit, or vegetables are ready to cut or pick: *The apple harvest is in September.*
2 all the grain, fruit, or vegetables that are cut or picked: *We had a good harvest this year.*
▶ **harvest** *verb* (harvests, harvesting, harvested): *When do they harvest the wheat?*

has *form of* HAVE

hasn't /'hæznt/ *short for* HAS NOT

hassle¹ /'hæsl/ *noun* (*informal*)
something that annoys you because it takes time or effort: *It's a real hassle having to change trains.*

hassle² /'hæsl/ *verb* (hassles, hassling, hassled /'hæsld/) (*informal*)
to annoy somebody by asking them many times to do something: *I wish he'd stop hassling me about that essay!*

haste /heɪst/ *noun* (no plural) (*formal*)
doing things too quickly, especially because you do not have enough time: *The letter was written in haste* (= quickly).

hasty /'heɪsti/ *adjective* (hastier, hastiest)
1 said or done quickly: *We ate a hasty lunch, then left.*
2 If you are **hasty**, you do something too quickly: *Don't be too hasty. This is a very important decision.*
▶ **hastily** /'heɪstɪli/ *adverb*: *He hastily changed the subject.*

hats

sun hats   hood

helmet   crash helmet

beret   baseball cap   cap

hat ⁰ₜ /hæt/ *noun*
a thing that you wear on your head: *She's wearing a hat.*

hatch /hætʃ/ *verb* (hatches, hatching, hatched /hætʃt/)
When baby birds, insects, or fish **hatch**, they come out of an egg.

hate¹ ⁰ₜ /heɪt/ *verb* (hates, hating, hated)
to have a very strong feeling of not liking somebody or something: *Most cats hate water.* ◇ *I hate waiting for buses.*
⊃ OPPOSITE **love**

hate² ⁰ₜ /heɪt/ *noun* (no plural)
a very strong feeling of not liking somebody or something ⊃ SAME MEANING **hatred**: *Her love for him had turned to hate.*
⊃ OPPOSITE **love**

hatred /'heɪtrɪd/ *noun* (no plural)
a very strong feeling of not liking somebody or something ⊃ SAME MEANING **hate**: *He had a deep hatred of injustice.*

haul /hɔːl/ *verb* (hauls, hauling, hauled /hɔːld/)
to pull something heavy: *They hauled the boat out of the river.*

haunt /hɔːnt/ *verb* (haunts, haunting, haunted)
1 If a place is **haunted**, people think that there are GHOSTS (= spirits of dead people) there: *A ghost haunts the castle.*
2 If something sad or unpleasant **haunts** you, you often think of it: *Her unhappy face still haunts me.*
▶ **haunted** /'hɔːntɪd/ *adjective*: *a haunted house*

have¹ ⁰ₜ /həv; hæv/ *verb*
a word that you use with parts of other verbs to show that something happened or started in the past: *I haven't seen that film.* ◇ *Have you ever been to Italy?* ◇ *We've been in England for six months.* ◇ *When we arrived, Paul had already left.*

have² ⁰ₜ /hæv/ *verb* (has /hæz/, having, had /hæd/, has had)
1 (*also* have got) to own or keep something: *She has blue eyes.* ◇ *They've got* (= have got) *a big car.* ◇ *Do you have any brothers and sisters?*
2 a word that you use with many nouns to talk about doing something: *What time do you have breakfast?* ◇ *Let's have a drink.* ◇ *I had a shower.* ◇ *Jill and I have had a fight.*
3 a word that you use with many nouns to talk about experiencing something: *Have fun!* ◇ *He has had an accident.* ◇ *Did you have*

A
B
C
D
E
F
G
H
I
J
K
L
M
N
O
P
Q
R
S
T
U
V
W
X
Y
Z

have

present tense		short forms		negative short forms	
I	**have**	I**'ve**		I	**haven't**
you	**have**	you**'ve**		you	**haven't**
he/she/it	**has** /hæz/	he**'s**/she**'s**/it**'s**		he/she/it	**hasn't**
we	**have**	we**'ve**		we	**haven't**
you	**have**	you**'ve**		you	**haven't**
they	**have**	they**'ve**		they	**haven't**

past tense short forms	past tense	present participle
I**'d**	**had** /hæd/	**having**
you**'d**		
he**'d**/she**'d**/it**'d**		past participle
we**'d**		**had**
you**'d**		
they**'d**		

a good holiday? ◇ I have an idea. ◇ Have you got time to help me?
4 (also **have got**) to be ill with something: She's got (= has got) a headache. ◇ I have flu.
have something done to let somebody do something for you: I had my hair cut yesterday. ◇ Have you had your car mended?

haven't /'hævnt/ short for HAVE NOT

have to 0🔟 /'hæv tə/ strong form and before vowels /'hæv tu:/ **modal verb** (British also **have got to**)
used for saying that somebody must do something or that something must happen: I have to go to school on Saturday mornings. ◇ We don't have to get up early tomorrow. ◇ Have we got to pay for this now? ◇ We had to do lots of boring exercises. ⊃ Look at the note at **must**.

hawk /hɔːk/ **noun**
a big bird that catches and eats other birds and small animals

hay /heɪ/ **noun** (no plural)
dry grass that is used as food for farm animals

hay fever /'heɪ fiːvə(r)/ **noun** (no plural)
an illness like a cold. Grass and other plants can cause **hay fever**.

hazard /'hæzəd/ **noun**
a danger: Ice is a hazard for drivers. ◇ a fire hazard

hazardous /'hæzədəs/ **adjective**
dangerous: Motor racing is a hazardous sport.

haze /heɪz/ **noun** (no plural)
air that is difficult to see through because of heat, dust or smoke

hazelnut /'heɪzlnʌt/ **noun**
a small nut that you can eat ⊃ Look at the picture at **nut**.

he 0🔟 /hiː/ **pronoun** (plural **they**)
the man or boy that the sentence is about: I saw Mike when he arrived. ◇ 'Where's John?' 'He's (= he is) at home.'

head¹ 0🔟 /hed/ **noun**
1 the part of your body above your neck: She turned her head to look at me. ⊃ Look at Picture Dictionary page **P4**.

🔎 **CULTURE**

In Britain and America you **nod your head** (= move it up and down) to say 'yes' or to show that you agree, and you **shake your head** (= move it from side to side) to say 'no' or to show that you disagree.

---

2 your mind or brain: A strange thought came into his head. ◇ **Use your head** (= think)!
3 the top, front or most important part: She sat **at the head of** the table.
4 the most important person: The Pope is **the head of** the Catholic church.
5 usually **Head** (British) the person in charge of a school or college ⊃ SAME MEANING **headmaster**, **headmistress**, **head teacher**: I've been called in to see the Head.
6 **heads** (plural) the side of a coin that has the head of a person on it

---

🔎 **SPEAKING**

You say '**heads or tails**?' when you are throwing a coin in the air to decide something, for example who will start a game.

---

a head, **per head** for one person: The meal cost €30 a head.
go to your head to make you too pleased with yourself: Stop telling him how clever he is, it will go to his head!
head first with your head before the rest of your body

head² /hed/ *verb* (heads, heading, headed)
1 to move in the direction mentioned: *Let's head for home.* ◇ *Where are you heading?*
2 to be at the front or top of a group: *Michael's name heads the list.*
3 to hit a ball with your head

headache /'hedeɪk/ *noun*
a pain in your head: *I've got a headache.*

heading /'hedɪŋ/ *noun*
the words at the top of a piece of writing to show what it is about

headlight /'hedlaɪt/ (*also* headlamp /'hedlæmp/) *noun*
one of the two big bright lights on the front of a car ➔ Look at Picture Dictionary page **P1.**

headline /'hedlaɪn/ *noun*
1 the words in big letters at the top of a newspaper story
2 the headlines (*plural*) the most important news on radio or television: *Here are the news headlines.*

headmaster /ˌhed'mɑːstə(r)/ *noun*
(*British*) (*American* principal)
a man who is in charge of a school

headmistress /ˌhed'mɪstrəs/ *noun*
(*plural* headmistresses) (*British*) (*American* principal)
a woman who is in charge of a school

headphones (*also* **earphones**)

headphones /'hedfəʊnz/ (*also* earphones) *noun* (*plural*)
things that you put over your head and ears so that you can listen to music without other people hearing it

headquarters /ˌhed'kwɔːtəz/ *noun*
(*plural*) (*abbr.* **HQ**)
the main offices where the leaders of an organization work: *The company's headquarters are in London.*

head teacher /ˌhed 'tiːtʃə(r)/ *noun*
(*British*) (*British also* Head) principal (*American*)
a person who is in charge of a school

headway /'hedweɪ/ *noun* (*no plural*)
make headway to go forward or make progress: *We haven't made much headway in our discussions.*

heal /hiːl/ *verb* (heals, healing, healed /hiːld/)
to become well again; to make something well again: *The cut on his leg healed slowly.*

health 0ー /helθ/ *noun* (*no plural*)
the condition of your body: *Smoking is bad for your health.* ➔ Look at Study Page **S13.**

healthy 0ー /'helθi/ *adjective* (healthier, healthiest)
1 well; not often ill: *healthy children*
2 helping to make or keep you well: *healthy food* ➔ OPPOSITE **unhealthy**

heap¹ /hiːp/ *noun*
1 a lot of things on top of one another in an untidy way: *She left her clothes in a heap on the floor.* ➔ Look at the note at **pile.**
2 heaps (*plural*) (*informal*) a lot
➔ SAME MEANING **loads**: *We've got heaps of time.*

heap² /hiːp/ *verb* (heaps, heaping, heaped /hiːpt/)
to put a lot of things on top of one another: *She heaped food onto my plate.*

hear 0ー /hɪə(r)/ *verb* (hears, hearing, heard /hɜːd/, has heard)

> *P* **PRONUNCIATION**
> The word **hear** sounds just like **here**.

1 to notice sounds with your ears: *Can you hear that noise?* ◇ *I heard somebody laughing in the next room.*

> *P* **WHICH WORD?**
> **Hear** or **listen**?
> **Hear** and **listen** are used in different ways. When you **hear** something, sounds come to your ears: *I heard the door close.* When you **listen to** something, you are trying to hear it: *I listen to the radio every morning.*

2 to be told about something: *Have you heard the news?*
hear from somebody to get a letter or a phone call from somebody: *Have you heard from your sister?*
hear of somebody or **something** to know about somebody or something: *Who is he? I've never heard of him.*
will not hear of something will not agree to something: *My father wouldn't hear of me paying for the meal.*

hearing /ˈhɪərɪŋ/ *noun* (no plural)
the ability to hear: *Speak louder – her hearing isn't very good.*

hearing aid /ˈhɪərɪŋ eɪd/ *noun*
a small machine that fits inside the ear and helps people to hear better

heart 0‑ₘ /hɑːt/ *noun*

> 🔍 **PRONUNCIATION**
> The word **heart** sounds like **start**.

1 the part of the body that makes the blood go round inside: *Your heart beats faster when you run.*
2 your feelings: *She has **a kind heart** (= she is kind).*
3 the centre; the middle part: *They live **in the heart of** the countryside.*
4 the shape ♥
5 hearts (*plural*) the group of playing cards (called a **suit**) that have red shapes like hearts on them: *the six of hearts* ➔ Look at the picture at **playing card**.
break somebody's heart to make somebody very sad: *It broke his heart when his wife died.*
by heart so that you know every word: *I have **learned** the poem by heart.*
lose heart to stop hoping: *Don't lose heart – you can still win if you try.*
your heart sinks you suddenly feel unhappy: *My heart sank when I saw the first question on the exam paper.*

heartache /ˈhɑːteɪk/ *noun* (no plural)
a strong feeling of sadness

heart attack /ˈhɑːt ətæk/ *noun*
a sudden dangerous illness, when your heart stops working properly: *She **had a heart attack** and died.*

heartbeat /ˈhɑːtbiːt/ *noun*
the movement or sound of your heart as it pushes blood around your body

heartbroken /ˈhɑːtbrəʊkən/ *adjective*
extremely sad because of something that has happened: *Maggie was heartbroken when her grandfather died.*

heartless /ˈhɑːtləs/ *adjective*
not kind; cruel

heat¹ 0‑ₘ /hiːt/ *noun*
1 (*no plural*) the feeling of something hot: *the heat of the sun*
2 (*no plural*) hot weather: *I love the heat.*
➔ OPPOSITE **cold**
3 (*plural* **heats**) one of the first parts of a race or competition

heat² 0‑ₘ /hiːt/ (*also* heat up) *verb* (heats, heating, heated)
to make something hot; to become hot: *I heated some milk in a saucepan.* ◇ *Wait for the oven to **heat up** before you put the food in.*

heater /ˈhiːtə(r)/ *noun*
a thing that makes a place warm or that heats water: *Switch on the heater if you feel cold.* ◇ *a water heater*

heating /ˈhiːtɪŋ/ *noun* (no plural)
a system for making a building warm: *What kind of heating do you have?* ➔ Look at **central heating**.

heave /hiːv/ *verb* (heaves, heaving, heaved /hiːvd/)
to lift or pull something heavy: *We heaved the suitcase up the stairs.*

heaven 0‑ₘ /ˈhevn/ *noun* (no plural)
the place where many people believe God lives and where good people go to when they die ➔ Look at **hell**.
Good Heavens! words that you use to show surprise: *Good Heavens! I've won £100!*

heavy

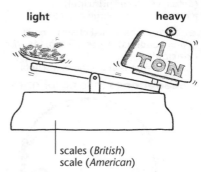

light   heavy

scales (*British*)
scale (*American*)

heavy 0‑ₘ /ˈhevi/ *adjective* (heavier, heaviest)
1 weighing a lot; difficult to lift or move: *I can't carry this bag – it's too heavy.*
➔ OPPOSITE **light**
2 larger, stronger or more than usual: *heavy rain* ◇ *The traffic was very heavy this morning.*
➔ OPPOSITE **light**
▸ **heavily** /ˈhevɪli/ *adverb*: *It was raining heavily.*

heavy metal /ˌhevi ˈmetl/ *noun* (no plural)
a kind of very loud rock music

hectare /ˈhekteə(r)/ *noun*
a measure of land. There are 10000 square metres in a **hectare**.

hectic /ˈhektɪk/ *adjective*
very busy: *I had a hectic day at work.*

he'd /hiːd/ *short for* HE HAD; HE WOULD

hedge /hedʒ/ *noun*
a line of small trees planted around the edge of a garden or field ⊃ Look at the picture at **fence**.

hedgehog /'hedʒhɒg/ *noun*
a small animal covered with sharp hairs (called **prickles**)

heel /hiːl/ *noun*
1 the back part of your foot ⊃ Look at the picture at **foot**.
2 the back part of a shoe under the **heel** of your foot ⊃ Look at the picture at **shoe**.
3 the part of a sock that covers the **heel** of your foot

height 0̶ᴍ /haɪt/ *noun*

🔍 **PRONUNCIATION**
The word **height** sounds like **white**.

1 (*plural* **heights**) how far it is from the bottom to the top of somebody or something: *What is the height of this mountain?* ◇ *The wall is two metres in height.* ◇ *She asked me my height, weight and age.* ⊃ The adjective is **high**.
2 (*plural* **heights**) a high place: *I'm afraid of heights.*
3 (*no plural*) the strongest or most important part of something: *the height of summer*

heir /eə(r)/ *noun*
a person who gets money or property when another person dies: *He's the heir to a large fortune.*
▶ **heiress** /'eəres/ *noun* (*plural* **heiresses**)
an HEIR who is a woman

held *form of* HOLD¹

helicopter /'helɪkɒptə(r)/ *noun*
a kind of small aircraft that can go straight up in the air. It has long metal parts on top that turn to help it fly. ⊃ Look at Picture Dictionary page **P1**.

hell /hel/ *noun* (*no plural*)
the place where some people believe that bad people go when they die ⊃ Look at **heaven**.

he'll /hiːl/ *short for* HE WILL

hello 0̶ᴍ /hə'ləʊ/ *exclamation*
a word that you say when you meet somebody or when you answer the telephone ⊃ Look at the note at **good afternoon**.

helmet /'helmɪt/ *noun*
a hard hat that keeps your head safe

help¹ 0̶ᴍ /help/ *verb* (**helps**, **helping**, **helped** /helpt/)
1 to do something useful for somebody; to make somebody's work easier: *Will you help me with the washing-up?* ◇ *She helped me to carry the box.*
2 a word that you shout when you are in danger: *Help! I can't swim!*
can't help If you **can't help** doing something, you cannot stop yourself doing it: *It was so funny that I couldn't help laughing.*
help yourself to take something that you want: *Help yourself to a drink.* ◇ *'Can I have a sandwich?' 'Of course. Help yourself!'*

help² 0̶ᴍ /help/ *noun* (*no plural*)
1 the act of helping somebody: *Thank you for all your help.* ◇ *Do you need any help?*
2 a person or thing that helps: *He was a great help to me when I was ill.*

helpful 0̶ᴍ /'helpfl/ *adjective*
A person or thing that is **helpful** wants to help you or be useful to you: *The woman in the shop was very helpful.* ◇ *helpful advice* ⊃ OPPOSITE **unhelpful**
▶ **helpfully** /'helpfəli/ *adverb*: *She helpfully suggested that I try the local library.*

helping /'helpɪŋ/ *noun*
the amount of food on your plate: *I had a big helping of pie.*

helpless /'helpləs/ *adjective*
not able to do things without help: *Babies are totally helpless.*

hem /hem/ *noun*
the bottom edge of something like a skirt or trousers, that is folded and sewn

hemisphere /'hemɪsfɪə(r)/ *noun*
one half of the earth: *the northern hemisphere* ⊃ Look at the picture at **earth**.

hen /hen/ *noun*
a female bird, especially a chicken, that people keep on farms for its eggs ⊃ Look at the note at **chicken**.

her¹ 0̶ᴍ /hɜː(r)/ *pronoun* (*plural* **them**)
a word that shows the woman or girl that you have just talked about: *Tell Jane that I'll see her tonight.* ◇ *I wrote to her yesterday.*

her² /hɜː(r)/ *adjective*
of or belonging to the woman or girl that you have just talked about: *That's her book.* ◇ *Jill has hurt her leg.*

herb /hɜːb/ *noun*
a plant whose leaves, seeds, etc. are used in medicine or in cooking ⊃ Look at **spice**. ⊃ Look at Picture Dictionary page **P6**.

herd¹ /hɜːd/ *noun*
a big group of animals of the same kind: *a herd of cows* ⊃ Look at **flock**.

A

herd² /hɜːd/ *verb* (herds, herding, herded)
to move people or animals somewhere in a group: *The prisoners were* **herded onto** *the train.*

here 0━ /hɪə(r)/ *adverb*

> 🔎 **PRONUNCIATION**
> The word **here** sounds just like **hear**.

in, at or to this place: *Your glasses are here.* ◇ *Come here, please.* ◇ *Here's my car.* ◇ **Here** *comes the bus.* ⊃ Look at **there**.
here and there in different places: *There were groups of people here and there along the beach.*
here goes (*informal*) words that you say before you do something exciting or dangerous: *'Here goes,' said Sue, and jumped into the river.*
here you are words that you say when you give something to somebody: *'Can I borrow a pen, please?' 'Yes, here you are.'*

hero /'hɪərəʊ/ *noun* (*plural* heroes)
1 a person, especially a man, who has done something brave or good: *Everybody said that Mark was a hero after he rescued his sister from the fire.*
2 the most important man or boy in a book, play or film ⊃ Look at **heroine**.

heroic /hə'rəʊɪk/ *adjective*
very brave

heroin /'herəʊɪn/ *noun* (*no plural*)
a very strong illegal drug

heroine /'herəʊɪn/ *noun*
1 a woman who has done something brave or good
2 the most important woman or girl in a book, play or film: *The heroine is played by Sandra Bullock.*

hers 0━ /hɜːz/ *pronoun*
something that belongs to her: *Gina says this book is hers.* ◇ *Are these keys hers?*

herself 0━ /hɜː'self/ *pronoun* (*plural* themselves /ðəm'selvz/)
1 a word that shows the same woman or girl that you have just talked about: *She fell and hurt herself.*
2 a word that makes 'she' stronger: *'Who told you that Jane was married?' 'She told me herself.'*
by herself
1 without other people ⊃ SAME MEANING **alone**: *She lives by herself.*
2 without help: *She can carry the box by herself.*

he's /hiːz/ *short for* HE IS; HE HAS

hesitate /'hezɪteɪt/ *verb* (hesitates, hesitating, hesitated)
to stop for a moment before you do or say something because you are not sure about it: *He hesitated before answering the question.*
▶ **hesitation** /ˌhezɪ'teɪʃn/ *noun* (*no plural*): *They agreed without hesitation.*

hexagon /'heksəgən/ *noun*
a shape with six sides
▶ **hexagonal** /heks'ægənl/ *adjective* with six sides: *a hexagonal box*

hey /heɪ/ *exclamation* (*informal*)
a word that you say to make somebody listen to you, or when you are surprised: *Hey! Where are you going?*

hi /haɪ/ *exclamation* (*informal*)
a word that you say when you meet somebody ⊃ SAME MEANING **hello**: *Hi Tony! How are you?*

hibernate /'haɪbəneɪt/ *verb* (hibernates, hibernating, hibernated)
When an animal **hibernates**, it goes to sleep for the winter.

hiccup (*also* hiccough) /'hɪkʌp/ *noun*
a sudden noise that you make in your throat. You sometimes get **hiccups** when you have eaten or drunk too quickly.

hide 0━ /haɪd/ *verb* (hides, hiding, hid /hɪd/, has hidden /'hɪdn/)
1 to put something where people cannot find it: *I hid the money under the bed.*
2 to be or get in a place where people cannot see or find you: *Somebody was hiding behind the door.*
3 to not tell or show something to somebody: *She tried to hide her feelings.*

hide-and-seek /ˌhaɪd n 'siːk/ *noun* (*no plural*)
a children's game in which one player covers his or her eyes while the other players hide, and then tries to find them

hideous /'hɪdiəs/ *adjective*
very ugly: *That shirt is hideous!*

hiding /'haɪdɪŋ/ *noun* (*no plural*)
be in hiding, go into hiding to be in, or to go into a place where people will not find you: *The escaped prisoners are believed to be in hiding.*

hi-fi /'haɪ faɪ/ *noun*
a machine for playing records, tapes and CDs

high[1] 0➔ /haɪ/ *adjective* (higher, highest)

> 🔍 **PRONUNCIATION**
> The word **high** sounds like **my**, because we don't say the letters **-gh** in this word.

1 Something that is **high** has a long distance between the top and the bottom: *a high wall* ◇ *Mount Everest is the highest mountain in the world.* ➔ The noun is **height**.
➔ OPPOSITE **low**
2 You use **high** to say or ask how far something is from the bottom to the top: *The table is 80 cm high.* ➔ The noun is **height**.

> 🔍 **WHICH WORD?**
> **Tall** or **high**?
> We use **tall**, not **high**, to talk about people: *How tall are you?* ◇ *He's 1.72 metres tall.*

3 far from the ground: *a high shelf*
➔ OPPOSITE **low**
4 more than the usual level or amount: *The car was travelling at high speed.* ◇ *high temperatures* ➔ OPPOSITE **low**
5 A **high** sound is not deep: *I heard the high voice of a child.* ➔ OPPOSITE **low**

high[2] /haɪ/ *adverb*
a long way above the ground: *The plane flew high above the clouds.* ➔ OPPOSITE **low**
high and low everywhere: *I've looked high and low for my keys, but I can't find them anywhere.*

higher education /ˌhaɪər edʒuˈkeɪʃn/ *noun* (no plural)
education at a college or university after the age of 18 ➔ Look at **further education**.

high jump /ˈhaɪ dʒʌmp/ *noun* (no plural)
a sport where people jump over a high bar

highlands /ˈhaɪləndz/ *noun* (plural)
the part of a country with hills and mountains: *the Scottish Highlands*

highlight /ˈhaɪlaɪt/ *noun*
the best or most exciting part of something: *The highlight of our holiday was a visit to the palace.*

highly 0➔ /ˈhaɪli/ *adverb*
1 very or very much: *Their children are highly intelligent.* ◇ *She has a highly paid job.*
2 very well: *I think very highly of your work* (= I think it is very good).

Highness /ˈhaɪnəs/ *noun* (plural Highnesses)
a word that you use when speaking to or about a royal person: *Yes, Your Highness.*

high school /ˈhaɪ skuːl/ *noun*
1 a school in the US and some other countries for young people between the ages of 14 and 18
2 often used in Britain in the names of schools for young people between the ages of 11 and 18 ➔ SAME MEANING **secondary school**

high street /ˈhaɪ striːt/ *noun* (British) (American **main street**)
the main street of a town, where most shops, banks, etc. are: *There is a butcher's on the high street.*

high-tech (also **hi-tech**) /ˌhaɪ ˈtek/ *adjective* (informal)
using the most modern methods and machines, especially electronic ones: *The country's future is in high-tech industries.*

highway /ˈhaɪweɪ/ *noun* (American)
a big road between towns

hijack /ˈhaɪdʒæk/ *verb* (hijacks, hijacking, hijacked /ˈhaɪdʒækt/)
to take control of a plane or a car and make the pilot or driver take you somewhere
▸ **hijacker** /ˈhaɪdʒækə(r)/ *noun*: *The hijackers threatened to blow up the plane.*

hike /haɪk/ *noun*
a long walk in the country: *We went on a ten-mile hike at the weekend.*
▸ **hike** *verb* (hikes, hiking, hiked /haɪkt/): *They went hiking in Wales for their holiday.*
➔ Look at Picture Dictionary page **P15**.

hill 0➔ /hɪl/ *noun*
a high piece of land that is not as high as a mountain: *I pushed my bike up the hill.* ◇ *Their house is at the top of the hill.* ➔ Look also at **uphill** and **downhill**.
▸ **hilly** /ˈhɪli/ *adjective* (hillier, hilliest): *The countryside is very hilly around here.*

him 0➔ /hɪm/ *pronoun* (plural them)
a word that shows a man or boy: *Where's Andy? I can't see him.* ◇ *I spoke to him yesterday.*

himself 0➔ /hɪmˈself/ *pronoun* (plural themselves /ðəmˈselvz/)
1 a word that shows the same man or boy that you have just talked about: *Paul looked at himself in the mirror.*
2 a word that makes 'he' stronger: *Did he make this cake himself?*
by himself
1 without other people ➔ SAME MEANING **alone**: *Dad went shopping by himself.*
2 without help: *He did it by himself.*

hinder /ˈhɪndə(r)/ *verb* (hinders, hindering, hindered /ˈhɪndəd/)
to make it more difficult to do something: *Teachers are hindered by a lack of resources.*

Hindu /'hɪndu:/ *noun*
a person who follows the religion of
HINDUISM

Hinduism /'hɪndu:ɪzəm/ *noun* (*no plural*)
the main religion of India

hinge /hɪndʒ/ *noun*
a piece of metal that joins a lid to a box or a
door to a frame so that you can open and
close it

hint¹ /hɪnt/ *noun*
1 something that you say, but not in a direct
way: *Sam keeps **dropping hints** (= making
hints) about wanting a bike for his birthday.*
2 a small amount of something: *There's a
hint of garlic in the soup.*

hint² /hɪnt/ *verb* (hints, hinting, hinted)
to say something, but not in a direct way:
*Sarah **hinted that** she might be leaving.*

hip /hɪp/ *noun*
the place where your leg joins the side of
your body ⊃ Look at Picture Dictionary
page **P4**.

hippie (*also* **hippy**) /'hɪpi/ *noun* (*plural*
hippies)
a person who refuses to accept the western
way of life. **Hippies** often have long hair,
wear brightly coloured clothes and take
illegal drugs.

hippopotamus /ˌhɪpə'pɒtəməs/ *noun*
(*plural* **hippopotamuses** or **hippopotami**
/ˌhɪpə'pɒtəmaɪ/) (*informal* **hippo** /'hɪpəʊ/)
a large African animal with thick skin that
lives near water ⊃ Look at Picture Dictionary
page **P3**.

hire /'haɪə(r)/ *verb* (hires, hiring, hired
/'haɪəd/)
1 to pay to use something for a short time:
We hired a car when we were on holiday.
2 to pay somebody to do a job for you: *We
hired somebody to mend the roof.*
hire something out to let somebody use
something for a short time, in return for
money: *They hire out bicycles.*
▶ **hire** *noun* (*no plural*): *Have you got any
boats **for hire**?* ⊃ Look at **rent**.

his¹ 0🛒 /hɪz/ *adjective*
of or belonging to the man or boy that you
have just talked about: *John came with his
sister. ◇ He has hurt his arm.*

his² 0🛒 /hɪz/ *pronoun*
something that belongs to him: *Are these
books yours or his?*

hiss /hɪs/ *verb* (hisses, hissing, hissed
/hɪst/)
to make a noise like a very long **S**: *The cat
hissed at me.*
▶ **hiss** *noun* (*plural* **hisses**): *the hiss of steam*

historian /hɪ'stɔːriən/ *noun*
a person who knows a lot about history

historic /hɪ'stɒrɪk/ *adjective*
important in history: *It was a historic moment
when man first walked on the moon.*

historical /hɪ'stɒrɪkl/ *adjective*
connected with real people or events in the
past: *She writes historical novels.*

history 0🛒 /'hɪstri/ *noun* (*no plural*)
1 all the things that happened in the past: *It
was an important moment in history.*
2 the study of things that happened in the
past: *History is my favourite subject.*

hit¹ 0🛒 /hɪt/ *verb* (hits, hitting, hit, has
hit)
to touch somebody or something hard: *He
hit me **on** the head **with** a book. ◇ The car hit a
wall. ◇ I **hit** my knee **on** the door.*

hit² 0🛒 /hɪt/ *noun*
1 touching somebody or something hard:
*That was a good hit! (= in a game of cricket or
baseball, for example)*
2 a person or a thing that a lot of people
like: *This song was a hit in the US.*
3 (*computing*) a result of a search on a
computer, especially on the Internet

hitchhike /'hɪtʃhaɪk/ *verb* (hitchhikes,
hitchhiking, hitchhiked /'hɪtʃhaɪkt/) (*also*
hitch /'hɪtʃ/) (hitches, hitching, hitched
/hɪtʃt/)
to travel by asking for free rides in cars and
lorries: *We **hitchhiked across** Europe.*
▶ **hitchhiker** /'hɪtʃhaɪkə(r)/ *noun*: *We
picked up a hitchhiker.*

HIV /ˌeɪtʃ aɪ 'viː/ *abbreviation*
the VIRUS (= a very small thing that can make
you ill) that causes AIDS (= a serious illness
which destroys the body's ability to fight
infection)
be HIV-positive to have HIV

hive /haɪv/ *noun* (*also* **beehive**)
a box where BEES (= black and yellow
insects) live

hoard /hɔːd/ *noun*
a secret store of something, for example
food or money
▶ **hoard** *verb* (hoards, hoarding,
hoarded) to save and keep things secretly:
*The old man hoarded the money in a box
under his bed.*

hoarse /hɔːs/ *adjective*
If your voice is **hoarse**, it is rough and quiet,
for example because you have a cold: *He
spoke in a hoarse whisper.*

hoax /həʊks/ *noun* (*plural* **hoaxes**)
a trick that makes somebody believe

something that is not true: *There wasn't really a bomb in the station – it was a hoax.*

hobby 0‑ᴡ /'hɒbi/ *noun* (*plural* hobbies)
something that you like doing in your free time: *My hobbies are reading and swimming.*

hockey /'hɒki/ *noun* (no plural)
1 (*British*) (*American* field hockey) a game for two teams of eleven players who hit a small hard ball with long curved sticks on a field (called a **pitch**)
2 *American English for* ICE HOCKEY

hold¹ 0‑ᴡ /həʊld/ *verb* (holds, holding, held /held/, has held)
1 to have something in your hand or arms: *She was holding a gun.* ◇ *He held the baby in his arms.*
2 to keep something in a certain way: *Hold your hand up.* ◇ *Try to hold the camera still.*
3 to support the weight of somebody or something: *Are you sure that branch will hold you?*
4 to have space for a certain number or amount: *The car holds five people.*
5 to make something happen: *The meeting was held in the town hall.* ◇ *It's impossible to hold a conversation with him.*
hold somebody or **something back** to stop somebody or something from moving forwards: *The police held back the crowd.*
Hold it! (*informal*) Wait! Don't move!
hold on
1 (*informal*) to wait ⊃ SAME MEANING **hang on**: *Hold on, I'm coming.*
2 to keep holding something tightly: *The child held on to her mother's hand.*
hold somebody or **something up**
1 to make somebody or something late: *The plane was held up for 40 minutes.*
2 to try to steal from a place, using a gun: *Two men held up a bank in Bristol today.*

hold² 0‑ᴡ /həʊld/ *noun* (no plural)
the part of a ship or plane where goods are kept
get hold of somebody to find somebody so that you can speak to them: *I'm trying to get hold of Peter but he's not at home.*
get hold of something
1 (*also* take hold of something) to take something in your hands: *Get hold of the rope!*
2 to find something: *I can't get hold of the book I need.*

hold-up /'həʊld ʌp/ *noun*
1 something that makes you wait ⊃ SAME MEANING **delay**: *There was a long hold-up on the motorway.*
2 when somebody tries to rob somebody

using a gun: *There's been a hold-up at the local supermarket.*

hole 0‑ᴡ /həʊl/ *noun*
an empty space or opening in something: *I'm going to **dig a hole** in the garden.* ◇ *My socks are full of holes.*

holiday 0‑ᴡ /'hɒlədeɪ/ *noun*
1 (*British*) (*American* vacation) a time when you do not go to work or school, and often go and stay away from home: *The school holidays start next week.* ◇ *We're going to the coast for our **summer holiday**.* ◇ *Mrs Smith isn't here this week. She's **on holiday**.*
2 a day when most people do not go to work or school, especially because of a religious or national celebration: *Next Monday is a holiday.*

🔎 **CULTURE**
A day when everybody has a holiday is called a **public holiday** in Britain and the US. In Britain it is also called a **bank holiday**.

hollow /'hɒləʊ/ *adjective*
with an empty space inside: *A drum is hollow.*

holly /'hɒli/ *noun* (no plural)
a plant that has leaves with a lot of sharp points, and red BERRIES (= small round fruit)

🔎 **CULTURE**
People often put **holly** in their houses at Christmas.

holy /'həʊli/ *adjective* (holier, holiest)
1 very special because it is about God or a god: *The Bible is the holy book of Christians.*
2 A **holy** person lives a good and religious life.

home¹ 0‑ᴡ /həʊm/ *noun*
1 the place where you live: *Simon **left home** (= stopped living in his parents' house) at the age of 18.*
2 a place where they look after people, for example children who have no parents, or old people: *My grandmother lives in an old people's home.*
at home in your house or flat: *I stayed at home yesterday.* ◇ *Is Sara at home?*

home² 0‑ᴡ /həʊm/ *adverb*
to the place where you live

🔎 **GRAMMAR**
Be careful! We do not use **to** before **home**: *Let's go home.* ◇ *What time did you get home last night?*

A B C D E F G **H** I J K L M N O P Q R S T U V W X Y Z

A

home³ /həʊm/ *adjective*
connected with your home or your country:
What is your home address? ◇ *home cooking*

B

homeless /ˈhəʊmləs/ *adjective*
If you are **homeless**, you have nowhere to
live: *The floods made many people homeless.*

C

home-made /ˌhəʊm ˈmeɪd/ *adjective*
made in your house, not bought in a shop:
home-made bread

D

E

home page /ˈhəʊm peɪdʒ/ *noun*
the first of a number of pages of information
on the Internet that belongs to a person or
an organization. A **home page** contains
connections to other pages of information.

F

G

homesick /ˈhəʊmsɪk/ *adjective*
sad because you are away from home

H

I

homework /ˈhəʊmwɜːk/ *noun (no plural)*
work that a teacher gives to you to do at
home: *Have you done your French homework?*
➜ Look at the note at **housework**.

J

K

homosexual /ˌhəʊməˈsekʃuəl/ *adjective*
attracted to people of the same sex

honest 0━ /ˈɒnɪst/ *adjective*
A person who is **honest** says what is true
and does not steal, lie or cheat: *She's a very
honest person.* ◇ *Be honest – do you really like
this dress?* ➜ OPPOSITE **dishonest**
▶ **honestly** /ˈɒnɪstli/ *adverb*: *Try to answer
the questions honestly.* ◇ *Honestly, I don't
know where your money is.*
▶ **honesty** /ˈɒnəsti/ *noun (no plural)*: *I have
serious doubts about his honesty.*

L

M

N

O

P

honey /ˈhʌni/ *noun (no plural)*
the sweet food that is made by insects
(called **bees**)

Q

honeymoon /ˈhʌnimuːn/ *noun*
a holiday for two people who have just got
married

R

S

honour (*British*) (*American* honor) /ˈɒnə(r)/
noun (no plural)
1 respect from other people for something
good that you have done: *They fought for the
honour of their country.*
2 something that makes you proud and
pleased: *It was a great honour to be invited to
Buckingham Palace.*
in honour of somebody or
something to show that you respect
somebody or something: *There is a party
tonight in honour of our visitors.*

T

U

V

W

X

Y

hood /hʊd/ *noun*
1 the part of a coat or jacket that covers
your head and neck ➜ Look at the picture at
hat.
2 *American English for* BONNET(1)

Z

hoof /huːf/ *noun (plural* hoofs *or* hooves
/huːvz/)
the hard part of the foot of horses and some
other animals ➜ Look at the picture at
horse.

hook 0━ /hʊk/
noun
a curved piece of
metal or plastic for
hanging things on,
or for catching fish
with: *Hang your coat
on that hook.* ◇ *a fish
hook*

hook

off the hook If a
telephone is **off the hook**, the part that you
speak into (called the **receiver**) is not in
place so that the telephone will not ring.

hooligan /ˈhuːlɪɡən/ *noun*
a young person who behaves in a noisy way
and fights other people: *football hooligans*

hooray (*also* hurray) /həˈreɪ/ *exclamation*
(*also* hurrah /həˈrɑː/)
a word that you shout when you are very
pleased about something: *Hooray! She's
won!*

hoot /huːt/ *noun*
the sound that a car's horn or an OWL (= a
type of bird) makes
▶ **hoot** *verb* (hoots, hooting, hooted):
The driver hooted at the dog.

hoover /ˈhuːvə(r)/ *verb* (*British*) (hoovers,
hoovering, hoovered /ˈhuːvəd/)
to clean a carpet or the floor with a machine
that sucks up the dirt ➜ SAME MEANING
vacuum
▶ **Hoover™** *noun* ➜ SAME MEANING
vacuum cleaner: *The Hoover needs a new
bag.*

hooves *plural of* HOOF

hop /hɒp/ *verb*
(hops, hopping,
hopped /hɒpt/)
1 (used about a
person) to jump on
one foot
2 (used about an
animal or bird) to
jump with two or all
feet together: *The
frog hopped onto the stone.*
▶ **hop** *noun* a short jump

hop

hope¹ 0━ /həʊp/ *verb* (hopes, hoping,
hoped /həʊpt/)
to want something to happen or be true: *I
hope that you have a nice holiday.* ◇ *I hope to
see you tomorrow.* ◇ *She's hoping for a bike
for her birthday.* ◇ *'Do you think it will rain?' 'I*

hope not.' ◇ *'Will you be at the party?' 'I'm not sure – I hope so.'*

hope² 0ᴿ /həʊp/ *noun*
1 (*plural* hopes) a feeling of wanting something to happen and thinking that it will: *There's little hope of finding survivors.* ◇ *Don't give up hope; you may still pass.*
2 (*no plural*) a person or thing that gives you hope: *Can you help me? You're my only hope.*

hopeful /'həʊpfl/ *adjective*
If you are **hopeful**, you think that something that you want will happen: *I'm hopeful about getting a job.*

hopefully /'həʊpfəli/ *adverb*
1 (*informal*) I hope; we hope: *Hopefully he won't be late.*
2 hoping that what you want will happen: *The cat looked hopefully at our plates.*

hopeless /'həʊpləs/ *adjective*
1 with no hope of success: *a hopeless situation* ◇ *It's hopeless trying to work with all this noise!*
2 (*informal*) very bad: *I'm hopeless at tennis.*
▶ **hopelessly** /'həʊpləsli/ *adverb*: *We got hopelessly lost in the forest.*

horizon /hə'raɪzn/ *noun*
the line between the earth or sea and the sky: *We could see a ship on the horizon.*

horizontal /ˌhɒrɪ'zɒntl/ *adjective*
going from side to side, not up and down: *a horizontal line* ⊃ Look at **vertical**. ⊃ Look at the picture at **line**.

hormone /'hɔːməʊn/ *noun*
a substance in your body that influences the way you grow and develop

horn 0ᴿ /hɔːn/ *noun*
1 one of the hard pointed things that some animals have on their heads ⊃ Look at the picture at **cow**.
2 a thing in a car or other vehicle that makes a loud sound to warn people: *Don't sound your horn late at night.*
3 a musical instrument with a curved metal tube that you blow into

horoscope /'hɒrəskəʊp/ *noun*
something that tells you what will happen, using the planets and your date of birth: *Have you read your horoscope today?* (= in a newspaper, for example)

horrible /'hɒrəbl/ *adjective* (*informal*)
very bad or unpleasant: *What horrible weather!* ◇ *I had a horrible dream.*

horrid /'hɒrɪd/ *adjective* (*informal*)
very bad or unpleasant ⊃ SAME MEANING **horrible**: *Don't be so horrid!*

horrific /hə'rɪfɪk/ *adjective*
very shocking or frightening: *a horrific accident*

horrify /'hɒrɪfaɪ/ *verb* (horrifies, horrifying, horrified /'hɒrɪfaɪd/, has horrified)
to shock and frighten somebody: *Everyone was horrified by the murders.*

horror /'hɒrə(r)/ *noun* (*no plural*)
a feeling of fear or shock: *They watched in horror as the child ran in front of the bus.*
horror film, **horror story** a film or a story which tries to frighten or shock you for entertainment

horse

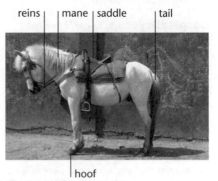

reins | mane | saddle | tail

hoof

horse 0ᴿ /hɔːs/ *noun*
a big animal that can carry people and pull heavy things: *Can you ride a horse?*

🔎 **WORD BUILDING**
A young horse is called a **foal**. The sound a horse makes is **neigh**.

horseback /'hɔːsbæk/ *noun*
on horseback sitting on a horse: *We saw a lot of policemen on horseback.*

horse riding /'hɔːs raɪdɪŋ/ (*British*) (*American* **horseback riding** /'hɔːsbæk raɪdɪŋ/) (*British and American also* **riding**) *noun* (*no plural*)
the sport or activity of riding a horse for pleasure: *She goes horse riding at the weekends.* ⊃ Look at Picture Dictionary page **P15**.

horseshoe /'hɔːsʃuː/ *noun*
a piece of metal like a U that a horse wears on its foot

hose /həʊz/ (*also* **hosepipe** /'həʊzpaɪp/) *noun*
a long soft tube that you use to bring water, for example in the garden or when there is a fire

hospitable /hɒ'spɪtəbl/ *adjective*
friendly and kind to visitors

A
B
C
D
E
F
G
H
I
J
K
L
M
N
O
P
Q
R
S
T
U
V
W
X
Y
Z

A
B
C
D
E
F
G
H
I
J
K
L
M
N
O
P
Q
R
S
T
U
V
W
X
Y
Z

hospital 0–┰ /'hɒspɪtl/ *noun*

a place where doctors and nurses look after people who are ill or hurt: *My brother is **in** hospital – he's broken his leg.* ◇ *The ambulance **took** her **to** hospital.*

> 🔎 **WORD BUILDING**
>
> If you are very ill or you **have an accident** you go **to hospital** (Be careful! In British English, you do not say **to the hospital**).
> A doctor gives you **treatment** and you are called a **patient**.
> You might need to **have an operation**. The room in a hospital where people sleep is called a **ward**.

hospitality /ˌhɒspɪ'tæləti/ *noun* (*no plural*)

being friendly to people who are visiting you, and looking after them well: *We thanked them for their hospitality.*

host /həʊst/ *noun*

a person who invites people to their house, for example to a party: *Ian, our host, introduced us to the other guests.* ➲ Look at **hostess**.

hostage /'hɒstɪdʒ/ *noun*

a prisoner that you keep until people give you what you want: *Several passengers were **taken hostage**.* ◇ *They **held** his daughter **hostage** until he paid them the money.*

hostel /'hɒstl/ *noun*

a place like a cheap hotel where people can stay: *a youth hostel*

hostess /'həʊstəs/ *noun* (*plural* hostesses)

a woman who invites people to her house, for example to a party ➲ Look at **host**. Look also at **air hostess**.

hostile /'hɒstaɪl/ *adjective*

very unfriendly: *a hostile crowd*

hot 0–┰ /hɒt/ *adjective* (hotter, hottest)

1 having a high temperature: *I'm hot. Can you open the window?* ◇ *It's hot today, isn't it?* ◇ *hot water* ➲ OPPOSITE **cold**

> 🔎 **WORD BUILDING**
>
> **Warm**, **hot** or **boiling**?
> **Warm** means quite hot, especially in a pleasant way: *Sit by the fire. You'll soon be warm.*
> **Boiling** means extremely hot, often in an unpleasant way: *Turn the heating down – it's boiling in here!*

2 Hot food has a strong, burning taste. ➲ SAME MEANING **spicy**: *a hot curry*

hot-air balloon /ˌhɒt 'eə bəluːn/ = BALLOON(2) ➲ Look at Picture Dictionary page **P1**.

hot dog /'hɒt dɒg/ *noun*

a hot SAUSAGE (= meat made into a long, thin shape) that you eat in a long bread roll ➲ Look at Picture Dictionary page **P7**.

hotel 0–┰ /həʊ'tel/ *noun*

a place where you pay to sleep and eat: *I stayed at a hotel near the airport.*

hotline /'hɒtlaɪn/ *noun*

a special telephone line that people can call to get advice or information

hour 0–┰ /'aʊə(r)/ *noun*

1 a measure of time. There are 60 minutes in an **hour**: *The journey took two hours.* ◇ *I've been waiting for an hour.* ◇ *half an hour*
2 hours (*plural*) the time when somebody is working, or when a shop or office is open: *Our office hours are 9 a.m. to 5 p.m.*
3 the hour (*no plural*) the time when a new **hour** starts (= 1 o'clock, 2 o'clock, etc.): *Buses are **on the hour** and at twenty past the hour.*

for hours (*informal*) for a long time: *I've been waiting for hours.*

hourly /'aʊəli/ *adjective, adverb*

happening or coming once an hour: *There is an hourly bus to the airport.* ◇ *Trains run hourly.*

house 0–┰ /haʊs/ *noun* (*plural* houses /'haʊzɪz/)

1 a building where a person or a family lives: *How many rooms are there in your house?* ◇ *We're having dinner at Jane's house tonight.*

house

chimney | drainpipe | roof

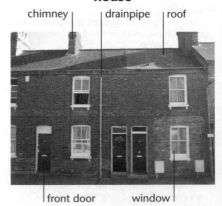

front door | window

> 🔎 **WORD BUILDING**
>
> A small house is called a **cottage**. A house with only one floor is called a **bungalow**:

My grandparents live in a bungalow near the sea.
A tall building where lots of people live is called a **block of flats** or an **apartment block**: *They live on the third floor of an apartment block.*

2 a building that has a special use: *an opera house*

housekeeper /'haʊskiːpə(r)/ *noun*
a person whose job is to look after somebody else's house

housewife /'haʊswaɪf/ *noun* (plural housewives /'haʊswaɪvz/)
a woman who stays at home and looks after her family

housework /'haʊswɜːk/ *noun* (no plural)
work that you do in your house, for example cleaning and washing

🔎 WHICH WORD?
Be careful! Work that a teacher gives you to do at home is called **homework**.

housing /'haʊzɪŋ/ *noun* (no plural)
flats and houses for people to live in: *We need more housing for young people.*

housing estate /'haʊzɪŋ ɪsteɪt/ *noun* (British)
a big group of houses that were built at the same time: *We live on a housing estate.*

hover /'hɒvə(r)/ *verb* (hovers, hovering, hovered /'hɒvəd/)
to stay in the air in one place: *A helicopter hovered above the building.*

hovercraft /'hɒvəkrɑːft/ *noun* (plural hovercraft)
a kind of boat that moves over the top of water on air that it pushes out

how 0̄⃛ /haʊ/ *adverb*
1 in what way: *How does this machine work?* ◇ *She told me **how to** get to the station.* ◇ *Do you know **how to** spell 'essential'?*
2 a word that you use to ask if somebody is well: *'How is your sister?' 'She's very well, thank you.'*

🔎 WHICH WORD?
You use **how** only when you are asking about somebody's health.
When you are asking somebody to describe another person or a thing you use **what ... like?**: *'What is your sister like?' 'She's tall with brown hair.'*

3 a word that you use to ask if something is good: *How was the film?*
4 a word that you use to ask questions about things like age, amount or time: *How old are*

you? ◇ *How many brothers and sisters have you got?* ◇ *How much does this cost?* ◇ *How long have you lived here?*
5 a word that shows surprise or strong feeling: *How kind of you to help!*

how about ...? words that you use when you suggest something: *How about a drink?* ◇ *How about going for a walk?*

how are you? do you feel well?: *'How are you?' 'Fine, thanks.'*

how do you do? polite words that you say when you meet somebody for the first time

🔎 SPEAKING
When somebody says **How do you do?**, you also answer **How do you do?** and you shake hands. Some people say **Pleased to meet you** when they meet.

however 0̄⃛ /haʊ'evə(r)/ *adverb*
1 it does not matter how: *I never win, however hard I try.*
2 but: *She's very intelligent. However, she's quite lazy.*
3 a way of saying 'how' more strongly

🔎 GRAMMAR
When **ever** is used like this to say **how** more strongly, we write it as a separate word: *How ever did you manage to find me?*

howl /haʊl/ *verb* (howls, howling, howled /haʊld/)
to make a long, loud sound, like a dog makes: *The dogs howled all night.* ◇ *The wind howled around the house.*
▶ **howl** *noun*: *He let out a howl of anger.*

HQ /ˌeɪtʃ 'kjuː/ *short for* HEADQUARTERS

huddle /'hʌdl/ *verb* (huddles, huddling, huddled /'hʌdld/)
to get close to other people because you are cold or frightened: *We **huddled together** for warmth.*

hug /hʌɡ/ *verb* (hugs, hugging, hugged /hʌɡd/)
to put your arms around somebody to show that you love them: *She hugged her parents and said goodbye.*
▶ **hug** *noun*: *Come and **give** me a **hug**.*

huge 0̄⃛ /hjuːdʒ/ *adjective*
very big ⊃ SAME MEANING **enormous**: *They live in a huge house.*
▶ **hugely** /'hjuːdʒli/ *adverb* very: *She is hugely popular.*

A

hullo = HELLO

hum /hʌm/ *verb* (hums, humming, hummed /hʌmd/)
1 to sing with your lips closed: *You can hum the tune if you don't know the words.*
2 to make a low continuous sound: *The overhead wires hummed with power.*
▸ **hum** *noun* (*no plural*): *The computer was making a low hum.*

human¹ 0🔑 /'hjuːmən/ *adjective*
connected with people, not animals or machines: *the human body*

human² 0🔑 /'hjuːmən/ (*also* **human being** /ˌhjuːmən 'biːɪŋ/) *noun*
a person: *Dogs can hear much better than humans.*

the human race /ðə ˌhjuːmən 'reɪs/ *noun*
(*no plural*)
all the people in the world

humble /'hʌmbl/ *adjective* (humbler, humblest)
1 A **humble** person does not think they are better or more important than other people: *Despite her success she is still very humble.*
2 simple or poor: *a humble cottage*

humid /'hjuːmɪd/ *adjective*
(used about the weather or climate) warm and wet ➍ SAME MEANING **damp**: *The island is hot and humid.*
▸ **humidity** /hjuː'mɪdəti/ *noun* (*no plural*): *high levels of humidity*

humor American English for HUMOUR

humorous /'hjuːmərəs/ *adjective*
making you smile or laugh ➍ SAME MEANING **funny**: *a humorous story*

humour 0🔑 (*British*) (*American* **humor**)
/'hjuːmə(r)/ *noun* (*no plural*)
1 the quality of being funny or amusing: *a story full of humour*
2 the ability to laugh and know that something is funny: *Dave has a good sense of humour.*

hump /hʌmp/ *noun*
a round lump on an animal's or a person's back: *A camel has a hump on its back.* ➍ Look at the picture at **camel**.

hundred 0🔑 /'hʌndrəd/ *number*
1 100: *We invited a hundred people to the party.* ◇ *two hundred pounds* ◇ *four hundred and twenty*
2 hundreds (*informal*) a lot: *I've got hundreds of things to do today.* ➍ Look at **Numbers** on Study Pages S6-S7.
▸ **hundredth** /'hʌndrədθ/ *pronoun, adjective, adverb* 100th

hung *form of* HANG(1)

hunger /'hʌŋgə(r)/ *noun* (*no plural*)
the feeling that you want or need to eat

> 🔍 **SPEAKING**
> Be careful! We say **I am hungry** not **I have hunger**.

➍ Look at **thirst**.

hungry 0🔑 /'hʌŋgri/ *adjective*
(hungrier, hungriest)
wanting to eat: *Let's eat soon – I'm hungry!*
➍ Look at **thirsty**.

hunt 0🔑 /hʌnt/ *verb* (hunts, hunting, hunted)
to chase animals to kill them as a sport or for food: *Young lions have to learn to hunt.*

> 🔍 **SPEAKING**
> When you talk about people spending time hunting as a sport, you say **go hunting**: *They went hunting in the forest.*

hunt for something to try to find something: *I've hunted everywhere for my watch but I can't find it.*
▸ **hunt** *noun*: *a fox hunt* ◇ *a hunt for the missing child*
▸ **hunting** /'hʌntɪŋ/ *noun* (*no plural*) the activity of chasing and killing animals

hunter /'hʌntə(r)/ *noun*
a person who HUNTS wild animals

hurl /hɜːl/ *verb* (hurls, hurling, hurled /hɜːld/)
to throw something very strongly: *She hurled the book across the room.*

hurrah, hurray = HOORAY

hurricane /'hʌrɪkən/ *noun*
a storm with very strong winds: *Hurricane Katrina caused chaos in the city of New Orleans.* ➍ Look at the note at **storm**.

hurry¹ 0🔑 /'hʌri/ *verb* (hurries, hurrying, hurried /'hʌrid/)
to move or do something quickly: *We hurried home after school.*
hurry up to move or do something more quickly because there is not much time: *Hurry up or we'll be late!*

hurry² 0🔑 /'hʌri/ *noun*
in a hurry needing or wanting to do something quickly: *I can't talk to you now – I'm in a hurry.*

hurt¹ 0🔑 /hɜːt/ *verb* (hurts, hurting, hurt, has hurt)
1 to make somebody or something feel pain: *I fell and hurt my leg.* ◇ *Did you hurt*

yourself? ◇ *These shoes hurt – they are too small.*
2 to feel pain: *My leg hurts.*
3 to make somebody unhappy: *I never meant to **hurt** your **feelings**.*

> 🔎 **WHICH WORD?**
>
> **Hurt** or **injured**?
> These words are similar in meaning. We usually use **injured** when someone has been hurt in an accident.

hurt² /hɜːt/ *adjective*
1 physically harmed ⊃ SAME MEANING
injured: *Was anyone hurt in the accident?*
2 upset: *I was very hurt by what you said.*

hurtful /ˈhɜːtfl/ *adjective*
making somebody feel upset
⊃ SAME MEANING **unkind**: *hurtful remarks*

husband 0━ /ˈhʌzbənd/ *noun*
the man that a woman is married to ⊃ Look at **wife**.

hush /hʌʃ/ *verb* (hushes, hushing, hushed /hʌʃt/)
a word that you use to tell somebody to be quiet: *Hush now, and go to sleep.*
▸ **hush** *noun* (no plural) a situation in which it is completely quiet ⊃ SAME MEANING **silence**: *A hush fell over the room.*

hut /hʌt/ *noun*
a small, simple building with one room

hydraulic /haɪˈdrɔːlɪk/ *adjective*
Hydraulic equipment is worked by liquid moving under pressure: *hydraulic brakes*

hydroelectric /ˌhaɪdrəʊˈlektrɪk/ *adjective*
using the power of water to produce electricity: *hydroelectric power*

hydrogen /ˈhaɪdrədʒən/ *noun* (no plural)
a light gas that you cannot see or smell: *Water is made of hydrogen and oxygen.*

hygiene /ˈhaɪdʒiːn/ *noun* (no plural)
keeping yourself and things around you clean: *Good hygiene is very important when you are preparing food.*
▸ **hygienic** /haɪˈdʒiːnɪk/ *adjective*: *hygienic conditions*

hymn /hɪm/ *noun*
a song that Christians sing in church

hype /haɪp/ *noun* (no plural) (informal)
advertisements that make you think something is better than it really is: *Don't believe the hype – the film's rubbish!*

hyphen /ˈhaɪfn/ *noun*
a mark (-) that you use in writing. It joins words together (for example '*left-handed*') or shows that a word continues on the next line.

hypnosis /hɪpˈnəʊsɪs/ *noun* (no plural)
when somebody's mind and actions can be controlled by another person because they are in a kind of deep sleep: *She spoke about the attack **under hypnosis**.*

hypocrite /ˈhɪpəkrɪt/ *noun*
a person who pretends to have moral beliefs that they do not really have
▸ **hypocrisy** /hɪˈpɒkrəsi/ *noun* (no plural): *He condemned the hypocrisy of those politicians who do one thing and say another.*

hysterical /hɪˈsterɪkl/ *adjective*
so excited or upset that you cannot control yourself: *hysterical laughter*

A
B
C
D
E
F
G
H
I
J
K
L
M
N
O
P
Q
R
S
T
U
V
W
X
Y
Z

I i

I, i ¹ /aɪ/ *noun* (*plural* I's, i's /aɪz/)
the ninth letter of the English alphabet:
'*Island*' *begins with an* '*I*'.

I ² 0̶ /aɪ/ *pronoun* (*plural* **we**)
the person who is speaking: *I phoned and
said I was busy.* ◇ *I'll* (= I will) *see you
tomorrow.* ◇ *I'm not going to fall, am I?*

ice 0̶ /aɪs/ *noun* (*no plural*)
water that has become hard because it is
frozen: *Do you want ice in your drink?*

iceberg /'aɪsbɜːg/ *noun*
a very big piece of ice in the sea

ice cream 0̶ /ˌaɪs 'kriːm/ *noun*
very cold sweet food made from milk: *Do you
like ice cream?* ◇ *Two chocolate ice creams,
please.* ➔ Look at Picture Dictionary page **P7**.

ice cube /'aɪs kjuːb/ *noun*
a small piece of ice that you put in a drink to
make it cold

ice hockey /'aɪs hɒki/ *noun* (*British*)
(*American* **hockey**) (*no plural*)
a game that is played on ice by two teams
who try to hit a small flat rubber thing
(called a **puck**) into a goal with long
wooden sticks

ice lolly /ˌaɪs 'lɒli/ *noun* (*plural* **ice lollies**)
(*British*) (*American* **Popsicle**™)
a piece of sweet ice on a stick

ice rink /'aɪs rɪŋk/ (*also* **skating rink, rink**)
noun
a special place where you can ICE-SKATE

ice-skate /'aɪs skeɪt/ *verb* (ice-skates, ice-
skating, ice-skated) (*also* **skate**)
to move on ice in special boots (called ice-
skates) that have long sharp pieces of metal
on the bottom ➔ Look at the picture at
skate.
▶ **ice-skating** /'aɪs skeɪtɪŋ/ (*also* **skating**)
noun (*no plural*): *We go ice-skating every
weekend in the winter.* ➔ Look at Picture
Dictionary pages **P14-P15**.

icicle /'aɪsɪkl/ *noun*
a long piece of ice that hangs down from
something ➔ Look at Picture Dictionary
page **P16**.

icing /'aɪsɪŋ/ *noun* (*no plural*) (*British*)
(*American* **frosting**)
a sweet substance that you use for covering
cakes: *a cake with pink icing*

icon /'aɪkɒn/ *noun*
(*computing*) a small picture on a computer

screen that you can use to start a program or
open a file: *Double-click on the icon.*

icy /'aɪsi/ *adjective* (**icier, iciest**)
1 covered with ice: *icy roads*
2 very cold: *an icy wind*

ID /ˌaɪ 'diː/ *abbreviation* (*informal*)
a document that shows who you are: *Do you
have any ID?* ◇ *an ID card* ➔ **ID** is short for
'identity' or 'identification'.

I'd /aɪd/ *short for* I HAD; I WOULD

idea 0̶ /aɪ'dɪə/ *noun*
1 a plan or new thought: *It was a good idea
to give Martin a pen for his birthday.* ◇ *I've got
an idea. Let's have a party!*
2 a picture in your mind: *The film gives you a
good idea of what Iceland is like.* ◇ *I've got no
idea* (= I do not know) *where she is.*

ideal /aɪ'diːəl/ *adjective*
the best or exactly right ➔ SAME MEANING
perfect: *This is an ideal place for a picnic.*

identical /aɪ'dentɪkl/ *adjective*
exactly the same: *These two cameras are
identical.* ◇ *identical twins*

identification /aɪˌdentɪfɪ'keɪʃn/ *noun*
(*no plural*)
1 the process of showing or finding out who
somebody or something is: *The
identification of bodies after the accident was
difficult.*
2 (*abbr.* **ID**) a document that shows who
you are: *Do you have any identification?*

identify 0̶ /aɪ'dentɪfaɪ/ *verb*
(identifies, identifying, identified
/aɪ'dentɪfaɪd/, has identified)
to say or know who somebody is or what
something is: *The police have not identified
the dead man yet.*

identity /aɪ'dentəti/ *noun* (*plural*
identities)
who or what a person or thing is: *The identity
of the killer is not known.*

identity card /aɪ'dentəti kɑːd/ *noun* (*also*
ID card)
a card that shows who you are

idiom /'ɪdiəm/ *noun*
a group of words with a special meaning:
*The idiom 'break somebody's heart' means 'to
make somebody very unhappy'.*

idiomatic /ˌɪdiə'mætɪk/ *adjective*
using language that contains natural
expressions: *She speaks fluent and idiomatic
English.*

idiot /'ɪdiət/ *noun*
a person who is stupid or does something silly: *I was an idiot to forget my key.*
▶ **idiotic** /ˌɪdi'ɒtɪk/ *adjective*: *an idiotic mistake*

idol /'aɪdl/ *noun*
1 a famous person that people love: *He was the pop idol of millions of teenagers.*
2 an object that people treat as a god

i.e. /ˌaɪ 'iː/ *abbreviation*
used in writing to mean 'that is' or 'in other words': *You can buy hot drinks, i.e. tea and coffee, on the train.*

if 0🔑 /ɪf/ *conjunction*
1 a word that you use to say what is possible or true when another thing happens or is true: *If you press this button, the machine starts.* ◇ *If you see him, give him this letter.* ◇ *If your feet were smaller, you could wear my shoes.* ◇ *If I had a million pounds, I would buy a big house.* ◇ *I may see you tomorrow. If not, I'll see you next week.*
2 a word that shows a question
⊃ SAME MEANING **whether**: *Do you know if Paul is at home?* ◇ *She asked me if I wanted to go to a party.*
3 every time ⊃ SAME MEANING **whenever**: *If I try to phone her she just hangs up.*
as if in a way that makes you think something: *She looks as if she has been on holiday.*
if only words that show that you want something very much: *If only I could drive!*

igloo /'ɪgluː/ *noun* (*plural* **igloos**)
a small house that is made out of blocks of snow

ignite /ɪg'naɪt/ *verb* (**ignites, igniting, ignited**) (*formal*)
to start burning or to make something start burning: *The gas ignited and caused an explosion.*

ignorance /'ɪgnərəns/ *noun* (*no plural*)
not knowing about something: *Her ignorance surprised me.*

ignorant /'ɪgnərənt/ *adjective*
not knowing about something: *I'm very ignorant about computers.*

ignore 0🔑 /ɪg'nɔː(r)/ *verb* (**ignores, ignoring, ignored** /ɪg'nɔːd/)
to know about somebody or something, but to not do anything about it: *He completely ignored his doctor's advice.* ◇ *I said hello to her, but she ignored me!*

> 🔎 **WHICH WORD?**
> Be careful! **Ignore** and **be ignorant** are not the same.

il- *prefix*
You can add **il-** to the beginning of some words to give them the opposite meaning, for example '*illegal*' (= not legal).

ill 0🔑 /ɪl/ *adjective* (British) (American **sick**)
not well; not in good health: *Mark is in bed because he is ill.* ◇ *I feel too ill to go to work.* ◇ *Josie was taken ill* (= became ill) *on holiday.*
⊃ The noun is **illness**. ⊃ Look at Study Page S13.

I'll /aɪl/ *short for* I SHALL; I WILL

illegal 0🔑 /ɪ'liːgl/ *adjective*
not allowed by law: *It's illegal to drive through a red light.* ⊃ OPPOSITE **legal**
▶ **illegally** /ɪ'liːgəli/ *adverb*: *She entered the country illegally.*

illegible /ɪ'ledʒəbl/ *adjective*
difficult or impossible to read: *Your handwriting is completely illegible.*
⊃ OPPOSITE **legible**

illiterate /ɪ'lɪtərət/ *adjective*
not able to read or write

illness 0🔑 /'ɪlnəs/ *noun*
1 (*no plural*) being ill: *I missed a lot of school because of illness last year.*
2 (*plural* **illnesses**) a type or period of illness: *She died after a long illness.*

ill-treat /ˌɪl 'triːt/ *verb* (**ill-treats, ill-treating, ill-treated**)
to do cruel things to a person or an animal: *This dog has been ill-treated.*

illusion /ɪ'luːʒn/ *noun*
a false idea or belief: *I have no illusions about the situation – I know it's serious.*

illustrate /'ɪləstreɪt/ *verb* (**illustrates, illustrating, illustrated**)
to add pictures to show something more clearly: *The book is illustrated with colour photographs.*

illustration /ˌɪlə'streɪʃn/ *noun*
a picture in a book: *This dictionary has a lot of illustrations.*

I'm /aɪm/ *short for* I AM

im- *prefix*
You can add **im-** to the beginning of some words to give them the opposite meaning, for example '*impatient*' (= not patient).

image 0🔑 /'ɪmɪdʒ/ *noun*
1 the impression that a person or an organization gives to the public: *He's very different from his public image.*
2 a picture in people's minds of somebody or something: *A lot of people have an image of London as cold and rainy.*

A

3 a picture on paper or in a mirror: *images of war*

B

imaginary /ɪ'mædʒɪnəri/ *adjective*
not real; only in your mind: *The film is about an imaginary country.*

C

D

imagination 0— /ɪ,mædʒɪ'neɪʃn/ *noun*
the ability to think of new ideas or make pictures in your mind: *He has a lively imagination.* ◇ *You didn't really see a ghost – it was just your imagination.*

E

F

imaginative /ɪ'mædʒɪnətɪv/ *adjective*
having or showing imagination: *imaginative ideas*

G

H

imagine 0— /ɪ'mædʒɪn/ *verb* (imagines, imagining, imagined /ɪ'mædʒɪnd/)
1 to make a picture of something in your mind: *Can you imagine life without electricity?* ◇ *I closed my eyes and imagined I was lying on a beach.*
2 to see, hear, or think something that is not true: *I never said that, you're imagining things.*

I

J

imitate /'ɪmɪteɪt/ *verb* (imitates, imitating, imitated)
to copy somebody or something: *Children learn by imitating adults.*

K

L

imitation /,ɪmɪ'teɪʃn/ *noun*
something that you make to look like another thing ⊃ SAME MEANING **copy**: *It's not a real diamond, it's only an imitation.* ◇ *imitation leather*

M

N

O

immature /,ɪmə'tjʊə(r)/ *adjective*
behaving in a way that is not sensible and is typical of younger people: *He's very immature for his age.* ⊃ OPPOSITE **mature**

P

Q

immediate 0— /ɪ'miːdiət/ *adjective*
happening now or very soon: *I can't wait – I need an immediate answer.*

R

S

immediately 0— /ɪ'miːdiətli/ *adverb*

T

U

🔎 **SPELLING**
Remember! You spell **immediately** with **MM**.

now ⊃ SAME MEANING **at once**: *Come to my office immediately!*

V

immense /ɪ'mens/ *adjective*
very big: *immense problems*

W

immensely /ɪ'mensli/ *adverb*
very or very much: *We enjoyed the party immensely.*

X

Y

immigrant /'ɪmɪgrənt/ *noun*
a person who comes to another country to live there: *Many immigrants to Britain have come from Asia.*

Z

immigration /,ɪmɪ'greɪʃn/ *noun* (no plural)
coming to another country to live there: *The government is trying to control immigration.*

immoral /ɪ'mɒrəl/ *adjective*
(used about people and their behaviour) not honest or good: *It's immoral to steal.*
⊃ OPPOSITE **moral**

immortal /ɪ'mɔːtl/ *adjective*
living or lasting for ever

immune /ɪ'mjuːn/ *adjective*
If you are **immune** to a disease, you cannot get it: *You're **immune to** measles if you've had it before.*

immunize /'ɪmjunaɪz/ *verb* (immunizes, immunizing, immunized /'ɪmjunaɪzd/)
to protect somebody from a disease by putting a substance that protects the body (called a **vaccine**) into their blood

impact /'ɪmpækt/ *noun*
the effect that something has: *I hope this campaign will **have an impact on** young people.*

impatient 0— /ɪm'peɪʃnt/ *adjective*
not wanting to wait for something: *Don't be so impatient! The bus will be here soon.*
⊃ OPPOSITE **patient**
▶ **impatience** /ɪm'peɪʃns/ *noun* (no plural): *He couldn't hide his impatience.*
▶ **impatiently** /ɪm'peɪʃntli/ *adverb*: *'Hurry up!' she said impatiently.*

imperative /ɪm'perətɪv/ *noun*
(*grammar*) the form of a verb that you use for telling somebody to do something: *'Listen!' and 'Go away!' are in the imperative.*

the imperfect /ði ɪm'pɜːfɪkt/ *noun* (no plural)
(*grammar*) the form of the verb that is used to talk about an action in the past that is not finished or that lasted for a long time: *In the sentence 'I was having a bath', the verb is in the imperfect.*

impertinent /ɪm'pɜːtɪnənt/ *adjective*
(*formal*)
rude and not showing respect
⊃ SAME MEANING **cheeky**: *Don't be impertinent!*

imply /ɪm'plaɪ/ *verb* (implies, implying, implied /ɪm'plaɪd/, has implied)
to suggest something without actually saying it: *He asked if I had any work to do. He was **implying that** I was lazy.*

impolite /,ɪmpə'laɪt/ *adjective*
rude: *It was **impolite of** him to ask you to leave.* ⊃ OPPOSITE **polite**

import /ɪmˈpɔːt/ *verb* (imports, importing, imported)
to buy things from another country and bring them into your country: *Britain imports oranges from Spain.* ⊃ OPPOSITE **export**
▶ **import** /ˈɪmpɔːt/ *noun*: *What are your country's main imports?* ⊃ OPPOSITE **export**
▶ **importer** /ɪmˈpɔːtə(r)/ *noun*: *an importer of electrical goods*

importance 0ᴡ /ɪmˈpɔːtns/ *noun* (no plural)
the quality of being important: *Oil is of great importance to industry.*

important 0ᴡ /ɪmˈpɔːtnt/ *adjective*
1 If something is **important**, you must do, have or think about it: *It is important to sleep well the night before an exam.* ◇ *I think that happiness is more important than money.*
2 powerful or special: *The prime minister is a very important person.*

impossible 0ᴡ /ɪmˈpɒsəbl/ *adjective*
If something is **impossible**, you cannot do it, or it cannot happen: *It's impossible for me to finish this work by five o'clock.* ◇ *The house was impossible to find.* ⊃ OPPOSITE **possible**

impractical /ɪmˈpræktɪkl/ *adjective*
not sensible or realistic: *It would be impractical to take our bikes on the train.*

impress /ɪmˈpres/ *verb* (impresses, impressing, impressed /ɪmˈprest/)
to make somebody admire and respect you: *We were very impressed by your work.*

impression 0ᴡ /ɪmˈpreʃn/ *noun*
feelings or thoughts you have about somebody or something: *What was your first impression of the city?* ◇ *I get the impression that she's not very happy.* ◇ *He made a good impression on his first day at work.*

impressive 0ᴡ /ɪmˈpresɪv/ *adjective*
If somebody or something is **impressive**, you admire them: *an impressive building* ◇ *Your work is very impressive.*

imprison /ɪmˈprɪzn/ *verb* (imprisons, imprisoning, imprisoned /ɪmˈprɪznd/)
to put somebody in prison: *He was imprisoned for killing his wife.*
▶ **imprisonment** /ɪmˈprɪznmənt/ *noun* (no plural): *two years' imprisonment*

improbable /ɪmˈprɒbəbl/ *adjective*
not likely to be true or to happen: *an improbable explanation*

improve 0ᴡ /ɪmˈpruːv/ *verb* (improves, improving, improved /ɪmˈpruːvd/)
to become better or to make something better: *Your English has improved a lot this year.* ◇ *You must improve your spelling.*

improvement 0ᴡ /ɪmˈpruːvmənt/ *noun*
a change that makes something better than it was before: *There has been a big improvement in Sam's work.*

impulse /ˈɪmpʌls/ *noun*
a sudden strong wish to do something: *She felt an impulse to run away.*

impulsive /ɪmˈpʌlsɪv/ *adjective*
doing things suddenly and without thinking carefully: *It was an impulsive decision.*

in¹ 0ᴡ /ɪn/ *preposition*
1 a word that shows where somebody or something is: *a country in Africa* ◇ *He put his hand in the water* ◇ *She was lying in bed.*
2 making all or part of something: *There are 100 centimetres in a metre.*
3 a word that shows when something happens: *My birthday is in May.* ◇ *He started school in 1987.*
4 a word that shows how long something takes: *I'll be ready in ten minutes.*
5 a word that shows what clothes somebody is wearing: *He was dressed in a suit.*
6 a word that shows how somebody or something is: *This room is in a mess.* ◇ *Jenny was in tears* (= she was crying). ◇ *Sit in a circle.*
7 a word that shows somebody's job: *He's in the army.*
8 a word that shows in what way or in what language: *Write your name in capital letters.* ◇ *They were speaking in French.*

in² 0ᴡ /ɪn/ *adverb*
1 to a place, from outside: *I opened the door and went in.*
2 at home or at work: *Nobody was in when we called.*

in- *prefix*
You can add **in-** to the beginning of some words to give them the opposite meaning, for example 'incomplete' (= not complete).

inability /ˌɪnəˈbɪləti/ *noun* (no plural)
not being able to do something: *He has an inability to talk about his problems.* ⊃ The adjective is **unable**.

inaccurate /ɪnˈækjərət/ *adjective*
not correct; with mistakes in it: *The report in the newspaper was inaccurate.* ⊃ OPPOSITE **accurate**

inadequate /ɪnˈædɪkwət/ *adjective*
not enough, or not good enough: *These shoes are inadequate for cold weather.* ⊃ OPPOSITE **adequate**

inappropriate /ˌɪnəˈprəʊpriət/ *adjective*
not suitable: *Isn't that dress rather*

A B C D E F G H I J K L M N O P Q R S T U V W X Y Z

inappropriate for a formal occasion?
➜ OPPOSITE **appropriate**

incapable /ɪnˈkeɪpəbl/ *adjective*
not able to do something: *He's incapable of lying.* ➜ OPPOSITE **capable**

incentive /ɪnˈsentɪv/ *noun*
something that makes you want to do something: *People need incentives to save money.*

inch /ɪntʃ/ *noun* (*plural* inches)
a measure of length (=2.54 centimetres). There are twelve **inches** in a **foot**: *I am five foot six inches tall.* ◇ *a twelve-inch ruler*
➜ Look at the note at **foot**.

incident /ˈɪnsɪdənt/ *noun*
something that happens, especially something bad or unusual: *There were a number of incidents after the football match.*

incidentally /ˌɪnsɪˈdentli/ *adverb*
a word that you say when you are going to talk about something different
➜ SAME MEANING **by the way**: *Incidentally, have you been to that new cinema yet?*

inclined /ɪnˈklaɪnd/ *adjective*
1 wanting to do something: *I'm inclined to agree with you.*
2 likely to do something: *She's inclined to change her mind a lot.*

include 0̶ₘ /ɪnˈkluːd/ *verb* (includes, including, included)
1 to have somebody or something as one part of the whole: *The price of the room includes breakfast.*
2 to make somebody or something part of a group: *Did you include the new girl in the list?* ➜ OPPOSITE **exclude**

including 0̶ₘ /ɪnˈkluːdɪŋ/ *preposition*
with; if you count: *There were five people in the car, including the driver.*
➜ OPPOSITE **excluding**

inclusive /ɪnˈkluːsɪv/ *adjective*
including everything or the thing mentioned: *The price is inclusive of meals.*

income /ˈɪnkʌm/ *noun*
all the money that you receive for your work, for example: *It's difficult for a family to live on one income.*

income tax /ˈɪnkʌm tæks/ *noun* (*no plural*)
the money that you pay to the government from the money that you earn

incomplete /ˌɪnkəmˈpliːt/ *adjective*
not finished; with parts missing: *This list is incomplete.* ➜ OPPOSITE **complete**

inconsiderate /ˌɪnkənˈsɪdərət/ *adjective*
(used about a person) not thinking or caring about other people and their feelings: *It's inconsiderate of you to make so much noise.*
➜ OPPOSITE **considerate**

inconsistent /ˌɪnkənˈsɪstənt/ *adjective*
not always the same: *She's so inconsistent – sometimes she's really friendly and sometimes she's not.* ➜ OPPOSITE **consistent**

inconvenient /ˌɪnkənˈviːniənt/ *adjective*
causing you problems or difficulty: *Is this an inconvenient time? I can call back later.*
➜ OPPOSITE **convenient**
▸ **inconvenience** /ˌɪnkənˈviːniəns/ *noun* (*no plural*): *We apologize for any inconvenience caused by the delay.*

incorrect /ˌɪnkəˈrekt/ *adjective*
not right or true: *There were several incorrect answers.* ➜ OPPOSITE **correct**
▸ **incorrectly** /ˌɪnkəˈrektli/ *adverb*: *Her name was spelled incorrectly.*
➜ OPPOSITE **correctly**

increase 0̶ₘ /ɪnˈkriːs/ *verb* (increases, increasing, increased /ɪnˈkriːst/)

> 🔎 **PRONUNCIATION**
> Be careful how you say this word. When **increase** is a verb, you say the second part of the word louder: **inCREASE**. When increase is a noun, you say the first part of the word louder: **INcrease**.

to become bigger or more; to make something bigger or more: *The number of women who go out to work has increased.* ◇ *I'm going to increase your pocket money to £5.*
▸ **increase** /ˈɪnkriːs/ *noun*: *There has been an increase in road accidents.* ◇ *a price increase* ➜ OPPOSITE **decrease**

increasingly /ɪnˈkriːsɪŋli/ *adverb*
more and more: *This city is becoming increasingly dangerous.*

incredible /ɪnˈkredəbl/ *adjective*
1 impossible or very difficult to believe
➜ SAME MEANING **unbelievable**: *I found his story completely incredible.*
2 (*informal*) very large or very good: *She earns an incredible amount of money.* ◇ *The hotel was incredible.*
▸ **incredibly** /ɪnˈkredəbli/ *adverb*
(*informal*) extremely: *He's incredibly clever.*

incubator /ˈɪŋkjubeɪtə(r)/ *noun*
a special machine that hospitals use to keep small or weak babies alive

indecisive /ˌɪndɪˈsaɪsɪv/ *adjective*
not able to make decisions easily
➜ OPPOSITE **decisive**

indeed 0̶ₘ /ɪnˈdiːd/ *adverb*
1 a word that makes a positive thing that

you say stronger ⊃ SAME MEANING
certainly: '*Did you have a good holiday?*' '*I
did indeed.*'
2 a word that makes 'very' stronger: *Thank
you very much indeed.* ◇ *She's very happy
indeed.*

indefinite /ɪnˈdefɪnət/ *adjective*
not clear or certain: *Our plans are still rather
indefinite.*

indefinite article /ɪnˌdefɪnət ˈɑːtɪkl/
noun
(*grammar*) the name for the words 'a' and
'an' ⊃ Look at **definite article**.

indefinitely /ɪnˈdefɪnətli/ *adverb*
for a long time, perhaps for ever: *I can't wait
indefinitely.*

independence /ˌɪndɪˈpendəns/ *noun* (*no
plural*)
being free from another person, thing or
country: *America declared its **independence**
from Britain in 1776.*

independent 0‑ₘ /ˌɪndɪˈpendənt/
adjective

> 🔍 SPELLING
> Remember! You spell **independent** with
> three **E**'s.

1 not controlled by another person, thing or
country: *Mozambique became independent in
1975.*
2 not needing or wanting help: *She lives
alone now and she is very independent.*

index /ˈɪndeks/ *noun* (*plural* indexes)
a list of words from A to Z at the end of a
book. It tells you what things are in the book
and where you can find them.

index finger /ˈɪndeks fɪŋɡə(r)/ *noun*
(*plural* index fingers)
the finger next to your thumb

indicate /ˈɪndɪkeɪt/ *verb* (indicates,
indicating, indicated)
1 to show that something is true, exists or
will happen: *Black clouds **indicate that** it's
going to rain.*
2 to make somebody notice something,
especially by pointing to it: *The receptionist
indicated the place where I should sign.*
3 (*British*) to show that your car is going
to turn by using a light: *You should indicate
left now.*

indication /ˌɪndɪˈkeɪʃn/ *noun*
something that shows something
⊃ SAME MEANING **sign**: *He gave no
indication that he was angry.*

indicator /ˈɪndɪkeɪtə(r)/ *noun*
a light on a car that shows that it is going to
turn left or right

indifferent /ɪnˈdɪfrənt/ *adjective*
not interested in or caring about somebody
or something: *He seemed completely
indifferent to my feelings.*

indigestion /ˌɪndɪˈdʒestʃən/ *noun* (*no
plural*)
pain in your stomach caused by something
you have eaten: *Onions **give** me **indigestion**.*

indignant /ɪnˈdɪɡnənt/ *adjective*
angry because somebody has done or said
something that you do not like or agree
with: *She was indignant when I said she
was lazy.*
▸ **indignantly** /ɪnˈdɪɡnəntli/ *adverb*: '*I'm
not late,*' *he said indignantly.*
▸ **indignation** /ˌɪndɪɡˈneɪʃn/ *noun* (*no
plural*) a feeling of anger and surprise

indirect /ˌɪndəˈrekt; ˌɪndaɪˈrekt/ *adjective*
not straight or direct: *We came by an indirect
route.* ◇ *These problems are an indirect result
of the war.* ⊃ OPPOSITE **direct**
▸ **indirectly** /ˌɪndəˈrektli; ˌɪndaɪˈrektli/
adverb: *These events affect us all, directly or
indirectly.*

indirect object /ˌɪndərekt ˈɒbdʒɪkt/
noun
(*grammar*) a person or thing that an action is
done to or for: *In the sentence 'I sent him a
letter', 'him' is the indirect object.* ⊃ Look at
direct object.

indirect speech /ˌɪndərekt ˈspiːtʃ/
another word for REPORTED SPEECH

individual¹ 0‑ₘ /ˌɪndɪˈvɪdʒuəl/
adjective
1 considered separately and not as part of a
group: *Each individual student gets their own
study plan.*
2 for only one person or thing: *an individual
portion of cheese*
▸ **individually** /ˌɪndɪˈvɪdʒuəli/ *adverb*:
The teacher spoke to each student individually.

individual² /ˌɪndɪˈvɪdʒuəl/ *noun*
one person: *Teachers must treat each child as
an individual.*

indoor /ˈɪndɔː(r)/ *adjective*
done or used inside a building: *an indoor
swimming pool* ◇ *indoor games*
⊃ OPPOSITE **outdoor**

indoors /ˌɪnˈdɔːz/ *adverb*
in or into a building: *Let's go indoors. I'm
cold.* ⊃ OPPOSITE **outdoors**

industrial /ɪnˈdʌstriəl/ *adjective*
1 connected with making things in
factories: *industrial machines*
2 with a lot of factories: *Leeds is an industrial
city.*

A
B
C
D
E
F
G
H
I
J
K
L
M
N
O
P
Q
R
S
T
U
V
W
X
Y
Z

A

industry 0🔑 /ˈɪndəstri/ *noun*
1 (*no plural*) the work of making things in factories: *Is there much industry in your country?*
2 (*plural* **industries**) all the companies that make the same thing: *Japan has a big car industry.*

inefficient /ˌɪnɪˈfɪʃnt/ *adjective*
A person or thing that is **inefficient** does not work well or in the best way: *This washing machine is very old and inefficient.*
➔ OPPOSITE **efficient**

inevitable /ɪnˈevɪtəbl/ *adjective*
If something is **inevitable**, it will certainly happen: *The accident was inevitable – he was driving too fast.*
▸ **inevitably** /ɪnˈevɪtəbli/ *adverb*: *Building the new hospital inevitably cost a lot of money.*

inexperienced /ˌɪnɪkˈspɪəriənst/ *adjective*
If you are **inexperienced**, you do not know about something because you have not done it many times before: *a young inexperienced driver*
➔ OPPOSITE **experienced**

inexplicable /ˌɪnɪkˈsplɪkəbl/ *adjective*
Something that is **inexplicable** cannot be explained or understood: *I found his behaviour inexplicable.*

infant /ˈɪnfənt/ *noun* (*formal*)
a baby or very young child

infant school /ˈɪnfənt skuːl/ *noun*
(*British*)
a school for children between the ages of five and seven

infect /ɪnˈfekt/ *verb* (**infects, infecting, infected**)
to give a disease to somebody: *Thousands of people have been infected with the virus.*

infected /ɪnˈfektɪd/ *adjective*
full of small living things (called **germs**) that can make you ill: *Clean that cut or it could become infected.*

infection 0🔑 /ɪnˈfekʃn/ *noun*
an illness that affects one part of the body: *Mike has an ear infection.*

infectious /ɪnˈfekʃəs/ *adjective*
An **infectious** disease goes easily from one person to another.

inferior /ɪnˈfɪəriə(r)/ *adjective*
not as good or important as another person or thing: *Lisa's so clever she always makes me feel inferior.* ➔ OPPOSITE **superior**

infinite /ˈɪnfɪnət/ *adjective*
with no end; too much or too many to count or measure: *There is an infinite number of stars in the sky.*

infinitely /ˈɪnfɪnətli/ *adverb*
very much: *DVDs are infinitely better than videos.*

infinitive /ɪnˈfɪnətɪv/ *noun*
(*grammar*) the simple form of a verb: '*Eat*', '*go*' and '*play*' are all infinitives.

> 🔎 **GRAMMAR**
> We sometimes use the **infinitive** with *to*, and sometimes without, depending on what comes before it: *He can sing.* ◇ *He wants to sing.*

infinity /ɪnˈfɪnəti/ *noun* (*no plural*)
space or time without end

inflammable /ɪnˈflæməbl/ *adjective*
An **inflammable** substance burns easily: *Petrol is **highly inflammable**.*

inflate /ɪnˈfleɪt/ *verb* (**inflates, inflating, inflated**) (*formal*)
to fill something with air or gas: *He inflated the tyre.*

> 🔎 **SPEAKING**
> It is more usual to say **blow up** or **pump up**: *I pumped up my bicycle tyres.*

inflation /ɪnˈfleɪʃn/ *noun* (*no plural*)
a general rise in prices in a country: *The government is trying to control inflation.*

influence¹ 0🔑 /ˈɪnfluəns/ *noun*
1 (*no plural*) the power to change what somebody believes or does: *Television has a strong influence on people.*
2 (*plural* **influences**) a person or thing that can change somebody or something: *Paul's new girlfriend is a good influence on him.*

influence² /ˈɪnfluəns/ *verb* (**influences, influencing, influenced** /ˈɪnfluənst/)
to change the way that somebody thinks or the way that something happens: *She is easily influenced by her friends.*

influential /ˌɪnfluˈenʃl/ *adjective*
having power or influence: *Her father's very influential.*

inform 0🔑 /ɪnˈfɔːm/ *verb* (**informs, informing, informed** /ɪnˈfɔːmd/)
to tell somebody something: *You should inform the police of the accident.*

informal 0🔑 /ɪnˈfɔːml/ *adjective*
relaxed and friendly; suitable for a relaxed occasion: *I wear informal clothes, like jeans and T-shirts, at weekends.* ◇ *an informal letter*

> 🔎 **SPEAKING**
>
> Some words and expressions in this dictionary are labelled **informal**. You use them when speaking and writing to people you know well, but not in serious writing or official letters.

▶ **informally** /ɪnˈfɔːməli/ *adverb*: *We have discussed the matter informally.*

information ௦ᵀ /ˌɪnfəˈmeɪʃn/ *noun* (*no plural*)

facts about people or things: *Can you give me some information about trains to London?*

> 🔎 **GRAMMAR**
>
> Be careful! You cannot say 'an information'. You can say **some information** or **a piece of information**: *She gave me an interesting piece of information.*

informative /ɪnˈfɔːmətɪv/ *adjective*

giving useful information: *The talk was very informative.*

ingredient /ɪnˈɡriːdiənt/ *noun*

one of the things that you put in when you make something to eat: *The ingredients for this cake are flour, butter, sugar and eggs.*

inhabit /ɪnˈhæbɪt/ *verb* (inhabits, inhabiting, inhabited)

to live in a place: *Is the island inhabited* (= does anybody live there)*?* ◇ *The South Pole is inhabited by penguins.*

inhabitant /ɪnˈhæbɪtənt/ *noun*

a person or an animal that lives in a place: *The town has 30 000 inhabitants.*

inhale /ɪnˈheɪl/ *verb* (inhales, inhaling, inhaled /ɪnˈheɪld/) (*formal*)

to take air, smoke, etc. into your body by breathing: *Be careful not to inhale the fumes from the paint.* ⊃ OPPOSITE **exhale**

inherit /ɪnˈherɪt/ *verb* (inherits, inheriting, inherited)

to get money or things from somebody who has died: *Sabine inherited some money from her grandmother.*
▶ **inheritance** /ɪnˈherɪtəns/ *noun* (*no plural*) money or things that you get from somebody who has died: *She spent her inheritance in just one year.*

initial¹ /ɪˈnɪʃl/ *adjective*

first: *My initial reaction was to say 'no'.*
▶ **initially** /ɪˈnɪʃəli/ *adverb*
⊃ SAME MEANING **at first**: *Initially, the system worked well.*

initial² /ɪˈnɪʃl/ *noun*

the first letter of a person's name: *John Waters' initials are J.W.*

inject /ɪnˈdʒekt/ *verb* (injects, injecting, injected)

to put a drug into a person's body using a special needle (called a **syringe**)
▶ **injection** /ɪnˈdʒekʃn/ *noun*: *The doctor gave the baby an injection.*

injure /ˈɪndʒə(r)/ *verb* (injures, injuring, injured /ˈɪndʒəd/)

to hurt yourself or somebody else, especially in an accident: *She injured her arm when she was playing tennis.* ◇ *Joe was injured in a car accident.*
▶ **injured** /ˈɪndʒəd/ *adjective*: *The injured woman was taken to hospital.*

injury ௦ᵀ /ˈɪndʒəri/ *noun* (*plural* injuries)

damage to the body of a person or an animal: *He had serious head injuries.*

injustice /ɪnˈdʒʌstɪs/ *noun* (*no plural*)

the fact of a situation not being fair or right: *the struggle against injustice*

ink /ɪŋk/ *noun* (*no plural*)

coloured liquid for writing and printing: *Please write in black or blue ink.* ⊃ Look at the picture at **pen**.

inland /ˌɪnˈlænd/ *adverb*

in or towards the middle of a country: *The village lies a few miles inland.*
▶ **inland** /ˈɪnlənd/ *adjective* in the middle of a country, not near the sea: *an inland lake*

inn /ɪn/ *noun* (British)

a pub, usually in the country and often one where you can stay the night

> 🔎 **CULTURE**
>
> **Inn** is an old word that we do not use much now, except in the names of pubs, hotels and restaurants.

inner /ˈɪnə(r)/ *adjective*

inside; towards or close to the centre: *the inner ear* ⊃ OPPOSITE **outer**

inner city /ˌɪnə ˈsɪti/ *noun* (*plural* inner cities)

the poor areas near the centre of a big city: *the problems of the inner cities*
▶ **inner-city** *adjective*: *an inner-city school*

innocent /ˈɪnəsnt/ *adjective*

If you are **innocent**, you have not done anything wrong: *He claims he's innocent of the crime.* ⊃ OPPOSITE **guilty**
▶ **innocence** /ˈɪnəsns/ *noun* (*no plural*): *The prisoner's family are convinced of her innocence.* ⊃ OPPOSITE **guilt**

input /ˈɪnpʊt/ *noun*

time, ideas or work that you put into something to make it successful: *Her specialist input to the discussions was very useful.*

A B C D E F G H I J K L M N O P Q R S T U V W X Y Z

A B C D E F G H **I** J K L M N O P Q R S T U V W X Y Z

inquest /'ɪŋkwest/ *noun*
an official process to find out how somebody died: *An inquest was held to discover the cause of death.*

inquire, inquiry /ɪn'kwaɪə(r)/, ɪn'kwaɪəri/ *another word for* ENQUIRE, ENQUIRY

inquisitive /ɪn'kwɪzətɪv/ *adjective*
wanting to find out as much as possible about things: *Don't be so inquisitive – it's none of your business!*

insane /ɪn'seɪn/ *adjective*
seriously mentally ill ➔ SAME MEANING **mad**: *The prisoners were slowly going insane.*

insect 0̄ /'ɪnsekt/ *noun*
a very small animal that has six legs: *Ants, flies, butterflies and beetles are all insects.*

> 🔎 **WORD BUILDING**
> There are many different types of **insect**. Here are some of them: ant, bee, butterfly, cockroach, flea, fly. Do you know any others?

insecure /ˌɪnsɪ'kjʊə(r)/ *adjective*
1 worried and not sure about yourself: *Many teenagers feel insecure about their appearance.*
2 not safe or firm: *This ladder looks a bit insecure.* ➔ OPPOSITE **secure**
▶ **insecurity** /ˌɪnsɪ'kjʊərəti/ *noun* (*no plural*): *She had feelings of insecurity.*

insensitive /ɪn'sensətɪv/ *adjective*
not knowing or caring how another person feels: *That was a very insensitive remark.* ◇ *She's completely insensitive to my feelings.* ➔ OPPOSITE **sensitive**

insert /ɪn'sɜːt/ *verb* (inserts, inserting, inserted) (*formal*)
to put something into something or between two things: *Insert the CD into the computer.*

inside¹ 0̄ /ɪn'saɪd/ *preposition, adverb, adjective*
in, on or to the inside of something: *What's inside the box?* ◇ *It's raining – let's go inside* (= into the building). ◇ *the inside pocket of a jacket* ➔ Look at **outside**.

inside² 0̄ /ɪn'saɪd/ *noun*
the part near the middle of something: *The door was locked from the inside.* ◇ *There's a label somewhere on the inside.* ➔ Look at **outside**.

inside out with the wrong side on the outside: *You've got your jumper on inside out.*

inside out

insignificant /ˌɪnsɪg'nɪfɪkənt/ *adjective*
of little value or importance: *an insignificant detail*
➔ OPPOSITE **significant**

insist /ɪn'sɪst/ *verb* (insists, insisting, insisted)
1 to say very strongly that something must happen or be done: *Paul insisted on driving me to the station.*
2 to say very strongly that something is true, when somebody does not believe you: *He insists that he didn't take the money.*

insolent /'ɪnsələnt/ *adjective* (*formal*)
not showing respect ➔ SAME MEANING **rude**: *He gave her an insolent stare.*

inspect /ɪn'spekt/ *verb* (inspects, inspecting, inspected)
to look at something carefully: *I inspected the car before I bought it.*
▶ **inspection** /ɪn'spekʃn/ *noun*: *The police made an inspection of the house.*

inspector /ɪn'spektə(r)/ *noun*
1 a person whose job is to see that things are done correctly: *a factory inspector*
2 a police officer

inspiration /ˌɪnspə'reɪʃn/ *noun*
a person or thing that makes you want to do something or gives you good ideas: *The beauty of the mountains is a great inspiration to many artists.*

inspire /ɪn'spaɪə(r)/ *verb* (inspires, inspiring, inspired /ɪn'spaɪəd/)
1 to make somebody want to do something: *His wife inspired him to write this poem.*
2 to make somebody feel or think something: *Her words inspired us all with hope.*
▶ **inspiring** /ɪn'spaɪərɪŋ/ *adjective*: *an inspiring teacher*

install /ɪn'stɔːl/ *verb* (installs, installing, installed /ɪn'stɔːld/)
to put a new thing in its place so it is ready to use: *They have installed a new computer system.*

instalment (*British*) (*American* **installment**) /ɪn'stɔːlmənt/ *noun*
1 a regular payment that you make for something: *She's paying for her new car in monthly instalments.*

2 one part of a story on radio or television, or in a magazine: *Don't miss next week's exciting instalment.*

instance /'ɪnstəns/ *noun*
for instance as an example: *There are several interesting places to visit around here – Warwick, for instance.*

instant¹ /'ɪnstənt/ *adjective*
1 happening very quickly: *The film was an instant success.*
2 (used about food) quick and easy to prepare: *an instant meal* ◇ *instant coffee*
▸ **instantly** /'ɪnstəntli/ *adverb*
immediately; at once: *The driver was killed instantly.*

instant² /'ɪnstənt/ *noun*
a very short time ➔ SAME MEANING **moment**: *She thought for an instant before she answered.*

instead 0🔑 /ɪn'sted/ *adverb, preposition*
in the place of somebody or something: *We haven't got any coffee. Would you like tea instead?* ◇ *He's been playing football all afternoon instead of studying.* ◇ *Can you go to the meeting instead of me?*

instinct /'ɪnstɪŋkt/ *noun*
something that makes people and animals do certain things without thinking or learning about them: *Birds build their nests by instinct.*
▸ **instinctive** /ɪn'stɪŋktɪv/ *adjective*:
Animals have an instinctive fear of fire.

institute /'ɪnstɪtjuːt/ *noun*
a group of people who meet to study or talk about a special thing; the building where they meet: *the Institute of Science*

institution /ˌɪnstɪ'tjuːʃn/ *noun*
a big organization like a bank, hospital, prison or school: *Many financial institutions are based in London.*

instruct /ɪn'strʌkt/ *verb* (instructs, instructing, instructed)
1 to tell somebody what they must do: *He instructed the driver to wait.*
2 (*formal*) to teach somebody something: *Children must be instructed in road safety.*

instruction 0🔑 /ɪn'strʌkʃn/ *noun*
1 instructions (*plural*) words that tell you what you must do or how to do something: *Read the instructions on the back of the packet carefully.* ◇ *You should always follow the instructions.*
2 (*no plural*) teaching or being taught something: *driving instruction*

instructor /ɪn'strʌktə(r)/ *noun*
a person who teaches you how to do something: *a driving instructor*

instrument 0🔑 /'ɪnstrəmənt/ *noun*
1 a thing that you use for doing a special job: *surgical instruments* (= used by doctors)
2 a thing that you use for playing music: *Violins and trumpets are musical instruments.* ◇ *What instrument do you play?*

insult 0🔑 /ɪn'sʌlt/ *verb* (insults, insulting, insulted)
to be deliberately rude to somebody: *She insulted my brother by saying he was fat.*
▸ **insult** /'ɪnsʌlt/ *noun*: *The boys shouted insults at each other.*

insurance /ɪn'ʃʊərəns/ *noun* (no plural)
an agreement where you pay money to a company so that it will give you a lot of money if something bad happens: *When I crashed my car, the insurance paid for the repairs.*

insure /ɪn'ʃʊə(r)/ *verb* (insures, insuring, insured /ɪn'ʃʊəd/)
1 to pay money to a company, so that it will give you money if something bad happens: *Have you insured your house against fire?*
2 American English for ENSURE

intellectual /ˌɪntə'lektʃuəl/ *adjective*
connected with a person's ability to think and understand things: *a child's intellectual development*

intelligence /ɪn'telɪdʒəns/ *noun* (no plural)
being able to think, learn and understand quickly and well: *He is a man of great intelligence.* ◇ *an intelligence test*

intelligent 0🔑 /ɪn'telɪdʒənt/ *adjective*
able to think, learn and understand quickly and well: *Their daughter is very intelligent.* ◇ *an intelligent question*
▸ **intelligently** /ɪn'telɪdʒəntli/ *adverb*:
They solved the problem very intelligently.

intend 0🔑 /ɪn'tend/ *verb* (intends, intending, intended)
to plan to do something: *When do you intend to go to London?* ➔ The noun is **intention**.
be intended for somebody or **something** to be planned or made for a particular person or reason: *This dictionary is intended for elementary learners of English.*

intense /ɪn'tens/ *adjective*
very great or strong: *intense pain* ◇ *The heat from the fire was intense.*
▸ **intensely** /ɪn'tensli/ *adverb*: *I found the film intensely boring.*

intensive /ɪn'tensɪv/ *adjective*
involving a lot of work in a short time: *an intensive English course*

A
B

intention 0➔ /ɪn'tenʃn/ *noun*
what you plan to do: *They **have no intention** of getting married.* ➔ The verb is **intend**.

C

intentional /ɪn'tenʃənl/ *adjective*
done on purpose, not by mistake
➔ SAME MEANING **deliberate**: *I'm sorry I upset you – it wasn't intentional!*
▶ **intentionally** /ɪn'tenʃənəli/ *adverb*
➔ SAME MEANING **deliberately**: *They broke the window intentionally.*

D
E

F

interactive /ˌɪntər'æktɪv/ *adjective*
(*computing*) involving direct communication both ways, between the computer and the person using it: *interactive computer games*

G

H

interest¹ 0➔ /'ɪntrəst/ *noun*
1 (*no plural*) wanting to know or learn about somebody or something: *He read the story **with interest**. ◇ He **takes** no **interest in** politics.*
2 (*plural* **interests**) something that you like doing or learning about: *His interests are computers and rock music.*
3 (*no plural*) the extra money that you pay back if you borrow money or that you receive if you put money in a bank

I

J

K

L

M

interest² 0➔ /'ɪntrəst/ *verb* (**interests**, **interesting**, **interested**)
to make somebody want to know more: *Religion doesn't interest her.*

N

O

interested 0➔ /'ɪntrəstɪd/ *adjective*
wanting to know more about somebody or something: *Are you **interested in** cars?*

P

Q

interesting 0➔ /'ɪntrəstɪŋ/ *adjective*
A person or thing that is **interesting** makes you want to know more about them: *This book is very interesting. ◇ That's an interesting idea!* ➔ OPPOSITE **boring**

R

S

interfere /ˌɪntə'fɪə(r)/ *verb* (**interferes**, **interfering**, **interfered** /ˌɪntə'fɪəd/)
1 to try to do something with or for somebody, when they do not want your help: *Don't interfere! Let John decide what he wants to do.*
2 to stop something from being done well: *His interest in football often **interferes with** his studies.*
▶ **interference** /ˌɪntə'fɪərəns/ *noun* (*no plural*): *I don't want any **interference in** my affairs!*

T

U

V

W

X

interior /ɪn'tɪəriə(r)/ *noun*
the inside part: *We painted the interior of the house white.*
▶ **interior** *adjective*: *interior walls*
➔ OPPOSITE **exterior**

Y

Z

intermediate /ˌɪntə'miːdiət/ *adjective*
coming between two things or levels: *She's in an intermediate class.*

internal /ɪn'tɜːnl/ *adjective*
of or on the inside: *He has internal injuries* (= inside his body). ➔ OPPOSITE **external**
▶ **internally** /ɪn'tɜːnəli/ *adverb*: *The matter was dealt with internally.*

international 0➔ /ˌɪntə'næʃnəl/ *adjective*
between different countries: *an international football match ◇ an international flight*
▶ **internationally** /ˌɪntə'næʃnəli/ *adverb*: *an internationally famous musician*

Internet 0➔ /'ɪntənet/ *noun* the Internet (*also informal* the Net) (*no plural*) (*computing*) the international system of computers that makes it possible for you to see information from all around the world on your computer and to send information to other computers: *You can find out almost anything **on the Internet**. ◇ Do you have Internet access?*

interpret /ɪn'tɜːprɪt/ *verb* (**interprets**, **interpreting**, **interpreted**)
1 to say in one language what somebody has said in another language: *I can't speak Italian – can you interpret for me?*
2 to explain the meaning of something: *You have to interpret the facts, not just repeat them.*

interpretation /ɪnˌtɜːprɪ'teɪʃn/ *noun*
an explanation of something: *What's your **interpretation of** these statistics?*

interpreter /ɪn'tɜːprɪtə(r)/ *noun*
a person whose job is to translate what somebody is saying into another language

interrupt 0➔ /ˌɪntə'rʌpt/ *verb* (**interrupts**, **interrupting**, **interrupted**)
1 to stop somebody speaking or doing something by saying or doing something yourself: *Please don't interrupt me when I'm speaking.*
2 to stop something for a time: *The game was interrupted by rain.*
▶ **interruption** /ˌɪntə'rʌpʃn/ *noun*: *I can't do my homework here. There are too many interruptions.*

interval /'ɪntəvl/ *noun*
1 a period of time between two events: *There was an **interval of** several weeks between the attacks.*
2 (*British*) a short time between two parts of a play or concert

interview¹ 0➔ /'ɪntəvjuː/ *noun*
1 a meeting when somebody asks you

questions to decide if you will get a job: *I've got a **job interview** tomorrow.*
2 a meeting when somebody answers questions for a newspaper or for a television or radio programme: *There was an **interview** with the Prime Minister on TV last night.*

interview² /'ɪntəvjuː/ *verb* (interviews, interviewing, interviewed /'ɪntəvjuːd/)
to ask somebody questions in an **interview**: *They **interviewed** six people **for** the job.*
▶ **interviewer** /'ɪntəvjuːə(r)/ *noun: The interviewer asked me why I wanted the job.*

intestine /ɪn'testɪn/ *noun*
the tube in your body that carries food away from your stomach to the place where it leaves your body

intimate /'ɪntɪmət/ *adjective*
(used about people) having a close relationship ⊃ SAME MEANING **close**: *They're intimate friends.*

into 0̄ᴿ /'ɪntə; 'ɪntu; 'ɪntuː/ *preposition*
1 to the middle or the inside of something: *Come **into** the house. ◇ I went **into** town. ◇ He fell **into** the river.*
2 in the direction of something: *Please speak **into** the microphone.*
3 against something: *The car crashed **into** a tree.*
4 a word that shows how somebody or something changes: *When it is very cold, water **changes into** ice. ◇ They **made** the room **into** a bedroom.*
5 a word that you use when you divide a number: *4 **into** 12 is 3.*
be into something (*informal*) to like something; to be interested in something: *What sort of music are you **into**?*

intolerable /ɪn'tɒlərəbl/ *adjective*
so bad or difficult that you cannot accept it ⊃ SAME MEANING **unbearable**: *The situation was intolerable.*

intranet /'ɪntrənet/ *noun*
(*computing*) a system of computers inside an organization that makes it possible for people to share information ⊃ Look at **Internet**.

intransitive /ɪn'trænsətɪv/ *adjective*
(*grammar*) An **intransitive** verb does not have an object. ⊃ Look at **transitive**.

intrigue /ɪn'triːg/ *verb* (intrigues, intriguing, intrigued /ɪn'triːgd/)
to make somebody very interested: *His story intrigued me.*

introduce 0̄ᴿ /ˌɪntrə'djuːs/ *verb*
(introduces, introducing, introduced /ˌɪntrə'djuːst/)
1 to bring people together for the first time

and tell each of them the name of the other: *She **introduced** me **to** her brother. ◇ He **introduced** himself **to** me (= told me his name).*

🔊 SPEAKING
When we introduce people we say **this is** not 'he is' or 'she is' and not 'here is': *Jane, **this is** Bob. ◇ Bob, **this is** Jane.*
When you meet someone for the first time, you can say **Hello, How do you do?** or **Pleased to meet you**.

2 to bring in something new: *This law was introduced in 2002.*

introduction 0̄ᴿ /ˌɪntrə'dʌkʃn/ *noun*
1 (*no plural*) bringing in something new: *the **introduction of** computers **into** schools*
2 (*plural* introductions) bringing people together to meet each other
3 (*plural* introductions) a piece of writing at the beginning of a book that tells you about the book

intruder /ɪn'truːdə(r)/ *noun*
a person who enters a place without permission: *Police say the intruder was not armed.*

invade /ɪn'veɪd/ *verb* (invades, invading, invaded)
to go into another country to attack it: *They invaded the country with tanks and guns.* ⊃ The noun is **invasion**.
▶ **invader** /ɪn'veɪdə(r)/ *noun: They prepared to repel the invaders.*

invalid¹ /ɪn'vælɪd/ *adjective*
not legally or officially acceptable: *I'm afraid your passport is invalid.* ⊃ OPPOSITE **valid**

invalid² /'ɪnvəlɪd/ *noun*
a person who has been very ill for a long time and needs another person to look after them

invaluable /ɪn'væljuəbl/ *adjective*
very useful: *Your help was invaluable.*

🔊 WHICH WORD?
Be careful! **Invaluable** is not the opposite of **valuable**. The opposite of **valuable** is **worthless**.

invariably /ɪn'veəriəbli/ *adverb*
always or almost always: *He invariably arrives late.*

invasion /ɪn'veɪʒn/ *noun*
a time when an army from one country goes into another country to attack it: *Germany's invasion of Poland in 1939* ⊃ The verb is **invade**.

A B C D E F G H I J K L M N O P Q R S T U V W X Y Z

A

invent 0⇌ /ɪn'vent/ *verb* (invents, inventing, invented)

B
1 to make or think of something for the first time: *Who invented the bicycle?*

C
2 to say something that is not true: *I realized that he had invented the whole story.*

D
▶ **inventor** /ɪn'ventə(r)/ *noun*: *Marconi was the inventor of the radio.*

E
invention /ɪn'venʃn/ *noun*
1 (*plural* inventions) a thing that somebody has made for the first time

F
2 (*no plural*) inventing something: *The invention of the telephone changed the world.*

G
inverted commas /ɪn,vɜːtɪd 'kɒməz/ *noun* (*plural*) (*British*)

H
the signs " " or ' ' that you use in writing before and after words that somebody said ⊃ SAME MEANING **quotation marks**

I

invest /ɪn'vest/ *verb* (invests, investing, invested)

J
to give money to a business or bank so that you will get more money back: *He invested all his money in the company.*

K
▶ **investment** /ɪn'vestmənt/ *noun*: *an investment of €10 000*

L

investigate 0⇌ /ɪn'vestɪgeɪt/ *verb* (investigates, investigating, investigated)

M
to try to find out about something: *The police are investigating the murder.*

N
▶ **investigation** /ɪn,vestɪ'geɪʃn/ *noun*: *They are carrying out an investigation into the fire.*

O

invisible /ɪn'vɪzəbl/ *adjective*

P
If something is **invisible**, you cannot see it: *Wind is invisible.* ⊃ OPPOSITE **visible**

Q

invitation 0⇌ /,ɪnvɪ'teɪʃn/ *noun*

R
If you have an **invitation** to go somewhere, somebody has spoken or written to you and asked you to go: *Joe sent me an invitation to his party.*

S

T
invite 0⇌ /ɪn'vaɪt/ *verb* (invites, inviting, invited)

U
to ask somebody to come to a party, to your house, etc.: *Anna invited me to her party.* ◇ *Let's invite them for dinner.*

V

invoice /'ɪnvɔɪs/ *noun*

W
a list that shows how much you must pay for things that somebody has sold you, or for work that somebody has done for you

X

Y
involve 0⇌ /ɪn'vɒlv/ *verb* (involves, involving, involved /ɪn'vɒlvd/)

Z
1 to have something as a part: *The job involves using a computer.*
2 If you **involve** somebody in something,

you make them take part in it: *I want to involve more people in the concert.*

involved /ɪn'vɒlvd/ *adjective*
taking part in something; being part of something or connected with something: *I'm very involved in local politics* ◇ *We need to interview the people involved.*

inwards /'ɪnwədz/ (*also* inward /'ɪnwəd/) *adverb*
towards the inside or centre: *The doors open inwards.* ⊃ OPPOSITE **outwards** or **outward**

IOU /,aɪ əʊ 'juː/ *noun* (*informal*)
a piece of paper that shows you promise to pay somebody the money you owe them
⊃ IOU is a way of writing 'I owe you'.

IPA /,aɪ piː 'eɪ/ *abbreviation*
a system of symbols to show how words sound ⊃ IPA is short for 'International Phonetic Alphabet'.

IQ /,aɪ 'kjuː/ *noun*
a way of measuring how intelligent somebody is: *She has an IQ of 128.*

ir- *prefix*
You can add **ir-** to the beginning of some words to give them the opposite meaning, for example *irregular* (= not regular).

iron¹ 0⇌ /'aɪən/ *noun*

> 🔎 **PRONUNCIATION**
> The word **iron** sounds like **lion**, because we don't say the letter **r** in this word.

1 (*no plural*) a strong hard metal: *The gates are made of iron.* ◇ *an iron bar*

iron

iron | ironing board

2 (*plural* irons) a piece of electrical equipment that gets hot and that you use for making clothes smooth: *a steam iron*

iron² 0⟶ /'aɪən/ *verb* (irons, ironing, ironed /'aɪənd/)
to make clothes smooth using an IRON: *Can you iron this shirt for me?*
▶ **ironing** /'aɪənɪŋ/ *noun* (no plural)
clothes that need to be IRONED: *I usually do the ironing on Sunday evening.*

ironic /aɪ'rɒnɪk/ *adjective*
If you are **ironic**, you say the opposite of what you mean because you want to make people laugh or show them you are annoyed: *When I said it was a beautiful day, I was being ironic.*

ironing board /'aɪənɪŋ bɔːd/ *noun*
a special long table where you IRON clothes ⊃ Look at the picture at **iron**.

irregular /ɪ'regjələ(r)/ *adjective*
1 happening at different times: *Their visits were irregular.* ⊃ OPPOSITE **regular**
2 A word that is **irregular** does not have the usual verb forms or plural: '*Catch*' *is an irregular verb.* ⊃ OPPOSITE **regular**

irrelevant /ɪ'reləvənt/ *adjective*
not connected with something and not important: *Your point is completely irrelevant to the discussion.* ⊃ OPPOSITE **relevant**

irritable /'ɪrɪtəbl/ *adjective*
becoming angry easily: *He's very irritable in the mornings.*

irritate /'ɪrɪteɪt/ *verb* (irritates, irritating, irritated)
1 to make somebody quite angry: *He irritates me when he asks so many questions.*
2 to make a part of your body hurt a little: *Cigarette smoke irritates my eyes.*
▶ **irritation** /ˌɪrɪ'teɪʃn/ *noun*: *This plant can cause irritation to your skin.*

is *form of* BE

Islam /'ɪzlɑːm/ *noun* (no plural)
the religion of Muslim people. **Islam** teaches that there is only one God and that Muhammad is his PROPHET (= the person that God has chosen to give his message to people).
▶ **Islamic** /ɪz'læmɪk/ *adjective*: *Islamic law*

island 0⟶ /'aɪlənd/ *noun*

> 🔎 PRONUNCIATION
> The word **island** sounds like **highland**, because we don't say the letter **s** in this word.

a piece of land with water all around it: *the Greek islands*

Isle /aɪl/ *noun*
an island: *the British Isles*

> 🔎 CULTURE
> **Isle** is usually used in names of islands.

isn't /'ɪznt/ *short for* IS NOT

isolated /'aɪsəleɪtɪd/ *adjective*
far from other people or things: *an isolated house in the mountains*

isolation /ˌaɪsə'leɪʃn/ *noun* (no plural)
being away from other people or things: *A lot of old people live in isolation.*

issue¹ 0⟶ /'ɪʃuː/ *noun*
1 an important problem that people talk about: *Pollution is a serious issue.*
2 a magazine or newspaper of a particular day, week, or month: *Have you read this week's issue?*

issue² /'ɪʃuː/ *verb* (issues, issuing, issued /'ɪʃuːd/)
to give or say something officially: *The soldiers were issued with uniforms.* ◇ *The police have issued a statement.*

IT /ˌaɪ 'tiː/ *noun* (no plural)
the study or use of computers and other electronic equipment to store and send information ⊃ **IT** is short for 'Information Technology'.

it 0⟶ /ɪt/ *pronoun* (plural they, them)
1 a word that shows a thing or animal: *I've got a new shirt. It's* (= it is) *blue.* ◇ *Where's the coffee? I can't find it.*
2 a word that points to an idea that follows: *It's difficult to learn Japanese.*
3 a word that shows who somebody is: '*Who's on the telephone?*' '*It's Jo.*'
4 a word at the beginning of a sentence about time, the weather or distance: *It's six o'clock.* ◇ *It's hot today.* ◇ *It's 100 kilometres to London.*

italics /ɪ'tælɪks/ *noun* (plural)
a type of writing or printing in which the letters do not stand straight up: *This sentence is in italics.*
▶ **italic** /ɪ'tælɪk/ *adjective*: *italic writing*

itch /ɪtʃ/ *verb* (itches, itching, itched /ɪtʃt/)
to have a feeling on your skin that makes you want to rub or scratch it: *My nose itches.* ◇ *This jumper makes me itch.*
▶ **itch** *noun* (plural itches): *I've got an itch.*
▶ **itchy** /'ɪtʃi/ *adjective*: *itchy skin*

it'd /'ɪtəd/ *short for* IT HAD; IT WOULD

item 0⟶ /'aɪtəm/ *noun*
1 one thing in a list or group of things: *She had the most expensive item on the menu.* ◇ *an item of clothing*
2 a piece of news: *There was an interesting news item about Spain.*

A B C D E F G H I J K L M N O P Q R S T U V W X Y Z

it'll /ˈɪtl/ *short for* IT WILL

its 0-π /ɪts/ *adjective*
of the thing or animal that you have just talked about: *The dog has hurt its leg.* ◇ *The company has its factory in Hull.*

> 🔎 **WHICH WORD?**
>
> **Its** or **it's**?
> Be careful! **It's** is a short way of saying *it is* or *it has*: *It's* (= it is) *cold today.* ◇ *It's* (= it has) *been raining.*
> **Its** means 'belonging to it': *The bird has broken its wing.*

it's /ɪts/ *short for* IT IS; IT HAS

itself 0-π /ɪtˈself/ *pronoun* (*plural* **themselves** /ðəmˈselvz/)
1 a word that shows the same thing or animal that you have just talked about: *The cat was washing itself.*
2 a word that makes 'it' stronger: *The hotel itself was nice but I didn't like the town.*

by itself
1 alone: *The house stands by itself in the forest.*
2 without being controlled by a person: *The machine will start by itself.*

I've /aɪv/ *short for* I HAVE

ivory /ˈaɪvəri/ *noun* (*no plural*)
the hard white substance that the long teeth (called **tusks**) of an ELEPHANT (= a very large grey animal with big ears) are made of

ivy

ivy /ˈaɪvi/ *noun* (*no plural*)
a plant with dark green leaves, that climbs up walls or trees

A B C D E F G H I J K L M N O P Q R S T U V W X Y Z

J j

J, j /dʒeɪ/ *noun* (*plural* J's, j's /dʒeɪz/)
the tenth letter of the English alphabet: '*Jam*' begins with a '*J*'.

jab /dʒæb/ *verb* (jabs, jabbing, jabbed /dʒæbd/)
to push at somebody with a sudden rough movement: *She **jabbed** me **in** the stomach with her elbow.*
▶ **jab** *noun*: *I felt a jab in my ribs.*

jack /dʒæk/ *noun*
the playing card that has a picture of a young man on it: *the jack of hearts*

jacket 0━┓ /ˈdʒækɪt/ *noun*
a short coat with sleeves ➷ Look at Picture Dictionary page **P5**.

jacket potato /ˌdʒækɪt pəˈteɪtəʊ/ *noun*
(*plural* jacket potatoes) another word for BAKED POTATO

jagged /ˈdʒægɪd/ *adjective*
rough, with a lot of sharp points: *jagged rocks*

jaguar /ˈdʒægjuə(r)/ *noun*
a large wild cat with black spots that lives in Central and South America ➷ Look at Picture Dictionary page **P3**.

jail /dʒeɪl/ *noun*
a prison: *He was **sent to jail** for two years.*
▶ **jail** *verb* (jails, jailing, jailed /dʒeɪld/): *She was **jailed for** killing her husband.*

jam¹ 0━┓ /dʒæm/ *noun*
1 (*no plural*) sweet food made from fruit and sugar. You eat **jam** on bread: *a jar of strawberry jam* ➷ Look at Picture Dictionary page **P6**.
2 (*plural* jams) a situation in which you cannot move because there are too many people or vehicles

jam² /dʒæm/ *verb* (jams, jamming, jammed /dʒæmd/)
1 to push something into a place where there is not much space: *She **jammed** all her clothes **into** a suitcase.*
2 to fix something or to become fixed so that you cannot move it: *I can't open the window. It's jammed.*

janitor /ˈdʒænɪtə(r)/ *American English for* CARETAKER

January 0━┓ /ˈdʒænjuəri/ *noun*
the first month of the year

jar /dʒɑː(r)/ *noun*
a glass container for food: *a **jar** of coffee* ◇ *a jam jar* ➷ Look at the picture at **container**.

javelin /ˈdʒævlɪn/ *noun*
a long pointed stick that people throw as a sport

jaw /dʒɔː/ *noun*
one of the two bones in the head of a person or animal that hold the teeth ➷ Look at Picture Dictionary page **P4**.

jazz /dʒæz/ *noun* (*no plural*)
a kind of music with a strong beat: *a jazz band*

jealous /ˈdʒeləs/ *adjective*
1 angry or sad because you are afraid of losing somebody's love: *Sarah's boyfriend gets jealous if she speaks to other boys.*
2 angry or sad because you want what another person has ➷ SAME MEANING **envious**: *Ben was **jealous of** his brother's new car.*
▶ **jealousy** /ˈdʒeləsi/ *noun* (*no plural*): *He felt sick with jealousy.*

jeans 0━┓ /dʒiːnz/ *noun* (*plural*)
trousers made of strong cotton material (called **denim**). **Jeans** are usually blue: *a pair of jeans* ◇ *He wore jeans and a T-shirt.* ➷ Look at Picture Dictionary page **P5**.

Jeep™ /dʒiːp/ *noun*
a strong car that can go well over rough land

jeer /dʒɪə(r)/ *verb* (jeers, jeering, jeered /dʒɪəd/)
to laugh or shout at someone in an unkind way that shows you do not respect them: *The crowd **jeered at** him.*

jelly /ˈdʒeli/ *noun* (British) (American jello, Jell-O™ /ˈdʒeləʊ/) (*no plural*)
a soft food made from fruit juice and sugar, that shakes when you move it

jellyfish /ˈdʒelifɪʃ/ *noun* (*plural* jellyfish *or* jellyfishes)
a sea animal with a body like JELLY and long thin parts that can STING (= hurt) you

jellyfish

jerk /dʒɜːk/ *verb* (jerks, jerking, jerked /dʒɜːkt/)
to move quickly or suddenly; to pull or make something move like this: *The*

A

B

C

D

E

F

G

H

I

J

K

L

M

N

O

P

Q

R

S

T

U

V

W

X

Y

Z

car jerked forward. ◊ *She jerked the door open.*
▶ **jerk** *noun*: *The bus started with a jerk.*

jersey /ˈdʒɜːzi/ *noun* (jerseys)
a warm piece of clothing with sleeves, that you wear on the top part of your body. **Jerseys** are often made of wool. ⊃ Look at the note at **sweater**.

Jesus /ˈdʒiːzəs/ (*also* Jesus Christ /ˌdʒiːzəs ˈkraɪst/ Christ) *noun*
the man who Christians believe is the Son of God

jet /dʒet/ *noun*
1 a type of fast modern plane
2 liquid or gas that comes very fast out of a small hole: *a jet of gas* ◊ *jets of water*

jet lag /ˈdʒet læg/ *noun* (*no plural*)
the feeling of being very tired after a long plane journey

jetty /ˈdʒeti/ *noun* (jetties)
a platform at the edge of a river, the sea, etc. where people get on and off boats

Jew /dʒuː/ *noun*
a person who follows the religion of Judaism
▶ **Jewish** /ˈdʒuːɪʃ/ *adjective*: *She is Jewish.*

jewel /ˈdʒuːəl/ *noun*
a beautiful stone that is very valuable
⊃ SAME MEANING **gem**

🔎 **WORD BUILDING**
There are many different types of **jewel**. Here are some of them: diamond, emerald, pearl, ruby.

jeweller (*British*) (*American* jeweler) /ˈdʒuːələ(r)/ *noun*
1 a person who sells, makes or repairs jewellery and watches
2 jeweller's a shop that sells jewellery and watches

jewellery 0🔑 (*British*) (*American* jewelry) /ˈdʒuːəlri/ *noun* (*no plural*)
objects that people wear to decorate their fingers, ears, arms, etc.: *a piece of gold jewellery*

jigsaw puzzle

jigsaw /ˈdʒɪgsɔː/ (*also* jigsaw puzzle /ˈdʒɪgsɔː pʌzl/) *noun*
a picture in many pieces that you put together

jingle /ˈdʒɪŋgl/ *verb* (jingles, jingling, jingled /ˈdʒɪŋgld/)
to make a pleasant sound like small bells; to cause something to make this sound: *She jingled the coins in her pocket.*

job 0🔑 /dʒɒb/ *noun*
1 the work that you do for money: *She got a job as a waitress.* ◊ *Peter's just lost his job.*

🔎 **WORD BUILDING**
When **you apply for a job** you fill in an **application form** or you send a letter and your **CV** (a list of your experience and education).
You **have an interview** and the **employer** asks for **references** (letters from other people saying what you can do). Some jobs are **full-time** and some are **part-time**.
If you **get the sack**, you lose your job because you are bad at it. When you reach a certain age, you **retire** (stop working). To find out what someone's job is, we say: **What do you do?**

2 something that you must do: *I have a lot of jobs to do in the house.* ⊃ Look at the note at **work**.
it's a good job (*informal*) it is a good or lucky thing: *It's a good job you reminded me – I had completely forgotten!*
make a good job of something to do something well: *You made a good job of the painting.*
out of a job without paid work
⊃ SAME MEANING **unemployed**

🔎 **WORD BUILDING**
There are many different types of **job**. Here are some of them: builder, chef, doctor, librarian, pilot, teacher. Do you know any others?

⊃ Look at Picture Dictionary page **P12**.

jockey /ˈdʒɒki/ *noun* (*plural* jockeys)
a person who rides horses in races

jog /dʒɒg/ *verb* (jogs, jogging, jogged /dʒɒgd/)
1 to run slowly for exercise: *I jogged round the park.* ◊ *I go jogging every morning.*
2 to push or touch something a little, so that it moves: *She jogged my arm and I spilled my drink.*
▶ **jog** *noun* a slow run for exercise: *She goes for a jog before breakfast.*

jogging

join 0️⃣ /dʒɔɪn/ *verb* (joins, joining, joined /dʒɔɪnd/)
1 to bring or fix one thing to another thing: *The tunnel **joins** Britain **to** France.* ◇ *Join the two pieces of wood **together**.*
2 to come together with somebody or something: *Will you join us for dinner?* ◇ *This road joins the motorway soon.*
3 to become a member of a group: *He joined the army.* ◇ *I've joined an aerobics class.*
join in to do something with other people: *Everyone started singing but Frank refused to join in.*

joint¹ /dʒɔɪnt/ *adjective*
involving two or more people together: *The report was a **joint effort** (= we worked on it together).* ◇ *My wife and I have a **joint account** (= a shared bank account)*

joint² /dʒɔɪnt/ *noun*
1 a part of your body where bones come together, for example your elbow or your knee
2 a place where two parts of something join together: *the joints of the pipe*
3 (*British*) a big piece of meat that you cook: *a joint of beef*

joke¹ 0️⃣ /dʒəʊk/ *noun*
something that you say or do to make people laugh, for example a funny story that you tell: *She **told** us a joke.* ◇ *I didn't **get the joke** (= understand it).*

joke² 0️⃣ /dʒəʊk/ *verb* (jokes, joking, joked /dʒəʊkt/)
to tell funny stories; to say things that are funny but not true: *They were laughing and joking together.* ◇ *I didn't mean what I said – I was **only joking**.*

jolly /ˈdʒɒli/ *adjective* (jollier, jolliest)
happy and full of fun

jolt /dʒəʊlt/ *verb* (jolts, jolting, jolted)
to move or to make somebody or something move in a sudden rough way

⭮ SAME MEANING **jerk**: *The bus jolted to a stop.* ◇ *The crash jolted us forwards.*
▶ **jolt** *noun*: *The train stopped with a jolt.*

jot /dʒɒt/ *verb* (jots, jotting, jotted)
jot something down to write something quickly: *I jotted down his phone number.*

journal /ˈdʒɜːnl/ *noun*
a magazine about one particular thing: *a medical journal*

journalism /ˈdʒɜːnəlɪzəm/ *noun* (no plural)
the work of collecting and reporting news for newspapers, television, etc.

journalist 0️⃣ /ˈdʒɜːnəlɪst/ *noun*
a person whose job is to collect and report news for newspapers, television, etc.

journey 0️⃣ /ˈdʒɜːni/ *noun* (plural journeys)
the act of travelling from one place to another: *Did you have a good journey?* ⭮ Look at the note at **travel**.

joy /dʒɔɪ/ *noun* (no plural)
a very happy feeling: *Their children give them so much joy.*
▶ **joyful** /ˈdʒɔɪfl/ *adjective* very happy: *a joyful occasion*

joyriding /ˈdʒɔɪraɪdɪŋ/ *noun* (no plural)
the crime of stealing a car and driving around in a fast, dangerous way
▶ **joyrider** /ˈdʒɔɪraɪdə(r)/ *noun* a person who steals a car and drives it in a fast, dangerous way

joystick /ˈdʒɔɪstɪk/ *noun*
a handle that you move to control something, for example a computer game

Judaism /ˈdʒuːdeɪɪzəm/ *noun* (no plural)
the religion of the Jewish people

judge¹ 0️⃣ /dʒʌdʒ/ *noun*
1 the person in a court of law who decides how to punish somebody: *The judge sent him to prison for 20 years.* ⭮ Look at Picture Dictionary page **P12**.
2 a person who chooses the winner of a competition

judge² 0️⃣ /dʒʌdʒ/ *verb* (judges, judging, judged /dʒʌdʒd/)
1 to have or to form an opinion about somebody or something: *It's difficult to judge how long the project will take.*
2 to decide who or what wins a competition: *The headmaster judged the painting competition.*

judgement 0️⃣ (*also* judgment) /ˈdʒʌdʒmənt/ *noun*
1 (*no plural*) your ability to form opinions or

make sensible decisions: *Use your judgement* (= you decide). ◇ *In my judgement, she will do the job very well.*
2 (*plural* **judgements**) the decision of a judge in a court of law

judo /ˈdʒuːdəʊ/ *noun* (*no plural*)
a sport where two people fight and try to throw each other onto the floor ➔ Look at Picture Dictionary page **P15**.

jug

jug /dʒʌɡ/ *noun* (*British*) (*American* **pitcher**)
a container with a handle that you use for holding or pouring liquids: *a milk jug* ◇ *a jug of water*

juggler

juggle /ˈdʒʌɡl/ *verb* (**juggles**, **juggling**, **juggled** /ˈdʒʌɡld/)
to keep two or more things in the air by throwing and catching them quickly
▶ **juggler** /ˈdʒʌɡlə(r)/ *noun* a person who JUGGLES

juice 0‑ɯ /dʒuːs/ *noun* (*no plural*)

> 🔎 **PRONUNCIATION**
> The word **juice** sounds like **loose**.

the liquid from fruit and vegetables: *a glass of orange juice* ➔ Look at Picture Dictionary page **P6**.

juicy /ˈdʒuːsi/ *adjective* (**juicier**, **juiciest**)
full of juice: *big juicy tomatoes*

jukebox /ˈdʒuːkbɒks/ *noun* (*plural* **jukeboxes**)
a machine in a pub, bar etc. that plays music when you put money in it

July 0‑ɯ /dʒuˈlaɪ/ *noun*
the seventh month of the year

jumble¹ /ˈdʒʌmbl/ *verb* (**jumbles**, **jumbling**, **jumbled** /ˈdʒʌmbld/)
jumble something up to mix things so that they are untidy or in the wrong place: *His clothes were all jumbled up in the cupboard.*

jumble² /ˈdʒʌmbl/ *noun* (*no plural*)
a lot of things that are mixed together in an untidy way: *a jumble of old clothes and books*

jumble sale /ˈdʒʌmbl seɪl/ *noun* (*British*) (*American* **rummage sale**)
a sale of things that people do not want any more. Clubs, churches and schools often have **jumble sales** to make money.

jumbo jet /ˌdʒʌmbəʊ ˈdʒet/ *noun*
a very big plane that can carry a lot of people

jump

jump 0‑ɯ /dʒʌmp/ *verb* (**jumps**, **jumping**, **jumped** /dʒʌmpt/)
1 to move quickly off the ground, using your legs to push you up: *The cat jumped onto the table.* ◇ *The horse jumped over the wall.*
2 to move quickly: *He jumped into the car and drove away.*
3 to move suddenly because you are surprised or frightened: *A loud noise made me jump.*
jump at something to accept an opportunity or an offer with enthusiasm: *Of course I jumped at the chance to work in New York for a year.*
▶ **jump** *noun*: *With a huge jump the horse cleared the fence.*

jumper /ˈdʒʌmpə(r)/ *noun*
a warm piece of clothing with sleeves, that you wear on the top part of your body. **Jumpers** are often made of wool. ➔ Look at the note at **sweater**. ➔ Look at Picture Dictionary page **P5**.

jump rope /ˈdʒʌmp rəʊp/ *American English for* SKIPPING ROPE

junction /ˈdʒʌŋkʃn/ *noun*
a place where roads or railway lines meet: *Turn right at the next junction.*

June ⊶ /dʒuːn/ *noun*
the sixth month of the year

jungle /'dʒʌŋgl/ *noun*
a thick forest in a hot part of the world: *the jungles of South America and Africa*

junior /'dʒuːniə(r)/ *adjective*
1 having a lower position in an organization: *a junior doctor*
2 of or for children below a particular age: *the junior athletics championships*
➾ OPPOSITE **senior**

junior school /'dʒuːniə skuːl/ *noun*
(*British*)
a school for children between the ages of seven and eleven

junk /dʒʌŋk/ *noun* (*no plural*)
things that are old or useless: *The cupboard is full of junk.*

junk food /'dʒʌŋk fuːd/ *noun* (*no plural*)
(*informal*)
food that is quick and easy to prepare and eat but that is bad for your health

jury /'dʒʊəri/ *noun* (*plural* **juries**)
a group of people in a court of law who decide if somebody has done something wrong or not: *The jury decided that the woman was guilty of killing her husband.*

just¹ ⊶ /dʒʌst/ *adverb*
1 exactly: *This jacket is just my size.* ◊ *You're just in time.* ◊ *She looks just like her mother.*

2 a very short time before: *I've just heard the news.* ◊ *Jim isn't here – he's just gone out.*
3 at this or that moment; now or very soon: *I'm just going to make some coffee.* ◊ *She phoned just as I was going to bed.*
4 by a small amount: *I got here just after nine.* ◊ *I only just caught the train.*
5 a word that makes what you say stronger: *Just look at that funny little dog!*
6 only: *It's just a small present.*

just about (*informal*) almost; very nearly: *I've met just about everyone.*

just a minute, **just a moment** used for asking somebody to wait for a short time: *Just a minute – there's someone at the door.*

just now
1 at this moment; now: *I can't talk to you just now. I'm busy.*
2 a short time before: *Where's Liz? She was here just now.*

just² /dʒʌst/ *adjective*
fair and right: *a just punishment*
➾ OPPOSITE **unjust**

justice /'dʒʌstɪs/ *noun* (*no plural*)
1 treatment of people in a fair way: *the struggle for justice* ➾ OPPOSITE **injustice**
2 the law: *the criminal justice system*

justify /'dʒʌstɪfaɪ/ *verb* (**justifies, justifying, justified** /'dʒʌstɪfaɪd/, **has justified**)
to be or give a good reason for something: *Can you justify what you did?*

A
B
C
D
E
F
G
H
I
J
K
L
M
N
O
P
Q
R
S
T
U
V
W
X
Y
Z

K k

K, k /keɪ/ *noun* (*plural* K's, k's /keɪz/)
the eleventh letter of the English alphabet:
'*King*' begins with a '*K*'.

kangaroo

kangaroo /ˌkæŋɡəˈruː/ *noun* (*plural* kangaroos)
an Australian animal that jumps on its strong back legs and carries its babies in a pocket on its front

karate /kəˈrɑːti/ *noun* (*no plural*)
a Japanese sport where people fight with their hands and feet

kebab /kɪˈbæb/ *noun*
small pieces of meat, vegetables, etc. that are cooked on a thin stick ⊃ Look at Picture Dictionary page **P7**.

keen /kiːn/ *adjective* (keener, keenest)
1 wanting to do something; interested in something: *Ian was **keen to** go out but I wanted to stay at home.* ◇ *Louise is a keen swimmer.*
2 very good or strong: *keen eyesight*
be keen on somebody or **something** (*informal*) to like somebody or something very much: *Tom's very keen on Anna.*

keep 0→ /kiːp/ *verb* (keeps, keeping, kept /kept/, has kept)
1 to stay in a particular state or condition: ***Keep still*** (= don't move) – *while I take your photo.* ◇ *We tried to **keep warm**.*
2 to make somebody or something stay in a particular state or condition: *Keep this door closed.* ◇ *I'm sorry to **keep** you **waiting**.*
3 to continue to have something: *You can keep that book – I don't need it.*
4 to put or store something in a particular place: *Where do you keep the coffee?*
5 to continue doing something; to do something many times: *Keep driving until you see the cinema, then turn left.* ◇ *She keeps forgetting my name.*
6 to look after and buy food and other things for a person or an animal: *It costs a lot to keep a family of four.* ◇ *They keep sheep and pigs on their farm.*
7 to stay fresh: *Will this fish keep until tomorrow?*
keep away from somebody or **something** to not go near somebody or something: *Keep away from the river, children.*
keep somebody from doing something to stop somebody from doing something: *You can't keep me from going out!*
keep going to continue: *I was very tired but I kept going to the end of the race.*
keep off something to not go on something: *Keep off the grass!*
keep on doing something to continue doing something; to do something many times: *We kept on driving all night!* ◇ *That man keeps on looking at me.*
keep out to stay outside: *The sign on the door said 'Danger. Keep out!'*
keep somebody or **something out** to stop somebody or something from going in: *We put a fence round the garden to keep the sheep out.*
keep up with somebody or **something** to go as fast as another person or thing so that you are together: *Don't walk so quickly – I can't keep up with you.*

kennel /ˈkenl/ *noun*
a small house where a dog sleeps

kerb

pavement (*British*)
sidewalk (*American*)

drain

kerb (*British*)
curb (*American*)

kept *form of* KEEP

kerb (*British*) (*American* **curb**) /kɜːb/ *noun*
the edge of a path next to a road: *They stood on the kerb waiting to cross the road.*

kerosene /'kerəsiːn/ *American English for*
PARAFFIN

ketchup /'ketʃəp/ *noun* (*no plural*)
a cold sauce made from tomatoes ⊃ Look at Picture Dictionary page **P7**.

kettle /'ketl/ *noun*
a container with a handle, for boiling water: *I'll go and put the kettle on* (= fill it with water and make it start to get hot).

kettle

key¹ 0̄ᵣ /kiː/ *noun*
1 a piece of metal that opens or closes a lock: *He turned the key and opened the door.*
2 one of the parts of a computer, a piano or other musical instrument that you press with your fingers: *Pianos have black and white keys.* ⊃ Look at the picture at **saxophone**.
3 answers to questions: *Check your answers with the key at the back of the book.*

keys

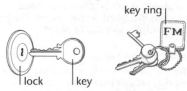

key ring

lock   key

key² /kiː/ *verb* (**keys, keying, keyed** /kiːd/)
key something in to put words or numbers into a computer by pressing the keys: *Key in your password.*

keyboard /'kiːbɔːd/ *noun*
1 all the keys on a computer or piano ⊃ Look at Picture Dictionary page **P11**.
2 a musical instrument like a small electrical piano: *a keyboard player*

keyhole /'kiːhəʊl/ *noun*
a hole in a lock where you put a key

key ring /'kiː rɪŋ/ *noun*
a metal ring that you keep keys on

kg *short way of writing* KILOGRAM

khaki /'kɑːki/ *adjective*
having the pale brown-green or brown-yellow colour of a soldier's uniform: *khaki uniforms*
▶ **khaki** *noun* (*no plural*)

kick¹ 0̄ᵣ /kɪk/ *verb* (**kicks, kicking, kicked** /kɪkt/)
1 to hit somebody or something with your foot: *I kicked the ball to Chris.*
2 to move your foot or feet up and down quickly: *The child was kicking and screaming.*
kick off to start a game of football
kick somebody out (*informal*) to make somebody leave a place: *The boys were kicked out of the cinema because they were noisy.*

kick² 0̄ᵣ /kɪk/ *noun*
1 a movement with your foot or your leg, usually to hit something with your foot: *If the door won't open, give it a kick.*
2 (*informal*) a feeling of excitement: *He gets a kick out of driving fast cars.*

kick-off /'kɪk ɒf/ *noun*
the start of a game of football: *Kick-off is at 2.30 this afternoon.*

kid¹ /kɪd/ *noun*
1 (*informal*) a child: *How old are your kids?*
2 a young GOAT (= a small animal with horns that lives in mountain areas) ⊃ Look at the picture at **goat**.

kid² /kɪd/ *verb* (**kids, kidding, kidded**) (*informal*)
to say something that it not true as a joke: *I didn't mean it. I was only kidding.*

kidnap /'kɪdnæp/ *verb* (**kidnaps, kidnapping, kidnapped** /'kɪdnæpt/)
to take somebody away and hide them, so that their family or friends will pay money to free them
▶ **kidnapper** /'kɪdnæpə(r)/ *noun*: *The kidnappers are demanding a ransom of $1 million.*

kidney /'kɪdni/ *noun* (*plural* **kidneys**)
one of the parts inside your body that takes waste liquid from your blood

kill 0̄ᵣ /kɪl/ *verb* (**kills, killing, killed** /kɪld/)
to make somebody or something die: *The police do not know who killed the old man.* ◇ *Three people were killed in the accident.*
▶ **killer** /'kɪlə(r)/ *noun* a person, animal or thing that kills

kilo /'kiːləʊ/ *noun* (**kilos**) *short way of writing* KILOGRAM

kilobyte /'kɪləbaɪt/ *noun* (*abbr.* **KB, Kb**)
a measure of computer memory or information. There are 1 024 **bytes** in a **kilobyte**.

kilogram 0̄ᵣ (*British also* **kilogramme**) /'kɪləɡræm/ (*also* **kilo** /'kiːləʊ/) (*plural* **kilos**) *noun* (*abbr.* **kg**)
a measure of weight. There are 1 000 **grams**

A B C D E F G H I J K L M N O P Q R S T U V W X Y Z

in a **kilogram**: *I bought two kilos of potatoes.* ◊ *1 kg of bananas*

kilometre 0ᵣ (*British*) kilometer (*American*) /'kɪləmiːtə(r); kɪ'lɒmɪtə(r)/ **noun** (*abbr.* km)

a measure of length. There are 1 000 **metres** in a kilometre: *They live 100 km from Paris.*

kilt /kɪlt/ **noun**

a skirt that men in Scotland sometimes wear

kin /kɪn/ **noun** (*no plural*) (*formal*)

the people in your family: *Who is your **next of kin** (= your closest relative)?*

kind¹ 0ᵣ /kaɪnd/ **noun**

a group of things or people that are the same in some way ⊃ SAME MEANING **sort** or **type**: *What **kind** of music do you like?* ◊ *The shop sells ten different **kinds** of bread.*
kind of (*informal*) words that you use when you are not sure about something: *He looks kind of tired.*

kind² 0ᵣ /kaɪnd/ **adjective** (kinder, kindest)

friendly and good to other people: *'Can I carry your bag?' 'Thanks. That's very **kind** of you.'* ◊ *Be **kind** to animals.*
⊃ OPPOSITE **unkind**

kind-hearted /ˌkaɪnd 'hɑːtɪd/ **adjective**

kind and generous to other people

kindly /'kaɪndli/ **adverb**

in a kind way: *She kindly drove me to the station.*

kindness 0ᵣ /'kaɪndnəs/ **noun**

the quality of being kind: *Thank you for your kindness.*

king 0ᵣ /kɪŋ/ **noun**

a man from a royal family who rules a country: *King Henry VIII* ⊃ Look at **queen**.

kingdom /'kɪŋdəm/ **noun**

a country where a king or queen rules: *the United Kingdom*

kiosk /'kiːɒsk/ **noun**

a small shop in a street where you can buy things like sweets and newspapers through a window

kiss 0ᵣ /kɪs/ **verb** (kisses, kissing, kissed /kɪst/)

to touch somebody with your lips to show love or to say hello or goodbye: *She kissed me on the cheek.* ◊ *They kissed, and then he left.*
► **kiss** (*plural* kisses) **noun**: *Give me a kiss!*

kit /kɪt/ **noun**

1 the clothes or things that you need to do something: *Where's my football kit?* ◊ *There's a hammer in the tool kit.*
2 a set of small pieces that you put together

to make something: *a kit for making a model aeroplane*

kitchen 0ᵣ /'kɪtʃɪn/ **noun**

a room where you cook food ⊃ Look at Picture Dictionary page **P10**.

kite /kaɪt/ **noun**

a toy that you fly in the wind on a long piece of string

kitten /'kɪtn/ **noun**

a young cat ⊃ Look at the picture at **cat**.

kiwi fruit /'kiːwiː fruːt/ (*also* kiwi) **noun** (*plural* kiwi fruit)

a small green fruit with black seeds and rough brown skin ⊃ Look at Picture Dictionary page **P8**.

km *short way of writing* KILOMETRE

knead /niːd/ **verb** (kneads, kneading, kneaded)

to press and stretch a mixture of flour and water (called **dough**) to make bread

> 🔎 **PRONUNCIATION**
>
> If a word starts with the letters **KN**, the **K** is always silent. So the word **knead** sounds like **need**, **know** sounds like **no** and **knight** sounds like **night**.

knee 0ᵣ /niː/ **noun**

the part in the middle of your leg where it bends: *I fell and cut my knee.* ⊃ Look at Picture Dictionary page **P4**.

kneecap /'niːkæp/ **noun**

the bone that covers the front of your knee

kneel /niːl/ **verb** (kneels, kneeling, knelt /nelt/ or kneeled /niːld/, has knelt or has kneeled)

to bend your legs and rest on one or both of your knees: *He knelt down to pray.* ◊ *Jane was kneeling on the floor.*

kite

string

kneel

knew *form of* KNOW

knickers /'nɪkəz/ **noun** (*plural*) (*British*) (*American* panties)

a piece of underwear for women that covers the lower part of the body but not the legs
⊃ SAME MEANING **pants**: *a pair of knickers*

knife

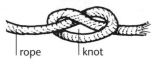

knife | blade

knife 0— /naɪf/ **noun** (plural **knives** /naɪvz/)
a sharp metal thing with a handle that you use to cut things or to fight: *a knife and fork*

knight /naɪt/ **noun**
a soldier of a high level who rode a horse and fought for his king a long time ago

knit

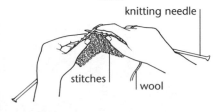

knitting needle

stitches | wool

knit /nɪt/ **verb** (knits, knitting, knitted)
to make clothes from wool using two long sticks (called **knitting needles**): *My grandmother knitted this hat for me.*
▸ **knitting** /'nɪtɪŋ/ **noun** (no plural):
I usually do some knitting while I'm watching television.

knitting needle /'nɪtɪŋ niːdl/ **noun**
one of two metal or plastic sticks that you use for making clothes from wool ⊃ Look at the picture at **knit**.

knives plural of KNIFE

knob /nɒb/ **noun**
1 a round thing that you turn to control part of a machine: *the volume control knob*
2 a round handle on a door or drawer
⊃ Look at the picture at **handle**.

knock¹ 0— /nɒk/ **verb** (knocks, knocking, knocked /nɒkt/)
1 to hit something and make a noise: *I knocked on the door, but nobody answered.*
2 to hit something hard, usually by accident: *I knocked my head on the door.* ◊ *She knocked a glass off the table.*
knock somebody down, knock somebody over to hit somebody so that they fall onto the ground: *The boy was knocked down by a car.*
knock something down to break a building so that it falls down
⊃ SAME MEANING **demolish**: *They're knocking down the old houses.*
knock somebody out to make somebody fall asleep or become unconscious: *The blow knocked him out.*

knock something over to hit something so that it falls over: *I knocked over a vase of flowers.*

knock² 0— /nɒk/ **noun**
the action of hitting something; the sound that this makes: *I heard a knock at the door.*

knot

rope | knot

knot¹ 0— /nɒt/ **noun**
a place where you have tied two pieces of rope, string, etc. tightly together: *I tied a knot in the rope.* ◊ *Can you undo this knot (= make it loose)?*

knot² /nɒt/ **verb** (knots, knotting, knotted)
to tie a knot in something: *He knotted the ends of the rope together.*

know 0— /nəʊ/ **verb** (knows, knowing, knew /njuː/, has known /nəʊn/)
1 to have information in your head: *I don't know her name.* ◊ *He knows a lot about cars.* ◊ *Do you know how to use this machine? ◊ Did you know that he's going to live abroad?*
2 to be familiar with a person or place: *I have known Mario for six years.* ◊ *I know Paris quite well.* ◊ *I liked him when I got to know him (= started to know him).*
I know (informal) used to agree with something somebody has just said: *'What a ridiculous situation!' 'I know.'*
let somebody know to tell somebody about something: *Let me know if you need any help.*
you know words that you use when you are thinking about what to say next: *Well, you know, it's hard to explain.*

know-all /'nəʊ ɔːl/ (British) (American **know-it-all** /'nəʊ ɪt ɔːl/) **noun**
an annoying person who behaves as if they know everything

knowledge 0— /'nɒlɪdʒ/ **noun** (no plural)
what you know and understand about something: *He has a good knowledge of European history.* ◊ *He did it without my knowledge (= I did not know).*

knowledgeable /'nɒlɪdʒəbl/ **noun**
knowing a lot: *She's very knowledgeable about history.*

known form of KNOW

knuckle /'nʌkl/ **noun**
one of the parts where your fingers bend or

A B C D E F G H I J **K** L M N O P Q R S T U V W X Y Z

where they join your hand ⊃ Look at the picture at **fist**.

koala /kəʊˈɑːlə/ *noun*
an Australian animal with large ears and thick grey fur that lives in trees ⊃ Look at Picture Dictionary page **P3**.

Koran (*also* Qur'an) /kəˈrɑːn/ *noun* (*no plural*)
the **Koran** the most important book in the Islamic religion

kph *abbreviation*
a way of measuring how fast something is moving. **Kph** is short for 'kilometres per hour'.

kung fu /ˌkʌŋ ˈfuː/ *noun* (*no plural*)
a Chinese style of fighting in which people use their hands and feet as weapons

L l

L, l¹ /el/ *noun* (*plural* L's, l's /elz/)
the twelfth letter of the English alphabet: *'Lake' begins with an 'L'.*

l² *short way of writing* LITRE

lab /læb/ (*informal*) *short for* LABORATORY

label¹ /'leɪbl/ *noun*
a piece of paper or material on something that tells you about it: *The label on the bottle says 'Made in Mexico'. ◇ The washing instructions are on the label.*

label

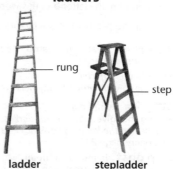

label

label² /'leɪbl/ *verb* (*British* **labels, labelling, labelled** /'leɪbld/) (*American* **labeling, labeled**)
to put a LABEL on something: *I labelled all the boxes with my name and address.*

labor *American English for* LABOUR

laboratory /lə'bɒrətri/ *noun* (*plural* **laboratories**) (*also informal* **lab**)
a special room where scientists work: *a research laboratory*

laborer *American English for* LABOURER

labour (*British*) (*American* **labor**) /'leɪbə(r)/ *noun* (*no plural*)
hard work that you do with your hands and body: *manual labour* (= work using your hands)

labourer (*British*) (*American* **laborer**) /'leɪbərə(r)/ *noun*
a person who does hard work with their hands and body: *a farm labourer*

the Labour Party / ðə 'leɪbə pɑːti/ *noun*
(*politics*) one of the important political parties in Britain ➔ Look at **the Conservative Party** and **the Liberal Democrats**.

lace

shoelaces

lace collar

lace /leɪs/ *noun*
1 (*no plural*) very thin cloth with holes that form a pretty pattern: *lace curtains ◇ a handkerchief with lace round the edge*
2 (*plural* **laces**) a string that you use for tying your shoe: *Do up your laces or you'll trip over them.*

lack¹ ⚬━ /læk/ *noun* (*no plural*)
the state of not having something or of not having enough of something: *There is a lack of good teachers.*

lack² /læk/ *verb* (**lacks, lacking, lacked** /lækt/)
to have none or not enough of something: *He lacked confidence.*

lad /læd/ *noun*
a boy or young man

ladders

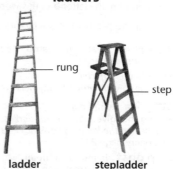

— rung

— step

ladder   stepladder

ladder /'lædə(r)/ *noun*
a thing that you climb up when you want to reach a high place. A **ladder** is made of two tall pieces of metal or wood with shorter pieces between them (called **rungs**).

ladies /'leɪdiz/ *noun* the ladies (*British*)
a public toilet for women: *Where is the ladies, please?* ➔ Look at **gents**.

ladle /'leɪdl/ *noun*
a spoon in the shape of a cup with a long handle, used for serving soup

ladle

lady ⚬━ /'leɪdi/ *noun* (*plural* **ladies**)
1 a polite way of saying 'woman': *an old lady* ➔ Look at **gentleman**.
2 **Lady** a title given to a woman with a high

A

social position: *The former prime minister became Lady Thatcher.* ➔ Look at **Lord.**

B

ladybird /'leɪdibɜːd/ (*British*) (*American* **ladybug** /'leɪdibʌg/) *noun*

C

a small red or yellow insect with black spots

lager /'lɑːgə(r)/ *noun*

D

1 (*no plural*) a light beer: *I'll have a pint of lager, please.*

2 (*plural* **lagers**) a glass, bottle or can of

E

lager

laid form of LAY¹

F

laid-back /ˌleɪd 'bæk/ *adjective* (*informal*) calm and relaxed; not worried

G

lain form of LIE¹

lake 0̄ /leɪk/ *noun*

H

a big area of water with land all around it: *Lake Victoria* ◇ *We went swimming in the lake.*

I

lamb /læm/ *noun*

1 (*plural* **lambs**)

J

🔎 **PRONUNCIATION**

K

The word **lamb** sounds like **ham**, because we don't say the letter **b** in this word.

L

a young sheep ➔ Look at the picture at **sheep.**

M

2 (*no plural*) meat from a **lamb**: *We had roast lamb for lunch.*

lame /leɪm/ *adjective*

N

not able to walk properly: *My horse is lame.*

lamp 0̄ /læmp/ *noun*

O

a thing that gives light: *It was dark, so I switched on the lamp.* ➔ Look at Picture Dictionary page **P10.**

P

lamp post /'læmp pəʊst/ *noun*

Q

a tall thing in the street with a light on the top: *The car skidded and hit a lamp post.*

R

lampshade /'læmpʃeɪd/ *noun*

a cover for a lamp ➔ Look at the picture at

S

light.

land¹ 0̄ /lænd/ *noun*

T

1 (*no plural*) the part of the earth that is not the sea: *After two weeks in a boat, we were happy to be back on land.*

U

2 (*no plural*) a piece of ground: *They bought a piece of land and built a house on it.* ◇ *farming land*

V

3 (*plural* **lands**) (*formal*) a country: *She returned to the land where she was born.*

W

land² 0̄ /lænd/ *verb* (**lands, landing, landed**)

X

1 to come down from the air or to bring something down to the ground: *The plane landed at Heathrow airport.* ◇ *The pilot landed the plane safely.* ◇ *He fell off the ladder and landed on his back.*

Y

Z

2 to go onto land or to put something onto land from a ship: *The soldiers landed on the beaches in Normandy.*

landing /'lændɪŋ/ *noun*

1 the area at the top of stairs in a building: *There's a telephone on the landing.* ➔ Look at the picture at **staircase.**

2 coming down onto the ground in a plane: *The plane made an emergency landing in a field.* ➔ OPPOSITE **take-off**

landlady /'lændleɪdi/ *noun* (*plural* **landladies**)

a woman who rents a house or room to people for money

landlord /'lændlɔːd/ *noun*

a man who rents a house or room to people for money

landmark /'lændmɑːk/ *noun*

a big building or another thing that you can see easily from far away: *Big Ben is one of London's most famous landmarks.*

landscape /'lændskeɪp/ *noun*

everything you can see in an area of land: *The Scottish landscape is very beautiful.*

lane /leɪn/ *noun*

1 a narrow road in the country

2 one part of a wide road: *We were driving in the middle lane of the motorway.*

language 0̄ /'læŋgwɪdʒ/ *noun*

1 (*plural* **languages**) words that people from a particular country say and write: '*Do you speak any foreign languages?' 'Yes, I speak French and Italian.'*

2 (*no plural*) words that people use to speak and write: *This word is not often used in spoken language.*

lantern /'læntən/ *noun*

a light in a container made of glass or paper, that usually has a handle so you can carry it ➔ Look at the picture at **light.**

lap /læp/ *noun*

1 the flat part at the top of your legs when you are sitting: *The child was sitting on his mother's lap.*

2 one journey around a track in a race: *There are three more laps to go in the race.*

laptop /'læptɒp/ *noun*

a small computer that is easy to carry

large 0̄ /lɑːdʒ/ *adjective* (**larger, largest**)

big: *They live in a large house.* ◇ *She has a large family.* ◇ *Have you got this shirt in a large size?* ➔ OPPOSITE **small**

largely /'lɑːdʒli/ *adverb*

mostly ➔ SAME MEANING **mainly**: *The room is largely used for meetings.*

laser /'leɪzə(r)/ *noun*
an instrument that makes a very strong line of light (called a **laser beam**). Some **lasers** are used to cut metal and others are used by doctors in operations.

lash *short for* EYELASH

last¹ 0̶ᴍ /lɑːst/ *adjective*
1 after all the others: *December is the last month of the year.* ⊃ OPPOSITE **first**
2 just before now; most recent: *It's June now, so last month was May.* ◇ *I was at school last week, but this week I'm on holiday.* ◇ *Did you go out last (= yesterday) night?*
3 the **last** person or thing is the only one left: *Who wants the last cookie?*
▸ **lastly** /'lɑːstli/ *adverb* finally, as the last thing: *Lastly, I want to thank my parents for all their help.*

last² 0̶ᴍ /lɑːst/ *adverb*
1 after all the others: *He finished last in the race.*
2 at a time that is nearest to now: *I last saw Penny in 2003.*

last³ 0̶ᴍ /lɑːst/ *noun*
the **last** (*plural* the **last**) a person or thing that comes after all the others; what comes at the end: *I was the last to arrive at the party.*
at last in the end; after some time ⊃ SAME MEANING **finally**: *She waited all week, and at last the letter arrived.*

last⁴ 0̶ᴍ /lɑːst/ *verb* (**lasts, lasting, lasted**)
1 to continue for a time: *The film lasted for three hours.* ◇ *How long did the game last?*
2 to be enough for a certain time: *We have enough food to last us till next week.*

lasting /'lɑːstɪŋ/ *adjective*
continuing for a long time: *Their trip to India made a lasting impression on them.*

last name /'lɑːst neɪm/ *noun*
the part of your name that other members of your family also have ⊃ SAME MEANING **surname**: *My first name's Alison, my last name's Waters.* ⊃ Look at the note at **name**.

late 0̶ᴍ /leɪt/ *adjective, adverb* (**later, latest**)
1 near the end of a time: *They arrived in the late afternoon.* ◇ *She's in her late twenties* (= between the age of 25 and 29).
⊃ OPPOSITE **early**
2 after the usual or right time: *I went to bed late last night.* ◇ *I was late for school today* (= I arrived late). ◇ *My train was late.*
⊃ OPPOSITE **early**
3 no longer alive; dead: *Her late husband was a doctor.*

a late night an evening when you go to bed later than usual
at the latest no later than a time or a date: *Please be here by twelve o'clock at the latest.*

lately /'leɪtli/ *adverb*
recently: *Have you seen Mark lately?* ◇ *The weather has been very bad lately.*

later¹ 0̶ᴍ /'leɪtə(r)/ *adverb*
at a time in the future; after the time you are talking about: *See you later.* ◇ *His father died later that year.* ⊃ OPPOSITE **earlier**
later on (*informal*) at a time in the future; after the time you are talking about: *I'm going out later on.*

later² 0̶ᴍ /'leɪtə(r)/ *adjective*
1 coming after something else or at a time in the future: *The match has been postponed to a later date.*
2 near the end of a period of time: *the later part of the twentieth century*
⊃ OPPOSITE **earlier**

latest /'leɪtɪst/ *adjective*
the newest or most recent: *the latest fashions*

Latin /'lætɪn/ *noun* (*no plural*)
the language that people used a long time ago in ancient Rome: *Do you study Latin at school?*
▸ **Latin** *adjective*: *Spanish, Italian and other Latin languages* (= that developed from Latin)

Latin American /ˌlætɪn ə'merɪkən/ *adjective*
from the parts of Central and South America where people speak Spanish or Portuguese

latitude /'lætɪtjuːd/ *noun* (*no plural*)
the distance of a place north or south of the line around the middle of the earth (called the **equator**). **Latitude** is measured in degrees. ⊃ Look at **longitude**. ⊃ Look at the picture at **earth**.

latter /'lætə(r)/ *noun* (*no plural*)
the **latter** the second of two things or people: *I studied both French and German, but I preferred the latter.* ⊃ Look at **former**.

laugh¹ 0̶ᴍ /lɑːf/ *verb* (**laughs, laughing, laughed** /lɑːft/)
to make sounds to show that you are happy or that you think something is funny: *His jokes always make me laugh.*
laugh at somebody or **something** to laugh to show that you think somebody or something is funny or silly: *The children laughed at the clown.* ◇ *They all laughed at me when I said I was afraid of dogs.*

laugh² 0̶ᴍ /lɑːf/ *noun*
the sound you make when you are happy or

A
B
C
D
E
F
G
H
I
J
K
L
M
N
O
P
Q
R
S
T
U
V
W
X
Y
Z

A
B
C
D
E
F
G
H
I
J
K
L
M
N
O
P
Q
R
S
T
U
V
W
X
Y
Z

when you think something is funny: *My brother has a loud laugh.* ◇ *She told us a joke and we all **had a good laugh*** (= laughed a lot).
for a laugh as a joke; for fun: *The boys put a spider in her bed for a laugh.*

laughter /'lɑːftə(r)/ *noun* (*no plural*)
the sound of laughing: *I could hear laughter in the next room.*

launch /lɔːntʃ/ *verb* (launches, launching, launched /lɔːntʃt/)
1 to start something new: *The magazine was launched last year.*
2 to put a ship into the water or a SPACECRAFT (= a vehicle that travels in space) into the sky: *This ship was launched in 2005.*

launderette /lɔːn'dret/ (*British*) (*American* Laundromat™ /'lɔːndrəmæt/) *noun*
a shop where you pay to wash and dry your clothes in machines

laundry /'lɔːndri/ *noun* (*no plural*)
clothes and sheets that you must wash or that you have washed ⊃ SAME MEANING **washing**: *a pile of dirty laundry*

lava /'lɑːvə/ *noun* (*no plural*)
hot liquid rock that comes out of a mountain with an opening at the top (called a volcano)

lavatory /'lævətri/ *noun* (*plural* lavatories) (*British, formal*)
a large bowl with a seat that you use when you need to empty waste from your body, or the room that it is in: *Where's the lavatory, please?* ⊃ Look at the note at **toilet**.

law 0̶ₘ /lɔː/ *noun*
1 the law (*no plural*) all the rules of a country: *Stealing is **against the law*** (= illegal). ◇ *You're **breaking the law*** (= doing something illegal).
2 a rule of a country that says what people may or may not do: *There is a **law against** carrying guns.*

law court /'lɔː kɔːt/ *noun* (*British*) = COURT OF LAW

lawn /lɔːn/ *noun*
an area of short grass in a garden or park: *They were sitting on the lawn.*

lawnmower /'lɔːnməʊə(r)/ (*also* mower) *noun*
a machine that you use to cut grass in a garden or park

lawnmower

lawnmower (*also* **mower**)

lawyer 0̶ₘ /'lɔːjə(r)/ *noun* (*American also* attorney)
a person who has studied the law and who helps people or talks for them in a court of law ⊃ Look at Picture Dictionary page **P12**.

lay¹ 0̶ₘ /leɪ/ *verb* (lays, laying, laid /leɪd/, has laid)
1 to put somebody or something carefully on another thing: *I laid the papers on the desk.*

> 🔎 **WHICH WORD?**
> **Lay** or **lie**?
> **Lay** has an object: *He is **laying a carpet** in our new house.* The past simple is **laid**: *She **laid the baby** down gently on the bed.*
> **Lie** does not have an object: *He is lying on the beach.* The past simple is **lay**: *She was tired so she **lay** on the bed.*

2 to make an egg: *Birds and insects lay eggs.*
lay the table (*British*) to put knives, forks, plates and other things on the table before you eat ⊃ SAME MEANING **set the table**

lay² *form of* LIE¹

layer 0̶ₘ /'leɪə(r)/ *noun*
something flat that lies on another thing or that is between other things: *The table was covered with a thin layer of dust.* ◇ *The cake has a layer of jam in the middle.* ⊃ Look also at **ozone layer**.

lazy 0̶ₘ /'leɪzi/ *adjective* (lazier, laziest)
A person who is **lazy** does not want to work: *Don't be so lazy – come and help me!* ◇ *My teacher said I was lazy.*
▶ **laziness** /'leɪzinəs/ *noun* (*no plural*)

lb *short way of writing* POUND(2)

lead¹ 0̶ₘ /liːd/ *verb* (leads, leading, led /led/, has led)

> 🔎 **PRONUNCIATION**
> The word **lead** usually sounds like **feed** or **need**.
> However, when it means a soft grey metal or the part inside a pencil, it sounds like **red** or **said**.

1 to take a person or an animal somewhere by going with them or in front of them: *He led me to the classroom.*
2 to go to a place: *This path leads to the river.*
3 to make something happen: *Smoking can **lead to** heart disease.*
4 to have a particular type of life: *They lead a very busy life.*
5 to be the first or the best, for example in a race or game: *Who's leading in the race?*
6 to control a group of people: *The team was led by Gwen Hollis.*

lead² /liːd/ *noun*
1 (*no plural*) the first place or position in front of other people: *The French runner has gone **into the lead**.* ◊ *Who is **in the lead** (= winning)?*
2 (*plural* **leads**) (*British*) (*American* **leash**) (*plural* **leashes**) a long piece of leather or a chain that you tie to a dog's neck so that it walks with you: *All dogs must be kept **on a lead**.*
3 (*plural* **leads**) a long piece of wire that brings electricity to things like lamps and machines

lead³ /led/ *noun*
1 (*no plural*) (*symbol* **Pb**) a soft grey metal that is very heavy. **Lead** is used to make things like water pipes and roofs.
2 (*plural* **leads**) the grey part inside a pencil

leader 0‑ₘ /ˈliːdə(r)/ *noun*
1 a person who controls a group of people: *They chose a new leader.*
2 a person or thing that is the first or the best: *The leader is ten metres in front of the other runners.*

leadership /ˈliːdəʃɪp/ *noun* (*no plural*)
the state or position of being the person who controls a group of people: *The country is **under** new **leadership** (= has new leaders).*

leading /ˈliːdɪŋ/ *adjective*
best or most important: *He's one of the leading experts in this field.*

leaf 0‑ₘ /liːf/ *noun* (*plural* **leaves** /liːvz/)
one of the flat green parts that grow on a plant or tree: *Leaves fall from the trees in autumn.*

leaflet /ˈliːflət/ *noun*
a piece of paper with writing on it that gives information about something: *I picked up a leaflet on local museums and art galleries.*

league /liːg/ *noun*
1 a group of teams that play against each other in a sport: *the football league*
2 a group of people or countries that work together to do something: *the League of Nations*

leak¹ /liːk/ *verb* (**leaks**, **leaking**, **leaked** /liːkt/)
1 to have a hole that liquid or gas can go through: *The roof of our house leaks when it rains.* ◊ *The boat is leaking.*
2 (used about liquid or gas) to go out through a hole: *Water is leaking from the pipe.*

leak² /liːk/ *noun*
a small hole that liquid or gas can get through: *There's a leak in the pipe.*
▶ **leaky** /ˈliːki/ *adjective*: *a leaky roof*

lean

She is **leaning** against a tree.   He is **leaning** out of a window.

lean¹ 0‑ₘ /liːn/ *verb* (**leans**, **leaning**, **leant** /lent/ *or* **leaned** /liːnd/, **has leant** *or* **has leaned**)
1 to not be straight; to bend forwards, backwards or to the side: *She leaned out of the window and waved.*
2 to put your body or a thing against another thing: *Lean your bike against the wall.*

lean² /liːn/ *adjective* (**leaner**, **leanest**)
1 thin and healthy: *He is tall and lean.*
2 **Lean** meat does not have very much fat.

leant *form of* LEAN¹

leap /liːp/ *verb* (**leaps**, **leaping**, **leapt** /lept/ *or* **leaped** /liːpt/, **has leapt** *or* **has leaped**)
to jump high or a long way: *The cat leapt onto the table.*
▶ **leap** *noun*: *With one leap, he was over the top of the wall.*

leapt *form of* LEAP

leap year /ˈliːp jɪə(r)/ *noun*
a year when February has 29 days. **Leap years** happen every four years.

learn 0‑ₘ /lɜːn/ *verb* (**learns**, **learning**, **learnt** /lɜːnt/ *or* **learned** /lɜːnd/, **has learnt** *or* **has learned**)

🔊 **PRONUNCIATION**
The word **learn** sounds like **turn**.

1 to find out something, or how to do something, by studying or by doing it often: *When did you **learn to** swim?* ◊ *I learnt English at school.* ◊ *Learn this list of words for homework (= so you can remember them).*
2 to hear about something: *I was sorry to **learn of** your father's death.*

learner /ˈlɜːnə(r)/ *noun*
a person who is learning: *This dictionary is for learners of English.*

leash /liːʃ/ *American English for* LEAD² (2)

least 0‑ₘ /liːst/ *adjective, pronoun, adverb*
1 the smallest amount of something: *Sue has*

A

a lot of money, Jane has less, and Kate has the least. ⇒ OPPOSITE **most**
2 less than all others: *I bought the least expensive tickets.* ⇒ OPPOSITE **most**
at least
1 not less than: *It will cost at least €150.*
2 although other things are bad: *We're not rich, but at least we're happy.*
not in the least not at all: *'Are you angry?' 'Not in the least!'*

leather 0⃞ /'leðə(r)/ *noun* (*no plural*)
the skin of an animal that is used to make things like shoes, jackets or bags: *a leather jacket*

leave¹ 0⃞ /liːv/ *verb* (leaves, leaving, left /left/, has left)
1 to go away from a place or a person: *The train leaves at 8.40.* ◇ *At what age do most people **leave school** in your country?* ◇ *We are **leaving for** France tomorrow.*
2 to let somebody or something stay in the same place or in the same way: *Leave the door open, please.*
3 to forget to bring something with you: *I left my books at home.* ◇ *I can't find my glasses. Maybe I **left** them **behind** at work.*
4 to make something stay; to not use something: *Leave some cake for me!*
5 to give something to somebody when you die: *She **left** all her money **to** her two sons.*
6 to give the responsibility for something to another person: *I'll **leave it to** you to organize the food.*
be left to still be there after everything else has gone: *There is only one piece of cake left.*
leave somebody or **something alone** to not touch, annoy or speak to somebody or something: *Leave me alone – I'm busy!* ◇ *Leave that bag alone – it's mine!*
leave somebody or **something out** to not put in or do something; to not include somebody or something: *The other children left him out of the game.* ◇ *I left out question 3 in the exam because it was too difficult.*

leave² /liːv/ *noun* (*no plural*)
a period of time when you are allowed to be away from work for a holiday or for a special reason: *I have 25 days' leave each year.* ◇ *She's not working – she's **on** sick **leave**.*

leaves plural of LEAF

lecture /'lektʃə(r)/ *noun*
a talk to a group of people to teach them about something: *She gave a fascinating **lecture on** Spanish history.*
▶ **lecture** *verb* (lectures, lecturing, lectured /'lektʃəd/): *Professor Sims **lectures** in Modern Art.*

lecturer /'lektʃərə(r)/ *noun*
a person who gives talks to teach people about a subject, especially as a job in a university: *He is a university lecturer.*

led form of LEAD¹

ledge /ledʒ/ *noun*
a long narrow flat place, for example under a window or on the side of a mountain: *a window ledge*

leek /liːk/ *noun*
a vegetable like a long onion that is white at one end and green at the other: *leek and potato soup*

left¹ form of LEAVE¹

left² 0⃞ /left/ *adjective, adverb*
on the side where your heart is in the body: *I've broken my left arm.* ◇ *Turn left at the church.* ⇒ OPPOSITE **right**

left³ 0⃞ /left/ *noun* (*no plural*)
the left side or direction: *In Britain we drive on **the left**.* ◇ *The house is **on your left**.* ⇒ OPPOSITE **right**

left-hand /'left hænd/ *adjective*
of or on the left: *Your heart is on **the left-hand side** of your body.* ⇒ OPPOSITE **right-hand**

left-handed /ˌleft 'hændɪd/ *adjective, adverb*
using your left hand more easily than your right hand, for example when you write: *Are you left-handed?* ◇ *I can't write left-handed.* ⇒ OPPOSITE **right-handed**

leg 0⃞ /leg/ *noun*
1 one of the long parts of the body of a person or an animal that is used for walking and standing: *A spider has eight legs.* ◇ *She sat down and crossed her legs.* ⇒ Look at Picture Dictionary **P4**.
2 one of the parts of a pair of trousers that covers your leg: *a trouser leg*
3 one of the long parts that a table or chair stands on: *a table leg*

legal 0⃞ /'liːgl/ *adjective*
1 using or connected with the law: *legal advice*
2 allowed by the law: *In many parts of the US it is **legal** to carry a gun.* ⇒ OPPOSITE **illegal** or **against the law**
▶ **legally** /'liːgəli/ *adverb*: *They are not legally married.*

legend /'ledʒənd/ *noun*
1 an old story that is perhaps not true: *the legend of Robin Hood*
2 a very famous person: *He was a legend in the world of music.*

legible /'ledʒəbl/ *adjective*
clear enough to read: *legible writing*
○ OPPOSITE **illegible**

leisure /'leʒə(r)/ *noun* (*no plural*)
the time when you are not working and can
do what you want: *leisure activities*

leisure centre /'leʒə sentə(r)/ (*British*)
noun
a public building where people can go to do
sports and other activities in their free time

lemon 0-π /'lemən/ *noun*
a yellow fruit with SOUR (= sharp tasting)
juice that is used for giving flavour to food
and drink: *lemon juice* ○ Look at Picture
Dictionary page **P8**.

lemonade /,lemə'neɪd/ *noun* (*no plural*)
1 (*British*) a sweet clear drink with bubbles in
it: *a glass of lemonade*
2 a drink that is made from fresh lemon
juice, sugar and water

lend 0-π /lend/ *verb* (lends, lending, lent
/lent/, has lent)
to give something to somebody for a short
time: *I lent the book to Jo.* ◇ *Rick lent me his
car for an hour.* ○ Look at the note and the
picture at **borrow**.

length 0-π /leŋθ/ *noun* (*no plural*)
how long something is: *The table is two
metres in length.* ◇ *We measured the length of
the garden.* ○ The adjective is **long**.

lengthen /'leŋθən/ *verb* (lengthens,
lengthening, lengthened /'leŋθnd/)
to become or to make something longer: *I
need to lengthen this skirt.*

lengthy /'leŋθi/ *adjective* (lengthier,
lengthiest)
very long: *a lengthy meeting*

lens /lenz/ *noun* (*plural* lenses)
a special piece of glass in things like cameras
or glasses. It makes things look bigger,
smaller or clearer when you look through it.
○ Look at the picture at **glasses**.

lent *form of* LEND

lentil /'lentl/ *noun*
a small round dried seed. You cook **lentils** in
water before you eat them: *lentil soup*

leopard /'lepəd/ *noun*
a wild animal like a big cat with yellow fur
and dark spots. **Leopards** live in Africa and
southern Asia. ○ Look at Picture Dictionary
page **P3**.

leotard /'liːətɑːd/ *noun*
a piece of clothing that fits the body tightly
from the neck to the tops of the legs.
Leotards are worn by dancers or by women

doing some sports. ○ Look at Picture
Dictionary page **P5**.

less¹ 0-π /les/ *adjective, pronoun*
a smaller amount of something: *A poor
person has less money than a rich person.* ◇
The doctor advised him to drink less beer.
○ OPPOSITE **more** ○ Look at **least**.

less² 0-π /les/ *adverb*
not so much: *It rains less in summer.* ◇ *I'm too
fat – I must try to eat less.* ◇ *He's less intelligent
than his sister.* ○ OPPOSITE **more** ○ Look at
least.

lessen /'lesn/ *verb* (lessens, lessening,
lessened /'lesnd/)
to become or to make something less: *This
medicine will lessen the pain.*

lesson 0-π /'lesn/ *noun*
a time when you learn something with a
teacher: *We have a French lesson after lunch.* ◇
She gives piano lessons. ◇ *I'm taking driving
lessons.*

let 0-π /let/ *verb* (lets, letting, let, has let)
1 to allow somebody or something to do
something: *Her parents won't let her stay out
after 11 o'clock.* ◇ *Let me carry your bag.* ◇ *Let
the dog in (= let it come in).*

> 🔎 **GRAMMAR**
> You cannot use **let** in the passive. You
> must use **allow** and **to**: *They let him take
> the exam again.* ◇ *He was allowed to take
> the exam again.*

○ Look at the note at **allow**.
2 **let's** used for making suggestions about
what you and other people can do: *Let's go
to the cinema tonight.*

> 🔎 **GRAMMAR**
> The negative is **let's not**: *Let's not go out
> this evening.*

3 to allow somebody to use your house or
land if they pay you: *Have you got any rooms
to let?*
let somebody down to not do
something that you promised to do for
somebody: *Claire has let me down. We agreed
to meet at eight o'clock but she didn't come.*
let go of somebody or **something**, **let
somebody** or **something go** to stop
holding somebody or something: *Let go of
my hand!* ◇ *Let me go. You're hurting me!*
let somebody off to not punish
somebody: *He wasn't sent to prison – the
judge let him off.*

lethal /'liːθl/ *adjective*
Something that is **lethal** can cause a lot of

damage or death. ⊃ SAME MEANING
deadly: *a lethal weapon*

letter 0—ᵣ /'letə(r)/ *noun*
1 a piece of writing that one person sends to another person: *He got a letter from his cousin this morning.* ◊ *I'm writing a **thank-you letter** for the flowers she sent me.*
2 a sign in writing that represents a sound in a language: *Z is the last letter in the English alphabet.*

> *ρ* WORD BUILDING
> A, B and C are **capital** letters, and a, b, and c are **small** letters.

letter box /'letə bɒks/ *noun* (*plural* **letter boxes**) (*British*) (*American* **mailbox**)
1 a private box outside a house or a building or a hole in a door for putting letters through ⊃ Look at Picture Dictionary page **P10**.
2 a small box near the main door of a building or by the road where letters are left for the owner to collect
3 (*British*) = POSTBOX

lettuce /'letɪs/ *noun*
a plant with big green leaves that you eat cold in salads ⊃ Look at Picture Dictionary page **P9**.

level¹ 0—ᵣ /'levl/ *noun*
1 the amount, size or number of something: *a low **level** of unemployment*
2 how high something is: *The town is 500 metres above **sea level**.* ◊ *an elementary-level English class*

level² 0—ᵣ /'levl/ *adjective*
1 with no part higher than another part ⊃ SAME MEANING **flat**: *We need level ground to play football on.* ◊ *This shelf isn't level.*
2 at the same height, standard or position: *The two teams are level with 40 points each.* ◊ *His head is **level with** his mother's shoulder.*

level crossing /ˌlevl 'krɒsɪŋ/ (*British*) (*American* **railroad crossing**) *noun*
a place where a railway line goes over a road

lever /'liːvə(r)/ *noun*
1 a handle that you pull or push to make a machine work: *Pull this lever.*
2 a bar for lifting something heavy or opening something. You put one end under the thing you want to lift or open, and push the other end.

liable /'laɪəbl/ *adjective*
be liable to do something to be likely to do something: *We're all liable to have accidents when we are very tired.*

liar /'laɪə(r)/ *noun*
a person who says or writes things that are

not true (called **lies**): *I don't believe her – she's a liar.* ⊃ The verb is **lie**.

liberal /'lɪbərəl/ *adjective*
A person who is **liberal** lets other people do and think what they want: *Kim's parents are very liberal, but mine are quite strict.*

the Liberal Democrats /ðə ˌlɪbərəl 'deməkræts/ *noun* (*plural*)
(*politics*) one of the important political parties in Britain ⊃ Look at **the Conservative Party** and **the Labour Party**.

liberate /'lɪbəreɪt/ *verb* (**liberates, liberating, liberated**)
to make somebody or something free: *The city was liberated by the advancing army.*

liberty /'lɪbəti/ *noun* (*no plural*)
being free to go where you want and do what you want ⊃ Look at **freedom**.

librarian /laɪ'breəriən/ *noun*
a person who works in a library

library 0—ᵣ /'laɪbrəri/ *noun* (*plural* **libraries**)
a room or building where you go to borrow or read books

> *ρ* WHICH WORD?
> Be careful! You cannot buy books from a **library**. The place where you buy books is called a **bookshop** or a **bookstore**.

lice *form of* LOUSE

licence /'laɪsns/ (*British*) (*American* **license**) *noun*
an official piece of paper that shows you are allowed to do or have something: *Do you have a licence for this gun?*

license /'laɪsns/ *verb* (**licenses, licensing, licensed** /'laɪsnst/)
to give somebody official permission to do or have something: *This shop is licensed to sell guns.*

license plate /'laɪsns pleɪt/ *American English for* NUMBER PLATE

lick /lɪk/ *verb* (**licks, licking, licked** /lɪkt/)
to move your tongue over something: *The cat was licking its paws.*
▶ **lick** *noun*: *Can I have a lick of your ice cream?*

lid 0—ᵣ /lɪd/ *noun*
the top part of a box, pot or other container that covers it and that you can take off ⊃ Look also at **eyelid**.

lie¹ 0—ᵣ /laɪ/ *verb* (**lies, lying, lay** /leɪ/, **has lain** /leɪn/)
1 to put your body flat on something so that

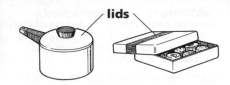

lids

you are not sitting or standing: *He lay on the bed.* ⊃ Look at the note at **lay**.

2 to have your body flat on something: *The baby was lying on its back.*

3 to be or stay in a position or state: *The hills lie to the north of the town.*

lie down to put or have your body flat so that you can rest: *She lay down on the bed.*

lie² 0— /laɪ/ *verb* (**lies**, **lying**, **lied** /laɪd/, has **lied**)

to say something that you know is not true: *He **lied about** his age. He said he was 16 but really he's 14.* ◇ *Don't ever **lie to** me again!* ⊃ A person who lies is a **liar**.

lie³ 0— /laɪ/ *noun*

something you say that you know is not true: *She **told** me **a lie**.*

lieutenant /lefˈtenənt/ (*abbr.* Lieut., Lt) *noun*

an officer at a middle level in the army or navy

life 0— /laɪf/ *noun* (*plural* **lives** /laɪvz/)

1 (*no plural*) People, animals and plants have **life** while they are alive, but things like stone, metal and water do not: *Do you believe there is life after death?* ◇ *Is there life on other planets?*

2 (*plural* **lives**) being alive: *Many people **lost** their **lives** (= died) in the fire.* ◇ *The doctor **saved** her **life** (= stopped her dying).*

3 (*plural* **lives**) the time that somebody is alive: *He has lived here **all his life**.*

4 (*plural* **lives**) the way that you live or the experiences that you have when you are alive: *They were very happy throughout their **married life**.* ◇ *They **lead** a busy **life**.*

5 (*no plural*) energy; being busy and interested: *Young children are **full of life**.*

lifebelt /ˈlaɪfbelt/ *noun*

a big ring that you hold or wear if you fall into water to stop you from dying in the water (**drowning**)

lifeboat /ˈlaɪfbəʊt/ *noun*

a boat that goes to help people who are in danger at sea

lifeguard /ˈlaɪfɡɑːd/ *noun*

a person at a beach or a swimming pool whose job is to help people who are in danger in the water

life jacket /ˈlaɪf dʒækɪt/ (*American also* **life vest** /ˈlaɪf vest/) *noun*

a special jacket with no sleeves that can be filled with air. You wear it to help you float if you fall in the water.

lifestyle /ˈlaɪfstaɪl/ *noun*

the way that you live: *They have a healthy lifestyle.*

lifetime /ˈlaɪftaɪm/ *noun*

all the time that you are alive: *There have been a lot of changes in my grandma's lifetime.*

lift¹ 0— /lɪft/ *verb* (**lifts**, **lifting**, **lifted**)

to move somebody or something to a higher position: *I can't lift this box. It's too heavy.* ◇ *Lift your arm up.*

lift² 0— /lɪft/ (*British*) *noun*

1 (*American* **elevator**) a machine that takes people and things up and down in a high building: *Shall we use the stairs or **take the lift**?*

2 (*American* **ride**) a free journey in another person's car: *Can you **give** me **a lift** to the station?*

lift-off /ˈlɪft ɒf/ *noun*

the moment when a SPACECRAFT (= a vehicle that can travel into space) leaves the ground

lights

lampshade

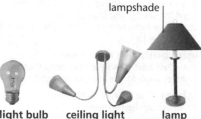

light bulb   ceiling light   lamp

lantern

torch (*British*)
flashlight (*American*)

light¹ 0— /laɪt/ *noun*

1 (*no plural*)

🔊 **PRONUNCIATION**
The word **light** sounds like **white**.

A B C D E F G H I J K **L** M N O P Q R S T U V W X Y Z

the energy from the sun, a lamp, etc. that allows us to see things: *Strong sunlight is bad for the eyes.* ◇ *The light was not very good so it was difficult to read.*
2 (*plural* **lights**) a thing that gives light, for example an electric lamp

> ### 🔎 WHICH WORD?
> A light can be **on** or **off**.
> You can **put**, **turn** or **switch** a light **on**, **off** or **out**: *Turn the lights off before you go to bed.* ◇ *It's getting dark. Shall I switch the light on?*

⊃ Look also at **traffic lights**.
3 (*plural* **lights**) something, for example a match, that you use to start a cigarette burning: *Do you have a light?*
set light to something to make something start to burn

light² 0⊸ /laɪt/ *adjective* (**lighter**, **lightest**)
1 full of natural light: *In summer it's light until about ten o'clock.* ◇ *The room has a lot of windows so it's very light.* ⊃ OPPOSITE **dark**
2 with a pale colour: *a light blue shirt* ⊃ OPPOSITE **dark**
3 easy to lift or move: *Will you carry this bag for me? It's very light.* ⊃ OPPOSITE **heavy** ⊃ Look at the picture at **heavy**.
4 not very much or not very strong: *light rain* ◇ *I had a light breakfast.*
▸ **lightly** /ˈlaɪtli/ *adverb*: *She touched me lightly on the arm.*

light³ 0⊸ /laɪt/ *verb* (**lights**, **lighting**, **lit** /lɪt/ *or* **lighted**, **has lit** *or* **has lighted**)
1 to make something start to burn: *Will you light the fire?* ◇ *She lit a candle.*
2 to give light to something: *The room is lit by two big lamps.*

light bulb /ˈlaɪt bʌlb/ *noun*
the glass part of an electric lamp that gives light ⊃ Look at the picture at **light**.

lighten /ˈlaɪtn/ *verb* (**lightens**, **lightening**, **lightened** /ˈlaɪtnd/)
to become lighter or to make something lighter in colour or weight
lighten up (*informal*) to become happier or less worried about something

lighter /ˈlaɪtə(r)/ *noun*
a thing for lighting cigarettes

lighthouse /ˈlaɪthaʊs/ *noun* (*plural* **lighthouses** /ˈlaɪthaʊzɪz/)
a tall building by or in the sea, with a strong light to show ships that there are rocks

lighting /ˈlaɪtɪŋ/ *noun* (*no plural*)
the kind of lights that a place has: *electric lighting*

lightning /ˈlaɪtnɪŋ/ *noun* (*no plural*)
a sudden bright light in the sky when there is a storm: *He was **struck** (= hit) **by lightning**.* ⊃ Look at Picture Dictionary page **P16**. ⊃ Look also at **thunder**.

like¹ 0⊸ /laɪk/ *verb* (**likes**, **liking**, **liked** /laɪkt/)
to feel that somebody or something is good or nice; to enjoy something: *Do you like your new teacher?* ◇ *I don't like carrots.* ◇ *I like playing tennis.* ⊃ OPPOSITE **dislike**
if you like used to agree with somebody or to suggest something: *'Shall we go out tonight?' 'Yes, if you like.'*

> ### 🔎 GRAMMAR
> **Would like** is a more polite way of saying **want**: *Would you like some coffee?* ◇ *I'd like to speak to the manager.*

like² 0⊸ /laɪk/ *preposition, conjunction*
1 the same as somebody or something: *She is wearing a dress like mine.* ◇ *John looks like his father.* ⊃ Look at **unlike**.
2 in the same way as somebody or something: *She acted like a child.*
3 for example: *I bought a lot of things, like books and clothes.*
what is ... like? words that you say when you want to know more about somebody or something: *'What's that book like?' 'It's very interesting.'*

likeable /ˈlaɪkəbl/ *adjective*
If a person is **likeable**, they are friendly and easy to like.

likelihood /ˈlaɪklihʊd/ *noun* (*no plural*)
the chance of something happening: *There is very little **likelihood of** you passing this exam* (= it is very unlikely that you will pass).

likely 0⊸ /ˈlaɪkli/ *adjective* (**likelier**, **likeliest**)
If something is **likely**, it will probably happen: *It's **likely that** she will agree.* ◇ *They are **likely to** be late.* ⊃ OPPOSITE **unlikely**

likeness /ˈlaɪknəs/ *noun* (*no plural*)
being or looking the same: *There's a **strong likeness** between John and his brother.*

likewise /ˈlaɪkwaɪz/ *adverb* (*formal*)
the same: *I sat down and John did likewise.*

liking /ˈlaɪkɪŋ/ *noun* (*no plural*)
the feeling that you like somebody or something: *She has a **liking for** spicy food.*

lily /ˈlɪli/ *noun* (*plural* **lilies**)
a plant with big white or coloured flowers

limb /lɪm/ *noun*
an arm or a leg

lime /laɪm/ *noun*
a small green fruit like a lemon ⊃ Look at Picture Dictionary page **P8**.

limit¹ ⟳ /'lɪmɪt/ *noun*
the most that is possible or allowed: *There is a **limit to** the amount of pain we can bear.* ◇ *What is the **speed limit** (= how fast are you allowed to go)?*

limit² ⟳ /'lɪmɪt/ *verb* (limits, limiting, limited)
to do or have no more than a certain amount or number: *There are only 100 seats, so we must limit the number of tickets we sell.*

limp¹ /lɪmp/ *adjective*
not firm or strong: *Her whole body went limp and she fell to the ground.*

limp² /lɪmp/ *verb* (limps, limping, limped /lɪmpt/)
to walk with difficulty because you have hurt your foot or leg
▶ **limp** *noun*: *He walks with a limp.*

lines

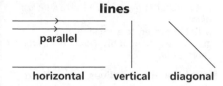

parallel   horizontal   vertical   diagonal

line¹ ⟳ /laɪn/ *noun*
1 a long thin mark like this ____: *Draw a straight line.* ◇ *The ball went over the line.*
2 people or things beside each other or one after the other ⊃ SAME MEANING **queue**: *There was a long **line of** people waiting at the Post Office.*
3 all the words that are beside each other on a page: *How many lines are there on this page?* ◇ *I don't know the next line of the poem.*
4 a long piece of string or rope: *Hang the washing on the line to dry.*
5 a very long wire for telephones or electricity: *I tried to phone him but the line was busy.*
6 a section of railway track that a train moves along: *The accident was caused by a cow on the line.*

line² /laɪn/ *verb* (lines, lining, lined /laɪnd/)
1 to cover the inside of something with a different material: *The boots are **lined with** fur.*
2 to stand or be in lines along something: *People lined the streets to watch the race.*
line up to stand in a line or make a line: *We lined up to buy tickets.*

linen /'lɪnɪn/ *noun* (no plural)
1 a kind of strong cloth: *a white linen jacket*

2 sheets and other things made of cloth that you use in the home: *bed linen*

liner /'laɪnə(r)/ *noun*
1 a big ship that carries people a long way ⊃ Look at Picture Dictionary page **P1**.
2 a bag that you put inside something to keep it clean: *a dustbin liner*

linger /'lɪŋɡə(r)/ *verb* (lingers, lingering, lingered /'lɪŋɡəd/)
to stay somewhere for a long time: *The smell of her perfume lingered in the room.*

lining /'laɪnɪŋ/ *noun*
material that covers the inside of something: *My coat has a thick lining so it's very warm.* ⊃ Look at Picture Dictionary page **P5**.

link¹ /lɪŋk/ *noun*
1 something that joins things or people together: *There's **a link between** smoking **and** heart disease.*
2 (*computing*) a place where one electronic document on the Internet is connected to another one: *To visit our other website, click on this link.*
3 one of the round parts in a chain ⊃ Look at the picture at **chain**.

link² /lɪŋk/ *verb* (links, linking, linked /lɪŋkt/)
to join one person or thing to another: *The computers are linked together in a network.*

lion

mane   coat   tail   paw   claw

lion /'laɪən/ *noun*
a large animal of the cat family that lives in parts of Africa and Asia. **Lions** have yellow fur, and the males have a lot of hair around their head and neck (called a **mane**).

🔎 **WORD BUILDING**
A female lion is called a **lioness** and a young lion is called a **cub**.

A B C D E F G H I J K L M N O P Q R S T U V W X Y Z

lip 0‑ᴡ /lɪp/ *noun*
one of the two soft red parts above and below your mouth: *to kiss somebody on the lips* ⊃ Look at Picture Dictionary page **P4**.

lipstick /'lɪpstɪk/ *noun* (no plural)
colour that women sometimes put on their lips: *She put on some lipstick.*

lipstick

liquid 0‑ᴡ
/'lɪkwɪd/ *noun*
anything that is not a solid or a gas. Water, oil and milk are **liquids**.
▶ **liquid** *adjective*: *liquid soap*

liquor store /'lɪkə stɔː(r)/ *noun* American English for OFF-LICENCE

list¹ 0‑ᴡ /lɪst/ *noun*
a lot of names or other things that you write or say, one after another: *a shopping list* (= of things that you must buy)

list² 0‑ᴡ /lɪst/ *verb* (lists, listing, listed)
to write or say things in a list: *Please list the items in alphabetical order.*

listen 0‑ᴡ /'lɪsn/ *verb* (listens, listening, listened /'lɪsnd/)
to hear something when you are trying to hear it: *I was **listening to** the radio.* ◇ *Listen! I want to tell you something.* ⊃ Look at the note at **hear**.

lit form of LIGHT³

liter American English for LITRE

literature 0‑ᴡ /'lɪtrətʃə(r)/ *noun* (no plural)
books, plays and poetry: *He is studying English literature.*

litre 0‑ᴡ (British) (American **liter**) /'liːtə(r)/ *noun* (abbr. l)
a measure of liquid: *three **litres of** water* ◇ *20 l*

litter¹ /'lɪtə(r)/ *noun*
1 (no plural) pieces of paper and other rubbish that people leave in a public place: *The park was full of litter after the concert.*
2 (plural **litters**) all the baby animals that are born to the same mother at the same time: *Our dog had a litter of six puppies.*

litter² /'lɪtə(r)/ *verb* (litters, littering, littered /'lɪtəd/)
to be or to make something untidy with **litter**: *My desk was **littered with** papers.*

litter bin /'lɪtə bɪn/ (British) (American **trash can**) *noun*
a container to put rubbish in, in the street or a public building

little¹ 0‑ᴡ /'lɪtl/ *adjective*
1 not big ⊃ SAME MEANING **small**: *a little table*
2 young: *a little girl* ◇ *my little* (= younger) *brother*
3 (used about distance or time) short: *Do you mind waiting **a little while**?*

little² 0‑ᴡ /'lɪtl/ *pronoun*, *adjective*
not much: *I did very little today.* ◇ *We have very little money.*
a little a small amount of something: *I've got some ice cream. Would you like a little?* ◇ *I speak a little French.*
little by little slowly: *Little by little she started to feel better.*

little³ 0‑ᴡ /'lɪtl/ *adverb*
not much: *I'm tired – I slept very little last night.*
a little rather; to a small degree
⊃ SAME MEANING **a bit**: *This skirt is a little too short for me.*

live¹ 0‑ᴡ /lɪv/ *verb* (lives, living, lived /lɪvd/)
1 to have your home somewhere: *Where do you live?* ◇ *He still lives with his parents.*
2 to be or stay alive: *You can't live without water.* ◇ *He lived to the age of 93.*
3 to spend your life in a certain way: *They live a quiet life in the country.*
live on something
1 to eat something as your only food: *Cows live on grass.*
2 to have enough money to buy what you need to live: *They live on £70 a week.*

live² /laɪv/ *adjective*
1 not dead: *Have you ever touched a **real live** snake?*
2 If a radio or television programme is **live**, you see or hear it at the same time as it happens: *The match is going out live on TV.*
3 with electricity passing through it: *Don't touch that wire – it's live!*

lively /'laɪvli/ *adjective* (livelier, liveliest)
full of life; always moving or doing things: *The children are very lively.*

liver /'lɪvə(r)/ *noun*
1 (plural **livers**) the part inside your body that cleans the blood
2 (no plural) the **liver** of an animal that you can cook and eat as food

lives *plural of* LIFE

living[1] 0-π /'lɪvɪŋ/ *adjective*
alive; not dead: *Some people say he is the greatest living writer.*

living[2] /'lɪvɪŋ/ *noun*
1 money to buy the things you need in life: *How did he **earn a living**?*
2 the way that you live: *The **cost of living** has risen in recent years.*

living room /'lɪvɪŋ ruːm/ *(British also* **sitting room**) *noun*
a room in a house where people sit together and watch television or talk, for example
‿ SAME MEANING **lounge** ‿ Look at Picture Dictionary page **P10**.

lizard

lizard /'lɪzəd/ *noun*
a small animal that has four legs, a long tail and rough skin

load[1] 0-π /ləʊd/ *noun*
1 something that is carried: *The truck brought another load of wood.*
2 loads *(plural)* *(informal)* a lot: *We've got loads of time.*

load[2] 0-π /ləʊd/ *verb* (**loads, loading, loaded**)
1 to put things in or on something, for example a car or a ship: *Two men loaded the furniture into the van.* ◊ *They're loading the plane now.* ‿ OPPOSITE **unload**
2 to put bullets in a gun or film in a camera

loaf /ləʊf/ *noun* (*plural* **loaves** /ləʊvz/)
bread that has been baked in one piece: *a loaf of bread* ‿ Look at the picture at **bread**.

loan[1] 0-π /ləʊn/ *noun*
money that somebody lends you: *to **take out** a bank **loan***

loan[2] /ləʊn/ *verb* (**loans, loaning, loaned** /ləʊnd/)
to give something to somebody for a period of time ‿ SAME MEANING **lend**: *A friend loaned me $1 000.*

loathe /ləʊð/ *verb* (**loathes, loathing, loathed** /ləʊðd/)
to hate somebody or something: *I loathe modern art.* ‿ OPPOSITE **love**

loaves *plural of* LOAF

lobby /'lɒbi/ *noun* (*plural* **lobbies**)
an area just inside a big building, where people can meet and wait: *a hotel lobby*

lobster /'lɒbstə(r)/ *noun*
a large sea animal with a hard shell and eight legs. Its shell is black but it turns red when it is cooked.

lobster

local 0-π /'ləʊkl/ *adjective*
of a place near you: *Her children go to the local school.* ◊ *a local newspaper* ◊ *local government*
▶ **locally** /'ləʊkəli/ *adverb*: *Do you work locally?*

located /ləʊ'keɪtɪd/ *adjective*
in a place: *The factory is located near Glasgow.*

location /ləʊ'keɪʃn/ *noun*
a place: *The house is in a quiet location on top of a hill.*

lock[1] 0-π /lɒk/ *verb* (**locks, locking, locked** /lɒkt/)
to close something with a key: *Don't forget to lock the door when you leave.*
‿ OPPOSITE **unlock**
lock something away to put something in a place that you close with a key: *The paintings are locked away at night.*
lock somebody in to lock a door so that somebody cannot get out: *The prisoners are locked in.*
lock somebody out to lock a door so that somebody cannot get in
lock up to lock all the doors and windows of a building: *Make sure you lock up before you leave.*

lock[2] 0-π /lɒk/ *noun*
a metal thing that keeps a door, gate or box closed so that you need a key to open it again: *I heard the key turn in the lock.* ‿ Look at the picture at **key**.

locker /'lɒkə(r)/ *noun*
a small cupboard with a lock for keeping things in, for example in a school or at a sports centre

locust /'ləʊkəst/ *noun*
a large insect that lives in hot countries and flies in very large groups, eating all the plants

lodge /lɒdʒ/ *verb* (**lodges, lodging, lodged** /lɒdʒd/)
to pay to live in a room in another person's house: *I **lodged with** a family when I was studying abroad.*

A B C D E F G H I J K **L** M N O P Q R S T U V W X Y Z

▶ **lodger** /ˈlɒdʒə(r)/ *noun* a person who pays to live in a room in another person's house

loft /lɒft/ *noun*
the room or space under the roof of a house ⊃ SAME MEANING **attic**: *My old books are in a box in the loft.* ⊃ Look at Picture Dictionary page **P10**.

log¹ /lɒg/ *noun*
a thick round piece of wood from a tree: *Put another log on the fire.*

log

log² /lɒg/ *verb* (**logs, logging, logged** /lɒgd/)
to keep an official record of things that happen ⊃ SAME MEANING **record**: *to log somebody's phone calls*
log in, log on to type your name, etc. so that you can start using a computer: *You need a password to log on.*
log off, log out to stop using a computer: *Make sure you log out before you switch off the computer.*

logical /ˈlɒdʒɪkl/ *adjective*
seeming natural or sensible: *There is only one logical conclusion.*

logo /ˈləʊgəʊ/ *noun* (*plural* **logos**)
a picture or a design that a company or an organization uses as its special sign: *You will find the company logo on all our products.*

lollipop /ˈlɒlipɒp/ (*British also, informal*) **lolly** /ˈlɒli/ (*plural* **lollies**) *noun*
a big sweet on a stick ⊃ Look also at **ice lolly**.

lonely 0̶🔑 /ˈləʊnli/ *adjective* (**lonelier, loneliest**)
1 unhappy because you are not with other people: *She felt very lonely when she first went to live in the city.*
2 far from other places: *a lonely house in the hills* ⊃ Look at **alone**.
▶ **loneliness** /ˈləʊnlinəs/ *noun* (*no plural*)

long¹ 0̶🔑 /lɒŋ/ *adjective* (**longer** /ˈlɒŋgə(r)/, **longest** /ˈlɒŋgɪst/)
1 far from one end to the other: *Which is the longest river in the world?* ◇ *She has long black hair.* ◇ *Tokyo is a long way from London.* ⊃ OPPOSITE **short** ⊃ Look at the note at **far**.
2 You use **long** to ask or talk about how far something is from one end to the other: *How long is the table?* ◇ *The wall is 5 m long.* ⊃ The noun is **length**.
3 continuing for a lot of time: *a long film* ◇ *He's lived here for a long time.*
⊃ OPPOSITE **short**
4 You use **long** to ask or talk about the time

from the beginning to the end of something: *How long is the lesson?*

long² 0̶🔑 /lɒŋ/ *adverb* (**longer** /ˈlɒŋgə(r)/, **longest** /ˈlɒŋgɪst/)
for a lot of time: *I can't stay long.* ◇ *How long have you been waiting?* ◇ *She moved to the city long after her children were born.* ◇ *My grandfather died long before I was born.*
as long as, so long as only if: *You can borrow the book as long as you promise not to lose it.*
for long for a lot of time: *She went shopping but she was not out for long.*
long ago many years in the past: *Long ago there were no cars.*
no longer, not any longer not now; not as before: *She doesn't live here any longer.*

long³ /lɒŋ/ *verb* (**longs, longing, longed** /lɒŋd/)
to want something very much, especially if this does not seem likely: *I long to see my family again.* ◇ *She's longing for a letter from her boyfriend.*

long-distance /ˌlɒŋ ˈdɪstəns/ *adjective*
travelling or communicating between places that are far from each other: *a long-distance phone call*

long-haul /ˈlɒŋ hɔːl/ *adjective*
travelling between places that are a long way from each other: *a long-haul flight* (= a journey on an airplane)

longing /ˈlɒŋɪŋ/ *noun*
a strong feeling of wanting something ⊃ SAME MEANING **desire**: *a longing for peace*

longitude /ˈlɒŋgɪtjuːd/ *noun* (*no plural*) (*abbr.* **long.**)
the distance of a place east or west of a line from the North Pole to the South Pole that passes through Greenwich in London. **Longitude** is measured in degrees. ⊃ Look at **latitude**. ⊃ Look at the picture at **earth**.

long jump /ˈlɒŋ dʒʌmp/ *noun* (*no plural*)
a sport where you try to jump as far as you can

loo /luː/ *noun* (*plural* **loos**) (*British, informal*)
toilet: *I need to go to the loo.* ⊃ Look at the note at **toilet**.

look¹ 0̶🔑 /lʊk/ *verb* (**looks, looking, looked** /lʊkt/)
1 to turn your eyes towards somebody or something and try to see them: *Look at this picture.* ◇ *You should look both ways before you cross the road.* ⊃ Look at the note at **see**.
2 to seem to be; to appear: *You look tired.* ◇ *It looks as if it's going to rain.*
3 You say **look** to make somebody listen to

you: *Look, I know you're busy, but I need your help.*

look after somebody or **something** to take care of somebody or something: *Can you look after my cat when I'm on holiday?*

look for somebody or **something** to try to find somebody or something: *I'm looking for my keys.*

look forward to something to wait for something with pleasure: *I'm looking forward to seeing you again.*

look into something to study or try to find out something: *We will look into the problem.*

look like somebody or **something**

1 to seem to be something: *That looks like a good film.*

2 words that you use to ask about somebody's appearance: '***What does he look like?***' '*He's tall with dark hair.*'

3 to have the same appearance as somebody or something: *She looks like her mother.*

look out! be careful: *Look out! There's a car coming!*

look out for somebody or **something** to pay attention and try to see or find somebody or something: *Look out for thieves!*

look round something to visit a place: *We looked round the museum.*

look² 0̄ /lʊk/ *noun*

1 turning your eyes towards somebody or something; looking: ***Have a look*** *at this article.* ◇ *Do you want to **take a look** around?*

2 trying to find somebody or something: *I've **had a look for** your pen, but I can't find it.*

3 the way somebody or something seems: *I don't like **the look of** this weather. I think it's going to rain.*

4 **looks** (*plural*) a person's appearance: *He has his father's good looks.*

loom /luːm/ *noun*

a machine that is used for making cloth by passing pieces of thread across and under other pieces

loop

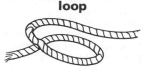

loop /luːp/ *noun*

a round shape made by something like string or rope

loose 0̄ /luːs/ *adjective* (**looser, loosest**)

> 🔎 SPELLING
>
> Remember! Don't confuse **loose** with **lose**, which is a verb: *We mustn't lose this game.*

1 not tied or fixed: *The dog broke its chain and got loose.* ◇ *One of his teeth is loose.*

2 not fitting closely: *a loose white shirt*
⊃ OPPOSITE **tight**

▶ **loosely** /'luːsli/ *adverb*: *The rope was tied loosely round a tree.*

loosen /'luːsn/ *verb* (**loosens, loosening, loosened** /'luːsnd/)

to become looser or to make something looser: *Can you loosen this knot? It's too tight.*
⊃ OPPOSITE **tighten**

lord /lɔːd/ *noun*

1 Lord (in Britain) a man who has a high position in society: *Lord Fraser* ⊃ Look at **Lady**.

2 the Lord (*no plural*) God or Jesus Christ

lorry 0̄ /'lɒri/ *noun* (*plural* **lorries**)

(*British*) (*American* **truck**)

a big vehicle for carrying heavy things
⊃ Look at Picture Dictionary page **P1**.

lose 0̄ /luːz/ *verb* (**loses, losing, lost** /lɒst/, has **lost**)

1 to not be able to find something: *I can't open the door because I've lost my key.*

2 to not have somebody or something that you had before: *I lost my job when the factory closed.*

3 to not win: *Our team lost the match.*

loser /'luːzə(r)/ *noun*

a person who does not win a game, race or competition ⊃ OPPOSITE **winner**

loss 0̄ /lɒs/ *noun* (*plural* **losses**)

1 losing something: *Has she told the police about **the loss of** her car?* ◇ *job losses*

2 how much money a business loses: *The company **made a loss** of £5 million.*
⊃ OPPOSITE **profit**

at a loss If you are **at a loss**, you do not know what to do or say.

lost¹ *form of* LOSE

lost² 0̄ /lɒst/ *adjective*

1 If you are **lost**, you do not know where you are: *I took the wrong road and now I'm lost.* ◇ *Take this map so you don't **get lost**!*

2 If something is **lost**, you cannot find it.

lost property /ˌlɒst 'prɒpəti/ *noun* (*no plural*) (*British*)

things that people have lost or left in a public place: *I left my bag on the train, so I went to the lost property office at the station.*

A B C D E F G H I J K L M N O P Q R S T U V W X Y Z

lot¹ 0🔊 /lɒt/ *pronoun* a lot (*also informal* lots)

very much; a large amount or number of things or people: *We ate a lot.*

a lot of, **lots of** a large number or amount of things or people: *She's got a lot of friends.* ◇ *Lots of love from Jane* (= words at the end of a letter).

lot² 0🔊 /lɒt/ *adverb*

a lot very much or often: *Your flat is a lot bigger than mine.* ◇ *I go to the cinema a lot.*

lotion /'ləʊʃn/ *noun*

liquid that you put on your skin: *suntan lotion*

lottery /'lɒtəri/ *noun* (*plural* lotteries)

a game where you buy a ticket with numbers on it. You win money if your numbers are chosen.

loud 0🔊 /laʊd/ *adjective, adverb* (louder, loudest)

making a lot of noise: *I couldn't hear what he said because the music was too loud.* ◇ *loud voices* ◇ *Please speak a bit louder – I can't hear you.* ⊃ OPPOSITE **quiet**

out loud so that other people can hear it: *I read the story out loud.*

▶ **loudly** /'laʊdli/ *adverb*: *She laughed loudly.*

loudspeaker /ˌlaʊd'spiːkə(r)/ *noun*

a piece of equipment that makes sounds or voices louder: *Music was coming from the loudspeakers.*

lounge /laʊndʒ/ *noun*

a room in a house where people sit together and watch television or talk, for example ⊃ SAME MEANING **living room**, **sitting room**

louse /laʊs/ *noun* (*plural* lice /laɪs/)

a small insect that lives on the bodies of people and animals

lousy /'laʊzi/ *adjective* (lousier, lousiest) (*informal*)

very bad ⊃ SAME MEANING **awful**: *The weather was lousy.*

lovable /'lʌvəbl/ *adjective*

easy to love: *a lovable little boy*

love¹ 0🔊 /lʌv/ *noun*

1 (*no plural*) the strong warm feeling you have when you like somebody or something very much: *Their love for each other was very strong.*

2 (*plural* loves) a person, a thing or an activity that you love: *Who was your first love?*

3 (*no plural*) a word in the game of TENNIS that means zero: *The score is 15-love.*

be in love with somebody to love somebody: *He says he is in love with her and they are going to get married.*

fall in love with somebody to begin to love somebody: *He fell in love with Anna the first time they met.*

love, **love from** (*informal*) a way of ending a letter to somebody that you know well: *See you soon. Love, Peter.*

love² 0🔊 /lʌv/ *verb* (loves, loving, loved /lʌvd/)

1 to have a very strong warm feeling for somebody: *I love him very much.* ◇ *She loves her parents.* ⊃ OPPOSITE **hate**

2 to like something very much: *I love skiing.* ◇ *I would love to go to America.*
⊃ OPPOSITE **hate**

love affair /'lʌv əfeə(r)/ *noun*

a romantic or sexual relationship between two people who love each other but who are not married

lovely /'lʌvli/ *adjective* (lovelier, loveliest)

beautiful or very nice: *That's a lovely dress.* ◇ *We had a lovely holiday.* ◇ *It's lovely to see you again.*

lover /'lʌvə(r)/ *noun*

1 If two people are **lovers**, they have a sexual relationship but they are not married.

2 a person who likes something very much: *a music lover*

loving /'lʌvɪŋ/ *adjective*

feeling or showing love: *loving parents*

low 0🔊 /ləʊ/ *adjective* (lower, lowest)

> 🔊 PRONUNCIATION
> The word **low** sounds like **go**.

1 near the ground: *There was a low wall round the garden.* ◇ *a low bridge*
⊃ OPPOSITE **high**

2 less than usual: *low temperatures* ◇ *low pay*
⊃ OPPOSITE **high**

3 deep or quiet: *a low sound* ◇ *I heard low voices in the next room.*

▶ **low** *adverb*: *The plane flew low over the fields.*

lower¹ /'ləʊə(r)/ *adjective*

that is under something or at the bottom of something: *She bit her lower lip.*
⊃ OPPOSITE **upper**

lower² /'ləʊə(r)/ *verb* (lowers, lowering, lowered /'ləʊəd/)

1 to move somebody or something down: *They lowered the boat into the water.*

2 to make something less: *Please lower your voice* (= speak more quietly).
⊃ OPPOSITE **raise**

lower case /ˌləʊə 'keɪs/ *noun* (*no plural*)

small letters: *My email address is all in lower case.* ⊃ OPPOSITE **upper case**

loyal /'lɔɪəl/ *adjective*
A person who is **loyal** does not change their friends or beliefs: *a loyal friend* ◇ *He is loyal to the company he works for.*
➔ OPPOSITE **disloyal**
▶ **loyalty** /'lɔɪəlti/ *noun* (*no plural*): *Loyalty to your friends is very important.*

L-plate /'el pleɪt/ *noun*
a sign with a big red letter L (for 'learner') on it, that you put on your car when you are learning to drive

Ltd *abbreviation* (*British*)
(used after the name of a British company or business) Limited: *Pierce and Co. Ltd*

luck ⚡ /lʌk/ *noun* (*no plural*)
1 good things that happen to you that you cannot control: *We wish you luck in your new career.*
2 things that happen to you that you cannot control; chance: *to have good luck*
bad luck, **hard luck** words that you say to somebody when you are sorry that they did not have good luck
be in luck to have good things happen to you: *I was in luck – the shop had the book I wanted.*
good luck words that you say to somebody when you hope that they will do well: *Good luck! I'm sure you'll get the job.*

lucky ⚡ /'lʌki/ *adjective* (**luckier**, **luckiest**)
1 having good luck: *She is lucky to be alive after the accident.* ➔ OPPOSITE **unlucky**
2 bringing success or good luck: *My lucky number is 3.* ➔ OPPOSITE **unlucky**
▶ **luckily** /'lʌkɪli/ *adverb* it is lucky that: *I was late, but luckily they waited for me.*

luggage ⚡ /'lʌgɪdʒ/ *noun* (*no plural*)
bags and suitcases that you take with you when you travel ➔ SAME MEANING **baggage**: *'How much luggage have you got?' 'Only one suitcase.'*

🔍 **GRAMMAR**

Luggage does not have a plural so you cannot say 'a luggage'. If you are talking about one suitcase or bag, you say **a piece of luggage**: *She brought five pieces of luggage with her and she was only staying for one week!*

lukewarm /ˌluːkˈwɔːm/ *adjective*
If a liquid is **lukewarm**, it is only slightly warm: *I had to have a lukewarm shower.*

lump ⚡ /lʌmp/ *noun*
1 a hard piece of something: *two lumps of sugar* ◇ *a lump of coal*
2 a part in or on your body which has become hard and bigger: *I've got a lump on my head where I hit it.*

lumpy /'lʌmpi/ *adjective* (**lumpier**, **lumpiest**)
full of or covered with LUMPS: *The sauce is rather lumpy.* ➔ OPPOSITE **smooth**

lunatic /'luːnətɪk/ *noun* (*informal*)
a person who does stupid and often dangerous things

lunch ⚡ /lʌntʃ/ *noun* (*plural* **lunches**)
a meal that you eat in the middle of the day: *What would you like for lunch?* ◇ *What time do you usually have lunch?*

lunchtime /'lʌntʃtaɪm/ *noun*
the time when you eat LUNCH: *I'll meet you at lunchtime.*

lung /lʌŋ/ *noun*
one of the two parts inside your body that you use for breathing

lurk /lɜːk/ *verb* (**lurks**, **lurking**, **lurked** /lɜːkt/)
to wait somewhere secretly, especially because you are going to do something bad: *I thought I saw somebody lurking among the trees.*

luxurious /lʌgˈʒʊəriəs/ *adjective*
very comfortable and expensive: *a luxurious hotel*

luxury /'lʌkʃəri/ *noun*
1 (*no plural*) a way of living when you have all the expensive and beautiful things you want: *They live in luxury in a beautiful house in Barbados.* ◇ *a luxury hotel*
2 (*plural* **luxuries**) something that is very nice and expensive that you do not really need: *Eating in a restaurant is a luxury for most people.*

lying *form of* LIE

lyrics /'lɪrɪks/ *noun* (*plural*)
the words of a song: *music and lyrics by Rodgers and Hart*

M m

M, m /em/ *noun* (*plural* M's, m's /emz/)
the thirteenth letter of the English alphabet:
'*Milk*' begins with an '*M*'.

m *short way of writing* METRE

mac /mæk/ *noun* (*British*)
a light coat that you wear when it rains
➔ SAME MEANING **raincoat**

machine 0➔ /mə'ʃiːn/ *noun*
a thing with moving parts that is made to do
a job. **Machines** often use electricity: *a
washing machine* ◇ *This machine does not
work.*

machine gun /mə'ʃiːn gʌn/ *noun*
a gun that can send out a lot of bullets very
quickly

machinery /mə'ʃiːnəri/ *noun* (*no plural*)
machines in general, especially large ones;
the moving parts of a machine: *industrial
machinery*

mad 0➔ /mæd/ *adjective* (madder,
maddest)
1 ill in your mind ➔ SAME MEANING **crazy**
2 (*British, informal*) very stupid
➔ SAME MEANING **crazy**: *I think you're mad
to go out in this snow!*
3 (*American, informal*) very angry: *He was
mad at me for losing his watch.*
be mad about somebody or
something (*informal*) to like somebody or
something very much: *Mina is mad about
computer games.* ◇ *He's mad about her.*
drive somebody mad to make
somebody very angry: *This noise is driving
me mad!*
go mad (*British, informal*)
1 to become ill in your mind: *He went mad
and killed himself.*
2 to become very angry: *Mum will go mad
when she finds out what you did at school.*
like mad (*informal*) very hard, fast, much,
etc.: *I had to run like mad to catch the bus.*

madam /'mædəm/ *noun* (*no plural*)
1 (*formal*) a polite way of speaking to a
woman: '*Can I help you, madam?*' *asked the
shop assistant.*
2 Madam a word that you use at the
beginning of a formal letter to a woman:
Dear Madam … ➔ Look at **sir**. ➔ Look at
Study Page **S14**.

made *form of* MAKE¹

madly /'mædli/ *adverb*
1 in a wild way: *They were rushing around
madly.*

2 (*informal*) very much: *Richard and Vanessa
are **madly in love**.*

madness /'mædnəs/ *noun* (*no plural*)
stupid behaviour that could be dangerous: *It
would be madness to take a boat out in this
terrible weather.*

magazine 0➔ /,mægə'ziːn/ *noun*
a kind of thin book with a paper cover that
you can buy every week or every month. It
has a lot of different stories and pictures
inside.

magic 0➔ /'mædʒɪk/ *noun* (*no plural*)
1 a special power that can make strange or
impossible things happen: *He suddenly
appeared **as if by magic**.*
2 clever tricks that somebody can do to
entertain people
▶ **magic** *adjective*: *magic tricks*

magical /'mædʒɪkl/ *adjective*
1 seeming to have special powers: *a herb
with **magical powers** to cure disease*
2 (*informal*) wonderful and exciting: *We
spent a magical week in Paris.*

magician /mə'dʒɪʃn/ *noun*
1 a person who does clever tricks to
entertain people ➔ SAME MEANING
conjuror
2 a man in stories who has strange, unusual
powers

magistrate /'mædʒɪstreɪt/ *noun*
a judge in a court of law who decides how to
punish people for small crimes

magnet
/'mægnət/ *noun*
a piece of metal that
can make other
metal things move
towards it

magnet

magnetic /mæg'netɪk/ *adjective*
having the ability to attract metal objects: *Is
this metal magnetic?*

magnificent /mæg'nɪfɪsnt/ *adjective*
very good or beautiful: *The Taj Mahal is a
magnificent building.*

> 🔎 **WORD BUILDING**
> Some similar words are **marvellous**,
> **remarkable**, **splendid** and **wonderful**.

magnify /'mægnɪfaɪ/ *verb* (magnifies, magnifying, magnified /'mægnɪfaɪd/, has magnified)
to make something look bigger than it really is: *We magnified the insect under a microscope.*

magnifying glass
/'mægnɪfaɪɪŋ glɑːs/
noun (*plural* magnifying glasses)
a round piece of glass, usually with a handle, that makes things look bigger than they are when you look through it

magnifying glass

maid /meɪd/ *noun*
a woman whose job is to clean in a hotel or a large house

maiden name /'meɪdn neɪm/ *noun*
a woman's family name before she is married

mail 0🔥 /meɪl/ (*British also* post) *noun* (*no plural*)
1 the way of sending and receiving letters and packages: *to send a letter by airmail*
2 letters and packages that you send or receive: *Is there any mail for me?* ➜ Look also at **email**.
▶ **mail** *verb* (mails, mailing, mailed /meɪld/) (*American*) to send something in the mail: *I'll mail the money to you.*

mailbox /'meɪlbɒks/ *noun* (*plural* mailboxes)
1 (*American*) (*British* letter box) a private box outside a house or a building or a hole in a door for putting letters through ➜ Look at Picture Dictionary page **P10**.
2 (*American*) (*British* postbox) a box in the street where you put letters that you want to send ➜ Look at the note at **foot**. ➜ Look at the picture at **postbox**.
2 (*computing*) a computer program that receives and stores email

mailman /'meɪlmæn/ *American English for* POSTMAN

main 0🔥 /meɪn/ *adjective*
most important: *My main reason for learning English is to get a better job.* ◊ *I had fish for the main course* (= the most important part of a meal).

mainly 0🔥 /'meɪnli/ *adverb*
mostly: *The students here are mainly from Japan.* ◊ *She eats mainly vegetables.*

main road /ˌmeɪn 'rəʊd/ *noun*
a big important road between towns

main street /ˌmeɪn 'striːt/ *noun American English for* HIGH STREET

maintain /meɪn'teɪn/ *verb* (maintains, maintaining, maintained /meɪn'teɪnd/)
1 to make something continue at the same level: *If he can maintain this speed, he'll win the race.*
2 to keep something working well: *The roads are well maintained.*

maintenance /'meɪntənəns/ *noun* (*no plural*)
keeping something in good condition: *car maintenance*

maize /meɪz/ (*British*) (*American* corn) *noun* (*no plural*)
a tall plant with big yellow seeds that you can eat (called **sweetcorn**)

majestic /mə'dʒestɪk/ *adjective*
impressive because of its size or beauty: *a majestic mountain view*

Majesty /'mædʒəsti/ *noun* (*plural* Majesties)
a word that you use to talk to or about a king or queen: *Her Majesty the Queen*

major[1] /'meɪdʒə(r)/ *adjective*
very large, important or serious: *There are airports in all the major cities.* ◊ *major problems* ➜ OPPOSITE **minor**

major[2] /'meɪdʒə(r)/ *noun*
an officer in the army

majority /mə'dʒɒrəti/ *noun* (*no plural*)
most things or people in a group: *The majority of people agreed with the new law.* ➜ OPPOSITE **minority**

make[1] 0🔥 /meɪk/ *verb* (makes, making, made /meɪd/, has made)
1 to produce or create something: *They make cars in that factory.* ◊ *He made a box out of some pieces of wood.* ◊ *This shirt is made of cotton.*
2 to cause something to be or to happen; to produce something: *The plane made a loud noise when it landed.* ◊ *Chocolate makes you fat.* ◊ *That film made me cry.* ◊ *I made a mistake.*
3 to force somebody to do something: *My father made me stay at home.*
4 to choose somebody to do a job: *They made him President.*
5 a word that you use with money, numbers and time: *She makes* (= earns) *a lot of money.* ◊ *Five and seven make twelve.* ◊ 'What's the time?' '**I make it** six o'clock.'
6 to be able to go somewhere: *I'm afraid I can't make the meeting on Friday.*
make do with something to use

A
B
C
D
E
F
G
H
I
J
K
L
M
N
O
P
Q
R
S
T
U
V
W
X
Y
Z

something that is not very good, because there is nothing better: *We didn't have a table, but we made do with some boxes.*
make something into something to change something so that it becomes a different thing: *They made the bedroom into an office.*
make something or somebody out to be able to see, hear or understand something or somebody: *It was dark and I couldn't make out the words on the sign.*
make something up to tell somebody something that is not true ➔ SAME MEANING **invent**: *Nobody believes that story – he made it up!*
make up to become friends again after an argument: *Jane and Tom had an argument last week, but they've made up now.* ◇ *Has she made up with him yet?* ➔ OPPOSITE **fall out with somebody**

make² 0┳ /meɪk/ *noun*
the name of the company that made something: *'What make is your car?' 'It's a Ford.'*

maker /'meɪkə(r)/ *noun*
a person, company or machine that makes something: *a film maker*

make-up /'meɪk ʌp/ *noun (no plural)*
special powders and creams that you put on your face to make yourself more beautiful. Actors also wear **make-up** when they are acting: *She put on her make-up.*

malaria /mə'leəriə/ *noun (no plural)*
a serious disease that you get in hot countries from the bite of a small flying insect (called a **mosquito**)

male 0┳ /meɪl/ *adjective*
A **male** animal or person belongs to the sex that does not have babies: *A cock is a male chicken.*
▶ **male** *noun*: *The males of this species are bigger than the females.* ➔ Look at **female**.

mall /mɔːl; mæl/ *(also* **shopping mall**) *(American) noun*
a large building that has a lot of shops, restaurants, etc. inside it

mammal /'mæml/ *noun*
any animal that drinks milk from its mother's body when it is young: *Dogs, horses, whales and people are all mammals.*

man 0┳ /mæn/ *noun*
1 *(plural* **men** /men/*)* an adult male person: *I saw a tall man with dark hair.*
2 *(no plural)* all humans; people: *the damage man has caused to the environment*
3 *(plural* **men**) any person: *All men are equal.*

manage 0┳ /'mænɪdʒ/ *verb* (**manages, managing, managed** /'mænɪdʒd/)
1 to be able to do something that is difficult: *The box was heavy but she managed to carry it to the car.*
2 to control somebody or something: *She manages a department of 30 people.*

management /'mænɪdʒmənt/ *noun (no plural)*
1 the control of something, for example a business, and the people who work in it: *Teachers must show good classroom management.*
2 all the people who control a business: *The hotel is now under new management.*

manager 0┳ /'mænɪdʒə(r)/ *noun*
a person who controls an organization, a business or a shop: *He is the manager of a shoe shop.* ◇ *a bank manager*

managing director /,mænɪdʒɪŋ də'rektə(r)/ *noun*
the person who controls a big business or company

mane /meɪn/ *noun*
the long hair on the neck of some animals, for example horses and LIONS ➔ Look at the pictures at **horse** and **lion**.

mango /'mæŋɡəʊ/ *noun (plural* **mangoes**)
a fruit that is yellow or red on the outside and yellow on the inside. **Mangoes** grow in hot countries. ➔ Look at Picture Dictionary page **P8**.

manic /'mænɪk/ *adjective (informal)*
full of activity and excitement: *Things are manic in the office at the moment.*

manipulate /mə'nɪpjuleɪt/ *verb* (**manipulates, manipulating, manipulated**)
to influence somebody so that they do or think what you want: *Politicians know how to manipulate people's opinions.*

mankind /mæn'kaɪnd/ *noun (no plural)*
all the people in the world

man-made /,mæn 'meɪd/ *adjective*
made by people; not formed in a natural way ➔ SAME MEANING **artificial**: *man-made materials*

manner /'mænə(r)/ *noun*
1 the way that you do something or the way that something happens: *Don't get angry. Let's try to talk about this in a calm manner.*
2 **manners** *(plural)* the way you behave when you are with other people: *It's bad manners to talk with your mouth full.*

mansion /'mænʃn/ *noun*
a very big house

Transport

hot-air balloon

wing

plane

helicopter

ship (*also* **liner**)

ferry

taxi (*also* **cab**)

train

underground (*British*)
subway (*American*)

lorry (*British*)
truck (*American*)

See more at

bicycle
boat
bus
motorbike
train

Car

headlight
(*also* headlamp)

bonnet (*British*)
hood (*American*)

windscreen (*British*)
windshield (*American*)

boot
(*British*)
trunk
(*American*)

number plate (*British*)
license plate (*American*)

bumper

tyre (*British*)
tire (*American*)

wheel

exhaust pipe (*British*)
tailpipe (*American*)

Animals

Farm animals

sheep | lamb

horse | foal

cow | calf

pig

turkey

donkey

chicken

goose

See more at	
bird	gorilla
fish	rabbit
goat	spider

Pets

dog

cat

peacock

guinea pigs

hamster

parrot

budgerigar

Wild animals

elephant

giraffe

buffalo

hippopotamus

rhinoceros

crocodile

lion

jaguar

koala

bear

leopard

tiger

wolf

polar bear

The body

finger

shoulder

arm

elbow

ankle

armpit

leg

hip

thigh

bottom

waist

back

head

knee

stomach

chest

foot

wrist

hand

hair

See more at

eye
foot
hair
hand

forehead

eye

ear

nose

cheek

nostril

tooth

mouth

lip

chin

neck

Clothes

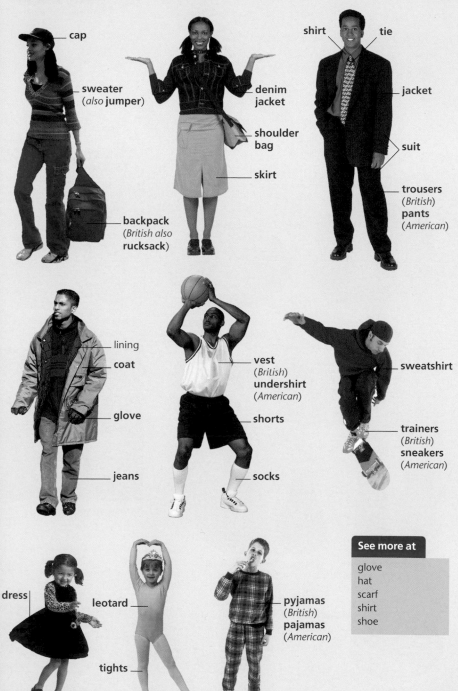

cap

sweater
(*also* **jumper**)

backpack
(*British also*
rucksack)

denim
jacket

shoulder
bag

skirt

shirt   tie

jacket

suit

trousers
(*British*)
pants
(*American*)

lining
coat

glove

jeans

vest
(*British*)
undershirt
(*American*)

shorts

socks

sweatshirt

trainers
(*British*)
sneakers
(*American*)

dress

leotard

tights

pyjamas
(*British*)
pajamas
(*American*)

See more at

glove
hat
scarf
shirt
shoe

Food and drink

eggs bread cracker cheese

butter

cake

biscuits (*British*)
cookies (*American*)

doughnut
(*American also* **donut**)

jam

noodles

olives

herbs and spices

salt and pepper vinegar olive oil

cup of tea

black
coffee

mineral
water

orange
juice

milk

milksha

Meals

cereal

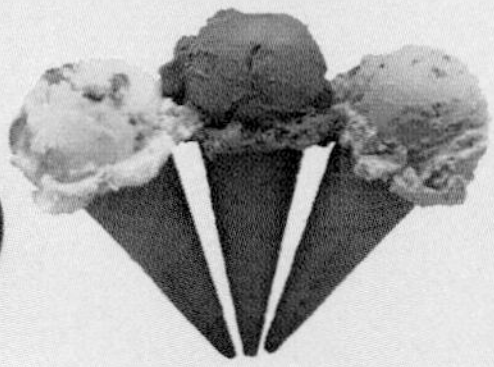

ice cream

pancake

fish and chips

soup

rice

curry

chicken

roast beef

fish

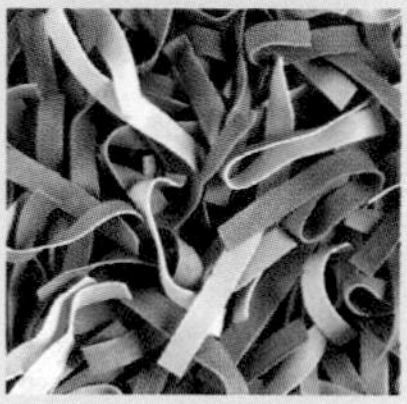

pasta

salad

quiche

sauce

spaghetti

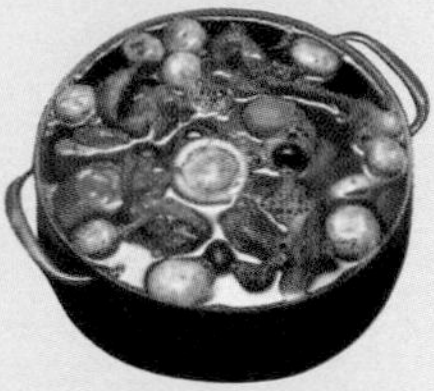

stew

kebab

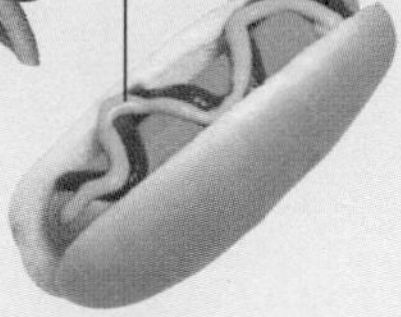

mustard | ketchup

hot dog

chips (*British*)
French fries (*American*) | burger

fast food

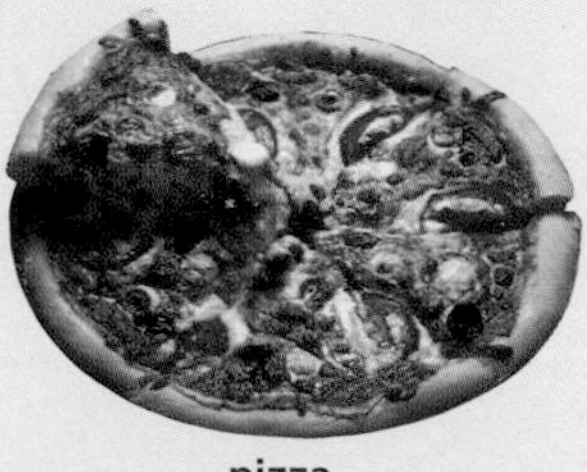

baked beans

pizza

baked potato
(*also* jacket potato)

sandwich

Fruit

dates

kiwi fruit

mango

pineapple

bananas

seed

melon

coconut

peel

pip

lime

lemon

orange

grapefruit

stone

apple

pear

peach

plum

blackcurrants

gooseberries

grapes

strawberry

cherry

Vegetables

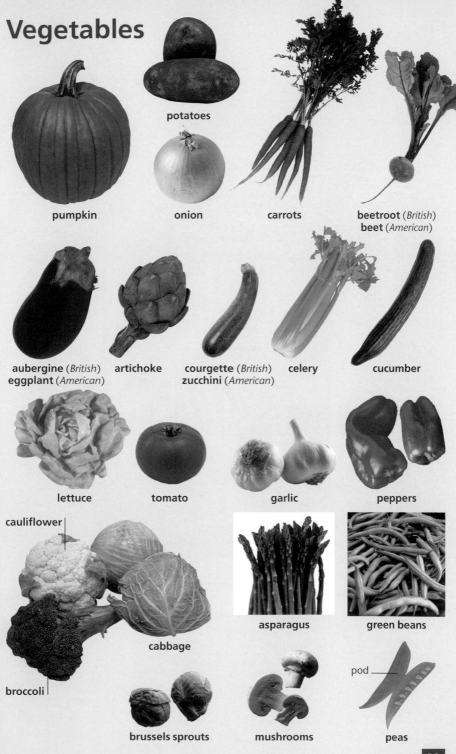

potatoes

pumpkin

onion

carrots

beetroot (*British*)
beet (*American*)

aubergine (*British*)
eggplant (*American*)

artichoke

courgette (*British*)
zucchini (*American*)

celery

cucumber

lettuce

tomato

garlic

peppers

cauliflower

asparagus

green beans

broccoli

cabbage

brussels sprouts

mushrooms

pod

peas

House

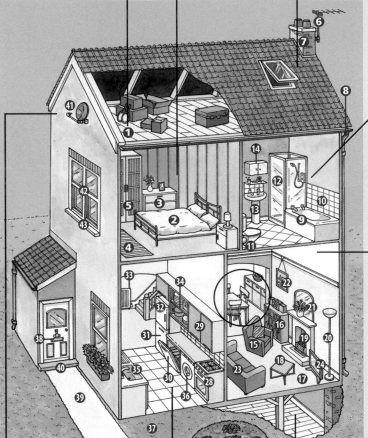

attic (also **loft**)
1 floorboards

bedroom
2 bed
3 chest of drawers
4 rug
5 wardrobe

roof
6 aerial (*British*)
   antenna (*American*)
7 chimney
8 drainpipe

bathroom
9 bath (*British*)
   bathtub (*America*
10 tiles
11 toilet
12 shower
13 washbasin
14 cabinet

living room
(*also* **sitting room**)
15 armchair
16 bookcase
17 carpet
18 coffee table
19 fireplace
20 lamp
21 mirror
22 picture
23 sofa
24 television

outside
37 garden (*British*)
   yard (*American*)
38 letter box (*British*)
   mailbox (*American*)
39 path
40 doorstep
41 satellite dish
42 window
43 windowsill

kitchen
28 cooker (*British*)
   stove (*American*)
29 cupboard
30 dishwasher
31 freezer
32 refrigerator (*British*)
   fridge (*American*)
33 radiator
34 shelf
35 sink
36 washing machine

cellar

dining room
25 chair
26 table
27 sideboard

School

ruler

classroom

1 blackboard
2 desk
3 pupil
4 teacher

nib

fountain pen

calculator

ballpoint

monitor

screen

hard disk
(*also* hard
drive)

keyboard

mouse mat | mouse

computer

dictionary

felt-tip pen

exercise book

pencil

textbook

file

sharpener

stapler

rubber (*British*)
eraser (*American*)

map

waste-paper basket (*British*)
wastebasket (*American*)

pencil case

paper clips

Jobs

painter   doctor   businesswoman   pilot   policeman

teacher

farmer

chef

plumber

judge   lawyer
(*American also*
attorney)

dentist

waiter

nurse

carpenter

shop assistant (*British*)
sales clerk (*American*)

vet (*British*)
veterinarian (*American*)

Shops

shopping centre (*British*)
mall (*American*)

supermarket

market

grocer's

baker's

butcher's

chemist's (*British*)
drugstore (*American*)

bookshop (*British*)
bookstore (*American*)

dry-cleaner's

florist's

optician's

clothes shop

Sports and hobbies

cricket

rugby

football (*British*)
soccer (*American*)

basketball

baseball

tennis

windsurfing

canoeing

swimming

surfboard

surfing

waterskiing

ice-skating

snowboarding

skateboarding

cycling

hang-gliding

hiking

gymnastics

horse riding (*British*)
horseback riding
(*American*)

yoga

judo

working out

golf

See more at

badminton
darts
dominoes
jogging
scuba-diving
skiing

snooker

bowling

Weather

Four seasons

spring

summer

clouds

snow

winter

autumn (*British*)
fall (*American*)

lightning

sunset

rainbow

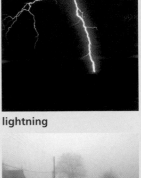

flood

It's raining.

It's foggy.

icicles

It's windy.

It's misty.

Study pages

Contents

Prepositions of place

1 Who's who?

Use the sentences on the right to work out the names of the people in the picture. One of them has been done for you.

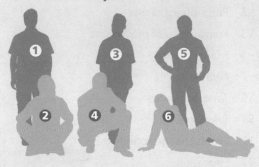

- Sarah is next to a boy.
- Tom has no one beside him on his right.
- James is in front of Diana.
- Jack is behind Jill.
- Diana is between Tom and another boy.

1 _Tom_
2 _____
3 _____
4 _____
5 _____
6 _____

2 Describing pictures

A Practise your shapes and prepositions. Complete the sentences with a preposition from the box.

between	~~in~~	below
on top of	above	

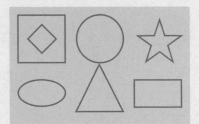

1 The diamond is _in_ the square.
2 The circle is _____ the triangle.
3 The square is _____ the oval.
4 The rectangle is _____ the star.
5 The triangle is _____ the oval and the rectangle.

B Describe the pictures using a preposition from the box to complete the sentences.

against	opposite	under
among	below	

1 The temperature is _____ zero.
2 The girl is leaning _____ the wall.
3 The cat is _____ the table.
4 The house is _____ the trees.
5 Kim is _____ Tom

Prepositions of movement

1 Where are they going?

All the prepositions in the box describe movement. Use each one to describe what the children are doing in the picture.

towards	through	out of
round	down	into
over	along	~~up~~
across		

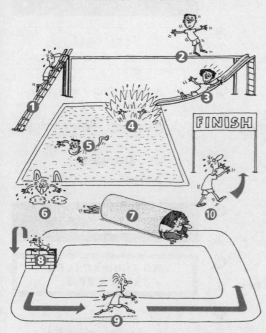

He's/she's...

1 going _____up_____ the ladder.

2 going _____ the pole.

3 going _____ the slide.

4 going _____ the pool.

5 swimming _____ the pool.

6 getting _____ the pool.

7 going _____ the tunnel.

8 climbing _____ the wall.

9 running _____ the track.

10 going _____ the finish.

2 Giving and following directions

Look at the map below. Use the words in the box to complete the paragraph, explaining how to get from the station to the café.

left again	down this road
~~right~~	on the right
turn left	take the second turning

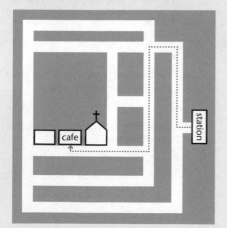

Go out of the station and turn

1 _right_____. Go to the end of

this road and **2**_____.

At the crossroads, turn **3**_____.

Walk **4**_____ and then

5_____ on the right.

Go straight on, past the first turning

on the right. The café is **6**_____,

next to the church.

Exam practice

These exercises can help you prepare for Cambridge Young Learners English Tests (Movers, Starters and Flyers), KET and ESOL Skills for Life Exams.

Part 1

Which notice (A–I) says this (1–6)?

▶ This trip is not possible because of bad weather.

   _G_

1 Be careful as you walk here. _____

2 You cannot leave your car here all day.

   _____

3 It is not safe to swim here. _____

4 You can get something without paying for it.

   _____

5 You must arrive early if you want to eat dinner here.

   _____

6 You can watch and listen to music here.

   _____

A Just add hot milk and stir

B ★ Jazz band playing ★
★ live tonight ★

C TAKE CARE
SLIPPERY PATH

D Car Parking – 1 hour maximum

E ⚠ Warning! – Very spicy

F Danger!
Jellyfish in the water

G Nature walk cancelled
because of rain

H NO FOOD SERVED
AFTER 8PM

I Buy two cups
of coffee and get
one **free**!

Part 2

Read the descriptions of some types of home. What is the word for each one? The first letter is already there. There is one space for each other letter in the word.

▶ You can attach this to the back of your car and take it to different places on holiday. You can sleep in it.

   c _a_ _r_ _a_ _v_ _a_ _n_

1 In Antarctica, people often live in this. It is made of blocks of snow.

   i _ _ _ _

2 When people go camping they sleep in this. It is made of cloth.

   t _ _ _

3 In this type of house, all the rooms are on one floor. There are no rooms upstairs.

   b _ _ _ _ _ _ _

4 A king or a queen lives in this.

   p _ _ _ _ _

5 A bird keeps its eggs in this. It is made from grass, leaves and straw.

   n _ _ _

6 People lived in these many years ago, before they lived in houses.

   c _ _ _ _

Photocopiable © Oxford University Press

Part 3

Read the text, then answer the questions.

Jessica Whitmore: Travel Writer

Jessica Whitmore spends most of her time travelling around the world. Newspapers and magazines pay her to go to different countries and write about them. Why? Because she is a travel writer.

Jessica explains how she became a travel writer. She says: 'It was an accident! After I finished university, I worked in a bank. But I hated it. One day I saw an advertisement for volunteers to teach in Africa. So I went! I was a teacher in a school in Tanzania for 2 years. While I was there, I also visited Uganda, Kenya and Zambia. It was fantastic. When I came back to England, I wrote articles about all the things that I saw. I sent the articles to a newspaper and they printed them. That was 20 years ago.'

Jessica has been to more than 70 countries and written thousands of articles about them. She says, 'I love my job. The best thing is that I meet lots of people from many countries. Every day is different. I'm so lucky.'

▶ Jessica Whitmore is 47 years old.

A Right   B Wrong   C Doesn't say

_C_

1 Jessica worked in a bookshop after she finished university.

A Right   B Wrong   C Doesn't say

_____

2 Jessica saw the advertisement for teachers in Africa in a newspaper.

A Right   B Wrong   C Doesn't say

_____

3 Jessica was a teacher in Tanzania for 2 years.

A Right   B Wrong   C Doesn't say

_____

4 When Jessica was in Africa, she visited Uganda, Ethiopia and Zambia.

A Right   B Wrong   C Doesn't say

_____

5 Jessica learnt how to speak the language in Tanzania.

A Right   B Wrong   C Doesn't say

_____

6 Jessica loves her job because she meets people from different countries.

A Right   B Wrong   C Doesn't say

_____

Part 4

Complete the letter. Write one word for each space.

Dear Dan,

I arrived ▶ _in_ Australia two weeks ago and I am having a fantastic time! The people here ¹_____ very friendly. It is very hot and ²_____ are many things to do. I was in Sydney for one week. I saw Sydney Opera House and the Botanical Gardens. Sydney ³_____ a beautiful and exciting city. Everyone here does lots of sport. People run in the parks and swim or surf ⁴_____ the sea.

Tomorrow I ⁵_____ going to visit a little island. I will go by boat with some other people. We will ⁶_____ in a tent on the beach. I hope we catch some fish for our ⁷_____ !

I ⁸_____ write again soon.

Love Elizabeth

Numbers

1 One or first?

*He has **three** children.*

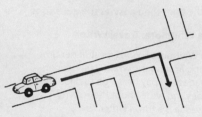

*Take the **third** turning on the right.*

A Write the missing numbers and words in this table.

1	one	*1st*	**first**
2	two	_____	**second**
3	three	_____	**third**
4	four	_____	**fourth**
5	five	**5th**	_____
6	six	6th	sixth
7	_____	7th	seventh
8	eight	**8th**	_____
9	nine	9th	ninth
10	ten	10th	tenth
11	eleven	11th	eleventh
12	twelve	**12th**	*twelfth*
13	thirteen	13th	thirteenth
14	_____	14th	fourteenth
15	fifteen	15th	fifteenth
16	sixteen	**16th**	_____
17	_____	17th	seventeenth
18	eighteen	18th	eighteenth
19	nineteen	19th	nineteenth
20	twenty	20th	twentieth
21	twenty-one	**21st**	_____
30	_____	30th	thirtieth
40	_____	40th	fortieth
50	fifty	50th	fiftieth
60	sixty	60th	sixtieth
70	seventy	70th	seventieth
80	eighty	**80th**	_____
90	ninety	90th	ninetieth
100	a/one hundred	_____	**hundredth**
101	_____	_____	**hundred and first**
200	two hundred	200th	two hundredth
_____	**a/one thousand**	**1 000th**	_____
_____	**a/one million**	1 000 000th	millionth

B One or first? Use the number at the end of each sentence to fill the ga and write the number out in full.

1 Their first two children were boys, but their ___*third*___ was a girl. (3)

2 'What number house do you live at?' 'At number ___*twelve*___.' (12)

3 I live on the _____ floor of that apartment building over there. (5)

4 We're planning a big party for our grandmother's _____ birthday. (60)

5 It's my father's birthday tomorrow. He's going to be _____. (49)

6 For the _____ time, pleas turn your music down! (100)

7 I've seen that film about _____ times, I think. (7)

8 They hold a market here on the _____ Sunday of every month. (2)

2 Large numbers

This is how we say large numbers

267   *two hundred and sixty-seven*
4302 *four thousand three hundred
and two*

Write out the answers to the questions below in full. Practise saying them.

1 There are seven days in a week. How many days are there in one year?

_____

2 There are ninety degrees (90°) in a right angle. How many degrees are there in a semicircle?

_____

3 What do you get if you subtract one hundred and fifty from ten thousand?

_____

3 Saying '0'

- We usually say **nought** or **zero**:
  nought point five (0.5)
  three, two, one, zero!

- In telephone numbers we usually say **o** (you say it like 'oh'):
  two nine oh three five

- When we talk about temperature we usually use **zero**:
  three degrees below zero

- In scores of games like football, we say **nil**:
  The score was two-nil.

4 Fractions and mathematical expressions

A Where should these diagrams go in the box below? Write the numbers 1–7 next to the correct written fractions.

____ ½   a half
____ ⅛   a/one eighth
____ ⅓   a/one third
____ 1/16   a/one sixteenth
____ ¼   a/one quarter
____ ¾   three quarters
____ 1²/₅   one and two fifths

B Here are the most common mathematical expressions:

Symbols		We write:	We say:
.	point	3.2	*three point two*
+	plus	5 + 6	*five plus six*
−	minus	10 − 4	*ten minus four*
×	multiplied by or times	4 × 6	*four multiplied by six* or *four times six*
÷	divided by	4 ÷ 2	*four divided by two*
%	per cent	78%	*seventy-eight per cent*
=	equals	1 + 3 = 4	*one plus three equals four*

What are the answers to these sums?

1 What is twenty divided by five? _____.

2 What is seventy-two plus thirteen? _____.

3 What is fifty per cent of three hundred? _____.

4 What is twelve minus four point two? _____.

5 What is six multiplied by nine? _____.

6 What is seventy-five per cent expressed as a fraction? _____.

Time and dates

1 What time is it?

There are usually two ways of telling the time.
Can you fill in the missing words below?

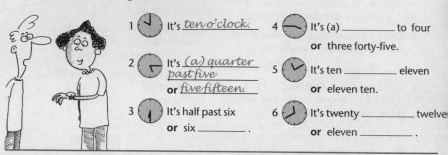

1 It's _ten o'clock._

2 It's _(a) quarter past five_ or _five fifteen._

3 It's half past six or six _____ .

4 It's (a) _____ to four or three forty-five.

5 It's ten _____ eleven or eleven ten.

6 It's twenty _____ twelve or eleven _____ .

2 What's the date?

- There are different ways to **say** dates:

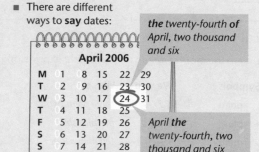

April 2006

M	01	8	15	22	29
T	02	9	16	23	30
W	03	10	17	24	31
T	04	11	18	25	
F	05	12	19	26	
S	06	13	20	27	
S	07	14	21	28	

the twenty-fourth *of* April, two thousand and six

April *the* twenty-fourth, two thousand and six

- We can **write** the date in any of these ways:

British English	American English
24 April	*April 24*
24th April	*April 24th*
24/4/06	*4/24/06*

- We say years like this:
  1706 *seventeen oh six*
  1800 *eighteen hundred*
  1998 *nineteen ninety-eight*
  2015 *twenty fifteen*

A Complete these sentences with the dates written out in full:

1 Today's date is

_____

_____ .

2 My date of birth is

_____

_____ .

B Match the events on the left with the correct date on the right, then practise reading the dates correctly.

1 Man landed on the moon on

2 William Shakespeare was born on

3 The first website appeared on

5 Queen Elizabeth II became Queen of the United Kingdom on

2 June, 1953

August 6, 1991

23rd April, 1564

20 July, 1969

3 Prepositions of time

Can you add more to each column?

in	at	on	—
the morning	6 o'clock	2nd June	next week
September	the weekend	my birthday	today
summer	Christmas	Wednesday	this afternoon

Telephoning

1 Asking for and saying telephone numbers

Which **three** of the following are correct ways of asking for somebody's phone number?

- What's your phone?
- What's your number?
- What number are you?
- What's your phone number?
- What's your mobile?
- What's your mobile number?

Notice how we usually answer the question:

- My (phone) number is...
  36920 three six nine two **oh**
- My mobile number is...
  25844 two five eight double four

Now write your own phone number(s) out in full here

_____

_____

2 Using the telephone

Choose the right word or phrase to complete the text below

When you want to **1 make a phone call / ~~do a phone call~~** , you **2 pick up / pick out** the receiver and **3 ring / dial** the number. The telephone **4 sounds / rings** and the person you are phoning answers it. When you have finished speaking, you **5 hang on / hang up** .

If the person you want to speak to is already **6 at the phone / on the phone** , it is **7 engaged / occupied** . If they are not at home, you can often **8 take a message / leave a message** , asking them to **9 talk you back / call you back** later.

3 Talking on the telephone

Put the sentences in the correct order. Write the numbers in the spaces.

A ___ Oh hello, Sally. It's John.
_1_ Hello. 56767.
___ Sally speaking.
___ Hello. Is Sally there, please?

B ___ I'm sorry – he's out. Can I take a message?
_1_ Good morning, Dr Lee's surgery.
___ Who's calling?
___ No, thank you. I'll call back later.
___ Hello. Can I speak to Dr Lee, please?
___ It's Mr White.

Words that go together

1 Prepositions

Many words are followed by a preposition. This dictionary helps you learn which preposition follows a word, so that you can learn them together.

about	for	on
at	in	with
by	of	

Choose prepositions from the box to complete the sentences. You can use each one more than once.

A Adjectives with prepositions

1 She's very good __*at*__ maths.
2 The room was full _____ people.
3 I don't think he's very interested _____ politics.
4 Are you excited _____ your birthday next week?
5 I'm tired _____ this game. Let's play something else.
6 Be careful _____ those plates – don't drop them!
7 She sleeps with the light on. She's afraid _____ the dark.
8 I'm worried _____ Tom. Do you think he'll be ok?

B Verbs with prepositions

1 I agree __*with*__ you – I think this one is too expensive.
2 She sat down and asked _____ a cup of coffee.
3 He smiled _____ her and walked away.
4 Thank you _____ all your help, I really appreciate it.
5 I'm not sure when I'll arrive. It depends _____ the traffic.
6 I'll be ten minutes. Will you wait _____ me?
7 They are always arguing _____ money.
8 Does your little brother believe _____ Santa Claus?

2 Verb + noun

A Match the verbs in column A with a noun in column B.

A	B
take	your exams
give	a cold
make	a lie
do	a mess
say	your homework
tell	goodbye
pass	somebody a call
catch	a photo

B Now use the same verbs and nouns to complete these sentences. Don't forget to put the verb into the correct tense!

1 I have to go now, but I'll __*give you a call*__ later.
2 What will you do if you don't _____ ?
3 Smile at the camera, I want to _____ .
4 I was surprised when he left without _____ .
5 Stop splashing the water, you're _____ .
6 I think she _____ .
   She's never been to New York.
7 Mum doesn't let me watch TV until I've _____ .
8 You keep sneezing – have you _____ ?

3 Finding information in the dictionary

You will find useful information on words that go together in this dictionary. Look at the entries for 'appetite' and 'bedside' below:

appetite /ˈæpɪtaɪt/ *noun*
the feeling that you want to eat: *Swimming always **gives** me **an appetite*** (= makes me hungry).

→ **appetite**
The words '**give** (somebody) **an appetite**' are printed in darker letters, which means that these words often go together.

bedside /ˈbedsaɪd/ *noun* (no plural)
the area that is next to a bed: *She sat at his bedside all night long. ◇ A book lay open on the **bedside table**.*

→ **bedside**
When the word 'bedside' is used, it is often in the phrase '**bedside table**'. The example sentence shows you this.

A Look up these words in the dictionary. What phrases are marked in the example sentences to show that these words often go together? The first one has been done for you.

answer *(noun)*	*answer to (something)* *no answer*
bed	
bread	
computer	
diet	
hardly	
holiday	
morning	

B Now use some of the phrases that you found in the last exercise to complete the sentences.

1 I tried calling her mobile phone but there was
   no answer .

2 It's eleven o'clock and I'm really tired. I think I'll
   _____ .

3 Mavis went to the shop to buy _____ .

4 Are you going to write the letter by hand or are you
   going to do it _____ ?

5 Rosa's only twelve, I think she's too young to
   _____ .

6 I _____ watch TV. I prefer to
   listen to the radio or read a book.

7 Where shall we go _____ this year?

8 He starts work at 10.30 _____
   and finishes at 9.30 at night.

Education

1 School subjects

A There are eleven school subjects hidden in the grid below. You can read them across [→] or down [↓]. Two have been found for you. Can you find the other **nine**?

```
I  B  W  A  M  U  B  E  J  Y  N  E
M  A  T  H  E  M  A  T  I  C  S  N
U  R  E  L  V  P  R  A  C  H  T  G
S  H  S  P  O  R  T  G  I  E  T  L
I  B  L  V  D  K  E  B  O  M  O  I
C  I  S  H  E  P  H  Y  S  I  C  S
W  O  D  I  M  U  N  Q  U  S  A  H
O  L  R  S  F  A  D  O  S  T  E  A
H  O  C  T  L  E  R  T  C  R  A  F
R  G  E  O  G  R  A  P  H  Y  P  Y
B  Y  H  R  O  A  M  X  N  U  K  E
G  P  S  Y  H  I  A  F  T  D  U  Z
```

B Complete the following sentences so that they are true for you.

- My favourite subject at school is/was

  _____ .

- I am/was not very good at

  _____ .

- I will always remember my _____

  teacher because _____ .

2 The Education System

A Here are the types of school in Britain and the US which children go to at different ages. Put the two sets into the correct order, starting with the one for the youngest children.

In Britain...	In the US...
___ secondary school	___ elementary school
_1_ nursery school	___ high school
___ college/ university	_4_ college/ university
___ primary school	___ nursery school

B Use the words or phrases from the box above each paragraph to complete the information about the education system in Britain and the US.

> terms   private school   attend

In Britain, children must ¹_____ school between the ages of five and sixteen. Most schools are free, but some parents choose to send their children to a ²_____ , which they pay for. The school year is divided into three ³_____ .

> GCSE   A level   pupils

When they are eleven, ⁴_____ move from primary to secondary school. At the age of sixteen everyone must take ⁵_____ (General Certificate of Secondary Education) exams. After this, they can take ⁶_____ (Advanced level) exams when they are eighteen.

> graduate   degree   university

Students who get good results in their A levels go to ⁷_____ , usually for three or four years. If they pass their exams, students ⁸_____ with a ⁹_____ in the subject they have studied.

> public schools   semesters   grades

In the US, school is compulsory between the ages of six and sixteen. Schools that are free are called ¹⁰_____ . All through the year, teachers give the students ¹¹_____ showing how well they have done in tests, homework and classroom work. The school year is divided into two ¹²_____ .

Health

1 How are you?

A Which of the following are ways of asking about somebody's health?

- [ ] How are you?
- [ ] How are your feelings?
- [ ] How are you feeling?
- [ ] How do you feel?
- [ ] What do you feel?

B Here are some answers to the questions. Choose a column for each answer. The first one has been done for you.

I'm sick.   I'm ill.
I'm ok.   I'm fine.
I feel great.   I'm not very well.
I feel awful.   I'm not too bad, thanks.
Very well, thank you.

	I'm not too bad, thanks.	

2 What's the matter?

A If you think somebody is not well, you can ask 'What's the matter?'. You can answer this question with one of the sentences below. Fill in the gap with a part of the body.

- My _____ hurts.
- My _____ aches.
- I've got a pain in my _____ .

B There are special words for pain in some parts of the body. Can you work out what they are from the example given?

▶ She's got a pain in her tooth.
  She's got toothache. _____ .

1 My head hurts.
  I've got a _____ .

2 My back ached.
  I had _____ .

3 His ear hurts.
  He's got _____ .

4 She had a pain in her stomach.
  She had _____ .

3 Going to the doctor's

Use these words and phrases to complete the paragraph.

- temperature
- ~~make an appointment~~
- examine
- symptoms
- get better
- medicine
- write a prescription

When you are ill, the best thing to do is **1** *make an appointment* to see a doctor. He or she will ask you to explain your **2** _____ , for example if you have any aches or pains. Your doctor might **3** _____ you, or take your **4** _____ . If you need treatment, the doctor will **5** _____ so that you can get some **6** _____ . If you do what the doctor says, you should **7** _____ soon.

Writing letters and emails

1 A formal letter

54 North Street ←— your address
Northampton   (but **not** your name)
NN9 5DB

23 March 2006 ←— the date

the name or title → Sarah Jackson
of the person   Rainbow Fashions
you are writing   42 High Street
to, and their   Northampton
address   NN3 4HY

Dear Ms Jackson

I am writing in response to your advertisement for a full-time sales assistant, and I enclose my CV in the hope that you will consider me for the position.

As you can see from my CV, I worked for two years at Stanwick's department store in London, where I was an assistant manager. I would be happy to attend an interview at any time.

I look forward to hearing from you.

Yours sincerely

your signature → *Victoria Dawson*

Victoria Dawson ←— your full name

2 An informal letter

54 North Street ←— your address
Northampton   (but **not** your name)
NN9 5DB

23/3/06 ←— the date

Dear Jason,

Just a quick note to thank you for dinner in Oxford last Saturday. It was great to see you, and I'm glad you're enjoying your course.

On Sunday morning, Alan and I went to the Science Museum, and then we went for a long walk along the river. We had a lovely time and we didn't want to come home!

Hope to see you soon.

Love Vicky ←—

PS Good luck with your exams next month.

You can also end with
■ Love from
■ Lots of love
■ Best wishes
■ Yours

Photocopiable © Oxford University Press

2 Formal beginnings and endings

Formal or informal?

A Which of the following can be used to begin and end **formal** letters? Mark each with ✔ or ✗.

___ Dear Sir

___ Dear Madam

___ Dear Sir or Madam

✗ Dear Miss

___ Dear Ms Jackson

___ Yours faithfully

✔ Yours sincerely

___ Your faithful

___ Yours hopefully

___ Yours truly

Formal or informal?

B Which of each pair of phrases is suitable for a **formal** letter and which for an **informal** letter? Write F for 'formal' or I for 'informal'. The first one has been done for you.

_I_ Lots of love, Vicky	_F_ Yours faithfully, Victoria Dawson
___ Dear Mr Khan	___ Dear Ali
___ I enclose a cheque for…	___ Here's some money for…
___ I'm writing to you…	___ I am writing to you…
___ Could you…?	___ I would be grateful if you could…
___ Write back soon!	___ I look forward to hearing from you.

Emails

Emails are often informal. Fill in the gaps in the email below with the informal phrases from the box.

Must go	keep in touch	Bye for now
~~Hi Carlos~~	what's more	to hear from you

Saying an email address
You say this email address as 'Vicky **dot** Dawson **at** freemail **dot** com'.

→ **From:** Vicky.Dawson@freemail.com
Sent: 23 March 2006 19:05
To: Carlos.Sanchez43@youserve.com
Subject: Re: Greetings from Thailand!

1 _Hi Carlos_

It was great 2 _____ . Thailand sounds fantastic, especially the beaches. I wish I was there too, because the weather's awful here and I'm worn out! I've got college most days and, 3 _____ , I'm working in the cafe four evenings a week. It's hard work!

4 _____ , I've got an essay to write, but 5 _____ .

6 _____

Vicky x   :-)

Filling in forms

1 Different types of form

A We often need to fill in forms. Match each verb on the left with the correct information on the right to find out some reasons why.

1 to **order** ____ A a job

2 to **apply** for ____ B a member of a club

3 to **become** ____ C something from a website or a catalogue

B These forms are called different names. Can you complete the words? The missing letters are in the boxes.

l p p t c a o i i

1 an **a** _ _ _ _ _ _ _ _ _ _ **n** form

e d r

2 an **o** _ _ _ **r** form

m h b r e e i s

3 a **m** _ _ _ _ _ _ _ _ _ **p** form

2 Understanding forms

Here are some words and phrases that you will see on forms. Fill in the gaps to find out what they mean.

nationality	last name	password
sign	in capitals	initials
signature	~~first name~~	tick

1 My name is Sara Esposito. Sara is my _first name_ , and Esposito is my _____ . My _____ are SE.

2 If you are born in Britain your _____ is British.

3 If you write something _____ , you use BIG LETTERS LIKE THIS.

4 A _____ is a secret word that only you should know.

5 A sign like this ✔ is called a _____ .

6 At the end of a form you usually have to _____ your name. This is called your _____ .

3 Filling in a form

You see this notice at your college. Read it and fill in the form.

Make new friends and improve your English!

Fill in this form and we will find you an English speaker who is learning your language.

You can then meet up for a language exchange.

Language exchange application

First name _____   Last name _____

Nationality _____   Age _____

Daytime telephone number _____

Email address _____

What is your first language? _____

How long have you been learning English? _____

What are your reasons for learning English?
(Write 10–20 words.)

_____

_____

What area of English would you most like to practise?
Please tick the one(s) that are important for you.

☐ speaking   ☐ listening   ☐ reading

☐ grammar   ☐ writing   ☐ pronunciation

Signature _____   Date _____

mantelpiece /'mæntlpi:s/ (British) (American **mantel** /'mæntl/) *noun*
a narrow shelf above the place where a fire is in a room (called the **fireplace**): *She has photographs of her children on the mantelpiece.* ⊃ Look at the picture at **fireplace**.

manual¹ /'mænjuəl/ *adjective*
using your hands: *Do you prefer **manual work** or office work?*
▸ **manually** /'mænjuəli/ *adverb*: *This machine is operated manually.*

manual² /'mænjuəl/ *noun*
a book that tells you how to do something: *Where is the instruction manual for the DVD player?*

manufacture /ˌmænjuˈfæktʃə(r)/ *verb*
(manufactures, manufacturing, manufactured /ˌmænjuˈfæktʃəd/)
to make things in a factory using machines: *The company manufactures radios.*
▸ **manufacture** *noun* (*no plural*): *the manufacture of cars*

manufacturer /ˌmænjuˈfæktʃərə(r)/ *noun*
a person or company that makes something: *If it doesn't work, send it back to the manufacturers.*

many 0₋ᵤ /'meni/ *adjective, pronoun*
(more, most)
1 a large number of people or things: *Many people in this country are very poor.* ◇ *There aren't many students in my class.* ◇ *Many of these books are very old.* ◇ *There are too many mistakes in your homework.*
2 a word that you use to ask or talk about the number of people or things: *How many brothers and sisters have you got?* ◇ *Take as many cakes as you want.* ⊃ Look at **much**.

map 0₋ᵤ /mæp/ *noun*
a drawing of a town, a country or the world that shows things like mountains, rivers and roads: *Can you find Glasgow on the map?* ◇ *a street map of Exeter*

> 🔎 WORD BUILDING
> A book of maps is called an **atlas**.

⊃ Look at Picture Dictionary page **P11**.

marathon /'mærəθən/ *noun*
a very long race when people run about 42 kilometres

marble /'mɑːbl/ *noun*
1 (*no plural*) a hard attractive stone that is used to make STATUES (= models of people) and parts of buildings: *Marble is always cold when you touch it.*
2 (*plural* **marbles**) a small glass ball that you

use in a children's game: *The children are playing marbles.*

March 0₋ᵤ /mɑːtʃ/ *noun*
the third month of the year

march¹ 0₋ᵤ /mɑːtʃ/ *verb* (marches, marching, marched /mɑːtʃt/)
1 to walk like a soldier: *The soldiers marched along the road.*
2 to walk somewhere quickly in a determined way: *She marched up to the manager and asked for her money back.*
3 to walk through the streets in a large group to show that you do not agree with something: *They marched through the town shouting 'Stop the war!'*

march² 0₋ᵤ /mɑːtʃ/ *noun* (*plural* marches)
1 an organized walk by a large group of people who want to show that they do not agree with something: *a peace march* ⊃ Look at **demonstration**.
2 a journey made by soldiers walking together: *The soldiers were tired after the long march.*

margarine /ˌmɑːdʒəˈriːn/ *noun* (*no plural*)
soft yellow food that looks like butter, but is not made of milk. You put it on bread or use it in cooking.

margin /'mɑːdʒɪn/ *noun*
the space at the side of a page that has no writing or pictures in it

mark¹ 0₋ᵤ /mɑːk/ *verb* (marks, marking, marked /mɑːkt/)
1 to put a sign on something by writing or drawing on it: *The price is marked on the bottom of the box.*
2 to show where something is: *This cross marks the place where he died.*
3 to look at school work to see how good it is: *The teacher marked all my answers wrong.*

mark² 0₋ᵤ /mɑːk/ *noun*
1 a spot or line that spoils the appearance of something: *There's a dirty mark on the front of your shirt.*
2 a shape or special sign on something: *This mark shows that the ring is made of silver.* ◇ *punctuation marks*
3 a number or letter that a teacher gives for your work to show how good it is: *She got very good marks in the exam.*

market¹ 0₋ᵤ /'mɑːkɪt/ *noun*
1 a place where people go to buy and sell things, usually outside: *There is a fruit and vegetable market in the town* ⊃ Look at Picture Dictionary page **P13**.
2 the people who want to buy something:

A B C D E F G H I J K L M N O P Q R S T U V W X Y Z

*There is a big **market for** personal computers in the USA.*

market² /'mɑːkɪt/ *verb* (markets, marketing, marketed)
to sell something using advertisements: *Companies spend millions marketing their products.*

marketing /'mɑːkɪtɪŋ/ *noun* (no plural)
using advertisements to help a company sell its products: *She works in the marketing department.*

marmalade /'mɑːməleɪd/ *noun* (no plural)
a type of soft sweet food (called **jam**) made from oranges or lemons: *We had toast and marmalade for breakfast.*

maroon /mə'ruːn/ *adjective*, *noun*
(having) a colour between brown and purple

marriage ⊶ /'mærɪdʒ/ *noun*
1 the time when two people are together as husband and wife: *They had a long and happy marriage.*
2 the time when a man and woman become husband and wife ⊃ SAME MEANING **wedding**: *The marriage will take place in church.*

married ⊶ /'mærid/ *adjective*
having a husband or a wife: *Ian is **married to** Helen.* ⊃ OPPOSITE **single** or **unmarried**
get married to take somebody as your husband or wife: *Fran and Paul **got married** last year.*

marry ⊶ /'mæri/ *verb* (marries, marrying, married /'mærid/, has married)
to take somebody as your husband or wife: *Will you marry me?* ◇ *They married when they were very young.*

> 🔎 **SPEAKING**
> It is more usual to say **get married**.

marsh /mɑːʃ/ *noun* (plural marshes)
soft wet ground

marvellous (*British*) (*American* marvelous) /'mɑːvələs/ *adjective*
very good ⊃ SAME MEANING **wonderful**: *I had a marvellous holiday.*

mascot /'mæskət/ *noun*
a person, animal or thing that people think brings them good luck

masculine /'mæskjəlɪn/ *adjective*
1 typical of a man or right for a man: *a masculine voice*
2 (*grammar*) (in some languages) belonging to a certain class of nouns, adjectives or pronouns: *The French word for 'sun' is masculine.* ⊃ Look at **feminine**.

mash /mæʃ/ *verb* (mashes, mashing, mashed /mæʃt/)
to press and mix food to make it soft: *mashed potatoes*

masks

mask /mɑːsk/ *noun*
a thing that you wear over your face to hide or protect it: *a gas mask* ◇ *The doctors and nurses all wore masks.*

Mass /mæs/ *noun* (plural Masses)
an important religious ceremony, especially in the Roman Catholic Church: *She goes to Mass every Sunday.*

mass /mæs/ *noun* (plural masses)
1 a large amount or quantity of something without a clear shape: *a **mass of** rock*
2 masses (*plural*) (*informal*) a large amount or number of something ⊃ SAME MEANING **lots**: *I've got **masses of** work to do.*

massacre /'mæsəkə(r)/ *noun*
the cruel killing of a lot of people
▶ **massacre** *verb* (massacres, massacring, massacred /'mæsəkəd/): *The army massacred hundreds of women and children.*

massage /'mæsɑːʒ/ *noun*
the act of rubbing somebody's body to get rid of pain or help them relax: *Do you want me to **give** you **a massage**?*
▶ **massage** *verb* (massages, massaging, massaged /'mæsɑːʒd/): *She massaged my back.*

massive /'mæsɪv/ *adjective*
very big ⊃ SAME MEANING **huge**: *The house is massive – it has 16 bedrooms!*

mast /mɑːst/ *noun*
1 a tall piece of wood or metal that holds the sails on a boat ⊃ Look at the picture at **boat**.
2 a very tall metal thing that sends out sounds or pictures for radio or television

master¹ /'mɑːstə(r)/ *noun*
1 a man who has people or animals in his control: *The dog ran to its master.*
2 a man who is very good at something: *paintings by the Italian masters*

master² /'mɑːstə(r)/ *verb* (masters, mastering, mastered /'mɑːstəd/)
to learn how to do something well: *It takes a long time to master a foreign language.*

masterpiece /'mɑːstəpiːs/ *noun*
a very good painting, book, film or play: '*War and Peace*' *was Tolstoy's masterpiece.*

mat /mæt/ *noun*
1 a small thing that covers a part of the floor: *Wipe your feet on the doormat before you go in.* ➲ Look at **rug**.
2 a small thing that you put under something on a table: *a table mat* (= that you put plates and dishes on) ◇ *a mouse mat* (= that you rest a computer mouse on) ➲ Look at Picture Dictionary page **P11**.

match¹ 0➟
/mætʃ/ *noun*
1 (*plural* matches)
a short thin piece of
wood that you use
to light a fire or a
cigarette: *He struck*
a match and lit his cigarette. ◇ *a box of matches*

matches

2 (*plural* matches) a game between two people or teams: *a football match* ◇ *a boxing match*
3 (*no plural*) something that looks good with something else, for example because it has the same colour, shape or pattern: *Your shoes and dress are a good match.*

match² 0➟ /mætʃ/ *verb* (matches, matching, matched /mætʃt/)
1 to have the same colour, shape or pattern as something else, or to look good with something else: *That scarf doesn't match your blouse.*
2 to find something that is like another thing or that you can put with it: *Match the word with the right picture.*
▶ **matching** /'mætʃɪŋ/ *adjective*: *She was wearing a blue skirt and matching jacket.*

matchbox /'mætʃbɒks/ *noun* (*plural* matchboxes)
a small box for matches

mate¹ /meɪt/ *noun*
1 (*British, informal*) a friend: *He went out with his mates last night.*
2 a person who lives, works or studies with you: *André is one of my classmates.* ◇ *a flatmate*
3 one of two animals that come together to make young animals: *In spring the birds look for mates.*

mate² /meɪt/ *verb* (mates, mating, mated)
When animals **mate**, they come together to make young animals.

material 0➟ /mə'tɪəriəl/ *noun*
1 cloth that you use for making clothes and other things such as curtains

➲ SAME MEANING **fabric**: *I don't have enough material to make a dress.*
2 what you use for making or doing something: *Wood and stone are building materials.* ◇ *writing materials* (= pens, pencils and paper, for example)

maternal /mə'tɜːnl/ *adjective*
1 behaving like a mother: *She's not very maternal.* ◇ *maternal love*
2 A **maternal** relation is from your mother's side of the family: *my maternal grandfather* ➲ Look at **paternal**.

mathematics 0➟ /ˌmæθə'mætɪks/ (*formal*) (*British, informal*) maths /mæθs/) (*American, informal*) math /mæθ/) *noun* (*no plural*)
the study of numbers, measurements and shapes: *Maths is my favourite subject.*
▶ **mathematical** /ˌmæθə'mætɪkl/ *adjective*: *a mathematical problem*

matter¹ 0➟ /'mætə(r)/ *noun*
something that you must talk about or do: *There is a matter I would like to discuss with you.*
as a matter of fact words that you use when you say something true, important or interesting: *I like Dave a lot. As a matter of fact, he's my best friend.*
the matter with somebody or **something** the reason for problems or unhappiness, for example: *Julie's crying. What's the matter with her?* ◇ *There is something the matter with my eye.*
no matter how, what, when, who, etc. words that you use to say that something is always true: *No matter how* (= however) *hard I try, I can't open the door.*

🔎 GRAMMAR
These expressions always come at the start of a phrase: *I'll help you, no matter what* (= whatever) *happens.* ◇ *You can't sit there, no matter who* (= whoever) *you are.*

matter² 0➟ /'mætə(r)/ *verb* (matters, mattering, mattered /'mætəd/)
to be important: *It doesn't matter if you're late – we'll wait for you.*

mattress /'mætrəs/ *noun* (*plural* mattresses)
the thick soft part of a bed ➲ Look at the picture at **bed**.

mature /mə'tjʊə(r)/ *adjective*
1 behaving in a sensible way like an adult
2 fully grown or fully developed
➲ OPPOSITE **immature**
▶ **mature** *verb* (matures, maturing,

matured /mə'tʃʊəd/): *He has matured a lot since he went to college.*

mauve /məʊv/ *adjective*
pale purple

maximum /'mæksɪməm/ *noun* (*no plural*)
the biggest possible size, amount or number: *This plane can carry a maximum of 150 people.*
▶ **maximum** *adjective*: *We drove at a maximum speed of 110 kilometres per hour.*
⊃ OPPOSITE **minimum**

May 0⟶ /meɪ/ *noun*
the fifth month of the year

may 0⟶ /meɪ/ *modal verb*
1 a word that shows what will perhaps happen or what is possible: *I may go to Spain next year.* ◇ *He may not be here.*
2 (*formal*) to be allowed to do something: *May I open the window?* ◇ *You may go now.*
⊃ Look at the note at **modal verb**.

maybe 0⟶ /'meɪbi/ *adverb*
a word that shows that something may happen or may be true ⊃ SAME MEANING **perhaps**: '*Are you going out tonight?*' '*Maybe.*' ◇ *Maybe you should phone him.*

> 🔎 SPEAKING
> You can say **perhaps** or **maybe** to sound more polite: *Perhaps/Maybe you could help me with the cooking.* (= Please help me with the cooking.)

mayonnaise /ˌmeɪə'neɪz/ *noun* (*no plural*)
a cold thick sauce made with eggs and oil

mayor /meə(r)/ *noun*
the leader of a group of people who control a town or city (called a **council**)

me 0⟶ /mi:/ *pronoun* (*plural* us)
the person who is speaking: *He telephoned me yesterday.* ◇ *Give it to me.* ◇ *Hello, it's me.*

meadow /'medəʊ/ *noun*
a field of grass

meal 0⟶ /mi:l/ *noun*
food that you eat at a certain time of the day: *What's your favourite meal of the day?* ◇ *We had a nice meal in that restaurant.*

> 🔎 CULTURE
> **Breakfast**, **lunch** and **dinner** (and sometimes **tea** and **supper**) are the usual meals of the day.
> **Dinner** is the main meal. Most people have this in the evening but some people eat their dinner in the middle of the day and call their evening meal **tea** or **supper**.

We do not usually say 'a breakfast/lunch/dinner': *Let's have lunch together tomorrow.*

mean¹ 0⟶ /mi:n/ *verb* (means, meaning, meant /ment/, has meant)
1 to have as a meaning: *What does 'medicine' mean?* ◇ *The red light means that you have to stop here.*
2 to plan or want to say something: *She said 'yes' but she really meant 'no'.* ◇ *I don't understand what you mean.* ◇ *We're going on Tuesday, I mean Thursday.*
3 to plan or want to do something ⊃ SAME MEANING **intend**: *I didn't mean to hurt you.* ◇ *I meant to phone you, but I forgot.*
4 to make something happen: *This snow means there will be no sport today.*
5 to be important to somebody: *My family means a lot to me.*
be meant to
1 If you **are meant to** do something, you should do it: *You're not meant to smoke on the train.*
2 If something **is meant to** be true, people say it is true: *This is meant to be a good film.*

mean² /mi:n/ *adjective* (meaner, meanest)
1 not liking to give things or to spend money: *Jim is very mean – he never buys anybody a drink.* ⊃ OPPOSITE **generous**
2 unkind: *It was mean of you to say that Peter was fat.*

meaning 0⟶ /'mi:nɪŋ/ *noun*
what something means or shows: *This word has two different meanings.*

means /mi:nz/ *noun* (*plural* means)
a way of doing something; a way of going somewhere: *Do you have any means of transport* (= a car, a bicycle etc.)?
by means of something by using something: *We crossed the river by means of a small bridge.*
by no means not at all: *I am by no means certain that I can come.*

meant *form of* MEAN¹

meantime /'mi:ntaɪm/ *noun* (*no plural*)
in the meantime in the time between two things happening: *Our house isn't ready, so we're living with my parents in the meantime.*

meanwhile /'mi:nwaɪl/ *adverb*
at the same time as another thing is happening or in the time between two things happening: *Peter was at home studying. Omar, meanwhile, was out with his friends.* ◇ *I'm going to buy a bed next week, but meanwhile I'm sleeping on the floor.*

measles /'miːzlz/ *noun* (*no plural*)
an illness that makes small red spots come on your skin: *My little brother has got measles.*

measure¹ 0̶ɯ /'meʒə(r)/ *verb*
(measures, measuring, measured /'meʒəd/)
1 to find the size, weight or amount of somebody or something: *Could you measure the window for me?*
2 to be a certain size or amount: *This room measures six metres across.*

measure² 0̶ɯ /'meʒə(r)/ *noun*
1 an action that somebody does in order to achieve something: *The government has* ***taken measures to*** *resolve the crisis.*
2 a way of showing the size or amount of something: *A metre is a* ***measure*** *of length.*

measurement 0̶ɯ /'meʒəmənt/ *noun*
the size of something that is found by measuring it: *What are the* ***measurements of*** *the kitchen* (= how long and wide is it)*?*

meat 0̶ɯ /miːt/ *noun* (*no plural*)

> 🔎 **PRONUNCIATION**
> The word **meat** sounds just like **meet**.

the parts of an animal or bird that you can eat: *You can buy meat at a butcher's* ◇ *I don't eat meat.*

mechanic /mə'kænɪk/ *noun*
a person whose job is to repair or work with machines: *a car mechanic*

mechanical /mə'kænɪkl/ *adjective*
moved, done or made by a machine: *a mechanical toy*
▶ **mechanically** /mə'kænɪkli/ *adverb*: *The pump is operated mechanically.*

mechanics /mə'kænɪks/ *noun* (*no plural*)
the study of how machines work

medal /'medl/ *noun*
a piece of metal with words and pictures on it that you get for doing something very good: *She won a gold medal in the Olympic Games.*

media /'miːdiə/ *noun* (*no plural*)
the media television, radio and newspapers: *The media always takes a great interest in the royal family.*

mediaeval (*British*) form of MEDIEVAL

medical 0̶ɯ /'medɪkl/ *adjective*
connected with medicine, hospitals or doctors: *a medical student* ◇ *medical treatment*

medicine 0̶ɯ /'medsn; 'medɪsn/ *noun*
1 (*no plural*) the science of understanding illnesses and making sick people well again: *He's studying medicine.*
2 (*plural* **medicines**) special liquids or pills that help you to get better when you are ill: ***Take*** *this* ***medicine*** *every morning.*

medieval (*British also* **mediaeval**) /ˌmedi'iːvl/ *adjective*
connected with the years between about 1100 and 1500 in Europe: *a medieval castle* ➔ Look at **the Middle Ages**.

medium 0̶ɯ /'miːdiəm/ *adjective*
not big and not small: *Would you like a small, medium or large Coke?* ◇ *He is of medium height.*

meet 0̶ɯ /miːt/ *verb* (meets, meeting, met /met/, has met)

> 🔎 **PRONUNCIATION**
> The word **meet** sounds just like **meat**.

1 to come together by chance or because you have planned it: *I met Kate in the library today.* ◇ *Let's meet outside the cinema at eight o'clock.*
2 to see and speak to somebody for the first time: *Have you met Anne?*
3 to go to a place and wait for somebody to arrive: *Can you* ***meet*** *me* ***at*** *the airport?*
4 to join together with something: *The two rivers meet in Oxford.*

meeting 0̶ɯ /'miːtɪŋ/ *noun*
1 a time when people come together for a special reason, usually to talk about something: *We* ***had a meeting*** *to talk about the plans for the new swimming pool.*
2 a time when two or more people come together: *Do you remember your first meeting with your husband?*

melody /'melədi/ *noun* (*plural* **melodies**)
a group of musical notes that make a nice sound when you play or sing them together ➔ SAME MEANING **tune**: *This song has a lovely melody.*

melon /'melən/ *noun*
a big round yellow or green fruit with a lot of seeds inside ➔ Look at Picture Dictionary page **P8**.

melt 0̶ɯ /melt/ *verb* (melts, melting, melted)
to warm something so that it becomes liquid; to get warmer so that it becomes liquid: *Melt the butter in a saucepan.* ◇ *The snow melted in the sunshine.*

member 0̶ɯ /'membə(r)/ *noun*
a person who is in a group: *I'm* ***a member of*** *the school football team.*

Member of Parliament /ˌmembər əv ˈpɑːləmənt/ (plural **Members of Parliament**) *noun* (*abbr.* **MP**)
a person that the people of a town or city choose to speak for them in politics

membership /ˈmembəʃɪp/ *noun* (*no plural*)
being in a group or an organization: *Membership of the club costs £80 a year.*

memo /ˈmeməʊ/ *noun* (*plural* memos)
a note that you write to a person who works with you: *I sent you a memo about the meeting on Friday.*

memorable /ˈmemərəbl/ *adjective*
easy to remember because it is special in some way: *Their wedding was a very memorable day.*

memorial /məˈmɔːriəl/ *noun*
something that people build or do to help us remember somebody, or something that happened: *The statue is a memorial to all the soldiers who died in the war.*

memorize /ˈmeməraɪz/ *verb* (memorizes, memorizing, memorized /ˈmeməraɪzd/)
to learn something so that you can remember it exactly: *We have to memorize a poem for homework.*

memory 0🔑 /ˈmeməri/ *noun* (*plural* memories)
1 the ability to remember things: *Ruth's got a very good memory – she never forgets people's names.*
2 something that you remember: *I have very happy memories of that holiday.*
3 the part of a computer that holds information

men *plural of* MAN

mend /mend/ *verb* (mends, mending, mended)
to make something that is broken or damaged good again ⊃ SAME MEANING **repair**: *Can you mend this chair?*

mental 0🔑 /ˈmentl/ *adjective*
of or in your mind: *mental illness* ◇ *mental arithmetic* (= done in your head)
▶ **mentally** /ˈmentəli/ *adverb*: *He is mentally ill.*

mention 0🔑 /ˈmenʃn/ *verb* (mentions, mentioning, mentioned /ˈmenʃnd/)
to speak or write about something without giving much information: *Liz mentioned that she was going to buy a new car.* ◇ *He didn't mention Anna in his letter.*
don't mention it polite words that you say when somebody says 'thank you': *'Thanks very much.' 'Don't mention it.'*

▶ **mention** *noun*: *There was no mention of the accident in the newspaper.*

menu /ˈmenjuː/ *noun* (*plural* menus)
1 a list of the food that you can choose in a restaurant: *What's on the menu tonight?* ◇ *Can I have the menu, please?*
2 (*computing*) a list on the screen of a computer that shows what you can do: *Go to the menu and click New.*

mercy /ˈmɜːsi/ *noun* (*no plural*)
being kind and not hurting somebody who has done wrong: *The prisoners begged for mercy.*
be at the mercy of somebody or **something** to have no power against somebody or something that is strong: *Farmers are at the mercy of the weather.*

mere /mɪə(r)/ *adjective*
only; not more than: *She was a mere child when her parents died.*

merely /ˈmɪəli/ *adverb*
only ⊃ SAME MEANING **just**: *I don't want to buy the book – I am merely asking how much it costs.*

merge /mɜːdʒ/ *verb* (merges, merging, merged /mɜːdʒd/)
to join together with something else: *Three small companies merged into one large one.*

merit[1] /ˈmerɪt/ *noun*
the thing or things that are good about somebody or something: *What are the merits of this plan?*

merit[2] /ˈmerɪt/ *verb* (merits, meriting, merited) (*formal*)
to be good enough for something ⊃ SAME MEANING **deserve**: *This suggestion merits further discussion.*

mermaid /ˈmɜːmeɪd/ *noun*
a woman in stories who has a fish's tail and lives in the sea

merry /ˈmeri/ *adjective* (merrier, merriest)
happy: *Merry Christmas!*

merry-go-round /ˈmeri gəʊ raʊnd/ *noun*
1 (*British*) (*also* roundabout) (*American* carousel) a big round machine with models of animals or cars on it. Children can ride on it as it turns.
2 *American English for* ROUNDABOUT(2)

mess[1] /mes/ *noun* (*no plural*)
1 a lot of untidy or dirty things all in the wrong place: *Your bedroom is in a mess.* ◇ *Don't make a mess in the kitchen.*
2 a person or thing that is untidy or dirty: *My hair is a mess!*
3 a difficult situation: *She's in a mess – she's got no money and nowhere to live.*

merry-go-round

merry-go-round
(*British also* **roundabout**)
carousel (*American*)

roundabout
(*British*)
merry-go-round
(*American*)

mess² /mes/ *verb* (messes, messing, messed /mest/)
mess about, **mess around** to behave in a silly way: *Stop messing around and finish your work!*
mess something up
1 to do something badly or make something go wrong: *The bad weather messed up our plans for the weekend.*
2 to make something untidy or dirty: *Don't mess my hair up!*

message 0̶ᴄ /'mesɪdʒ/ *noun*
words that one person sends to another: *Could you give a message to Jane, please?* ◇ *Mr Willis is not here at the moment. Can I take a message?*

messenger /'mesɪndʒə(r)/ *noun*
a person who brings a message

messy /'mesi/ *adjective* (messier, messiest)
1 untidy or dirty: *a messy kitchen*
2 making you untidy or dirty: *Painting is a messy job.*

met *form of* MEET

metal 0̶ᴄ /'metl/ *noun*
a solid substance that is usually hard and shiny, such as iron, tin or gold: *This chair is made of metal.* ◇ *a metal box*

metallic /mə'tælɪk/ *adjective*
looking like metal or making a noise like one piece of metal hitting another: *metallic paint*

meter /'miːtə(r)/ *noun*
1 a machine that measures or counts something: *an electricity meter*
2 American English for METRE

method 0̶ᴄ /'meθəd/ *noun*
a way of doing something: *What is the best method of cooking beef?*

metre 0̶ᴄ (*British*) (*American* meter) /'miːtə(r)/ (*abbr.* m) *noun*
a measure of length. There are 100 **centimetres** in a **metre**: *The wall is eight metres long.*

metric /'metrɪk/ *adjective*
using the system of metres, grams and litres to measure things

miaow /mi'aʊ/ *noun*
a sound that a cat makes
▶ **miaow** *verb* (miaows, miaowing, miaowed /mi'aʊd/): *Why is the cat miaowing?* ➸ Look at **purr**.

mice *plural of* MOUSE

microchip /'maɪkrəʊtʃɪp/ *noun*
a very small thing inside a computer or a machine that makes it work

microphone

microphone /'maɪkrəfəʊn/ *noun*
a piece of electrical equipment that makes sounds louder or records them so you can listen to them later

microscope /'maɪkrəskəʊp/ *noun*
a piece of equipment with special glass in it, that makes very small things look much bigger: *We looked at the hair under a microscope.*

microwave /'maɪkrəweɪv/ (*also* microwave oven /ˌmaɪkrəweɪv 'ʌvn/) *noun*
a type of oven that cooks or heats food very quickly using electric waves

mid- /mɪd/ *adjective*
(in) the middle of: *My mother's in her mid-thirties.* ◇ *mid-morning coffee*

midday 0̶ᴄ /ˌmɪd'deɪ/ *noun* (no plural)
twelve o'clock in the day: *We met at midday.* ➸ Look at **midnight**.

middle 0̶ᴄ /'mɪdl/ *noun*
1 the part that is the same distance from the sides, edges or ends of something: *A peach has a stone in the middle.*
2 the time after the beginning and before the end: *The phone rang in the middle of the night.*

A
B
C
D
E
F
G
H
I
J
K
L
M
N
O
P
Q
R
S
T
U
V
W
X
Y
Z

be in the middle of doing something
to be busy doing something: *I can't speak to you now – I'm in the middle of cooking dinner.*
▶ **middle** *adjective*: *There are three houses and ours is the middle one.*

middle-aged /ˌmɪdl ˈeɪdʒd/ *adjective*
not old and not young; between the ages of about 40 and 60: *a middle-aged man*

the Middle Ages /ðə ˌmɪdl ˈeɪdʒɪz/ *noun*
(*plural*)
the years between about 1100 and 1500 in Europe ⊃ Look at **medieval**.

middle name /ˈmɪdl neɪm/ *noun*
a name that comes between your first name and your family name

middle school /ˈmɪdl skuːl/ *noun* (*British*)
a school for children between the ages of 9 and 13

midnight ⟐ /ˈmɪdnaɪt/ *noun* (*no plural*)
twelve o'clock at night: *We left the party at midnight.* ⊃ Look at **midday**.

midway /ˌmɪdˈweɪ/ *adverb*
in the middle ⊃ SAME MEANING **halfway**: *The village is midway between Girona and Barcelona.*

midwife /ˈmɪdwaɪf/ *noun* (*plural midwives* /ˈmɪdwaɪvz/)
a person whose job is to help women give birth to babies

might ⟐ /maɪt/ *modal verb*
1 used as the form of 'may' when you repeat later what somebody has said: *He said he might be late* (= his words were 'I may be late'), *but he was early.*
2 a word that shows what will perhaps happen or what is possible: *Don't run because you might fall.* ◇ *'Where's Anne?' 'I don't know – she might be in the kitchen.'*
3 (*British*, *formal*) a word that you use to ask something in a very polite way: *Might I say something?* ⊃ Look at the note at **modal verb**.

mighty /ˈmaɪti/ *adjective* (**mightier**, **mightiest**) (*formal*)
very great, strong or powerful: *He hit him with a mighty blow across his shoulder*

migrate /maɪˈɡreɪt/ *verb* (**migrates**, **migrating**, **migrated**)
1 (used about animals and birds) to move from one part of the world to another every year
2 (used about large numbers of people) to go to live and work in another place
▶ **migration** /maɪˈɡreɪʃn/ *noun*: *the annual migration of the reindeer*

mild /maɪld/ *adjective* (**milder**, **mildest**)
1 not strong: *This cheese has a mild taste.*
2 not too hot and not too cold: *a mild winter*

mile ⟐ /maɪl/ *noun*
a measure of length that is used in Britain and the USA (=1.6 kilometres): *We live three miles from the sea.* ⊃ Look at the note at **foot**.

military /ˈmɪlətri/ *adjective*
connected with soldiers or the army, navy, etc.: *a military camp* ◇ *military action*

milk¹ ⟐ /mɪlk/ *noun* (*no plural*)
the white liquid that a mother makes in her body to give to her baby. People drink the **milk** of cows and some other animals: *Do you want milk in your coffee?* ⊃ Look at Picture Dictionary page **P6**.

milk² /mɪlk/ *verb* (**milks**, **milking**, **milked** /mɪlkt/)
to take milk from a cow or another animal

milkman /ˈmɪlkmən/ *noun* (*plural milkmen* /ˈmɪlkmən/)
(in Britain) a person who takes milk to people's houses every day

milkshake /ˈmɪlkʃeɪk/ *noun*
a drink made of milk with the flavour of chocolate or fruit added to it: *a strawberry milkshake* ⊃ Look at Picture Dictionary page **P6**.

milky /ˈmɪlki/ *adjective* (**milkier**, **milkiest**)
with a lot of milk in it: *milky coffee*

mill /mɪl/ *noun*
1 a building where a machine makes flour from grain ⊃ Look also at **windmill**.
2 a factory where one material is made, for example cloth or paper: *a paper mill*

millennium /mɪˈleniəm/ *noun* (*plural millennia* /mɪˈleniə/ *or* **millenniums**)

> ✎ SPELLING
>
> Remember! You spell **millennium** with **LL** and **NN**.

a period of a thousand years

millimetre (*British*) (*American* **millimeter**) /ˈmɪlimiːtə(r)/ (*abbr.* mm) *noun*
a measure of length. There are ten millimetres in a **centimetre**: *60 mm*

million ⟐ /ˈmɪljən/ *number*
1 1 000 000; one thousand thousand: *About 56 million people live in this country.* ◇ *millions of dollars* ◇ *six million pounds*

> ✎ GRAMMAR
>
> We say **six million pounds** (without 's'), but **millions of** pounds.

2 millions (*informal*) a lot: *I have **millions of** things to do.*

millionaire /ˌmɪljə'neə(r)/ *noun*
a person who has more than a million pounds, dollars, etc.; a very rich person

millionth 0ᴸ /'mɪljənθ/ *adjective, pronoun, noun*
1 000 000th: *Our millionth customer will receive a prize.* ◇ *three millionths of a second*

mime /maɪm/ *noun* (*no plural*)
a way of telling a story or telling somebody something by moving your face, hands and body, without speaking: *The show is a combination of dance and mime.*
▶ **mime** *verb* (mimes, miming, mimed /maɪmd/): *He **mimed that** he was hungry.*

mimic /'mɪmɪk/ (mimics, mimicking, mimicked /'mɪmɪkt/) *verb*
to copy the way somebody moves and speaks in an amusing way
▶ **mimic** *noun*: *Sally's a brilliant mimic.*

mince /mɪns/ *noun* (*no plural*) (*British*)
meat that has been cut into very small pieces
▶ **mince** *verb* (minces, mincing, minced /mɪnst/): *Mince the beef finely.*

mind¹ 0ᴸ /maɪnd/ *noun*
the part of you that thinks and remembers: *He has a very quick mind.*
be or **go out of your mind** (*informal*) to be or become mad or very worried: *Where were you? I was going out of my mind with worry.*
change your mind to have an idea, then decide to do something different: *I planned a holiday in France and then changed my mind and went to Italy.*
have something on your mind to be worried about something: *I've got a lot on my mind at the moment.*
make up your mind to decide something: *Shall I buy the blue shirt or the red one? I can't make up my mind.*

mind² 0ᴸ /maɪnd/ *verb* (minds, minding, minded)
1 to feel unhappy or angry about something: ***Do you mind if** I smoke?* ◇ *I **don't** mind the heat at all.*
2 to be careful of somebody or something
◐ SAME MEANING **watch**: *Mind the step!*
do you mind ...?, would you mind ...? please could you...?: *It's cold – would you mind closing the window?*
I don't mind it is not important to me which thing: *'Do you want tea or coffee?' 'I don't mind.'*

mind out (*British, informal*) used to tell somebody to get out of the way or to be careful: *Mind out! There's a dog in the road.*
never mind don't worry; it doesn't matter: *'I forgot your book.' 'Never mind, I don't need it today.'*

mine¹ 0ᴸ /maɪn/ *pronoun*
something that belongs to me: *That bike is mine.* ◇ *Are those books mine or yours?*

mine² 0ᴸ /maɪn/ *noun*
1 a very big hole in the ground where people work to get things like coal, gold or diamonds: *a coal mine*
2 a bomb that is hidden under the ground or under water
▶ **mine** *verb* (mines, mining, mined /maɪnd/): *Diamonds are mined in South Africa.*

miner /'maɪnə(r)/ *noun*
a person who works in a mine

mineral /'mɪnərəl/ *noun*
Minerals are things like coal, gold, salt or oil that come from the ground and that people use.

mineral water /'mɪnərəl wɔːtə(r)/ *noun* (*no plural*)
water with MINERALS in it, that comes from the ground: *a bottle of mineral water* ◐ Look at Picture Dictionary page **P6**.

mingle /'mɪŋgl/ *verb* (mingles, mingling, mingled /'mɪŋgld/)
to mix with other things or people: *The colours **mingled together** to make brown.* ◇ *Policemen **mingled with** the crowd.*

mini- /'mɪni/ *prefix*
very small: *The school has a minibus that can carry twelve people.*

miniature /'mɪnətʃə(r)/ *adjective*
very small; much smaller than usual: *a miniature railway*

minimize /'mɪnɪmaɪz/ *verb* (minimizes, minimizing, minimized /'mɪnɪmaɪzd/)
to make something as small as possible: *We want to minimize the risk to the public.*

minimum /'mɪnɪməm/ *noun* (*no plural*)
the smallest size, amount or number that is possible: *We need **a minimum of** six people to play this game.*
▶ **minimum** *adjective*: *What is the minimum age for leaving school in your country?* ◐ OPPOSITE **maximum**

miniskirt /'mɪniskɜːt/ *noun*
a very short skirt

minister /'mɪnɪstə(r)/ *noun*
1 one of the most important people in a government: *the **Minister of** Education* ◐ Look at **prime minister**.
2 a priest in some Christian churches

A

ministry /'mɪnɪstri/ *noun* (*plural*
ministries)
a part of the government that controls one
special thing: *the **Ministry** of Defence*

B

C

minor /'maɪnə(r)/ *adjective*
not very big or important: *Don't worry – it's
only a minor problem.* ◇ *a minor road*
⊃ OPPOSITE **major**

D

E

minority /maɪ'nɒrəti/ *noun* (*plural*
minorities)
the smaller part of a group: *Only **a minority**
of the students speak English.*
⊃ OPPOSITE **majority**.

F

G

mint /mɪnt/ *noun*
1 (*no plural*) a small plant with a strong
fresh taste and smell, that you put in food
and drinks: *mint sauce*
2 (*plural* mints) a sweet made from this

H

I

minus¹ /'maɪnəs/ *preposition*
1 (*maths*) less; when you take away: *Six
minus two is four* (6 − 2 = 4). ⊃ Look at **plus**.
2 below zero: *The temperature will fall to
minus ten degrees.*

J

K

minus² /'maɪnəs/ *adjective*
(*maths*) lower than zero: *a minus number*

L

M

minute¹ 0̶ /'mɪnɪt/ *noun*
1 a measure of time. There are 60 seconds in
a **minute** and 60 **minutes** in an hour: *It's
nine **minutes** past six.* ◇ *The train leaves **in** ten
minutes.*
2 a short time ⊃ SAME MEANING **moment**:
Just a minute – I'll get my coat. ◇ *Have you got
a minute? I'd like to talk to you.*
in a minute very soon: *I'll be ready in a
minute.*
the minute as soon as: *Phone me the
minute you arrive.*

N

O

P

Q

minute² /maɪ'njuːt/ *adjective*
very small ⊃ SAME MEANING **tiny**: *I can't
read his writing – it's minute.*

R

S

miracle /'mɪrəkl/ *noun*
a wonderful and surprising thing that
happens and that you cannot explain: *It's a
miracle that he wasn't killed.*

T

U

miraculous /mɪ'rækjələs/ *adjective*
wonderful and surprising: *a miraculous
escape*
▸ **miraculously** *adverb*: *Miraculously, no
one was hurt.*

V

W

mirror 0̶ /'mɪrə(r)/ *noun*
a piece of special glass where you can see
yourself: *Look in the mirror.* ⊃ Look at Picture
Dictionary page **P10**.

X

Y

Z

mis- *prefix*
You can add **mis-** to the beginning of some
words to show that something is done

wrong or badly, for example *misunderstand*
(= not understand correctly).

misbehave /ˌmɪsbɪ'heɪv/ *verb*
(misbehaves, misbehaving, misbehaved
/ˌmɪsbɪ'heɪvd/)
to behave badly: *Children who misbehaved
were punished.* ⊃ OPPOSITE **behave**

mischief /'mɪstʃɪf/ *noun* (*no plural*)
bad behaviour that is not very serious: *Don't
get into mischief while I'm out!*

mischievous /'mɪstʃɪvəs/ *adjective*
A **mischievous** child likes to annoy people,
but not in a serious way. ⊃ SAME MEANING
naughty: *He gave a mischievous grin.*

miserable /'mɪzrəbl/ *adjective*
1 feeling very sad: *I waited in the rain for an
hour, feeling cold, wet and miserable.*
2 making you feel sad: *miserable weather*

misery /'mɪzəri/ *noun* (*no plural*)
great unhappiness: *the misery of war*

misfortune /ˌmɪs'fɔːtʃuːn/ *noun* (*formal*)
something bad that happens; bad luck: *He
has known great misfortune.*

mislead /ˌmɪs'liːd/ *verb* (misleads,
misleading, misled /ˌmɪs'led/, has misled)
to make somebody believe something that is
not true: *You misled me when you said you
could give me a job.*

Miss 0̶ /mɪs/ *noun*
a word that you use before the name of a girl
or woman who is not married: *Dear Miss
Smith, …* ⊃ Look at the note at **Ms**.

miss 0̶ /mɪs/ *verb* (misses, missing,
missed /mɪst/)
1 to not hit or catch something: *I tried to hit
the ball but I missed.*
2 to not see or hear something: *You missed a
good programme on TV last night.* ◇ *Our house
is the one on the corner – you can't miss it.*
3 to be too late for a train, bus, plane or
boat: *I just missed my bus.* ⊃ OPPOSITE **catch**
4 to feel sad about somebody or something
that has gone: *I'll miss you when you leave.*
miss something out to not put in or do
something; to not include something: *I
didn't finish the exam – I missed out two
questions.*

missile /'mɪsaɪl/ *noun*
1 a powerful weapon that can be sent long
distances through the air and then explodes:
nuclear missiles
2 a thing that you throw at somebody to
hurt them

missing 0̶ /'mɪsɪŋ/ *adjective*
lost, or not in the usual place: *The police are*

looking for the missing child. ◇ *My purse is missing. Have you seen it?*

mission /ˈmɪʃn/ ***noun***
a journey to do a special job: *They were sent* ***on a mission*** *to the moon.*

missionary /ˈmɪʃənri/ ***noun*** (*plural* **missionaries**)
a person who goes to another country to teach people about a religion

mist /mɪst/ ***noun***
thin cloud near the ground, that is difficult to see through: *Early in the morning, the fields were covered in mist.*
▶ **misty** ***adjective*** (**mistier**, **mistiest**): *a misty morning* ➲ Look at Picture Dictionary page **P16**.

mistake[1] 0‑╥ /mɪˈsteɪk/ ***noun***
something that you think or do that is wrong: *You have* ***made*** *a lot of* ***spelling mistakes*** *in this letter.* ◇ *It was* ***a mistake to*** *go by bus – the journey took two hours!*

> **WHICH WORD?**
> **Mistake** or **fault**?
> When you **make a mistake** you do something wrong: *Try not to make any mistakes in your exam.*
> If you do something bad it is **your fault**: *It's my fault we're late. I lost the tickets.*

by mistake when you did not plan to do it: *Sorry, I took your book by mistake.*

mistake[2] 0‑╥ /mɪˈsteɪk/ ***verb*** (**mistakes**, **mistaking**, **mistook** /mɪˈstʊk/, **has mistaken** /mɪˈsteɪkən/)
to think that somebody or something is a different person or thing: *I'm sorry – I* ***mistook*** *you* ***for*** *my cousin.*

mistaken /mɪˈsteɪkən/ ***adjective***
wrong: *I said she was Spanish but I was mistaken – she's Portuguese.* ◇ *a case of* ***mistaken identity*** (= when people think that a person is somebody else)

misunderstand /ˌmɪsʌndəˈstænd/ ***verb*** (**misunderstands**, **misunderstanding**, **misunderstood** /ˌmɪsʌndəˈstʊd/, **has misunderstood**)
to not understand something correctly: *I'm sorry, I misunderstood what you said.*

misunderstanding /ˌmɪsʌndəˈstændɪŋ/ ***noun***
a situation in which somebody does not understand something correctly: *I think* ***there's been a misunderstanding****. I ordered two tickets, not four.*

mitten /ˈmɪtn/ ***noun***
a thing that you wear to keep your hand warm. It has one part for your thumb and another part for your other fingers. ➲ Look at **glove**.

mix 0‑╥ /mɪks/ ***verb*** (**mixes**, **mixing**, **mixed** /mɪkst/)
1 to put different things together to make something new: ***Mix*** *yellow and blue paint* ***together*** *to make green.*
2 to join together to make something new: *Oil and water don't mix.*
3 to be with and talk to other people: *In my job, I* ***mix with*** *a lot of different people.*
mix somebody or **something up** to think that one person or thing is a different person or thing: *People often mix Mark up with his brother.*
mix something up to make things untidy: *Don't mix up my papers!*

mixed 0‑╥ /mɪkst/ ***adjective***
containing different kinds of people or things: *a mixed salad* ◇ *Is their school mixed* (= with boys and girls together)*?*

mixer /ˈmɪksə(r)/ ***noun***
a machine that mixes things together: *a food mixer*

mixture 0‑╥ /ˈmɪkstʃə(r)/ ***noun***
something that you make by mixing different things together: *Air is* ***a mixture of*** *gases.* ◇ *a cake mixture*

mm *short way of writing* MILLIMETRE

moan /məʊn/ ***verb*** (**moans**, **moaning**, **moaned** /məʊnd/)
1 to make a long sad sound when you are hurt or very unhappy: *He was* ***moaning with*** *pain.*
2 (*informal*) to talk a lot about something in a way that annoys other people
➲ SAME MEANING **complain**: *He's always* ***moaning about*** *the weather.*
▶ **moan** ***noun***: *I heard a loud moan.*

mob /mɒb/ ***noun***
a big noisy group of people who are shouting or fighting

mobile /ˈməʊbaɪl/ ***adjective***
able to move easily from place to place: *A mobile library visits the village every week.*

mobile phone 0‑╥ /ˌməʊbaɪl ˈfəʊn/ (*British*) (*British also* **mobile** /ˈməʊbaɪl/) (*American* **cellphone**) ***noun***

mobile phone

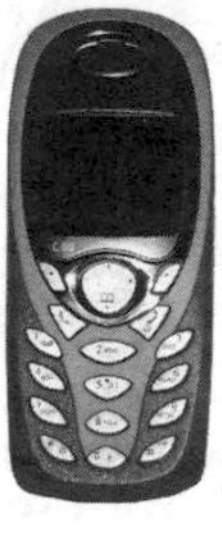

A B C D E F G H I J K L M N O P Q R S T U V W X Y Z

a telephone that you can carry around with you: *I'll ring you on your mobile tonight.*

mock /mɒk/ *verb* (mocks, mocking, mocked /mɒkt/) (*formal*)
to laugh at somebody or something in an unkind way: *The other children mocked her old-fashioned clothes.*

modal verb /ˌməʊdl ˈvɜːb/ *noun*
a verb, for example 'might', 'can' or 'must', that you use with another verb

> 🔎 **GRAMMAR**
>
> **Can**, **could**, **may**, **might**, **should**, **must**, **will**, **shall**, **would** and **ought to** are modal verbs.
> Modal verbs do not have an 's' in the 'he/she' form: *She can drive* (NOT *She cans drive*).
> After modal verbs (except **ought to**), you use the infinitive without 'to': *I must go now* (NOT *I must to go*).
> You make questions and negative sentences without 'do' or 'did': *Will you come with me?* (NOT *Do you will come?*)
> ◊ *They might not know* (NOT *They don't might know*).

model¹ 0ᴍ /ˈmɒdl/ *noun*
1 a small copy of something: *a model of the Taj Mahal* ◊ *a model aeroplane*
2 one of the cars, machines, etc. that a certain company makes: *Have you seen their latest model?*
3 a person who wears clothes at a special show or for photographs, so that people will see them and buy them
4 a person who sits or stands so that an artist can draw, paint or photograph them

model² /ˈmɒdl/ *verb* (models, modelling, modelled /ˈmɒdld/)
to wear and show clothes as a model: *Kate modelled swimsuits at the fashion show.*

modem /ˈməʊdem/ *noun*
a piece of equipment that uses a telephone line to connect two computers

moderate /ˈmɒdərət/ *adjective*
not too much and not too little: *Cook the vegetables over a moderate heat.*

modern 0ᴍ /ˈmɒdn/ *adjective*
of the present time; of the kind that is usual now: *modern art* ◊ *The airport is very modern.*

modest /ˈmɒdɪst/ *adjective*
not talking much about good things that you have done or about things that you can do well: *You didn't tell me you could sing so well – you're very modest!*

▶ **modestly** *adverb*: *He spoke quietly and modestly about his success.*
▶ **modesty** /ˈmɒdəsti/ *noun* (*no plural*): *She accepted the prize with her usual modesty.*

moist /mɔɪst/ *adjective*
a little wet: *Keep the earth moist or the plant will die.*

moisture /ˈmɔɪstʃə(r)/ *noun* (*no plural*)
small drops of water on something or in the air

mold, moldy *American English for* MOULD, MOULDY

mole /məʊl/ *noun*
1 a small grey or brown animal that lives under the ground and makes tunnels
2 a small dark spot on a person's skin

molecule /ˈmɒlɪkjuːl/ *noun*
the smallest part into which a substance can be divided without changing its chemical nature ⟹ Look at **atom**.

mom /mɒm/ *American English for* MUM

moment 0ᴍ /ˈməʊmənt/ *noun*
a very short time ⟹ SAME MEANING **minute**: *He thought for a moment before he answered.* ◊ *Can you wait a moment?*
at the moment now: *She's on holiday at the moment, but she'll be back next week.*
in a moment very soon: *He'll be here in a moment.*
the moment as soon as: *Tell Jim to phone me the moment he arrives.*

mommy /ˈmɒmi/ (*also* momma /ˈmɒmə/) *American English for* MUMMY

monarch /ˈmɒnək/ *noun*
a king or queen

monarchy /ˈmɒnəki/ *noun* (*plural* monarchies)
a country that has a king or queen

monastery /ˈmɒnəstri/ *noun* (*plural* monasteries)
a place where religious men (called **monks**) live together

Monday 0ᴍ /ˈmʌndeɪ/ *noun*
the day of the week after Sunday and before Tuesday, the first day of the working week ⟹ Look at the note at **day**.

money 0ᴍ /ˈmʌni/ *noun* (*no plural*)

> 🔎 **PRONUNCIATION**
> The word **money** sounds like **funny**.

what you use when you buy or sell something: *How much money did you spend?* ◊ *This jacket cost a lot of money.* ◊ *The film made a lot of money.*

money

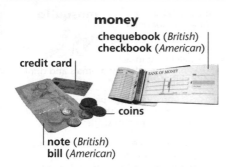

credit card

chequebook (*British*)
checkbook (*American*)

coins

note (*British*)
bill (*American*)

🔍 **WORD BUILDING**

Money consists of **coins** (small round metal things) and **notes** (pieces of paper). This is called **cash**: *I haven't got much cash. Can I pay by cheque?*
The coins that you have in your purse are called **change**: *Have you got any change for the phone?*
The money somebody gives you in a shop if you pay too much is also called **change**: *Here's your change.*

monitor /'mɒnɪtə(r)/ *noun*
a machine that shows pictures or information on a screen like a television: *a PC with a 17-inch colour monitor* ➪ Look at Picture Dictionary page **P11**.

monk /mʌŋk/ *noun*
a religious man who lives with other religious men in a special building (called a monastery)

monkey

monkey /'mʌŋki/ *noun* (*plural* monkeys)
an animal with a long tail, that can climb trees

monotonous /mə'nɒtənəs/ *adjective*
always the same and therefore very boring: *It's a very monotonous job.*

monsoon /ˌmɒn'suːn/ *noun*
the season when very heavy rain falls in Southern Asia

monster /'mɒnstə(r)/ *noun*
an animal in stories that is big, ugly and frightening

month 0̶ᴡ /mʌnθ/ *noun*
1 one of the twelve parts of a year: *December is the last month of the year.* ◇ *We went on holiday* **last month**.

🔍 **WORD BUILDING**

The **months** of the year are: January, February, March, April, May, June, July, August, September, October, November, December.

2 about four weeks: *She was in hospital* **for a month**.

monthly /'mʌnθli/ *adjective, adverb*
happening or coming every month or once a month: *a monthly magazine* ◇ *I am paid monthly.*

monument /'mɒnjumənt/ *noun*
a thing that is built to help people remember a person or something that happened: *This is* **a monument** *to Queen Victoria.*

moo /muː/ *noun*
the sound that a cow makes
▶ **moo** *verb* (moos, mooing, mooed /muːd/): *Cows were mooing in the barn.*

mood 0̶ᴡ /muːd/ *noun*
the way that you feel at a particular time: *Dad is* **in a bad mood** *because he's lost his glasses.* ◇ *Our teacher was* **in a** *very* **good mood** *today.* ◇ *I'm not* **in the mood for** *a party.*

moody /'muːdi/ *adjective* (moodier, moodiest)
If you are **moody**, you often change and become angry or unhappy without warning: *Teenagers can be very moody.*

moon 0̶ᴡ /muːn/ *noun* the moon (*no plural*)
the big object that shines in the sky at night: *When was the first landing* **on the moon**?

moonlight /'muːnlaɪt/ *noun* (*no plural*)
the light from the moon

moor¹ /mʊə(r)/ *noun*
wild land on hills that has grass and low plants, but not many trees: *We went walking on the Yorkshire moors.*

moor² /mʊə(r)/
verb (moors, mooring, moored /mʊəd/)
to tie a boat or ship to something so that it will stay in one place

mop

mop /mɒp/ *noun*
a thing with a long handle that you use for washing floors

▶ **mop** *verb* (mops, mopping, mopped /mɒpt/): *I mopped the floor.*

moped /'məʊped/ *noun*
a vehicle like a bicycle with a small engine
⊃ Look at the picture at **motorcycle**.

moral¹ 0🔑 /'mɒrəl/ *adjective*
connected with what people think is right or wrong: *Some people do not eat meat for moral reasons.* ◇ *a moral problem*
▶ **morally** /'mɒrəli/ *adverb*: *It's morally wrong to tell lies.*

moral² /'mɒrəl/ *noun*
1 morals (*plural*) ideas about what is right and wrong: *These people have no morals.*
2 a lesson about what is right and wrong, that you can learn from a story or from something that happens: *The moral of the story is that we should be kind to animals.*

more¹ 0🔑 /mɔː(r)/ *adjective, pronoun*
a bigger amount or number of something: *You've got more money than I have.* ◇ *Can I have some more sugar in my tea?* ◇ *We need two more chairs.* ◇ *There aren't any more chocolates.* ⊃ Look at **most**. ⊃ OPPOSITE **less** or **fewer**

more² 0🔑 /mɔː(r)/ *adverb*
1 a word that makes an adjective or adverb stronger: *Your book was more expensive than mine.* ◇ *Please speak more slowly.*
2 a bigger amount or number: *I like Anna more than her brother.* ⊃ Look at **most**.
⊃ OPPOSITE **less**
more or less almost, but not exactly
⊃ SAME MEANING **roughly**: *We are more or less the same age.*
not any more not any longer: *They don't live here any more.*
once more (*formal*) again: *Spring will soon be here once more.*

morning 0🔑 /'mɔːnɪŋ/ *noun*
the first part of the day, between the time when the sun comes up and the middle of the day (**midday**): *I went swimming this morning.* ◇ *I'm going to London tomorrow morning.* ◇ *The letter arrived on Tuesday morning.* ◇ *I felt ill all morning.* ◇ *I start work at nine o'clock in the morning.*
in the morning tomorrow during the morning: *I'll see you in the morning.*

mortgage /'mɔːɡɪdʒ/ *noun*
money that you borrow to buy a house

Moslem /'mɒzləm/ = MUSLIM

mosque /mɒsk/ *noun*
a building where Muslims go to say their prayers

mosquito /mə'skiːtəʊ/ *noun* (*plural* mosquitoes)
a small flying insect that bites people and animals and drinks their blood

mosquito

moss /mɒs/ *noun* (*no plural*)
a soft green plant that grows like a carpet on things like trees and stones

most¹ 0🔑 /məʊst/ *adjective, pronoun*
the biggest amount or number of something: *Jo did a lot of work, but I did the most.* ◇ *He was ill for most of last week.*
⊃ Look at **more**. ⊃ OPPOSITE **least**
at most, at the most not more than a certain number, and probably less: *We can stay two days at the most.*
make the most of something to use something in the best way: *We only have one free day, so let's make the most of it.*

most² 0🔑 /məʊst/ *adverb*
more than all others: *It's the most beautiful garden I have ever seen.* ◇ *Which part of your holiday did you enjoy most?*
⊃ OPPOSITE **least**

mostly 0🔑 /'məʊstli/ *adverb*
almost all: *The students in my class are mostly Japanese.*

motel /məʊ'tel/ *noun*
a hotel for people who are travelling by car

moth /mɒθ/ *noun*
an insect with big wings that flies at night

mother 0🔑 /'mʌðə(r)/ *noun*
a woman who has a child: *My mother is a doctor.* ⊃ Look at **mum** and **mummy**.

motherhood /'mʌðəhʊd/ *noun* (*no plural*)
the state of being a mother

mother-in-law /'mʌðər ɪn lɔː/ *noun* (*plural* mothers-in-law)
the mother of your husband or wife

motion /'məʊʃn/ *noun* (*no plural*)
movement: *The motion of the boat made her feel sick.* ◇ *Please remain seated while the bus is in motion* (= moving).

motivate /'məʊtɪveɪt/ *verb* (motivates, motivating, motivated)
to make somebody want to do something: *The best teachers know how to motivate children to learn.*

motive /'məʊtɪv/ *noun*
a reason for doing something: *Was there a motive for the murder?*

motor /ˈməʊtə(r)/ *noun*
the part inside a machine that makes it move or work: *an electric motor* ◇ *The washing machine doesn't work. It needs a new motor.*

> 🔊 **SPEAKING**
> We usually use **engine**, not **motor**, when we are talking about cars and motorbikes.

motorbike

motorbike   moped

scooter

motorbike 0̶ᵣ /ˈməʊtəbaɪk/ (*also formal* **motorcycle** /ˈməʊtəsaɪkl/) *noun*
a vehicle with two wheels and an engine

motorboat /ˈməʊtəbəʊt/ *noun*
a small fast boat that has a MOTOR ⊃ Look at the picture at **boat**.

motorcyclist /ˈməʊtəsaɪklɪst/ *noun*
a person who rides a motorbike

motorist /ˈməʊtərɪst/ *noun*
a person who drives a car

motor racing /ˈməʊtə reɪsɪŋ/ *noun* (*no plural*)
a sport where people drive cars very fast on a special road (called a **track**) to try to win races: *He watched motor racing on TV.*

motorway /ˈməʊtəweɪ/ (*British*) (*American* **expressway, freeway**) *noun*
a wide road where vehicles can travel fast: *The motorway around London is called the M25.*

mould¹ /məʊld/ (*British*) (*American* **mold**) *noun*
1 (*plural* **moulds**) a container that you pour liquid into. The liquid then becomes hard (**sets**) and takes the shape of the container: *They poured the chocolate into a heart-shaped mould.*
2 (*no plural*) a soft green, grey or blue substance that grows on food that is too old
▶ **mouldy** /ˈməʊldi/ *adjective*: *mouldy cheese*

mould

mould

mould² /məʊld/ (*British*) (*American* **mold**) *verb* (**moulds, moulding, moulded**)
to make something soft into a certain shape: *The children moulded animals out of clay.*

mound /maʊnd/ *noun*
1 a small hill; a large pile of earth
2 a pile of things: *a mound of newspapers*

Mount /maʊnt/ (*abbr.* **Mt**) *noun*
You use **Mount** before the name of a mountain: *Mount Everest* ◇ *Mt Etna*

mount /maʊnt/ *verb* (**mounts, mounting, mounted**)
1 (*also* **mount up**) to increase: *Tension in the area is mounting.* ◇ *My debts were beginning to mount up.*
2 to get on a horse or a bicycle

mountain

mountain 0̶ᵣ /ˈmaʊntən/ *noun*
a very high hill: *Everest is the highest mountain in the world.* ◇ *We climbed the mountain.*

mountain bike /ˈmaʊntən baɪk/ *noun*
a bicycle with a strong frame and wide tyres that you can use to ride over rough ground

mountaineer /ˌmaʊntəˈnɪə(r)/ *noun*
a person who climbs mountains
▶ **mountaineering** /ˌmaʊntəˈnɪərɪŋ/ *noun* (*no plural*): *He took up mountaineering as a boy.*

mourn /mɔːn/ *verb* (**mourns, mourning, mourned** /mɔːnd/)
to feel very sad, usually because somebody has died: *She is still mourning for her husband.*

▶ **mourning** /'mɔ:nɪŋ/ *noun* (*no plural*): *They are in mourning for their son.*

mouse 0️⃣ /maʊs/ *noun* (*plural* mice /maɪs/)
1 a small animal with a long tail: *Our cat caught a mouse.*
2 a thing that you move with your hand to tell a computer what to do

mice

moustache (*British*) (*American* mustache) /mə'stɑ:ʃ/ *noun*
the hair above a man's mouth, below his nose: *He has got a moustache.* ⊃ Look at the picture at **hair**.

mouth 0️⃣ /maʊθ/ *noun* (*plural* mouths /maʊðz/)
1 the part of your face below your nose that you use for eating and speaking: *Open your mouth, please!* ⊃ Look Picture Dictionary page **P4**.
2 the place where a river goes into the sea: *the mouth of the Thames*

mouthful /'maʊθfʊl/ *noun*
the amount of food or drink that you can put in your mouth at one time: *She only had a mouthful of cake.*

move¹ 0️⃣ /mu:v/ *verb* (moves, moving, moved /mu:vd/)
1 to go from one place to another; to change the way you are standing or sitting: *Don't get off the bus while it's moving.* ◇ *We moved to the front of the cinema.*
2 to put something in another place or another way: *Can you move your car, please?*
3 to go to live in another place: *They sold their house in London and moved to Liverpool.* ◇ *We are moving house soon.*
move in to go to live in a house or flat: *I've got a new flat – I'm moving in next week.*
move out to leave a house or flat where you were living

move² 0️⃣ /mu:v/ *noun*
1 a change of place or position: *The police are watching every move she makes.*
2 a change in the place where you live: *We need a big van for the move.*

get a move on (*informal*) hurry: *Get a move on or you'll be late for work!*

movement 0️⃣ /'mu:vmənt/ *noun*
1 moving or being moved: *The old man's movements were slow and painful.*
2 a group of people who have the same ideas or beliefs: *a political movement*

movie 0️⃣ /'mu:vi/ *noun* (*American*)
1 (*British* film) a film that you see at the cinema: *Would you like to see a movie?*
2 the movies (*plural*) (*British* the cinema) (*no plural*) the place where you go to watch a film: *We went to the movies last night.*

moving /'mu:vɪŋ/ *adjective*
making you feel something strongly, especially sadness: *It's a very moving story.*

mow /məʊ/ *verb* (mows, mowing, mowed /məʊd/, has mown /məʊn/)
to cut grass with a machine: *Sally is mowing the grass.*

mower /'məʊə(r)/ *noun*
a machine that cuts grass ⊃ SAME MEANING **lawnmower** ⊃ Look at the picture at **lawnmower**.

MP /,em 'pi:/ *short for* MEMBER OF PARLIAMENT

MP3 /,em pi: 'θri:/ *noun* (*also* MP3 file /,em pi: 'θri: faɪl/)
a type of computer file which holds music

MP3 player /,em pi: 'θri: pleɪə(r)/ *noun*
a piece of computer equipment that can play MP3 FILES

mph /,em pi: 'eɪtʃ/ *abbreviation*
a way of measuring how fast something is moving. **Mph** is short for **miles per hour**: *The train was travelling at 125 mph.*

Mr 0️⃣ /'mɪstə(r)/ *noun*
a word that you use before the name of a man: *Mr Richard Waters* ◇ *Mr Holland*

Mrs 0️⃣ /'mɪsɪz/ *noun*
a word that you use before the name of a woman who is married: *Mrs Sandra Garcia* ◇ *Mrs Nolan*

Ms /məz; mɪz/ *noun*
a word that you can use before the name of any woman, instead of **Mrs** or **Miss**: *Ms Fiona Green*

🔎 **GRAMMAR**

Miss, **Mrs**, **Ms** and **Mr** are all titles that we use in front of somebody's family name, NOT their first name, unless it is included with the family name: *Is there a Miss (Tamsin) Hudson here?* ◇ *Hello, Miss Hudson, come this way* (NOT Miss Tamsin).

MSc /ˌem es 'siː/ *abbreviation*
a second university degree that you get by doing a course or a piece of research in a science subject. **MSc** is short for **Master of Science**.

Mt *short way of writing* MOUNT

much¹ 0̄ᴍ /mʌtʃ/ *adjective, pronoun* (more, most)
a big amount of something; a lot of something: *I haven't got much money.* ◇ *There was so much food that we couldn't eat it all.* ◇ *Eat as much as you can.* ◇ *How much paper do you want?* ◇ *How much is this shirt?*

> 🔎 **GRAMMAR**
>
> We usually use **much** only in negative sentences, in questions, and after 'too', 'so', 'as' and 'how'.
> In other sentences we use **a lot (of)**: *She's got a lot of money.*

⊃ Look at **many**.

much² 0̄ᴍ /mʌtʃ/ *adverb*
a lot: *I don't like him very much.* ◇ *Your flat is much bigger than mine.* ◇ *'Do you like it?' 'No, not much.'*

muck /mʌk/ *verb* (mucks, mucking, mucked /mʌkt/) (*British, informal*)
muck about, **muck around** to behave in a silly way: *Stop mucking about and come and help me!*

mud 0̄ᴍ /mʌd/ *noun* (no plural)
soft wet earth: *Phil came home from the football match covered in mud.*

muddle /ˈmʌdl/ *verb* (muddles, muddling, muddled /ˈmʌdld/)
1 (*also* muddle something up) to put things in the wrong order or mix them up: *Their letters were all muddled up together in a drawer.*
2 (*also* muddle somebody up) (*informal*) to mix somebody's ideas so that they cannot understand or think clearly
⊃ SAME MEANING **confuse**: *Don't ask so many questions – you're muddling me.*
muddle somebody or **something up** to think that one person or thing is a different person or thing: *I always muddle Jane up with her sister.*
▶ **muddle** *noun*: *I was in such a muddle that I couldn't find anything.*

muddy /ˈmʌdi/ *adjective* (muddier, muddiest)
covered with mud: *When it rains, the roads get very muddy.*

muesli /ˈmjuːzli/ *noun* (no plural)
food made from grain, fruit and nuts that you eat with milk for breakfast

mug¹ /mʌg/ *noun*
a big cup with straight sides: *a mug of tea*
⊃ Look at the picture at **cup**.

mug² /mʌg/ *verb* (mugs, mugging, mugged /mʌgd/)
to attack somebody in the street and take their money
▶ **mugger** *noun*: *Watch out for muggers, especially at night.*

mule /mjuːl/ *noun*
an animal that is used for carrying heavy loads and whose parents are a horse and a DONKEY (= an animal like a small horse with long ears)

multicultural /ˌmʌltiˈkʌltʃərəl/ *adjective*
for or including people from many different countries and cultures: *We live in a multicultural society.*

multimedia /ˌmʌltiˈmiːdiə/ *adjective*
using sound, pictures and film as well as words on a screen: *The firm produces multimedia software for schools.*

multiple-choice /ˌmʌltɪpl ˈtʃɔɪs/ *adjective*
A **multiple-choice** exam or question gives you three or four different answers and you have to choose the right one.

multiply 0̄ᴍ /ˈmʌltɪplaɪ/ *verb* (multiplies, multiplying, multiplied /ˈmʌltɪplaɪd/, has multiplied)
to make a number bigger by a certain number of times: *Two multiplied by three is six* ($2 \times 3 = 6$). ◇ *Multiply three and seven together.* ⊃ Look at **divide**.
▶ **multiplication** /ˌmʌltɪplɪˈkeɪʃn/ *noun* (no plural): *Today we did multiplication and division.*

multi-storey /ˌmʌlti ˈstɔːri/ *adjective* (*British*)
with many floors: *a multi-storey car park*

mum /mʌm/ (*British*) (*American* mom) *noun* (*informal*)
mother: *This is my mum.* ◇ *Can I have an apple, Mum?*

mumble /ˈmʌmbl/ *verb* (mumbles, mumbling, mumbled /ˈmʌmbld/)
to speak quietly in a way that is not clear, so that people cannot hear you well: *She mumbled something, but I didn't hear what she said.*

mummy /ˈmʌmi/ (*British*) (*American* mommy) *noun* (*plural* mummies) (*informal*)
a word for 'mother' that children use

A
B
C
D
E
F
G
H
I
J
K
L
M
N
O
P
Q
R
S
T
U
V
W
X
Y
Z

A B C D E F G H I J K L M N O P Q R S T U V W X Y Z

mumps /mʌmps/ *noun* (*no plural*)
an illness that children get which makes your neck swell (= get bigger)

murder¹ 0⇥ /'mɜːdə(r)/ *noun*
the crime of killing somebody deliberately: *He was sent to prison for the murder of a police officer.*

murder² 0⇥ /'mɜːdə(r)/ *verb* (**murders, murdering, murdered** /'mɜːdəd/)
to kill somebody deliberately: *She was murdered with a knife.*
▶ **murderer** /'mɜːdərə(r)/ *noun*: *The police have caught the murderer.*

murmur /'mɜːmə(r)/ *verb* (**murmurs, murmuring, murmured** /'mɜːməd/)
to speak in a low quiet voice: '*I love you,'* she murmured.
▶ **murmur** *noun*: *I heard the murmur of voices from the next room.*

muscle 0⇥ /'mʌsl/ *noun*
one of the parts inside your body that are connected to the bones and which help you to move: *Riding a bicycle is good for developing the leg muscles.*

museum 0⇥ /mjuˈziːəm/ *noun*
a building where people can look at old or interesting things: *Have you ever been to the British Museum?*

mushroom /'mʌʃrʊm/ *noun*
a plant with a flat top and no leaves that you can eat as a vegetable ➲ Look at Picture Dictionary page **P9**.

music 0⇥ /'mjuːzɪk/ *noun* (*no plural*)
1 the sounds that you make by singing, or by playing instruments: *What sort of music do you like?*
2 signs on paper to show people what to sing or play: *Can you read music?*

> ♫ **WORD BUILDING**
> There are many different types of **music**. Here are some of them: classical, heavy metal, jazz, opera, reggae, rock. Do you know any others?

musical¹ 0⇥ /'mjuːzɪkl/ *adjective*
1 connected with music: *musical instruments* (= the piano, the guitar or the trumpet, for example)
2 good at making music: *Sophie's very musical.*

musical² /'mjuːzɪkl/ *noun*
a play or film that has singing and dancing in it: *We went to see the musical 'Chicago'.*

musician 0⇥ /mjuˈzɪʃn/ *noun*
a person who writes music or plays a musical instrument

Muslim /'mʊzlɪm/ *noun*
a person who follows the religion of Islam
▶ **Muslim** *adjective*: *the Muslim way of life*

must 0⇥ /məst; mʌst/ *modal verb*
1 a word that you use to tell somebody what to do or what is necessary: *You must look before you cross the road.*

> ♫ **GRAMMAR**
> You use **must not** or the short form **mustn't** /'mʌsnt/ to tell people **not** to do something: *You mustn't be late.*
> When you want to say that somebody can do something if they want, but that it is not necessary, you use **don't have to**: *You don't have to do your homework today* (= you can do it today if you want, but it is not necessary).

2 a word that shows that you are sure something is true: *You must be tired after your long journey.* ◊ *I can't find my keys. I must have left them at home.* ➲ Look at the note at **modal verb**.

mustache *American English for* MOUSTACHE

mustard /'mʌstəd/ *noun* (*no plural*)
a thick yellow sauce with a very strong taste, that you eat with meat ➲ Look at Picture Dictionary page **P7**.

mustn't /'mʌsnt/ *short for* MUST NOT

mutter /'mʌtə(r)/ *verb* (**mutters, muttering, muttered** /'mʌtəd/)
to speak in a low quiet voice that is difficult to hear: *He muttered something about going home, and left the room.*

my 0⇥ /maɪ/ *adjective*
of or belonging to me: *Where is my watch?* ◊ *These are my books, not yours.* ◊ *I've hurt my arm.*

myself 0⇥ /maɪˈself/ *pronoun* (*plural* **ourselves**)
1 a word that shows the same person as the one who is speaking: *I hurt myself.* ◊ *I bought myself a new shirt.*
2 a word that makes 'I' stronger: '*Did you buy this cake?' 'No, I made it myself.'*
by myself
1 without other people ➲ SAME MEANING **alone**: *I live by myself.*
2 without help: *I made dinner by myself.*

mysterious 0⇥ /mɪˈstɪəriəs/ *adjective*
Something that is **mysterious** is strange and you do not know about it or understand

it: *Several people said they had seen mysterious lights in the sky.*
▶ **mysteriously** *adverb*: *The plane disappeared mysteriously.*

mystery /'mɪstri/ *noun* (*plural* mysteries) something strange that you cannot understand or explain: *The police say that the man's death is still a mystery.*

myth /mɪθ/ *noun*
1 a very old story: *Greek myths*
2 a story or belief that is not true: *It's a myth that money makes you happy.*

A
B
C
D
E
F
G
H
I
J
K
L
M
N
O
P
Q
R
S
T
U
V
W
X
Y
Z

Nn

N, n /en/ *noun* (*plural* N's, n's /enz/)
the fourteenth letter of the English alphabet: '*Nice*' begins with an '*N*'.

nag /næg/ *verb* (nags, nagging, nagged /nægd/)
to keep asking somebody to do something: *My parents are always **nagging** me to work harder.*

nail 0— /neɪl/ *noun*
1 the hard part at the end of a finger or toe: *toenails* ◇ *fingernails*
2 a small thin piece of metal with one sharp end which you hit into wood (with a tool called a **hammer**) to fix things together
▶ **nail** *verb* (nails, nailing, nailed /neɪld/): *I nailed the pieces of wood together.*

nail

nail polish /'neɪl pɒlɪʃ/ (*British also* nail varnish /'neɪl vɑːnɪʃ/) *noun*
a coloured liquid that people put on their nails

naked /'neɪkɪd/ *adjective*
not wearing any clothes. ⇒ SAME MEANING **nude**

name¹ 0— /neɪm/ *noun*
a word or words that you use to call or talk about a person or thing: *My name is Chris Eaves.* ◇ *What's your name?* ◇ *Do you know the name of this flower?*

> 🔎 **WHICH WORD?**
>
> Your **first name**, **given name** or **forename** is the name that your parents give you when you are born.
> Many people also have a **middle name**.
> Your **surname**, **last name** or **family name** is the name that everybody in your family has.
> A **nickname** is a name that your friends or family sometimes call you instead of your real name: *Her real name is Rachel, but her nickname is Binty.*

call somebody names to say bad, unkind words about somebody: *Joe cried because the other children were calling him names.*

name² 0— /neɪm/ *verb* (names, naming, named /neɪmd/)
1 to give a name to somebody or something: *They named their baby Sophie.* ◇

They **named** him Michael **after** his grandfather (= gave him the same name as his grandfather).
2 to know and say the name of somebody or something: *The headmaster could name every one of his 600 pupils.*

namely /'neɪmli/ *adverb*
You use **namely** when you are going to name a person or thing that you have just said something about: *Only two students were late, namely Sergio and Antonio.*

nanny /'næni/ *noun* (*plural* nannies)
a woman whose job is to look after the children of a family

nap /næp/ *noun*
a short sleep that you have during the day: *I had a nap after lunch.*

napkin /'næpkɪn/ *noun* (*British*)
a piece of cloth or paper that you use when you are eating to clean your mouth and hands and to keep your clothes clean
⇒ SAME MEANING **serviette**

nappy /'næpi/ *noun* (*British*) (*plural* nappies) (*American* diaper)
a piece of cloth or strong paper that a baby wears around its bottom and between its legs: *Does his nappy need changing?*

narrow 0— /'nærəʊ/ *adjective* (narrower, narrowest)
1 not far from one side to the other: *The bridge was very narrow.* ◇ *a narrow ribbon*
⇒ OPPOSITE **broad** or **wide**
2 by a small amount: *We had a narrow escape – the car nearly hit a tree.* ◇ *a narrow defeat*

narrowly /'nærəʊli/ *adverb*
only by a small amount: *They narrowly escaped injury.*

narrow-minded /ˌnærəʊ 'maɪndɪd/ *adjective*
not wanting to accept ideas or opinions that are different from your own: *The people in this town are very narrow-minded.*
⇒ OPPOSITE **broad-minded**

nasty /'nɑːsti/ *adjective* (nastier, nastiest)
bad; not nice ⇒ SAME MEANING **horrible**: *There's a nasty smell in this room.* ◇ *Don't be so nasty!*

nation /'neɪʃn/ *noun*
a country and all the people who live in it
⇒ Look at the note at **country**.

national ⊶ /'næʃnəl/ *adjective*
connected with all of a country; typical of a
country: *She wore Greek national costume.* ◇
national newspapers

national anthem /ˌnæʃnəl 'ænθəm/
noun
the official song of a country

nationality /ˌnæʃə'næləti/ *noun* (*plural*
nationalities)
the state of belonging to a certain country:
'What nationality are you?' 'I'm Australian.'

national park /ˌnæʃnəl 'pɑːk/ *noun*
a large area of beautiful land that is
protected by the government so that people
can enjoy it

native¹ /'neɪtɪv/ *adjective*
connected with the place where you were
born: *I returned to my native country.* ◇ *My
native language is German.*

native² /'neɪtɪv/ *noun*
a person who was born in a place: *He's a
native of Liverpool.*

Native American /ˌneɪtɪv ə'merɪkən/
noun
a member of the group of people who were
living in America before people from Europe
arrived there

native speaker /ˌneɪtɪv 'spiːkə(r)/ *noun*
a person who speaks a language as their first
language: *All our teachers are Spanish native
speakers.*

natural ⊶ /'nætʃrəl/ *adjective*
1 made by nature, not by people: *This part of
Scotland is an area of great natural beauty.* ◇
*Earthquakes and floods are **natural disasters**.*
2 normal or usual: *It's **natural for** parents **to**
feel sad when their children leave home.*
Ɔ OPPOSITE **unnatural**

naturally /'nætʃrəli/ *adverb*
1 in a way that you would expect
Ɔ SAME MEANING **of course**: *Naturally, I get
upset when things go wrong.*
2 in a way that is not made or caused by
people: *Is your hair naturally curly?*
3 in a normal way: *Try to stand naturally
while I take a photo.*

nature ⊶ /'neɪtʃə(r)/ *noun*
1 (*no plural*) all the plants, animals, etc. in
the world and all the things that happen in it
that are not made or caused by people: *the
beauty of nature*
2 (*plural* **natures**) the way a person or thing
is: *Our cat has a very friendly nature.*

naughty /'nɔːti/ *adjective* (**naughtier,
naughtiest**)
A **naughty** child does bad things or does

not do what you ask them to do: *She's the
naughtiest child in the class.*

naval /'neɪvl/ *adjective*
connected with a navy: *a naval officer*

navigate /'nævɪgeɪt/ *verb* (**navigates,
navigating, navigated**)
to use a map or some other method to find
which way a ship, a plane or a car should go:
Long ago, explorers used the stars to navigate.
▶ **navigation** /ˌnævɪ'geɪʃn/ *noun* (*no
plural*) deciding which way a ship or other
vehicle should go by using a map, etc.:
navigation skills
▶ **navigator** /'nævɪgeɪtə(r)/ *noun* a person
who decides which way a ship, etc. should
go: *Dad's usually the navigator when we go
somewhere in the car.*

navy ⊶ /'neɪvi/ *noun* (*plural* **navies**)
the ships that a country uses when there is a
war, and the people who work on them:
*Mark is **in the navy**.*

navy blue /ˌneɪvi 'bluː/ (*also* **navy** /'neɪvi/)
adjective
dark blue

near ⊶ /nɪə(r)/ *adjective, adverb,
preposition* (**nearer, nearest**)
not far away; close to somebody or
something: *Let's walk to my house. It's quite
near.* ◇ *Where's the nearest hospital?* ◇ *My
parents live quite near.* ◇ *I don't need a car
because I live near the city centre.*

nearby ⊶ /'nɪəbaɪ/ *adjective*
not far away; close: *We took her to a nearby
hospital.*
▶ **nearby** /ˌnɪə'baɪ/ *adverb*: *Let's go and see
Tim – he lives nearby.*

nearly ⊶ /'nɪəli/ *adverb*
almost; not quite: *I'm nearly 16 – it's my
birthday next week.* ◇ *She was so ill that she
nearly died.*
not nearly not at all: *The book wasn't
nearly as good as the film.*

neat /niːt/ *adjective* (**neater, neatest**)
1 with everything in the right place and
done carefully Ɔ SAME MEANING **tidy**: *Keep
your room **neat and tidy**.* ◇ *She has very neat
handwriting.*
2 (*American, informal*) good; nice: *That's a
really neat car!*
▶ **neatly** *adverb*: *Write your name neatly.*

necessarily /ˌnesə'serəli/ *adverb*
not necessarily not always: *Big men aren't
necessarily strong.*

necessary ⊶ /'nesəsəri/ *adjective*
If something is **necessary**, you must have it
or do it: *Warm clothes are necessary in winter.*

A B C D E F G H I J K L M **N** O P Q R S T U V W X Y Z

necessity /nə'sesəti/ *noun* (*plural* necessities)
something that you must have: *Food and clothes are necessities of life.*

neck 0— /nek/ *noun*
1 the part of your body between your shoulders and your head: *Helen wore a thick scarf round her neck.* ⇒ Look at Picture Dictionary page **P4**.
2 the part of a piece of clothing that goes round your neck: *The neck's too tight.*
3 the thin part at the top of a bottle

necklaces

necklace /'nekləs/ *noun*
a piece of jewellery that you wear round your neck: *a diamond necklace*

need¹ 0— /niːd/ *verb* (needs, needing, needed)
1 If you **need** something, you must have it: *All plants and animals need water.* ◇ *You don't need your coat – it's not cold.*
2 If you **need** to do something, you must do it: *James is very ill. He needs to go to hospital.* ◇ *'Do we need to pay now, or can we pay next week?' 'You don't need to pay now.'*

need² 0— /niːd/ *noun*
a situation in which you must have something or do something: *the growing need for new books and equipment* ◇ *There's no need for you to come.* ◇ *She's in need of a rest.*

needle 0— /'niːdl/ *noun*
1 a small thin piece of metal that you use for sewing cloth: *Put the thread through the eye* (= hole) *of the needle.* ⇒ Look at the picture at **sew**. ⇒ Look also at **knitting needle**.
2 a small thin piece of metal that forms part of an instrument: *The compass needle points north.* ◇ *a hypodermic needle* (= for taking blood or giving drugs)
3 a very thin pointed leaf on a tree that stays green all year: *pine needles*

needless /'niːdləs/ *adjective*
not necessary; able to be avoided: *needless suffering* ◇ *The problem is the cost,* **needless to say** (= it is not necessary to say this, because it is obvious).
▶ **needlessly** *adverb*: *Many people died needlessly.*

needn't /'niːdnt/ *short for* NEED NOT: *You needn't go if you don't want to.*

negative¹ 0— /'negətɪv/ *adjective*
1 bad or harmful: *The whole experience was definitely more positive than negative.*
⇒ OPPOSITE **positive**
2 only thinking about the bad qualities of somebody or something: *If you go into the match with a negative attitude, you'll never win.* ⇒ OPPOSITE **positive**
3 using words like 'no', 'not' and 'never': *'I don't like British food' is a negative sentence.*

negative² /'negətɪv/ *noun*
a piece of film that we use to make a photograph. On a **negative**, dark things are light and light things are dark.

neglect /nɪ'glekt/ *verb* (neglects, neglecting, neglected)
to not take care of somebody or something: *The dog was dirty and thin because its owner had neglected it.*
▶ **neglect** *noun* (*no plural*): *The house was in a state of neglect.*
▶ **neglected** *adjective*: *neglected children*

negotiate /nɪ'gəʊʃieɪt/ (negotiates, negotiating, negotiated) *verb*
to reach an agreement by talking with other people: *We have negotiated a deal.* ◇ *The unions were* **negotiating with** *the management* **over** *pay.*

neigh /neɪ/ *verb* (neighs, neighing, neighed /neɪd/)
When a horse **neighs**, it make a long high sound.
▶ **neigh** *noun*

neighbor, neighboring *American English for* NEIGHBOUR, NEIGHBOURING

neighborhood *American English for* NEIGHBOURHOOD

neighbour 0— (*British*) (*American* neighbor) /'neɪbə(r)/ *noun*
a person who lives near you: *Don't make so much noise or you'll wake the neighbours.*

🔎 **WHICH WORD?**
Your **next-door neighbour** is the person who lives in the house next door to your house

neighbourhood (British) (American **neighborhood**) /'neɪbəhʊd/ *noun*
a part of a town; the people who live there: *They live in a friendly neighbourhood.*

neighbouring (British) (American **neighboring**) /'neɪbərɪŋ/ *adjective*
near or next to: *people from neighbouring villages*

neither¹ 0🔑 /'naɪðə(r); 'niːðə(r)/ *adjective, pronoun*
not one and not the other of two things or people: *Neither book is very interesting.* ◇ *Neither of the boys was there.*

neither² 0🔑 /'naɪðə(r); 'niːðə(r)/ *adverb*
also not: *Lydia can't swim and neither can I.* ◇ *'I don't like rice.' 'Neither do I.'*
neither ... nor not ... and not: *Neither Paul nor I went to the party.*

neon /'niːɒn/ *noun* (no plural) (symbol Ne)
a type of gas that is used in bright lights and signs

nephew /'nefjuː/ *noun*
the son of your brother or sister

nerd /nɜːd/ *noun* (informal)
a person who spends a lot of time on a particular interest and who is not popular or fashionable ⊃ SAME MEANING **geek**

nerve 0🔑 /nɜːv/ *noun*
1 (plural **nerves**) one of the long thin things inside your body that carry feelings and messages to and from your brain
2 nerves (plural) a feeling of worry or fear: *John breathed deeply to **calm** his **nerves**.*
3 (no plural) the state of being brave or calm when there is danger: *You need a lot of nerve to be a racing driver.*
get on somebody's nerves to annoy somebody: *Stop making that noise – you're getting on my nerves!*

nerve-racking /'nɜːv rækɪŋ/ *adjective*
making you very nervous or worried: *It was a nerve-racking drive up the mountain.*

nervous 0🔑 /'nɜːvəs/ *adjective*
1 worried or afraid: *I'm quite nervous about starting my new job.*
2 connected with the NERVES in your body: *the nervous system*
▶ **nervously** /'nɜːvəsli/ *adverb*: *He laughed nervously, not knowing know what to say.*
▶ **nervousness** /'nɜːvəsnəs/ *noun* (no plural): *He tried to hide his nervousness.*

nest¹ /nest/ *noun*
a place where a bird, snake, insect, etc. keeps its eggs or its babies: *a bird's nest*

nest² /nest/ *verb* (nests, nesting, nested)
to make and live in a **nest**: *The ducks are nesting by the river.*

nets

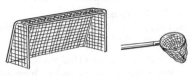

net 0🔑 /net/ *noun*
1 material that has very large spaces between the threads; a piece of this material that we use for a particular purpose: *a fishing net* ◇ *a tennis net* ◇ *He kicked the ball into the back of the net.*
2 the Net (informal) = THE INTERNET

netball /'netbɔːl/ *noun* (no plural)
a game where two teams of seven players, usually women, try to throw a ball through a high round net

nettle /'netl/ *noun*
a wild plant covered with hairs that can hurt you if you touch them

network /'netwɜːk/ *noun*
a number of things or people that form a single system or that are closely connected: *the rail network* ◇ *computer networks* ◇ *a network of friends*

neutral¹ /'njuːtrəl/ *adjective*
1 not supporting either side in an argument or war: *I don't take sides when my brothers argue – I remain neutral.*
2 having or showing no strong qualities, emotions or colour: *a neutral tone of voice* ◇ *neutral colours*

neutral² /'njuːtrəl/ *noun* (no plural)
the position in which no power is being sent from a vehicle's engine to its wheels: *Put the car in neutral.*

never 0🔑 /'nevə(r)/ *adverb*
not at any time; not ever: *She never works on Saturdays.* ◇ *I've never been to America.* ◇ *I will never forget you.*

nevertheless /ˌnevəðə'les/ *adverb* (formal)
but ⊃ SAME MEANING **however**: *They played very well. Nevertheless, they didn't win.*

new 0🔑 /njuː/ *adjective* (newer, newest)
1 not existing before: *Have you seen his new film?* ◇ *I bought a new pair of shoes yesterday.*
2 different from before: *Our new flat is much bigger than our old one.* ◇ *The teacher usually explains the new words to us.*
3 doing something for the first time: *New*

parents are often tired. ◇ *He's new to the job and still needs help.*

newcomer /'nju:kʌmə(r)/ *noun*
a person who has just come to a place

newly /'nju:li/ *adverb*
not long ago ⊃ SAME MEANING **recently**: *Our school is newly built.*

news 0̶ₓ /nju:z/ *noun (no plural)*
1 information about things that have just happened: *Have you heard the news? Stewart is getting married.* ◇ *I've got some good news for you.*

> 🔎 GRAMMAR
>
> Be careful! You cannot say 'a news'. To talk about a single item, you can say **some news** or **a piece of news**: *Julie told us an interesting piece of news.*

2 the news (*no plural*) a programme on television or radio that tells people about important things that have just happened: *We heard about the plane crash on the news.*
break the news to be the first person to tell somebody about something important: *Have you broken the news to your wife?*

newsagent /'nju:zeɪdʒənt/ *noun*
1 a person who sells things like newspapers, magazines, sweets and cigarettes
2 newsagent's a shop that sells things like newspapers, magazines, sweets and cigarettes

newspaper 0̶ₓ /'nju:speɪpə(r)/ *noun*
1 (*plural*) (newspapers) large pieces of paper with news, advertisements and other things printed on them: *a daily newspaper*
2 (*no plural*) paper taken from old **newspapers**: *We wrapped the plates in newspaper before packing them.*

new year (*also* New Year) /ˌnju: 'jɪə(r)/ *noun (no plural)*
the beginning of the year: *Happy New Year!* ◇ *We will get in touch in the new year.*

> 🔎 WHICH WORD?
>
> 1 January is called **New Year's Day** and 31 December is called **New Year's Eve**.

next[1] 0̶ₓ /nekst/ *adjective*
1 coming after this one: *I'm going on holiday next week.* ◇ *Take the next road on the right.*
2 nearest to this one: *I live in the next village.*
next to somebody or something at the side of somebody or something
⊃ SAME MEANING **beside**: *The bank is next to the post office.*

next[2] 0̶ₓ /nekst/ *adverb*
straight after this: *I've finished this work. What shall I do next?*

next[3] 0̶ₓ /nekst/ *noun (no plural)*
the person or thing that comes after this one: *Susy came first and Paul was the next to arrive.*

next door /ˌnekst 'dɔ:(r)/ *adverb*
in or to the nearest house: *Who lives next door?*
▶ **next-door** *adjective*: *They're my next-door neighbours.*

nib /nɪb/ *noun*
the metal point of a pen, where the coloured liquid (called **ink**) comes out ⊃ Look at Picture Dictionary page **P11**.

nibble /'nɪbl/ *verb* (nibbles, nibbling, nibbled /'nɪbld/)
to eat something in very small bites: *The mouse nibbled the cheese.*

nice 0̶ₓ /naɪs/ *adjective* (nicer, nicest)
pleasant, good or kind: *Did you have a nice holiday?* ◇ *I met a nice boy at the party.* ◇ *It's nice to see you.*

> 🔎 SPEAKING
>
> We often say **great**, **lovely** or **wonderful** instead of 'very nice': *The party was great.* ◇ *We had a lovely weekend.* ◇ *It was a wonderful show.*

nice and ... words that show that you like something: *It's nice and warm by the fire.*
▶ **nicely** *adverb*: *You can have a cake if you ask nicely* (= in a polite way).

nickname /'nɪkneɪm/ *noun*
a name that your friends or family sometimes call you instead of your real name
▶ **nickname** *verb* (nicknames, nicknaming, nicknamed /'nɪkneɪmd/): *She was nicknamed 'The Ice Queen'.*

nicotine /'nɪkəti:n/ *noun (no plural)*
a poisonous chemical in cigarettes that makes it difficult to stop smoking

niece /ni:s/ *noun*
the daughter of your brother or sister ⊃ Look at **nephew**.

night 0̶ₓ /naɪt/ *noun*
1 the part of the day when it is dark and most people sleep: *These animals come out at night.* ◇ *The baby cried all night.* ◇ *She stayed at my house last night.*
2 the part of the day between the afternoon and when you go to bed: *We went to a party on Saturday night.* ◇ *He doesn't get home until 8 o'clock at night.* ⊃ **Tonight** means the night or evening of today.

nightclub /ˈnaɪtklʌb/ *noun*
a place where you can go late in the evening to drink and dance ➲ SAME MEANING **club**

nightdress /ˈnaɪtdres/ (*plural* **nightdresses**) (*also* **nightie** /ˈnaɪti/) *noun*
a loose dress that a woman or girl wears in bed

nightlife /ˈnaɪtlaɪf/ *noun* (*no plural*)
things to do in the evenings in a particular area, such as dancing or going to bars: *What's the nightlife like round here?*

nightly /ˈnaɪtli/ *adjective, adverb*
happening or coming every night: *a nightly TV show*

nightmare /ˈnaɪtmeə(r)/ *noun*
1 a dream that frightens you: *I had a nightmare last night.*
2 something that is very bad or frightening: *Travelling through the snow was a nightmare.*

night-time /ˈnaɪt taɪm/ *noun* (*no plural*)
the time when it is dark: *She is afraid to go out at night-time.* ➲ OPPOSITE **daytime**

nil /nɪl/ *noun* (*no plural*)
the number 0, especially when it is the score in games such as football: *Our team won the match by two goals to nil.*

nine 0̶ᴡ /naɪn/ *number* 9
▶ **ninth** /naɪnθ/ *pronoun, adjective, adverb* 9th

nineteen 0̶ᴡ /ˌnaɪnˈtiːn/ *number* 19
▶ **nineteenth** /ˌnaɪnˈtiːnθ/ *pronoun, adjective, adverb* 19th

ninety 0̶ᴡ /ˈnaɪnti/ *number*
1 90
2 the nineties (*plural*) the numbers, years or temperatures between 90 and 99
in your nineties between the ages of 90 and 99: *My grandmother is in her nineties.*
▶ **ninetieth** /ˈnaɪntiəθ/ *pronoun, adjective, adverb* 90th

nip /nɪp/ *verb* (**nips**, **nipping**, **nipped** /nɪpt/)
1 to give somebody a quick painful bite: *The dog nipped his leg.*
2 (*British*) to go somewhere quickly: *I'm just nipping to the shops.*

nipple /ˈnɪpl/ *noun*
one of the two small dark circles on either side of your chest. A baby can get milk from its mother through the **nipples**.

nitrogen /ˈnaɪtrədʒən/ *noun* (*no plural*) (*symbol* N)
the gas that forms about 80% of the air

No. (*also* **no.**) *short way of writing* NUMBER(1)

no¹ 0̶ᴡ /nəʊ/ *exclamation*
1 used for giving a negative reply or statement ➲ OPPOSITE **yes**: *'Do you want a drink?' 'No, thank you.'* ◇ *'He's Italian.' 'No he isn't. He's French.'*
2 something that you say when something bad happens or to show you are surprised or shocked: *Oh no! I've broken my watch!*

no² 0̶ᴡ /nəʊ/ *adjective*
1 not one; not any: *I have no money – my purse is empty.* ◇ *No visitors may enter without a ticket.*
2 used for saying that something is not allowed: *The sign said 'No Smoking'.*

no³ /nəʊ/ *adverb*
not any: *My flat is no bigger than yours.*

noble /ˈnəʊbl/ *adjective* (**nobler**, **noblest**)
1 good, honest and caring about other people: *noble thoughts*
2 belonging to the highest social class: *a man of noble birth*

nobody 0̶ᴡ /ˈnəʊbədi/ *pronoun*
no person; not anybody ➲ SAME MEANING **no one**: *Nobody in our class speaks Greek.* ◇ *There was nobody at home.*

nod /nɒd/ *verb* (**nods**, **nodding**, **nodded**)
to move your head down and up again quickly as a way of saying 'yes' or 'hello' to somebody: *'Do you understand?' asked the teacher, and everybody nodded.*
nod off to go to sleep: *Grandma nodded off in her chair.*
▶ **nod** *noun*: *Jim gave me a nod when I arrived.*

noise 0̶ᴡ /nɔɪz/ *noun*
a sound, especially one that is loud or unpleasant: *I heard a noise upstairs.* ◇ *Don't make so much noise!*

noisy 0̶ᴡ /ˈnɔɪzi/ *adjective* (**noisier**, **noisiest**)
making a lot of noise; full of noise ➲ OPPOSITE **quiet**: *The children are very noisy.* ◇ *The restaurant was too noisy.*
▶ **noisily** /ˈnɔɪzɪli/ *adverb*: *He ate his dinner noisily.*

nomad /ˈnəʊmæd/ *noun*
a member of a group of people that moves with its animals from place to place
▶ **nomadic** /nəʊˈmædɪk/ *adjective*: *nomadic tribes*

non- /nɒn/ *prefix*
You can add **non-** to the beginning of some words to give them the opposite meaning, for example: *non-alcoholic* drinks (= drinks containing no alcohol) ◇ *a non-smoker* (= a person who does not smoke)

A

◇ *This train is non-stop* (= does not stop before the end of the journey).

B

none 0̶ₘ /nʌn/ *pronoun*

C

not any; not one: *She has eaten all the chocolates – there are none in the box.* ◇ *I went to four shops, but none of them had the book I wanted.*

D

E

nonsense 0̶ₘ /'nɒnsns/ *noun* (*no plural*)
words or ideas that have no meaning or that are not true: *It's nonsense to say that Jackie is lazy.*

F

noodles /'nu:dlz/ *noun* (*plural*)

G

long thin lines of food made from flour, eggs and water (called pasta), which are used especially in Chinese and Italian cooking: *Would you prefer rice or noodles?* ➔ Look at Picture Dictionary page **P6**.

H

I

noon /nu:n/ *noun* (*no plural*)
twelve o'clock in the middle of the day ➔ SAME MEANING **midday**: *I met him at noon.*

J

K

no one 0̶ₘ /'nəʊ wʌn/ *pronoun*
no person; not anybody ➔ SAME MEANING **nobody**: *There was no one in the classroom.* ◇ *No one saw me go into the house.*

L

M

nor 0̶ₘ /nɔː(r)/ *conjunction*
used after 'neither' and 'not' to mean 'also not': *If Alan doesn't go, nor will Lucy.* ◇ *'I don't like eggs.' 'Nor do I.'* ◇ *Neither Tom nor I eat meat.*

N

O

normal 0̶ₘ /'nɔːml/ *adjective*
usual and ordinary; not different or special: *I will be home at the normal time.*

P

Q

normally 0̶ₘ /'nɔːməli/ *adverb*
1 usually: *I normally go to bed at about eleven o'clock.*
2 in the usual or ordinary way: *He isn't behaving normally.*

R

S

north 0̶ₘ /nɔːθ/ *noun* (*no plural*) (*abbr.* N)
the direction to your left when you watch the sun rise; a place in this direction: *the north of England* ➔ Look at the picture at **compass**.
▶ **north** *adjective, adverb*: *They live in North London.* ◇ *a north wind* (= that comes from the north) ◇ *We travelled north from London to Scotland.*

T

U

V

W

north-east /ˌnɔːθ 'iːst/ *noun* (*no plural*) (*abbr.* NE)
the direction between north and east; a place in this direction: *He lives in the north-east.* ➔ Look at the picture at **compass**.
▶ **north-east** *adjective, adverb*: *north-east Scotland*

X

Y

Z

▶ **north-eastern** /ˌnɔːθ 'iːstən/ *adjective*: *north-eastern regions*

northern 0̶ₘ /'nɔːðən/ *adjective*
connected with, in or from the north: *Newcastle is in northern England.*

the North Pole /ðə ˌnɔːð 'pəʊl/ *noun* (*no plural*)
the point on the Earth's surface which is furthest north ➔ Look at **the South Pole**. ➔ Look at the picture at **earth**.

north-west /ˌnɔːθ 'west/ *noun* (*no plural*)
the direction between north and west; a place in this direction: *She's from the north-west.* ➔ Look at the picture at **compass**.
▶ **north-west** *adjective, adverb*: *north-west London*
▶ **north-western** /ˌnɔːθ 'westən/ *adjective*: *north-western France*

nose 0̶ₘ /nəʊz/ *noun*
1 the part of your face, above your mouth, that you use for breathing and smelling: *Blow your nose!* (= Clear your nose by blowing through it.) ➔ Look at Picture Dictionary page **P4**.
2 the front part of a plane

nostril /'nɒstrəl/ *noun*
one of the two holes in your nose ➔ Look at Picture Dictionary page **P4**.

nosy /'nəʊzi/ *adjective* (**nosier, nosiest**)
too interested in other people's lives, in a way which is annoying: *'Where are you going?' 'Don't be so nosy!'*

not 0̶ₘ /nɒt/ *adverb*
used for forming negative sentences or phrases: *I'm not hungry.* ◇ *They did not arrive.* ◇ *I can come tomorrow, but not on Tuesday.* ◇ *'Are you angry with me?' 'No, I'm not.'*

> 🔎 GRAMMAR
> We often say and write **n't**: *John isn't* (= is not) *here.* ◇ *I haven't* (= have not) *got any sisters.*

not at all
1 used as a reply when somebody has thanked you for something: *'Thanks for your help.' 'Oh, not at all.'*
2 no; not a little bit: *'Are you tired?' 'Not at all.'*

note¹ 0̶ₘ /nəʊt/ *noun*
1 words that you write quickly to help you remember something: *I made a note of her address.* ◇ *The teacher told us to take notes.*
2 a short letter: *Dave sent me a note to thank me for the present.*
3 (*British*) (*American* **bill**) a piece of paper money: *He gave me a $20 note.* ➔ Look at the picture at **money**.

4 a short piece of extra information about something in a book: *Look at the note on page 39.*
5 one sound in music; the written symbol for one sound: *I can play a few notes.* ◇ *What's this note?*

note² 0̅̅̅ /nəʊt/ *verb* (notes, noting, noted)
to notice and remember something: *Please note that all the shops are closed on Mondays.*
note something down to write something so that you can remember it: *The police officer noted down my name and address.*

notebook /'nəʊtbʊk/ *noun*
1 a small book that you can write in
2 a very small computer that you can carry with you and use anywhere

notepad /'nəʊtpæd/ *noun*
pieces of paper that you can write on, joined together in a block

notepaper /'nəʊtpeɪpə(r)/ *noun* (*no plural*)
paper that you write letters on

nothing 0̅̅̅ /'nʌθɪŋ/ *pronoun*
not anything; no thing: *There's nothing in this bottle – it's empty.* ◇ *I've finished all my work and I've got nothing to do.* ◇ *Don't leave the baby there with nothing on* (= not wearing any clothes) *– he'll get cold.*
be or **have nothing to do with somebody** or **something** to have no connection with somebody or something: *That question has nothing to do with what we're discussing.* ◇ *Keep out of this – it's nothing to do with you.*
for nothing
1 for no money ◐ SAME MEANING **free**: *You can have these books for nothing. I don't want them.*
2 without a good result: *I went to the station for nothing – she wasn't on the train.*
nothing but only: *He eats nothing but salad.*
nothing like not the same as somebody or something in any way: *He's nothing like his brother.*

notice¹ 0̅̅̅ /'nəʊtɪs/ *noun*
1 (*plural* **notices**) a piece of writing that tells people something: *The notice on the wall says 'NO SMOKING'.*
2 (*no plural*) a warning that something will happen; the amount of time before it happens: *We only had two weeks' notice of the exam.* ◇ *We left for Scotland at very short notice and I forgot my coat.* ◇ *He's handed in his notice* (= he has said officially that he will leave his job).

take no notice to not pay attention to something ◐ SAME MEANING **ignore**: *Take no notice of what she said.*

notice² 0̅̅̅ /'nəʊtɪs/ *verb* (notices, noticing, noticed /'nəʊtɪst/)
to see or pay attention to somebody or something: *Did you notice what she was wearing?* ◇ *I noticed that he was driving a new car.*

noticeable /'nəʊtɪsəbl/ *adjective*
easy to see: *I've got a mark on my shirt. Is it noticeable?*

noticeboard /'nəʊtɪsbɔːd/ (*British*) (*American* **bulletin board**) *noun*
a board on a wall for information: *The teacher put the exam results on the noticeboard.*

notorious /nəʊ'tɔːriəs/ *adjective*
well known for being bad: *a notorious criminal*
▸ **notoriously** *adverb*: *This road is notoriously dangerous.*

nought /nɔːt/ *noun*
the number 0: *We say 0.5 as 'nought point five'.*

noun /naʊn/ *noun*
(*grammar*) a word that is the name of a person, place, thing or idea: *'Anne', 'London', 'cat' and 'happiness' are all nouns.*

novel¹ 0̅̅̅ /'nɒvl/ *noun*
a book that tells a story about people and things that are not real: *'David Copperfield' is a novel by Charles Dickens.*

novel² /'nɒvl/ *adjective*
new, different and interesting: *a novel idea*

novelist /'nɒvəlɪst/ *noun*
a person who writes novels

November 0̅̅̅ /nəʊ'vembə(r)/ *noun*
the eleventh month of the year

now¹ 0̅̅̅ /naʊ/ *adverb*
1 at this time: *I can't see you now – can you come back later?* ◇ *She was in Paris but she's living in Rome now.* ◇ *Don't wait – do it now!* ◇ *From now on* (= after this time) *your teacher will be Mr Hancock.*
2 used when you start to talk about something new, or to make people listen to you: *I've finished writing this letter. Now, what shall we have for dinner?* ◇ *Be quiet, now!*
now and again, now and then sometimes, but not often: *We go to the cinema now and again.*

now² /naʊ/ (*also* **now that**) *conjunction*
because something has happened: *Now that Mark has arrived we can start dinner.*

A
B
C
D
E
F
G
H
I
J
K
L
M
N
O
P
Q
R
S
T
U
V
W
X
Y
Z

nowadays /ˈnaʊədeɪz/ *adverb*
at this time: *A lot of people work with computers nowadays.*

nowhere 0-ᴴ /ˈnəʊweə(r)/ *adverb*
not anywhere; at, in or to no place: *There's nowhere to stay in this village.*
nowhere near not at all: *Ruichi's English is nowhere near as good as yours.*

nuclear 0-ᴴ /ˈnjuːklɪə(r)/ *adjective*
1 using the energy that is made when the central part of an ATOM (= one of the very small things that everything is made of) is broken: *nuclear energy* ◇ *nuclear weapons*
2 connected with the centre of ATOMS (= one of the very small things that everything is made of): *nuclear physics*

nucleus /ˈnjuːklɪəs/ (*plural* nuclei /ˈnjuːklɪaɪ/) *noun*
the centre of a cell or an ATOM (= one of the very small things that everything is made of)

nude /njuːd/ *adjective*
not wearing any clothes ➔ SAME MEANING **naked**

nudge /nʌdʒ/ *verb* (nudges, nudging, nudged /nʌdʒd/)
to touch or push somebody or something with your elbow (= the pointed part where your arm bends): *Nudge me if I fall asleep in the film.*
▸ **nudge** *noun: Liz gave me a nudge.*

nuisance /ˈnjuːsns/ *noun*
a person or thing that causes you trouble: *I've lost my keys. What a nuisance!*

numb /nʌm/ *adjective*
not able to feel anything: *My fingers were numb with cold.*

number¹ 0-ᴴ /ˈnʌmbə(r)/ *noun*
1 (*abbr.* No. or no.) a word or symbol that represents a quantity, for example 'two' or '130': *Choose a number between ten and one hundred.* ◇ *My phone number is Oxford 56767.* ◇ *I live at no. 47.*
2 a group of more than one person or thing: *A large number of our students come from Japan.* ◇ *There are a number of ways you can cook an egg.*

number² /ˈnʌmbə(r)/ *verb* (numbers, numbering, numbered /ˈnʌmbəd/)
to give a number to something: *Number the pages from one to ten.*

number plate /ˈnʌmbə pleɪt/ (*British*) (*American* license plate) *noun*
the flat piece of metal on the front and back of a car that has numbers and letters on it (its **registration number**) ➔ Look at Picture Dictionary page **P1**.

numerous /ˈnjuːmərəs/ *adjective* (*formal*)
many

nun /nʌn/ *noun*
a woman who has given her life to God instead of getting married. Most **nuns** live together in a special building (called a convent). ➔ Look at **monk**.

nurse¹ 0-ᴴ /nɜːs/ *noun*
a person whose job is to look after people who are sick or hurt: *My sister works as a nurse in a hospital.* ➔ Look at Picture Dictionary page **P12**.

nurse² /nɜːs/ *verb* (nurses, nursing, nursed /nɜːst/)
to look after somebody who is sick or hurt: *I nursed my father when he was ill.*

nursery /ˈnɜːsəri/ *noun* (*plural* nurseries)
1 a place where small children and babies can stay when their parents are at work
2 a place where people grow and sell plants

nursery rhyme /ˈnɜːsəri raɪm/ *noun*
a song or poem for young children

nursery school /ˈnɜːsəri skuːl/ *noun*
a school for children between the ages of about two and five

nursing /ˈnɜːsɪŋ/ *noun* (*no plural*)
the job of being a nurse: *He has decided to go into nursing when he leaves school.*

nuts

almond   walnut

shell

peanut   hazelnut

nut 0-ᴴ /nʌt/ *noun*
1 a dry fruit that has a hard outside part with a seed inside. Many types of **nut** can be eaten: *walnuts, hazelnuts and peanuts*
2 a metal ring that you put on the end of a long piece of metal (called a **bolt**) to fix things together ➔ Look at the picture at **bolt** (sense 2).

nutritious /njuˈtrɪʃəs/ *adjective*
(used about food) good for you: *tasty and nutritious meals*

nylon /ˈnaɪlɒn/ *noun* (*no plural*)
very strong material that is made by machines and is used for making clothes, rope, brushes and other things: *a nylon fishing line*

O o

O, o[1] /əʊ/ *noun* (*plural* O's, o's /əʊz/)
the fifteenth letter of the English alphabet: '*Orange*' *begins with an* '*O*'.

O[2] /əʊ/ *exclamation, noun*
1 = OH
2 a way of saying the number '0'

oak /əʊk/ *noun*
1 (*plural* oaks) a kind of large tree
2 (*no plural*) the wood of an **oak** tree: *an oak table*

OAP /ˌəʊ eɪ 'piː/ (*British*) *short for* OLD-AGE PENSIONER

oar /ɔː(r)/ *noun*
a long stick with a flat end that you use for moving a boat through water (called **rowing**) ⊃ Look at the picture at **rowing**.

oasis /əʊ'eɪsɪs/ *noun* (*plural* oases /əʊ'eɪsiːz/)
a place in a desert with that has trees and water

oath /əʊθ/ *noun*
a formal promise: *He swore an* **oath** *of loyalty.*

oats /əʊts/ *noun* (*plural*)
a plant with seeds that we use as food for people and animals: *We make porridge from oats.*

obedient /ə'biːdiənt/ *adjective*
doing what somebody tells you to do: *He was an obedient child.*
⊃ OPPOSITE **disobedient**
▶ **obedience** /ə'biːdiəns/ *noun* (*no plural*): *Teachers expect complete obedience from their pupils.*
▶ **obediently** /ə'biːdiəntli/ *adverb*: *I called the dog and it followed me obediently.*

obese /əʊ'biːs/ *adjective*
(used about people) very fat, in a way that is not healthy

obey /ə'beɪ/ *verb* (obeys, obeying, obeyed /ə'beɪd/)
to do what somebody tells you to do; to follow an order or rule: *He always obeyed his parents.* ◇ *You must obey the law.*

object[1] 0-ᴙ /'ɒbdʒɪkt/ *noun*

> 🔎 PRONUNCIATION
> When the word **object** is a noun, you say the first part of the word louder: **OB**ject. When the word **object** is a verb, you say the second part of the word louder: ob**JECT**.

1 a thing that you can see and touch: *There was a small round object on the table.*
2 what you plan to do ⊃ SAME MEANING **aim**: *His object in life is to become as rich as possible.*
3 (*grammar*) the person or thing that is affected by an action. In the sentence '*Jane painted the door*', the **object** of the sentence is '*the door*'.

object[2] /əb'dʒekt/ *verb* (objects, objecting, objected)
to not like something; to not agree with something: *I objected to their plan.*

objection /əb'dʒekʃn/ *noun*
a reason why you do not like something or do not agree with something: *I have no objections to the plan.*

objective /əb'dʒektɪv/ *noun*
something that you are trying to achieve ⊃ SAME MEANING **aim**

obligation /ˌɒblɪ'geɪʃn/ *noun*
something that you must do: *We have an obligation to help.*

obligatory /ə'blɪɡətri/ *adjective* (*formal*)
If something is **obligatory**, you must do it because it is the law or a rule.
⊃ SAME MEANING **compulsory**

oblige /ə'blaɪdʒ/ *noun* (obliges, obliging, obliged /ə'blaɪdʒd/)
to force somebody to do something: *The law obliges parents to send their children to school.*

obliged /ə'blaɪdʒd/ *adjective*
forced to do something; feeling that you must do something: *We felt obliged to offer our help.*

oblivious /ə'blɪviəs/ *adjective*
not noticing or realizing something: *She was completely oblivious of all the trouble she had caused.*

oblong /'ɒblɒŋ/ *noun*
a shape with two long sides, two short sides and four angles of 90° ⊃ SAME MEANING **rectangle**
▶ **oblong** *adjective*: *This page is oblong.*

obnoxious /əb'nɒkʃəs/ *adjective*
extremely unpleasant: *He really is an obnoxious person.*

observant /əb'zɜːvənt/ *adjective*
good at noticing things: *That's very observant of you!*

A

observation /ˌɒbzə'veɪʃn/ *noun* (*no plural*)
when you watch somebody or something carefully: *The police kept the house* **under observation**. ◇ *His powers of observation are excellent.*

observe /əb'zɜːv/ *verb* (**observes, observing, observed** /əb'zɜːvd/) (*formal*)
to watch or see somebody or something: *The police observed a man leaving the house.*

obsess /əb'ses/ *verb* (**obsesses, obsessing, obsessed** /əb'sest/)
to completely fill your mind: *Debbie is* **obsessed with** *football.*

obsession /əb'seʃn/ *noun*
a person or thing that you think about all the time: *Cars are his obsession.*

obstacle /'ɒbstəkl/ *noun*
something that makes it difficult for you to do something or go somewhere: *Not speaking a foreign language was a major* **obstacle to** *her career.*

obstinate /'ɒbstɪnət/ *adjective*
not changing your ideas; not doing what other people want you to do
⊃ SAME MEANING **stubborn**: *He's too obstinate to say he's sorry.*

obstruct /əb'strʌkt/ *verb* (**obstructs, obstructing, obstructed**)
to be in the way so that somebody or something cannot go past: *Please move your car – you're obstructing the traffic.*
▶ **obstruction** /əb'strʌkʃn/ *noun* a thing that stops somebody or something from going past: *The train had to stop because there was an obstruction on the line.*

obtain 0ᴟ /əb'teɪn/ *verb* (**obtains, obtaining, obtained** /əb'teɪnd/) (*formal*)
to get something: *Where can I obtain tickets for the play?*

obtuse angle /əbˌtjuːs 'æŋgl/ *noun*
an angle between 90° and 180° ⊃ Look at **acute angle** and **right angle**.

obvious 0ᴟ /'ɒbviəs/ *adjective*
easy to see or understand ⊃ SAME MEANING **clear**: *It's obvious that she's not happy.*
▶ **obviously** /'ɒbviəsli/ *adverb*: *There has obviously been a mistake.*

occasion 0ᴟ /ə'keɪʒn/ *noun*
1 a time when something happens: *I've been to Paris* **on** *three or four* **occasions**.
2 a special time: *A wedding is a big family occasion.*

occasional /ə'keɪʒənl/ *adjective*
happening sometimes, but not very often: *We get the occasional visitor.*

occasionally /ə'keɪʒnəli/ *adverb*
sometimes, but not often: *I go to London occasionally.*

occupation /ˌɒkju'peɪʃn/ *noun*
1 (*plural* **occupations**) (*formal*) a job: *What is your mother's occupation?*
2 (*plural* **occupations**) something that you do in your free time: *Fishing is his favourite occupation.*
3 (*no plural*) when a country or army takes or has control of an area or building: *the Roman occupation of Britain*
4 (*no plural*) (*formal*) the fact of living in a house, room, etc.: *The new house is now ready for occupation.*

occupy /'ɒkjupaɪ/ *verb* (**occupies, occupying, occupied** /'ɒkjupaɪd/, has **occupied**)
1 to fill a space or period of time
⊃ SAME MEANING **take up**: *The bed seemed to occupy most of the room.*
2 to keep somebody busy: *She occupied herself reading.*
3 (*formal*) to live or work in a room or building: *Who occupies these offices?*
4 to take or have control of an area or building: *Protestors occupied the TV station.*
▶ **occupied** /'ɒkjupaɪd/ *adjective*
1 busy: *This work will keep me occupied all week.*
2 being used: *Excuse me – is this seat occupied?*

occur 0ᴟ /ə'kɜː(r)/ *verb* (**occurs, occurring, occurred** /ə'kɜːd/) (*formal*)
to happen: *The accident occurred this morning.*
occur to somebody to come into somebody's mind: *It occurred to me that you might like to come.*

ocean 0ᴟ /'əʊʃn/ *noun*
a very big sea: *the Atlantic Ocean*

o'clock 0ᴟ /ə'klɒk/ *adverb*
used after the numbers one to twelve for saying the time: *I left home at four o'clock and arrived in London at half past five.*

> 🔎 GRAMMAR
> Be careful! **O'clock** is only used with full hours. You cannot say 'at half past five o'clock').

octagon /'ɒktəgən/ *noun*
a shape with eight straight sides
▶ **octagonal** /ɒk'tægənl/ *adjective*: *an octagonal coin*

October 0ᴟ /ɒk'təʊbə(r)/ *noun*
the tenth month of the year

octopus

/'ɒktəpəs/ *noun*
(*plural* octopuses)
a sea animal with
eight arms

octopus

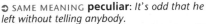

tentacle

odd 0━ /ɒd/

adjective (odder,
oddest)
1 strange or
unusual
⊃ SAME MEANING **peculiar**: *It's odd that he
left without telling anybody.*
2 not able to be divided by two: *1, 3, 5 and 7
are all **odd numbers**.* ⊃ OPPOSITE **even**
3 not with the pair or set it belongs to; not
matching: *You're wearing **odd socks!***
the odd one out one that is different from
all the others: *'Apple', 'orange', 'cabbage' –
which is the odd one out?*

oddly /'ɒdli/ *adverb*

in a strange or unusual way: *She behaved very
oddly.*

odds /ɒdz/ *noun*

the odds used for saying how likely
something is: *The **odds are that** he'll win
(= he'll probably win).* ◇ *The **odds are against**
us (= we will probably not succeed).*

odds and ends /ˌɒdz ənd 'endz/ *noun*

(*plural*) (*British, informal*)
different small things that are not important:
a box of odds and ends

of 0━ /əv; ɒv/ *preposition*

1 belonging to or connected with
somebody or something: *the back of the chair*
◇ *What's the name of this mountain?* ◇ *the
plays of Shakespeare* ◇ *the arrival of the
president*
2 used after an amount, etc.: *a litre of water*
◇ *the fourth of July*
3 used for saying what something is or what
something is made of: *a piece of wood* ◇ *a cup
of tea* ◇ *Is this shirt made of cotton?*
4 used for giving your opinion about
somebody's behaviour: *That's very kind of
you.*
5 used for showing that somebody or
something is part of a group: ***one of** the girls*
◇ ***some of** his friends*
6 used with some adjectives and verbs: *I'm
proud of you.* ◇ *This perfume smells of roses.*

off¹ 0━ /ɒf/ *preposition, adverb*

1 away from a place; at a distance in space
or time: *My birthday is not far off.* ◇ *I must be
off soon (= leave).*
2 down or away from something: *He fell off
the roof.* ◇ *We got off the bus.* ◇ *The thief ran
off.*
3 used for talking about removing

something: *If you're hot, take your coat off.* ◇
Can you clean that paint off the carpet?
⊃ OPPOSITE **on**
4 not connected; not working: *Make sure the
lights are off before you go.* ⊃ OPPOSITE **on**
5 not at work or school: *I had the day off
yesterday.*
6 joined to something and leading from it:
The bathroom is off the bedroom.

off² 0━ /ɒf/ *adjective*

not fresh enough to eat or drink: *The milk's
off.*

offence 0━ (*British*) (*American* offense)

/ə'fens/ *noun*
1 (*plural* offences) an illegal action
⊃ SAME MEANING **crime**: *He has **committed**
an **offence**.*
2 (*no plural*) when a person is angry or
unhappy because of what somebody has
said or done: *He **took offence** when I refused
his help.*

offend /ə'fend/ *verb* (offends, offending,

offended)
to make somebody feel angry or unhappy;
to hurt somebody's feelings: *I hope they
won't be offended if I don't come.*

offense *American English for* OFFENCE

offensive /ə'fensɪv/ *adjective*

rude in a way that makes somebody feel
upset, angry or insulted: *offensive language*

offer¹ 0━ /'ɒfə(r)/ *verb* (offers, offering,

offered /'ɒfəd/)
to say or show that you will give or give
something if another person wants it: *She
offered me a cake.* ◇ *I **offered to** help her.*

offer² 0━ /'ɒfə(r)/ *noun*

1 when you offer to do or give something if
another person wants it: *Thanks for the offer,
but I don't need any help.*
2 an amount of money that you say you will
give for something: *They've **made an offer for**
the house.*
on offer
1 for sale or available: *The college has a wide
range of courses on offer.*
2 (*British*) for sale at a lower price than usual
for a certain time

office 0━ /'ɒfɪs/ *noun*

1 a place where people work, usually at
desks: *I work in an office*
2 a place where you can buy something or
get information ⊃ Look at **post office** and
ticket office.
3 Office one part of the government: *the
Foreign Office*

A
B
C
D
E
F
G
H
I
J
K
L
M
N
O
P
Q
R
S
T
U
V
W
X
Y
Z

officer 0— /'ɒfɪsə(r)/ noun

1 a person in the army, navy or air force who gives orders to other people: *a naval officer*
2 a person who does important work, especially for the government: *a prison officer* ◊ *police officers*

official¹ 0— /ə'fɪʃl/ adjective

connected with government or with a particular organization or a person in authority: *an official government report* ◊ *an official announcement*
▶ **officially** /ə'fɪʃəli/ **adverb**: *He has now heard officially that he's got the job.*

official² /ə'fɪʃl/ noun

a person who does important work, especially for the government: *government officials*

off-licence /'ɒf laɪsns/ (British) (American liquor store) noun

a shop where you can buy drinks like beer and wine

often 0— /'ɒfn/ adverb

many times: *We often play football on Sundays.* ◊ *I've often seen her on the train.* ◊ *I don't write to him very often.* ◊ **How often** *do you visit her?*
every so often sometimes, but not often: *Every so often she phones me.*

oh 0— /əʊ/ exclamation

1 used for showing a strong feeling, like surprise or fear: *Oh no! I've lost my keys!*
2 used before other words, for example when you are thinking what to say: '*What time is it?*' '*Oh, about two o'clock.*'
Oh dear used for showing that you are surprised or unhappy: *Oh dear – have you hurt yourself?*
Oh well used when you are not happy about something, but you cannot change it: '*I'm too busy to go out tonight.*' '*Oh well, I'll see you tomorrow then.*'

oil 0— /ɔɪl/ noun (no plural)

1 a thick liquid that comes from under the ground or the sea. We use **oil** for energy and to make machines work smoothly.
2 a thick liquid that comes from plants or animals and that we use in cooking: *Fry the onions in oil.*

oil painting /'ɔɪl peɪntɪŋ/ noun

a picture that has been done with paint made from oil

oil rig /'ɔɪl rɪg/ noun

a special building or a platform with machines that dig for oil under the sea or on land

oil slick /'ɔɪl slɪk/ noun

a large amount of oil on the sea after an accident

oil well /'ɔɪl wel/ noun

a hole that is made deep in the ground or under the sea in order to get oil

oily /'ɔɪli/ adjective (oilier, oiliest)

like oil or covered with oil: *an oily liquid* ◊ *oily hands*

ointment /'ɔɪntmənt/ noun

a smooth substance that you put on sore skin or on an injury to help it get better

OK¹ 0— (also okay) /əʊ'keɪ/ exclamation (informal)

yes ⊃ SAME MEANING **all right**: '*Shall we go to the party?*' '*OK.*'

OK² 0— (also okay) /əʊ'keɪ/ adjective, adverb (informal)

1 safe and well; calm or happy
⊃ SAME MEANING **all right**: '*How's your mum?*' '*OK, thanks.*'
2 all right; acceptable: *Is it okay to sit here?*

old 0— /əʊld/ adjective (older, oldest)

1 having lived for a long time: *My grandfather is very old.* ◊ *My sister is older than me.* ⊃ OPPOSITE **young**
2 made or bought a long time ago: *an old house* ⊃ OPPOSITE **new**
3 You use **old** to show the age of somebody or something: *He's nine years old.* ◊ *How old are you?* ◊ *a six-year-old boy*
4 done or had before now: *My old job was more interesting than this one.*
⊃ OPPOSITE **new**
5 known for a long time: *Jane is an old friend – we were at school together.*
▶ **the old noun** (*plural*) old people

old age /,əʊld 'eɪdʒ/ noun (no plural)

the part of your life when you are old: *He's enjoying life in his old age.*
⊃ OPPOSITE **youth**

old-age pension /,əʊld eɪdʒ 'penʃn/ noun (no plural)

money that you get from a government or a company when you are old and do not work any more (when you are **retired**)
▶ **old-age pensioner** /,əʊld eɪdʒ 'penʃənə(r)/ **noun** (*abbr.* **OAP**) a person who has an OLD-AGE PENSION

old-fashioned 0— /,əʊld 'fæʃnd/ adjective

not modern ⊃ OPPOSITE **fashionable**: *old-fashioned clothes* ◊ *My parents are rather old-fashioned.*

olive /'ɒlɪv/ noun

a small green or black fruit, that people eat

or make into oil ⊃ Look at Picture Dictionary page **P6**.

olive oil /ˌɒlɪv ˈɔɪl/ *noun* (*no plural*)
oil that is produced from OLIVES: *Fry the onions in a little olive oil.* ⊃ Look at Picture Dictionary page **P6**.

the Olympic Games /ði əˌlɪmpɪk ˈɡeɪmz/ (*also* **the Olympics** /ði əˈlɪmpɪks/) *noun* (*plural*)
an international sports competition that is organized every four years in a different country

omelette /ˈɒmlət/ *noun*
a dish made of eggs mixed together and then fried: *a cheese omelette*

omit /əˈmɪt/ *verb* (omits, omitting, omitted) (*formal*)
to not include something ⊃ SAME MEANING **leave out**: *Omit question 2 and do question 3.*

on 0̶̅ᴡ /ɒn/ *preposition, adverb*
1 used for showing where something is: *Your book is on the table.* ◇ *The number is on the door.* ◇ *There is a good film on TV tonight.* ◇ *I've got a cut on my hand.*
2 used for showing when: *My birthday is on 6 May.* ◇ *I'll see you on Monday.* ⊃ Look at Study Page **S8**.
3 used with ways of travelling and types of travel: *He got on the train.* ◇ *I came here on foot* (= walking).
4 used for showing that somebody or something continues: *You can't stop here – drive on.*
5 working; being used: *All the lights were on.* ⊃ OPPOSITE **off**
6 using something: *I bought it on the Internet.* ◇ *I was on the phone to Jania.* ◇ *He saw it on TV.*
7 about: *a book on cars*
8 covering your body: *Put your coat on.*
9 happening: *What's on at the cinema?*
10 when something happens: *She telephoned me on her return from New York.*
on and on without stopping: *He went* (= talked) *on and on about his girlfriend.*

once¹ 0̶̅ᴡ /wʌns/ *adverb*
1 one time: *I've only been to Spain once.* ◇ *He phones us once a week* (= once every week).
2 at some time in the past: *This house was once a school.*
at once
1 immediately ⊃ SAME MEANING **now**: *Come here at once!*
2 at the same time: *I can't do two things at once!*
for once this time only: *For once I agree with you.*

once again, **once more** again; one more time: *Can you explain it to me once more?*
once or twice a few times; not often: *I've only met them once or twice.*
once upon a time (used at the beginning of a children's story) a long time ago: *Once upon a time there was a beautiful princess …*

once² /wʌns/ *conjunction*
as soon as; when: *Once you've finished your homework you can go out.*

one¹ 0̶̅ᴡ /wʌn/ *number, adjective*
1 the number 1: *One and one make two* (*1 + 1 = 2*). ◇ *Only one person spoke.*
2 a person or thing, especially when they are part of a group: *One of my friends is ill.* ◇ *I've lost one of my books.*
3 only: *You are the one person I can trust.*
4 used for talking about a particular time, without saying exactly when: *I'll come over one evening.*
one by one first one, then the next, etc.; separately: *Please come in one by one.*

one² 0̶̅ᴡ /wʌn/ *pronoun*
1 used instead of the name of a person or thing: *I've got some bananas. Do you want one?* ◇ *'Can I borrow a book?' 'Yes. Which one?'* ◇ *The questions are hard – leave the ones you can't do.*
2 (*formal*) people in general; I: *One feels quite helpless.*

🔎 SPEAKING
It is very formal to use **one** in this way and it sounds rather old-fashioned.
We usually say 'you' for 'people in general' and 'I' when you are talking about yourself.

one another 0̶̅ᴡ /ˌwʌn əˈnʌðə(r)/ *pronoun*
each other: *We looked at one another.*

oneself /wʌnˈself/ *pronoun* (*formal*)
used with 'one' for saying that an action involves the person doing it: *One has to ask oneself if such action is necessary.*
by oneself
1 alone; without other people
2 without help

one-way /ˌwʌn ˈweɪ/ *adjective*
allowing travel in one direction only: *a one-way street* ◇ *a one-way ticket*

onion 0̶̅ᴡ /ˈʌnjən/ *noun*
a round vegetable with many layers and a strong smell. Cutting **onions** can make you cry. ⊃ Look at Picture Dictionary page **P9**.

online /ˌɒnˈlaɪn/ *adjective, adverb*
using a computer or the Internet: *Online*

A B C D E F G H I J K L M N **O** P Q R S T U V W X Y Z

shopping is both cheap and convenient. ◇ Bookings can be made online.

only¹ 0⇝ /ˈəʊnli/ *adjective*
with no others: *She's the only girl in her class.*

only² 0⇝ /ˈəʊnli/ *adverb*
and nobody or nothing else; no more than: *I invited twenty people to the party, but only five came.* ◇ *We can't have dinner now. It's only four o'clock!* ◇ *We only waited five minutes.*
only just
1 not long ago: *We've only just arrived.*
2 almost not: *We only just had enough money to pay for the meal.*

only³ /ˈəʊnli/ *conjunction* (*informal*)
but: *I like this bag, only it's too expensive.*

only child /ˌəʊnli ˈtʃaɪld/ *noun* (*plural* only children)
a child who has no brothers or sisters: *I'm an only child.*

onto 0⇝ (*also* on to) /ˈɒntə; ˈɒntu/ *preposition*
to a place on somebody or something: *The bottle fell onto the floor.* ◇ *The cat jumped onto the table.*

onwards /ˈɒnwədz/ (*also* onward /ˈɒnwəd/) *adverb*
1 and after: *I shall be at home from eight o'clock onwards.*
2 forward; further: *The soldiers marched onwards until they came to a bridge.*

oops /ʊps/ *exclamation*
a word you say when something has gone wrong, for example when somebody has fallen over or has dropped something: *Oops! Are you ok?*

ooze /uːz/ *verb* (oozes, oozing, oozed)
1 If a thick liquid **oozes** from something, it comes out slowly: *Blood was oozing from the wound.*
2 to show a lot of a particular quality: *She walked into the party oozing confidence.*

open¹ 0⇝ /ˈəʊpən/ *adjective*
1 not closed, so that people or things can go in or out: *Leave the windows open.* ◇ *The book lay open on the table.* ◇ *an open box*
2 able to be used or done; available: *The bank is open from 9 a.m. to 4 p.m.* ◇ *The competition is open to all children under the age of 14.*
3 not hiding your thoughts and feelings: *She's a very open person.*
4 away from towns and people; with not many buildings or trees: *We were in open country.*
5 not yet decided: *'Where shall we go on Friday?' 'Let's leave it open.'*

in the open air outside: *We had our lunch in the open air.*

open² 0⇝ /ˈəʊpən/ *verb* (opens, opening, opened /ˈəʊpənd/)
1 to move, or to move something, so that something is not closed or covered: *The door opened and a man came in.* ◇ *It was hot, so I opened a window.* ◇ *Open your eyes!* ◇ *Open your books at page 10.*
2 to make it possible for people to enter a place: *Banks don't open on Sundays.* ◇ *The President opened the new hospital.*
3 to start something; to start: *I'd like to open a bank account.* ◇ *How do you open a file in this program?* ◇ *The story opens with a murder.* ⊅ **close** or **shut**

open³ /ˈəʊpən/ *noun* (*no plural*)
out in the open outside; in the countryside: *Children need to play out in the open.*
into the open not hidden or secret: *They intend to bring their complaints out into the open.*

open-air /ˌəʊpən ˈeə(r)/ *adjective*
outside: *an open-air concert*

opener /ˈəʊpnə(r)/ *noun*
a small tool that you use for opening tins or bottles: *a tin-opener*

opening /ˈəʊpnɪŋ/ *noun*
1 a space in something where people or things can go in and out ⊃ SAME MEANING **hole**: *The cattle got out through an opening in the fence.*
2 a ceremony to celebrate the start of a public event or the first time a new building, road, etc. is used: *the opening of the Olympic Games*

openly /ˈəʊpənli/ *adverb*
not secretly; without trying to hide anything: *She told me openly that she didn't agree.*

opera /ˈɒprə/ *noun*
a play where the actors sing most of the words to music: *Do you like opera?* ◇ *We went to see an opera by Verdi.*

opera house /ˈɒprə haʊs/ *noun*
a building where you can see OPERAS

operate 0⇝ /ˈɒpəreɪt/ *verb* (operates, operating, operated)
1 to work; to make something work: *I don't know how this machine operates.* ◇ *These switches operate the heating.*
2 to cut into somebody's body to take out or repair a part inside: *Doctors will operate on her leg tomorrow.*

🔍 **WORD BUILDING**

A doctor who **operates** on people in hospital is called a **surgeon**. A surgeon's work is called **surgery**.

operation 0̶ⱳ /ˌɒpəˈreɪʃn/ *noun*
1 cutting into somebody's body to take out or repair a part inside: *He had an operation on his eye.*
2 an event that needs a lot of people or planning: *a military operation*

operator /ˈɒpəreɪtə(r)/ *noun*
1 a person who makes a machine work: *a machine operator*
2 a person who works for a telephone company and helps to connect people making calls: *What number do you dial for the operator?*
3 a person or company that runs a particular business: *a tour operator* ◇ *a bus operator*

opinion 0̶ⱳ /əˈpɪniən/ *noun*
what you think about something
⊃ SAME MEANING **view**: *In my opinion, she's wrong.* ◇ *What's your opinion of his work?* ◇ *He had strong opinions on everything.*

opponent /əˈpəʊnənt/ *noun*
the person against you in a fight or competition: *The first team beat their opponents easily.*

opportunity 0̶ⱳ /ˌɒpəˈtjuːnəti/ *noun*
(*plural* **opportunities**)
a chance to do something; a time when you can do something that you want to do: *I didn't get the opportunity to visit them.* ◇ *It was a golden (= perfect) opportunity and I decided to take it.*

oppose /əˈpəʊz/ *verb* (**opposes, opposing, opposed** /əˈpəʊzd/)
to try to stop or change something because you do not like it: *A lot of people opposed the new law.*

opposed /əˈpəʊzd/ *adjective*
disagreeing strongly with something and trying to stop it: *I am opposed to the plan.*
as opposed to (*formal*) words that you use to show that you are talking about one thing, not something different: *She teaches at the college, as opposed to the university.*

opposite¹ 0̶ⱳ /ˈɒpəzɪt/ *adjective, adverb, preposition*

🖉 **SPELLING**
Remember! You spell **opposite** with **PP**.

1 across from where somebody or something is; on the other side: *The church is on the opposite side of the road from my flat.* ◇ *You sit here, and I'll sit opposite.* ◇ *The bank is opposite the supermarket.*
2 as different as possible: *North is the opposite direction to south.*

opposite² 0̶ⱳ
/ˈɒpəzɪt/ *noun*
a word or thing that is as different as possible from another word or thing: *'Hot' is the opposite of 'cold'.*

opposite

They're sitting **opposite** each other.

opposition /ˌɒpəˈzɪʃn/ *noun* (*no plural*)
disagreeing with something and trying to stop it: *There was a lot of opposition to the plan.*

opt /ɒpt/ *verb* (**opts, opting, opted**)
to choose to do something: *She opted for a career in medicine.*

optician /ɒpˈtɪʃn/ *noun*
1 a person who examines your eyes to find out how well you can see and who sells glasses
2 **optician's** the shop where an **optician** works and where you can buy glasses ⊃ Look at Picture Dictionary page **P13**.

optimism /ˈɒptɪmɪzəm/ *noun* (*no plural*)
the feeling that good things will happen
⊃ OPPOSITE **pessimism**

optimist /ˈɒptɪmɪst/ *noun*
a person who thinks that good things will happen ⊃ OPPOSITE **pessimist**

optimistic /ˌɒptɪˈmɪstɪk/ *adjective*
If you are **optimistic**, you think that good things will happen ⊃ OPPOSITE **pessimistic**: *I'm optimistic about winning.*

option /ˈɒpʃn/ *noun*
a thing that you can choose
⊃ SAME MEANING **choice**: *You have the option of studying full-time or part-time.*

optional /ˈɒpʃənl/ *adjective*
If something is **optional**, you can choose it or not choose it: *All students must learn English, but German is optional.*
⊃ OPPOSITE **compulsory**

or 0̶ⱳ /ɔː(r)/ *conjunction*
1 a word that joins possibilities: *Is it blue or green?* ◇ *Are you coming or not?* ◇ *You can have soup, salad or sandwiches.* ◇ *She hasn't phoned or written for weeks.*
2 if not ⊃ SAME MEANING **otherwise**: *Go now, or you'll be late.*

oral /ˈɔːrəl/ *adjective*
spoken; not written: *the oral exam*

A **orange¹** 0‑🔊 /ˈɒrɪndʒ/ *noun*
1 a round fruit with a colour between red
B   and yellow, and a thick skin: *orange juice*
    ➲ Look at Picture Dictionary page **P8**.
C   **2** a colour between red and yellow

orange² 0‑🔊 /ˈɒrɪndʒ/ *adjective*
D   with a colour that is between red and yellow:
    orange paint

E **orbit** /ˈɔːbɪt/ *noun*
    the path of a planet or an object that is
F   moving around another thing in space
    ▶ **orbit** *verb* (**orbits, orbiting, orbited**)
G   to move around something in space: *The*
    spacecraft is orbiting the moon.

H **orchard** /ˈɔːtʃəd/ *noun*
    a piece of land where fruit trees grow

I **orchestra** /ˈɔːkɪstrə/ *noun*
    a big group of people who play different
J   musical instruments together

ordeal /ɔːˈdiːl/ *noun*
K   a very bad or unpleasant thing that happens
    to somebody: *He was lost in the mountains for*
L   *a week without food or water – it was a terrible*
    ordeal.

M **order¹** 0‑🔊 /ˈɔːdə(r)/ *noun*
    1 (*no plural*) the way that you place people
N   or things together: *The names are in*
    ***alphabetical order**. ◇ List the jobs in order of*
    importance.
O   **2** (*no plural*) when everything is in the right
    place or everybody is doing the right thing:
    Our teacher likes order in the classroom. ◇ Are
P   *these papers in order* (= correct and tidy)?
    3 (*plural* **orders**) words that tell somebody
Q   to do something: *He **gave** the **order** for work*
    *to begin. ◇ Soldiers have to **obey** orders.*
R   **4** (*plural* **orders**) when you ask a company
    to send or supply goods to you: *I'd like to*
S   ***place** an **order** for some books.*
    5 (*plural* **orders**) when you ask for food or
    drink in a restaurant, bar, etc.: *The waiter*
T   ***took** our **order**.*
    in order to so that you can do something:
U   *We arrived early in order to buy our tickets.*
    out of order (used about a machine, etc.)
    not working: *I couldn't ring you – the phone*
V   *was out of order.*

W **order²** 0‑🔊 /ˈɔːdə(r)/ *verb* (**orders,**
    ordering, ordered /ˈɔːdəd/)
X   **1** to tell somebody that they must do
    something: *The student was ordered to leave*
Y   *the classroom.*
    2 to ask a company to send or supply goods
    to you: *The shop didn't have your book – I*
Z   *ordered it.*
    3 to ask for food or drink in a restaurant, bar,
    etc.: *I ordered some coffee.*

ordinary 0‑🔊 /ˈɔːdnri/ *adjective*
not special or unusual ➲ SAME MEANING
normal: *Simon was wearing a suit, but I was*
in my ordinary clothes.
out of the ordinary unusual
➲ SAME MEANING **strange**: *Did you see*
anything out of the ordinary?

ore /ɔː(r)/ *noun*
rock or earth from which you get metal:
iron ore

organ /ˈɔːgən/ *noun*
1 a part of your body that has a special
purpose, for example your heart: *the body's*
internal organs
2 a musical instrument, usually in a church,
that is played like a piano

organic /ɔːˈgænɪk/ *adjective*
1 grown in a natural way, without using
chemicals: *organic vegetables*
2 containing living things: *Improve the soil*
by adding organic matter.

organism /ˈɔːgənɪzəm/ *noun*
a living thing, especially a very small one
that you can only see with a special
instrument (called a **microscope**)

organization 0‑🔊 /ˌɔːgənaɪˈzeɪʃn/
noun
1 (*plural* **organizations**) a group of people
who work together for a special purpose: *He*
works for an organization that helps old
people.
2 (*no plural*) the activity of planning or
arranging something; the way that
something is planned or arranged: *She's*
busy with the organization of her daughter's
wedding.

organize 0‑🔊 /ˈɔːgənaɪz/ *verb*
(**organizes, organizing, organized**
/ˈɔːgənaɪzd/)
to plan or arrange something: *Our teacher*
has organized a visit to the museum.

organized 0‑🔊 /ˈɔːgənaɪzd/ *adjective*
with everything planned or arranged: *She's*
very organized. ➲ OPPOSITE **disorganized**

oriental /ˌɔːriˈentl/ *adjective*
connected with the eastern part of the world,
especially China and Japan: *oriental art*

origin /ˈɒrɪdʒɪn/ *noun*
1 the time, way or place that something first
existed: *the origins of life on earth*
2 the country, race, culture, etc. that a
person comes from: *His family is of French*
origin.

original 0‑🔊 /əˈrɪdʒənl/ *adjective*
1 first; earliest: *I have the car now, but my*
sister was the original owner.

2 new and different: *His poems are very original.*
3 real, not copied: *original paintings*
▶ **original** *noun*: *This is a copy of the painting – the original is in the National Gallery.*

originally /əˈrɪdʒənəli/ *adverb*
in the beginning: *The school was originally very small.* ◇ *I'm from London originally.*

ornament /ˈɔːnəmənt/ *noun*
a thing that we have because it is beautiful, not because it is useful: *china ornaments* ⊃ Look at the picture at **fireplace**.
▶ **ornamental** /ˌɔːnəˈmentl/ *adjective*: *There is an ornamental pond in the garden.*

orphan /ˈɔːfn/ *noun*
a child whose parents are dead

orphanage /ˈɔːfənɪdʒ/ *noun*
a home for children whose parents are dead

ostrich /ˈɒstrɪtʃ/ *noun* (*plural* **ostriches**)
a very big bird from Africa that cannot fly but can run fast because it has long legs

other 0➔ /ˈʌðə(r)/ *adjective, pronoun*
as well as or different from the one or ones I have said: *Carmen is Spanish, but the other students in my class are Japanese.* ◇ *I can only find one shoe. Have you seen the other one?* ◇ *I saw her on the other side of the road.* ◇ *John and Claire arrived at nine o'clock, but the others* (= the other people) *were late.*
other than except; apart from: *I haven't told anybody other than you.*
some... or other (*informal*) words that show you are not sure: *I can't find my glasses. I know I put them somewhere or other.*
the other day not many days ago ⊃ SAME MEANING **recently**: *I saw your brother the other day.*

otherwise¹ 0➔ /ˈʌðəwaɪz/ *adverb*
1 in all other ways: *The house is a bit small, but otherwise it's very nice.*
2 in a different way: *Most people agreed, but Rachel thought otherwise.*

otherwise² /ˈʌðəwaɪz/ *conjunction*
if not ⊃ SAME MEANING **or**: *Hurry up, otherwise you'll be late.*

ouch /aʊtʃ/ *exclamation*
You say '**ouch**' when you suddenly feel pain: *Ouch! That hurts!*

ought to 0➔ /ˈɔːt tə; ˈɔːt tu/ *modal verb*

> 🔎 **PRONUNCIATION**
> The word **ought** sounds like **sport**.

1 words that you use to tell or ask somebody what is the right thing to do

⊃ SAME MEANING **should**: *It's late – you ought to go home.* ◇ *You oughtn't to argue.*
2 words that you use to say what you think will happen or what you think is true
⊃ SAME MEANING **should**: *Tim has worked very hard, so he ought to pass the exam.* ◇ *That film ought to be good.* ⊃ Look at the note at **modal verb**.

ounce /aʊns/ *noun* (*abbr.* **oz**)
a measure of weight (= 28.35 grams). There are 16 **ounces** in a **pound**: *four ounces of flour* ⊃ Look at the note at **pound**

our 0➔ /ɑː(r); ˈaʊə(r)/ *adjective*
belonging to us: *This is our house.*

ours 0➔ /ɑːz; ˈaʊəz/ *pronoun*
something that belongs to us: *Your car is the same as ours.*

ourselves 0➔ /ɑːˈselvz; ˌaʊəˈselvz/ *pronoun* (*plural*)
1 used when you and another person or other people do an action and are also affected by it: *We made ourselves some coffee.*
2 a word that makes 'we' stronger: *We built the house ourselves.*
by ourselves
1 alone; without other people: *We went on holiday by ourselves.*
2 without help

out 0➔ /aʊt/ *adjective, adverb*
1 away from the inside of a place: *When you go out, please close the door.* ◇ *She opened the box and took out a picture.* ⊃ OPPOSITE **in**
2 not at home or not in the place where you work: *I phoned Steve but he was out.* ◇ *I went out to the cinema last night.* ⊃ OPPOSITE **in**
3 not burning or shining: *The fire went out.*
4 not hidden; that you can see: *Look! The sun is out!* ◇ *All the flowers are out* (= open).
5 in a loud voice: *She cried out in pain.*
⊃ Look also at **out of**.

outbreak /ˈaʊtbreɪk/ *noun*
the sudden start of something bad: *the outbreak of war*

outdoor /ˈaʊtdɔː(r)/ *adjective*
happening, existing or used outside a building: *an outdoor swimming pool* ◇ *Bring outdoor clothing.* ⊃ OPPOSITE **indoor**

outdoors 0➔ /ˌaʊtˈdɔːz/ *adverb*
not in a building ⊃ SAME MEANING **outside**: *In summer we sometimes eat outdoors.*
⊃ OPPOSITE **indoors**

outer /ˈaʊtə(r)/ *adjective*
on the outside; far from the centre: *Remove the outer leaves from the cabbage.* ◇ *outer London* ⊃ OPPOSITE **inner**

A

outfit /ˈaʊtfɪt/ *noun*
a set of clothes that you wear together: *I've bought a new outfit for the party.*

B

outgrow /ˌaʊtˈɡrəʊ/ *verb* (outgrows, outgrowing, outgrew /ˌaʊtˈɡruː/, has outgrown /ˌaʊtˈɡrəʊn/)
to become too big or too old for something
◇ SAME MEANING **grow out of**: *She's outgrown her school uniform again.*

C

D

E

outing /ˈaʊtɪŋ/ *noun*
an organized visit that lasts for less than a day ◇ SAME MEANING **trip**: *Year Two are going on an outing to the zoo.*

F

G

outline /ˈaʊtlaɪn/ *noun*
a line that shows the shape or edge of something: *It was dark, but we could see the dim outline of the castle.*

H

I

outlook /ˈaʊtlʊk/ *noun*
what will probably happen: *The outlook for the economy is not good.*

J

K

out of 0🔑 /ˈaʊt əv/ *preposition*
1 words that show where from: *She took a cake out of the box.* ◇ *She got out of bed.*
◇ OPPOSITE **into**
2 not in: *Fish can't live out of water.*
3 using something; from: *He made a table out of some old pieces of wood.*
4 from a number or set: *Nine out of ten people think that the government is right.*
5 because of a particular feeling: *I was just asking out of curiosity.*
6 without: *We're out of coffee.* ◇ *She's been out of work for six months.*

L

M

N

O

out of date /ˌaʊt əv ˈdeɪt/ *adjective*
old; not useful, wanted or allowed now: *This map is out of date.*

P

output /ˈaʊtpʊt/ *noun* (no plural)
the amount of things that somebody or something has made or done: *What was the factory's output last year?*

Q

R

outside¹ 0🔑 /ˌaʊtˈsaɪd/ *noun*
the part of something that is away from the middle: *the outside of the packet* ◇ *We've only seen the building from the outside.*
◇ OPPOSITE **inside**

S

T

U

outside² 0🔑 /ˌaʊtˈsaɪd/ *adjective*
away from the middle of something: *the outside walls of the house* ◇ *an outside toilet*
◇ OPPOSITE **inside**

V

W

outside³ 0🔑 /ˌaʊtˈsaɪd/ *preposition, adverb*
in or to a place that is not inside a building: *I left my bicycle outside the shop.* ◇ *Come outside and see the garden!*
◇ OPPOSITE **inside**

X

Y

Z

outskirts /ˈaʊtskɜːts/ *noun* (plural)
the edges of a town or city: *They live on the outskirts of town.*

outstanding /aʊtˈstændɪŋ/ *adjective*
very good; much better than others
◇ SAME MEANING **excellent**: *Her work is outstanding.*

outward /ˈaʊtwəd/ *adjective*
1 connected with the way things seem to be: *Despite her cheerful outward appearance, she was in fact very unhappy.*
2 travelling away from a place that you will return to later: *There were no delays on the outward journey.*

outwards /ˈaʊtwədz/ (also outward /ˈaʊtwəd/) *adverb*
towards the outside: *The windows open outwards.* ◇ OPPOSITE **inwards** or **inward**

oval /ˈəʊvl/ *adjective*
with a shape like an egg: *an oval mirror*
◇ Look at the picture at **shape**.
▶ **oval** *noun*: *Draw an oval.*

oven 0🔑 /ˈʌvn/ *noun*
the part of a cooker shaped like a box with a door on the front. You put food in the **oven** to cook or heat it: *Take the bread out of the oven.*

over¹ 0🔑 /ˈəʊvə(r)/ *adverb, preposition*
1 on somebody or something so that it covers them: *She put a blanket over the sleeping child.*
2 above something; higher than something: *A plane flew over our heads.* ◇ *There is a picture over the fireplace.*
3 across; to the other side of something: *The dog jumped over the wall.*
4 to or in a place: *Come over and see us on Saturday.* ◇ *Come over here!* ◇ *Go over there and see if you can help.*
5 down or sideways: *I fell over in the street.* ◇ *He leaned over to speak to her.*
6 so that the other side is on top: *You may turn your papers over and begin.*
7 more than a number, price, etc.: *She lived in Spain for over 20 years.* ◇ *This game is for children of ten and over.*
8 not used; remaining: *There are a lot of cakes left over from the party.*
9 used for saying that somebody repeats something: *He said the same thing over and over again* (= many times). ◇ *You'll have to start all over again* (= from the beginning).
all over everywhere; in every part: *Have you seen my glasses? I've looked all over.* ◇ *She travels all over the world.*

over² /ˈəʊvə(r)/ *adjective*
finished: *The exams are over now.*

over- /ˈəʊvə(r)/ *prefix*
more than is good; too much: *He's been* **overeating.** ◇ *You're being* **over-optimistic** – *she won't pass all her exams.*

overall¹ /ˌəʊvərˈɔːl/ *adjective*
including everything ➔ SAME MEANING **total:** *The overall cost of the repairs will be about $350.*
▸ **overall** *adverb:* *How much will it cost overall?*

overall² /ˈəʊvərɔːl/ *noun* (*British*)
a kind of coat that you wear over your clothes to keep them clean when you are working: *The laboratory assistant was wearing a white overall.*

overalls
/ˈəʊvərɔːlz/ (*British*)
(*American*
coveralls)
noun
(*plural*)
a piece of clothing that covers your legs, body and arms. You wear it over your other clothes to keep them clean when you are working.

overalls

overboard
/ˈəʊvəbɔːd/ *adverb*
over the side of a boat and into the water: *She fell overboard.*

overcoat /ˈəʊvəkəʊt/ *noun*
a long warm coat: *Although it was a hot day, he was wearing an overcoat.*

overcome /ˌəʊvəˈkʌm/ *verb* (overcomes, overcoming, overcame /ˌəʊvəˈkeɪm/, has overcome)
to find an answer to a difficult thing in your life; to control something: *He overcame his fear of flying.*

overcrowded /ˌəʊvəˈkraʊdɪd/ *adjective*
too full of people: *The trains are overcrowded on Friday evenings.*

overdue /ˌəʊvəˈdjuː/ *adjective*
not done by the expected time
➔ SAME MEANING **late:** *We had no money and the rent was overdue.*

overflow /ˌəʊvəˈfləʊ/ *verb* (overflows, overflowing, overflowed /ˌəʊvəˈfləʊd/)
to be so full that there is no space: *Someone left the tap on and the bath overflowed.*

overgrown /ˌəʊvəˈɡrəʊn/ *adjective*
covered with plants that have grown too big: *The house was empty and the garden was overgrown.*

overhead /ˈəʊvəhed/ *adjective*
above your head: *an overhead light*
▸ **overhead** /ˌəʊvəˈhed/ *adverb:* *A plane flew overhead.*

overhear /ˌəʊvəˈhɪə(r)/ *verb* (overhears, overhearing, overheard /ˌəʊvəˈhɜːd/, has overheard)
to hear what somebody is saying when they are speaking to another person: *I overheard Louise saying that she was unhappy.*

overlap /ˌəʊvəˈlæp/ *verb* (overlaps, overlapping, overlapped /ˌəʊvəˈlæpt/)
When two things **overlap**, part of one thing covers part of the other thing: *The tiles on the roof overlap.*

overlook /ˌəʊvəˈlʊk/ *verb* (overlooks, overlooking, overlooked /ˌəʊvəˈlʊkt/)
1 to not see or notice something: *He overlooked one important fact.*
2 to have a view over something: *My room overlooks the garden.*

overnight /ˌəʊvəˈnaɪt/ *adjective, adverb*
for or during the night: *an overnight journey*
◇ *They stayed at our house overnight.*

overpass /ˈəʊvəpɑːs/ *American English for* FLYOVER

overseas /ˌəʊvəˈsiːz/ *adjective, adverb*
in, to or from another country across the sea: *There are many overseas students in Britain.* ◇ *She travels overseas a lot.*

oversleep /ˌəʊvəˈsliːp/ *verb* (oversleeps, oversleeping, overslept /ˌəʊvəˈslept/, has overslept)
to sleep too long and not wake up at the right time: *I overslept and was late for work.*

overtake /ˌəʊvəˈteɪk/ *verb* (overtakes, overtaking, overtook /ˌəʊvəˈtʊk/, has overtaken /ˌəʊvəˈteɪkən/)
to go past somebody or something that is going more slowly: *The car overtook a bus.*

overtime /ˈəʊvətaɪm/ *noun* (*no plural*)
extra time that you spend at work: *I have* **done** *a lot of* **overtime** *this week.*

overweight /ˌəʊvəˈweɪt/ *adjective*
too heavy or fat: *The doctor said I was overweight and that I should eat less.*

overwhelming /ˌəʊvəˈwelmɪŋ/ *adjective*
very great or strong: *an overwhelming feeling of loneliness*

ow /aʊ/ *exclamation*
You say '**ow**' when you suddenly feel pain: *Ow! You're standing on my foot.*

owe 0➞ /əʊ/ *verb* (owes, owing, owed /əʊd/)

🔎 **PRONUNCIATION**
The word **owe** sounds like **go**.

A B C D E F G H I J K L M N O P Q R S T U V W X Y Z

1 to have to pay money to somebody: *I lent you $10 last week and $10 the week before, so you owe me $20.*
2 to have something because of a particular person or thing: *He owes his life to the man who pulled him out of the river.* ◇ *She owes her success to hard work.*

owing to /ˈəʊɪŋ tu/ *preposition*
because of: *The train was late owing to the bad weather.*

owl

owl /aʊl/ *noun*
a bird that flies at night and eats small animals

own¹ 0🔑 /əʊn/ *adjective, pronoun*

🔎 **PRONUNCIATION**
The word **own** sounds like **bone**.

used for emphasizing that something belongs to a particular person: *Is that your own camera or did you borrow it?* ◇ *I have my own room now that my sister has left home.* ◇ *I want a home of my own.*

🔎 **GRAMMAR**
Be careful! You cannot use **own** after 'a' or 'the'. You cannot say: *I would like an own room.* You say: *I would like my own room* or: *I would like a room of my own.*

get your own back on somebody to do something bad to somebody who has done something bad to you: *He said he would get his own back on me for breaking his watch.*
on your own
1 alone: *She lives on her own.*
2 without help: *I can't move this box on my own – can you help me?*

own² 0🔑 /əʊn/ *verb* (owns, owning, owned /əʊnd/)
to have something that is yours: *We don't own our flat – we rent it.* ◇ *I don't own a car.*
own up to say that you have done something wrong: *Nobody owned up to breaking the window.*

owner 0🔑 /ˈəʊnə(r)/ *noun*
a person who has something that belongs to them: *Who is the owner of that red car?*

ox /ɒks/ *noun* (*plural* oxen /ˈɒksn/)
a large male cow that is used for pulling or carrying heavy things ⊃ Look at the picture at **plough**.

oxygen /ˈɒksɪdʒən/ *noun* (*no plural*) (*symbol* O)
a gas in the air. Animals and plants need **oxygen** to live.

oyster /ˈɔɪstə(r)/ *noun*
a small sea animal with a shell. You can eat some types of **oyster** and others produce shiny white things used to make jewellery (called **pearls**).

oz short way of writing OUNCE

ozone /ˈəʊzəʊn/ *noun* (*no plural*)
a poisonous gas which is a form of OXYGEN

ozone-friendly /ˌəʊzəʊn ˈfrendli/ *adjective*
(used about cleaning products, etc.) not containing chemicals that could harm the OZONE LAYER: *Most aerosol sprays are now ozone-friendly.*

the ozone layer /ði ˈəʊzəʊn leɪə(r)/ *noun* (*no plural*)
the layer of OZONE high above the surface of the earth, which helps to protect the earth from the bad effects of the sun

A B C D E F G H I J K L M N O P Q R S T U V W X Y Z

Pp

P, p [1] /piː/ *noun* (*plural* **P's, p's** /piːz/)
the sixteenth letter of the English alphabet:
'*Pencil*' begins with a '*P*'.

p [2]
1 /piː/ *short for* PENCE
2 *short way of writing* PAGE

pace [1] /peɪs/ *noun*
1 (*no plural*) how fast you do something or
how fast something happens: *We started at a
steady pace.*
2 (*plural* **paces**) a step: *Take two paces
forward.*
keep pace with somebody or
something to go as fast as somebody or
something: *She couldn't keep pace with the
other runners.*

pace [2] /peɪs/ *verb*
to walk around nervously or angrily: *She
paced up and down outside.*

pacifier /'pæsɪfaɪə(r)/ *American English for*
DUMMY

pack [1] 0ᴍ /pæk/ *noun*
1 a set of things: *I bought a pack of five
exercise books.* ◇ *an information pack*
2 (*British*) (*American* **deck**) a set of 52 cards
for playing games ➔ Look at the picture at
playing card.
3 a group of wild dogs or similar animals: *a
pack of wolves*
3 *American English for* PACKET: *a pack of
cigarettes*

pack [2] 0ᴍ /pæk/ *verb* (**packs, packing,
packed** /pækt/)
1 to put things into a bag or suitcase before
you go somewhere: *Have you packed your
suitcase?* ◇ *Don't forget to pack your
toothbrush.*
2 to put things into a box, bag, etc.: *Pack all
these books into boxes.* ➔ OPPOSITE **unpack**
pack up
1 to stop doing something: *At two o'clock we
packed up and went home.*
2 (*British, informal*) If a machine **packs up**, it
stops working.

package 0ᴍ /'pækɪdʒ/ *noun*
something that is wrapped in paper,
cardboard or plastic ➔ SAME MEANING
parcel

package holiday /,pækɪdʒ 'hɒlədeɪ/
(*British*) (*American* **package tour** /'pækɪdʒ
tʊə(r)/) *noun*
a complete holiday that you buy from a

single company, instead of paying different
companies for your travel, hotel, etc.

packaging /'pækɪdʒɪŋ/ *noun* (*no plural*)
material like paper, cardboard or plastic that
is used to wrap things that you buy or that
you send

packed /pækt/ *adjective*
full: *The train was packed.*

packed lunch /,pækt 'lʌntʃ/ *noun* (*British*)
food that you take to school or work to eat in
the middle of the day

packet 0ᴍ /'pækɪt/ (*British*) (*American*
pack) *noun*
a small box or bag that you buy things in: *a
packet of biscuits* ◇ *an empty crisp packet*

packing /'pækɪŋ/ *noun* (*no plural*)
1 the act of putting things into a bag or
suitcase before you go somewhere: *Have you
done your packing?*
2 material like paper, cardboard or plastic
that is used to wrap things that you buy or
that you send: *The price includes postage and
packing.*

pact /pækt/ *noun*
an important agreement to do something:
They made a pact not to tell anyone.

pad /pæd/ *noun*
1 a thick flat piece of soft material:
*Footballers wear pads on their legs to protect
them.* ◇ *I used a pad of cotton wool to clean
the cut.*
2 pieces of paper that are joined together at
one end: *a writing pad*

padded /'pædɪd/ *adjective*
covered with or containing a layer of thick
soft material: *a padded jacket*

paddle [1] /'pædl/ *noun*
a piece of wood with a flat end, that you use
for moving a small boat through water

paddle [2] /'pædl/ *verb* (**paddles, paddling,
paddled** /'pædld/)
1 to move a small boat through water with a
PADDLE: *We paddled up the river.*
2 to walk in water that is not deep: *The
children were paddling in the sea.*

padlock /'pædlɒk/ *noun*
a lock that you use on things like gates and
bicycles ➔ Look at the picture on the next
page.

page 0ᴍ /peɪdʒ/ (*abbr.* p) *noun*
one or both sides of a piece of paper in a
book, magazine or newspaper: *Please turn to*

A

page 120. ◇ *What page is the story on?* ◇ *I'm reading a 600-page novel.*

B

paid form of PAY¹

C

pain 0–ᴛ /peɪn/ *noun*

D

1 (*plural* **pains**) the feeling that you have in your body when you are hurt or ill: *I've got a pain in my leg.* ◇ *He's in terrible pain.*

E

F

G

2 (*no plural*) unhappiness: *Her eyes were full of pain.*

H

be a pain or **a pain in the neck** (*informal*) a person, thing or situation that makes you angry or annoyed: *She can be a real pain when she's in a bad mood.*

I

J

painful 0–ᴛ /ˈpeɪnfl/ *adjective*
giving pain: *I've cut my leg – it's very painful.* ⊃ OPPOSITE **painless**

K

painkiller /ˈpeɪnkɪlə(r)/ *noun*
a drug that makes pain less strong: *She's on painkillers.*

L

M

painless /ˈpeɪnləs/ *adjective*
not causing pain: *a painless injection* ⊃ OPPOSITE **painful**

N

O

paint¹ 0–ᴛ /peɪnt/ *noun*
a coloured liquid that you put on things with a brush, to change the colour or to make a picture: *red paint* ◇ *Is the paint dry yet?*

P

paint

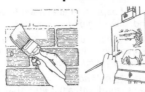

Q

R

S

T

paint² 0–ᴛ /peɪnt/ *verb* (**paints, painting, painted**)

U

1 to put **paint** on something to change the colour: *We painted the walls grey.*
2 to make a picture of somebody or something using **paints**: *I'm painting a picture of some flowers.* ◇ *My sister paints very well.*

V

W

X

paintbrush /ˈpeɪntbrʌʃ/ *noun* (*plural* **paintbrushes**)
a brush that you use for painting ⊃ Look at the picture at **brush**.

Y

Z

painter 0–ᴛ /ˈpeɪntə(r)/ *noun*
1 a person whose job is to paint things like

padlock

walls or houses ⊃ Look at Picture Dictionary page **P12**.
2 a person who paints pictures: *Picasso was a famous painter.* ⊃ SAME MEANING **artist**

painting 0–ᴛ /ˈpeɪntɪŋ/ *noun*
a picture that somebody makes with paint: *a painting by Rembrandt* ◇ *He did a painting of the bridge.*

pair 0–ᴛ /peə(r)/ *noun*

🔎 **PRONUNCIATION**
The word **pair** sounds just like **pear**.

1 two things of the same kind that you use together: *a pair of shoes* ◇ *a new pair of earrings*
2 a thing with two parts that are joined together: *a pair of glasses* ◇ *a pair of scissors* ◇ *I bought two pairs of trousers.*
3 two people or animals together: *a pair of ducks* ⊃ Look at **couple**.
in pairs with two things or people together: *Shoes are only sold in pairs.* ◇ *The students are working in pairs.*

pajamas /pəˈdʒɑːməz/ *American English for* PYJAMAS

pal /pæl/ *noun* (*informal*)
a friend

palace

walls or houses ⊃ Look at Picture Dictionary

palace /ˈpæləs/ *noun*
a very large house where a king or queen lives: *The Queen lives at Buckingham Palace.*

pale 0–ᴛ /peɪl/ *adjective* (**paler, palest**)
1 with not much colour in your face ⊃ SAME MEANING **white**: *Are you ill? You look pale.* ◇ *She has very pale skin.*
2 with a light colour; not strong or dark ⊃ SAME MEANING **light**: *a pale blue dress* ⊃ OPPOSITE **dark**

palm /pɑːm/ *noun*
1 the flat part of the front of your hand ⊃ Look at the picture at **hand**.
2 (*also* **palm tree** /ˈpɑːm triː/) a tree that grows in hot countries, with no branches

and a lot of big leaves at the top: *a coconut palm*

pamphlet /ˈpæmflət/ *noun*
a very thin book with a paper cover that gives information about something

pan 0ᵐ /pæn/ *noun*
a metal pot that you use for cooking: *a frying pan* ➲ Look at the picture at **saucepan**.

pancake /ˈpænkeɪk/ *noun*
a very thin round thing that you eat. You make **pancakes** with flour, eggs and milk and cook them in a frying pan ➲ Look at Picture Dictionary page **P7**.

panda

panda /ˈpændə/ *noun* (*plural* pandas)
a large black and white animal that lives in China

pane /peɪn/ *noun*
a piece of glass in a window: *a windowpane*

panel /ˈpænl/ *noun*
1 a flat piece of wood, metal or glass that is part of a door, wall or ceiling
2 a group of people who give their opinions about something or discuss something: *Do you have any questions for our panel?* ◇ *a panel of experts*
3 a flat part on a machine, where there are things to help you control it: *the TV's control panel*

pang /pæŋ/ *noun*
a sudden strong and painful feeling: *hunger pangs* ◇ *a pang of jealousy*

panic /ˈpænɪk/ *noun*
a sudden feeling of fear that you cannot control and that makes you do things without thinking carefully: *There was panic in the shop when the fire started.*
▶ **panic** *verb* (panics, panicking, panicked /ˈpænɪkt/): *Don't panic!*

panic-stricken /ˈpænɪk strɪkən/ *adjective*
very frightened in a way that stops you thinking clearly: *Panic-stricken shoppers fled from the scene.*

pant /pænt/ *verb* (pants, panting, panted)
to take in and let out air quickly through your mouth, for example after running or

because you are very hot: *The dog was panting.*

panther /ˈpænθə(r)/ *noun*
a wild animal like a big cat with black fur

panties /ˈpæntiz/ *American English for* KNICKERS

pantomime /ˈpæntəmaɪm/ *noun* (*British*)
a funny play for children, with singing and dancing. You can usually see **pantomimes** at Christmas.

pants /pænts/ *noun* (*plural*)
1 (*British*) (*American* **panties, underpants**) a small piece of clothing that you wear under your other clothes, around the middle of your body to cover your bottom
➲ SAME MEANING **knickers, underpants**: *a pair of pants*
2 *American English for* TROUSERS

paper 0ᵐ /ˈpeɪpə(r)/ *noun*
1 (*no plural*) thin material for writing or drawing on or for wrapping things in: *a sheet of paper* ◇ *a paper bag*
2 (*plural* **papers**) a newspaper: *Have you seen today's paper?*
3 **papers** (*plural*) important pieces of paper with writing on them: *Her desk was piled high with papers.*
4 (*plural* **papers**) a group of questions in an exam: *The English paper was easy.*

paperback /ˈpeɪpəbæk/ *noun*
a book with a paper cover ➲ Look at **hardback**.

paper clip /ˈpeɪpə klɪp/ *noun*
a small metal object that you use for holding pieces of paper together ➲ Look at Picture Dictionary page **11**.

paperwork /ˈpeɪpəwɜːk/ *noun* (*no plural*)
the written work that you have to do as part of your job: *Teachers have far too much paperwork.*

parachute

parachute /ˈpærəʃuːt/ *noun*
a thing that you have on your back when you jump out of a plane and that opens, so that you fall to the ground slowly

A B C D E F G H I J K L M N O **P** Q R S T U V W X Y Z

A B C D E F G H I J K L M N O **P** Q R S T U V W X Y Z

parade /pə'reɪd/ *noun*
a line of people who are walking together for a special reason, while other people watch them: *a military parade*

paradise /'pærədaɪs/ *noun* (*no plural*)
the place where some people think good people go after they die ⇒ SAME MEANING **heaven**

paraffin /'pærəfɪn/ (*British*) (*American* **kerosene**) *noun* (*no plural*)
a type of oil that people burn to produce heat or light

paragraph /'pærəgrɑːf/ *noun*
a group of lines of writing. A **paragraph** always begins on a new line.

parallel /'pærəlel/ *adjective*
Parallel lines are straight lines that are always the same distance from each other. ⇒ Look at the picture at **line**.

paralyse /'pærəlaɪz/ (*British*) (*American* **paralyze**) *verb* (**paralysing, paralyses, paralysed** /'pærəlaɪzd/)
to make a person unable to move all or part of their body: *After the accident she was paralysed from the waist down.*
▶ **paralysis** /pə'ræləsɪs/ *noun* (*no plural*): *The disease can cause paralysis.*

paramedic /ˌpærə'medɪk/ *noun*
a person who is not a doctor or a nurse, but who looks after people who are hurt or ill until they get to a hospital

parcel

parcel /'pɑːsl/ (*American also* **package**) *noun*
something with paper around it, that you send or carry: *She sent a parcel of books to her aunt.*

pardon¹ /'pɑːdn/ *exclamation*
1 (*British*) (*American* **pardon me**) What did you say?: *'You're very quiet.' 'Pardon?' 'I said, you're very quiet.'*
2 (*British and American also* **pardon me**) I'm sorry: *Pardon me, I didn't see you standing there.*

pardon² /'pɑːdn/ *verb* (**pardons, pardoning, pardoned** /'pɑːdnd/) (*formal*)
to officially decide not to punish somebody for something bad that they have done: *Two*

hundred prisoners were pardoned by the king. ⇒ SAME MEANING **forgive**

parent 0̄ᴡ /'peərənt/ *noun*
a mother or father: *Her parents live in Italy.*

parenthood /'peərənthʊd/ *noun* (*no plural*)
being a parent

parish /'pærɪʃ/ *noun* (*plural* **parishes**)
an area that has its own church and priest

park¹ 0̄ᴡ /pɑːk/ *noun*
a place with grass and trees, where anybody can go to walk, play games or relax: *We had a picnic in the park.* ◇ *Hyde Park*

park² 0̄ᴡ /pɑːk/ *verb* (**parks, parking, parked** /pɑːkt/)
to stop and leave a vehicle somewhere for a time: *You can't park in this street.* ◇ *My car is parked opposite the bank.*
▶ **parking** /'pɑːkɪŋ/ *noun* (*no plural*): *The sign says 'No Parking'. ◇ I can't find a parking space.*

parking lot /'pɑːkɪŋ lɒt/ *American English* for CAR PARK

parking meter /'pɑːkɪŋ miːtə(r)/ *noun*
a machine beside the road that you put money into when you park your car next to it

parking ticket /'pɑːkɪŋ tɪkɪt/ *noun*
a piece of paper that orders you to pay money (called a **fine**) for parking your car where it is not allowed

parliament /'pɑːləmənt/ *noun*
the people who make the laws in a country: *the French parliament*

> 🔎 CULTURE
>
> In the United Kingdom, the group of people who make the laws meet in the **Houses of Parliament** in London. The two parts of the Houses of Parliament are called the **House of Commons** (where the **Members of Parliament** meet) and the **House of Lords**.

parrot /'pærət/ *noun*
a bird with very bright feathers that can copy what people say ⇒ Look at Picture Dictionary page **P2**.

parsley /'pɑːsli/ *noun* (*no plural*)
a type of plant (called a **herb**) with small green leaves that you use in cooking or for decorating food

part¹ 0̄ᴡ /pɑːt/ *noun*
1 some, but not all of something; one of the pieces of something: *We spent part of the day on the beach.* ◇ *Which part of Spain do you come from?*

2 a piece of a machine: *Is there a shop near here that sells bicycle parts?*
3 the person you are in a play or film: *She played the part of Ophelia.*
4 *American for* PARTING (2)
take part in something to do something together with other people: *All the students took part in the concert.*

part² /pɑːt/ *verb* (parts, parting, parted) (*formal*)
to go away from each other: *We parted at the airport.*
part with something to give something to somebody else, especially something that you would prefer to keep: *Read the contract very carefully before you part with any money.*

partial /ˈpɑːrʃl/ *adjective*
not complete: *The evening was only a partial success.*
▶ **partially** *adverb* ⊃ SAME MEANING **partly**: *The road was partially blocked by a fallen tree.*

participant /pɑːˈtɪsɪpənt/ *noun*
a person who does something together with other people: *All participants in the event will receive a certificate.*

participate /pɑːˈtɪsɪpeɪt/ *verb*
(participates, participating, participated) (*formal*)
to do something together with other people ⊃ SAME MEANING **take part**: *Ten countries participated in the discussions.*
▶ **participation** /pɑːˌtɪsɪˈpeɪʃn/ *noun* (*no plural*): *Your participation is greatly appreciated.*

participle /pɑːˈtɪsɪpl/ *noun*
(*grammar*) a form of a verb: *The present participle of 'eat' is 'eating' and the past participle is 'eaten'.*

particular ⚬ᴏ /pəˈtɪkjələ(r)/ *adjective*
1 one only, and not any other: *You need a particular kind of flour to make bread.*
2 more than usual ⊃ SAME MEANING **special**: *The road is very icy, so take particular care when you are driving.*
3 If you are **particular**, you want something to be exactly right: *He's very particular about the food he eats.*
in particular more than others ⊃ SAME MEANING **especially**: *Is there anything in particular you want to do this weekend?*

particularly ⚬ᴏ /pəˈtɪkjələli/ *adverb*
more than usual or more than others ⊃ SAME MEANING **especially**: *I'm particularly tired today.* ◇ *I don't particularly like fish.*

parties *plural of* PARTY

parting /ˈpɑːtɪŋ/ *noun*
1 a time when people leave each other: *We had a sad parting at the airport.*
2 (*British*) (*American* **part**) a line in your hair that you make by brushing it in different directions using a plastic or metal thing (called a **comb**): *He has a side parting.*

partly ⚬ᴏ /ˈpɑːtli/ *adverb*
not completely but in some way: *The window was partly open.* ◇ *The accident was partly my fault.*

partner ⚬ᴏ /ˈpɑːtnə(r)/ *noun*
1 your husband, wife, boyfriend or girlfriend
2 one of the people who owns a business
3 a person you are dancing with, or playing a game with

partnership /ˈpɑːtnəʃɪp/ *noun*
being partners: *The two sisters **went into partnership** and opened a shop.*

part of speech /ˌpɑːt əv ˈspiːtʃ/ *noun*
(*plural* **parts of speech**)
(*grammar*) one of the groups that words are divided into, for example 'noun', 'verb', 'adjective', etc.

part-time /ˌpɑːt ˈtaɪm/ *adjective, adverb*
for only a part of the day or week: *I've got a **part-time job** as a secretary.* ◇ *Jane **works part-time**.* ⊃ Look at **full-time**.

party ⚬ᴏ /ˈpɑːti/ *noun* (*plural* **parties**)
1 a time when friends meet, usually in somebody's home, to eat, drink and enjoy themselves: *We're **having a party** this Saturday. Can you come?* ◇ *a birthday party*
2 (*politics*) a group of people who have the same ideas about politics: *He's a member of the Labour Party.*

> 🔎 **CULTURE**
> The main **political parties** in Britain are the **Labour Party**, the **Conservative Party** (also called the **Tory Party**) and the **Liberal Democrats**.
> In the US the main **parties** are the **Republicans** and the **Democrats**.

---

3 a group of people who are travelling or working together: *a party of tourists*

pass¹ ⚬ᴏ /pɑːs/ *verb* (passes, passing, passed /pɑːst/)
1 to go by somebody or something: *She passed me in the street.* ◇ *Do you pass any shops on your way to the station?*
2 to go or move in a particular direction: *A plane **passed overhead**.* ◇ *The train **passes through** Oxford on its way to London.*

A B C D E F G H I J K L M N O P Q R S T U V W X Y Z

3 to give something to somebody: *Could you pass me the salt, please?*
4 (in some sports) to kick, hit or throw the ball to somebody on your team
5 If time **passes**, it goes by: *A week passed before his letter arrived.*
6 to spend time: *How did you pass the time in hospital?*
7 to do well enough in an examination or test: *Did you pass your driving test?*
➔ OPPOSITE **fail**

pass away to die: *The old man passed away in his sleep.*

pass something on to give or tell something to another person: *Will you pass on a message to Mike for me?*

pass out to suddenly become unconscious
➔ SAME MEANING **faint**

pass² /paːs/ *noun* (*plural* passes)
1 doing well enough in an exam: *How many passes did you get in your exams?*
➔ OPPOSITE **fail**
2 a special piece of paper or card that says you can go somewhere or do something: *You need a pass to get into the factory.*
3 kicking, throwing or hitting a ball to somebody in a game
4 a road or way through mountains: *the Brenner Pass*

passage 0─┓ /ˈpæsɪdʒ/ *noun*
1 a narrow way, for example between two buildings
2 a short part of a book, a speech or a piece of music: *We studied a passage from the story for homework.*

passenger 0─┓ /ˈpæsɪndʒə(r)/ *noun*
a person who is travelling in a car, bus, train or plane but not driving or flying it: *The plane was carrying 200 passengers.*

passer-by /ˌpɑːsə ˈbaɪ/ *noun* (*plural* passers-by)
a person who is walking past you in the street: *I asked a passer-by where the Science Museum was.*

passion /ˈpæʃn/ *noun*
a very strong feeling, usually of love, but sometimes of anger or hate

passionate /ˈpæʃənət/ *adjective*
having or showing very strong feelings: *a passionate kiss*

passive /ˈpæsɪv/ *noun* (*no plural*)
(*grammar*) the form of a verb that shows that the action is done by a person or thing to another person or thing: *In the sentence 'The car was stolen', the verb is in the passive.*
➔ OPPOSITE **active**

passport 0─┓ /ˈpɑːspɔːt/ *noun*
a small book with your name and photograph in it. You must take it with you when you travel to other countries.

password /ˈpɑːswɜːd/ *noun*
a secret word that allows you to go into a place or start using a computer: *Never tell anybody your password.*

past¹ 0─┓ /pɑːst/ *adjective*
1 connected with the time that has gone: *We will forget your past mistakes.*
2 just before now ➔ SAME MEANING **last**: *He has been ill for the past week.*

past² 0─┓ /pɑːst/ *noun* (*no plural*)
1 the time before now, and the things that happened then: *We learn about the past in history lessons.* ◇ *In the past, many people had large families.*
2 (*also the past tense*) the form of a verb that you use to talk about the time before now: *The past tense of the verb 'go' is 'went'.*
➔ Look at **future** and **present**.

past³ 0─┓ /pɑːst/ *preposition, adverb*
1 a word that shows how many minutes after the hour: *It's two minutes past four.* ◇ *It's half past seven.*
2 from one side to the other of somebody or something; on the other side of somebody or something: *Go past the cinema, then turn left.* ◇ *The bus went past without stopping.*

pasta /ˈpæstə/ *noun* (*no plural*)
an Italian food that is made from flour, water and sometimes eggs, which comes in many different shapes: *pasta with tomato sauce*
➔ Look at Picture Dictionary page **P7**.

paste¹ /peɪst/ *noun*
a soft wet substance, usually made from powder and liquid, and sometimes used for sticking paper to things: *Mix the flour with milk to make a paste.*

paste² /peɪst/ *verb* (pastes, pasting, pasted)
1 to stick something to something else using **paste**: *Paste the picture into your books.*
2 (*computing*) to copy or move writing or pictures into a computer document from somewhere else: *You can cut and paste the tables into your essay.*

pastime /ˈpɑːstaɪm/ *noun*
something that you like doing when you are not working ➔ SAME MEANING **hobby**: *Painting is her favourite pastime.*

past participle /ˌpɑːst ˈpɑːtɪsɪpl/ *noun*
(*grammar*) the form of a verb that in English is used with 'have' to make a tense (called

the **perfect tense**): '*Gone*' *is the past participle of '*go*'.*

the past perfect /ðə ˌpɑːst ˈpɜːfɪkt/ *noun* (*no plural*)
(*grammar*) the form of a verb that describes an action that was finished before another thing happened: *The film had already started when we got there.*

pastry /ˈpeɪstri/ *noun*
1 (*no plural*) a mixture of flour, fat and water that is rolled flat and used for making a special type of food (called a **pie**) ⊃ Look at the picture at **pie**.
2 (*plural* **pastries**) a small cake made with pastry

the past tense /ðə ˌpɑːst ˈtens/ *noun* (*no plural*)
(*grammar*) the form of a verb that you use to talk about the time before now: *The past tense of '*sing*' is '*sang*'.*

pat /pæt/ *verb* (**pats**, **patting**, **patted**)
to touch somebody or something lightly with your hand flat: *She **patted** the dog **on** the head.* ⊃ Look at the picture at **stroke**.
▶ **pat** *noun*: *He gave me **a pat on the** shoulder.*

patch /pætʃ/ *noun* (*plural* **patches**)
1 a small piece of something that is not the same as the other parts: *a black cat with a white patch on its back*
2 a piece of cloth that you use to cover a hole in things like clothes: *I sewed a patch on my jeans.*

pâté /ˈpæteɪ/ *noun* (*no plural*)
thick food made from meat, fish or vegetables, that you eat on bread: *duck paté*

paternal /pəˈtɜːnl/ *adjective*
1 like a father or connected with being a father: *paternal love*
2 A **paternal** relation is part of your father's family: *my paternal grandmother* (= my father's mother)

path

path ___ cottage

path 0─┐ /pɑːθ/ *noun* (*plural* **paths** /pɑːðz/)
a way across a piece of land, where people can walk: *a path through the woods*

pathetic /pəˈθetɪk/ *adjective* (*informal*)
very bad or weak: *That was a pathetic performance – they deserved to lose!*

patience /ˈpeɪʃns/ *noun* (*no plural*)
staying calm and not getting angry when you are waiting for something, or when you have problems: *Learning to play the piano takes hard work and patience.* ◇ *She was walking so slowly that her sister finally **lost patience with** her* (= became angry with her).
⊃ OPPOSITE **impatience**

patient¹ 0─┐ /ˈpeɪʃnt/ *adjective*
able to stay calm and not get angry when you are waiting for something or when you have problems: *Just sit there and be patient. Your mum will be here soon.*
⊃ OPPOSITE **impatient**
▶ **patiently** /ˈpeɪʃntli/ *adverb*: *She waited patiently for the bus.*

patient² 0─┐ /ˈpeɪʃnt/ *noun*
a sick person that a doctor is looking after

patio /ˈpætiəʊ/ *noun* (*plural* **patios**)
a flat hard area outside a house where people can sit and eat

patriotic /ˌpeɪtriˈɒtɪk/ *adjective*
having or showing a great love for your country

patrol /pəˈtrəʊl/ *noun*
a group of people or vehicles that go round a place to see that everything is all right: *an army patrol*
on patrol the act of going round a place to see that everything is all right: *During the carnival there will be 30 police officers **on patrol**.*
▶ **patrol** *verb* (**patrols**, **patrolling**, **patrolled** /pəˈtrəʊld/): *A guard patrols the gate at night.*

patter /ˈpætə(r)/ *noun* (*no plural*)
quick light sounds: *I heard **the patter of** children's feet on the stairs.*
▶ **patter** *verb* (**patters**, **pattering**, **pattered** /ˈpætəd/): *Rain pattered against the window.*

pattern 0─┐ /ˈpætn/ *noun*
1 the way in which something happens or develops: *Her days all seemed to follow the same pattern.*
2 shapes and colours on something: *The curtains had **a pattern of** flowers and leaves.*
3 a thing that you copy when you make something: *I bought some material and a pattern to make a new skirt.*

A B C D E F G H I J K L M N O **P** Q R S T U V W X Y Z

A B C D E F G H I J K L M N O **P** Q R S T U V W X Y Z

patterned /'pætənd/ *adjective*
with shapes and colours on it: *a patterned shirt*

pause /pɔːz/ *verb* (pauses, pausing, paused /pɔːzd/)
to stop talking or doing something for a short time: *He **paused for** a moment before answering my question.*
▶ **pause** *noun* a period of time when you stop talking or stop what you are doing: *There was a long pause before she spoke.*

pave /peɪv/ *verb* (paves, paving, paved /peɪvd/)
to cover an area of ground with flat stones (called **paving stones**) or bricks: *There is a paved area near the house.*

pavement /'peɪvmənt/ (*British*) (*American* **sidewalk**) *noun*
the part at the side of a road where people can walk ⊃ Look at the picture at **kerb**.

paw /pɔː/ *noun*
the foot of an animal, for example a dog or a cat ⊃ Look at the pictures at **cat** and **lion**.

pay¹ 0— /peɪ/ *verb* (pays, paying, paid /peɪd/, has paid)
to give somebody money for something, for example something they are selling you or work that they do: *How much did you **pay for** your car?* ◇ *I **paid** the builder **for** mending the roof.* ◇ *She has a very **well-paid** job.*
pay somebody back to hurt somebody who has hurt you: *One day I'll pay her back for lying to me!*
pay somebody or something back to give back the money that somebody has lent to you: *Can you lend me £10? I'll pay you back (= pay it back to you) next week.*

pay² 0— /peɪ/ *noun* (no plural)
the money that you get for working: *There are millions of workers on low pay.*

🔎 **WORD BUILDING**
Pay is the general word for money that you **earn** (= get regularly for work that you have done).
If you are paid each week you get **wages**.
If you are paid each month you get a **salary**.

payment 0— /'peɪmənt/ *noun*
1 (*no plural*) paying or being paid: *This cheque is **in payment for** the work you have done.*
2 (*plural* **payments**) an amount of money that you pay: *I make monthly **payments of** £50.*

pay phone /'peɪfəʊn/ *noun*
a telephone that you put money in to make a call

PC /ˌpiː 'siː/ *noun*
1 a small computer. PC is short for 'personal computer'.
2 (*British*) a police officer. PC is short for 'police constable': *PC Smith*

PE /ˌpiː 'iː/ *noun* (*no plural*)
sport and exercise that are done as a subject at school. PE is short for 'physical education': *We have PE on Tuesdays.*

pea /piː/ *noun*
a very small round green vegetable. **Peas** grow in long, thin cases (called **pods**). ⊃ Look at Picture Dictionary page **P9**.

peace 0— /piːs/ *noun* (*no plural*)
1 a time when there is no war or fighting between people or countries: *The two countries eventually **made peace** (= agreed to stop fighting).*
2 the state of being quiet and calm: *the **peace and quiet** of the countryside* ◇ *Go away and leave me **in peace**!*

peaceful 0— /'piːsfl/ *adjective*
1 with no fighting: *a peaceful demonstration*
2 quiet and calm: *It's so peaceful here.*
▶ **peacefully** /'piːsfəli/ *adverb*: *She's sleeping peacefully.*

peach /piːtʃ/ *noun* (*plural* **peaches**)
a soft round fruit with a yellow and red skin and a large stone in the centre ⊃ Look at Picture Dictionary page **P8**.

peacock /'piːkɒk/ *noun*
a large bird with beautiful long blue and green feathers in its tail ⊃ Look at Picture Dictionary page **P3**.

peak /piːk/ *noun*
1 the time when something is highest, biggest, etc.: *The traffic is **at its peak** between five and six in the evening.*
2 the pointed top of a mountain: *snowy mountain peaks*
3 the front part of a hat that sticks out above your eyes

peanut /'piːnʌt/ *noun*
a nut that you can eat: *salted peanuts* ⊃ Look at the picture at **nut**.

peanut butter /ˌpiːnʌt 'bʌtə(r)/ *noun* (*no plural*)
a thick soft substance made from PEANUTS that you eat on bread

pear /peə(r)/ *noun*

🔎 **PRONUNCIATION**
The word **pear** sounds just like **pair**.

a fruit that is green or yellow on the outside and white on the inside ⊃ Look at Picture Dictionary page **P8**.

pearl /pɜːl/ *noun*
a small round white thing that grows inside the shell of a fish (called an **oyster**). **Pearls** are valuable and are used to make jewellery: *a pearl necklace*

peasant /ˈpeznt/ *noun*
a poor person who lives in the country and works on a small piece of land

pebble /ˈpebl/ *noun*
a small round stone

peck /pek/ *verb* (pecks, pecking, pecked /pekt/)
When a bird **pecks** something, it eats or bites it quickly: *The hens were pecking at the corn.*

peculiar /pɪˈkjuːliə(r)/ *adjective*
strange; not usual ⊃ SAME MEANING **odd**: *What's that peculiar smell?*

pedal /ˈpedl/ *noun*
a part of a bicycle or other machine that you move with your feet ⊃ Look at the picture at **bicycle**.

pedestrian /pəˈdestriən/ *noun*
a person who is walking in the street

pedestrian crossing /pəˌdestriən ˈkrɒsɪŋ/ (British) (American **crosswalk**) *noun*
a place where cars must stop so that people can cross the road

peel¹ /piːl/ *verb* (peels, peeling, peeled /piːld/)
1 to take the outside part off a fruit or vegetable: *Can you peel the potatoes?*
2 to come off in thin pieces: *The paint is peeling off the walls.*

peel² /piːl/ *noun* (no plural)
the outside part of some fruit and vegetables: *orange peel ◊ potato peel* ⊃ Look at Picture Dictionary page **P8**.

peep /piːp/ *verb* (peeps, peeping, peeped /piːpt/)
to look at something quickly or secretly: *I peeped through the window and saw her.*
▶ **peep** *noun* (no plural): *Have a peep in the bedroom and see if the baby is awake.*

peer /pɪə(r)/ *verb* (peers, peering, peered /pɪəd/)
to look closely at something because you cannot see well: *I peered outside but I couldn't see anything because it was dark.*

peg /peg/ *noun*
1 a small thing on a wall or door where you can hang things: *Your coat is on the peg.*
2 a small wooden or plastic thing that holds wet clothes on a line when they are drying: *a clothes peg*

pen

pen
ink

pen 0— /pen/ *noun*
1 a thing that you use for writing with a coloured liquid (called **ink**)
2 a small piece of ground with a fence around it for keeping farm animals in

penalty /ˈpenlti/ *noun* (plural **penalties**)
1 a punishment: *The penalty for travelling without a ticket is £300* (= you must pay £300).
2 (in sport) a punishment for one team and an advantage for the other team because a player has broken a rule: *Beckham stepped forward to take the penalty* (= try to score the goal).

pence *plural of* PENNY

pencil

sharpener
pencil

pencil 0— /ˈpensl/ *noun*
a thin object that you use for writing or drawing. **Pencils** are usually made of wood and have a black or coloured point. ⊃ Look at **pen**

penetrate /ˈpenɪtreɪt/ *verb* (penetrates, penetrating, penetrated)
to go through or into something: *The knife penetrated deep into his chest.*

penfriend /ˈpenfrend/ (British) (American **pen pal** /ˈpen pæl/) *noun*
a person that you make friends with by writing letters but you have probably never met them

penguin

penguin /ˈpeŋgwɪn/ *noun*

A B C D E F G H I J K L M N O **P** Q R S T U V W X Y Z

a black and white bird that lives in very cold places. **Penguins** can swim but they cannot fly.

penicillin /ˌpenɪˈsɪlɪn/ ***noun*** (*no plural*)
a drug that is used to stop infections and to treat illnesses

penis /ˈpiːnɪs/ ***noun*** (*plural* **penises**)
the part of a man's or a male animal's body that is used for getting rid of waste liquid and for having sex

penknife /ˈpennaɪf/ ***noun*** (*plural* **penknives** /ˈpennaɪvz/)
a small knife that you can carry in your pocket

penknife

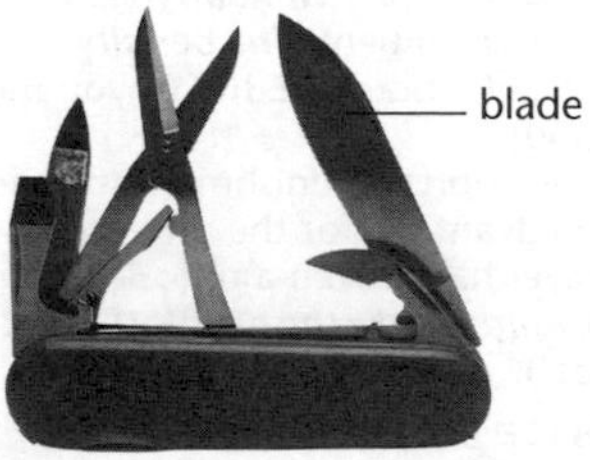

penny /ˈpeni/ (*abbr.* **p**) ***noun*** (*plural* **pence** /pens/ *or* **pennies**)
a small coin that people use in Britain. There are 100 **pence** in a **pound**: *These pencils cost 40 pence each.* ◇ *Can you lend me 50p?*

pension /ˈpenʃn/ ***noun***
money that you get from a government or a company when you are old and do not work any more (when you are **retired**)
▸ **pensioner** /ˈpenʃənə(r)/ (*British*) (*British also* **old-age pensioner** /ˌəʊld eɪdʒ ˈpenʃənə(r)/) ***noun***: *Many pensioners live in poverty.*

people /ˈpiːpl/ ***noun*** (*plural*)
more than one person: *How many people came to the meeting?* ◇ *People often arrive late at parties.*

pepper /ˈpepə(r)/ ***noun***
1 (*no plural*) powder with a hot taste that you put on food: *salt and pepper* ➲ Look at Picture Dictionary page **P6**.
2 (*plural* **peppers**) a red, green or yellow vegetable that is almost empty inside ➲ Look at Picture Dictionary page **P9**.

peppermint /ˈpepəmɪnt/ ***noun***
1 (*no plural*) a plant with a strong fresh taste and smell. It is used to make things like sweets and medicines.
2 (*plural* **peppermints**) a sweet with the flavour of **peppermint**

per /pə(r)/ ***preposition***
for each; in each: *These apples cost 40p per pound.* ◇ *I was driving at 60 miles per hour.*

perceive /pəˈsiːv/ ***verb*** (**perceives, perceiving, perceived** /pəˈsiːvd/) (*formal*)
to understand or think of something or somebody in a particular way: *My comments were **perceived as** criticism.*

per cent /pə ˈsent/ ***noun*** (*no plural*) (*symbol* %) in each hundred: *90 per cent of the people who work here are men* (= in 100 people there are 90 men). ◇ *You get 10% off if you pay cash.*
▸ **percentage** /pəˈsentɪdʒ/ ***noun***: *'What **percentage of** students passed the exam?' 'Oh, about eighty per cent.'*

perch[1] /pɜːtʃ/ ***verb*** (**perches, perching, perched** /pɜːtʃt/)
to sit on something narrow or uncomfortable: *The bird **perched on** a branch.* ◇ *We perched on high stools.*

perch[2] /pɜːtʃ/ ***noun*** (*plural* **perches**)
a place where a bird sits

perfect /ˈpɜːfɪkt/ ***adjective***
1 so good that it cannot be better; with nothing wrong: *Her English is perfect.* ◇ *It's **perfect** weather **for** a picnic.*
2 made from 'has', 'have' or 'had' and the PAST PARTICIPLE of a verb: *perfect tenses*

the perfect /ðə ˈpɜːfɪkt/ (*also* **the perfect tense** /ðə ˌpɜːfɪkt ˈtens/) ***noun*** (*no plural*) (*grammar*) the form of the verb that is made with 'has', 'have' or 'had' and the PAST PARTICIPLE: *'I've finished' is in the perfect tense.* ➲ Look at **the past perfect** and **the present perfect**.

perfection /pəˈfekʃn/ ***noun*** (*no plural*)
the state of being perfect: *The meat was cooked **to perfection**.*

perfectly /ˈpɜːfɪktli/ ***adverb***
1 completely ➲ SAME MEANING **quite**: *I'm perfectly all right.*
2 in a perfect way: *She played the piece of music perfectly.*

perform /pəˈfɔːm/ ***verb*** (**performs, performing, performed** /pəˈfɔːmd/)
1 to do something such as a piece of work or a task: *Doctors **performed** a complicated **operation** to save her life.*
2 to be in something such as a play or a concert: *The band is performing at the Odeon tonight.* ◇ *The play will be performed every night next week.*

performance /pəˈfɔːməns/ ***noun***
1 (*plural* **performances**) a time when a play, etc. is shown, or music is played in front of a lot of people: *We went to the evening performance of the play.*

2 (*no plural*) how well you do something: *My parents were pleased with my performance in the exam.*

performer /pəˈfɔːmə(r)/ *noun*
a person who is in something such as a play or a concert

perfume /ˈpɜːfjuːm/ *noun*
1 a liquid with a nice smell that you put on your body: *a bottle of perfume*
2 a nice smell

perhaps 0̅ /pəˈhæps/ *adverb*
a word that you use when you are not sure about something ➔ SAME MEANING **maybe**: *I don't know where she is – perhaps she's still at work. ◊ There were three men, or perhaps four.*

period 0̅ /ˈpɪəriəd/ *noun*
1 an amount of time: *This is a difficult period for him. ◊ What period of history are you studying?*
2 a lesson in school: *We have five periods of German a week.*
3 the time when a woman loses blood from her body each month
4 *American English for* FULL STOP

perm /pɜːm/ *noun*
the treatment of hair with special chemicals to make it curly: *I think I'm going to have a perm.*
▸ **perm** *verb* (perms, perming, permed /pɜːmd/): *Have you had your hair permed?*

permanent 0̅ /ˈpɜːmənənt/ *adjective*
continuing for ever or for a very long time without changing: *I'm looking for a permanent job.* ➔ Look at **temporary**.
▸ **permanently** /ˈpɜːmənəntli/ *adverb*: *Has he left permanently?*

permission 0̅ /pəˈmɪʃn/ *noun* (*no plural*)
allowing somebody to do something: *She gave me permission to leave early. ◊ You may not leave the school without permission.*

permit¹ /pəˈmɪt/ *verb* (permits, permitting, permitted) (*formal*)
to let somebody do something
➔ SAME MEANING **allow**: *You are not permitted to smoke in the hospital.*

permit² /ˈpɜːmɪt/ *noun*
a piece of paper that says you can do something or go somewhere: *Have you got a work permit?*

persevere /ˌpɜːsɪˈvɪə(r)/ *verb*
(perseveres, persevering, persevered /ˌpɜːsɪˈvɪəd/)
to continue trying to do something that is

difficult: *If you persevere with your studies, you could go to university.*

persistent /pəˈsɪstənt/ *adjective*
1 determined to continue doing something even though people tell you to stop: *She's a very persistent child – she just never gives up.*
2 lasting for a long time: *a persistent cough*

person 0̅ /ˈpɜːsn/ *noun* (*plural* **people** /ˈpiːpl/)
a man or woman: *I think she's the best person for the job. ◊ We've invited a few people to dinner.*
in person seeing somebody, not just speaking on the telephone or writing a letter: *I want to speak to her in person.*

personal 0̅ /ˈpɜːsənl/ *adjective*
of or for one person: *That letter is personal and you have no right to read it. ◊ Please keep all your personal belongings with you.*

personal computer /ˌpɜːsənl kəmˈpjuːtə(r)/ = PC

personality /ˌpɜːsəˈnæləti/ *noun* (*plural* personalities)
1 the qualities that a person has that make them different from other people: *Mark has a great personality.*
2 a famous person: *a television personality*

personally /ˈpɜːsənəli/ *adverb*
1 You say **personally** when you are saying what you think about something: *Personally, I like her, but a lot of people don't.*
2 done by you yourself, and not by somebody else acting for you: *I will deal with this matter personally.*

personal stereo /ˌpɜːsənl ˈsteriəʊ/ *noun* (*plural* personal stereos)
a small machine for listening to music. You can carry it with you and listen through wires (called headphones) that go in your ears.

personnel /ˌpɜːsəˈnel/ *noun* (*plural*)
the people who work for a large business or organization: *military personnel*

persuade 0̅ /pəˈsweɪd/ *verb*
(persuades, persuading, persuaded)
to make somebody think or do something by talking to them: *The shop assistant persuaded me to buy the most expensive pair of jeans.*

persuasion /pəˈsweɪʒn/ *noun* (*no plural*)
the process of making somebody think or do something: *After a lot of persuasion she agreed to come.*

pessimism /ˈpesɪmɪzəm/ *noun* (*no plural*)
thinking that bad things will happen
➔ OPPOSITE **optimism**

▶ **pessimist** /'pesɪmɪst/ *noun*: Lisa's such a pessimist. ⊃ OPPOSITE **optimist**

▶ **pessimistic** /ˌpesɪ'mɪstɪk/ *adjective*: Don't be so pessimistic – of course it's not going to rain! ⊃ OPPOSITE **optimistic**

pest /pest/ *noun*
1 an insect or animal that damages plants or food
2 (*informal*) a person or thing that makes you a little angry: My little sister's a real pest!

pester /'pestə(r)/ *verb* (pesters, pestering, pestered) /'pestəd/
to annoy somebody by asking them for something many times: Journalists **pestered** the neighbours **for** information.

pet 0➡ /pet/ *noun*
1 an animal that you keep in your home: I've got two pets – a cat and a goldfish. ⊃ Look at Picture Dictionary page **P2**.
2 a child that a teacher or a parent likes best: She's the **teacher's pet**.

petal /'petl/ *noun*
one of the coloured parts of a flower ⊃ Look at the picture at **plant**.

petition /pə'tɪʃn/ *noun*
a special letter from a group of people that asks for something: Hundreds of people signed the **petition for** a new pedestrian crossing.

petrol 0➡ /'petrəl/ (*British*) (*American* gas, gasoline) *noun* (*no plural*)
a liquid that you put in a car to make it go

petrol station /'petrəl steɪʃn/ (*American* gas station) *noun*
a place where you can buy PETROL

phantom /'fæntəm/ *noun*
a spirit of a dead person that people think they see ⊃ SAME MEANING **ghost**

pharmacist /'fɑːməsɪst/ = CHEMIST(1)

pharmacy /'fɑːməsi/ *noun* (*plural* pharmacies)
a shop, or part of a shop, which sells medicines and drugs

phase /feɪz/ *noun*
a time when something is changing or growing: She's going through a difficult phase just now.

PhD /ˌpiː eɪtʃ 'diː/ *abbreviation*
a high level university degree that you get by doing an important piece of work in a particular subject ⊃ 'PhD' is short for **Doctor of Philosophy**.

philosopher /fə'lɒsəfə(r)/ *noun*
a person who studies PHILOSOPHY

philosophy /fə'lɒsəfi/ *noun*
1 (*no plural*) the study of ideas about the meaning of life

2 (*plural philosophies*) a set of beliefs that a person has about life: Enjoy yourself and don't worry about tomorrow – that's my philosophy!

phone[1] 0➡ /fəʊn/ (*also* telephone) *noun*
an instrument that you use for talking to somebody who is in another place: The phone's ringing – can you answer it?
be on the phone to be using the phone: Anna was **on the phone** for an hour.

phone[2] 0➡ /fəʊn/ *verb* (phones, phoning, phoned /fəʊnd/) (*British also* phone up)
to speak to somebody by phone
⊃ SAME MEANING **call**: I phoned Di last night. ◇ I was just phoning up for a chat. ◇ Could you **phone back** later?

phone book /'fəʊn bʊk/ (*also* telephone book, telephone directory) *noun*
a book of people's names, addresses and telephone numbers

phone box /'fəʊn bɒks/ (*plural* phone boxes) (*also* telephone box) *noun*
a public telephone in the street

phone call /'fəʊn kɔːl/ (*also* telephone call) *noun*
when you use the phone to talk to somebody: I need to **make a phone call**.

phonecard /'fəʊnkɑːd/ *noun*
a small plastic card that you can use to pay for a call to somebody from a phone box

phone number /'fəʊn nʌmbə(r)/ (*also* telephone number) *noun*
the number of a particular phone that you use when you want to make a call to it: What's your phone number?

phonetic /fə'netɪk/ *adjective*
using special signs to show how to say words: The phonetic alphabet is on a chart on the classroom wall.

phonetics /fə'netɪks/ *noun* (*no plural*)
the study of the sounds that people make when they speak

photo 0➡ /'fəʊtəʊ/ *noun* (*plural* photos) (*informal*) = PHOTOGRAPH

photocopier /'fəʊtəʊkɒpiə(r)/ *noun*
a machine that makes copies of documents by photographing them

photocopy /'fəʊtəʊkɒpi/ *noun* (*plural* photocopies)
a copy of something on paper that you make with a PHOTOCOPIER

▶ **photocopy** *verb* (photocopies, photocopying, photocopied /'fəʊtəʊkɒpid/, has photocopied): Can you photocopy this letter for me?

photograph 0━┱ /'fəʊtəɡrɑːf/ *noun*
(*also* **photo**) *noun*
a picture that you take with a camera: *I took
a photo of the Eiffel Tower.*
▶ **photograph** (photographs,
photographing, photographed
/'fəʊtəɡrɑːft/): *The winner was photographed
holding his prize.*

photographer 0━┱ /fə'tɒɡrəfə(r)/
noun
a person who takes photographs, especially
as a job

photographic /ˌfəʊtə'ɡræfɪk/ *adjective*
connected with photographs or
photography: *photographic equipment*

photography /fə'tɒɡrəfi/ *noun* (*no
plural*)
taking photographs

phrasal verb /ˌfreɪzl 'vɜːb/ *noun*
(*grammar*) a verb that joins with another
word or words to make a verb with a new
meaning: '*Look after*' and '*take off*' are phrasal
verbs.

phrase 0━┱ /freɪz/ *noun* (*grammar*)

> 🔎 **PRONUNCIATION**
> The word **phrase** sounds like **days**.

a group of words that you use together as
part of a sentence: '*First of all*' and '*a bar of
chocolate*' are phrases.

physical 0━┱ /'fɪzɪkl/ *adjective*
connected with things that you feel or do
with your body: *physical exercise*
▶ **physically** /'fɪzɪkli/ *adverb*: *I'm not
physically fit.*

physical education /ˌfɪzɪkl edʒu'keɪʃn/
(*abbr.* **PE**) *noun* (*no plural*)
sport and exercise that are done as a subject
at school

physicist /'fɪzɪsɪst/ *noun*
a person who studies or knows a lot about
PHYSICS

physics /'fɪzɪks/ *noun* (*no plural*)
the scientific study of things like heat, light
and sound

pianist /'pɪənɪst/ *noun*
a person who plays the piano

piano 0━┱ /pi'ænəʊ/ *noun* (*plural* **pianos**)
a big musical instrument that you play by
pressing black and white bars (called **keys**):
Can you play the piano?

pick[1] 0━┱ /pɪk/ *verb* (picks, picking,
picked /pɪkt/)
1 to take the person or thing you like best

piano

|pedal

⊃ SAME MEANING **choose**: *They picked
Simon as their captain.*
2 to take a flower, fruit or vegetable from
the place where it grows: *I've picked some
flowers for you.*
pick on somebody (*informal*) to treat
somebody in an unfair or cruel way: *Sally gets
picked on by the other kids.*
pick somebody or something out to
be able to see somebody or something
among a lot of others: *Can you pick out my
father in this photo?*
pick somebody up to come to get
somebody, especially in a car: *My father picks
me up from school.*
pick somebody or something up to
take and lift somebody or something: *She
picked up the kitten and stroked it.* ◇ *The
phone stopped ringing just as I picked it up.*
pick something up to learn something
without really studying it: *Did you pick up any
Japanese while you were in Tokyo?*

pick[2] /pɪk/ *noun* (*no plural*)
the one that you choose; your choice
take your pick to choose what you like:
*We've got orange juice, lemonade or milk.
Take your pick.*

pickaxe (*British*) (*American* **pickax**)
/'pɪkæks/ *noun*
a large sharp metal tool with a wooden
handle which is used for breaking rocks or
hard ground

picket /'pɪkɪt/ *noun*
a person or group of people who stand
outside the place where they work when
there is a STRIKE (= an organized protest),
and try to stop other people going in
▶ **picket** *verb* (pickets, picketing,
picketed): *Workers were picketing the factory.*

pickpocket /'pɪkpɒkɪt/ *noun*
a person who steals things from people's
pockets

picnic /'pɪknɪk/ *noun*
a meal that you eat outside, away from
home: *We had a picnic by the river.*
▶ **picnic** *verb* (picnics, picnicking,

picnicked /'pɪknɪkt/): *We picnicked on the beach yesterday.*

picture¹ 0ᴍ /'pɪktʃə(r)/ *noun*
a drawing, painting or photograph: *Julie drew a picture of her dog.* ◇ *They showed us some pictures* (= photographs) *of their wedding.* ◇ *I took a picture* (= a photograph) *of the house.* ➔ Look at Picture Dictionary page **P10**.

picture² /'pɪktʃə(r)/ *verb* (pictures, picturing, pictured /'pɪktʃəd/)
to imagine something in your mind: *I can just picture them lying on the beach.*

pie

pastry — — filling

pie /paɪ/ *noun*
a type of food made of meat, fruit or vegetables covered with PASTRY (= a mixture of flour, butter and water): *an apple pie*

piece 0ᴍ /piːs/ *noun*

> 🔎 **SPELLING**
>
> Remember! **I** comes before **E** in **piece**. Use the phrase **a piece of pie** to help you remember.

1 a part of something: *Would you like another piece of cake?* ◇ *a piece of broken glass*
2 one single thing: *Have you got a piece of paper?* ◇ *That's an interesting piece of news.*
3 a coin: *a 50p piece*
fall to pieces to become very old and in bad condition; to break: *The chair fell to pieces when I sat on it.*
in pieces broken: *The teapot lay in pieces on the floor.*
take something to pieces to divide something into its parts: *I took the bed to pieces because it was too big to go through the door.*

pier /pɪə(r)/ *noun*
a long structure that is built from the land into the sea, where people can walk or get on and off boats

pierce /pɪəs/ *verb* (pierces, piercing, pierced /pɪəst/)
to make a hole in something with a sharp point: *The nail pierced her skin.* ◇ *I'm going to have my ears pierced.*

pier

piercing /'pɪəsɪŋ/ *adjective*
A **piercing** sound is very loud and unpleasant: *a piercing cry*

pig 0ᴍ /pɪg/ *noun*
1 a fat animal that people keep on farms for its meat
➔ Look at Picture Dictionary page **P2**.

> 🔎 **WORD BUILDING**
>
> A young pig is called a **piglet**. Meat from a pig is called **pork**, **bacon** or **ham**.

2 an unkind person or a person who eats too much: *You've eaten all the biscuits, you pig!*

pigeon /'pɪdʒɪn/ *noun*
a grey bird that you often see in towns

piglet /'pɪglət/ *noun*
a young pig

pigsty /'pɪgstaɪ/ (*also* sty) *noun* (*plural* pigsties)
a small building where pigs live

pigtail /'pɪgteɪl/ *noun*
hair that you twist together (**plait**) and tie at the sides or at the back of your head ➔ Look at the picture at **hair**.

pile¹ 0ᴍ /paɪl/ *noun*
a lot of things on top of one another; a large amount of something: *Clothes lay in piles on the floor.* ◇ *a pile of earth*

pile

> 🔎 **WHICH WORD?**
>
> **Pile** or **heap**?
> A **pile** may be tidy or untidy. A **heap** is untidy.

pile² 0ᴍ /paɪl/ *verb* (piles, piling, piled /paɪld/)
to put a lot of things on top of one another: *She piled the boxes on the table.*

pilgrim /ˈpɪlɡrɪm/ *noun*
a person who travels a long way to a place because it has a special religious meaning

pilgrimage /ˈpɪlɡrɪmɪdʒ/ *noun*
a journey that a PILGRIM makes

pill /pɪl/ *noun*
a small round hard piece of medicine that you swallow ➪ SAME MEANING **tablet**: *Take one of these **pills** before every meal.*

pillar

pillar

pillar /ˈpɪlə(r)/ *noun*
a tall strong piece of stone, wood or metal that holds up a building

pillow /ˈpɪləʊ/ *noun*
a soft thing that you put your head on when you are in bed

pillowcase /ˈpɪləʊkeɪs/ *noun*
a cover for a PILLOW

pilot 0➔ /ˈpaɪlət/ *noun*
a person who flies a plane ➪ Look at Picture Dictionary page **P12**.

pimple /ˈpɪmpl/ *noun*
a small spot on your skin

pins

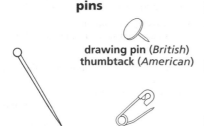

drawing pin (*British*)
thumbtack (*American*)

pin   safety pin

pin[1] 0➔ /pɪn/ *noun*
a small thin piece of metal with a flat part at one end and a sharp point at the other. You use a **pin** for holding things together or fixing one thing to another. ➪ Look also at **drawing pin** and **safety pin**.

pin[2] /pɪn/ *verb* (pins, pinning, pinned /pɪnd/)
1 to fix things together with a pin or pins: *Could you **pin** this notice to the board?*
2 to hold somebody or something so that they cannot move: *He tried to get away, but they pinned him against the wall.*

pinch

pinch[1] /pɪntʃ/ *verb* (pinches, pinching, pinched /pɪntʃt/)
1 to press somebody's skin tightly between your thumb and finger: *Don't pinch me – it hurts!*
2 (*British*, *informal*) to steal something: *Who's pinched my pen?*

pinch[2] /pɪntʃ/ *noun* (*plural* pinches)
1 the act of pressing somebody's skin tightly between your thumb and finger: *He gave me a pinch on the arm to wake me up.*
2 an amount of something you can hold between your thumb and finger: *Add a pinch of salt to the soup.*

pine /paɪn/ (*also* pine tree /ˈpaɪn triː/) *noun*
a tall tree with thin sharp leaves (called needles) that do not fall off in winter

pineapple /ˈpaɪnæpl/ *noun*
a big fruit that is yellow inside and has a rough brown skin ➪ Look at Picture Dictionary page **P8**.

ping-pong /ˈpɪŋ pɒŋ/ *noun* (*no plural*)
a game where players hit a small light ball over a net on a big table ➪ SAME MEANING **table tennis**

pink 0➔ /pɪŋk/ *adjective*
with a light red colour: *a pink jumper*
▶ **pink** *noun* (*no plural*): *She was dressed in pink.*

pins and needles /ˌpɪnz ən ˈniːdlz/ *noun* (*plural*)
a feeling that you sometimes get in a part of your body when you have not moved it for a long time

pint /paɪnt/ (*abbr.* pt) *noun*
a measure of liquid (=0.57 litres). There are eight **pints** in a **gallon**: *a pint of beer ◊ two pints of milk*

A
B
C
D
E
F
G
H
I
J
K
L
M
N
O
P
Q
R
S
T
U
V
W
X
Y
Z

A
B
C
D
E
F
G
H
I
J
K
L
M
N
O
P
Q
R
S
T
U
V
W
X
Y
Z

pioneer /ˌpaɪə'nɪə(r)/ *noun*
a person who goes somewhere or does something before other people: *the pioneers of the American West*

pip /pɪp/ *noun* (*British*)
the seed of some fruits. Lemons, oranges and apples have **pips**. ⊃ Look at Picture Dictionary page **P8**.

pipe 0ⲡ /paɪp/ *noun*
1 a long tube that takes something such as water, oil or gas from one place to another: *A water pipe is leaking under the ground.*
2 a tube with a small bowl at one end that is used for smoking TOBACCO (= the dried leaves used for making cigarettes): *My grandfather smoked a pipe.*

pipeline /'paɪplaɪn/ *noun*
a line of pipes that carry oil or gas a long way
in the pipeline Something that is **in the pipeline** is being planned or prepared and will happen soon.

pirate /'paɪrət/ *noun*
a person on a ship who robs other ships

pistol /'pɪstl/ *noun*
a small gun

pit /pɪt/ *noun*
1 a deep hole in the ground
2 a deep hole that people make in the ground to take out coal ⊃ SAME MEANING **mine**

pitch¹ /pɪtʃ/ *noun*
1 (*plural* **pitches**) a piece of ground where you play games like football: *a cricket pitch*

🔎 **WORD BUILDING**

You also play **hockey** and **rugby** on a **pitch**.
You play **badminton** and **tennis** on a **court**.

2 (*no plural*) how high or low a sound is

pitch² /pɪtʃ/ *verb* (**pitches**, **pitching**, **pitched** /pɪtʃt/)
to put up a tent: *We pitched our tent under a big tree.*

pitcher /'pɪtʃə(r)/ *American English for* JUG

pity¹ 0ⲡ /'pɪti/ *noun* (*no plural*)
1 a feeling of sadness for a person or an animal who is in pain or who has problems: *I feel no **pity** for him – it's his own fault.*
2 something that makes you feel a little sad or disappointed ⊃ SAME MEANING **shame**: *It's **a pity** you can't come to the party.*
take pity on somebody to help somebody because you feel sad for them: *I took pity on her and gave her some money.*

pity² /'pɪti/ *verb* (**pities**, **pitying**, **pitied**, **has pitied** /'pɪtid/)
to feel sad for somebody who is in pain or who has problems: *I really pity people who haven't got anywhere to live.*

pizza /'piːtsə/ *noun* (*plural* **pizzas**)
a flat round piece of bread with tomatoes, cheese and other things on top, that is cooked in an oven ⊃ Look at Picture Dictionary page **P7**.

place¹ 0ⲡ /pleɪs/ *noun*
1 a particular area or position: *Put the book back in the right place.*
2 a particular building, town or country: *Budapest is a very interesting place.* ◇ *Do you know **a good place to** have lunch?*
3 a seat or space for one person: *An old man was sitting **in** my place.*
4 the position that you have in a race, competition or test: *Alice finished **in** second place.*
in place where it should be; in the right place: *Use tape to hold the picture in place.*
in place of somebody or **something** instead of somebody or something: *You can use milk in place of cream.*
take place to happen: *The wedding of John and Sara will take place on 22 May.*

place² 0ⲡ /pleɪs/ *verb* (**places**, **placing**, **placed** /pleɪst/) (*formal*)
to put something somewhere: *The waiter placed the meal in front of me.*

plague /pleɪg/ *noun*
a disease that spreads quickly and kills many people

plain¹ 0ⲡ /pleɪn/ *adjective* (**plainer**, **plainest**)
1 easy to see, hear or understand ⊃ SAME MEANING **clear**: *It's **plain that** he's unhappy.*
2 simple and ordinary: *plain food*
3 with no pattern; all one colour: *She wore a plain blue dress.*
4 not pretty: *She was a plain child.*

plain² /pleɪn/ *noun*
a large piece of flat land

plainly /'pleɪnli/ *adverb*
in a way that is easy to see, hear or

understand ⊃ SAME MEANING **clearly**: *They were plainly very angry.*

plait /plæt/ (*British*) (*American* braid) *noun*
a long piece of hair that somebody has divided into three parts and put over and under each other: *She wears her hair in plaits.* ⊃ Look at the picture at **hair**.
▸ **plait** *verb* (plaits, plaiting, plaited): *She plaited her hair.*

plan¹ 0-π /plæn/ *noun*
1 something that you have decided to do and how you are going to do it: *What are your holiday plans?* ◇ *They have plans to build a new school.*
2 a map showing a building or a town: *a street plan of London*
3 a drawing that shows how a new building, room or machine will be made: *Have you seen the plans for the new shopping centre?*

plan² 0-π /plæn/ *verb* (plans, planning, planned /plænd/)
to decide what you are going to do and how you are going to do it: *They're planning a holiday in Australia next summer.* ◇ *I'm planning to go to university.*

plane 0-π /pleɪn/ *noun* (*British also* aeroplane) (*American* airplane)
a vehicle with wings that can fly through the air: *I like travelling by plane.* ◇ *What time does your plane land?* ◇ *Our plane took off three hours late.* ◇ *I caught the next plane to Dublin.*

> 🔎 **WORD BUILDING**
> A plane **lands** and **takes off** at an **airport**.

⊃ Look at Picture Dictionary page **P1**.

planet 0-π /'plænɪt/ *noun*
a large round object in space that moves around the sun or another star: *Earth, Mars and Venus are planets.*

plank /plæŋk/ *noun*
a long flat piece of wood

plant¹ 0-π /plɑːnt/ *noun*
anything that grows from the ground: *Don't forget to water the plants.*

> 🔎 **WORD BUILDING**
> There are many different types of **plant**. Here are some of them: bamboo, cactus, grass, moss, seaweed, tree. Do you know any others?

plant² 0-π /plɑːnt/ *verb* (plants, planting, planted)
to put plants or seeds in the ground: *We planted some roses in the garden.*

plant

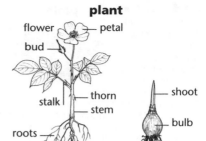

plantation /plɑːn'teɪʃn/ *noun*
a piece of land where things like tea, bananas or rubber grow: *a sugar plantation*

plaster¹ /'plɑːstə(r)/ *noun*
1 (*no plural*) a substance that is used for covering walls inside buildings

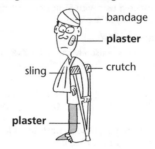

2 (*no plural*) a hard covering around a broken bone; the substance that the covering is made of: *My leg was in plaster.*
3 (*plural* plasters) (*British*) (*American* Band-Aid™) a small piece of sticky material that you put over a cut on your body to keep it clean

plaster² /'plɑːstə(r)/ *verb* (plasters, plastering, plastered)
1 to cover a wall with PLASTER¹(1) to make it smooth
2 to cover a surface with a large amount of something: *She plastered herself in suntan lotion.*

plastic 0-π /'plæstɪk/ *noun* (*no plural*)
an artificial material that is used for making many different things: *These chairs are made of plastic.* ◇ *plastic cups*

plastic surgery /ˌplæstɪk 'sɜːdʒəri/ *noun* (*no plural*)
medical operations that doctors can do to improve a person's appearance

plate 0-π /pleɪt/ *noun*
a round dish that you put food on ⊃ Look at the picture on the next page. ⊃ Look also at **number plate**.

platform 0→ /'plætfɔ:m/ *noun*
1 the part of a railway station where people get on and off trains: *The train to London leaves from platform 5.*
2 a surface that is higher than the floor, where people stand so that other people can see and hear them: *The headmaster went up to the platform to make his speech.*

play¹ 0→ /pleɪ/ *verb* (plays, playing, played /pleɪd/)
1 to have fun; to do something to enjoy yourself: *The children were playing with their toys.*
2 to take part in a game: *I like playing tennis.* ◇ *Do you know how to play chess?*
3 to make music with a musical instrument: *My sister plays the piano very well.*

> 🔎 **GRAMMAR**
> Note that we usually say 'play **the** violin, **the** piano, etc.': *I'm learning to play the clarinet.*

4 to put a record, CD, DVD, etc. in a machine and listen to it: *Shall I play the CD again?*
5 to act the part of somebody in a play: *Who wants to play the policeman?*

play² 0→ /pleɪ/ *noun*
1 (*plural* plays) a story that you watch in the theatre or on television, or listen to on the radio: *We went to see a play at the National Theatre.*
2 (*no plural*) games; what children do for fun: *work and play*

> 🔎 **GRAMMAR**
> Be careful! We **play** football, cards, etc. or we **have a game of** football, cards, etc. (NOT **a play**).

player 0→ /'pleɪə(r)/ *noun*
1 a person who plays a game: *football players*
2 a person who plays a musical instrument: *a trumpet player*

playful /'pleɪfl/ *adjective*
full of fun; not serious: *a playful puppy* ◇ *a playful remark*

playground /'pleɪɡraʊnd/ *noun*
an area where children can play, for example at school

playing card /'pleɪɪŋ kɑ:d/ (*also* card) *noun*
one of a set of 52 cards with numbers and

plate

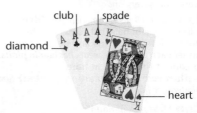

playing cards

club | spade

diamond

heart

pictures on them that you use for playing games: *a pack of playing cards*

playing field /'pleɪɪŋ fi:ld/ *noun*
a large area of grass where people play sports like football

playtime /'pleɪtaɪm/ *noun* (*British*) (*American* **recess**)
the time at school between lessons when you can go out and play: *She fell over at playtime.*

plea /pli:/ *noun*
asking for something with strong feeling: *He made a plea for help.*

plead /pli:d/ *verb* (pleads, pleading, pleaded)
1 to ask for something in a very strong way: *He pleaded with his parents to buy him a guitar.*
2 to say in a court of law that you did or did not do a crime: *She pleaded not guilty to murder.*

pleasant 0→ /'pleznt/ *adjective*
nice, enjoyable or friendly: *The weather here is very pleasant.* ◇ *He's a very pleasant person.* ⊃ OPPOSITE **unpleasant**
▶ **pleasantly** /'plezntli/ *adverb*: *a pleasantly cool room*

please¹ 0→ /pli:z/ *exclamation*
a word that you use when you ask for something politely: *What's the time, please?* ◇ *Two cups of coffee, please.* ◇ *'Would you like a cake?' 'Yes, please.'*

please² 0→ /pli:z/ *verb* (pleases, pleasing, pleased /pli:zd/)
to make somebody happy: *I wore my best clothes to please my mother.*

pleased 0→ /pli:zd/ *adjective*
happy: *He wasn't very pleased to see me.* ◇ *Are you pleased with your new watch?* ⊃ Look at the note at **glad**.

pleasure 0→ /'pleʒə(r)/ *noun*
1 (*no plural*) the feeling of being happy or enjoying something: *She gets a lot of pleasure from her music.*

2 (*plural* **pleasures**) something that makes you happy: *It was a pleasure to meet you.*
it's a pleasure You say 'it's a pleasure' as a polite way of answering somebody who thanks you: '*Thank you for your help.*' '*It's a pleasure.*'
with pleasure You say 'with pleasure' to show in a polite way that you are happy to do something: '*Can you help me move these boxes?*' '*Yes, with pleasure.*'

pleat /pliːt/ *noun*
a fold that is part of a skirt, a pair of trousers, etc.

pled /pled/ *American English for* PLEADED

plenty 0🔑 /'plenti/ *pronoun*
as much or as many as you need; a lot: '*Do we need more chairs?*' '*No, there are plenty.*' ◇ *We've got **plenty of** time to get there.*

pliers /'plaɪəz/ *noun* (*plural*)
a tool for holding things tightly or for cutting wire: *Have you got **a pair of pliers**?*

plod /plɒd/ *verb* (**plods, plodding, plodded**)
to walk slowly in a heavy tired way: *We plodded up the hill in the rain.*

plot¹ /plɒt/ *noun*
1 what happens in a story, play or film: *This book has a very exciting plot.*
2 a secret plan to do something bad: *a plot to kill the President*
3 a small piece of land that you use or you plan to use for a special purpose: *She bought a small plot of land to build a house on.* ◇ *a vegetable plot*

plot² /plɒt/ *verb* (**plots, plotting, plotted**)
to make a secret plan to do something bad: *They plotted to rob the bank.*

plough

plough (*British*) (*American* **plow**) /plaʊ/ *noun*
a large farm tool that is pulled across a field to dig the soil
▶ **plough** *verb*: *The farmer ploughed his fields.*

pluck /plʌk/ *verb* (**plucks, plucking, plucked** /plʌkt/)
to remove something by pulling it quickly: *He plucked the letter from her hands.* ◇ *We needed to pluck the chicken* (= remove its feathers).

plugs

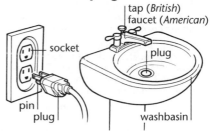

tap (*British*)
faucet (*American*)
socket
plug
pin plug
washbasin

plug¹ /plʌg/ *noun*
1 a thing with metal pins that joins a lamp, machine, etc. to a place in the wall (called a **socket**) where there is electricity
2 a round thing that you put in the hole in a bath, to keep the water in

plug² /plʌg/ *verb* (**plugs, plugging, plugged** /plʌgd/)
to fill a hole, so that nothing can get out: *He plugged the hole in the pipe with an old rag.*
plug something in to join a lamp, machine, etc. to the electricity, using a PLUG: *Can you plug in the television, please?*
⊃ OPPOSITE **unplug**

plughole /'plʌghəʊl/ (*British*) *noun*
a hole in a bath where water flows away

plum /plʌm/ *noun*
a soft round fruit with a stone in the middle
⊃ Look at Picture Dictionary page **P8**.

plumber /'plʌmə(r)/ *noun*
a person whose job is to put in and repair things like water pipes and baths ⊃ Look at Picture Dictionary page **P12**.

plumbing /'plʌmɪŋ/ *noun* (*no plural*)
1 the pipes that carry water into and around a building: *The builders are putting in the plumbing and central heating.*
2 the work of a PLUMBER

plump /plʌmp/ *adjective* (**plumper, plumpest**)
quite fat, in a nice way: *a plump baby*

plunge /plʌndʒ/ *verb* (**plunges, plunging, plunged** /plʌndʒd/)
1 to jump or fall suddenly into something: *She plunged into the pool.*
2 to push something suddenly and strongly into something else: *I plunged my hand into the water.*

plural 0🔑 /'plʊərəl/ *noun*
(*grammar*) the form of a word that shows there is more than one: *The plural of 'child' is 'children'.*
▶ **plural** *adjective*: *Most plural nouns in English end in 's'.* ⊃ OPPOSITE **singular**

plus /plʌs/ *preposition*
added to; and: *Two plus three is five*
(2 + 3 = 5). ◇ *All of our class plus half of Class*
Four are going. ➔ Look at **minus**.

p.m. /ˌpiː ˈem/ *abbreviation*
You use **p.m.** after a time to show that it is
between midday and midnight: *The plane*
leaves at 3 p.m. ➔ We use **a.m.** for times
between midnight and midday.

pneumonia /njuːˈməʊniə/ *noun* (no
plural)
a serious illness of the LUNGS (= the parts of
your body that you breathe with)

poach /pəʊtʃ/ *verb* (poaches, poaching,
poached /pəʊtʃt/)
1 to cook food gently in liquid: *I had a*
poached egg for breakfast.
2 to kill and steal animals, birds or fish from
another person's land
▸ **poacher** *noun* a person who kills or steals
animals, etc. from another person's land: *The*
elephant had been shot by poachers.

PO Box /ˌpiː ˈəʊ bɒks/ *noun* (*plural* PO
Boxes)
a box in a post office for keeping the letters
of a person or office: *The address is PO Box*
63, Bristol BS7 1JN.

pocket 0➔ /ˈpɒkɪt/ *noun*
the part of a piece of clothing that you can
put things in: *I put the key in my pocket.*
➔ Look at the picture at **shirt**.
pick somebody's pocket to steal money
from somebody's pocket or bag

pocketbook /ˈpɒkɪtbʊk/ *American English*
for WALLET

pocket money /ˈpɒkɪt mʌni/ *noun* (no
plural)
money that parents give to a child each
week to buy things: *How much pocket money*
do you get?

pod /pɒd/ *noun*
a long thin case that some plants have,
which is filled with seeds: *Peas grow in pods.*
➔ Look at Picture Dictionary page **P9**.

poem 0➔ /ˈpəʊɪm/ *noun*
words arranged in lines in an artistic way,
often with sounds repeated at the ends of
lines: *He wrote poems about the beauty of the*
countryside.

poet /ˈpəʊɪt/ *noun*
a person who writes poems

poetic /pəʊˈetɪk/ *adjective*
like a poem: *poetic language*

poetry 0➔ /ˈpəʊətri/ *noun* (no plural)
poems: *Wordsworth wrote beautiful poetry.*

point[1] 0➔ /pɔɪnt/ *noun*
1 a fact, an idea or an opinion: *You* **made**
some interesting **points** (= said some
interesting things) *in your essay.* ➔ Look at
point of view.
2 the purpose of, or the reason for, doing
something: ***The point of** going to school is to*
learn. ◇ ***What's the point** of going to her*
house? She's not at home. ◇ ***There's no point***
in waiting for Julie – she isn't coming.
3 a particular moment in time: *It started to*
rain and **at that point** *we decided to go home.*
4 a particular place: *No parking beyond this*
point.
5 a small round mark (.) that we use when
writing part of a number (called a **decimal**):
2.5 (= two point five)
6 the sharp end of something: *the point of a*
needle
7 a mark that you win in a game or sport:
Our team scored six points.
be on the point of doing something
If you **are on the point of doing**
something, you are going to do it very
soon: *I was on the point of leaving when he*
turned up.

point[2] 0➔ /pɔɪnt/ *verb* (points, pointing,
pointed)
1 to show where something is using your
finger, a stick, etc.: *I asked him where the*
bank was and he **pointed** *across the road.* ◇
There was a sign **pointing towards** *the city*
centre.
2 to hold something towards somebody or
something: *She was* **pointing** *a gun* **at** *his*
head.
point something out to tell or show
somebody something: *Eva* **pointed out** *that*
my bag was open.

pointed 0➔ /ˈpɔɪntɪd/ *adjective*
with a sharp end: *a long pointed nose*

pointless /ˈpɔɪntləs/ *adjective*
with no use or purpose: *It's pointless telling*
Paul anything – he never listens.

point of view /ˌpɔɪnt əv ˈvjuː/ (*plural*
points of view) *noun*
an opinion or way of thinking about
something: *The book was written* **from** *the*
father's **point of view**.

poison[1] 0➔ /ˈpɔɪzn/ *noun* (no plural)
something that will kill you or make you very
ill if you eat or drink it: *rat poison*

poison[2] 0➔ /ˈpɔɪzn/ *verb* (poisons,
poisoning, poisoned /ˈpɔɪznd/)
to use **poison** to kill or hurt somebody or
something

A
B
C
D
E
F
G
H
I
J
K
L
M
N
O
P
Q
R
S
T
U
V
W
X
Y
Z

poisonous 0–π /ˈpɔɪzənəs/ *adjective*
Something that is **poisonous** will kill you or make you very ill if you eat or drink it: *Some mushrooms are poisonous.*

poke /pəʊk/ *verb*
(pokes, poking, poked /pəʊkt/)

poke

1 to push somebody or something hard with your finger or another long thin thing: *She poked me in the eye with a pencil.*
2 to push something quickly somewhere: *Jeff poked his head out of the window.*
▸ **poke** *noun*: *I gave her a poke to wake her up.*

poker /ˈpəʊkə(r)/ *noun*
1 (*no plural*) a game that people play with cards, usually for money
2 (*plural* pokers) a metal stick that you use for moving the wood in a fire ⊃ Look at the picture at **fireplace**.

polar /ˈpəʊlə(r)/ *adjective*
connected with the areas around the top and bottom of the earth (called the **North Pole** and the **South Pole**): *the polar regions*

polar bear /ˌpəʊlə ˈbeə(r)/ *noun*
a large white animal that lives near the North Pole ⊃ Look at Picture Dictionary page **P3**.

pole /pəʊl/ *noun*
1 a long thin piece of wood or metal. **Poles** are often used to hold something up: *a flag pole* ◇ *tent poles* ⊃ Look at the picture at **ski**.
2 one of two places at the top and bottom of the earth: *the North Pole* ◇ *the South Pole*

police 0–π /pəˈliːs/ *noun* (*plural*)
the official organization whose job is to make sure that people do not break the laws of a country: *Have the police found the murderer?* ◇ *a police car*

police constable /pəˌliːs ˈkʌnstəbl/ (*abbr.* PC) *noun*
an ordinary police officer: *PC Nolan*

police force /pəˈliːs fɔːs/ *noun*
all the police officers in a country or part of a country

policeman /pəˈliːsmən/ *noun* (*plural* policemen /pəˈliːsmən/)
a man who is a police officer ⊃ Look at Picture Dictionary page **P12**.

police officer /pəˈliːs ɒfɪsə(r)/ *noun*
a man or woman who works in the police

police station /pəˈliːs steɪʃn/ *noun*
an office where police officers work: *They*

took the men to the police station for questioning.

policewoman /pəˈliːswʊmən/ *noun* (*plural* policewomen)
a woman who is a police officer

policy /ˈpɒləsi/ *noun* (*plural* policies)
the plans of a government or organization: *What is the government's policy on education?*

polish¹ /ˈpɒlɪʃ/ *noun* (*no plural*)
a cream or liquid that you put on something to make it shine: *furniture polish*

polish² /ˈpɒlɪʃ/ *verb* (polishes, polishing, polished /ˈpɒlɪʃt/)
to rub something so that it shines: *Have you polished your shoes?*

polite 0–π /pəˈlaɪt/ *adjective*
speaking or behaving in a way that shows respect: *It is polite to say 'please' when you ask for something.* ⊃ OPPOSITE **impolite** or **rude**
▸ **politely** /pəˈlaɪtli/ *adverb*: *He asked politely for a glass of water.*
▸ **politeness** /pəˈlaɪtnəs/ *noun* (*no plural*): *He stood up out of politeness and offered her his seat.*

political 0–π /pəˈlɪtɪkl/ *adjective*
connected with politics or the government: *political parties* ◇ *his political beliefs*
▸ **politically** /pəˈlɪtɪkli/ *adverb*: *a politically powerful country*

politician 0–π /ˌpɒləˈtɪʃn/ *noun*
a person who works in politics: *Politicians of all parties supported us.*

politics 0–π /ˈpɒlətɪks/ *noun* (*no plural*)
1 the work and ideas that are connected with government: *Are you interested in politics?*
2 the study of government: *She studied Politics at university.* ⊃ Look at the notes at **Congress**, **election** and **party**.

poll /pəʊl/ *noun*
1 a way of discovering opinions by asking a group of people questions: *A recent poll showed that 73% were unhappy with the government.*
2 an election; the number of votes in an election: *The country will go to the polls* (= vote) *in June.*

pollen /ˈpɒlən/ *noun* (*no plural*)
the yellow powder in flowers that is taken to other flowers by insects or by the wind

pollute /pəˈluːt/ *verb* (pollutes, polluting, polluted)
to make the air, rivers, etc. dirty and dangerous: *Many of Britain's rivers are polluted with chemicals from factories.*

pollution /pəˈluːʃn/ *noun* (*no plural*)
1 the action of making the air, rivers, etc. dirty and dangerous: *We must stop the pollution of our beaches.*
2 dirty and dangerous chemicals, gases, etc. that harm the environment

polystyrene /ˌpɒliˈstaɪriːn/ *noun* (*no plural*)
soft white plastic that is used for packing things so that they do not get broken

pond /pɒnd/ *noun*
a small area of water: *We have a fish pond in our garden.*

pony /ˈpəʊni/ *noun* (*plural* ponies)
a small horse

ponytail /ˈpəʊniteɪl/ *noun*
long hair that you tie at the back of your head so that it hangs down ⊃ Look at the picture at **hair**.

pool¹ 0̶ᴡ /puːl/ *noun*
1 (*also* swimming pool) a place that has been built for people to swim in: *Karen dived into the pool.*
2 a small area of liquid or light on the ground: *She was lying in a pool of blood.*

pool² /puːl/ *verb* (pools, pooling, pooled /puːld/)
to collect money or ideas together from different people: *First we'll work in pairs, then we'll pool our ideas.*

poor 0̶ᴡ /pɔː(r)/ *adjective* (poorer, poorest)
1 with very little money: *She was too poor to buy clothes for her children.* ◇ *She gave her life to helping the poor* (= poor people). ⊃ The noun is **poverty**. ⊃ OPPOSITE **rich**
2 a word that you use when you feel sad because somebody has problems: *Poor Tina! She's feeling ill.*
3 bad: *My grandfather is in very poor health.*

poorly¹ /ˈpɔːli/ *adverb*
badly: *The street is poorly lit.*

poorly² /ˈpɔːli/ *adjective* (British, informal)
ill: *She felt poorly.*

pop¹ /pɒp/ *noun*
1 (*no plural*) (*also* pop music) modern music that is most popular among young people: *What's your favourite pop group?* ◇ *a pop singer*
2 (*plural* pops) a short sharp sound: *The cork came out of the bottle with a loud pop.*

pop² /pɒp/ *verb* (pops, popping, popped /pɒpt/)
1 to burst, or to make something burst, with a short sharp sound: *The balloon will pop if you put a pin in it.*

2 to come or go somewhere quickly: *She's just popped out to the shops.*
3 to put something somewhere quickly: *Katie popped a sweet into her mouth.*
pop in to make a short visit: *We were near Tim's house so we popped in for a cup of coffee.*
pop up (*informal*) to appear suddenly: *The menu pops up when you double-click on the link.* ◇ *New restaurants were popping up everywhere.*

popcorn /ˈpɒpkɔːn/ *noun* (*no plural*)
light white balls of cooked grain (from a plant called maize), which are covered in salt or sugar

pope /pəʊp/ *noun*
the head of the Roman Catholic Church: *Pope Benedict*

Popsicle™ /ˈpɒpsɪkl/ *American English for* ICE LOLLY

popular 0̶ᴡ /ˈpɒpjələ(r)/ *adjective*
liked by a lot of people: *Football is a popular sport in Britain.* ⊃ OPPOSITE **unpopular**

popularity /ˌpɒpjuˈlærəti/ *noun* (*no plural*)
being liked by many people

population /ˌpɒpjuˈleɪʃn/ *noun*
the number of people who live in a place: *What is the population of your country?*

porch /pɔːtʃ/ *noun*
1 (*British*) a small area at the door of a house or a church, that is covered by a roof and often has walls
2 *American English for* VERANDAH

pork /pɔːk/ *noun* (*no plural*)
meat from a pig: *pork sausages* ⊃ Look at the note at **pig**.

porridge /ˈpɒrɪdʒ/ *noun* (*no plural*)
a soft food made by boiling grain with liquid: *porridge oats*

port 0̶ᴡ /pɔːt/ *noun*
a town or city by the sea, where ships arrive and leave: *Liverpool is a large port in the North of England.*

portable /ˈpɔːtəbl/ *adjective*
able to be moved or carried easily: *a portable television*

porter /ˈpɔːtə(r)/ *noun*
1 a person whose job is to carry people's bags in places like railway stations and hotels
2 (*British*) a person whose job is to look after the entrance of a hotel or other large building

portion /ˈpɔːʃn/ *noun*
a part of something that one person gets: *He*

gave a **portion of** the money to each of his children. ◇ a large portion of chips

portrait /'pɔːtreɪt/ *noun*
a painting or picture of a person

posh /pɒʃ/ *adjective* (posher, poshest)
1 expensive and of good quality: a posh restaurant
2 (British) connected with a high social class, in a way that ordinary people do not like: They thought she was too posh.

position 0̄ₜ /pə'zɪʃn/ *noun*
1 the place where somebody or something is: Can you show me the **position of** your village on the map? ◇ Is everyone **in position** (= in the right place)?
2 the way that somebody or something is sitting, standing, facing, etc.: She was still sitting **in** the same **position** when I came back. ◇ Keep the box in an upright position.
3 how things are at a certain time: He's **in a** difficult **position** – he hasn't got enough money to finish his studies.
4 a job: There have been over a hundred applications for the **position of** Sales Manager.

positive 0̄ₜ /'pɒzətɪv/ *adjective*
1 thinking or talking about the good parts of a situation: It's important to stay positive. ◇ The teacher was very **positive about** my work. ⊃ OPPOSITE **negative**
2 completely certain: Are you **positive that** you closed the door? ⊃ SAME MEANING **sure**

positively *adverb* /'pɒzətɪvli/ (informal)
really; extremely: The idea is positively stupid.

possess /pə'zes/ *verb* (possesses, possessing, possessed /pə'zest/) (formal)
to have or own something: He lost everything that he possessed in the fire.

possession /pə'zeʃn/ *noun*

> 🔍 **SPELLING**
> Remember! You spell **possession** with **SS** and **SS**.

1 (no plural) (formal) the fact of having or owning something: The possession of drugs is a crime.
2 possessions (plural) the things that you have or own ⊃ SAME MEANING **belongings**

possibility 0̄ₜ /ˌpɒsə'bɪləti/ *noun* (plural possibilities)
something that might happen: There's a **possibility that** it will rain, so take your umbrella.

possible 0̄ₜ /'pɒsəbl/ *adjective*
able to happen or to be done: Is it possible to get to Birmingham by train? ◇ I'll phone you **as soon as possible**. ⊃ OPPOSITE **impossible**

possibly 0̄ₜ /'pɒsəbli/ *adverb*
1 perhaps: 'Will you be free tomorrow?' 'Possibly.'
2 in a way that can be done: I'll come as soon as I possibly can.

post¹ 0̄ₜ /pəʊst/ *noun*
1 (British) (American **mail**) (no plural) the official system for sending and receiving letters, packages, etc.: I sent your present **by post**.
2 (British) (American **mail**) (no plural) all the letters and packages that you send or receive: Did you get any post this morning?
3 (plural **posts**) a job, especially an important one in a large organization: a government post
4 (plural **posts**) a piece of wood or metal that stands in the ground to hold something or to show where something is: The sign had fallen off the post. ◇ a lamp post ⊃ Look at **goalpost** and **signpost**.

post² 0̄ₜ /pəʊst/ *verb* (posts, posting, posted)
1 (British) (American **mail**) to send a letter or package by post: Could you **post** this **letter** for me?
2 to send somebody to a place to do a job: Sara's company have **posted** her **to** Japan for two years.

postage /'pəʊstɪdʒ/ *noun* (no plural)
money that you pay to send a letter or package

postal /'pəʊstl/ *adjective*
connected with sending and receiving letters, packages, etc.: postal collections

postbox

postbox   **mailbox**
(British)   (American)

postbox /'pəʊstbɒks/ *noun* (plural postboxes) (British) (British also **letter box**) (American **mailbox**)
a box in the street where you put letters that you want to send

postcard

postcard /'pəʊstkɑːd/ *noun*
a card with a picture on one side, that you write on and send by post: *She sent me a postcard from California.*

postcode /'pəʊstkəʊd/ (*British*) (*American* **zip code**) *noun*
a group of numbers and letters that you write at the end of an address

poster /'pəʊstə(r)/ *noun*
a big piece of paper on a wall, with a picture or words on it

postgraduate /ˌpəʊstˈgrædʒuət/ *noun*
a student at a university who has already done a degree

postman /'pəʊstmən/ (*plural* **postmen** /'pəʊstmən/) (*American* **mailman**) *noun*
a person whose job is to take (**deliver**) letters and packages to people's homes

pots

plant pot

yogurt pot

coffee pot

post office 0﹏ /'pəʊst ɒfɪs/ *noun*
a building where you go to send letters and packages and to buy stamps

postpone /pə'spəʊn/ *verb* (**postpones, postponing, postponed** /pə'spəʊnd/)
to say that something will happen later than you planned: *The match was postponed because of the weather.*

pot 0﹏ /pɒt/ *noun*
1 a deep round container for cooking: *a big pot of soup*
2 a container that you use for a special thing: *a teapot* ◇ *a pot of paint* ◇ *a plant pot*

potato 0﹏ /pə'teɪtəʊ/ *noun* (*plural* **potatoes**)
a white vegetable with a brown or red skin that grows underground: *a baked potato* ◇ *mashed potato* ⊃ Look at Picture Dictionary page **P9**.

potato chip /pə'teɪtəʊ tʃɪp/ (*American*) *noun* = CRISP²

potential¹ /pə'tenʃl/ *adjective*
possible; likely to happen or exist: *potential students*

potential² /pə'tenʃl/ *noun* (*no plural*)
qualities or possibilities that exist and can be developed: *She has great potential as a musician.*

pottery /'pɒtəri/ *noun* (*no plural*)
1 cups, plates and other things that are made from CLAY (= heavy earth that becomes hard when it is baked in an oven): *This shop sells beautiful pottery.*
2 the activity of making cups, plates and other things from CLAY: *Her hobby is pottery.*

poultry /'pəʊltri/ *noun* (*plural*)
birds such as chickens that people keep on farms for their eggs or their meat

pounce /paʊns/ *verb* (**pounces, pouncing, pounced** /paʊnst/)
to jump on somebody or something suddenly: *The cat pounced on the bird.*

pound 0﹏ /paʊnd/ *noun*
1 (*symbol* £) money that people use in Britain. There are 100 **pence** in a **pound**: *The computer cost six hundred pounds.* ◇ *a ten-pound note* ◇ *a pound coin* ◇ *I spent £40 today.*
2 (*symbol* lb) a measure of weight (=0.454 kilograms). There are 16 **ounces** in a **pound**: *You need half a pound of flour.* ◇ *2lbs sugar*

> **CULTURE**
> Many older people in Britain still use **ounces**, **pounds** and **stones** instead of **grams** and **kilograms** to measure weight.
> In the US, people use **ounces** and **pounds**, but not **stones**.

pour 0‑ /pɔː(r)/ *verb* (**pours**, **pouring**, **poured** /pɔːd/)
1 to make liquid flow out of or into something: *She poured water into the teapot.* ◇ *She poured me a cup of tea.* ◇ *Pour the sauce over the meat.*
2 to flow quickly: *Oil poured out of the damaged ship.* ◇ *Tears were* ***pouring down*** *her cheeks.*
3 to rain very hard: *It's pouring.* ◇ *It* ***poured with rain*** *all day.*

pour

poverty /ˈpɒvəti/ *noun* (*no plural*)
the state of being poor: *There are many people living* ***in poverty*** *in this city.*

powder 0‑ /ˈpaʊdə(r)/ *noun*
a dry substance like flour that is made of a lot of very small pieces: *Crush the spices to a powder.* ◇ *Can you get some more* ***washing powder*** (= for washing clothes)*?*

power 0‑ /ˈpaʊə(r)/ *noun*
1 (*no plural*) the ability to control people or things; the ability to do things: *The president has a lot of power.* ◇ *I did* ***everything in my power*** (= everything I could do) *to help her.*
2 (*plural* **powers**) the right to do something: *Police officers have the* ***power to*** *arrest people.*
3 (*plural* **powers**) a strong person or country: *There is a meeting of* ***world powers*** *in Rome next week.*
4 (*no plural*) the energy or strength that somebody or something has: *The ship was helpless against the* ***power of*** *the storm.*
5 (*no plural*) energy that can be collected and used for making machines work, making electricity, etc.: *nuclear power*

powerful 0‑ /ˈpaʊəfl/ *adjective*
1 having a lot of strength or power: *The car has a very powerful engine.* ◇ *The president is very powerful.*
2 having a strong effect: *a powerful drug*

powerless /ˈpaʊələs/ *adjective*
not able to do anything: *I was* ***powerless to*** *help.*

power point /ˈpaʊə pɔɪnt/ (*British*) *noun*
a place in a wall where you connect a lamp, machine, etc. to the electricity
➲ SAME MEANING **socket**

power station /ˈpaʊə steɪʃn/ *noun*
a place where electricity is made

PR /ˌpiː ˈɑː(r)/ *abbreviation* = PUBLIC RELATIONS

practical 0‑ /ˈpræktɪkl/ *adjective*
1 connected with doing or making things, not just with ideas: *Have you got any* ***practical experience*** *of teaching?*
2 sensible or suitable; likely to be successful: *Your plan isn't practical.*
➲ OPPOSITE **impractical**
3 good at making and repairing things: *She's a very practical person and has made a lot of improvements to the house.*

practically /ˈpræktɪkli/ *adverb*
almost; nearly: *Don't go out – lunch is practically ready!* ◇ *It rained practically every day of our holiday.*

practice 0‑ /ˈpræktɪs/ *noun* (*no plural*)

> **SPELLING**
> Remember! Don't confuse **practice**, which is a noun in British English, with **practise**, which is a verb: *Our football practice is on Monday, but we should practise every day.*
> In American English you spell both the verb and the noun **practice**.

1 doing something many times so that you will do it well: *You need lots of practice when you're learning to play a musical instrument.*
2 *American English for* PRACTISE
out of practice not good at something, because you have not done it for a long time

practise 0‑ /ˈpræktɪs/ (*British*) (*American* **practice**) *verb* (**practises**, **practising**, **practised** /ˈpræktɪst/)
to do something many times so that you will do it well: *If you want to play the piano well, you must practise every day.* ➲ Look at the note at **practice**.

praise /preɪz/ *verb* (**praises**, **praising**, **praised** /preɪzd/)
to say that somebody or something is good: *She was* ***praised for*** *her hard work.*
▶ **praise** *noun* (*no plural*): *The book has received a lot of praise.*

pram /præm/ (*British*) (*American* **baby carriage**) *noun*
a thing that a baby lies in to go out. It has wheels so that you can push it. ➲ Look at the picture at **pushchair**.

A B C D E F G H I J K L M N O P Q R S T U V W X Y Z

A

prawn /prɔːn/ *noun* (*British*) (*American* **shrimp**)
a small sea animal that is pink after it has been cooked

B

pray /preɪ/ *verb* (prays, praying, prayed /preɪd/)
to speak to God or a god: *They **prayed to** God for help.*

C

D

prayer 0‑ᵐ /preə(r)/ *noun*
1 (*plural* **prayers**) words that you say when you speak to God or a god: *They **said a prayer for** world peace.*
2 (*no plural*) the act of PRAYING: *the power of prayer* ◇ *They knelt **in prayer**.*

E

F

G

preach /priːtʃ/ *verb* (preaches, preaching, preached /priːtʃt/)
to talk about God or a god to a group of people

H

I

preacher /ˈpriːtʃə(r)/ *noun*
a person who gives religious talks in public: *Our preacher tonight is Reverend Jones.*

J

precaution /prɪˈkɔːʃn/ *noun*
something that you do so that bad things will not happen: *I **took the precaution of** locking all the windows when I went out.*

K

L

precious /ˈpreʃəs/ *adjective*
1 very valuable or expensive: *Diamonds are precious stones.*
2 that you consider to be very special: *My family is very precious to me.*

M

N

precise /prɪˈsaɪs/ *adjective*
exactly right: *I gave him precise instructions on how to get to my house.*

O

precisely /prɪˈsaɪsli/ *adverb*
exactly: *They arrived at two o'clock precisely.*

P

predict /prɪˈdɪkt/ *verb* (predicts, predicting, predicted)
to say what you think will happen: *She **predicted that** it would rain, and she was right.*
▶ **prediction** /prɪˈdɪkʃn/ *noun*: *The results confirmed our predictions.*

Q

R

S

T

prefect /ˈpriːfekt/ *noun* (*British*)
an older student in a school who has duties such as making sure that younger students behave

U

V

prefer 0‑ᵐ /prɪˈfɜː(r)/ *verb* (prefers, preferring, preferred /prɪˈfɜːd/)
to like one thing or person better than another: *Would you **prefer** tea or coffee?* ◇ *I would **prefer to** stay at home.* ◇ *He **prefers** going out **to** studying.*

W

X

Y

preferable /ˈprefrəbl/ *adjective*
better or more suitable: *I think living in the country is **preferable to** living in the city.*
▶ **preferably** /ˈprefrəbli/ *adverb*: *Phone

Z

me on Sunday morning, but preferably not too early!*

preference /ˈprefrəns/ *noun*
a feeling that you like one thing or person better than another: *We have lemonade and orange juice – do you have a preference?*

prefix /ˈpriːfɪks/ *noun* (*plural* **prefixes**)
(*grammar*) a group of letters that you add to the beginning of a word to make another word: *The prefix 'im-' means 'not', so 'impossible' means 'not possible'.* ➔ Look at **suffix**.

pregnancy /ˈpregnənsi/ (*plural* **pregnancies**) *noun*
the state of being pregnant: *Many women feel sick **during pregnancy**.*

pregnant 0‑ᵐ /ˈpregnənt/ *adjective*
If a woman is **pregnant**, she has a baby growing in her body: *She's five months pregnant.*

prejudice /ˈpredʒudɪs/ *noun*
a strong idea that you do not like somebody or something, for a reason that is wrong or unfair: *She was a victim of racial prejudice.*

prejudiced /ˈpredʒədɪst/ *adjective*
having a strong idea that you do not like somebody or something, for a reason that is wrong or unfair: *He is **prejudiced against** me because I'm a woman.*

preparation 0‑ᵐ /ˌprepəˈreɪʃn/ *noun*
1 (*no plural*) making something ready: *I packed my bags **in preparation for** the journey.*
2 **preparations** (*plural*) what you do to get ready for something: *They began to **make preparations for** the wedding last year.*

prepare 0‑ᵐ /prɪˈpeə(r)/ *verb* (prepares, preparing, prepared /prɪˈpeəd/)
to make somebody or something ready; to make yourself ready: *Martin is in the kitchen preparing the dinner.* ◇ *I prepared well for the exam.*

prepared 0‑ᵐ /prɪˈpeəd/ *adjective*
ready; able to deal with something: *I wasn't **prepared for** all these problems.*
prepared to do something happy to do something: *I'm not **prepared to** give you any money.* ➔ SAME MEANING **willing**

preposition /ˌprepəˈzɪʃn/ *noun*
(*grammar*) a word that you use before a noun or pronoun to show where, when, how, etc.: *In the sentence 'He travelled from London to Munich','from' and 'to' are prepositions.*

prescribe /prɪˈskraɪb/ *verb* (prescribes, prescribing, prescribed /prɪˈskraɪbd/)
to say that somebody must take a medicine: *The doctor prescribed some tablets.*

prescription /prɪˈskrɪpʃn/ *noun*
a piece of paper that a doctor gives to you with the name of your medicine on it

presence /ˈprezns/ *noun* (*no plural*)
the fact of being in a place: *an experiment to test for the **presence of** oxygen* ◇ *Mother did not allow arguing **in** her **presence*** (= when she was there).

present¹ 0-ᵣ /ˈpreznt/ *adjective*

> 🔎 **PRONUNCIATION**
>
> When the word **present** is a noun or an adjective, you say the first part of the word louder: **PRESent**.
> When the word **present** is a verb, you say the second part of the word louder: **preSENT**.

1 in a place: *The whole class was present.*
➡ OPPOSITE **absent**
2 being or happening now
➡ SAME MEANING **current**: *What is your present job?*

presents

bow | ribbon

wrapping paper

present² 0-ᵣ /ˈpreznt/ *noun*
1 (*plural* presents) something that you give to somebody or get from somebody
➡ SAME MEANING **gift**: *What can I get him for a **birthday present**?*
2 (*no plural*) the time now: *I can't help you **at present** – I'm too busy.*
3 the present (*also* the present tense) (*no plural*) (*grammar*) the form of a verb that you use to talk about what is happening or what exists now ➡ Look at **future** and **past**.

present³ 0-ᵣ /prɪˈzent/ *verb* (presents, presenting, presented)
to give something to somebody, especially in a formal ceremony: *The prizes were **presented to** the winners.* ◇ *They **presented** their teacher **with** some flowers.*

presentation /ˌpreznˈteɪʃn/ *noun*
1 the act of giving something to somebody, especially in a formal ceremony: *The presentation of the prizes will take place at 7.30.*
2 a meeting where somebody shows or explains something to the people listening: *Each student has to **give** a short **presentation** on a subject of their choice.*

presenter /prɪˈzentə(r)/ *noun*
a person whose job is to introduce programmes on TV or radio

presently /ˈprezntli/ *adverb*
1 soon: *He will be here presently.*
2 now: *She's presently working in a cafe.*

present participle /ˌpreznt ˈpɑːtɪsɪpl/ *noun*
(*grammar*) the form of a verb that ends in *-ing*

the present perfect /ðə ˌpreznt ˈpɜːfɪkt/ *noun* (*no plural*)
(*grammar*) the form of a verb for things that began in the past and continue now. We make it with the present tense of *have* and a past participle of the verb: '*They have finished*' is in the present perfect.

the present tense /ðə ˌpreznt ˈtens/ (*also* the present) *noun* (*no plural*)
(*grammar*) the form of a verb that you use to talk about what is happening or what exists now

preservation /ˌprezəˈveɪʃn/ *noun* (*no plural*)
the act of keeping something safe or in good condition: *the preservation of rare birds*

preserve /prɪˈzɜːv/ *verb* (preserves, preserving, preserved /prɪˈzɜːvd/)
to keep something safe or in good condition: *They managed to preserve most of the paintings.*

president 0-ᵣ /ˈprezɪdənt/ *noun*
1 the leader of a country that does not have a king or queen (called a republic): *the President of the United States of America*
2 the person with the highest position in an organization or a company
▶ **presidential** /ˌprezɪˈdenʃl/ *adjective*: *the presidential elections*

press¹ 0-ᵣ /pres/ *noun*
1 the press (*no plural*) newspapers and magazines and the people who write them: *She told her story to the press.*
2 (*plural* presses) a machine for printing things like books and newspapers
3 (*plural* presses) the act of pushing something: *Give the doorbell a press.*

A B C D E F G H I J K L M N O **P** Q R S T U V W X Y Z

press² 0—ᵣ /pres/ *verb* (presses, pressing, pressed /prest/)
1 to push something: *If you press this button, the door will open.* ◇ *She pressed her face against the window.* ⮡ Look at the picture at **squeeze**.
2 to make clothes flat and smooth using an iron: *This suit needs pressing.*

press conference /'pres kɒnfərəns/ *noun*
a meeting when a famous or important person answers questions from newspaper and TV journalists

press-up /'pres ʌp/ (*British*) (*American* **push-up**) *noun*
a type of exercise in which you lie on your front and push your body up with your arms: *I do twenty press-ups every morning.*

pressure 0—ᵣ /'preʃə(r)/ *noun*
1 the force that presses on something: *The pressure of the water caused the dam to crack.*
2 the force that a gas or liquid has when it is contained inside something: *He has high blood pressure* (= the force with which blood travels round your body). ◇ *You should check the tyre pressures* (= the amount of air in the car tyres) *regularly.*
3 a feeling of worry because of the things you have to do: *She's under a lot of pressure at work.* ◇ *financial pressures*

presume /prɪ'zjuːm/ *verb* (presumes, presuming, presumed /prɪ'zjuːmd/)
to think that something is true, although you are not certain: *She's not home yet so I presume he's still at work.*

pretend 0—ᵣ /prɪ'tend/ *verb* (pretends, pretending, pretended)
to try to make somebody believe something that is not true: *He didn't want to talk, so he pretended to be asleep.* ◇ *I pretended that I was enjoying myself.*

pretty¹ 0—ᵣ /'prɪti/ *adverb* (*informal*)
quite; fairly: *It's pretty cold today.*

pretty² 0—ᵣ /'prɪti/ *adjective* (prettier, prettiest)
nice to look at: *a pretty little girl* ◇ *These flowers are very pretty.* ⮡ Look at the note at **beautiful**.

prevent 0—ᵣ /prɪ'vent/ *verb* (prevents, preventing, prevented)
to stop somebody from doing something; to stop something happening: *Her parents want to prevent her from getting married.* ◇ *It is easier to prevent disease than to cure it.*

prevention /prɪ'venʃn/ *noun* (*no plural*)
stopping somebody from doing something or stopping something from happening: *crime prevention* ◇ *the prevention of cruelty to animals*

preview /'priːvjuː/ *noun*
1 a chance to see a play, film, etc. before it is shown to the general public
2 a chance to see what something will be like before it happens or is shown: *Click on the print preview button.*

previous 0—ᵣ /'priːviəs/ *adjective*
coming or happening before or earlier: *Who was the previous owner of the car?*
▶ **previously** *adverb*: *I work in a factory now, but previously I was a secretary.*

prey /preɪ/ *noun* (*no plural*)
an animal or bird that another animal or bird kills for food: *Zebra are prey for lions.*

price 0—ᵣ /praɪs/ *noun*
how much money you pay to buy something: *The price is £15.* ◇ *Prices in this country are very high.*

> 🔎 **WHICH WORD?**
>
> **Price, cost** or **charge**?
> The **price** of something is the amount of money that you must pay to buy something. We usually say *How much?* or *How much is it?* if we want to know the **price** of something.
> You use **cost** when you are talking about paying for services or about prices without saying an exact sum of money: *The cost of electricity is going up.*
> A **charge** is the amount of money that you must pay to use something: *Is there a charge for parking here?*

priceless /'praɪsləs/ *adjective*
extremely valuable: *priceless jewels*

prick /prɪk/ *verb* (pricks, pricking, pricked /prɪkt/)
to make a very small hole in something, or to hurt somebody, with a sharp point: *I pricked my finger on a needle.*
▶ **prick** *noun*: *She felt the prick of a needle.*

prickle /'prɪkl/ *noun*
a sharp point on a plant or an animal: *A hedgehog has prickles.*

prickly /'prɪkli/ *adjective*
covered with PRICKLES: *a prickly cactus*

pride /praɪd/ *noun* (*no plural*)
1 the feeling that you are proud of something that you or others have got or have done: *She showed us her painting with great pride.*
2 the feeling that you are better than other people

priest 0⃣ /priːst/ *noun*
a person who leads people in their religion: *a Buddhist priest*

primary /ˈpraɪməri/ *adjective*
first; most important: *The primary aim of this course is to improve your spoken English.*

primary school /ˈpraɪməri skuːl/ (*British*) *noun*
a school for children between the ages of five and eleven ⊃ Look at **secondary school**.

prime minister 0⃣ /ˌpraɪm ˈmɪnɪstə(r)/ *noun*
the leader of the government in some countries, for example in Britain

primitive /ˈprɪmətɪv/ *adjective*
very simple; not developed: *The cooking facilities were very primitive.* ◇ *primitive beliefs*

prince /prɪns/ *noun*
1 a man in a royal family, especially the son of a king or queen: *the Prince of Wales*
2 a man from a royal family who is the ruler of a small country

princess /ˌprɪnˈses/ *noun* (*plural* princesses)
a woman in a royal family, especially the daughter of a king or queen or the wife of a PRINCE

principal¹ /ˈprɪnsəpl/ *adjective*
most important: *My principal reason for going to Rome was to learn Italian.*

principal² /ˈprɪnsəpl/ *noun*
a person who is in charge of a school or college

principally /ˈprɪnsəpli/ *adverb*
mainly; mostly: *She sometimes travels to Europe, but she works principally in Africa.*

principle /ˈprɪnsəpl/ *noun*
1 a rule about how you should live: *He has very strong principles.* ◇ *I refuse to lie about it; it's against my principles.*
2 a rule or fact about how something happens or works: *scientific principles*

print¹ 0⃣ /prɪnt/ *verb* (prints, printing, printed)
1 to put words or pictures onto paper using a machine. Books, newspapers and magazines are **printed**.
2 to write with letters that are not joined together: *Please print your name and address clearly.*

print² /prɪnt/ *noun*
1 (*no plural*) letters that a machine makes on paper: *The print is too small to read without my glasses.*
2 (*plural* prints) a mark where something

has pressed on something: *footprints in the snow* ◇ *The police are looking for prints* (= fingerprints).
3 (*plural* prints) a copy on paper of a painting or photograph

printer /ˈprɪntə(r)/ *noun*
1 a machine that prints words from a computer
2 a person or company that prints things like books or newspapers

priority 0⃣ /praɪˈɒrəti/ *noun*
1 (*plural* priorities) something that you think is more important than other things and that you must do first: *Education is a top priority.*
2 (*no plural*) being more important than somebody or something or coming before somebody or something else: *We give priority to families with small children.* ◇ *Emergency cases take priority over other patients in hospital.*

prison 0⃣ /ˈprɪzn/ *noun*
a place where criminals must stay as a punishment ⊃ SAME MEANING **jail**: *He was sent to prison for robbing a bank.* ◇ *She was in prison for 15 years.*

prisoner 0⃣ /ˈprɪznə(r)/ *noun*
a person who is in prison as a punishment; a person who is not free: *The number of prisoners serving life sentences has fallen.* ◇ *He was taken prisoner by rebel soldiers.*

private 0⃣ /ˈpraɪvət/ *adjective*
1 for one person or a small group of people only, and not for anybody else: *You shouldn't read his letters – they're private.* ◇ *This is private property*
2 alone; without other people there: *I would like a private meeting with the manager.*
3 not connected with your job: *She never talks about her private life at work.*
4 not controlled or paid for by the government: *a private hospital* ◇ *private schools*
in private alone; without other people there: *Can I speak to you in private?*
▶ **privately** /ˈpraɪvətli/ *adverb*: *Let's go into my office – we can talk more privately there.*

privilege /ˈprɪvəlɪdʒ/ *noun*
something special that only one person or a few people may do or have: *Prisoners who behave well have special privileges.*
▶ **privileged** /ˈprɪvəlɪdʒd/ *adjective*: *I feel very privileged to be playing for the national team.*

prize 0⃣ /praɪz/ *noun*
something that you give to the person who

A
B
C
D
E
F
G
H
I
J
K
L
M
N
O
P
Q
R
S
T
U
V
W
X
Y
Z

A B C D E F G H I J K L M N O P Q R S T U V W X Y Z

wins a game, race, etc.: *I won first prize* in the painting competition. ◇ *Did you win a prize?*

probable 0-¬ /'prɒbəbl/ *adjective*
likely to happen or to be true: *It is probable that he will be late.* ⊃ OPPOSITE **improbable**

probably 0-¬ /'prɒbəbli/ *adverb*
almost certainly: *I will probably see you on Thursday.*

problem 0-¬ /'prɒbləm/ *noun*
1 something that is difficult; something that makes you worry: *She has a lot of problems. Her husband is ill and her son is in prison.* ◇ *There is a problem with my telephone – it doesn't work.*
2 a question that you must answer by thinking about it: *I can't solve this problem.*

proceed /prə'siːd/ *verb* (**proceeds, proceeding, proceeded**) (*formal*)
1 to continue doing something: *We're not sure whether we want to proceed with the sale of the house.*
2 to do something next, after having done something else first: *Once he had calmed down, he proceeded to tell us what had happened.*

process 0-¬ /'prəʊses/ *noun* (*plural* **processes**)
a number of actions, one after the other, for doing or making something: *He explained the process of building a boat.* ◇ *Learning a language is usually a slow process.*

procession /prə'seʃn/ *noun*
a line of people or cars that are moving slowly along: *We watched the carnival procession.*

produce¹ 0-¬ /prə'djuːs/ *verb* (**produces, producing, produced** /prə'djuːst/)
1 to make or grow something: *This factory produces cars.* ◇ *What does the farm produce?*
2 to make something happen: *His hard work produced good results.*
3 to bring something out to show it: *She produced a ticket from her pocket.*
4 to organize something like a play or film: *The play was produced by Peter Gordon.*

produce² /'prɒdjuːs/ *noun* (*no plural*)
food that you grow on a farm or in a garden to sell: *fresh farm produce*

producer /prə'djuːsə(r)/ *noun*
1 a person who organizes something like a play or film: *a television producer*
2 a company or country that makes or grows something: *Brazil is an important producer of coffee.*

product 0-¬ /'prɒdʌkt/ *noun*
something that people make or grow to sell: *The company has just launched a new product.*

production 0-¬ /prə'dʌkʃn/ *noun*
1 (*no plural*) the action of making or growing something: *the production of oil*
2 (*plural* **productions**) a play, film, etc.

productive /prə'dʌktɪv/ *adjective*
doing, achieving or producing a lot: *The meeting was very productive.*

profession 0-¬ /prə'feʃn/ *noun*
a job that needs a lot of studying and special training: *She's a doctor by profession.*

professional 0-¬ /prə'feʃənl/ *adjective*
1 connected with a profession: *I got professional advice from a lawyer.*
2 doing something for money as a job: *a professional footballer* ⊃ OPPOSITE **amateur**
▶ **professionally** /prə'feʃənəli/ *adverb*: *He plays the piano professionally.*

professor /prə'fesə(r)/ *noun*
1 (*British*) a university teacher of the highest level: *Professor Oliver* ◇ *He's professor of Psychology at Birmingham University.*
2 (*American*) a teacher at a college or university

profile /'prəʊfaɪl/ *noun*
the shape of a person's face when you see it from the side

profit 0-¬ /'prɒfɪt/ *noun*
money that you get when you sell something for more than it cost to buy or make: *They made a profit of £10.*

profitable /'prɒfɪtəbl/ *adjective*
If something is **profitable**, it brings you money: *a profitable business*

program¹ 0-¬ /'prəʊgræm/ *noun*
1 (*computing*) a set of instructions that you give to a computer: *Load the program into the computer.*
2 American English for PROGRAMME

program² /'prəʊgræm/ *verb* (**programs, programming, programmed** /'prəʊgræmd/)
to give a set of instructions to a computer

programme 0-¬ (*British*) (*American* **program**) /'prəʊgræm/ *noun*
1 something on television or radio: *Did you watch that programme about Japan on TV last night?*
2 a piece of paper or a little book that tells people at a play or concert what they are going to see or hear

3 a plan of things to do: *What is your programme for tomorrow?*

programmer (*British*) (*American programer*) /'prəʊgræmə(r)/ *noun*
a person whose job is to write programs for a computer

progress¹ 0‑ᴡ /prə'gres/ *verb*
(progresses, progressing, progressed /prə'grest/)
1 to improve or develop: *Students can progress at their own speed.*
2 to move forwards; to continue: *She became more tired as the evening progressed.*

progress² 0‑ᴡ /'prəʊgres/ *noun* (*no plural*)
1 improvement or development: *Jo has made good progress in maths this year.*
2 movement forward: *She watched her father's slow progress down the steps.*
in progress happening now: *Quiet please – examination in progress.*

prohibit /prə'hɪbɪt/ *verb* (prohibits, prohibiting, prohibited) (*formal*)
to say that people must not do something
➲ SAME MEANING **forbid**: *Smoking is prohibited in the theatre.*

project 0‑ᴡ /'prɒdʒekt/ *noun*
1 a big plan to do something: *a project to build a new airport ◊ The research project will be funded by the government.*
2 a piece of work that you do at school. You find out a lot about something and write about it: *We did a project on Africa.*

projector /prə'dʒektə(r)/ *noun*
a machine that shows films or pictures on a wall or screen

prominent /'prɒmɪnənt/ *adjective*
1 easy to see, for example because it is bigger than usual: *prominent teeth*
2 important and famous: *a prominent writer*

promise¹ 0‑ᴡ /'prɒmɪs/ *verb* (promises, promising, promised /'prɒmɪst/)
to say that you will certainly do or not do something: *She promised to give me the money today. ◊ I promise that I'll come. ◊ Promise me you won't be late!*

promise² 0‑ᴡ /'prɒmɪs/ *noun*
when you say that you will certainly do or not do something: *He kept his promise (= did what he said). ◊ You broke your promise – how can I trust you?*

promote /prə'məʊt/ *verb* (promotes, promoting, promoted)
1 to help to sell a product or make it more popular by advertising it or offering it at a

special price: *The band has gone on tour to promote their new album.*
2 to give somebody a more important job: *She worked hard, and after a year she was promoted to manager.*
▶ **promotion** /prə'məʊʃn/ *noun*: *The new job is a promotion for me.*

prompt /prɒmpt/ *adjective*
quick: *She gave me a prompt answer.*

promptly /'prɒmptli/ *adverb*
quickly; not late: *We arrived promptly at two o'clock.*

pronoun /'prəʊnaʊn/ *noun*
(*grammar*) a word that you use in place of a noun: '*He*', '*it*', '*me*' and '*them*' are all pronouns.

pronounce 0‑ᴡ /prə'naʊns/ *verb*
(pronounces, pronouncing, pronounced /prə'naʊnst/)
to make the sound of a letter or word: *How do you pronounce your name? ◊ You don't pronounce the 'b' at the end of 'comb'.*

pronunciation /prə,nʌnsi'eɪʃn/ *noun*
how you say a word or words: *What's the correct pronunciation of this word? ◊ His pronunciation is very good.*

proof 0‑ᴡ /pruːf/ *noun* (*no plural*)
something that shows that an idea is true: *Do you have any proof that you are the owner of this car?* ➲ The verb is **prove**.

propeller /prə'pelə(r)/ *noun*
a part that is connected to the engine on a ship or a plane. It turns round very fast to make the ship or plane move. ➲ Look at the picture at **toy**.

proper 0‑ᴡ /'prɒpə(r)/ *adjective*
1 right or correct: *I haven't got the proper tools to mend the car.*
2 (*British, informal*) real: *He hasn't got any proper friends.*

properly 0‑ᴡ /'prɒpəli/ *adverb*
well or correctly: *Close the door properly. ◊ I can't see properly without my glasses.*

property 0‑ᴡ /'prɒpəti/ *noun*
1 (*no plural*) something that you have or own: *This book is the property of James Waters.*
2 (*plural* properties) a building and the land around it

prophet /'prɒfɪt/ *noun*
a person that God chooses to give his message to people

proportion /prə'pɔːʃn/ *noun*
1 a part of something: *A large proportion of (= many) people agree.*

2 the amount or size of one thing compared to another thing: *What is the **proportion of** men **to** women in the factory?*

proposal /prə'pəʊzl/ *noun*
1 a plan or idea about how to do something: *a proposal to build a new station*
2 when you ask somebody to marry you

propose /prə'pəʊz/ *verb* (proposes, proposing, proposed /prə'pəʊzd/)
1 (*formal*) to say what you think should happen or be done ⊃ SAME MEANING **suggest**: *I **proposed that** we should meet again on Monday.*
2 to ask somebody to marry you: *He **proposed** to me!*

prose /prəʊz/ *noun* (*no plural*)
(*language*) writing that is not poetry: *He wrote poetry and prose.*

prosecute /'prɒsɪkjuːt/ *verb* (prosecutes, prosecuting, prosecuted)
to say officially in a court of law that somebody has done something illegal: *He was **prosecuted** for theft.*

prosperous /'prɒspərəs/ *adjective*
rich and successful

protect 0ᴍ /prə'tekt/ *verb* (protects, protecting, protected)
to keep somebody or something safe: *Parents try to **protect** their children **from** danger.* ◇ *Wear a hat to **protect** your head **against** the sun.*

protection 0ᴍ /prə'tekʃn/ *noun* (*no plural*)
keeping somebody or something safe: *He was put **under** police **protection**.*

protein /'prəʊtiːn/ *noun*
a substance in foods such as meat, fish and beans. **Protein** helps you to grow and stay healthy.

protest¹ 0ᴍ /'prəʊtest/ *noun*
an action that shows publicly that you do not like or approve of something: *She took part in a **protest against** the war.*

protest² 0ᴍ /prə'test/ *verb* (protests, protesting, protested)
to say or show strongly that you do not like something: *They **protested against** the government's plans.*

Protestant /'prɒtɪstənt/ *noun*
a person who believes in the Christian God and who is not a Roman Catholic

proud 0ᴍ /praʊd/ *adjective* (prouder, proudest)
1 pleased about something that you or others have done or about something that

you have: *They are very **proud of** their new house.*
2 thinking that you are better than other people: *She was too proud to say she was sorry.* ⊃ The noun is **pride**.
▸ **proudly** *adverb*: '*I made this myself,*' he said proudly.

prove 0ᴍ /pruːv/ *verb* (proves, proving, proved /pruːvd/, has proved or has proven /'pruːvn/)
to show that something is true: *The blood on his shirt **proves that** he is the murderer.* ⊃ The noun is **proof**.

proverb /'prɒvɜːb/ *noun*
a short sentence that people often say, that gives help or advice: '*Waste not, want not*' is an English proverb.

provide 0ᴍ /prə'vaɪd/ *verb* (provides, providing, provided)
to give something to somebody who needs it: *I'll **provide** the food for the party.* ◇ *The company have **provided** me **with** a car.*

provided /prə'vaɪdɪd/ (*also* providing /prə'vaɪdɪŋ/) *conjunction*
only if: *I'll go **provided that** the children can come with me.* ◇ *Phone me when you get home, providing it's not too late.*

province /'prɒvɪns/ *noun*
a part of a country: *Canada has ten provinces.*
▸ **provincial** /prə'vɪnʃl/ *adjective*
connected with a PROVINCE: *the provincial government*

provision /prə'vɪʒn/ *noun* (*no plural*)
when something is given to somebody who needs it: *The government is responsible for the provision of health care.*

provoke /prə'vəʊk/ *verb* (provokes, provoking, provoked /prə'vəʊkt/)
to cause particular feelings or behaviour: *Dairy products may provoke allergic reactions in some people.*

prowl /praʊl/ *verb* (prowls, prowling, prowled /praʊld/)
(used about an animal that is hunting or a person who is waiting for a chance to do something bad) to move around an area quietly so that you nobody sees or hears you: *I could hear someone prowling around outside.*

PS /ˌpiː 'es/ *noun*
You write **PS** at the end of a letter, after your name, when you want to add something: *... Love from Paul. PS I'll bring the car.*

psychiatrist /saɪ'kaɪətrɪst/ *noun*
a doctor who helps people who have a mental illness

psychologist /saɪˈkɒlədʒɪst/ *noun*
a person who studies PSYCHOLOGY

psychology /saɪˈkɒlədʒi/ *noun* (*no plural*)
the study of the mind and how it works

psychopath /ˈsaɪkəpæθ/ *noun*
a person who has a serious mental illness
that makes them behave in a violent way
towards other people

pt *short way of writing* PINT

PTO /ˌpiː tiː ˈəʊ/ *abbreviation*
the abbreviation for 'please turn over';
written at the bottom of a page to tell you to
turn to the next page

pub 0̅ᴛ /pʌb/ *noun* (*British*)
a place where people go to drink and meet
their friends: *They've gone to the pub for a
drink.* ◇ *On Sundays, we often go out for a
pub lunch.*

> 🔎 CULTURE
> In Britain, you can buy alcoholic drinks
> like **beer** or **wine** in a **pub** if you are over
> the age of 18. In a lot of pubs you can also
> buy food.

public¹ 0̅ᴛ /ˈpʌblɪk/ *adjective*
connected with everybody; for everybody: *a
public telephone* ◇ *Smoking is not allowed in
public places.*
▶ **publicly** *adverb* to everybody; not
secretly: *She spoke publicly about her
friendship with the Prince.*

public² 0̅ᴛ /ˈpʌblɪk/ *noun* **the public** (*no
plural*)
people in general; everybody: *The palace is
open to the public between 10 a.m. and 4 p.m.*
in public when other people are there: *I
don't want to talk about it in public.*

publication /ˌpʌblɪˈkeɪʃn/ *noun*
1 (*no plural*) when a book, magazine, etc. is
made and sold: *He became very rich after the
publication of his first book.*
2 (*plural* publications) a book, magazine,
etc.

publicity /pʌbˈlɪsəti/ *noun* (*no plural*)
giving information about something so that
people know about it: *There was a lot of
publicity for the new film.*

public relations /ˌpʌblɪk rɪˈleɪʃnz/ *noun*
(*no plural*) (*abbr.* PR)
the business of providing information about
somebody or something, in order to give
people a good impression of them: *She works
in public relations.*

public school /ˌpʌblɪk ˈskuːl/ *noun*
1 (in Britain, especially in England) a private
school for young people between the ages

of 13 and 18, whose parents pay for their
education. The students often live at the
school while they are studying.
2 (in the US, Australia, Scotland and other
countries) a free local school paid for by the
government

public transport /ˌpʌblɪk ˈtrænspɔːt/
noun (*no plural*)
buses and trains that everybody can use:
I usually travel by public transport.

publish 0̅ᴛ /ˈpʌblɪʃ/ *verb* (publishes,
publishing, published /ˈpʌblɪʃt/)
1 to prepare and print a book, magazine or
newspaper for selling: *This dictionary was
published by Oxford University Press.*
2 to make information available to the
public, especially on the Internet
▶ **publisher** /ˈpʌblɪʃə(r)/ *noun*: *The
publisher is OUP.*

pudding /ˈpʊdɪŋ/ *noun* (*British*)
1 something sweet that you eat at the end
of a meal ⟹ SAME MEANING **dessert**: '*What's
for pudding?*' '*Fruit.*'
2 a hot sweet dish, often like a cake, that you
eat at the end of a meal: *Christmas pudding*

puddle /ˈpʌdl/ *noun*
a small pool of rain or other liquid on the
ground

puff¹ /pʌf/ *verb* (puffs, puffing, puffed
/pʌft/)
1 to smoke a cigarette, pipe, etc.: *He sat
puffing his cigar.*
2 (used about air, smoke, wind, etc.) to
blow or come out in clouds: *Smoke was
puffing out of the chimney.* ◇ *Stop puffing
cigarette smoke in my face.*
3 (*informal*) to breathe quickly or loudly,
especially after you have been running: *She
was puffing as she ran up the hill.*

puff² /pʌf/ *noun*
a small amount of air, wind, smoke, etc. that
is blown from somewhere: *a puff of smoke*

pull

pull¹ 0̅ᴛ /pʊl/ *verb* (pulls, pulling, pulled
/pʊld/)
1 to move somebody or something strongly
towards you: *She pulled the drawer open.*

2 to go forward, moving something behind you: *The cart was pulled by two horses.*
3 to move something somewhere: *He pulled up his trousers.*

pull down to destroy a building: *The old school has been pulled down.*

pull in to drive a car to the side of the road and stop: *I pulled in to look at the map.*

pull somebody's leg (*informal*) to try to make somebody believe something that is not true, for fun: *I didn't really see an elephant – I was only pulling your leg!*

pull yourself together to control your feelings after being upset: *Pull yourself together and stop crying.*

pull up to stop a car: *The driver pulled up at the traffic lights.*

pull² 0ᴍ /pʊl/ *noun*
an action of pulling something: *Give the rope a pull.*

pullover /'pʊləʊvə(r)/ *noun*
a warm piece of clothing with sleeves, that you wear on the top part of your body. **Pullovers** are often made of wool. ⊃ Look at the note at **sweater**.

pulse /pʌls/ *noun*
the beating of your heart that you feel in different parts of your body, especially in your wrist: *The nurse **felt** (= measured) his **pulse**.*

pump¹ /pʌmp/ *noun*
a machine that moves a liquid or gas into or out of something: *a bicycle pump ◇ a petrol pump*

pump² /pʌmp/ *verb* (pumps, pumping, pumped /pʌmpt/)
to force a gas or a liquid to go in a particular direction: *Your heart **pumps** blood **around** your body.*

pump something up to fill something with air, using a **pump**: *I pumped up my bicycle tyres.*

pumpkin /'pʌmpkɪn/ *noun*
a very large round vegetable with a thick orange skin ⊃ Look at Picture Dictionary page **P9**.

pun /pʌn/ *noun*
a funny use of a word that has two meanings, or that sounds the same as another word

punch /pʌntʃ/ *verb* (punches, punching, punched /pʌntʃt/)
1 to hit somebody or something hard with your closed hand (your **fist**): *He punched me on the nose.*
2 to make a hole in something with a special tool: *The ticket collector punched my ticket.*

punch

▸ **punch** *noun* (*plural* **punches**): *a punch on the chin*

punctual /'pʌŋktʃuəl/ *adjective*
arriving or doing something at the right time; not late: *Please try to be punctual for your classes.*
▸ **punctually** /'pʌŋktʃuəli/ *adverb*: *They arrived punctually at seven o'clock.*

punctuate /'pʌŋktʃueɪt/ *verb* (punctuates, punctuating, punctuated)
to put full stops, question marks, etc. in your writing

punctuation /ˌpʌŋktʃu'eɪʃn/ *noun* (*no plural*)
using PUNCTUATION MARKS when you are writing

punctuation mark /pʌŋktʃu'eɪʃn mɑːk/ *noun*
one of the marks that you use in your writing, for example a full stop or question mark

puncture /'pʌŋktʃə(r)/ *noun* (*British*)
a hole in a tyre, that lets the air go out: *My bike has got a puncture.*
▸ **puncture** *verb* (punctures, puncturing, punctured /'pʌŋktʃəd/)
make a PUNCTURE in something: *A piece of glass punctured the tyre.*

punish 0ᴍ /'pʌnɪʃ/ *verb* (punishes, punishing, punished /'pʌnɪʃt/)
to make somebody suffer because they have done something wrong: *The children were **punished for** telling lies.*

punishment 0ᴍ /'pʌnɪʃmənt/ *noun*
an act or a way of punishing somebody: *What is the **punishment for** murder in your country? ◇ The child was sent to bed **as a punishment** for being naughty.*

pupil 0ᴍ /'pjuːpl/ *noun*
1 a person who is learning at school: *There are 30 pupils in the class.* ⊃ Look at the note at **student**. ⊃ Look at Picture Dictionary page **P11**.
2 the round black hole in the middle of your eye ⊃ Look at the picture at **eye**.

puppet /'pʌpɪt/ *noun*
a small model of a person or animal that you

move by pulling strings or by putting your hand inside

puppet

puppy /'pʌpi/ *noun*
(*plural* **puppies**)
a young dog ➋ Look at the picture at **dog**.

purchase¹ /'pɜːtʃəs/ *noun*
(*formal*)
the action of buying something; something that you have bought: *She made several purchases and then left the store.*

purchase² /'pɜːtʃəs/ *verb* (**purchases, purchasing, purchased** /'pɜːtʃəst/)
(*formal*)
to buy something: *The company has purchased three new shops.*

pure 0🔑 /pjʊə(r)/ *adjective* (**purer, purest**)
1 not mixed with anything else: *This shirt is pure cotton.*
2 clean and healthy: *pure mountain air*
2 complete or total: *What she said was pure nonsense.*

purely /'pjʊəli/ *adverb*
only or completely: *He doesn't like his job – he does it purely for the money.*

purple 0🔑 /'pɜːpl/ *adjective*
with a colour between red and blue
▶ **purple** *noun*: *She often wears purple.*

purpose 0🔑 /'pɜːpəs/ *noun*
the reason for doing something: *What is the purpose of your visit?*
on purpose because you want to; not by accident ➋ SAME MEANING **deliberately**: *'You've broken my pen!' 'I'm sorry, I didn't do it on purpose.'*

purposely /'pɜːpəsli/ *adverb*
on purpose; deliberately

purse

| strap
handbag
purse (*American*)

wallet

purse

purr /pɜː(r)/ *verb* (**purrs, purring, purred** /pɜːd/)
When a cat **purrs**, it makes a low sound that shows that it is happy.

purse /pɜːs/ *noun*
1 (*British*) a small bag made of leather, plastic, etc. for carrying money, credit cards, etc., used especially by women
2 *American English for* HANDBAG

pursue /pə'sjuː/ *verb* (**pursues, pursuing, pursued** /pə'sjuːd/) (*formal*)
to follow somebody or something because you want to catch them ➋ SAME MEANING **chase**: *The police pursued the stolen car for several kilometres.*

push

push 0🔑 /pʊʃ/ *verb* (**pushes, pushing, pushed** /pʊʃt/)
1 to use force to move somebody or something forward or away from you: *The car broke down so we had to push it to a garage.* ◇ *He pushed me over!*
2 to press something with your finger: *Push the red button to stop the bus.*
▶ **push** *noun* (*plural* **pushes**): *She gave him a push and he fell.*

pushchair

pushchair   **pram**

pushchair /'pʊʃtʃeə(r)/ (*British*) (*American* **stroller**) *noun*
a chair on wheels in which a young child is pushed along ➋ SAME MEANING **buggy**

push-up /'pʊʃ ʌp/ *noun American English for* PRESS-UP

pussy /'pʊsi/ *noun* (*plural* **pussies**)
a word for 'cat' that children use

put 0—/pʊt/ *verb* (puts, putting, put, has put)

1 to move something to a place or position: *She put the book on the table.* ◊ *He put his hand in his pocket.*

2 to write something: *Put your name at the top of the page.*

put something away to put something back in its usual place: *She put the box away in the cupboard.*

put something down to stop holding something and put it on another thing, for example on the floor or a table: *Let me put my bags down first.*

put somebody off to make somebody not like someone or something: *The accident put me off driving.*

put something off to not do something until later ➔ SAME MEANING **delay**: *He put off his holiday because the children were ill.*

put something on

1 to take clothes and wear them: *Put on your coat.* ◊ *Put your shoes on.* ➔ OPPOSITE **take something off**

2 to make a piece of electrical equipment start to work: *I put on the TV.* ◊ *Put the lights on.* ◊ *Shall we put some music on?*

put something out to stop a fire or to stop a light shining: *She put out the fire with a bucket of water.* ◊ *Put the lights out before you go.*

put somebody through to connect somebody on the telephone to the person they want to speak to: *Can you put me through to the manager, please?*

put somebody up to let somebody sleep in your home: *Can you put me up for the night?*

put up with somebody or **something** to have pain or problems without complaining: *We can't change the bad weather, so we have to put up with it.*

puzzle¹ /'pʌzl/ *noun*

1 something that is difficult to understand or explain: *Janet's reason for leaving her job is a puzzle to me.*

2 a game that is difficult and makes you think a lot ➔ Look also at **crossword puzzle** and **jigsaw puzzle**.

puzzle² /'pʌzl/ *verb* (puzzles, puzzling, puzzled /'pʌzld/)

to make you feel that you cannot understand or explain something: *Tim's illness puzzled his doctors.*

puzzled /'pʌzld/ *adjective*

not able to understand or explain something: *She had a puzzled look on her face.*

puzzling /'pʌzlɪŋ/ *adjective*

difficult to understand or explain

pyjamas (*British*) (*American* pajamas) /pə'dʒɑːməz/ *noun* (*plural*)

a loose jacket and trousers that you wear in bed ➔ Look at Picture Dictionary page **P5**.

pyramid

pyramid /'pɪrəmɪd/ *noun*

a shape with a flat bottom and three or four sides that come to a point at the top: *the pyramids of Egypt*

Q q

Q, q /kjuː/ *noun* (plural Q's, q's /kjuːz/)
the seventeenth letter of the English alphabet: *'Queen' begins with a 'Q'*

quack /kwæk/ *noun*
the sound that a DUCK (= a bird that lives on or near water) makes
▶ **quack** *verb* (quacks, quacking, quacked /kwækt/)

quaint /kweɪnt/ *adjective* (quainter, quaintest)
old-fashioned, usually in an attractive way: *a quaint little cottage*

qualification /ˌkwɒlɪfɪˈkeɪʃn/ *noun*
an examination that you have passed, or training or knowledge that you need to do a special job: *He left school with no qualifications.*

qualified /ˈkwɒlɪfaɪd/ *adjective*
having passed the exams or done the training necessary to do a particular job: *She's a qualified nurse.*

qualify /ˈkwɒlɪfaɪ/ *verb* (qualifies, qualifying, qualified /ˈkwɒlɪfaɪd/, has qualified)
to get the right knowledge and training and pass exams so that you can do a certain job: *Anna has **qualified as** a doctor.*

quality 0ᵐ /ˈkwɒləti/ *noun* (no plural)
how good or bad something is: *The **quality** of her work is excellent.* ◊ *This furniture isn't very **good quality.***

quantity 0ᵐ /ˈkwɒntəti/ *noun* (plural quantities)
how much of something there is
⊃ SAME MEANING **amount**: *I only bought a small **quantity of** cheese.*

quarrel¹ /ˈkwɒrəl/ *noun*
an argument or a disagreement with somebody: *He had a **quarrel with** his wife **about** money.*

quarrel² /ˈkwɒrəl/ *verb* (British) (quarrels, quarrelling, quarrelled /ˈkwɒrəld/) (American quarreling, quarreled)
to argue or disagree with somebody: *He **quarrelled with** his wife **about** money.* ◊ *The children are always quarrelling.*

quarry /ˈkwɒri/ *noun* (plural quarries)
a place where people cut stone, sand, etc. out of the ground

quarter 0ᵐ /ˈkwɔːtə(r)/ *noun*
1 one of four equal parts of something; ¼:

a mile and a quarter ◊ *The film starts in three quarters of an hour.*
2 three months: *You get a telephone bill every quarter.*
3 a part of a town: *the Chinese quarter*
(a) quarter past (British) 15 minutes after the hour: *It's quarter past two.* ◊ *I'll meet you at a quarter past.* ⊃ In American English you say **a quarter after**: *It's a quarter after seven.*
(a) quarter to (British) 15 minutes before the hour: *It's quarter to nine.* ⊃ In American English you say **a quarter of**: *It's a quarter of four now.*

quarter-final /ˌkwɔːtə ˈfaɪnl/ *noun*
one of the four matches between the eight players or teams left in a competition ⊃ Look at **semi-final**.

quay /kiː/ *noun* (plural quays)
a place in a port where ships go so that people can move things on and off them

queen 0ᵐ /kwiːn/ *noun*
1 a woman from a royal family who rules a country: *Queen Elizabeth II (= the second), the Queen of England.*
2 the wife of a king

quench /kwentʃ/ *verb* (quenches, quenching, quenched /kwentʃt/)
quench your thirst to drink as much as you need so that you stop feeling thirsty

query¹ /ˈkwɪəri/ *noun* (plural queries)
a question: *Phone me if you have any queries.*

query² /ˈkwɪəri/ *verb* (queries, querying, queried /ˈkwɪərid/)
to ask a question about something that you think is wrong: *We queried the bill but the waitress said it was correct.*

question¹ 0ᵐ /ˈkwestʃən/ *noun*
1 something that you ask: *They **asked** me a lot of **questions**.* ◊ *She didn't **answer** my question.* ◊ *What is the answer to question 3?*
2 something that you need to deal with; something that is being discussed: *The question is, how can we raise the money?* ◊ *It's a question of time – we need to finish the work today.*
in question that we are talking about: *On the day in question I was in London.*
out of the question not possible: *No, I won't give you any more money. It's out of the question!*

A B C D E F G H I J K L M N O P Q R S T U V W X Y Z

question² 0─ /ˈkwestʃən/ *verb*
(questions, questioning, questioned
/ˈkwestʃənd/)
1 to ask somebody questions about
something: *The police* **questioned** *him* **about**
the stolen car.
2 to feel doubt about something: *She told*
me she was the child's mother so I didn't
question her right to be there.

question mark /ˈkwestʃən mɑːk/ *noun*
the sign (**?**) that you write at the end of a
question

questionnaire /ˌkwestʃəˈneə(r)/ *noun*
a list of questions for people to answer so
that information can be collected from the
answers: *Please* **fill in** (= write the answers
on) *the* **questionnaire.**

question tag /ˈkwestʃən tæg/ *noun*
(*grammar*) words such as 'is it?' or 'didn't
you?' that you put on the end of a sentence
to make it into a question: *In the sentence*
'You're French, aren't you?', 'aren't you' is a
question tag.

queue¹ /kjuː/ *noun* (*British*) (*American* line)
a line of people who are waiting to do
something: *We stood* **in the queue** *for the*
cinema.

queue² /kjuː/ (*also* queue up) *verb*
(queues, queuing, queued /kjuːd/)
(*British*)
to stand in a QUEUE: *We* **queued for** *a bus.*

quiche /kiːʃ/ *noun* (*plural* quiches /ˈkiːʃɪz/)
a type of food made of PASTRY (= a mixture
of flour, fat and water) filled with egg and
milk with cheese, onion, etc. and cooked in
the oven. You can eat **quiche** hot or cold.
➲ Look at Picture Dictionary page **P7.**

quick 0─ /kwɪk/ *adjective, adverb*
(quicker, quickest)
taking little time ➲ SAME MEANING **fast**: *It's*
quicker to travel by plane than by train. ◇ *Can I*
make a quick telephone call?
➲ OPPOSITE **slow**
▶ **quickly** *adverb*: *Come as quickly as you*
can!

quid /kwɪd/ *noun* (*plural* quid) (*British,*
informal)
(money) a pound: *It costs five quid.*

quiet¹ 0─ /ˈkwaɪət/ *adjective* (quieter,
quietest)
1 making very little noise: *Be quiet – the*
baby's asleep. ◇ *a quiet voice*
➲ OPPOSITE **loud** or **noisy**
2 without many people or without many

things happening: *London is very quiet on*
Sundays.
▶ **quietly** /ˈkwaɪətli/ *adverb*: *Please close*
the door quietly.

quiet² /ˈkwaɪət/ *noun* (*no plural*)
when there is no noise: *I need quiet when I'm*
working. ◇ *I go to the library for a little* **peace**
and quiet.

quilt /kwɪlt/ *noun*
a bed cover with soft material inside

quit /kwɪt/ *verb* (quits, quitting, quit, has
quit) (*informal*)
to leave a job or place; to stop doing
something: *She* **quit** *as coach.* ◇ *We've nearly*
finished – we're not going to quit now!

quite 0─ /kwaɪt/ *adverb*
1 not very; rather ➲ SAME MEANING **fairly**:
It's quite warm today, but it's not hot. ◇ *He*
plays the guitar quite well. ◇ *We waited quite a*
long time.
2 completely: *Dinner is* **not quite** *ready.*
quite a few or **quite a lot** a fairly large
amount or number: *There were* **quite a few**
people at the party. ◇ *They drank* **quite a lot** *of*
wine.

quiver /ˈkwɪvə(r)/ *verb* (quivers,
quivering, quivered /ˈkwɪvəd/)
to shake slightly ➲ SAME MEANING **tremble**:
Her lip quivered and then she started to cry.

quiz /kwɪz/ *noun* (*plural* quizzes)
a game where you try to answer questions: *a*
quiz on television

quota /ˈkwəʊtə/ *noun*
the limited number or amount of people or
things that is officially allowed: *We have*
already reached our quota – we cannot take
any more people.

quotation /kwəʊˈteɪʃn/ (*also* quote
/kwəʊt/) *noun*
words that you say or write, that another
person said or wrote before: *That's a*
quotation from a poem by Keats.

quotation marks /kwəʊˈteɪʃn mɑːks/
(*also* quotes) *noun* (*plural*)
the signs (" ") or (' ') that you use in writing
before and after the exact words that
someone has said

quote /kwəʊt/ *verb* (quotes, quoting,
quoted)
to repeat exactly something that another
person said or wrote: *She* **quoted from** *the*
Bible. ◇ *Don't* **quote** *me, but she's wrong.*

the Qu'ran /ðə kəˈrɑːn/ *noun* (*no plural*)
= THE KORAN

R r

R, r /ɑː(r)/ *noun* (*plural* R's, r's /ɑːz/)
the eighteenth letter of the English
alphabet: '*Rose' begins with an 'R'.*

rabbi /'ræbaɪ/ *noun* (*plural* rabbis)
a teacher or leader of the Jewish religion

rabbit

hare   rabbit

rabbit /'ræbɪt/ *noun*
a small animal with long ears. **Rabbits** live in
holes under the ground.

rabies /'reɪbiːz/ *noun* (*no plural*)
a serious disease that people can get if a dog
or another animal with the disease bites
them: *The dog had rabies.*

race¹ 0— /reɪs/ *noun*
1 a competition to see who can run, drive,
ride, etc. fastest: *Who **won** the **race**? ◇ a horse
race*
2 the races (*British*) (*plural*) horse races or
dog races: *He likes **going to the races**.*
3 a group of people of the same kind, for
example with the same colour skin,
language or customs: *People of many
different races live together in this country.*

race² 0— /reɪs/ *verb* (races, racing, raced
/reɪst/)
1 to run, drive, ride, etc. in a competition to
see who is the fastest: *The cars raced round
the track. ◇ I'll race you to the other end of the
pool.*
2 to move, or to move somebody or
something, very fast: *He raced up the stairs. ◇
The ambulance raced the injured woman to
hospital.*

racecourse /'reɪskɔːs/ (*also* racetrack
/'reɪstræk/) *noun*
a place where you go to see horse races

racial /'reɪʃl/ *adjective*
connected with people's race; happening

between people of different races: *racial
differences*

racing /'reɪsɪŋ/ *noun* (*no plural*)
the sport of taking part in races: *a racing car*

racism /'reɪsɪzəm/ *noun* (*no plural*)
the belief that some groups (**races**) of
people are better than others
▸ **racist** *noun*: *He's a terrible racist.*
▸ **racist** *adjective*: *a racist comment*

rack /ræk/ *noun*
a kind of shelf, made of bars, that you put
things on: *I got on the train and put my bag on
the **luggage rack**.*

racket (*also*   **racket**
racquet /'rækɪt/)
noun
a thing that you use
for hitting the ball in
sports such as
TENNIS,
BADMINTON and
SQUASH

radar /'reɪdɑː(r)/ *noun* (*no plural*)
a way of finding where a ship or an aircraft is
and how fast it is travelling by using radio
waves

radiation /ˌreɪdi'eɪʃn/ *noun* (*no plural*)
dangerous energy that some substances
send out: *High levels of radiation have been
recorded near the nuclear power station.*

radiator /'reɪdieɪtə(r)/ *noun*
1 a metal thing with hot water inside that
makes a room warm ⊃ Look at Picture
Dictionary page **P10**.
2 a part of a car that has water in it to keep
the engine cold

radio 0— /'reɪdiəʊ/ *noun*
1 (*no plural*) sending or receiving sounds
that travel a long way through the air by
special waves: *The captain of the ship sent a
message **by radio**.*
2 (*plural* radios) a piece of equipment that
brings voices or music from far away so that
you can hear them: *We listened to an
interesting programme **on the radio**. ◇ Can
you **turn on the radio**?*

radioactive /ˌreɪdiəʊ'æktɪv/ *adjective*
sending out dangerous energy: *the disposal
of **radioactive waste**

A

radius /'reɪdiəs/ *noun* (*plural* radii /'reɪdiaɪ/)
the length of a straight line from the centre of a circle to the outside ⊃ Look at **diameter**. ⊃ Look at the picture at **circle**.

B

C

raffle /'ræfl/ *noun*
a way of making money for a charity by selling tickets with numbers on them. Later some numbers are chosen and the tickets with these numbers on them win prizes.

D

E

raft /rɑːft/ *noun*
a flat boat with no sides and no engine

F

rag /ræg/ *noun*
1 a small piece of old cloth that you use for cleaning
2 rags (*plural*) clothes that are very old and torn: *She was dressed in rags.*

G

H

rage /reɪdʒ/ *noun*
very strong anger: *Sue stormed out of the room in a rage.*

I

J

raid /reɪd/ *noun*
a sudden attack on a place: *a bank raid*
▶ **raid** *verb* (raids, raiding, raided): *Police raided the house looking for drugs.*

K

L

rail /reɪl/ *noun*
1 (*plural* rails) a long piece of wood or metal that is fixed to the wall or to something else: *Hang your towel on the rail in the bathroom.*
2 rails (*plural*) the long pieces of metal that trains go on
3 (*no plural*) trains as a way of travelling: *We decided to travel by rail.*

M

N

O

railings /'reɪlɪŋz/ *noun* (*plural*)
a fence made of long pieces of metal

P

railroad /'reɪlrəʊd/ *American English for* RAILWAY

Q

railroad crossing /'reɪlrəʊd krɒsɪŋ/ *American English for* LEVEL CROSSING

R

railway 0→ /'reɪlweɪ/ *noun*
1 (*also* railway line) the metal lines that trains go on from one place to another
2 a train service that carries people and things: *a railway timetable*

S

T

railway station /'reɪlweɪ steɪʃn/ *noun*
a place where trains stop so that people can get on and off

U

V

rain[1] 0→ /reɪn/ *noun* (*no plural*)
the water that falls from the sky

W

X

rain[2] 0→ /reɪn/ *verb* (rains, raining, rained /reɪnd/)
When it **rains**, water falls from the sky: *It's raining.* ◇ *It rained all day.* ⊃ Look at Picture Dictionary page **P16**.

Y

Z

rainbow /'reɪnbəʊ/ *noun*
a half circle of colours in the sky when rain and sun come together ⊃ Look at Picture Dictionary page **P16**.

raincoat /'reɪnkəʊt/ *noun*
a light coat that you wear when it rains
⊃ SAME MEANING **mac**

raindrop /'reɪndrɒp/ *noun*
one drop of rain

rainforest /'reɪnfɒrɪst/ *noun*
a forest in a hot part of the world where there is a lot of rain: *the Amazon rainforest*

rainy /'reɪni/ *adjective* (rainier, rainiest)
with a lot of rain: *a rainy day*

raise 0→ /reɪz/ *verb* (raises, raising, raised /reɪzd/)
1 to move something or somebody up: *Raise your hand if you want to ask a question.*
⊃ OPPOSITE **lower**
2 to make something bigger, higher, stronger, etc.: *They've raised the price of petrol.* ◇ *She raised her voice* (= spoke more loudly). ⊃ OPPOSITE **lower**
3 to get money from other people for a particular purpose: *We raised £1 000 for the hospital.*
4 to start to talk about something: *He raised an interesting question.*
5 to look after a child or an animal until they are an adult: *It's difficult to raise a family with so little money.*

raisin /'reɪzn/ *noun*
a small dried fruit (called a grape)

rake /reɪk/ *noun*
a tool with a long handle that you use in a garden for collecting leaves or for making the soil flat
▶ **rake** *verb* (rakes, raking, raked /reɪkt/): *Rake up the dead leaves.*

rally /'ræli/ *noun* (*plural* rallies)
1 a group of people walking or standing together to show that they feel strongly about something: *a peace rally*
2 a race for cars or motorcycles

RAM /ræm/ *noun* (*no plural*)
(*computing*) the type of memory that allows a computer to work: *32 megabytes of RAM*

ram /ræm/ *noun*
a male sheep

ramp /ræmp/ *noun*
a path that you use instead of steps to go up or down: *I pushed the wheelchair up the ramp.*

ran *form of* RUN[1]

ranch /rɑːntʃ/ *noun*
a very large farm, especially in the US or Australia, where cows, horses or sheep are kept

random /'rændəm/ *adjective*
without any special plan: *She chose a few books at random.*

rang form of RING²

range¹ /reɪndʒ/ *noun*
1 different things of the same kind: *This shop sells a range of bicycles.*
2 how far you can see, hear, shoot, travel, etc.: *The gun has a range of five miles.*
3 the amount between the highest and the lowest: *The age range of the children is between eight and twelve.*
4 a line of mountains or hills

range² /reɪndʒ/ *verb* (ranges, ranging, ranged /reɪndʒd/)
to be at different points between two things: *The ages of the students in the class range from 18 to 50.*

rank /ræŋk/ *noun*
how important somebody is in a group of people, for example in an army: *General is one of the highest ranks in the army.*

ransom /'rænsəm/ *noun*
the money that you must pay so that a criminal will free a person that they have taken: *The kidnappers have demanded a ransom of a million pounds.*

rap¹ /ræp/ *noun*
1 a quick knock: *I heard a rap on the door.*
2 (*music*) a type of modern music in which singers speak the words of a song very quickly: *a rap song*

rap² /ræp/ *verb* (raps, rapping, rapped /ræpt/)
1 to hit something quickly and lightly, making a noise: *She rapped on the door.*
2 (*music*) to speak the words of a **rap** song

rape /reɪp/ *verb* (rapes, raping, raped /reɪpt/)
to force somebody to have sex when they do not want to
▶ **rape** *noun*: *He was sent to prison for rape.*

rapid /'ræpɪd/ *adjective*
happening or moving very quickly: *She made rapid progress and was soon the best in the class.* ⊃ OPPOSITE **slow**
▶ **rapidly** *adverb*: *The snow rapidly disappeared.*

rare 0— /reə(r)/ *adjective* (rarer, rarest)
1 If something is **rare**, you do not find or see it often: *Pandas are rare animals.* ◇ *It's rare to see snow in April.* ⊃ OPPOSITE **common**
2 Meat that is **rare** is not cooked for very long, so that the inside is still red.

rarely 0— /'reəli/ *adverb*
not very often: *We rarely agree with each other.*

rash¹ /ræʃ/ *noun* (*plural* rashes)
a lot of small red spots on your skin

rash² /ræʃ/ *adjective* (rasher, rashest)
If you are **rash**, you do things too quickly and without thinking about the possible result: *You were very rash to leave your job before you had found a new one.*

raspberry /'rɑːzbəri/ *noun* (*plural* raspberries)
a small soft red fruit that grows on bushes: *raspberry jam*

rat

rat /ræt/ *noun*
an animal like a big mouse

rate /reɪt/ *noun*
1 the speed of something or how often something happens: *The crime rate was lower in 2004 than in 2005.*
2 the amount that something costs or that somebody is paid: *The basic rate of pay is £10 an hour.*
at any rate (*informal*) anyway; whatever happens: *I hope to be back before ten o'clock – I won't be late at any rate.*

rather 0— /'rɑːðə(r)/ *adverb*
more than a little but not very
⊃ SAME MEANING **quite**: *We were rather tired after our long journey.* ◇ *It's rather a small room.*

> 🔎 **SPEAKING**
> If you use **rather** with a positive word, it sounds as if you are surprised and pleased: *The new teacher is rather nice.*

rather than in the place of; instead of: *Could I have tea rather than coffee?*
would rather would prefer to do something: *I'd rather go by train than by bus.*

ration¹ /'ræʃn/ *noun*
a small amount of something that you are allowed to have when there is not enough for everybody to have what they want: *food rations*

ration² /'ræʃn/ *verb* (rations, rationing, rationed /'ræʃnd/)
to control the amount of something that somebody is allowed to have, for example because there is not enough for everyone to have as much as they want: *Eggs were rationed during the war.*

A B C D E F G H I J K L M N O P Q **R** S T U V W X Y Z

A

rational /'ræʃnəl/ *adjective*
based on facts; sensible: *There must be a
rational explanation for why he's behaving
like this.*

rattle¹ /'rætl/ *verb* (rattles, rattling,
rattled /'rætld/)
to make a sound like hard things hitting each
other or to shake something so that it makes
this sound: *The windows were rattling all night
in the wind.* ◇ *She rattled the money in the tin.*

rattle² /'rætl/ *noun*
1 the noise of hard things hitting each
other: *the rattle of empty bottles*
2 a toy that a baby can shake to make a
noise

rattlesnake /'rætlsneɪk/ *noun*
a poisonous American snake that makes a
noise like a RATTLE with its tail when it is
angry or afraid

raw /rɔː/ *adjective*

🔍 **PRONUNCIATION**
The word **raw** sounds like **more**.

1 not cooked: *raw meat*
2 in its natural state; not yet made into
anything: *raw sugar*

ray /reɪ/ *noun* (plural rays)
a line of light or heat: *the sun's rays*

razor /'reɪzə(r)/ *noun*
a sharp thing that people use to cut hair off
their bodies (to **shave**): *an electric razor*

razor blade /'reɪzə bleɪd/ *noun*
the thin metal part of a RAZOR that cuts

Rd *short way of writing* ROAD

re- /riː/ *prefix*
You can add **re-** to the beginning of some
words to give them the meaning 'again': *We
had to **rebuild** (= build again) the fence after
the storm.* ◇ *Your homework is all wrong.
Please **redo** it (= do it again).*

reach¹ 0—┱ /riːtʃ/ *verb* (reaches,
reaching, reached /riːtʃt/)
1 to arrive somewhere: *It was dark when we
reached Paris.* ◇ *Have you reached the end of
the book yet?*
2 to put out your hand to do or get
something: *I **reached for** the telephone.*
3 to be able to touch something: *Can you
get that book from the top shelf for me? I **can't**
reach.*

reach² /riːtʃ/ *noun* (no plural)
beyond reach, out of reach too far
away to touch: *Keep this medicine out of
children's reach.*
within reach near enough to touch or go
to: *Is the beach within reach of the hotel?*

react /ri'ækt/ *verb* (reacts, reacting,
reacted)
to say or do something because something
has happened: *How did Paul **react to** the
news?*

reaction 0—┱ /ri'ækʃn/ *noun*
what you say or do because of something
that has happened: *What was her reaction
when you told her about the accident?* ◇ *What
was his **reaction to** the news?*

read 0—┱ /riːd/ *verb* (reads, reading, read
/red/, has read)
1 to look at words and understand them:
Have you read this book? It's very interesting.
2 to say words that you can see: *I **read** a
story **to** the children.*
read something out to read something
to other people: *The teacher read out the list
of names.*
▶ **reading** *noun* (no plural): *My interests are
reading and football.*

reader /'riːdə(r)/ *noun*
1 a person who reads something
2 a book for reading at school

readily /'redɪli/ *adverb*
quickly and easily: *Most vegetables are
readily available at this time of year.*

ready 0—┱ /'redi/ *adjective*
1 prepared and able to do something: *I'll be
ready to leave in five minutes.* ◇ *I must go and
get ready to go out.*
2 finished so that you can use it: *Dinner will
be ready soon.*
3 happy to do something ⊃ SAME MEANING
willing: *He's always **ready to** help.*

ready-made /,redi 'meɪd/ *adjective*
already prepared and ready to use: *ready-
made meals*

real 0—┱ /rɪəl/ *adjective*
1 existing, not just imagined: *The film is
about events that happened **in real life**.*
2 actually true, not only what people think is
true: *The name he gave to the police wasn't his
real name.*
3 natural; not false or a copy: *This ring is real
gold.*
4 big or complete: *I've got a real problem.*

real estate agent /'rɪəl ɪsteɪt eɪdʒənt/
American English for ESTATE AGENT

realistic /,riːə'lɪstɪk/ *adjective*
sensible and accepting what is possible in a
particular situation: *We have to **be realistic**
about our chances of winning.*

reality 0—┱ /ri'æləti/ *noun* (no plural)
the way that something really is, not how
you would like it to be: *I enjoyed my holiday,*

R

but now it's back to reality. ◇ She looked very confident but **in reality** she was extremely nervous.

realize 0☞ /'ri:əlaɪz/ **verb** (realizes, realizing, realized /'rɪəlaɪzd/)
to understand or know something: When I got home, I realized that I had lost my key. ◇ I didn't realize you were American.
▶ **realization** /,ri:əlaɪ'zeɪʃn/ **noun** (no plural): the sudden realization of what he had done

really 0☞ /'rɪəli/ **adverb**
1 in fact; actually: Do you really love him?
2 very or very much: I'm really hungry. ◇ 'Do you like this music?' 'Not really.'
3 a word that shows you are interested or surprised: 'I'm going to China next year.' 'Really?'

rear¹ /rɪə(r)/ **noun** (no plural)
the back part of something: The kitchen is at **the rear of** the house. ⊃ OPPOSITE **front**

rear² /rɪə(r)/ **adjective**
at the back of something: the rear window of a car

rear³ /rɪə(r)/ **verb** (rears, rearing, reared /rɪəd/)
to care for and educate young children ⊃ SAME MEANING **bring somebody up, raise**: She reared three children without any help.

reason 0☞ /'ri:zn/ **noun**
a cause or an explanation for why you do something or why something happens: The reason I didn't come to the party was that I was ill. ◇ Is there any **reason why** you were late? ◇ She gave no **reasons for** her decision.

reasonable 0☞ /'ri:znəbl/ **adjective**
1 fair and ready to listen to what other people say: I tried to be reasonable even though I was very angry.
2 fair or right in a particular situation: I think $100 is a reasonable price.
⊃ OPPOSITE **unreasonable**

reasonably /'ri:znəbli/ **adverb**
1 quite, but not very ⊃ SAME MEANING **fairly**: The food was reasonably good.
2 in a reasonable way: Don't get angry – let's talk about this reasonably.

reassure /,ri:ə'ʃʊə(r)/ **verb** (reassures, reassuring, reassured /,ri:ə'ʃʊəd/)
to say or do something to make somebody feel safer or happier: The doctor reassured her that she was not seriously ill.
▶ **reassurance** /,ri:ə'ʃʊərəns/ **noun** (no plural): He needs reassurance that he is right.

rebel¹ /'rebl/ **noun**
a person who fights against the people in control, for example the government

rebel² /rɪ'bel/ **verb** (rebels, rebelling, rebelled /rɪ'beld/)
to fight against the people in control, for example the government or your parents: She **rebelled against** her parents by refusing to go to university.

rebellion /rɪ'beljən/ **noun**
a time when some of the people in a country fight against their government: Hundreds of people died in the rebellion.

recall /rɪ'kɔ:l/ **verb** (recalls, recalling, recalled /rɪ'kɔ:ld/) (formal)
to remember something: I don't recall the name of the hotel.

receipt /rɪ'si:t/ **noun**
a piece of paper that shows you have paid for something: Can I have a receipt?

receive 0☞ /rɪ'si:v/ **verb** (receives, receiving, received /rɪ'si:vd/) (formal)

> 🔎 SPELLING
>
> Remember! When the sound is /i:/, there is a spelling rule: **I before E, except after C**, so you spell **receive** with **EI** (not **IE**).

to get or accept something that somebody has given or sent to you ⊃ SAME MEANING **get**: Did you receive my letter?

receiver /rɪ'si:və(r)/ **noun**
the part of a telephone that you use for listening and speaking

recent 0☞ /'ri:snt/ **adjective**
that happened or began only a short time ago: Is this a recent photo of your son?

recently 0☞ /'ri:sntli/ **adverb**
not long ago: She worked here until quite recently.

reception /rɪ'sepʃn/ **noun**
1 (no plural) the place where you go first when you arrive at a hotel or an office building: Leave your key **in reception** if you go out.
2 (plural receptions) a big important party: The wedding reception will be held at the castle.

receptionist /rɪ'sepʃənɪst/ **noun**
a person in a hotel, an office, etc. whose job is to answer the telephone and to help people when they arrive

recess /rɪ'ses/ American English for PLAYTIME

recipe /'resəpi/ **noun**
a piece of writing that tells you how to cook something

A B C D E F G H I J K L M N O P Q R S T U V W X Y Z

A

reckless /'rekləs/ *adjective*
A person who is **reckless** does dangerous things without thinking about what could happen: *reckless driving*

B

C

reckon /'rekən/ *verb* (reckons, reckoning, reckoned /'rekənd/)
1 (*informal*) to believe something because you have thought about it: *It's very late. I reckon she isn't coming.*

D

E

2 to use numbers to find an answer
➔ SAME MEANING **calculate**: *We reckoned the journey would take about half an hour.*

F

recognition /ˌrekəg'nɪʃn/ *noun* (no plural)
1 knowing what something is or who somebody is when you see it or them: *I said hello to her, but there was no sign of recognition on her face.*

G

H

I

2 knowing that something is true: *There is a general recognition of the need to change the law.*

J

recognize 0— /'rekəgnaɪz/ *verb* (recognizes, recognizing, recognized /'rekəgnaɪzd/)
1 to know again somebody or something that you have seen or heard before: *I didn't recognize you without your glasses.*

K

L

M

2 to know that something is true: *They recognize that there is a problem.*

N

recommend 0— /ˌrekə'mend/ *verb* (recommends, recommending, recommended)

O

> 🔎 SPELLING
> Remember! You spell **recommend** with one **C** and **MM**.

P

Q

1 to tell somebody that a person or thing is good or useful: *Can you recommend a hotel near the airport?*
2 to tell somebody in a helpful way what you think they should do ➔ SAME MEANING **advise**: *I recommend that you see a doctor.*

R

S

recommendation /ˌrekəmen'deɪʃn/ *noun*
saying that something is good or useful: *We stayed at this hotel on their recommendation* (= because they said it was good).

T

U

record¹ 0— /'rekɔːd/ *noun*

V

> 🔎 PRONUNCIATION
> When the word **record** is a noun, you say the first part of the word louder: **REcord**.
> When the word **record** is a verb, you say the second part of the word louder: **reCORD**.

W

X

Y

Z

1 notes about things that have happened: *Keep a record of all the money you spend.*

2 a thin, round piece of plastic that makes music when you play it on a special machine: *Put another record on.* ◇ *a record company*
3 the best, fastest, highest, lowest, etc. that has been done in a sport: *She holds the world record for long jump.* ◇ *He did it in record time* (= very fast). ◇ *She's hoping to break the record for the 100 metres* (= to do it faster than anyone has done before).

record² 0— /rɪ'kɔːd/ *verb* (records, recording, recorded)
1 to write notes about or make pictures of things that happen so you can remember them later: *In his diary he recorded everything that he did.*
2 to put music or a film on a tape, a CD or a DVD so that you can listen to or watch it later: *I recorded a programme from the TV.*

record-breaking /'rekɔːd breɪkɪŋ/ *adjective*
the best, fastest, highest, etc. ever: *We did the journey in record-breaking time.*

recorder

recorder /rɪ'kɔːdə(r)/ *noun*
a musical instrument that children often play. You blow through it and cover the holes in it with your fingers. ➔ Look also at **tape recorder** and **video recorder**.

recording /rɪ'kɔːdɪŋ/ *noun*
sounds or pictures on a tape, CD or film: *a new recording of Mozart's 'Don Giovanni'*

record player /'rekɔːd pleɪə(r)/ *noun*
a machine that you use for playing records

recover 0— /rɪ'kʌvə(r)/ *verb* (recovers, recovering, recovered /rɪ'kʌvəd/)
1 to become well or happy again after you have been ill or sad: *She is slowly recovering from her illness.*
2 to get back something that was lost: *Police never recovered the stolen car.*

recovery /rɪ'kʌvəri/ *noun* (no plural)
when you feel well or happy again after you have been ill or sad: *He made a quick recovery after his operation.*

recreation /ˌrekri'eɪʃn/ *noun* (no plural)
relaxing and enjoying yourself, when you are not working: *recreation activities such as swimming and yoga*

recruit¹ /rɪˈkruːt/ *verb* (recruits, recruiting, recruited)
to find new people to join a company or an organization: *The army are recruiting new officers.*

recruit² /rɪˈkruːt/ *noun*
a person who has just joined the army, the navy or the police: *the training of new recruits*

rectangle /ˈrektæŋgl/ *noun*
a shape with two long sides, two short sides and four angles of 90 degrees
▶ **rectangular** /rekˈtæŋgjələ(r)/ *adjective*: *This page is rectangular.*

recycle /ˌriːˈsaɪkl/ *verb* (recycles, recycling, recycled /ˌriːˈsaɪkld/)
to do something to materials like paper and glass so that they can be used again: *Old newspapers can be recycled.*

recycled /ˌriːˈsaɪkld/ *adjective*
Something that is **recycled** has been used before: *recycled paper*

red 0̶ /red/ *adjective* (redder, reddest)
1 having the colour of blood: *She's wearing a bright red dress.* ◇ *red wine*
2 Red hair has a colour between red, orange and brown.
▶ **red** *noun*: *Lucy was dressed in red.*

reduce 0̶ /rɪˈdjuːs/ *verb* (reduces, reducing, reduced /rɪˈdjuːst/)
to make something smaller or less: *I bought this shirt because the price was reduced from £20 to £12.* ◇ *Reduce speed now* (= words on a road sign). ⊃ OPPOSITE **increase**

reduction /rɪˈdʌkʃn/ *noun*
making something smaller or less: *price reductions* ◇ *There has been some reduction in unemployment.*

redundant /rɪˈdʌndənt/ *adjective*
without a job because you are not needed any more: *When the factory closed, 300 people were made redundant.*

reed /riːd/ *noun*
a tall plant, like grass, that grows in or near water

reel /riːl/ *noun*
a thing with round sides that holds cotton for sewing, film for cameras, etc.: *a reel of cotton*

reel

a reel of cotton

refer 0̶ /rɪˈfɜː(r)/ *verb* (refers, referring, referred /rɪˈfɜːd/)
refer to somebody or **something**
1 to talk about somebody or something:

When I said that some people are stupid, I wasn't referring to you!
2 to describe or be connected with somebody or something: *The word 'child' here refers to anybody under the age of 16.*
3 to look in a book or ask somebody for information ⊃ SAME MEANING **consult**: *If you don't understand a word, you may refer to your dictionaries.*

referee /ˌrefəˈriː/ *noun*
a person who watches a game such as football to make sure the players obey the rules ⊃ Look at **umpire**.

reference /ˈrefrəns/ *noun*
1 (*plural* references) what somebody says or writes about something: *The book is full of references to her childhood in India.*
2 (*no plural*) looking at something for information: *Keep these instructions for future reference.*
3 (*plural* references) If somebody gives you a **reference**, they write about you to somebody who may give you a new job: *Did your boss give you a good reference?*

reference book /ˈrefrəns bʊk/ *noun*
a book where you look for information: *A dictionary is a reference book.*

reflect /rɪˈflekt/ *verb* (reflects, reflecting, reflected)
1 to show a picture of somebody or something in a mirror, water or glass: *She could see herself reflected in the mirror.*
2 to send back light, heat or sound: *The windows reflected the bright morning sunshine.*
3 to show something: *His music reflects his interest in African culture.*

reflection /rɪˈflekʃn/ *noun*
1 (*plural* reflections) a picture that you see in a mirror or on a shiny surface: *He admired his reflection in the mirror.*
2 (*no plural*) sending back light, heat or sound
3 a thing that shows what somebody or something is like: *Your clothes are a reflection of your personality.*

reform¹ /rɪˈfɔːm/ *verb* (reforms, reforming, reformed /rɪˈfɔːmd/)
to change something to make it better: *The government wants to reform the education system in this country.*

reform² /rɪˈfɔːm/ *noun*
a change to something to make it better: *economic reform*

refresh /rɪˈfreʃ/ *verb* (refreshes, refreshing, refreshed /rɪˈfreʃt/)
to make somebody feel less tired, less hot or

A

full of energy again: *A sleep will refresh you after your long journey.*

B **refreshed** /rɪˈfreʃt/ *adjective*
If you feel **refreshed**, you feel less tired, less
C hot or full of energy again: *He looked refreshed after a good night's sleep.*

D **refreshing** /rɪˈfreʃɪŋ/ *adjective*
making you feel less tired or less hot: *a cool,*
E *refreshing drink*

refreshments /rɪˈfreʃmənts/ *noun*
F (*plural*)
food and drinks that are available in a place
G like a cinema or theatre, or at a public event:
Light refreshments will be served during the
break.

H **refrigerator** /rɪˈfrɪdʒəreɪtə(r)/ *noun*
American English for FRIDGE

I **refuge** /ˈrefjuːdʒ/ *noun*
a place where you are safe from somebody
J or something: *We took refuge from the hot*
sun under a tree.

K **refugee** /ˌrefjuˈdʒiː/ *noun*
a person who must leave their country
L because of danger, for example a war

refund /ˈriːfʌnd/ *noun*
M money that is paid back to you, because you
have paid too much or because you are not
N happy with something you have bought: *The*
watch didn't work properly so I took it back to
O *the shop and got a refund.*
▸ **refund** /rɪˈfʌnd/ *verb* (refunds,
refunding, refunded): *We will refund your*
P *money in full.*

refusal /rɪˈfjuːzl/ *noun*
Q saying 'no' when somebody asks you to do
or have something: *a refusal to pay*

R **refuse**[1] 0🔑 /rɪˈfjuːz/ *verb* (refuses,
refusing, refused /rɪˈfjuːzd/)
S to say 'no' when somebody asks you to do or
have something: *I asked Matthew to help, but*
T *he refused.* ◇ *The shop assistant refused to*
give me my money back.

refuse[2] /ˈrefjuːs/ *noun* (no plural) (formal)
U things that you throw away
➔ SAME MEANING **rubbish**

V **regard**[1] /rɪˈɡɑːd/ *verb* (regards,
regarding, regarded)
W to think about somebody or something in a
certain way: *I regard her as my best friend.*

X **regard**[2] /rɪˈɡɑːd/ *noun*
1 (*no plural*) (*formal*) attention to or care for
Y somebody or something: *She shows no*
regard for other people's feelings.
Z **2** (*no plural*) what you feel when you admire
or respect somebody or something: *I have*
great regard for his work (= I think it is very
good).

3 regards (*plural*) used to send good
wishes to somebody at the end of a letter or
an email, or when you ask somebody to give
your good wishes to another person who is
not there: *With kind regards, Yours...* ◇ *Please*
give my regards to your parents.

regarding /rɪˈɡɑːdɪŋ/ *preposition* (*formal*)
about somebody or something
➔ SAME MEANING **concerning**: *Please*
contact us if you require further information
regarding this matter.

regardless /rɪˈɡɑːdləs/ *adverb*
in spite of problems or difficulties: *The*
weather was terrible, but we **carried on**
regardless.

reggae /ˈreɡeɪ/ *noun* (*no plural*)
(*music*) a type of West Indian music

regiment /ˈredʒɪmənt/ *noun*
a group of soldiers in an army

region 0🔑 /ˈriːdʒən/ *noun*
a part of a country or of the world: *tropical*
regions of the world

regional /ˈriːdʒənl/ *adjective*
belonging to a certain REGION

register[1] /ˈredʒɪstə(r)/ *verb* (registers,
registering, registered /ˈredʒɪstəd/)
1 to put a name on an official list: *I would like*
to register for the English course.
2 to show a number or amount: *The*
thermometer registered 30°C.

register[2] /ˈredʒɪstə(r)/ *noun*
an official list of names: *The teacher keeps a*
register of all the students in the class.

registration /ˌredʒɪˈstreɪʃn/ *noun* (*no*
plural)
putting a name on an official list: *the*
registration of births, marriages and deaths

registration number /ˌredʒɪˈstreɪʃn
nʌmbə(r)/ (*British*) *noun*
the numbers and letters on the front and
back of a car or other vehicle

regret[1] /rɪˈɡret/ *verb* (regrets, regretting,
regretted)
to feel sorry about something that you did or
did not do: *He regrets selling his car.* ◇ *I don't*
regret what I said to her.

regret[2] /rɪˈɡret/ *noun*
a sad feeling about something that you did
or did not do: *Do you* **have** any **regrets** about
leaving your job?

regular 0🔑 /ˈreɡjələ(r)/ *adjective*
1 happening again and again with the same
amount of space or time in between: *a*
regular heartbeat ◇ *A light flashed* **at regular**
intervals. ➔ OPPOSITE **irregular**
2 going somewhere or doing something

often: *I've never seen him before – he's not one of my regular customers.*
3 usual: *Who is your regular doctor?*
4 (*grammar*) A word that is **regular** has the usual verb forms or plural: '*Work*' *is a regular verb.* ⊃ OPPOSITE **irregular**
▶ **regularly** /'reɡjələli/ *adverb*: *We meet regularly every Friday.*

regulation /ˌreɡju'leɪʃn/ *noun*
an official rule that controls what people do: *You can't smoke here – it's **against** fire regulations.*

rehearsal /rɪ'hɜːsl/ *noun*
a time when you practise something such as a play or a piece of music before you do it in front of other people: *There's a rehearsal for the play tonight.*

rehearse /rɪ'hɜːs/ *verb* (rehearses, rehearsing, rehearsed /rɪ'hɜːst/)
to practise something such as a play or a piece of music before you do it in front of other people: *We are rehearsing for the concert.*

reign¹ /reɪn/ *noun*
a time when a king or queen rules a country: *The reign of Queen Elizabeth II began in 1952.*

reign² /reɪn/ *verb* (reigns, reigning, reigned /reɪnd/)
to be king or queen of a country: *Queen Victoria reigned for over sixty years.*

rein /reɪn/ *noun*
a long thin piece of leather that a horse wears on its head so that the person riding it can control it ⊃ Look at the picture at **horse**.

reindeer

reindeer /'reɪndɪə(r)/ *noun* (plural **reindeer**)
a big animal that lives in very cold countries. **Reindeer** are brown and have long horns on their heads.

reject /rɪ'dʒekt/ *verb* (rejects, rejecting, rejected)
to say that you do not want somebody or something: *He rejected my offer of help.*
▶ **rejection** /rɪ'dʒekʃn/ *noun*: *David got a rejection from Leeds University.*

relate /rɪ'leɪt/ *verb* (relates, relating, related)
to show or to make a connection between two or more things: *I found it difficult to relate the two ideas in my mind.*
relate to somebody or **something** to be connected to somebody or something: *We don't need to listen to this, as it doesn't relate to our situation.*

related /rɪ'leɪtɪd/ *adjective*
in the same family; connected: '*Are those two boys related?*' '*Yes, they're brothers.*'

relation 0— /rɪ'leɪʃn/ *noun*
1 a connection between two things: *There is no **relation between** the size of the countries and the number of people who live there.*
2 a person in your family ⊃ SAME MEANING **relative**

relationship 0— /rɪ'leɪʃnʃɪp/ *noun*
the way people, groups or countries behave with each other or how they feel about each other: *I **have a** good **relationship with** my parents.* ◇ *The book is about the **relationship between** an Indian boy **and** an English girl.*

relative 0— /'relətɪv/ *noun*
a person in your family ⊃ SAME MEANING **relation**

relatively /'relətɪvli/ *adverb*
quite, especially when compared to others: *This room is relatively small.*

relax 0— /rɪ'læks/ *verb* (relaxes, relaxing, relaxed /rɪ'lækst/)
1 to rest and be calm; to become less worried or angry: *After a hard day at work I spent the evening relaxing in front of the television.*
2 to become less tight or to make something become less tight: *Let your body relax.*

relaxation /ˌriːlæk'seɪʃn/ *noun* (no plural)
time spent resting and being calm: *You need more rest and relaxation.*

relaxed 0— /rɪ'lækst/ *adjective*
calm and not worried: *She felt relaxed after her holiday.*

relaxing /rɪ'læksɪŋ/ *adjective*
helping you to rest and become less worried: *a quiet, relaxing holiday*

release¹ 0— /rɪ'liːs/ *verb* (release, releasing, released /rɪ'liːst/)
to let a person or an animal go free: *He was **released from** prison last month.*

release² /rɪ'liːs/ *noun*
when a person or an animal is allowed to go free: *the **release of** the prisoners*

A B C D E F G H I J K L M N O P Q R S T U V W X Y Z

relevant 0̶ /'reləvənt/ *adjective*
connected with what you are talking or writing about; important: *We need somebody who can do the job well – your age is not relevant.* ⟶ OPPOSITE **irrelevant**

reliable /rɪ'laɪəbl/ *adjective*
that you can trust: *My car is very reliable.* ◇ *He is a reliable person.* ⟶ OPPOSITE **unreliable** ⟶ The verb is **rely**.

relied form of RELY

relief 0̶ /rɪ'liːf/ *noun* (no plural)
1 the good feeling you have when pain or worry stops: *It was a great relief to know she was safe.*
2 food or money that is given to people who need it: *Many countries sent relief to the victims of the disaster.*

relies form of RELY

relieve /rɪ'liːv/ *verb* (relieve, relieving, relieved /rɪ'liːvd/)
to make a bad feeling or a pain stop or get better: *These pills should relieve the pain.*

relieved /rɪ'liːvd/ *adjective*
feeling happy because a problem or danger has gone away: *I was relieved to hear that you weren't hurt in the accident.*

religion 0̶ /rɪ'lɪdʒən/ *noun*
1 (no plural) believing in a god or gods and the activities connected with this
2 (plural **religions**) one of the ways of believing in a god or gods: *Christianity, Islam and other world religions*

religious 0̶ /rɪ'lɪdʒəs/ *adjective*
1 connected with religion: *a religious leader*
2 having a strong belief in a religion: *My parents are very religious.*

reluctance /rɪ'lʌktəns/ *noun* (no plural)
not wanting to do something: *He agreed, but with great reluctance.*

reluctant /rɪ'lʌktənt/ *adjective*
If you are **reluctant** to do something, you do not want to do it: *He was reluctant to give me the money.*
▶ **reluctantly** *adverb*: *She reluctantly agreed to help with the cleaning.*

rely 0̶ /rɪ'laɪ/ *verb* (relies, relying, relied /rɪ'laɪd/, has relied)
rely on somebody or **something**
1 to need somebody or something ⟶ SAME MEANING **depend on somebody** or **something**: *I rely on my parents for money.*
2 to feel sure that somebody or something will do what they say they will do: *You can rely on him to help you.* ⟶ The adjective is **reliable**.

remain 0̶ /rɪ'meɪn/ *verb* (remains, remaining, remained /rɪ'meɪnd/) (formal)
1 to stay in the same way; to not change: *I asked her a question but she remained silent.*
2 to stay after other people or things have gone: *After the fire, very little remained of the house.*

remaining /rɪ'meɪnɪŋ/ *adjective*
continuing to exist or stay after other people or things have gone or been used: *They spent the remaining two days of their holiday on the beach.*

remains /rɪ'meɪnz/ *noun* (plural)
what is left when most of something has gone: *the remains of an old church*

remark¹ 0̶ /rɪ'mɑːk/ *noun*
something that you say ⟶ SAME MEANING **comment**: *He made a remark about the food.*

remark² /rɪ'mɑːk/ *verb* (remarks, remarking, remarked /rɪ'mɑːkt/)
to say something ⟶ SAME MEANING **comment**: *'It's cold today,' he remarked.*

remarkable /rɪ'mɑːkəbl/ *adjective*
unusual and surprising in a good way: *a remarkable discovery*
▶ **remarkably** /rɪ'mɑːkəbli/ *adverb*: *She speaks French remarkably well.*

remedy /'remədi/ *noun* (plural **remedies**)
something that makes you better when you are sick or in pain: *He gave me a remedy for toothache.*

remember 0̶ /rɪ'membə(r)/ *verb* (remembers, remembering, remembered /rɪ'membəd/)
to keep something in your mind or bring something back into your mind: *Can you remember his name?* ◇ *I remember posting the letter.* ◇ *Did you remember to go to the bank?* ⟶ OPPOSITE **forget**

remind 0̶ /rɪ'maɪnd/ *verb* (reminds, reminding, reminded)
1 to help somebody remember something that they must do: *Please remind me to buy some bread on the way home.*
2 to make somebody remember somebody or something: *She reminds me of her mother.*

reminder /rɪ'maɪndə(r)/ *noun*
something that makes you remember something: *Eddie kept the ring as a reminder of happier days.*

remorse /rɪ'mɔːs/ *noun* (no plural)
the feeling you have when you are sorry for doing something wrong: *She was filled with remorse for what she had done.* ⟶ Look at **guilt**.

remote /rɪ'məʊt/ *adjective* (remoter, remotest)
far away from where other people live: *a remote island in the Pacific Ocean*

remote control

remote control /rɪ,məʊt kən'trəʊl/ *noun* (*no plural*)
1 a way of controlling something from a distance: *The doors can be opened by remote control.*
2 (*also informal* **remote**) a piece of equipment that you use for controlling something from a distance: *Pass me the remote control – I'll see what's on the other channel.*

remotely /rɪ'məʊtli/ *adverb*
at all; in any way: *I'm not remotely interested in your opinions.*

removal /rɪ'muːvl/ *noun*
when you take something off or away: *the removal of a car that was blocking the exit*

remove 0ᴛ /rɪ'muːv/ *verb* (removes, removing, removed /rɪ'muːvd/)
to take somebody or something off or away from somebody or something: *The statue was removed from the museum.* ◇ *Please remove your shoes before entering the temple.* ⊃ SAME MEANING Less formal verbs are **take away** or **take off**.

renew /rɪ'njuː/ *verb* (renews, renewing, renewed /rɪ'njuːd/)
to get or give something new in the place of something old: *If you want to stay in the country for another month you must renew your visa.*

rent¹ 0ᴛ /rent/ *noun*
the money that you pay to live in a place or to use something that belongs to another person: *How much is your rent?*

rent² 0ᴛ /rent/ *verb* (rents, renting, rented)
1 to pay to live in a place or to use something that belongs to another person: *I rent a house on the edge of town.*
2 to let somebody live in a place or use something that belongs to you, if they pay you: *He rents rooms in his house to students.* ⊃ Look at the note at **hire**.

rep /rep/ *noun* (*informal*)
a person whose job is to travel around an area selling their company's products

repaid *form of* REPAY

repair¹ 0ᴛ /rɪ'peə(r)/ *verb* (repairs, repairing, repaired /rɪ'peəd/)
to make something that is broken or damaged good again ⊃ SAME MEANING **mend**: *Can you repair my bike?*

repair² /rɪ'peə(r)/ *noun*
something you do to fix something that is broken or damaged: *The school is closed for repairs to the roof.*

repay /rɪ'peɪ/ *verb* (repays, repaying, repaid /rɪ'peɪd/, has repaid)
1 to pay back money to somebody: *to repay a loan*
2 to do something for somebody to show your thanks: *How can I repay you for all your help?*

repayment /rɪ'peɪmənt/ *noun*
paying somebody back, or the money that you pay them: *monthly repayments*

repeat 0ᴛ /rɪ'piːt/ *verb* (repeats, repeating, repeated)
1 to say or do something again: *He didn't hear my question, so I repeated it.*
2 to say what another person has said: *Repeat this sentence after me.*
▶ **repeat** *noun*: *I think I've seen this programme before – it must be a repeat.*

repeated /rɪ'piːtɪd/ *adjective*
happening or done many times: *There have been repeated accidents on this stretch of road.*
▶ **repeatedly** /rɪ'piːtɪdli/ *adverb*: *I've asked him repeatedly not to leave his bicycle here.*

repetition /,repə'tɪʃn/ *noun*
saying or doing something again: *to learn by repetition*

replace 0ᴛ /rɪ'pleɪs/ *verb* (replaces, replacing, replaced /rɪ'pleɪst/)
1 to take the place of somebody or something: *Teachers will never be replaced by computers in the classroom.*
2 to put a new or different person or thing in the place of another: *The watch was broken so the shop replaced it with a new one.*
3 to put something back in the place where it was before: *Please replace the books on the shelf when you have finished with them.*

replacement /rɪ'pleɪsmənt/ *noun*
a new or different person or thing that takes the place of another: *Sue is leaving the company next month so we need to find a replacement.*

replay /'riːpleɪ/ *noun* (*British*)
(*sport*) a game that is played again because nobody won the first time

A
B
C
D
E
F
G
H
I
J
K
L
M
N
O
P
Q
R
S
T
U
V
W
X
Y
Z

reply¹ 0—π /rɪˈplaɪ/ *verb* (replies, replying, replied /rɪˈplaɪd/, has replied)
to say or write something as an answer to somebody or something: *I wrote to Jane but she hasn't replied.*

reply² 0—π *noun* (*plural* replies)
an answer: *Have you had a reply to your letter?* ◇ *What did you say in reply to his question?*

report¹ 0—π /rɪˈpɔːt/ *verb* (reports, reporting, reported)
to give people information about something that has happened: *We reported the accident to the police.*

report² 0—π /rɪˈpɔːt/ *noun*
1 something that somebody says or writes about something that has happened: *Did you read the newspaper reports about the earthquake?*
2 (*British*) something that teachers write about a student's work

reported speech /rɪˈpɔːtɪd spiːtʃ/ *noun* (*no plural*) (*also* indirect speech)
(*grammar*) saying what somebody has said, rather than repeating their exact words. In **reported speech**, 'I'll come later' becomes 'He said he'd (= he would) come later'. ⊃ Look at **direct speech**.

reporter /rɪˈpɔːtə(r)/ *noun*
a person who writes in a newspaper or speaks on the radio or television about things that have happened ⊃ Look at **journalist**.

represent 0—π /ˌreprɪˈzent/ *verb* (represents, representing, represented)
1 to speak or do something in place of another person or other people: *It is an honour for athletes to represent their country.*
2 to be an example or a sign of something: *The yellow lines on the map represent roads.*

representative /ˌreprɪˈzentətɪv/ *noun*
a person who speaks or does something for a group of people: *There were representatives from every country in Europe at the meeting.*

reproduce /ˌriːprəˈdjuːs/ *verb* (reproduces, reproducing, reproduced /ˌriːprəˈdjuːst/)
1 to make a copy of something
2 When people, animals or plants **reproduce**, they have young ones.

reproduction /ˌriːprəˈdʌkʃn/ *noun* (*no plural*)
producing babies or young animals or plants: *We are studying plant reproduction at school.*

reptile /ˈreptaɪl/ *noun*
any animal with cold blood that lays eggs. Snakes are **reptiles**.

> ⌕ **WORD BUILDING**
> There are many different types of **reptile**. Here are some of them: alligator, crocodile, lizard, snake, tortoise, turtle. Do you know any others?

republic /rɪˈpʌblɪk/ *noun*
a country where people choose the government and the leader (the **president**): *the Republic of Ireland* ⊃ Look at **monarchy**.

republican /rɪˈpʌblɪkən/ *noun*
1 a person who wants a REPUBLIC
2 Republican (*politics*) a person in THE REPUBLICAN PARTY in the US ⊃ Look at **Democrat**.

the Republican Party /ðə rɪˈpʌblɪkən pɑːti/ *noun* (*no plural*)
(*politics*) one of the two main political parties in the US ⊃ Look at **the Democratic Party**.

repulsive /rɪˈpʌlsɪv/ *adjective*
making you feel disgusted; very unpleasant: *What a repulsive smell!*

reputation /ˌrepjuˈteɪʃn/ *noun*
what people think or say about somebody or something: *This restaurant has a good reputation.*

request¹ 0—π /rɪˈkwest/ *noun*
asking for something in a polite or formal way: *They made a request for money.*

request² 0—π /rɪˈkwest/ *verb* (requests, requesting, requested) (*formal*)
to ask for something: *Passengers are requested not to smoke* (= a notice in a bus).

> ⌕ **SPEAKING**
> It is more usual to say **ask for**.

require 0—π /rɪˈkwaɪə(r)/ *verb* (requires, requiring, required /rɪˈkwaɪəd/) (*formal*)
to need something: *Do you require anything else?*

> ⌕ **SPEAKING**
> **Need** is the word that we usually use.

requirement /rɪˈkwaɪəmənt/ *noun*
something that you need or that you must have

rescue¹ 0—π /ˈreskjuː/ *verb* (rescues, rescuing, rescued)
to save somebody or something from danger: *She rescued the child when he fell in the river.*

rescue² 0→ /'reskjuː/ *noun*
saving somebody or something from
danger: *The police came to his rescue.*

research¹ 0→ /rɪ'sɜːtʃ; 'riːsɜːtʃ/ *noun*
(*no plural*)
studying something carefully to find out
more about it: *scientific research*

research² 0→ /rɪ'sɜːtʃ/ *verb*
(researches, researching, researched
/rɪ'sɜːtʃt/)
to study something carefully to find out
more about it: *Scientists are researching the
causes of the disease.*
▸ **researcher** /rɪ'sɜːtʃə(r)/ *noun*

resemblance /rɪ'zembləns/ *noun*
looking like somebody or something else:
*There's no resemblance between my two
brothers.*

resemble /rɪ'zembl/ *verb* (resembles,
resembling, resembled /rɪ'zembld/)
to look like somebody or something else: *Lisa
resembles her mother.*

🔎 SPEAKING
It is more usual to say **look like**.

resent /rɪ'zent/ *verb* (resents, resenting,
resented)
to feel angry about something because you
think it is not fair: *I resented her criticism of my
work.*

resentment /rɪ'zentmənt/ *noun* (*no
plural*)
a feeling of anger about something that you
think is not fair

reservation /ˌrezə'veɪʃn/ *noun*
a room, seat, table or another thing that you
have asked somebody to keep for you:
*I called the restaurant and made a reservation
for a table for two.*

reserve¹ 0→ /rɪ'zɜːv/ *verb* (reserves,
reserving, reserved /rɪ'zɜːvd/)
1 to keep something for a special reason or
to use later: *Those seats are reserved.*
2 to ask for a seat, table, room, etc. to be
kept for you at a future time
⊃ SAME MEANING **book**: *I would like to
reserve a single room for tomorrow night,
please.*

reserve² /rɪ'zɜːv/ *noun*
1 something that you keep to use later:
reserves of food
2 an area of land where the animals and
plants are protected by law: *a nature reserve*
3 (*sport*) a person who will play in a game if
another person cannot play

in reserve for using later: *Don't spend all
the money – keep some in reserve.*

reserved /rɪ'zɜːvd/ *adjective*
If you are **reserved**, you keep your feelings
hidden from other people.

reservoir /'rezəvwɑː(r)/ *noun*
a big lake where a town or city keeps water
to use later

residence /'rezɪdəns/ *noun*
1 (*plural* residences) (*formal*) a large
house, usually where an important or
famous person lives: *The Prime Minister's
official residence is 10 Downing Street.*
2 (*no plural*) having your home in a
particular place: *The family applied for
permanent residence in the United States.* ◇ *a
university hall of residence* (= a place where
students live)

resident /'rezɪdənt/ *noun*
a person who lives in a place

residential /ˌrezɪ'denʃl/ *adjective*
A **residential** area is one where there are
houses rather than offices or factories.

resign /rɪ'zaɪn/ *verb* (resigns, resigning,
resigned /rɪ'zaɪnd/)
to leave your job: *The director has resigned.*
resign yourself to something to
accept something that you do not like but
that you cannot change: *There were a lot of
people at the doctor's so John resigned himself
to a long wait.*

resignation /ˌrezɪg'neɪʃn/ *noun*
saying that you want to leave your job: *a
letter of resignation* ◇ *to hand in your
resignation* (= to give your employer a letter
saying that you want to leave your job)

resist /rɪ'zɪst/ *verb* (resists, resisting,
resisted)
1 to try to stop something happening or to
fight against somebody or something: *The
government are resisting pressure to change
the law.*
2 to stop yourself doing or having
something that you want to do or have:
I can't resist chocolate.

resistance /rɪ'zɪstəns/ *noun* (*no plural*)
when people try to stop something
happening; fighting against somebody or
something: *There was a lot of resistance to
the plan to build a new airport.*

resolution /ˌrezə'luːʃn/ *noun*
something that you decide to do or not to
do: *Julie made a resolution to study harder.*

resolve /rɪ'zɒlv/ *verb* (resolves,
resolving, resolved /rɪ'zɒlvd/) (*formal*)
to decide to do or not to do something: *He
resolved never to do it again.*

A
B
C
D
E
F
G
H
I
J
K
L
M
N
O
P
Q
R
S
T
U
V
W
X
Y
Z

A
B
C
D
E
F
G
H
I
J
K
L
M
N
O
P
Q
R
S
T
U
V
W
X
Y
Z

resort /rɪˈzɔːt/ *noun*
a place where a lot of people go on holiday: *a popular seaside resort*
a last resort the only person or thing left that can help: *Nobody else will lend me the money, so I am asking you as a last resort.*

resource /rɪˈsɔːs; rɪˈzɔːs/ *noun*
something that a person, an organization or a country has and can use: *Oil is one of our most important natural resources.*

respect¹ 0⃞ /rɪˈspekt/ *noun* (*no plural*)
1 thinking that somebody or something is very good or clever: *I have a lot of respect for your father.*
2 being polite to somebody or something: *You should treat old people with more respect.*

respect² 0⃞ /rɪˈspekt/ *verb* (respects, respecting, respected)
to have a good opinion of somebody or something ⊃ SAME MEANING **admire**: *I respect him for his honesty.*

respectable /rɪˈspektəbl/ *adjective*
If a person or thing is **respectable**, people think they are good or correct: *She comes from a respectable family.*

respectful /rɪˈspektfl/ *adjective*
If you are **respectful**, you are polite to other people and in different situations: *The crowd listened in respectful silence.*

respond /rɪˈspɒnd/ *verb* (responds, responding, responded) (*formal*)
to do or say something to answer somebody or something ⊃ SAME MEANING **reply**: *I said 'hello', but he didn't respond.*

response /rɪˈspɒns/ *noun*
an answer to somebody or something ⊃ SAME MEANING **reply**: *I wrote to them but I've had no response.*

responsibility 0⃞ /rɪˌspɒnsəˈbɪləti/ *noun*
a duty to deal with or take care of somebody or something, so that it is your fault if something goes wrong: *Who has responsibility for the new students?* ◊ *The dog is my brother's responsibility.*

responsible 0⃞ /rɪˈspɒnsəbl/ *adjective*
1 having the duty to take care of somebody or something, so that it is your fault if something goes wrong: *The driver is responsible for the lives of the people on the bus.*
2 being the person who made something bad happen: *Who was responsible for the accident?*
2 A **responsible** person is somebody that

you can trust: *We need a responsible person to look after our son.*

rest¹ 0⃞ /rest/ *noun*
1 **the rest** the part that is left or the ones that are left: *If you don't want the rest, I'll eat it.* ◊ *I liked the beginning, but the rest of the film wasn't very good.* ◊ *Jason watched TV and the rest of us went for a walk.*
2 a time when you relax, sleep or do nothing: *After walking for an hour, we stopped for a rest.*

rest² 0⃞ /rest/ *verb* (rests, resting, rested)
1 to relax, sleep or do nothing after an activity or an illness: *We worked all morning and then rested for an hour before starting work again.*
2 to be on something; to put something on or against another thing: *His arms were resting on the table.*

restaurant 0⃞ /ˈrestrɒnt/ *noun*
a place where you buy a meal and eat it

🔎 **WORD BUILDING**

You usually go to a **restaurant** for a special meal.
You can get a quick or cheap meal at a **cafe**, a **sandwich bar**, a **takeaway** or a **fast-food restaurant**.

---

restful /ˈrestfl/ *adjective*
making you feel relaxed and calm: *a restful holiday*

restless /ˈrestləs/ *adjective*
not able to stay still or relax because you are bored or nervous: *The children always get restless on long journeys.*

restore /rɪˈstɔː(r)/ *verb* (restores, restoring, restored /rɪˈstɔːd/)
to make something as good as it was before: *The old palace has been restored.*

restrain /rɪˈstreɪn/ *verb* (restrains, restraining, restrained /rɪˈstreɪnd/)
to stop somebody or something from doing something; to control somebody or something: *I couldn't restrain my anger.*

restrict /rɪˈstrɪkt/ *verb* (restricts, restricting, restricted)
to allow only a certain amount, size, sort, etc. ⊃ SAME MEANING **limit**: *Our house is very small, so we had to restrict the number of people we invited to the party.*

restriction /rɪˈstrɪkʃn/ *noun*
a rule to control somebody or something: *There are a lot of parking restrictions in the city centre.*

restroom /'restruːm/ *noun* (*American*)
a room with a toilet in a public place, for example a restaurant or theatre

result¹ ⊶ /rɪˈzʌlt/ *noun*
1 something that happens because of something else: *The accident was a result of bad driving.* ◇ *I woke up late and as a result I was late for school.*
2 the score at the end of a game, competition or exam: *football results* ◇ *When will you know your exam results?*

result² ⊶ /rɪˈzʌlt/ *verb* (results, resulting, resulted)
result in something to make something happen ⊃ SAME MEANING **cause**: *The accident resulted in the death of two drivers.*

resume /rɪˈzjuːm/ *verb* (resumes, resuming, resumed) /rɪˈzjuːmd/ (*formal*)
to start something again after stopping for a period of time: *to resume negotiations*

résumé /'rezjumeɪ/ *noun American English* for CV

retire /rɪˈtaɪə(r)/ *verb* (retires, retiring, retired /rɪˈtaɪəd/)
to stop working because you are a certain age: *My grandfather retired when he was 65.*
▶ **retired** *adjective*: *a retired teacher*

retirement /rɪˈtaɪəmənt/ *noun* (*no plural*)
the time in a person's life after they have reached a certain age and have stopped working: *We all wish you a long and happy retirement.*

retreat /rɪˈtriːt/ *verb* (retreats, retreating, retreated)
to move back or away from somebody or something, for example because you have lost a fight: *The enemy is retreating.*
▶ **retreat** *noun*: *The army is now in retreat.*

return¹ ⊶ /rɪˈtɜːn/ *verb* (returns, returning, returned /rɪˈtɜːnd/)
1 to come or go back to a place: *They returned from Italy last week.*
2 to give, put, send or take something back: *Will you return this book to the library?*

return² ⊶ /rɪˈtɜːn/ *noun*
1 (*no plural*) coming or going back to a place: *They met me at the airport on my return to Britain.*
2 (*no plural*) giving, putting, sending or taking something back: *the return of the stolen money*
3 (*plural* **returns**) (*British*) (*British also* **return ticket**) (*American* **round trip**, **round-trip ticket**) a ticket to travel to a place and back again: *A return to London, please.* ⊃ OPPOSITE **single**
in return as a way of thanking somebody

for something they have done for you or paying them for something they have given you: *Can I buy you lunch in return for all your help?*
many happy returns words that you say to wish somebody a happy birthday

reunion /ˌriːˈjuːniən/ *noun*
a meeting of people who have not seen each other for a long time: *We had a family reunion on my aunt's birthday.*

reunite /ˌriːjuːˈnaɪt/ *verb* (reunites, reuniting, reunited)
to come together or to bring people together again: *The missing child was found and reunited with his parents.*

Rev. *short way of writing* REVEREND

reveal /rɪˈviːl/ *verb* (reveals, revealing, revealed /rɪˈviːld/)
to tell something that was a secret or show something that was hidden: *She refused to reveal any names to the police.*

revenge /rɪˈvendʒ/ *noun* (*no plural*)
something bad that you do to somebody who has done something bad to you: *He wants to take his revenge on his enemies.*

Reverend /'revərənd/ *adjective* (*abbr.* Rev.)
the title of a Christian priest

reverse¹ /rɪˈvɜːs/ *verb* (reverses, reversing, reversed /rɪˈvɜːst/)
1 to turn something the other way round: *Writing is reversed in a mirror.*
2 to go backwards in a car, etc.; to make a car, etc. go backwards: *I reversed the car into the garage.*
reverse the charges (*British*) to make a telephone call that the person you are telephoning will pay for: *I want to reverse the charges, please.*

reverse² /rɪˈvɜːs/ *noun* (*no plural*)
1 the complete opposite of what somebody just said, or of what you expect: *Of course I don't dislike you – quite the reverse* (= I like you very much).
2 the control in a car or other vehicle that allows it to move backwards: *Leave the car in reverse while it's parked on this hill.*

review¹ /rɪˈvjuː/ *noun*
1 looking at something or thinking about something again to see if it needs changing: *There will be a review of your contract after six months.*
2 a piece of writing in a newspaper or magazine that says what somebody thinks about a book, film, play, etc.: *The film got very good reviews.*

A B C D E F G H I J K L M N O P Q **R** S T U V W X Y Z

A

review² /rɪ'vjuː/ *verb* (reviews, reviewing, reviewed /rɪ'vjuːd/)
1 to look at something or think about something again to see if it needs changing: *Your salary will be reviewed after one year.*
2 to write about a new book, film, etc., giving your opinion of it: *The play was reviewed in the national newspapers*

revise /rɪ'vaɪz/ *verb* (revises, revising, revised /rɪ'vaɪzd/)
1 to change something to make it better or more correct: *The book has been revised for this new edition.*
2 (*British*) to study again something that you have learnt, before an exam: *I'm revising for the Geography test.*

revision /rɪ'vɪʒn/ *noun* (*no plural*) (*British*)
studying something again that you have already learnt, in order to prepare for an exam: *I need to do some revision for the History exam.*

revive /rɪ'vaɪv/ *verb* (revives, reviving, revived /rɪ'vaɪvd/)
to become or make somebody or something well or strong again: *They tried to revive him, but he was already dead.*

revolt /rɪ'vəʊlt/ *verb* (revolts, revolting, revolted)
to fight against the people in control: *The army is revolting against the government.*
▶ **revolt** *noun*: *The army quickly stopped the revolt.*

revolting /rɪ'vəʊltɪŋ/ *adjective*
extremely unpleasant; so bad that it makes you feel sick ➾ SAME MEANING **disgusting**: *This meat tastes revolting.*

revolution /ˌrevə'luːʃn/ *noun*
1 a fight by people against their government in order to put a new government in its place: *The French Revolution was in 1789.*
2 a big change in the way of doing things: *the Industrial Revolution*

revolutionary /ˌrevə'luːʃənəri/ *adjective*
1 connected with a political REVOLUTION(1)
2 producing great changes; very new and different: *a revolutionary new scheme to ban cars from the city centre*

revolve /rɪ'vɒlv/ *verb* (revolves, revolving, revolved /rɪ'vɒlvd/)
to move around in a circle: *The earth revolves around the sun.*

revolver /rɪ'vɒlvə(r)/ *noun*
a type of small gun

reward¹ /rɪ'wɔːd/ *noun*
a present or money that somebody gives you because you have done something good or worked hard: *She is offering a £50 reward to anyone who finds her dog.*

reward² /rɪ'wɔːd/ *verb* (rewards, rewarding, rewarded)
to give something to somebody because they have done something well or worked hard: *His parents bought him a bike to reward him for passing his exam.*

rewind /ˌriː'waɪnd/ *verb* (rewinds, rewinding, rewound /ˌriː'waʊnd/, has rewound)
to make a video or a tape go backwards: *Please rewind the tape at the end of the film.*

rheumatism /'ruːmətɪzəm/ *noun* (*no plural*)
an illness that causes pain in the muscles and where your bones join together (your joints)

rhino /'raɪnəʊ/ *noun* (*plural* rhinos) (*informal*) *short for* RHINOCEROS

rhinoceros

horn

rhinoceros /raɪ'nɒsərəs/ *noun* (*plural* rhinoceros *or* rhinoceroses)
a big wild animal from Africa or Asia, with thick skin and a horn on its nose

rhyme¹ /raɪm/ *noun*
1 a word that has the same sound as another sound, for example 'bell' and 'well'
2 a short piece of writing where the lines end with the same sounds: *a children's rhyme*

rhyme² /raɪm/ *verb* (rhymes, rhyming, rhymed /raɪmd/)
1 to have the same sound as another word: *'Chair' rhymes with 'bear'.*
2 to have lines that end with the same sounds: *This poem doesn't rhyme.*

rhythm /'rɪðəm/ *noun*
a regular pattern of sounds that come again and again: *This music has a good rhythm.*

rib /rɪb/ *noun*
one of the bones around your chest

ribbon /'rɪbən/ *noun*
a long thin piece of material for tying things or making something look pretty: *She wore a pink ribbon in her hair.*

rice 0— /raɪs/ *noun* (*no plural*)
short, thin white or brown grain from a plant that grows on wet land in hot countries. We cook and eat **rice**: *Would you like rice or potatoes with your chicken?* ⊃ Look at Picture Dictionary page **P7**.

rich 0— /rɪtʃ/ *adjective* (richer, richest)
1 having a lot of money: *a rich family* ◇ *It's a favourite resort for **the rich** (= people who are rich) and famous.* ⊃ **poor**
2 containing a lot of something: *Oranges are rich in vitamin C.*
3 Food that is **rich** has a lot of fat or sugar in it and makes you feel full quickly: *a rich chocolate cake*

rid 0— /rɪd/ *adjective*
get rid of somebody or **something** to make yourself free of somebody or something that you do not want; to throw something away: *This dog is following me – I can't get rid of it.* ◇ *I got rid of my old coat and bought a new one.*

ridden *form of* RIDE¹

riddle /'rɪdl/ *noun*
a difficult question that has a clever or funny answer: *Here's a riddle: What has four legs but can't walk? The answer is a chair!*

ride¹ 0— /raɪd/ *verb* (rides, riding, rode /rəʊd/, has ridden /'rɪdn/)
1 to sit on a horse or bicycle and control it as it moves: *I'm learning to ride (= a horse).* ◇ *Don't ride your bike on the grass!*

> 🔎 **SPEAKING**
> When you talk about spending time riding a horse for pleasure, you say **go riding** or **go horse riding** in British English: *I went riding today.*
> In American English, you say **go horseback riding**.

2 to travel in a car, bus or train: *We rode in the back of the car.* ⊃ When you control a car, bus or train, you **drive** it.

ride² 0— /raɪd/ *noun*
1 a journey on a horse or bicycle, or in a car, bus or train: *We went for a ride in the woods.* ◇ *I had a ride in his new car.*
2 *American English for* LIFT² (2): *We managed to get a ride into town when we missed the bus.*

rider /'raɪdə(r)/ *noun*
a person who rides a horse or bicycle

ridge /rɪdʒ/ *noun*
a long thin part of something that is higher than the rest, for example along the top of

hills or mountains: *We walked along the ridge looking down at the valley below.*

ridiculous /rɪ'dɪkjələs/ *adjective*
so silly that it makes people laugh: *I look ridiculous in this hat.*

riding /'raɪdɪŋ/ (*British also* **horse riding**) (*American* **horseback riding**) *noun* (*no plural*)
the sport of riding a horse

rifle /'raɪfl/ *noun*
a long gun that you hold against your shoulder to shoot with

right¹ 0— /raɪt/ *adjective*

> 🔎 **PRONUNCIATION**
> The word **right** sounds like **quite**.

1 good; fair or what the law allows: *It's not right to leave young children alone in the house.*
2 correct or true: *That's not the right answer.* ◇ '*Are you Mr Johnson?*' '*Yes, **that's** right.*'
3 best: *Is she the right person for the job?* ⊃ OPPOSITE **wrong**
4 on or of the side of the body that faces east when a person faces north: *Most people write with their right hand.* ⊃ OPPOSITE **left**

right² 0— /raɪt/ *adverb*
1 exactly: *He was sitting right next to me.*
2 all the way; completely: *Go right to the end of the road.*
3 immediately: *Wait here – I'll be right back.* ◇ *Phone the doctor right away.*
4 correctly: *Have I spelt your name right?* ⊃ OPPOSITE **wrong**
5 to the right side: *Turn right at the end of street.* ⊃ OPPOSITE **left**

right³ 0— /raɪt/ *noun*
1 (*no plural*) what is good or fair: *Young children have to learn the difference between right and wrong.* ⊃ OPPOSITE **wrong**
2 (*plural* **rights**) what you are allowed to do, especially by law: *In Britain, everyone **has the right to** vote at 18.*
3 (*no plural*) the right side or direction: *We live in the first house **on the right**.* ⊃ OPPOSITE **left**

right⁴ 0— /raɪt/ *exclamation* (*British, informal*)
1 yes, I agree; yes, I will: '*I'll see you tomorrow.*' '*Right.*'
2 You say 'right' to make somebody listen to you: *Are you ready? Right, let's go.*

right angle /'raɪt æŋgl/ *noun*
(*maths*) an angle of 90 degrees. A square has four **right angles**. ⊃ Look at the picture at **angle**.

A B C D E F G H I J K L M N O P Q R S T U V W X Y Z

A B C D E F G H I J K L M N O P Q R S T U V W X Y Z

right-hand /'raɪt hænd/ *adjective*
of or on the right: *The supermarket is on the* ***right-hand side*** *of the road.*

right-handed /ˌraɪt 'hændɪd/ *adjective*
If you are **right-handed**, you use your right hand more easily than your left hand, for example for writing.

rightly /'raɪtli/ *adverb*
correctly: *If I remember rightly, the party was on 15 June.*

rigid /'rɪdʒɪd/ *adjective*
1 not able or not wanting to be changed: *The school has very rigid rules.*
2 hard and not easy to bend or move: *She was rigid with fear.*

rim /rɪm/ *noun*
the edge of something round: *the rim of a cup*

rind /raɪnd/ *noun*
the thick hard skin of some fruits, or some types of cheese and meat: *lemon rind*

ring¹ 0-ₘ /rɪŋ/ *noun*

rings

1 a circle of metal that you wear on your finger: *a wedding ring*
2 a circle: *The coffee cup left a ring on the table top.*
3 a space with seats around it, used for a competition or a performance: *a boxing ring*
4 the sound that a bell makes: *There was a ring at the door.*
give somebody a ring (*British, informal*) to telephone somebody: *I'll give you a ring later.*

ring² 0-ₘ /rɪŋ/ *verb* (rings, ringing, rang /ræŋ/, has rung /rʌŋ/)
1 (*British*) to telephone somebody
⊃ SAME MEANING **call** and **phone**: *I'll ring you on Sunday.* ◇ *She **rang up** yesterday and cancelled the order.*
2 to make a sound like a bell: *The telephone is ringing.*
3 to press or move a bell so that it makes a sound: *We rang the doorbell again but nobody answered.*
ring somebody back (*British*) to telephone somebody again: *He isn't here now – can you ring back later?*

ringtone /'rɪŋtəʊn/ *noun*
the sound a mobile phone makes when somebody is calling you: *You can download ringtones from the Internet.*

rink /rɪŋk/ *noun*
1 short for ICE RINK
2 short for SKATING RINK

rinse /rɪns/ *verb* (rinses, rinsing, rinsed /rɪnst/)
to wash something with water to take away dirt or soap: *Wash your hair and rinse it well.*

riot /'raɪət/ *noun*
when a group of people fight and make a lot of noise and trouble: *There were riots in the streets after the football match.*
▶ **riot** *verb* (riots, rioting, rioted): *The prisoners are rioting.*

rip /rɪp/ *verb* (rips, ripping, ripped /rɪpt/)
to pull or tear something quickly and suddenly: *I ripped my shirt on a nail.* ◇ *Joe ripped the letter open.*
rip somebody off (*informal*) to cheat somebody by making them pay too much for something: *Tourists complained that they were being ripped off by local taxi drivers.*
⊃ The noun is **rip-off**.
rip something up to tear something into small pieces: *She ripped the photo up.*

ripe /raɪp/ *adjective* (riper, ripest)
Fruit that is **ripe** is ready to eat: *These bananas aren't ripe – they're still green.*

rip-off /'rɪp ɒf/ *noun* (*informal*)
something that costs a lot more than it should: *$70 for a T-shirt! What a rip-off!*

ripple¹ /'rɪpl/ *noun*
a small wave or movement on the surface of water

ripple

ripple² /'rɪpl/ *verb* (ripples, rippling, rippled /'rɪpld/)
to move in small waves: *The sea rippled and sparkled in the sun.*

rise¹ 0-ₘ /raɪz/ *noun*
when the amount, number or level of something goes up ⊃ SAME MEANING **increase**: *There has been a **sharp rise in** the price of oil.* ◇ *a pay rise*

rise² 0-ₘ /raɪz/ *verb* (rises, rising, rose /rəʊz/, has risen /'rɪzn/)
1 to go up; to become higher or more: *Smoke was rising from the chimney.* ◇ *Prices have risen by 20 %.*
2 to get up from a sitting or lying position: *She rose to her feet.*
3 If the sun or moon rises, it moves up in the sky: *The sun rises in the east and sets (= goes down) in the west.*

risk¹ 0-ₘ /rɪsk/ *noun*
the possibility that something bad may happen; a dangerous situation: *Smoking can increase the **risk of** heart disease.*

at risk in danger: *Children are most at risk from this disease.*

take a risk *or* **risks** to do something when you know that something bad may happen because of it: *Don't take risks when you're driving.*

risk² 0‑ᴡ /rɪsk/ *verb* (risks, risking, risked /rɪskt/)

1 to put something or yourself in danger: *He risked his life to save the child from the burning house.*

2 to do something when you know that something bad may happen because of it: *If you don't work harder, you risk failing the exam.*

risky /'rɪski/ *adjective* (riskier, riskiest) dangerous

rival /'raɪvl/ *noun*
a person who wants to do better than you or who is trying to take what you want: *John and Lucy are rivals for the manager's job.*

river 0‑ᴡ /'rɪvə(r)/ *noun*
a long wide line of water that flows into the sea: *the River Amazon*

road 0‑ᴡ /rəʊd/ *noun*
the way from one place to another, where cars can go: *Is this the road to the city centre?* ◇ *My address is 34a Windsor Road, London NW2.* ᴓ The short way of writing 'Road' in addresses is **Rd**: *30 Welton Rd.*

🔎 **WORD BUILDING**

Street is another word for **road**.
A country road is often called a **lane**.
A **motorway** *(British)* or a **freeway** *(American)* is a fast road which you use to travel between cities.

---

by road in a car, bus, etc.: *It's a long journey by road – the train is faster.*

roadworks /'rəʊdwɜːks/ *noun* (plural) (British)
work that involves repairing or building roads

roam /rəʊm/ *verb* (roams, roaming, roamed /rəʊmd/)
to walk or travel with no special plan: *Dogs were roaming the streets looking for food.*

roar¹ /rɔː(r)/ *verb* (roars, roaring, roared /rɔːd/)
to make a loud deep sound: *The lion roared.* ◇ *Everybody roared with laughter.*

roar² /rɔː(r)/ *noun*
a loud deep sound: *the lion gave a huge roar* ◇ *the roar of an aeroplane's engines*

roast /rəʊst/ *verb* (roasts, roasting, roasted)
to cook or be cooked in an oven or over a fire: *Roast the chicken in a hot oven.*
▶ **roast** *adjective*: *roast beef and roast potatoes*

rob 0‑ᴡ /rɒb/ *verb* (robs, robbing, robbed /rɒbd/)
to take something that is not yours from a person or place: *They robbed a bank.* ᴓ Look at the note at **steal**.

robber /'rɒbə(r)/ *noun*
a person who steals things from a person or a place: *a bank robber* ᴓ Look at the note at **thief**.

robbery /'rɒbəri/ *noun* (plural robberies)
taking something that is not yours from a person or a place: *What time did the robbery take place?*

robe /rəʊb/ *noun*
1 a long loose thing that you wear on your body, for example at a special ceremony: *a graduation robe*
2 *American English* for DRESSING GOWN

robin /'rɒbɪn/ *noun*
a small brown bird with a red front

robot /'rəʊbɒt/ *noun*
a machine that can work like a person: *This car was built by robots.*

rock¹ 0‑ᴡ /rɒk/ *noun*
1 *(no plural)* the very hard material that is in the ground and in mountains
2 *(plural rocks)* a big piece of rock: *The ship hit the rocks.*
3 *(no plural)* *(also rock music)* a sort of modern music with a strong rhythm: *a rock concert*

rock² /rɒk/ *verb* (rocks, rocking, rocked /rɒkt/)
to move slowly backwards and forwards or from side to side; to make somebody or something do this: *The boat was rocking gently on the lake.* ◇ *I rocked the baby until she went to sleep.*

rock and roll *(also rock 'n' roll)* /ˌrɒk ən 'rəʊl/ *noun* *(no plural)*
a type of music with a strong rhythm that was most popular in the 1950s

rocket /'rɒkɪt/ *noun*
1 a vehicle that is used for travelling into space: *to launch a rocket* ◇ *a space rocket*
2 a weapon that travels through the air and carries a bomb ᴓ SAME MEANING **missile**
3 an object that shoots high into the air and then explodes with pretty coloured lights (a type of **firework**)

rock music /ˈrɒk mjuːzɪk/ = ROCK¹(3)

rocky /ˈrɒki/ *adjective* (rockier, rockiest)
with a lot of rocks: *a rocky path*

rod /rɒd/ *noun*
a long thin straight piece of wood or metal: *a fishing rod*

rode *form of* RIDE¹

rodent /ˈrəʊdnt/ *noun*
a type of small animal that has strong sharp front teeth, for example a mouse or a RABBIT

role 0️⃣ /rəʊl/ *noun*
1 what a person does, for example in an organization or a relationship: *Your role is to welcome guests as they arrive.*
2 a person's part in a play or film: *He played the role of the King.*

rolls

bread rolls

toilet roll

roll of tape

roll¹ 0️⃣ /rəʊl/ *noun*
1 something made into a long round shape by turning it around itself many times: *a roll of material* ◊ *a roll of film*
2 a small round piece of bread made for one person: *a roll and butter*

roll² 0️⃣ /rəʊl/ *verb* (rolls, rolling, rolled /rəʊld/)
1 to move along by turning over and over; to make something move in this way: *The pencil rolled off the table on to the floor.* ◊ *We rolled the rock down the path.*
2 to turn your body over when you are lying down: *She rolled over onto her back.*
3 to move on wheels: *The car rolled down the hill.*
4 to make something into a long round shape or the shape of a ball: *Can you help me to roll up this carpet?*
5 to make something flat by moving something heavy on top of it: *Roll the pastry into a large circle.*

Rollerblade™ (*American* Roller Blade™) /ˈrəʊləbleɪd/ (*British*) *noun*
a boot with a line of small wheels on the bottom ➔ Look at **roller skate**. ➔ Look at the picture at **skate**.
▶ **Rollerblading** *noun* (*no plural*): *to go Rollerblading*

roller coaster /ˈrəʊlə ˈkəʊstə(r)/ *noun*
a metal track that goes up and down and around bends, and that people ride on in a small train for fun

roller skate /ˈrəʊlə skeɪt/ (*also* skate) *noun*
a boot with small wheels on the bottom ➔ Look at **Rollerblade**. ➔ Look at the picture at **skate**.
▶ **roller skate** (*also* skate) *verb* to move over a hard surface wearing **roller skates**
▶ **roller skating** (*also* skating) *noun* (*no plural*): *At the weekend, they go roller skating at the local skating rink.*

Roman Catholic /ˌrəʊmən ˈkæθəlɪk/ *noun*
a member of the Christian church that has the Pope as its head
▶ **Roman Catholic** *adjective*: *a Roman Catholic priest*

romance /rəʊˈmæns/ *noun*
1 a time when two people are in love: *a romance between a doctor and a nurse*
2 a story about love: *She writes romances.*

romantic 0️⃣ /rəʊˈmæntɪk/ *adjective*
about love; full of feelings of love: *a romantic film*

roof 0️⃣ /ruːf/ *noun* (*plural* roofs)
the top of a building or car, that covers it ➔ Look at Picture Dictionary page **P10**.

room 0️⃣ /ruːm/ *noun*
1 (*plural* rooms) one of the spaces in a building that has walls around it: *How many rooms are there in the new house?* ◊ *a classroom*

> 🔎 **WORD BUILDING**
>
> A house or flat usually has a **living room** (or **sitting room** or **lounge**), **bedrooms**, a **bathroom**, a **toilet**, a **kitchen**, a **hall** and perhaps a **dining room**.

➔ Look at Picture Dictionary page **P10**.
2 (*no plural*) space; enough space: *There's no room for you in the car.*

rooster /ˈruːstə(r)/ *American English for* COCK

root 0️⃣ /ruːt/ *noun*
the part of a plant that is under the ground ➔ Look at the picture at **plant**.

rope 0️⃣ /rəʊp/ *noun*
very thick strong string

rose¹ *form of* RISE²

rose² /rəʊz/ *noun*
a flower with a sweet smell. It grows on a

rope

coil of rope

bush that has sharp points (called **thorns**) on it.

rosy /ˈrəʊzi/ *adjective* (rosier, rosiest)
pink and looking healthy: *rosy cheeks*

rot /rɒt/ *verb* (rots, rotting, rotted)
to become bad and soft, as things do when they die ⊃ SAME MEANING **decay**: *the smell of rotting fruit*

rotate /rəʊˈteɪt/ *verb* (rotates, rotating, rotated)
to move in circles: *The earth rotates around the sun.*
▶ **rotation** /rəʊˈteɪʃn/ *noun*: *the rotation of the earth*

rotten /ˈrɒtn/ *adjective*
1 old and not fresh; bad: *These eggs are rotten – they smell horrible!*
2 (*informal*) very bad; not nice or kind: *That was a rotten thing to say!*

rough 0🔑 /rʌf/ *adjective* (rougher, roughest)

> 🔊 **PRONUNCIATION**
>
> The word **rough** sounds like **stuff** because sometimes the letters **-gh** sound like **f**, in words like **enough** and **tough**.

1 not smooth or flat: *It was difficult to walk on the rough ground.*
2 not exactly correct; made or done quickly: *Can you give me a rough idea how much it will cost?* ◇ *a rough drawing*
3 not gentle or calm: *rough seas*

roughly /ˈrʌfli/ *adverb*
1 about; not exactly ⊃ SAME MEANING **approximately**: *The journey should take roughly two hours.* ⊃ OPPOSITE **exactly**
2 not gently: *He pushed me roughly away.*

round¹ 0🔑 /raʊnd/ *adjective*
having the shape of a circle or a ball: *a round table*

round² 0🔑 /raʊnd/ (*also* around) *adverb, preposition*
1 on or to all sides of something, often in a circle: *The earth moves round the sun.* ◇ *We sat round the table.* ◇ *The bird flew round and round the room.*

2 in the opposite direction or in another direction: *I turned round and went home again.* ◇ *Turn your chair round.*
3 in or to different parts of a place: *We travelled round France last summer.*
4 to or on the other side of something: *There's a bank just round the corner.*
5 from one person or place to another: *Pass these photos round the class.*
6 (*informal*) to or at somebody's house: *Come round* (= to my house) *at eight o'clock.*
go round to be enough for everybody: *Are there enough cakes to go round?*
round about nearly; not exactly: *It will cost round about £90.*

round³ /raʊnd/ *noun*
1 one part of a game or competition: *the third round of the boxing match*
2 a lot of visits, one after another, for example as part of your job: *The postman starts his round at seven o'clock.*
3 drinks for all the people in a group: *I'll buy this round. What would you all like?*

roundabout /ˈraʊndəbaʊt/ (*British*) *noun*
1 (*American* **traffic circle**) a place where roads meet, where cars must drive round in a circle
2 (*American* **merry-go-round**) a round platform for children to play on. They sit or stand on it and somebody pushes it round.
3 another word for MERRY-GO-ROUND ⊃ Look at the picture at **merry-go-round**.

round trip /ˌraʊnd ˈtrɪp/ *noun*
1 a journey to a place and back again: *It's a four-mile round trip to the centre of town.*
2 (*American also* **round-trip ticket**) American English for RETURN² (3)

route 0🔑 /ruːt/ *noun*
a way from one place to another: *What is the quickest route from London to Edinburgh?*

routine /ruːˈtiːn/ *noun*
your usual way of doing things: *Make exercise a part of your daily routine.*

row¹ 0🔑 /rəʊ/ *noun*

> 🔊 **PRONUNCIATION**
> This meaning of **row** sounds like **no**.

a line of people or things: *We sat in the front row of the theatre* (= the front line of seats). ◇ *a row of houses*

row² /rəʊ/ *verb* (rows, rowing, rowed /rəʊd/)

> 🔊 **PRONUNCIATION**
> This meaning of **row** sounds like **no**.

to move a boat through water using long

pieces of wood with flat ends (called oars): *We rowed across the lake.*

> 🔎 **SPEAKING**
>
> When you talk about spending time rowing as a sport, you say **go rowing**: *We went rowing on the river.*

row³ /raʊ/ *noun* (*British*)

> 🔎 **PRONUNCIATION**
>
> This meaning of **row** sounds like **how**.

1 (*plural* **rows**) a noisy talk between people who do not agree about something
➲ SAME MEANING **argument**: *She had a row with her boyfriend.*
2 (*no plural*) a loud noise: *The children were making a terrible row.*

rowing boat

oar

rowing boat

rowing boat /ˈrəʊɪŋ bəʊt/ *noun*
a small boat that you move through water using long thin pieces of wood with flat ends (called oars)

royal 0— /ˈrɔɪəl/ *adjective*
connected with a king or queen: *the royal family*

royalty /ˈrɔɪəlti/ *noun* (*no plural*)
kings, queens and their families

rub 0— /rʌb/ *verb* (rubs, rubbing, rubbed /rʌbd/)
to move something backwards and forwards on another thing: *I rubbed my hands together to keep them warm.* ◇ *The cat rubbed its head against my leg.*
rub something out (*British*) to take writing or marks off something by using a rubber or a cloth: *I rubbed the word out and wrote it again.*
▶ **rub** *noun* (*no plural*): *Give your shoes a rub.*

rubber 0— /ˈrʌbə(r)/ *noun*
1 (*no plural*) a strong material that we use to make things like car tyres
2 (*plural* **rubbers**) (*British*) (*American* **eraser**) a small piece of rubber that you use for taking away marks that you have made with a pencil ➲ Look at Picture Dictionary page **P11**.

rubber band /ˌrʌbə ˈbænd/ (*British also* **elastic band**) *noun*
a thin circle of rubber that you use for holding things together

rubbish 0— /ˈrʌbɪʃ/ (*British*) *noun* (*no plural*)
1 (*American* **garbage**, **trash**) things that you do not want any more: *old boxes, bottles and other rubbish* ◇ *Throw this rubbish in the bin.*
2 something that you think is bad, stupid or wrong: *You're talking rubbish!*

ruby /ˈruːbi/ *noun* (*plural* **rubies**)
a dark red stone that is used in jewellery: *a ruby ring*

rucksack /ˈrʌksæk/ *noun* (*British*)
a bag that you carry on your back, for example when you are walking or climbing ➲ SAME MEANING **backpack** ➲ Look at the picture at **backpack**.

rudder /ˈrʌdə(r)/ *noun*
a flat piece of wood or metal at the back of a boat or a plane. It moves to make the boat or plane go left or right.

rude 0— /ruːd/ *adjective* (ruder, rudest)
1 not polite ➲ SAME MEANING **impolite**: *It's rude to walk away when someone is talking to you.*
2 about things like sex or using the toilet: *rude words*
▶ **rudely** *adverb*: '*Shut up!*' *she said rudely.*
▶ **rudeness** *noun* (*no plural*): *I would like to apologize for my rudeness.*

rug

rug /rʌg/ *noun*
1 a small piece of thick material that you put on the floor ➲ Look at **carpet**.
2 a thick piece of material that you put round your body to keep you warm

rugby /ˈrʌgbi/ *noun* (*no plural*)
a game like football for two teams of 13 or 15 players. In **rugby**, you can kick and carry the ball. ➲ Look at Picture Dictionary page **P14**.

rugged /ˈrʌgɪd/ *noun*
Rugged land is not smooth, and has a lot of rocks and not many plants on it.

ruin¹ 0̶ᵐ /ˈruːɪn/ *verb* (ruins, ruining, ruined /ˈruːɪnd/)
to damage something badly so that it is no longer good; to destroy something completely: *I spilled coffee on my jacket and ruined it.* ◇ *The rain ruined our picnic.*

ruin

ruin² /ˈruːɪn/ *noun*
a building that has been badly damaged: *The old castle is now a ruin.*
in ruins badly damaged or destroyed: *The city was in ruins after the war.*

rule¹ 0̶ᵐ /ruːl/ *noun*
1 (*plural* **rules**) something that tells you what you must or must not do: *It's against the school rules to smoke.* ◇ *to break a rule* (= do something that you should not do)
2 (*no plural*) government: *The country is under military rule.*

rule² 0̶ᵐ /ruːl/ *verb* (rules, ruling, ruled /ruːld/)
to control a country: *Queen Victoria ruled for many years.*

ruler /ˈruːlə(r)/ *noun*
1 a long piece of plastic, metal or wood that you use for drawing straight lines or for measuring things ⊃ Look at Picture Dictionary page **P11**.
2 a person who rules a country

rum /rʌm/ *noun*
a strong alcoholic drink that is made from the sugar plant

rumble /ˈrʌmbl/ *verb* (rumbles, rumbling, rumbled /ˈrʌmbld/)
to make a long deep sound: *I'm so hungry that my stomach is rumbling.*
▶ **rumble** *noun* (*no plural*): *the rumble of thunder*

rummage sale /ˈrʌmɪdʒ seɪl/ *noun*
American English for JUMBLE SALE

rumour (*British*) (*American* **rumor**) /ˈruːmə(r)/ *noun*
something that a lot of people are talking about that is perhaps not true: *There's a rumour that our teacher is leaving.*

run¹ 0̶ᵐ /rʌn/ *verb* (runs, running, ran /ræn/, has run)
1 to move very quickly on your legs: *I was late, so I ran to the bus stop.*
2 to control something and make it work: *Who runs the business?*
3 to work: *The car had stopped but the engine was still running.*
4 to go; to make a journey: *The buses don't run on Sundays.*
5 to move something somewhere: *He ran his fingers through his hair.*
6 to pass or go somewhere: *The road runs across the fields.*
7 to flow: *The river runs into the North Sea.*
run after somebody or **something** to try to catch a person or an animal
⊃ SAME MEANING **chase**: *The dog ran after a rabbit.*
run away to go quickly away from a place
⊃ SAME MEANING **escape**: *She ran away from home when she was 14.*
run into somebody to meet somebody by chance: *Guess who I ran into today?*
run into somebody or **something** to crash into somebody or something: *The bus went out of control and ran into a line of people.*
run out of something to have no more of something: *We've run out of coffee. Will you go and buy some?*
run over somebody or **something** to hit a person or an animal with your car or other vehicle: *The dog was run over by a bus.*

run² 0̶ᵐ /rʌn/ *noun*
1 moving very quickly on your legs: *I go for a run every morning.*
2 a point in the games of BASEBALL and CRICKET: *Our team won by two runs.*

rung¹ *form of* RING²

rung² /rʌŋ/ *noun*
one of the steps of a LADDER (= a piece of equipment that is used for climbing up something) ⊃ Look at the picture at **ladder**.

runner /ˈrʌnə(r)/ *noun*
a person who runs

runner-up /ˌrʌnər ˈʌp/ *noun* (*plural* **runners-up** /ˌrʌnəzˈʌp/)
a person or team that comes second in a race or competition

running[1] /'rʌnɪŋ/ *noun* (*no plural*)
the sport of running: *Let's go running tomorrow morning.*

running[2] /'rʌnɪŋ/ *adjective*
one after another: *We won the competition for three years running.*

runny /'rʌni/ *adjective* (runnier, runniest)
1 If you have a **runny** nose, a lot of liquid comes out of it, for example because you have a cold.
2 If a substance is **runny**, it has more liquid than is usual: *Omelettes should be runny in the middle.*

runway /'rʌnweɪ/ *noun* (*plural* runways)
a long piece of ground where planes take off and land

rural /'rʊərəl/ *adjective*
connected with the country, not the town: *The book is about life in rural France.* ⊃ Look at **urban**.

rush[1] 0-ᴡ /rʌʃ/ *verb* (rushes, rushing, rushed /rʌʃt/)
1 to move or do something very quickly or too quickly: *The children rushed out of school.* ◇ *We rushed to finish the work on time.*
2 to take somebody or something quickly to a place: *She was rushed to hospital.*

rush[2] 0-ᴡ /rʌʃ/ *noun* (*no plural*)
1 a sudden quick movement: *At the end of the film there was a rush for the exits.*

2 a situation when you need to move or do something very quickly ⊃ SAME MEANING **hurry**: *I can't stop now – I'm in a rush.*

rush hour /'rʌʃ aʊə(r)/ *noun*
the time when the roads are busy because a lot of people are going to or coming from work

rust /rʌst/ *noun* (*no plural*)
a red-brown substance that you sometimes see on metal that has been wet
▶ **rust** *verb* (rusts, rusting, rusted): *My bike rusted because I left it out in the rain.*

rustle /'rʌsl/ *verb* (rustles, rustling, rustled /'rʌsld/)
to make a sound like dry leaves moving together; to make something make this sound: *Stop rustling your newspaper – I can't hear the film!*
▶ **rustle** *noun* (*no plural*): *the rustle of leaves*

rusty *adjective* (rustier, rustiest)
(used about things made of metal) covered with a red-brown substance (called **rust**) because it has got wet: *a rusty nail*

rut /rʌt/ *noun*
a deep track that a wheel makes in the ground
be in a rut to have a boring life that is difficult to change: *I gave up my job because I felt I was stuck in a rut.*

S s

S,s /es/ *noun* (plural S's, s's /'esɪz/)
the nineteenth letter of the English alphabet:
'*Sun*' begins with an '*S*'.

sack¹ /sæk/ *noun*
a big strong bag for carrying heavy things: *a
sack of potatoes*
get the sack (*British, informal*) to lose your
job: *She got the sack for being late.*
give somebody the sack (*British,
informal*) to say that somebody must leave
their job: *Tony's work wasn't good enough
and he was given the sack.*

sack² /sæk/ *verb* (sacks, sacking, sacked
/sækt/)
to say that somebody must leave their job:
*The manager sacked her because she was
always late.*

sacred /'seɪkrɪd/ *adjective*
with a special religious meaning: *A church is a
sacred building.*

sacrifice /'sækrɪfaɪs/ *verb* (sacrifices,
sacrificing, sacrificed /'sækrɪfaɪst/)
1 to stop doing or having something
important so that you can help somebody or
to get something else: *During the war, many
people sacrificed their lives for their country.*
2 to kill an animal as a present to a god: *They
sacrificed a lamb.*
▶ **sacrifice** *noun*: *They made a lot of
sacrifices to pay for their son to go to
university.*

sad 0̄ /sæd/ *adjective* (sadder, saddest)
unhappy or making you feel unhappy: *We
are very sad to hear that you are leaving.* ◇ *a
sad story*
▶ **sadly** /'sædli/ *adverb*: *She looked sadly at
the empty house.*
▶ **sadness** /'sædnəs/ *noun* (*no plural*):
Thoughts of him filled her with sadness.

saddle /'sædl/ *noun*
a seat on a horse or bicycle ⊃ Look at the
pictures at **bicycle** and **horse**.

safari /sə'fɑːri/ *noun* (plural safaris)
a journey to look at or hunt wild animals,
usually in Africa

safe¹ 0̄ /seɪf/ *adjective* (safer, safest)
1 not in danger; not hurt: *Don't go out alone
at night – you won't be safe.*
2 not dangerous: *Is it safe to swim in this
river?* ◇ *Always keep medicines in a safe place.*
safe and sound not hurt or broken: *The
child was found safe and sound.*

▶ **safely** /'seɪfli/ *adverb*: *Phone your parents
to tell them you have arrived safely.*

safe² /seɪf/ *noun*
a strong metal box with a lock where you
keep money or things like jewellery

safety 0̄ /'seɪfti/ *noun* (*no plural*)
being safe: *He is worried about the safety of his
children.*

safety belt /'seɪfti belt/ *noun*
a long thin piece of material that you put
round your body in a car or a plane to keep
you safe in an accident ⊃ SAME MEANING
seat belt

safety pin /'seɪfti pɪn/ *noun*
a pin that you use for joining pieces of cloth
together. It has a cover over the point so
that it is not dangerous. ⊃ Look at the
picture at **pin¹**.

sag /sæg/ *verb* (sags, sagging, sagged
/sægd/)
to bend or hang down: *The bed is very old
and it sags in the middle.*

said *form of* SAY¹

sail¹ 0̄ /seɪl/ *verb* (sails, sailing, sailed
/seɪld/)

> 🔎 **PRONUNCIATION**
> The word **sail** sounds just like **sale**.

1 to travel on water: *The ship sailed along the
coast.*
2 to control a boat with sails: *We sailed the
yacht down the river.*

> 🔎 **SPEAKING**
> When you talk about spending time
> sailing a boat, you say **go sailing**: *We
> often go sailing on the lake at weekends.*

▶ **sailing** /'seɪlɪŋ/ *noun* (*no plural*) the
sport of controlling a boat with sails

sail² 0̄ /seɪl/ *noun*
a big piece of cloth on a boat that catches
the wind and moves the boat along ⊃ Look
at the picture at **boat**.

sailor 0̄ /'seɪlə(r)/ *noun*
a person who sails ships or boats as their job
or as a sport

saint /seɪnt/ *noun*
(in the Christian religion) a dead person who
lived their life in a very good way: *Saint
Nicholas* ⊃ Look at the note on the next
page.

🔎 **PRONUNCIATION**
You usually say /snt/ before names. The short way of writing **Saint** before names is **St**: *St George's church*

sake /seɪk/ *noun*
for goodness' sake, for Heaven's sake (*informal*) something that you say to show you are annoyed
for the sake of somebody or **something, for somebody's** or **something's sake** to help somebody or something; because of somebody or something: *The couple stayed together for the sake of their children.*

salad 0🔨 /'sæləd/ *noun*
a dish of cold vegetables that have not been cooked: *Do you want chips or salad with your chicken?* ⟳ Look at Picture Dictionary page **P7**.

salary /'sæləri/ *noun* (*plural* salaries)
money that you receive every month for the work that you do

sale 0🔨 /seɪl/ *noun*

🔎 **PRONUNCIATION**
The word **sale** sounds just like **sail**.

1 (*no plural*) selling something
2 (*plural* sales) a time when a shop sells things for less money than usual: *In the sale, everything is half-price.*
for sale If something is **for sale**, its owner wants to sell it: *Is this house for sale?*
on sale If something is **on sale**, you can buy it in shops: *The magazine is on sale at most newsagents.*

sales clerk /'seɪlz klɜːrk/ *American English for* SHOP ASSISTANT

salesman /'seɪlzmən/ *noun* (*plural* salesmen /'seɪlzmən/)
a man whose job is to sell things

salesperson /'seɪlzpɜːsn/ *noun* (*plural* salespeople)
a man or a woman whose job is to sell things

saleswoman /'seɪlzwʊmən/ *noun* (*plural* saleswomen)
a woman whose job is to sell things

saliva /sə'laɪvə/ *noun* (*no plural*)
the liquid in your mouth that helps you to swallow food

salmon /'sæmən/ *noun* (*plural* salmon)
a big fish with pink meat that lives in the sea and in rivers

salt 0🔨 /sɔːlt/ *noun* (*no plural*)
a white substance that comes from sea water and from the earth. We put it on food to make it taste better: *Add a little salt and pepper.* ⟳ Look at Picture Dictionary page **P6**.

▶ **salty** /'sɔːlti/ *adjective* (saltier, saltiest)
tasting of salt or containing salt: *Sea water is salty.*

salute /sə'luːt/ *verb* (salutes, saluting, saluted)
to make the special sign that soldiers make, by lifting your hand to your head: *The soldiers saluted as the Queen walked past.*
▶ **salute** *noun*: *The soldier gave a salute.*

same¹ 0🔨 /seɪm/ *adjective*
the same not different; not another: *Emma and I like the same kind of music.* ◇ *I've lived in the same town all my life.* ◇ *He went to the same school as me.*

same² 0🔨 /seɪm/ *pronoun*
all or **just the same** in spite of this: *I understand why you're angry. All the same, I think you should say sorry.*
same to you (*informal*) words that you use for saying to somebody what they have said to you: 'Have a good weekend.' 'Same to you.'
the same not a different person or thing: *Do these two words mean the same?* ◇ *I'd like one the same as yours.*
▶ **same** *adverb* the same in the same way: *We treat boys exactly the same as girls.*

sample /'sɑːmpl/ *noun*
a small amount of something that shows what the rest is like: *a free sample of perfume* ◇ *a blood sample*

sand 0🔨 /sænd/ *noun* (*no plural*)
powder made of very small pieces of rock, that you find on beaches and in deserts: *Concrete is a mixture of sand and cement.*

sandal /'sændl/ *noun*
a light open shoe that you wear in warm weather ⟳ Look at the picture at **shoe**.

sandwich /'sænwɪtʃ; 'sænwɪdʒ/ *noun* (*plural* sandwiches)
two pieces of bread with other food between them: *a cheese sandwich* ⟳ Look at Picture Dictionary page **P7**.

sandy /'sændi/ *adjective* (sandier, sandiest)
with sand: *a sandy beach*

sane /seɪm/ *adjective* (saner, sanest)
with a normal healthy mind; not mad
⟳ OPPOSITE **insane**

sang *form of* SING

sank *form of* SINK[1]

Santa Claus /'sæntə klɔːz/ *another name for* FATHER CHRISTMAS

sarcasm /'sɑːkæzəm/ *noun* (*no plural*)
saying the opposite of what you mean because you want to be rude to somebody or to show them you are angry
▶ **sarcastic** /sɑːˈkæstɪk/ *adjective*: *There's no need to be sarcastic.*

sardine /ˌsɑːˈdiːn/ *noun*
a very small sea fish that you can eat. You often buy **sardines** in tins.

sari /'sɑːri/ *noun* (*plural* saris)
a long piece of material that women, particularly Indian women, wear around their bodies as a dress

sat *form of* SIT

satchel /'sætʃəl/ *noun*
a bag that children use for carrying books to and from school

satellite /'sætəlaɪt/ *noun*
a piece of electronic equipment that people send into space. **Satellites** travel round the earth and send back pictures or television and radio signals: *satellite television*

satellite dish /'sætəlaɪt dɪʃ/ *noun*
a piece of equipment that people put on the outside of their houses so that they can receive television signals from a SATELLITE
⊃ Look at Picture Dictionary page **P10**.

satin /'sætɪn/ *noun* (*no plural*)
very shiny smooth cloth

satire /'sætaɪə(r)/ *noun*
1 (*no plural*) using humour to attack somebody or something that you think is bad or silly: *political satire*
2 (*plural* satires) a piece of writing or a play, film, etc. that uses **satire**: *The play is a satire on political life.*

satisfaction 0━ /ˌsætɪsˈfækʃn/ *noun* (*no plural*)
being pleased with what you or other people have done: *She finished painting the picture and looked at it with satisfaction.*

satisfactory /ˌsætɪsˈfæktəri/ *adjective*
good enough, but not very good: *Her work is not satisfactory.* ⊃ OPPOSITE **unsatisfactory**

satisfied 0━ /'sætɪsfaɪd/ *adjective*
pleased because you have had or done what you wanted: *The teacher was not satisfied with my work.*

satisfy /'sætɪsfaɪ/ *verb* (satisfies, satisfying, satisfied /'sætɪsfaɪd/, has satisfied)
to give somebody what they want or need; to be good enough to make somebody pleased: *Nothing he does satisfies his father.*

satisfying /'sætɪsfaɪɪŋ/ *adjective*
Something that is **satisfying** makes you pleased because it is what you want: *a satisfying result*

Saturday 0━ /'sætədeɪ/ *noun*
the day of the week after Friday and before Sunday ⊃ Look at the note at **day**.

sauce 0━ /sɔːs/ *noun*
a thick liquid that you eat on or with other food: *pasta with tomato sauce* ⊃ Look at Picture Dictionary page **P7**.

saucepans

lid

saucepan /'sɔːspən/ *noun* (*also* pan)
a round metal container for cooking

saucer /'sɔːsə(r)/ *noun*
a small round plate that you put under a cup
⊃ Look at the picture at **cup**.

sauna /'sɔːnə/ *noun*
a room that is hot and filled with steam where people sit to relax and feel healthy: *a hotel with a swimming pool and sauna*

sausage /'sɒsɪdʒ/ *noun*
a mixture of meat, spices, etc. that is pressed into a long, thin skin: *garlic sausage* ◇ *sausages and chips*

savage /'sævɪdʒ/ *adjective*
wild or violent: *He was the victim of a savage attack by a large dog.*

save 0━ /seɪv/ *verb* (saves, saving, saved /seɪvd/)
1 to take somebody or something away from danger: *He saved me from the fire.* ◇ *The doctor saved her life.*
2 (*also* save up) to keep or not spend money so that you can buy something later: *I've saved enough money to buy a car.* ◇ *I'm saving up for a new bike.*
3 to keep something to use in the future: *Save some of the meat for tomorrow.*
4 to use less of something: *She saves money by making her own clothes.*
5 to stop somebody from scoring a goal, for example in football
6 (*computing*) to store information in a computer by giving it a special instruction: *Don't forget to save the file before you close it.*

A B C D E F G H I J K L M N O P Q R S T U V W X Y Z

savings /ˈseɪvɪŋz/ *noun* (*plural*)
money that you are keeping to use later:
I keep my savings in the bank.

saw¹ *form of* SEE

saw

saw² /sɔː/ *noun*
a metal tool for cutting wood
▸ **saw** *verb* (saws, sawing, sawed /sɔːd/,
has sawn /sɔːn/): *She sawed a branch off
the tree.*

sawdust /ˈsɔːdʌst/ *noun* (*no plural*)
powder that falls when you saw SAW wood

saxophone
/ˈsæksəfəʊn/ *noun*
a musical
instrument made of
metal that you play
by blowing into it

saxophone

— key

say¹ 0‒ᴛ /seɪ/ *verb*
(says /sez/, saying,
said /sed/, has
said)
1 to make words
with your mouth:
*You say 'please'
when you ask for
something.* ◇ *'This is
my room,' he said.* ◇
She said that she was cold.

> 🔎 **WHICH WORD?**
>
> **Say** or **tell**?
> We use **say** with the actual words that are
> spoken, or before **that** in reported
> speech: *'I'm ready,' Tim said.* ◇ *Tim said
> that he was ready.*
> Notice that you **say** something **to**
> somebody: *Tim said to Kate that he was
> ready,* but you **tell** somebody something
> (without **to**): *Tim told Kate that he was
> ready.*

2 to give information in writing, numbers or
pictures: *The notice on the door said 'Private'.*
◇ *The clock says half past three.*

that is to say what I mean is …: *I'll see you
in a week, that's to say next Monday.*

say² /seɪ/ *noun*
have a say to have the right to help decide
something: *I'd like to have a say in who we
invite to the party.*

saying /ˈseɪɪŋ/ *noun*
a sentence that people often say, that gives

advice about something: *'Love is blind' is an
old saying.*

scab /skæb/ *noun*
a hard covering that grows over your skin
where it is cut or broken

scaffolding /ˈskæfəldɪŋ/ *noun* (*no plural*)
metal bars and pieces of wood joined
together, where people like painters can
stand when they are working on high parts
of a building

scald /skɔːld/ *verb* (scalds, scalding,
scalded)
to burn somebody or something with very
hot liquid

scales

bathroom scales   **scale**

kitchen scales   **fish scales**

scale 0‒ᴛ /skeɪl/ *noun*
1 the size or level of something: *It was not
until morning that the full scale of the damage
could be seen.*
2 a set of levels or numbers used for
measuring something: *Their work is assessed
on a scale from 1 to 10.*
3 scales (*plural*) (*British*) (*American* **scale**) a
machine for showing how heavy people or
things are: *bathroom scales*
4 how distances are shown on a map: *This
map has a scale of one centimetre to ten
kilometres.*
5 one of the flat hard things that cover the
body of animals like fish and snakes

scalp /skælp/ *noun*
the skin on the top of your head, under your
hair

scan /skæn/ *verb* (scans, scanning,
scanned /skænd/)
1 to look at or read every part of something
quickly until you find what you are looking
for: *Vic scanned the list until he found his own
name.*
2 to pass light over a picture or document
using an electronic machine (called a

scanner) in order to copy it and put it in the memory of a computer

scandal /ˈskændl/ *noun*
1 (*plural* **scandals**) something that shocks people and makes them talk about it because they think it is bad: *a sex scandal*
2 (*no plural*) unkind talk about somebody that gives you a bad idea of them

scanner /ˈskænə(r)/ *noun*
1 (*computing*) a piece of equipment that copies words or pictures from paper into a computer
2 a machine that gives a picture of the inside of something. Doctors use one kind of **scanner** to look inside people's bodies.

scar /skɑː(r)/ *noun*
a mark that is left on your skin by an old cut or wound: *The operation didn't leave a very big scar.*
▶ **scar** *verb* (**scars**, **scarring**, **scarred** /skɑːd/): *His face was badly scarred by the accident.*

scarce /skeəs/ *adjective* (**scarcer**, **scarcest**)
difficult to find; not enough: *Food for birds and animals is scarce in the winter.*

scarcely /ˈskeəsli/ *adverb*
almost not; only just: *He was so frightened that he could scarcely speak.*

scare¹ /skeə(r)/ *verb* (**scares**, **scaring**, **scared** /skeəd/)
to make somebody frightened: *That noise scared me!*

scare² /skeə(r)/ *noun*
1 a feeling of being frightened: *You gave me a scare!*
2 a situation where many people are afraid or worried about something: *a health scare*

scarecrow /ˈskeəkrəʊ/ *noun*
a thing that looks like a person, that farmers put in their fields to frighten birds

scared *adjective*
frightened: *Claire is scared of the dark.*

scarves

scarf
scarf

scarf /skɑːf/ *noun* (*plural* **scarves** /skɑːvz/)
a piece of material that you wear around your neck or head

scarlet /ˈskɑːlət/ *adjective*
with a bright red colour

scary /ˈskeəri/ *adjective* (**scarier**, **scariest**) (*informal*)
frightening: *a scary ghost story*

scatter /ˈskætə(r)/ *verb* (**scatters**, **scattering**, **scattered** /ˈskætəd/)
1 to throw things so that they fall in a lot of different places: *Scatter the grass seed over the lawn.*
2 to move quickly in different directions: *The crowd scattered when it started to rain.*

scene 0ᵤ /siːn/ *noun*
1 a place where something happened: *The police arrived at the scene of the crime.*
2 part of a play or film: *Act 1, Scene 2 of 'Hamlet'*
3 what you see in a place ⊃ SAME MEANING **view**: *He painted scenes of life in the countryside.*

scenery /ˈsiːnəri/ *noun* (*no plural*)
1 the things like mountains, rivers and forests that you see around you in the countryside: *What beautiful scenery!*
2 things on the stage of a theatre that make it look like a real place

scent /sent/ *noun*
1 (*plural* **scents**) a smell: *These flowers have no scent.*
2 (*no plural*) a liquid with a nice smell, that you put on your body ⊃ SAME MEANING **perfume**: *a bottle of scent*
▶ **scented** /ˈsentɪd/ *adjective* having a nice smell: *scented candles*

sceptical /ˈskeptɪkl/ *adjective*
having doubts that something is true or that something will happen: *I am sceptical about his chances of winning.*

schedule /ˈʃedjuːl/ *noun*
a plan or list of times when things will happen or be done: *I've got a busy schedule next week.* ◇ *We're behind schedule (= late) with the project.* ◇ *Filming began on schedule (= at the planned time).*

scheme¹ /skiːm/ *noun* (*British*)
a plan or a system for doing or organizing something: *a local scheme for recycling newspapers*

scheme² /skiːm/ *verb* (**schemes**, **scheming**, **schemed** /skiːmd/)
to make secret plans to do something: *She felt that they were all scheming against her.*

scholar /ˈskɒlə(r)/ *noun*
a person who has learned a lot about something: *a famous history scholar*

scholarship /ˈskɒləʃɪp/ *noun*
money that is given to a good student to help them to continue studying: *Adrian won a scholarship to university.*

A
B
C
D
E
F
G
H
I
J
K
L
M
N
O
P
Q
R
S
T
U
V
W
X
Y
Z

school 0ᴙ /skuːl/ *noun*
1 (*plural* **schools**) a place where children go to learn: *Lucy is at school.* ◇ *Which school do you go to?*
2 (*no plural*) being at **school**: *I hate school!* ◇ *He left school when he was 16.* ◇ *School starts at nine o'clock.*

> 🔎 **GRAMMAR**
> You usually talk about **school** without 'the' or 'a': *I enjoyed being at school.* ◇ *Do you walk to school?*
> You use 'a' or 'the' when more information about the school is given: *Harry goes to the school that his father went to.* ◇ *She teaches at a school for deaf children.*

➲ Look at Study Page S12.
3 (*plural* **schools**) (*American, informal*) a college or university, or the time that you spend there
4 (*plural* **schools**) a place where you go to learn a special thing: *a language school*

schoolboy /'skuːlbɔɪ/ *noun*
a boy who goes to school

schoolchild /'skuːltʃaɪld/ (*plural* **schoolchildren**) *noun*
a boy or girl who goes to school

schooldays /'skuːldeɪz/ *noun* (*plural*)
the time in your life when you are at school

schoolgirl /'skuːlgɜːl/ *noun*
a girl who goes to school

science 0ᴙ /'saɪəns/ *noun*
the study of natural things: *I'm interested in science.* ◇ *Biology, chemistry and physics are all sciences.*

science fiction /ˌsaɪəns 'fɪkʃn/ *noun* (*no plural*)
stories about things like travel in space, life on other planets or life in the future

scientific 0ᴙ /ˌsaɪən'tɪfɪk/ *adjective*
of or about science: *We need more grants for scientific research.*

scientist 0ᴙ /'saɪəntɪst/ *noun*
a person who studies science or works with science

scissors 0ᴙ /'sɪzəz/ *noun* (*plural*)
a tool for cutting that has two sharp parts that are joined together: *These scissors aren't very sharp.*

scissors

a pair of scissors

> 🔎 **GRAMMAR**
> Be careful! You cannot say 'a scissors'. You can say a **pair of scissors**: *I need a pair of scissors.* (or: *I need some scissors.*)

scold /skəʊld/ *verb* (**scolds**, **scolding**, **scolded**)
to tell a child in an angry way that they have done something wrong: *His mother scolded him for being so naughty.*

scoop /skuːp/ *verb* (**scoops**, **scooping**, **scooped** /skuːpt/)
to use a spoon or your hands to take something up or out: *I scooped some ice cream out of the bowl.*

scooter /'skuːtə(r)/ *noun*
a light motorcycle with a small engine
➲ Look at the picture at **motorbike**.

score¹ 0ᴙ /skɔː(r)/ *noun*
the number of points, goals, etc. that you win in a game or competition: *The winner got a score of 320.* ◇ *What's the score now?*

score² 0ᴙ /skɔː(r)/ *verb* (**scores**, **scoring**, **scored** /skɔːd/)
to win points, goals, etc. in a game or competition: *Brazil scored three goals against France.*

scoreboard /'skɔːbɔːd/ *noun*
a large board that shows the score during a game or competition

scorn /skɔːn/ *noun* (*no plural*)
a strong feeling that somebody or something is stupid or not good enough: *He was full of scorn for my idea.*
▶ **scornful** /'skɔːnfl/ *adjective*: *She gave him a scornful look.*

scorpion
/'skɔːpiən/ *noun*
a small animal that looks like an insect and has a sting in its tail

scorpion

sting

Scout /skaʊt/ *noun*
1 the Scouts (*plural*) a special club for boys, and sometimes girls too, which does a lot of activities with them, for example camping
2 (*British*) (*American* **Boy Scout**) a boy or girl who is a member of the **Scouts**

scowl /skaʊl/ *verb* (**scowls**, **scowling**, **scowled** /skaʊld/)
to look at somebody in an angry way: *His teacher scowled at him for being late.*
▶ **scowl** *noun*: *He looked up at me with a scowl.*

scramble /'skræmbl/ *verb* (scrambles, scrambling, scrambled /'skræmbld/)
to move quickly up or over something, using your hands to help you: *They scrambled over the wall.*

scrambled eggs /ˌskræmbld 'egz/ *noun* (plural)
eggs that you mix together with milk and cook in a pan with butter

scrap /skræp/ *noun*
1 (*plural* scraps) a small piece of something: *a scrap of paper*
2 (*no plural*) something you do not want any more but that is made of material that can be used again: *scrap paper*

scrapbook /'skræpbʊk/ *noun*
a large book with empty pages that you can stick pictures or newspaper articles in

scrape /skreɪp/ *verb* (scrapes, scraping, scraped /skreɪpt/)
1 to move a rough or sharp thing across something: *I scraped the mud off my shoes with a knife.*
2 to hurt or damage something by moving it against a rough or sharp thing: *I fell and scraped my knee on the wall.*

scratch¹ 0➡ /skrætʃ/ *verb* (scratches, scratching, scratched /skrætʃt/)
1 to move your nails across your skin: *She scratched her head.*
2 to cut or make a mark on something with a sharp thing: *The cat scratched me!*

scratch² /skrætʃ/ *noun* (*plural* scratches)
a cut or mark that a sharp thing makes: *Her hands were covered in scratches from the cat.*
from scratch from the beginning: *I threw away the letter I was writing and started again from scratch.*

scream¹ /skriːm/ *verb* (screams, screaming, screamed /skriːmd/)
to make a loud high cry that shows you are afraid or hurt: *She saw the snake and screamed.* ◇ *He screamed for help.*

scream² /skriːm/ *noun*
a loud high cry: *a scream of pain*

screech /skriːtʃ/ *verb* (screeches, screeching, screeched /skriːtʃt/)
to make a loud high sound: *The car's brakes screeched as it stopped suddenly.*

screen 0➡ /skriːn/ *noun*
1 the flat square part of a television or computer where you see pictures or words
➔ Look at Picture Dictionary page **P11**.
2 the flat thing on the wall of a cinema, where you see films
3 a kind of thin wall that you can move around. **Screens** are used to keep away

cold, light, etc. or to stop people from seeing something: *The nurse put a screen around the bed.*

screw¹ /skruː/ *noun*
a small metal thing with a sharp end, that you use for fixing things together. You push it into something by turning it with a special tool (called a **screwdriver**).

screw

screw² /skruː/ *verb* (screws, screwing, screwed /skruːd/)
1 to fix something to another thing using a SCREW: *The cupboard is screwed to the wall.*
2 to turn something to fix it to another thing: *Screw the lid on the jar.*
screw something up to make paper or material into a ball with your hand: *He screwed up the letter and threw it in the bin.*

screwdriver /'skruːdraɪvə(r)/ *noun*
a tool for turning SCREWS

scribble /'skrɪbl/ *verb* (scribbles, scribbling, scribbled /'skrɪbld/)
to write something or make marks on paper quickly and without care: *The children scribbled in my book.*

script /skrɪpt/ *noun*
the written words that actors speak in a play or film

scripture /'skrɪptʃə(r)/ *noun*
the book or books that a particular religion is based on

scroll /skrəʊl/ *verb* (scrolls, scrolling, scrolled /skrəʊld/)
to move what you can see on a computer screen up or down so that you can look at different parts of it: *Scroll down to the bottom of the document.*

scrub /skrʌb/ *verb* (scrubs, scrubbing, scrubbed /skrʌbd/)
to rub something hard to clean it, usually with a brush and soap and water: *He scrubbed the floor.*

scruffy /'skrʌfi/ *adjective* (scruffier, scruffiest)
untidy and perhaps dirty: *She was wearing scruffy jeans.*

scuba-diving /'skuːbə daɪvɪŋ/ *noun*
swimming underwater using special equipment for breathing: *You should never go scuba-diving alone.* ➔ Look at the picture on the next page.

sculptor /'skʌlptə(r)/ *noun*
a person who makes shapes from things like stone or wood

A B C D E F G H I J K L M N O P Q R S T U V W X Y Z

scuba-diving

tank

flipper

scuba-diving

seal

flipper

mask

snorkel

snorkelling

sculpture /'skʌlptʃə(r)/ *noun*
1 (*no plural*) making shapes from things like stone or wood
2 (*plural* **sculptures**) a shape made from things like stone or wood

sea 0▬ /siː/ *noun*

> 🔍 **PRONUNCIATION**
> The word **sea** sounds just like **see**.

1 (*no plural*) the salt water that covers large parts of the earth: *We went for a swim in the sea.* ◇ *The sea is very rough today.*
2 Sea (*plural* Seas) a big area of salt water: *the Black Sea* ➪ Look at **ocean**.
at sea travelling on the sea: *We spent three weeks at sea.*

the seabed /ðə 'siːbed/ *noun* (*no plural*)
the floor of the sea

seafood /'siːfuːd/ *noun* (*no plural*)
fish and small animals from the sea that we eat, especially SHELLFISH (= animals with shells that live in water)

seagull /'siːgʌl/
noun
a big grey or white bird with a loud cry, that lives near the sea

seal¹ /siːl/ *noun*
an animal with short fur that lives in and near the sea, and that eats fish

seagull

seal² /siːl/ *verb* (**seals**, **sealing**, **sealed** /siːld/)
to close something tightly by sticking two parts together: *She sealed the envelope.*

seam /siːm/ *noun*
a line where two pieces of cloth are joined together

search¹ 0▬ /sɜːtʃ/ *verb* (**searches**, **searching**, **searched** /sɜːtʃt/)
to look carefully because you are trying to find somebody or something: *I searched everywhere for my pen.*

search² 0▬ /sɜːtʃ/ *noun* (*plural* **searches**)
when you try to find somebody or something: *I found my key after a long search.*
◇ *We drove round the town in search of a cheap hotel.* ◇ *The search for the murder weapon goes on.*

seashell /'siːʃel/ *noun*
the empty shell of a small animal that lives in the sea

seashore /'siːʃɔː(r)/ *noun* the seashore (*no plural*)
the land next to the sea: *We were looking for seashells on the seashore.*

seasick /'siːsɪk/ *adjective*
If you are **seasick**, you feel ill in your stomach because the boat you are on is moving a lot.

seaside /'siːsaɪd/ *noun* (*no plural*)
an area or a place next to the sea where people often go on holiday: *Let's go to the seaside today.*

season 0▬ /'siːzn/ *noun*
1 one of the four parts of the year

> 🔍 **WORD BUILDING**
> The four seasons are **spring**, **summer**, **autumn** and **winter**.

➪ Look at Picture Dictionary page **P16**.
2 a special time of the year for something: *The football season starts in August.*

seat 0▬ /siːt/ *noun*
something that you sit on: *the back seat of a car* ◇ *We had seats at the front of the theatre.*
◇ *Please take a seat (= sit down).*

seat belt /'si:t belt/ *noun*
a long thin piece of material that you put round your body in a car, bus or plane to keep you safe in an accident

seaweed /'si:wi:d/ *noun* (*no plural*)
a plant that grows in the sea. There are many different types of **seaweed**.

second[1] 0→ /'sekənd/ *adjective, adverb*
next after first: *February is the second month of the year.* ◇ *She came second in the race.*

second[2] 0→ /'sekənd/ *noun* (*no plural*)
a person or thing that comes next after the first: *Today is the second of April* (= April 2nd). ◇ *I was the first to arrive, and Jim was the second.*

second[3] 0→ /'sekənd/ *noun*
1 a measure of time. There are 60 **seconds** in a minute.
2 a very short time: *Wait a second!* ◇ *I'll be ready in a second.*

secondary school /'sekəndri sku:l/ *noun* (*British*)
a school for children between the ages of 11 and 16 or 18

second class /ˌsekənd 'klɑːs/ *noun* (*no plural*)
1 the part of a train, plane, etc. that it is cheaper to travel in: *We sat in second class.*
2 (*British*) the cheapest but the slowest way of sending letters ⊃ Look at the note at **stamp**.
▶ **second-class** *adjective*: *a second-class ticket*
▶ **second class** *adverb*: *I sent the letter second class.*

second-hand /ˌsekənd 'hænd/ *adjective, adverb*
not new; used by another person before: *second-hand books* ◇ *I bought this car second-hand.*

secondly /'sekəndli/ *adverb*
a word that you use when you are giving the second thing in a list: *Firstly, it's too expensive and secondly, we don't really need it.*

secrecy /'si:krəsi/ *noun* (*no plural*)
not telling other people: *They worked in secrecy.*

secret[1] 0→ /'si:krət/ *noun*
something that you do not or must not tell other people: *I can't tell you where I'm going – it's a secret.* ◇ *Can you keep a secret* (= not tell other people)?
in secret without other people knowing: *They met in secret.*

secret[2] 0→ /'si:krət/ *adjective*
If something is **secret**, other people do not

or must not know about it: *They kept their wedding secret* (= they did not tell anybody about it). ◇ *a secret meeting*

secretarial /ˌsekrə'teəriəl/ *adjective*
connected with the work of a secretary: *a secretarial college*

secretary 0→ /'sekrətri/ *noun* (*plural* secretaries)
1 a person who types letters, answers the telephone and does other things in an office
2 an important person in the government: *the Secretary of State* (= head of the department) *for Education*
3 *American English for* MINISTER(1)

secretive /'si:krətɪv/ *adjective*
If you are **secretive**, you do not like to tell other people about yourself or your plans: *Mark is very secretive about his job.*

secretly 0→ /'si:krətli/ *adverb*
without other people knowing: *We are secretly planning a big party for her.*

section 0→ /'sekʃn/ *noun*
one of the parts of something: *This section of the road is closed.*

secure /sɪ'kjʊə(r)/ *adjective*
1 If you are **secure**, you feel safe and you are not worried: *Do you feel secure about the future?* ⊃ OPPOSITE **insecure**
2 safe: *Don't climb that ladder – it's not very secure* (= it may fall). ◇ *Her job is secure* (= she will not lose it).
3 well locked or protected so that nobody can go in or out: *This gate isn't very secure.*
▶ **securely** /sɪ'kjʊəli/ *adverb*: *Are all the windows securely closed?*

security /sɪ'kjʊərəti/ *noun* (*no plural*)
1 the feeling of being safe: *Children need love and security.* ⊃ OPPOSITE **insecurity**
2 things that you do to keep a place safe: *We need better security at airports.*

see 0→ /si:/ *verb* (sees, seeing, saw /sɔː/, has seen /si:n/)

> 🔊 **PRONUNCIATION**
> The word **see** sounds just like **sea**.

1 to know or notice something using your eyes: *It was so dark that I couldn't see anything.* ◇ *Can you see that plane?*

> 🔊 **WHICH WORD?**
> **See, look** or **watch**?
> When you **see** something, you know about it with your eyes, without trying: *Suddenly, I saw a bird fly past the window.* When you **watch** something, you look at it for some time: *They watched the carnival procession.*

A B C D E F G H I J K L M N O P Q R S T U V W X Y Z

When you **look at** something, you turn your eyes towards it because you want to see it: *She looked at all the pictures in the room.*

2 to watch a film, play or television programme: *I'm going to see a film tonight.*
3 to find out about something: *Go and see what time the train leaves.*
4 to visit or meet somebody: *We're going to see my grandma at the weekend.* ◊ *I'll see you outside the station at ten o'clock.*
5 to understand something: *'You have to turn the key this way.' 'I see.'*
6 to make certain about something: *Please see that you lock the door.*
I'll see, we'll see I will think about what you have said and tell you what I have decided later: *'Will you lend me the money?' 'I'll see.'*
let's see, let me see words that you use when you are thinking or trying to remember something: *Let's see, where did I put the keys?*
seeing that, seeing as (*informal*) because: *Seeing that you've got nothing to do, you can help me!*
see somebody off to go to an airport or a station to say goodbye to somebody who is leaving
see to somebody or **something** to do what you need to do for somebody or something: *Sit down – I'll see to the dinner.*
see you, see you later (*informal*) goodbye: *'Bye Dave!' 'See you!'*

seed 0🔑 /siːd/ *noun*
the small hard part of a plant from which a new plant grows ➔ Look at Picture Dictionary page **P8**.

seek /siːk/ *verb* (seeks, seeking, sought /sɔːt/, has sought) (*formal*)
to try to find or get something: *You should seek help.*

seem 0🔑 /siːm/ *verb* (seems, seeming, seemed /siːmd/)
to give the impression of being or doing something: *She seems tired.* ◊ *My mother seems to like you.* ◊ *Helen seems like* (= seems to be) *a nice girl.*

seen form of SEE

see-saw /ˈsiː sɔː/ *noun*
a piece of equipment for children to play on which is made of a piece of wood that moves up and down when a child sits on each end

segment /ˈseɡmənt/ *noun*
one of the sections of an orange, a lemon, etc.

seize /siːz/ *verb* (seizes, seizing, seized /siːzd/)
to take something quickly and firmly ➔ SAME MEANING **grab**: *The thief seized her bag and ran away.*

seldom /ˈseldəm/ *adverb*
not often ➔ SAME MEANING **rarely**: *It seldom snows in Athens.*

select /sɪˈlekt/ *verb* (selects, selecting, selected) (*formal*)
to take the person or thing that you like best ➔ SAME MEANING **choose**: *We select only the finest fruits.*

selection /sɪˈlekʃn/ *noun*
1 (*no plural*) taking the person or thing you like best: *The manager is responsible for team selection.*
2 (*plural* **selections**) a group of people or things that somebody has chosen, or a group of things that you can choose from: *The shop has a good selection of CDs.*

self /self/ *noun* (*plural* **selves** /selvz/)
a person's own nature or qualities: *It's good to see you back to your old self again* (= well or happy again).

self- /self/ *prefix*
by yourself; for yourself: *He is self-taught – he never went to university.*

self-confident /ˌself ˈkɒnfɪdənt/ *adjective*
sure about yourself and what you can do
▶ **self-confidence** /ˌself ˈkɒnfɪdəns/ *noun* (*no plural*): *Failing that exam made her lose a lot of self-confidence.*

self-conscious /ˌself ˈkɒnʃəs/ *adjective*
worried about what other people think of you: *She walked into her new school feeling very self-conscious.*

self-control /ˌself kənˈtrəʊl/ *noun* (*no plural*)
the ability to control yourself and your emotions

self-defence (*British*) (*American* **self-defense**) /ˌself dɪˈfens/ *noun* (*no plural*)
the use of force to protect yourself: *I only hit him in self-defence.*

self-employed /ˌself ɪmˈplɔɪd/ *adjective*
working for yourself, not for somebody else: *He's a self-employed electrician.*

selfish /ˈselfɪʃ/ *adjective*
thinking too much about what you want and not about what other people want: *I'm sick of your selfish behaviour!*
➔ OPPOSITE **unselfish**
▶ **selfishly** /ˈselfɪʃli/ *adverb*: *He behaved very selfishly.*

▶ **selfishness** /'selfɪʃnəs/ *noun* (*no plural*): *Her selfishness made me very angry.*

self-pity /ˌself 'pɪti/ *noun* (*no plural*)
when you think too much about your own problems and feel sorry for yourself

self-service /ˌself 'sɜ:vɪs/ *adjective*
In a **self-service** shop or restaurant you take what you want and then pay for it: *The cafe is self-service.*

sell 0🔑 /sel/ *verb* (**sells**, **selling**, **sold** /səʊld/, **has sold**)
to give something to somebody who pays you money for it: *I sold my guitar for £200. ◇ He sold me a ticket. ◇ Newsagents usually sell chocolates and cigarettes.* ➔ Look at **buy**.
sell out, **be sold out** to be sold completely so that there are no more left: *I went to the shop to buy a newspaper, but they had all sold out. ◇ The concert was sold out weeks ago.*
sell out of something to sell all that you have of something: *I'm afraid we've sold out of milk.*

Sellotape™ /'seləteɪp/ (*British*) *noun* (*no plural*)
a type of clear tape that you use for sticking things like paper and cardboard together

semester /sɪ'mestə(r)/ *noun* (*American*)
one of the two periods that the school or college year is divided into ➔ Look at **term**.

semi- /'semi/ *prefix*
half or part: *She's semi-retired now* (= she only works some of the time).

semicircle /'semisɜ:kl/ *noun*
half a circle: *The children sat in a semicircle.* ➔ Look at the picture at **circle**.

semicolon /ˌsemi'kəʊlən/ *noun*
a mark (;) that you use in writing to separate parts of a sentence

semi-detached /ˌsemi dɪ'tætʃt/ *adjective*
A **semi-detached** house is joined to another house on one side.

semi-final /ˌsemi 'faɪnl/ *noun*
one of the two games that are played in a competition to find out who will play in the last part of the competition (the **final**)

senate /'senət/ *noun*
the Senate one of the parts of the government in some countries, for example the US ➔ Look at **Congress**.

senator /'senətə(r)/ *noun*
Senator a member of the SENATE

send 0🔑 /send/ *verb* (**sends**, **sending**, **sent** /sent/, **has sent**)
1 to make something go somewhere,

especially a letter or a message: *I sent a message to John. ◇ Have you sent your parents a postcard?*
2 to make somebody go somewhere: *My company is sending me to New York. ◇ He was sent to prison for ten years.*
send for somebody or **something** to ask for somebody or something to come to you: *Send for an ambulance!*
send something off to post something: *I'll send the letter off today.*

senior 0🔑 /'si:niə(r)/ *adjective*
1 more important than others: *a senior officer in the army*
2 older than others: *a senior pupil*
➔ OPPOSITE **junior**

senior citizen /ˌsi:niə 'sɪtɪzn/ *noun*
a person who has reached the age when you can stop work ➔ SAME MEANING **pensioner**

🔊 SPEAKING
Some people think it is polite to say **senior citizens** or **pensioners** instead of **old people**.

sensation /sen'seɪʃn/ *noun*
1 a physical feeling: *I felt a burning sensation on my skin.*
2 great excitement or interest: *The film caused a sensation.*

sensational /sen'seɪʃənl/ *adjective*
very exciting or interesting: *sensational news*

sense¹ 0🔑 /sens/ *noun*
1 (*plural* **senses**) the power to see, hear, smell, taste or touch: *Dogs have a very good sense of smell.*
2 (*no plural*) the ability to feel or understand something: *The boy had no sense of right and wrong. ◇ I like him – he's got a great sense of humour.*
3 (*no plural*) the ability to think carefully about something and to do the right thing: *Did anybody have the sense to call the police?*
4 (*plural* **senses**) a meaning: *This word has four senses.*
make sense to be possible to understand: *What does this sentence mean? It doesn't make sense to me.*

sense² /sens/ *verb* (**senses**, **sensing**, **sensed** /senst/)
to understand or feel something: *I sensed that he was worried.*

sensible 0🔑 /'sensəbl/ *adjective*
able to think carefully about something and to do the right thing: *It wasn't very sensible of you to run away. ◇ a sensible answer*
➔ OPPOSITE **silly**

A B C D E F G H I J K L M N O P Q R S T U V W X Y Z

A

▶ **sensibly** /'sensəbli/ *adverb*: I hope you'll act sensibly.

B

sensitive 0ᵣ /'sensətɪv/ *adjective*
1 understanding other people's feelings and being careful about them: *He's a very sensitive man.* ➾ OPPOSITE **insensitive**
2 easily becoming worried or unhappy about something, or about things in general: *Don't say anything about her hair – she's very sensitive about it.*
➾ OPPOSITE **insensitive**
3 easily hurt or damaged: *She's got very sensitive skin.*

C

D

E

F

G

sent *form of* SEND

sentence¹ 0ᵣ /'sentəns/ *noun*
1 a group of words that tells you something or asks a question. When a **sentence** is written, it always begins with a capital letter and usually ends with a full stop: *You don't need to write a long letter. A couple of sentences will be enough.*
2 the punishment that a judge gives to somebody in a court of law: *20 years in prison was a very harsh sentence.*

H

I

J

K

sentence² /'sentəns/ *verb* (sentences, sentencing, sentenced /'sentənst/)
to tell somebody in a court of law what their punishment will be: *The judge sentenced the man to two years in prison.*

L

sentimental /ˌsentɪ'mentl/ *adjective*
producing or showing feelings such as romantic love or pity that are too strong or not appropriate: *a sentimental love story* ◇ *I'm so sentimental – I always cry at weddings!*

M

N

O

P

separate¹ 0ᵣ /'seprət/ *adjective*
1 away from something; not together or not joined: *The cup broke into three separate pieces.* ◇ *In my school, the older children are separate from the younger ones.*
2 different; not the same: *We stayed in separate rooms in the same hotel.*
▶ **separately** /'seprətli/ *adverb*: Shall we pay separately or together?

Q

R

S

T

separate² 0ᵣ /'sepəreɪt/ *verb*
(separates, separating, separated)
1 to stop being together ➾ SAME MEANING **split up**: *My parents separated when I was a baby.*
2 to divide people or things; to keep people or things away from each other
➾ SAME MEANING **split**: *The teacher separated the class into two groups.*
3 to be between two things: *The Mediterranean separates Europe and Africa.*
▶ **separation** /ˌsepə'reɪʃn/ *noun*: The separation from my family and friends made me very unhappy.

U

V

W

X

Y

Z

September 0ᵣ /sep'tembə(r)/ *noun*
the ninth month of the year

sequence /'si:kwəns/ *noun*
a number of things that happen or come one after another: *an extraordinary sequence of events* ◇ *Complete the following sequence: 2, 4, 8…*

sergeant /'sɑ:dʒənt/ *noun*
an officer in the army or the police

serial /'sɪəriəl/ *noun*
a story that is told in parts on television or radio, or in a magazine ➾ Look at **series**(2).

series 0ᵣ /'sɪəri:z/ *noun* (*plural* series)
1 a number of things of the same kind that come one after another: *I heard a series of shots and then silence.*
2 a number of television or radio programmes, often on the same subject, that come one after another: *The first episode of the new series is on Saturday.* ◇ *a TV series on dinosaurs* ➾ Look at **serial**.

serious 0ᵣ /'sɪəriəs/ *adjective*
1 very bad: *That was a serious mistake.* ◇ *They had a serious accident.*
2 important: *a serious decision*
3 not funny: *a serious film*
4 If you are **serious**, you are not joking or playing: *Are you serious about going to live in Spain?* ◇ *You look very serious. Is something wrong?*
▶ **seriousness** /'sɪəriəsnəs/ *noun* (no plural): The boy didn't understand the seriousness of his crime.

seriously 0ᵣ /'sɪəriəsli/ *adverb*
in a serious way: *She's seriously ill.* ◇ *You're not seriously expecting me to believe that?* ◇ *Smoking can seriously damage your health.*
take somebody or **something seriously** to show that you know somebody or something is important: *Don't take what he says too seriously – he's always joking.*

sermon /'sɜ:mən/ *noun*
a talk that a priest gives in church

servant /'sɜ:vənt/ *noun*
a person who works in another person's house, doing work like cooking and cleaning

serve 0ᵣ /sɜ:v/ *verb* (serves, serving, served /sɜ:vd/)
1 to give food or drink to somebody: *Breakfast is served from 7.30 to 9.00 a.m.*
2 to help somebody in a shop to buy things: *Excuse me, Madam. Are you being served?*
3 to do work for other people: *During the war he served in the army.*
it serves you right words that you use to

tell somebody that it is right that a bad thing has happened to them: '*I feel ill.*' '*It serves you right for eating so much!*'

service 0̶ᴚ /'s3:vɪs/ *noun*

1 (*plural* **services**) a business that does useful work for all the people in a country or an area: *This town has a good bus service.* ◇ *the postal service*

2 (*no plural*) the work that somebody does for customers in a shop, restaurant or hotel: *The food was good but the service was very slow.*

3 (*no plural*) help or work that you do for somebody: *She left the company after ten years of service.*

4 (*plural* **services**) the time when somebody looks at a car or machine to see that it is working well: *She takes her car to the garage for a service every six months.*

5 **the services** (*plural*) the army, navy and air force

6 (*plural* **services**) a meeting in a church with prayers and singing: *We went to the evening service.*

7 **services** (*plural*) (*British*) a place at the side of a big road where you can stop to buy petrol and food and use the toilets ⊃ SAME MEANING **service station**

service station /'s3:vɪs steɪʃn/ *noun* (*British*)

a place at the side of a big road where you can stop to buy food and petrol and use the toilets

serviette /ˌs3:vi'et/ *noun*

a piece of cloth or paper that you use when you are eating to clean your mouth and hands and to keep your clothes clean ⊃ SAME MEANING **napkin**

session /'seʃn/ *noun*

a period of time spent doing a particular activity: *The first swimming session is at nine o'clock.*

set¹ 0̶ᴚ /set/ *verb* (**sets, setting, set, has set**)

1 to put something somewhere: *Dad set the plate in front of me.*

2 to put the action of a play, book or film in a particular time and place: *The film is set in India in the 1920s.*

3 to make something ready to use or to start working: *I set my alarm clock for seven o'clock.* ◇ *Can you set the video recorder* (= make it record a programme)*?*

4 to make something happen: *They set the school on fire* (= made it start to burn).

5 When the sun **sets**, it goes down from the sky. ⊃ OPPOSITE **rise**

6 to decide what something will be; to fix something: *Let's set a date for the meeting.*

7 to give somebody work to do: *Our teacher set us a lot of homework.*

8 to become hard or solid: *Wait for the cement to set.*

set off, set out to start a journey: *We set off for Oxford at two o'clock.*

set the table (*British*) to put knives, forks, plates and other things on the table before you eat ⊃ SAME MEANING **lay the table**

set something up to start something: *The company was set up in 1981.*

set² 0̶ᴚ /set/ *noun*

a group of things of the same kind, or a group of things that you use together: *a set of six glasses* ◇ *a tool set*

settee /se'ti:/ *noun* (*British*)

a long soft seat for more than one person ⊃ SAME MEANING **sofa** ⊃ Look at the picture at **sofa**.

setting /'setɪŋ/ *noun*

the place where something is or where something happens: *The house is in a beautiful setting on top of a hill.*

settle 0̶ᴚ /'setl/ *verb* (**settles, settling, settled** /'setld/)

1 to decide something after talking with somebody; to end a discussion or an argument: *That's settled then, we'll go on Monday.* ◇ *Have you settled your argument with Rajit?*

2 to go to live in a new place and stay there: *Ruth left England and settled in America.*

3 to come down and rest somewhere: *The bird settled on a branch.*

4 to pay something: *Have you settled your bill?*

settle down

1 to sit down or lie down so that you are comfortable: *I settled down in front of the television.*

2 to become calm and quiet: *The children settled down and went to sleep.*

3 to begin to have a calm life in one place: *When are you going to get married and settle down?*

settle in to start to feel happy in a new place: *We only moved to this flat last week and we haven't settled in yet.*

settlement /'setlmənt/ *noun*

1 an agreement about something after talking or arguing: *After days of talks, the two sides reached a settlement.*

2 a group of homes in a place where no people have lived before: *a settlement in the forest*

A
B
C
D
E
F
G
H
I
J
K
L
M
N
O
P
Q
R
S
T
U
V
W
X
Y
Z

A
B
C
D
E
F
G
H
I
J
K
L
M
N
O
P
Q
R
S
T
U
V
W
X
Y
Z

seven 0⚓ /'sevn/ *number* 7

seventeen 0⚓ /,sevn'ti:n/ *number* 17

seventeenth 0⚓ /,sevn'ti:nθ/ *adjective, adverb, noun* 17th

seventh 0⚓ /'sevnθ/ *adjective, adverb, noun*
1 7th
2 one of seven equal parts of something; ¹/₇

seventieth 0⚓ /'sevntiəθ/ *adjective, adverb, noun* 70th

seventy 0⚓ /'sevnti/ *number*
1 70
2 the seventies (*plural*) the numbers, years or temperature between 70 and 79
in your seventies between the ages of 70 and 79

several 0⚓ /'sevrəl/ *adjective, pronoun*
more than two but not many: *I've read this book several times.* ◇ *Several letters arrived this morning.* ◇ *If you need a pen, there are several on the table.*

severe /sɪ'vɪə(r)/ *adjective* (severer, severest)
1 not kind or gentle: *a severe punishment*
2 very bad: *She suffers from severe headaches.* ◇ *We're expecting a severe* (= very cold) *winter.*
▶ **severely** /sɪ'vɪəli/ *adverb*: *They punished him severely.* ◇ *She was severely injured in the accident.*

sewing

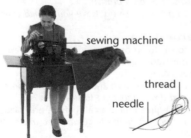

sewing machine

thread
needle

sew 0⚓ /səʊ/ *verb* (sews, sewing, sewed /səʊd/, has sewed *or* has sewn /səʊn/)

🔎 **PRONUNCIATION**
The word **sew** sounds just like **so**.

to use a needle and cotton to join pieces of material together or to join something to material: *He sewed a button on his shirt.* ◇ *Can you sew?*

sewing 0⚓ /'səʊɪŋ/ *noun* (no plural)
the activity of sewing; something that you sew

sewing machine /'səʊɪŋ məʃi:n/ *noun*
a machine that you use for sewing ➔ Look at the picture at **sew**.

sex 0⚓ /seks/ *noun*
1 (*plural* **sexes**) the state of being a male or a female: *What sex is your dog?* ◇ *the male sex*
2 (*no plural*) when two people put their bodies together, sometimes to make a baby: *to have sex*

sexual 0⚓ /'sekʃuəl/ *adjective*
connected with sex: *a campaign for sexual equality* ◇ *the sexual organs*
▶ **sexually** /'sekʃuəli/ *adverb*: *to be sexually active*

sh! /ʃ/ *exclamation*
be quiet!: *Sh! You'll wake the baby up!*

shabby /'ʃæbi/ *adjective* (shabbier, shabbiest)
old and untidy or dirty because it has been used a lot: *This coat's getting a bit shabby.*
▶ **shabbily** /'ʃæbɪli/ *adverb*: *She was shabbily dressed.*

shade

shadow   shade

shade¹ 0⚓ /ʃeɪd/ *noun*
1 (*no plural*) a place where it is dark and cool because the sun doesn't shine there: *We sat in the shade of a big tree.*
2 (*plural* **shades**) a thing that keeps strong light from your eyes: *I bought a new shade for the lamp.*
3 (*plural* **shades**) how light or dark a colour is: *I'm looking for a shirt in a darker shade of green.*
4 shades (*plural*) (*informal*) = SUNGLASSES

shade² /ʃeɪd/ *verb* (shades, shading, shaded)
to stop light from shining on something: *He shaded his eyes with his hand.*

shadow 0⚓ /'ʃædəʊ/ *noun*
a dark shape that you see near somebody or something that is in front of the light: *The*

dog was chasing its own shadow. ➲ Look at the picture at **shade**.

shady /ˈʃeɪdi/ *adjective* (shadier, shadiest)
not in the sun: *We sat in a shady part of the garden.*

shake

They shook hands.   He shook his head.

shake 0ᴍ /ʃeɪk/ *verb* (shakes, shaking, shook /ʃʊk/, has shaken /ˈʃeɪkən/)
to move quickly from side to side or up and down; to make something do this: *The house shakes when trains go past.* ◇ *He was shaking with fear.* ◇ *Shake the bottle before opening it.* ◇ *An explosion shook the windows.*
shake hands to hold somebody's hand and move it up and down when you meet them
shake your head to move your head from side to side to say 'no'

shaken *form of* SHAKE

shaky /ˈʃeɪki/ *adjective* (shakier, shakiest)
1 shaking because you are ill or frightened: *You've got shaky hands.*
2 not firm; not strong: *That ladder looks a little shaky.*

shall 0ᴍ /ʃəl; ʃæl/ *modal verb*

> 🔎 **GRAMMAR**
> The negative form of **shall** is **shall not** or the short form **shan't** /ʃɑːnt/: *I shan't be there.*
> The short form of **shall** is **'ll**. We often use this: *I'll* (= I shall) *see you tomorrow.*

1 a word that you use when you are asking, offering or suggesting something: *What time shall I come?* ◇ *Shall I close the window?* ◇ *What shall we do tomorrow?* ◇ *Shall we go now?*
2 (*formal*) a word that you use instead of 'will' with 'I' and 'we' to show the future: *I shall see you tomorrow.* ➲ Look at the note at **modal verb**.

shallow /ˈʃæləʊ/ *adjective* (shallower, shallowest)
not deep; with not much water: *This part of the river is shallow – we can walk across.*
➲ OPPOSITE **deep**

shame 0ᴍ /ʃeɪm/ *noun* (no plural)
1 the unhappy feeling that you have when

shallow

shallow   deep

you have done something wrong or stupid: *I was filled with* (= felt a lot of) *shame after I lied to my parents.* ➲ The adjective is **ashamed**.
2 a fact or situation that makes you feel sad or disappointed ➲ SAME MEANING **pity**: *It's a shame you can't come to the party.* ◇ *'Sally's not well.' 'What a shame!'*

shameless /ˈʃeɪmləs/ *adjective*
doing bad things without caring what other people think: *It was a shameless attempt to copy somebody else's work.*

shampoo /ʃæmˈpuː/ *noun* (plural shampoos)
a special liquid for washing your hair: *a bottle of shampoo*
▶ **shampoo** *verb* (shampoos, shampooing, shampooed /ʃæmˈpuːd/): *How often do you shampoo your hair?*

shan't /ʃɑːnt/ *short for* SHALL NOT

shapes

square   circle

rectangle   star   oval

crescent   triangle   diamond

shape¹ 0ᴍ /ʃeɪp/ *noun*
1 (*plural* shapes) what you see if you draw a line round something; the form of something: *What shape is the table – round or square?* ◇ *I bought a bowl in the shape of a fish.* ◇ *Circles, squares and triangles are all different shapes.*
2 (*no plural*) the physical condition of somebody or something: *He was in bad*

shape *after the accident.* ◇ *I like to* **keep in shape** (= keep fit) *by exercising every day.*

out of shape

1 not having the right shape: *My jumper went out of shape when I washed it.*
2 (used about a person) not in good physical condition: *I didn't realize how out of shape I was!*

shape² 0⃞ /ʃeɪp/ *verb* (shapes, shaping, shaped /ʃeɪpt/)
to give a certain shape to something: *She* **shaped** *the clay* **into** *a pot.*

shaped 0⃞ /ʃeɪpt/ *adjective*
having a certain shape: *He gave me a birthday card* **shaped like** *a cat.* ◇ *a heart-shaped box of chocolates*

share¹ 0⃞ /ʃeə(r)/ *verb* (shares, sharing, shared /ʃeəd/)

1 to divide something between two or more people: **Share** *these sweets* **with** *your friends.* ◇ *We* **shared** *a large pizza* **between** *three of us.*
2 to have or use something with another person: *I* **share** *a bedroom* **with** *my sister.*

share² 0⃞ /ʃeə(r)/ *noun*

1 a part of something bigger that each person has: *Here is your* **share** *of the money.* ◇ *I did my* **share** *of the work.*
2 one of equal parts which the value of a company is divided into and that are sold to people who want to own part of the company: *a fall in share prices*

shark

fin

shark /ʃɑːk/ *noun*
a big fish that lives in the sea. Some **sharks** have sharp teeth and are dangerous.

sharp¹ 0⃞ /ʃɑːp/ *adjective* (sharper, sharpest)

1 with an edge or point that cuts or makes holes easily: *a sharp knife* ◇ *a sharp needle* ⊃ OPPOSITE **blunt**
2 strong and sudden: *a sharp bend in the road* ◇ *I felt a sharp pain in my leg.*
3 clear and easy to see: *We could see the sharp outline of the mountains against the sky.*
4 able to see, hear or learn well: *She's got a very sharp mind.* ◇ *sharp eyes*
5 sudden and angry: *sharp words*

▶ **sharply** /ʃɑːpli/ *adverb*: *The road bends sharply to the left.* ◇ *'Go away!' he said sharply.*

sharp² /ʃɑːp/ *adverb*

1 exactly: *Be here at six o'clock sharp.*
2 with a big change of direction: *Turn sharp right at the next corner.*

sharpen /ʃɑːpən/ *verb* (sharpens, sharpening, sharpened /ʃɑːpənd/)
to make something sharp or sharper: *They sharpened all the knives.*

sharpener /ʃɑːpnə(r)/ *noun*
a thing that you use for making something sharp: *a pencil sharpener* ⊃ Look at Picture Dictionary page **P11**.

shatter /ʃætə(r)/ *verb* (shatters, shattering, shattered /ʃætəd/)
to break into very small pieces; to break something into very small pieces: *The glass hit the floor and shattered.* ◇ *The explosion shattered the windows.*

shave /ʃeɪv/ *verb* (shaves, shaving, shaved /ʃeɪvd/)
to cut hair off your face or body by cutting it very close with a special knife (called a **razor**): *He shaves every morning.*
▶ **shave** *noun*: *I haven't* **had a shave** *today.*

shaver /ʃeɪvə(r)/ *noun*
an electric tool that you use for SHAVING ⊃ Look at **razor**.

shawl /ʃɔːl/ *noun*
a big piece of cloth that a woman wears round her shoulders, or that you put round a baby

she 0⃞ /ʃiː/ *pronoun* (plural they)
a woman or girl who the sentence is about: *'Where's your sister?' 'She's (= she is) at work.'*

shears

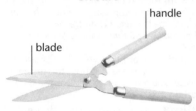

handle

blade

shears /ʃɪəz/ *noun* (plural)
a tool like a very large pair of scissors that you use for cutting things in the garden

shed¹ /ʃed/ *noun*
a small building where you keep things or animals: *We keep our tools in the garden shed.*

shed² /ʃed/ *verb* (sheds, shedding, shed, has shed)
to lose something because it falls off: *The snake shed its skin.*

she'd /ʃiːd/ *short for* SHE HAD; SHE WOULD

sheep

sheep   lamb

sheep 0̄ /ʃiːp/ *noun* (*plural* sheep)
an animal that people keep on farms for its meat and its wool

> 🔎 **WORD BUILDING**
>
> A young sheep is called a **lamb**. Meat from a young sheep is also called **lamb**.

sheer /ʃɪə(r)/ *adjective*
1 complete: *sheer nonsense*
2 very steep: *It was a sheer drop to the sea.*

sheet 0̄ /ʃiːt/ *noun*
1 a big piece of thin material for a bed: *I put some clean sheets on the bed.* ⊃ Look at the picture at **bed**.
2 a thin flat piece of something like paper, glass or metal: *a sheet of writing paper*

shelf 0̄ /ʃelf/ *noun* (*plural* shelves /ʃelvz/)
a long flat piece of wood on a wall or in a cupboard, where things can stand: *Put the plates on the shelf.* ◇ *bookshelves* ⊃ Look at Picture Dictionary page **P10**.

shell 0̄ /ʃel/ *noun*
the hard outside part of birds' eggs and nuts and of some animals ⊃ Look also at **seashell**.

she'll /ʃiːl/ *short for* SHE WILL

shellfish /'ʃelfɪʃ/ *noun* (*plural* shellfish)
a kind of animal that lives in water and that has a shell

shelter¹ /'ʃeltə(r)/ *noun*
1 (*no plural*) protection from bad weather or danger: *We took shelter from the rain under a tree.* ◇ *People ran for shelter when the bombs started to fall.*
2 (*plural* shelters) a place that protects you

shells

shell

seashell   snail

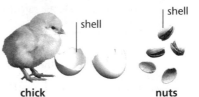

shell   shell

chick   nuts

from bad weather or danger: *a bus shelter* (= for people who are waiting at a bus stop)

shelter² /'ʃeltə(r)/ *verb* (shelters, sheltering, sheltered /'ʃeltəd/)
1 to make somebody or something safe from bad weather or danger: *The trees shelter the house from the wind.*
2 to go to a place where you will be safe from bad weather or danger: *Let's shelter from the rain under that tree.*

shelves *plural of* SHELF

shepherd /'ʃepəd/ *noun*
a person who looks after sheep

she's /ʃiːz/ *short for* SHE IS; SHE HAS

shield¹ /ʃiːld/ *noun*
a big piece of metal, wood or leather that soldiers carried in front of their bodies when they were fighting in wars long ago. Some police officers carry **shields** now.

shield² /ʃiːld/ *verb* (shields, shielding, shielded)
to keep somebody or something safe from danger or from being hurt: *She shielded her eyes from the sun with her hand.*

shift¹ /ʃɪft/ *verb* (shifts, shifting, shifted)
to move something from one place to another: *Can you help me to shift the bed? I want to sweep the floor.*

shift² /ʃɪft/ *noun*
1 a change in what people think about something: *There has been a shift in public opinion away from the war.*
2 a group of workers who begin work when another group finishes: *the night shift*

shin /ʃɪn/ *noun*
the bone in the front part of your leg from your knee and your foot

shine 0̶ /ʃaɪn/ verb (shines, shining, shone /ʃɒn/, has shone)
1 to give out light: *The sun is shining.*
2 to be bright: *I polished the silver until it shone.*
3 to direct a light at somebody or something: *Don't **shine** your torch **in** my eyes!*

shiny 0̶ /'ʃaɪni/ adjective (shinier, shiniest)
causing a bright effect when in the sun or in light: *The new shampoo leaves your hair soft and shiny.* ◊ *He's got a shiny new car.*

ship 0̶ /ʃɪp/ noun
a big boat for long journeys on the sea: *We went to India **by ship**.*
▶ **ship** *verb* (ships, shipping, shipped /ʃɪpt/): *New Zealand **ships** meat to Britain.*
⊃ Look at Picture Dictionary page **P1**.

shipping /'ʃɪpɪŋ/ noun (no plural)
ships in general or the carrying of goods by ships: *The port is now open to shipping.* ◊ *a shipping company*

shipwreck /'ʃɪprek/ noun
an accident at sea when a ship breaks in bad weather or on rocks
be shipwrecked to be on a ship when it is in a **shipwreck**: *They were shipwrecked off the coast of Portugal.*

shirt 0̶ /ʃɜːt/ noun

> 🔊 **PRONUNCIATION**
> The word **shirt** sounds like **hurt**.

a thin piece of clothing that you wear on the top part of your body

shiver /'ʃɪvə(r)/ verb (shivers, shivering, shivered /'ʃɪvəd/)
to shake because you are cold, frightened or ill: *We were shivering with cold.*

shoes

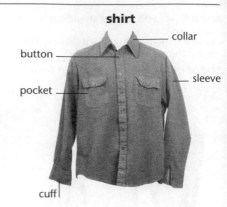

shirt

- collar
- button
- sleeve
- pocket
- cuff

▶ **shiver** *noun*: *Sue **gave a shiver** and pulled her coat around her.*

shock¹ 0̶ /ʃɒk/ noun
1 a very bad surprise: *The news of his death **came as a shock to** all of us.*
2 a sudden pain when electricity goes through your body: *Don't touch that wire – you'll get an **electric shock**.*

shock² 0̶ /ʃɒk/ verb (shocks, shocking, shocked /ʃɒkt/)
to give somebody a very bad surprise; to upset somebody: *I was shocked by his behaviour.*
▶ **shocked** /ʃɒkt/ *adjective*: *Don't look so shocked – I did warn you!*

shocking 0̶ /'ʃɒkɪŋ/ adjective
making you feel upset, angry, or surprised in a very bad way: *a shocking crime*

shoe 0̶ /ʃuː/ noun

> 🔊 **PRONUNCIATION**
> The word **shoe** sounds like **who**.

slippers

sandal

sole — **wellingtons** (*British*) **rubber boots** (*American*)

buckle — **boot**

shoelace (*also* lace) — **trainers** (*British*) **sneakers** (*American*)

shoes

flip-flops (*British*) **thongs** (*American*)

heel — **shoe**

a covering made of leather or plastic that you wear on your foot: *a pair of shoes* ◇ *What size shoes do you take?* ◇ *a shoe shop*

shoelace /'ʃuːleɪs/ (*also* **lace**) (*American also* **shoestring** /'ʃuːstrɪŋ/) *noun*
a long thin piece of material like string that you tie to close a shoe: *Tie your shoelaces.* ➲ Look at the picture at **shoe**.

shone *form of* SHINE

shook *form of* SHAKE

shoot¹ 0̶̶̶̶ /ʃuːt/ *verb* (**shoots, shooting, shot** /ʃɒt/, **has shot**)
1 to fire a gun or another weapon; to hurt or kill a person or an animal with a gun: *She shot a bird.* ◇ *The police officer was shot in the arm.*
2 to move quickly or suddenly: *The car shot past us.*
3 to make a film: *They are shooting a film about the war.*

shoot² /ʃuːt/ *noun*
a new part of a plant: *The first shoots appear in spring.* ➲ Look at the picture at **plant**.

shop¹ 0̶̶̶̶ /ʃɒp/ (*British*) (*American* **store**) *noun*
a building where you buy things: *a bookshop* ◇ *Do you need anything from the shops?*

shop² 0̶̶̶̶ /ʃɒp/ *verb* (**shops, shopping, shopped** /ʃɒpt/)
to go to buy things from shops: *I'm **shopping** for some new clothes.*

> 🔎 SPEAKING
> It is more usual to say **go shopping**.

▶ **shopper** *noun* /'ʃɒpə(r)/ *The streets were full of shoppers.*

shop assistant /'ʃɒp əsɪstənt/ (*British*) (*American* **sales clerk, clerk**) *noun*
a person who works in a shop ➲ Look at Picture Dictionary page **P12**.

shopkeeper /'ʃɒpkiːpə(r)/ (*British*) (*American* **storekeeper**) *noun*
a person who owns a small shop

shoplifting /'ʃɒplɪftɪŋ/ *noun* (*no plural*)
the crime of stealing things from shops: *He was accused of shoplifting.*
▶ **shoplifter** /'ʃɒplɪftə(r)/ *noun*: *Shoplifters will be prosecuted.*

shopping 0̶̶̶̶ /'ʃɒpɪŋ/ *noun* (*no plural*)
1 buying things from shops: *She **does** her **shopping** after work.* ◇ *I usually **go shopping** at the weekend.*
2 the things that you have bought in a shop: *Will you carry my shopping for me?*

shopping centre /'ʃɒpɪŋ sentə(r)/ (*British*) (*American* **shopping mall, mall**) *noun*
a large building that has a lot of shops, restaurants, etc. inside it ➲ Look at Picture Dictionary page **P13**.

shore /ʃɔː(r)/ *noun*
the land next to the sea or a lake: *The swimmer kept close to the shore.*

short 0̶̶̶̶ /ʃɔːt/ *adjective* (**shorter, shortest**)
1 a small distance from one end to the other: *Her hair is very short.* ◇ *We live a short distance from the beach.* ➲ OPPOSITE **long**
2 less tall than most people: *I'm too short to reach the top shelf.* ◇ *a short fat man* ➲ OPPOSITE **tall**
3 lasting for only a little time: *The film was very short.* ◇ *a short holiday* ➲ OPPOSITE **long**
be short of something to not have enough of something: *I'm short of money this month.*
for short as a short way of saying or writing something: *My sister's name is Deborah, but we call her 'Deb' for short.*
short for something a short way of saying or writing something: *'Tom' is short for 'Thomas'.*

shortage /'ʃɔːtɪdʒ/ *noun*
a situation when there is not enough of something: *a water shortage* ◇ *There is a **shortage of** good teachers.*

short cut /ˌʃɔːt 'kʌt/ *noun*
a shorter way to get somewhere: *We took a **short cut** to school across the field.*

shorten /'ʃɔːtn/ *verb* (**shortens, shortening, shortened** /'ʃɔːtnd/)
to become shorter or to make something shorter: *The trousers were too long, so I shortened them.*

shortly /'ʃɔːtli/ *adverb*
soon: *The doctor will see you shortly, Mr Smith.* ◇ *We left shortly after six o'clock.*

shorts /ʃɔːts/ *noun* (*plural*)
1 short trousers that end above your knees: *a pair of shorts* ➲ Look at Picture Dictionary page **P5**.
2 (*American*) a piece of loose clothing that men wear under their trousers

shot¹ *form of* SHOOT¹

shot² 0̶̶̶̶ /ʃɒt/ *noun*
1 the action of firing a gun, or the noise that this makes: *He fired a shot.*
2 the action of kicking or hitting a ball in a sport like football: *a shot at goal*
3 a photograph: *This is a good shot of you.*

A
B
C
D
E
F
G
H
I
J
K
L
M
N
O
P
Q
R
S
T
U
V
W
X
Y
Z

A
B
C
D
E
F
G
H
I
J
K
L
M
N
O
P
Q
R
S
T
U
V
W
X
Y
Z

should 0🔑 /ʃʊd/ *modal verb*

> 🔍 **PRONUNCIATION**
> The word **should** sounds like **good**, because we don't say the letter **l** in this word.

> 🔍 **GRAMMAR**
> The negative form of **should** is **should not** or the short form **shouldn't** /'ʃʊdnt/.

1 a word that you use to tell or ask somebody what is the right thing to do ⊃ SAME MEANING **ought to**: *If you feel ill, you should stay in bed.* ◇ *You shouldn't eat so much chocolate.* ◇ *I'm tired. I shouldn't have gone to bed so late.*
2 a word that you use to give or ask somebody for advice: *You should try that new restaurant.* ◇ *Should I invite him to the party?*
3 a word that you use to say what you think will happen or what you think is true: *They should be here soon.*
4 the word that we use for 'shall' in the past, when we say what somebody said: *We asked if we should help her.* ⊃ Look at the note at **modal verb**.

shoulder 0🔑 /'ʃəʊldə(r)/ *noun*

> 🔍 **PRONUNCIATION**
> The word **shoulder** sounds like **older**.

the part of your body between your neck and your arm ⊃ Look at Picture Dictionary page **P4**.

shoulder bag /'ʃəʊldə bæg/ *noun*
a type of bag that you carry over one shoulder with a long narrow piece of cloth or leather ⊃ Look at Picture Dictionary page **P5**.

shouldn't /'ʃʊdnt/ *short for* SHOULD NOT

should've /'ʃʊdəv/ *short for* SHOULD HAVE

shout 0🔑 /ʃaʊt/ *verb* (shouts, shouting, shouted)
to speak very loudly: *Don't shout at me!* ◇ *'Go back!' she shouted.*
▶ **shout** *noun*: *We heard a shout for help.*

shove /ʃʌv/ *verb* (shoves, shoving, shoved /ʃʌvd/)
to push somebody or something in a rough way: *They shoved him through the door.*

shovel¹ /'ʃʌvl/ *noun*
a tool that you use for picking up and moving earth, sand or snow

shovel² *verb* (British shovels, shovelling, shovelled /'ʃʌvld/) (American shoveling, shoveled)
to move something with a **shovel**: *We shovelled the snow off the path.*

show¹ 0🔑 /ʃəʊ/ *verb* (shows, showing, showed /ʃəʊd/, has shown /ʃəʊn/ *or* has showed)

> 🔍 **PRONUNCIATION**
> The word **show** sounds like **go**.

1 to let somebody see something: *She showed me her holiday photos.* ◇ *You have to show your ticket on the train.*
2 to make something clear; to explain something to somebody: *Can you show me how to use the computer?* ◇ *Research shows that most people get too little exercise.*
3 to appear or be seen: *The anger showed in his face.*
show off to talk loudly or do something silly to make people notice you: *Joyce was showing off by driving too fast.*
show something off to let people see something that is new or beautiful: *James wanted to show off his new jacket.*
show somebody round to go with somebody and show them everything in a building: *David showed me round the school.*
show up (*informal*) to arrive: *What time did they show up?*

show² 0🔑 /ʃəʊ/ *noun*
1 something that you watch at the theatre or on television: *a comedy show* ◇ *Did you enjoy the show?*
2 a group of things in one place that people go to see: *a flower show* ◇ *The paintings are on show at the National Gallery until 15 May.*

shower 0🔑 /'ʃaʊə(r)/ *noun*
1 a place where you can wash by standing under water that falls from above you: *There's a shower in the bathroom.* ⊃ Look at Picture Dictionary page **P10**.
2 the act of washing yourself in a shower: *I had a shower after the tennis match.*
3 rain that falls for a short time: *The day will be cloudy, with occasional heavy showers.*

shown *form of* SHOW¹

shrank *form of* SHRINK

shred /ʃred/ *noun*
a small thin piece of material that has been cut or torn off: *shreds of paper*

shrewd /ʃruːd/ *adjective* (shrewder, shrewdest)
able to make good decisions because you understand people or situations well: *She's a very shrewd businesswoman.*

shriek /ʃriːk/ *verb* (shrieks, shrieking, shrieked /ʃriːkt/)
to make a loud high cry: She **shrieked with fear** (= because she was afraid).
▶ **shriek** *noun*: He **gave a shriek** of pain.

shrill /ʃrɪl/ *adjective* (shriller, shrillest)
A **shrill** sound is high and loud: a shrill whistle

shrimp /ʃrɪmp/ *noun*
1 (British) a small sea animal with a shell and a lot of legs that turns pink when you cook it. **Shrimps** are smaller than PRAWNS.
2 American English for PRAWN

shrine /ʃraɪn/ *noun*
a special place that is important to people for religious reasons

shrink

'Oh no! My T-shirt has shrunk!'

shrink /ʃrɪŋk/ *verb* (shrinks, shrinking, shrank /ʃræŋk/ or shrunk /ʃrʌŋk/, has shrunk)
to become smaller or to make something smaller: My jeans shrank when I washed them.

shrivel /ʃrɪvl/ *verb* (British shrivels, shrivelling, shrivelled /ʃrɪvld/) (American shriveling, shriveled)
to become smaller, especially because of dry conditions: The plants shrivelled up and died in the hot weather

shrub /ʃrʌb/ *noun*
a plant like a small low tree

shrug /ʃrʌg/ *verb* (shrugs, shrugging, shrugged /ʃrʌgd/)
to move your shoulders to show that you do not know or do not care

shrug

He shrugged his shoulders.

about something: I asked her where Sam was but she just shrugged.
▶ **shrug** *noun*: He answered my question with a shrug.

shrunk *form of* SHRINK

shudder /ʃʌdə(r)/ *verb* (shudders, shuddering, shuddered /ʃʌdəd/)
to shake because you are cold or frightened, or because of a strong feeling: He shuddered when he saw the snake.
▶ **shudder** *noun*: She felt a shudder of fear.

shuffle /ʃʌfl/ *verb* (shuffles, shuffling, shuffled /ʃʌfld/)
1 to walk slowly, without taking your feet off the ground: The old man shuffled along the road.
2 to mix playing cards before a game: She shuffled the cards carefully before dealing them.

shut[1] 0→ /ʃʌt/ *verb* (shuts, shutting, shut, has shut)
1 to move, or to move something, so that it is not open ⊃ SAME MEANING **close**: Could you shut the door, please? ◇ The door shut behind me.
2 to stop being open, so that people cannot go there ⊃ SAME MEANING **close**: The shops shut at 5.30.
shut down to close and stop working; to make something close and stop working ⊃ SAME MEANING **close down**: The factory shut down last year.
shut up (informal) to stop talking: Shut up and listen!

> 🔊 SPEAKING
> This expression is quite rude. It is more polite to say 'be quiet'.

shut[2] 0→ /ʃʌt/ *adjective*
not open ⊃ SAME MEANING **closed**: The restaurant is shut today. ◇ Is the door shut?

shutter /ʃʌtə(r)/ *noun*
a wooden or metal thing that covers the outside of a window: Close the shutters at night.

shuttle /ʃʌtl/ *noun*
1 a plane, bus or train that travels regularly between two places
2 = SPACE SHUTTLE

shy 0→ /ʃaɪ/ *adjective* (shyer, shyest)
not able to talk easily to people you do not know: He was too shy to speak to her. ◇ a shy smile
▶ **shyness** /ʃaɪnəs/ *noun* (no plural): As a child she suffered from terrible shyness.

A B C D E F G H I J K L M N O P Q R **S** T U V W X Y Z

sick 0🔑 /sɪk/ *adjective* (sicker, sickest)
not well ⊃ SAME MEANING **ill**: *She's looking after her sick mother.* ◊ *Joe's been off sick (= away because of illness) all week.*
be sick (*British*) When you **are sick**, food comes up from your stomach and out of your mouth. ⊃ SAME MEANING **vomit**
be sick of something to have had or done too much of something, so that you do not want it any longer: *I'm sick of watching TV – let's go out.*
feel sick (*British*) to feel that food is going to come up from your stomach

sickness /'sɪknəs/ *noun* (*no plural*)
being ill: *He could not work for a long time because of sickness.*

side 0🔑 /saɪd/ *noun*
1 one of the flat outside parts of something: *A box has six sides.*
2 the part of something that is not the front, back, top or bottom: *There is a door at the side of the house.* ◊ *There's a scratch on the side of my car.* ⊃ Look at the picture at **back**.
3 the part of something that is near the edge and away from the middle: *I stood at the side of the road.*
4 the right or left part of something: *He lay on his side.* ◊ *We drive on the left side of the road in Britain.*
5 one of two groups of people who fight, argue or play a game against each other: *I thought you were on my side (= agreed with me).* ◊ *Which side won?*
side by side next to each other: *They walked side by side.*
take sides to show that you agree with one person, and not the other, in a fight or an argument

sideboard /'saɪdbɔːd/ *noun*
a type of cupboard that you use for storing plates and dishes in the room where you eat (called a **dining room**) ⊃ Look at Picture Dictionary page **P10**.

sidewalk /'saɪdwɔːk/ *American English for* PAVEMENT

sideways /'saɪdweɪz/ *adjective, adverb*
1 to or from the side: *She looked sideways at the girl next to her.*
2 with one of the sides first: *We carried the table sideways through the door.*

siege /siːdʒ/ *noun*
a situation when an army stays outside a town or police stay outside a building for a long time so that no one can get in or out

sieve /sɪv/ *noun*
a type of kitchen tool that you use to remove lumps from food such as flour or soup

sieve

sigh /saɪ/ *verb* (sighs, sighing, sighed /saɪd/)
to let out a deep breath, for example because you are sad, tired or pleased
▶ **sigh** *noun*: '*I wish I had more money,' he said with a sigh.*

sight 0🔑 /saɪt/ *noun*
1 (*no plural*) the ability to see ⊃ SAME MEANING **eyesight**: *She has poor sight (= she cannot see well).*
2 (*no plural*) seeing somebody or something: *We had our first sight of London from the plane.*
3 (*plural* sights) something that you see: *The mountains were a beautiful sight.*
4 sights (*plural*) the interesting places, especially in a town or city, that are often visited by tourists: *When you come to Paris I'll show you the sights.*
5 (*no plural*) a position where you can see somebody or something: *We watched until they were out of sight (= we could not see them).* ◊ *Eventually the town came into sight (= we could see it).*
at first sight when you see somebody or something for the first time: *He fell in love with her at first sight.*
catch sight of somebody or **something** to see somebody or something suddenly: *I caught sight of Fiona in the crowd.*
lose sight of somebody or **something** to no longer be able to see somebody or something: *After an hour at sea we lost sight of land.*

sightseeing /'saɪtsiːɪŋ/ *noun* (*no plural*)
the activity of visiting interesting buildings and places as a tourist: *to go sightseeing* ◊ *Did you have a chance to do any sightseeing?*
▶ **sightseer** /'saɪtsiːə(r)/ *noun*
⊃ SAME MEANING **tourist**: *The town was full of sightseers.*

sign[1] 0🔑 /saɪn/ *noun*
1 something that tells you that something exists, is happening or may happen in the future: *Dark clouds are a sign of rain.*
2 a thing with writing or a picture

sign

on it that tells you something: *The sign said 'No Smoking'.* ◇ *a road sign*
3 a mark, shape or movement that has a special meaning: *In mathematics, a cross is a plus sign.* ◇ *I put up my hand as a sign for him to stop.*

sign² 0🔑 /saɪn/ *verb* (signs, signing, signed /saɪnd/)
to write your name in your own way on something: *Sign here, please.* ◇ *I signed the cheque.* ⊃ The noun is **signature**.

signal 0🔑 /'sɪɡnəl/ *noun*
a light, sound or movement that tells you something without words: *A red light is a signal for cars to stop.*
▶ **signal** *verb* (*British* **signals**, **signalling**, **signalled** /'sɪɡnəld/) (*American* **signaling**, **signaled**) *The policeman* **signalled to** *the children* **to** *cross the road.*

signature /'sɪɡnətʃə(r)/ *noun*
your name as you usually write it, for example at the end of a letter ⊃ The verb is **sign**.

significance /sɪɡ'nɪfɪkəns/ *noun* (*no plural*)
the importance or meaning of something: *What is* **the significance of** *this discovery?*

significant /sɪɡ'nɪfɪkənt/ *adjective*
important; with a special meaning: *The police say that the time of the robbery was very significant.*

sign language /'saɪn læŋɡwɪdʒ/ *noun* (*no plural*)
a language that uses movements of the hands. It is used especially by people who cannot hear.

signpost

signpost /'saɪnpəʊst/ *noun*
a sign beside a road, that shows the way to a place and how far it is

Sikh /siːk/ *noun*
a person who follows one of the religions of India (called **Sikhism**)

silence 0🔑 /'saɪləns/ *noun*
1 (*no plural*) a situation in which there is no sound: *I can only work* **in** *complete* **silence**.
2 (*plural* **silences**) a time when nobody speaks or makes a noise: *There was a long silence before she answered the question.* ◇ *We ate our dinner* **in silence**.

silent /'saɪlənt/ *adjective*
1 with no sound; completely quiet: *Everyone was asleep, and the house was silent.*
2 If you are **silent**, you are not speaking: *I asked him a question and he was silent for a moment before he answered.*
▶ **silently** /'saɪləntli/ *adverb*: *The cat moved silently towards the bird.*

silk /sɪlk/ *noun* (*no plural*)
a type of thin smooth cloth that is made from the threads that an insect (called a **silkworm**) makes: *This scarf is made of silk.* ◇ *a silk shirt*

silky /'sɪlki/ *adjective* (silkier, silkiest)
soft, smooth and shiny, like SILK: *silky hair*

silly 0🔑 /'sɪli/ *adjective* (sillier, silliest)
not sensible or clever; stupid: *Don't be so silly!* ◇ *It was silly of you to leave the door open when you went out.*

silver¹ 0🔑 /'sɪlvə(r)/ *noun* (*no plural*)
1 a shiny grey metal that is valuable: *a silver necklace*
2 things that are made of silver, for example knives, forks and dishes: *The thieves stole some valuable silver.*

silver² /'sɪlvə(r)/ *adjective*
with the colour of silver: *silver paper*

similar 0🔑 /'sɪmələ(r)/ *adjective*
the same in some ways but not completely the same: *Rats are* **similar to** *mice, but they are bigger.* ◇ *Jane and her sister look very similar.*

similarity /ˌsɪmə'lærəti/ *noun* (*plural* **similarities**)
a way that people or things are the same: *There are a lot of* **similarities between** *the two countries.* ⊃ OPPOSITE **difference**

simmer /'sɪmə(r)/ *verb* (simmers, simmering, simmered /'sɪməd/)
to cook gently in water that is almost boiling: *Simmer the vegetables for ten minutes.*

simple 0🔑 /'sɪmpl/ *adjective* (simpler, simplest)
1 easy to do or understand: *This dictionary is written in simple English.* ◇ *'How do you open this?' 'I'll show you – it's simple.'*
⊃ OPPOSITE **difficult**
2 without a lot of different parts or extra

A
B
C
D
E
F
G
H
I
J
K
L
M
N
O
P
Q
R
S
T
U
V
W
X
Y
Z

things ➔ SAME MEANING **plain**: *She wore a simple black dress.* ◇ *a simple meal*

simplicity /sɪm'plɪsəti/ *noun* (*no plural*)
the quality of being simple: *I like the simplicity of these paintings.*

simplify /'sɪmplɪfaɪ/ *verb* (simplifies, simplifying, simplified /'sɪmplɪfaɪd/, has simplified)
to make something easier to do or understand: *The story has been simplified so that the children can understand it.*

simply /'sɪmpli/ *adverb*
1 a word that you use when you want to show how easy or basic something is ➔ SAME MEANING **just**: *Simply add water and stir.*
2 in a simple way: *Please explain it more simply.*
3 really: *The weather was simply terrible – it rained every day!*

simultaneous /ˌsɪml'teɪniəs/ *adjective*
happening at exactly the same time: *The city was hit by three simultaneous explosions.*
▶ **simultaneously** /ˌsɪml'teɪniəsli/ *adverb*: *'I'm sorry!' they said simultaneously.*

sin /sɪn/ *noun*
something that your religion says you should not do, because it is very bad: *Stealing is a sin.*
▶ **sin** *verb* (sins, sinning, sinned /sɪnd/): *He knew that he had sinned.*

since 0̶ /sɪns/ *adverb, preposition, conjunction*
1 from a time in the past until a later time in the past or until now: *He has been ill since Sunday.* ◇ *I haven't seen him since 1987.* ◇ *She has lived here since she was a child.* ◇ *George went to Canada in 1974 and he has lived there ever since* (= in all the time from then until now). ◇ *Andy left three years ago and we haven't seen him since.*

> 🔎 **WHICH WORD?**
> **For** or **since**?
> We use **for** to say how long something has continued, for example in **hours**, **days** or **years**: *She has been ill for three days.* ◇ *I've lived in this house for ten months.* ◇ *We have been married for ten years.*
> We use **since** with points of time in the past, for example a **time** on the clock, a **date** or an **event**: *I have been here since six o'clock.* ◇ *She has been alone since her husband died.* ◇ *We have been married since 1996.*

2 because ➔ SAME MEANING **as**: *Since it's your birthday, I'll buy you a drink.*

3 at a time after another time in the past: *They got married five years ago and have since had three children.*

sincere /sɪn'sɪə(r)/ *adjective*
being honest and meaning what you say: *Were you being sincere when you said that you loved me?*

sincerely /sɪn'sɪəli/ *adverb*
in a sincere way: *I am sincerely grateful to you.*
Yours sincerely words that you write at the end of a formal letter, before your name ➔ Look at Study Page **S14**.

sing 0̶ /sɪŋ/ *verb* (sings, singing, sang /sæŋ/, has sung /sʌŋ/)
to make music with your voice: *She sang a song.* ◇ *The birds were singing.*

singer 0̶ /'sɪŋə(r)/ *noun*
a person who sings, or whose job is singing, especially in public: *an opera singer*

single¹ 0̶ /'sɪŋgl/ *adjective*
1 only one: *He gave her a single red rose.*
2 a word that makes 'every' stronger: *You answered every single question correctly.*
3 not married: *Are you married or single?*
4 for one person: *I would like to book a single room, please.* ◇ *a single bed* ➔ Look at **double¹**.
5 (*British*) for a journey to a place, but not back again: *How much is a single ticket to London, please?* ➔ Look at **return²**.

single² /'sɪŋgl/ *noun*
1 a ticket for a journey to a place, but not back again: *A single to Brighton, please.* ➔ Look at **return²**.
2 a CD, tape, etc. that has only one song on each side; the main song on this CD or tape: *Have you heard Joss Stone's new single?* ➔ Look at **album**.

single parent /ˌsɪŋgl 'peərənt/ *noun*
a person who looks after his or her child or children alone, without help from the other parent

singular /'sɪŋgjələ(r)/ *noun* (*no plural*)
(*grammar*) the form of a word that you use for one person or thing: *The singular of 'men' is 'man'.*
▶ **singular** *adjective*: *'Table' is a singular noun.* ➔ Look at **plural**.

sink¹ 0̶ /sɪŋk/ *verb* (sinks, sinking, sank /sæŋk/, has sunk /sʌŋk/)
1 to go down under water: *If you throw a stone into water, it sinks.* ◇ *The fishing boat sank to the bottom of the sea.* ➔ Look at **float**.
2 to make a ship go down under water: *The ship was sunk by a torpedo.*

3 to go down: *The sun sank slowly behind the hills.*

sink² /sɪŋk/ *noun*
the place in a kitchen where you wash dishes
➣ Look at Picture Dictionary page **P10**.

sip /sɪp/ *verb* (sips, sipping, sipped /sɪpt/)
to drink something slowly, taking only a little each time: *She sipped her coffee.*
▶ **sip** *noun*: *Can I have **a sip of** your lemonade?*

sir 0ᴍ /sɜː(r)/ *noun*
1 (*no plural*) a polite way of speaking to a man, instead of using his name: *'Can I help you, sir?' asked the shop assistant.* ➣ Look at **madam**.
2 Sir (*no plural*) a word that you use at the beginning of a business letter to a man: *Dear Sir...* ➣ Look at **madam**.
3 Sir (*no plural*) the title that is used in front of the name of a man who has received one of the highest British honours: *Sir Bob Geldof* ➣ Look at **Lady**.

siren /'saɪrən/ *noun*
a machine that makes a long loud sound to warn people about something. Police cars and fire engines have **sirens**.

sister 0ᴍ /'sɪstə(r)/ *noun*
1 a girl or woman who has the same parents as you: *I've got two sisters and one brother.* ◇ *Jane and Anne are sisters.*
2 Sister (*British*) a nurse who has an important job in a hospital
3 Sister a female member of religious group

sister-in-law /'sɪstər ɪn lɔː/ *noun* (*plural* sisters-in-law)
1 the sister of your wife or husband
2 the wife of your brother

sit 0ᴍ /sɪt/ *verb* (sits, sitting, sat /sæt/, has sat)
1 to rest your weight on your bottom, for example in a chair: *We sat in the garden all afternoon.* ◇ *Come and sit next to me.* ◇ *She was **sitting on** the sofa.*
2 (*British*) to take an examination: *The students will sit their exams in June.*
sit down to move your body downwards so you are sitting: *She came into the room and sat down.*
sit up to sit when you have been lying: *He sat up in bed and looked at the clock.*

site /saɪt/ *noun*
1 a place where a building is, was, or will be: *a building site* ◇ *This house was built **on the site of** an old theatre.*
2 a place where something happened: *the **site of** a famous battle*
3 = WEBSITE

sitting room /'sɪtɪŋ ruːm/ *noun* (*British*)
another word for LIVING ROOM

situated /'sɪtʃueɪtɪd/ *adjective*
in a place: *The hotel is situated close to the beach.*

situation 0ᴍ /ˌsɪtʃu'eɪʃn/ *noun*
the things that are happening in a certain place or at a certain time: *We are **in a** difficult situation at the moment.*

sit-up /'sɪt ʌp/ *noun*
an exercise for the stomach muscles in which you lie on your back with your legs bent, then lift the top half of your body from the floor: *To keep fit, she does twenty sit-ups every morning.*

six 0ᴍ /sɪks/ *number* (*plural* sixes) 6

sixteen 0ᴍ /ˌsɪks'tiːn/ *number* 16

sixteenth 0ᴍ /ˌsɪks'tiːnθ/ *pronoun, adjective, adverb, noun*
1 16th
2 one of sixteen equal parts of something; ¹⁄₁₆

sixth 0ᴍ /sɪksθ/ *pronoun, adjective, adverb, noun*
1 6th
2 one of six equal parts of something; ¹⁄₆

sixth form /'sɪksθ fɔːm/ *noun* (*British*)
the classes in the last two years of secondary school, for students between the ages of 16 and 18

sixtieth 0ᴍ /'sɪkstiəθ/ *pronoun, adjective, adverb*
60th

sixty 0ᴍ /'sɪksti/ *number*
1 60
2 the sixties (*plural*) the numbers, years or temperatures between 60 and 69
in your sixties between the ages of 60 and 69: *My mum's in her sixties.*

size 0ᴍ /saɪz/ *noun*
1 (*no plural*) how big or small something is: *My bedroom is **the same size as** yours.*
2 (*plural* sizes) an exact measurement: *Have you got these shoes **in a** bigger **size**?*

skate¹ /skeɪt/ *verb* (skates, skating, skated)
1 (*also* ice-skate) to move on ice wearing **skates**: *Can you skate?* ◇ *They skated across the frozen lake.*

🔊 **SPEAKING**
We usually say **go skating** when we talk about skating for pleasure: *We **go skating** every weekend.*

A B C D E F G H I J K L M N O P Q R S T U V W X Y Z

skates

ice skates   Rollerblades™   roller skates

2 = ROLLER SKATE

skate² /skeɪt/ *noun*
1 a boot with a long sharp piece of metal under it, that you wear for moving on ice ⊃ SAME MEANING **ice skate**
2 a boot with wheels on the bottom, that you wear for moving quickly on smooth ground ⊃ SAME MEANING **roller skate**

skateboard

skateboard /'skeɪtbɔːd/ *noun*
a long piece of wood or plastic on wheels. You stand on it as it moves over the ground.
▶ **skateboarding** /'skeɪtbɔːdɪŋ/ *noun* (*no plural*): Dave **goes skateboarding** every weekend. ⊃ Look at Picture Dictionary page **P14**.

skating rink /'skeɪtɪŋ rɪŋk/ (*also* rink) *noun*
1 a special place where you can SKATE on ice
2 a special place where you can ROLLER SKATE (= move over a hard surface wearing boots with small wheels on the bottom)

skeleton /'skelɪtn/ *noun*
the bones of a whole animal or person

sketch /sketʃ/ *noun* (*plural* sketches)
a picture that you draw quickly: The artist is making sketches for his next painting.
▶ **sketch** *verb* (sketches, sketching, sketched /sketʃt/): He quickly sketched the view from the window.

ski /skiː/ *noun* (*plural* skis)
one of a pair of long flat pieces of wood, metal or plastic that you fix to boots so that you can move over snow: a pair of skis
▶ **ski** *verb* (skis, skiing /'skiːɪŋ/, skied /skiːd/, has skied): Can you ski? ◇ We **went skiing** in Austria.
▶ **skier** /'skiːə(r)/ *noun*: Marie's a good skier.

skid /skɪd/ *verb* (skids, skidding, skidded)
If a vehicle such as a car or lorry **skids**, it moves suddenly and in a dangerous way to the side, for example because the road is wet: The lorry skidded on the icy road.

skies *plural of* SKY

skilful (*British*) (*American* skillful) /'skɪlfl/ *adjective*
very good at doing something: a very skilful tennis player
▶ **skilfully** (*British*) (*American* skillfully) /'skɪlfəli/ *adverb*: He chopped the vegetables quickly and skilfully.

skill 0─┓ /skɪl/ *noun*
1 (*no plural*) the ability to do something well: Flying a plane takes great skill.
2 (*plural* skills) a thing that you can do well: What skills do you need for this job?

skilled /skɪld/ *adjective*
good at something because you have learned about or done it for a long time: skilled workers

skillful, skillfully American English for SKILFUL, SKILFULLY

skin 0─┓ /skɪn/ *noun*
1 the substance that covers the outside of a person or an animal's body: She has dark skin. ◇ animal skins
2 the outside part of some fruits and vegetables: a banana skin

skinny /'skɪni/ *adjective* (skinnier, skinniest)
too thin: He's so skinny – he doesn't eat enough. ⊃ Look at the note at **thin**.

skip /skɪp/ *verb* (skips, skipping, skipped /skɪpt/)
1 to move along quickly with little jumps from one foot to the other: The children were skipping along the road.
2 to jump many times over a rope that is turning
3 to not do or have something that you

skiing

skier
pole
goggles
boot
ski

should do or have: *I skipped my class today and went swimming.*
▶ **skip** *noun*: *She gave a skip and a jump and was off down the street.*

skipping rope /ˈskɪpɪŋ rəʊp/ (*British*) (*American* **jump rope**) *noun*
a rope that you use for SKIPPING

skirt ⊶ /skɜːt/ *noun*

a piece of clothing for a woman or girl that hangs from the waist and covers part of the legs ➲ Look at Picture Dictionary page **P5**.

ski slope /ˈskiː sləʊp/ *noun*
a part of a mountain where you can SKI (= move over snow on special pieces of wood, metal or plastic)

skull /skʌl/ *noun*
the bones in the head of a person or an animal

sky ⊶ /skaɪ/ *noun* (*plural* **skies**)
the space above the earth where you can see the sun, moon and stars: *a beautiful blue sky* ◇ *There are no clouds in the sky.*

skyscraper /ˈskaɪskreɪpə(r)/ *noun*
a very tall building: *He works on the 49th floor of a skyscraper.*

slab /slæb/ *noun*
a thick flat piece of something: *stone slabs* ◇ *a big slab of cheese*

slack /slæk/ *adjective*
1 loose: *Suddenly the rope went slack.*
➲ OPPOSITE **tight**
2 not busy: *Business has been very slack.*

slam /slæm/ *verb* (**slams, slamming, slammed** /slæmd/)
to close something or put something down with a loud noise: *She slammed the door angrily.* ◇ *He slammed the book on the table and went out.*

slang /slæŋ/ *noun* (*no plural*)
informal words that people use when they are talking. You do not use **slang** when you need to be polite, and you do not usually use it in writing: *In British English, 'quid' is slang for 'pound'.*

slant /slɑːnt/ *verb* (**slants, slanting, slanted**)
Something that **slants** has one side higher than the other or does not stand straight up: *My handwriting slants to the left.*
▶ **slant** *noun* (*no plural*): *Cut the flower stems on the slant.*

slap

slap /slæp/ *verb* (**slaps, slapping, slapped** /slæpt/)
to hit somebody with the flat inside part of your hand: *He slapped me on the face.*
▶ **slap** *noun*: *She gave me a slap across the face.*

slaughter /ˈslɔːtə(r)/ *verb* (**slaughters, slaughtering, slaughtered** /ˈslɔːtəd/)
1 to kill an animal for food
2 to kill a lot of people in a cruel way
▶ **slaughter** *noun* (*no plural*): *We must act to stop this slaughter.*

slave¹ /sleɪv/ *noun*
a person who belongs to another person and must work for that person for no money
▶ **slavery** /ˈsleɪvəri/ *noun* (*no plural*): *When did slavery end in America?*

slave² /sleɪv/ *verb* (**slaves, slaving, slaved** /sleɪvd/)
to work very hard: *I've been slaving away all day.*

sledge

sledge   sleigh

sledge /sledʒ/ (*American also* **sled** /sled/) *noun*
a small vehicle with pieces of metal or wood instead of wheels that you sit in to move over snow ➲ Look at **sleigh**.

sleep¹ ⊶ /sliːp/ *verb* (**sleeps, sleeping, slept** /slept/, **has slept**)
to rest with your eyes closed, as you do at night: *I sleep for eight hours every night.* ◇ *Did you sleep well?*

A

B

C

D

E

F

G

H

I

J

K

L

M

N

O

P

Q

R

S

T

U

V

W

X

Y

Z

sleep[2] 0ᴛ /sli:p/ *noun* (*no plural*)
the natural condition of rest when your eyes are closed and your mind and body are not active or conscious: *I didn't get any sleep last night.*
go to sleep to start to sleep
⊃ SAME MEANING **fall asleep**: *I got into bed and soon went to sleep.*

sleeping bag /'sli:pɪŋ bæg/ *noun*
a big warm bag that you sleep in when you go camping

sleepless /'sli:pləs/ *adjective*
without sleep: *I had a sleepless night.*

sleepy /'sli:pi/ *adjective* (**sleepier, sleepiest**)
1 tired and ready to sleep: *I felt sleepy after that big meal.*
2 quiet, with not many things happening: *a sleepy little village*

sleet /sli:t/ *noun* (*no plural*)
snow and rain together

sleeve 0ᴛ /sli:v/ *noun*
the part of a coat, dress or shirt, for example, that covers your arm: *a shirt with short sleeves* ⊃ Look at the picture at **shirt**.

sleigh /sleɪ/ *noun*
a large vehicle with pieces of metal or wood instead of wheels that you sit in to move over snow. A **sleigh** is usually pulled by animals. ⊃ Look at the picture at **sledge**.

slender /'slendə(r)/ *adjective*
thin, in an attractive way: *She has long, slender legs.*

slept *form of* SLEEP

slice 0ᴛ /slaɪs/ *noun*
a thin piece that you cut off bread, meat or other food: *Would you like a slice of cake?* ◇ *She cut the bread into slices.* ⊃ Look at the picture at **bread**.
▶ **slice** *verb* (**slices, slicing, sliced** /slaɪst/): *Slice the onions.*

slide[1] 0ᴛ /slaɪd/ *verb* (**slides, sliding, slid** /slɪd/, **has slid**)
to move smoothly or to make something move smoothly across something: *She fell and slid along the ice.*

slide[2] /slaɪd/ *noun*
1 a long metal thing that children play on. They climb up steps, sit down, and then SLIDE down the other side. ⊃ Look at the picture at **swing**[2].
2 a small photograph that you show on a screen, using a special machine (called a **projector**): *a slide show*

slight /slaɪt/ *adjective* (**slighter, slightest**)
small; not important or serious: *I've got a slight problem.* ◇ *a slight headache*

slightly 0ᴛ /'slaɪtli/ *adverb*
a little: *I'm feeling slightly better today.*

slim[1] /slɪm/ *adjective* (**slimmer, slimmest**)
thin, but not too thin: *a tall slim man* ⊃ Look at the note at **thin**.

slim[2] /slɪm/ *verb* (**slims, slimming, slimmed** /slɪmd/)
to become thinner: *I've been trying to slim.*

🔎 SPEAKING
The more usual expression is **lose weight**.

slime /slaɪm/ *noun* (*no plural*)
a thick liquid that looks or smells bad: *The pond was covered in green slime.*
▶ **slimy** /'slaɪmi/ *adjective* (**slimier, slimiest**): *a slimy surface*

sling[1] /slɪŋ/ *noun*
a piece of cloth that you wear to hold up an arm that is hurt: *She's got her arm in a sling.* ⊃ Look at the picture at **plaster**[1].

sling[2] /slɪŋ/ *verb* (**slings, slinging, slung** /slʌŋ/, **has slung**) (*British, informal*)
to throw something without care: *He got angry and slung the book at me.*

slip[1] 0ᴛ /slɪp/ *verb* (**slips, slipping, slipped** /slɪpt/)
1 to move smoothly over something by accident and fall or almost fall: *He slipped on the ice and broke his leg.*
2 to go quickly and quietly so that nobody sees you: *Ann slipped out of the room.* ◇ *We slipped away when no one was looking.*
3 to put something in a place quickly and quietly: *He slipped the money into his pocket.*
slip up (*informal*) to make a mistake

slip[2] /slɪp/ *noun*
1 a small mistake: *It was just a slip.*
2 a small piece of paper: *Write your address on this slip of paper.*

slipper /'slɪpə(r)/ *noun*
a light soft shoe that you wear in the house: *a pair of slippers* ⊃ Look at the picture at **shoe**.

slippery /'slɪpəri/ *adjective*
so smooth or wet that you cannot move on it or hold it easily: *a slippery floor* ◇ *The road was wet and slippery.*

slit /slɪt/ *noun*
a long thin hole or cut
▶ **slit** *verb* (**slits, slitting, slit, has slit**): *I slit the envelope open with a knife.*

slither /'slɪðə(r)/ *verb* (slithers, slithering, slithered /'slɪðəd/)
to move by sliding from side to side along the ground like a snake: *I saw a snake slithering down a rock.*

slob /slɒb/ *noun* (*informal*)
a lazy, untidy person: *My brother's such a slob – he never tidies his room.*

slogan /'sləʊgən/ *noun*
a short sentence or group of words that is easy to remember. **Slogans** are used to make people believe something or buy something: *anti-government slogans* ◇ *an advertising slogan*

slope[1] /sləʊp/ *noun*
a piece of ground that has one end higher than the other, like the side of a hill: *We walked down the mountain slope.* ⊃ Look also at **ski slope**.

slope[2] /sləʊp/ *verb* (slopes, sloping, sloped /sləʊpt/)
to have one end higher than the other: *The field slopes down to the river.* ◇ *a sloping roof*

sloppy /'slɒpi/ *adjective* (sloppier, sloppiest)
1 showing a lack of care or effort: *a sloppy piece of work*
2 Sloppy clothes are loose and comfortable: *a sloppy sweater*

slot /slɒt/ *noun*
a long thin hole that you push something through: *Put your money in the slot and take your ticket.*

slot machine /'slɒt məʃiːn/ *noun*
a machine that gives you things like drinks or sweets when you put money in

slow[1] 0— /sləʊ/ *adjective* (slower, slowest)

> 🔎 **PRONUNCIATION**
> The word **slow** sounds like **go**.

1 not moving or doing something quickly: *a slow train* ◇ *She hasn't finished her work yet – she's very slow.*
2 If a clock or watch is **slow**, it shows a time that is earlier than the real time: *My watch is five minutes slow.* ⊃ Look at **fast** and **quick**.
▶ **slowly** /'sləʊli/ *adverb*: *The old lady walked slowly up the hill.*

slow[2] /sləʊ/ *adverb*
slowly: *Please drive slower.* ◇ *slow-moving traffic*

slow[3] /sləʊ/ *verb* (slows, slowing, slowed /sləʊd/)
slow down, **slow somebody** or **something down** to start to go more slowly; to make somebody or something start to go more slowly: *The train slowed down as it came into the station.* ◇ *Don't talk to me when I'm working – it slows me down.*

slug /slʌg/ *noun*
a small soft animal that moves slowly and eats plants

slug

slum /slʌm/ *noun*
a poor part of a city where people live in old dirty buildings

slump /slʌmp/ *verb* (slumps, slumping, slumped /slʌmpt/)
1 (used about prices, sales and the economy) to fall suddenly and by a large amount: *Shares slumped to their lowest ever level.*
2 to fall or sit down suddenly because you are ill, weak or tired: *Suddenly the old man slumped to the floor.*

slung form of SLING[2]

sly /slaɪ/ *adjective*
A person who is **sly** tricks people or does things secretly. ⊃ SAME MEANING **cunning**

smack /smæk/ *verb* (smacks, smacking, smacked /smækt/)
to hit somebody with the inside part of your hand: *They never smack their children.*
▶ **smack** *noun*: *She gave her son a smack.*

small 0— /smɔːl/ *adjective* (smaller, smallest)
1 not big; little: *This dress is too small for me.* ◇ *My house is smaller than yours.*
2 young: *They have two small children.*

smart /smɑːt/ *adjective* (smarter, smartest)
1 (*British*) right for a special or an important time; clean and tidy: *a smart new suit* ◇ *He looks very smart in his new jacket.*
2 (*American*) clever: *She's not as smart as her sister.*
▶ **smartly** /'smɑːtli/ *adverb*: *She was very smartly dressed.*

smash /smæʃ/ *verb* (smashes, smashing, smashed /smæʃt/)
1 to break something into many pieces: *The boys smashed the window with their ball.*
2 to break into many pieces: *The plate fell on the floor and smashed.*
▶ **smash** *noun*: *The glass hit the floor with a smash.*

smashing /'smæʃɪŋ/ *adjective* (*British, informal*)
very good ⊃ SAME MEANING **great**: *The food was smashing.*

A
B
C
D
E
F
G
H
I
J
K
L
M
N
O
P
Q
R
S
T
U
V
W
X
Y
Z

smear /smɪə(r)/ *verb* (smears, smearing, smeared /smɪəd/)
to spread a soft substance on something, making it dirty: *The child had **smeared** chocolate all **over** his clothes.*
▶ **smear** *noun*: *She had smears of paint on her dress.*

smell 0⟶ /smel/ *verb* (smells, smelling, smelt /smelt/ or smelled /smeld/, has smelt or has smelled)
1 to have a particular smell: *Dinner smells good!* ◇ *The perfume **smells of** roses.*
2 to notice something with your nose: *Can you **smell** smoke?*
3 to have a bad smell: *Your feet smell!*
▶ **smell** *noun*: *There's a smell of gas in this room.*

smelly /'smeli/ *adjective* (smellier, smelliest)
having a bad smell: *smelly socks*

smile 0⟶ /smaɪl/ *verb* (smiles, smiling, smiled /smaɪld/)
to move your mouth to show that you are happy or that you think something is funny: *He **smiled at** me.*
▶ **smile** *noun*: *She had a big smile on her face.*

smog /smɒg/ *noun* (no plural)
dirty poisonous air that can cover a whole city

smoke¹ 0⟶ /sməʊk/ *noun* (no plural)
the grey, white or black gas that you see in the air when something is burning: *The room was full of smoke.* ◇ *cigarette smoke*

smoke² 0⟶ /sməʊk/ *verb* (smokes, smoking, smoked /sməʊkt/)
to breathe in smoke through a cigarette, etc. and let it out again; to use cigarettes, etc. in this way, as a habit: *He was smoking a cigar.* ◇ *Do you smoke?*
▶ **smoker** /'sməʊkə(r)/ *noun*: *Her parents are both **heavy smokers** (= they smoke a lot).*
⊃ OPPOSITE **non-smoker**
▶ **smoking** /'sməʊkɪŋ/ *noun* (no plural): *No smoking in the theatre.*

smoked /sməʊkt/ *adjective*
Smoked food is put over a wood fire to give it a special taste: *smoked salmon*

smoky /'sməʊki/ (smokier, smokiest) *adjective*
full of smoke: *a smoky room*

smolder *verb* American English for SMOULDER

smooth 0⟶ /smuːð/ *adjective* (smoother, smoothest)
1 having a completely flat surface: *Babies have such smooth skin.* ◇ *The surface should be completely smooth.* ⊃ OPPOSITE **rough**
2 with no big pieces in it: *Beat the sauce until it is smooth.* ⊃ OPPOSITE **lumpy**
3 A **smooth** movement or journey is even and comfortable: *The weather was good so we had a very smooth flight.*
⊃ OPPOSITE **bumpy**
▶ **smoothly** /'smuːðli/ *adverb*: *The plane landed smoothly.*

smother /'smʌðə(r)/ *verb* (smothers, smothering, smothered /'smʌðəd/)
1 to kill somebody by covering their face so that they cannot breathe
2 to cover a thing with too much of something: *He smothered his cake with cream.*

smoulder (British) (American **smolder**) /'sməʊldə(r)/ *verb* (smoulders, smouldering, smouldered /'sməʊldəd/)
to burn slowly without a flame: *A fire smouldered in the grate.*

smudge /smʌdʒ/ *verb* (smudges, smudging, smudged /smʌdʒd/)
If something **smudges** or you **smudge** it, it becomes dirty or untidy because you have touched it: *Leave the painting to dry or you'll smudge it.* ◇ *My lipstick has smudged.*
▶ **smudge** *noun*: *There's a smudge on your cheek.*

smug /smʌg/ *adjective* (smugger, smuggest)
too pleased with yourself, in a way that annoys other people: *He gave her a smug look.*

smuggle /'smʌgl/ *verb* (smuggles, smuggling, smuggled /'smʌgld/)
to take things secretly into or out of a country when this is against the law: *They were trying to **smuggle** drugs **into** France.*
▶ **smuggler** /'smʌglə(r)/ *noun*: *drug smugglers*

snack /snæk/ *noun*
a small quick meal: *We had a snack on the train.*

snack bar /'snæk bɑː(r)/ *noun*
a place where you can buy and eat SNACKS

snag /snæg/ *noun*
a small problem: *It's a beautiful bike – the only snag is, it's very expensive.*

snail /sneɪl/ *noun*
a small soft animal with a hard shell on its back. **Snails** move very slowly.

snail

shell

snake

snake 0🔴 /sneɪk/ *noun*
an animal with a long thin body and no legs: *Do these snakes bite?*

snap¹ /snæp/ *verb* (snaps, snapping, snapped /snæpt/)
1 to break something suddenly with a sharp noise; to be broken in this way: *He snapped the pencil in two.* ◊ *Suddenly, the rope snapped.*
2 to say something in a quick angry way: *'Go away – I'm busy!' she snapped.*
3 to try to bite somebody or something: *The dog snapped at my leg.*

snap² /snæp/ *noun*
1 a sudden sound of something breaking
2 (*also* **snapshot** /'snæpʃɒt/) a photograph: *She showed us her holiday snaps.*

snarl /snɑːl/ *verb* (snarls, snarling, snarled /snɑːld/)
When an animal **snarls**, it shows its teeth and makes a low angry sound: *The dogs snarled at the stranger.*

snatch /snætʃ/ *verb* (snatches, snatching, snatched /snætʃt/)
to take something with a quick rough movement ➔ SAME MEANING **grab**: *A thief snatched her handbag and ran away.*

sneak /sniːk/ *verb* (sneaks, sneaking, sneaked /sniːkt/)
to go somewhere very quietly so that nobody sees or hears you: *She sneaked out of the house without telling her parents.*

sneaker /'sniːkə(r)/ *noun* American English for TRAINER(1)

sneer /snɪə(r)/ *verb* (sneers, sneering, sneered /snɪəd/)
to speak or smile in an unkind way to show that you do not like somebody or something, or that you think they are not good enough: *I told her about my idea, but she just sneered at it.*
▶ **sneer** *noun*: *His lips curled in a sneer.*

sneeze

sneeze /sniːz/ *verb* (sneezes, sneezing, sneezed /sniːzd/)
to make air come out of your nose

and mouth with a sudden loud noise, for example because you have a cold: *Pepper makes you sneeze.*
▶ **sneeze** *noun*: *She gave a loud sneeze.*

sniff /snɪf/ *verb* (sniffs, sniffing, sniffed /snɪft/)
1 to make a noise by suddenly taking in air through your nose. People sometimes **sniff** when they have a cold or when they are crying: *I wish you'd stop sniffing!*
2 to smell something: *The dog was sniffing the meat.*
▶ **sniff** *noun*: *I heard a loud sniff.*

snob /snɒb/ *noun*
a person who likes people with a high social position and thinks they are better than other people: *Jack's such a snob – he's always going on about his rich relations.*

snooker /'snuːkə(r)/ *noun* (no plural)
a game in which two players try to hit coloured balls into pockets on the edge of a large table, using a long stick (called a **cue**) ➔ Look at Picture Dictionary page **P15**.

snooze /snuːz/ *verb* (snoozes, snoozing, snoozed /snuːzd/) (*informal*)
to sleep for a short time
▶ **snooze** *noun*: *I had a snooze after lunch.*

snore /snɔː(r)/ *verb* (snores, snoring, snored /snɔːd/)
to make a noise in your nose and throat when you are asleep: *He was snoring loudly.*

snorkel /'snɔːkl/ *noun*
a short tube that a person swimming just below the surface of the water can use to breathe through
▶ **snorkelling** (*British*) (*American* **snorkeling**) /'snɔːklɪŋ/ *noun* (no plural): *to go snorkelling* ➔ Look at the picture at **scuba-diving**.

snort /snɔːt/ *verb* (snorts, snorting, snorted)
to make a noise by blowing air through the nose: *The horse snorted.*

snow 0🔴 /snəʊ/ *noun* (no plural)

> 🔍 **PRONUNCIATION**
> The word **snow** sounds like **go**.

soft white pieces of frozen water that fall from the sky when it is very cold
▶ **snow** *verb* (snows, snowing, snowed /snəʊd/): *It often snows in Scotland in winter.* ◊ *It's snowing!* ➔ Look at Picture Dictionary page **P16**.

snowball /'snəʊbɔːl/ *noun*
a ball of snow that children throw at each other: *The kids were having a snowball fight* (= throwing snowballs at each other).

A
B
C
D
E
F
G
H
I
J
K
L
M
N
O
P
Q
R
S
T
U
V
W
X
Y
Z

snowboarding /'snəʊbɔːdɪŋ/ *noun* (*no plural*)
the sport of moving down mountains that are covered in snow using a large board that you fasten to both your feet ➷ Look at Picture Dictionary page **P15**.

snowflake /'snəʊfleɪk/ *noun*
one piece of falling snow

snowman /'snəʊmæn/ *noun* (*plural* snowmen) /'snəʊmen/
the figure of a person that children make out of snow

snowplough (*British*) (*American* snowplow) /'snəʊplaʊ/ *noun*
a large vehicle that clears snow away from roads

snowy /'snəʊi/ *adjective* (snowier, snowiest)
with a lot of snow: *snowy weather*

so[1] 0ₘ /səʊ/ *adverb*
1 a word that makes an adjective or adverb stronger, especially when this produces a particular result: *This bag is so heavy that I can't carry it.* ◊ *I'm so tired I can't keep my eyes open.* ◊ *Why are you so late?*

> 🔎 **GRAMMAR**
> **So** or **such**?
> You use **so** before an adjective that is used without a noun: *It was so cold that we stayed at home.* ◊ *This book is so exciting.*
> You use **such** before a noun that has an adjective in front of it: *It was such a cold night that we stayed at home.* ◊ *This is such an exciting book.*

3 You use 'so' instead of saying words again: *'Is John coming?' 'I think so (= I think that he is coming).'* ◊ *'I got it wrong, didn't I?' 'I'm afraid so (= you did get it wrong).'*
2 also: *Julie is a teacher and so is her husband.* ◊ *'I like this music.' 'So do I.'*

> 🔎 **GRAMMAR**
> In negative sentences, we use **neither** or **nor**: *Lydia can't swim and neither can I.* ◊ *If Alan doesn't go, nor will Lucy.*

and so on and other things like that: *The shop sells pens, paper and so on.*
not so ... as words that show how two people or things are different: *He's not so tall as his brother.*
or so words that you use to show that a number is not exactly right: *Forty or so people came to the party.*

so[2] 0ₘ /səʊ/ *conjunction*
1 because of this or that: *The shop is closed so I can't buy any bread.*

2 (*also* so that) in order that: *Speak louder so that everybody can hear you.* ◊ *I'll give you a map so you can find my house.*
so what? (*informal*) why is that important or interesting?: *'It's late.' 'So what? There's no school tomorrow.'*

soak /səʊk/ *verb* (soaks, soaking, soaked /səʊkt/)
1 to make somebody or something very wet: *Soak the plants thoroughly once a week.*
2 to be in a liquid; to let something stay in a liquid: *Leave the dishes to soak in hot water.*
soak something up to take in a liquid: *Soak the water up with a cloth.*

soaked /səʊkt/ *adjective*
very wet: *You're soaked! Come in and get dry.*

soaking /'səʊkɪŋ/ *adjective*
very wet: *This towel is soaking.*

soap 0ₘ /səʊp/ *noun* (*no plural*)

> 🔎 **PRONUNCIATION**
> The word **soap** sounds like **rope**.

a substance that you use with water for washing and cleaning: *a bar of soap* ➷ Look at the picture at **bar**.
▶ **soapy** /'səʊpi/ *adjective*: *soapy water*

soap opera /'səʊp ɒprə/ (*also informal* soap) *noun*
a story about the lives of a group of people, that is on the TV or radio every day or several times each week: *Do you watch the soaps?*

soap powder /'səʊp paʊdə(r)/ *noun* (*no plural*)
powder that you use for washing clothes

soar /sɔː(r)/ *verb* (soars, soaring, soared /sɔːd/)
1 to fly high in the sky
2 to go up very fast: *Prices are soaring.*

sob /sɒb/ *verb* (sobs, sobbing, sobbed /sɒbd/)
to cry loudly, making short sounds
▶ **sob** *noun*: *I could hear her sobs through the wall.*

sober /'səʊbə(r)/ *adjective*
not drunk

so-called /ˌsəʊ 'kɔːld/ *adjective*
a word that you use to show that you do not think another word is correct: *Her so-called friends did not help her (= they are not really her friends).*

soccer /'sɒkə(r)/ *noun* (*no plural*) another word for FOOTBALL

sociable /'səʊʃəbl/ *adjective*
friendly and enjoying being with other people

social 0—ᴑ /'səʊʃl/ *adjective*
connected with people together in society; connected with being with other people: *the social problems of big cities ◇ Anne has a busy social life* (= she goes out with friends a lot).

socialize /'səʊʃəlaɪz/ *verb* (socializes, socializing, socialized /'səʊʃəlaɪzd/)
to meet and spend time with people in a friendly way: *I enjoy socializing with friends.*

social security /,səʊʃl sɪ'kjʊərəti/ *noun* (no plural) (British)
money that a government pays to somebody who is poor, for example because they have no job

social worker /'səʊʃl wɜːkə(r)/ *noun*
a person whose job is to help people who have problems, for example because they are poor or ill

society 0—ᴑ /sə'saɪəti/ *noun*
1 (*no plural*) a large group of people who live in the same country or area and have the same ideas about how to live: *They carried out research into the roles of men and women in today's society.*
2 (*plural* societies) a group of people who are interested in the same thing: *a music society*

sock 0—ᴑ /sɒk/ *noun*
a thing that you wear on your foot, inside your shoe: *a pair of socks* ⊃ Look at Picture Dictionary page **P5**.

socket /'sɒkɪt/ *noun*
a place in a wall where you can connect electrical equipment to a power supply ⊃ Look at the picture at **plug**.

soda /'səʊdə/ (*also* soda water /'səʊdə wɔːtə(r)/) *noun* (no plural)
1 water with bubbles in it that is used for mixing with other drinks: *whisky and soda*
2 (*American*) a sweet drink with bubbles in it that is made from soda water and a fruit flavour

sofa

sofa /'səʊfə/ (*also* couch) (*British also* settee) *noun*
a long soft seat for more than one person: *Jane and Bob were sitting on the sofa.*

soft 0—ᴑ /sɒft/ *adjective* (softer, softest)
1 not hard or firm; that moves when you press it: *Warm butter is soft.* ◇ *a soft bed*
2 smooth and nice to touch; not rough: *soft skin* ◇ *My cat's fur is very soft.*
3 not bright or strong: *the soft light of a candle*
4 quiet or gentle; not loud: *soft music* ◇ *He has a very soft voice.*
5 kind and gentle; not strict: *She's too soft with her class and they don't do any work.*

soft drink /,sɒft 'drɪŋk/ *noun*
a cold sweet drink that does not have alcohol in it, for example orange juice

soften /'sɒfn/ *verb* (softens, softening, softened /'sɒfnd/)
to become softer or to make something softer: *This cream softens the skin.*

softly /'sɒftli/ *adverb*
gently or quietly: *She spoke very softly.*

software /'sɒftweə(r)/ *noun* (no plural)
programs for a computer: *There's a lot of new educational software available now.*

soggy /'sɒgi/ *adjective* (soggier, soggiest)
very wet

soil 0—ᴑ /sɔɪl/ *noun* (no plural)
what plants and trees grow in; earth

solar /'səʊlə(r)/ *adjective*
of or using the sun: *solar energy*

the solar system /ðə 'səʊlə sɪstəm/ *noun* (no plural)
the sun and the planets that move around it

sold *form of* SELL

soldier 0—ᴑ /'səʊldʒə(r)/ *noun*
a person in an army

sole¹ /səʊl/ *adjective*
only: *His sole interest is football.*

sole² /səʊl/ *noun*
1 (*plural* soles) the bottom part of your foot or of a shoe: *These boots have leather soles.* ⊃ Look at the picture at **foot**.
2 (*plural* sole) a flat sea fish that we eat

solely /'səʊlli/ *adverb*
only, and not involving anybody or anything else: *I agreed to come solely because of Frank.*

solemn /'sɒləm/ *adjective*
serious: *slow, solemn music*
▶ **solemnly** /'sɒləmli/ *adverb*: *'I've got some bad news for you,' he said solemnly.*

solicitor /sə'lɪsɪtə(r)/ *noun* (British)
a lawyer whose job is to give legal advice, prepare legal documents and arrange the buying and selling of land, etc.

solid¹ 0—ᴑ /'sɒlɪd/ *adjective*
1 hard, not like a liquid or a gas: *Water becomes solid when it freezes.*

A B C D E F G H I J K L M N O P Q R S T U V W X Y Z

2 with no empty space inside; made of the same material inside and outside: *a solid rubber ball* ◊ *This ring is solid gold.*

solid² 0̅̅ᴡ /'sɒlɪd/ *noun*
not a liquid or gas: *Milk is a liquid and cheese is a solid.*

solitary /'sɒlətri/ *adjective*
without others; alone: *She went for a long solitary walk.*

solo¹ /'səʊləʊ/ *adjective, adverb*
alone; without other people: *She flew solo across the Atlantic.*

solo² /'səʊləʊ/ *noun* (*plural* **solos**)
a piece of music for one person to sing or play: *a guitar solo*

solution 0̅̅ᴡ /sə'luːʃn/ *noun*
the answer to a question or problem: *I can't find a solution to this problem.*

solve 0̅̅ᴡ /sɒlv/ *verb* (**solves, solving, solved** /sɒlvd/)
to find the answer to a question or problem: *The police are still trying to solve the crime.*

some 0̅̅ᴡ /sʌm/ *adjective, pronoun*

> 🔎 **PRONUNCIATION**
> The word **some** sounds just like **sum**.

1 a number or an amount of something: *I bought some tomatoes and some butter.* ◊ *This cake is nice. Do you want some?*

> 🔎 **WHICH WORD?**
> **Some** or **any**?
> We use **some** in statements and in questions where we expect the answer to be 'Yes': *He gave me some good advice.* ◊ *Would you like some cake?*
> We use **any** in questions and after 'not' and 'if': *Did you buy any apples?* ◊ *I didn't buy any meat.* ◊ *If you have any questions, please ask me at the end of the lesson.*

2 part of a number or an amount of something: *Some of the children can swim, but the others can't.*
3 I do not know which: *There's some man at the door who wants to see you.*
some more a little more or a few more: *Have some more coffee.* ◊ *Some more people arrived.*
some time quite a long time: *We waited for some time but she did not come.*

somebody 0̅̅ᴡ /'sʌmbədi/ (*also* **someone**) *pronoun*
a person; a person that you do not know: *There's somebody at the door.* ◊ *Someone has broken the window.* ◊ *Ask somebody else* (= another person) *to help you.*

somehow 0̅̅ᴡ /'sʌmhaʊ/ *adverb*
in some way that you do not know: *We must find her somehow.*

someone 0̅̅ᴡ /'sʌmwʌn/ *another word for* SOMEBODY

someplace /'sʌmpleɪs/ *American English for* SOMEWHERE

somersault /'sʌməsɔːlt/ *noun*
a movement when you turn your body with your feet going over your head: *The children were doing somersaults on the carpet.*

something 0̅̅ᴡ /'sʌmθɪŋ/ *pronoun*
a thing; a thing you cannot name: *There's something under the table. What is it?* ◊ *I want to tell you something.* ◊ *Would you like something else* (= another thing) *to eat?*
something like the same as somebody or something in some ways, but not in every way: *A rat is something like a mouse, but bigger.*

sometime 0̅̅ᴡ /'sʌmtaɪm/ *adverb*
at a time that you do not know exactly: *I'll phone sometime tomorrow.*

sometimes 0̅̅ᴡ /'sʌmtaɪmz/ *adverb*
not very often: *He sometimes writes to me.* ◊ *Sometimes I drive to work and sometimes I go by bus.*

somewhere 0̅̅ᴡ /'sʌmweə(r)/ *adverb*
(*British*) (*American* **someplace**)
at, in or to a place that you do not know exactly: *They live somewhere near London.* ◊ *'Did she go to Spain last year?' 'No, I think she went somewhere else* (= to another place).'

son 0̅̅ᴡ /sʌn/ *noun*

> 🔎 **PRONUNCIATION**
> The word **son** sounds just like **sun**.

a boy or man who is somebody's child: *They have a son and two daughters.*

song 0̅̅ᴡ /sɒŋ/ *noun*
1 (*plural* **songs**) a piece of music with words that you sing: *a pop song*
2 (*no plural*) singing; music that a person or bird makes: *The story is told through song and dance.*

son-in-law /'sʌn ɪn lɔː/ *noun* (*plural* **sons-in-law**)
the husband of your daughter

soon 0̅̅ᴡ /suːn/ *adverb*
not long after now, or not long after a certain time: *John will be home soon.* ◊ *She arrived soon after two o'clock.* ◊ *Goodbye! See you soon!*

as soon as at the same time that; when: *Phone me as soon as you get home.*
sooner or later at some time in the future: *Don't worry – I'm sure he'll write to you sooner or later.*

soot /sʊt/ *noun* (no plural)
black powder that comes from smoke

soothe /suːð/ *verb* (soothes, soothing, soothed /suːðd/)
to make somebody feel calmer and less unhappy: *The baby was crying, so I tried to soothe her by singing to her.*
▸ **soothing** /'suːðɪŋ/ *adjective*: *soothing music*

sophisticated /sə'fɪstɪkeɪtɪd/ *adjective*
1 having a lot of experience of the world and social situations; knowing about things like fashion and culture: *She's a very sophisticated young woman.*
2 (used about machines, systems etc.) clever and complicated: *highly sophisticated computer systems*

sore 0̴ /sɔː(r)/ *adjective*
If a part of your body is **sore**, it gives you pain: *My feet were sore after the long walk.* ◇ *I've got a sore throat.*

sorrow /'sɒrəʊ/ *noun* (no plural)
sadness

sorry 0̴ /'sɒri/ *adjective*
1 feeling sad: *I'm sorry you can't come to the party.*
2 a word that you use when you feel bad about something you have done: *I'm sorry I didn't phone you.* ◇ *Sorry I'm late!* ◇ *I'm sorry for losing your pen.*
3 a word that you use to say 'no' politely: *I'm sorry – I can't help you.*
4 a word that you use when you did not hear what somebody said and you want them to say it again: *'My name is Linda Willis.' 'Sorry? Linda who?'*
feel sorry for somebody to feel sad because somebody has problems: *I felt sorry for her and gave her some money.*

sort¹ 0̴ /sɔːt/ *noun*
a group of things or people that are the same in some way; a type or kind: *What sort of music do you like best – pop or classical?* ◇ *We found all sorts of shells on the beach.*
sort of (informal) words that you use when you are not sure about something: *It's sort of long and thin, a bit like a sausage.*

sort² 0̴ /sɔːt/ *verb* (sorts, sorting, sorted)
to put things into groups: *The machine sorts the eggs into large ones and small ones.*

sort something out
1 (informal) to make something tidy: *I sorted out my clothes and put the old ones in a bag.*
2 to find an answer to a problem: *I haven't found a flat yet but I hope to sort something out soon.*

SOS /ˌes əʊ 'es/ *noun*
a call for help from a ship or a plane that is in danger

sought *form of* SEEK

soul /səʊl/ *noun*
1 (plural souls) the part of a person that some people believe does not die when the body dies: *Christians believe that your soul goes to heaven when you die.*
2 (also soul music /'səʊl mjuːzɪk/) (no plural) a kind of music that was made popular by African American musicians: *a soul singer*
not a soul not one person: *I looked everywhere, but there wasn't a soul in the building.*

sound¹ 0̴ /saʊnd/ *noun*
something that you hear: *I heard the sound of a baby crying.* ◇ *Light travels faster than sound.*

sound² 0̴ /saʊnd/ *verb* (sounds, sounding, sounded)
to seem a certain way when you hear it: *He sounded angry when I spoke to him on the phone.* ◇ *That sounds like a good idea.* ◇ *She told me about the book – it sounds interesting.*

sound³ /saʊnd/ *adjective*
1 right and good: *She gave me some sound advice.*
2 healthy or strong: *sound teeth*

sound⁴ /saʊnd/ *adverb*
sound asleep sleeping very well: *The children are sound asleep.*

soundly /'saʊndli/ *adverb*
completely and deeply: *I slept very soundly last night.*

soup 0̴ /suːp/ *noun* (no plural)

> 🔍 **PRONUNCIATION**
> The word **soup** sounds like **loop**.

liquid food that you make by cooking things like vegetables or meat in water: *tomato soup* ➔ Look at Picture Dictionary page **P7**.

sour /'saʊə(r)/ *adjective*
1 with a sharp taste like a lemon: *If it's too sour, put some sugar in it.*
2 **Sour** milk tastes bad because it is not fresh: *This milk has gone sour.*

source /sɔːs/ *noun*
a place where something comes from: *Our information comes from many sources.*

A B C D E F G H I J K L M N O P Q R S T U V W X Y Z

A
B
C
D
E
F
G
H
I
J
K
L
M
N
O
P
Q
R
S
T
U
V
W
X
Y
Z

south 0️⃣ /saʊθ/ *noun* (no plural) (abbr. S)
the direction that is on your right when you watch the sun come up in the morning
⊃ Look at the picture at **compass**.
▶ **south** *adjective, adverb*: *Brazil is in South America.* ◇ *the south coast of England* ◇ *Birds fly south in the winter.*

south-east /ˌsaʊθ 'iːst/ *noun* (no plural) (abbr. SE)
the direction between south and east; a place in this direction: *He lives in the south-east.* ⊃ Look at the picture at **compass**.
▶ **south-east** *adjective, adverb*: *south-east London*
▶ **south-eastern** /ˌsaʊθ 'iːstən/ *adjective*: *the south-eastern states of the US*

southern 0️⃣ /'sʌðən/ *adjective*
connected with, in or from the south: *Italy is in southern Europe.*

the South Pole /ðə ˌsaʊθ 'pəʊl/ *noun* (no plural)
the point on the Earth's surface which is furthest south ⊃ Look at the picture at **earth**.

south-west /ˌsaʊθ 'west/ *noun* (no plural) (abbr. SW)
the direction between south and west; a place in this direction: *He's from the south-west.* ⊃ Look at the picture at **compass**.
▶ **south-west** *adjective, adverb*: *Our garden faces south-west.*
▶ **south-western** /ˌsaʊθ 'westən/ *adjective*

souvenir /ˌsuːvə'nɪə(r)/ *noun*
something that you keep to remember a place or a special event: *I brought back this cowboy hat as a souvenir of Texas.*

sow /səʊ/ *verb* (sows, sowing, sowed /səʊd/, has sown /səʊn/ or has sowed)
to put seeds in the ground: *The farmer sowed the field with corn.*

space 0️⃣ /speɪs/ *noun*
1 (no plural) a place that is big enough for somebody or something to go into or onto ⊃ SAME MEANING **room**: *Is there space for me in your car?*
2 (plural spaces) an empty place between things: *a parking space* ◇ *There is a space here for you to write your name.*
3 (also outer space) (no plural) the area outside the Earth's atmosphere where all the other planets and stars are: *space travel*

spacecraft /'speɪskrɑːft/ *noun* (plural spacecraft)
a vehicle that travels in space

spaceship /'speɪsʃɪp/ *noun*
a vehicle that travels in space

space shuttle /'speɪs ʃʌtl/ (*also* shuttle) *noun*
a vehicle that can travel into space and land like a plane when it returns to Earth

spacious /'speɪʃəs/ *adjective*
with a lot of space inside: *a spacious kitchen*

spade /speɪd/ *noun*
1 a tool that you use for digging ⊃ Look at the picture at **dig**.
2 spades (*plural*) the playing cards that have the shape ♠ on them: *the queen of spades* ⊃ Look at the picture at **playing card**.

spaghetti /spə'geti/ *noun* (no plural)
a kind of food made from flour and water, that looks like long pieces of string: *Shall we have some spaghetti?* ⊃ Look at Picture Dictionary page **P7**.

spam /spæm/ *noun* (no plural) (informal)
advertisements that companies send by email to people who have not asked for them

span¹ /spæn/ *noun*
1 the length of time that something continues: *We are looking at a **time span** of several months.*
2 the length of something from one end to another: *The bird's wingspan is 60cm.*

span² /spæn/ *verb* (spans, spanning, spanned /spænd/)
1 to continue for a particular length of time: *His career spanned more than 50 years.*
2 to form a bridge over something: *The river is spanned by a beautiful iron bridge.*

spanner

spanner /'spænə(r)/ (*British*) (*American* wrench) *noun*
a tool that you use for turning small metal rings (called **nuts**) and pins (called **bolts**) that are used for holding things together

spare¹ /speə(r)/ *adjective*
1 If something is **spare**, you do not use or need it all the time: *Have you got a **spare tyre** in your car?* ◇ *You can stay with us tonight. We've got a **spare room**.*
2 **Spare** time is time when you are not working: *What do you do **in your spare time**?*

spare² /speə(r)/ *verb* (spares, sparing, spared /speəd/)
to be able to give something to somebody: *I can't spare the time to help you today.* ◇ *Can you spare any change?*

spark /spɑːk/ *noun*
a very small piece of something that is burning

sparkle /'spɑːkl/ *verb* (sparkles, sparkling, sparkled /'spɑːkld/)
to shine with a lot of very small points of light: *The sea sparkled in the sunlight.* ◇ *Her eyes sparkled with excitement.*
▸ **sparkle** *noun* (*no plural*): *the sparkle of diamonds*

sparkling /'spɑːklɪŋ/ *adjective*
1 shining with a lot of very small points of light: *sparkling blue eyes*
2 Sparkling wine or water has a lot of small bubbles in it. ➷ SAME MEANING **fizzy**

sparrow /'spærəʊ/ *noun*
a small brown bird

spat *form of* SPIT

speak 0̶ᴛ /spiːk/ *verb* (speaks, speaking, spoke /spəʊk/, has spoken /'spəʊkən/)
1 to say things; to talk to somebody: *Please speak more slowly.* ◇ *Can I speak to John Smith, please?* (= words that you say on the telephone) ◇ *The head teacher spoke for over an hour.* ➷ Look at the note at **talk**.
2 to know and use a language: *I can speak French and Italian.*
speak up to talk louder: *Can you speak up? I can't hear you!* ➷ The noun is **speech**.

speaker 0̶ᴛ /'spiːkə(r)/ *noun*
1 a person who is talking to a group of people
2 the part of something such as a radio or CD player where the sound comes out

spear /spɪə(r)/ *noun*
a long stick with a sharp point at one end, used for hunting or fighting

special 0̶ᴛ /'speʃl/ *adjective*
1 not usual or ordinary; important for a reason: *It's my birthday today so we are having a special dinner.*
2 for a particular person or thing: *He goes to a special school for deaf children.*

specialist /'speʃəlɪst/ *noun*
a person who knows a lot about something: *She's a specialist in Chinese art.*

specialize /'speʃəlaɪz/ *verb* (specializes, specializing, specialized /'speʃəlaɪzd/)
specialize in something to study or know a lot about one special thing: *He specialized in criminal law.*

specially /'speʃəli/ (*also* especially) *adverb*
1 for a particular person or thing: *I made this cake specially for you.*
2 very; more than usual or more than others ➷ SAME MEANING **particularly**: *The food was not specially good.*

species /'spiːʃiːz/ *noun* (*plural* species)
a group of animals or plants that are the same and can BREED (= make new animals or plants) together: *a rare species of frog*

specific /spə'sɪfɪk/ *adjective*
1 exact and clear: *He gave us specific instructions on how to get there.*
2 particular: *Is there anything specific that you want to talk about?*
▸ **specifically** /spə'sɪfɪkli/ *adverb*:
I specifically asked you to buy butter, not margarine.

specify /'spesɪfaɪ/ *verb* (specifies, specifying, specified /'spesɪfaɪd/)
to say something clearly or in detail: *He said he'd be arriving in the morning, but didn't specify the time.*

specimen /'spesɪmən/ *noun*
1 one example of a group of things: *specimens of different types of rock*
2 a small amount or part of something that shows what the rest is like ➷ SAME MEANING **sample**: *The doctor took a specimen of blood for testing.*

speck /spek/ *noun*
a very small bit of something: *specks of dust*

spectacles /'spektəklz/ *noun* (*plural*) (*formal*)
pieces of special glass that you wear over your eyes to help you see better
➷ SAME MEANING **glasses**: *a pair of spectacles*

spectacular /spek'tækjələ(r)/ *adjective*
wonderful to see: *There was a spectacular view from the top of the mountain.*
▸ **spectacularly** /spek'tækjələli/ *adverb*:
This is a spectacularly beautiful area.

spectator /spek'teɪtə(r)/ *noun*
a person who is watching an event, especially a sports event: *There were 2 000 spectators at the football match.*

sped *form of* SPEED²

speech 0̶ᴛ /spiːtʃ/ *noun*
1 (*plural* speeches) a talk that you give to a group of people: *The President made a speech.*
2 (*no plural*) the power to speak, or the way that you speak: *He has problems with his speech.*

speed¹ 0̶ᴛ /spiːd/ *noun*
how fast something goes: *The car was travelling at a speed of 50 miles an hour.* ◇ *a high-speed train* (= that goes very fast)

speed² /spiːd/ *verb* (speeds, speeding, sped /sped/ *or* speeded, has sped *or* has speeded)
1 to go or move very quickly: *He sped past me on his bike.*

A B C D E F G H I J K L M N O P Q R S T U V W X Y Z

2 to drive too fast: *The police stopped me because I was speeding.*
speed up, **speed something up** to go faster; to make something go faster: *What can we do to speed up the process?*

speed limit /'spiːd lɪmɪt/ *noun*
the fastest that you are allowed to travel on a road: *The speed limit on motorways is 100 kilometres an hour.*

spell¹ /spel/ *verb* (spells, spelling, spelt /spelt/ or **spelled** /speld/, has spelt or has spelled)
to use the right letters to make a word: '*How do you spell your name?*' '*A-Z-I-Z.*' ◇ *You have spelt this word wrong.*

spell² /spel/ *noun*
magic words that make somebody change or make them do what you want: *The witch cast a spell on the prince.*

spelling /'spelɪŋ/ *noun*
1 (*plural* **spellings**) the right way of writing a word: *Look in your dictionary to find the right spelling.*
2 (*no plural*) the ability to spell correctly: *You need to work on your spelling.*

spend 0→ /spend/ *verb* (spends, spending, spent /spent/, has spent)
1 to pay money for something: *Louise spends a lot of money on clothes.*
2 to pass time: *I spent the summer in Italy.* ◇ *He spent a lot of time sleeping.*

sphere /sfɪə(r)/ *noun*
any round object that is like a ball: *The earth is a sphere.*

spice 0→ /spaɪs/ *noun*
a powder of the seeds from a plant, that you can put in food to give it a stronger taste: *They use a lot of spices, such as chilli and ginger.* ➲ Look at Picture Dictionary page **P6**.
▶ **spicy** /'spaɪsi/ *adjective* (spicier, spiciest): *spicy food*

spider 0→
/'spaɪdə(r)/ *noun*
a small animal with eight legs, that catches and eats insects: *Spiders spin webs to catch flies.*

spider

web

spider

spied form of SPY²

spies
1 *plural* of SPY¹
2 form of SPY²

spike /spaɪk/ *noun*
a piece of metal with a sharp point: *The fence has spikes along the top.*

spiky /'spaɪki/
adjective (spikier, spikiest)
1 having sharp points: *spiky leaves*
2 Spiky hair sticks straight up in the air.

spiky

spiky hair

spill /spɪl/ *verb*
(spills, spilling, spilt /spɪlt/ or spilled /spɪld/, has spilt or has spilled)
If you **spill** a liquid, it flows out of something by accident: *I've spilt my coffee!*

spill

He **spilled** his milk.

spin /spɪn/ *verb* (spins, spinning, spun /spʌn/, has spun)
1 to turn round quickly; to turn something round quickly: *She spun round as he entered the room.* ◇ *Spin the wheel.*
2 to make thread from wool or cotton: *She spun and dyed the wool herself.*
3 If a spider **spins** a WEB (= a thin net that it makes to catch flies), it produces thread from its own body to make it.

spinach /'spɪnɪtʃ/ *noun* (no plural)
a vegetable with big green leaves

spine /spaɪn/ *noun*
the line of bones in your back

spiral

spiral staircase   spiral

spiral /'spaɪrəl/ *noun*
a long shape that goes round and round as it goes up: *A spring is a spiral.*
▶ **spiral** *adjective*: *a spiral staircase*

spire /'spaɪə(r)/ *noun*
a tall pointed tower on top of a church

spirit 0→ /'spɪrɪt/ *noun*
1 the part of a person that is not the body. Some people think that your **spirit** does not die when your body dies.
2 spirits (*plural*) strong alcoholic drinks such as WHISKY
3 spirits (*plural*) the way that a person feels: *She's* **in high spirits** (= happy) *today.*

spiritual /'spɪrɪtʃuəl/ *adjective*
connected with deep feelings and beliefs rather than the physical body: *Our society often neglects people's spiritual needs.*

spit /spɪt/ *verb* (spits, spitting, spat /spæt/, has spat)
to send liquid or food out from your mouth: *He spat on the ground.* ◇ *The baby spat her food* **out.**

spite 0→ /spaɪt/ *noun* (*no plural*)
when somebody deliberately says or does unkind things: *She broke my watch* **out of** *spite.*
in spite of something although something is true; not noticing or caring about something ➲ SAME MEANING **despite**: *I slept well in spite of the noise.* ◇ *In spite of the bad weather, we went out.*

spiteful /'spaɪtfl/ *adjective*
saying or doing unkind things

splash¹ /splæʃ/ *verb* (splashes, splashing, splashed /splæʃt/)
to throw drops of liquid over somebody or something; to make this happen: *The car splashed us as it drove past.* ◇ *The children were splashing around in the pool.*

splash² /splæʃ/ *noun* (*plural* splashes)
1 the sound that a person or thing makes when they fall into water: *Tom jumped into the river with a big splash.*
2 a small amount of liquid: *There were splashes of paint on the floor.*

splendid /'splendɪd/ *adjective*
very beautiful or very good: *a splendid palace* ◇ *What a splendid idea!*

splinter /'splɪntə(r)/ *noun*
a small thin sharp piece of wood, metal or glass that has broken off a bigger piece: *I've got a splinter in my finger.*

split¹ /splɪt/ *verb* (splits, splitting, split, has split)
1 to divide or separate; to make this happen: *I split the wood with an axe.* ◇ *We* **split** *the money* **between** *us.* ◇ *The teacher told us to* **split into** *groups.*
2 to tear or break apart; to make this happen: *His jeans split when he sat down.* ◇ *How did you split your lip?*
split up to stop being together: *He has split up* **with** *his girlfriend.*

split² /splɪt/ *noun*
a long cut or hole in something: *There's a big split in the tent.*

spoil 0→ /spɔɪl/ *verb* (spoils, spoiling, spoilt /spɔɪlt/ *or* spoiled /spɔɪld/, has spoilt *or* has spoiled)
1 to make something less good than before: *The mud spoiled my shoes.* ◇ *Did the bad weather spoil your holiday?*
2 to give a child too much so that they think they can always have what they want: *She spoils her grandchildren.*

spoilt /spɔɪlt/ *adjective*
(used about a child) rude and badly behaved because people give them everything they ask for: *a spoilt child*

spoke¹ *form of* SPEAK

spoke² /spəʊk/ *noun*
one of the thin bars that join the middle part of a wheel to the outside part ➲ Look at the picture at **bicycle.**

spoken 0→ *form of* SPEAK

spokesman /'spəʊksmən/ *noun* (*plural* spokesmen /'spəʊksmən/) (*also* spokeswoman /'spəʊkswʊmən/, *plural* spokeswomen /'spəʊkswɪmɪn/)
a person who tells somebody what a group of people has decided

sponge /spʌndʒ/ *noun*
1 a soft thing with a lot of small holes in it, that you use for washing yourself or cleaning things
2 (*British*) (*also* sponge cake /'spʌndʒ keɪk/) a soft light cake: *a chocolate sponge*

spongy /'spʌndʒi/ *adjective*
soft, like a SPONGE: *The ground was quite spongy.*

sponsor¹ /'spɒnsə(r)/ *noun*
1 a person or a company that gives money so that an event will take place: *The race organizers are trying to attract sponsors.*
2 a person who agrees to pay money to a charity if somebody else completes a particular activity: *I need sponsors for a bike ride to Brighton in aid of Cancer Research.*

sponsor² /'spɒnsə(r)/ *verb* (sponsors, sponsoring, sponsored /'spɒnsəd/)
1 to give money so that an event will take place: *The local football team were sponsored by a large firm.*
2 to agree to pay money to a charity if somebody else completes a particular activity: *a sponsored walk to raise money for children in need*

spoon 0→ /spuːn/ *noun*
a thing with a round end that you use for

spoons

tablespoon

soup spoon

dessertspoon teaspoon

eating, serving or mixing food: *a wooden spoon* ◇ *You need a knife, fork and spoon.*

spoonful /'spuːnfʊl/ *noun*
the amount that you can put in one spoon: *a spoonful of sugar*

sport 0─╖ /spɔːt/ *noun*
a physical game or activity that you do to keep your body strong or because you enjoy it: *Jane **does** a lot of **sport**.* ◇ *Football, swimming, and tennis are all sports.*

> 🔎 **WORD BUILDING**
>
> There are many different types of **sport**. Here are some of them: baseball, football, karate, motor racing, rugby, snowboarding. Do you know any others?

➲ Look at Picture Dictionary pages **P14–15**.

sports car /'spɔːts kɑː(r)/ *noun*
a fast car, usually with a roof that you can open

sports centre /'spɔːts sentə(r)/ *noun*
a big building where you can play a lot of different sports

sportsman /'spɔːtsmən/ *noun* (*plural* sportsmen /'spɔːtsmən/) (*also* sportswoman /'spɔːtswʊmən/, *plural* sportswomen /'spɔːtswɪmɪn/)
a person who plays sport

sporty /'spɔːti/ *adjective* (sportier, sportiest)
liking or good at sport

spot¹ 0─╖ /spɒt/ *noun*
1 a small round mark: *a red dress with white spots*
2 (*British*) a small red mark on your skin: *A lot of teenagers get spots on their faces.*
3 a place: *This is a good spot for a picnic.*

spot

spot

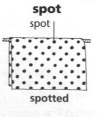

spotted

spot² /spɒt/ *verb* (spots, spotting, spotted)
to see somebody or something suddenly: *She spotted her friend in the crowd.*

spotless /'spɒtləs/ *adjective*
completely clean: *She keeps the house spotless.*

spotted /'spɒtɪd/ *adjective*
with small round marks on it: *a spotted shirt* ➲ Look at the picture at **spot**¹.

spotty /'spɒti/ *adjective* (spottier, spottiest) (*British*)
with small red marks on your skin: *He's got a very spotty face.*

spout /spaʊt/ *noun*
the narrow part of a container that you pour liquid out of ➲ Look at the picture at **teapot**.

sprain /spreɪn/ *verb* (sprains, spraining, sprained /spreɪnd/)
to hurt part of your body by turning it suddenly: *Scott fell and sprained his ankle.*

sprang *form of* SPRING²

spray¹ /spreɪ/
noun (*no plural*)
1 liquid in very small drops that flies through the air: *spray from the sea*
2 liquid in a container that comes out in very small drops when you press a button: *a can of hairspray*

spray

spray

can

spray² /spreɪ/ *verb* (sprays, spraying, sprayed /spreɪd/)
to make very small drops of liquid fall on something: *Somebody has sprayed paint on my car.*

spread 0─╖ /spred/ *verb* (spreads, spreading, spread, has spread)
1 to open something so that you can see all of it: *The bird spread its wings and flew away.* ◇ ***Spread out** the map on the table.*
2 to put a soft substance all over something: *I spread butter on the bread.*
3 to reach more people or places; to make something do this: *Fire quickly spread to other parts of the building.* ◇ *Rats spread disease.*
▶ **spread** *noun* (*no plural*): *Doctors are trying to stop the spread of the disease.*

spreadsheet /'spredʃiːt/ *noun*
(*computing*) a computer program for working with rows of numbers, used especially for doing accounts

spring¹ 0─╖ /sprɪŋ/ *noun*
1 the part of the year after winter, when

plants start to grow: *flowers that bloom in spring* ⊃ Look at Picture Dictionary page **P16**.

2 a long thin piece of metal that is bent round and round. A **spring** will go back to the same size and shape after you push or pull it.

spring

3 a place where water comes out of the ground: *a mountain spring*

spring² /sprɪŋ/ *verb* (springs, springing, sprang /spræŋ/, has sprung /sprʌŋ/)
to jump or move suddenly: *He **sprang to his feet**.* ◇ *Everyone **sprang into action**.*

spring onion /ˌsprɪŋ ˈʌnjən/ (British) (American **green onion**) *noun*
a very small onion with long leaves, often eaten raw

sprinkle /ˈsprɪŋkl/ *verb* (sprinkles, sprinkling, sprinkled /ˈsprɪŋkld/)
to shake small pieces of something or drops of a liquid on another thing: *Sprinkle some sugar on the fruit.*

sprint /sprɪnt/ *verb* (sprints, sprinting, sprinted)
to run a short distance very fast

sprout¹ /spraʊt/ *verb* (sprouts, sprouting, sprouted)
to start to grow: *New leaves are sprouting on the trees.*

sprout² /spraʊt/ *noun* = BRUSSELS SPROUT

sprung *form of* SPRING²

spun *form of* SPIN

spy¹ /spaɪ/ *noun* (*plural* spies)
a person who tries to learn secrets about another country, person or company

spy² /spaɪ/ *verb* (spies, spying, spied /spaɪd/, has spied)
to watch a country, person or company and try to learn their secrets: *He spied for his government for more than ten years.*
spy on somebody or **something** to watch somebody or something secretly: *Have you been spying on me?*

squabble /ˈskwɒbl/ *verb* (squabbles, squabbling, squabbled /ˈskwɒbld/)
to argue about something that is not important: *The children were squabbling over the last cake.* ◇ *Stop squabbling with your brother!*
▶ **squabble** *noun*: *It was a silly squabble about what game to play.*

squad /skwɒd/ *noun*
a small group of people who work together: *England's football squad* ◇ *a squad of police officers*

square¹ 0ᵀ /skweə(r)/ *adjective*

> 🔍 **PRONUNCIATION**
> The word **square** ends with the same sound as **stair**.

1 with four straight sides that are the same length: *a square table*
2 (*abbr.* sq) used for talking about the area of something: *If a room is 5 metres long and 4 metres wide, its area is 20 square metres.*
3 (used about something that is square in shape) having sides of a particular length: *The picture is twenty centimetres square* (= each side is 20cm long).

square² 0ᵀ /skweə(r)/ *noun*
1 a shape with four straight sides that are the same length ⊃ Look at the picture at **shape**.
2 an open space in a town with buildings around it: *Trafalgar Square is in London.* ◇ *the town square*
3 (maths) the number that you get when you multiply another number by itself: *Four is the **square** of two (2 × 2 = 4).*

squash¹ /skwɒʃ/ *verb* (squashes, squashing, squashed /skwɒʃt/)
1 to press something hard and make it flat: *She sat on my hat and squashed it.* ⊃ Look at the picture at **squeeze**.
2 to push a lot of people or things into a small space: *We **squashed** five people **into** the back of the car.*

squash² /skwɒʃ/ *noun* (no plural)
1 a game where two players hit a small ball against the wall in a special room: *the squash courts*
2 (British) a drink made from fruit juice and sugar. You add water before you drink it: *a glass of orange squash*

squat /skwɒt/ *verb* (squats, squatting, squatted)

squat

1 to sit with your feet on the ground, your legs bent and your bottom just above the ground: *I **squatted down** to light the fire.*
2 to live in an empty building that is not yours and that you do not pay for

A
B
C
D
E
F
G
H
I
J
K
L
M
N
O
P
Q
R
S
T
U
V
W
X
Y
Z

squatter /'skwɒtə(r)/ *noun*
a person who is living in an empty building without the owner's permission

squeak /skwiːk/ *verb* (squeaks, squeaking, squeaked /skwiːkt/)
to make a short high sound like a mouse: *The door was squeaking, so I put some oil on it.*
▶ **squeak** *noun*: *the squeak of a mouse*
▶ **squeaky** /'skwiːki/ *adjective*: *He's got a squeaky voice.*

squeal /skwiːl/ *verb* (squeals, squealing, squealed /skwiːld/)
to make a loud high sound: *The children squealed with excitement.*
▶ **squeal** *noun*: *squeals of delight*

squeeze

squeeze   crush

squash   press

squeeze /skwiːz/ *verb* (squeezes, squeezing, squeezed /skwiːzd/)
1 to press something hard: *Squeeze the lemons and add the juice to the mixture.* ◇ *She squeezed his hand.*
2 to go into a small space; to push too much into a small space: *Fifty people squeezed into the small room.* ◇ *Can you squeeze another person into your car?*
▶ **squeeze** *noun*: *She gave my arm a squeeze.*

squid /skwɪd/ *noun*
(*plural* **squid** or **squids**)
a sea animal that we eat, with a soft body and ten long parts (called **tentacles**)

squid

squirrel /'skwɪrəl/ *noun*
a small grey or brown animal with a big thick tail. **Squirrels** live in trees and eat nuts.

squirrel

squirt /skwɜːt/ *verb* (squirts, squirting, squirted)
(used about a liquid) to suddenly come out and go onto something or towards something; to make this happen: *I bit into the orange and juice squirted out.* ◇ *He squirted me with water.*

St
1 short way of writing SAINT
2 short way of writing STREET

stab /stæb/ *verb* (stabs, stabbing, stabbed /stæbd/)
to push a knife or another sharp thing into somebody or something: *He was stabbed in the back.*

stable¹ /'steɪbl/ *adjective*
not likely to move, fall or change: *Don't stand on that table – it's not very stable.*
つ OPPOSITE **unstable**

stable² /'steɪbl/ *noun*
a building where you keep horses

stack¹ /stæk/ *noun*
a lot of things on top of one another
つ SAME MEANING **pile**: *a stack of books*

stack² /stæk/ *verb* (stacks, stacking, stacked /stækt/)
to put things on top of one another: *I stacked the chairs after the concert.*

stadium /'steɪdiəm/ *noun*
a place with seats around it where you can watch sport: *a football stadium*

staff /stɑːf/ *noun* (*plural*)
the people who work in a place: *The hotel staff were very friendly.*

staffroom /'stɑːfruːm/ *noun*
a room in a school where teachers can work and rest

stage ०▬ /steɪdʒ/ *noun*
1 a certain time in a longer set of things that happen: *The first stage of the course lasts for two weeks.* ◇ *At this stage I don't know what I'll do when I leave school.*
2 the part of a theatre where the actors, dancers, etc. perform: *The audience threw flowers onto the stage.* ◇ *There were more than 50 people on stage in one scene.*

stagger /'stægə(r)/ *verb* (staggers, staggering, staggered /'stægəd/)
to walk as if you are going to fall: *He staggered across the room with the heavy box.*

stain /steɪn/ *verb* (stains, staining, stained /steɪnd/)
to leave a dirty mark that is difficult to remove on something: *The wine stained the carpet red.*

▶ **stain** *noun*: *She had **blood stains** on her shirt.*

stair 0–📐 /steə(r)/ *noun*
1 **stairs** (*plural*) steps that lead up and down inside a building: *I ran **up the stairs** to the bedroom.* ➷ Look also at **downstairs** and **upstairs**.
2 one of the steps in a set of **stairs**: *How many stairs are there up to the top floor?*

staircase

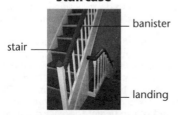

banister
stair
landing

staircase /'steəkeɪs/ (*also* **stairway**) /'steəweɪ/ *noun*
a big set of stairs

stale /steɪl/ *adjective* (**staler, stalest**)
not fresh: *stale bread ◇ stale air*

stalk /stɔːk/ *noun*
one of the long thin parts of a plant that the flowers, leaves or fruit grow on ➷ Look at the picture at **plant**.

stall /stɔːl/ *noun*
a big table with things on it that somebody wants to sell, for example in a street or market: *a fruit stall*

stammer /'stæmə(r)/ *verb* (**stammers, stammering, stammered** /'stæməd/)
to say the same sound many times when you are trying to say a word ➷ SAME MEANING **stutter**: *'B-b-b-but wait for me,' she stammered.*

stamp[1] 0–📐 /stæmp/ *noun*
1 a small piece of paper that you put on a letter to show that you have paid to send it: *Could I have three first-class stamps, please? ◇ He has been collecting stamps since he was eight.*

> 🔎 **CULTURE**
> There are two kinds of **stamp** for sending letters to other parts of Britain: **first-class stamps** and **second-class stamps**. First-class stamps are more expensive and the letters arrive more quickly.
> In Britain and the US you can buy stamps and send letters at a **post office**.

2 a small piece of wood or metal that you press on paper to make marks or words: *a date stamp*

stamp

She **stamped** her foot.

stamp[2] /stæmp/ *verb* (**stamps, stamping, stamped** /stæmpt/)
1 to put your foot down very hard: *She stamped on the spider and killed it.*
2 to walk by putting your feet down hard and loudly: *Mike stamped angrily out of the room.*
3 to press a small piece of wood or metal on paper to make marks or words: *They stamped my passport at the airport.*

stand[1] 0–📐 /stænd/ *verb* (**stands, standing, stood** /stʊd/, **has stood**)
1 to be on your feet: *She was standing by the door. ◇ **Stand still** while I take your photograph.*
2 (*also* **stand up**) to get up on your feet: *The teacher asked us all to stand up.*
3 to be in a place: *The castle stands on a hill.*
4 to put something somewhere: *I stood the ladder against the wall.*
can't stand somebody or **something**
to hate somebody or something: *I can't stand this music.*
stand by
1 to watch but not do anything: *How can you stand by while those boys kick the cat?*
2 to be ready to do something: *Stand by until I call you!*
stand by somebody to help somebody when they need it: *Julie's parents stood by her when she was in trouble.*
stand for something to be a short way of saying or writing something: *USA stands for 'the United States of America'.*
stand out to be easy to see: *Joe stands out in a crowd because of his red hair.*
stand up for somebody or **something**
to say that somebody or something is right; to support somebody or something: *Everyone else said I was wrong, but my sister stood up for me.*
stand up to somebody to argue or fight with a more powerful person who is attacking you

stand[2] 0–📐 /stænd/ *noun*
1 a table or small shop where you can buy things or get information: *a news-stand*

A
B
C
D
E
F
G
H
I
J
K
L
M
N
O
P
Q
R
S
T
U
V
W
X
Y
Z

A
B
C
D
E
F
G
H
I
J
K
L
M
N
O
P
Q
R
S
T
U
V
W
X
Y
Z

(= where you can buy newspapers and magazines)

2 a piece of furniture that you can put things on: *an umbrella stand*

3 a large structure where people can watch sport from seats arranged in rows that are low near the front and high near the back

standard¹ 0🔑 /'stændəd/ *noun*

1 how good somebody or something is: *Her work is of a very high standard.*

2 standards (*plural*) a level of behaviour that people think is acceptable: *Many people are worried about falling standards in modern society.*

standard² /'stændəd/ *adjective*

normal; not special: *Clothes are sold in standard sizes.*

standard of living /ˌstændəd əv 'lɪvɪŋ/ *noun* (*plural* standards of living)

how rich or poor you are: *They have a low standard of living* (= they are poor).

stank *form of* STINK

staple /'steɪpl/ *noun*

a small straight piece of metal that you use for fixing pieces of paper together. You press the **staples** through the paper, using a STAPLER.

▶ **staple** *verb* (staples, stapling, stapled /'steɪpld/): *Staple the pieces of paper together.*

stapler /'steɪplə(r)/ *noun*

a tool that you use for fixing pieces of paper together with metal STAPLES ⊃ Look at Picture Dictionary page **P11**.

star¹ 0🔑 /stɑː(r)/ *noun*

1 one of the small bright lights that you see in the sky at night

2 a shape with points: *a horse with a white star on its forehead* ⊃ Look at the picture at **shape**.

3 a famous person, for example an actor or a singer: *a film star*

star² 0🔑 /stɑː(r)/ *verb* (stars, starring, starred /stɑːd/)

1 to be the main actor in a play or film: *He has starred in many films.*

2 to have somebody as a star: *The film stars Julia Roberts.*

stare 0🔑 /steə(r)/ *verb* (stares, staring, stared /steəd/)

to look at somebody or something for a long time: *Everybody stared at her hat.* ◇ *He was staring out of the window.*

start¹ 0🔑 /stɑːt/ *verb* (starts, starting, started)

1 to begin to do something: *I start work at nine o'clock.* ◇ *It started raining.* ◇ *She started to cry.*

2 to begin to happen; to make something begin to happen: *The film starts at 7.30.* ◇ *The police do not know who started the fire.*

3 to begin to work or move; to make something begin to work or move: *The engine won't start.* ◇ *I can't start the car.*

start off to begin: *The teacher started off by asking us our names.*

start² 0🔑 /stɑːt/ *noun*

1 the beginning or first part of something: *She arrived after the start of the meeting.*

2 the act of starting something: *There's lots of work to do, so let's make a start.*

for a start (*informal*) words that you use when you give your first reason for something: *'Why can't we go on holiday?' 'Well, for a start, we don't have any money.'*

starter /'stɑːtə(r)/ (*British*) (*American* appetizer) *noun*

a small amount of food that you eat as the first part of a meal: *What would you like as a starter – soup or melon?*

startle /'stɑːtl/ *verb* (startles, startling, startled /'stɑːtld/)

to make somebody suddenly surprised or frightened: *You startled me when you knocked on the window.*

starve /stɑːv/ *verb* (starves, starving, starved /stɑːvd/)

to die because you do not have enough to eat: *Millions of people are starving in some parts of the world.*

be starving (*informal*) to be very hungry: *When will dinner be ready? I'm starving!*

▶ **starvation** /stɑː'veɪʃn/ *noun* (no plural): *The child died of starvation.*

state¹ 0🔑 /steɪt/ *noun*

1 how somebody or something is: *The house was in a terrible state.* ◇ *What state of mind is he in?*

2 a country and its government: *Many schools are owned by the state.*

3 (*also* State) a part of a country: *Texas is a state in the USA.*

4 the States (*plural*) (*informal*) the United States of America

state² ⚬┱ /steɪt/ *verb* (states, stating, stated)
to formally say or write something: *I stated in my letter that I was looking for a job.*

statement ⚬┱ /'steɪtmənt/ *noun*
something that you say or write, especially formally: *The driver made a statement to the police about the accident.*

station ⚬┱ /'steɪʃn/ *noun*
1 (*also* railway station) a place where trains stop so that people can get on and off
2 a place where buses or coaches start and end their journeys: *the bus station*
3 a building for some special work: *the police station* ◇ *the fire station* ◇ *a petrol station*
4 a television or radio company

stationary /'steɪʃənri/ *adjective*
not moving: *a stationary vehicle*

stationery /'steɪʃənri/ *noun* (*no plural*)
paper, pens and other things that you use for writing

station wagon /'steɪʃn wægən/
American English for ESTATE CAR

statistics /stə'tɪstɪks/ *noun* (*plural*)
numbers that give information about something: *Statistics show that women live longer than men.*

statue /'stætʃuː/ *noun*
a model of a person or an animal, made from stone or metal: *the Statue of Liberty in New York*

stay¹ ⚬┱ /steɪ/ *verb* (stays, staying, stayed /steɪd/)
1 to be in the same place and not go away: *Stay here until I come back.* ◇ *I stayed in bed until ten o'clock.*
2 to continue in the same way and not change: *I tried to stay awake.*
3 to live somewhere for a short time: *I stayed with my friend in Dublin.* ◇ *Which hotel are you staying at?*
stay behind to be somewhere after other people have gone: *The teacher asked me to stay behind after the lesson.*
stay in to be at home and not go out: *I'm staying in this evening because I'm tired.*
stay up to not go to bed: *We stayed up until after midnight.*

stay² ⚬┱ /steɪ/ *noun* (*plural* stays)
a short time when you live somewhere: *Did you enjoy your stay in London?*

steady ⚬┱ /'stedi/ *adjective* (steadier, steadiest)
1 developing or changing at a regular speed: *a steady increase*
2 not changing or stopping: *Father now had a steady job.* ◇ *His breathing was steady.*
3 not moving or shaking: *Hold the ladder steady while I stand on it.*
▶ **steadily** /'stedɪli/ *adverb*: *Prices are falling steadily.*

steak /steɪk/ *noun*
a wide flat piece of meat, especially meat from a cow (called beef): *I'd like steak and chips, please.*

steal ⚬┱ /stiːl/ *verb* (steals, stealing, stole /stəʊl/, has stolen /'stəʊlən/)
to secretly take something that is not yours: *Her money has been stolen.*

🔎 **WHICH WORD?**
A person who steals is called a **thief**. A thief **steals** things, but **robs** people and places: *They stole my camera.* ◇ *I've been robbed.* ◇ *They robbed a bank.*

steam¹ ⚬┱ /stiːm/ *noun* (*no plural*)
the gas that water becomes when it gets very hot: *There was steam coming from my coffee.*

steam² /stiːm/ *verb* (steams, steaming, steamed /stiːmd/)
1 to send out STEAM: *a steaming bowl of soup*
2 to cook something in STEAM: *steamed vegetables*

steel /stiːl/ *noun* (*no plural*)
very strong metal that is used for making things like knives, tools and machines

steep /stiːp/ *adjective* (steeper, steepest)
A **steep** hill, mountain or road goes up quickly from a low place to a high place: *I can't cycle up the hill – it's too steep.*
▶ **steeply** /'stiːpli/ *adverb*: *The path climbed steeply up the side of the mountain.*

steeple /'stiːpl/ *noun*
a tall pointed tower on a church

steer /stɪə(r)/ *verb* (steers, steering, steered /stɪəd/)
to make a car, boat, bicycle, etc. go left or right by turning a wheel or handle

steering wheel /'stɪərɪŋ wiːl/ *noun*
the wheel that you turn to make a car go left or right

stem /stem/ *noun*
the long thin part of a plant that the flowers and leaves grow on ⮕ Look at the picture at **plant**.

A B C D E F G H I J K L M N O P Q R **S** T U V W X Y Z

step[1] 0—₮ /step/ *noun*

1 a movement when you move your foot up and put it down in another place to walk, run or dance: *She took a step forward and then stopped.*

2 a place to put your foot when you go up or down: *These steps go down to the garden.*
➲ Look at Picture Dictionary page **P10**.

3 one thing in a list of things that you must do: *What is the first step in planning a holiday?*

step by step doing one thing after another; slowly: *This book shows you how to play the guitar, step by step.*

step[2] 0—₮ /step/ *verb* (steps, stepping, stepped /stept/)

to move your foot up and put it down in another place when you walk, run or dance: *You stepped on my foot!*

stepfather /'stepfɑːðə(r)/ *noun*

a man who has married your mother but who is not your father ➲ Look at the note at **stepmother**.

stepladder /'steplædə(r)/ *noun*

a type of LADDER (= a thing that helps you to climb up something) with two parts, one with steps. The parts are joined together at the top so that it can stand on its own and be folded up when you are not using it. ➲ Look at the picture at **ladder**.

stepmother /'stepmʌðə(r)/ *noun*

a woman who has married your father but who is not your mother

> 🔎 **WORD BUILDING**
>
> The child of your stepmother or stepfather is called your **stepbrother** or **stepsister**.

stereo /'steriəʊ/ *noun* (plural stereos)

a machine for playing CDs, tapes or records, with two parts (called **speakers**) where the sound comes from: *a car stereo*

▶ **stereo** *adjective*: *a stereo cassette player*

sterling /'stɜːlɪŋ/ *noun* (no plural)

the system of money that is used in Britain; the pound: *You can pay in pounds sterling or in American dollars.*

stern /stɜːn/ *adjective* (sterner, sternest)

serious and strict with people; not smiling or friendly: *a stern expression*

stew /stjuː/ *noun*

food that you make by cooking meat or vegetables in liquid for a long time: *beef stew*
➲ Look at Picture Dictionary page **P7**.

▶ **stew** *verb* (stews, stewing, stewed /stjuːd/): *stewed fruit*

steward /'stjuːəd/ *noun*

a man whose job is to look after people on a

plane or a ship ➲ SAME MEANING **flight attendant**

stewardess /ˌstjuːəˈdes/ *noun* (plural stewardesses)

a woman whose job is to look after people on a plane or a ship ➲ SAME MEANING **air hostess**, **flight attendant**

stick[1] 0—₮ /stɪk/ *verb* (sticks, sticking, stuck /stʌk/, has stuck)

1 to push a pointed thing into something: *Stick a fork into the meat to see if it's cooked.*

2 to join something to something else with a sticky substance; to become joined in this way: *I stuck a stamp on the envelope.*

3 to be fixed in one place; to not be able to move: *This door always sticks.*

4 (*informal*) to put something somewhere: *Stick that box on the floor.*

stick out to come out of the side or top of something so that you can see it easily: *The boy's head was sticking out of the window.*

stick something out to push something out: *Don't stick your tongue out!*

stick to something to continue with something and not change it: *We're sticking to Peter's plan.*

stick up for somebody or **something** to say that somebody or something is right: *Everyone else said I was wrong, but Kim stuck up for me.*

stick[2] 0—₮ /stɪk/ *noun*

1 a long thin piece of wood: *We found some sticks and made a fire.*

2 (*British*) = WALKING STICK: *The old man walked with a stick.*

3 a long thin object that is used in some sports to hit or control the ball: *a hockey stick*

4 a long thin piece of something: *a stick of chalk*

sticker /'stɪkə(r)/ *noun*

a small piece of paper with a picture or words on it, that you can stick onto things

sticky 0—₮ /'stɪki/ *adjective* (stickier, stickiest)

able to stick to things; covered with a substance that can stick to things: *Glue is sticky.* ◇ *sticky fingers*

stiff /stɪf/ *adjective* (stiffer, stiffest)

not easy to bend or move: *stiff cardboard*

still[1] 0—₮ /stɪl/ *adverb*

1 a word that you use to show that something has not changed: *Do you still live in London?* ◇ *Is it still raining?*

2 although that is true: *She felt ill, but she still went to the party.*

3 a word that you use to make another word

stronger: *It was cold yesterday, but today it's colder still.*

still² 0̶ᴡ /stɪl/ *adjective*
1 without moving: *Please **stand still** while I take a photo.* ◇ *The water was perfectly still.*
2 (*British*) (used about a drink) not containing any bubbles or gas: *still mineral water* ➋ OPPOSITE **fizzy, sparkling**
▸ **stillness** /'stɪlnəs/ *noun* (*no plural*): *the stillness of the night*

sting¹ /stɪŋ/ *verb* (stings, stinging, stung /stʌŋ/, has stung)
1 If an insect or a plant **stings** you, it hurts you by pushing a small sharp part into your skin: *I've been stung by a bee!*
2 to feel a sudden sharp pain: *The smoke made my eyes sting.*

sting² /stɪŋ/ *noun*
1 the sharp part of some insects, that can hurt you: *A wasp's sting is in its tail.* ➋ Look at the picture at **scorpion**.
2 a hurt place on your skin where an insect or a plant has **stung** you: *a bee sting*

stink¹ /stɪŋk/ *verb* (stinks, stinking, stank /stæŋk/, has stunk /stʌŋk/) (*informal*)
to have a very bad smell: *That fish stinks!*

stink² /stɪŋk/ *noun* (*informal*)
a very bad smell: *What a terrible stink!*

stir /stɜː(r)/ *verb* (stirs, stirring, stirred /stɜːd/)
1 to move a spoon or another thing round and round to mix something: *He put sugar in his coffee and stirred it.*
2 to move a little; to make something move a little: *The wind stirred the leaves.*

stitch¹ /stɪtʃ/ *noun* (*plural* stitches)
1 a small line or circle of thread that joins or decorates cloth ➋ Look at the picture at **embroidery**.
2 a circle of wool that you put round a needle when you are KNITTING (= making clothes from wool) ➋ Look at the picture at **knit**.
3 a short piece of special thread that doctors use to sew the edges of a cut together: *The cut needed eight stitches.*

stitch² /stɪtʃ/ *verb* (stitches, stitching, stitched /stɪtʃt/)
to sew something: *I stitched a button on my skirt.*

stock¹ /stɒk/ *noun*
1 things that a shop keeps ready to sell: *We have a large stock of tables and chairs.* ◇ *I'll see if we have your size **in stock**.* ◇ *I'm afraid that book's **out of stock** at the moment.*
2 (*business*) a share in a company or business that somebody has bought, or the

value of those shares: *stocks and shares*
➋ Look at **stock exchange**.

stock² /stɒk/ *verb* (stocks, stocking, stocked /stɒkt/)
to keep something ready to sell: *I'm afraid we don't stock umbrellas.*

stockbroker /'stɒkbrəʊkə(r)/ *noun*
(*business*) a person whose job is to buy and sell shares in companies for other people

stock exchange /'stɒk ɪkstʃeɪndʒ/ (*also* stock market /'stɒk mɑːkɪt/) *noun* (*no plural*)
(*business*) a place where people buy and sell shares in companies; the business of doing this: *the London Stock Exchange* ◇ *to lose money on the stock market*

stocking /'stɒkɪŋ/ *noun*
a long thin thing that a woman wears over her leg and foot: *a pair of stockings*

stole, stolen *forms of* STEAL

stomach 0̶ᴡ /'stʌmək/ *noun*
1 the part inside your body where food goes after you eat it ➋ Look at Picture Dictionary page **P4**.
2 the front part of your body below your chest and above your legs

stomach ache /'stʌmək eɪk/ *noun* (*no plural*)
a pain in your stomach: *I've got stomach ache.*

stone 0̶ᴡ /stəʊn/ *noun*
1 (*no plural*) the very hard material that is in the ground. **Stone** is sometimes used for building: *a stone wall*
2 (*plural* stones) a small piece of **stone**: *The children were throwing stones into the river.*
3 (*plural* stones) the hard part in the middle of some types of fruit: *Peaches, plums, cherries and olives all have stones.* ➋ Look at Picture Dictionary page **P8**.
4 (*plural* stones) a small piece of beautiful rock that is very valuable: *A diamond is a precious stone.*
5 (*plural* stone) (*British*) a measure of weight equal to 6.35 kg. There are 14 **pounds** in a **stone**: *I weigh ten stone.* ➋ Look at the note at **pound**.

stony /'stəʊni/ *adjective* (stonier, stoniest)
containing a lot of stones; covered with a lot of stones: *stony ground*

stood *form of* STAND¹

stool /stuːl/ *noun*
a small seat with no back ➋ Look at the picture at **bar¹**.

A
B
C
D
E
F
G
H
I
J
K
L
M
N
O
P
Q
R
S
T
U
V
W
X
Y
Z

stoop /stuːp/ *verb* (stoops, stooping, stooped /stuːpt/)
If you **stoop**, you bend your body forward and down: *She stooped to pick up the baby.*

stop¹ 0̅ /stɒp/ *verb* (stops, stopping, stopped /stɒpt/)
1 to finish moving or working; to become still: *The train stopped at every station.* ◇ *The clock has stopped.* ◇ *I stopped to post a letter.*
2 to not do something any more; to finish: *Stop making that noise!*
3 to make somebody or something finish moving or doing something: *Ring the bell to stop the bus.*
stop somebody (from) doing something to not let somebody do something: *My dad stopped me from going out.*

stop² 0̅ /stɒp/ *noun*
1 the moment when somebody or something finishes moving: *The train came to a stop.*
2 a place where buses or trains stop so that people can get on and off: *I'm getting off at the next stop.*
put a stop to something to make something finish: *A teacher put a stop to the fight.*

store¹ 0̅ /stɔː(r)/ *noun*
1 a big shop that sells many different types of things: *Harrods is a famous London store.*
2 (*American*) a shop, large or small: *a health food store*
3 things that you are keeping to use later: *a secret store of food*

store² 0̅ /stɔː(r)/ *verb* (stores, storing, stored /stɔːd/)
to keep something to use later: *The information is stored on a computer.*

storekeeper /ˈstɔːkiːpə(r)/ *American English for* SHOPKEEPER

storey (*British*) (*American* **story**) /ˈstɔːri/ *noun* (*British plural* **storeys**) (*American plural* **stories**)
one level in a building: *The building has four storeys.*

storm¹ 0̅ /stɔːm/ *noun*
very bad weather with strong winds and rain: *a thunderstorm*

> 🔎 **WORD BUILDING**
>
> When there is a storm, you hear **thunder** and see **lightning** in the sky. **Cyclones**, **hurricanes**, **tornadoes** and **typhoons** are large violent storms.

⊃ Look at Picture Dictionary page **P16**.

storm² /stɔːm/ *verb* (storms, storming, stormed /stɔːmd/)
to move in a way that shows you are angry: *He stormed out of the room.*

stormy /ˈstɔːmi/ *adjective* (stormier, stormiest)
with strong wind and rain: *a stormy night*

story 0̅ /ˈstɔːri/ *noun* (*plural* **stories**)
1 words that tell you about people and things that are not real: *Hans Christian Andersen wrote stories for children.* ◇ *a ghost story*
2 words that tell you about things that really happened: *My grandmother told me stories about when I was a child.*
3 *American English for* STOREY

stove /stəʊv/ *noun*
1 a closed metal box in which you burn wood and coal to heat a room: *a wood-burning stove*
2 *American English for* COOKER

straight¹ 0̅ /streɪt/ *adverb*
1 in a straight line: *Look straight in front of you.* ◇ *Go straight on until you come to the bank, then turn left.*
2 without stopping or doing anything else; directly: *Come straight home.* ◇ *She walked straight past me.*
straight away immediately; now: *I'll do it straight away.*

straight

straight   crooked

straight² 0̅ /streɪt/ *adjective* (straighter, straightest)
1 with no curve or bend: *Use a ruler to draw a straight line.* ◇ *His hair is curly and mine is straight.* ⊃ Look at the picture at **hair**.
2 with one side as high as the other: *This picture isn't straight.*
3 honest and direct: *a straight answer to a straight question*
get something straight to make sure that you understand something completely: *Let's get this straight. Are you sure you left your bike by the cinema?*

straighten /ˈstreɪtn/ *verb* (straightens, straightening, straightened /ˈstreɪtnd/)
to become or to make something straight

straightforward /ˌstreɪtˈfɔːwəd/
adjective
easy to understand or do: *a straightforward question*

strain¹ /streɪn/ *noun*
1 physical force: *The rope broke **under the strain**.*
2 worry; problems caused by worry: *His illness **put** a great **strain on** their marriage.*
3 an injury to part of your body, caused by making it work too hard: *back strain*

strain² /streɪn/ *verb* (strains, straining, strained /streɪnd/)
1 to try very hard: *Her voice was so quiet that I had to strain to hear her.*
2 to hurt a part of your body by making it work too hard: *Don't read in the dark. You'll strain your eyes.*
3 to pour a liquid through something with small holes in it, to remove any solid bits

strand /strænd/ *noun*
one piece of thread or hair

stranded /ˈstrændɪd/ *adjective*
left in a place that you cannot get away from: *The car broke down and I was stranded on a lonely road.*

strange 0̱⊸ /streɪndʒ/ *adjective* (stranger, strangest)
1 unusual or surprising: *Did you hear that strange noise?*
2 that you do not know: *We were lost in a strange town.*

> 🔎 **WHICH WORD?**
>
> Be careful! We use **foreign**, not **strange**, to talk about a person or thing that comes from another country.

strangely /ˈstreɪndʒli/ *adverb*
in a surprising or an unusual way: *He was acting very strangely.* ◇ *She was strangely quiet.*

stranger /ˈstreɪndʒə(r)/ *noun*
1 a person who you do not know
2 a person who is in a place that they do not know: *I'm a stranger to this city.*

> 🔎 **WHICH WORD?**
>
> Be careful! We use the word **foreigner**, not **stranger**, for a person who comes from another country.

strangle /ˈstræŋgl/ *verb* (strangles, strangling, strangled /ˈstræŋgld/)
to kill somebody by pressing their neck very tightly

strap¹ /stræp/ *noun*
a long flat piece of material that you use for carrying something or for keeping

something in place: *a leather watch strap*
⊃ Look at the picture at **purse**.

strap² /stræp/ *verb* (straps, strapping, strapped /stræpt/)
to hold something in place with a STRAP: *I strapped the bag onto the back of my bike.*

strategy /ˈstrætədʒi/ *noun* (plural strategies)
a plan; planning: *What's your **strategy for** passing the exam?*

straw /strɔː/ *noun*
1 (*no plural*) dried plants that animals sleep on or that people use for making things like hats and floor coverings: *a straw hat*
2 (*plural* straws) a thin paper or plastic tube that you can drink through
the last straw, the final straw the last of several bad things; the thing that finally makes a situation impossible for you

strawberry /ˈstrɔːbəri/ *noun* (plural strawberries)
a soft red fruit with seeds near the surface
⊃ Look at Picture Dictionary page **P8**.

stray /streɪ/ *adjective*
A **stray** animal is lost or does not have a home: *a stray dog*
▶ **stray** *noun* (plural strays) an animal that has no home

streak /striːk/ *noun*
a long thin line that is a different colour from the surface it is on: *She's got **streaks of** grey in her hair.* ◇ *a **streak of** lightning*

stream¹ /striːm/ *noun*
1 a small river: *a mountain stream*
2 moving liquid, or moving things or people: *a **stream of** blood* ◇ *I've had a **steady stream of** visitors.*

stream² /striːm/ *verb* (streams, streaming, streamed /striːmd/)
to move like water: *Tears were **streaming down** his face.*

streamline /ˈstriːmlaɪn/ *verb* (streamlines, streamlining, streamlined /ˈstriːmlaɪnd/)
1 to give something like a car or boat a long smooth shape so that it can go fast through air or water
2 to make an organization or a way of doing things work better by making it simpler

street 0̱⊸ /striːt/ *noun* (abbr. St)
a road in a city, town or village with buildings along the sides: *I saw Anna walking down the street.* ◇ *I live in Hertford Street.* ◇ *91 Oxford St, London*

streetcar /ˈstriːtkɑː(r)/ *noun* American English for TRAM

street light /ˈstriːt laɪt/ *noun*
a light on a tall post in the street

strength 0️⃣ /streŋθ/ *noun* (no plural)
how strong or powerful you are: *I don't have the strength to lift this box – it's too heavy.*

strengthen /ˈstreŋθn/ *verb* (strengthens, strengthening, strengthened /ˈstreŋθnd/)
to become or to make somebody or something stronger: *The wind had strengthened overnight.*

stress¹ /stres/ *noun* (no plural)
1 a feeling of worry because of problems in your life: *Mum's been suffering from stress since Dad's been ill.*
2 saying one word or part of a word more strongly than another: *In the word 'dictionary', the stress is on the first part of the word.*

stress² /stres/ *verb* (stresses, stressing, stressed /strest/)
1 to say something strongly to show that it is important: *I must stress how important this meeting is.*
2 to say one word or part of a word more strongly than another: *You should stress the first part of the word 'happy'.*

stressful /ˈstresfl/ *adjective*
causing a lot of worry: *a stressful job*

stretch¹ 0️⃣ /stretʃ/ *verb* (stretches, stretching, stretched /stretʃt/)
1 to pull something to make it longer or wider; to become longer or wider: *The T-shirt stretched when I washed it.*
2 to push your arms and legs out as far as you can: *Joe got out of bed and stretched.* ◇ *The cat stretched out in front of the fire and went to sleep.*
3 to cover a large area of land or a long period of time: *The beach stretches for miles.*

stretch² /stretʃ/ *noun* (plural stretches)
a piece of land or water: *This is a beautiful stretch of countryside.*

stretcher /ˈstretʃə(r)/ *noun*
a kind of bed for carrying somebody who is ill or hurt: *They carried him to the ambulance on a stretcher.*

strict 0️⃣ /strɪkt/ *adjective* (stricter, strictest)
If you are **strict**, you make people do what you want and do not allow them to behave badly: *Her parents are very strict – she always has to be home before ten o'clock.* ◇ *strict rules*

strictly /ˈstrɪktli/ *adverb*
1 definitely; in a strict way: *Smoking is strictly forbidden.*
2 exactly: *That is not strictly true.*

stride /straɪd/ *verb* (strides, striding, strode /strəʊd/)
to walk with long steps: *The police officer strode across the road.*
▸ **stride** *noun*: *He walked with long strides.*

strike¹ /straɪk/ *verb* (strikes, striking, struck /strʌk/, has struck)
1 (formal) to hit somebody or something: *A stone struck me on the back of the head.*

🔍 **SPEAKING**

Hit is the more usual word, but when you talk about **lightning** (= the flashes of light that you see in the sky when there is a storm), you always use **strike**: *The tree was struck by lightning.*

2 to stop working because you want more money or are angry about something: *The nurses are striking for better pay.*
3 to come suddenly into your mind: *It suddenly struck me that she looked like my sister.*
4 If a clock **strikes**, it rings a bell a certain number of times so that people know what time it is: *The clock struck nine.*
strike a match to make fire with a match

strike² /straɪk/ *noun*
a time when people are not working because they want more money or are angry about something: *There are no trains today because the drivers are on strike.*

striking /ˈstraɪkɪŋ/ *adjective*
If something is **striking**, you notice it because it is very unusual or interesting: *That's a very striking hat.*

string 0️⃣ /strɪŋ/ *noun*

string

1 very thin rope that you use for tying things: *I tied up the parcel with string.* ◇ *The key was hanging on a string.*
2 a line of things on a piece of thread: *a string of blue beads*
3 a piece of thin wire on a musical instrument: *guitar strings*

strip¹ /strɪp/ *verb* (strips, stripping, stripped /strɪpt/)
1 (also **strip off**) to take off your clothes; to take off another person's clothes: *She stripped off and ran into the sea.* ◇ *They were stripped and searched by the police officers.*
2 to take off something that is covering

something: *I stripped the wallpaper off the walls.*

strip² /strɪp/ *noun*
a long thin piece of something: *a strip of paper*

stripe /straɪp/
noun
a long thin line of colour: *Zebras have black and white stripes.*
▶ **striped** /straɪpt/ *adjective*: *He wore a blue and white striped shirt.*

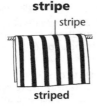

stripe

| stripe

striped

strode *form of* STRIDE

stroke¹ /strəʊk/ *noun*
1 a movement that you make with your arms, for example when you are swimming or playing sports such as TENNIS
2 a sudden serious illness when the brain stops working properly: *He had a stroke.*
3 a sudden successful action or event: *It was a stroke of luck finding your ring again so quickly.*
4 a gentle movement of your hand over a surface: *He gave the cat a stroke.*

stroke

pat

stroke² /strəʊk/ *verb* (**strokes, stroking, stroked** /strəʊkt/)
to move your hand gently over somebody or something to show love: *She stroked his hair.*

stroll /strəʊl/ *verb* (**strolls, strolling, strolled** /strəʊld/)
to walk somewhere in a slow relaxed way: *We strolled along the beach.*
▶ **stroll** *noun*: *We went for a stroll by the river.*

stroller /ˈstrəʊlə(r)/ *noun* American English for PUSHCHAIR

strong 0̶ᴡ /strɒŋ/ *adjective* (**stronger, strongest**)
1 A **strong** person has a powerful body, and

can carry heavy things: *I need somebody strong to help me move this piano.*
2 A **strong** object does not break easily: *Don't stand on that chair – it's not very strong.*
3 A **strong** opinion or belief is not easy to change: *There was strong opposition to the plan.*
4 powerful: *strong winds* ◇ *The current was very strong.*
5 having a big effect on the mind or the body: *I like strong tea* (= with not much milk in it). ◇ *a strong smell of oranges*
▶ **strongly** /ˈstrɒŋli/ *adverb*: *I strongly believe that he is wrong.*

struck *form of* STRIKE¹

structure 0̶ᴡ /ˈstrʌktʃə(r)/ *noun*
1 (*no plural*) the way that something is made: *We are studying the structure of a bird's wing.*
2 (*plural* **structures**) a building or another thing that people have made with many parts: *The new post office is a tall glass and brick structure.*

struggle /ˈstrʌɡl/ *verb* (**struggles, struggling, struggled** /ˈstrʌɡld/)
1 to try very hard to do something that is not easy: *We struggled to lift the heavy box.*
2 to move your arms and legs a lot when you are fighting or trying to get free: *She struggled with her attacker.*
▶ **struggle** *noun*: *In 1862 the American slaves won their struggle for freedom.*

stubborn /ˈstʌbən/ *adjective*
A **stubborn** person does not change their ideas easily or do what other people want them to do. ⊃ SAME MEANING **obstinate**: *She's too stubborn to say sorry.*
▶ **stubbornly** /ˈstʌbənli/ *adverb*: *He stubbornly refused to apologize.*

stuck¹ *form of* STICK¹

stuck² /stʌk/ *adjective*
1 not able to move: *This drawer is stuck – I can't open it.* ◇ *I was stuck in Italy with no money.*
2 not able to do something because it is difficult: *If you get stuck, ask your teacher for help.*

student 0̶ᴡ /ˈstjuːdnt/ *noun*
a person who is studying at a school, college or university: *Tim is a history student.*

> 🔎 **WHICH WORD?**
>
> **Student** or **pupil**?
> We usually say **student**. We often say **pupil** when talking about children at school.

studio /'stju:diəʊ/ *noun* (*plural* studios)
1 a room where an artist works
2 a room where people make films, radio and television programmes or records: *a television studio*

study¹ 0— /'stʌdi/ *noun* (*plural* studies)
1 the activity of learning about something: *He's doing a course in Business Studies.* ◇ *Biology is the study of living things.*
2 a room in a house where you go to study, read or write

study² 0— /'stʌdi/ *verb* (studies, studying, studied /'stʌdid/, has studied)
1 to spend time learning about something: *He studied French at university.*
2 to look at something carefully: *We must study the map before we leave.*

stuff¹ 0— /stʌf/ *noun* (no plural) (*informal*)
any material, substance or group of things: *What's this blue stuff on the carpet?* ◇ *Put your stuff in this bag.*

stuff² /stʌf/ *verb* (stuffs, stuffing, stuffed /stʌft/)
1 to fill something with something: *The pillow was stuffed with feathers.*
2 (*informal*) to push something quickly into another thing: *He took the money quickly and stuffed it into his pocket.*

stuffy /'stʌfi/ *adjective* (stuffier, stuffiest)
If a room is **stuffy**, it has no fresh air in it: *Open the window – it's very stuffy in here.*

stumble /'stʌmbl/ *verb* (stumbles, stumbling, stumbled /'stʌmbld/)
to hit your foot against something when you are walking or running, and almost fall: *The old lady stumbled as she was going upstairs.*

stump /stʌmp/ *noun*
the small part that is left when something is cut off or broken: *a tree stump*

stun /stʌn/ *verb* (stuns, stunning, stunned /stʌnd/)
1 to hit a person or an animal on the head so hard that they cannot see, think or make a sound for a short time
2 to make somebody very surprised: *His sudden death stunned his family and friends.*

stung form of STING¹

stunk form of STINK¹

stunning /'stʌnɪŋ/ *adjective*
very beautiful; wonderful: *a stunning dress* ◇ *a stunning victory*

stunt /stʌnt/ *noun*
something dangerous or difficult that a person does, especially as part of a film: *James Bond films are full of exciting stunts.*

stupid 0— /'stju:pɪd/ *adjective*
not intelligent; silly: *Don't be so stupid!* ◇ *What a stupid question!*
▶ **stupidity** /stju:'pɪdəti/ *noun* (no plural): *There are no limits to his stupidity!*
▶ **stupidly** /'stju:pɪdli/ *adverb*: *I stupidly forgot to close the door.*

sturdy /'stɜːdi/ *adjective* (sturdier, sturdiest)
strong and healthy; not easy to break: *sturdy legs* ◇ *sturdy shoes*

stutter /'stʌtə(r)/ *verb* (stutters, stuttering, stuttered /'stʌtəd/)
to say the same sound many times when you are trying to say a word ⊃ SAME MEANING **stammer**: '*I d-d-don't understand,*' he stuttered.

sty /staɪ/ *noun* (*plural* sties) = PIGSTY

style 0— /staɪl/ *noun*
1 a way of doing, making or saying something: *I don't like his style of writing.*
2 the shape or kind of something: *This shop has all the latest styles.* ◇ *a new hairstyle*

stylish /'staɪlɪʃ/ *adjective*
fashionable and attractive: *Jane's very stylish.*

subject 0— /'sʌbdʒɪkt/ *noun*
1 the person or thing that you are talking or writing about: *What is the subject of the talk?*
2 something you study at school, university or college: *I'm studying three subjects: Maths, Physics and Chemistry.*
3 (*grammar*) the word in a sentence that does the action of the verb: *In the sentence 'Sue ate the cake', 'Sue' is the subject.* ⊃ Look at **object**.
4 a person who belongs to a certain country: *British subjects*

submarine /ˌsʌbmə'riːn/ *noun*
a ship that can travel underwater

subscription /səb'skrɪpʃn/ *noun*
money that you pay, for example to get the same magazine each month or to join a club: *I've got a subscription to 'Vogue' magazine.*

substance 0— /'sʌbstəns/ *noun*
any solid, liquid or gas: *Stone is a hard substance.* ◇ *chemical substances*

substitute /'sʌbstɪtjuːt/ *noun*
a person or thing that you put in the place of another: *One player was injured, so a substitute came on.*
▶ **substitute** *verb* (substitutes, substituting, substituted): *You can substitute margarine for butter.*

subtitles /'sʌbtaɪtlz/ *noun* (*plural*)
words at the bottom of a film or TV

programme that tell you what people are saying: *It was a French film with English subtitles.*

subtle /'sʌtl/ *adjective*
not large, bright or easy to notice: *subtle colours* ◇ *There has been a subtle change in her behaviour.*

subtract /səb'trækt/ *verb* (subtracts, subtracting, subtracted)
to take a number away from another number ⊃ SAME MEANING **take away**: *If you subtract 6 from 9, you get 3.*
⊃ OPPOSITE **add**
▶ **subtraction** /səb'trækʃn/ *noun*: *The children are learning how to do subtraction.*
⊃ Look at **addition**.

suburb /'sʌbɜːb/ *noun*
one of the parts of a town or city outside the centre: *We live in the suburbs.*
▶ **suburban** /sə'bɜːbən/ *adjective*: *suburban areas*

subway /'sʌbweɪ/ *noun* (plural subways)
1 *American English for* UNDERGROUND²: *the New York subway* ◇ *a subway station*
2 (*British*) a path that goes under a busy road, so that people can cross safely

succeed 0—ₐ /sək'siːd/ *verb* (succeeds, succeeding, succeeded)
to do or get what you wanted to do or get: *She finally succeeded in getting a job.* ◇ *I tried to get a ticket for the concert but I didn't succeed.* ⊃ OPPOSITE **fail**

success 0—ₐ /sək'ses/ *noun*
1 (*no plural*) doing or getting what you wanted; doing well: *I wish you success with your studies.*
2 (*plural* successes) somebody or something that does well or that people like a lot: *The film 'The Matrix' was a great success.*
⊃ OPPOSITE **failure**

successful 0—ₐ /sək'sesfl/ *adjective*

🔎 SPELLING
Remember! You spell **successful** with **CC** and **SS**.

If you are **successful**, you have got or done what you wanted, or you have become popular, rich, etc.: *a successful actor* ◇ *The party was very successful.*
⊃ OPPOSITE **unsuccessful**
▶ **successfully** /sək'sesfəli/ *adverb*: *He completed his studies successfully.*

such 0—ₐ /sʌtʃ/ *adjective*
1 a word that makes another word stronger: *He wears such strange clothes.* ◇ *It was such a*

nice day that we decided to go to the beach.
⊃ Look at the note at **so¹**.
2 like this or that: '*Can I speak to Mrs Graham?*' '*I'm sorry. There's no such person here.*'
such as words that you use to give an example ⊃ SAME MEANING **like**: *Sweet foods such as chocolate can make you fat.*

suck 0—ₐ /sʌk/ *verb* (sucks, sucking, sucked /sʌkt/)
1 to pull something into your mouth, using your lips: *The baby sucked milk from its bottle.*
2 to hold something in your mouth and touch it a lot with your tongue: *She was sucking a sweet.*

sudden 0—ₐ /'sʌdn/ *adjective*
happening quickly when you do not expect it: *His death was very sudden.* ◇ *a sudden change in the weather*
all of a sudden suddenly: *We were watching TV when all of a sudden the lights went out.*

suddenly 0—ₐ /'sʌdənli/ *adverb*
quickly and unexpectedly: *He left very suddenly.* ◇ *Suddenly there was a loud noise.*

sue /suː/ *verb* (sues, suing, sued /suːd/)
to go to a court of law and ask for money from a person who has done something bad to you: *She sued the company for loss of earnings.*

suede /sweɪd/ *noun* (no plural)
a type of soft leather with a rough surface: *suede boots*

suffer 0—ₐ /'sʌfə(r)/ *verb* (suffers, suffering, suffered /'sʌfəd/)
to feel pain, sadness or another unpleasant feeling: *She suffers from bad headaches.* ◇ *It's not right for children to suffer.*
▶ **suffering** /'sʌfərɪŋ/ *noun* (no plural): *They have experienced so much suffering.*

sufficient /sə'fɪʃnt/ *adjective* (formal)
as much or as many as you need or want
⊃ SAME MEANING **enough**: *There was sufficient food to last two weeks.*

suffix /'sʌfɪks/ *noun* (plural suffixes)
letters that you add to the end of a word to make another word: *If you add the suffix '-ly' to the adjective 'quick', you make the adverb 'quickly'.* ⊃ Look at **prefix**.

suffocate /'sʌfəkeɪt/ *verb* (suffocates, suffocating, suffocated)
to die or to make somebody die because there is no air to breathe

sugar 0—ₐ /'ʃʊɡə(r)/ *noun*
1 (*no plural*) a sweet substance that comes

A

from certain plants: *Do you take sugar in your coffee?*

2 (*plural* sugars) the amount of **sugar** that a small spoon can hold: *Two sugars, please.*

B

suggest 0⊸ /sə'dʒest/ *verb* (suggests, suggesting, suggested)
to say what you think somebody should do or what should happen: *I suggest that you stay here tonight.* ◇ *Simon suggested going for a walk.* ◇ *What do you suggest?*

C

D

E

suggestion 0⊸ /sə'dʒestʃən/ *noun*
a plan or an idea that somebody thinks of for somebody else to discuss and consider: *I don't know what to buy Alison for her birthday. Have you got any suggestions?* ◇ *May I make a suggestion?*

F

G

H

suicide /'su:ɪsaɪd/ *noun*
the act of killing yourself: *He committed suicide at the age of 23.*

I

J

suit¹ 0⊸ /su:t/ *noun*

K

L

1 a jacket and trousers, or a jacket and skirt, that you wear together and that are made from the same material ⊃ Look at Picture Dictionary page **P5**.
2 one of the 4 sets that PLAYING CARDS (= cards with numbers and pictures on them that you use for playing games) are divided into: *The four suits are hearts, clubs, diamonds and spades.* ⊃ Look at the picture at **playing card**.

M

N

O

P

suit² 0⊸ /su:t/ *verb* (suits, suiting, suited)
1 If something **suits** you, it looks good on you: *Does this hat suit me?*
2 to be right for you; to be what you want or need: *Would it suit you if I came at five o'clock?*

Q

R

S

suitable 0⊸ /'su:təbl/ *adjective*
right for somebody or something: *This film isn't suitable for children.*
⊃ OPPOSITE **unsuitable**
▶ **suitably** /'su:təbli/ *adverb*: *Tony wasn't suitably dressed for a party.*

T

U

V

suitcase 0⊸
/'su:tkeɪs/ *noun*
a large bag with flat sides that you carry your clothes in when you travel

W

suitcase

X

Y

sulfur *noun American English for* SULPHUR

Z

sulk /sʌlk/ *verb* (sulks, sulking, sulked /sʌlkt/)

to not speak because you are angry about something: *She's been sulking all day because her mum wouldn't let her go to the party.*
▶ **sulky** /'sʌlki/ *adjective* (sulkier, sulkiest): *I can't stand sulky teenagers.*

sullen /'sʌlən/ *adjective*
looking bad-tempered and not wanting to speak to people: *a sullen expression*

sulphur (*British*) (*American* **sulfur**)
/'sʌlfə(r)/ *noun* (*no plural*) (*symbol* S)
a natural yellow substance that smells like bad eggs

sum 0⊸ /sʌm/ *noun*

1 an amount of money: *£200 000 is a large sum of money.*
2 the answer that you have when you add numbers together: *The sum of two and five is seven.*
3 a simple piece of work with numbers, for example adding or dividing: *Children have to learn how to do sums.*

summary /'sʌməri/ *noun* (*plural* summaries)
a short way of telling something by giving only the most important facts: *Here is a summary of the news ...*

summer 0⊸ /'sʌmə(r)/ *noun*
the season that comes between spring and autumn: *I am going to Spain in the summer.* ◇ *the summer holidays* ⊃ Look at Picture Dictionary page **P16**.

summit /'sʌmɪt/ *noun*
the top of a mountain

summon /'sʌmən/ *verb* (summon, summoning, summoned /'sʌmənd/) (*formal*)
to order a person to come to a place: *The boys were summoned to the head teacher's office.*

sun 0⊸ /sʌn/ *noun* (*no plural*)
1 the sun

the big round object in the sky that gives us light in the day, and heat: *The sun is shining.*
2 light and heat from the sun: *We sat in the sun all morning.*

sunbathe /'sʌnbeɪð/ *verb* (sunbathes, sunbathing, sunbathed /'sʌnbeɪðd/)
to lie in the sun so that your skin becomes darker: *We sunbathed on the beach.*

▶ **sunbathing** /'sʌnbeɪðɪŋ/ *noun* (*no plural*): *Sunbathing is bad for your skin.*

sunburn /'sʌnbɜːn/ *noun* (*no plural*)
red painful skin that you get when you have been in the hot sun for too long ⊃ Look at **suntan**.
▶ **sunburned** /'sʌnbɜːnd/ (*also* **sunburnt** /'sʌnbɜːnt/) *adjective*: *sunburned shoulders*

Sunday 0–ਜ਼ /'sʌndeɪ/ *noun*
the day of the week after Saturday and before Monday, thought of as either the first or the last day of the week ⊃ Look at the note at **day**.

sunflower

/'sʌnflaʊə(r)/ *noun*
a very tall plant with large yellow flowers, which farmers grow for its seeds and their oil, which are used in cooking

sung *form of* SING

sunglasses
/'sʌnglɑːsɪz/ (*also informal* **shades**)
noun (*plural*)
glasses with dark glass in them that you wear in strong light: *a pair of sunglasses* ⊃ Look at the picture at **glasses**.

sunk *form of* SINK¹

sunlight /'sʌnlaɪt/ *noun* (*no plural*)
the light from the sun: *The room was full of sunlight.*

sunny /'sʌni/ *adjective* (**sunnier, sunniest**)
bright and warm with light from the sun: *a sunny day* ◊ *Tomorrow will be warm and sunny.*

sunrise /'sʌnraɪz/ *noun* (*no plural*)
the time in the morning when the sun comes up ⊃ SAME MEANING **dawn**: *They were up before sunrise.* ⊃ Look at **sunset**.

sunset /'sʌnset/ *noun*
the time in the evening when the sun goes down: *The park closes at sunset.* ⊃ Look at **sunrise**. ⊃ Look at Picture Dictionary page **P16**.

sunshine /'sʌnʃaɪn/ *noun* (*no plural*)
the light and heat from the sun: *We sat outside in the sunshine.*

suntan /'sʌntæn/ (*also* **tan**) *noun*
When you have a **suntan**, your skin is brown because you have been in the hot sun: *I'm trying to get a suntan.* ⊃ Look at **sunburn**.
▶ **suntanned** /'sʌntænd/ (*also* **tanned**) *adjective*: *suntanned arms*

super /'suːpə(r)/ *adjective* (*informal*)
very good ⊃ SAME MEANING **lovely**: *That was a super meal.*

superb /suː'pɜːb/ *adjective*
very good or beautiful: *a superb holiday* ◊ *The view from the window is superb.*

superintendent /ˌsuːpərɪn'tendənt/ *noun*
1 a person who manages and controls a large building: *the superintendent of schools in Dallas*
2 a police officer with a high position: *Detective Superintendent Nolan*

superior /suː'pɪəriə(r)/ *adjective*
better or more important than another person or thing: *I think ground coffee is superior to instant coffee.*
⊃ OPPOSITE **inferior**

superlative /suː'pɜːlətɪv/ *noun*
(*grammar*) the form of an adjective or adverb that shows the most of something: *'Most intelligent', 'best' and 'fastest' are all superlatives.*
▶ **superlative** *adjective*: *'Youngest' is the superlative form of 'young'.* ⊃ Look at **comparative**.

supermarket /'suːpəmɑːkɪt/ *noun*
a big shop where you can buy food and other things for your home

> 🔎 **WORD BUILDING**
> In a supermarket you put the things you want to buy in a **basket** or a **trolley** (*British*) (*American* **cart**) and pay for them all at the **checkout**.

⊃ Look at Picture Dictionary page **P13**.

supersonic /ˌsuːpə'sɒnɪk/ *adjective*
faster than the speed of sound: *a supersonic aeroplane*

superstar /'sjuː-/ *noun*
a person such as a singer or film star who is very famous and successful: *Madonna is a global superstar.*

superstition /ˌsuːpə'stɪʃn/ *noun*
a belief in good and bad luck and other things that cannot be explained: *People say that walking under a ladder brings bad luck, but it's just a superstition.*
▶ **superstitious** /ˌsuːpə'stɪʃəs/ *adjective*: *A lot of people are superstitious about the number 13.*

superstore /'suːpəstɔː(r)/ *noun*
a very big shop: *There's a new computer superstore on the edge of town.*

supervise /'suːpəvaɪz/ *verb* (**supervises, supervising, supervised** /'suːpəvaɪzd/)
to watch somebody or something in order

A
B
C
D
E
F
G
H
I
J
K
L
M
N
O
P
Q
R
S
T
U
V
W
X
Y
Z

supervise (continued)

to see that people are working or behaving correctly: *It was his job to supervise the builders.*

▶ **supervision** /ˌsuːpə'vɪʒn/ *noun* (no plural): *Children must not use the pool without supervision.*

▶ **supervisor** /'suːpəvaɪzə(r)/ *noun*: *a factory supervisor*

supper /'sʌpə(r)/ *noun*

the last meal of the day: *We had supper and then went to bed.* ➔ Look at the note at **meal**.

supply¹ 0🔑 /sə'plaɪ/ *noun* (plural supplies)

a store or an amount of something that you need: *Food supplies were dropped by helicopter.* ◇ *The water supply was cut off.*

supply² /sə'plaɪ/ *verb* (supplies, supplying, supplied /sə'plaɪd/, has supplied)

to give or sell something that somebody needs: *The school supplies us with books.* ◇ *The lake supplies water to thousands of homes.*

▶ **supplier** /sə'plaɪə(r)/ *noun*: *We are the region's biggest supplier of computer equipment.*

support¹ 0🔑 /sə'pɔːt/ *verb* (supports, supporting, supported)

1 to say that somebody or something is right or the best: *Everybody else said I was wrong but Paul supported me.* ◇ *Which football team do you support?*
2 to help somebody to live by giving things like money, a home or food: *She has three children to support.*
3 to hold somebody or something up, so that they do not fall: *The bridge isn't strong enough to support heavy lorries.*

support² /sə'pɔːt/ *noun*

1 (no plural) help: *Thank you for all your support.*
2 (plural supports) something that holds up another thing: *a roof support*

supporter /sə'pɔːtə(r)/ *noun*

a person who supports a political party or a sports team: *football supporters*

suppose 0🔑 /sə'pəʊz/ *verb* (supposes, supposing, supposed /sə'pəʊzd/)

1 to think that something is probably true or will probably happen: *'Where's Jenny?' 'I don't know – I suppose she's still at work.'*
2 a word that you use when you agree with something but are not happy about it: *'Can I borrow your pen?' 'Yes, I suppose so – but don't lose it.'*

be supposed to

1 If you **are supposed to** do something, you should do it: *They were supposed to meet us here.* ◇ *You're not supposed to smoke in this room.*
2 (*informal*) If something **is supposed to** be true, people say it is true: *This is supposed to be a good restaurant.*

supposing /sə'pəʊzɪŋ/ *conjunction*

if something happens or is true: *Supposing we miss the bus, how will we get to the airport?*

supreme /suː'priːm/ *adjective*

highest or most important: *the Supreme Court*

supremely /suː'priːmli/ *adverb*

extremely: *He is supremely confident that he can win.*

sure 0🔑 /ʃɔː(r)/ *adjective* (surer, surest) *adverb*

1 knowing that something is true or right ➔ SAME MEANING **certain**: *I'm sure I've seen that man before.* ◇ *If you're not sure how to do it, ask your teacher.*
2 If you are **sure** to do something, you will certainly do it: *If you work hard, you're sure to pass the exam.*

for sure without any doubt: *I think he's coming to the party but I don't know for sure.*

make sure to check something so that you are certain about it: *I think the party starts at eight, but I'll phone to make sure.* ◇ *Make sure you don't leave your bag on the bus.*

sure (*American, informal*) yes: *'Can I borrow this book?' 'Sure.'*

sure enough as I thought: *I said they would be late, and sure enough they were.*

surely /'ʃɔːli/ *adverb*

a word that you use when you think that something must be true, or when you are surprised: *This will surely cause problems.* ◇ *Surely you know where your brother works!*

surf¹ /sɜːf/ *noun* (no plural)

the white part on the top of waves in the sea

surf² /sɜːf/ *verb* (surfs, surfing, surfed /sɜːft/) (*also* go surfing)

to stand or lie on a long piece of wood or plastic (called a **surfboard**) and ride on a wave: *We went surfing in Hawaii.*

surf the Net, surf the Internet to use the Internet: *He spends hours every day surfing the Net.*

▶ **surfer** /'sɜːfə(r)/ *noun*: *The beach is popular with surfers.*

surface 0🔑 /'sɜːfɪs/ *noun*

1 the outside part of something: *the earth's surface*
2 the top of water: *She dived below the surface.*

surfboard /'sɜːfbɔːd/ *noun*
a long piece of wood or plastic that you sit or lie on to ride on a wave ➷ Look at Picture Dictionary page **P14**.

surfing /'sɜːfɪŋ/ *noun (no plural)*
the sport of riding on waves while standing on a SURFBOARD: *His hobbies include surfing and photography.* ➷ Look at Picture Dictionary page **P14**.

surgeon /'sɜːdʒən/ *noun*
a doctor who cuts your body to take out or repair a part inside. (This is called an **operation**): *a brain surgeon*

surgery /'sɜːdʒəri/ *noun*
1 (*no plural*) cutting a person's body to take out or repair a part inside: *He needed surgery after the accident.*
2 (*plural* **surgeries**) a place or time when a doctor or dentist sees patients: *There is no surgery on Saturdays.*

surname /'sɜːneɪm/ *noun*
the name that a family has ➷ SAME MEANING **last name, family name**: *Her name is Kate Smith; Smith is her surname.* ➷ Look at the note at **name**.

surprise¹ 0̄ₘ /sə'praɪz/ *noun*
1 (*no plural*) the feeling that you have when something happens suddenly that you did not expect: *He looked up in surprise when I walked in.* ◇ *To my surprise, everyone agreed with me.*
2 (*plural* **surprises**) something that happens when you do not expect it: *Don't tell him about the party – it's a surprise!*
take somebody by surprise to happen when somebody does not expect it: *The news took me completely by surprise.*

surprise² 0̄ₘ /sə'praɪz/ *verb*
(**surprises, surprising, surprised** /sə'praɪzd/)
to do something that somebody does not expect: *I arrived early to surprise her.*

surprised 0̄ₘ /sə'praɪzd/ *adjective*
If you are **surprised**, you feel or show surprise: *I was surprised to see Tim yesterday – I thought he was in Canada.*

surprising 0̄ₘ /sə'praɪzɪŋ/ *adjective*
If something is **surprising**, it makes you feel surprise: *The news was surprising.*
▶ **surprisingly** /sə'praɪzɪŋli/ *adverb*: *The exam was surprisingly easy.*

surrender /sə'rendə(r)/ *verb* (**surrenders, surrendering, surrendered** /sə'rendəd/)
to stop fighting because you cannot win: *After six hours on the roof, the man surrendered to the police.*
▶ **surrender** *noun (no plural)*: *We will not even consider surrender.*

surround 0̄ₘ /sə'raʊnd/ *verb*
(**surrounds, surrounding, surrounded**)
to be or go all around something: *The lake is surrounded by trees.*

surroundings /sə'raʊndɪŋz/ *noun* (*plural*)
everything around you, or the place where you live: *I don't like seeing animals in a zoo – I prefer to see them in their natural surroundings.*

survey /'sɜːveɪ/ *noun* (*plural* **surveys**)
asking questions to find out what people think or do: *We did a survey of people's favourite TV programmes.*

survive 0̄ₘ /sə'vaɪv/ *verb* (**survives, surviving, survived** /sə'vaɪvd/)
to continue to live in or after a difficult or dangerous time: *Camels can survive for many days without water.* ◇ *Only one person survived the plane crash.*
▶ **survival** /sə'vaɪvl/ *noun (no plural)*: *Food and water are necessary for survival.*
▶ **survivor** /sə'vaɪvə(r)/ *noun*: *The government sent help to the survivors of the earthquake.*

suspect¹ /sə'spekt/ *verb* (**suspects, suspecting, suspected**)
1 to think that something is true, but not be certain: *John wasn't at college today – I suspect that he's ill.*
2 to think that somebody has done something wrong but not be certain: *They suspect Helen of stealing the money.* ➷ The noun is **suspicion** and the adjective is **suspicious**.

suspect² /'sʌspekt/ *noun*
a person who you think has done something wrong: *The police have arrested two suspects.*

suspend /sə'spend/ *verb* (**suspends, suspending, suspended**)
1 to hang something from something else: *Coloured flags were suspended from the ceiling.*
2 to stop or delay something for a time: *Rail services were suspended for 24 hours.*

suspense /sə'spens/ *noun (no plural)*
a feeling of excitement or worry that you have when you are waiting for news or for something to happen: *Don't keep me in suspense – did you pass?*

suspicion /sə'spɪʃn/ *noun*
1 a feeling that somebody has done something wrong: *He was arrested on suspicion of murder.*
2 an idea that is not totally certain: *We have a suspicion that she is unhappy.* ➷ The verb is **suspect**.

A
B
C
D
E
F
G
H
I
J
K
L
M
N
O
P
Q
R
S
T
U
V
W
X
Y
Z

A

suspicious /sə'spɪʃəs/ *adjective*
1 If you are **suspicious**, you do not believe somebody or something, or you feel that something is wrong: *The police are **suspicious** of her story.*
2 A person or thing that is **suspicious** makes you feel that something is wrong: *Anyone who sees anything suspicious should contact the police.*
▸ **suspiciously** /sə'spɪʃəsli/ *adverb*: *'What are you doing here?' the woman asked suspiciously.*

swallow¹ ⊶ /'swɒləʊ/ *verb*
(swallows, swallowing, swallowed /'swɒləʊd/)
to make food or drink move down your throat from your mouth: *I can't swallow these tablets without water.*

swallow² /'swɒləʊ/ *noun*
a small bird with a long tail

swam *form of* SWIM

swamp /swɒmp/ *noun*
an area of soft wet ground

swan /swɒn/ *noun*
a big white bird with a very long neck. **Swans** live on rivers and lakes.

swan

swap (*also* **swop**) /swɒp/ *verb*
(swaps, swapping, swapped /swɒpt/)
to change one thing for another thing; to give one thing and get another thing for it: *Do you want to **swap** chairs **with** me* (= you have my chair and I'll have yours)*? ◊ I **swapped** my CD **for** Tom's* (= I had his and he had mine).
▸ **swap** *noun*: *Why don't we **do a swap**?*

swarm¹ /swɔːm/ *noun*
a big group of flying insects: *a swarm of bees*

swarm² /swɔːm/ *verb* (swarms, swarming, swarmed /swɔːmd/)
to fly or move quickly in a big group: *The fans swarmed into the stadium.*

sway /sweɪ/ *verb* (sways, swaying, swayed /sweɪd/)
to move slowly from side to side: *The trees were swaying in the wind.*

swear ⊶ /sweə(r)/ *verb* (swears, swearing, swore /swɔː(r)/, has sworn /swɔːn/)
1 to say bad words: *Don't **swear** at your mother!*
2 to make a serious promise: *He **swears that** he is telling the truth.*

swear word /'sweə wɜːd/ *noun*
a bad word

sweat ⊶ /swet/ *verb* (sweats, sweating, sweated)
to produce liquid through your skin because you are hot, ill or afraid: *The room was so hot that everyone was sweating.*
▸ **sweat** *noun* (*no plural*): *He wiped the sweat from his forehead.*

sweater /'swetə(r)/ *noun*
a warm piece of clothing with long sleeves, which you wear on the top part of your body

🔎 **WORD BUILDING**
Other words for **sweater** are **jersey**, **jumper** and **pullover**. **Sweaters** are often made of wool. A **cardigan** is a sweater that fastens at the front like a jacket.

⊃ Look at Picture Dictionary page **P5**.

sweatshirt /'swetʃɜːt/ *noun*
a warm piece of clothing with long sleeves made of thick cotton, which you wear on the top part of your body ⊃ Look at Picture Dictionary page **P5**.

sweaty /'sweti/ *adjective* (sweatier, sweatiest)
covered with sweat: *sweaty socks ◊ I'm all hot and sweaty – I need a shower.*

sweep /swiːp/ *verb* (sweeps, sweeping, swept /swept/, has swept)
1 to clean something by moving dirt or rubbish away with a brush: *I've swept the floor.*
2 to push something along or away quickly and strongly: *The bridge was **swept away** by the floods.*
sweep up, **sweep something up** to remove dirt or rubbish using a brush: *I swept up the broken glass.*

sweet¹ ⊶ /swiːt/ *adjective* (sweeter, sweetest)
1 containing or tasting of sugar: *Honey is sweet.*
2 with a good smell: *the sweet smell of roses*
3 attractive; pretty ⊃ SAME MEANING **cute**: *What a sweet little girl!*
4 having or showing a kind character: *It was **sweet of** you to help me.*

sweet² ⊶ /swiːt/ *noun*
1 (*British*) (*American* **candy**) a small piece of sweet food: *He bought a packet of sweets for the children.*
2 sweet food that you eat at the end of a meal ⊃ SAME MEANING **dessert**: *Do you want a sweet?*

sweetcorn /'swiːtkɔːn/ (British) (American **corn**) noun (no plural)
the sweet yellow seeds of a tall plant (called **maize**) that you eat as a vegetable

sweetheart /'swiːthɑːt/ noun (no plural)
a word that you use when speaking to a person that you love: Do you want a drink, sweetheart?

sweetly /'swiːtli/ adverb
in a pretty, kind or nice way: She smiled sweetly.

swell /swel/ verb (swells, swelling, swelled /sweld/, has swollen /'swəʊlən/ or has swelled)
swell up to become bigger or thicker than normal: After he hurt his ankle it began to swell up.

swelling /'swelɪŋ/ noun
a place on the body that is bigger or fatter than it usually is: He's got a swelling on his head where he fell and hit it.

swept form of SWEEP

swerve /swɜːv/ verb (swerves, swerving, swerved /swɜːvd/)
to change direction suddenly so that you do not hit somebody or something: The driver swerved when he saw the child in the road.

swift /swɪft/ adjective (swifter, swiftest)
quick or fast: We made a swift decision.
▶ **swiftly** /'swɪftli/ adverb: She ran swiftly up the stairs.

swim 0— /swɪm/ verb (swims, swimming, swam /swæm/, has swum /swʌm/)
to move your body through water: Can you swim? ◇ I swam across the lake.

> 𝒫 **GRAMMAR**
> When you talk about spending time swimming as a sport, you usually say **go swimming**: I go swimming every day.

▶ **swim** noun (no plural): Let's go for a swim.
▶ **swimmer** /'swɪmə(r)/ noun: He's a good swimmer.
▶ **swimming** /'swɪmɪŋ/ noun (no plural): Swimming is my favourite sport. ⊃ Look at Picture Dictionary page **P14**.

swimming costume /'swɪmɪŋ kɒstjuːm/ (also **swimsuit**) noun
a piece of clothing that a woman or girl wears for swimming ⊃ Look at the picture at **dive**.

swimming pool 0— /'swɪmɪŋ puːl/ (also **pool**) noun
a place that is built for people to swim in: an open-air swimming pool

swimming trunks /'swɪmɪŋ trʌŋks/ (also **trunks**) noun (plural)
short trousers that a man or boy wears for swimming

swimsuit /'swɪmsuːt/ another word for SWIMMING COSTUME

swing¹ /swɪŋ/ verb (swings, swinging, swung /swʌŋ/, has swung)
1 to move backwards and forwards or from side to side through the air; to make somebody or something do this: Monkeys were swinging from the trees. ◇ He swung his arms as he walked.
2 to move in a curve: The door swung open.

swing

slide   swings

swing² /swɪŋ/ noun
a seat that hangs down and that children can sit on to move backwards and forwards through the air

swipe /swaɪp/ verb (swipes, swiping, swiped /swaɪpt/) (informal)
1 to hit or try to hit something by swinging your arm: He swiped at the ball and missed.
2 to steal something

switch¹ 0— /swɪtʃ/ noun (plural switches)
a small thing that you press to turn electricity on or off: Where is the light switch?

switch

switch² 0— /swɪtʃ/ verb (switches, switching, switched /swɪtʃt/)
to change to something different: I switched to another seat because I couldn't see the film.
switch something off to make a light or a machine stop working by pressing a SWITCH ⊃ SAME MEANING **turn something off**: I switched the TV off. ◇ Don't forget to switch off the lights!
switch something on to make a light or a machine work by pressing a SWITCH ⊃ SAME MEANING **turn something on**: Switch the radio on.

switchboard /'swɪtʃbɔːd/ noun
the place in a large company where somebody answers telephone calls and sends them to the right people

A B C D E F G H I J K L M N O P Q R S T U V W X Y Z

swollen¹ *form of* SWELL

swollen² /'swəʊlən/ *adjective*
(used about a part of the body) thicker or fatter than it usually is: *a swollen ankle*

swoop /swu:p/ *verb* (swoops, swooping, swooped /swu:pt/)
to fly down quickly: *The plane swooped down low over the buildings.*

swop /swɒp/ *verb* = SWAP

sword /sɔːd/ *noun*

> 🔍 **PRONUNCIATION**
> The word **sword** sounds like **cord**, because we don't say the **w**.

a weapon that looks like a very long sharp knife

swore, sworn *forms of* SWEAR

swot¹ /swɒt/ (*British, informal*)
a person who spends too much time studying

swot² /swɒt/ *verb* (swots, swotting, swotted) (*British, informal*)
to study hard before an exam: *Debbie is swotting for her test next week.*

swum *form of* SWIM

swung *form of* SWING¹

syllable /'sɪləbl/ *noun*
a part of a word that has one VOWEL sound when you say it. 'Swim' has one **syllable** and 'system' has two **syllables**.

syllabus /'sɪləbəs/ *noun* (*plural* syllabuses)
a list of all the things that you must study on a course

symbol ⍾ /'sɪmbl/ *noun*
a mark, sign or picture that has a special meaning: *O is the symbol for oxygen. ◇ A dove is the symbol of peace.*

symmetrical /sɪ'metrɪkl/ (*also* symmetric /sɪ'metrɪk/) *adjective*
having two halves that are exactly the same: *symmetrical patterns*

sympathetic /ˌsɪmpə'θetɪk/ *adjective*
showing that you understand other people's feelings when they have problems: *Everyone was very sympathetic when I was ill.*
➲ OPPOSITE **unsympathetic**

▸ **sympathetically** /ˌsɪmpə'θetɪkli/ *adverb*: *He smiled sympathetically.*

sympathize /'sɪmpəθaɪz/ *verb* (sympathizes, sympathizing, sympathized /'sɪmpəθaɪzd/)
to show that you understand somebody's feelings when they have problems:
I sympathize with you – I've got a lot of work to do too.

sympathy /'sɪmpəθi/ *noun* (*no plural*)
understanding of another person's feelings and problems: *Everyone feels a lot of sympathy for the victims.*

symphony /'sɪmfəni/ *noun* (*plural* symphonies)
a long piece of music for a lot of musicians playing together: *Beethoven's fifth symphony*

symptom /'sɪmptəm/ *noun*
something that shows that you have an illness: *A sore throat is often a symptom of a cold.*

synagogue /'sɪnəgɒg/ *noun*
a building where Jewish people go to say prayers and learn about their religion

synonym /'sɪnənɪm/ *noun*
a word that means the same as another word: *'Big' and 'large' are synonyms.*

synthesizer /'sɪnθəsaɪzə(r)/ *noun*
an electronic musical instrument that can produce a lot of different sounds

synthetic /sɪn'θetɪk/ *adjective*
made by people, not natural
➲ SAME MEANING **artificial**: *Nylon is a synthetic material, but wool is natural.*

syringe /sɪ'rɪndʒ/ *noun*
a plastic or glass tube with a needle that is used for taking blood out of the body or putting drugs into the body

syrup /'sɪrəp/ *noun* (*no plural*)
a thick sweet liquid made by boiling sugar with water or fruit juice: *peaches in syrup*

system ⍾ /'sɪstəm/ *noun*
1 a group of things or parts that work together: *the railway system ◇ We have a new computer system at work.*
2 a group of ideas or ways of doing something: *What system of government do you have in your country?*

T t

T, t /ti:/ *noun* (*plural* T's, t's /ti:z/)
the twentieth letter of the English alphabet: *'Table' begins with a 'T'.*

table 0‒ /'teɪbl/ *noun*
1 a piece of furniture with a flat top on legs: *a coffee table* ⊃ Look at Picture Dictionary page **P10**.
2 a list of facts or numbers: *There is a table of irregular verbs at the back of this dictionary.*

tablecloth /'teɪblklɒθ/ *noun*
a cloth that you put over a table when you have a meal

tablespoon /'teɪblspu:n/ *noun*
a big spoon that you use for putting food on plates ⊃ Look at the picture at **spoon**.

tablet /'tæblət/ *noun*
a small hard piece of medicine that you swallow ⊃ SAME MEANING **pill**: *Take two of these tablets before every meal.*

table tennis /'teɪbl tenɪs/ (*also informal* ping pong) *noun* (*no plural*)
a game where players use a small round BAT (= a piece of wood) to hit a small light ball over a net on a big table

tabloid /'tæblɔɪd/ *noun*
a newspaper with small pages

tackle¹ /'tækl/ *verb* (tackles, tackling, tackled /'tækld/)
1 to try to deal with a difficult problem or situation: *How shall we tackle this problem?*
2 to try to take the ball from somebody in a game like football
3 to try to catch and hold somebody: *The police officer tackled one of the robbers as he ran out.*

tackle² /'tækl/ *noun*
trying to get the ball from somebody in a game like football: *a rugby tackle*

tacky /'tæki/ *adjective* (tackier, tackiest) (*informal*)
cheap and of bad quality: *a shop selling tacky souvenirs*

tact /tækt/ *noun* (*no plural*)
knowing how and when to say things so that you do not hurt people: *She handled the situation with great tact.*

tactful /'tæktfl/ *adjective*
careful not to say or do things that may make people unhappy or angry: *That wasn't a very tactful thing to say!*
⊃ OPPOSITE **tactless**
▶ **tactfully** /'tæktfəli/ *adverb*: *He tactfully suggested I should lose some weight.*

tactless /'tæktləs/ *adjective*
saying or doing things that may make people unhappy or angry: *It was tactless of you to ask how old she was.*
⊃ OPPOSITE **tactful**

tag /tæg/ *noun*
a small piece of paper or material fixed to something, that tells you about it
⊃ SAME MEANING **label**: *I looked at the price tag to see how much the dress cost.*

tail 0‒ /teɪl/ *noun*
1 the long thin part at the end of an animal's body: *The dog wagged its tail.* ⊃ Look at the pictures at **cat**, **fish**, **horse** and **lion**.
2 the part at the back of something: *the tail of an aeroplane*
3 **tails** (*plural*) the side of a coin that does not have the head of a person on it
⊃ OPPOSITE **heads**

tailor /'teɪlə(r)/ *noun*
a person whose job is to make clothes for men

tailpipe /'teɪlpaɪp/ *American English for* EXHAUST¹(2)

take 0‒ /teɪk/ *verb* (takes, taking, took /tʊk/, has taken /'teɪkn/)
1 to move something or go with somebody to another place: *Take your coat with you – it's cold.* ◇ *Mark took me to the station.*
⊃ Look at the note at **bring**.
2 to put your hand round something and hold it: *Take this money – it's yours.* ◇ *She took my hand and led me outside.*
3 to remove something from a place or a person, often without asking them: *Somebody has taken my bike.*
4 to eat or drink something: *Don't forget to take your medicine.*
5 to agree to have something; to accept something: *If you take my advice you'll forget all about him.*
6 to need an amount of time: *The journey took four hours.* ◇ *It takes a long time to learn a language.*
7 to travel in a bus, train, etc.: *I took a taxi to the hospital.*

take after somebody to be or look like an older member of your family: *She takes after her mother.*

take something away to remove somebody or something: *I took the scissors away from the child.*

A B C D E F G H I J K L M N O P Q R S **T** U V W X Y Z

take something down to write something that somebody says: *He took down my address.*

take off When a plane **takes off**, it leaves the ground and starts to fly.
⊃ OPPOSITE **land**

take something off
1 to remove clothes from your body: *Take off your coat.* ⊃ OPPOSITE **put something on**
2 to have time as a holiday, not working: *I am taking a week off in June.*

take over, take something over to get control of something or look after something when another person stops: *Robert took over the business when his father died.*

take up something to use or fill time or space: *The bed takes up half the room.* ◇ *The new baby takes up all her time.*

takeaway /'teɪkəweɪ/ *noun* (plural **takeaways**) (*British*) (*American* **takeout**)
1 a restaurant that sells hot food that you take out with you to eat somewhere else: *a Chinese takeaway*
2 food that you buy at this kind of restaurant: *Let's have a takeaway tonight.*
▶ **takeaway** *adjective*: *a takeaway pizza*

take-off /'teɪk ɒf/ *noun*
the time when a plane leaves the ground and starts to fly ⊃ OPPOSITE **landing**

takeout /'teɪkaʊt/ *American English for* TAKEAWAY

tale /teɪl/ *noun*
a story, usually about things that are not true: *fairy tales*

talent /'tælənt/ *noun*
a natural ability to do something very well: *She has a talent for drawing.*

talented /'tæləntɪd/ *adjective*
having a natural ability to do something well: *a talented musician*

talk¹ 0ᵤ /tɔːk/ *verb* (talks, talking, talked /tɔːkt/)
to speak to somebody; to say words: *She is talking to her friend on the telephone.* ◇ *We talked about our holiday.*

talk² 0ᵤ /tɔːk/ *noun*
1 when two or more people talk about something: *Dave and I had a long talk about the problem.* ◇ *The two countries are holding talks to try and end the war.*
2 when a person speaks to a group of people: *Professor Wilson gave an interesting talk on Chinese art.*

talkative /'tɔːkətɪv/ *adjective*
A person who is **talkative** likes to talk a lot.

tall 0ᵤ /tɔːl/ *adjective* (taller, tallest)
1 higher than other people or things: *a tall tree* ◇ *Richard is taller than his brother.*
⊃ OPPOSITE **short**
2 You use **tall** to say or ask how far it is from the bottom to the top of somebody or something: *How tall are you?* ◇ *She's 1.62 metres tall.* ⊃ Look at the note at **high**.

tame¹ /teɪm/ *adjective* (tamer, tamest)
A **tame** animal is not wild and is not afraid of people: *The birds are so tame they will eat from your hand.*

tame² /teɪm/ *verb* (tames, taming, tamed /teɪmd/)
to make a wild animal easy to control; to make something TAME

tan¹ /tæn/ *verb* (tans, tanning, tanned /tænd/)
If your skin **tans**, it becomes brown because you have spent time in the sun: *My skin tans really easily.*
▶ **tanned** /tænd/ *adjective*: *a tanned face*

tan² /tæn/ (*also* **suntan**) *noun*
the brown colour that your skin goes when you have spent time in the sun: *to get a tan*

tangerine /ˌtændʒə'riːn/ *noun*
a fruit like a small sweet orange, with a skin that is easy to take off

tangle /'tæŋgl/ *noun*
many things that have become twisted together so that you cannot easily separate the different parts: *My hair is full of tangles.*
▶ **tangle** *verb* (tangles, tangling, tangled /'tæŋgld/): *Does your hair tangle easily?*

tangled /'tæŋgld/ *adjective*
twisted together in an untidy way: *The string is all tangled.*

tank /tæŋk/ *noun*
1 a large container for holding liquid or gas: *a fuel tank* (= in a car) ⊃ Look at the picture at **scuba-diving**.
2 a strong heavy vehicle with big guns. **Tanks** are used by armies in wars.

tanker /'tæŋkə(r)/ *noun*
a ship or lorry that carries oil, petrol or gas in large amounts: *an oil tanker*

tantrum /'tæntrəm/ *noun*
If a child has a **tantrum**, they cry and shout because they are angry.

tap¹ 0ᵤ /tæp/ *verb* (taps, tapping, tapped /tæpt/)
to hit or touch somebody or something quickly and lightly: *She tapped me on the shoulder.* ◇ *I tapped on the window.*

tap² 0🔊 /tæp/ (British) (American **faucet**) noun

1 a thing that you turn to make something like water or gas come out of a pipe: *Turn the tap off.* ⟳ Look at the picture at **plug**.
2 a light hit with your hand or fingers: *They heard a tap at the door.*

tape¹ 0🔊 /teɪp/ noun

1 a long thin piece of plastic material, that is used for recording sound, music or moving pictures so that you can listen to or watch it later: *I have got the concert on tape.* ◇ *Will you play your new music tape?*
2 a long thin piece of material or paper, used for sticking things together: *sticky tape*

tape² /teɪp/ verb (tapes, taping, taped /teɪpt/)

to put sound, music or moving pictures on TAPE so that you can listen to or watch it later ⟳ SAME MEANING **record**: *I taped the film that was on TV last night.*

tape measure /'teɪp meʒə(r)/ noun

a long thin piece of plastic, cloth or metal for measuring things

tape recorder /'teɪp rɪˌkɔːdə(r)/ noun

a machine that you use for recording and playing sound or music on tape

tapestry /'tæpəstri/ noun (plural tapestries)

a piece of cloth with pictures on it made from coloured thread

tar /tɑː(r)/ noun (no plural)

a black substance that is thick and sticky when it is hot, and hard when it is cold. Tar is used for making roads.

target /'tɑːɡɪt/ noun

1 a result that you are trying to achieve: *Our target is to finish the job by Friday.*
2 a person, place or thing that you try to hit when you are shooting or attacking: *The bomb hit its target.*

Tarmac™ /'tɑːmæk/ noun (no plural)

a black material that is used for making the surfaces of roads. It is made with TAR.

tart /tɑːt/ noun

an open PIE (= a type of baked food) filled with sweet food such as fruit: *Would you like a piece of apple tart?*

tartan /'tɑːtn/ noun

a special pattern on material that comes from Scotland: *a tartan skirt*

task 0🔊 /tɑːsk/ noun

a piece of work that you must do; a job: *I had the task of cleaning the floors.*

taste¹ 0🔊 /teɪst/ noun

1 (plural tastes) the feeling that a certain food or drink gives in your mouth: *Sugar has a sweet taste and lemons have a sour taste.* ◇ *I don't like the taste of this cheese.*
2 (no plural) the power to know about food and drink with your mouth: *When you have a cold, you often lose your sense of taste.*
3 (plural tastes) a little bit of food or drink: *Have a taste of the fish to see if you like it.*
4 (no plural) being able to choose nice things: *She has good taste in clothes.*

taste² 0🔊 /teɪst/ verb (tastes, tasting, tasted)

1 to have a certain flavour: *This tastes of oranges.* ◇ *Honey tastes sweet.*
2 to feel or know a certain food or drink in your mouth: *Can you taste onions in this soup?*
3 to eat or drink a little of something, to test its flavour: *Taste this cheese to see if you like it.*

tasteful /'teɪstfl/ adjective

attractive and of good quality, and showing that you can choose nice things: *tasteful furniture* ⟳ OPPOSITE **tasteless**
▸ **tastefully** /'teɪstfəli/ adverb: *The room was tastefully decorated.*

tasteless /'teɪstləs/ adjective

1 having little or no flavour: *a bowl of tasteless soup* ⟳ OPPOSITE **tasty**
2 of bad quality and not attractive, showing that you cannot choose nice things: *tasteless furniture* ⟳ OPPOSITE **tasteful**

tasty /'teɪsti/ adjective (tastier, tastiest)

good to eat: *The soup was very tasty.*

tattoo¹ /tə'tuː/ noun (plural tattoos)

a picture on somebody's skin, made with a needle and coloured liquid: *She has a tattoo of a tiger on her shoulder.*

tattoo² /tə'tuː/ verb (tattoos, tattooing, tattooed /tə'tuːd/)

to mark somebody's skin with a picture, made with a needle and coloured ink: *He had a snake tattooed on his arm.*

taught form of TEACH

tax¹ 0🔊 /tæks/ noun (plural taxes)

money that you have to pay to the government. You pay **tax** from the money you earn or when you buy things: *There is a tax on cigarettes in this country.*

tax² /tæks/ verb (taxes, taxing, taxed /tækst/)

to make somebody pay TAX

taxi 0🔊 /'tæksi/ (also **cab**) noun

a car that you can travel in if you pay the driver: *I took a taxi to the airport.* ◇ *I came by taxi.* ⟳ Look at Picture Dictionary page **P1**.

A B C D E F G H I J K L M N O P Q R S T U V W X Y Z

tea 0📖 /tiː/ *noun*

1 (*no plural*) the dry leaves of a special plant that you use to make **tea** to drink

2 (*no plural*) a brown drink that you make with hot water and the dry leaves of a special plant: *Would you like a cup of tea?* ⊃ Look at Picture Dictionary page **P6**.

3 (*plural* **teas**) a cup of this drink: *Two teas, please.*

4 (*plural* **teas**) (*British*) a small afternoon meal of SANDWICHES (= two slices of bread with food between them), cakes and cups of tea

> *P* CULTURE
>
> Some people call their evening meal **tea**, especially when it is eaten early in the evening.

⊃ Look at the note at **meal**.

tea bag /'tiː bæg/ *noun*

a small paper bag with tea leaves inside. You use it to make tea.

teach 0📖 /tiːtʃ/ *verb* (**teaches**, **teaching**, **taught** /tɔːt/, **has taught**)

1 to give lessons to students, for example in a school or college: *He teaches English as a foreign language.*

2 to show somebody how to do something: *My mother taught me how to drive.*

▶ **teaching** /'tiːtʃɪŋ/ *noun* (*no plural*): *modern teaching methods*

teacher 0📖 /'tiːtʃə(r)/ *noun*

a person whose job is to teach: *He's my English teacher.* ⊃ Look at Picture Dictionary page **P12**.

team 0📖 /tiːm/ *noun*

1 a group of people who play a sport or a game together against another group: *Which team do you play for?* ◊ *a football team*

2 a group of people who work together: *a team of doctors*

teapot

spout

teapot /'tiːpɒt/ *noun*

a container for making and pouring tea

tear

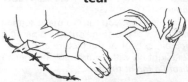

'Oh no! I just **tore** my shirt!'   She **tore** the letter in half.

tear¹ 0📖 /teə(r)/ *verb* (**tears**, **tearing**, **tore** /tɔː(r)/, **has torn** /tɔːn/)

> *P* PRONUNCIATION
>
> The verb and noun **tear¹** and **tear²** sound like **hair** or **care**.

1 to damage something by pulling it apart or making an untidy hole in it: *She tore her dress on a nail.* ◊ *I tore the piece of paper in half.* ◊ *I can't use this bag – it's torn.*

2 to come apart; to break: *Paper tears easily.*

3 to take something from somebody or something in a quick and violent way: *He tore the bag out of her hands.*

4 to move somewhere very fast: *He tore down the street.*

tear something up to destroy something by pulling it into small pieces: *I tore the letter up and threw it away.*

tear² 0📖 /teə(r)/ *noun*

an untidy hole in something like paper or material: *You've got a tear in your jeans.*

tear³ 0📖 /tɪə(r)/ *noun*

> *P* PRONUNCIATION
>
> With this meaning, **tear** sounds like **near** or **cheer**.

a drop of water that comes from your eye when you cry: *I was in tears* (= crying) *at the end of the film.* ◊ *She read the letter and burst into tears* (= suddenly started to cry).

tease /tiːz/ *verb* (**teases**, **teasing**, **teased** /tiːzd/)

to laugh at somebody in a friendly way or in order to upset them: *Don't take any notice of him – he's only teasing you.*

teaspoon /'tiːspuːn/ *noun*

a small spoon that you use for putting sugar into tea or coffee ⊃ Look at the picture at **spoon**.

tea towel /'tiː taʊəl/ *noun*

a small cloth that you use for drying things like plates and cups after you wash them

technical 0📖 /'teknɪkl/ *adjective*

connected with the machines and materials

used in science and in making things: *The train was delayed due to a technical problem.*

technician /tek'nɪʃn/ *noun*
a person who works with machines or instruments: *a laboratory technician*

technique /tek'ni:k/ *noun*
a special way of doing something: *new techniques for learning languages*

technology 0‑╖ /tek'nɒlədʒi/ *noun* (*no plural*)
knowing about science and about how things work, and using this to build and make things: *science and technology ◇ developments in computer technology*

teddy bear

teddy bear /'tedi beə(r)/ (*plural* **teddy bears**) (*also* **teddy** /'tedi/, *plural* **teddies**) *noun*
a toy for children that looks like a BEAR (= a big wild animal with thick fur)

tedious /'ti:diəs/ *adjective*
very long and not interesting
↻ SAME MEANING **boring**: *a tedious journey*

teenager /'ti:neɪdʒə(r)/ *noun*
a person who is between 13 and 19 years old
▸ **teenage** /'ti:neɪdʒ/ *adjective*: *comic books for teenage boys*

teens /ti:nz/ *noun* (*plural*)
the time when you are between the ages of 13 and 19: *She is in her teens.*

teeth *plural of* TOOTH

telephone[1] 0‑╖ /'telɪfəʊn/ (*also* **phone**) *noun*
a piece of equipment that you use for talking to somebody who is in another place: *What's your telephone number? ◇ Can I make a telephone call? ◇ The telephone's ringing – can you answer it?*
on the telephone using a telephone to speak to somebody: *He's on the telephone to his wife.* ↻ Look at Study Page **S9**.

telephone[2] 0‑╖ /'telɪfəʊn/ *verb*
(**telephones, telephoning, telephoned** /'telɪfəʊnd/) (*British, formal*)
to use a telephone to speak to somebody
↻ SAME MEANING **call**, **phone**: *I must telephone my parents.* ↻ Look at Study Page **S9**.

telephone box /'telɪfəʊn bɒks/ *noun* (*plural* **telephone boxes**) another word for PHONE BOX

telephone directory /'telɪfəʊn dɪrektəri/ *noun* (*plural* **telephone directories**)
a book of people's names, addresses and telephone numbers

telescope

telescope
/'telɪskəʊp/ *noun*
a long round piece of equipment with special glass inside it. You look through it to make things that are far away appear bigger.

television 0‑╖
/'telɪvɪʒn/ *noun*
(*abbr.* TV)
1 (*plural* **televisions**) (*also* **television set**) (*British also, informal* **telly**) a piece of electrical equipment with a screen that shows moving pictures with sound: *to turn the television on* ↻ Look at Picture Dictionary page **P10**.
2 (*no plural*) things that you watch on a television: *I watched television last night. ◇ What's on television? ◇ a television programme*
3 a way of sending pictures and sounds so that people can watch them on television: *satellite television*

tell 0‑╖ /tel/ *verb* (**tells, telling, told** /təʊld/, **has told**)
1 to give information to somebody by speaking or writing: *I told her my new address. ◇ This book tells you how to make bread. ◇ He told me that he was tired.*
2 to say what somebody must do: *Our teacher told us to read this book.*
3 to know, guess or understand something: *I can tell that she's been crying because her eyes are red. ◇ I can't tell the difference between James and his brother. They look exactly the same!* ↻ Look at the note at **say**.
tell somebody off to speak to somebody in an angry way because they have done something wrong: *I told the children off for making so much noise.*

A
B
C
D
E
F
G
H
I
J
K
L
M
N
O
P
Q
R
S
T
U
V
W
X
Y
Z

telly /'teli/ *noun* (*plural* **tellies**) (*British, informal*) short for TELEVISION

temper /'tempə(r)/ *noun*
1 If you have a **temper**, you get angry very easily: *She must learn to control her temper.*
2 the way you are feeling at a certain time ➔ SAME MEANING **mood**: *Why are you in a bad temper?*
in a temper angry: *She's in a temper because she's tired.*
lose your temper to suddenly become angry: *She lost her temper with a customer and shouted at him.*

temperature 0️⃣ /'temprətʃə(r)/ *noun*
how hot or cold a thing or a place is: *On a hot day, the temperature can reach 35° C.* ◇ *a high temperature*
have a temperature to feel very hot because you are ill
take somebody's temperature to see how hot somebody is, using a special instrument (called a **thermometer**)

temple /'templ/ *noun*
a building where people go to say prayers to a god or gods

temporarily /'temprərəli; ,tempə'rerəli/ *adverb*
for a short time only: *The road is temporarily closed for repairs.* ➔ OPPOSITE **permanently**

temporary 0️⃣ /'temprəri/ *adjective*
Something that is **temporary** lasts for a short time: *I had a temporary job in the summer holidays.* ➔ OPPOSITE **permanent**

tempt /tempt/ *verb* (**tempts, tempting, tempted**)
to make somebody want to do or have something, especially something that is wrong: *He saw the money on the table, and he was tempted to take it.*

temptation /temp'teɪʃn/ *noun*
1 (*no plural*) a feeling that you want to do something that you know is wrong: *I couldn't resist the temptation to open the letter.*
2 (*plural* **temptations**) a thing that makes you want to do something wrong: *Don't leave the money on your desk – it's a temptation to thieves.*

tempting /'temptɪŋ/ *adjective*
Something that is **tempting** makes you want to do or have it: *That cake looks very tempting!*

ten 0️⃣ /ten/ *number* 10

tenant /'tenənt/ *noun*
a person who pays money (called **rent**) to live in or use a place

tend 0️⃣ /tend/ *verb* (**tends, tending, tended**)
to usually do or be something: *Men tend to be taller than women.*

tendency /'tendənsi/ *noun* (*plural* **tendencies**)
something that a person or thing usually does: *He has a tendency to be late.*

tender /'tendə(r)/ *adjective*
1 kind, gentle and loving: *a tender look*
2 **Tender** meat is soft and easy to cut or bite. ➔ OPPOSITE **tough**
3 If a part of your body is **tender**, it hurts when you touch it. ➔ SAME MEANING **sore**
▶ **tenderly** /'tendəli/ *adverb* in a kind and gentle way: *He touched her arm tenderly.*
▶ **tenderness** /'tendənəs/ *noun* (*no plural*): *a feeling of tenderness*

tennis /'tenɪs/ *noun* (*no plural*)
a game for two or four players who hit a ball to each other over a net using a piece of equipment (called a **racket**): *Let's play tennis.* ◇ *a tennis court* (= a place where you play tennis) ➔ Look at Picture Dictionary page **P14**.

tense¹ /tens/ *adjective*
1 worried or nervous and not able to relax: *I always feel very tense before exams.* ➔ OPPOSITE **relaxed**
2 pulled tightly, not relaxed: *tense muscles*

tense² /tens/ *noun*
(*grammar*) the form of a verb that shows if something happens in the past, present or future

tension /'tenʃn/ *noun* (*no plural*)
being worried or nervous and not able to relax: *Tension can give you headaches.*

tent

tent 0️⃣ /tent/ *noun*
a kind of small house made of cloth. You sleep in a **tent** when you go camping: *We put up our tent.*

tentacle /'tentəkl/ *noun*
one of the long thin parts like legs on the

body of some sea animals: *An octopus has eight tentacles.* ➩ Look at the picture at **octopus**.

tenth 0-ᴙ /tenθ/ *pronoun, adjective, adverb*
1 10th
2 one of ten equal parts of something; ¹⁄₁₀

term /tɜːm/ *noun*
1 a word or group of words connected with a special subject: *a computing term*
2 (*British*) (*American* **trimester**) one of the three periods that the school or college year is divided into: *The summer term is from April to July.*

terminal /'tɜːmɪnl/ *noun*
a building where people begin and end their journeys by bus, train, plane or ship: *All remaining passengers for Nairobi should go to Terminal 2.*

terms /tɜːmz/ *noun* (*plural*)
the things that people must agree to when they make an arrangement or an agreement: **Under the terms of** *the contract you must complete all work by the end of the year.*

terrace /'terəs/ *noun*
1 (*British*) a line of houses that are joined together
2 a flat place outside a house or restaurant: *We had our lunch on the terrace.*

terraced house /ˌterəst 'haʊs/ *noun* (*British*)
a house that is part of a line of houses that are all joined together ➩ Look at the picture at **house**.

terrible 0-ᴙ /'terəbl/ *adjective*
very bad: *She had a terrible accident.* ◇ *The food in that restaurant is terrible!*

terribly /'terəbli/ *adverb*
1 very: *I'm terribly sorry!*
2 very badly: *He played terribly.*

terrific /tə'rɪfɪk/ *adjective* (*informal*)
very good; excellent: *What a terrific idea!*

terrified /'terɪfaɪd/ *adjective*
very frightened: *He is terrified of dogs.*

terrify /'terɪfaɪ/ *verb* (**terrifies, terrifying, terrified** /'terɪfaɪd/, **has terrified**)
to make somebody feel very frightened: *Spiders terrify me!*

territory /'terətri/ *noun* (*plural* **territories**)
the land that belongs to one country: *This island was once French territory.*

terror /'terə(r)/ *noun* (*no plural*)
very great fear: *He screamed in terror as the rats came towards him.*

terrorism /'terərɪzəm/ *noun* (*no plural*)
when a group of people hurt or kill other people, for example by putting a bomb in a public place, in order to try to make a government do what they want: *the fight against terrorism*

terrorist /'terərɪst/ *noun*
a person who hurts or kills people, for example by putting a bomb in a public place, in order to try to make the government do what they want: *a terrorist attack*

test¹ 0-ᴙ /test/ *noun*
an exam that you do in order to show what you know or what you can do: *We have a spelling test every Friday.* ◇ *Did you pass your driving test?*

test² 0-ᴙ /test/ *verb* (**tests, testing, tested**)
1 to ask somebody questions to find out what they know or what they can do: *The teacher tested us on our spelling.*
2 to use or look at something carefully to find out how good it is or if it works well: *I don't think drugs should be tested on animals.* ◇ *The doctor tested my eyes.*

test tube /'test tjuːb/ *noun*
a long thin glass tube that you use in chemical experiments

text¹ 0-ᴙ /tekst/ *noun*
1 (*no plural*) the words in a book, newspaper or magazine: *This book has a lot of pictures but not much text.*
2 (*plural* **texts**) another word for TEXT MESSAGE
3 (*plural* **texts**) a book or a short piece of writing that you study: *Read the text and answer the questions.*

text² /tekst/ *verb* (**texts, texting, texted**)
to send someone a message on a mobile phone: *He texted me to say he'd arrived in Prague.*

textbook /'tekstbʊk/ *noun*
a book that teaches you about something: *a biology textbook* ➩ Look at Picture Dictionary page **P11**.

text message /'tekst mesɪdʒ/ (*also* **text**) *noun*
a message that you send in writing from one mobile phone to another

texture /'tekstʃə(r)/ *noun*
the way that something feels when you touch it: *Silk has a smooth texture.*

than 0-ᴙ /ðən; ðæn/ *conjunction, preposition*
You use 'than' when you compare people or

A

things: *I'm older than him.* ◇ *You speak Spanish much better than she does.* ◇ *We live less than a kilometre from the beach.*

B

thank 0ᴍ /θæŋk/ *verb* (thanks, thanking, thanked /θæŋkt/)
to tell somebody that you are pleased because they gave you something or helped you: *I thanked her for my birthday present.* ⊃ Look at **thanks** and **thank you**.

C

D

E

thankful /'θæŋkfl/ *adjective*
happy that something good has happened or that something bad has not happened: *I was thankful for a rest after the long walk.*
▶ **thankfully** /'θæŋkfəli/ *adverb*: *There was an accident, but thankfully nobody was hurt.*

F

G

H

thanks 0ᴍ /θæŋks/ *noun* (plural)
a word that shows you are pleased because somebody gave you something or helped you: *Please give my thanks to your sister for her help.*
thanks to somebody or **something** because of somebody or something: *We're late, thanks to you!* ⊃ Look at **thank** and **thank you**.

I

J

K

L

Thanksgiving /ˌθæŋks'gɪvɪŋ/ (*also* **Thanksgiving Day** /ˌθæŋks'gɪvɪŋ deɪ/) *noun* (no plural)
a public holiday in November in the US or October in Canada. In the past, people thanked God on this day for their food.

M

N

O

thank you 0ᴍ /'θæŋk ju/ *noun*
words that show you are pleased because somebody gave you something or helped you ⊃ SAME MEANING **thanks**: *Thank you for your letter.* ◇ '*How are you?*' '*I'm fine, thank you.*'
no, thank you, **no**, **thanks** You use these words to say that you do not want something: '*Would you like some more tea?*' '*No, thank you.*'

P

Q

R

S

T

that¹ 0ᴍ /ðæt/ *adjective, pronoun* (plural those)
a word that you use to talk about a person or thing that is there or then: '*Who is that boy in the garden?*' '*That's my brother.*' ◇ *She got married two years ago. At that time, she was a teacher.* ⊃ Look at the picture at **this**.

U

V

W

that² 0ᴍ /ðət/ *pronoun*
which, who or whom: *A lion is an animal that lives in Africa.* ◇ *The people (that) I met were very nice.* ◇ *I'm reading the book (that) you gave me.*

X

Y

Z

that³ 0ᴍ /ðət; ðæt/ *conjunction*
a word that you use to join two parts of a sentence: *Jo said (that) she was unhappy.* ◇

I'm sure (that) he will come. ◇ *I was so hungry (that) I ate all the food.*

that⁴ /ðæt/ *adverb*
as much as that ⊃ SAME MEANING **so**: *The next village is ten kilometres from here. I can't walk that far.*

thaw /θɔː/ *verb* (thaws, thawing /'θɔːɪŋ/, thawed /θɔːd/)
to warm something that is frozen so that it becomes soft or liquid; to get warmer so that it becomes soft or liquid: *The ice is thawing.*
⊃ OPPOSITE **freeze**

the 0ᴍ /ðə; ði; ðiː/ *article*
1 a word that you use before the name of somebody or something when it is clear what person or thing you mean: *I bought a shirt and some trousers. The shirt is blue.* ◇ *The sun is shining.*
2 a word that you use before numbers and dates: *Monday the sixth of May*
3 a word that you use to talk about a group of people or things of the same kind: *the French* (= all French people) ◇ *Do you play the piano?*
4 a word that you use before the names of rivers, seas, etc. and some countries: *the Seine* ◇ *the Atlantic* ◇ *the United States of America*

🔎 GRAMMAR
Before the names of most countries, we do not use **the**: *I went to France.* (NOT *I went to the France*).

the..., the... words that you use to talk about two things happening together because of each other: *The more you eat, the fatter you get.*

the Antarctic /ði æn'tɑːktɪk/ *noun* (no plural)
the very cold lands in the most southern part of the world ⊃ Look at **Arctic**. ⊃ Look at the picture at **earth**.

the Arctic /ði 'ɑːktɪk/ *noun* (no plural)
the very cold land and countries in the most northern part of the world ⊃ Look at **Antarctic**. ⊃ Look at the picture at **earth**.

theatre 0ᴍ (*British*) (*American* **theater**) /'θɪətə(r)/ *noun*
a building where you go to see plays: *I'm going to the theatre this evening.*

theft /θeft/ *noun*
the crime of stealing something from a person or a place: *She was sent to prison for theft.* ◇ *I told the police about the theft of my car.* ⊃ Look at **thief**.

their 0ᵣ /ðeə(r)/ *adjective*

> 🔎 **PRONUNCIATION**
>
> The word **their** sounds just like **there** and **they're**.

of or belonging to them: *What is their address?*

theirs 0ᵣ /ðeəz/ *pronoun*

something that belongs to them: *Our house is smaller than theirs.*

them 0ᵣ /ðəm; ðem/ *pronoun (plural)*

1 a word that shows more than one person, animal or thing: *I wrote them a letter and then I phoned them.* ◇ *I'm looking for my keys. Have you seen them?*
2 him or her: *If anybody phones, tell them I'm busy.*

theme /θiːm/ *noun*

something that you talk or write about: *The theme of his speech was 'the future of our planet'.*

themselves 0ᵣ /ðəm'selvz/ *pronoun* (plural)

1 a word that shows the same people, animals or things that you have just talked about: *They bought themselves a new car.*
2 a word that makes 'they' stronger: *Did they build the house themselves?*
by themselves
1 alone; without other people: *The children went out by themselves.*
2 without help: *They cooked dinner by themselves.*

then 0ᵣ /ðen/ *adverb*

1 at that time: *I became a teacher in 1999. I lived in London then, but now I live in Paris.* ◇ *I'm going tomorrow. Can you wait until then?*
2 next; after that: *We had dinner and then watched a movie.*
3 if that is true: *If you miss that train then you'll have to get a bus.*

theory /'θɪəri/ *noun (plural* **theories***)*

an idea that tries to explain something: *There are a lot of different theories about how life began.*

therapy /'θerəpi/ *noun (no plural)*

a way of helping people who are ill in their body or mind, usually without drugs: *speech therapy*

there 0ᵣ /ðeə(r)/ *adverb, pronoun*

> 🔎 **PRONUNCIATION**
>
> The word **there** sounds just like **their** and **they're**.

1 a word that you use with verbs like 'be', 'seem' and 'appear' to show that something is true or that something is happening: *There is a man at the door.* ◇ *Is there a film on TV tonight?* ◇ *There aren't any shops in this village.*
2 in, at or to that place: *Don't put the box there – put it here.* ◇ *Have you been to Bonn? I'm going there next week.*
3 a word that makes people look or listen: *Oh look, there's Kate.*
there you are words that you say when you give something to somebody: *'There you are,' she said, giving me a cake.*

therefore 0ᵣ /'ðeəfɔː(r)/ *adverb*

for that reason: *Simon was busy and therefore could not come to the meeting.*

thermometer /θə'mɒmɪtə(r)/ *noun*

an instrument that shows how hot or cold something is

thesaurus /θɪ'sɔːrəs/ *noun (plural* **thesauruses***)*

a book that has lists of words and phrases with similar meanings

these 0ᵣ /ðiːz/ *adjective, pronoun* (plural)

> 🔎 **GRAMMAR**
>
> **These** is the plural form of **this**.

a word that you use to talk about people or things that are here or now: *These books are mine.* ◇ *Do you want these?* ⊃ Look at the picture at **this**.

they 0ᵣ /ðeɪ/ *pronoun (plural)*

1 the people, animals or things that the sentence is about: *Jo and David came at two o'clock and they left at six o'clock.* ◇ *'Where are my keys?' 'They're (= they are) on the table.'*
2 a word that you use instead of 'he' or 'she': *Someone phoned for you – they said they would phone again later.*
3 people: *They say it will be cold this winter.*

they'd /ðeɪd/ *short for* THEY HAD; THEY WOULD

they'll /ðeɪl/ *short for* THEY WILL

they're /ðeə(r)/ *short for* THEY ARE

they've /ðeɪv/ *short for* THEY HAVE

thick 0ᵣ /θɪk/ *adjective (* **thicker, thickest** *)*

1 far from one side to the other: *The walls are very thick.* ◇ *It's cold outside, so wear a thick coat.* ⊃ OPPOSITE **thin**
2 You use **thick** to say or ask how far something is from one side to the other: *The ice is six centimetres thick.*
3 with a lot of people or things close together: *thick dark hair*

A B C D E F G H I J K L M N O P Q R S T U V W X Y Z

A
B
C
D
E
F
G
H
I
J
K
L
M
N
O
P
Q
R
S
T
U
V
W
X
Y
Z

4 If a liquid is **thick**, it does not flow easily: *This paint is too thick.* ➔ OPPOSITE **thin**
5 difficult to see through: *thick smoke*
▸ **thickness** /'θɪknəs/ *noun* (no plural): *The wood is 3 cm in thickness.*

thief 0👂 /θiːf/ *noun* (*plural* **thieves** /θiːvz/)
a person who steals something: *A thief stole my car.*

> 🔎 WORD BUILDING
>
> A **thief** is a general word for a person who steals things, usually secretly and without violence. The name of the crime is **theft**.
> A **robber** steals from a bank, shop, etc. and often uses violence or threats.
> A **burglar** takes things from your house when you are out or asleep: *We had burglars while we were on holiday and all my jewellery was stolen.*

thigh /θaɪ/ *noun*
the part of your leg above your knee ➔ Look at Picture Dictionary page **P4**.

thin 0👂 /θɪn/ *adjective* (**thinner**, **thinnest**)
1 not far from one side to the other: *The walls in this house are very thin.* ◇ *I cut the bread into thin slices.* ➔ OPPOSITE **thick**
2 not fat: *He's tall and thin.* ➔ OPPOSITE **fat**

> 🔎 WORD BUILDING
>
> We say **slim** to talk about people who are **thin** in an attractive way: *How do you manage to stay so slim?*
> If you say somebody is **skinny**, you mean that he or she is too thin.

3 not close together: *My father's hair is getting thin.* ➔ OPPOSITE **thick**
4 If a liquid is **thin**, it flows easily like water. ➔ SAME MEANING **runny**: *The soup was very thin.* ➔ OPPOSITE **thick**

thing 0👂 /θɪŋ/ *noun*
1 an object: *What's that red thing?*
2 **things** (*plural*) objects, clothes or tools that belong to you or that you use for something: *Have you packed your things for the journey?*
3 what happens or what you do: *A strange thing happened to me yesterday.* ◇ *That was a difficult thing to do.*
4 an idea or a subject: *We talked about a lot of things.*

think 0👂 /θɪŋk/ *verb* (**thinks**, **thinking**, **thought** /θɔːt/, **has thought**)
1 to have an opinion about something; to believe something: *I think it's going to rain.* ◇ *'Do you think Sara will come tomorrow?' 'Yes, I think so.'* (= I think that she will come) ◇ *I*

think they live in Rome but I'm not sure. ◇ *What do you **think of** this music?*
2 to use your mind: *Think before you answer the question.* ◇ *I often **think about** that day.*
think about doing something to consider doing something: *He's thinking about leaving his job.*
think of something, think of doing something
1 to have something in your mind: *I can't think of her name.*
2 to try to decide whether to do something: *We're thinking of going to America.*

thinly /'θɪnli/ *adverb*
in a way that makes a thin piece of something: *Slice the potatoes thinly.*

third 0👂 /θɜːd/ *pronoun, adjective, adverb*
1 3rd
2 one of three equal parts of something; ⅓

thirst /θɜːst/ *noun* (no plural)
the feeling you have when you want to drink something

> 🔎 GRAMMAR
>
> Be careful! We say **I am thirsty** not **I have thirst**.

thirsty 0👂 /'θɜːsti/ *adjective* (**thirstier**, **thirstiest**)
If you are **thirsty**, you want to drink something: *I'm thirsty. Can I have a drink of water, please?* ➔ Look at **hungry**.

thirteen 0👂 /ˌθɜːˈtiːn/ *number* 13
▸ **thirteenth** /ˌθɜːˈtiːnθ/ *pronoun, adjective, adverb* 13th

thirtieth 0👂 /'θɜːtiəθ/ *pronoun, adjective, adverb*
30th

thirty 0👂 /'θɜːti/ *number*
1 30
2 **the thirties** (*plural*) the numbers, years or temperatures between 30 and 39
in your thirties between the ages of 30 and 39

this¹ 0👂 /ðɪs/ *adjective, pronoun* (*plural* **these**)
1 a word that you use to talk about a person or thing that is close to you in time or space: *Come and look at this photo.* ◇ *This is my sister.* ◇ *These boots are really comfortable.* ◇ *How much does this cost?*
2 a word that you use with periods of time that are connected to the present time: *I am on holiday this week.* ◇ *What are you doing **this evening** (= today in the evening)?*

this

this   these   that   those

He caught **this fish**.

He didn't catch
that fish.

this² /ðɪs/ *adverb*
so: *The road is not usually this busy* (= not as
busy as it is now).

thistle /'θɪsl/ *noun*
a plant with sharp pointed leaves and purple
flowers

thong /θɒŋ/ *noun* American English for FLIP-
FLOP

thorn /θɔːn/ *noun*
a sharp point that grows on a plant: *Rose
bushes have thorns.* ➔ Look at the picture at
plant.

thorough /'θʌrə/ *adjective*
careful and complete: *We gave the room a
thorough clean.*

thoroughly /'θʌrəli/ *adverb*
1 carefully and completely: *He cleaned the
room thoroughly.*
2 completely; very or very much:
I thoroughly enjoyed the film.

those 0̄ /ðəʊz/ *adjective, pronoun*
(*plural*)

> ℗ **GRAMMAR**
> **Those** is the plural form of **that**.

a word that you use to talk about people or
things that are there or then: *I don't know
those boys.* ◇ *Her grandfather was born in
1850. In those days, there were no cars.* ◇ *Can
I have those?* ➔ Look at the picture at **this**.

though¹ 0̄ /ðəʊ/ *conjunction*

> ℗ **PRONUNCIATION**
> The word **though** sounds like **go**.

1 in spite of something ➔ SAME MEANING
although: *I was very cold, though I was
wearing my coat.* ◇ *Though she was in a hurry,*
she stopped to talk. ◇ *I went to the party, even
though I was tired.*
2 but: *I thought it was right, though I wasn't
sure.*

as though in a way that makes you think
something: *The house looks as though nobody
lives there.* ◇ *I'm so hungry – I feel as though I
haven't eaten for days!*

though² 0̄ /ðəʊ/ *adverb*
however: *I like him very much. I don't like his
wife, though.*

thought¹ *form of* THINK

thought² 0̄ /θɔːt/ *noun*
1 (*no plural*) thinking: *After a lot of thought, I
decided not to take the job.*
2 (*plural* **thoughts**) an idea: *Have you had
any thoughts about what you want to do
when you leave school?*

thoughtful /'θɔːtfl/ *adjective*
1 thinking carefully: *She listened with a
thoughtful look on her face.*
2 thinking about other people
➔ SAME MEANING **kind**, **considerate**: *It was
very thoughtful of you to cook us dinner.*

thoughtless /'θɔːtləs/ *adjective*
not thinking about other people
➔ SAME MEANING **inconsiderate**: *It was
very thoughtless of them to leave the room in
such a mess.*

thousand 0̄ /'θaʊznd/ *number*
1 000: *a thousand people* ◇ *two thousand and
fifteen* ◇ *There were thousands of birds on
the lake.*
▶ **thousandth** /'θaʊznθ/ *pronoun,
adjective, adverb* 1 000th

thread¹ 0̄ /θred/ *noun*

> ℗ **PRONUNCIATION**
> The word **thread** sounds like **red**.

a long thin piece of cotton, wool, etc.: *I need
a needle and thread.* ➔ Look at the picture
at **sew**.

thread² /θred/ *verb* (**threads, threading,
threaded**)
to put THREAD through the hole in a needle:
to thread a needle

threat 0̄ /θret/ *noun*
1 a promise that you will hurt somebody if
they do not do what you want
2 a person or thing that may damage or
hurt somebody or something: *Pollution is a
threat to the lives of animals and people.*

threaten 0̄ /'θretn/ *verb* (**threatens,
threatening, threatened** /'θretnd/)
1 to say that you will hurt somebody if they

do not do what you want: *They* **threatened to** kill everyone on the plane. ◇ *She* **threatened** him **with** a knife.

2 to seem ready to do something bad: *The dark clouds* **threatened** *rain.*

three 0→ /θriː/ *number* 3

threw *form of* THROW

thrill[1] /θrɪl/ *noun*
a sudden strong feeling of excitement: *It* **gave me a big thrill** *to meet my favourite footballer in person.*

thrill[2] /θrɪl/ *verb* (thrills, thrilling, thrilled /θrɪld/)
to make somebody feel very excited or pleased: *This band has thrilled audiences all over the world.*

thrilled /θrɪld/ *adjective*
very happy and excited: *We are all thrilled that you have won the prize.*

thriller /ˈθrɪlə(r)/ *noun*
an exciting book, film or play about a crime

thrilling /ˈθrɪlɪŋ/ *adjective*
very exciting: *a thrilling adventure*

throat 0→ /θrəʊt/ *noun*
1 the front part of your neck
2 the part inside your neck that takes food and air down from your mouth into your body: *I've got a sore throat.*

throb /θrɒb/ *verb* (throbs, throbbing, throbbed /θrɒbd/)
to make strong regular movements or noises; to beat strongly: *His heart was throbbing with excitement.*

throne /θrəʊn/ *noun*
a special chair where a king or queen sits

through 0→ /θruː/ *preposition, adverb*

🔊 **PRONUNCIATION**
The word **through** sounds like **who**, because we don't say the letters **-gh** in this word.

1 from one side or end of something to the other side or end: *We drove through the tunnel.* ◇ *What can you see through the window?* ◇ *She opened the gate and we walked through.*
2 from the beginning to the end of something: *We travelled through the night.*
3 connected by telephone: *Can you* **put me through** *to Jill Knight, please?* ◇ *I tried to phone you but I couldn't* **get through***.*
4 (*American*) (*also informal* **thru**) until, and including: *We'll be in New York Tuesday through Friday.*

5 because of somebody or something: *She got the job through her father.*

throughout /θruːˈaʊt/ *preposition, adverb*
1 in every part of something: *We painted the house throughout.* ◇ *She is famous throughout the world.*
2 from the beginning to the end of something: *They talked throughout the film.*

throw 0→ /θrəʊ/ *verb* (throws, throwing, threw /θruː/, has thrown /θrəʊn/)

🔊 **PRONUNCIATION**
The word **throw** sounds like **go**.

1 to move your arm quickly to send something through the air: *Throw the ball to Alex.* ◇ *The boys were* **throwing** *stones* **at** *people.*
2 to do something quickly and without care: *She threw on her coat* (= put it on quickly) *and ran out of the house.*
3 to move your body or part of it quickly: *He threw his arms up.*
throw something away or **out** to get rid of rubbish or something that you do not want: *Don't throw that box away.*
▶ **throw** *noun*: *What a good throw!*

thru /θruː/ (*informal*) American English for THROUGH(4)

thrust /θrʌst/ *verb* (thrusts, thrusting, thrust, has thrust)
to push somebody or something suddenly and strongly: *She* **thrust** *the money* **into** *my hand.*
▶ **thrust** *noun*: *He killed her with a thrust of the knife.*

thud /θʌd/ *noun*
the sound that a heavy thing makes when it hits something: *The book hit the floor* **with a thud***.*

thug /θʌɡ/ *noun*
a violent person

thumb 0→ /θʌm/ *noun*

🔊 **PRONUNCIATION**
The word **thumb** sounds like **come**, because we don't say the letter **b** in this word.

the short thick finger at the side of your hand ⊅ Look at the picture at **hand**.

thumbtack /ˈθʌmtæk/ American English for DRAWING PIN

thump /θʌmp/ *verb* (thumps, thumping, thumped /θʌmpt/)
1 to hit somebody or something hard with

your hand or a heavy thing: *He thumped on the door.*
2 to make a loud sound by hitting or beating hard: *Her heart was thumping with fear.*

thunder[1] /'θʌndə(r)/ *noun* (*no plural*)
a loud noise in the sky when there is a storm: *There was **thunder and lightning**.* ➔ Look at the note at **storm**.

thunder[2] /'θʌndə(r)/ *verb* (**thunders, thundering, thundered** /'θʌndəd/)
1 When it **thunders**, there is a loud noise in the sky during a storm: *It thundered all night.*
2 to make a very loud deep noise: *The lorries thundered along the road.*

thunderstorm /'θʌndəstɔːm/ *noun*
a storm with a lot of rain, THUNDER and flashes of light (called **lightning**) in the sky ➔ Look at the note at **storm**.

Thursday 0-🠒 /'θɜːzdeɪ/ *noun*
the day of the week after Wednesday and before Friday ➔ Look at the note at **day**.

thus /ðʌs/ *adverb* (*formal*)
1 in this way: *Hold the wheel in both hands, thus.*
2 because of this: *He was very busy and was thus unable to come to the meeting.*

tick[1] /tɪk/ *verb* (**ticks, ticking, ticked** /tɪkt/)
1 (used about a clock) to make short repeated sounds: *I could hear a clock ticking.*
2 (*British*) (*American* **check**) to make a mark like this ✓ by something: *Tick the right answer.*

tick[2] /tɪk/ *noun*
1 (*British*) (*American* **check mark, check**) a small mark like this ✓: *Put a tick by the correct answer.*
2 one of the short repeated sounds that a clock makes

ticket

```
Oxford – London
ADULT RETURN
0813 030400
```

ticket 0-🠒 /'tɪkɪt/ *noun*
a piece of paper or card that you buy to travel, or to go into a cinema, theatre, etc.: *Do you want a single or a return ticket?* ◇ *a theatre ticket*

ticket office /'tɪkɪt ɒfɪs/ *noun*
a place where you buy tickets

tickle /'tɪkl/ *verb* (**tickles, tickling, tickled** /'tɪkld/)
1 to touch somebody lightly with your

fingers to make them laugh: *She tickled the baby's feet.*
2 to have the feeling that something is touching you lightly: *My nose tickles.*

tide /taɪd/ *noun*
the movement of the sea towards the land and away from the land: *The tide is **coming in**.* ◇ *The tide is **going out**.*

> 🔎 **WORD BUILDING**
> **High tide** is when the sea is nearest the land, and **low tide** is when the sea is furthest from the land.

tidy[1] 0-🠒 /'taɪdi/ *adjective* (**tidier, tidiest**)
1 with everything in the right place: *Her room is very tidy.*
2 liking to have everything in the right place: *a tidy boy* ➔ OPPOSITE **untidy**
▸ **tidily** /'taɪdɪli/ *adverb*: *Put the books back tidily when you've finished with them.*
▸ **tidiness** /'taɪdinəs/ *noun* (*no plural*)

tidy[2] 0-🠒 /'taɪdi/ (*also* **tidy up**) *verb* (**tidies, tidying, tidied** /'taɪdid/, **has tidied**)
to make something tidy: *I tidied the house before my parents arrived.* ◇ *Can you help me to tidy up?*

tie[1] 0-🠒 /taɪ/ *verb* (**ties, tying, tied** /taɪd/, **has tied**)
1 to fasten or fix something using rope, string, etc.: *I tied my hair back with a ribbon.* ◇ *I tied a scarf round my neck.* ◇ *The prisoner was tied to a chair.*
2 to end a game or competition with the same number of points for both teams or players: *France **tied with** Spain for second place.*
tie somebody up to put a piece of rope around somebody so that they cannot move: *The robbers tied up the owner of the shop.*
tie something up to put a piece of string or rope around something to hold it in place: *I tied up the parcel with string.* ◇ *The dog was tied up in the garden.*

tie[2] 0-🠒 /taɪ/ *noun*
1 a long thin piece of cloth that you wear round your neck with a shirt ➔ Look at Picture Dictionary page **P5**.
2 when two teams or players have the same number of points at the end of a game or competition: *The match ended in a tie.*
3 **ties** (*plural*) a connection between people or organizations: *Our school has **ties with** a school in France.*

tiger /'taɪgə(r)/ *noun*
a wild animal like a big cat, with yellow fur

A

and black stripes. **Tigers** live in Asia. ➔ Look
at Picture Dictionary page **P3**.

B

tight 0̶ͫ /taɪt/ *adjective* (tighter,
tightest)

C

🔎 PRONUNCIATION
The word **tight** sounds like **white**.

D

1 fixed firmly so that you cannot move it
easily: *a tight knot* ◊ *I can't open this jar of jam
– the lid is too tight.* ➔ OPPOSITE **loose**
2 **Tight** clothes fit very closely in a way that
is often uncomfortable: *These shoes are too
tight.* ◊ *tight trousers*
▶ **tight** (*also* **tightly** /'taɪtli/) *adverb*: *Hold
tight!* ◊ *I tied the string tightly around the box.*

E

F

G

tighten /'taɪtn/ *verb* (tightens,
tightening, tightened /'taɪtnd/)
to become tighter or to make something
tighter: *Can you tighten this screw?*
➔ OPPOSITE **loosen**

H

I

J

tightrope /'taɪtrəʊp/ *noun*
a rope or wire high above the ground.
People (called **acrobats**) walk along
tightropes as a form of entertainment.

K

tights /taɪts/ *noun* (*plural*)
a thin piece of clothing that a woman or girl
wears over her feet and legs: *a pair of tights*
➔ Look at Picture Dictionary page **P5**.

L

M

N

tile /taɪl/ *noun*
a flat square object. We use **tiles** for
covering roofs, walls and floors. ➔ Look at
Picture Dictionary page **P10**.
▶ **tile** *verb* (tiles, tiling, tiled): *Dad is tiling
the bathroom.*

O

P

Q

till¹ 0̶ͫ /tɪl/ *conjunction, preposition*
(*informal*) = UNTIL: *Let's wait till the rain stops.*
◊ *I'll be here till Monday.* ◊ *They didn't arrive till
six o'clock.*

R

till² /tɪl/ *noun*
a drawer or machine for money in a shop

S

tilt /tɪlt/ *verb* (tilts, tilting, tilted)
to have one side higher than the other; to
move something so that it has one side
higher than the other: *She tilted the tray and
all the glasses fell off.*

T

U

V

timber /'tɪmbə(r)/ *noun* (no plural)
wood that we use for building and making
things

W

X

time¹ 0̶ͫ /taɪm/ *noun*
1 (*no plural*) a period of seconds, minutes,
hours, days, weeks, months or years: *Time
passes quickly when you're busy.* ◊ *They have
lived here for some time* (= for quite a long
time). ◊ *I haven't got time to help you now –
I'm late for school.* ◊ *It takes a long time to
learn a language.*

Y

Z

2 (*plural* **times**) a certain point in the day or
night, that you say in hours and minutes:
'*What time is it?*' '*It's twenty past six.*' ◊
What's the time? ◊ *Can you tell me the times
of trains to Brighton, please?* ◊ *It's time to* go
home. ◊ *By the time* (= when) *we arrived they
had eaten all the food.*
3 (*plural* **times**) a certain moment or
occasion: *I've seen this film four times.* ◊ *Come
and visit us next time you're in England.*
4 (*plural* **times**) an experience; something
that you do: *We had a great time on holiday.*
5 (*plural* **times**) certain years in history: *In
Shakespeare's time, not many people could
read.*

at a time together; on one occasion: *The
lift can carry six people at a time.*

at one time in the past, but not now: *We
were in the same class at one time.*

at the time then: *My family moved to
London in 1986 – I was four at the time.*

at times sometimes: *A teacher's job can be
very difficult at times.*

for the time being now, but not for long:
*You can stay here for the time being, until you
find a flat.*

from time to time sometimes; not often:
I see my cousin from time to time.

have a good time enjoy yourself: *Have a
good time at the party!*

**in a week's, two months', a year's
time** after a week, two months, a year: *I'll
see you in two weeks' time.*

in good time at the right time or early: *I
want to get to the station in good time.*

in time not late: *If you hurry, you'll arrive in
time for the film.*

it's about time (*informal*) words that you
use to say that something should be done
now: *It's about time you started studying if you
want to pass the exam.*

on time not late or early: *My train was on
time.*

spare time, free time time when you do
not have to work or study: *What do you do in
your spare time?*

spend time to use time to do something: *I
spend a lot of time playing tennis.*

take your time to do something slowly

tell the time to read the time from a clock
or watch: *Can your children tell the time?*

time after time, time and time again
many times

time² /taɪm/ *verb* (times, timing, timed
/taɪmd/)
1 to plan something so that it will happen
when you want: *The bomb was timed to
explode at six o'clock.*
2 to measure how much time it takes to do

something: *We timed the journey – it took half an hour.*

times[1] /taɪmz/ *preposition* (*symbol* x)
multiplied by: *Three times four is twelve* (3 x 4 = 12).

times[2] /taɪmz/ *noun* (*plural*)
a word that you use to show how much bigger, smaller, more expensive, etc. one thing is than another: *Edinburgh is five times bigger than Oxford.*

timetable /'taɪmteɪbl/ (*British*) (*American* **schedule**) *noun*
a list of times when something happens: *a train timetable ◇ a school timetable* (= showing when lessons start and finish)

timid /'tɪmɪd/ *adjective*
shy and easily frightened
▸ **timidly** /'tɪmɪdli/ *adverb*: *She opened the door timidly and came in.*

tin 0ᴍ /tɪn/ *noun*
1 (*no plural*) (*symbol* Sn) a soft white metal
2 (*plural* tins) (*British*) (*American* can) a metal container for food and drink that keeps it fresh: *I opened a **tin** of beans.*
▸ **tinned** /tɪnd/ *adjective*: *tinned peaches*
➔ Look at the picture at **container**.

tin-opener /'tɪn əʊpnə(r)/ *noun*
a tool for opening tins

tin-opener

tiny /'taɪni/ *adjective* (tinier, tiniest)
very small: *Ants are tiny in*

tip[1] /tɪp/ *noun*
1 the pointed or thin end of something: *the tips of your fingers*
2 a small, extra amount of money that you give to somebody who has done a job for you: *I **left a tip** on the table.*
3 a small piece of advice: *She gave me some useful **tips on** how to pass the exam.*

tip[2] /tɪp/ *verb* (tips, tipping, tipped /tɪpt/)
1 to move so that one side goes up or down; to move something so that one side goes up or down: *Don't tip your chair back.*
2 to turn something so that the things inside fall out: *She opened a tin of beans and tipped them into a bowl.*
3 to give somebody an extra amount of money to thank them for something they have done for you as part of their job: *Do you tip taxi drivers in your country?*
tip over, **tip something over** to turn over; to make something turn over: *The boat tipped over and we all fell in the water. ◇ Don't tip your drink over!*

tiptoe /'tɪptəʊ/ *verb* (tiptoes, tiptoeing, tiptoed /'tɪptəʊd/)
to walk quietly on your toes: *He tiptoed into the bedroom.*
on tiptoe standing or walking on your toes with the rest of your feet off the ground: *She stood on tiptoe.*

tire *American English for* **TYRE**

tired 0ᴍ /'taɪəd/ *adjective*
needing to rest or sleep: *I've been working all day and I'm **tired out** (= extremely tired). ◇ He's feeling tired.*
be tired of something to have had or done too much of something, so that you do not want it any longer: *I'm tired of watching TV – let's go out.*

tiring 0ᴍ /'taɪərɪŋ/ *adjective*
making you feel tired: *a tiring journey*

tissue /'tɪʃuː/ *noun*
1 (*plural* tissues) a thin piece of soft paper that you use to clean your nose: *a box of tissues*
2 (*no plural*) all the cells that form the bodies of humans, animals and plants

tissue paper /'tɪʃuː peɪpə(r)/ *noun* (*no plural*)
thin paper that you use for wrapping things

title 0ᴍ /'taɪtl/ *noun*
1 the name of something, for example a book, film or picture: *What is the **title of** this poem?*
2 a word like 'Mr', 'Mrs' or 'Doctor' that you put in front of a person's name

to 0ᴍ /tə; tu; tuː/ *preposition*
1 a word that shows direction: *She went to Italy. ◇ James has gone to school. ◇ This bus goes to the city centre.*
2 a word that shows the person or thing that receives something: *I gave the book to Paula. ◇ He sent a letter to his parents. ◇ Be kind to animals.*
3 a word that shows the end or limit of something: *The museum is open from 9.30 to 5.30. ◇ Jeans cost from £20 to £45.*
4 on or against something: *He put his hands to his ears. ◇ They were sitting back to back.*
5 a word that shows how something changes: *The sky changed from blue to grey.*
6 a word that shows why: *I came to help.*
7 a word that you use for comparing things: *I prefer football to tennis.*
8 a word that shows how many minutes it is before the hour: *It's two minutes to six.*
9 a word that you use before verbs to make the INFINITIVE (= the simple form of a verb): *I want to go home. ◇ Don't forget to write. ◇ She asked me to go but I didn't want to* (= to go).

A

toad /təʊd/ *noun*
a small animal with
rough skin that lives
in or near water
➲ Look at **frog**.

toad

toast /təʊst/ *noun*
(*no plural*)
1 a thin piece of bread that you have cooked
so that it is brown: *I had a **slice of toast** and
jam for breakfast.*

toast

toast

))

toaster

2 the act of holding up a glass of wine and
wishing somebody happiness or success
before you drink: *They **drank a toast** to the
Queen.*
▶ **toast** *verb* (toasts, toasting, toasted):
toasted sandwiches ◇ *We all toasted the bride
and groom (= at a wedding).*

toaster /ˈtəʊstə(r)/ *noun*
a machine for making TOAST(1)

tobacco /təˈbækəʊ/ *noun* (*no plural*)
special dried leaves that people smoke in
cigarettes and pipes

toboggan /təˈbɒɡən/ *noun*
a type of flat board that people use for
travelling down hills on snow for fun ➲ Look
also at **sledge**.

today 0̶ /təˈdeɪ/ *adverb, noun* (*no plural*)
1 this day; on this day: *What shall we do
today?* ◇ *Today is Friday.*
2 the present time; at the present time
➲ SAME MEANING **nowadays**: *Most families
in Britain today have a car.*

toddler /ˈtɒdlə(r)/ *noun*
a young child who has just started to walk

toe 0̶ /təʊ/ *noun*
1 one of the five parts at the end of your foot
➲ Look at the picture at **foot**.
2 the part of a shoe or sock that covers the
end of your foot

toenail /ˈtəʊneɪl/ *noun*
the hard part at the end of your toe ➲ Look
at the picture at **foot**.

toffee /ˈtɒfi/ *noun*
a hard brown sweet made from sugar and
butter

together 0̶ /təˈɡeðə(r)/ *adverb*
1 with each other or close to each other:
John and Lisa usually walk home together. ◇
Stand with your feet together. ◇ *They live
together.*
2 so that two or more things are joined to or
mixed with each other: *Tie the ends of the
rope together.* ◇ *Add these numbers together.*
◇ *Mix the eggs and sugar together.*

toilet 0̶ /ˈtɔɪlət/ *noun*
1 a large bowl with a seat, that you use
when you need to empty waste from your
body
2 (*British*) (*American* **bathroom**) a room
that contains a **toilet**: *I'm **going to the toilet**.*
➲ Look at Picture Dictionary page **P10**.

> **🔎 WORD BUILDING**
>
> In their houses, British people usually say
> **the toilet** or, informally, **the loo**.
> **Lavatory** and **WC** are formal and old-
> fashioned words.
> In public places in Britain, the toilets are
> called the **Ladies** or the **Gents**.
> In American English, people say **the
> bathroom** in their homes and **the
> restroom**, **ladies' room** or **men's room**
> in public places.

toilet paper /ˈtɔɪlət peɪpə(r)/ *noun* (*no
plural*)
paper that you use in the toilet

toilet roll /ˈtɔɪlət rəʊl/ *noun*
a roll of paper that you use in the toilet

token /ˈtəʊkən/ *noun*
1 a piece of paper, plastic or metal that you
use instead of money to pay for something: *a
book token*
2 a small thing that you use to show
something else: *This gift is **a token of** our
friendship.*

told form of TELL

tolerant /ˈtɒlərənt/ *adjective*
letting people do things even though you do
not like or understand them: *We must be
tolerant of other people's beliefs.*
▶ **tolerance** /ˈtɒlərəns/ *noun* (*no plural*):
tolerance of other religions

tolerate /ˈtɒləreɪt/ *verb* (tolerates,
tolerating, tolerated)
to let people do something even though you
do not like or understand it: *He won't tolerate
rudeness.*

tomato 0̶ /təˈmɑːtəʊ/ *noun* (*plural
tomatoes*)
a soft red fruit that you cook or eat cold in
salads: *tomato soup* ➲ Look at Picture
Dictionary page **P9**.

B C D E F G H I J K L M N O P Q R S **T** U V W X Y Z

tomb /tuːm/ *noun*
a thing made of stone where a dead person's body is buried

tombstone /'tuːmstəʊn/ *noun*
a large flat stone on the place where a person is buried (their **grave**) showing their name and the dates when they lived

tomorrow 0─┅ /tə'mɒrəʊ/ *adverb, noun* (*no plural*)
the day after today; on the day after today: *Let's go swimming tomorrow.* ◊ *I'll see you tomorrow morning.* ◊ *We are going home* **the day after tomorrow.**

ton /tʌn/ *noun*
1 a unit for measuring weight. There are 2240 pounds (=1016 kilos) in a British **ton**. In the US, a **ton** is 2000 pounds.
2 tons (*plural*) (*informal*) a lot: *He's got tons of money.*

tone /təʊn/ *noun*
the way that something sounds: *I knew he was angry by the tone of his voice.*

tongs /tɒŋz/ *noun*
(*plural*)
a tool with two parts that you use for holding things or picking things up

tongs

tongue 0─┅ /tʌŋ/ *noun*

🔍 **PRONUNCIATION**
The word **tongue** sounds like **young**.

the soft part inside your mouth that moves when you talk or eat

tongue-twister /'tʌŋ twɪstə(r)/ *noun*
words that are difficult to say together quickly: '*Red lorry, yellow lorry*' is a tongue-twister.

tonight 0─┅ /tə'naɪt/ *adverb, noun* (*no plural*)
the evening or night of today; on the evening or night of today: *I'm going to a party tonight.* ◊ *Tonight is the last night of our holiday.*

tonne /tʌn/ *noun*
a measure of weight. There are 1000 kilograms in a **tonne**.

too 0─┅ /tuː/ *adverb*
1 more than you want or need: *These shoes are too big.* ◊ *She put too much milk in my coffee.*
2 also ⟳ SAME MEANING **as well**: *Green is my favourite colour but I like blue too.*

took *form of* TAKE

too

Tom's sweater is   **Kevin's sweater**
not big enough.   **is too big.**

tool 0─┅ /tuːl/ *noun*
a thing that you hold in your hand and use to do a special job: *Hammers and saws are tools.*

🔍 **WORD BUILDING**
There are many different types of **tool**. Here are some of them: **drill**, **hammer**, **knife**, **saw**, **screwdriver**. Do you know any others?

tooth 0─┅ /tuːθ/ *noun* (*plural* **teeth** /tiːθ/)
1 one of the hard white things in your mouth that you use for eating: *I brush my teeth after every meal.* ⟳ Look at Picture Dictionary page **P4**.

🔍 **WORD BUILDING**
A **dentist** is a person whose job is to look after teeth.
If a tooth is bad, the dentist may **fill** it (= put a substance in the hole) or **take** it **out**.
People who have lost their own teeth can wear **false teeth**.

2 one of the long narrow pointed parts of an object such as a COMB (= an object that you use for making your hair tidy)

toothache /'tuːθeɪk/ *noun* (*no plural*)
a pain in your tooth: *I've got toothache.*

toothbrush /'tuːθbrʌʃ/ *noun* (*plural* **toothbrushes**)
a small brush for cleaning your teeth ⟳ Look at the picture at **brush**.

toothpaste /'tuːθpeɪst/ *noun* (*no plural*)
a substance that you put on your TOOTHBRUSH and use for cleaning your teeth

top[1] 0─┅ /tɒp/ *noun*
1 the highest part of something: *There's a*

A

church **at the top of** the hill.
➲ OPPOSITE **bottom**
2 a cover that you put on something to close it: *Where's the top of this jar?*
3 a piece of clothing that you wear on the top part of your body: *I like your top – is it new?*
on top on its highest part: *The cake had cream on top.*
on top of something on or over something: *A tree fell on top of my car.*

top² 0–ᴡ /tɒp/ *adjective*
highest or best: *Put this book on the top shelf.*
◇ *She's one of the country's top athletes.*

topic /'tɒpɪk/ *noun*
something that you talk, learn or write about
➲ SAME MEANING **subject**: *The topic of the discussion was war.*

torch /tɔːtʃ/ *noun* (*plural* **torches**) (*British*) (*American* **flashlight**)
a small electric light that you can carry
➲ Look at the picture at **light**.

tore, torn *forms of* TEAR¹

tornado /tɔː'neɪdəʊ/ *noun* (*plural* **tornadoes**)
a violent storm with a very strong wind that blows in a circle

torpedo /tɔː'piːdəʊ/ *noun* (*plural* **torpedoes**)
a type of bomb in the shape of a long tube that is fired from a ship that travels under the water (a **submarine**)

torrent /'tɒrənt/ *noun*
a strong fast flow of water: *The rain was coming down **in torrents**.*
▶ **torrential** /tə'renʃl/ *adjective*: *torrential rain*

tortoise /'tɔːtəs/ *noun* (*American also* **turtle**)
an animal with a hard shell on its back, that moves very slowly

tortoise
shell

torture /'tɔːtʃə(r)/ *noun* (*no plural*)
the act of making somebody feel great pain, often to make them give information: *His confession was obtained **under torture**.*
▶ **torture** *verb* (**tortures, torturing, tortured** /'tɔːtʃəd/): *Many of the prisoners had been tortured.*

the Tory Party /ðə 'tɔːri pɑːti/ *another word for* THE CONSERVATIVE PARTY

toss /tɒs/ *verb* (**tosses, tossing, tossed** /tɒst/)
1 to throw something quickly and without care: *I tossed the paper into the bin.*
2 to move quickly up and down or from side to side; to make something do this: *The boat was being tossed by the huge waves.*
3 to decide something by throwing a coin in the air and seeing which side shows when it falls: *We **tossed a coin** to see who would pay for the meal.*

total¹ 0–ᴡ /'təʊtl/ *adjective*
complete; if you count everything or everybody: *There was total silence in the classroom.* ◇ *What was the total number of people at the meeting?*

total² 0–ᴡ /'təʊtl/ *noun*
the number you have when you add everything together: *Enter the total at the bottom of the page.*

totally 0–ᴡ /'təʊtəli/ *adverb*
completely: *I totally agree.*

touch¹ 0–ᴡ /tʌtʃ/ *verb* (**touches, touching, touched** /tʌtʃt/)

🔎 **PRONUNCIATION**
The word **touch** sounds like **much**.

1 to put your hand or finger on somebody or something: *Don't touch the paint – it's still wet.* ◇ *He touched me on the arm.*
2 to be so close to another thing or person that there is no space in between: *The two wires were touching.* ◇ *Her coat was so long that it **touched the ground**.*

touch² 0–ᴡ /tʌtʃ/ *noun*
1 (*plural* **touches**) the action of putting a hand or finger on somebody or something: *I felt the **touch of** his hand on my arm.*
2 (*no plural*) the feeling in your hands and skin that tells you about something: *We had to feel our way **by touch**.*
be or **keep in touch with somebody** to meet, telephone or write to somebody often: *Are you still in touch with Kevin?* ◇ *Let's keep in touch.*
get in touch with somebody to write to, or telephone somebody: *I'm trying to get in touch with my cousin.*
lose touch with somebody to stop meeting, telephoning or writing to somebody: *I've lost touch with all my old friends from school.*

tough /tʌf/ *adjective* (**tougher, toughest**)
1 difficult ➲ SAME MEANING **hard**: *This is a tough job.*
2 strict or firm ➲ SAME MEANING **hard**: *He's very tough on his children.* ➲ OPPOSITE **soft**

3 very strong: *You need to be tough to go climbing in winter.*
4 Tough meat is difficult to cut and eat. ⊃ OPPOSITE **tender**
5 difficult to break or tear: *a tough pair of boots*

tour 0📺 /tʊə(r)/ *noun*
1 a journey to see a lot of different places: *We went on a tour of Scotland.*
2 a short visit to see a building or city: *They gave us a tour of the house.*
▶ **tour** *verb* (**tours, touring, toured** /tʊəd/): *We toured France for three weeks.*

tourism /'tʊərɪzəm/ *noun* (*no plural*)
the business of arranging holidays for people: *The country earns a lot of money from tourism.*

tourist 0📺 /'tʊərɪst/ *noun*
a person who visits a place on holiday

tournament /'tʊənəmənt; 'tɔːnəmənt/ *noun*
a sports competition with a lot of players or teams: *a tennis tournament*

tow /təʊ/ *verb* (**tows, towing, towed** /təʊd/)
to pull a vehicle using a rope or chain: *My car was towed to a garage.*

towards 0📺 /tə'wɔːdz/ (*also* **toward** /tə'wɔːd/) *preposition*
1 in the direction of somebody or something: *We walked towards the river.* ◇ *I couldn't see her face – she had her back towards me.*
2 near a time or a date: *Let's meet towards the end of the week.* ◇ *It gets cooler towards evening.*
3 to somebody or something: *The people in the village are always very friendly towards tourists.*
4 to help pay for something: *Tom gave me £10 towards Sam's birthday present.*

towel 0📺 /'taʊəl/ *noun*
a piece of cloth that you use for drying yourself: *I washed my hands and dried them on a towel.*

tower 0📺 /'taʊə(r)/ *noun*
a tall narrow building or a tall part of a building: *the Eiffel Tower* ◇ *a church tower*

tower block /'taʊə(r) blɒk/ *noun* (*British*)
a very tall building with a lot of flats or offices inside

town 0📺 /taʊn/ *noun*
a place where there are a lot of houses, shops and other buildings: *Banbury is a town near Oxford.* ◇ *I'm going into town to do some shopping.*

---

town hall /,taʊn 'hɔːl/ *noun*
a large building that contains the local government offices of a town or city

toxic /'tɒksɪk/ *adjective*
containing poison ⊃ SAME MEANING **poisonous**: *Toxic waste had been dumped on the site.*

toys

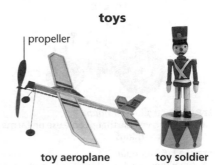

| propeller

toy aeroplane   **toy soldier**

toy 0📺 /tɔɪ/ *noun*
a thing for a child to play with

trace[1] /treɪs/ *verb* (**traces, tracing, traced** /treɪst/)
1 to look for and find somebody or something: *The police traced the gang to a house in Manchester.*
2 to put thin paper over a picture and draw over the lines to make a copy

trace[2] /treɪs/ *noun*
a mark or sign that shows that a person or thing has been in a place: *The police could not find any trace of the missing child.*

track[1] 0📺 /træk/ *noun*
1 a rough path or road: *We drove along a track through the woods.*
2 **tracks** (*plural*) a line of marks that an animal, a person or a vehicle makes on the ground: *We saw tracks in the snow.*
3 the metal lines that a train runs on: *The train had left the tracks.* ⊃ Look at the picture at **train**[1].
4 a special road for races: *a racing track*
5 one song or piece of music on a tape, CD or record: *Which is your favourite track?*
lose track of somebody or **something** to not have information about what is happening or where somebody or something is: *I lost all track of time* (= forgot what time it was).

A

track² /træk/ *verb* (tracks, tracking, tracked /trækt/)
to follow signs or marks to find somebody or something
track somebody or **something down**
to find somebody or something after looking in several different places: *The police have so far failed to track down the attacker.*

tracksuit /'træksu:t/ *noun*
a special jacket and trousers that you wear for sport

tractor

tractor /'træktə(r)/ *noun*
a big strong vehicle that people use on farms to pull heavy things

trade¹ /treɪd/ *noun*
1 (*no plural*) the buying and selling of things: *trade between Britain and the US*
2 (*plural* **trades**) a particular type of business: *the building trade*
3 (*plural* **trades**) a job for which you need special skills, especially with your hands: *Dave is a plumber **by trade**.* ◇ *to learn a trade*

trade² /treɪd/ *verb* (trades, trading, traded)
to buy and sell things: *Japan **trades with** many different countries.*

trademark /'treɪdmɑ:k/ *noun* (*abbr.* TM)
a special mark or name that a company puts on the things it makes and that other companies must not use

tradesman /'treɪdzmən/ *noun* (*plural* tradesmen /'treɪdzmən/) (*British*)
a person who sells things, especially in a small shop: *Local tradesmen are opposed to the new supermarket.*

trade union /,treɪd 'ju:niən/ (*also* union) *noun*
a group of workers who have joined together to try to get better pay and working conditions

tradition 0— /trə'dɪʃn/ *noun*
something that people in a certain place have done or believed for a long time: *In Britain it's a tradition to give chocolate eggs at Easter.*
▶ **traditional** /trə'dɪʃənl/ *adjective*: *traditional English food*

▶ **traditionally** /trə'dɪʃənəli/ *adverb*: *Driving trains was traditionally a man's job.*

traffic 0— /'træfɪk/ *noun* (*no plural*)
all the cars and other vehicles that are on a road: *There was a lot of traffic on the way to work this morning.*

traffic circle /'træfɪk sɜ:kl/ *American English for* ROUNDABOUT(1)

traffic jam /'træfɪk dʒæm/ *noun*
a long line of cars and other vehicles that cannot move or can only move slowly

traffic lights /'træfɪk laɪts/ *noun* (*plural*)
lights that change from red to orange to green, to tell cars and other vehicles when to stop and start

traffic warden /'træfɪk wɔ:dn/ *noun* (*British*)
a person whose job is to check that cars park in the right places and for the right time

tragedy /'trædʒədi/ *noun* (*plural* tragedies)
1 a very sad thing that happens: *The child's death was a tragedy.*
2 a serious and sad play: *Shakespeare's 'King Lear' is a tragedy.* ➔ Look at **comedy**.

tragic /'trædʒɪk/ *adjective*
very sad: *a tragic accident*
▶ **tragically** /'trædʒɪkli/ *adverb*: *He died tragically at the age of 25.*

trail¹ /treɪl/ *noun*
1 a line of marks that show which way a person or thing has gone: *There was a trail of blood across the floor.*
2 a path in the country: *We followed the trail through the forest.*

trail² /treɪl/ *verb* (trails, trailing, trailed /treɪld/)
to pull something along behind you; to be pulled along behind somebody or something: *Her skirt was too long and it trailed along the ground.*

trailer /'treɪlə(r)/ *noun*
1 a container with wheels that a vehicle pulls along: *The car was towing a boat on a trailer.*
2 (*American*) a vehicle without an engine, that can be pulled by a car or truck or used as a home when it is parked
3 a short piece from a film that shows you what it is like

train¹ 0— /treɪn/ *noun*
a vehicle that is pulled by an engine along a railway line: *I'm going to Bristol **by train**.* ◇ *We **caught** the 7.15 **train** to Leeds.* ◇ *You have to **change trains** at Reading.*

train

carriage (British)
car (American) | engine

track

🔍 **WORD BUILDING**
You get **on** and **off** trains at a **station**.
A **goods train** or a **freight train** carries
things and a **passenger train** carries
people.

train² 0🔊 /treɪn/ *verb* (trains, training,
trained /treɪnd/)
1 to teach a person or an animal to do
something: *He was **trained as** a pilot.*
2 to make yourself ready for something by
studying or doing something a lot: *Ann is
training to be a doctor.* ◇ *She's **training for**
the Olympics.*

trainer /'treɪnə(r)/ *noun*
1 trainers (*plural*) (*British*) (*American*
sneakers) soft shoes that you wear for
doing sport or with informal clothes ⊃ Look
at Picture Dictionary page **P5**.
2 a person who teaches people or animals to
do something: *teacher trainers*

training 0🔊 /'treɪnɪŋ/ *noun* (*no plural*)
the process of getting ready for a sport or
job: *She is **in training** for the Olympic Games.*

traitor /'treɪtə(r)/ *noun*
a person who harms their own country in
order to help another country

tram /træm/ (*British*) (*American* **streetcar**)
noun
an electric bus that runs along metal tracks
(called **rails**) in the road

tramp /træmp/ *noun*
a person with no home or job, who goes
from place to place

trample /'træmpl/ *verb* (tramples,
trampling, trampled /'træmpld/)
to walk on something and damage it with
your feet: *Don't **trample on** the flowers!*

trampoline /'træmpəliːn/ *noun*
a piece of equipment for jumping up and
down on

transfer /træns'fɜː(r)/ *verb* (transfers,
transferring, transferred /træns'fɜːd/)
to move somebody or something to a
different place: *I want to **transfer** £500 **to** my
savings account.*
▶ **transfer** /'trænsfɜː(r)/ *noun*: *Barnes has
asked for **a transfer to** a different team.*

transform /træns'fɔːm/ *verb*
(transforms, transforming, transformed
/træns'fɔːmd/)
to change a person or thing completely:
Electricity has transformed people's lives.
▶ **transformation** /ˌtrænsfə'meɪʃn/
noun: *The city's transformation has been
amazing.*

transistor /træn'zɪstə(r)/ *noun*
a small electronic part inside something
such as a radio, a television or a computer

transitive /'trænsətɪv/ *adjective*
(*grammar*) A **transitive** verb has an object:
*In the sentence 'Jane opened the door',
'opened' is a transitive verb.*
⊃ OPPOSITE **intransitive**

translate 0🔊 /træns'leɪt/ *verb*
(translates, translating, translated)
to change what somebody has said or
written in one language to another
language: *Can you **translate** this letter **into**
English for me?*
▶ **translation** /træns'leɪʃn/ *noun*: *a
translation **from** English **into** French* ◇ *I've only
read his books **in translation**.*
▶ **translator** /træns'leɪtə(r)/ *noun*: *She
works as a translator.*

transparent 0🔊 /træns'pærənt/
adjective
If something is **transparent**, you can see
through it: *Glass is transparent.*

transport 0🔊 /'trænspɔːt/ *noun* (*no
plural*)
a way of carrying people or things from one
place to another: *road transport* ◇ *I travel to
school by **public transport** (= bus or train).*
▶ **transport** /træn'spɔːt/ *verb*
(transports, transporting, transported):
The goods were transported by air.

trap¹ /træp/ *noun*
1 a thing that you use for catching animals:
The rabbit's leg was caught in a trap.
2 a plan to trick somebody: *I knew the
question was a trap, so I didn't answer it.*

trap² /træp/ *verb* (traps, trapping,
trapped /træpt/)
1 to keep somebody in a place that they

cannot escape from: *They were trapped in the burning building.*
2 to catch or trick somebody or something: *Police are hoping this new evidence could help trap the killer.*

trash /træʃ/ *American English for* RUBBISH

trash can /'træʃ kæn/ *American English for* DUSTBIN, LITTER BIN

travel 0-π /'trævl/ *verb* (British **travels**, **travelling**, **travelled** /'trævld/) (*American* **traveling**, **traveled**)

to go from one place to another: *I would like to travel round the world.* ◇ *I travel to school by bus.* ◇ *She travelled 800 km in one day.*
▶ **travel** *noun* (*no plural*): *My hobbies are music and travel.*

> 🔎 **WHICH WORD?**
>
> **Journey, trip or travel?**
> You say **journey** to talk about going from one particular place to another. A journey can be long: *the journey across Canada* or short: *the journey to work.*
> You often use **trip** when you are thinking about the whole visit, including your stay in a place: *We're just back from a trip to Japan. We had a wonderful time.* A trip can be short: *a school trip* ◇ *a shopping trip.*
> You say **travel** to talk about the general activity of moving from place to place: *Foreign travel is very popular these days.* **Travel** has no plural, so you cannot say 'go on a travel'. You **go on a journey** or **a trip**.

travel agency /'trævl eɪdʒənsi/ *noun* (*plural* **travel agencies**)
a company that plans holidays and journeys for people

travel agent /'trævl eɪdʒənt/ *noun*
a person who works in a TRAVEL AGENCY

traveller (*British*) (*American* **traveler**) /'trævələ(r)/ *noun*
a person who is travelling

traveller's cheque (*British*) (*American* **traveler's check**) /'trævələz tʃek/ *noun*
a special cheque that you can use when you go to other countries

trawler /'trɔːlə(r)/ *noun*
a large fishing boat

tray /treɪ/ *noun*
a flat object that you use for carrying food or drinks

treacle /'triːkl/ *noun* (*no plural*)
a thick, dark, sticky liquid that is made from sugar

tray

tread /tred/ *verb* (**treads**, **treading**, **trod** /trɒd/, **has trodden** /'trɒdn/)
to put your foot down while you are walking: *He **trod on** my foot.*

treason /'triːzn/ *noun* (*no plural*)
the crime of harming your country by helping its enemies

treasure /'treʒə(r)/ *noun* (*no plural*)
a collection of gold, silver, jewellery or other things that are worth a lot of money: *They were searching for **buried treasure**.*

treasurer /'treʒərə(r)/ *noun*
a person who looks after the money of a club or an organization

treat¹ 0-π /triːt/ *verb* (**treats**, **treating**, **treated**)
1 to behave in a certain way towards somebody or something: *How does your boss treat you?* ◇ *Treat these glasses **with** care.*
2 to think about something in a certain way: *They **treated** my idea **as** a joke.*
3 to try to make a sick person well again: *Several people are being **treated for** burns.*
4 to give yourself or another person something special or enjoyable: *I **treated** the children **to** an ice cream.*

treat² /triːt/ *noun*
something special or enjoyable that makes somebody happy: *My parents took me to the theatre **as a treat** for my birthday.*

treatment 0-π /'triːtmənt/ *noun*
1 (*plural* **treatments**) the things that a doctor does to try to make a sick person well again: *a new **treatment for** cancer*
2 (*no plural*) the way that you behave towards somebody or something: *Their **treatment of** the animals was very cruel.*

treaty /'triːti/ *noun* (*plural* **treaties**)
a written agreement between countries: *The two countries signed a peace treaty.*

tree 0-π /triː/ *noun*
a big plant that can live for a long time. Trees have a central part (called a **trunk**) and many smaller parts (called **branches**): *an oak tree* ◇ *Apples grow on trees.*

tremble /ˈtrembl/ *verb* (**trembles**,
trembling, **trembled** /ˈtrembld/)
to shake, for example because you are cold,
afraid or ill: *She was **trembling** with fear.*

tremendous /trəˈmendəs/ *adjective*
1 very big or very great: *The new trains travel
at a tremendous speed.*
2 very good: *The match was tremendous.*
▸ **tremendously** /trəˈmendəsli/ *adverb*:
The film was tremendously exciting.

trench /trentʃ/ *noun* (*plural* **trenches**)
a long narrow hole that is dug in the ground,
for example to put pipes or wires in

trend /trend/ *noun*
a change to something different: *new trends
in science*

trendy /ˈtrendi/ *adjective* (**trendier**,
trendiest) (*informal*)
fashionable: *a trendy new bar*

trespass /ˈtrespəs/ *verb* (**trespasses**,
trespassing, **trespassed** /ˈtrespəst/)
to go on somebody's land without asking
them if you can
▸ **trespasser** /ˈtrespəsə(r)/ *noun*: *A sign on
the gate said 'No Trespassers'.*

trial 0̄ /ˈtraɪəl/ *noun*
1 the process in a court of law when people
(called the **judge** and the **jury**) can decide if
a person has done something wrong and
what the punishment will be: *He was **on trial**
for murder.*
2 the process of testing something to see if
it is good or bad: *They are conducting trials of
a new drug.*

triangle 0̄ /ˈtraɪæŋgl/ *noun*
a shape with three straight sides ➔ Look at
the picture at **shape**.
▸ **triangular** /traɪˈæŋgjələ(r)/ *adjective*:
triangular shapes

tribe /traɪb/ *noun*
a small group of people who have the same
language and customs: *the Zulu tribes of
Africa*
▸ **tribal** /ˈtraɪbl/ *adjective*: *tribal dances*

tribute /ˈtrɪbjuːt/ *noun*
something that you do, say or give to show
that you respect or admire somebody: *They
built a statue in London as a **tribute to** Nelson
Mandela.*

trick¹ 0̄ /trɪk/ *noun*
1 a clever plan that makes somebody

believe something that is not true: *They used
a trick to get past the guards.*
2 something clever that you have learned to
do: *Do you know any **card tricks**?*
play a trick on somebody to do
something that makes somebody look silly,
in order to make other people laugh: *The
children played a trick on their teacher by
hiding her books.*

trick² 0̄ /trɪk/ *verb* (**tricks**, **tricking**,
tricked /trɪkt/)
to do something that is not honest to get
what you want from somebody: *He **tricked**
the old lady **into** giving him all her money.*

trickle /ˈtrɪkl/ *verb* (**trickles**, **trickling**,
trickled /ˈtrɪkld/)
to move slowly like a thin line of water: *Tears
trickled down her cheeks.*
▸ **trickle** *noun*: *a trickle of blood*

tricky /ˈtrɪki/ *adjective* (**trickier**, **trickiest**)
difficult; hard to do: *a tricky question*

tricycle

tricycle /ˈtraɪsɪkl/ *noun*
a type of bicycle with three wheels

tried *form of* TRY

tries
1 *form of* TRY
2 *plural of* TRY

trigger /ˈtrɪgə(r)/ *noun*
the part of a gun that you pull with your
finger to fire it

trim /trɪm/ *verb* (**trims**, **trimming**,
trimmed /trɪmd/)
to cut a small amount off something to make
it tidy: *He trimmed my hair.*
▸ **trim** *noun*: *My hair needs a trim.*

trimester /traɪˈmestə(r)/ *noun* American
English *for* TERM

trip¹ 0̄ /trɪp/ *noun*
a journey to a place and back again: *We went
on a trip to the mountains.* ➔ Look at the
note at **travel**.

trip² 0̄ /trɪp/ *verb* (**trips**, **tripping**,
tripped /trɪpt/)
to hit your foot against something so that

A

you fall or nearly fall: *She **tripped over** the step.*

trip somebody up to make somebody fall or nearly fall: *Gary put out his foot and tripped me up.*

B

C

triple /'trɪpl/ *adjective*
with three parts, happening three times or containing three times as much as usual: *a triple murder* (= in which three people were killed)
▶ **triple** *verb* (triples, tripling, tripled /'trɪpld/) to become or to make something three times bigger: *Sales have tripled this year.*

D

E

F

G

triumph /'traɪʌmf/ *noun*
great success: *The race ended in triumph for the German team.*

H

triumphant /traɪˈʌmfənt/ *adjective*
very happy because you have won or succeeded at something
▶ **triumphantly** /traɪˈʌmfəntli/ *adverb*: *The winning team ran triumphantly round the stadium.*

I

J

K

trivial /'trɪviəl/ *adjective*
not important: *She gets angry about trivial things.*

L

trod, trodden forms of TREAD

M

trolleys

N

O

P

Q

R

supermarket trolley   **luggage trolley**

S

trolley /'trɒli/ *noun* (plural **trolleys**) (*British*) (*American* **cart**)
a thing on wheels that you use for carrying things: *a supermarket trolley*

T

U

trombone
/trɒmˈbəʊn/ *noun*
a large musical instrument. You play it by blowing and moving a long tube up and down.

trombone

V

W

X

Y

troops /truːps/
noun (plural)
soldiers

Z

trophy /'trəʊfi/ *noun* (plural **trophies**)
a thing, for example a silver cup, that you

get when you win a competition: *a tennis trophy*

the tropics /ðə ˈtrɒpɪks/ *noun* (plural)
the part of the world where it is very hot and wet
▶ **tropical** /'trɒpɪkl/ *adjective*: *tropical fruit*

trot /trɒt/ *verb* (trots, trotting, trotted)
to run with short quick steps: *The horse trotted along the road.*

trouble¹ 0— /'trʌbl/ *noun*
1 (plural **troubles**) difficulty, problems or worry: *We **had** a lot of **trouble** finding the book you wanted.*
2 (no plural) extra work: *'Thanks for your help!' 'Oh, it was no trouble.'*
3 (plural **troubles**) a situation in which people are fighting or arguing: *There was trouble after the football match last Saturday.*
4 (no plural) pain or illness: *He's got heart trouble.*
be in trouble to have problems, for example because you have done something wrong: *I'll be in trouble if I'm late home again.*
get into trouble to get into a situation which is dangerous or in which you may be punished: *He got into trouble **with** the police.*
go to a lot of trouble to do extra work: *They went to a lot of trouble to help me.*

trouble² /'trʌbl/ *verb* (troubles, troubling, troubled /'trʌbld/)
1 to worry somebody: *I was troubled by the news.*
2 (formal) a word that you use when you need to disturb somebody by asking them something ⊃ SAME MEANING **bother**: *I'm sorry to trouble you, but you're sitting in my seat.*

troublemaker /'trʌblmeɪkə(r)/ *noun*
a person who deliberately causes trouble

trough /trɒf/ *noun*
a long open container that holds food or water for animals

trousers 0— /'traʊzəz/ (*British*) (*American* **pants**) *noun* (plural)
a piece of clothing for your legs and the lower part of your body: *Your trousers are on the chair.* ⊃ Look at Picture Dictionary page **P5**.

> 🔎 **GRAMMAR**
> Be careful! You cannot say 'a trousers'. You can say **a pair of trousers**: *I bought a new pair of trousers* or: *I bought some new trousers.*

trout /traʊt/ *noun* (plural **trout**)
a fish that lives in rivers and that you can eat

truant /ˈtruːənt/ *noun*
a child who stays away from school when they should be there
play truant to stay away from school when you should be there

truce /truːs/ *noun*
an agreement to stop fighting for a short time

truck 0━ /trʌk/ *noun* (*American*) (*British* **lorry**)
a big vehicle for carrying heavy things: *a truck driver*

true 0━ /truː/ *adjective*
1 right or correct: *Is it **true that** you are leaving?* ◇ *Glasgow is in England: true or false?*
⊃ OPPOSITE **untrue**, **false**
2 real: *A true friend will always help you.* ◇ *It's a true story* (= it really happened).
⊃ The noun is **truth**.
come true to happen in the way that you hoped or imagined: *Her dream came true.*

truly /ˈtruːli/ *adverb*
really: *I'm truly sorry.*
Yours truly (*American, formal*) words that you can use at the end of a formal letter before you write your name

trumpet
/ˈtrʌmpɪt/ *noun*
a musical instrument that is made of metal and that you blow

trumpet

truncheon
/ˈtrʌntʃən/ *noun*
(*British*)
a short thick stick that a police officer carries as a weapon

trunk /trʌŋk/ *noun*
1 the thick part of a tree, that grows up from the ground
2 *American English for* BOOT(2)
3 the long nose of an ELEPHANT (= a very large grey animal)
4 **trunks** (*plural*) = SWIMMING TRUNKS
5 a big strong box for carrying things when you travel

trust¹ 0━ /trʌst/ *noun* (*no plural*)
the belief that somebody is honest and good and will not hurt you in any way: *Put your trust in God.*

trust² 0━ /trʌst/ *verb* (**trusts**, **trusting**, **trusted**)
to believe that somebody is honest and good and will not hurt you in any way: *I just don't trust him.* ◇ *You can trust Penny to do the job well.*

trunks

trunk

trunk

trunk

trustworthy /ˈtrʌstwɜːði/ *adjective*
A **trustworthy** person is somebody that you can trust.

truth 0━ /truːθ/ *noun* (*no plural*)
being true; what is true: *There is **no truth in** these rumours.* ◇ *We need to find out the **truth about** what happened.* ◇ *Are you **telling** me the truth?*

truthful /ˈtruːθfl/ *adjective*
1 true: *a truthful answer*
2 A person who is **truthful** tells the truth.
▶ **truthfully** /ˈtruːθfəli/ *adverb*: *You must answer me truthfully.*
▶ **truthfulness** /ˈtruːθflnəs/ *noun* (*no plural*): *I have doubts about the truthfulness of her story.*

try 0━ /traɪ/ *verb* (**tries**, **trying**, **tried** /traɪd/, **has tried**)
1 to make an effort to do something: *I **tried to** remember her name but I couldn't.* ◇ *I'm not sure if I can help you, but I'll try.*
2 to use or do something to find out if you like it: *Have you ever **tried** Japanese food?*
3 to ask somebody questions in a court of law to decide if they have done something wrong: *He was **tried for** murder.*

A
B
C
D
E
F
G
H
I
J
K
L
M
N
O
P
Q
R
S
T
U
V
W
X
Y
Z

try and do something (*informal*) to try to do something: *I'll try and come early tomorrow.*

try something on to put on a piece of clothing to see if you like it and if it is big enough: *I tried the jeans on but they were too small.*

▶ **try** *noun* (*plural* **tries**): *I can't open this door – will you have a try?*

T-shirt /'tiː ʃɜːt/ *noun*
a kind of shirt with short sleeves and no COLLAR (= the folded part round the neck)

tsunami /tsuːˈnɑːmi/ *noun* (*plural* **tsunamis**)
a very large wave in the sea, usually caused by the sudden strong shaking of the ground (called an **earthquake**)

tub /tʌb/ *noun*
a round container: *a tub of ice cream*

tube 0ₘ /tjuːb/ *noun*
1 (*plural* **tubes**) a long thin pipe for liquid or gas
2 (*plural* **tubes**) a long thin soft container with a hole and a lid at one end: *a tube of toothpaste* ⊃ Look at the picture at **container**.
3 (*no plural*) (*British, informal*) the underground railway in London: *Shall we go by bus or by tube?*

tuck /tʌk/ *verb* (**tucks, tucking, tucked** /tʌkt/)
to put or push the edges of something inside or under something else: *He **tucked** his shirt **into** his trousers.*
tuck somebody in, tuck somebody up to make somebody feel comfortable in bed by pulling the covers around them: *I'll come up later and tuck you in.*

Tuesday 0ₘ /'tjuːzdeɪ/ *noun*
the day of the week after Monday and before Wednesday ⊃ Look at the note at **day**.

tuft /tʌft/ *noun*
a small amount of something such as hair or grass growing together

tug¹ /tʌɡ/ *verb* (**tugs, tugging, tugged** /tʌɡd/)
to pull something hard and quickly: *I tugged at the rope and it broke.*

tug² /tʌɡ/ *noun*
1 a sudden hard pull: *The little girl gave my hand a tug.*
2 (*also* **tugboat** /'tʌɡbəʊt/) a small strong boat that pulls big ships

tuition /tjuˈɪʃn/ *noun* (*no plural*)
teaching, especially to a small group: *A lot of students have extra tuition before their exams.*

tulip /'tjuːlɪp/ *noun*
a brightly coloured flower that comes in spring and is shaped like a cup

tumble /'tʌmbl/ *verb* (**tumbles, tumbling, tumbled** /'tʌmbld/)
to fall suddenly: *He tumbled down the steps.*

tummy /'tʌmi/ *noun* (*plural* **tummies**) (*informal*)
the part of your body between your chest and your legs ⊃ SAME MEANING **stomach**

tuna /'tjuːnə/ *noun* (*plural* **tuna**)
a large fish that lives in the sea and that you can eat

tune¹ 0ₘ /tjuːn/ *noun*
a group of musical notes that make a nice sound when you play or sing them together: *I know the tune but I don't know the words.*

tune² /tjuːn/ *verb* (**tunes, tuning, tuned** /tjuːnd/)
to make small changes to a musical instrument so that it makes the right sounds: *She tuned her guitar.*

tunnel

tunnel 0ₘ /'tʌnl/ *noun*
a long hole under the ground or sea for a road or railway

turban /'tɜːbən/ *noun*
a covering that some men wear on their heads. You make a **turban** by folding a long piece of material round and round.

turkey /'tɜːki/ *noun* (*plural* **turkeys**)
a big bird that people keep on farms and that you can eat. People eat **turkeys** especially at Christmas in Britain, and at Thanksgiving in the US. ⊃ Look at Picture Dictionary page **P2**.

turn¹ 0ₘ /tɜːn/ *verb* (**turns, turning, turned** /tɜːnd/)
1 to move round, or to move something round: *The wheels are turning.* ◇ *Turn the key.* ◇ *She turned round and walked towards the door.*
2 to move in a different direction: *Turn left at the traffic lights.*

tulip

3 to become different: *The weather has turned cold.*
4 to make somebody or something change: *The sun turned her hair blond.*
5 to find a certain page in a book: *Turn to page 97.*
turn something down
1 to say no to what somebody wants to do or to give you: *They offered me the job but I turned it down.*
2 to make something produce less sound or heat by moving a switch: *I'm too hot – can you turn the heating down?*
turn into something to become different; to change somebody or something into something different: *Water turns into ice when it gets very cold.*
turn something off to move the handle or switch that controls something, so that it stops: *Turn the tap off.* ◇ *She turned off the television.*
turn something on to move the handle or switch that controls something, so that it starts: *Could you turn the light on?*
turn out to be something in the end: *It has turned out to be a lovely day.*
turn something out to switch off a light: *Can you turn the lights out before you leave?*
turn over to move so that the other side is on top: *She turned over and went back to sleep.*
turn something over to move something so that the other side is on top: *If you turn over the page you'll find the answers on the other side.*
turn up (used about a person) to arrive: *Has David turned up yet?*
turn something up to make something produce more sound or heat by moving a switch: *Turn up the TV – I can't hear it properly.*

turn² 0̶ᴡ /tɜːn/ *noun*
1 the action of turning something round: *Give the screw a few turns.*
2 a change of direction: *Take a left turn at the end of this road.*
3 the time when you can or should do something: *It's your turn to do the washing-up!*
in turn one after the other: *I spoke to each of the students in turn.*
take turns at something, take it in turns to do something to do something one after the other: *You can't both use the computer at the same time. Why don't you take it in turns?*

turning /'tɜːnɪŋ/ (*British*) *noun*
a place where one road joins another road: *Take the first turning on the right.*

turnip /'tɜːnɪp/ *noun*
a round white vegetable that grows under the ground

turquoise /'tɜːkwɔɪz/ *adjective*
with a bright colour between blue and green

turtle /'tɜːtl/ *noun*   **turtle**
1 an animal that lives in the sea and has a hard shell on its back
2 (*informal*) American English for TORTOISE

tusk /tʌsk/ *noun*
a long pointed tooth that grows beside the mouth of an ELEPHANT (= a very big grey animal that lives in Africa and Asia) ➜ Look at the picture at **elephant**.

tutor /'tjuːtə(r)/ *noun*
a teacher who teaches one person or a small group

TV 0̶ᴡ /ˌtiː ˈviː/ *abbreviation* short for TELEVISION: *All rooms have a bathroom and colour TV.*

tweezers /'twiːzəz/ *noun* (*plural*)
a small tool made of two pieces of metal joined at one end. You use **tweezers** for holding or pulling out very small things: *She pulled the splinter out of her finger with a pair of tweezers.*

twelfth 0̶ᴡ /twelfθ/ *adjective, adverb, pronoun* 12th

twelve 0̶ᴡ /twelv/ *number* 12

twentieth 0̶ᴡ /'twentiəθ/ *adjective, adverb, pronoun* 20th

twenty 0̶ᴡ /'twenti/ *number*
1 20
2 **the twenties** (*plural*) the numbers, years or temperatures between 20 and 29
in your twenties between the ages of 20 and 29

twice 0̶ᴡ /twaɪs/ *adverb*
two times: *I have been to Japan twice.* ◇ *He ate twice as much as I did.*

twig /twɪg/ *noun*
a small thin branch of a tree

twilight /'twaɪlaɪt/ *noun* (*no plural*)
the time after the sun has gone down and before it gets completely dark ➜ Look at **dusk**.

twin /twɪn/ *noun*
1 one of two people who have the same mother and were born at the same time:

A
B
C
D
E
F
G
H
I
J
K
L
M
N
O
P
Q
R
S
T
U
V
W
X
Y
Z

David and John are twins. ◇ *I have a twin sister.*

2 one of two things that are the same: *a room with twin beds*

twinkle /'twɪŋkl/ *verb* (twinkles, twinkling, twinkled /'twɪŋkld/)
to shine with a small bright light that comes and goes: *Stars twinkled in the night sky.*

twist 0‑ᴡ /twɪst/ *verb* (twists, twisting, twisted)

1 to change the shape of something by turning it in different directions; to turn in many directions: *She twisted the metal into strange shapes.* ◇ *The path twists and turns through the forest.*

2 to turn something with your hand: *Twist the lid off the jar.*

3 to turn something round another object many times: *They twisted the sheets into a rope and escaped through the window.*

4 to hurt part of your body by suddenly turning it in a way that is not natural: *She fell and twisted her ankle.*

▶ **twist** *noun*: *the twists and turns of the river* ◇ *She gave the handle a hard twist.*

twitch /twɪtʃ/ *verb* (twitches, twitching, twitched /twɪtʃt/)
to make a sudden quick movement with a part of your body: *Rabbits twitch their noses.*

two 0‑ᴡ /tuː/ *number* 2
in two into two pieces: *The cup fell on the floor and broke in two.*

tying *form of* TIE¹

type¹ 0‑ᴡ /taɪp/ *noun*

1 (*plural* types) a group of things that are the same in some way ⊃ SAME MEANING **kind**, **sort**: *An almond is a type of nut.* ◇ *What type of music do you like?*

2 (*no plural*) the letters that a machine makes on paper: *The type was so small I couldn't read it.*

type² 0‑ᴡ /taɪp/ *verb* (types, typing, typed /taɪpt/)
to write something using a machine that has keys, such as a computer or a TYPEWRITER: *Her secretary types all her letters.* ◇ *Can you type?*

typewriter /'taɪpraɪtə(r)/ *noun*
a machine with keys that you use for writing: *an electric typewriter*

typhoon /taɪ'fuːn/ *noun*
a violent storm with strong winds in a hot country ⊃ Look at the note at **storm**.

typical 0‑ᴡ /'tɪpɪkl/ *adjective*
Something that is **typical** is a good example of its kind: *We had a typical English breakfast – bacon, eggs, toast and tea.*

▶ **typically** /'tɪpɪkli/ *adverb*: *She is typically British.*

typist /'taɪpɪst/ *noun*
a person who works in an office typing letters and documents

tyrant /'taɪrənt/ *noun*
a person with a lot of power who uses it in a cruel way

▶ **tyrannical** /tɪ'rænɪkl/ *adjective*: *a tyrannical ruler*

tyre 0‑ᴡ (*British*) (*American* tire) /'taɪə(r)/ *noun*
a circle of rubber around the outside of a wheel, for example on a car or bicycle: *I think we've got a flat tyre* (= a tyre with not enough air inside). ⊃ Look at the picture at **bicycle**.

U u

U, u /juː/ *noun* (*plural* U's, u's /juːz/)
the twenty-first letter of the English alphabet: '*Ugly* begins with a '*U*'.

UFO /ˌjuː ef ˈəʊ/ *abbreviation* (*plural* UFOs)
a strange object that some people think they have seen in the sky and that may come from another planet. **UFO** is short for 'unidentified flying object'.

ugly 0━┳ /ˈʌgli/ *adjective* (uglier, ugliest)
not pleasant to look at: *an ugly face* ◇ *The house was really ugly.* ➔ OPPOSITE **beautiful**

> 🔎 SPEAKING
> It is not polite to say somebody is **ugly**. It is better to say **unattractive**.

ulcer /ˈʌlsə(r)/ *noun*
a painful area on your skin or inside your body: *a mouth ulcer*

ultimate /ˈʌltɪmət/ *adjective*
happening at the end of a long process: *Our ultimate goal is independence.*

ultraviolet /ˌʌltrəˈvaɪələt/ *adjective*
Ultraviolet light cannot be seen and makes your skin go darker: *You must protect your skin from harmful ultraviolet rays.*

umbrella

umbrella /ʌmˈbrelə/ *noun*
a thing that you hold over your head to keep you dry when it rains: *It started to rain, so I put my umbrella up.*

umpire /ˈʌmpaɪə(r)/ *noun*
a person who watches a game such as TENNIS or CRICKET to make sure the players obey the rules
▶ **umpire** *verb* (umpires, umpiring, umpired /ˈʌmpaɪəd/): *The match was umpired by an Italian.* ➔ Look at **referee**.

the UN /ðə ˌjuː ˈen/ *abbreviation* short for THE UNITED NATIONS

un- /ʌn/ *prefix*
You can add **un-** to the beginning of some words to give them the opposite meaning, for example: *unhappy* (= not happy) ◇ *untrue* (= not true) ◇ *undress* (= to take clothes off)

unable 0━┳ /ʌnˈeɪbl/ *adjective*
not able to do something: *John is unable to come to the meeting because he is ill.* ➔ The noun is **inability**.

unacceptable /ˌʌnəkˈseptəbl/ *adjective*
If something is **unacceptable**, you cannot accept or allow it: *This behaviour is completely unacceptable.* ➔ OPPOSITE **acceptable**

unanimous /juˈnænɪməs/ *adjective*
with the agreement of every person: *The decision was unanimous.*

unarmed /ˌʌnˈɑːmd/ *adjective*
not carrying a gun or any weapon: *an unarmed police officer* ➔ OPPOSITE **armed**

unattractive /ˌʌnəˈtræktɪv/ *adjective*
not nice to look at ➔ OPPOSITE **attractive** ➔ Look at the note at **ugly**.

unavoidable /ˌʌnəˈvɔɪdəbl/ *adjective*
If something is **unavoidable**, you cannot stop it or get away from it: *This tragic accident was unavoidable.*

unaware /ˌʌnəˈweə(r)/ *adjective*
not knowing about or not noticing somebody or something: *I was unaware of the danger.* ➔ OPPOSITE **aware**

unbearable /ʌnˈbeərəbl/ *adjective*
If something is **unbearable**, you cannot accept it because it is so bad: *Everyone left the room because the noise was unbearable.*
▶ **unbearably** /ʌnˈbeərəbli/ *adverb*: *It was unbearably hot.*

unbelievable /ˌʌnbɪˈliːvəbl/ *adjective*
very surprising or difficult to believe ➔ SAME MEANING **incredible**

unborn /ˌʌnˈbɔːn/ *adjective*
not yet born: *an unborn child*

uncertain /ʌnˈsɜːtn/ *adjective*
not sure; not decided ➔ SAME MEANING **unsure**: *I'm uncertain about what to do.* ◇ *an uncertain future* ➔ OPPOSITE **certain**
▶ **uncertainty** /ʌnˈsɜːtnti/ *noun* (*plural* uncertainties): *This decision should put an end to all the uncertainty.*

uncle 0➡ /ˈʌŋkl/ *noun*
the brother of your mother or father, or the husband of your aunt: *Uncle Paul*

uncomfortable 0➡ /ʌnˈkʌmftəbl/ *adjective*
not pleasant to wear, sit on, lie on, etc.: *The chair was hard and uncomfortable.*
⊃ OPPOSITE **comfortable**
▸ **uncomfortably** /ʌnˈkʌmftəbli/ *adverb*: *The room was uncomfortably hot.*

uncommon /ʌnˈkɒmən/ *adjective*
not usual ⊃ SAME MEANING **rare**: *This tree is uncommon in Britain.* ⊃ OPPOSITE **common**

unconscious 0➡ /ʌnˈkɒnʃəs/ *adjective*
1 If you are **unconscious**, you are in a kind of sleep and you do not know what is happening: *She hit her head and was unconscious for three days.*
2 If you are **unconscious** of something, you do not know about it: *Mike seemed unconscious that I was watching him.*
⊃ OPPOSITE **conscious**
▸ **unconsciousness** /ʌnˈkɒnʃəsnəs/ *noun* (no plural): *She slipped into unconsciousness.*

uncontrollable /ˌʌnkənˈtrəʊləbl/ *adjective*
If a feeling is **uncontrollable**, you cannot control or stop it: *I suddenly got an uncontrollable urge to sneeze.*
▸ **uncontrollably** /ˌʌnkənˈtrəʊləbli/ *adverb*: *He started laughing uncontrollably.*

uncountable /ʌnˈkaʊntəbl/ *adjective*
(*grammar*) **Uncountable** nouns are ones that have no plural and cannot be used with 'a' or 'an', for example *advice* and *furniture*.

uncover /ʌnˈkʌvə(r)/ *verb* (uncovers, uncovering, uncovered /ʌnˈkʌvəd/)
1 to take something from on top of another thing: *Uncover the pan and cook the soup for 30 minutes.* ⊃ OPPOSITE **cover**
2 to find out something that was secret: *Police uncovered a plot to steal the painting.*

undeniable /ˌʌndɪˈnaɪəbl/ *adjective*
clear, true or certain: *It is undeniable that girls mature faster than boys.*

under 0➡ /ˈʌndə(r)/ *preposition, adverb*
1 in or to a place that is lower than or below something: *The cat is under the table.* ◇ *We sailed under the bridge.* ◇ *The boat filled with water, then went under.*
2 less than something: *If you are under 17 you are not allowed to drive a car.*
3 covered by something ⊃ SAME MEANING **underneath**: *I'm wearing a vest under my shirt.*

4 controlled by somebody or something: *The team are playing well under their new captain.*

under- /ˈʌndə(r)/ *prefix*
1 You can add **under-** to the beginning of some words to show that something is under another thing: *underwater* (= below the surface of the water) ◇ *underwear* (= clothes that you wear under your other clothes)
2 You can add **under-** to the beginning of some words to show that something is not enough: *undercooked* (= not cooked enough) ◇ *underpaid* (= not paid enough)

underage /ˈʌndəreɪdʒ/ *adjective*
too young to be allowed by law to do something: *underage drinking*

undergo /ˌʌndəˈgəʊ/ *verb* (undergoes, undergoing, underwent /ˌʌndəˈwent/, has undergone /ˌʌndəˈgɒn/)
to have a difficult or unpleasant experience: *Laura is in hospital undergoing an operation.*

undergraduate /ˌʌndəˈgrædʒuət/ *noun*
a student at a university who is studying for his or her first degree ⊃ Look at **graduate**.

underground¹ 0➡ /ˈʌndəgraʊnd/ *adjective, adverb*
under the ground: *an underground car park* ◇ *Moles spend much of their time underground.*

underground² /ˈʌndəgraʊnd/ (*also* the **Underground**) (*British*) (*American* **subway**) *noun* (no plural)
an underground railway system in a city: *I go to work by underground.* ◇ *We took the Underground to Piccadilly Circus.* ⊃ Look at Picture Dictionary page **P1**.

undergrowth /ˈʌndəgrəʊθ/ *noun* (no plural)
bushes and other plants that grow under trees: *There was a path through the undergrowth.*

underline /ˌʌndəˈlaɪn/ *verb* (underlines, underlining, underlined /ˌʌndəˈlaɪnd/)
to draw a line under a word or words. This sentence is underlined.

underneath 0➡ /ˌʌndəˈniːθ/ *preposition, adverb*
under or below something: *The dog sat underneath the table.* ◇ *She wore a black jacket with a red jumper underneath.*

underpants /ˈʌndəpænts/ *noun* (plural)
1 (*British*) (*British also, informal* **pants**) a piece of clothing that a man or boy wears under his trousers: *a pair of underpants*
2 (*American*) a piece of clothing that men or women wear under trousers, a skirt, etc.

A
B
C
D
E
F
G
H
I
J
K
L
M
N
O
P
Q
R
S
T
U
V
W
X
Y
Z

undershirt /'ʌndəʃɜːt/ *American English for* VEST(1)

understand 0→ /ˌʌndə'stænd/ *verb* (understands, understanding, understood /ˌʌndə'stʊd/, has understood)

1 to know what something means or why something happens: *I didn't understand what the teacher said.* ◇ *He doesn't understand Spanish.* ◇ *I don't understand why you're so angry.*

2 to know something because somebody has told you about it ⊃ SAME MEANING **believe**: *I understand that the plane from Geneva will be late.*

make yourself understood to make people understand you: *My German isn't very good but I can usually make myself understood.*

understanding¹ /ˌʌndə'stændɪŋ/ *noun* (no plural)
knowing about something: *He's got a good understanding of computers.*

understanding² /ˌʌndə'stændɪŋ/ *adjective*
ready to listen to other people's problems and try to understand them ⊃ SAME MEANING **sympathetic**: *My parents are very understanding.*

understood *form of* UNDERSTAND

undertaker /'ʌndəteɪkə(r)/ *noun*
a person whose job is to organize FUNERALS (= the time when dead people are buried or burned)

underwater 0→ /ˌʌndə'wɔːtə(r)/ *adjective, adverb*
below the surface of water: *Can you swim underwater?* ◇ *an underwater camera*

underwear 0→ /'ʌndəweə(r)/ *noun* (no plural)
clothes that you wear next to your body, under your other clothes

underwent *form of* UNDERGO

undo /ʌn'duː/ *verb* (undoes /ʌn'dʌz/, undoing, undid /ʌn'dɪd/, has undone /ʌn'dʌn/)
to open something that was tied or fixed: *I can't undo this zip.* ◇ *to undo a jacket* ⊃ OPPOSITE **do something up**

undone /ʌn'dʌn/ *adjective*
not tied or fixed: *Your shoelaces are undone.*

undoubtedly /ʌn'daʊtɪdli/ *adverb*
certainly; without doubt: *She is undoubtedly very intelligent.*

undress /ʌn'dres/ *verb* (undresses, undressing, undressed /ʌn'drest/)
to take clothes off yourself or another person: *He undressed and got into bed.* ◇ *She undressed her baby.* ⊃ OPPOSITE **dress**
▶ **undressed** /ʌn'drest/ *adjective*: *I got undressed and had a shower.*

uneasy /ʌn'iːzi/ *adjective*
worried that something is wrong: *I started to feel uneasy when the children were late coming home.*
▶ **uneasily** /ʌn'iːzɪli/ *adverb*: *She looked uneasily around the room.*

unemployed /ˌʌnɪm'plɔɪd/ *adjective*
If you are **unemployed**, you can work but you do not have a job: *She has been unemployed for over a year.*
⊃ OPPOSITE **employed**

unemployment 0→ /ˌʌnɪm'plɔɪmənt/ *noun* (no plural)
when there are not enough jobs for the people who want to work: *If the factory closes, unemployment in the town will increase.* ⊃ OPPOSITE **employment**

uneven /ʌn'iːvn/ *adjective*
not smooth or flat: *We had to drive slowly because the road was so uneven.*
⊃ OPPOSITE **even**

unexpected 0→ /ˌʌnɪk'spektɪd/ *adjective*
surprising because you did not expect it: *an unexpected visit*
▶ **unexpectedly** /ˌʌnɪk'spektɪdli/ *adverb*: *She arrived unexpectedly.*

unfair 0→ /ˌʌn'feə(r)/ *adjective*
Something that is **unfair** does not treat people in the same way or in the right way: *It was unfair to give chocolates to some of the children and not to the others.*
⊃ OPPOSITE **fair**
▶ **unfairly** /ˌʌn'feəli/ *adverb*: *He left his job because the boss was treating him unfairly.*

unfamiliar /ˌʌnfə'mɪliə(r)/ *adjective*
that you do not know; strange: *I woke up in an unfamiliar room.* ⊃ OPPOSITE **familiar**

unfashionable /ʌn'fæʃnəbl/ *adjective*
not popular at a particular time: *unfashionable clothes*
⊃ OPPOSITE **fashionable**

unfasten /ʌn'fɑːsn/ *verb* (unfastens, unfastening, unfastened /ʌn'fɑːsnd/)
to open something that was tied or fixed: *to unfasten your seatbelt* ⊃ OPPOSITE **fasten**

unfit /ʌn'fɪt/ *adjective*
1 not good enough or not right for something: *This house is unfit for people to live in.*

A B C D E F G H I J K L M N O P Q R S T U V W X Y Z

2 not healthy or strong: *She never takes any exercise – that's why she's so unfit.*
➔ OPPOSITE **fit**

unfold /ʌnˈfəʊld/ *verb* (unfolds, unfolding, unfolded)
to open something to make it flat; to open out and become flat: *Marie unfolded the newspaper and started to read.* ◇ *The sofa unfolds to make a bed.* ➔ OPPOSITE **fold**

unfortunate /ʌnˈfɔːtʃənət/ *adjective*
not lucky: *It's unfortunate that you were ill on your birthday.* ➔ OPPOSITE **fortunate**

unfortunately 0̶ᴡ /ʌnˈfɔːtʃənətli/ *adverb*
a word that you use to show that you are not happy about a situation or fact: *I'd like to give you some money, but unfortunately I haven't got any.* ➔ OPPOSITE **fortunately**

unfriendly 0̶ᴡ /ʌnˈfrendli/ *adjective*
not friendly; not kind or helpful to other people ➔ OPPOSITE **friendly**

ungrateful /ʌnˈɡreɪtfl/ *adjective*
If you are **ungrateful**, you do not show thanks when somebody helps you or gives you something: *Don't be so ungrateful! I spent all morning looking for this present.* ➔ OPPOSITE **grateful**

unhappy 0̶ᴡ /ʌnˈhæpi/ *adjective* (unhappier, unhappiest)
not happy ➔ SAME MEANING **sad**: *He was very unhappy when his wife left him.* ➔ OPPOSITE **happy**
▸ **unhappily** / ʌnˈhæpɪli/ *adverb*: '*I failed the exam,*' *she said unhappily.*
▸ **unhappiness** /ʌnˈhæpinəs/ *noun* (no plural): *John has had a lot of unhappiness in his life.*

unhealthy /ʌnˈhelθi/ *adjective* (unhealthier, unhealthiest)
1 not well; often ill: *an unhealthy child*
2 that can make you ill: *unhealthy food*
➔ OPPOSITE **healthy**

unhelpful /ʌnˈhelpfl/ *adjective*
not wanting to help somebody; not useful: *I'm afraid the shop assistant was rather unhelpful.* ➔ OPPOSITE **helpful**

uniform 0̶ᴡ /ˈjuːnɪfɔːm/ *noun*
the special clothes that everybody in the same job, school, etc. wears: *Police officers wear blue uniforms.*

unimportant /ˌʌnɪmˈpɔːtnt/ *adjective*
not important ➔ OPPOSITE **important**

uninhabited /ˌʌnɪnˈhæbɪtɪd/ *adjective*
where nobody lives: *an uninhabited island*

union 0̶ᴡ /ˈjuːniən/ *noun*
1 (*plural* **unions**) (*also* **trade union**) a group of workers who have joined together to talk to their managers about things like pay and the way they work: *the National Union of Teachers*
2 (*plural* **unions**) a group of people or countries that have joined together: *the European Union*
3 (*no plural*) coming together: *The union of England and Scotland was in 1707.*

unique /juˈniːk/ *adjective*
not like anybody or anything else: *Everybody in the world is unique.*

unit 0̶ᴡ /ˈjuːnɪt/ *noun*
1 one complete thing or group that may be part of something larger: *The book has twelve units.*
2 a measurement: *A metre is a unit of length and a kilogram is a unit of weight.*

unite 0̶ᴡ /juˈnaɪt/ *verb* (unites, uniting, united)
to join together to do something together; to put two things together: *We must unite to defeat our enemies.*
▸ **united** /juˈnaɪtɪd/ *adjective*: *the United States of America*

the United Nations /ðə juˌnaɪtɪd ˈneɪʃnz/ *noun* (no plural) (*abbr.* **UN**)
the organization that tries to stop world problems and to give help to countries that need it

universal /ˌjuːnɪˈvɜːsl/ *adjective*
connected with, done by or for everybody: *The environment is a universal issue.*
▸ **universally** /ˌjuːnɪˈvɜːsəli/ *adverb*: *to be universally accepted* (= accepted everywhere and by everybody)

the universe 0̶ᴡ /ðə ˈjuːnɪvɜːs/ *noun* (no plural)
the earth and all the stars, planets and everything else in space

university 0̶ᴡ /ˌjuːnɪˈvɜːsəti/ *noun* (*plural* **universities**)
a place where people go to study more difficult subjects after they have left school: *I'm hoping to go to university next year.* ◇ *My sister is at university studying Chemistry.*

🔎 **WORD BUILDING**
If you pass all your exams at a university, you get a **degree**.

unjust /ˌʌnˈdʒʌst/ *adjective*
not fair or right ➔ SAME MEANING **unfair**: *This tax is unjust because poor people pay as much as rich people.*

unkind 0⟶ /ˌʌnˈkaɪnd/ *adjective*
unpleasant and not friendly: *It was unkind of you to laugh at her.* ➔ OPPOSITE **kind**

unknown 0⟶ /ˌʌnˈnəʊn/ *adjective*
1 that you do not know ➔ SAME MEANING **unfamiliar**: *an unknown face*
2 not famous: *an unknown actor*
➔ OPPOSITE **famous, well known**

unleaded /ˌʌnˈledɪd/ *adjective*
Unleaded petrol is less harmful to the environment because it does not contain any LEAD (= a soft heavy grey metal).

unless 0⟶ /ənˈles/ *conjunction*
if not; except if: *You will be late unless you leave now.* ◇ *Unless you work harder you'll fail the exam.*

unlike /ˌʌnˈlaɪk/ *preposition*
different from: *She is unlike anyone I've ever met.* ➔ OPPOSITE **like**

unlikely 0⟶ /ʌnˈlaɪkli/ *adjective*
(unlikelier, unlikeliest)
If something is **unlikely**, it will probably not happen: *It is unlikely that it will rain.* ◇ *He is unlikely to pass the exam.* ➔ OPPOSITE **likely**

unload /ˌʌnˈləʊd/ *verb* (unloads, unloading, unloaded)
to take things that have been carried somewhere off or out of a car, lorry, ship or plane: *I unloaded the shopping from the car.* ◇ *They unloaded the ship at the dock.*

unlock /ˌʌnˈlɒk/ *verb* (unlocks, unlocking, unlocked /ˌʌnˈlɒkt/)
to open something with a key: *I unlocked the door and went in.*

unlucky /ʌnˈlʌki/ *adjective* (unluckier, unluckiest)
having or bringing bad luck: *They were unlucky to lose because they played very well.* ◇ *Some people think the number 13 is unlucky.* ➔ OPPOSITE **lucky**
▶ **unluckily** /ʌnˈlʌkɪli/ *adverb*: *Unluckily, I missed the bus.*

unmarried /ˌʌnˈmærid/ *adjective*
not married; without a husband or wife
➔ SAME MEANING **single**

unmistakable /ˌʌnmɪˈsteɪkəbl/ *adjective*
If something is **unmistakable**, it is easy to recognize and will not be confused with anything else: *Her Australian accent was unmistakable.*

unnatural /ʌnˈnætʃrəl/ *adjective*
different from what is normal or expected: *There was an unnatural silence.*
➔ OPPOSITE **natural**

unnecessary /ʌnˈnesəsəri/ *adjective*

> 🔎 **SPELLING**
> Remember! You spell **unnecessary** with **NN**, one **C** and **SS**.

not needed, or more than is needed: *All this fuss is totally unnecessary.*

unofficial /ˌʌnəˈfɪʃl/ *adjective*
not accepted or approved by a person in authority: *Unofficial reports say that four people died in the explosion.*

unpack /ˌʌnˈpæk/ *verb* (unpacks, unpacking, unpacked /ˌʌnˈpækt/)
to take all the things out of a bag, suitcase, etc.: *Have you unpacked your suitcase?* ◇ *We arrived at the hotel, unpacked, and then went to the beach.*

unpaid /ˌʌnˈpeɪd/ *adjective*
not yet paid: *unpaid bills*

unpleasant 0⟶ /ʌnˈpleznt/ *adjective*
not pleasant; not nice: *There was an unpleasant smell of bad fish.*
▶ **unpleasantly** /ʌnˈplezntli/ *adverb*: *It was unpleasantly hot in that room.*

unplug /ˌʌnˈplʌg/ *verb* (unplugs, unplugging, unplugged /ˌʌnˈplʌgd/)
to take out a piece of electrical equipment (called a **plug**) from the electricity supply: *Could you unplug the TV?* ➔ OPPOSITE **plug something in**

unpopular /ʌnˈpɒpjələ(r)/ *adjective*
not liked by many people; not popular: *He's unpopular at work because he's lazy.*

unpredictable /ˌʌnprɪˈdɪktəbl/ *adjective*
If something is **unpredictable**, you cannot say how it will change in the future: *The weather is very unpredictable at this time of year.*

unreasonable /ʌnˈriːznəbl/ *adjective*
expecting too much: *an unreasonable request*

unreliable /ˌʌnrɪˈlaɪəbl/ *adjective*
If something or somebody is **unreliable**, you cannot trust it or them: *Don't lend her any money – she's very unreliable.* ◇ *an unreliable car*

unruly /ʌnˈruːli/ *adjective*
difficult to control: *an unruly crowd*

unsafe /ˌʌnˈseɪf/ *adjective*
dangerous; not safe: *Don't climb on that wall – it's unsafe.*

unsatisfactory /ˌʌnˌsætɪsˈfæktəri/ *adjective*
not good enough; not acceptable: *Your work is unsatisfactory. Please do it again.*

A B C D E F G H I J K L M N O P Q R S T U V W X Y Z

A
B
C
D
E
F
G
H
I
J
K
L
M
N
O
P
Q
R
S
T
U
V
W
X
Y
Z

unstable /ʌnˈsteɪbl/ *adjective*
Something that is **unstable** may fall, move or change: *This bridge is unstable.* ◇ *an unstable government*

unsuccessful /ˌʌnsəkˈsesfl/ *adjective*
If you are **unsuccessful**, you have not done what you wanted and tried to do: *I tried to repair the bike but I was unsuccessful.*
▸ **unsuccessfully** /ˌʌnsəkˈsesfəli/ *adverb*: *He tried unsuccessfully to lift the box.*

unsuitable /ʌnˈsuːtəbl/ *adjective*
not suitable; not right for somebody or something: *This film is unsuitable for children.*

unsure /ˌʌnˈʃʊə(r)/ *adjective*
not sure about something: *We were unsure what to do.*

unsympathetic /ˌʌnˌsɪmpəˈθetɪk/ *adjective*
If you are **unsympathetic**, you are not kind to somebody who is hurt or sad, and you show that you do not understand their feelings and problems.

untidy 0➡ /ʌnˈtaɪdi/ *adjective* (untidier, untidiest)
not tidy; not with everything in the right place ⊃ SAME MEANING **messy**: *Your room is always so untidy!*
▸ **untidiness** /ʌnˈtaɪdinəs/ *noun* (no plural): *I hate untidiness!*

untie /ʌnˈtaɪ/ *verb* (unties, untying, untied /ʌnˈtaɪd/, has untied)
to remove a knot; to take off the string or rope that is holding something: *Can you untie this knot?* ◇ *I untied the parcel.*

until 0➡ /ənˈtɪl/ (*also informal* till) *conjunction, preposition*

🔎 SPELLING
Remember! You spell **until** with one **L** (but you spell **till** with **LL**).

up to a certain time or event: *The shop is open until 6.30.* ◇ *Stay in bed until you feel better.* ◇ *I can't come until tomorrow.*

untrue /ʌnˈtruː/ *adjective*
not true or correct: *What you said was completely untrue.*

unusual 0➡ /ʌnˈjuːʒuəl/ *adjective*
If something is **unusual**, it does not often happen or you do not often see it: *It's unusual to see a cat without a tail.* ◇ *What an unusual name!*
▸ **unusually** /ʌnˈjuːʒuəli/ *adverb*: *It was an unusually hot summer.*

unwanted /ˌʌnˈwɒntɪd/ *adjective*
not wanted: *an unwanted gift*

unwelcome /ʌnˈwelkəm/ *adjective*
If somebody or something is **unwelcome**, you are not happy to have or see them: *an unwelcome visitor*

unwell /ʌnˈwel/ *adjective*
not well; ill

unwilling /ʌnˈwɪlɪŋ/ *adjective*
If you are **unwilling** to do something, you are not ready or happy to do it: *He was unwilling to lend me any money.*

unwind /ˌʌnˈwaɪnd/ *verb* (unwinds, unwinding, unwound /ˌʌnˈwaʊnd/, has unwound)
1 to open out something that is wrapped into a ball or around something else: *to unwind a ball of string*
2 to start to relax, after working hard or worrying about something: *Watching television helps me unwind after a busy day.*

unwise /ˌʌnˈwaɪz/ *adjective*
showing that you do not make good decisions ⊃ SAME MEANING **foolish**: *It would be unwise to tell anybody about our plan yet.*
▸ **unwisely** /ˌʌnˈwaɪzli/ *adverb*: *Perhaps unwisely, I agreed to help her.*

unwrap /ʌnˈræp/ *verb* (unwraps, unwrapping, unwrapped /ʌnˈræpt/)
to take off the paper or cloth that is around something: *I unwrapped the parcel.*
⊃ OPPOSITE **wrap something up**

up 0➡ /ʌp/ *preposition, adverb*
1 in or to a higher place: *We climbed up the mountain.* ◇ *Put your hand up if you know the answer.* ⊃ OPPOSITE **down**
2 from sitting or lying to standing: *Stand up, please.* ◇ *What time do you get up* (= out of bed)? ◇ '*Is Joe up* (= out of bed)?' '*No, he's still asleep.*'
3 to the place where somebody or something is: *She came up to me and asked me the time.*
4 a word we use to show an increase in something: *Prices are going up.* ◇ *Please turn the radio up – I can't hear it.*
⊃ OPPOSITE **down**
5 into pieces: *Cut the meat up.*
6 so that it is finished: *Eat up, I want you to finish this food.*
7 in a certain direction: *We walked up the road.* ⊃ OPPOSITE **down**
8 (*informal*) a word that you use to show that something unusual or unpleasant is happening: *I could tell something was up by the looks on their faces.* ◇ *What's up* (= What's the matter)?
be up to somebody to be the person who should do or decide something: '*What*

shall we do this evening?' 'I don't mind. It's up to you.'

up to

1 as far as; until: *Up to now, she has worked very hard.*

2 as much or as many as: *Up to 300 people came to the meeting.*

3 doing something, especially something bad: *What is that man up to?*

update /ˌʌpˈdeɪt/ *verb* (updates, updating, updated)
to make something more modern or add new things to it: *The information on our website is updated every week.*

upgrade /ˌʌpˈɡreɪd/ *verb* (upgrades, upgrading, upgraded)
to change something so that it is better: *I've just upgraded my PC.*
▶ **upgrade** /ˈʌpɡreɪd/ *noun*: *to install an upgrade*

uphill /ˌʌpˈhɪl/ *adverb*
going up, towards the top of a hill: *It's difficult to ride a bicycle uphill.*
⊃ OPPOSITE **downhill**

upon /əˈpɒn/ *preposition* (formal)
on: *The decision was based upon the doctor's evidence.*

🔎 SPEAKING
On is the word that we usually use.

upper 0️⃣ /ˈʌpə(r)/ *adjective*
in a higher place than something else: *the upper lip* ⊃ OPPOSITE **lower**

upper case /ˌʌpə ˈkeɪs/ *noun* (no plural)
the large form of letters, for example A, B, C (not a, b, c): *'BBC' is written in upper case.*
⊃ OPPOSITE **lower case**

upright /ˈʌpraɪt/ *adjective*, *adverb*
standing straight up, not lying down: *Put the ladder upright against the wall.*

upset¹ 0️⃣ /ˌʌpˈset/ *verb* (upsets, upsetting, upset, has upset)
1 to make somebody feel unhappy or worried: *You upset Tom when you said he was fat.*
2 to make something go wrong: *The bad weather upset our plans for the weekend.*
3 to knock something so that it turns over and things fall out: *I upset a glass of wine all over the table.*

upset² 0️⃣ /ˌʌpˈset/ *adjective*
1 unhappy or worried: *The children were very upset when their dog died.*
2 ill: *I've got an upset stomach.*
▶ **upset** /ˈʌpset/ *noun* an illness in your stomach: *Sara has got a stomach upset.*

upsetting /ʌpˈsetɪŋ/ *adjective*
making you feel unhappy or worried: *The experience was very upsetting for all of us.*

upside down

The painting is upside down.

upside down /ˌʌpsaɪd ˈdaʊn/ *adverb*
with the top part at the bottom: *The picture is upside down.*

upstairs 0️⃣ /ˌʌpˈsteəz/ *adverb*
to or on a higher floor of a building: *I went upstairs to bed.*
▶ **upstairs** /ˈʌpsteəz/ *adjective*: *An upstairs window was open.* ⊃ OPPOSITE **downstairs**

up to date /ˌʌp tə ˈdeɪt/ *adjective*
modern; using new information: *Is this information up to date?*

upwards 0️⃣ /ˈʌpwədz/ (*also* **upward** /ˈʌpwəd/) *adverb*
up; towards a higher place: *We climbed upwards, towards the top of the mountain.*
⊃ OPPOSITE **downwards**

urban /ˈɜːbən/ *adjective*
connected with a town or city: *urban areas*

urge¹ /ɜːdʒ/ *verb* (urges, urging, urged /ɜːdʒd/)
to try to make somebody do something: *I urged him to stay for dinner.*

urge² /ɜːdʒ/ *noun*
a strong feeling that you want to do something: *I had a sudden urge to laugh.*

urgency /ˈɜːdʒənsi/ *noun* (no plural)
the need to do something quickly because it is very important

urgent 0️⃣ /ˈɜːdʒənt/ *adjective*
so important that you must do it or answer it quickly: *The doctor received an urgent telephone call.*
▶ **urgently** /ˈɜːdʒəntli/ *adverb*: *I must see you urgently.*

us 0️⃣ /əs; ʌs/ *pronoun* (plural)
me and another person or other people; me and you: *We were pleased when she invited us to dinner.* ◇ *Come with us.*

A
B
C
D
E
F
G
H
I
J
K
L
M
N
O
P
Q
R
S
T
U
V
W
X
Y
Z

A

use[1] /juːz/ *verb* (uses, using, used /juːzd/)

> 🔎 **PRONUNCIATION**
>
> When the word **use** is a verb, it sounds like **shoes** or **choose**.
> When the word **use** is a noun, it sounds like **juice** or **loose**.

1 to do a job with something: *Could I use your telephone?* ◇ *Do you know how to use this machine?* ◇ *Wood is used to make paper.*
2 to take something: *Don't use all the milk.*
use something up to use something until you have no more: *I've used up all the coffee, so I need to buy some more.*

use[2] /juːs/ *noun*
1 (*no plural*) using something or being used: *This pool is for the use of hotel guests only.*
2 (*plural* **uses**) what you can do with something: *This machine has many uses.*
3 (*no plural*) the opportunity to use something, for example something that belongs to somebody else: *I've got the use of Jim's car while he's on holiday.*
it's no use doing something it will not help to do something: *It's no use telling her anything – she never listens.*
make use of something to find a way of using something: *If you don't want that box, I can make use of it.*

used[1] /juːst/ *adjective*
be used to something to know something well because you have seen, heard, tasted, done, etc. it a lot: *I'm used to walking because I don't have a car.*
get used to something to begin to know something well after a time: *I'm getting used to my new job.*

used[2] /juːzd/ *adjective*
that had another owner before; not new ⊃ SAME MEANING **second-hand**: *The garage sells used cars.* ⊃ OPPOSITE **new**

used to /ˈjuːst tə; ˈjuːst tu/ *modal verb*
words that tell us about something that happened often or that was true in the past:

She used to smoke when she was young. ◇ *I used to be afraid of dogs, but now I like them.*

> 🔎 **GRAMMAR**
>
> To form questions we use **did** with **use to**: *Did she use to smoke when she was young?*
> We form negatives with **didn't use to**: *I didn't use to like fish, but I do now.*

useful /ˈjuːsfl/ *adjective*
good and helpful for doing something: *This bag will be useful for carrying my books.*

useless /ˈjuːsləs/ *adjective*
1 not good for anything: *A car is useless without petrol.*
2 that does not do what you hoped: *It was useless asking my brother for money – he didn't have any.*

user /ˈjuːzə(r)/ *noun*
a person who uses something: *computer users*

user-friendly /ˌjuːzə ˈfrendli/ *adjective*
easy to understand and use: *Computers are much more user-friendly now than they used to be.*

usual /ˈjuːʒuəl/ *adjective*
that happens most often ⊃ SAME MEANING **normal**: *He arrived home later than usual.*
as usual in the way that happens most often: *Julie was late, as usual.*

usually /ˈjuːʒuəli/ *adverb*
in the way that is usual; most often: *I'm usually home by six o'clock.*

utensil /juːˈtensl/ *noun*
a tool that is used in the home: *cooking utensils*

utter[1] /ˈʌtə(r)/ *adjective*
complete: *He felt an utter fool.*

utter[2] /ˈʌtə(r)/ *verb* (utters, uttering, uttered /ˈʌtəd/) (*formal*)
to say something or make a sound with your mouth: *She did not utter a word.*

utterly /ˈʌtəli/ *adverb*
completely or very: *That's utterly impossible!*

B
C
D
E
F
G
H
I
J
K
L
M
N
O
P
Q
R
S
T
U
V
W
X
Y
Z

V v

V, v /viː/ *noun*
1 (*plural* V's, v's /viːz/) the twenty-second letter of the English alphabet: *'Voice' begins with a 'V'.*
2 V *short for* VOLT
3 v (*British*) (*American* vs) *short for* VERSUS: *Liverpool v Manchester United*

vacancy /'veɪkənsi/ *noun* (*plural* **vacancies**)
1 a job that nobody is doing: *We have a* **vacancy for** *a secretary in our office.*
2 a room in a hotel that nobody is using: *The sign outside the hotel says 'no vacancies'* (= the hotel is full).

vacant /'veɪkənt/ *adjective*
1 empty or not being used: *a vacant room*
2 If a job in a company is **vacant**, nobody is doing it and it is available for somebody to do.

vacation 0━ /və'keɪʃn/ *noun* (*American*) (*British* **holiday**)
a period of time when you are not working or studying: *They're* **on vacation** *in Hawaii.*

vaccinate /'væksɪneɪt/ *verb* (**vaccinates, vaccinating, vaccinated**)
to put a substance into a person's or an animal's blood using a needle, to stop them getting a disease: *Have you been* **vaccinated against** *measles?*

vaccination /,væksɪ'neɪʃn/ *adjective*
when a substance is put into a person's or an animal's blood with a needle, to stop them getting a disease: *a vaccination against measles*

vaccine /'væksiːn/ *noun*
a substance that is put into a person's or an animal's blood using a needle, to stop them getting a disease

vacuum
/'vækjuəm/ *noun*
a space with no air, gas or anything else in it

vacuum cleaner
/'vækjuəm kliːnə(r)/ *noun*
a machine that cleans carpets by sucking up dirt

vacuum cleaner

vagina /və'dʒaɪnə/ *noun*
the part of a woman's or a female animal's body that leads to the place where a baby grows (called the **womb**)

vague /veɪɡ/ *adjective* (**vaguer, vaguest**)
not clear or not exact: *I couldn't find the house because he gave me very vague directions.*
▸ **vaguely** /'veɪɡli/ *adverb*: *I vaguely remember what happened.*

vain /veɪn/ *adjective* (**vainer, vainest**)
1 too proud of what you can do or how you look ⊃ The noun is **vanity**.
2 useless; without success: *They made a* **vain attempt** *to save his life.*
in vain without success: *I tried in vain to sleep.*

valid /'vælɪd/ *adjective*
able to be used; acceptable: *Your bus ticket is valid for one week.* ⊃ OPPOSITE **invalid**

valley 0━ /'væli/ *noun* (*plural* **valleys**)
the low land between mountains; the land that a river flows through

valuable 0━ /'væljuəbl/ *adjective*
1 worth a lot of money: *Is this ring valuable?*
2 very useful: *The book contains some valuable information.*

value¹ 0━ /'vælju:/ *noun*
1 (*plural* **values**) how much money you can sell something for: *The thieves stole goods with a total value of $100 000.*
2 (*no plural*) (*British*) how much something is worth compared with its price: *The meal was* **good value** *at only €8.50.*
3 (*no plural*) how useful or important something is: *Their help was* **of great value**.

value² /'vælju:/ *verb* (**values, valuing, valued** /'vælju:d/)
1 to think that something is very important: *I value my freedom.*
2 to say how much money something is worth: *The house was* **valued at** *$800 000.*

valve /vælv/ *noun*
a part in a pipe or tube which lets air, liquid or gas flow in one direction only

vampire /'væmpaɪə(r)/ *noun*
a person in stories who drinks people's blood

van /væn/ *noun*
a kind of big car or small lorry for carrying things ⊃ Look at the picture on the next page.

van

vandal /'vændl/ *noun*
a person who deliberately damages public property: *Vandals have damaged the benches in the park.*

vandalism /'vændəlɪzəm/ *noun* (no plural)
the crime of destroying or damaging public property deliberately and for no good reason: *Vandalism is a problem in this part of the city.*

vandalize /'vændəlaɪz/ *verb* (vandalizes, vandalizing, vandalized /'vændəlaɪzd/)
to damage public property deliberately

vanilla /və'nɪlə/ *noun* (no plural)
a substance from a plant that gives a taste to some sweet foods: *vanilla ice cream*

vanish /'vænɪʃ/ *verb* (vanishes, vanishing, vanished /'vænɪʃt/)
to go away; to stop being seen
➜ SAME MEANING **disappear**: *The thief ran into the crowd and vanished.*

vanity /'vænəti/ *noun* (no plural)
being too proud of what you can do or how you look ➜ The adjective is **vain**.

vapour (British) (American **vapor**) /'veɪpə(r)/ *noun*
very small drops of liquid that look like a gas: *water vapour*

varied[1] ⊶ /'veərid/ *adjective*
including a lot of different things: *I try to make my lessons as varied as possible.*

varied[2] form of VARY

varies form of VARY

variety ⊶ /və'raɪəti/ *noun*
1 (no plural) a lot of different things: *There's a wide variety of dishes on the menu.*
2 (no plural) the fact that you are not always doing the same things: *There's a lot of variety in my new job.*
3 (plural **varieties**) a type of something: *This variety of apple is very sweet.*

various ⊶ /'veəriəs/ *adjective*
several different: *We sell this shirt in various colours and sizes.*

varnish /'vɑːnɪʃ/ *noun* (no plural)
a clear paint with no colour, that you put on something to make it shine
▶ **varnish** *verb* (varnishes, varnishing, varnished /'vɑːnɪʃt/): *The doors are then stained and varnished.*

vary ⊶ /'veəri/ *verb* (varies, varying, varied /'veərid/, has varied)
1 to be different from each other or to change according to the situation: *Class sizes vary from 8 to 15.* ◇ *The price varies according to the quality.*
2 to make something different by changing it often in some way: *We try to vary the course to suit students' needs.*

vase

— vase

vase /vɑːz/ *noun*
a pot that you put cut flowers in

vast /vɑːst/ *adjective*
very big ➜ SAME MEANING **enormous, huge**: *Australia is a vast country.*

VCR /ˌviː siː 'ɑː(r)/ *noun*
a machine connected to a television, that you use for recording or showing programmes. **VCR** is short for 'video cassette recorder'.

VDU /ˌviː diː 'juː/ *noun*
a computer screen. **VDU** is short for 'visual display unit'.

veal /viːl/ *noun* (no plural)
meat from a young cow (a **calf**) ➜ Look at the note at **cow**.

vegan /'viːgən/ *noun*
a person who does not eat meat or any other foods that come from animals, such as eggs or milk

vegetable ⊶ /'vedʒtəbl/ *noun*
a plant or part of a plant that we eat: *The students grow vegetables such as cabbages, beans and carrots.* ➜ Look at Picture Dictionary page **P9**.

vegetarian /ˌvedʒə'teəriən/ *noun*
a person who does not eat meat or fish

▶ **vegetarian** *adjective*: *a vegetarian restaurant*

vehicle 0— /'vi:əkl/ *noun* (*formal*)
a car, bus, lorry, bicycle, etc.; a thing that takes people or things from place to place: *Are you the owner of this vehicle?*

veil /veɪl/ *noun*
a piece of material that a woman puts over her head and face

vein /veɪn/ *noun*
one of the small tubes in your body that carry blood to the heart

Velcro™ /'velkrəʊ/ *noun* (*no plural*)
two bands of special material that stick together to fasten clothes, shoes, etc.

velvet /'velvɪt/ *noun* (*no plural*)
cloth that is soft and thick on one side: *red velvet curtains*

ventilate /'ventɪleɪt/ *verb* (**ventilates, ventilating, ventilated**)
to allow air to move through a building
▶ **ventilation** /ˌventɪ'leɪʃn/ *noun* (*no plural*): *The only ventilation was one tiny window.*

veranda (*also* **verandah**) /və'rændə/ (*British*) (*American* **porch**) *noun*
a covered area with an open front, which is joined to a house on the ground floor

verb /vɜːb/ *noun*
(*grammar*) a word that tells you what somebody does or what happens. 'Go', 'sing', 'do' and 'be' are all **verbs**.

verdict /'vɜːdɪkt/ *noun*
a decision in a court of law about whether somebody is guilty or not: *The jury returned a verdict of* 'not guilty'.

verse /vɜːs/ *noun*
1 (*no plural*) words arranged in lines with a definite beat, often with sounds repeated at the ends of lines ⊃ SAME MEANING **poetry**: *The play is written in verse.*
2 (*plural* **verses**) a group of lines in a song or poem: *This song has five verses.*

version /'vɜːʃn/ *noun*
1 a form of something that is different in some way: *the latest version of the software*
2 what one person says or writes about something that happened: *His version of the accident is different from mine.*

versus /'vɜːsəs/ (*abbr.* **v, vs**) *preposition*
on the other side in a sport
⊃ SAME MEANING **against**: *There's a good football match on TV tonight – England versus Brazil.*

vertical /'vɜːtɪkl/ *adjective*
going straight up or down at an angle of 90°

from the ground: *a vertical line* ⊃ Look at **horizontal**. ⊃ Look at the picture at **line**.

very¹ 0— /'veri/ *adverb*
You use 'very' before another word to make it stronger: *Very few people know that.* ◇ *She speaks very quietly.* ◇ *I like chocolate very much.* ◇ *I'm not very hungry.*

very² /'veri/ *adjective*
exact; same: *You are the very person I wanted to see!* ◇ *We climbed to the very top of the mountain.*

vest /vest/ *noun*
1 (*British*) (*American* **undershirt**) a piece of clothing that you wear under your other clothes on the top part of your body ⊃ Look at Picture Dictionary page **P5**.
2 *American English for* WAISTCOAT

vet /vet/ (*British*) (*American* **veterinarian** /ˌvetərɪ'neəriən/) (*British also, formal* **veterinary surgeon** /'vetrənri sɜːdʒən/) *noun*
a doctor for animals ⊃ Look at Picture Dictionary page **P12**.

via /'vaɪə/ *preposition*
going through a place: *We flew from London to Sydney via Bangkok.*

vibrate /vaɪ'breɪt/ *verb* (**vibrates, vibrating, vibrated**)
to move very quickly from side to side or up and down: *The house vibrates every time a train goes past.*
▶ **vibration** /vaɪ'breɪʃn/ *noun*: *You can feel the vibrations from the engine when you are in the car.*

vicar /'vɪkə(r)/ *noun*
a priest in some Christian churches

vice /vaɪs/ *noun*
1 (*no plural*) criminal activities involving sex or drugs: *detectives from the vice squad*
2 (*plural* **vices**) a moral weakness or bad habit

vice- /vaɪs/ *prefix*
next to the leader in importance; able to represent the leader: *He's vice-captain of the team.* ◇ *the vice-president*

vicinity /və'sɪnəti/ *noun*
in the vicinity (*formal*) in an area; near a place: *There are three parks in the vicinity of the school.*

vicious /'vɪʃəs/ *adjective*
violent and cruel: *a vicious attack*

victim /'vɪktɪm/ *noun*
a person or thing that is hurt, damaged or killed by somebody or something: *the innocent victims of crime*

A B C D E F G H I J K L M N O P Q R S T U **V** W X Y Z

victorious /vɪk'tɔːriəs/ *adjective*
successful in a fight, game or war: *the victorious team*

victory /'vɪktəri/ *noun* (*plural* victories)
success in a fight, game or war: *the team's 3–2 victory against Poland*

video 0⃘̈ /'vɪdiəʊ/ *noun* (*plural* videos)
1 (*also* **videotape**) tape in a plastic box (called a **cassette**) on which a film, TV programme or real event is recorded: *You can get this film on video or on DVD.* ◊ *We stayed at home and watched a video.* ◊ *They made a video of the wedding.*
2 (*British*) (*also* **video recorder**) a machine connected to a television, that you use for recording or showing programmes: *Have you set the video?*

video game /'vɪdiəʊ ɡeɪm/ *noun*
a game that you play using a TV or computer screen

view 0⃘̈ /vjuː/ *noun*
1 what you believe or think about something ➔ SAME MEANING **opinion**: *He has strong views on marriage.* ◊ *In my view, she has done nothing wrong.*
2 what you can see from a place: *There were beautiful views of the mountains all around.* ◊ *At the top of the hill, the lake came into view* (= could be seen).
in view of something because of something: *In view of the bad weather we decided to cancel the match.*
on view in a place for people to see: *Her paintings are on view at the museum.*

viewer /'vjuːə(r)/ *noun*
a person who watches a television programme

vigorous /'vɪɡərəs/ *adjective*
strong and active: *vigorous exercise*
▸ **vigorously** /'vɪɡərəsli/ *adverb*: *She shook my hand vigorously.*

vile /vaɪl/ *adjective* (viler, vilest)
extremely unpleasant ➔ SAME MEANING **horrible**: *What a vile smell!*

villa /'vɪlə/ *noun*
a house with a garden in the countryside, especially in southern Europe

village 0⃘̈ /'vɪlɪdʒ/ *noun*
a very small town in the countryside: *She lives in a village in the mountains.* ➔ Look at the note at **town**.

villager /'vɪlɪdʒə(r)/ *noun*
a person who lives in a village

villain /'vɪlən/ *noun*
a bad person, usually in a book, play or film

vine /vaɪn/ *noun*
the plant that produces GRAPES (= small fruits that we eat or use to make wine)

vinegar /'vɪnɪɡə(r)/ *noun* (*no plural*)
a liquid with a strong sharp taste that is used in cooking: *I mixed some oil and vinegar to put on the salad.* ➔ Look at Picture Dictionary page **P6**.

vineyard /'vɪnjəd/ *noun*
a piece of land where GRAPES are grown to make wine

viola /vi'əʊlə/ *noun*
a musical instrument like a large VIOLIN

violence 0⃘̈ /'vaɪələns/ *noun* (*no plural*)
1 violent behaviour: *There's too much violence on TV.*
2 force or power: *the violence of the storm*

violent 0⃘̈ /'vaɪələnt/ *adjective*
strong and dangerous; causing physical harm: *Her husband was a violent man.* ◊ *The protest march started peacefully but later turned violent.*
▸ **violently** /'vaɪələntli/ *adverb*: *Did she behave violently towards you?*

violet /'vaɪələt/ *noun*
1 a small purple flower
2 a colour that is between dark blue and purple
▸ **violet** *adjective*: *violet eyes*

violin /ˌvaɪə'lɪn/ *noun*
a musical instrument that you hold under your chin and play by moving a stick (called a **bow**) across the strings

violin

bow

VIP /ˌviː aɪ 'piː/ *noun*
a person who is famous or important. **VIP** is short for 'very important person'.

virtual /'vɜːtʃuəl/ *adjective*
1 being almost or very nearly something: *He married a virtual stranger.*
2 made to appear to exist by a computer

virtually /'vɜːtʃuəli/ *adverb*
almost: *The two boys look virtually the same.*

virtual reality /ˌvɜːtʃuəl ri'æləti/ *noun* (*no plural*)
computer images that seem to be all around you and seem almost real

virtue /'vɜ:tʃu:/ *noun*
behaviour that shows high moral standards; a good quality or habit: *a life of virtue* ◇ *He has many virtues.*

virus /'vaɪrəs/ *noun* (*plural* **viruses**)
1 a living thing that is too small to see but that can make you ill: *a flu virus*
2 (*computing*) a program that enters your computer and stops it from working properly

visa /'vi:zə/ *noun*
an official piece of paper or mark in your passport to show that you can go into a country

visible /'vɪzəbl/ *adjective*
If something is **visible**, you can see it: *Stars are only visible at night.*
➲ OPPOSITE **invisible**

vision /'vɪʒn/ *noun*
1 (*no plural*) the power to see
➲ SAME MEANING **sight**: *He wears glasses because he has poor vision.*
2 (*plural* **visions**) a picture in your mind; a dream: *They **have a vision of** a world without war.*

visit 0️⃣ /'vɪzɪt/ *verb* (visits, visiting, visited)
to go to see a person or place for a short time: *When you go to London you must visit the Science Museum.* ◇ *She visited me in hospital.*
▶ **visit** *noun*: *This is my first **visit to** New York.* ◇ *He promised to **pay us a visit** next year.*

visitor 0️⃣ /'vɪzɪtə(r)/ *noun*
a person who goes to see another person or a place for a short time: *The old lady never has any visitors.* ◇ *Millions of visitors come to Rome every year.*

visual /'vɪʒuəl/ *adjective*
connected with seeing: *Painting and cinema are visual arts.*

visual aid /ˌvɪʒuəl 'eɪd/ *noun*
an object that a teacher shows you in lessons to help you learn something

vital /'vaɪtl/ *adjective*
very important: *It's **vital that** she sees a doctor – she's very ill.*

vitamin /'vɪtəmɪn/ *noun*
one of the things in food that you need to be healthy: *Oranges are full of vitamin C.*

vivid /'vɪvɪd/ *adjective*
1 making a very clear picture in your mind: *I had a very vivid dream last night.*
2 having a strong bright colour: *vivid yellow*
▶ **vividly** /'vɪvɪdli/ *adverb*: *I remember my first day at school vividly.*

vocabulary /və'kæbjələri/ *noun*
1 (*plural* **vocabularies**) all the words that somebody knows or that are used in a particular book or subject: *He has an amazing vocabulary for a five-year-old.*
2 (*no plural*) all the words in a language: *New words are always entering the vocabulary.*

voice 0️⃣ /vɔɪs/ *noun*
the sounds that you make when you speak or sing: *Steve has a very deep voice.*
at the top of your voice very loudly: *'Come here!' she shouted at the top of her voice.*
raise your voice to speak more loudly

voicemail /'vɔɪsmeɪl/ *noun* (*no plural*)
an electronic system that lets you leave or listen to telephone messages: *Have you checked your voicemail?*

volcano /vɒl'keɪnəʊ/ *noun* (*plural* **volcanoes**)
a mountain with a hole in the top where fire, gas and hot liquid rock (called **lava**) sometimes come out
▶ **volcanic** /vɒl'kænɪk/ *adjective*: *volcanic rocks*

volleyball /'vɒlibɔ:l/ *noun* (*no plural*)
a game where two teams try to hit a ball over a high net with their hands: *We played volleyball on the beach.*

volt /vəʊlt/ (*abbr.* **V**) *noun*
a measure of electricity

volume /'vɒlju:m/ *noun*
1 (*no plural*) the amount of space that something fills, or the amount of space inside something: *What is the volume of this box?*
2 (*no plural*) the amount of sound that something makes: *I can't hear the radio. Can you turn the volume up?*
3 (*plural* **volumes**) a book, especially one of a set: *The dictionary is in two volumes.*

voluntarily /'vɒləntrəli/ *adverb*
because you want to, not because you must: *She left the job voluntarily.*

voluntary /'vɒləntri/ *adjective*
1 If something is **voluntary**, you do it because you want to, not because you must: *She made a voluntary decision to leave the job.*
2 without payment: *He does **voluntary work** at a children's hospital.*

volunteer¹ /ˌvɒlən'tɪə(r)/ *noun*
a person who says that they will do a job without being forced or without being paid: *They're asking for volunteers to help at the Christmas party.*

A B C D E F G H I J K L M N O P Q R S T U V W X Y Z

A

volunteer² /ˌvɒlən'tɪə(r)/ *verb*
(volunteers, volunteering, volunteered
/ˌvɒlən'tɪəd/)
to say that you will do a job without being
forced or without being paid: *I volunteered to
do the washing-up.*

B

C

vomit /'vɒmɪt/ *verb* (vomits, vomiting,
vomited)
When you **vomit**, food comes up from your
stomach and out of your mouth.
➲ SAME MEANING **be sick**
▶ **vomit** noun (*no plural*) the food that
comes up from your stomach when you
VOMIT

D

E

F

G

vote 0➡ /vəʊt/ *noun*
when you choose somebody or something
by writing on a piece of paper or by putting
up your hand: *There were 96 votes for the
plan, and 25 against.*
▶ **vote** verb (votes, voting, voted): *Who
did you vote for in the election?*

H

I

J

voter /'vəʊtə(r)/ *noun*
a person who votes in a political election

K

voucher /'vaʊtʃə(r)/ *noun* (*British*)
a piece of paper that you can use instead of
money to pay for something

L

vowel /'vaʊəl/ *noun*
1 one of the letters *a, e, i, o* or *u*

M

N

2 a sound represented by one of the letters
a, e, i, o, u or *y*, or by a set of letters such as
ea, ow or *oy*. ➲ Look at **consonant**.

voyage /'vɔɪɪdʒ/ *noun*
a long journey by boat or in space: *a voyage
from London to New York*

vs *short way of writing* VERSUS

vulgar /'vʌlɡə(r)/ *adjective*
not showing good judgement about what is
attractive or appropriate; not polite or well
behaved: *She found their behaviour rather
vulgar.*

vulnerable /'vʌlnərəbl/ *adjective*
likely to be hurt or damaged: *The soldiers'
position meant that they were vulnerable to
attack.*

vulture

vulture /'vʌltʃə(r)/ *noun*
a type of bird that eats dead animals

O

P

Q

R

S

T

U

V

W

X

Y

Z

W w

W, w /'dʌblju:/ *noun*
1 (*plural* **W's, w's** /'dʌblju:z/) the twenty-third letter of the English alphabet: '*Water*' begins with a '*W*'.
2 **W** short for **WATT**

wade /weɪd/ *verb* (**wades, wading, waded**)
to walk through water: *Can we wade across the river, or is it too deep?*

wag /wæg/ *verb* (**wags, wagging, wagged** /wægd/)
to move or make something move from side to side or up and down: *The dog wagged its tail.*

wages /'weɪdʒɪz/ *noun* (*plural*)
the money that you receive every week for the work that you do: *Our wages are paid every Friday.* ◇ *low wages*

wagon /'wægən/ *noun*
1 a vehicle with four wheels that a horse pulls
2 (*British*) (*American* **freight car**) a part of a train where things like coal are carried

wail /weɪl/ *verb* (**wails, wailing, wailed** /weɪld/)
to make a long sad noise: *The little boy started wailing for his mother.*

waist /weɪst/ *noun*
the narrow part around the middle of your body ◑ Look at Picture Dictionary page **P4**.

waistcoat
/'weɪskəʊt/ (*British*)
(*American* **vest**)
noun
a piece of clothing
like a jacket with no
sleeves

waistcoat

wait¹ 0— /weɪt/
verb (**waits, waiting, waited**)
to stay in one place
until something
happens or until somebody or something comes: *If I'm late, please wait for me.* ◇ *Have you been waiting long?* ◇ *The doctor kept me waiting* (= made me wait) *for half an hour.*
can't wait used when somebody is very excited about something that is going to happen: *I can't wait to see you again!*
wait and see to be patient and find out later: '*What are we having for dinner?*' '*Wait and see!*'

wait up to not go to bed until somebody comes home: *I'll be home late tonight so don't wait up for me.*

wait² /weɪt/ *noun*
a time when you wait: *We had a long wait for the bus.*

waiter /'weɪtə(r)/ *noun*
a man who brings food and drink to your table in a restaurant ◑ Look at Picture Dictionary page **P12**.

waiting room /'weɪtɪŋ ruːm/ *noun*
a room where people can sit and wait, for example to see a doctor or to catch a train

waitress /'weɪtrəs/ *noun* (*plural* **waitresses**)
a woman who brings food and drink to your table in a restaurant

wake 0— /weɪk/ (*also* **wake up**) *verb* (**wakes, waking, woke** /wəʊk/, has **woken** /'wəʊkən/)
1 to stop sleeping: *What time did you wake up this morning?*
2 to make somebody stop sleeping: *The noise woke me up.* ◇ *Don't wake the baby.*

> 🔎 **SPEAKING**
> It is more usual to say **wake up** than **wake**.

walk¹ 0— /wɔːk/ *verb* (**walks, walking, walked** /wɔːkt/)
to move on your legs, but not run: *I usually walk to work.* ◇ *We walked 20 kilometres today.*
walk out to leave suddenly because you are angry: *He walked out of the meeting.*

walk² 0— /wɔːk/ *noun*
a journey on foot: *The beach is a short walk from our house.* ◇ *I took the dog for a walk.* ◇ *It was a lovely day so we went for a walk in the park.*

walker /'wɔːkə(r)/ *noun*
a person who is walking

walking stick /'wɔːkɪŋ stɪk/ *noun*
a stick that you use to help you walk

wall 0— /wɔːl/ *noun*
1 a side of a building or room: *There's a picture on the wall.*
2 a thing made of stones or bricks that is built around an area: *He went through a gate in the wall.* ◇ *Tom sat on the garden wall.*
◑ Look at the picture at **fence**.

wallet /'wɒlɪt/ *noun* (British) (American **billfold, pocketbook**)
a small flat case for money and bank cards: *A pickpocket stole my wallet.*

wallpaper /'wɔːlpeɪpə(r)/ *noun* (no plural)
special paper that you use for covering the walls of a room
▶ **wallpaper** *verb* (wallpapers, wallpapering, wallpapered /'wɔːlpeɪpəd/) to put WALLPAPER onto the walls of a room: *We wallpapered the living room ourselves.*

walnut /'wɔːlnʌt/ *noun*
a type of nut that we eat ⊃ Look at the picture at **nut**.

wander /'wɒndə(r)/ *verb* (wanders, wandering, wandered /'wɒndəd/)
to walk slowly with no special plan: *We wandered around the town until the shops opened.*

want 0̃ /wɒnt/ *verb* (wants, wanting, wanted)
1 to wish to have or do something: *Do you want a chocolate?* ◇ *I want to go out tonight.* ◇ *She wanted me to give her some money.*

🔊 **SPEAKING**
Would like is more polite than **want**: *Would you like a cup of tea?*

2 (*informal*) to need something: *Your car wants a wash!* ◇ *You want to be careful of that dog.*

war 0̃ /wɔː(r)/ *noun*
fighting between countries or between groups of people: *War had broken out* (= started). ◇ *The two countries have been at war* (= fighting) *for five years.* ◇ *Britain declared war on Germany.*

ward /wɔːd/ *noun*
a room in a hospital that has beds for the patients: *He worked as a nurse on the children's ward.*

warden /'wɔːdn/ *noun*
a person whose job is to look after a place and the people in it: *the warden of a youth hostel* ⊃ Look also at **traffic warden**.

wardrobe /'wɔːdrəʊb/ *noun*
a cupboard where you hang your clothes ⊃ Look at Picture Dictionary page **P10**.

warehouse /'weəhaʊs/ *noun* (plural warehouses /'weəhaʊzɪz/)
a big building where people keep things before they sell them: *a furniture warehouse*

warfare /'wɔːfeə(r)/ *noun* (no plural)
the activity of fighting a war: *naval warfare*

warm¹ 0̃ /wɔːm/ *adjective* (warmer, warmest)

🔊 **PRONUNCIATION**
The word **warm** sounds like **storm**.

1 having a pleasant temperature that is fairly high, between cool and hot: *It's warm by the fire.* ⊃ Look at the note at **hot**.
2 **Warm** clothes are clothes that stop you feeling cold: *It's cold in the mountains, so take some warm clothes with you.*
3 friendly and kind: *Martha is a very warm person.* ⊃ OPPOSITE **cold**
▶ **warmly** /'wɔːmli/ *adverb*: *The children were warmly dressed.* ◇ *He thanked me warmly.*

warm² 0̃ /wɔːm/ *verb* (warms, warming, warmed /wɔːmd/)
warm up, **warm somebody** or **something up** to become warmer, or to make somebody or something warmer: *I warmed up some soup for lunch.* ◇ *It was cold this morning, but it's warming up now.*

warmth /wɔːmθ/ *noun* (no plural)
1 a pleasant temperature that is not too hot: *the warmth of the sun*
2 the quality of being kind and friendly: *the warmth of his smile*

warn 0̃ /wɔːn/ *verb* (warns, warning, warned /wɔːnd/)
to tell somebody about danger or about something bad that may happen: *I warned him not to go too close to the fire.*

warning 0̃ /'wɔːnɪŋ/ *noun*
something that tells you about danger or about something bad that may happen: *There is a warning on every packet of cigarettes.* ◇ *The storm came without warning.*

warrant /'wɒrənt/ *noun*
an official document giving somebody permission to do something: *Police have issued a warrant for his arrest.*

was *form of* BE

wash¹ 0̃ /wɒʃ/ *verb* (washes, washing, washed /wɒʃt/)
1 to clean somebody, something or yourself with water: *Have you washed the car?* ◇ *Wash your hands before you eat.* ◇ *I washed and dressed quickly.*
2 (used about water) to flow somewhere: *The waves washed over my feet.*
wash somebody or **something away** (used about water) to move or carry somebody or something to another place: *The house was washed away by the river.*

wash up
1 (*British*) to clean the plates, knives, forks, and pans after a meal: *I washed up after dinner.*
2 (*American*) to wash your face and hands

wash² /wɒʃ/ *noun* (*no plural*)
cleaning something with water: *She gave the car a wash.* ◇ *I had a quick wash before dinner.*
in the wash being washed: *All my socks are in the wash!*

washbasin /'wɒʃbeɪsn/ (*also* **basin**) *noun*
the place in a bathroom where you wash your hands and face ➔ Look at Picture Dictionary page **P10**.

washing 0➡ /'wɒʃɪŋ/ *noun* (*no plural*)
clothes that you need to wash or that you have washed: *I've done the washing.* ◇ *Shall I hang the washing outside to dry?*

washing machine /'wɒʃɪŋ məʃiːn/ *noun*
a machine that washes clothes ➔ Look at Picture Dictionary page **P10**.

washing powder /'wɒʃɪŋ paʊdə(r)/ *noun* (*no plural*)
soap powder for washing clothes

washing-up /ˌwɒʃɪŋ 'ʌp/ *noun* (*no plural*) (*British*)
the work of washing the plates, knives, forks, and pans after a meal: *I'll do the washing-up if you cook the meal.*

washing-up liquid /ˌwɒʃɪŋ 'ʌp lɪkwɪd/ *noun* (*no plural*) (*British*)
liquid soap that you use for washing dishes

washroom /'wɒʃruːm/ *noun* (*American*)
a room with a toilet in it

wasn't /'wɒznt/ *short for* WAS NOT

wasp /wɒsp/ *noun*
a yellow and black insect that flies and can sting people

waste¹ 0➡ /weɪst/ *verb* (wastes, wasting, wasted)
to use too much of something or not use something in a good way: *She wastes a lot of money on sweets.* ◇ *He wasted his time at university – he didn't do any work.*

waste² 0➡ /weɪst/ *noun* (*no plural*)
1 not using something in a useful way: *It's a waste to throw away all this food!* ◇ *This watch was a waste of money – it's broken already!*
2 things that people throw away because they are not useful: *A lot of waste from the factories goes into this river.*

waste³ 0➡ /weɪst/ *adjective*
not useful or needed: *There's an area of waste ground outside the town where people dump their rubbish.* ◇ *waste paper*

waste-paper basket /ˌweɪst 'peɪpə bɑːskɪt/ *noun* (*British*) (*American* **wastebasket** /'weɪstbɑːskɪt/)
a container where you put things like paper that you do not want ➔ Look at Picture Dictionary page **P11**.

watch¹ 0➡ /wɒtʃ/ *verb* (watches, watching, watched /wɒtʃt/)
1 to look at somebody or something for some time: *We watched television all evening.* ◇ *Watch how I do this.* ➔ Look at the note at **see**.
2 to look after something or somebody: *Could you watch my bags while I buy a ticket?*
watch out to be careful because of somebody or something dangerous ➔ SAME MEANING **look out**: *Watch out! There's a car coming.*
watch out for somebody or **something** to look carefully and be ready for somebody or something dangerous ➔ SAME MEANING **look out for somebody or something**: *Watch out for ice on the roads.*

watches

strap

watch   digital watch

watch² 0➡ /wɒtʃ/ *noun*
1 (*plural* **watches**) a thing that you wear on your wrist so you know what time it is: *She kept looking at her watch nervously.* ➔ Look at the note at **clock**.
2 (*no plural*) the action of watching something in case of danger or problems: *The soldier was keeping watch at the gate.*

water¹ 0➡ /'wɔːtə(r)/ *noun* (*no plural*)
the liquid that is in rivers, lakes and seas: *I'd like a glass of water.* ◇ *After the heavy rain a lot of the fields were under water.*

water² /'wɔːtə(r)/ *verb* (waters, watering, watered /'wɔːtəd/)
1 to give water to plants: *Have you watered the plants?*
2 When your eyes **water**, they fill with tears: *The smoke made my eyes water.*

A B C D E F G H I J K L M N O P Q R S T U V W X Y Z

A
B
C
D
E
F
G
H
I
J
K
L
M
N
O
P
Q
R
S
T
U
V
W
X
Y
Z

watercolour /'wɔːtəkʌlə(r)/ *noun*
1 **watercolours** (*plural*) paints that you mix with water
2 a picture that you paint with **watercolours**

waterfall

waterfall /'wɔːtəfɔːl/ *noun*
a place where water falls from a high place to a low place

watering can /'wɔːtərɪŋ kæn/ *noun*
a container that you use for watering plants

watermelon /'wɔːtəmelən/ *noun*
a big round fruit with a thick green skin. It is pink inside with a lot of black seeds.

waterproof /'wɔːtəpruːf/ *adjective*
If something is **waterproof**, it does not let water go through it: *a waterproof jacket*

waterskiing /'wɔːtəskiːɪŋ/ *noun* (*no plural*)
the sport of moving fast over water on long boards (called **waterskis**), pulled by a boat ⊃ Look at Picture Dictionary page **P14**.

watt /wɒt/ *noun* (*abbr.* W)
a unit of electrical power: *a 60-watt light bulb*

wave¹ 0⊸ /weɪv/ *noun*
1 one of the lines of water that moves across the top of the sea: *Waves crashed against the cliffs.*
2 a movement of your hand from side to side in the air, to say hello or goodbye, or to make a sign to somebody: *As she turned the corner, she **gave** me **a wave**.*
3 a gentle curve in hair
4 the form that some types of energy such as heat, light and sound take: *radio waves*

wave

wave² 0⊸ /weɪv/ *verb* (waves, waving, waved /weɪvd/)
1 to move your hand from side to side in the air to say hello or goodbye, or to make a sign to somebody: *She **waved to** me as the train left the station.* ◇ *Who are you **waving at**?*
2 to move something quickly from side to side in the air: *The children waved flags as the President's car drove past.*
3 to move up and down or from side to side: *The flags were waving in the wind.*

wavelength /'weɪvleŋθ/ *noun*
the size of a radio wave that a particular radio station uses to send out its programmes
be on the same wavelength (*informal*) to have the same way of thinking as another person: *We get on OK, but we're not really on the same wavelength.*

wavy /'weɪvi/ *adjective* (wavier, waviest)
having curves; not straight: *a wavy line* ◇ *She has wavy black hair.* ⊃ Look at the picture at **hair**.

wavy

a wavy line

a straight line

a dotted line

wax /wæks/ *noun* (*no plural*)
the substance that is used for making CANDLES (= tall sticks that you burn to give light) or for making things shine: *wax floor polish*

way 0⊸ /weɪ/ *noun*
1 (*plural* **ways**) a method or style of doing something: *What is the best way to learn a language?* ◇ *He smiled in a friendly way.*
2 (*plural* **ways**) a road or path that you must follow to go to a place: *Can you tell me **the way to** the station, please?* ◇ *I **lost** my **way** and I had to look at the map.* ◇ *We stopped for a meal **on the way to** Bristol.* ◇ *Here's the museum. Where's **the way in**?* ◇ *I can't find **the way out**.*
3 (*plural* **ways**) a direction; where somebody or something is going or looking: *Come this way.* ◇ *She was looking **the other way**.* ◇ *Is this picture **the right way up**?* ◇ *Those two words are **the wrong way round**.*
4 (*no plural*) distance: *It's **a long way** from Glasgow to London.*
by the way words that you say when you are going to talk about something different: *By the way, I had a letter from Ann yesterday.*
give way
1 to stop and let somebody or something go before you: *You must give way to traffic coming from the right.*
2 to agree with somebody when you did not

agree before: *My parents finally gave way and said I could go on holiday with my friends.*
3 to break: *The ladder gave way and Ben fell to the ground.*
in the way in front of somebody so that you stop them from seeing something or moving: *I can't see – you're in the way.*
no way (*informal*) a way of saying 'no' more strongly: *'Can I borrow your bike?' 'No way!'*
out of the way no longer stopping somebody from moving or doing something: *Get out of the way! There's a car coming!*
way of life how people live: *Is the way of life in Europe different from America?*

WC /,dʌblju: 'si:/ *noun* (*British, formal*) (often written on signs and doors in public places) a toilet ➔ Look at the note at **toilet**.

we 0━ /wi:/ *pronoun* (*plural*) I and another person or other people; you and I: *Mick and I went out last night – we went to the theatre.* ◇ *Are we late?*

weak 0━ /wi:k/ *adjective* (weaker, weakest)

🔎 **PRONUNCIATION**
The word **weak** sounds just like **week**.

1 not powerful or strong: *She felt very weak after her long illness.* ◇ *He is too weak to be a good leader.* ➔ OPPOSITE **strong**
2 Something that is **weak** can break easily: *The bridge is too weak to carry heavy traffic.*
3 (used about a drink) containing a lot of water; not strong in taste: *I like my tea quite weak.* ➔ OPPOSITE **strong**
▶ **weakly** /'wi:kli/ *adverb*: *She smiled weakly at them.*

weaken /'wi:kən/ *verb* (weakens, weakening, weakened /'wi:kənd/) to become less strong or to make somebody or something less strong: *He was weakened by the illness.*

weakness 0━ /'wi:knəs/ *noun*
1 (*no plural*) the state of not being strong: *He thought that crying was a sign of weakness.*
2 (*plural* weaknesses) something that is wrong or bad in a person or thing ➔ OPPOSITE **strength**

wealth /welθ/ *noun* (*no plural*) a lot of money, land, or property: *He is a man of great wealth.*
▶ **wealthy** /'welθi/ *adjective* (wealthier, wealthiest) ➔ SAME MEANING **rich**: *a wealthy family*

weapon 0━ /'wepən/ *noun* something such as a gun that is used for

fighting or killing people: *nuclear weapons* ◇ *The police still haven't found the* **murder weapon**.

wear¹ 0━ /weə(r)/ *verb* (wears, wearing, wore /wɔ:(r)/, has worn /wɔ:n/)

🔎 **PRONUNCIATION**
The word **wear** sounds just like **where**.

to have clothes, jewellery, etc. on your body: *She was wearing a red dress.* ◇ *I wear glasses.*
wear off to become less strong: *The pain is wearing off.*
wear out to become thin or damaged because you have used it a lot; to make something do this: *Children's shoes usually wear out very quickly.*
wear somebody out to make somebody very tired: *She wore herself out by working too hard.*

wear² /weə(r)/ *noun* (*no plural*)
1 clothes: *sportswear*
2 long use which damages something: *This carpet is showing signs of wear.*

weary /'wɪəri/ *adjective* (wearier, weariest) very tired: *a weary traveller*
▶ **wearily** /'wɪərəli/ *adverb*: *She sank wearily into a chair.*

weather 0━ /'weðə(r)/ *noun* (*no plural*) how much sun, rain or wind there is at a certain time, or how hot or cold it is: *What's the weather like where you are?* ◇ *We had bad weather last week.* ➔ Look at Picture Dictionary page **P16**.

weather forecast /'weðə fɔ:kɑ:st/ *noun* words on television, radio or in a newspaper that tell you what the weather will be like: *The weather forecast says it will be sunny and dry tomorrow.*

weave /wi:v/ *verb* (weaves, weaving, wove /wəʊv/, has woven /'wəʊvn/) to make cloth by putting threads over and under one other: *These scarves are woven by hand.*

web /web/ *noun*
1 (*plural* webs) a thin net that a spider makes to catch flies ➔ Look at the picture at **spider**.
2 the Web (*no plural*) (*computing*) the system that makes it possible for you to see information from all over the world on your computer ➔ SAME MEANING **the World Wide Web**

webcam (*British*) (*American* Webcam™) /'webkæm/ *noun* a video camera that is connected to a

A B C D E F G H I J K L M N O P Q R S T U V W X Y Z

A B C D E F G H I J K L M N O P Q R S T U V **W** X Y Z

computer so that you can watch what it records on a website as it is happening

web page /'web peɪdʒ/ *noun*
a part of a website that you can see on your computer screen: *We learned how to create and register a new web page.*

website 0️⃣ /'websaɪt/ *noun*
a place on the Internet that you can look at to find out information about something: *I found this information on their website.* ◇ *Visit our website to learn more.*

we'd /wiːd/ *short for* WE HAD; WE WOULD

wedding 0️⃣ /'wedɪŋ/ *noun*
a time when a man and a woman get married: *Billy and Elena invited me to their wedding.* ◇ *She wore a long white wedding dress.*

> 🔎 **WORD BUILDING**
> At a **wedding**, two people **get married**. On their **wedding day**, the woman is called the **bride** and the man is the **groom** (or **bridegroom**). They are helped during the **wedding ceremony** by the **best man** and the **bridesmaids**. After the ceremony, there is usually a **wedding reception** (= a formal party). Many **couples** go on a **honeymoon** (= a holiday) after getting married. **Marriage** is the relationship between a **husband** and a **wife**: *They had a long and happy marriage.*

Wednesday 0️⃣ /'wenzdeɪ/ *noun*
the day of the week after Tuesday and before Thursday ⮕ Look at the note at **day**.

weed[1] /wiːd/ *noun*
a wild plant that grows where you do not want it: *The garden of the old house was full of weeds.*

weed[2] /wiːd/ *verb* (weeds, weeding, weeded)
to pull WEEDS out of the ground

week 0️⃣ /wiːk/ *noun*
1 a time of seven days, usually from Sunday to the next Saturday: *I'm going on holiday next week.* ◇ *I play tennis twice a week.* ◇ *I saw him two weeks ago.*

> 🔎 **WORD BUILDING**
> In British English, a period of two weeks is called a **fortnight**.

2 the part of the week when people go to work, especially Monday to Friday: *I work during the week but not at weekends.*

weekday /'wiːkdeɪ/ *noun*
any day except Saturday or Sunday: *I only work on weekdays.*

weekend 0️⃣ /ˌwiːk'end/ *noun*
Saturday and Sunday: *What are you doing at the weekend?*

weekly /'wiːkli/ *adjective, adverb*
happening or coming every week or once a week: *a weekly magazine* ◇ *I am paid weekly.*

weep /wiːp/ *verb* (weeps, weeping, wept /wept/, has wept) (*formal*)
to cry, usually because you are sad

> 🔎 **SPEAKING**
> **Cry** is the word that we usually use.

weigh 0️⃣ /weɪ/ *verb* (weighs, weighing, weighed /weɪd/)

> 🔎 **PRONUNCIATION**
> The word **weigh** sounds just like **way**.

1 to measure how heavy somebody or something is using a machine (called scales): *The shop assistant weighed the tomatoes.*
2 to have or show a certain weight: '*How much do you weigh?*' '*I weigh 55 kilos.*'

weight 0️⃣ /weɪt/ *noun*
1 (*no plural*) how heavy somebody or something is: *Do you know the weight of the parcel?* ◇ *I'm getting fat – I need to lose weight* (= get thinner)*!* ◇ *He's put on weight* (= got fatter) *lately.*
2 (*plural* weights) a piece of metal that weighs a particular amount and is used to measure the weight of something, or which people lift in order to improve their strength and as a sport: *She lifts weights as part of her training.*

weightlifting /'weɪtlɪftɪŋ/ *noun* (*no plural*)
a sport in which people lift heavy metal weights

weird /wɪəd/ *adjective* (weirder, weirdest)
very strange: *I had a weird dream.*

welcome[1] 0️⃣ /'welkəm/ *verb* (welcome, welcoming, welcomed /'welkəmd/)
to show that you are happy to have or see somebody or something: *He came to the door to welcome us.*
▶ **welcome** *noun*: *They gave us a great welcome.*

welcome[2] 0️⃣ /'welkəm/ *adjective*
1 If somebody or something is **welcome**,

you are happy to see them or it: *The cool drinks were welcome on such a hot day.* ◇ *Welcome to Oxford!*

2 (*informal*) used to say that you are happy for somebody to do something if they want to: *If you come to England again, you're welcome to stay with us.*

make somebody welcome to show a visitor that you are happy to see them

you're welcome polite words that you say when somebody has said 'thank you': '*Thank you.*' '*You're welcome.*'

welfare /'welfeə(r)/ *noun* (*no plural*)
the health and happiness of a person: *The school looks after the welfare of its students.*

well¹ 0— /wel/ *adverb* (**better, best**)
1 in a good or right way: *You speak English very well.* ◇ *These shoes are very well made.* ⊃ OPPOSITE **badly**
2 completely or very much: *I don't know Cathy very well.* ◇ *Shake the bottle well before you open it.*

as well also ⊃ SAME MEANING **too:** '*I'm going out.*' '*Can I come as well?*' ⊃ Look at the note at **also.**

as well as and also: *She has a flat in London as well as a house in Edinburgh.*

do well to be successful: *He did well in his exams.*

may or **might as well** words that you use to say that you will do something, often because there is nothing else to do: *If you've finished your work, you may as well go home.*

well done! words that you say to somebody who has done something good: '*I got the job!*' '*Well done!*'

well² 0— /wel/ *adjective* (**better, best**)
healthy: '*How are you?*' '*I'm very well, thanks.*' ⊃ OPPOSITE **ill**

well³ 0— /wel/ *exclamation*
1 a word that you often say when you are starting to speak: '*Do you like it?*' '*Well, I'm not really sure.*'
2 a word that you use to show surprise: *Well, that's strange!*

well⁴ /wel/ *noun*
a deep hole for getting water or oil from under the ground: *an oil well*

we'll /wi:l/ *short for* WE WILL, WE SHALL

well behaved /,wel bɪ'heɪvd/ *adjective*
behaving in a way that most people think is good: *Their children are very well behaved.*

well dressed /,wel 'drest/ *adjective*
wearing attractive or expensive clothes

wellingtons /'welɪŋtənz/ (*also* **wellington boots** /,welɪŋtən 'bu:ts/) (*British*) (*British also, informal*) **wellies** /'weliz/ (*American* **rubber boots**) *noun* (*plural*)
long rubber boots that you wear to keep your feet and part of your legs dry ⊃ Look at the picture at **shoe.**

well known /,wel 'nəʊn/ *adjective*
famous: *a well-known writer*
⊃ OPPOSITE **unknown**

well off /,wel 'ɒf/ *adjective*
rich ⊃ SAME MEANING **wealthy:** *They must be very well off – their house is huge.*

went *form of* GO¹

wept *form of* WEEP

were *form of* BE

we're /wɪə(r)/ *short for* WE ARE

weren't /wɜ:nt/ *short for* WERE NOT

west 0— /west/ *noun* (*no plural*)
1 (*abbr.* W) the direction you look in to see the sun go down: *Which way is west?* ◇ *They live in the west of England.* ⊃ Look at the picture at **compass.**
2 **the West** the countries of North America and Western Europe
▶ **west** *adjective, adverb*: *I live in west London.* ◇ *The town is five miles west of here.*

western¹ 0— /'westən/ *adjective*
in or of the west of a place: *Western parts of the country will be very cold.*

western² /'westən/ *noun*
a film or book about life in the west of the US in the past

wet 0— /wet/ *adjective* (**wetter, wettest**)
1 covered in water or another liquid: *This towel is wet – can I have a dry one?* ◇ *There was a strong smell of wet paint.*
2 with a lot of rain: *a wet day*
⊃ OPPOSITE **dry**

we've /wi:v; wɪv/ *short for* WE HAVE

whale

whale /weɪl/ *noun*
a very big animal that lives in the sea and looks like a very big fish

A B C D E F G H I J K L M N O P Q R S T U V W X Y Z

A

what 0🔊 /wɒt/ *pronoun, adjective*

1 a word that you use when you ask about somebody or something: *What's your name?* ◊ *What are you reading?* ◊ *What time is it?* ◊ *What kind of music do you like?*

2 the thing that: *I don't know what this word means.* ◊ *Tell me what to do.*

3 a word that you use to show surprise or other strong feelings: *What a terrible day!* ◊ *What beautiful flowers!*

what about ...? words that you use when you suggest something ➔ SAME MEANING **how about...?**: *What about going to the cinema tonight?*

what ... for? for what purpose or reason?: *What did you say that for?* ◊ *What's this machine for?*

what is ... like? words that you use when you want to know more about somebody or something: *'What's her brother like?' 'He's very nice.'*

what's on? words that you use when you want to know what television programmes or films are being shown: *What's on TV tonight?*

what's up? what is wrong? ➔ SAME MEANING **what's the matter?**: *You look sad. What's up?*

whatever 0🔊 /wɒt'evə(r)/ *adjective, pronoun, adverb*

1 any or every; anything or everything: *These animals eat whatever food they can find.* ◊ *I'll do whatever I can to help you.*

2 it does not matter what: *Whatever you do, don't be late.*

3 (*informal*) a word that you say to show that you do not mind what you do or have: *'What shall we do tomorrow?' 'Whatever.'*

what's /wɒts/ *short for* WHAT IS; WHAT HAS

wheat /wiːt/ *noun* (no plural)
a type of grain that can be made into flour

wheel¹ 0🔊 /wiːl/ *noun*
a thing like a circle that turns round to move something such as a car or a bicycle: *His favourite toy is a dog on wheels.* ➔ Look at the picture at **bicycle**.

wheel² /wiːl/ *verb* (wheels, wheeling, wheeled /wiːld/)

to push along something that has wheels: *I wheeled my bicycle up the hill.*

wheelbarrow

wheelbarrow
/'wiːlbærəʊ/ *noun*

a container with one wheel and two handles that you use outside for carrying things

wheelchair
/'wiːltʃeə(r)/ *noun*
a chair with wheels for somebody who cannot walk

wheelchair

when 0🔊 /wen/
adverb, conjunction

1 at what time: *When did she arrive?* ◊ *I don't know when his birthday is.*

2 at the time that: *It was raining when we left school.* ◊ *I saw her in May, when she was in London.* ◊ *He came when I called him.*

whenever 0🔊 /wen'evə(r)/ *conjunction*

1 at any time that: *Come and see us whenever you want.*

2 every time that: *Whenever I see her, she talks about her boyfriend.*

where 0🔊 /weə(r)/ *adverb, conjunction*

1 in or to what place: *Where do you live?* ◊ *I asked her where she lived.* ◊ *Where is she going?*

2 in which; at which: *This is the street where I live.*

whereas 0🔊 /ˌweər'æz/ *conjunction*
a word that you use between two different ideas: *John likes travelling, whereas I don't.*

wherever 0🔊 /weər'evə(r)/ *adverb, conjunction*

1 at, in or to any place: *Sit wherever you like.*
2 a way of saying 'where' more strongly: *Wherever did I put my keys?*

whether 0🔊 /'weðə(r)/ *conjunction*

1 a word that we use to talk about choosing between two things: *I don't know whether to go or not.*

2 if: *She asked me whether I was Spanish.*

which 0🔊 /wɪtʃ/ *pronoun, adjective*

🔎 **PRONUNCIATION**
The word **which** sounds just like **witch**.

1 what person or thing: *Which colour do you like best – blue or green?* ◊ *Which flat do you live in?*

2 a word that shows exactly what thing or things you are talking about: *Did you read the poem (which) Louise wrote?*

3 a word that you use before you say more about something: *Her new dress, which she bought in London, is beautiful.*

whichever /wɪtʃ'evə(r)/ *adjective, pronoun*
any person or thing: *Here are two books – take whichever you want.*

while¹ 0-ᴡ /waɪl/ (*also formal* **whilst** /waɪlst/) *conjunction*
1 during the time that; when: *The telephone rang while I was having a shower.*
2 at the same time as: *I listen to the radio while I'm eating my breakfast.*

while² 0-ᴡ /waɪl/ *noun* (*no plural*)
a period of time: *Let's sit here for a while.* ◇ *I'm going home in a while* (= soon).

whilst /waɪlst/ (*formal*) = WHILE¹: *He waited whilst I looked for my keys.*

whimper /'wɪmpə(r)/ *verb* (whimpers, whimpering, whimpered /'wɪmpəd/)
to make a soft crying noise, because you are hurt or afraid: *'Don't leave me alone,' he whimpered.*
▶ **whimper** *noun*: *The dog gave a whimper.*

whine /waɪn/ *verb* (whines, whining, whined /waɪnd/)
to make a long high sad sound: *The dog was whining outside the door.*

whinge /wɪndʒ/ *verb* (whinges, whingeing, whinged /wɪndʒd/) (*British, informal*)
to complain about things in an annoying way: *She's always whingeing about how much homework she has to do.*
▶ **whinge** *noun*

whip¹ /wɪp/ *noun*
a long piece of leather or rope with a handle, used for making animals move or for hitting people

whip² *verb* (whips, whipping, whipped /wɪpt/)
1 to hit an animal or a person with a WHIP: *The rider whipped the horse to make it go faster.*
2 to mix food very quickly with a fork, for example, until it is light and thick: *whipped cream*

whirl /wɜːl/ *verb* (whirls, whirling, whirled /wɜːld/)
to move round and round very quickly: *The dancers whirled around the room.*

whisk¹ /wɪsk/ *verb* (whisks, whisking, whisked /wɪskt/)
1 to mix eggs or cream very quickly with a fork or a WHISK
2 to take somebody or something somewhere very quickly: *The President was whisked away in a helicopter.*

whisk² /wɪsk/ *noun*
a tool that you use for mixing eggs or cream very quickly

whisker /'wɪskə(r)/ *noun*
one of the long hairs that grow near the mouth of cats, mice and some other animals ⊃ Look at the picture at **cat**.

whisky /'wɪski/ *noun* (*British*)

> 🔎 SPELLING
> In the US and in Ireland the spelling is **whiskey**.

1 (*no plural*) a strong alcoholic drink
2 (*plural* whiskies) a glass of **whisky**

whisper /'wɪspə(r)/ *verb* (whispers, whispering, whispered /'wɪspəd/)
to speak very quietly to somebody, so that other people cannot hear what you are saying: *He whispered so that he would not wake the baby up.*
▶ **whisper** *noun*: *She spoke in a whisper.*

whistle¹ /'wɪsl/ *noun*
1 a small musical instrument that makes a long high sound when you blow it: *The referee blew his whistle to end the match.*
2 the long high sound that you make when you blow air out between your lips or when you blow a **whistle**

whistle² /'wɪsl/ *verb* (whistles, whistling, whistled /'wɪsld/)
to make a long high sound by blowing air out between your lips or through a WHISTLE: *He whistled a tune to himself.*

white¹ 0-ᴡ /waɪt/ *adjective* (whiter, whitest)
1 with the colour of snow or milk: *He wore a white shirt and a blue tie.*
2 with pale skin
3 (*British*) **White** coffee is made with milk: *I'd like a white coffee.*
4 **White** wine is wine with a light colour.

white² 0-ᴡ /waɪt/ *noun*
1 (*no plural*) the colour of snow or milk: *She was dressed in white.*
2 (*plural* whites) a person with pale skin
3 (*plural* whites) the part inside an egg that is around the yellow middle part: *Add the whites of two eggs.* ⊃ Look at the picture at **egg**.

whizz (*British*) (*American* whiz) /wɪz/ *verb* (whizzes, whizzing, whizzed /wɪzd/) (*informal*)
to move very quickly: *The bullet whizzed past his head.*

who 0-ᴡ /huː/ *pronoun*
1 a word we use in questions to ask about

the name, position, etc. of one or more people: *Who is that girl?* ◇ *I don't know who did it.*

2 a word that shows which person or people you are talking about: *I like people who say what they think.* ◇ *The woman (who) I work for is very nice.*

who'd /hu:d/ *short for* WHO HAD; WHO WOULD

whoever 0— /hu:'evə(r)/ *pronoun*

1 the person who; any person who: *Whoever broke the glass must pay for it.*

2 a way of saying 'who' more strongly: *Whoever could have done that?*

whole¹ 0— /həʊl/ *adjective*

> 🔎 **PRONUNCIATION**
>
> The word **whole** sounds just like **hole**, because we don't say the **w** in this word.

complete; with no parts missing: *He ate the whole cake!* ◇ *We are going to Australia for a whole month.*

whole² 0— /həʊl/ *noun* (*no plural*)

1 a thing that is complete: *Two halves make a whole.*

2 all of something: *I spent the whole of the weekend in bed.*

on the whole generally, but not always completely true: *On the whole, I think it's a good idea.*

who'll /hu:l/ *short for* WHO WILL

wholly /'həʊlli/ *adverb* (*formal*)

completely ⊃ SAME MEANING **totally**: *He is not wholly to blame for the situation.*

whom 0— /hu:m/ *pronoun* (*formal*)

a word we use instead of 'who' as the object of a verb or PREPOSITION: *To whom did you give the money?* ◇ *She's the woman (whom) I met in Greece.*

> 🔎 **SPEAKING**
>
> **Whom** is very formal. **Who** is the word that we usually use.

who's /hu:z/ *short for* WHO IS; WHO HAS

whose 0— /hu:z/ *adjective, pronoun*

1 used to ask who something belongs to: *Whose car is this?*

2 used to say exactly which person or thing you mean, or to give extra information about a person or thing: *That's the boy whose sister is a singer.*

who've /hu:v/ *short for* WHO HAVE

why 0— /waɪ/ *adverb*

for what reason: *Why are you late?* ◇ *I don't know why she's angry.*

why not? words that you use to make or agree to a suggestion: *Why not ask Kate to go with you?*

wicked /'wɪkɪd/ *adjective*

1 very bad ⊃ SAME MEANING **evil**: *a story about a wicked witch*

2 (*informal*) very good: *This song is wicked!*

wide¹ 0— /waɪd/ *adjective* (**wider, widest**)

1 far from one side to the other: *We drove down a wide road.* ⊃ OPPOSITE **narrow**

2 You use **wide** to say or ask how far something is from one side to the other: *The table was 2 m wide.* ◇ *How wide is the river?*

3 completely open: *The children's eyes were wide with excitement.* ⊃ The noun is **width**.

wide² /waɪd/ *adverb*

completely; as far or as much as possible: *Open your mouth wide.* ◇ *I'm wide awake!* ◇ *She stood with her feet wide apart.*

widely /'waɪdli/ *adverb*

by a lot of people; in or to a lot of places: *He has travelled widely in Asia.*

widen /'waɪdn/ *verb* (**widens, widening, widened** /'waɪdnd/)

to become wider; to make something wider: *They are widening the road.*

widespread /'waɪdspred/ *adjective*

If something is **widespread**, it is happening in many places: *The disease is becoming more widespread.*

widow /'wɪdəʊ/ *noun*

a woman whose husband is dead

widower /'wɪdəʊə(r)/ *noun*

a man whose wife is dead

width /wɪdθ/ *noun*

how far it is from one side of something to the other; how wide something is: *The room is five metres in width.* ⊃ The adjective is **wide**.

wife 0— /waɪf/ *noun* (*plural* **wives** /waɪvz/)

the woman that a man is married to

wig /wɪg/ *noun*

a covering for your head made of hair that is not your own

wild 0— /waɪld/ *adjective* (**wilder, wildest**)

1 **Wild** plants and animals live or grow in nature, not with people: *We picked some wild flowers.*

2 excited; not controlled: *She was wild with anger.* ◊ *The crowd went wild with excitement.*

wildlife /'waɪldlaɪf/ *noun* (*no plural*)
animals and plants in nature

will¹ 0—ᵣ /wɪl/ *modal verb*

> 🔎 **GRAMMAR**
> The negative form of **will** is **will not** or the short form **won't** /wəʊnt/ : *They won't be there.*
> The short form of **will** is **'ll**. We often use this: *You'll* (= you will) *be late.* ◊ *He'll* (= he will) *drive you to the station.*

1 a word that shows the future: *Do you think she will come tomorrow?*
2 a word that you use when you agree or promise to do something: *I'll carry your bag.*
3 a word that you use when you ask somebody to do something: *Will you open the window, please?* ➮ Look at the note at **modal verb**.

will² 0—ᵣ /wɪl/ *noun*
1 (*no plural*) the power of your mind that makes you choose, decide and do things: *She has a very strong will and nobody can stop her doing what she wants.*
2 (*no plural*) what somebody wants to happen: *The man made him get into the car against his will* (= when he did not want to).
3 (*plural* **wills**) a piece of paper that says who will have your money, house, etc. when you die: *My grandmother left me £2 000 in her will.*

willing /'wɪlɪŋ/ *adjective*
ready and happy to do something: *I'm willing to work at weekends.*
➮ OPPOSITE **unwilling**
▶ **willingly** /'wɪlɪŋli/ *adverb*: *I'll willingly help you.*
▶ **willingness** /'wɪlɪŋnəs/ *noun* (*no plural*): *He showed no willingness to help.*

win 0—ᵣ /wɪn/ *verb* (**wins, winning, won** /wʌn/, **has won**)
1 to be the best or the first in a game, race or competition: *Who won the race?* ◊ *Tom won and I was second.* ➮ OPPOSITE **lose**
2 to receive something because you did well or tried hard: *I won a prize in the competition.* ◊ *Who won the gold medal?*

> 🔎 **WHICH WORD?**
> Be careful! You **earn** (not **win**) money by working.

▶ **win** *noun*: *Our team has had five wins this year.*

wind¹ 0—ᵣ /wɪnd/ *noun*
air that moves: *The wind blew his hat off.* ◊ *Strong winds caused a lot of damage to buildings.*

wind² /waɪnd/ *verb* (**winds, winding, wound** /waʊnd/, **has wound**)

> 🔎 **PRONUNCIATION**
> The verb **wind** sounds like **find** and the past forms sound like **found**.

1 A road or river that **winds** has a lot of bends and turns: *The path winds through the forest.*
2 to make something long go round and round another thing: *The nurse wound the bandage around my knee.*
3 to turn a key or handle to make something work or move: *The clock will stop if you don't wind it up.* ◊ *The driver wound her car window down.*
wind somebody up (*British, informal*) to deliberately say things that make somebody angry: *You're just trying to wind me up!*

windmill
/'wɪndmɪl/ *noun*
a tall building with long flat parts that turn in the wind

windmill

window 0—ᵣ
/'wɪndəʊ/ *noun*
an opening in a building or in a car door, for example, with glass in it: *It was cold, so I closed the window.* ◊ *She looked out of the window.*
➮ Look at Picture Dictionary page **P10**.

windowpane /'wɪndəʊpeɪn/ *noun*
a piece of glass in a window

windowsill /'wɪndəʊsɪl/ (*also* **window ledge** /'wɪndəʊ ledʒ/) *noun*
a shelf under a window ➮ Look at Picture Dictionary page **P10**.

windscreen /'wɪndskriːn/ (*British*) (*American* **windshield**) *noun*
the big window at the front of a car ➮ Look at Picture Dictionary page **P1**.

windscreen wiper /'wɪndskriːn waɪpə(r)/ (*British*) (*American* **windshield wiper** /'wɪndʃiːld waɪpə(r)/) *noun*
a thing that cleans rain and dirt off the WINDSCREEN while you are driving

windshield /'wɪndʃiːld/ *American English for* WINDSCREEN

windsurfer /'wɪndsɜːfə(r)/ *noun*
1 a special board with a sail. You stand on it as it moves over the water.

A B C D E F G H I J K L M N O P Q R S T U V **W** X Y Z

A
B
C
D
E
F
G
H
I
J
K
L
M
N
O
P
Q
R
S
T
U
V
W
X
Y
Z

2 a person who rides on a board like this

windsurfing /'wɪndsɜːfɪŋ/ *noun* (*no plural*)

the sport of moving over water on a special board with a sail: *We like to go windsurfing at the weekend.* ➲ Look at Picture Dictionary page **P14**.

windy /'wɪndi/ *adjective* (windier, windiest)

with a lot of wind: *It's very windy today!* ➲ Look at Picture Dictionary page **P16**.

wine 0➔ /waɪn/ *noun*

an alcoholic drink made from small green or purple fruit (called **grapes**): *Would you like red or white wine? ◊ She ordered a glass of wine.*

wing 0➔ /wɪŋ/ *noun*

1 one of the two parts that a bird or an insect uses to fly: *The chicken ran around flapping its wings.* ➲ Look at the picture at **bird**.

2 one of the two long parts at the sides of a plane that support it in the air ➲ Look at Picture Dictionary page **P1**.

wink /wɪŋk/ *verb* (winks, winking, winked /wɪŋkt/)

to close and open one eye quickly as a friendly or secret sign to somebody: *She winked at me.*
▸ **wink** *noun*: *He gave me a wink.* ➲ Look also at **blink**.

winner 0➔ /'wɪnə(r)/ *noun*

a person or an animal that wins a game, race or competition: *The winner was given a prize.* ➲ OPPOSITE **loser**

winning /'wɪnɪŋ/ *adjective*

The **winning** person or team is the one that wins a game, race or competition: *the winning team*

winter 0➔ /'wɪntə(r)/ *noun*

the coldest part of the year: *It often snows in winter.* ➲ Look at Picture Dictionary page **P16**.

wipe¹ /waɪp/ *verb* (wipes, wiping, wiped /waɪpt/)

1 to make something clean or dry with a cloth: *The waitress wiped the table. ◊ I washed my hands and wiped them on a towel.*

2 to take away something by rubbing it: *She wiped the writing off the blackboard. ◊ I wiped up the milk on the floor.*

wipe something out to destroy a place completely: *The bombs wiped out whole towns.*

wipe² /waɪp/ *noun*

1 the action of wiping something: *He gave the table a quick wipe.*

2 a piece of paper or thin cloth with a special liquid on it that you use for cleaning things: *a box of face wipes* (= for cleaning your face)

wire 0➔ /'waɪə(r)/ *noun*

a long piece of very thin metal: *The box was fastened with a piece of wire. ◊ The telephone wires had been cut.*

wisdom /'wɪzdəm/ *noun* (*no plural*)

knowing and understanding a lot about many things: *Some people think that old age brings wisdom.* ➲ The adjective is **wise**.

wise /waɪz/ *adjective* (wiser, wisest)

knowing and understanding a lot about many things: *a wise old man ◊ Do you think this is wise?*
▸ **wisely** /'waɪzli/ *adverb*: *Many people wisely stayed at home in the bad weather.*

wish¹ 0➔ /wɪʃ/ *verb* (wishes, wishing, wished /wɪʃt/)

1 to want something that is not possible or that will probably not happen: *I wish I could fly! ◊ I wish I had passed the exam! ◊ I wish we were rich.*

2 to say to yourself that you want something and hope that it will happen: *You can't have everything you wish for.*

3 (*formal*) to want to do or have something: *I wish to see the manager.*

🔎 SPEAKING

This is very formal. It is more usual to say **want** or **would like**.

4 to say that you hope somebody will have something: *I wished her a happy birthday.*

wish² 0➔ /wɪʃ/ *noun* (*plural* wishes)

1 a feeling that you want to do or have something: *I have no wish to go.*

2 an act of trying to make something happen by saying you want it to happen or hoping that it will happen: *Close your eyes and make a wish!*

best wishes words that you write at the end of a letter, before your name, to show that you hope somebody is well and happy: *See you soon. Best wishes, Lucy.*

wit /wɪt/ *noun* (*no plural*)

speaking or writing in a clever and funny way

witch /wɪtʃ/ *noun* (*plural* witches)

🔊 PRONUNCIATION

The word **witch** sounds just like **which**.

a woman in stories who uses magic to do bad things ➔ Look also at **wizard**.

with 0🔫 /wɪð/ *preposition*
1 a word that shows people or things are together: *I live with my parents.* ◇ *Mix the flour with milk.* ◇ *I agree with you.*
2 having or carrying: *He's an old man with grey hair.* ◇ *I want to live in a house with a garden.* ◇ *I passed a woman with an enormous suitcase.*
3 using: *I cut it with a knife.* ◇ *Fill the bottle with water.*
4 against: *I played tennis with my sister.*
5 because of: *Her hands were blue with cold.*

withdraw /wɪð'drɔː/ *verb* (withdraws, withdrawing, withdrew /wɪð'druː/, has withdrawn /wɪð'drɔːn/)
1 to move back or away: *The army withdrew from the town.*
2 to say that you will not take part in something: *Rob has withdrawn from the race.*
3 to take something out or away: *I withdrew $100 from my bank account.*

wither /'wɪðə(r)/ *verb* (withers, withering, withered /'wɪðəd/)
If a plant **withers**, it becomes dry and dies: *The plants withered in the hot sun.*

within 0🔫 /wɪ'ðɪn/ *preposition*
1 before the end of: *I'll be back within an hour.*
2 not further than: *We live within a mile of the station.*
3 (*formal*) inside: *There are 400 prisoners within the prison walls.*

without 0🔫 /wɪ'ðaʊt/ *preposition, adverb*
1 not having, showing or using something: *It's cold – don't go out without your coat.* ◇ *I drink coffee without sugar.*
2 not being with somebody or something: *He left without me.*
do without to manage when something is not there: *There isn't any tea so we will have to do without.*
without doing something not doing something: *They left without saying goodbye.*

witness /'wɪtnəs/ *noun* (plural witnesses)
1 a person who sees something happen and can tell other people about it later: *There were two witnesses to the accident.*
2 a person who goes to a court of law to tell people what they saw: *a witness for the defence*
▶ **witness** *verb* (witnesses, witnessing, witnessed /'wɪtnəst/): *She witnessed a murder.*

witty /'wɪti/ *adjective* (wittier, wittiest)
clever and funny: *a witty answer*

wives *plural of* WIFE

wizard /'wɪzəd/ *noun*
a man in stories who has magic powers ➔ Look at **witch**.

wobble /'wɒbl/ *verb* (wobbles, wobbling, wobbled /'wɒbld/)
to move a little from side to side: *That chair wobbles when you sit on it.*
▶ **wobbly** /'wɒbli/ *adjective*: *a wobbly table*

woke, woken *forms of* WAKE

wolf /wʊlf/ *noun* (plural wolves /wʊlvz/)
a wild animal like a big dog ➔ Look at Picture Dictionary page **P3**.

woman 0🔫 /'wʊmən/ *noun* (plural women /'wɪmɪn/)
an adult female person: *men, women and children* ◇ *Would you prefer to see a woman doctor?*

womb /wuːm/ *noun*
the part of a woman's body where a baby grows

won *form of* WIN

wonder¹ 0🔫 /'wʌndə(r)/ *verb* (wonders, wondering, wondered /'wʌndəd/)
to ask yourself something; to want to know something: *I wonder what that noise is.* ◇ *I wonder why he didn't come.*
I wonder if... words that you use to ask a question politely: *I wonder if I could use your phone.*

wonder² /'wʌndə(r)/ *noun*
1 (*no plural*) a feeling that you have when you see or hear something very strange, surprising or beautiful: *The children stared in wonder at the elephants.*
2 (*plural wonders*) something that gives you this feeling: *the wonders of modern medicine*
it's a wonder... it is surprising that...: *It's a wonder you weren't killed in the accident.*
no wonder it is not surprising: *She didn't sleep last night, so no wonder she's tired.*

wonderful 0🔫 /'wʌndəfl/ *adjective*
very good ➔ SAME MEANING **fantastic**: *What a wonderful present!* ◇ *This food is wonderful.*

won't /wəʊnt/ *short for* WILL NOT

wood 0🔫 /wʊd/ *noun*
1 (*no plural*) the hard substance that trees are made of: *Put some more wood on the fire.* ◇ *The table is made of wood.*
2 (*also* woods) a big group of trees, smaller

A B C D E F G H I J K L M N O P Q R S T U V W X Y Z

than a forest: *a large wood* ◇ *a walk in the woods*

wooden 0—☞ /'wʊdn/ *adjective*
made of wood: *The toys are kept in a wooden box.*

wool 0—☞ /wʊl/ *noun* (*no plural*)
1 the soft thick hair of sheep
2 thread or cloth that is made from the hair of sheep: *The cat was playing with a ball of wool.* ◇ *This jumper is made of pure wool.*
➲ Look at the picture at **knit**.

woollen (*British*) (*American* **woolen**)
/'wʊlən/ *adjective*
made of wool: *woollen socks*

woolly (*British*) (*American* **wooly**) /'wʊli/
adjective
made of wool, or like wool: *a woolly hat*

word 0—☞ /wɜːd/ *noun*
1 (*plural* **words**) a sound that you make, or a letter or group of letters that you write, which has a meaning: *What's the Italian word for 'dog'?* ◇ *Do you know the words of this song?*
2 something that you say: *Can I have a word with you?* ◇ *Don't say a word about this to anybody.*
3 (*no plural*) a promise: *She gave me her word that she wouldn't tell anyone.* ◇ *Claire said she would come, and she kept her word* (= did what she had promised).
in other words saying the same thing in a different way: *Joe doesn't like hard work – in other words, he's lazy!*
take somebody's word for it to believe what somebody says
word for word using exactly the same words: *Ian repeated word for word what you told him.*

word processor /'wɜːd ,prəʊsesə(r)/
noun
a small computer that you can use for writing

wore form of WEAR¹

work¹ 0—☞ /wɜːk/ *verb* (**works, working, worked** /wɜːkt/)
1 to be busy doing or making something: *You will need to work hard if you want to pass the exam.* ◇ *I'm going to work on my essay this evening.*
2 to do something as a job and get money for it: *Susy works for the BBC.* ◇ *I work at the car factory.*
3 to go correctly or to do something correctly: *We can't watch TV – it isn't working.* ◇ *How does this camera work?*
4 to make something do something: *Can you show me how to work the coffee machine?*

5 to have the result you wanted: *I don't think your plan will work.*
work out
1 to have the result you wanted: *I hope things work out for you.*
2 to do exercises to keep your body strong and well: *She works out every day.* ➲ Look at Picture Dictionary page **P15**.
work something out to find the answer to something: *We worked out the cost of the holiday.* ◇ *Why did she do it? I can't work it out.*

work² 0—☞ /wɜːk/ *noun*
1 (*no plural*) the job that you do to earn money: *I'm looking for work.* ◇ *What time do you start work?* ◇ *How long have you been out of work* (= without a job)?

> 🔎 **WHICH WORD?**
>
> **Work** or **job**?
> **Work** has no plural, so you cannot say 'a work' or 'works'. You can say: *I'm looking for work* or you have to say **a job** or **jobs**: *I'm looking for a job.*

2 (*no plural*) the place where you have a job: *I phoned him at work.* ◇ *I'm not going to work today.*
3 (*no plural*) doing or making something: *Digging the garden is hard work.* ◇ *She's so lazy – she never does any work.* ◇ *The group are at work on* (= making) *a new album.*
4 (*no plural*) something that you make or do: *The teacher marked our work.* ◇ *The artist only sells her work to friends.*
5 (*plural* **works**) a book, painting or piece of music: *He's read the complete works of Shakespeare.* ◇ *A number of priceless works of art were stolen from the gallery.*
6 **works** (*plural*) a place where people make things with machines: *My grandfather worked at the steelworks.*
get to work to start doing something: *Let's get to work on this washing-up.*

workbook /'wɜːkbʊk/ *noun*
a book where you write answers to questions, that you use when you are studying something

worker 0—☞ /'wɜːkə(r)/ *noun*
a person who works: *The factory workers all went out on strike.* ◇ *an office worker*

workman /'wɜːkmən/ *noun* (*plural* **workmen** /'wɜːkmən/)
a man who works with his hands to build or repair something

worksheet /'wɜːkʃiːt/ *noun*
a piece of paper where you write answers to questions, which you use when you are studying something

workshop /'wɜːkʃɒp/ *noun*
1 a place where people make or repair things
2 a time when people meet and work together to learn about something: *We went to a drama workshop.*

world 0̶ᵣ /wɜːld/ *noun*
1 (*no plural*) the earth with all its countries and people: *There was a map of the world on the classroom wall.* ◇ *Which is the biggest city in the world?*
2 (*plural* **worlds**) all the people who do the same kind of thing: *the world of politics*
think the world of somebody or **something** to like somebody or something very much: *She thinks the world of her grandchildren.*

world-famous /ˌwɜːld 'feɪməs/ *adjective*
known everywhere in the world: *a world-famous writer*

worldwide /ˌwɜːld'waɪd/ *adjective, adverb*
existing or happening everywhere in the world: *Pollution is a worldwide problem.* ◇ *They sell their computers worldwide.*

the World Wide Web /ðə ˌwɜːld waɪd 'web/ (*also* **the Web**) *noun* (*no plural*) (*abbr.* **WWW**)
the system of computers that makes it possible to see information from all over the world on your computer ➜ Look at **the Internet.**

worm /wɜːm/ *noun*
a small animal with a long thin body and no legs

worn *form of* WEAR¹

worn out /ˌwɔːn 'aʊt/ *adjective*
1 old and completely finished because you have used it a lot: *These shoes are completely worn out.* ◇ *worn-out carpets*
2 very tired ➜ SAME MEANING **exhausted**: *He's worn out after his long journey.*

worried 0̶ᵣ /'wʌrid/ *adjective*
unhappy because you think that something bad will happen or has happened: *Fiona is worried that she's going to fail the exam.* ◇ *I'm worried about my brother – he looks ill.*

worry¹ 0̶ᵣ /'wʌri/ *verb* (**worries, worrying, worried** /'wʌrid/, **has worried**)
to feel that something bad will happen or has happened; to make somebody feel this: *I always worry when Mark doesn't come home at the usual time.* ◇ *Don't worry if you don't know the answer.* ◇ *There's nothing to worry*

about. ◇ *What worries me is how we are going to get home.*

worry² 0̶ᵣ /'wʌri/ *noun*
1 (*no plural*) a feeling that something bad will happen or has happened: *Her face showed signs of worry.*
2 (*plural* **worries**) something that makes you feel worried: *I have a lot of worries.*

worse 0̶ᵣ /wɜːs/ *adjective, adverb* (**bad, worse, worst**)
1 not as good or as well as something else: *The weather today is worse than yesterday.* ◇ *Her Spanish is bad but her Italian is even worse.*
2 more ill: *If you get worse, you must go to the doctor's.* ➜ OPPOSITE **better**

worship /'wɜːʃɪp/ *verb* (**worships, worshipping, worshipped** /'wɜːʃɪpt/)
1 to show that you believe in God or a god by saying prayers: *Christians usually worship in churches.*
2 to love somebody very much or think that somebody is wonderful: *She worships her grandchildren.*
▶ **worship** *noun* (*no plural*): *A mosque is a place of worship.*

worst¹ 0̶ᵣ /wɜːst/ *adjective, adverb* (**bad, worse, worst**)
the least pleasant or suitable; the least well: *He's the worst player in the team!* ◇ *That was the worst day of my life.* ◇ *Everyone played badly, but I played worst of all.*
➜ OPPOSITE **best**

worst² 0̶ᵣ /wɜːst/ *noun* (*no plural*)
something or somebody that is as bad as it or they can be: *I'm the worst in the class at grammar.* ➜ OPPOSITE **best**
if the worst comes to the worst if something very bad happens: *If the worst comes to the worst and I fail the exam, I'll take it again next year.*

worth¹ 0̶ᵣ /wɜːθ/ *adjective*
1 having a particular value: *This house is worth $700 000.*
2 good or useful enough to do or have: *Is this film worth seeing?* ◇ *It's not worth asking Lyn for money – she never has any.*

worth² /wɜːθ/ *noun* (*no plural*)
1 value: *The painting is of little worth.*
2 how much or how many of something an amount of money will buy: *I'd like twenty pounds' worth of petrol, please.*

worthless /'wɜːθləs/ *adjective*
having no value or use: *A cheque is worthless if you don't sign it.*

A B C D E F G H I J K L M N O P Q R S T U V **W** X Y Z

worthwhile /ˌwɜːθ'waɪl/ *adjective*
good or useful enough for the time that you spend or the work that you do: *Passing the exam **made** all my hard work **worthwhile**.*

worthy /'wɜːði/ *adjective* (**worthier, worthiest**)
good enough for something or to have something: *He always felt he was not **worthy of** her.*

would 0⃞ /wʊd/ *modal verb*

> 🔍 **GRAMMAR**
> The negative form of **would** is **would not** or the short form **wouldn't** /'wʊdnt/: *He wouldn't help me.* The short form of **would** is **'d**. We often use **to** like this: *I'd* (= I would) *like to meet her.* ◇ *They'd* (= they would) *help if they had the time.*

1 a word that you use to talk about a situation that is not real: *If I had a million pounds, I would buy a big house.*
2 a word that you use to ask something in a polite way: *Would you close the door, please?*
3 a word that you use with 'like' or 'love' to ask or say what somebody wants: *Would you like a cup of tea?* ◇ *I'd love to go to Africa.*
4 the past form of 'will': *He said he would come.* ◇ *They wouldn't tell us where she was.*
5 a word that you use to talk about something that happened many times in the past: *When I was young, my grandparents would visit us every Sunday.* ⟳ Look at the note at **modal verb**.

would've /'wʊdəv/ *short for* WOULD HAVE

wound¹ /wuːnd/ *noun*
a hurt place in your body made by something like a gun or a knife: *He had knife wounds in his chest.*

wound² /wuːnd/ *verb* (**wounds, wounding, wounded**)
to hurt somebody with a weapon: *The bullet wounded him in the leg.*
▶ **wounded** /'wuːndɪd/ *adjective*: *She nursed the wounded soldier.*

wound³ *form of* WIND²

wove, woven *forms of* WEAVE

wow /waʊ/ *exclamation* (*informal*)
a word that shows surprise and pleasure: *Wow! What a lovely car!*

wrap 0⃞ /ræp/ *verb* (**wraps, wrapping, wrapped** /ræpt/)
to put paper or cloth around somebody or something: *The baby was **wrapped in** a blanket.* ◇ *She **wrapped** the glasses **up in** paper.* ⟳ OPPOSITE **unwrap**

wrapper /'ræpə(r)/ *noun*
a piece of paper or plastic that covers something like a sweet or a packet of cigarettes: *Don't throw your wrappers on the floor!*

wrapping /'ræpɪŋ/ *noun*
a piece of paper or plastic that covers a present or something that you buy: *I took the shirt out of its wrapping.*

wrapping paper /'ræpɪŋ peɪpə(r)/ *noun* (*no plural*)
special paper that you use to wrap presents ⟳ Look at the picture at **present²**.

wreath /riːθ/ *noun* (*plural* **wreaths** /riːðz/)
a circle of flowers or leaves: *She put a wreath on the grave.*

wreck¹ /rek/ *noun*
a ship, car or plane that has been very badly damaged in an accident: *a shipwreck* ◇ *The car was a wreck, but no one was hurt.*

wreck² /rek/ *verb* (**wrecks, wrecking, wrecked** /rekt/)
to break or destroy something completely: *The fire had completely wrecked the hotel.* ◇ *Our holiday was wrecked by the strike.*

wreckage /'rekɪdʒ/ *noun* (*no plural*)
the broken parts of something that has been badly damaged: *A few survivors were pulled from the wreckage of the train.*

wrench /rentʃ/ *American English for* SPANNER

wrestle /'resl/ *verb* (**wrestles, wrestling, wrestled** /'resld/)
to fight by trying to throw somebody to the ground, especially as a sport
▶ **wrestler** /'reslə(r)/ *noun*: *He used to be a professional wrestler.*
▶ **wrestling** /'reslɪŋ/ *noun* (*no plural*): *a wrestling match*

wriggle /'rɪgl/ *verb* (**wriggles, wriggling, wriggled** /'rɪgld/)
to turn your body quickly from side to side: *The teacher told the children to stop wriggling.*

wring /rɪŋ/ *verb* (**wrings, wringing, wrung** /rʌŋ/, **has wrung**)
to press and twist something with your hands to make water come out: *He **wrung** the towel **out** and put it outside to dry.*

wring

wrinkle /ˈrɪŋkl/   **wrinkle**
noun
a small line in
something, for
example in the skin
of your face: *My
grandmother has a
lot of wrinkles.*
▶ **wrinkled**
/ˈrɪŋkld/ *adjective*:
*His face is very
wrinkled.*

wrist /rɪst/ *noun*
the part of your body where your arm joins
your hand ⊃ Look at Picture Dictionary page
P4.

write 0‑ᴡ /raɪt/ *verb* (writes, writing,
wrote /rəʊt/, has written /ˈrɪtn/)

> *𝒫* **PRONUNCIATION**
> The word **write** sounds just like **right.**

1 to make letters or words on paper using a
pen or pencil: *Write your name at the top of
the page.* ◇ *He can't read or write.*
2 to create a story, book, song, piece of
music, etc.: *Shakespeare wrote plays.* ◇ *I've
written a poem for you.*
3 to write and send a letter to somebody: *My
mother **writes to** me every week.* ◇ *I wrote her
a postcard.*
write something down to write
something on paper, so that you can
remember it: *I wrote down his telephone
number.*

writer 0‑ᴡ /ˈraɪtə(r)/ *noun*
a person who writes books, stories, etc.:
Charles Dickens was a famous writer.

writing 0‑ᴡ /ˈraɪtɪŋ/ *noun* (no plural)
1 the activity or skill of putting words on
paper: *Today we're going to practise our
writing.*
2 words that somebody puts on paper; the

way a person writes: *I can't read your writing
– it's so small.*
in writing written on paper: *They have
offered me the job on the telephone but not in
writing.*

writing paper /ˈraɪtɪŋ peɪpə(r)/ *noun* (no
plural)
paper for writing letters on

written *form of* WRITE

wrong¹ 0‑ᴡ /rɒŋ/ *adjective*
1 not true or not correct: *She gave me the
wrong key, so I couldn't open the door.* ◇ *This
clock is wrong.* ⊃ OPPOSITE **right**
2 not the best: *We took the wrong road and
got lost.* ⊃ OPPOSITE **right**
3 not as it should be, or not working well:
*There's something **wrong with** my car – it
won't start.* ◇ *'What's **wrong with** Judith?'
'She's got a cold.'*
4 bad, or not what the law allows: *Stealing is
wrong.* ◇ *I haven't **done** anything **wrong.***
⊃ OPPOSITE **right**

wrong² 0‑ᴡ /rɒŋ/ *adverb*
not correctly; not right: *You've spelt my name
wrong.* ⊃ OPPOSITE **right**
go wrong
1 to not happen as you hoped or wanted: *All
our plans went wrong.*
2 to stop working well: *My watch keeps going
wrong.*

wrong³ /rɒŋ/ *noun* (no plural)
what is bad or not right: *Babies don't know
the difference between right and wrong.*

wrongly /ˈrɒŋli/ *adverb*
not correctly: *He was wrongly accused of
stealing the money.*

wrote *form of* WRITE

wrung *form of* WRING

WWW /ˌdʌbljuː dʌbljuː ˈdʌbljuː/
abbreviation short for THE WORLD WIDE WEB

A
B
C
D
E
F
G
H
I
J
K
L
M
N
O
P
Q
R
S
T
U
V
W
X
Y
Z

X x

X, x /eks/ *noun* (*plural* X's, x's /'eksɪz/)
the twenty-fourth letter of the English alphabet: *'X-ray begins with an 'X'.*

Xmas /'krɪsməs; 'eksməs/ (*informal*) *short way of writing* CHRISTMAS

🔍 **SPEAKING**
Xmas is used mainly in writing: *Happy Xmas and New Year!*

X-ray /'eks reɪ/ *noun*
a photograph of the inside of your body that is made by using a special light that you cannot see: *The doctor **took an X-ray** of my shoulder.*
▶ **X-ray** *verb* (X-rays, X-raying, X-rayed /'eksreɪd/): *She had her leg X-rayed.*

xylophone /'zaɪləfəʊn/ *noun*
a musical instrument with metal or wooden bars that you hit with small hammers

Y y

Y, y /waɪ/ *noun* (*plural* Y's, y's /waɪz/)
the twenty-fifth letter of the English alphabet: *'Yawn' begins with a 'Y'.*

yacht /jɒt/ *noun*

🔍 **PRONUNCIATION**
The word **yacht** sounds like **hot**.

1 a boat with sails that people go on for pleasure: *a yacht race*
2 a big boat with an engine that people go on for pleasure: *a millionaire's yacht* ➪ Look at the picture at **boat**.

yard /jɑːd/ *noun*
1 an area next to a building, usually with a fence or wall around it: *The children were playing in the school yard.* ◇ *a farmyard*
2 *American English for* GARDEN
3 (*abbr.* yd) a measure of length (=91 centimetres). There are three feet in a **yard**. ➪ Look at the note at **foot**.

yawn /jɔːn/ *verb* (yawns, yawning, yawned /jɔːnd/)
to open your mouth wide and breathe in deeply because you are tired
▶ **yawn** *noun*: *'I'm going to bed now,' she said with a yawn.*

yd *short way of writing* YARD(3)

yeah /jeə/ *exclamation* (*informal*)
yes

year 0️⃣ /jɪə(r)/ *noun*
1 a period of 365 or 366 days from 1 January to 31 December. A year has twelve months and 52 weeks: *Where are you going on holiday*
this year? ◇ *'What year were you born?' '1973.'* ◇ *I left school last year.*
2 any period of twelve months: *I've known Chris for three years.* ◇ *My son is five years old.* ◇ *I have a five-year-old son.* ◇ *I've got a two-year-old.*

🔍 **GRAMMAR**
Be careful! You can say: **She's ten** or **She's ten years old** (BUT NOT *'She's ten years'*).

3 (*British*) the level that a student is at in school or university: *I'm in year nine.* ◇ *They're third-year students.*
all year round for the whole year: *The swimming pool is open all year round.* ➪ Look also at **leap year** and **new year**.

yearly /'jɪəli/ *adjective, adverb*
happening or coming every year or once a year: *a yearly visit* ◇ *We meet twice yearly.*

yeast /jiːst/ *noun* (*no plural*)
a substance that you use for making bread rise

yell /jel/ *verb* (yells, yelling, yelled /jeld/)
to shout loudly: *Stop **yelling** at me!*
▶ **yell** *noun*: *He gave a yell of pain.*

yellow 0️⃣ /'jeləʊ/ *adjective*
with the colour of a lemon or of butter: *She was wearing a yellow shirt.*
▶ **yellow** *noun*: *Yellow is my favourite colour*

yes 0️⃣ /jes/ *exclamation*
a word that you use for answering a question. You use 'yes' to agree, to say that something is true, or to say that you would

like something: '*Have you got the key?*' '*Yes,
here it is.*' ◇ '*Would you like some coffee?*' '*Yes,
please.*'

yesterday 0̶ /ˈjestədeɪ/ *adverb, noun*
(*no plural*)
(on) the day before today: *Did you see Tom
yesterday?* ◇ *I phoned you yesterday afternoon
but you were out.* ◇ *I sent the letter* **the day
before yesterday.** ⊃ Look at **tomorrow**.

yet 0̶ /jet/ *adverb, conjunction*
1 a word that you use for talking about
something that has not happened but that
you expect to happen: *I haven't finished the
book yet.* ◇ *Have you seen that film yet?*
⊃ Look at the note at **already**.
2 now; as early as this: *You don't need to go
yet – it's only seven o'clock.*
3 in the future: *They may win yet.*
4 but; in spite of that: *We arrived home tired
yet happy.*
yet again once more: *John is late yet again!*

yield /jiːld/ *verb* (yields, yielding,
yielded)
1 to produce something such as crops or
results: *The survey yielded some interesting
information.*
2 to allow somebody to have power or
control ⊃ SAME MEANING **give in**: *The
government eventually yielded to the rebels.*

yob /jɒb/ *noun* (British, informal)
a young man who is rude and sometimes
violent

yoga /ˈjəʊgə/ *noun* (*no plural*)
a system of exercises that helps you relax
both your body and your mind ⊃ Look at
Picture Dictionary page **P15**.

yogurt (*also* **yoghurt**) /ˈjɒgət/ *noun*
a thick liquid food made from milk:
strawberry yogurt ◇ *Do you want a yogurt?*

yolk /jəʊk/ *noun*
the yellow part in an egg ⊃ Look at the
picture at **egg**.

you 0̶ /juː; ju/ *pronoun*
1 the person or people that I am speaking
to: *You are late.* ◇ *I phoned you yesterday.*
2 any person; a person: *You can buy stamps
at a post office.*

you'd /juːd/ *short for* YOU HAD; YOU WOULD

you'll /juːl/ *short for* YOU WILL

young¹ 0̶ /jʌŋ/ *adjective* (younger
/ˈjʌŋgə(r)/, youngest /ˈjʌŋgɪst/)
in the early part of life; not old: *They have two
young children.* ◇ *You're younger than me.*
⊃ OPPOSITE **old**

young² /jʌŋ/ *noun* (*plural*)
1 baby animals: *Birds build nests for their
young.*
2 **the young** children and young people: *a
television programme for the young*

youngster /ˈjʌŋstə(r)/ *noun*
a young person: *There isn't much for
youngsters to do here.*

your 0̶ /jɔː(r)/ *adjective*
1 of or belonging to the person or people
you are talking to: *Where's your car?* ◇ *Do you
all have your books?* ◇ *Show me your hands.*
2 belonging to or connected with people in
general: *You should have your teeth checked
every six months.*

you're /jɔː(r)/ *short for* YOU ARE

yours 0̶ /jɔːz/ *pronoun*
1 something that belongs to you: *Is this pen
yours or mine?*
2 **Yours** a word that you write at the end of
a letter: *Yours sincerely …* ◇ *Yours faithfully …*

yourself 0̶ /jɔːˈself/ *pronoun* (*plural*
yourselves /jɔːˈselvz/)
1 a word that shows 'you' when I have just
talked about you: *Did you hurt yourself?* ◇ *Buy
yourselves a drink.*
2 a word that makes 'you' stronger: *Did you
make this cake yourself?* ◇ *'Who told you?'* '*You
told me yourself!*'
by yourself, by yourselves
1 alone; without other people: *Do you live by
yourself?*
2 without help: *You can't carry all those bags
by yourself.*

youth 0̶ /juːθ/ *noun*
1 (*no plural*) the part of your life when you
are young: *She regrets that she spent her
youth travelling and not studying.* ◇ *He was
a fine musician in his youth.* ⊃ OPPOSITE
old age
2 (*plural* youths /juːðz/) a boy or young
man: *The fight was started by a gang of
youths.*
3 **the youth** (*no plural*) young people: *We
must do more for the youth of this country.*

youth club /ˈjuːθ klʌb/ *noun*
a club for young people

youth hostel /ˈjuːθ hɒstl/ *noun*
a cheap place where people can stay when
they are travelling

you've /juːv/ *short for* YOU HAVE

yo-yo /ˈjəʊ jəʊ/ *noun* (*plural* yo-yos)
a toy which is a round piece of wood or
plastic with a string round the middle. You
put the string on your finger and make the
yo-yo go up and down.

A
B
C
D
E
F
G
H
I
J
K
L
M
N
O
P
Q
R
S
T
U
V
W
X
Y
Z

A
B
C
D
E
F
G
H
I
J
K
L
M
N
O
P
Q
R
S
T
U
V
W
X
Y
Z

yuck /jʌk/ *exclamation* (*informal*)
a word that you say when you think
something looks or tastes disgusting: *Yuck! I
hate cabbage!*

yummy /ˈjʌmi/ *adjective* (*informal*)
tasting very good ➲ SAME MEANING
delicious: *This cake is yummy.*

Z z

Z, z /zed/ *noun* (*plural Z's, z's* /zedz/)

🔎 **PRONUNCIATION**

In American English, the letter 'Z' is
pronounced /ziː/.

the twenty-sixth and last letter of the English
alphabet: '*Zoo' begins with a 'Z'.*

zebra

zebra /ˈzebrə/ *noun* (*plural zebras or zebra*)
an African wild animal like a horse, with
black and white lines on its body

zebra crossing /ˌzebrə ˈkrɒsɪŋ/ *noun*
(*British*)
a black and white path across a road. Cars
must stop there to let people cross the road
safely.

zero 0🔔 /ˈzɪərəʊ/ *noun* (*plural zeros or
zeroes*)
1 the number 0
2 freezing point; 0° C: *The temperature is five
degrees **below zero**.*

zigzag /ˈzɪgzæg/
noun
a line that goes up
and down, like a lot
of letter W's, one
after the other

zigzag

zinc /zɪŋk/ *noun* (*no plural*) (*symbol Zn*)
a blue-white metal

zip /zɪp/ (*British*)
(*American* **zipper**)
noun
a long metal or
plastic thing with a
small part that you
pull to close and
open things like
clothes and bags
▶ **zip** *verb* (zips,
zipping, zipped
/zɪpt/)
**zip something
up** to fasten
something together with a ZIP: *She zipped up
her dress.*

zip

zip code (*also* ZIP code) /ˈzɪp kəʊd/
American English for POSTCODE

zipper /ˈzɪpə(r)/ *American English for* ZIP

zone /zəʊn/ *noun*
a place where something special happens:
Do not enter the danger zone!

zoo /zuː/ *noun* (*plural zoos*)
a place where wild animals are kept and
people can go and look at them

zoom /zuːm/ *verb* (zooms, zooming,
zoomed /zuːmd/)
to move very fast: *The traffic zoomed past us.*

zucchini /zuˈkiːni/ (*plural zucchini or
zucchinis*) *American English for* COURGETTE

Geographical names

If there are different words for the adjective and the person who comes from a particular place, we also give the word for the person, for example **Finland**; **Finnish** (*person*) **Finn**.

Geographical name	Adjective
Afghanistan /æfˈɡænɪstæn/	Afghan /ˈæfɡæn/
Africa /ˈæfrɪkə/	African /ˈæfrɪkən/
Albania /ælˈbeɪniə/	Albanian /ælˈbeɪniən/
Algeria /ælˈdʒɪəriə/	Algerian /ælˈdʒɪəriən/
America /əˈmerɪkə/	American /əˈmerɪkən/
Angola /æŋˈɡəʊlə/	Angolan /æŋˈɡəʊlən/
Antarctica /ænˈtɑːktɪkə/	Antarctic /ænˈtɑːktɪk/
Antigua and Barbuda /ænˌtiːɡə ən bɑːˈbjuːdə/	Antiguan /ænˈtiːɡən/ Barbudan /bɑːˈbjuːdən/
the Arctic /ði ˈɑːktɪk/	Arctic /ˈɑːktɪk/
Argentina /ˌɑːdʒənˈtiːnə/	Argentinian /ˌɑːdʒənˈtɪniən/ (*person*) Argentine /ˈɑːdʒəntaɪn/
Armenia /ɑːˈmiːniə/	Armenian /ɑːˈmiːniən/
Asia /ˈeɪʃə, ˈeɪʒə/	Asian /ˈeɪʃn, ˈeɪʒn/
the Atlantic /ði ətˈlæntɪk/	Atlantic /ətˈlæntɪk/
Australia /ɒˈstreɪliə/	Australian /ɒˈstreɪliən/
Austria /ˈɒstriə/	Austrian /ˈɒstriən/
Azerbaijan /ˌæzəbaɪˈdʒɑːn/	Azerbaijani /ˌæzəbaɪˈdʒɑːni/ Azeri /əˈzeəri/
the Bahamas /ðə bəˈhɑːməz/	Bahamian /bəˈheɪmiən/
Bahrain, Bahrein /bɑːˈreɪn/	Bahraini, Bahreini /bɑːˈreɪmi/
Bangladesh /ˌbæŋɡləˈdeʃ/	Bangladeshi /ˌbæŋɡləˈdeʃi/
Barbados /bɑːˈbeɪdɒs/	Barbadian /bɑːˈbeɪdiən/
Belarus /ˌbeləˈruːs/	Belorussian /ˌbeləˈrʌʃn/
Belgium /ˈbeldʒəm/	Belgian /ˈbeldʒən/
Belize /bəˈliːz/	Belizean /bəˈliːziən/
Benin /beˈniːn/	Beninese /ˌbenɪˈniːz/
Bhutan /buːˈtɑːn/	Bhutanese /ˌbuːtəˈniːz/
Bolivia /bəˈlɪviə/	Bolivian /bəˈlɪviən/
Bosnia-Herzegovina /ˌbɒzniə ˌhɜːtsəɡəˈviːnə/	Bosnian /ˈbɒzniən/
Botswana /bɒtˈswɑːnə/	Botswanan /bɒtˈswɑːnən/ (*person*) Motswana /mɒtˈswɑːnə/ (*people*) Batswana /bætˈswɑːnə/
Brazil /brəˈzɪl/	Brazilian /brəˈzɪliən/
Britain /ˈbrɪtn/ → the United Kingdom	
Bulgaria /bʌlˈɡeəriə/	Bulgarian /bʌlˈɡeəriən/
Burkina /bɜːˈkiːnə/	Burkinese /ˌbɜːkɪˈniːz/
Burma /ˈbɜːmə/ (now officially MYANMAR)	Burmese /bɜːˈmiːz/
Burundi /bʊˈrʊndi/	Burundian /bʊˈrʊndiən/
Cambodia /kæmˈbəʊdiə/	Cambodian /kæmˈbəʊdiən/
Cameroon /ˌkæməˈruːn/	Cameroonian /ˌkæməˈruːniən/
Canada /ˈkænədə/	Canadian /kəˈneɪdiən/
the Caribbean /ðə ˌkærəˈbiːən/	Caribbean /ˌkærəˈbiːən/
Central African Republic (CAR) /ˌsentrəl ˌæfrɪkən rɪˈpʌblɪk/	Central African /ˌsentrəl ˈæfrɪkən/
Chad /tʃæd/	Chadian /ˈtʃædiən/
Chile /ˈtʃɪli/	Chilean /ˈtʃɪliən/
China /ˈtʃaɪnə/	Chinese /tʃaɪˈniːz/
Colombia /kəˈlɒmbiə/	Colombian /kəˈlɒmbiən/
Congo /ˈkɒŋɡəʊ/	Congolese /ˌkɒŋɡəˈliːz/
the Democratic Republic of the Congo (DROC) /ðə ˌdeməˌkrætɪk rɪˌpʌblɪk əv ðə ˈkɒŋɡəʊ/	Congolese /ˌkɒŋɡəˈliːz/

Geographical name	Adjective
Costa Rica /ˌkɒstə ˈriːkə/	Costa Rican /ˌkɒstə ˈriːkən/
Côte d'Ivoire /ˌkəʊt diːˈvwɑː/	Ivorian /aɪˈvɔːriən/
Croatia /krəʊˈeɪʃə/	Croatian /krəʊˈeɪʃn/
Cuba /ˈkjuːbə/	Cuban /ˈkjuːbən/
Cyprus /ˈsaɪprəs/	Cypriot /ˈsɪpriət/
the Czech Republic /ðə ˌtʃek rɪˈpʌblɪk/	Czech /tʃek/
Denmark /ˈdenmɑːk/	Danish /ˈdeɪnɪʃ/ (person) a Dane /deɪn/
Djibouti /dʒɪˈbuːti/	Djiboutian /dʒɪˈbuːtiən/
East Timor /ˌiːst ˈtiːmɔː(r)/	East Timorese /ˌiːst tɪməˈriːz/
Ecuador /ˈekwədɔː(r)/	Ecuadorian /ˌekwəˈdɔːriən/
Egypt /ˈiːdʒɪpt/	Egyptian /iˈdʒɪpʃn/
El Salvador /el ˈsælvədɔː(r)/	Salvadorean /ˌsælvəˈdɔːriən/
England /ˈɪŋɡlənd/	English /ˈɪŋɡlɪʃ/ (person) an Englishman /ˈɪŋɡlɪʃmən/ an Englishwoman /ˈɪŋɡlɪʃwʊmən/
Equatorial Guinea /ˌekwətɔːriəl ˈɡɪni/	Equatorial Guinean /ˌekwətɔːriəl ˈɡɪniən/
Eritrea /ˌerɪˈtreɪə/	Eritrean /ˌerɪˈtreɪən/
Estonia /eˈstəʊniə/	Estonian /eˈstəʊniən/
Ethiopia /ˌiːθiˈəʊpiə/	Ethiopian /ˌiːθiˈəʊpiən/
Europe /ˈjʊərəp/	European /ˌjʊərəˈpiːən/
Fiji /ˈfiːdʒiː/	Fijian /fiːˈdʒiːən/
Finland /ˈfɪnlənd/	Finnish /ˈfɪnɪʃ/ (person) a Finn /fɪn/
France /frɑːns/	French /frentʃ/ (person) a Frenchman /ˈfrentʃmən/ a Frenchwoman /ˈfrentʃwʊmən/
FYROM /ˈfaɪrɒm/ → (the) Former Yugoslav Republic of Macedonia	
Gabon /ɡæˈbɒn/	Gabonese /ˌɡæbəˈniːz/
the Gambia /ðə ˈɡæmbiə/	Gambian /ˈɡæmbiən/
Georgia /ˈdʒɔːdʒə/	Georgian /ˈdʒɔːdʒən/
Germany /ˈdʒɜːməni/	German /ˈdʒɜːmən/
Ghana /ˈɡɑːnə/	Ghanaian /ɡɑːˈneɪən/
Great Britain /ˌɡreɪt ˈbrɪtn/	British /ˈbrɪtɪʃ/ (person) a Briton /ˈbrɪtn/
Greece /ɡriːs/	Greek /ɡriːk/
Grenada /ɡrəˈneɪdə/	Grenadian /ɡrəˈneɪdiən/
Guatemala /ˌɡwɑːtəˈmɑːlə/	Guatemalan /ˌɡwɑːtəˈmɑːlən/
Guinea /ˈɡɪni/	Guinean /ˈɡɪniən/
Guinea-Bissau /ˌɡɪni bɪˈsaʊ/	Guinean /ˈɡɪniən/
Guyana /ɡaɪˈænə/	Guyanese /ˌɡaɪəˈniːz/
Haiti /ˈheɪti/	Haitian /ˈheɪʃn/
Holland /ˈhɒlənd/ → the Netherlands	
Honduras /hɒnˈdjʊərəs/	Honduran /hɒnˈdjʊərən/
Hungary /ˈhʌŋɡəri/	Hungarian /hʌŋˈɡeəriən/
Iceland /ˈaɪslənd/	Icelandic /aɪsˈlændɪk/ (person) an Icelander /ˈaɪsləndə(r)/
India /ˈɪndiə/	Indian /ˈɪndiən/
Indonesia /ˌɪndəˈniːʒə/	Indonesian /ˌɪndəˈniːʒn/
Iran /ɪˈrɑːn/	Iranian /ɪˈreɪniən/
Iraq /ɪˈrɑːk/	Iraqi /ɪˈrɑːki/
the Republic of Ireland /ðə rɪˌpʌblɪk əv ˈaɪələnd/	Irish /ˈaɪrɪʃ/ (person) an Irishman /ˈaɪrɪʃmən/ an Irishwoman /ˈaɪrɪʃwʊmən/
Israel /ˈɪzreɪl/	Israeli /ɪzˈreɪli/
Italy /ˈɪtəli/	Italian /ɪˈtæliən/
the Ivory Coast /ði ˌaɪvəri ˈkəʊst/ → Côte d'Ivoire	
Jamaica /dʒəˈmeɪkə/	Jamaican /dʒəˈmeɪkən/
Japan /dʒəˈpæn/	Japanese /ˌdʒæpəˈniːz/
Jordan /ˈdʒɔːdn/	Jordanian /dʒɔːˈdeɪniən/

Geographical name	Adjective
Kazakhstan /ˌkæzæk'stæn/	Kazakh /'kæzæk/
Kenya /'kenjə/	Kenyan /'kenjən/
Korea, North /ˌnɔːθ kə'rɪə/	North Korean /ˌnɔːθ kə'rɪən/
Korea, South /ˌsaʊθ kə'rɪə/	South Korean /ˌsaʊθ kə'rɪən/
Kuwait /kʊ'weɪt/	Kuwaiti /kʊ'weɪti/
Kyrgyzstan /ˌkɜːgɪ'stæn/	Kyrgyz /'kɜːgɪz/
Laos /laʊs/	Laotian /'laʊʃn/
Latvia /'lætviə/	Latvian /'lætviən/
Lebanon /'lebənən/	Lebanese /ˌlebə'niːz/
Lesotho /lə'suːtuː/	Sotho /'suːtuː/ (person) Mosotho /mə'suːtuː/ (people) Basotho /bə'suːtuː/
Liberia /laɪ'bɪəriə/	Liberian /laɪ'bɪəriən/
Libya /'lɪbiə/	Libyan /'lɪbiən/
Lithuania /ˌlɪθju'eɪniə/	Lithuanian /ˌlɪθju'eɪniən/
Luxembourg /'lʌksəmbɜːg/	Luxembourg (person) a Luxembourger /'lʌksəmbɜːgə(r)/
the Former Yugoslav Repulic of Macedonia /ðə ˌfɔːmə ˌjuːgəʊslɑːv rɪˌpʌblɪk əv ˌmæsə'dəʊniə/	Macedonian /ˌmæsə'dəʊniən/
Madagascar /ˌmædə'gæskə/	Madagascan /ˌmædə'gæskən/ Malagasy /ˌmælə'gæsi/
Malawi /mə'lɑːwi/	Malawian /mə'lɑːwiən/
Malaysia /mə'leɪzə/	Malaysian /mə'leɪzn/
Mali /'mɑːli/	Malian /'mɑːliən/
Mauritania /ˌmɒrɪ'teɪniə/	Mauritanian /ˌmɒrɪ'teɪniən/
the Mediterranean /ðə ˌmedɪtə'reɪniən/	Mediterranean /ˌmedɪtə'reɪniən/
Mexico /'meksɪkəʊ/	Mexican /'meksɪkən/
Moldova /mɒl'dəʊvə/	Moldovan /mɒl'dəʊvən/
Mongolia /mɒŋ'gəʊliə/	Mongolian /mɒŋ'gəʊliən/ Mongol /'mɒŋgl/
Morocco /mə'rɒkəʊ/	Moroccan /mə'rɒkən/
Mozambique /ˌməʊzæm'biːk/	Mozambican /ˌməʊzæm'biːkən/
Myanmar /miˌæn'mɑː(r)/ (see also BURMA)	
Namibia /nə'mɪbiə/	Namibian /nə'mɪbiən/
Nepal /nə'pɔːl/	Nepalese /ˌnepə'liːz/
the Netherlands /ðə 'neðələndz/	Dutch /dʌtʃ/ (person) a Dutchman /'dʌtʃmən/ a Dutchwoman /'dʌtʃwʊmən/
New Zealand /ˌnjuː 'ziːlənd/	New Zealand (person) a New Zealander /ˌnjuː 'ziːləndə(r)/
Nicaragua /ˌnɪkə'rægjuə/	Nicaraguan /ˌnɪkə'rægjuən/
Niger /niː'ʒeə(r)/	Nigerien /niː'ʒeəriən/
Nigeria /naɪ'dʒɪəriə/	Nigerian /naɪ'dʒɪəriən/
Northern Ireland /ˌnɔːðən 'aɪələnd/	Northern Irish /ˌnɔːðən 'aɪrɪʃ/
Norway /'nɔːweɪ/	Norwegian /nɔː'wiːdʒən/
Oman /əʊ'mɑːn/	Omani /əʊ'mɑːni/
the Pacific /ðə pə'sɪfɪk/	Pacific /pə'sɪfɪk/
Pakistan /ˌpækɪ'stæn/	Pakistani /ˌpækɪ'stæni/
Panama /'pænəmɑː/	Panamanian /ˌpænə'meɪniən/
Papua New Guinea /ˌpæpjuə ˌnjuː 'gɪmiː/	Papuan /'pæpjuən/
Paraguay /'pærəgwaɪ/	Paraguayan /ˌpærə'gwaɪən/
Peru /pə'ruː/	Peruvian /pə'ruːviən/
the Philippines /ðə 'fɪlɪpiːnz/	Philippine /'fɪlɪpiːn/ Filipino /ˌfɪlɪ'piːnəʊ/
Poland /'pəʊlənd/	Polish /'pəʊlɪʃ/ (person) a Pole /pəʊl/
Portugal /'pɔːtʃʊgl/	Portuguese /ˌpɔːtʃʊ'giːz/
Puerto Rico /ˌpwɜːtəʊ 'riːkəʊ/	Puerto Rican /ˌpwɜːtəʊ 'riːkən/

Geographical name	Adjective
Qatar /ˈkʌtɑː(r), kæˈtɑː(r)/	Qatari /ˈkʌtɑːri, kæˈtɑːri/
Romania /ruˈmeɪniə/	Romanian /ruˈmeɪniən/
Russia /ˈrʌʃə/	Russian /ˈrʌʃn/
Rwanda /ruˈændə/	Rwandan /ruˈændən/
Samoa /səˈməʊə/	Samoan /səˈməʊən/
Saudi Arabia /ˌsaʊdi əˈreɪbiə/	Saudi /ˈsaʊdi/ Saudi Arabian /ˌsaʊdi əˈreɪbiən/
Scotland /ˈskɒtlənd/	Scottish /ˈskɒtɪʃ/ Scots /skɒts/ (person) a Scot /skɒt/ a Scotsman /ˈskɒtsmən/ a Scotswoman /ˈskɒtswʊmən/
Senegal /ˌsenɪˈgɔːl/	Senegalese /ˌsenɪɡəˈliːz/
Serbia and Montenegro /ˌsɜːbiə ən mɒntɪˈniːɡrəʊ/	Serbian /ˈsɜːbiən/ (person) a Serb /sɜːb/ Montenegrin /ˌmɒntrˈniːɡrɪn/
Sierra Leone /siˌerə liˈəʊn/	Sierra Leonean /siˌerə liˈəʊniən/
Singapore /ˌsɪŋəˈpɔː(r)/	Singaporean /ˌsɪŋəˈpɔːriən/
Slovakia /sləˈvækiə/	Slovak /ˈsləʊvæk/
Slovenia /sləˈviːniə/	Slovene /ˈsləʊviːn/ Slovenian /sləˈviːniən/
Somalia /səˈmɑːliə/	Somali /səˈmɑːli/
South Africa /ˌsaʊθ ˈæfrɪkə/	South African /ˌsaʊθ ˈæfrɪkən/
Spain /speɪn/	Spanish /ˈspænɪʃ/ (person) a Spaniard /ˈspæniəd/
Sri Lanka /ˌsri ˈlæŋkə/	Sri Lankan /ˌsri ˈlæŋkən/
Sudan /suˈdɑːn/	Sudanese /ˌsuːdəˈniːz/
Suriname /ˌsʊərɪˈnɑːm/	Surinamese /ˌsʊərəməˈmiːz/
Swaziland /ˈswɑːzilænd/	Swazi /ˈswɑːzi/
Sweden /ˈswiːdn/	Swedish /ˈswiːdɪʃ/ (person) a Swede /swiːd/
Switzerland /ˈswɪtsələnd/	Swiss /swɪs/
Syria /ˈsɪriə/	Syrian /ˈsɪriən/
Taiwan /taɪˈwɒn/	Taiwanese /ˌtaɪwəˈniːz/
Tajikistan /tæˌdʒiːkɪˈstæn/	Tajik /tæˈdʒiːk/
Tanzania /ˌtænzəˈniːə/	Tanzanian /ˌtænzəˈniːən/
Thailand /ˈtaɪlænd/	Thai /taɪ/
Togo /ˈtəʊgəʊ/	Togolese /ˌtəʊɡəˈliːz/
Trinidad and Tobago /ˌtrɪnɪdæd ən təˈbeɪɡəʊ/	Trinidadian /ˌtrɪnɪˈdædiən/ Tobagan /təˈbeɪɡən/
Tunisia /tjuˈnɪziə/	Tunisian /tjuˈnɪziən/
Turkey /ˈtɜːki/	Turkish /ˈtɜːkɪʃ/ (person) a Turk /tɜːk/
Turkmenistan /tɜːkˌmenɪˈstæn/	Turkmen /ˈtɜːkmen/
Uganda /juːˈɡændə/	Ugandan /juːˈɡændən/
Ukraine /juːˈkreɪn/	Ukrainian /juːˈkreɪniən/
the United Arab Emirates /ðə juːˌnaɪtɪd ˌærəb ˈemɪrəts/	Emirian /ɪˈmɪəriən/
the United Kingdom /ðə juːˌnaɪtɪd ˈkɪŋdəm/	British /ˈbrɪtɪʃ/ (person) a Briton /ˈbrɪtn/
the United States of America /ðə juːˌnaɪtɪd ˌsteɪts əv əˈmerɪkə/ (also the USA and the US)	American /əˈmerɪkən/
Uruguay /ˈjʊərəgwaɪ/	Uruguayan /ˌjʊərəˈgwaɪən/
Uzbekistan /ʊzˌbekɪˈstæn/	Uzbek /ˈʊzbek/
Venezuela /ˌvenəˈzweɪlə/	Venezuelan /ˌvenəˈzweɪlən/
Vietnam /ˌvjetˈnæm/	Vietnamese /ˌvjetnəˈmiːz/
Wales /weɪlz/	Welsh /welʃ/ (person) a Welshman /ˈwelʃmən/ a Welshwoman /ˈwelʃwʊmən/
Yemen Republic /ˌjemən rɪˈpʌblɪk/	Yemeni /ˈjeməni/
Zambia /ˈzæmbiə/	Zambian /ˈzæmbiən/
Zimbabwe /zɪmˈbɑːbwi/	Zimbabwean /zɪmˈbɑːbwiən/

2000 keywords

This is a list of the 2000 most important words to learn at this stage in your language learning. If you know these words, then you will be able to understand all the definitions in this dictionary, as well as most of the words you will come across in your listening and reading.

Keywords which are marked in the dictionary, but not included in this list are numbers, days of the week and the months of the year. For more information about how to use those important words, look at Study Pages **S6–8**.

A

a, an *indefinite article*
ability *n.*
able *adj.*
about *adv., prep.*
above *prep., adv.*
abroad *adv.*
absolutely *adv.*
accept *v.*
acceptable *adj.*
accident *n.*
  by accident
account *n.*
achieve *v.*
acid *n.*
according to *prep.*
accuse *v.*
across *adv., prep.*
act *n., v.*
action *n.*
active *adj.*
activity *n.*
actor, actress *n.*
actual *adj*
  actually *adv.*
add *v.*
address *n.*
admire *v.*
admit *v.*
adult *n., adj.*
advantage *n.*
adventure *n.*
advertisement *n.*
advice *n.*
advise *v.*
affect *v.*
afford *v.*
afraid *adj.*
after *prep., conj., adv.*
afternoon *n.*
afterwards *adv.*
again *adv.*
against *prep.*
age *n.*
aged *adj.*
ago *adv.*
agree *v.*
agreement *n.*
ahead *adv.*
aim *n., v.*

air *n.*
aircraft *n.*
airport *n.*
alcohol *n.*
alcoholic *adj.*
alive *adj.*
all *adj., pron., adv.*
all right *adj., adv., exclamation.*
allow *v.*
almost *adv.*
alone *adj., adv.*
along *prep., adv.*
alphabet *n.*
already *adv.*
also *adv.*
although *conj.*
always *adv..*
among *prep.*
amount *n.*
amuse *v.*
  amusing *adj.*
ancient *adj.*
and *conj.*
anger *n.*
angle *n.*
angry *adj.*
  angrily *adv.*
animal *n.*
announce *v.*
annoy *v.*
  annoying *adj.*
  annoyed *adj.*
another *adj., pron.*
answer *n., v.*
any *adj., pron., adv.*
anyone *pron.*
anything *pron.*
anyway *adv.*
anywhere *adv.*
apart *adv*
  apart from
apparently *adv.*
appear *v.*
appearance *n.*
apple *n.*
apply *v.*
appropriate *adj.*
approval *n.*
approve *v.*
area *n.*

argue *v.*
argument *n.*
arm *n.*
army *n.*
around *adv., prep.*
arrange *v.*
arrangement *n.*
arrest *v.*
arrive *v.*
arrow *n.*
art *n.*
article *n.*
artificial *adj.*
artist *n.*
artistic *adj.*
as *prep., adv., conj.*
ashamed *adj.*
ask *v.*
asleep *adj.*
at *prep.*
atmosphere *n.*
attach *v.*
attack *n., v.*
attention *n.*
attitude *n.*
attract *v.*
attractive *adj.*
aunt *n.*
authority *n.*
autumn *n.*
available *adj.*
avoid *v.*
awake *adj.*
aware *adj.*
away *adv.*

B

baby *n.*
back *n., adj., adv.*
backwards *adv.*
bad *adj.*
  go bad
badly *adv.*
bad-tempered *adj.*
bag *n.*
balance *n.*
ball *n.*
band *n.*
bank *n.*
bar *n.*
base *n., v.*

basic *adj.*
basis *n.*
bath *n.*
bathroom *n.*
be *v.*
beach *n.*
bear *v.*
beard *n.*
beat *v.*
beautiful *adj.*
beauty *n.*
because *conj.*
become *v.*
bed *n.*
bedroom *n.*
been *v.*
beer *n.*
before *prep., conj.*
begin *v.*
beginning *n.*
behave *v.*
behaviour *n.*
behind *prep., adv.*
belief *n.*
believe *v.*
bell *n.*
belong *v.*
below *prep., adv.*
belt *n.*
bend *v.*
  bent *adj.*
beneath *prep., adv.*
benefit *n.*
beside *prep.*
between *prep., adv.*
beyond *prep., adv.*
bicycle *n.*
big *adj.*
bill *n.*
bird *n.*
birth *n.*
birthday *n.*
biscuit *n.*
bit *n.*
bite *v.*
bitter *adj.*
black *adj.*
blame *v., n.*
block *n.*
blood *n.*
blow *v.*
blue *adj., n.*
board *n.*
boat *n.*
body *n.*
boil *v.*
bomb *n.*
bone *n.*

book *n.*
boot *n.*
border *n.*
bored *adj.*
boring *adj.*
born: be born *v.*
borrow *v.*
both *adj., pron.*
bottle *n.*
bottom *n.*
box *n.*
boy *n.*
boyfriend *n.*
brain *n.*
branch *n.*
brave *adj.*
bread *n.*
break *v.*
breakfast *n.*
breath *n.*
breathe *v.*
brick *n.*
bridge *n.*
brief *adj.*
bright *adj.*
brightly *adv.*
bring *v.*
broken *adj*
brother *n.*
brown *adj., n.*
brush *n., v.*
bubble *n.*
build *v.*
building *n.*
bullet *n.*
burn *v.*
burst *v.*
bury *v.*
bus *n.*
bush *n.*
business *n.*
busy *adj.*
but *conj.*
butter *n.*
button *n.*
buy *v.*
by *prep.*

C

cake *n.*
calculate *v.*
call *v., n.*
  be called
calm *adj.*
camera *n.*
camp *n., v.*
camping *n.*
can *modal v., n.*
  cannot
  could *modal v.*
capable *adj.*
capital *n.*
car *n.*

card n.
cardboard n.
care n., v.
  take care
  care for
career n.
careful adj.
carefully adv.
careless adj.
carelessly adv.
carpet n.
carry v
case n.
  in case of
cash n.
castle n.
cat n.
catch v.
cause n., v.
CD n.
ceiling n.
celebrate v.
celebration n.
cell n.
cent n.
  (abbr. c, ct)
centimetre
  (AmE centimeter)
  n. (abbr. cm)
central adj.
centre (AmE
  center) n.
century n.
ceremony n.
certain adj.
certainly adv.
certificate n.
chain n.
chair n.
challenge n.
chance n.
change v., n.
character n.
characteristic n.
charge n., v.
  in charge of
charity n.
chase v., n.
cheap adj.
cheat v., n.
check v., n.
cheek n.
cheese n.
chemical adj., n.
chemistry n.
cheque n.
chest n.
chicken n.
chief adj., n.
child n.
chin n.
chocolate n.
choice n.
choose v.
church n.
cigarette n.
cinema n.

circle n.
city n.
class n.
clean adj., v.
clear adj., v.
clearly adv.
clever adj.
climate n.
climb v.
clock n.
close /kləʊs / adj.
close /kləʊz/ v.
closed adj.
closely adv.
cloth n.
clothes n.
clothing n.
cloud n.
club n.
coal n.
coast n.
coat n.
coffee n.
coin n.
cold adj., n.
collect v.
collection n.
college n.
colour
  (AmE color) n.
coloured (AmE
  colored) adj.
column n.
combination n.
combine v.
come v.
comfortable adj.
command n.
comment n., v.
common adj.
communicate v.
communication n.
community n.
competition n.
company n.
compare v.
comparison n.
competition n.
complain v.
complaint n.
complete adj., v.
completely adv.
complicated adj.
computer n.
concentrate v.
concert n.
conclusion n.
condition n.
confidence n.
confident adj.
confuse v.
  confusing adj.
confused adj.
connect v.
connection n.
conscious adj.
consider v.

consist v.
contact n., v.
contain v.
container n.
continue v.
continuous adj.
contract n.
contrast n., v.
contribute v.
control n., v.
  in control
  under control
conversation n.
convince v.
cook v.
cooker n.
  (AmE stove)
cookie n.
cooking n.
cool adj.
copy n., v.
corner n.
correct adj., v.
correctly adv.
cost n. v.
cotton n.
cough v., n.
count v.
country n.
countryside n.
couple n.
course n.
  of course
court n.
cousin n.
cover v., n.
covering n.
cow n.
crash n., v.
crazy adj.
cream n., adj.
create v.
credit card n.
crime n.
criminal adj., n.
crisis n.
criticism n.
cross n.
crowd n.
crowded adj.
cruel adj.
crush v.
cry v., n.
culture n.
cup n.
cupboard n.
curly adj.
curtain n.
curve n.
custom n.
customer n.
cut v., n.

D
damage n., v.
dance n., v.
  dancing n.

dancer n.
danger n.
dangerous adj.
dark adj., n.
date n.
daughter n.
day n.
dead adj.
deal v.
dear adj.
death n.
debt n.
decide v.
decision n.
declare v.
decorate v.
deep adj.
deeply adv.
defeat v., n.
definite adj.
definitely adv.
degree n.
deliberately adv.
deliver v.
demand n., v.
dentist n.
department n.
depend v.
describe v.
description n.
desert n.
design n., v.
desire n.
desk n.
destroy v.
detail n.
  in detail
determination n.
determined adj.
develop v.
development n.
diagram n.
diamond n.
dictionary n.
die v.
difference n.
different adj.
difficult adj.
difficulty n.
dig v.
dinner n.
direct adj., adv., v.
direction n.
directly adv.
dirt n.
dirty adj.
disadvantage n.
disagree v.
disagreement n.
disappear v.
disappoint v.
disappointed adj.
disappointing adj.
disappointment n.
disaster n.
discover v.
discuss v.

discussion n.
disease n.
disgust n., v.
disgusted adj.
disgusting adj.
dish n.
dishonest adj.
disk n.
distance n.
disturb v.
divide v.
division n.
do v.
doctor n.
  (abbr. Dr)
document n.
dog n.
dollar n.
door n.
double adj.
doubt n.
down adv., prep.
downstairs adv.
downwards adv.
draw v.
drawer n.
drawing n.
dream n.,v.
dress n., v.
drink v., n.
drive v., n.
driver n.
drop v., n.
drug n.
drunk adj.
dry adj., v.
during prep.
dust n.
duty n.
DVD n.

E
each adj., pron.
each other pron.
ear n.
early adj., adv.
earn v.
earth n.
easily adv.
east n., adj., adv.
eastern adj.
easy adj.
eat v.
edge n.
educate v.
education n.
effect n.
effort n.
egg n.
either adj.,
  pron., adv.
election n.
electric adj.
electrical adj.
electricity n.
electronic adj.
else adv.

email *n., v.*
embarrass *v.*
embarrassed *adj.*
embarrassing *adj.*
embarrassment *n.*
emergency *n.*
emotion *n.*
employ *v.*
empty *adj., v.*
encourage *v.*
end *n., v.*
  in the end
enemy *n.*
energy *n.*
engine *n.*
enjoy *v.*
enjoyable *adj.*
enjoyment *n.*
enough *adj.,*
  pron., adv.
enter *v.*
entertain *v.*
entertainment *n.*
enthusiasm *n.*
enthusiastic *adj.*
entrance *n.*
environment *n.*
equal *adj., v.*
equally *adv.*
equipment *n.*
error *n.*
escape *v.*
especially *adv.*
etc. *abbr.*
euro *n.*
even *adv.*
evening *n.*
event *n.*
eventually *adv.*
ever *adv.*
every *adj.*
everybody *pron.*
everyone *pron.*
everything *pron.*
everywhere *adv.*
evidence *n.*
evil *adj.*
exact *adj.*
exactly *adv.*
exaggerate *v.*
exam *n.*
examination *n.*
examine *v.*
example *n.*
excellent *adj.*
except *prep.*
exchange *n , v*
  in exchange
excited *adj.*
excitement *n.*
exciting *adj.*
excluding *prep.*
excuse *n., v.*
exercise *n.*
exhibition *n.*
exist *v.*
expect *v.*
expensive *adj.*

experience *n., v.*
experiment *n., v.*
expert *n.*
explain *v.*
explanation *n.*
explode *v.*
explore *v.*
explosion *n.*
expression *n.*
extra *adj., adv.*
extreme *adj.*
extremely *adv.*
eye *n.*

F
face *n., v.*
fact *n.*
factory *n.*
fail *v.*
failure *n.*
fair *adj.*
fairly *adv.*
fall *v., n.*
familiar *adj.*
family *n.*
famous *adj.*
far *adv., adj.*
farm *n.*
farmer *n.*
farming *n.*
fashion *n.*
fashionable *adj.*
fast *adj., adv.*
fasten *v.*
fat *adj., n.*
father *n.*
fault *n.*
favour *n.*
  in favour
favourite *adj., n.*
fear *n*
feather *n.*
feature *n.*
feed *v.*
feel *v.*
feeling *n.*
female *adj., n.*
fence *n.*
festival *n.*
few *adj., pron.*
  a few
field *n.*
fight *v., n.*
figure *n.*
file *n.*
fill *v.*
film *n., v.*
final *adj., n.*
finally *adv.*
financial *adj.*
find *v.*
  find sth out
fine *adj.*
finger *n.*
finish *v.*
fire *n., v.*
firm *n., adj.*
firmly *adv.*

first *adj., adv., n.*
  at first
fish *n., v.*
fit *v., adj.*
fix *v.*
fixed *adj.*
flag *n.*
flame *n.*
flash *v., n.*
flat *adj., n.*
flavour *n.*
flight *n.*
float *v.*
flood *n.*
floor *n.*
flour *n.*
flow *n., v.*
flower *n.*
fly *v., n.*
flying *adj.*
fold *v., n.*
follow *v.*
following *adj.*
food *n.*
foot *n.*
football *n.*
for *prep.*
force *n., v.*
foreign *adj.*
forest *n.*
forget *v.*
forgive *v.*
fork *n.*
form *n., v.*
formal *adj.*
forward *adv.*
frame *n.*
free *adj., adv., v.*
freedom *n.*
freeze *v.*
fresh *adj.*
friend *n.*
friendly *adj.*
friendship *n.*
frighten *v.*
frightened *adj.*
frightening *adj.*
from *prep.*
front *n., adj.*
  in front
frozen *adj.*
fruit *n.*
fry *v.*
fuel *n.*
full *adj.*
fully *adv.*
fun *n.*
funny *adj.*
fur *n.*
furniture *n.*
further *adj., adv.*
future *n., adj.*

G
gain *v.*
game *n.*
garden *n.*
gas *n.*

gate *n.*
general *adj.*
  in general
generally *adv.*
generous *adj.*
gentle *adj.*
  gently *adv.*
get *v.*
  get on
  get off
gift *n.*
girl *n.*
girlfriend *n.*
give *v*
  give sth away
  give (sth) up.
glass *n.*
glasses *n.*
glove *n.*
go *v.*
  be going to
goal *n.*
god *n.*
gold *n., adj.*
good *adj., n.*
  good at
  good for
goodbye
  exclamation
goods *n.*
government *n.*
grade *n.*
grain *n.*
gram *n.*
grammar *n.*
granddaughter *n.*
grandfather *n.*
grandmother *n.*
grandson *n.*
grass *n.*
grateful *adj.*
great *adj.*
green *adj.*
grey *adj., n.*
ground *n.*
group *n.*
grow *v.*
  grow up
growth *n.*
guard *n., v.*
guess *v., n.*
guest *n.*
guide *n., v.*
guilty *adj.*
gun *n.*

H
habit *n.*
hair *n.*
half *n., adj., pron.,*
  adv.
hall *n.*
hammer *n.*
hand *n.*
handle *n., v.*
hang *v.*
happen *v.*
happiness *n.*

happy *adj.*
hard *adj., adv.*
hardly *adv.*
harm *n., v.*
harmful *adj.*
hat *n.*
hate *v., n.*
have *v.*
  have to *modal v.*
he *pron.*
head *n.*
health *n.*
healthy *adj.*
hear *v.*
heart *n.*
heat *n., v.*
heaven *n.*
heavy *adj.*
height *n.*
hello
  exclamation
help *v., n.*
helpful *adj.*
her *pron.*
here *adv.*
hers *pron.*
herself *pron.*
hide *v.*
high *adj.*
highly *adv.*
hill *n.*
him *pron.*
himself *pron.*
his *adj., pron.*
history *n.*
hit *v., n.*
hobby *n.*
hold *v., n.*
hole *n.*
holiday *n.*
home *n., adv..*
honest *adj.*
hook *n.*
hope *v., n.*
horn *n.*
horse *n.*
hospital *n.*
hot *adj.*
hotel *n.*
hour *n.*
house *n.*
how *adv.*
however *adv.*
huge *adj.*
human *adj., n.*
humour *n.*
hungry *adj.*
hunt *v., n.*
hurry *v., n.*
hurt *v.*
husband *n.*

I
I *pron.*
ice *n.*
ice cream *n.*
idea *n.*
identify *v.*

if *conj.*
ignore *v.*
ill *adj.*
illegal *adj.*
  illegally *adv.*
illness *n.*
image *n.*
imagination *n.*
imagine *v.*
immediate *adj.*
immediately *adv.*
impatient *adj.*
importance *n.*
important *adj.*
impossible *adj.*
impression *n.*
impressive *adj.*
improve *v.*
improvement *n.*
in *prep., adv.*
include *v.*
including *prep.*
increase *v., n.*
indeed *adv.*
independent
  adj.
individual *adj.*
industry *n.*
infection *n.*
influence *n.*
inform *v.*
informal *adj.*
information *n.*
injury *n.*
insect *n.*
inside *prep.,*
  adv., adj., n.
instead *adv., prep.*
instruction *n.*
instrument *n.*
insult *v., n.*
intelligent *adj.*
intend *v.*
intention *n.*
interest *n., v.*
interested *adj.*
interesting *adj.*
international *adj.*
Internet *n.*
interrupt *v.*
interview *n.*
into *prep.*
introduce *v.*
introduction *n.*
invent *v.*
investigate *v.*
invitation *n.*
invite *v.*
involve *v.*
iron *n., v.*
island *n.*
issue *n.*
it *pron.*
item *n.*
its *adj.*
itself *pron.*

J
jacket *n.*
jam *n.*
jeans *n.*
jewellery *n.*
job *n.*
join *v.*
joke *n., v.*
journalist *n.*
journey *n.*
judge *n., v.*
judgement *n.*
juice *n.*
jump *v., n.*
just *adv.*

K
keep *v.*
key *n.*
kick *v., n.*
kill *v.*
kilogram *n.*
  (abbr. kg)
kilometre *(BrE)*
  (AmE kilometer)
  n. (abbr. k, km)
kind *n., adj.*
kindness *n.*
king *n.*
kiss *v., n.*
kitchen *n.*
knee *n.*
knife *n.*
knock *v., n.*
knot *n.*
know *v.*
knowledge *n.*

L
lack *n.*
lady *n.*
lake *n.*
lamp *n.*
land *n., v.*
language *n.*
large *adj.*
last *adj., adv.,*
  n., v.
late *adj., adv.*
later *adv., adj.*
laugh *v., n.*
law *n.*
lawyer *n.*
lay *v.*
layer *n.*
lazy *adj.*
lead /liːd/ *v*
leader *n.*
leaf *n.*
lean *v.*
learn *v.*
least *adj., pron.,*
  adv.
  at least
leather *n.*
leave *v.*
left *adj., adv., n.*

leg *n.*
legal *adj.*
  legally *adv.*
lemon *n.*
lend *v.*
length *n.*
less *adj., pron.,*
  adv.
lesson *n.*
let *v.*
letter *n.*
level *n., adj.*
library *n.*
lid *n.*
lie *v., n.*
life *n.*
lift *v., n.*
light *n., adj., v.*
  lightly *adv.*
like *v., prep., conj.*
likely *adj.*
limit *n., v.*
line *n.*
lip *n.*
liquid *n., adj.*
list *n., v.*
listen *v.*
literature *n.*
litre *(AmE* liter) *n.*
  (abbr. l)
little *adj.,*
  pron., adv.
  a little
live /lɪv/ *v.*
living *adj.*
load *n., v.*
loan *n.*
local *adj.*
lock *v., n.*
lonely *adj.*
long *adj., adv.*
look *v., n.*
  look after
  look for
  look forward to
loose *adj.*
lorry *n.*
lose *v.*
loss *n.*
lost *adj.*
lot: a lot (of)
  pron., adv.
loud *adj., adv.*
  loudly *adv.*
love *n., v.*
low *adj., adv.*
luck *n.*
lucky *adj.*
luggage *n*
lump *n.*
lunch *n.*

M
machine *n.*
mad *adj.*
magazine *n.*
magic *n., adj.*

mail *n., v.*
main *adj.*
mainly *adv.*
make *v., n.*
male *adj., n.*
man *n.*
manage *v.*
manager *n.*
many *adj., pron.*
map *n.*
march *v., n.*
mark *n. v.*
market *n.*
marriage *n.*
married *adj.*
marry *v.*
match *n., v.*
material *n.*
mathematics *n.*
matter *n., v.*
may *modal v.*
maybe *adv.*
me *pron.*
meal *n.*
mean *v.*
meaning *n.*
measure *v., n.*
measurement *n.*
meat *n.*
medical *adj.*
medicine *n.*
medium *adj.*
meet *v.*
meeting *n.*
melt *n.*
member *n.*
memory *n.*
mental *adj.*
mention *v.*
message *n.*
metal *n.*
method *n.*
metre *(BrE*
  (AmE meter) *n.*
midday *n.*
middle *n., adj.*
midnight *n.*
might *modal v.*
mile *n.*
milk *n.*
mind *n., v*
mine *pron., n.*
minute *n.*
mirror *n.*
Miss *n.*
miss *v.*
missing *adj.*
mistake *n., v.*
mix *v.*
mixed *adj.*
mixture *n.*
mobile phone *n.*
model *n.*
modern *adj.*
moment *n.*
money *n.*
month *n.*

mood *n.*
moon *n.*
moral *adj.*
  morally *adv.*
more *adj., pron.,*
  adv.
morning *n.*
most *adj., pron.,*
  adv.
mostly *adv.*
mother *n.*
motorbike *n.*
mountain *n.*
mouse *n.*
mouth *n.*
move *v., n.*
movement *n.*
movie *n.*
Mr *n.*
Mrs *n.*
much *adj., pron.,*
  adv.
mud *n.*
multiply *v.*
murder *n., v.*
muscle *n.*
museum *n.*
music *n.*
musical *adj.*
musician *n.*
must *modal v.*
my *adj.*
myself *pron.*
mysterious *adj.*

N
nail *n.*
name *n., v.*
narrow *adj.*
national *adj.*
natural *adj.*
nature *n.*
navy *n.*
near *adj., adv.,*
  prep.
nearby *adj.*
nearly *adv.*
necessary *adj.*
neck *n.*
need *v., n.*
needle *n.*
negative *adj.*
neighbour *n.*
neither *adj.,*
  pron., adv.
nerve *n.*
nervous *adj.*
net *n.*
never *adv.*
new *adj.*
news *n.*
newspaper *n.*
next *adj., adv., n.*
nice *adj.*
night *n.*
no *exclamation, adj.*
nobody *pron.*

noise *n.*
noisy *adj.*
  noisily *adv.*
none *pron.*
nonsense *n.*
no one *pron.*
nor *conj.*
normal *adj.*
normally *adv.*
north *n., adj., adv.*
northern *adj.*
nose *n.*
not *adv.*
note *n., v.*
nothing *pron.*
notice *n., v.*
novel *n.*
now *adv.*
nowhere *adv.*
nuclear *adj.*
number
  (*abbr.* No., no.) *n.*
nurse *n.*
nut *n.*

O
object *n.*
obtain *v.*
obvious *adj.*
occasion *n.*
occur *v.*
ocean *n.*
o'clock *adv.*
odd *adj.*
of *prep.*
off *prep., adv., adj.*
offence (*AmE*
  offense) *n.*
offer *v., n.*
office *n.*
officer *n.*
official *adj.*
  officially *adv.*
often *adv.*
oh *exclam.*
oil *n.*
OK *exclam., adj.*
old *adj.*
old-fashioned *adj.*
on *prep., adv.*
once *adv.*
one *number, adj.,*
  pron.
one another *pron.*
onion *n.*
only *adj., adv.*
onto *prep.*
open *adj., v.*
operate *v.*
operation *n.*
opinion *n.*
opportunity *n.*
opposite *adj., adv.,*
  prep., n.
or *conj.*
orange *n., adj.*
order *n., v.*

ordinary *adj.*
organization *n.*
organize *v.*
organized *adj.*
original *adj., n.*
other *adj., pron.*
otherwise *adv.*
ought to *modal v.*
our *n.*
ours *pron.*
ourselves *pron.*
out *adj., adv.*
outdoors *adv.*
out of *prep.*
outside *n., adj.,*
  prep., adv.
oven *n.*
over *adv., prep.*
owe *v.*
own *adj., pron., v.*
owner *n.*

P
pack *v., n.*
package *n.*
packet *n.*
page *n.*
pain *n.*
painful *adj.*
paint *n., v.*
painter *n.*
painting *n.*
pair *n.*
pale *adj.*
pan *n.*
paper *n.*
parent *n.*
park *n., v.*
part *n.*
  take part (in)
particular *adj.*
particularly *adv.*
partly *adv.*
partner *n.*
party *n.*
pass *v.*
passage *n.*
passenger *n.*
passport *n.*
past *adj., n.,*
  prep., adv.
path *n.*
patient *n., adj.*
pattern *n.*
pay *v., n.*
payment *n.*
peace *n.*
peaceful *adj.*
pen *n.*
pencil *n.*
penny *n.* (*abbr.* p)
people *n.*
perfect *adj.*
perform *v.*
performance *n.*
perhaps *adv.*
period *n.*

permanent *adj.*
permission *n.*
person *n.*
personal *adj.*
persuade *v.*
pet *n.*
petrol *n.*
phone *n., v.*
photograph *n., v.*
photographer *n.*
phrase *n.*
physical *adj.*
  physically *adv.*
piano *n.*
pick *v.*
  pick sth up
picture *n.*
piece *n.*
pig *n.*
pile *n., v.*
pilot *n.*
pin *n.*
pink *adj., n.*
pipe *n.*
pity *n.*
place *n., v.*
  take place
plain *adj.*
plan *n., v.*
plane *n.*
planet *n.*
plant *n., v.*
plastic *n.*
plate *n.*
platform *n.*
play *v., n.*
player *n.*
pleasant *adj.*
please
  exclamation, v.
pleased *adj.*
pleasure *n.*
plenty *pron.*
plural *adj., n.*
pocket *n.*
poem *n.*
poetry *n.*
point *n., v.*
pointed *adj.*
poison *n., v.*
poisonous *adj.*
police *n.*
polite *adj.*
  politely *adv.*
political *adj.*
politician *n.*
politics *n.*
pool *n.*
poor *adj..*
popular *adj.*
port *n.*
position *n.*
positive *adj.*
possibility *n.*
possible *adj.*
possibly *adv.*
post *n., v.*

post office *n.*
pot *n.*
potato *n.*
pound *n.*
pour *v.*
powder *n.*
power *n.*
powerful *adj.*
practical *adj.*
practice *n.* (*BrE,*
  AmE), *v.* (*AmE*)
practise *v.* (*BrE*)
prayer *n.*
prefer *v.*
pregnant *adj.*
preparation *n.*
prepare *v.*
prepared *adj.*
present *adj., n., v.*
president *n.*
press *n., v.*
pressure *n.*
pretend *v.*
pretty *adv., adj.*
prevent *v.*
previous *adj.*
price *n.*
priest *n.*
prime minister *n.*
print *v.*
priority *n.*
prison *n.*
prisoner *n.*
private *adj.*
prize *n.*
probable *adj.*
probably *adv.*
problem *n.*
process *n.*
produce *v.*
product *n.*
production *n.*
profession *n.*
professional *adj.*
profit *n.*
program *n., v.*
programme *n.*
progress *v., n.*
project *n.*
promise *v., n.*
pronounce *v.*
proof *n.*
proper *adj.*
properly *adv.*
property *n.*
protect *v.*
protection *n.*
protest *n., v.*
proud *adj.*
prove *v.*
provide *v.*
pub *n.*
public *adj., n.*
  in public
  publicly *adv.*
publish *v.*
pull *v., n.*

punish *v.*
punishment *n.*
pupil *n.*
pure *adj.*
purple *adj., n.*
purpose *n.*
  on purpose
push *v., n.*
put *v.*
  put sth on

Q
quality *n.*
quantity *n.*
quarter *n.*
queen *n.*
question *n., v.*
quick *adj., adv.*
  quickly *adv.*
quiet *adj.*
  quietly *adv.*
quite *adv.*

R
race *n., v.*
radio *n.*
railway *n.*
rain *n., v.*
raise *v.*
rare *adj.*
rarely *adv.*
rather *adv.*
reach *v.*
reaction *n.*
read *v.*
ready *adj.*
real *adj.*
reality *n.*
realize *v.*
really *adv.*
reason *n.*
reasonable
  adj.
receive *v.*
recent *adj.*
recently *adv.*
recognize *v.*
recommend *v.*
record *n., v.*
recover *v.*
red *adj., n.*
reduce *v.*
refer to *v.*
refuse *v.*
region *n.*
regular *adj.*
  regularly *adv.*
relation *n.*
relationship *n.*
relative *n.*
relax *v.*
relaxed *adj.*
release *v.*
relevant *adj.*
relief *n.*
religion *n.*
religious *adj.*

rely v.
remain v.
remark n.
remember v.
remind v.
remove v.
rent n., v.
repair v.
repeat v., n.
replace v.
reply n., v.
report v., n.
represent v.
request n., v.
require v.
rescue v., n.
research n., v.
reserve v.
respect n., v.
responsibility n.
responsible
　adj.
rest n., v.
restaurant n.
result n., v.
return v., n.
rice n.
rich adj.
rid adj.: get rid of
ride v., n.
right adj., adv., n.,
　exclam.
ring n., v.
rise n., v.
risk n., v.
river n.
road n.
rob v.
rock n.
role n.
roll n., v.
romantic adj.
roof n.
room n.
root n.
rope n.
rough adj.
round adj.,
　adv., prep.
route n.
row /rəʊ/ n.
royal adj.
rub v.
rubber n.
rubbish n.
rude adj.
　rudely adv.
ruin v.
rule n., v.
run v., n.
rush v., n.

S
sad adj.
　sadness n.
safe adj.
　safely adv.

safety n.
sail v., n.
sailor n.
salad n.
sale n.
salt n.
same adj., pron.
sand n.
satisfaction n
satisfied adj.
sauce n.
save v.
say v.
scale n.
scene n.
school n.
science n.
scientific adj.
scientist n.
scissors n.
score n., v.
scratch v.
screen n.
sea n.
search v., n.
season n.
seat n.
second adj.,
　adv., n.
secret n., adj.
secretary n.
secretly adv.
section n.
see v.
seed n.
seem v.
sell v.
send v.
senior adj.
sense n.
sensible adj.
sensitive adj.
sentence n.
separate adj., v.
　separately adv.
series n.
serious adj.
seriously adv.
serve v.
service n.
set v., n.
settle v.
several adj., pron.
sew v.
sewing n.
sex n.
sexual adj.
shade n.
shadow n.
shake v.
shall modal v.
shame n.
shape n., v.
shaped adj.
share v., n.
sharp adj.
she pron.

sheep n.
sheet n.
shelf n.
shell n.
shine v.
shiny adj.
ship n.
shirt n.
shock n., v.
　shocked adj.
shocking adj.
shoe n.
shoot v.
shop n., v.
shopping n.
short adj.
shot n.
should modal v.
shoulder n.
shout v., n.
show v., n.
shower n.
shut v., adj.
shy adj.
sick adj.
　be sick
　feel sick
side n.
sight n.
sign n., v.
signal n., v.
silence n.
silly adj.
silver n.
similar adj.
simple adj.
since adv., prep.,
　conj.
sing v.
singer n.
single adj.
sink v.
sir n.
sister n.
sit v.
　sit down
situation n.
size n.
skill n.
skin n.
skirt n.
sky n.
sleep v., n.
sleeve n.
slice n. v.
slide v.
slightly adv.
slip v.
slow adj.
　slowly adv.
small adj.
smell v., n.
smile v., n.
smoke n., v.
smooth adj.
　smoothly adv.
snake n.

snow n., v.
so adv., conj.
soap n.
social adj.
society n.
sock n.
soft adj.
soil n.
soldier n.
solid adj., n.
solution n.
solve v.
some adj., pron.
somebody pron.
somehow adv.
someone pron.
something
　pron.
sometimes adv.
somewhere adv.
son n.
song n.
soon adv.
　as soon as
sore adj.
sorry adj.
sort n., v.
sound n., v.
soup n.
south n., adj., adv.
southern adj.
space n.
speak v.
speaker n.
special adj.
speech n.
speed n.
spend v.
spice n.
spider n.
spirit n.
spite n.: in spite of
spoil v.
spoon n.
sport n.
spot n.
spread v.
spring n.
square adj., n.
stage n.
stair n.
stamp n
stand v., n.
　stand up
standard n.
star n., v.
stare v.
start v., n.
state n., v.
statement n.
station n.
stay v., n.
steady adj.
steal v.
steam n.
step n., v
stick v., n.

sticky adj.
still adv., adj.
stomach n.
stone n.
stop v., n.
store n., v.
storm n.
story n.
straight adv.,
　adj.
strange adj.
street n.
strength n.
stretch v.
strict adj.
string n.
strong adj.
　strongly adv.
structure n.
student n.
study n., v.
stuff n.
stupid adj.
style n.
subject n.
substance n.
succeed v.
success n.
successful adj.
successfully adv.
such adj.
　such as
suck v.
sudden adj.
suddenly adv.
suffer v.
sugar n.
suggest v.
suggestion n.
suit n., v.
suitable adj.
suitcase n.
sum n.
summer n.
sun n.
supply n.
support v.
suppose v.
sure adj., adv.
　make sure
surface n.
surprise n., v.
surprised adj.
surprising adj.
surround v.
survive v.
swallow v.
swear v.
sweat v., n.
sweet adj., n.
swim v.
swimming pool n.
switch n., v.
　switch sth off
　switch sth on
symbol n.
system n.

T

table n.
tail n.
take v.
  take sth off
talk v., n.
tall adj.
tap v., n.
tape n.
task n.
taste n., v.
tax n.
taxi n.
tea n.
teach v.
teacher n.
team n.
tear /teə(r)/ v., n.
tear /tɪə(r)/ n.
technical adj.
technology n.
telephone n., v.
television n.
tell v.
temperature n.
temporary adj.
tend v.
tent n.
terrible adj.
test n., v.
text n.
than conj., prep.
thank v.
thanks n.
thank you n.
that adj., pron.,
  conj.
the definite article
theatre (AmE
  theater) n.
their adj.
theirs pron.
them pron.
themselves pron.
then adv.
there adv., pron.
therefore adv.
they pron.
thick adj.
thief n.
thin adj.
thing n.
think v.
thirsty adj.
this adj., pron.
those adj., pron.
though conj., adv.
thought n.
thread n.
threat n.
threaten v.
throat n.
through prep.,
  adv.

throw v.
  throw sth away
thumb n.
ticket n.
tidy adj., v.
tie v., n.
tight adj., adv.
time n.
tin n.
tired adj.
tiring adj.
title n.
to prep.
today adv., n.
toe n.
together adv.
toilet n.
tomato n.
tomorrow adv., n.
tongue n.
tonight adv., n.
too adv.
tool n.
tooth n.
top n., adj.
total adj., n.
totally adv.
touch v., n.
tour n.
tourist n.
towards prep.
towel n.
tower n.
town n.
toy n.
track n.
tradition n.
traffic n.
train n., v.
  training n.
translate v.
transparent adj.
transport n., v.
travel v., n.
treat v.
treatment n.
tree n.
trial n.
triangle n.
trick n., v.
trip n., v.
trouble n.
trousers n.
truck n.
true adj.
trust n., v.
truth n.
try v.
tube n.
tune n.
tunnel n.
turn v., n.
twice adv.
twist v.

type n., v.
typical adj.
tyre n

U

ugly adj.
unable adj.
uncle n.
uncomfortable adj.
unconscious adj.
under prep., adv.
underground adj.,
  adv.
underneath prep.,
  adv.
understand v.
underwater adj.,
  adv.
underwear n.
unemployment n.
unexpected adj.
  unexpectedly adv.
unfair adj.
unfortunately adv.
unfriendly adj.
unhappy adj.
  unhappiness n.
uniform n.
union n.
unit n.
unite v.
universe n.
university n.
unkind adj.
unknown adj.
unless conj.
unlikely adj.
unpleasant adj.
untidy adj.
until conj., prep.
unusual adj.
up prep., adv.
upper adj.
upset v., adj.
upstairs adv., adj.
upwards adv.
urgent adj.
us pron.
use v., n.
  used adj.
  used to sth/to
    doing sth
  used to modal v.
useful adj.
useless adj.
user n.
usual adj.
usually adv.

V

vacation n.
valley n.
valuable adj.
value n.

varied adj.
variety n.
various adj.
vary v.
vegetable n.
vehicle n.
very adv.
video n.
view n.
village n.
violence n.
violent adj.
visit v., n.
visitor n..
voice n.
vote n., v.

W

wait v.
wake (up) v.
walk v., n.
wall n.
want v.
war n.
warm adj., v.
warn v.
warning n.
wash v.
washing n.
waste v., n.,
  adj.
watch v., n.
water n.
wave n., v.
way n.
we pron.
weak adj.
weakness n.
weapon n.
wear v.
weather n.
website n.
wedding n.
week n.
weekend n.
weigh v.
weight n.
welcome v.,
  adj., n.
well adv., adj.,
  exclamation
  as well (as)
west n., adj., adv.
western adj.
wet adj.
what pron., adj.
whatever adj.,
  pron., adv.
wheel n.
when adv., conj.
whenever conj.
where adv., conj.
whereas conj.
wherever adv., conj.

whether conj.
which pron., adj.
while conj., n.
white adj., n.
who pron.
whoever pron.
whole adj., n.
whom pron
whose adj., pron.
why adv.
wide adj.
wife n.
wild adj.
will modal v., n.
win v.
wind /wɪnd/ n.
window n.
wine n.
wing n.
winner n.
winter n.
wire n.
wish v., n.
with prep.
within prep.
without prep.
woman n.
wonder v
wonderful adj.
wood n.
wooden adj.
wool n.
word n.
work v., n.
worker n.
world n.
worried adj.
worry v., n.
worse adj., adv.
worst adj.,
  adv., n.
worth adj.
would modal v.
wrap v.
write v.
writer n.
writing n.
wrong adj., adv.
  go wrong

Y

year n.
yellow adj., n.
yes exclamation
yesterday adv., n.
yet adv., conj.
you pron.
young adj.
your adj.
yours pron.
yourself pron.
youth n.

Irregular verbs

Infinitive	Past tense	Past participle	Infinitive	Past tense	Past participle
arise	arose	arisen	fling	flung	flung
babysit	babysat	babysat	fly	flew	flown
be	was/were	been	forbid	forbade	forbidden
bear	bore	borne	forecast	forecast	forecast
beat	beat	beaten	foresee	foresaw	foreseen
become	became	become	forget	forgot	forgotten
begin	began	begun	forgive	forgave	forgiven
bend	bent	bent	freeze	froze	frozen
bet	bet	bet	get	got	got;
bid	bid	bid			(*American*) gotte
bind	bound	bound	give	gave	given
bite	bit	bitten	go	went	gone
bleed	bled	bled	grind	ground	ground
blow	blew	blown	grow	grew	grown
break	broke	broken	hang	hung,	hung,
breed	bred	bred		hanged	hanged
bring	brought	brought	have	had	had
broadcast	broadcast	broadcast	hear	heard	heard
build	built	built	hide	hid	hidden
burn	burnt,	burnt,	hit	hit	hit
	burned	burned	hold	held	held
burst	burst	burst	hurt	hurt	hurt
buy	bought	bought	keep	kept	kept
catch	caught	caught	kneel	knelt,	knelt,
choose	chose	chosen		kneeled	kneeled
cling	clung	clung	know	knew	known
come	came	come	lay	laid	laid
cost	cost	cost	lead	led	led
creep	crept	crept	lean	leant,	leant,
cut	cut	cut		leaned	leaned
deal	dealt	dealt	leap	leapt, leaped	leapt, leaped
dig	dug	dug	learn	learnt,	learnt,
do	did	done		learned	learned
draw	drew	drawn	leave	left	left
dream	dreamt,	dreamt,	lend	lent	lent
	dreamed	dreamed	let	let	let
drink	drank	drunk	lie	lay	lain
drive	drove	driven	light	lit, lighted	lit, lighted
eat	ate	eaten	lose	lost	lost
fall	fell	fallen	make	made	made
feed	fed	fed	mean	meant	meant
feel	felt	felt	meet	met	met
fight	fought	fought	mislead	misled	misled
find	found	found	mistake	mistook	mistaken
flee	fled	fled	misunderstand	misunderstood	misunderstood

Infinitive	Past tense	Past participle	Infinitive	Past tense	Past participle
mow	mowed	mown	spell	spelt, spelled	spelt, spelled
outgrow	outgrew	outgrown	spend	spent	spent
overcome	overcame	overcome	spill	spilt, spilled	spilt, spilled
overhear	overheard	overheard	spin	spun	spun
oversleep	overslept	overslept	spit	spat	spat
overtake	overtook	overtaken	split	split	split
pay	paid	paid	spoil	spoilt, spoiled	spoilt, spoiled
prove	proved	proved, proven	spread	spread	spread
put	put	put	spring	sprang	sprung
quit	quit	quit	stand	stood	stood
read	read	read	steal	stole	stolen
repay	repaid	repaid	stick	stuck	stuck
rewind	rewound	rewound	sting	stung	stung
ride	rode	ridden	stink	stank	stunk
ring	rang	rung	stride	strode	—
rise	rose	risen	strike	struck	struck
run	ran	run	swear	swore	sworn
saw	sawed	sawn	sweep	swept	swept
say	said	said	swell	swelled	swollen, swelled
see	saw	seen	swim	swam	swum
seek	sought	sought	swing	swung	swung
sell	sold	sold	take	took	taken
send	sent	sent	teach	taught	taught
set	set	set	tear	tore	torn
sew	sewed	sewed, sewn	tell	told	told
shake	shook	shaken	think	thought	thought
shed	shed	shed	throw	threw	thrown
shine	shone	shone	thrust	thrust	thrust
shoot	shot	shot	tread	trod	trodden
show	showed	shown, showed	undergo	underwent	undergone
shrink	shrank, shrunk	shrunk	understand	understood	understood
shut	shut	shut	undo	undid	undone
sing	sang	sung	unwind	unwound	unwound
sink	sank	sunk	upset	upset	upset
sit	sat	sat	wake	woke	woken
sleep	slept	slept	wear	wore	worn
slide	slid	slid	weave	wove	woven
sling	slung	slung	weep	wept	wept
slit	slit	slit	win	won	won
smell	smelt, smelled	smelt, smelled	wind	wound	wound
sow	sowed	sown, sowed	withdraw	withdrew	withdrawn
speak	spoke	spoken	wring	wrung	wrung
speed	sped, speeded	sped, speeded	write	wrote	written

Key to study pages

Prepositions of place [S2]

1 Who's who?

1 Tom	3 Diana	5 Jack
2 Sarah	4 James	6 Jill

2 Describing pictures

A	B
1 in	1 below
2 on top of	2 against
3 above	3 under
4 below	4 among
5 between	5 opposite

Prepositions of movement [S3]

1 Where are they going?

1 up the ladder	6 out of the pool
2 along the pole	7 through the tunnel
3 down the slide	8 over the wall
4 into the pool	9 round the track
5 across the pool	10 towards the finish

2 Giving and following directions

1 right	4 down this road
2 turn left	5 take the second turning
3 left again	6 on the right

Exam practice [S4–5]

Part 1

1 C 2 D 3 F 4 I 5 H 6 B

Part 2

1 igloo	3 bungalow	5 nest
2 tent	4 palace	6 caves

Part 3

1 B wrong	4 B wrong
2 C doesn't say	5 C doesn't say
3 A right	6 A right

Part 4

1 are
2 there
3 is
4 in
5 am
6 sleep/stay/camp
7 breakfast/lunch/dinner/supper/tea
8 will

Numbers [S6–7]

1 One or first?

A

1 one		1st	first
2 two		2nd	second
3 three		3rd	third
4 four		4th	fourth
5 five		5th	fifth
6 six		6th	sixth
7 seven		7th	seventh
8 eight		8th	eighth
9 nine		9th	ninth
10 ten		10th	tenth
11 eleven		11th	eleventh
12 twelve		12th	twelfth
13 thirteen		13th	thirteenth
14 fourteen		14th	fourteenth
15 fifteen		15th	fifteenth
16 sixteen		16th	sixteenth
17 seventeen		17th	seventeenth
18 eighteen		18th	eighteenth
19 nineteen		19th	nineteenth
20 twenty		20th	twentieth
21 twenty-one		21st	twenty-first
30 thirty		30th	thirtieth
40 forty		40th	fortieth
50 fifty		50th	fiftieth
60 sixty		60th	sixtieth
70 seventy		70th	seventieth
80 eighty		80th	eightieth
90 ninety		90th	ninetieth
100 a/one hundred		100th	hundredth
101 a/one hundred and one		101st	hundred and first
200 two hundred		200th	two hundredth
1 000 a/one thousand		1 000th	thousandth
1 000 000 a/one million		1 000 000th	millionth

B

1 third	4 sixtieth	7 seven
2 twelve	5 forty-nine	8 second
3 fifth	6 hundredth	

2 Large numbers

1 three hundred and sixty-five (365)
2 one hundred and eighty (180)
3 nine thousand eight hundred and fifty (9850)

4 Fractions and mathematical expressions

A

1 $\frac{1}{2}$	a half	3 $\frac{1}{4}$	a/one quarter
4 $\frac{1}{8}$	an/one eighth	7 $\frac{3}{4}$	three quarters
2 $\frac{1}{3}$	a/one third	6 $1\frac{2}{5}$	one and two fifths
5 $\frac{1}{16}$	a/one sixteenth		

B

1 four	4 seven point eight
2 eighty-five	5 fifty-four
3 one hundred and fifty	6 three quarters

Time and dates [S8]

What's the time?

3 six **thirty**
4 (a) **quarter** to four
5 ten **past** eleven
6 twenty **to** twelve or eleven **forty**

What's the date?

1 Man landed on the moon
  on 20 July, 1969.
2 William Shakespeare was born
  on 23rd April, 1564.
3 The first ever website appeared
  on August 6, 1991.
4 Queen Elizabeth II became Queen of the
  United Kingdom on 2 June, 1953.

We say

1 the twentieth of July, nineteen sixty-nine
2 the twenty-third of April, fifteen sixty-four
3 August the sixth, nineteen ninety one
4 the second of June, nineteen fifty-three

Telephoning [S9]

Asking for and saying telephone numbers

What's your number?
What's your phone number?
What's your mobile number?

Using the telephone

1 make a phone call   6 on the phone
2 pick up   7 engaged
3 dial   8 leave a message
4 rings   9 call you back
5 hang up

Talking on the telephone

1 Hello. 56767
2 Hello. Is Sally there, please?
3 Sally speaking.
4 Oh hello, Sally. It's John.

1 Good morning, Dr Lee's surgery.
2 Hello. Can I speak to Dr Lee, please?
3 Who's calling?
4 It's Mr White.
5 I'm sorry – he's out. Can I take a message?
6 No thank you. I'll call back later.

Words that go together [S10]

Adjectives with prepositions

1 at   4 about   7 of
2 of   5 of   8 about
3 in   6 with

Verbs with prepositions

1 with   4 for   7 about
2 for   5 on   8 in
3 at   6 for

Verb + noun

A take a photo   tell a lie
   make a mess   pass your exams
   do your homework   catch a cold
   say goodbye

B 1 give somebody a call   5 making a mess
   2 pass your exams   6 told a lie
   3 take a photo   7 done my homework
   4 saying goodbye   8 caught a cold

3 Finding information in the dictionary

A Bed: go to bed, in bed, make the bed,
              single bed, double bed, bunk beds
   Bread: loaf of bread
   Computer: by computer, on the computer,
              computer program, computer games
   Diet: go on a diet
   Hardly: could hardly, hardly any, hardly ever
   Holiday: summer holiday, on holiday,
              public holiday, bank holiday
   Morning: this morning, tomorrow morning,
              on Tuesday morning, all morning,
              in the morning

B 1 no answer   5 go on a diet
   2 go to bed   6 hardly ever
   3 a loaf of bread   7 on holiday
   4 on the computer   8 in the morning

Education [S12]

1 School subjects

2 The Education System

A In Britain...   In the US...

   1 nursery school   1 nursery school
   2 primary school   2 elementary school
   3 secondary school   3 high school
   4 college/university   4 college/university

B
1. attend
2. private school
3. terms
4. pupils
5. GCSE
6. A level
7. university
8. graduate
9. degree
10. public schools
11. grades
12. semesters

Health [S13]

1 How are you?

A How are you?
How are you feeling?
How do you feel?

B 😊
Very well, thank you.
I feel great.
I'm fine.

😐
I'm not too bad, thanks.
I'm ok.

☹️
I'm sick.
I feel awful.
I'm not very well.
I'm ill.

2 What's the matter?

A
1. headache
2. backache
3. earache
4. stomach ache

3 Going to the doctor's

1. make an appointment
2. symptoms
3. examine
4. temperature
5. write a prescription
6. medicine
7. get better

Writing letters and emails [S14–15]

1 Formal beginnings and endings

- ✔ Dear Sir
- ✔ Dear Madam
- ✔ Dear Sir or Madam
- ✗ Dear Miss
- ✔ Dear Ms Jackson
- ✔ Yours faithfully
- ✔ Yours sincerely
- ✗ Your faithful
- ✗ Yours hopefully
- ✔ Yours truly

2 Formal or informal

I Lots of love, Vicky
F Yours faithfully, Victoria Dawson

F Dear Mr Khan
I Dear Ali

F I enclose a cheque for...
I Here's some money for...

I I'm writing to you...
F I am writing to you...

I Could you...?
F I would be grateful if you could...

I Write back soon!
F I look forward to hearing from you.

3 Emails

1. Hi Carlos
2. to hear from you
3. what's more
4. Must go
5. keep in touch
6. Bye for now

Filling in forms [S14]

1 Different forms

A 1 C 2 A 3 B

B
1. application
2. order
3. membership

2 Understanding forms

1. last name, initials
2. nationality
3. in capitals
4. password
5. tick/check (*American*)
6. sign, signature

3 Filling in a form

Language Exchange Application
(example answer)

First name *Sara*   Last name *Esposito*

Nationality *Mexican* Age *19*

Daytime telephone number *80610 415353*

Email address *sesposito5@newmail.com*

What is your first language? *Spanish*

How long have you been learning English?
5 years

What are your reasons for learning English?
(Write in 10–20 words.)
I would like to visit the UK. I like watching English and American films.

What area of English would you most like to practise? Please tick the one(s) that are important for you.

- ✔ speaking
- listening
- ✔ reading
- grammar
- writing
- pronunciation

Signature *SMEsposito*

Date *8th March, 2006*